Heath

Teacher's Edition

ALGEBRA 1

Clyde A. Dilley

Steven P. Meiring

John E. Tarr

Ross Taylor

HEATH

D.C. Heath and Company
Lexington, Massachusetts   Toronto

Authors

Clyde A. Dilley
Author in residence; formerly Professor of Education,
University of Toledo, Ohio; and formerly mathematics teacher
in Iowa and Illinois

Steven P. Meiring
Supervisor of Mathematics, State of Ohio;
formerly mathematics teacher in Indiana

John E. Tarr
Professor, University of Northern Iowa;
and Mathematics Teacher, Malcolm Price Laboratory School

Ross Taylor
Supervisor of Mathematics, Minneapolis Public Schools;
formerly mathematics teacher in Illinois

Contents

1 Algebraic Expressions

2 Real Numbers

3 Solving Equations

4 Polynomials

5 Graphing Linear Equations and Functions

6 Systems of Linear Equations

7 Multiplying and Factoring Polynomials

8 Algebraic Fractions and Applications

9 Inequalities and Their Graphs

10 Rational and Irrational Numbers

11 Solving Quadratic Equations

Supplementary Topics

In the student's text, Selected Answers are on pages 649–689.

A Letter to the Student

Algebra 1 is the first in a series of high-school mathematics courses that can prepare you for promising opportunities in higher education and in future careers. Algebra is like arithmetic because it deals with numbers; but it is a more general way (and a more powerful way) to think about relationships among numbers. It takes time and practice to become used to this new way of thinking, but the time and effort are well spent. Algebra provides a deeper understanding not only of mathematics but also of the world in which we live.

You will now be expected to take greater responsibility for your own learning. You will need to learn how to read mathematics, how to study mathematics, and how to use a textbook effectively. To help you develop these new learning skills we have provided study hints called *Strategies for Success*.

Expect to be successful in this algebra course. Believe in yourself, apply yourself, enjoy the work, and in all likelihood you will be successful.

Clyde A. Dilley   *John E. Tarr*

Steven P. Meiring   *Ross Taylor*

Strategy for Success   Reading Mathematics

To read mathematics with understanding you need to use skills different from those you use when reading a novel, a poem, or even a science lesson. Part of the power of mathematics lies in using a very abbreviated notation to express ideas that in ordinary English might require long sentences. Since big ideas are expressed very compactly, mathematics must be read very slowly, and frequently must be reread many times to get the full meaning. Keep paper and pencil handy as you read mathematics and try to illustrate or write an example for each new idea.

Motivation . . .

"Students who see that algebra is important in their lives are more likely to persevere and to succeed. I need a textbook that helps make algebra relevant to my students."

Walter Shields
Needham High School
Needham, Massachusetts

In HEATH ALGEBRA 1 . . .

■ A Preview (introduction) for every lesson relates the lesson to the student and the student's world.

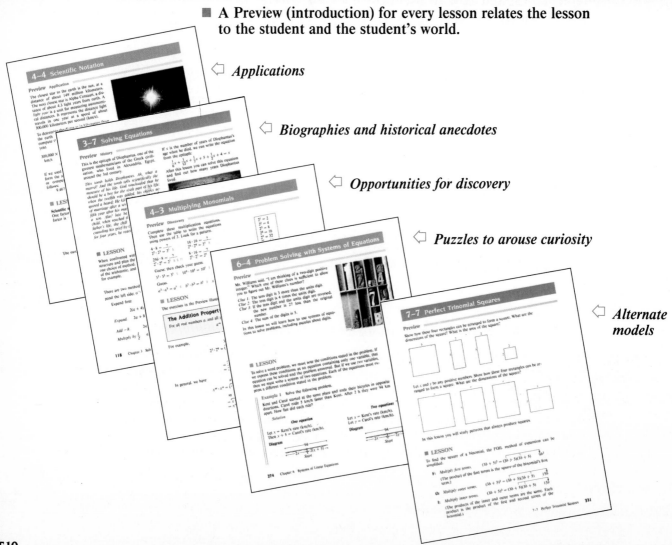

◁ *Applications*

◁ *Biographies and historical anecdotes*

◁ *Opportunities for discovery*

◁ *Puzzles to arouse curiosity*

◁ *Alternate models*

■ Chapter introductions

- *illustrate an interesting topic related to the chapter.*
- *explain the topic in a short paragraph.*
- *illustrate the mathematical application with a technical drawing.*

■ Exercises are interesting, developmental, and thought-provoking.

◁ *Applications*

◁ *Exercises related to student activities*

◁ *Puzzles*

◁ *Geometry exercises*

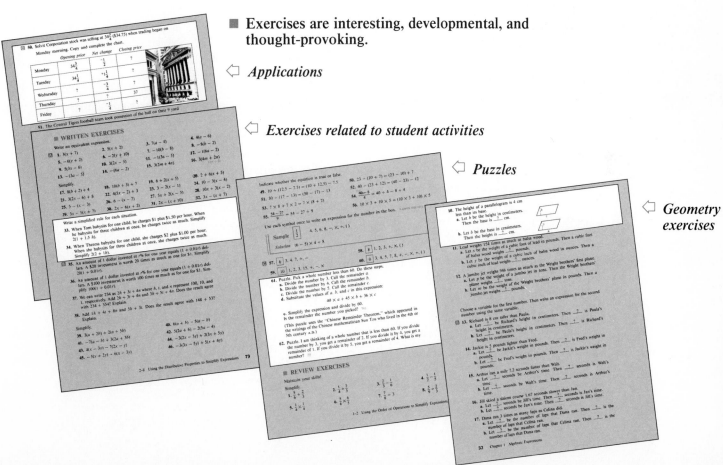

Problem Solving/Applications . . .

"I need a textbook that helps students understand algebra well enough to apply it and solve challenging problems."

Larry Luck
Southwest High School
Minneapolis, Minnesota

In HEATH ALGEBRA 1 . . .

■ **Problem-solving skills are introduced early and developed carefully.**

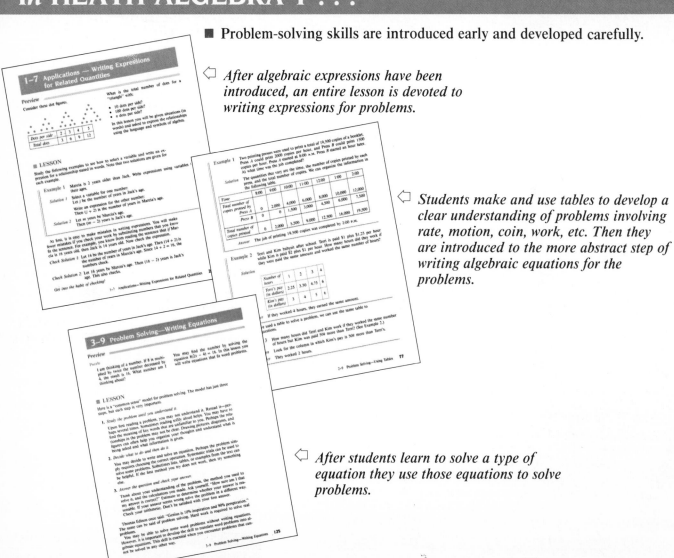

◁ *After algebraic expressions have been introduced, an entire lesson is devoted to writing expressions for problems.*

◁ *Students make and use tables to develop a clear understanding of problems involving rate, motion, coin, work, etc. Then they are introduced to the more abstract step of writing algebraic equations for the problems.*

◁ *After students learn to solve a type of equation they use those equations to solve problems.*

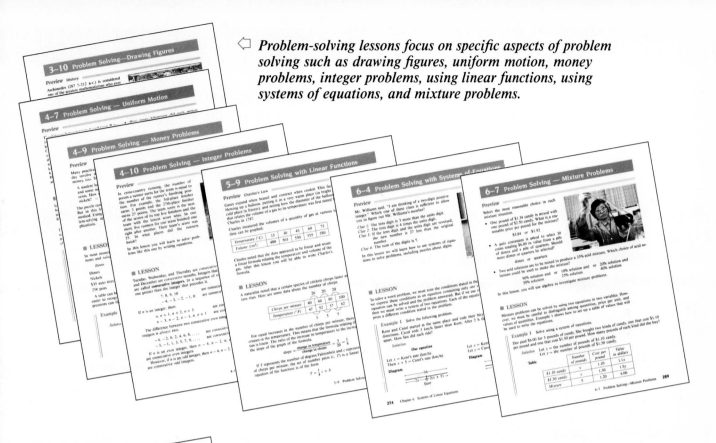

◁ *Problem-solving lessons focus on specific aspects of problem solving such as drawing figures, uniform motion, money problems, integer problems, using linear functions, using systems of equations, and mixture problems.*

■ Problem-solving practice is incorporated into other skill lessons.

■ Higher-order thinking skills are developed throughout the text, especially in C-level exercises and in Practice for College Entrance Tests.

"I need a text that challenges the best students and helps all students attain maximum proficiency and understanding."

Don Wiederanders
Northern University High School
Cedar Falls, Iowa

In HEATH ALGEBRA 1 . . .

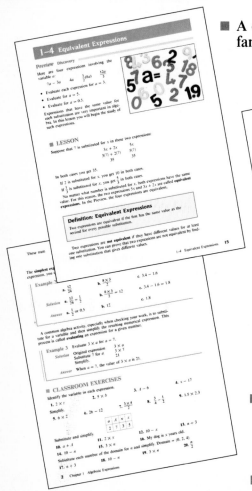

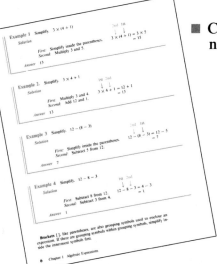

■ A carefully-sequenced development of algebra is based on familiar ideas in arithmetic.

■ Clear Examples illustrate each new idea and skill.

■ Classroom Exercises insure that all students will be successful with the written assignment.

■ Abundant Written Exercises are on three levels of difficulty (A, B, and C). The A exercises are in equivalent pairs to provide for alternate assignments. The C exercises are a thoughtful challenge for the best students.

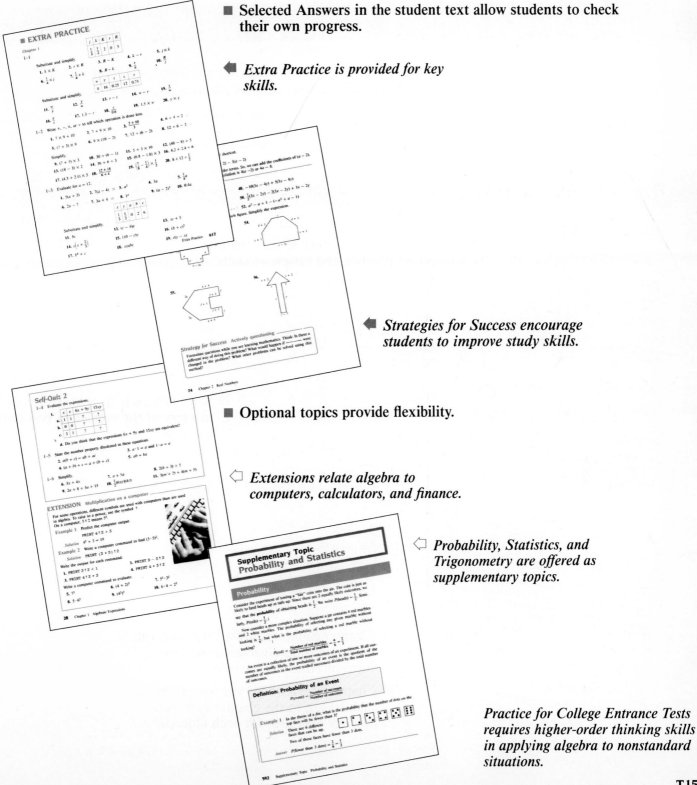

■ Selected Answers in the student text allow students to check their own progress.

◀ *Extra Practice is provided for key skills.*

◀ *Strategies for Success encourage students to improve study skills.*

■ Optional topics provide flexibility.

◁ *Extensions relate algebra to computers, calculators, and finance.*

◁ *Probability, Statistics, and Trigonometry are offered as supplementary topics.*

Practice for College Entrance Tests requires higher-order thinking skills in applying algebra to nonstandard situations.

"I am always concerned that students will not remember what they have learned and will not do well on tests."

Susan Stevenson
Charles D. Owen High School
Swannanoa, North Carolina

In HEATH ALGEBRA 1 . . .

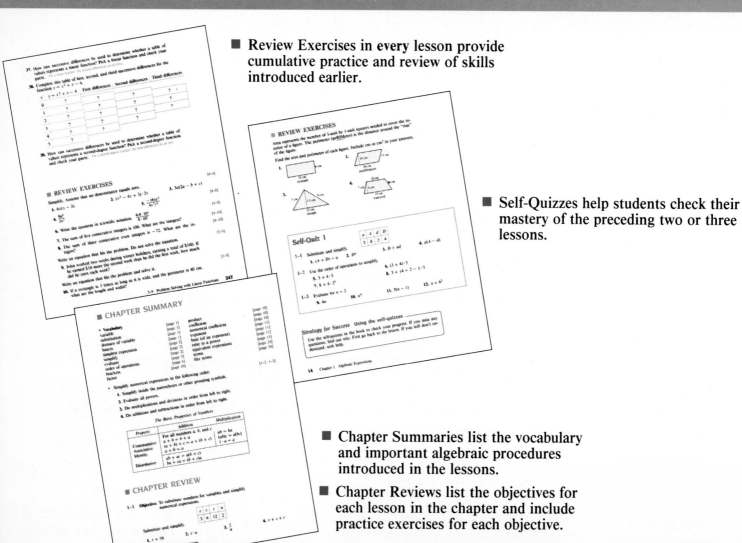

■ **Review Exercises in every lesson provide cumulative practice and review of skills introduced earlier.**

■ **Self-Quizzes help students check their mastery of the preceding two or three lessons.**

■ **Chapter Summaries list the vocabulary and important algebraic procedures introduced in the lessons.**

■ **Chapter Reviews list the objectives for each lesson in the chapter and include practice exercises for each objective.**

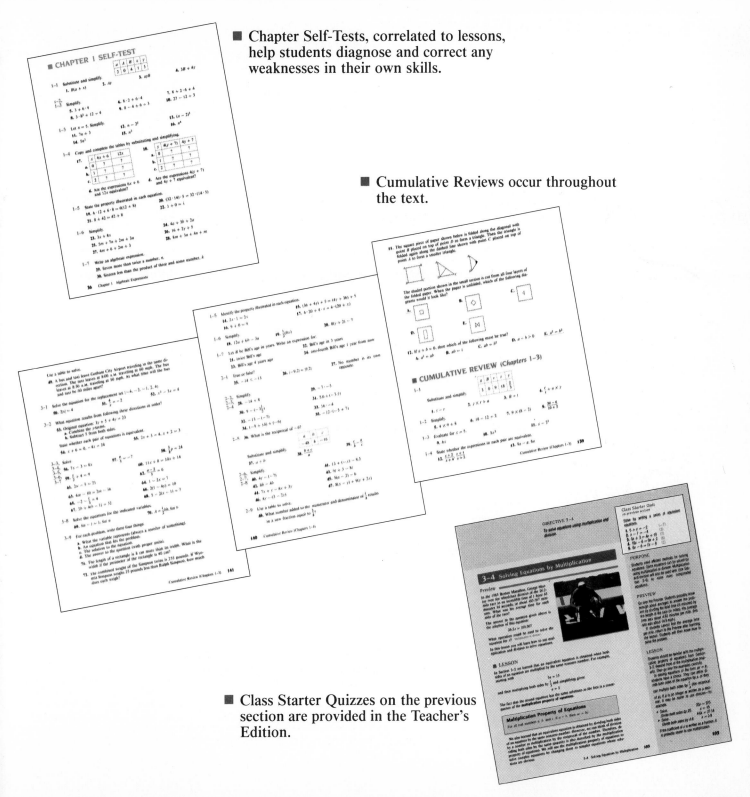

■ Chapter Self-Tests, correlated to lessons, help students diagnose and correct any weaknesses in their own skills.

■ Cumulative Reviews occur throughout the text.

■ Class Starter Quizzes on the previous section are provided in the Teacher's Edition.

Teaching Resources . . .

"There are always so many things to be done. I wish my textbook would save me time by providing many varied ideas for planning effective lessons."

Frank DeGeorge
Melrose High School
Melrose, Massachusetts

In HEATH ALGEBRA 1 . . .

■ A consistent lesson structure (Preview—Lesson—Examples —Classroom Exercises—Written Exercises—Review Exercises) is convenient and efficient.

■ A wide Teacher's Edition provides additional support right where you need it.

Objective for each Section

Class Starter Quiz on Previous Section

Purpose for each Section

Background for the Previews and Lessons

Classroom Strategies

Additional Examples

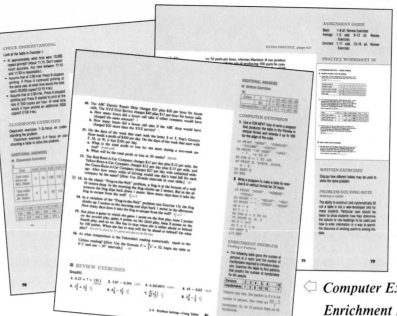

Questions to Check
Understanding prior
to using Classroom
Exercises

Notes on the
Classroom Exercises

Assignment Guides ⇦

Reduced Copies of the
Worksheets and Tests

Notes on the Written
Exercises

Problem-Solving Notes

Computer Extensions ⇦
Enrichment Problems

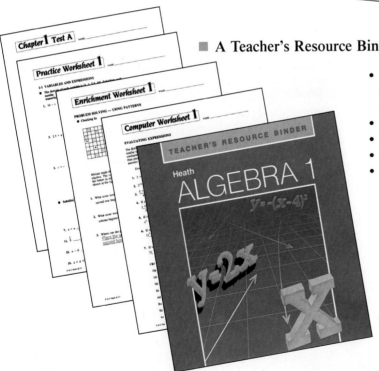

■ A Teacher's Resource Binder (copymasters) provides:

- Tests (2 forms for each chapter, cumulative tests every three chapters)
- Practice Worksheets
- Enrichment Worksheets
- Computer Worksheets
- Teaching Aids

▨ A complete Solution Key
▨ Tests on duplicating masters
▨ Worksheets on duplicating masters
▨ A computer bank of test questions allows teachers to quickly construct and print out tests in various forms.

Philosophy of Heath Algebra

HEATH ALGEBRA is organized so that students experience algebra as a cumulative, unified subject rather than as a series of disjointed topics. Relationships between concepts and skills are stressed. References to the uses and users of mathematics are woven into the lessons rather than left as disconnected, separate ideas.

Likewise, problem solving is an integral part of the development of the course.

Problem Solving

HEATH ALGEBRA provides activities that help students become good problem solvers. Good problem solvers are very active—planning, checking, reviewing, extending. They distinguish relevant from irrelevant information. They see quickly the mathematical structure of a problem. They generalize across wide ranges of problems. And they remember a problem's mathematical structure for purposes of relating it to other problems. Happily, research is clear in finding that students of all ages and achievement levels can learn behaviors and thought processes that make them better problem solvers.

To improve student problem-solving skills, evidence suggests that teachers should integrate problem solving within two instructional roles: (1) they should teach and regularly reinforce aspects of problem solving, such as drawing diagrams, constructing tables, and building equations; and (2) they should develop attitudes toward problem solving that are not easily taught but that must be nurtured over a period of time—attitudes like risk-taking and questioning. ("What if . . . ?" "How is that related to . . . ?" etc.)

Problem-solving strategies (for example, looking for a pattern, writing an open sentence, working backward) provide students with problem-solving tools that help them interact with problem elements in an organized way. Students should be aware of how a strategy or other organized attack upon a problem brings their thinking to bear upon the concepts of the problem. Research suggests that regular encouragement to verbalize problem solving thinking can help students become more aware of their own thinking processes and those of others. Verbalization requires students to bring their thinking to the conscious level for evaluation and refinement. Some students have recommended small-group activities for this purpose, particularly for students of average to below-average ability.

In the broader context of outcomes, it is perhaps too limiting to view problem solving as a discrete activity or a particular part of the curriculum. Problem solving is a way of viewing mathematics and of thinking mathematically. It is a way of relating ideas within one's mind and building structures of mathematical concepts. Evidence confirms the relationship between students' perception of the mathematical structure of a problem and their problem-solving competence. Good problem solvers are even characterized as having mathematical frames of mind that they tend to impose structurally on their perceptions of the world. Effective problem-solving teachers strive toward this level of understanding. They employ a problem-solving approach to their instruction every day, encouraging such thinking among their students. These teachers are problem-solving minded. The questions they pose, the instructional tasks they set, and the attitudes and values they convey bespeak problem solving as a way of understanding and using mathematics.

The HEATH ALGEBRA program approaches the teaching of problem solving both from a specific point of view and from the broader point of view as described above. In the specific context, some lessons and parts of lessons directly teach problem-solving skills, such as making a table, selecting and assigning variables, writing an equation, and the like. In the broader context, each lesson is carefully written to help students understand mathematical structures and recognize those structures in problem situations. Further, the Teacher's Edition provides suggestions for helping students grow toward this level of understanding in sections headed Lesson, Concept Extension, and Problem-Solving Notes.

Instruction

Several research-based models for instruction have been developed in recent years. In general, these models share the following elements:

1. Motivating students to focus on the lesson
2. Making students aware of the objective and purpose of the lesson
3. Teaching the content of the lesson
4. Providing worked-out examples for students to follow
5. Checking for student understanding
6. Providing guided practice
7. Providing independent practice
8. Providing frequent, spaced review

Each of these elements for effective instruction is carefully addressed in HEATH ALGEBRA.

1. The Preview actively involve students in an exploration activity, state an interesting historical anecdote, or relate an application of the lesson.
2. The Previews make students aware of the objectives of the lesson in terms they can easily understand. The objectives are stated in the Chapter Review and in the Teacher's Edition. The Purpose in the Teachers Edition states the relationship between the lesson and other lessons.
3. New content is clearly and interestingly developed. Further, teaching suggestions are provided in the wide margins of the Teacher's Edition.
4. Worked-out examples are provided in the text. Parallel worked-out examples are provided in the Teacher's Edition in case they are needed for some students.
5. Questions for determining whether students have the fundamental understandings needed for successfully beginning the Classroom Exercises are provided in the Teacher's Edition in the Check Understanding sections.
6. The Classroom Exercises provided guided practice. These exercises are equivalent to the A-level Written Exercises.
7. The Written Exercises provide independent practice on three levels of difficulty.
8. Review of prior lessons is provided in the Review Exercises, Self-Quizzes, Chapter Reviews, Chapter Self-Tests, Cumulative Reviews, and in the Class Starter Quiz given in the Teacher's Edition.

For teachers who wish to obtain more information about what recent research implies about the teaching of algebra, we suggest the following publications:

Classroom Ideas from Research on Secondary School Mathematics by Donald Dessart and Marilyn Suydam
Research within Reach: Secondary School Mathematics by Mark Driscoll

Both of these publications can be purchased from the National Council of Teachers of Mathematics, 1906 Association Drive, Reston, Virginia 22091.

The publications *Every Minute Counts* and *Making Minutes Count Even More* by David R. Johnson contain a wealth of practical ideas for keeping students on task and teaching mathematics effectively. They can be obtained from Dale Seymour Publications, P.O. Box 10888, Palo Alto, CA 94303.

HEATH ALGEBRA frequently uses rectangles as models for multiplying and factoring polynomials. Manipulatives that facilitate demonstration of this model on the overhead projector and that can be used by individual students are available from Cuisenaire Co. of America, Inc., 12 Church St., P.O. D, New Rochelle, NY 10802, and from Nasco, 901 Jamesville Ave., Fort Atkinson, WI 53538.

Cooperative Learning

Teachers can consider having students work together in groups of two to five students for at least part of the time. This gives students the opportunity to learn from each other. Students also clarify their ideas about algebra by having the opportunity to express them. Small-group work can help the teacher meet the needs of individual students. A teacher may have difficulty getting around the classroom to provide individual attention to 30 students. Attending to 15 groups of 2 students or 10 groups of 3 students or 6 groups of 5 students is more manageable, provided the teacher insists that the students first seek help within the group. Then when the group asks for help, the teacher will be providing help not to just one student but to all of the students in the group.

In cooperative learning, the environment is structured so that each member of the group benefits when *all* members of the group learn. For example, if the group is assigned a problem, the group's work is not complete until the group can certify that each member of the group can do the problem. The teacher usually selects the groups. In most cases the groups are made as heterogeneous as possible, including different ability levels, boys and girls, and students from different backgrounds.

Small-group work is particularly effective for problem solving. Through talking to each other in small groups, students are able to clarify their thinking. In small groups, students are able to take risks and say things that they might be afraid to say in front of the whole class. There is a considerable body of research that indicates that cooperative learning results in higher achievement, more positive attitudes, and greater understanding and acceptance of other students regardless of ability, sex, race, ethnic background, social class, or handicapping conditions.

Information about cooperative learning can be obtained from the Cooperative Learning Center, 202 Pattee Hall, 150 Pillsbury Drive S.E., Minneapolis, MN 55455, or The Center for Social Organization of Schools, The Johns Hopkins University, 3505 N. Charles Street, Baltimore, MD 21218.

Pacing Algebra 1

The following chart suggests how 170 class days might be allocated to the chapters in the text (including reviews and tests) for three levels of ability, and suggests the sections that are appropriate for each level.

Basic Course

Chapter	1	2	3	4	5	6	7	8	9	10	11	Supplementary Topics
Days	12	14	19	17	17	16	19	23	10	11	12	0
Sections	all	all	all	all	all	all	all	all	all but 9-6, 9-8	all but 10-8	all but 11-4, 11-6, 11-7	none

Average Course

Chapter	1	2	3	4	5	6	7	8	9	10	11	Supplementary Topics
Days	11	13	17	16	16	15	18	22	11	12	15	4
Sections	all	all	all	all	all	all	all	all	all but 9-6, 9-8	all	all	Probability & Statistics

Enriched Course

Chapter	1	2	3	4	5	6	7	8	9	10	11	Supplementary Topics
Days	11	12	16	15	15	14	18	21	14	12	14	8
Sections	all	all	all	all	all	all	all	all	all	all	all	all

Based on the above allocation of class days, the chart on the following pages suggests the sections that might be taught over two days and an effective way to split those sections. The assignment guides that are provided with each lesson (in the side margin) should be used with each section that is taught in one day.

PACING CHART

Day	Basic Course	Average Course	Enriched Course
1	1-1	1-1	1-1
2	1-2	1-2	1-2
3	1-3 Discuss all examples & Class Ex.; Assign 1–47 odd	1-3	1-3
4	Assign 22–48 even, Review Ex., *Self-Quiz 1*	1-4	1-4
5	1-4	1-5	1-5
6	1-5	1-6 Discuss all examples & Class Ex.; Assign 1–39 odd	1-6 Discuss all examples & Class Ex.; Assign 1–41 odd, 42
7	1-6 Discuss examples 1–3 & Class Ex. 1–10; Assign 1–23 odd	Assign 22–40 even, 41–47, Review Ex. *Self-Quiz 2*	Assign 22–40 even, 43–56, Review Ex., *Self-Quiz 2*
8	Discuss examples 4–6 & Class Ex. 11–15; Assign 22, 24, 27–39 odd, Review Ex., *Self-Quiz 2*	1-7 Discuss all examples & Class Ex.; Assign 1–23 odd	1-7 Discuss all examples & Class Ex.; Assign 1–23 odd
9	1-7 Discuss all examples & Class Ex.; Assign 1–6	Assign 2–22 even, Review Ex.	Assign 14–22 even, 24–30, Review Ex.
10	Assign 7–12, Review Ex.	*Chapter Review*	*Chapter Review*
11	*Chapter Review*	*Chapter Test*	*Chapter Test*
12	*Chapter Test*	2-1	2-1
13	2-1	2-2	2-2
14	2-2	2-3	2-3
15	2-3	2-4	2-4
16	2-4	2-5	2-5
17	2-5	2-6	2-6
18	2-6 Discuss all examples & Class Ex.; Assign 1–35 odd	2-7	2-7
19	Assign 14–36 even, Review Ex., *Self-Quiz 2*	2-8 Discuss all examples & Class Ex.; Assign 17–37 odd	2-8
20	2-7	Assign 18–46 even, Review Ex., *Self-Quiz 3*	2-9 Discuss all examples & Class Ex.; Assign 1–11 odd
21	2-8 Discuss example 1 & Class Ex. 1–12; Assign 1–16	2-9 Discuss all examples & Class Ex.; Assign 1–11 odd	Assign 8–12 even, 13–16, Review Ex.
22	Discuss examples 2–3 & Class Ex. 13–24; Assign 17–34, Review Ex., *Self-Quiz 3*	Assign 8–12 even, Review Ex.	*Chapter Review*
23	2-9 Discuss all examples & Class Ex.; Assign 1–7 odd	*Chapter Review*	*Chapter Test*
24	Assign 2–8 even, Review Ex.	*Chapter Test*	3-1
25	*Chapter Review*	3-1	3-2

Day	Basic Course	Average Course	Enriched Course
26	*Chapter Test*	3-2	3-3
27	3-1	3-3	3-4
28	3-2	3-4	3-5
29	3-3 Discuss all examples & Class Ex.; Assign 1–23 odd	3-5 Discuss all examples & Class Ex.; Assign 5–45 odd	3-6
30	Assign 2–24 even, Review Ex., *Self-Quiz 1*	Assign 18–46 even, 47–56, Review Ex.	3-7
31	3-4	3-6	3-8
32	3-5 Discuss examples 1–3 & Class Ex.; Assign 1–27 odd	3-7	3-9 Discuss all examples & Class Ex.; Assign 9–21 odd, Review Ex.
33	Discuss example 4; Assign 18–28 even, 29–45 odd, Review Ex.	3-8	Assign 10–22 even, 23–27, *Self-Quiz 3*
34	3-6	3-9 Discuss all examples & Class Ex.; Assign 1–17 odd	3-10 Discuss all examples & Class Ex.; Assign 9–21 odd
35	3-7	Assign 10–18 even, 19–23, Review Ex., *Self-Quiz 3*	Assign 10–22 even, Review Ex.
36	3-8 Discuss all examples & Class Ex.; Assign 1–23 odd	3-10 Discuss all examples & Class Ex.; Assign 1–17 odd	*Chapter Review*
37	Assign 2–24 even, Review Ex.	Assign 10–18 even, Review Ex.	*Chapter Test*
38	3-9 Discuss all examples & Class Ex.; Assign 1–13 odd	*Chapter Review*	*Cumulative Review*
39	Assign 2–14 even, 15–18, Review Ex., *Self-Quiz 3*	*Chapter Test*	*Cumulative Test*
40	3-10 Discuss all examples & Class Ex.; Assign 1–9	*Cumulative Review*	4-1
41	Assign 10–14, Review Ex.	*Cumulative Test*	4-2
42	*Chapter Review*	4-1 Discuss all examples & Class Ex.; Assign 1–27 odd	4-3
43	*Chapter Test*	Assign 22–28 even, 29–38, Review Ex.	4-4
44	*Cumulative Review*	4-2	4-5
45	*Cumulative Test*	4-3	4-6
46	4-1 Discuss all examples & Class Ex.; Assign 1–27 odd	4-4	4-7 Discuss all examples & Class Ex.; Assign 1–29 odd
47	Assign 2–28 even, Review Ex.	4-5	Assign 26, 28, 30–33, Review Ex.
48	4-2	4-6	4-8
49	4-3 Discuss all examples & Class Ex.; Assign 1–33 odd	4-7 Discuss all examples & Class Ex.; Assign 1–23 odd	4-9 Discuss all examples & Class Ex.; Assign 7–27 odd
50	Assign 14–34 even, Review Ex., *Self-Quiz 1*	Assign 18–32 even, Review Ex.	Assign 18–28 even, 29–31, Review Ex., *Self-Quiz 3*
51	4-4	4-8	4-10 Discuss all examples & Class Ex.; Assign 1–25 odd

Day	Basic Course	Average Course	Enriched Course
52	4-5	4-9 Discuss all examples & Class Ex.; Assign 1–21 odd	Assign 14–24 even, 26–33, Review Ex.
53	4-6	Assign 18–22 even, 23–28, Review Ex., *Self-Quiz 3*	*Chapter Review*
54	4-7 Discuss all examples & Class Ex.; Assign 1–15 odd	4-10 Discuss all examples & Class Ex.; Assign 1–21 odd	*Chapter Test*
55	Assign 6–16 even, 17–25 odd, Review Ex.	Assign 2–22 even, 23–28, Review Ex.	5-1
56	4-8	*Chapter Review*	5-2
57	4-9 Discuss all examples & Class Ex.; Assign 1–16	*Chapter Test*	5-3
58	Assign 17–22, Review Ex., *Self-Quiz 3*	5-1	5-4 Discuss all examples & Class Ex.; Assign 7–21 odd
59	4-10 Discuss all examples & Class Ex.; Assign 1–21 odd	5-2	Assign 23–30, Review Ex.
60	Assign 2–22 even, Review Ex.	5-3	5-5
61	*Chapter Review*	5-4 Discuss all examples & Class Ex.; Assign 7–21 odd	5-6 Discuss all examples & Class Ex.; Assign 35–59 odd
62	*Chapter Test*	Assign 16–22 even, 23–28, Review Ex.	Assign 42–60 even, 64–66, Review Ex.
63	5-1	5-5 Discuss all examples & Class Ex.; Assign 17–35 odd	5-7
64	5-2	Assign 18–34 even, Review Ex., *Self-Quiz 2*	5-8 Discuss all examples & Class Ex.; Assign 17–41 odd
65	5-3 Discuss all examples & Class Ex.; Assign 1–21 odd	5-6 Discuss examples 1–2 & Class Ex. 1–4; Assign 15–21 odd, 41–55 odd	Assign 36–42 even, 43–51, Review Ex., *Self-Quiz 3*
66	Assign 12–22 even, Review Ex., *Self-Quiz 1*	Discuss examples 3–5 & Class Ex. 5–7; Assign 23–39 odd, 56–60, Review Ex.	5-9 Discuss all examples & Class Ex.; Assign 9–27 odd
67	5-4 Discuss all examples & Class Ex.; Assign 1–13 odd	5-7	Assign 29–39, Review Ex.
68	Assign 2–14 even, Review Ex.	5-8 Discuss all examples & Class Ex.; Assign 1–41 odd	*Chapter Review*
69	5-5 Discuss all examples & Class Ex.; Assign 1–23 odd	Assign 18–42 even, Review Ex., *Self-Quiz 3*	*Chapter Test*
70	Assign 2–24 even, Review Ex., *Self-Quiz 2*	5-9 Discuss all examples & Class Ex.; Assign 9–27 odd	6-1 Discuss all examples & Class Ex.; Assign 3–30 multiples of 3
71	5-6 Discuss examples 1–2 & Class Ex. 1–4; Assign 1–21 odd	Assign 24–28 even, 29–35 Review Ex.	Assign 31–39, Review Ex.
72	Discuss examples 3–5 & Class Ex. 5–7; Assign 16–22 even, 23–39 odd, Review Ex.	*Chapter Review*	6-2
73	5-7	*Chapter Test*	6-3

Day	Basic Course	Average Course	Enriched Course
74	5-8 Discuss all examples & Class Ex.; Assign 1–15 odd	6-1 Discuss all examples & Class Ex.; Assign 3–30 multiples of 3	6-4 Discuss all examples & Class Ex.; Assign 1–23 odd
75	Assign 2–16 even, Review Ex., *Self-Quiz 3*	Assign 25, 26, 28, 29, 31–36, Review Ex.	Assign 22, 24–29, Review Ex.
76	5-9 Discuss all examples & Class Ex.; Assign 1–21 odd	6-2 Discuss all examples & Class Ex.; Assign 1–29 odd	6-5
77	Assign 10–22 even, Review Ex.	Assign 28, 30–42, Review Ex.	6-6
78	*Chapter Review*	6-3	6-7 Discuss all examples & Class Ex.; Assign 3–17 odd
79	*Chapter Test*	6-4 Discuss all examples & Class Ex.; Assign 1–19 odd	Assign 18–23, Review Ex.
80	6-1 Discuss all examples & Class Ex.; Assign 1–21 odd	Assign 18, 20, 21–26, Review Ex.	*Chapter Review*
81	Assign 12–22 even, 23–30, Review Ex.	6-5	*Chapter Test*
82	6-2 Discuss examples 1–2 & all Class Ex.; Assign 1–23 odd	6-6	*Cumulative Review*
83	Discuss example 3, Assign 10–24 even, 27, 28, 32, Review Ex.	6-7 Discuss all examples & Class Ex.; Assign 1–13 odd	*Cumulative Test*
84	6-3	Assign 14–19, Review Ex.	7-1
85	6-4 Discuss all examples & Class Ex.; Assign 1–15 odd	*Chapter Review*	7-2
86	Assign 8–14 even, 16–20, Review Ex.	*Chapter Test*	7-3
87	6-5	*Cumulative Review*	7-4
88	6-6 Discuss all examples & Class Ex.; Assign 1–17 odd	*Cumulative Test*	7-5 Discuss all examples & Class Ex.; Assign 1–27 odd, 29–34
89	Assign 17–25, Review Ex., *Self-Quiz 2*	7-1	Assign 35–51, Review Ex.
90	6-7 Discuss all examples & Class Ex.; Assign 1–9 odd	7-2	7-6 Discuss all examples & Class Ex.; Assign 4–32 multiples of 4, 33–53 odd
91	Assign 8, 10–13, Review Ex.	7-3	Assign 54–64, Review Ex., *Self-Quiz 2*
92	*Chapter Review*	7-4	7-7 Discuss all examples & Class Ex.; Assign 27–61 odd
93	*Chapter Test*	7-5 Discuss all examples & Class Ex.; Assign 1–27 odd	Assign 63–70, Review Ex.
94	*Cumulative Review*	Assign 29–43, Review Ex.	7-8 Discuss all examples & Class Ex.; Assign 1–57 multiples of 3
95	*Cumulative Test*	7-6 Discuss all examples & Class Ex.; Assign 1–45 odd	Assign 58–73, Review Ex.

Day	Basic Course	Average Course	Enriched Course
96	7-1	Assign 47–53 odd, 54–60, Review Ex., *Self-Quiz 2*	7-9 Discuss all examples & Class Ex.; Assign 15–51 multiples of 3
97	7-2	7-7 Discuss all examples & Class Ex.; Assign 11–49 odd	Assign 53–62, Review Ex., *Self-Quiz 3*
98	7-3 Discuss all examples & Class Ex.; Assign 1–17 odd	Assign 28–50 even, 51–61 odd, Review Ex.	7-10 Discuss all examples & Class Ex.; Assign 15–48 multiples of 3
99	Assign 2–18 even, Review Ex., *Self-Quiz 1*	7-8 Discuss all examples & Class Ex.; Assign 1–35 odd	Assign 51–58, Review Ex.
100	7-4	Assign 37–63 odd, Review Ex.	*Chapter Review*
101	7-5 Discuss all examples & Class Ex.; Assign 1–27 odd	7-9 Discuss all examples & Class Ex.; Assign 7–39 odd	*Chapter Test*
102	Assign 8–28 even, Review Ex.	Assign 41–52, Review Ex., *Self-Quiz 3*	8-1
103	7-6 Discuss examples 1–4 & Class Ex. 1–15, Assign 1–31 odd	7-10 Discuss all examples & Class Ex.; Assign 9–39 odd	8-2
104	Discuss examples 5–6 & Class Ex. 16–18, Assign 22–32 even, 37–45 odd, Review Ex., *Self-Quiz 2*	Assign 41–51, Review Ex.	8-3
105	7-7 Discuss examples 1–4 & Class Ex. 1–15, Assign 1–37 odd	*Chapter Review*	8-4 Discuss all examples & Class Ex.; Assign 9–45 odd
106	Discuss example 5 & Class Ex. 16–17; Assign 28–38 even, 39–49 odd, Review Ex.	*Chapter Test*	Assign 47–59 odd, Review Ex.
107	7-8 Discuss examples 1–2 & Class Ex. 1–9; Assign 1–23 odd	8-1	8-5
108	Discuss examples 3–4 & Class Ex. 10–12; Assign 14–36 even, Review Ex.	8-2	8-6 Discuss all examples & Class Ex.; Assign 7–27 odd
109	7-9 Discuss all examples & Class Ex.; Assign 1–35 odd	8-3 Discuss all examples & Class Ex.; Assign 1–23 odd	Assign 30–35, Review Ex., *Self-Quiz 2*
110	Assign 14–40 even, Review Ex., *Self-Quiz 3*	Assign 25–36, Review Ex., *Self-Quiz 1*	8-7
111	7-10 Discuss all examples & Class Ex.; Assign 1–27 odd	8-4 Discuss examples 1–3 & Class Ex. 1–4, 6–9; Assign 1–11 odd, 17–37 odd	8-8 Discuss all examples & Class Ex.; Assign 1–47 odd
112	Assign 29–39 odd, Review Ex.	Discuss examples 4–5 & Class Ex. 5, 10; Assign 13–16, 39–50, Review Ex.	Assign 49–58, Review Ex.
113	*Chapter Review*	8-5	8-9 Discuss all examples & Class Ex.; Assign 11–35 odd
114	*Chapter Test*	8-6 Discuss all examples & Class Ex.; Assign 3–23 odd	Assign 34, 36–41, Review Ex.
115	8-1	Assign 24–31, Review Ex., *Self-Quiz 2*	8-10 Discuss all examples & Class Ex.; Assign 21–43 odd

Day	Basic Course	Average Course	Enriched Course
116	8-2	8-7	Assign 44–52, Review Ex., *Self-Quiz 3*
117	8-3 Discuss all examples & Class Ex.; Assign 1–23 odd	8-8 Discuss all examples & Class Ex.; Assign 1–41 odd	8-11 Discuss all examples & Class Ex.; Assign 3–45 multiples of 3
118	Assign 10–24 even, Review Ex., *Self-Quiz 1*	Assign 40, 42–52, Review Ex.	Assign 46–51, Review Ex.
119	8-4 Discuss examples 1–3 & Class Ex. 1–4, 6–9; Assign 1–11 odd, 17–31 odd	8-9 Discuss all examples & Class Ex.; Assign 1–25 odd	*Chapter Review*
120	Assign 18–32 even, 33, 34, Review Ex.	Assign 27–36, Review Ex.	*Chapter Test*
121	8-5 Discuss examples 1–3 & Class Ex. 1–5; Assign 1–31 odd	8-10 Discuss all examples & Class Ex.; Assign 3–39 multiples of 3	*Cumulative Review*
122	Discuss example 4 & Class Ex. 6–7; Assign 10–36 even, Review Ex.	Assign 41–48, Review Ex. *Self-Quiz 3*	*Cumulative Test*
123	8-6 Discuss examples 1–2 & Class Ex. 1–4; Assign 1–15 odd	8-11 Discuss all examples & Class Ex.; Assign 1–39 odd	9-1
124	Discuss example 3 & Class Ex. 5; Assign 14, 16–20, Review Ex., *Self-Quiz 2*	Assign 41–48, Review Ex.	9-2 Discuss all examples & Class Ex.; Assign 3–60 multiples of 3
125	8-7	*Chapter Review*	Assign 62–69, Review Ex., *Self-Quiz 1*
126	8-8 Discuss all examples & Class Ex.; Assign 1–41 odd	*Chapter Test*	9-3
127	Assign 24–42 even, Review Ex.	*Cumulative Review*	9-4
128	8-9 Discuss all examples & Class Ex.; Assign 1–19 odd	*Cumulative Test*	9-5
129	Assign 12–26 even, Review Ex.	9-1	9-6 Discuss all examples & Class Ex.; Assign 1–37 odd
130	8-10 Discuss all examples & Class Ex.; Assign 1–25 odd	9-2 Discuss all examples & Class Ex.; Assign 1–43 odd	Assign 39–55 odd, Review Ex.
131	Assign 27–39 odd, Review Ex., *Self-Quiz 3*	Assign 45–61 odd, Review Ex., *Self-Quiz 1*	9-7 Discuss all examples & Class Ex.; Assign 15–35 multiples of 3
132	8-11 Discuss all examples & Class Ex.; Assign 1–39 odd	9-3	Assign 41–44, Review Ex., *Self-Quiz 3*
133	Assign 26–40 even, Review Ex.	9-4	9-8 Discuss all examples & Class Ex.; Assign 9–30 multiples of 3
134	*Chapter Review*	9-5 Discuss all examples & Class Ex.; Assign 1–27 odd	Assign 31–43, Review Ex.
135	*Chapter Test*	Assign 29–41 odd, Review Ex., *Self-Quiz 2*	*Chapter Review*
136	*Cumulative Review*	9-7 Discuss all examples & Class Ex.; Assign 1–27 odd	*Chapter Test*
137	*Cumulative Test*	Assign 29–38, Review Ex.	10-1

Day	Basic Course	Average Course	Enriched Course
138	9-1	*Chapter Review*	10-2
139	9-2 Discuss all examples & Class Ex.; Assign 1–43 odd	*Chapter Test*	10-3
140	Assign 20–44 even, Review Ex., *Self-Quiz 1*	10-1	10-4
141	9-3	10-2	10-5
142	9-4	10-3	10-6
143	9-5 Discuss examples 1–2 & all Class Ex.; Assign 1–17 odd	10-4	10-7
144	Discuss example 3; Assign 19–29, Review Ex., *Self-Quiz 2*	10-5	10-8 Discuss all examples & Class Ex.; Assign 3–39 multiples of 3, 28
145	9-7	10-6	Discuss example 4; Assign 41–46, Review Ex., *Self-Quiz 3*
146	*Chapter Review*	10-7	10-9
147	*Chapter Test*	10-8 Discuss all examples & Class Ex.; Assign 1–27 odd, 28	*Chapter Review*
148	10-1	Assign 29–40, Review Ex., *Self-Quiz 3*	*Chapter Test*
149	10-2	10-9	11-1
150	10-3 Discuss all examples & Class Ex.; Assign 1–19 odd	*Chapter Review*	11-2
151	Assign 21–33 odd, Review Ex., *Self-Quiz 1*	*Chapter Test*	11-3
152	10-4	11-1	11-4 Discuss all examples & Class Ex.; Assign 15–48 multiples of 3
153	10-5	11-2 Discuss all examples & Class Ex; Assign 3–24 multiples of 3, 25	Assign 50–54, Review Ex., *Self-Quiz 2*
154	10-6	Assign 27–34, 36, 38, Review Ex., *Self-Quiz 1*	11-5
155	10-7	11-3	11-6
156	10-9	11-4 Discuss examples 1–3 & Class Ex. 1–8,; Assign 3–36 multiples of 3	11-7
157	*Chapter Review*	Discuss example 4 & Class Ex. 9; Assign 37–49 odd, Review Ex., *Self-Quiz 2*	*Chapter Review*
158	*Chapter Test*	11-5	*Chapter Test*
159	11-1	11-6	*Cumulative Review*
160	11-2 Discuss all examples & Class Ex.; Assign 1–11 odd	11-7	
161	11-2 Assign 13–25 odd, Review Ex., *Self-Quiz 1*	*Chapter Review*	*Cumulative Test*

Day	Basic Course	Average Course	Enriched Course
162	11-3	*Chapter Test*	
163	11-5 Discuss all examples & Class Ex.; Assign 1–25 odd	*Cumulative Review*	*Probability*
164	Assign 26–36, Review Ex.		*Compound Events*
165	*Chapter Review*	*Cumulative Test*	*Statistics*
166	*Chapter Test*		*Variation*
167	*Cumulative Review*	*Probability*	*Similar Triangles*
168		*Compound Events*	*The Tangent Ratio*
169	*Cumulative Test*	*Statistics*	*Sine and Cosine*
170		*Variation*	*Using Trigonometric Ratios*

Order of Chapters

If you wish to teach factoring earlier in the year, you may wish to use Chapter 7 before Chapters 5 and 6. To help you plan other organizations of the course, the arrows in the following chart indicate which chapters are prerequisites for other chapters.

$$1 \rightarrow 2 \rightarrow 3 \rightarrow 4 \rightarrow 7 \rightarrow 8 \rightarrow 10 \rightarrow 11$$
$$5 \rightarrow 6 \rightarrow 9$$

When using chapters out of sequence, assign only those Review Exercises that apply to chapters that have been taught.

Teaching Algebra 1 over Two Years

If you wish to use this text for a two-year course you might teach Chapters 1–6 the first year. You could spend an average of three days on each section, using the A-level exercises, Practice Worksheets, and Review Exercises.

For the second year, you could review the first six chapters by using their Chapter Summaries, Chapter Reviews, Chapter Tests, and Cumulative Reviews. However, don't spend an excessive time on the first six chapters. Get started on new material as soon as possible and use the Review Exercises in each section to rebuild skills taught the first year.

Using Computers in Teaching Algebra

Simple computer programs that use, investigate, or extend the algebra topic being studied can be a useful supplement to an algebra course. Students with little programming experience can use programs that are provided for them; students with more experience can improve and extend those programs; and other students can write their own programs. These kinds of computer activities are provided in three places in HEATH ALGEBRA: (1) Extensions in the student text (see page 28 for an example), (2) Computer Worksheets in the Teacher's Resource Binder, and (3) Computer Extensions for appropriate lessons as suggested in the wide margin of the Teacher's Edition (see page 4 for an example).

The Computer Worksheets in the Teacher's Resource Binder are shown here in reduced format.

Computer Worksheet 1

NAME _____

EVALUATING EXPRESSIONS

The BASIC computer language uses rules of computation that are similar to the rules of algebra. The following table will illustrate these similarities. Execute each BASIC statement by typing the statement and then pressing the Return key. These exercises will verify that the answers are the same.

	Evaluate in algebra		Execute in BASIC†
1.	$3 \div 2 + 5 \cdot 8$	41.5	PRINT 3 / 2 + 5 * 8
2.	2^{10}	1024	PRINT 2 ↑ 10
3.	$\frac{5+7}{4}$	3	PRINT (5 + 7) / 4
4.	If x is 8, find $\frac{x+7}{5}$	3	X = 8 PRINT (X + 7) / 5
5.	If x is 7, find $x^2 + 5x - 8$	76	X = 7 PRINT X ↑ 2 + 5 * X - 8
6.	If x is 3, find $\frac{(x^3 - 2x + 3)}{3x}$	2.66	X = 3 PRINT (X ↑ 3 - 2 * X + 3) / (3 * X)
7.	If x is 2, find $\frac{(x+2)(x-3)}{(x-4)}$	2	X = 2 PRINT ((X + 2) * (X - 3)) / (X - 4)

†BASIC programming notes

Operator	Algebra symbol	BASIC symbol
Grouping	( )	( )
Multiply	·	*
Divide	÷	/
Add	+	+
Raise to a power	x^2	X ↑ 2
Subtract	−	−
Assignment	=	=

© D.C. Heath & Co.

Use anytime after Section 1-6

Computer Worksheet 2

NAME _____

DEFINITION OF ABSOLUTE VALUE

The following program will help you learn about the *absolute value* of numbers. The program will print three columns of numbers labeled "X", "−X", and "| X |". Enter and run the program.

```
10  PRINT "X", "−X", "| X |"
↑20  FOR X = −5 TO 5
30  PRINT X, −X, ABS (X)
↑40  NEXT X
50  END
```

■ Examine the three columns of numbers produced by this program and answer the following questions.

1. For which values of X is the column labeled X equal to the column labeled | X |? X = 0, 1, 2, 3, 4, 5 _____

2. For which values of X is the column labeled −X equal to the column labeled | X |? X = −5, −4, −3, −2, −1, 0 _____

3. For which values of X are the column labeled X and the column labeled −X both equal to the column labeled | X |? X = 0 _____

4. From the above statements, write a formal definition of absolute value by using < and ≥ to fill in the blanks in the following statements.

| X | = X when X ≥ 0.

| X | = −X when X < 0.

†BASIC programming note
The FOR and NEXT statements are used in pairs to define a loop which repeatedly executes the statements enclosed by the FOR and NEXT statements. In this FOR statement −5 is the initial value of X and each repetition of the loop increases X by 1. When the loop has been executed for the upper limit 5, the program jumps to the statement below the NEXT statement.

Use anytime after Section 2-1
© D.C. Heath & Co.

Computer Worksheet 3

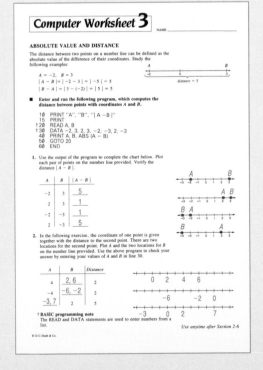

Computer Worksheet 4

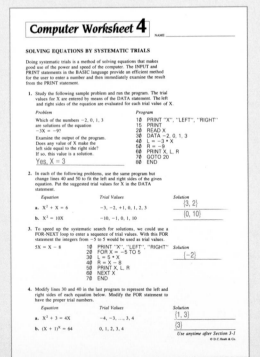

Computer Worksheet 5

NAME _____

EVALUATING FORMULAS

To evaluate a formula, you can write a short BASIC program. The INPUT command enables you to enter values for variables. Algebraic problems are stated below and the first two BASIC programs are given. Run the programs and analyze the output.

Algebraic Problem

BASIC Program

1. Find the areas A of a square with sides S equal to 1, 2, 4, 10, 100.
   Formula: $A = S^2$

   $A = 1, 4, 16, 100, 10000$

```
10  PRINT "ENTER S";
†20  INPUT S
†30  A = S ↑ 2
40  PRINT A
50  END
```

2. Find the areas A and perimeters P for rectangles with the following dimensions:

Length	L	2	4	10	100
Width	W	1	3	4	90

   Formulas: $A = LW$, $P = 2(L + W)$

   $A = 2, 12, 40, 9000$;

   $P = 6, 14, 28, 380$

```
10  PRINT "ENTER L, W";
20  INPUT L, W
30  A = L • W
40  P = 2 • (L + W)
50  PRINT A, P
60  END
```

3. Find the surface areas A and volumes V of cubes with edges E equal to 1, 2, 4, 10, 12.
   Formulas: $A = 6E^2$, $V = E^3$

   $A = 6, 24, 96, 600, 864$;

   $V = 1, 8, 64, 1000, 1728$

   Using problems 1 and 2 as models, write and run a BASIC program to solve this problem.
```
10  PRINT "ENTER E";
20  INPUT E
30  A = 6 • E ↑ 2
40  V = E ↑ 3
50  PRINT E, A, V
60  END
```

4. Find the areas A for triangles with the given bases B and heights H.

B	3	4	5	100
H	6	9	6	100

   Formula: $A = \dfrac{BH}{2}$

   $A = 9, 18, 15, 5000$

   Write and run a BASIC program to solve this problem.
```
10  PRINT "ENTER B, H";
20  INPUT B, H
30  A = (B • H) / 2
40  PRINT B, H, A
50  END
```

† *BASIC programming notes*

INPUT S   The computer will type a question mark, then wait for you to type a numerical value for S and press Return. $A = S ↑ 2$ The value of S is placed in the formula and the calculated result is placed in variable A.

Use anytime after Section 3-8

© D.C. Heath & Co.

Computer Worksheet 6

NAME _____

SCIENTIFIC NOTATION

Computers and calculators use scientific notation to express large and small numbers. It is interesting to experiment with a computer or a calculator to learn when its representation of numbers changes from standard decimal notation to scientific notation. Enter and run the programs below to find out.

```
5   PRINT "X", "10 ↑ I"
10  FOR I = 0 TO 12
20  X = 9.87654321987 • 10 ↑ I
30  PRINT X, 10 ↑
40  NEXT I
50  END
```

```
5   PRINT "X", "10 ↑ -I"
10  FOR I = 0 TO 12
20  X = 9.876543219 • 10 ↑ (−I)
30  PRINT X, 10 ↑ (−I)
40  NEXT I
50  END
```

1. How many digits does your computer print for each number?
   Answers will vary. (Check your computer manual.)

2. How large is the number when the computer switches from standard decimal notation to scientific notation? Answers will vary.

3. How small is the number when the computer switches from standard decimal notation to scientific notation? Answers will vary.

■ **Modify the above programs to research the following questions:**

4. On the first program, increase the upper limit of the FOR statement to find the largest number the computer handles before it prints an overflow error. 10 FOR I = 0 TO 50

5. Make a similar change on the second program to find the smallest number the computer handles before it no longer prints an answer.
   10 FOR I = 0 TO 50

6. Continue your research by changing the base factor from 10 to a smaller number n. Does a change in base affect the answers above?
   Yes, because $10^I \neq n^J$ for all positive integers n, I, and J, $n \neq 10$.

Use anytime after Section 4-4

© D.C. Heath & Co.

Computer Worksheet 7

NAME _____

GRAPHING EQUATIONS

When graphing an equation in two variables, the tables of values can be generated by a computer. The following program produces such a table for the equation $y = 2x + 5$. Notice that the equation is used in line 30. Run the given program and complete the table. Then draw the graph.

```
10  PRINT "X", "Y"
15  PRINT
†20  FOR X = −4 TO 4 STEP 2
30  Y = 2 • X + 5
40  PRINT X, Y
50  NEXT X
60  END
```

x	y
−4	−3
−2	1
0	5
2	9
4	13

■ **Graph the following equations by solving each equation for *y* and using this form of the equation to modify line 30. Then complete the tables and draw the graphs.**

1. $x − y = 6$

x	y
−4	−10
−2	−8
0	−6
2	−4
4	−2

2. $2x − y = 8$

x	y
−4	−16
−2	−12
0	−8
2	−4
4	0

3. $x + y + 5 = 0$

x	y
−4	−1
−2	−3
0	−5
2	−7
4	−9

4. $x − 3y − 6 = 0$

x	y
−4	3.33...
−2	−2.66...
0	−2
2	−1.33...
4	−0.66...

■ **Modify line 20 so that the amount of increase is 0.5. Then modify line 30, complete the tables, and draw the graphs.**

5. $y = x^2$

x	−4.0	−3.5	−3.0	−2.5	−2.0	−1.5	−1.0	−0.5	0	0.5	1.0	1.5	2.0	2.5	3.0	3.5	4.0
y	16	12.25	9	6.25	4	2.25	1	0.25	0	0.25	1	2.25	4	6.25	9	12.25	16

6. $y = x^2 − 4$

x	−4.0	−3.5	−3.0	−2.5	−2.0	−1.5	−1.0	−0.5	0	0.5	1.0	1.5	2.0	2.5	3.0	3.5	4.0
y	12.0	8.25	5.0	2.25	0	−1.75	−3.0	−3.75	−4.0	−3.75	−3.0	−1.75	0	2.25	5.0	8.25	12.0

† *BASIC programming note:* The FOR statement normally increases the first value by 1 until the last value is reached; but the amount of the increase can be changed, for example to 2, by adding "STEP 2."

Use anytime after Section 5-3

© D.C. Heath & Co.

Computer Worksheet 8

NAME _____

SLOPE OF A LINEAR EQUATION

Linear equations are easily graphed when they are in the form $Y = MX + B$. Use the following program to help you see how the values of M are related to the graphs of the functions.

```
10  PRINT "FOR Y = M • X + B ENTER M, B";
20  INPUT M, B
30  PRINT "X", "Y"
40  FOR X = −5 TO 5
50  Y = M • X + B
60  PRINT X, Y
70  NEXT X
80  END
```

1. Run the program for B = 0 and M equal to 2, 1, 0 +1, and −2. Draw graphs of these five linear functions.

2. For each linear function you have graphed, tell whether the values of Y increase or decrease as the values of X increase from −5 to 5.

M	B	Does Y increase or decrease?
2	0	Increases
1	0	Increases
0	0	Stays the same
−1	0	Decreases
−2	0	Decreases

3. Which values of M give increasing values for Y? M = 1, M = 2 (M > 0)

4. Which values of M give decreasing values for Y? M = −1, M = −2 (M < 0)

5. Which value of M gives no change in the value for Y? M = 0

Use anytime after Section 5-6

© D.C. Heath & Co.

T33

Computer Worksheet 9

NAME _____

INTERCEPT OF A LINEAR EQUATION

Linear equations are easily graphed when they are in the form
Y = MX + B. Use the following program to help you see how
the values of B are related to the graphs of the functions.

```
10  PRINT "FOR Y = M * X + B ENTER M, B";
20  INPUT M, B
30  PRINT "X", "Y"
40  FOR X = −5 TO 5
50  Y = M * X + B
60  PRINT X, Y
70  NEXT X
80  END
```

1. Run the program for M = 2 and B equal to −6, −2, 0 3, and 5.
   Draw graphs of these five linear functions.

2. Describe in your own words how the value of B is related to the
   graph of the linear function.

   The value of B is the same as the y-intercept of
   each graph.

3. Use the above program to help you determine and write the
   equation for each line shown.

Line a −X + Y = 4
Line b −X + Y = −4
Line c X + Y = 4
Line d X + Y = −4

Use anytime after Section 5-7

© D.C. Heath & Co.

Computer Worksheet 10

NAME _____

EQUATIONS FOR PARALLEL OR PERPENDICULAR LINES

The following program takes an equation of a line in variables X and Y
in the form DX + EY = F and calculates the slope M and Y-intercept
B. Enter and run this program to find the slope and Y-intercept of the
following equations.

```
10  PRINT "FOR DX + EY = F, ENTER D, E, F";
20  INPUT D, E, F
†30  IF E = 0 THEN 80
40  M = −D / E
50  B = F / E
60  PRINT "SLOPE = "; M; " Y-INTERCEPT = "; B
70  GOTO 90
80  PRINT "VERTICAL LINE AT X = "; F / D
90  END
```

	Equation	Slope	Y-intercept
1.	2X + 3Y = 6	−0.66...	2
2.	3X + 2Y = 6	−1.5	3
3.	2X − 3Y = 6	0.66...	−2
4.	−4X + 6Y = −9	0.66...	−1.5
5.	3X = 5	Vertical line	None
6.	2Y = 12	0	6

■ Use the completed chart.

7. Which pairs of equations have the same slope? Equations 3
   and 4

8. Which lines are parallel? Lines 3 and 4

9. Which pairs of equations have slopes that are negative reciprocals?
   Equations 2 and 3; Equations 2 and 4

10. Which lines are perpendicular? Lines 2 and 3; 2 and 4

11. Which lines are vertical? Line 5

12. Which lines are horizontal? Line 6

†**BASIC programming note**
The IF-THEN statement allows the program to make decisions. If
the condition between the words IF and THEN is true, the
computer executes the THEN-part of the statement. If the condition
between the words IF and THEN is false, the computer goes on to
the next line.

Use anytime after Section 6-3

© D.C. Heath & Co.

Computer Worksheet 11

NAME _____

SOLVING SYSTEMS OF EQUATIONS BY GRAPHING

This program computes the slope and Y-intercept for an equation in the
form DX + EY = F.

```
10  PRINT "FOR DX + EY = F, ENTER D, E, F";
20  INPUT D, E, F
30  IF E = 0 THEN 80
40  M = −D / E
50  B = F / E
60  PRINT "SLOPE = "; M;" Y-INTERCEPT = "; B
70  GOTO 90
80  PRINT "VERTICAL LINE AT X = "; F / D
90  END
```

■ Use the program to find the slope and Y-intercept of the
following equations. Sketch the graphs of the equations to
solve each system.

1. Equations	Slope	Y-intercept
2X + Y = 6	−2	6
X + Y = 3	−1	3

The solution of the system of equations is {(3, 0)}

2. Equations	Slope	Y-intercept
X + 2Y = 5	−0.5	2.5
−5X − 10Y = −25	−0.5	2.5

The solution of the system of equations is {(X, Y): X + 2Y = 5}

3. Equations	Slope	Y-intercept
X + Y = 6	−1	6
X − Y = 4	1	−4

The solution of the system of equations is {(5, 1)}

4. Equations	Slope	Y-intercept
3X − 5Y = 14	0.6	−2.8
1.2X − 2.59 = 7	Vertical line	None

The solution of the system of equations is {(8, 2)}

Use anytime after Section 6-7

© D.C. Heath & Co.

Computer Worksheet 12

NAME _____

GREATEST COMMON FACTOR

The Euclidean algorithm uses successive divisions to find the greatest
common factor (GCF) of two integers. The following program uses the
Euclidean algorithm to find the GCF of two positive integers A and B.

```
10  PRINT "ENTER INTEGERS A, B";
20  INPUT A, B
30  IF A > B THEN N = B: D = A: GOTO 60
40  IF A < B THEN N = A: D = B: GOTO 60
50  D = A: GOTO 100
†60  Q = INT (N / D)
70  R = N − D * Q
80  IF R = 0 THEN 100
90  N = D: D = R: GOTO 60
100 PRINT "GCF OF ";A;" AND ";B;" IS ";D
110 END
```

■ Use the program to find the GCF of each pair of integers.

	A	B	GCF		A	B	GCF
1.	35	49	7	2.	116	20	4
3.	1024	400	16	4.	17	34	17
5.	15	63	3				

■ Suppose each pair of integers in exercises 1–5 is used to define
a rational number $\frac{A}{B}$. Use the GCF you found to write each
rational number in its lowest terms.

6. $\frac{35}{49}$ = 5/7   7. $\frac{116}{20}$ = 29/5   8. $\frac{1024}{400}$ = 64/25

9. $\frac{17}{34}$ = 1/2   10. $\frac{15}{63}$ = 5/21

The least common multiple (LCM) of two integers A and B can be
computed by multiplying A and B and dividing by their GCF.

$$LCM \text{ of } A, B = \frac{AB}{GCF \text{ of } A, B}$$

11. Modify the above program to print the LCM of A and B by adding
    a statement, numbered 95, that uses the formula above.

    95 PRINT "LCM OF ";A;" AND"; B; "IS"; (A * B) / D

†**BASIC programming note**
In this program, INT (N / D) indicates that the greatest whole
number of N ÷ D is accepted as the quotient.

Use anytime after Section 7-2

© D.C. Heath & Co.

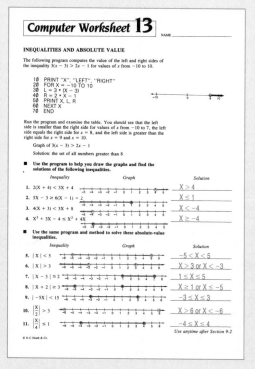

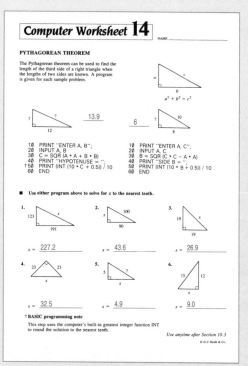

Computer Worksheet 13

NAME _____

INEQUALITIES AND ABSOLUTE VALUE

The following program computes the value of the left and right sides of
the inequality $3(x - 3) > 2x - 1$ for values of x from -10 to 10.

```
10  PRINT "X", "LEFT", "RIGHT"
20  FOR X = -10 TO 10
30  L = 3 * (X - 3)
40  R = 2 * X - 1
50  PRINT X, L, R
60  NEXT X
70  END
```

Run the program and examine the table. You should see that the left
side is smaller than the right side for values of x from -10 to 7, the left
side equals the right side for $x = 8$, and the left side is greater than the
right side for $x = 9$ and $x = 10$.

Graph of $3(x - 3) > 2x - 1$

Solution: the set of all numbers greater than 8

■ Use the program to help you draw the graphs and find the
solutions of the following inequalities.

	Inequality	Graph	Solution
1.	$2(X + 4) < 3X + 4$		$X > 4$
2.	$5X - 3 \geq 6(X - 1) + 2$		$X \leq 1$
3.	$4(X < 3X + 8$		$X < -4$
4.	$X^2 + 3X - 4 \leq X^2 + 4X$		$X \geq -4$

■ Use the same program and method to solve these absolute-value
inequalities.

	Inequality	Graph	Solution
5.	$|X| < 5$		$-5 < X < 5$
6.	$|X| > 3$		$X > 3$ or $X < -3$
7.	$|X - 3| \leq 2$		$1 \leq X \leq 5$
8.	$|X + 2| \geq 3$		$X \geq 1$ or $X \leq -5$
9.	$|-5X| < 15$		$-3 \leq X \leq 3$
10.	$\left|\frac{X}{2}\right| > 3$		$X > 6$ or $X < -6$
11.	$\left|\frac{X}{4}\right| \leq 1$		$-4 \leq X \leq 4$

Use anytime after Section 9-2

© D.C. Heath & Co.

Computer Worksheet 14

NAME _____

PYTHAGOREAN THEOREM

The Pythagorean theorem can be used to find the
length of the third side of a right triangle when
the lengths of two sides are known. A program
is given for each sample problem.

$$a^2 + b^2 = c^2$$

```
10  PRINT "ENTER A, B";
20  INPUT A, B
30  C = SQR (A * A + B * B)
40  PRINT "HYPOTENUSE = ";
†50 PRINT (INT (10 * C + 0.5)) / 10
60  END
```

```
10  PRINT "ENTER A, C";
20  INPUT A, C
30  B = SQR (C * C - A * A)
40  PRINT "SIDE B = ";
50  PRINT (INT (10 * B + 0.5)) / 10
60  END
```

■ Use either program above to solve for x to the nearest tenth.

1. $x = 227.2$ 2. $x = 43.6$ 3. $x = 26.9$

4. $x = 32.5$ 5. $x = 4.9$ 6. $x = 9.0$

† **BASIC programming note**
This step uses the computer's built-in greatest integer function INT
to round the solution to the nearest tenth.

Use anytime after Section 10.3

© D.C. Heath & Co.

Computer Worksheet 15

NAME _____

DISTANCE FORMULA

The distance between two points with coordinates (X_1, Y_1) and
(X_2, Y_2) is given by the formula:

$$D = \sqrt{(X_2 - X_1)^2 + (Y_2 - Y_1)^2}$$

The following program asks you to enter the coordinates of the vertices
of a triangle. It then calculates and prints the lengths of the three sides.
Use the results to classify the triangle as isosceles (two congruent
sides), equilateral (three congruent sides), or scalene (no congruent
sides). Then calculate the perimeter.

```
10  PRINT "VERTEX 1";
20  INPUT X1, Y1
30  PRINT "VERTEX 2";
40  INPUT X2, Y2
50  PRINT "VERTEX 3";
60  INPUT X3, Y3
70  S1 = SQR((X2 - X1) ↑ 2 + (Y2 - Y1) ↑ 2)
80  S2 = SQR((X3 - X2) ↑ 2 + (Y3 - Y2) ↑ 2)
90  S3 = SQR((X1 - X3) ↑ 2 + (Y1 - Y3) ↑ 2)
100 PRINT S1, S2, S3
110 END
```

■ Modify the above program in order to compute and print the
perimeter round to the nearest tenth. Complete the table below.

```
110 P = S1 + S2 + S3
120 PRINT (INT (10 * P + 0.5)) / 10
130 END
```

	Vertex 1	Vertex 2	Vertex 3	Type	Perimeter
1.	$(-6, -3)$	$(-2, 5)$	$(4, -3)$	Isosceles	28.9
2.	$(-1, 6)$	$(1, 7)$	$(-4, 2)$	Scalene	14.3
3.	$(2, -2)$	$(2, 4)$	$(-1, -2)$	Scalene	15.7
4.	$(7, 0)$	$(1, -4)$	$(3, -8)$	Scalene	20.6

Use anytime after Section 10-9

© D.C. Heath & Co.

Computer Worksheet 16

NAME _____

SIMULATING PROBABILITY EXPERIMENTS

The BASIC command RND generates a random number between 0
and 1. The following program uses that command to simulate drawing
a marble from a bag containing 9 marbles: 3 red, 4 white, and 2 blue.
The theoretical probabilities are P (red) $= \frac{3}{9} = 0.\overline{3}\%$, P (white) $= \frac{4}{9} =$
$0.\overline{4}\%$, and P (blue) $= \frac{2}{9} = 0.\overline{2}\%$. The experiment is repeated 30 times
(line 10).

```
  5  R = 0: W = 0: B = 0
 10  FOR I = 1 to 30
 20  LET X = RND (I)
†30  IF X < = 1 / 3 THEN R = R + 1
†40  IF (X > 1 / 3) AND (X < 7 / 9) THEN W = W + 1
†50  IF X > 7 / 9 THEN B = B + 1
 60  NEXT I
 70  PRINT "NUMBER", "PERCENT"
 80  PRINT "R: "; R, R / 0.3; "%"
 90  PRINT "W: "; W, W / 0.3; "%"
100  PRINT "B: "; B, B / 0.3; "%"
110  END
```

Answers will vary.

1. Run the program to simulate drawing 30 marbles, one at a time,
with replacement. How do the results compare to the stated

   probabilities? _____

2. Repeat the experiment several times and compare the results to the

   stated probabilities. _____

3. Since each of the experiments in exercises 1 and 2 have the same
   number of trials, you can average the results. How does the

   average compare to the stated probabilities? _____

4. Change the program to draw a sample of 300 marbles. (Change
   lines 10, 80, 90, and 100.) Run the program several times. How
   do the results of samples of 300 compare to the results of samples
   of 30? In lines 80, 90, and 100 divide by 3 instead of 0.3.

5. Predict the results of a sample of 900 marbles. Change the program

   and test your prediction. In lines 80, 90, and 100 divide by 9.

† **BASIC programming notes**
Line 30 assigns the value "red" to one third of the random numbers.
Line 40 assigns the value "white" to the next $\frac{4}{9}$ of the random numbers.
Line 50 assigns the value "blue" to the remaining $\frac{2}{9}$ of the random numbers.

Use anytime after Probability

© D.C. Heath & Co.

Graphing Software

Graphing programs are a very useful tool for classroom demonstrations and for use by individuals or small groups. These programs quickly and dramatically show how a change in an equation changes the graph. Effective graphing programs can be found in the literature (for example, see page 195 of the March 1985 issue of *The Mathematics Teacher*), or graphing programs can be purchased from a number of software publishers.

You or your students may wish to use the following short graphing program which runs on an Apple. Any function of the form $y = \dots$ can be entered on line 60.

```
10 HOME : HGR : HCOLOR = 3
20 HPLOT 0,80 TO 279,80: HPLOT
   140,0 TO 140,191
30 FOR X = -10 TO 10 STEP .05
40 P = 140 + 15 * X: IF P < 0 OR
   P > 279 THEN 90
60 Y = 2 * X - 3
70 Q = 80 - 15 * Y: IF Q < 0 OR
   Q > 191 THEN 90
80 HPLOT P, Q
90 NEXT X
```

The function is graphed for values of x between -10 and 10 (line 30) but these values are easily changed.

To graph two functions on the same axis, the above program can be modified by adding the following lines where any second function can be inserted in line 45.

```
45 Y = 2 * (X - 3) ↑ 2
50 R = 80 - 15 * Y: IF R < 0 OR
   R > 191 THEN 60
55 HPLOT P, R
```

Correlated Software

HEATH ALGEBRA SOFT-WARE is a series of nine educational programs providing drill and practice, tutorial activities, and remedial instruction to supplement and enrich any algebra course. Each package of HEATH ALGEBRA SOFTWARE contains a disk, a backup disk, a student workbook, and a teacher's manual. The following is a correlation of the sections of HEATH ALGEBRA 1 to the software.

Student Textbook   **HEATH ALGEBRA SOFTWARE**

SECTION	PAGE	PACKAGE	LESSON	OBJECTIVE
1–2	5	Signed Number Operations	1. Order of Operations	1a. Order of Operations
2–2	43	Signed Number Operations	2. Addition	2a. Additive Inverses 2b. Adding Integers 2c. Adding Rationals
2–3	48	Signed Number Operations	3. Subtraction	3a. Subtracting Integers 3b. Subtracting Rationals
2–4	52	Signed Number Operations	4. Multiplication	4a. Multiplying Integers 4b. Multiplying Rationals
2–5	56	Signed Number Operations Polynomials Rational Expressions	5. Division 1. Addition 1. Basic Concepts	5a. Dividing Integers 5b. Multiplicative Inverses 5c. Dividing Rationals 1a. Evaluating Expressions 1a. Evaluating Expressions
3–3	98	Equations and Inequalities	1. Linear Equations Part 1	1a. Equations: $x \pm a = b$
3–4	103	Equations and Inequalities	1. Linear Equations Part 1	1b. Equations: $ax = b$
3–5	107	Equations and Inequalities	2. Linear Equations Part 2	2a. Equations: $ax \pm b = c$ 2b. Equations: $ax \pm b = cx \pm d$
4–1	143	Polynomials	1. Addition 2. Subtraction	1b. Adding Monomials 1c. Adding Polynomials 2a. Additive Inverses 2b. Subtracting Monomials 2c. Subtracting Polynomials
4–3	153	Exponents, Roots, & Radicals Polynomials	2. Exponential Expressions: Multiplication and Division 3. Multiplication Part 1	2a. Multiplying Exponential Expressions 3a. Multiplying Monomials
4–6	165	Polynomials	3. Multiplication Part 1 4. Multiplication Part 2	3b. Monomial × Polynomial 4a. Simplifying Polynomial Expressions
4–8	175	Exponents, Roots, & Radicals Polynomials	1. Integer Exponents 5. Division Part 1	1a. Whole-Number Exponents 5a. Dividing Monomials
5–1	197	Graphing Lines on a Plane	1. Points on a Plane	1a. Points as Ordered Pairs 1b. Ordered Pairs as Points 1c. Graphing Ordered Pairs
5–4	211	Graphing Lines on a Plane	2. Graphing Linear Equations	2a. Graphing Linear Equations
5–5	216	Graphing Lines on a Plane	3. Lines: Slope and y-intercept	3a. Slope of a Line

SECTION	PAGE	PACKAGE	LESSON	OBJECTIVE
5–6	223	Graphing Lines on a Plane	3. Lines: Slope and y-intercept 4. Equations: y = mx + b Form	3b. y-intercept of a Line 4a. y = mx + b Form
6–1	257	Systems of Equations	1. Graphing Method	1a. Graphing Method
6–2	263	Systems of Equations	2. Substitution Method	2a. Substitution Method
6–5	279	Systems of Equations	3. Addition Method	3a. Addition Method
7–2	310	Factoring	1. Common Monomial Factors	1a. Greatest Common Factors
7–4	318	Factoring Quadratic Equations	1. Common Monomial Factors 1. Special Cases	1b. Removing the GCF 1a. Equations: $ax^2 \pm bx = 0$
7–5	322	Polynomials	4. Multiplication Part 2	4b. Multiplying Binomials
7–6	326	Factoring Quadratic Equations	3. Special Cases 1. Special Cases	3a. Difference of Squares 1b. Equations: $x^2 - a^2 = 0$
7–7	331	Factoring Quadratic Equations	3. Special Cases 2. The General Case	3b. Perfect Square Trinomial 2b. Factorable Forms: One Solution
7–9	342	Quadratic Equations Factoring	2. The General Case 2. Factoring Trinomials	2a. Factorable Forms: Two Solutions 2a. Trinomials: One Variable 2b. Trinomials: Two Variables
8–1	359	Rational Expressions	1. Basic Concepts	1b. Simplification
8–2	365	Rational Expressions	3. Multiplication and Division	3a. Multiplication 3b. Division
8–3	371	Rational Expressions	2. Addition and Subtraction: Common Denominator	2a. Addition: Common Denominators 2b. Subtraction: Common Denominators
8–4	375	Rational Expressions	4. Addition and Subtraction: Monomial Denominators 5. Addition and Subtraction: Polynomial Denominators	4a. LCD: Monomials 4b. Addition: Monomial Denominators 4c. Subtraction: Monomial Denominators 5a. LCD: Polynomials 5b. Addition: Polynomial Denominators 5c. Subtraction: Polynomial Denominators
9–1	435	Equations & Inequalities	3. Linear Inequalities Part 1	3a. Graphing Real Numbers
9–3	447	Equations & Inequalities	3. Linear Inequalities Part 1	3b. Inequalities: + and − Rules
9–4	452	Equations & Inequalities	4. Linear Inequalities Part 2	4a. Inequalities: × and ÷ Rules
9–5	458	Equations & Inequalities	4. Linear Inequalities Part 2	4b. Inequalities: General Case
10–1	487	Exponents, Roots, & Radicals	3. Radical Expressions Part 1	3a. Square Roots
10–4	506	Exponents, Roots, & Radicals	4. Radical Expressions Part 2	4a. Simplifying Square Root Expressions
10–5	510	Exponents, Roots, & Radicals	3. Radical Expressions Part 1	3b. Square Root Expressions: × 3c. Square Root Expressions: ÷
10–6	515	Exponents, Roots, & Radicals	4. Radical Expressions Part 2	4b. Square Root Expressions: + 4c. Square Root Expressions: −
11–5	569	Quadratic Equations	3. The Quadratic Formula	3a. The Quadratic Formula

Heath
ALGEBRA 1

CLASSROOM STRATEGY
Advanced organizers

Research indicates that students learn better if they receive an **overview** of what is to be learned. This overview should describe what is to be learned, how it is related to knowledge previously learned, and why the new knowledge is important. Such an overview is sometimes called an **advanced organizer.**

To help teachers provide an overview of each section, this Teacher's Edition includes a statement of the **objective,** which indicates what is to be learned, and a statement of the **purpose,** which tells how the section relates to other sections. Students will learn algebra better if they are continuously able to integrate new knowledge into a meaningful, purposeful whole.

To help teachers provide students with the "big picture" of what they are learning in this course, the Teacher's Edition has a Chapter Overview for each chapter. Each overview describes what is to be learned in the chapter and how the new knowledge is related to knowledge previously learned. Chapter overviews also describe how the new knowledge is related to further learning in mathematics and how the new knowledge can be applied outside of mathematics. Teachers may wish to use information from the chapter overviews to help set the stage for learning the mathematics contained in the chapter.

ENRICHMENT WORKSHEETS

These Enrichment Worksheets are available as blackline copymasters in the Teacher's Resource Binder. They are also available as duplicating masters. You may assign these activity sheets at any time during the year after the prerequisite skill has been covered.

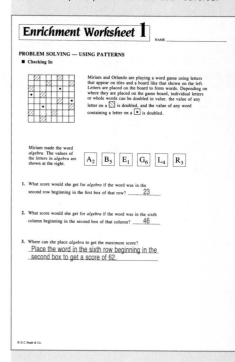

CHAPTER 1

CHAPTER OVERVIEW

A major difference between arithmetic and algebra is the use in algebra of variables (letters or other symbols that can be replaced by numbers). Chapter 1 focuses on the understanding of variables and algebraic expressions that contain variables.

In Chapter 1, students learn to evaluate algebraic expressions by substituting numbers for the variables and then simplifying the resulting numerical expressions. To accomplish this, students need to be able to compute accurately with whole numbers, fractions, and decimals. Skill in evaluating algebraic expressions is essential for all further work in algebra.

In Chapter 1, students learn basic properties for addition and multiplication of real numbers. These properties, which are stated using variables, apply to both arithmetic and algebra. Students learn to use these properties to simplify algebraic expressions. The basic properties and the simplification techniques learned in this chapter are fundamental to all further work in algebra.

In this chapter, students also learn to use algebraic expressions to express relationships that are stated in words. This skill is important for later work in using equations to solve problems. Facility in translating between verbal and algebraic expressions is necessary for applying algebra in real-life situations.

1 Algebraic Expressions

In skydiving, algebra is used to calculate information the skydiver needs to know before attempting a jump. The jumper must determine the altitude of the plane, the wind velocity, and a safe time interval in which to freefall.

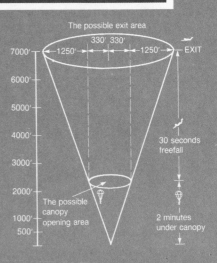

PURPOSE

The use of variables is one of the major differences between algebra and the mathematics the students have studied prior to this time. It is essential that students quickly learn to substitute numbers for variables and simplify the results.

1–1 Variables and Expressions

Preview

Diana Briggs is a skydiver. This table shows how far she traveled during the first few seconds of freefall.

Number of seconds	Distance fallen
1	16 ft
3	144 ft
5	400 ft
7	784 ft
9	1296 ft

• How many feet did she fall in the first three seconds? 144
• How many feet did she fall during the second and third seconds? 128
• Estimate how many feet she fell in the first two seconds.

Most people estimate that she fell 80 feet in the first two seconds because 80 is halfway between 16 and 144. The actual distance fallen is 64 feet. The table does not provide enough information for you to give an accurate estimate. By the end of this lesson you will be able to use algebra skills to answer these kinds of questions.

PREVIEW

Have the questions in the Preview answered. Ask these questions.
• Is the skydiver falling at a constant rate? (No)
• How do you know that? (She falls farther in the 4th and 5th seconds than in the 2nd and 3rd seconds.)
• Does the skydiver continue to gain speed, or does she reach a terminal velocity? (Students may not know the answer to this question. Air resistance eventually counteracts the force of gravity, and the skydiver reaches a terminal velocity of about 120 mph, or 176 ft/s.)

LESSON

Go over the exposition carefully. The concepts and vocabulary introduced in this lesson are very important and will be used daily.

Note that variables are symbols that are used in place of other things. Variables in algebra are usually letters such as x, y, a, b, c, and n. Occasionally, however, a box ($\square$), blank (___), question mark (?) or other symbol may be used as a variable by teachers.

Note that {3, 4½, 5.2} is read "the set consisting of the numbers 3, 4½, and 5.2." The word *number* is used to refer to both the value of a numerical expression and the expression itself. *Numeral*, *symbol*, and *name for a number* may also be used to refer to the expression.

■ LESSON

Letters such as x, y, A, and g are used in expressions in place of numbers. When letters are used in this way, they are called **variables.** Here are some expressions with variables:

$$9 + x \qquad y - 17 \qquad A \times \frac{3}{4} \qquad \frac{g}{0.7}$$

Variables can be replaced by numbers. This process is called **substitution.** The set of numbers to be substituted is called the **domain of the variable. Braces { }** are used to indicate a set of numbers.

Example 1   Let the domain of x be $\{3, 4\frac{1}{2}, 5.2\}$. Substitute each number of the domain for x in this expression:

$$9 + x$$

Solution

Original expression	$9 + x$
Substitute 3 for x.	$9 + 3$
Substitute $4\frac{1}{2}$ for x.	$9 + 4\frac{1}{2}$
Substitute 5.2 for x.	$9 + 5.2$

ADDITIONAL EXAMPLES

Example 1.
Let the domain of c be {0, ½, 2}.
Substitute each number in the domain for c in this expression.

$10 \times c$	10×0
	$10 \times \frac{1}{2}$
	10×2

Example 2.
Simplify each of the following.
a. $10 + 20 + 30$ 60
b. $^{25}/_{100}$ 0.25 or ¼

Example 3.
Evaluate $5 - a$ for $a = 3$.

Substitute.	$5 - 3$
Simplify.	2

CHECK UNDERSTANDING

- List three examples of variables.
- Write an expression for "the set that contains 3, 4, and 5." ({3, 4, 5})
- Give an example of a numerical expression in simplest form.
- Give an example of a numerical expression not in simplest form.

CLASSROOM EXERCISES

In classroom exercises 10–16 the students combine two skills—substituting numbers for variables and simplifying numerical expressions. The two steps can be performed mentally and only the final result stated.

Although it is usually obvious what the simplest name for a number is, sometimes more than one expression may be considered simplest. For example, fractions and their decimal equivalents are considered to be equally simple. The simplest name for $^5/_{10}$ is either ½ or 0.5. Simplified improper fractions and equivalent mixed numbers are considered to be equally simple. The simplest name for $^{24}/_{10}$ is either $^{12}/_5$, $2^2/_5$, or 2.4.

In classroom exercise 10, it should be noted that a and A are different variables. Uppercase (capital) letters and lowercase letters are different variables, and students should be especially careful when both types of letters are in the same expression.

Answers to all Classroom Exercises will be found in the "Answers to Selected Exercises" section of the student text.

ASSIGNMENT GUIDE

Basic	1–33 odd, Review Exercises
Average	1–39 odd, Review Exercises
Enriched	21–43 all, Review Exercises

These numerical expressions represent the same number.

$$12 - 4 \qquad \frac{6 \times 4}{3} \qquad 5 + 2 + 1 \qquad 8$$

The **simplest expression** is 8. Whenever you are asked to **simplify** a numerical expression, you are to write the simplest expression that represents the number.

Example 2 Simplify each of the following.

a. $\dfrac{12}{24}$ **b.** $\dfrac{8 \times 3}{2}$ **c.** $3.4 - 1.6$

Solution   **a.** $\dfrac{12}{24} = \dfrac{1}{2}$ **b.** $\dfrac{8 \times 3}{2} = 12$ **c.** $3.4 - 1.6 = 1.8$

Answer   **a.** $\dfrac{1}{2}$ or 0.5   **b.** 12   **c.** 1.8

A common algebra activity, especially when checking your work, is to substitute for a variable and then simplify the resulting numerical expression. This process is called **evaluating** an expression for a given number.

Example 3 Evaluate $3 \times a$ for $a = 7$.

Solution
Original expression	$3 \times a$
Substitute 7 for a.	3×7
Simplify.	21

Answer When $a = 7$, the value of $3 \times a$ is 21.

■ CLASSROOM EXERCISES

Identify the variable in each expression.

1. $2 \times t$ t   **2.** $5 \times b$ b   **3.** $A - 6$ A   **4.** $x - 17$ x

Simplify.

5. 6×2 12   **6.** $26 - 12$ 14   **7.** $\dfrac{3 \times 4}{2}$ 6   **8.** $\dfrac{3}{4} - \dfrac{1}{2}$ $\frac{1}{4}$ **9.** 1.5×2.3 3.45

a	A	n	x
2	7	3	5

Substitute and simplify.

10. $a + A$ 9   **11.** $2 \times x$ 10   **12.** $10 - x$ 5   **13.** $n \div 3$ 1

14. $10 - n$ 7   **15.** $3 \times n$ 9   **16.** My dog is x years old.   My dog is 5 years old.

Substitute each number of the domain for n and simplify. Domain = {0, 2, 4}

17. $n + 3$ 3, 5, 7   **18.** $10 - n$ 10, 8, 6   **19.** $3 \times n$ 0, 6, 12   **20.** $\dfrac{n}{2}$ 0, 1, 2

Students are better able to absorb new ideas when they have a context or setting into which they can fit the new ideas. Use the Previews or other short introductions to provide the setting.

■ WRITTEN EXERCISES

The domain of each variable is {1, 4, 3.7}. Substitute each number of the domain for the variable. Do *not* simplify the numerical expression.

A
1. $17 - x$
$17 - 1, 17 - 4, 17 - 3.7$

2. $11 - t$
$11 - 1, 11 - 4, 11 - 3.7$

3. $\dfrac{2}{a}$ $\dfrac{2}{1}, \dfrac{2}{4}, \dfrac{2}{3.7}$

4. $\dfrac{b}{2}$ $\dfrac{1}{2}, \dfrac{4}{2}, \dfrac{3.7}{2}$

5. $1 + y$
$1 + 1, 1 + 4, 1 + 3.7$

6. $c + 3$

7. $6 \times N$

8. $10 \times P$

6. $1 + 3, 4 + 3, 3.7 + 3$
7. $6 \times 1, 6 \times 4, 6 \times 3.7$
8. $10 \times 1, 10 \times 4, 10 \times 3.7$

a	b	m	T	x
3	5	6	3	2

Substitute and simplify.

9. $a + 7$ 10
10. $9 + m$ 15
11. $12 - b$ 7
12. $6 - m$ 0

13. $4 \times T$ 12
14. $5 \times x$ 10
15. $T \div a$ 1
16. $m \div a$ 2

17. $m \times b$ 30
18. $b \times x$ 10
19. $m + m$ 12
20. $a + a$ 6

B	c	n	x	y
4	2	1	$\frac{2}{3}$	0

Substitute and simplify.

21. $\dfrac{24}{c}$ 12
22. $\dfrac{44}{B}$ 11
23. $n \times x$ $\frac{2}{3}$
24. $x \times y$ 0
25. $\dfrac{B}{n}$ 4

26. $\dfrac{c}{n}$ 2
27. $c + n + x$ $3\frac{2}{3}$
28. $x + c + n$ $3\frac{2}{3}$
29. $y \times c \times 5$ 0
30. $B \times c \times y$ 0

Copy the expression and substitute the given values. Do *not* simplify.

31. Substitue 10 for l and 5 for w.
  a. The area of a rectangle is $l \times w$. 10×5
  b. The perimeter of a rectangle is $l + w + l + w$. $10 + 5 + 10 + 5$

32. Substitute your age in years for A.   Answers will vary.
  a. I am A years old.
  b. In 5 years I will be $(A + 5)$ years old.
  c. Six years ago I was $(A - 6)$ years old.
  d. In A years I will be $(2 \times A)$ years old.

33. Substitute your height in inches for h.   Answers will vary.
  a. I am h inches tall.
  b. If I grow 3 inches taller, I will be $(h + 3)$ inches tall.

34. Substitute your weight in pounds for w.   Answers will vary.
  a. I weigh w pounds.
  b. If I lose 10 pounds, I will weigh $(w - 10)$ pounds.
  c. My brother weighs $\frac{3}{4}$ as much as I do. He weighs $\left(\frac{3}{4} \times w\right)$ pounds.
  d. Last year I weighed $(w - 12)$ pounds.

These Practice Worksheets are available as blackline copymasters in the Teacher's Resource Binder. They are also available as duplicating masters.

1-1 VARIABLES AND EXPRESSIONS

■ The domain of each variable is {1, 2, 7.5, 10}. Substitute each number of the domain for the variable. Write the simplified numerical expression in the answer blank.

1. $10 - t$ 9 / 8 / 2.5 / 0

2. $\dfrac{150}{n}$ 150 / 75 / 20 / 15

3. $2.5 + a$ 3.5 / 4.5 / 10.0 / 12.5

4. $r - 1$ 0 / 1 / 6.5 / 9

5. $c + c$ 2 / 4 / 15 / 20

6. $y \times y$ 1 / 4 / 56.25 / 100

■ Substitute and simplify.

n	N	a	A	y
$\frac{1}{2}$	$\frac{1}{4}$	0	3	100

7. $a + n$ 1/2
8. $A + N$ 31/4
9. $\dfrac{300}{A}$ 100
10. $\dfrac{100}{y}$ 1

11. $\dfrac{y}{4}$ 25
12. $1 - N$ 3/4
13. $A - n$ 21/2
14. $n + N$ 3/4

15. $n - N$ 1/4
16. $12 \times n$ 6
17. $\dfrac{y}{A}$ 331/3
18. $a + A + y$ 103

19. $a \times A \times y$ 0
20. $n \times N - a$ 1/8
21. $y - A - n$ 961/2
22. $4 \times N \times A$ 3

WRITTEN EXERCISES

In exercise 14, students may notice that the letter x and the multiplication sign $\times$ could be confused. The meaning of the symbol will usually be clear from the context in which it appears. The dot is first used as a multiplication sign in Section 1–3.

In exercises 38–40, it may be noted that sometimes order makes a difference ($\dfrac{m}{n}$ and $\dfrac{n}{m}$ are not equal) and sometimes it makes no difference ($x \times y$ and $y \times x$ are equal).

Answers to odd-numbered Written Exercises will be found in the "Answers to Selected Exercises" section of the student text.

REVIEW EXERCISES

It is highly recommended that the Review Exercises be assigned to all students. Answers to all Review Exercises will be found in the "Answers to Selected Exercises" section of the student text.

COMPUTER EXTENSION

Write and run a program that makes a table showing how far a skydiver falls for up to 20 seconds of the fall. (See Section 1–1, exercise 37.) The output should look like this:

Seconds	Feet
1	16
2	64
3	144
⋮	⋮
20	6400

```
10 PRINT "SECONDS", "FEET"
20 FOR T = 1 TO 20
30 PRINT T, 16*T*T
40 NEXT T
50 END
```

PROBLEM-SOLVING NOTE

In the Preview, the *systematic recording of results in a table* permits one to examine the data easily to obtain additional information. As one variable increases or decreases regularly (in this case, time), the effect of that change upon another variable (distance fallen) can be examined easily. In creating their own tables in subsequent lessons, students should be encouraged to list the value of one variable in increasing or decreasing order.

ENRICHMENT PROBLEM

The Enrichment Problems for each section are provided on copymasters in the Teacher's Resource Binder so that you can easily distribute copies to your students.

Solving simpler problems

• How many league games are there in all if each team in your school's athletic conference plays every other team exactly once during the regular football season?

Don't tell the students that they can get the result by substituting in the expression $\frac{n(n-1)}{2}$. Let them struggle to come up with it. However, you might help them by suggesting that they approach the problem by starting with a 2-team league, then a 3-team league, then a 4-team league, etc., and then making a table and looking for patterns.

4

EXTRA PRACTICE, page 617

B 35. Substitute the number of girls in your algebra class for g and the number of boys for b. Simplify. Answers will vary.
  a. There are g girls in my class.
  b. There are $(g + b)$ students in my class.
  c. If one girl moves away, there will be $(g - 1)$ girls and $(g + b - 1)$ students in my class.
  d. If two classmates move away, there will be $(g + b - 2)$ students in my class.

36. Substitute the number of hours of class you have in the morning for a and the number of hours of class you have in the afternoon for b. Simplify.
  a. I have b hours of class in the afternoon. Answers will vary.
  b. I have $(a + b)$ hours of class each day.
  c. If I get out of school an hour early, I will have $(b - 1)$ hours of class in the afternoon and $(a + b - 1)$ hours of class for the day.
  d. If school is dismissed at noon after I arrive an hour late, I will have $(a - 1)$ hours of class for the day.

37. In the Preview, we can find the number of feet fallen by the skydiver by the expression $16 \times t \times t$.
  a. How many feet did the skydiver fall in the first 8 seconds? [*Hint:* Evaluate $16 \times t \times t$ for $t = 8$.] 1024
  b. How many feet did she fall in the first 2 seconds? 64
  c. How many feet did she fall in the first 6 seconds? 576
  d. How many feet did she fall by the time she pulled the rip cord, assuming a freefall of 10 seconds? 1600

Copy and complete the following tables.

38.

a	b	$a + b$	$a - 7$
7	4	?	?

11   0

39.

x	y	$x \times y$	$y \times x$
0.5	7	?	?

3.5   3.5

40.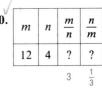

3    $\frac{1}{3}$

C 41.

c	d	$c + d$	$c - d$
7	?	10	?

3   4

42.

r	s	$r + s$	$r - s$	$\frac{r}{s}$
?	5	?	5	?

10   15   2

43.

p	q	$p + q$	$p - q$	$\frac{p}{q}$
?	?	10	6	?

8 2   4

■ REVIEW EXERCISES

Keep your arithmetic skills sharp!

Simplify.

1. $\frac{3}{8} + \frac{1}{4}$ $\frac{5}{8}$

2. $\frac{2}{5} + \frac{1}{3}$ $\frac{11}{15}$

3. $\frac{5}{6} - \frac{1}{2}$ $\frac{1}{3}$

4. $\frac{7}{8} - \frac{2}{5}$ $\frac{19}{40}$

5. $\frac{1}{2} \times \frac{1}{3}$ $\frac{1}{6}$

6. $\frac{1}{6} \times \frac{3}{5}$ $\frac{1}{10}$

7. $\frac{2}{3} \div 3$ $\frac{2}{9}$

8. $\frac{4}{5} \div \frac{1}{3}$ $2\frac{2}{5}$

Class Starter Quiz
on previous section

Have this quiz for Section 1–1 written on the board or on a transparency. Copies of these quizzes are provided in the Teacher's Resource Binder so that you can prepare transparencies on a copying machine. When the bell rings, have students immediately begin answering the questions on paper.

Substitute and simplify.

n	N	a	x
2	1	0	½

1. $n + x$ 2½
2. $N - a$ 1
3. $n \times N$ 2
4. $n + n + n$ 6
5. $x + a + N$ 1½

1–2 Using the Order of Operations to Simplify Expressions

Preview   **Multiplication on a computer**

When Greg Mason was learning about a computer at school, he tried to use it to add 6 and 4 and then multiply the result by 9.

He typed:

PRINT 4 + 6 * 9   " * " is the computer symbol for multiplication.

The computer screen displayed this number:

58

That was not the answer that Greg expected. What do you think happened?

4 was added to the product 6 · 9.

In this lesson you will learn some rules mathematicians have agreed on to be sure that an expression has just one meaning.

PURPOSE

Without an agreement about the order in which operations are to be performed, some mathematical expressions could be interpreted in more than one way. To avoid ambiguous notation, it is essential that all students perform operations in the same order and that this order be consistent with common usage.

■ LESSON

In the Preview you saw that the expression

$$4 + 6 \times 9$$

could be considered to represent either of two numbers, depending on the order in which the operations (addition and multiplication) were done.

Multiplication first	Addition first
$4 + 6 \times 9 = 58$	$4 + 6 \times 9 = 90$
↑ ↑	↑ ↑
2nd 1st	1st 2nd

To avoid this confusing situation, mathematicians have agreed on the following rules for the **order of operations.**

Order of Operations

1. Simplify inside parentheses and other grouping symbols first.
2. Do multiplications and divisions next, in order from left to right.
3. Do additions and subtractions next, in order from left to right.

PREVIEW

How can the PRINT statement be changed so the output will be 90? (PRINT (4 + 6)*9)

LESSON

Using the order-of-operation conventions may seem unnatural to students at times. The English language is nearly always written and read from left to right. Therefore, it may seem awkward to evaluate the expression

$$2 + 3 \times (4 - 1)$$

since the 2 is the last number operated on.

The following mnemonic device may be used to help students remember the order of operations:

Pardon My Dear Aunt Sally (PMDAS):
Parentheses, Multiply and Divide,
Add and Subtract.

Note that multiplications and divisions are done in order from left to right. Neither operation takes precedence over the other. Addition and subtraction behave similarly.

Grouping symbols are used to indicate when the desired order of operations is different from that which would result from using the standard rules of order. If we want to first add 4 and 6 and then multiply the sum by 9, we could draw a loop around the first step:

$$\overparen{(4 + 6)} \times 9$$

Parentheses can be thought of as "remnants" of the loop.

$$(4 + 6) \times 9$$

This conception of grouping symbols can be helpful in interpreting the case of grouping symbols within grouping symbols.

$$(\,(8 - 3) - 4) \times 7$$

It should be pointed out that the rules given refer only to addition, subtraction, multiplication, and division. Other operations will be introduced later (raising to a power, taking the square root, etc.), and each time it will be necessary to indicate what place that operation takes in the order of operations.

ADDITIONAL EXAMPLES

Example 1. Simplify. $2 \times (3 + 4)$ 14
Example 2. Simplify. $2 \times 3 + 4$ 10
Example 3. Simplify. $10 - (6 - 2)$ 6
Example 4. Simplify. $10 - 6 - 2$ 2

Example 1   Simplify. $3 \times (4 + 1)$

Solution

First: Simplify inside the parentheses.
Second: Multiply 3 and 5.

$$3 \times (4 + 1) = 3 \times 5$$
$$= 15$$

Answer   15

Example 2.   Simplify. $3 \times 4 + 1$

Solution

First: Multiply 3 and 4.
Second: Add 12 and 1.

$$3 \times 4 + 1 = 12 + 1$$
$$= 13$$

Answer   13

Example 3   Simplify. $12 - (8 - 3)$

Solution

First: Simplify inside the parentheses.
Second: Subtract 5 from 12.

$$12 - (8 - 3) = 12 - 5$$
$$= 7$$

Answer   7

Example 4   Simplify. $12 - 8 - 3$

Solution

First: Subtract 8 from 12.
Second: Subtract 3 from 4.

$$12 - 8 - 3 = 4 - 3$$
$$= 1$$

Answer   1

Brackets [ ], like parentheses, are also grouping symbols used to enclose an expression. If there are grouping symbols within grouping symbols, simplify inside the innermost symbols first.

Example 5   Simplify. $26 - [(2 \times 3) \times 3]$

Solution

$$\overset{\text{3rd}\quad\text{1st}\quad\text{2nd}}{\downarrow\quad\downarrow\quad\downarrow}$$

First: Multiply 2 and 3. $26 - [(2 \times 3) \times 3] = 26 - [6 \times 3]$
Second: Multiply 6 and 3. $= 26 - 18$
Third: Subtract 18 from 26. $= 8$

Answer   8

Example 6   Simplify. $7 \times 5 + 9 \times 4 \div 3$

Solution

$$\overset{\text{1st}\ \text{4th}\ \text{2nd}\ \text{3rd}}{\downarrow\ \downarrow\ \downarrow\ \downarrow}$$

First: Multiply 7 and 5. $7 \times 5 + 9 \times 4 \div 3 = 35 + 9 \times 4 \div 3$
Second: Multiply 9 and 4. $= 35 + 36 \div 3$
Third: Divide 36 by 3. $= 35 + 12$
Fourth: Add 35 and 12. $= 47$

Answer   47

Example 7   Simplify. $\dfrac{8 + 5 \times 2}{12}$

Solution   The "fraction bar" in this example does two jobs. It indicates the operation division and it is also a grouping symbol. It indicates that $8 + 5 \times 2$ is divided by 12.

$$\overset{\text{2nd}\ \text{1st}\quad\text{3rd}}{\downarrow\ \downarrow}$$

First: Multiply 5 and 2. $\dfrac{8 + 5 \times 2}{12} = \dfrac{8 + 10}{12}$

Second: Add 8 and 10. $= \dfrac{18}{12}$

Third: Divide 18 by 12. $= 1.5$

Answer   1.5

■ CLASSROOM EXERCISES

1. State the rules for order of operations.   See page 5.

Indicate the order of operations. Then simplify.

$$\overset{2}{?}\ \overset{1}{?}\qquad\qquad \overset{1}{?}\ \overset{2}{?}\qquad\qquad \overset{2}{?}\ \overset{1}{?}\ \overset{3}{?}$$
$$\downarrow\ \downarrow\qquad\qquad \downarrow\ \downarrow\qquad\qquad \downarrow\ \downarrow\ \downarrow$$

2. $2 + 3 \times 7$ 23   **3.** $(2 + 3) \times 7$ 35   **4.** $3 \times (2 + 2) \times 4$ 48

ADDITIONAL EXAMPLES

Example 5.
Simplify. $50 - [(2 \times 4) \times 5]$ 10
Example 6.
Simplify. $5 \times 3 + 6 \times 4 \div 2$ 27
Example 7. Simplify. $\dfrac{9 + 6 \times 5}{3}$ 13

CHECK UNDERSTANDING
• Why are there rules for order of operations?

CONCEPT EXTENSION

Have students make up three order-of-operations exercises and give them to a classmate. Three things will be accomplished: (1) Students will focus more specific attention on the way such exercises are structured, since the objective is *not* to produce an answer. (2) If students give their problems to classmates to solve, peer teaching and evaluation are likely to result as they try to find answers. (3) You will get a chance to assess informally their levels of understanding and comfort with such problems by examining the types of exercises and levels of difficulty created by individual students .

CLASSROOM EXERCISES

If the students seem to need more group work before starting on their assignment, written exercises 1–12 could be started orally.

PRACTICE WORKSHEET 2

1-2 USING THE ORDER OF OPERATIONS TO SIMPLIFY EXPRESSIONS

■ Write +, −, ×, or ÷ on the answer blank to identify the operation to be done first.

1. $10 + 2 \times 6$ ___×___   2. $7 - 3 + 2$ ___−___   3. $3 \div 2 \times 3$ ___÷___
4. $12 - 6 \div 2$ ___÷___   5. $(24 - 6) \div 3$ ___−___   6. $12 \div 6 - 2$ ___÷___
7. $(4 + 5) \times 2$ ___+___   8. $(3.5 - 0.5) \times 5$ ___−___   9. $3.5 \div (0.5 \times 5)$ ___×___

■ Simplify.

10. $3 + 4 \times 2$ ___11___   11. $(3 + 4) \times 2$ ___14___   12. $(1 + 2) \times (4 + 5)$ ___27___
13. $\frac{8 + 6}{2}$ ___7___   14. $8 + 6 \div 2$ ___11___   15. $5 \times 2 + 3 \times 2$ ___16___
16. $10 - 2 \times 4$ ___2___   17. $30 \div 2 \times 4$ ___60___   18. $\frac{30}{2 + 4}$ ___5___
19. $\frac{15 + 9}{5 + 3}$ ___3___   20. $7 \times (8 - 5)$ ___21___   21. $15 - (8 - 3)$ ___10___
22. $24 \times 4 + 4$ ___100___   23. $22 - 4 + 18$ ___36___   24. $22 - (4 + 18)$ ___0___

WRITTEN EXERCISES

In exercises 25 and 26, the horizontal bar is used both as a grouping symbol and to indicate division. For example, exercise 25

$$\frac{70}{2 + 5}$$

could have been written $70 \div (2 + 5)$.

In exercises 49–56, students should notice that the same numbers are used on both sides of the equation. They should carry out the computation only when they are not certain whether the statement is true or false.

COMPUTER EXTENSION

1. Write and run simple PRINT statement programs for exercises 1 and 3.

```
1. 10 PRINT (8 + 4)/2
   20 END
3. 10 PRINT 8 + 2*5
   20 END
```

2. Write and run simple programs for exercises 29 and 31.

```
29. 10 P = 5
    20 PRINT 4*(P + 2)
    30 END
31. 10 B = 30
    20 H = 3
    30 PRINT 2*B*H
    40 END
```

8

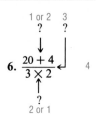

5. $4 \times [(3 + 4) \div 2]$ 14

6. $\dfrac{20 + 4}{3 \times 2}$ 4

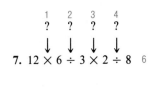

7. $12 \times 6 \div 3 \times 2 \div 8$ 6

■ WRITTEN EXERCISES

Write +, −, ×, or ÷ to identify the operation to be done first.

A
1. $(8 + 4) \div 2$ +   2. $(6 + 12) \div 3$ +   3. $8 + 2 \times 5$ ×
4. $4 + 3 \times 6$ ×   5. $8 + 4 \div 2$ ÷   6. $6 + 12 \div 3$ ÷
7. $(10 \div 2) \times 4$ ÷   8. $(15 - 2) \times 5$ −   9. $13 - 1 \times 6$ ×
10. $4 + 7 \times 2 - 2$ ×   11. $12 \div 4 + 15 \times 3$ ÷   12. $8 \times [2 \div (2 - 1)]$ −

Simplify.

13. $4 + 5 \times 6$ 34   14. $5 + 6 \times 4$ 29   15. $20 - 8 \div 4$ 18
16. $30 - 10 \div 5$ 28   17. $4 \times 5 + 6$ 26   18. $6 \times [5 + 4]$ 54
19. $(20 - 8) \div 4$ 3   20. $(30 \div 10) + 5$ 8   21. $3 \times 4 + 6 \times 4$ 36
22. $5 \times [(2 + 5) \times 3]$ 105   23. $(3 + 6) \times 4$ 36   24. $5 \times (2 + 3)$ 25
25. $\dfrac{70}{2 + 5}$ 10   26. $\dfrac{18}{3 + 6}$ 2

h	B	p	c
3	30	5	100

Substitute and simplify.

27. $4 \times p + 2$ 22   28. $5 \times h + 4$ 19   29. $4 \times (p + 2)$ 28
30. $5 \times (B + 1)$ 155   31. $2 \times B \times h$ 180   32. $3 \times B \times p$ 450
33. $B \times (h + 4)$ 210   34. $c \times (p + 5)$ 1000   35. $5 + B \times p$ 155
36. $200 + 3 \times B$ 290   37. $c - (70 - B)$ 60   38. $(B - h) + (c - h)$ 124

Simplify.

B
39. $8 \times 2 - 3 \times 4 + 5$ 9   40. $7 \times 3 - 5 \times 4 + 6$ 7
41. $18 \times (12 - 9) + 2$ 56   42. $15 \times (10 - 8) + 1$ 31
43. $27 + 18 \div 9 - 3 + 1$ 27   44. $40 + 24 \div 8 - 3 + 1$ 41
45. $(27 + 18) \div 9 - (3 + 1)$ 1   46. $(40 + 24) \div 8 - (3 + 1)$ 4
47. $\dfrac{27 + 18}{9 - (3 + 1)}$ 9   48. $\dfrac{40 + 24}{8 - (3 + 1)}$ 16

Indicate whether the equation is true or false.

49. $10 + (12.5 - 7.5) = (10 + 12.5) - 7.5$ T   **50.** $23 - (10 + 7) = (23 - 10) + 7$ F

51. $30 - (17 - 13) = (30 - 17) - 13$ F   **52.** $40 - (23 + 12) = (40 - 23) - 12$ T

53. $7 \times 8 + 7 \times 2 = 7 \times (8 + 2)$ T   **54.** $\dfrac{40 - 8}{4} = 40 \div 4 - 8 \div 4$ T

55. $\dfrac{54 - 27}{9} = 54 - 27 \div 9$ F   **56.** $10 \times 3 + 10 \times 5 = (10 \times 3 + 10) \times 5$ F

Use each symbol once to write an expression for the number in the box.   Answers may vary.

> **Sample** $\boxed{\dfrac{1}{2}}$ $4, 5, 6, 8, -, \times, \div, (\,)$
>
> *Solution* $(6 - 5) \times 4 \div 8$

C **57.** $\boxed{6}$ $3, 4, 7, +, -$ $7 + 3 - 4$ **58.** $\boxed{8}$ $1, 2, 3, +, \times, (\,)$ $(3 + 1) \times 2$

59. $\boxed{10}$ $1, 2, 3, 15, +, -, \times$ $15 + 1 - 2 \times 3$ **60.** $\boxed{0}$ $3, 4, 5, 7, 8, +, -, \times, \div, (\,)$
                                                     $8 \times 5 \div 4 - (7 + 3)$

61. Puzzle. Pick a whole number less than 60. Do these steps.
   a. Divide the number by 3. Call the remainder a.
   b. Divide the number by 4. Call the remainder b.
   c. Divide the number by 5. Call the remainder c.
   d. Substitute the values of a, b, and c in this expression:

$$40 \times a + 45 \times b + 36 \times c$$

   e. Simplify the expression and divide by 60.
   Is the remainder the number you picked?   Yes

(This puzzle uses the "Chinese Remainder Theorem," which appeared in the writings of the Chinese mathematician Sun Tzu who lived in the 4th or 5th century A.D.)

62. Puzzle. I am thinking of a whole number that is less than 60. If you divide the number by 3, you get a remainder of 2. If you divide it by 4, you get a remainder of 1. If you divide it by 5, you get a remainder of 4. What is my number?   29

■ REVIEW EXERCISES

Maintain your skills!

Simplify.

1. $\dfrac{5}{6} + \dfrac{2}{3}$ $1\dfrac{1}{2}$ **2.** $\dfrac{1}{4} + \dfrac{2}{5}$ $\dfrac{13}{20}$ **3.** $\dfrac{2}{3} - \dfrac{1}{6}$ $\dfrac{1}{2}$ **4.** $\dfrac{1}{2} - \dfrac{1}{5}$ $\dfrac{3}{10}$

5. $\dfrac{1}{4} \times \dfrac{1}{4}$ $\dfrac{1}{16}$ **6.** $\dfrac{5}{6} \times \dfrac{6}{5}$ 1 **7.** $\dfrac{7}{8} \div 3$ $\dfrac{7}{24}$ **8.** $\dfrac{5}{9} \div \dfrac{2}{3}$ $\dfrac{5}{6}$

1–2   Using the Order of Operations to Simplify Expressions   **9**

Computer Extension *continued*

3. Write and run a program for the Chinese Remainder Theorem (exercise 61) that uses INPUT statements.

```
10 PRINT "PICK A WHOLE
   NUMBER LESS THAN 60"
20 PRINT "WHAT IS THE
   REMAINDER WHEN YOU DIVIDE
   IT BY 3";
30 INPUT A
40 PRINT "WHAT IS THE
   REMAINDER WHEN YOU DIVIDE
   IT BY 4";
50 INPUT B
60 PRINT "WHAT IS THE
   REMAINDER WHEN YOU DIVIDE
   IT BY 5";
70 INPUT C
80 N = 40*A + 45*B + 36*C
90 Q = N/60
100 R = N - 60*INT(Q)
110 PRINT R; ''IS THE NUMBER''
```

ENRICHMENT PROBLEM
Systematic trials

• How many of the numbers from 0 to 9 can you name using the digit 4 four times, any of the four operation signs $(+, -, \times, \div)$, and parentheses? For example, $4 \div 4 + (4 - 4) = 1$.

This problem can be generalized into naming other numbers. Students may ask if writing 44 is permissible. That is up to you. The problem can be generalized further using exponents and square-root signs. Additional problems can be generated by using a number other than 4.

Some possible answers
$0 = (4 - 4)(4 + 4)$
$1 = 4 \div 4 + (4 - 4)$
$2 = 4 - (4 + 4) \div 4$
$3 = (4 + 4 + 4) \div 4$
$4 = 4 + (4 - 4) \div 4$
$5 = ((4 \times 4) + 4) \div 4$
$6 = (4 + 4) \div 4 + 4$
$7 = (4 + 4) - 4 \div 4$
$8 = (4 \times 4) - (4 + 4)$
$9 = (4 + 4) + 4 \div 4$

9

Simplify.

1. $3 + 7 \times 10$ 73

2. $\dfrac{4+6}{2}$ 5

Substitute and simplify.

a	n	N
5	0	10

3. $(a + N) \div a$ 3
4. $a + N \div a$ 7
5. $a + n \times N$ 5

PURPOSE

To avoid confusion and to aid communication, various notations for representing multiplication have been developed. It is important that students recognize these notations. The use of exponents to represent repeated factors is an essential part of the language of mathematics.

PREVIEW

The intent of the historical previews is to help students realize that mathematics has been created by humans over a long period of time. Various notations were invented by individuals to solve specific problems. As time passed, some of the notations became widely accepted while others disappeared. New notations are still being invented as new mathematics and new uses of mathematics are discovered. For example, the development of computers required a new notation for multiplication.

LESSON

Since the content of this lesson is almost entirely made up of definitions, it is ideally suited to lecture/recitation.

Although several acceptable ways of indicating multiplication are presented, students should know that preference is usually given to the shortest or simplest. For example, $5n$, xy, and abc would usually be preferred to other alternatives.

OBJECTIVE 1–3

To understand and use common algebraic notation for multiplication.

You may wish to spend two days on this section. Refer to the Pacing Chart.

1–3 Symbols for Multiplication in Expressions

Preview **Historical note: Multiplication signs**

The use of "$\times$" for multiplication may have come from an early printing custom of using crossed lines to indicate multiplication steps. An early book might have set out the problem of multiplying 52 by 38 as

By the year 1600, the symbol $\times$ was employed in England but did not come into wide use until the late 1800's.

In this lesson you will learn ways of expressing multiplication in algebra.

■ LESSON

Mathematicians use several different ways to indicate multiplication. Each of the following expressions means 7 times m.

$$7 \times m \qquad 7 * m \qquad 7 \cdot m \qquad 7m \qquad 7(m)$$

We avoid using "$\times$" to show multiplication in algebra because it is easily confused with the variable "x". We use "$7 * m$" only with computers.

The following expressions are used in algebra:

7 times m	m times n	5 times a times b	2 times 6
$7 \cdot m$	$m \cdot n$	$5 \cdot a \cdot b$	$2 \cdot 6$
$7m$	mn	$5 \cdot ab$	$2(6)$
$7(m)$		$5a \cdot b$	
		$5ab$	

In a multiplication expression, numbers that are multiplied are called **factors.** The result is called the **product.**

$$\underset{\text{product}}{\underbrace{3 \cdot a \cdot b}}^{\overset{\text{factors}}{\downarrow\ \downarrow\ \downarrow}}$$

For a product that includes a number and variables, the number is called the **coefficient** (or **numerical coefficient**) of the remaining expression.

For $3a$, 3 is the coefficient of a.

For $\left(\dfrac{1}{5}\right)xy$, $\left(\dfrac{1}{5}\right)$ is the coefficient of xy.

For $7(a + b)$, 7 is the coefficient of $(a + b)$.

Discuss the Strategies for Success feature given in the student text in order to give students hints about how to take tests, reduce test anxiety, and pretest themselves.

Mathematicians invent simpler ways to write expressions. Omitting multiplication signs in expressions like $3ab$ is an example of using shortened notation. Another shortened notation allows us to write $2 \cdot 2 \cdot 2 \cdot 2 \cdot 2$ more simply:

Long way	Short way
$2 \cdot 2 \cdot 2 \cdot 2 \cdot 2$	2^5 ← exponent
	↑———base

The **exponent** (5) indicates how many times the **base** (2) is used as a factor.

Read as:

$4 \cdot 4 \cdot 4 = 4^3$ "4 cubed"

$7 \cdot 7 \cdot 7 \cdot 7 = 7^4$ "7 to the 4th power"

$m \cdot m \cdot m \cdot m \cdot m = m^5$ "m to the 5th power"

$(a + 1)(a + 1) = (a + 1)^2$ "the quantity $(a + 1)$ squared"

If expressions such as $3 \cdot 4^2$ and $(1 + 2)^2$ are to have a clearly understood meaning, we must agree on an *order of operations* that includes **raising to a power.**

Order of Operations

After simplifying inside parentheses, evaluate powers before doing the multiplication and division.

Example 1   Simplify. $7 \cdot 2^2$

Solution

                                              2nd 1st

First: Evaluate the power. $7 \cdot 2^2 = 7 \cdot 4$
Second: Multiply 7 and 4. $= 28$

Answer   28

Example 2   Simplify. $(7 \cdot 2)^2$

Solution

                                              1st 2nd

First: Simplify inside the parentheses. $(7 \cdot 2)^2 = (14)^2$
Second: Evaluate the power. $= 196$

Answer   196

The word *coefficient* is used in this book to refer to the numerical coefficient. However, in an expression such as ax, the coefficient of x is a.

The coefficient of x (or a^2, or rs, or $(a + b)$) is 1, even though 1 is not written. However, that question is not raised in this section. The question is raised in Section 1–5 at the time when the identity property for multiplication is introduced.

The mnemonic device for remembering the order of operations can be extended to include exponents:

Please Excuse My Dear Aunt Sally (PEMDAS): Parentheses, Exponents, Multiplication and Division, Addition and Subtraction.

ADDITIONAL EXAMPLES

Example 1. Simplify. $2 \cdot 5^2$ 50
Example 2. Simplify. $(2 \cdot 5)^2$ 100

CHECK UNDERSTANDING

- Give an example of a numerical coefficient.
- Give an example of an exponent.
- Give an example of a power.

If students confuse "exponent" and "power," this diagram can be used:

$$\text{④} \leftarrow \text{exponent}$$
$$6$$
$$\text{⑥}^4 \leftarrow \text{power}$$

- Write symbols for "the fourth power of x" and "the fourth power of $2x$." (x^4, $(2x)^4$)
- In the expression $3a^2$, which operation is done first, squaring or multiplying by 3? (Squaring)

CLASSROOM EXERCISES

In classroom exercises 6–10, check that students understand what they are reading. For example, in classroom exercise 7 the symbol 6^4 is read as "the fourth power of six," or "six to the fourth power."

If additional practice is needed before the students start their assignment, have them write expressions that are read to them. Written exercises 9–24 provide suitable examples, and the students can correct their own work.

ASSIGNMENT GUIDE

Basic   1–47 odd, Review Exercises, Self-Quiz 1
Average   1–11 odd, 29–63 odd, Review Exercises, Self-Quiz 1
Enriched   1–11 odd, 29–47 odd, 49–67 all, Review Exercises, Self-Quiz 1

Example 3   Simplify. $2^3 + (4 + 1)^2$

Solution

First: Simplify inside the parentheses.
Second and third: Evaluate the powers.
Fourth: Add 8 and 25.

$$\overset{\text{2nd 4th 1st 3rd}}{2^3 + (4 + 1)^2} = 2^3 + 5^2$$
$$= 8 + 25$$
$$= 33$$

Answer   33

■ CLASSROOM EXERCISES

Give two factors of each product.   Answers will vary.

1. $2xy$ 2, x, y, 2x, 2y, xy, 2xy, 1   **2.** $5a^2$ 5, a, 5a, a², 5a², 1   **3.** $4(a + 1)$ 4, (a + 1), 4(a + 1), 1, 2

Identify the coefficient in each expression.

4. For $7mn$, what is the coefficient of mn? 7   **5.** For $3y^2$, what is the coefficient of y^2? 3

Read.

6. m^2 m squared   **7.** 6^4 6 to the fourth power   **8.** y^3 y cubed   **9.** $4 + a^2$ 4 plus a squared   **10.** $(4 + a)^2$ the quantity (four plus a) squared

Simplify.

11. 4^2 16   **12.** 5^3 125   **13.** 10^5 100,000

14. $3 + 2^3$ 11   **15.** $3^2 + 4^2$ 25   **16.** $(3 + 4)^2$ 49

Strategy for Success   **Doing assignments**

When you have time in class to begin an assignment, complete as many problems as possible. Then if you get "stuck" on a problem you can ask for help.

■ WRITTEN EXERCISES

Ⓐ Simplify.

1. 3^2 9   **2.** 2^3 8   **3.** 10^6 1,000,000   **4.** 10^5 100,000

5. $10 \cdot 3^2$ 90   **6.** $10 \cdot 4^2$ 160   **7.** $6 + 2^3$ 14   **8.** $2 + 3^3$ 29

9. $(2 + 3)^2$ 25   **10.** $(5 - 2)^2$ 9   **11.** 3.5^2 12.25   **12.** 4.5^2 20.25

Evaluate for $n = 3$.

13. $2n$ 6   **14.** $4n$ 12   **15.** n^2 9   **16.** n^4 81

17. 2^n 8   **18.** 4^n 64   **19.** $5n^2$ 45   **20.** $4n^2$ 36

EXTRA PRACTICE, page 617

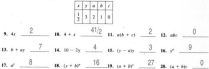

Evaluate for $n = 10$.

21. $6n$ 60   **22.** $3n$ 30   **23.** n^6 1,000,000   **24.** n^3 1,000

25. $n + 2^3$ 18   **26.** $n + 3^2$ 19   **27.** $(n + 2)^2$ 144   **28.** $(n - 2)^2$ 64

a	b	t	r	s
0	1	4	$\frac{2}{3}$	3

Substitute and simplify.

29. $3(2 + t)^2$ 108   **30.** $10(1 + t)^2$ 250   **31.** b^8 1   **32.** b^{10} 1

33. $(rs)^2$ 4   **34.** rs^2 6   **35.** $(t - b)^2$ 9   **36.** $(b - r)^2$ $\frac{1}{9}$

The expression e^3 is used to find the volume of a cube when the length of an edge e is known. Find the volumes of cubes with these edges.

37. 5 cm   125 cm³   **38.** 4 cm   64 cm³   **39.** 10 m   1000 m³   **40.** 15 m   3375 m³

41. 1.5 cm   3.375 cm³   **42.** 1.2 m   1.728 m³   **43.** $\frac{1}{2}$ in. $\frac{1}{8}$ in.³   **44.** $\frac{1}{3}$ in. $\frac{1}{27}$ in.³

The expression $16t^2$ is used to find the distance in feet that an object falls in t seconds. Find the distance an object falls in these times.

45. $\frac{1}{2}$ second   4 ft   **46.** 1 second   16 ft   **47.** 5 seconds   400 ft   **48.** 10 seconds   1600 ft

The expression $1000(1.1)^t$ is used to find the current value of a $1000 investment that earns 10% interest per year, compounded annually for t years. Find the current value of a $1000 investment after the following periods:

B   **49.** 2 years $1210   **50.** 3 years $1331   **51.** 4 years $1464.10   **52.** 5 years $1610.51

The expression $0.01E + 0.003E^2$ gives the required thickness in millimeters for an electrical insulation material. If E is the number of kilovolts required to puncture the insulation, find the thickness of insulation material for these voltages:

53. 1 kilovolt   0.013 mm   **54.** 2 kilovolts   0.032 mm   **55.** 10 kilovolts   0.4 mm   **56.** 20 kilovolts   1.4 mm

x	y	z	R	S
2	4	6	8	10

Substitute and simplify.

57. $z^x + R^x - S^x$ 0   **58.** $y^x + R^x$ 80   **59.** $z^3 - y^3$ 152   **60.** $R^x - x^y$ 48

61. $(z + R - S)^x$ 16   **62.** $(x + R - z)^x$ 16   **63.** $(z - y)^3$ 8   **64.** $(S - R)^3$ 8

C   Copy and complete each table.

65.

a	n	a^n
4	3	?

64

66.

a	n	a^n
2	?	64

6

67.

a	n	a^n
?	4	81

3

1–3   Symbols for Multiplication in Expressions   **13**

WRITTEN EXERCISES

Calculators may be used whenever the computations seem unduly cumbersome. Nearly all of the exercises, however, require little more than simple arithmetic.

Students should be encouraged to use mental arithmetic and estimation to check the reasonableness of their answers.

COMPUTER EXTENSION

1. Write and run simple PRINT statement programs for exercises 1 and 5.

```
1. 10 PRINT 3 ↑ 2
   20 END
5. 10 PRINT 10*3 ↑ 2
   20 END
```

2. Write and run simple programs for exercises 17, 25, and 35.

```
17. 10 N = 3
    20 PRINT 2 ↑ N
    30 END
25. 10 N = 10
    20 PRINT N + 2 ↑ 3
    30 END
35. 10 T = 4
    20 B = 1
    30 PRINT (T - B) ↑ 2
    40 END
```

SELF-QUIZ 1

Students may check their understanding of the major concepts in Sections 1–1, 1–2, and 1–3 by taking the self-quiz. Answers to all Self-Quiz exercises are given in the "Answers to Selected Exercises" section of the student text.

ENRICHMENT PROBLEM
Applying definitions

- Show that $(10^3)^2 = (10^2)^3$

$(10^3)^2 = (10^3)(10^3)$
$\quad = (10 \cdot 10 \cdot 10)(10 \cdot 10 \cdot 10) = 10^6$
$(10^2)^3 = (10^2)(10^2)(10^2)$
$\quad = (10 \cdot 10)(10 \cdot 10)(10 \cdot 10) = 10^6$

Therefore, $(10^3)^2 = (10^2)^3$

■ REVIEW EXERCISES

Area represents the number of 1-unit by 1-unit squares needed to cover the interior of a figure. The **perimeter** (pe<u>RIM</u>eter) is the distance around the "rim" of the figure.

Find the area and perimeter of each figure. Include cm or cm^2 in your answers.

1.
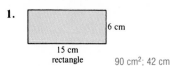
15 cm
rectangle   90 cm^2; 42 cm

2.
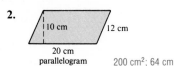
20 cm
parallelogram   200 cm^2; 64 cm

3.
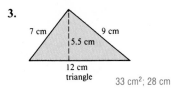
12 cm
triangle   33 cm^2; 28 cm

4.
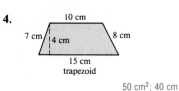
15 cm
trapezoid   50 cm^2; 40 cm

Self-Quiz 1

a	A	d	D
3	8	2	4

1–1   Substitute and simplify.

1. $(A + D) \div a$ 4   **2.** D^a 64   **3.** $5 \times d$ 10   **4.** $2 \times A + d$ 18

1–2   Use the order of operations to simplify.

5. $3 + 4 \cdot 5$ 23   **6.** $(3 + 4) \cdot 5$ 35

7. $8 + 4 \cdot 2^3$ 40   **8.** $3 + 14 \div 2 - 1 \cdot 5$ 5

1–3   Evaluate for $n = 2$.

9. $4n$ 8   **10.** n^4 16   **11.** $5(n - 1)$ 5   **12.** $n + 6^2$ 38

Strategy for Success   Using the self-quizzes

Use the self-quizzes in the book to check your progress. If you miss any questions, find out why. First go back to the lesson. If you still don't understand, seek help.

1–4 Equivalent Expressions

Preview   Discovery

Here are four expressions involving the variable a:

$$7a - 3a \qquad 4a \qquad \frac{1}{2}(8a) \qquad \frac{12a}{3}$$

- Evaluate each expression for $a = 3$.
- Evaluate for $a = 5$. 20, 20, 20, 20
- Evaluate for $a = 0.5$. 2, 2, 2, 2

12, 12, 12, 12

Expressions that have the same value for each substitution are very important in algebra. In this lesson you will begin the study of such expressions.

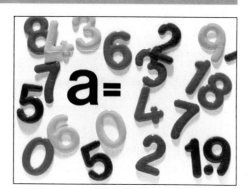

■ LESSON

Suppose that 7 is substituted for x in these two expressions:

$$3x + 2x \qquad 5x$$
$$3(7) + 2(7) \qquad 5(7)$$
$$35 \qquad\qquad 35$$

In both cases you get 35.

If 2 is substituted for x, you get 10 in both cases.

If $\frac{1}{3}$ is substituted for x, you get $\frac{5}{3}$ in both cases.

No matter what number is substituted for x, both expressions have the same value. For this reason, the two expressions $5x$ and $3x + 2x$ are called **equivalent expressions**. In the Preview, the four expressions are equivalent.

Definition: Equivalent Expressions

Two expressions are equivalent if the first has the same value as the second for every possible substitution.

Two expressions are **not equivalent** if they have different values for at least one substitution. You can prove that two expressions are not equivalent by finding one substitution that gives different values.

Simplify.

1. $4 + 3^2$ 13
2. $(1 + 4)^2$ 25

Substitute and simplify.

b	c
2	8

3. bc^2 128
4. $(b + c)^2$ 100
5. $b + c^2$ 66

PURPOSE

In later sections the concept of equivalent expressions is used in simplifying, in proof, and in equation solving.

PREVIEW

A table can be used to organize the answers in the Preview.

a	$7a - 3a$	$4a$	$\frac{1}{2}(8a)$	$\frac{12a}{3}$
3				
5				
0.5				

After the table is completed, it will be readily apparent that the four entries in each row are equal. The table could be extended to include 0, 100, and ⅓.

LESSON

Use the examples from the Preview to illustrate the definition of *equivalent expressions*. Students should first substitute several values into each expression. Students should then be encouraged to substitute large numbers and fractions as they explore equivalent expressions. Special numbers such as 0 and 1 should also be tried.

After some experience, students will begin to make hypotheses about which expressions are equivalent without actually making substitutions. Encourage such experimenting. However, frequently (and always when there are disagreements) ask students to justify their answers.

Lesson *continued*

Go over the examples in the text. Note that we can *prove* that two expressions are *not* equivalent by finding just *one* substitution for which the two expressions do not have the same value. On the other hand, finding *one* substitution for which the two expressions have the same value does *not prove* that the two expressions are equivalent. However, finding *several* substitutions that give the same value for both expressions can convince us that the expressions are equivalent. In later lessons, students will learn how to actually *prove* that two expressions are equivalent.

ADDITIONAL EXAMPLES

Example 1.
Are $5a - a$ and $5a$ equivalent?
Substitute 1: $5a - a$ $5a$
$$5 \cdot 1 - 1 \qquad 5 \cdot 1$$
$$4 \leftarrow different \rightarrow 5$$
$5a - a$ and $5a$ are *not* equivalent.

Example 2.
Are $4a - a$ and $3a$ equivalent?

Substitute 1, 10, 0, and $\frac{1}{2}$.

a	$4a - a$	$3a$
1	$4 \cdot 1 - 1 = 3$	$3 \cdot 1 = 3$
10	$4 \cdot 10 - 10 = 30$	$3 \cdot 10 = 30$
0	$4 \cdot 0 - 0 = 0$	$3 \cdot 0 = 0$
$\frac{1}{2}$	$4 \cdot \frac{1}{2} - \frac{1}{2} = 1\frac{1}{2}$	$3 \cdot \frac{1}{2} = 1\frac{1}{2}$

The expressions appear to be equivalent.

Example 3.
Are a^3 and aaa equivalent?
The two expressions are known to be equivalent because of the definition of exponents.

Example 4.
Are $2(b + c)$ and $2b + c$ equivalent?
Substitute 3 for b and 10 for c.
$$2(b + c) \qquad\qquad 2b + c$$
$$2(3 + 10) \qquad\qquad 2 \cdot 3 + 10$$
$$2 \cdot 13 \qquad\qquad\qquad 6 + 10$$
$$26 \leftarrow different \rightarrow 16$$
The expressions are not equivalent.

Example 1   Are $4a + 1$ and $5a$ equivalent?

Solution   Substitute 1:
$$4a + 1 \qquad\qquad 5a$$
$$4 \cdot 1 + 1 \qquad\qquad 5 \cdot 1$$
$$5 \quad \leftarrow same \rightarrow \quad 5$$

Substitute 3:
$$4a + 1 \qquad\qquad 5a$$
$$4 \cdot 3 + 1 \qquad\qquad 5 \cdot 3$$
$$13 \leftarrow different \rightarrow 15$$

Answer   We know that $4a + 1$ and $5a$ are not equivalent because they have different values when 3 is substituted for a.

Example 2   Are $4a + a$ and $5a$ equivalent?

Solution   Substitute the following values: 2, 7, 12, and $\frac{1}{2}$.

a	$4a + a$	$5a$
2	$4 \cdot 2 + 2 = 10$	$5 \cdot 2 = 10$
7	$4 \cdot 7 + 7 = 35$	$5 \cdot 7 = 35$
12	$4 \cdot 12 + 12 = 60$	$5 \cdot 12 = 60$
$\frac{1}{2}$	$4 \cdot \frac{1}{2} + \frac{1}{2} = 2\frac{1}{2}$	$5 \cdot \frac{1}{2} = 2\frac{1}{2}$

In each case the values are the same.

Answer   This information strongly suggests that the expressions are equivalent but does *not prove* it.

Example 3   Are aa and a^2 equivalent?

Answer   No substitutions are necessary. We know that these two expressions are equivalent by the definition of exponents.

Example 4   Are $2a + b$ and $a + 2b$ equivalent?

Solution   Substitute 0 for a and 0 for b.
$$2a + b \qquad\qquad a + 2b$$
$$2 \cdot 0 + 0 \qquad\qquad 0 + 2 \cdot 0$$
$$0 \quad \leftarrow same \rightarrow \quad 0$$

Substitute 3 for a and 4 for b.
$$2a + b \qquad\qquad a + 2b$$
$$2 \cdot 3 + 4 \qquad\qquad 3 + 2 \cdot 4$$
$$10 \leftarrow different \rightarrow 11$$

Answer   The expressions are not equivalent.

CLASSROOM STRATEGY   *Effective questioning*

Ask students to explain or defend their answers to yes-no or true-false questions, so you will know whether their reasoning is correct.

CHECK UNDERSTANDING

- State two expressions that are equivalent.
- State two expressions that are not equivalent. Prove that the expressions are not equivalent.

In the above activity, encourage students to give expressions involving different operations and involving more than one operation.

■ CLASSROOM EXERCISES

1. How can you prove that two expressions are not equivalent?   Two expressions are not equivalent if they have different values for at least one substitution.

Copy and complete the tables by substituting and simplifying.

2.

x	$3x - 1$	$2x$
a. 1	? 2	? 2
b. 3	? 8	? 6
c. 4	? 11	? 8

d. Do you think that $3x - 1$ and $2x$ are equivalent?   No

3.

a	b	a^2b^2	$(ab)^2$
a. 2	3	? 36	? 36
b. 4	1	? 16	? 16
c. 3	3	? 81	? 81

d. Do you think that a^2b^2 and $(ab)^2$ are equivalent?   Yes

CLASSROOM EXERCISES

Classroom exercise 3 provides a good opportunity to review the order-of-operations agreement involving both parentheses and exponents. If additional classroom exercises are needed, written exercises 1 and 2 may be discussed as a class activity.

■ WRITTEN EXERCISES

Copy and complete the tables by substituting and simplifying. Then state whether you think the two expressions are equivalent.

A **1.**

x	$x + 3x$	$2x + 2x$
a. 0	? 0	? 0
b. 1	? 4	? 4
c. 10	? 40	? 40

Yes

2.

a	$3 + a$	$4a$
a. 0	? 3	? 0
b. 1	? 4	? 4
c. 3	? 6	? 12

No

For each pair of expressions, substitute 0, 2, and 5 for the variable. Simplify the expressions and state whether you think they are equivalent.

3. $3(a + 5)$ 15, 21, 30
$3a + 5$ 5, 11, 20   No

4. $4(a + 10)$ 40, 48, 60
$4a + 10$ 10, 18, 30   No

5. $x^2 + 10$ 10, 14, 35
$7x$ 0, 14, 35   No

6. $2x$ 0, 4, 10
x^2 0, 4, 25   No

State whether you think the expressions in each pair are equivalent. If the expressions are not equivalent, find one number that produces different values when substituted for the variable.

7. $5 + a$
$a + 5$ Yes

8. $10 + z$
$z + 10$ Yes

9. $2x + 3$
$5x$ No, 0

10. $x + 4x$
$3x + 2x$ Yes

11. x^3
$x \cdot 3$ No, 1

12. $3x - 1$
$2x$ No, 0

13. $2x^2$
$(2x)^2$ No, 1

14. $2 + b$
$3b$ No, 0

15. Steve thinks that $2x + 1$ and $3x$ are equivalent. Show that he is wrong. $x = 0$ gives different values.

16. Al thinks that $3x + 2$ and $10x$ are equivalent. Show that he is wrong. $x = 0$ gives different values.

17. Jo believes that $(5x)^2$ and $5x^2$ are equivalent. Do you agree with her?   No

18. Ed believes that $(3x)^2$ and $9x^2$ are equivalent. Do you agree with him?   Yes

PRACTICE WORKSHEET 3

1-4 EQUIVALENT EXPRESSIONS

■ Complete the tables by substituting and simplifying. Then state whether you think the two expressions are equivalent.

1.

x	$3(2 + x)$	$6 + x$
0	6	6
1	9	7
10	36	16

Are the expressions $3(2 + x)$ and $6 + x$ equivalent?   No

2.

x	$2(x + 4)$	$2x + 8$
0	8	8
1	10	10
10	28	28

Are the expressions $2(x + 4)$ and $2x + 8$ equivalent?   Yes

3.

x	$\frac{3x + 3}{3}$	$x + 1$
0	1	1
2	3	3
5	6	6

Are the expressions $\frac{3x + 3}{3}$ and $x + 1$ equivalent?   Yes

4.

x	$3^2 + x^2$	$(3 + x)^2$
0	9	9
2	13	25
5	34	64

Are the expressions $3^2 + x^2$ and $(3 + x)^2$ equivalent?   No

5.

a	b	$\frac{a + 2}{b + 2}$	$\frac{a}{b}$
0	1	2/3	0
1	1	1	1
2	10	1/3	1/5

Are the expressions $\frac{a + 2}{b + 2}$ and $\frac{a}{b}$ equivalent?   No

6.

a	b	$\frac{2a}{2b}$	$2\left(\frac{a}{b}\right)$
0	3	0	0
1	1	1	2
5	10	1/2	1

Are the expressions $\frac{2a}{2b}$ and $2\left(\frac{a}{b}\right)$ equivalent?   No

■ For each pair of expressions, substitute numbers for the variable and simplify the expressions. State whether you think the expressions in each pair are equivalent.

7. $10a$
$a \cdot 10$ Yes

8. a^2
$2a$ No

9. $(3a)^2$
$a \cdot (9a)$ Yes

10. $(a + 5)^2$
$a^2 + 25$ No

11. $a^2 + a$
$3a$ No

12. $a^2 + 2a$
$a(a + 2)$ Yes

13. $2a + 4$
$2(a + 4)$ No

14. $\frac{2a + 4}{2}$
$a + 2$ Yes

WRITTEN EXERCISES

After some experience, students should examine pairs of expressions looking for ways to predict (before testing) whether the expressions are equivalent. Guessing before substituting and evaluating should be encouraged.

Some exercises show common *false* generalizations that some students make: Note exercises 2, 3, 6, 9, 11, 12, 13, and 14. Some exercises are examples of properties that are introduced in later lessons. Note exercises 7, 8, 18, 21, 22, 23, and 24.

PROBLEM-SOLVING NOTE
Understanding the problem

Considering specific values is a powerful tool used in the first stage of addressing a problem—becoming familiar with the characteristics of the problem situation. When examining several specific cases before tackling the more general situation, convenient values should be chosen.

ENRICHMENT PROBLEM
Exploration

- Simplify, looking for shortcuts.
1. $478 + 994 + 1006$
2. $673 \cdot 25 \cdot 4$
3. $432 \cdot 83 + 432 \cdot 17$
4. $77 \cdot 963 + 23 \cdot 963$

The first two answers, 2478 and 67,300, are easily found by using the associative properties and calculating from right to left. The last two answers, 43,200 and 96,300, can be calculated mentally using the distributive property. Doing these problems can help students see the usefulness of the properties they will learn in the next lesson.

EXTRA PRACTICE, page 618

Substitute the values of a and b in each expression. State whether you think the expressions are equivalent.

19. Yes

a	b	$(2a)b$	$2(ab)$
5	10	? 100	? 100
1	1	? 2	? 2
3	0	? 0	? 0

20. No

a	b	$5(a + b)$	$(5a) + b$
4	0	? 20	? 20
10	0	? 50	? 50
1	1	? 10	? 6

State whether you think the two expressions are equivalent. If the expressions are not equivalent, find one pair of numbers that produces different values when substituted for the variables.

B **21.** $\left(\frac{1}{2}b\right)h$ **22.** $\left(\frac{1}{2}h\right)(a + b)$ **23.** $6(ab)$ **24.** $\left(\frac{1}{2}a\right)(2b)$

$\frac{bh}{2}$ Yes $\frac{h(a + b)}{2}$ Yes $(2a)(3b)$ Yes $(2a)\left(\frac{1}{2}b\right)$ Yes

25. $\frac{2}{3} + \frac{a}{b}$ **26.** $\frac{a}{b} + \frac{1}{2}$ **27.** $(a + b)(a + b)$ **28.** $(p + 2)q + 3$

$\frac{2 + a}{3 + b}$ No, 1 and 1 $\frac{a + 1}{b + 2}$ No, 1 and 1 $a^2 + b^2$ No, 1 and 1 $pq + 6$ No, 1 and 1

In each exercise, two of the three expressions are equivalent. Write the equivalent expressions.

29. $\frac{5x + 10y}{15xy}$ **30.** $\frac{x^2 \cdot x^3}{x^6}$ **31.** $10 - a - b$, **32.** $a - (b - 1)$
$5(x + 2y)$ $x \cdot x^4$ $10 - (a - b)$ $(a - b) - 1$
                              $(10 - a) + b$ $(a - b) + 1$

C **33.** These expressions can be put into three groups of equivalent expressions. List the expressions in each group.

$2x + 2y$ I $x + 2y$ II $x + y + x$ III $2(x + y)$ I $x + y + y$ II

$2y + 2x$ I $y + y + x + x$ I $x + y + x + y$ I $2y + x$ II $y + x + x$ III

34. Show that these expressions are not equivalent.

$$\frac{x^2 - 4}{x - 2} \quad \text{and} \quad x + 2 \quad \text{x cannot equal 2 in the first expression.}$$

■ REVIEW EXERCISES

Simplify each numerical expression.   [1–2, 1–3]

1. $3 + 4 \cdot 5$ 23   **2.** $7 - 1 \cdot 4$ 3   **3.** $5(7 - 4)$ 15   **4.** $5 \cdot 7 - 5 \cdot 4$ 15

5. $2 \cdot 3^2$ 18   **6.** $2 + 2^3$ 10   **7.** $(2 + 3)^2$ 25   **8.** $2^2 + 3^2$ 13

To identify and use the basic properties of addition and multiplication.

State whether you think the two expressions are equivalent.

1. *aaaa* and 4*a* — No
2. *aaa* and a^3 — Yes
3. $2(x + 5)$ and $2x + 5$ — No
4. $3x - 1$ and $2x$ — No
5. $5x + 10y$ and $5(x + 2y)$ — Yes

1–5 Basic Properties of Numbers

Preview

Pick any 3-digit number. Multiply it by 7. Multiply the product by 11. Multiply the new product by 13. Look at the number you picked and the final product. You should see something unexpected.

Can you explain why the two numbers are related in this way? $7 \cdot 11 \cdot 13 = 1001$

This lesson will help you understand what happened.

■ LESSON

In earlier grades, you discovered that the order of two addends does not affect their sum. You also discovered that the order of two factors does not affect their product.

$$6 + 5 = 5 + 6 \qquad 7 \cdot 2 = 2 \cdot 7$$

$$3\frac{1}{2} + \frac{1}{4} = \frac{1}{4} + 3\frac{1}{2} \qquad 9.5 \cdot 3 = 3 \cdot 9.5$$

These are examples of general properties of numbers.

Commutative Property of Addition

For all numbers *a* and *b*,

$$a + b = b + a$$

Commutative Property of Multiplication

For all numbers *a* and *b*,

$$ab = ba$$

Commutative property of addition

$$2x + 3 = 3 + 2x$$
$$m + n^2 = n^2 + m$$
$$4x + (3 + 2x) = (3 + 2x) + 4x$$

Commutative property of multiplication

$$(5a)4 = 4(5a)$$
$$rs^2 = s^2r$$
$$5(3y + 1) = (3y + 1)5$$

You also learned that the way three addends are grouped or associated does not affect their sum, and that the way three factors are grouped does not affect their product.

$$(4 + 6) + 3 = 4 + (6 + 3) \qquad (2 \cdot 5) \cdot 4 = 2 \cdot (5 \cdot 4)$$

$$3.2 + (5.7 + 2.1) = (3.2 + 5.7) + 2.1 \qquad \frac{1}{2} \cdot (2 \cdot 3) = \left(\frac{1}{2} \cdot 2\right) \cdot 3$$

PURPOSE

Algebra is a highly structured, systematic subject. A few basic properties form the foundation of the system. Knowledge of these properties allows students to understand why the techniques of algebra are valid. The properties provide a means for explaining and expanding algebraic procedures.

PREVIEW

Since $7 \cdot 11 \cdot 13 = 1001$, the number picked is multiplied by 1001. Suppose the three-digit number picked is 532. Multiplying by 1001 has the effect of repeating the three-digit sequence.

$$532 \times 1001 = 532(1000 + 1)$$
$$= 532000 + 532$$
$$= 532532$$

Discussions of how the puzzle works may be delayed until after the distributive property has been introduced in the lesson.

LESSON

The words *commutative* and *associative* are often confused by students. It may help to think of people who commute to work on commuter trains. They go to work and later turn around to return home. In the commutative properties the numbers or expressions can "turn around":

$$a + b \qquad b + a \qquad a \cdot b \qquad b \cdot a$$

Lesson *continued*

To better remember the associative property it may help to think of the fact that the middle of three addends (or middle of three factors) can be "associated" with either of the other addends (or factors).

$$a + b + c \qquad a \cdot b \cdot c$$

$$\widehat{(a + b)} + c \qquad \widehat{(a \cdot b)} \cdot c$$

$$a + \widehat{(b + c)} \qquad a \cdot \widehat{(b \cdot c)}$$

Parentheses can be used instead of things.

The following diagrams can be used to show how multiplication is distributed over addition.

$$\overbrace{a \cdot (b + c)} = a \cdot b + a \cdot c$$

$$a \cdot (b + c)$$

$$a \cdot b + a \cdot c$$

$$\overbrace{(b + c) \cdot a} = b \cdot a + c \cdot a$$

$$(b + c) \cdot a$$

$$b \cdot a + c \cdot a$$

We make no distinction between the left-hand distributive property and the right-hand distributive property. Both are simply called the distributive property of multiplication over addition.

Note the similarities between the identity properties for addition and multiplication. Zero and one are sometimes called the additive identity element and the multiplicative identity element respectively. Adding zero does not affect the sum; multiplying by 1 does not affect the product.

Note the introduction of coefficients for variable expressions that appear to have no numerical coefficient. Although 1 may not be written, 1 is the coefficient of x, a^2, and rs. This follows because $x = 1x$, $a^2 = 1a^2$, and $rs = 1rs$.

These properties may be stated generally for numbers.

The Associative Property of Addition

For all numbers a, b, and c,

$$(a + b) + c = a + (b + c)$$

The Associative Property of Multiplication

For all numbers a, b, and c,

$$(ab)c = a(bc)$$

Associative property of addition

$$3a + (4a + 1) = (3a + 4a) + 1$$

$$(5x + 2) + 7 = 5x + (2 + 7)$$

$$2 + [3x + (4x + 1)] = (2 + 3x) + (4x + 1)$$

Associative property of multiplication

$$(2x^2)x = 2(x^2 x)$$

$$\frac{1}{2}(4a) = \left(\frac{1}{2} \cdot 4\right)a$$

$$3[6(4y - 5)] = (3 \cdot 6)(4y - 5)$$

Applied together, the commutative and associative properties of addition show that a collection of addends can be rearranged in any way without affecting the sum. The commutative and associative properties of multiplication show that a collection of factors can be rearranged in any way without affecting the product.

$$2x + 5 + 7x + 2 = (2x + 7x) + (5 + 2)$$

$$\left(\frac{1}{3}a\right)(6)(b) = \left(\frac{1}{3} \cdot 6\right)(ab)$$

The operations of addition and multiplication are combined in the following property.

The Distributive Property of Multiplication over Addition

For all numbers a, b, and c,

$$ab + ac = a(b + c) \qquad \text{and} \qquad ba + ca = (b + c)a$$

These equations are examples of the distributive property of multiplication over addition.

$$7 \cdot 2 + 7 \cdot 3 = 7(2 + 3)$$

$$8x + 5x = (8 + 5)x$$

Here are two other important properties.

Identity Property for Addition

For all numbers a,
$$a + 0 = a \quad \text{and} \quad 0 + a = a$$

Identity Property for Multiplication

For all numbers a,
$$1a = a \quad \text{and} \quad a \cdot 1 = a$$

Identity property for addition	*Identity property for multiplication*
$7 + 0 = 7$	$1 \cdot 9 = 9$
$0 + y = y$	$x \cdot 1 = x$

Some algebraic expressions are written without a numerical coefficient. In those cases, we say the coefficient is 1. Each of these expressions has a coefficient of 1:

$$b \qquad xy \qquad z^2 \qquad (c - d)$$

■ CLASSROOM EXERCISES

Give an example of each property.   Examples will vary.

1. The associative property of multiplication. $5(3 \cdot 2) = (5 \cdot 3)2$

2. The commutative property of addition. $3 + 4 = 4 + 3$

3. The distributive property of multiplication over addition.

4. The identity property for addition. $8(4 + 5b) = 8 \cdot 4 + 8 \cdot 5b$ $6b + 0 = 6b$

5. The identity property for multiplication. $6 \cdot 1 = 6$

Each equation illustrates one property. Name the property.

6. $(7a + 3) + 2a = 7a + (3 + 2a)$
Associative property of addition

7. $y \cdot 7 + y \cdot 3 = y(7 + 3)$
Distributive property

8. $(8b)\frac{1}{2} = \frac{1}{2}(8b)$
Commutative property of multiplication

9. $x(3 + 4) = (3 + 4)x$
Commutative property of multiplication

■ WRITTEN EXERCISES

Each equation illustrates the commutative property of addition or the associative property of addition. Name the property.

A **1.** $17 + (30 + 15) = (17 + 30) + 15$ Associative (addition)

2. $(4 + 5x) + x = 4 + (5x + x)$ Associative (addition)

CHECK UNDERSTANDING

- State an example of the commutative property of addition.
- Which property does the equation $3x + 2x = x \cdot 3 + 2x$ illustrate? (Commutative property of multiplication)

CLASSROOM EXERCISES

As additional exercises, the students could do these computations mentally and state the property they found to be useful.

1. $163 + 899 + 101$
1163; Associative (addition)

2. $2\frac{7}{8} + 3\frac{1}{4} + \frac{3}{4}$

$6\frac{7}{8}$; Associative (addition)

3. $68.34 \cdot 25 \cdot 4$
6834; Associative (multiplication)

4. $2\frac{3}{4} \cdot \frac{5}{2} \cdot \frac{2}{5}$

$2\frac{3}{4}$; Associative (multiplication)

5. $6 \cdot 996 + 6 \cdot 4$
6000; Distributive property

6. $7.9 \cdot 4.3 + 7.9 \cdot 5.7$
79; Distributive property

7. $45 \cdot (100 + 2)$
4590; Disributive property

Students should know:

1. The commutative properties involve reversing the order of the addends or factors.
2. The associative properties involve reassociating addends or factors.
3. The distributive property involves both multiplication and addition. Multiplication is distributive over addition.
4. The identity properties involve operations with 0 or 1.

Basic   1–23 odd, 25–33 all, Review
          Exercises
Average   1–43 odd, Review Exercises
Enriched   1–39 odd, 40–48 all, Review
          Exercises

PRACTICE WORKSHEET 4

1-5 BASIC PROPERTIES OF NUMBERS

■ Write in the answer blank the letter of the property illustrated in each equation.

d	**1.** $5(x + y) = 5x + 5y$	a. Commutative property of addition
c	**2.** $(5 + x) + y = 5 + (x + y)$	b. Commutative property of multiplication
e	**3.** $(7 + a) + 0 = 7 + a$	c. Associative property of addition
a	**4.** $7 + a = a + 7$	d. Distributive property of multiplication over addition
b	**5.** $1 \cdot a = a \cdot 1$	e. Identity property for addition

■ Name the property illustrated in each equation.

6. $5a + 7a = 7a + 5a$	Comm. (add.)
7. $10 \cdot 27 = 27 \cdot 10$	Comm. (mult.)
8. $7x + 7y = 7(x + y)$	Distributive
9. $4 \cdot (25x) = (4 \cdot 25)x$	Assoc. (mult.)
10. $3a + a = 3a + 1a$	Identity (mult.)

WRITTEN EXERCISES

Exercises 9–16 show that the identity properties of zero and one do not depend on how the numbers are written. Zero may be written $(1 - 1)$, $(5 - 5)$, or 0. One may be written $\frac{3}{3}$, $\frac{5}{5}$, or 1.

    Exercises 40–44 relate to the Preview.

    Exercise 45 is a discovery exercise for the distributive property of multiplication over subtraction. This property is formally stated in Section 1–6.

    The property stated in exercise 46 can be proved later.

Each equation illustrates the commutative property of addition or the associative property of addition. Name the property.

3. $6 + 3x = 3x + 6$ Commutative (addition)

4. $14 + 0 = 0 + 14$ Commutative (addition)

5. $12 + (4x + 2x) = (4x + 2x) + 12$ Commutative (addition)

6. $(13 + 22) + 5x = 5x + (13 + 22)$ Commutative (addition)

7. $(2 + 3x) + 7x = 2 + (3x + 7x)$ Associative (addition)

8. $23 + (47 + 2x) = (23 + 47) + 2x$ Associative (addition)

Each equation illustrates the identity property for addition or multiplication. Name the property.

9. $17 + 0 = 17$ addition   **10.** $13 + (1 - 1) = 13$ addition

11. $(5 - 5) + 6 = 6$ addition   **12.** $0 + 11 = 11$ addition

13. $6 \cdot \frac{3}{3} = 6$ multiplication   **14.** $1 \cdot 4\frac{2}{3} = 4\frac{2}{3}$ multiplication

15. $(5.3)1 = 5.3$ multiplication   **16.** $\frac{5}{5} \cdot \frac{3}{8} = \frac{3}{8}$ multiplication

Name the property illustrated in each equation.

17. $5 \cdot 7 = 7 \cdot 5$
Commutative property of multiplication

18. $6000 \cdot 438 = 438 \cdot 6000$
Commutative property of multiplication

19. $(17 \cdot 25) \cdot 4 = 17 \cdot (25 \cdot 4)$
Associative property of multiplication

20. $\left(\frac{4}{5} \cdot \frac{2}{3}\right) \cdot \frac{3}{1} = \frac{4}{5} \cdot \left(\frac{2}{3} \cdot \frac{3}{1}\right)$
Associative property of multiplication

21. $5 \cdot (10 + 3) = 5 \cdot 10 + 5 \cdot 3$
Distributive property of multiplication over addition

22. $(3 + 8) \cdot 10 = 3 \cdot 10 + 8 \cdot 10$
Distributive property of multiplication over addition

23. $(6 + 4.7) + 5.3 = 6 + (4.7 + 5.3)$
Associative property of addition

24. $(17.2 + 5.4) + 4.6 = 17.2 + (5.4 + 4.6)$
Associative property of addition

Use the property listed to write an expression equivalent to $5x + 2x$.

25. Commutative property of addition. $2x + 5x$

26. Distributive property of multiplication over addition. $(5 + 2)x$ or $x(5 + 2)$

Use the property listed to write an expression equivalent to $5(x + 2)$.

27. Distributive property of multiplication over addition. $5x + 5 \cdot 2$

28. Commutative property of addition. $5(2 + x)$

29. Commutative property of multiplication. $(x + 2)5$

Name the property illustrated in each equation.

30. $5x + (7 + x \cdot 2) = 5x + (7 + 2x)$
Commutative property of multiplication

31. $5x + (7 + 2x) = 5x + (2x + 7)$
Commutative property of addition

32. $5x + (2x + 7) = (5x + 2x) + 7$
Associative property of addition

33. $(5x + 2x) + 7 = (5 + 2)x + 7$
Distributive property of multiplication over addition

Use the distributive property of multiplication over addition to write an equivalent expression.

Sample: $5(100 + 3) = 5 \cdot 100 + 5 \cdot 3$

B **34.** $8\left(1 + \frac{1}{2}\right)$ $8 \cdot 1 + 8 \cdot \frac{1}{2}$ **35.** $6\left(3 + \frac{1}{3}\right)$ $6 \cdot 3 + 6 \cdot \frac{1}{3}$ **36.** $52(100 + 1)$
$52 \cdot 100 + 52 \cdot 1$

37. $43(100 + 1)$ $43 \cdot 100 + 43 \cdot 1$ **38.** $67(1000 + 1)$ $67 \cdot 1000 + 67 \cdot 1$ **39.** $29(1000 + 1)$
$29 \cdot 1000 + 29 \cdot 1$

Multiply in the order indicated. Simplify within parentheses first.

40. $[(123 \cdot 7) \cdot 11] \cdot 13$ 123,123   **41.** $(123 \cdot 7) \cdot (11 \cdot 13)$ 123,123

42. $123 \cdot (7 \cdot 11) \cdot 13$ 123,123   **43.** $123 \cdot [(7 \cdot 11) \cdot 13]$ 123,123

44. Explain why the puzzle in the Preview works. [*Hint:* What is $7 \cdot 11 \cdot 13$?]
For every 3-digit number abc, the product is (abc)(7 · 11 · 13) = abc(1001) = abcabc.
Evaluate the following expressions for $a = 2$, $b = 60$, and $c = 10$. Decide if there are other "distributive" properties.

C **45.** $a(b - c)$ $ab - ac$
       100   100
Is multiplication distributive over subtraction? Yes

46. $(b + c) \div a$ $b \div a + c \div a$ $\frac{a + b}{c}$ $\frac{a}{c} + \frac{b}{c}$
       35   35   6.2   6.2
Is division distributive over addition? Yes

47. $a(b \div c)$ $ab \div ac$
       12   600
Is multiplication distributive over division? No

48. $(b + c)^a$ $b^a + c^a$
       4900   3700
Is raising to a power distributive over addition? No

■ REVIEW EXERCISES

Simplify.

1. $4.23 + 6.7$ 10.93   **2.** $5 - 1.39$ 3.61   **3.** $0.05 \cdot 7.3$ 0.365

4. $72 - 0.6$ 71.4   **5.** $\frac{1}{4} + \frac{2}{3}$ $\frac{11}{12}$ **6.** $\frac{1}{4} \cdot \frac{2}{3}$ $\frac{1}{6}$

7. a. Copy and complete the table by substituting and simplifying.

a	b	$a^2 + b^2$	$(a + b)^2$	$b^2 - a^2$	$(b - a)^2$
2	3	? 13	? 25	? 5	? 1
1	4	? 17	? 25	? 15	? 9
5	5	? 50	? 100	? 0	? 0

b. Do you think that $a^2 + b^2$ and $(a + b)^2$ are equivalent? No
c. Do you think that $b^2 - a^2$ and $(b - a)^2$ are equivalent? No

• Suppose that you know these facts:

$$\square + \bigcirc = 59$$
$$(\square + \triangle) + \bigcirc = 106$$

Evaluate these expressions:

a. $\square + (\triangle + \bigcirc)$ 106 **b.** $\bigcirc + \square$ 59

c. $\triangle$ 47   **d.** $\square$

Students should recognize that they can answer the first two questions even though they don't know the values of the variables. Some students may recognize that $\triangle = 47$ because $\square$ and $\bigcirc$ together in the second equation are equal to 59. Don't talk about methods of solving equations at this time. The value of $\square$ cannot be found.

Emphasize that we can evaluate the first two expressions because numbers have certain general properties.

State which property is illustrated in each
equation.

1. $11 \cdot (100 + 3) = 11 \cdot 100 + 11 \cdot 3$
        Distributive Property

2. $5x + 3 = 3 + 5x$
        Commutative (addition)

3. $\frac{5}{5} \cdot \frac{x}{3} = \frac{x}{3}$
        Identity (multiplication)

4. $4 \cdot (25 \cdot 17) = (4 \cdot 25) \cdot 17$
        Associative (multiplication)

5. $57 + 0 = 57$
        Identity (addition)

PURPOSE

Using the language of mathematics effectively requires skill in simplifying algebraic expressions. This skill is widely used throughout algebra in such tasks as solving equations.

PREVIEW

Before having students look at the Preview, use the following number trick.
- Think of a number. Multiply it by 6. Add 30. Divide the result by 3. Subtract 12 from the quotient. Divide that result by 2. Then add 1. Tell me your result, and I will tell you the number you started with. (The result is the number you started with.)

If 0 is selected as the starting number, the chain of operations involves negative numbers. If you wish to avoid that at this time, instruct students to think of numbers that are greater than 0.

You may wish to let students try to explain why the series of operations takes them back to the starting number. However, their explanations are likely to be intuitive and unclear.

OBJECTIVE 1–6

To simplify algebraic expressions by using the basic properties and combining like terms.

You may wish to spend two days on this section. Refer to the Pacing Chart.

1–6 Using Basic Properties to Simplify Expressions

Preview

To explore a number trick, a student substituted different numbers for n into the expression:

$$[(6n + 30) \div 3 - 12] \div 2 + 1$$

The student kept getting the substituted number as a result. It seemed that the expression was equivalent to n, but the student didn't know how to show it.

In this lesson you will learn how to change complicated algebraic expressions into simpler ones.

■ LESSON

The expression shown below has four **terms**. Terms are parts of an expression "connected" by addition or subtraction signs.

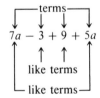

The terms $7a$ and $5a$ are called **like terms** because they contain the same variable factors. The terms 3 and 9 are also like terms because they contain no variable factors.

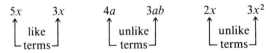

Exercise 45 in Section 1–5 showed that there is a distributive property of multiplication over subtraction.

Distributive Property of Multiplication over Subtraction

For all numbers a, b, and c,

$$ca - cb = c(a - b) \qquad \text{and} \qquad ac - bc = (a - b)c$$

Research indicates that students frequently think primitively in terms of symbols instead of thinking about the meanings of the symbols. For example, a student may think that 5x − x = 5 because when the variable "x" is taken away from the "5x," the symbol "5" is left. Therefore, it is important to repeatedly emphasize the meanings of the symbols. In the above case, have students do much substituting and simplifying.

The basic properties can be used to change an algebraic expression to a simpler *equivalent* expression.

Study these examples.

Example 1   Simplify. $4x + 3x$

Solution $4x + 3x = (4 + 3)x$ *Distributive property*
        $= 7x$ *Computation (4 + 3 = 7)*

Example 2   Simplify. $7y - 2y$

Solution $7y - 2y = (7 - 2)y$ *Distributive property*
        $= 5y$ *Computation*

Example 3   Simplify. $\frac{1}{2}(6y)$

Solution $\frac{1}{2}(6y) = \left(\frac{1}{2} \cdot 6\right)y$ *Associative property of multiplication*
        $= 3y$ *Computation*

Example 4   Simplify. $7a + a$

Solution $7a + a = 7a + 1a$ *Identity property for multiplication*
        $= (7 + 1)a$ *Distributive property*
        $= 8a$ *Computation*

Example 5   Simplify. $2x + 3y + 4x + y$

Solution $2x + 3y + 4x + y$
     $= 2x + 3y + 4x + 1y$ *Identity property for multiplication*
     $= (2x + 4x) + (3y + 1y)$ *Commutative and associative properties of addition*
     $= 6x + 4y$ *Distributive property and computation*

Example 6   Simplify. $2(4x + 1) + 3x$

Solution $2(4x + 1) + 3x$
     $= 2(4x) + 2(1) + 3x$ *Distributive property*
     $= (2 \cdot 4)x + (2 \cdot 1) + 3x$ *Associative property of multiplication*
     $= 8x + 2 + 3x$ *Computation*
     $= (8x + 3x) + 2$ *Commutative and associative properties of addition*
     $= 11x + 2$ *Distributive property and computation*

When simplifying expressions, you often combine steps as in Examples 5 and 6.

LESSON

Use examples to define *term, like terms,* and *unlike terms.* Then write this expression on the board.

$$3x + 2y + 4 + 5x + 6 + y$$

- How many terms are in the expression? (6)
- What are the like terms ($3x$ and $5x$ are like terms. So are $2y$ and y. And so are 4 and 6.)

After introducing the distributive property of multiplication over subtraction, ask students to complete these examples of the property:

$3(10 - 6) = ?$	$3 \cdot 10 - 3 \cdot 6$
$(7 - 5) \cdot 3 = ?$	$7 \cdot 3 - 5 \cdot 3$
$5x - 2x = ?$	$(5 - 2)x$

ADDITIONAL EXAMPLES

Example 1. Simplify. $5a + 3a$ $8a$
Example 2. Simplify. $6x - 2x$ $4x$
Example 3. Simplify. $\frac{1}{3}(12a)$ $4a$
Example 4. Simplify. $5x + x$ $6x$
Example 5.
Simplify. $4x + 3y + x + 5y$ $5x + 8y$
Example 6.
Simplify. $3(2a + 3) + 4a$ $10a + 9$

CHECK UNDERSTANDING

- State two like terms.
- State two unlike terms.
- State a term like $3x^2$. And a term like 7.

CLASSROOM EXERCISES

Students should explain how they know when terms are (or are not) like terms.

ASSIGNMENT GUIDE

Basic   1–39 odd, Review Exercises, Self-Quiz 2

Average 21–47 odd, Review Exercises, Self-Quiz 2

Enriched 21–39 odd, 41–56 all, Review Exercises, Self-Quiz 2

PRACTICE WORKSHEET 4

1-6 USING BASIC PROPERTIES TO SIMPLIFY EXPRESSIONS

■ Simplify these expressions.

1. $6a + 4a$ $10a$
2. $10b - b$ $9b$
3. $12a + a$ $13a$
4. $20a - 15a$ $5a$
5. $a + b + 2a$ $3a + b$
6. $3b + 5 + 6b$ $9b + 5$
7. $8 + 7b - 3$ $7b + 5$
8. $2(5a) + 3a$ $13a$
9. $5a - 5 - a$ $4a - 5$
10. $3a + a + 3$ $4a + 3$
11. $7a + 2b - b$ $7a + b$
12. $3b + 2(6b)$ $15b$
13. $2(a + 3) + 4$ $2a + 10$
14. $2 + 3(b + 1)$ $3b + 5$
15. $8(2 + b) + 2b$ $10b + 16$
16. $2a + 3(2 + a)$ $5a + 6$
17. $5(2b + a) + a$ $6a + 10b$
18. $3(a - b) - 2a$ $a - 3b$
19. $9a + b + 2b + a$ $10a + 3b$
20. $5b - a - b + a$ $4b$
21. $a^2 + a + 2a^2$ $3a^2 + a$
22. $3b + b^2 - 3b$ b^2
23. $3(a + b) - 3a$ $3b$
24. $2(a + 3) - 4$ $2a + 2$
25. $2a + 3b - a + b$ $a + 4b$
26. $2(3a + 2b) + a$ $7a + 4b$
27. $3(2a + 2b) - 2b$ $6a + 4b$
28. $a(a + 2) - a$ $a^2 + a$
29. $a(a + b) - ab$ a^2
30. $3(a - b) + 3b$ $3a$

EXTRA PRACTICE, page 618
COMPUTER WORKSHEET 1

■ CLASSROOM EXERCISES

1. What are the terms in this expression?

$2x - 2y + 7 + 4y$ 2x, 2y, 7, 4y

2. Are $2x$ and 7 like terms? No

3. Are $3x$ and $2yx$ like terms? No

4. Are $2ab$ and $5ba$ like terms? Yes

5. What are the like terms in this expression?

$$\boxed{3a} + \boxed{2b} + \boxed{5a} + \underline{9} - \underline{7} + \boxed{3b}$$

Simplify.

6. $3(4x)$ 12x
7. $\frac{1}{2}(8c)$ 4c
8. $2x + 3x$ 5x
9. $5y + 4y$ 9y
10. $2ab + 5ba$ 7ab
11. $2a + 6 + 3a$ 5a + 6
12. $3x + 2y + 4y$ 3x + 6y
13. $3 + 2(x + 5)$ 2x + 13
14. $6m + 3(4 + 2m)$ 12m + 12
15. $2a + 5$ 2a + 5

■ WRITTEN EXERCISES

State the number of terms in each expression.

A
1. $5x + 3$ Two
2. $7 + 4x$ Two
3. $5 + x + 3$ Three
4. $7 + 4 + x$ Three
5. $2xy + x$ Two
6. $2x + xy$ Two
7. $x - y - xy$ Three
8. $xy - x + y$ Three

List the terms in each expression.

9. $2x + 3y - 4x + 5xy$ 2x, 3y, 4x, 5xy
10. $5x^2 - 3y^2 + x + y$ 5x², 3y², x, y
11. $7a^2 + 8b^2 - 6 + 3ab$ 7a², 8b², 6, 3ab
12. $17 - a^2 + b^2 + 12ab$ 17, a², b², 12ab

State whether the terms are like or unlike.

13. $5a$ and a Like
14. $6b$ and 6   Unlike
15. $8c$ and 8   Unlike
16. d and $12d$ Like
17. $3xy$ and $7x$ Unlike
18. $10y$ and $20xy$ Unlike
19. $3x^2$ and $3x$ Unlike
20. $13x$ and $2x^2$ Unlike

Simplify these expressions.

21. $3m + 2m$ 5m
22. $5n + 4n$ 9n
23. $6x - 2x$ 4x
24. $5y - 2y$ 3y
25. $2a + a$ 3a
26. $3a + a$ 4a
27. $5b - b$ 4b
28. $9c - c$ 8c
29. $5a + 3a + 4b$ 8a + 4b
30. $2a + 3b + 4b$ 2a + 7b
31. $3 + 4a + 5$ 4a + 8
32. $8 + 2a + 4$ 12 + 2a
33. $8a + 3 + 6a + 2b$ 14a + 2b + 3
34. $5a + 2b + 2a + b$ 7a + 3b
35. $2(4x) + 3x$ 11x
36. $3(5x) + 2x$ 17x
37. $5(x + 2) + x$ 6x + 10
38. $3(x + 7) - 6$ 3x + 15
39. $3(2x + 5) + x + 1$ 7x + 16
40. $2(3x + 10) + x + 9$ 7x + 29

26   Chapter 1   Algebraic Expressions

26

Exercise 41–42 and 55–56 may be used for those wishing to use the properties in a more formal setting.

You might ask students to provide the correct simplifications for exercises 43–48 or to indicate when no further simplification is possible. (Answers: **43.** impossible; **44.** 4x; **45.** impossible; **46.** impossible; **47.** impossible; **48.** $x^2 + 4x + 4$)

B **41.** List the properties used to simplify the expression.

$$5(2x + 7) + x + 4 = 5 \cdot 2x + 5 \cdot 7 + x + 4$$
$$= (5 \cdot 2)x + 5 \cdot 7 + x + 4$$
$$= 10x + 35 + x + 4$$
$$= 10x + x + 35 + 4$$
$$= 10x + 1 \cdot x + 35 + 4$$
$$= (10 + 1)x + 35 + 4$$
$$= 11x + 39$$

a. _____?_____ Distributive property
b. _____?_____ Associative property of
Computation multiplication
c. _____?_____ Commutative property of addition
d. _____?_____ Identity property for multiplication
e. _____?_____ Distributive property
Computation

42. List the reason for each step used to simplify the expression.

$$7x + 3 + 8x + 2 = 7x + 8x + 3 + 2$$
$$= (7 + 8)x + 3 + 2$$
$$= 15x + 5$$

a. _____?_____ Commutative property of addition
b. _____?_____ Distributive property
c. _____?_____ Computation

43. Carmen simplified $2x + 1$ to $3x$. Show that she was wrong. $x = 0$ gives different values.

44. John simplified $5x - x$ to 5. Show that he was wrong. $x = 0$ gives different values.

45. Leonard simplified $x^2 + x$ to $3x$. Show that he was wrong. $x = 1$ gives different values.

46. Estela simplified $x^2 + x$ to $2x^2$. Show that she was wrong. $x = 3$ gives different values.

47. Amy simplified $3x^2 - x$ to $2x^2$. Show that she was wrong. $x = 3$ gives different values.

48. William simplified $(x + 2)^2$ to $x^2 + 4$. Show that he was wrong. $x = 1$ gives different values.

Simplify.

C **49.** $5(x + 2) + 3(x + 1)$ $8x + 13$ **50.** $x(x + 5x) + x^2$ $7x^2$ **51.** $\frac{1}{3}(6x + 12) - x$ $x + 4$

52. $\frac{1}{4}(x + 3) + \frac{3}{4}(x + 3)$ $x + 3$ **53.** $x(3 + x) + 3(5 - x)$ $x^2 + 15$**54.** $2(x + 7) + x(x + 5)$
$x^2 + 7x + 14$

Simplify. List the reason for each step.

55. $5(x + 3) + 10x$ $5x + 15 + 10x$ Distributive
$5x + 10x + 15$ Commutative, add
$15x + 15$ Distributive

56. $2(3x + 8) + 5$ $6x + 16 + 5$ Distributive
$6x + 21$ Computation

■ REVIEW EXERCISES

Simplify.   [1–2]

1. $8 + 4 - 2$ 10   **2.** $2 + 3 \cdot 10$ 32   **3.** $\frac{3}{4} - \frac{1}{3} + \frac{1}{2}$ $\frac{11}{12}$ **4.** $\frac{3}{5} + \frac{1}{2} - \frac{2}{3}$ $\frac{13}{30}$

Prove that the following pairs of expressions are not equivalent.   [1–4]

5. $5(a + 2)$ $a = 0$ gives   **6.** $(a - b)^2$ $a = 2$ and $b = 1$ **7.** $6x + 1$ $x = 0$ gives
$5a + 2$ different values $a^2 - b^2$ gives different values $7x$ different values

State the property illustrated in each equation.   [1–5]

8. $(3a + 4) + 5a = 3a + (4 + 5a)$ **9.** $2a + 3 = 3 + 2a$
Associative property of addition   Commutative property of addition
10. $5a + a = 5a + 1a$ Identity property for multiplication**11.** $5a + 1a = (5 + 1)a$ Distributive property

ENRICHMENT PROBLEM
Make up a problem

• Make up a number trick similar to the one in the Preview and then simplify the resulting expression to show why it works.

You could make a contest out of this to see who comes up with the most interesting or the most complicated puzzle.

In addition to the Computer Extensions in the student text, Computer Worksheets are supplied in the Teacher's Resource Binder. You may wish to assign Computer Worksheet 1 at this time. See the reduced copies of the Computer Worksheets in the front of this teacher's edition.

Self-Quiz 2

1–4 Evaluate the expressions.

1.

	x	y	$6x + 9y$	$15xy$
a.	1	1	? 15	? 15
b.	0	0	? 0	? 0
c.	3	1	? 27	? 45

d. Do you think that the expressions $6x + 9y$ and $15xy$ are equivalent?   No

1–5 State the number property illustrated in these equations.

2. $a(b + c) = ab + ac$ Distributive property

3. $a \cdot 1 = a$ and $1 \cdot a = a$
Identity property for multiplication

4. $(a + b) + c = a + (b + c)$
Associative property of addition

5. $ab = ba$
Commutative property of multiplication

1–6 Simplify.

6. $3x + 4x$ 7x

7. $a + 5a$ 6a

8. $2(b + 3) + 5$ 2b + 11

9. $2a + 8 + 5a + 15$
7a + 23

10. $\frac{1}{2}(6xy)(4z)$ 12xyz

11. $3(m + 2) + 4(m + 5)$
7m + 26

EXTENSION   Multiplication on a computer

For some operations, different symbols are used with computers than are used in algebra. To raise to a power, use the symbol ↑.
On a computer, 5↑2 means 5^2.

Example 1   Predict the computer output.

PRINT 4↑2 + 3

Solution $4^2 + 3 = 19$

Example 2   Write a computer command to find $(3 \cdot 5)^2$.

Solution   PRINT (3 * 5)↑2

Write the output for each command.

1. PRINT 3↑2 + 1   10

2. PRINT 9 − 2↑3   1

3. PRINT 4↑2 * 3   48

4. PRINT 4 * 3↑2   36

Write a computer command to evaluate.

5. 7^2 PRINT 7↑2

6. $(4 + 2)^3$
PRINT (4 + 2)↑3

7. $5^2 \cdot 3^2$
PRINT 5↑2 * 3↑2

8. $5 \cdot 6^2$ PRINT 5 * 6↑2

9. $(4^2)^3$ PRINT (4 ↑ 2)↑3

10. $6 \cdot 4 − 2^3$
PRINT 6 * 4 − 2↑3

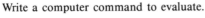

You may wish to spend two days on this section. Refer to the Pacing Chart.

Class Starter Quiz
on previous section

Simplify these expressions.
1. $2x + 4x$ $6x$
2. $a + 10a$ $11a$
3. $5 + y + 3y + 10$ $15 + 4y$
4. $2x + 3(x + 4)$ $5x + 12$
5. $5(x - 2) + 3x$ $8x - 10$

1–7 Applications — Writing Expressions for Related Quantities

Preview

Consider these dot figures.

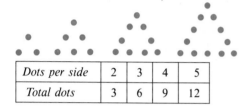

Dots per side	2	3	4	5
Total dots	3	6	9	12

What is the total number of dots for a "triangle" with:

- 10 dots per side?   27
- 100 dots per side?   297
- n dots per side? $3(n - 1)$

In this lesson you will be given situations (in words) and asked to express the relationships using the language and symbols of algebra.

■ LESSON

Study the following examples to see how to select a variable and write an expression for a relationship stated in words. Note that two solutions are given for each example.

> **Example 1**   Marcia is 2 years older than Jack. Write expressions using variables for their ages.
>
> *Solution 1*   Select a variable for one number:
> Let j be the number of years in Jack's age.
>
> Write an expression for the other number:
> Then $(j + 2)$ is the number of years in Marcia's age.
>
> *Solution 2*   Let m years be Marcia's age.
> Then $(m - 2)$ years is Jack's age.

At first, it is easy to make mistakes in writing expressions. You will make fewer mistakes if you check your work by substituting numbers that you *know* fit the sentence. For example, you know from reading the sentence that *if* Marcia is 16 years old, then Jack is 14 years old. Now check the expression.

Check Solution 1:   Let 14 be the number of years in Jack's age. Then $(14 + 2)$ is the number of years in Marcia's age. Since $14 + 2 = 16$, the numbers check.

Check Solution 2:   Let 16 years be Marcia's age. Then $(16 - 2)$ years is Jack's age. This also checks.

Get into the habit of checking!

PURPOSE

One of the principal reasons for studying algebra is to solve practical problems. To apply algebra to practical situations, it is often necessary to translate from the English language (in the real world) to the language of algebra (in the world of mathematics) and vice versa.

PREVIEW

Students may answer the first question by drawing a picture and counting the dots. However, that technique is too time consuming and boring for the second question. Students may notice one of the following relationships that simplify the work:

1. The number of dots is always a multiple of 3. The other factor is 1 less than the number of dots per side. Therefore, if there are 100 dots per side, the total number of dots is 3(99) or 297. If there are n dots per side, the total number of dots is $3(n - 1)$.

2. The total number of dots when there are 6 dots per side can be found by counting as shown in the figure.

$6 + 5 + 4 = 15$

Similar counting when there are 100 dots per side gives this result.

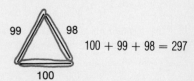

$100 + 99 + 98 = 297$

When there are n dots per side the total is $n + (n - 1) + (n - 2)$.

If both of the above techniques are discovered, have students show that these answers
to the third question are equivalent.

Do not *expect* students to answer the third
question. You may wish to return to the Preview for that question after the exercises have
been completed.

LESSON

Emphasize that the domain of a variable in all
examples and exercises in this lesson (and
throughout the book) is a set of numbers.
Therefore, the variable always represents a
number of something.

ADDITIONAL EXAMPLES

Example 1.
Neal is 10 pounds heavier than Kevin.

a. If k is Kevin's weight in pounds, what is
Neal's weight in pounds?

$$k + 10$$

b. If n is Neal's weight in pounds, what is
Kevin's weight in pounds?

$$n - 10$$

Example 2.
Suzanne has 5 times as many dimes as
quarters.

a. If q represents the number of quarters,
how many dimes does Suzanne have?

$$5q$$

b. If d represents the number of dimes, how
many quarters does Suzanne have?

$$\frac{d}{5}$$

Example 3.
The boiling point of water is 100° Kelvin
more than the freezing point of water.

a. If the boiling point of water is $x°$ Kelvin,
what is the freezing point of water in degrees Kelvin?

$$x - 100$$

b. If the freezing point of water is $y°$ Kelvin,
what is the boiling point of water in degrees Kelvin?

$$y + 100$$

Example 2 A rectangle is 3 times as long as it is wide. Write expressions using a variable
for its dimensions.

Solution 1

Let w be the width in centimeters.
Then $3w$ is the length in centimeters.

Solution 2

Let l be the length in centimeters.
Then $\frac{l}{3}$ or $\frac{1}{3}l$ is the width in centimeters.

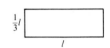

Example 3 The melting point of lead is 90°C (degrees Celsius) less than the melting
point of zinc. Write an expression for the melting point of each metal in degrees Celsius.

Solution 1

Let m be the melting point of lead in degrees Celsius.
Then $(m + 90)$ is the melting point of zinc in degrees Celsius.

Solution 2

Let n be the melting point of zinc in degrees Celsius.
Then $(n - 90)$ is the melting point of lead in degrees Celsius.

■ CLASSROOM EXERCISES

1. Let t be a number.
   a. What number is 3 greater than t? $(t + 3)$
   b. What number is 5 less than t? $(t - 5)$
   c. What number is 4 times as great as t? $4t$
   d. What number is $\frac{1}{2}$ as great as t? $\frac{1}{2}t$

2. A bicyclist pedals twice as fast as a marathoner runs.
   a. If r is the speed of the runner in miles per hour, then
   __?__ is the speed of the bicyclist in miles per hour. $2r$
   b. If b is the speed of the bicyclist in miles per hour, then
   __?__ is the speed of the runner in miles per hour. $\frac{1}{2}b$

3. Let n be a number.
   a. What number results if you increase n by 7? $(n + 7)$
   b. What number results if you decrease n by 10? $(n - 10)$
   c. What number results if n is tripled? $3n$
   d. What number results if n is halved? $\frac{1}{2}n$

■ WRITTEN EXERCISES

Complete.

A

1. Al is 3 years younger than Mary.
  a. If Al is 17 years old, then Mary is __?__ years old. 20
  b. Let A be Al's age in years. Then __?__ is Mary's age in years. $(A + 3)$

2. Juan is 4 cm taller than Jean.
  a. Let u be Juan's height in centimeters. Then __?__ is Jean's height in centimeters. $(u - 4)$
  b. Let e be Jean's height in centimeters. Then __?__ is Juan's height in centimeters. $(e + 4)$

3. John weighs 3 pounds more than Ted.
  a. Let d be John's weight in pounds. Then __?__ is Ted's weight in pounds. $(d - 3)$
  b. Let t be Ted's weight in pounds. Then __?__ is John's weight in pounds. $(t + 3)$

4. Jennifer scored 8 points more than Sarah.
  a. Let j be the number of points scored by Jennifer. Then Sarah scored __?__ points. $(j - 8)$
  b. Let s be Sarah's score. Then Jennifer scored __?__ points. $(s + 8)$

5. Susan lost 5 pounds more than Maria did.
  a. If Susan lost 12 pounds, then Maria lost __?__ pounds. 7
  b. Let s pounds be Susan's weight loss. Then Maria lost __?__ pounds. $(s - 5)$

6. The increase in Steve's height was 3 inches more than the increase in Barbara's height.
  a. If Barbara's height increased by 4 inches, then Steve grew __?__ inches. 7
  b. Let b inches be Barbara's increase in height. Then __?__ inches is Steve's increase in height. $(b + 3)$
  c. Let s inches be Steve's increase in height. Then __?__ inches is Barbara's increase in height. $(s - 3)$

7. a. If Mike is 17 years old, then 4 years ago he was __?__ years old. 13
  b. Let m be Mike's age in years. Then 4 years ago he was __?__ years old. $(m - 4)$
  c. In 5 years Mike will be __?__ years old. $(m + 5)$

8. a. If Kelly has 50 dollars and earns 10 dollars, then she has __?__ dollars. 60
  b. If Kelly has k dollars and earns 10 dollars, then she has __?__ dollars. $(k + 10)$
  c. If Kelly has y dollars and spends 10 dollars, then she has __?__ dollars. $(y - 10)$

9. A rectangle is 3 cm longer than it is wide.
  a. Let w be the width in centimeters. Then __?__ cm is the length. $(w + 3)$
  b. Let l be the length in centimeters. Then __?__ cm is the width. $(l - 3)$

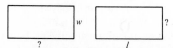

CLASSROOM EXERCISES

If the students have difficulty with the classroom exercises, the first few written exercises can be done orally as a group activity.

Sometimes a label should be used in a problem or in an answer to clarify the units used. For example, *x* centimeters, *x* meters, *x* miles, or *x* inches would clarify a measurement in a distance problem (where just *x* might be ambiguous). Sometimes the units are clear from the problem and need not be stated in the answer. In the beginning stages, however, students should be encouraged to use proper labels wherever they are appropriate.

ASSIGNMENT GUIDE

Basic   1–12 all, Review Exercises
Average 1–23 odd, Review Exercises
Enriched 9–17 odd, 19–30 all, Review Exercises

PRACTICE WORKSHEET 5

1-7 APPLICATIONS: WRITING EXPRESSIONS FOR RELATED QUANTITIES

■ Write an expression using the given variable.

1. Maria is 20 years older than Angela.
  a. Let x be Maria's age in years. What is Angela's age? **1a.** $x - 20$
  b. Let y be Angela's age in years. What is Maria's age? **b.** $y + 20$

2. Scott is 2 cm shorter than Brad.
  a. Let s be Scott's height in centimeters. What is Brad's height? **2a.** $s + 2$
  b. Let b be Brad's height in centimeters. What is Scott's height? **b.** $b - 2$

3. Mr. Cooper has x dollars.
  a. If Mr. Cooper receives ten more dollars, how many dollars will he have? **1a.** $x + 10$
  b. If Mr. Cooper spends two dollars, how many dollars will he have? **b.** $x - 2$
  c. If Mr. Cooper doubles his money, how many dollars will he have? **c.** $2x$

4. Mrs. Steele has s stamps.
  a. If Mrs. Steele uses 5 stamps, how many will she have left? **4a.** $s - 5$
  b. If each stamp is worth 25 cents, what is the value in cents of all the stamps? **b.** $25s$
  c. If Mrs. Steele uses half of the stamps, how many stamps will she have left? **c.** $s/2$

5. A secretary has s sheets of paper.
  a. Each sheet weighs 4.5 g. What is the weight in grams of all the paper? **5a.** $4.5s$
  b. The area of one side of a sheet of paper is 600 cm². What area in square centimeters can be covered using all the paper? **b.** $600s$
  c. Each sheet is 0.01 cm thick. How high in centimeters is the stack of all the paper? **c.** $0.01s$

6. A student has q quarters.
  a. If the student receives 5 more quarters, what will be the total number of quarters? **6a.** $q + 5$
  b. If 3 quarters are spent, what is the value in cents of those quarters remaining? **b.** $25(q - 3)$
  c. If 2 more quarters are received, what is the value in cents of all the quarters? **c.** $25(q + 2)$

WRITTEN EXERCISES

In exercises 13–30 the letters chosen for use as variables are arbitrary. However, it is often customary to use the first letter of the quantity being represented—for example, *h* for height, *b* for base, *j* for Jackie's weight in pounds, and so on. It is common to use *x* and *y* as variables when no obvious choice is evident.

The statement in exercise 30 is true. Many good students occasionally have difficulty translating into the language of algebra. Many errors can be avoided by quickly substituting numbers that are known to be correct.

PROBLEM-SOLVING NOTE
Developing understanding

Findings do not support emphasizing mathematical equivalents for word expressions (such as *addition* for *more than*). The teaching of word cues may give students temporary success. However, this practice is counterproductive eventually because it steers the students' thinking away from the ideas of the problem. This practice substitutes an unreliable crutch for the more powerful reasoning required for more difficult situations.

EXTRA PRACTICE, page 618

10. The height of a parallelogram is 4 cm less than its base.
    a. Let *h* be the height in centimeters. Then the base is __?__ cm. (h + 4)

    b. Let *b* be the base in centimeters. Then the height is __?__ cm. (b − 4)

11. Lead weighs 154 times as much as balsa wood.
    a. Let *x* be the weight of a cubic foot of lead in pounds. Then a cubic foot of balsa wood weighs __?__ pounds. $\frac{1}{154}x$
    b. Let *y* be the weight of a cubic inch of balsa wood in ounces. Then a cubic inch of lead weighs __?__ ounces. 154y

12. A jumbo jet weighs 946 times as much as the Wright brothers' first plane.
    a. Let *p* be the weight of a jumbo jet in tons. Then the Wright brothers' plane weighs __?__ tons. $\frac{1}{946}p$
    b. Let *m* be the weight of the Wright brothers' plane in pounds. Then a jumbo jet weighs __?__ pounds. 946m

Choose a variable for the first number. Then write an expression for the second number using the same variable.

B 13. Richard is 8 cm taller than Paula.
    a. Let __?__ be Richard's height in centimeters. Then __?__ is Paula's height in centimeters. r;(r − 8)
    b. Let __?__ be Paula's height in centimeters. Then __?__ is Richard's height in centimeters. p;(p + 8)

14. Jackie is 5 pounds lighter than Fred.
    a. Let __?__ be Jackie's weight in pounds. Then __?__ is Fred's weight in pounds. j;(j + 5)
    b. Let __?__ be Fred's weight in pounds. Then __?__ is Jackie's weight in pounds. f;(f − 5)

15. Arthur ran a mile 7.2 seconds faster than Walt.
    a. Let __?__ seconds be Arthur's time. Then __?__ seconds is Walt's time. a;(a + 7.2)
    b. Let __?__ seconds be Walt's time. Then __?__ seconds is Arthur's time. w;(w − 7.2)

16. Jill skied a slalom course 1.67 seconds slower than Jan.
    a. Let __?__ seconds be Jill's time. Then __?__ seconds is Jan's time. t;(t − 1.67)
    b. Let __?__ seconds be Jan's time. Then __?__ seconds is Jill's time. n;(n + 1.67)

17. Dana ran 3 times as many laps as Celina did.
    a. Let __?__ be the number of laps that Dana ran. Then __?__ is the number of laps that Celina ran. d;$\frac{1}{3}$d
    b. Let __?__ be the number of laps that Celina ran. Then __?__ is the number of laps that Dana ran. c;3c

Choose a variable for one number. Write an expression for the other number using the same variable. Answers may vary.

18. Meaghan and Sue are skydivers. In one jump Meaghan was in freefall twice as long as Sue. Susan: s; Meaghan: 2s

19. Morris and Ken ride motorcycles in hillclimbs. In one run Ken climbed three times as far as Morris. Morris: m; Ken: 3m

20. Pam and Sharon were running laps after school. Pam ran 0.7 as many laps as Sharon. Sharon: s; Pam: 0.7s

21. Chris practiced gymnastics 3 hours longer than Frank did. Frank: f; Chris: (f + 3)

22. Pam and Sharon were running laps after school. Pam ran 0.8 as many minutes as Sharon. Sharon: s; Pam: 0.8s

23. Frank practiced 3 more piano pieces than Chris did. Chris: c; Frank: (c + 3)

C **24.** Steve and Martin swam a total of 60 lengths of the pool. [*Remember:* It can be helpful to think of numbers that satisfy the conditions. For example, suppose that Steve swam 25 lengths.] Steve: s; Martin: (60 − s)

25. Millie and Janell pitched a total of 48 minutes in a softball game. Millie: m; Janell: (48 − m)

26. Kevin and James spent a total of $15.20. Kevin: k; James: (15.20 − k)

27. Phil and Sandy sold a total of 47 boxes of candy for the school band. Phil: p; Sandy: (47 − p)

28. a. Jane scored twice as many points as Pat did. Pat: p; Jane: 2p
b. If Sharon had scored 1 more point, she would have scored 3 times as many points as Pat did. Sharon: (3p − 1)

29. a. Jack earned half as much as Bill earned. Bill: b; Jack: $\frac{1}{2}b$
b. Howard earned 1 dollar more than half as much as Bill earned. Howard: $\frac{1}{2}b + 1$

30. Half of the mathematics students in a university class wrote incorrect expressions for this sentence because they didn't bother to check by substituting numbers that they *knew* worked. Try it.
    There are 12 students for every professor at this university.
Students: s; Professors: $\frac{s}{12}$ or Professors: p; Students: 12p

▪ REVIEW EXERCISES

Substitute 1 for a and $\frac{1}{3}$ for b and simplify.   [1–2, 1–3]

1. $(a + b)(a - b)$ $\frac{8}{9}$ **2.** $a^2 - b^2$ $\frac{8}{9}$

Show that the following pairs of expressions are not equivalent.   [1–4, 1–6]

3. $6x + 1$ and $7x$ Let x = 0.   **4.** $3a - 1$ and $2a$ Let x = 0.

5. $3x + 4y$ and $(3 + 4)xy$ Let x = 0 and y = 1.   **6.** $(a + b)^2$ and $a^2 + b^2$ Let a = 1 and b = 1.

State the property illustrated in each equation.   [1–5]

7. $a \cdot 2 + 3 = 2a + 3$
Commutative property of multiplication   **8.** $1 \cdot a + 1 \cdot a = (1 + 1) \cdot a$
Distributive property

COMPUTER EXTENSION

There is research evidence that computer programming can help clarify the concept of variables for students.
    Have the students use the following programs for exercise 30.

1. The input is the number of professors, and the output is the number of students.

```
10  PRINT "HOW MANY PROFESSORS";
20  INPUT P
30  S = 12*P
40  PRINT "THERE ARE "; S;
    "STUDENTS."
50  END
```

2. The input is the number of students, and the output is the number of professors.

```
10  PRINT "HOW MANY STUDENTS";
20  INPUT S
30  P = S/12
40  PRINT "THERE ARE "; P;
    "PROFESSORS."
50  END
```

ENRICHMENT PROBLEM
Logical reasoning

    Aardvark is $(a + 2)$ years old.
    Monique is $(b - 3)$ years old.
    Fuddletter is $(a + b)$ years old.

- Who is oldest?
- How does Fuddletter's age compare with the sum of Aardvark's age and Monique's age?

The value of b must be greater than 3, since Monique's age is $(b - 3)$; so Fuddletter $(a + b)$ is older than Aardvark $(a + 2)$ or Monique $(b - 3)$. Since $(a + 2) + (b - 3) = (a + b) - 1$, Fuddletter's age is greater than the sum of the other two ages.

■ CHAPTER SUMMARY

• **Vocabulary**

variable	[page 1]	product	[page 10]
substitution	[page 1]	coefficient	[page 10]
domain of variable	[page 1]	numerical coefficient	[page 10]
braces	[page 1]	exponent	[page 11]
simplest expression	[page 2]	base (of an exponent)	[page 11]
simplify	[page 2]	raise to a power	[page 11]
evaluate	[page 2]	equivalent expressions	[page 15]
order of operations	[page 5]	terms	[page 24]
brackets	[page 6]	like terms	[page 24]
factor	[page 10]		

• Simplify numerical expressions in the following order: [1–2, 1–3]

    1. Simplify inside the parentheses or other grouping symbols.

    2. Evaluate all powers.

    2. Do multiplications and divisions in order from left to right.

    4. Do additions and subtractions in order from left to right.

The Basic Properties of Numbers

Property	Addition	Multiplication
Commutative Associative Identity	For all numbers a, b, and c $a + b = b + a$ $(a + b) + c = a + (b + c)$ $a + 0 = a$	$ab = ba$ $(ab)c = a(bc)$ $1 \cdot a = a$
Distributive	$ab + ac = a(b + c)$ $ba + ca = (b + c)a$	

■ CHAPTER REVIEW

1–1 **Objective:** To substitute numbers for variables and simplify numerical expressions.

r	s	t	u
3	6	12	2

Substitute and simplify.

1. $r + 10$ 13   **2.** $t \cdot u$ 24   **3.** $\dfrac{t}{u}$ 6   **4.** $r + s + t$ 21

1–2 **Objective:** To simplify numerical expressions that have more than one operation.

Simplify.

5. $3 + 4 \cdot 5$ 23   **6.** $2 \cdot 5 + 4 \cdot 5$ 30   **7.** $(7 - 3) \cdot (7 + 3)$ 40   **8.** $\dfrac{20 - 8}{4}$ 3

1–3 **Objective:** To use algebraic notation for multiplication.

Simplify.

9. 3^4 81   **10.** $2 \cdot 5^2$ 50   **11.** $(2 \cdot 5)^2$ 100   **12.** $(10 - 5)^2$ 25

1–4 **Objective:** To decide whether expressions are equivalent.

13. a. Copy and complete the table by substituting and simplifying.

x	$3(x + 2)$	$3x + 2$
0	? 6	? 2
1	? 9	? 5
5	? 21	? 17

b. Do you think that $3(x + 2)$ and $3x + 2$ are equivalent?   No

1–5 **Objective:** To identify and use basic properties of addition and multiplication.

Identify the property illustrated in each equation.

14. $3 + x = x + 3$
Commutative property of addition
16. $4x + x = 4x + 1x$
Identity property for multiplication

15. $3x + 4x = (3 + 4)x$
Distributive property of multiplication over addition
17. $(67 \cdot 25) \cdot 4 = 67 \cdot (25 \cdot 4)$
Associative property of multiplication

1–6 **Objective:** To simplify algebraic expressions by combining like terms.

Simplify these expressions.

18. $x + 4x$ 5x   **19.** $4x + 5 + 3x$ 7x + 5   **20.** $3a + 4b + 5a$ 8a + 4b   **21.** $5(x + 3) + 2x$ 7x + 15
22. $4(x + 2) + 3$ 4x + 11   **23.** $3(x + 6) + 2$ 3x + 20   **24.** $3a + 6 + 4$ 3a + 10   **25.** $4b + 3 + 2b$ 6b + 3

1–7 **Objective:** To use algebraic expressions to express relationships that are stated in words.

Complete.

26. Mary has five dollars more than Carla.
   a. If Carla has c dollars, then Mary has   ?   dollars.   (c + 5)
   b. If Mary has m dollars, then Carla has   ?   dollars.   (m − 5)

27. A rectangle is three times as long as it is wide.
   a. If it is w cm wide, then it is   ?   cm long.   3w
   b. If it is l cm long, then it is   ?   cm wide. $\frac{1}{3}l$

TESTS

These tests are available as blackline copy-masters in the Teacher's Resource Binder. They are also available as duplicating masters.

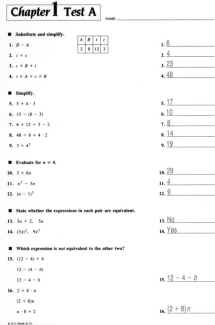

Chapter 1 Test A   NAME _____

■ **Substitute and simplify.**

	A	B	t	c
	2	8	12	3

1. $B - A$ 1. 6
2. $t \div c$ 2. 4
3. $c + B + t$ 3. 23
4. $t \times A + c \times B$ 4. 48

■ **Simplify.**

5. $5 + 4 \cdot 3$ 5. 17
6. $15 - (8 - 3)$ 6. 10
7. $6 + 12 \div 3 - 2$ 7. 8
8. $48 \div 8 + 4 \cdot 2$ 8. 14
9. $3 + 4^2$ 9. 19

■ **Evaluate for $n = 4$.**

10. $5 + 6n$ 10. 29
11. $n^2 - 3n$ 11. 4
12. $(n - 1)^2$ 12. 9

■ **State whether the expressions in each pair are equivalent.**

13. $3a + 2$, $5a$ 13. No
14. $(3x)^2$, $9x^2$ 14. Yes

■ **Which expression is *not* equivalent to the other two?**

15. $(12 - 4) + b$
    $12 - (4 - b)$
    $12 - 4 - b$ 15. $12 - 4 - b$

16. $2 + 8 \cdot n$
    $(2 + 8)n$
    $n \cdot 8 + 2$ 16. $(2 + 8)n$

© D.C. Heath & Co.

Chapter 1 Test A *(page 2)*   NAME _____

■ **Identify the property illustrated.**

17. $9 + 2x = 2x + 9$ 17. Commutative (add.)
18. $y \cdot 1 = y$ 18. Identity (mult.)
19. $4x + 3x = (4 + 3)x$ 19. Distributive
20. $8a + (3a + 7) = (8a + 3a) + 7$ 20. Associative (add.)

■ **Simplify.**

21. $7y - 3y$ 21. $4y$
22. $5(x + 3) + x$ 22. $6x + 15$

■ **Write an expression.**

23. Steve is 5 years older than Erin. Let E be Erin's age in years. Then ___?___ is Steve's age in years.   23. $E + 5$

24. Mary is 30 pounds lighter in weight than Jerry. Let j be Jerry's weight in pounds. Then ___?___ is Mary's weight in pounds.   24. $j - 30$

25. A rectangle is 4 times as long as it is wide. Let w be the width in centimeters. Then the perimeter in centimeters is ___?___.   25. $w + 4w + w + 4w$

26. Farley spends half as much time eating as Glenda does. Let f be Farley's eating time in minutes. Then Glenda's time in minutes is ___?___.   26. $2f$

★ **BONUS**

Consider these dot figures.

Dots per side	2	3	4	5
Total dots	4	8	12	16

How many dots per side does a "square" dot figure have with 812 total dots?   BONUS 204

© D.C. Heath & Co.

36

■ CHAPTER 1 SELF-TEST

a	A	B	x	y
2	0	4	1	3

1–1 Substitute and simplify.

1. $B(a + x)$ 12   2. Ay 0   3. ayB 24   4. $3B + 4y$ 24

1–2, 1–3 Simplify.

5. $3 + 6 \cdot 9$ 57   6. $8 \cdot 2 + 6 \cdot 4$ 40   7. $8 + 2 \cdot 6 + 4$ 24

8. $3 \cdot 8^2 + 12 \div 4$ 195   9. $8 - 4 + 6 \div 3$ 6   10. $27 - 12 \div 3$ 23

1–3 Let $n = 5$. Simplify.

11. $7n + 3$ 38   12. $n - 2^2$ 1   13. $(n - 2)^2$ 9

14. $5n^2$ 125   15. n^3 125   16. n^4 625

1–4 Copy and complete the tables by substituting and simplifying.

17.

x	$6x + 6$	$12x$
a. 0	? 6	? 0
b. 1	? 12	? 12
c. 2	? 18	? 24

d. Are the expressions $6x + 6$ and $12x$ equivalent? No

18.

y	$4(y + 7)$	$4y + 7$
a. 0	? 28	? 7
b. 1	? 32	? 11
c. 2	? 36	? 15

d. Are the expressions $4(y + 7)$ and $4y + 7$ equivalent? No

1–5 State the property illustrated in each equation.

19. $6 \cdot 12 + 6 \cdot 8 = 6(12 + 8)$
    Distributive property
20. $(32 \cdot 14) \cdot 5 = 32 \cdot (14 \cdot 5)$
    Associative property of multiplication
21. $8 + 42 = 42 + 8$
    Commutative property of addition
22. $1 + 0 = 1$ Identity property for addition

1–6 Simplify.

23. $3x + 8x$ 11x   24. $4a + 3b + 2a$ 6a + 3b

25. $5m + 7n + 2m + 3n$ 7m + 10n   26. $16 + 2y + 5$ 2y + 21

27. $4m + 6 + 2m + 3$ 6m + 9   28. $8m + 3n + 4n + m$ 9m + 7n

1–7 Write an algebraic expression.

29. Seven more than twice a number, n. 2n + 7

30. Sixteen less than the product of three and some number, k. 3k − 16

36   Chapter 1 Algebraic Expressions

■ PRACTICE FOR COLLEGE ENTRANCE TESTS

Choose the best answer for each question.

1. If $y = 3^2$, then $y^2 = \underline{\ ?\ }$.
   A. 3   **B.** 9   **C.** 27   <u>**D.** 81</u>   **E.** 243

2.

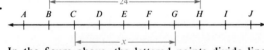

In the figure above, the lettered points divide line segment BH into segments of equal length. If $BH = 24$, then $x = \underline{\ ?\ }$.
   A. 4   **B.** 8   **C.** 12   <u>**D.** 16</u>   **E.** 20

3. If $y = \dfrac{(a+b)^2}{a^2-b}$, what is the value of y when $a = 2$ and $b = 1$?
   A. 1   **B.** 2   <u>**C.** 3</u>   **D.** 4   **E.** 6

4. If the average of two numbers is 9 and their product is 72, then the difference between the numbers is $\underline{\ ?\ }$.
   A. 2   **B.** 3   **C.** 4   **D.** 5   <u>**E.** 6</u>

5. If 2 dozen eggs cost $1.68, what is the cost of 7 dozen eggs?
   A. $2.52   **B.** $3.36   **C.** $4.20   **D.** $5.04   <u>**E.** $5.88</u>

6. If m and n are whole numbers and $m + n$ is divisible by 3, then which of the following must also be divisible by 3?
   A. $m^2 + n^2$ **B.** $m - n$ **C.** mn

   D. Either m or n, but not necessarily both   <u>**E.** None of these</u>

7. Juan, Henri, Erika, and Stasha each have a hamburger special lunch. Henri and Erika each also have a shake to drink. If the total bill is $15 and shakes cost $1.00, how much should Erika pay?
   A. $3.00   **B.** $3.25   **C.** $3.75   **D.** $4.00   <u>**E.** $4.25</u>

8. In the equation $5 + a + b = 17$, if a and b are positive 1-digit whole numbers, what is the smallest value that b can have?
   A. 1   <u>**B.** 3</u>   **C.** 5   **D.** 7   **E.** 9

9. If the height of the figure is 9 cm and the area of the square is 4 cm², what is the area of the triangle in square centimeters?
   A. 5   <u>**B.** 7</u>   **C.** 10

   D. 14   **E.** 28

9 cm

10. In a class of 30 algebra students, 16 are boys and 24 are ninth graders. There are 2 boys who are not ninth graders. How many girls are ninth graders?
   A. 4   **B.** 6   <u>**C.** 8</u>   **D.** 10   **E.** 12

11. If the perimeter of a rectangle is 40 cm and the width is 8 cm, what is the area?
   A. 64 cm²   **B.** 72 cm²   **C.** 80 cm²   **D.** 88 cm²   **E.** 96 cm²

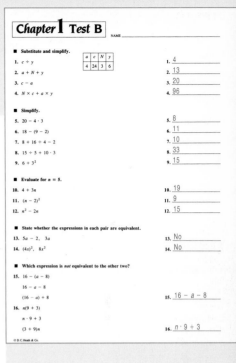

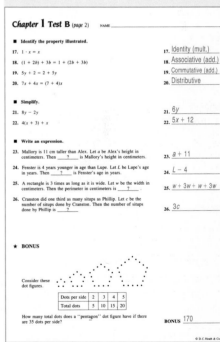

CHAPTER 2

CHAPTER OVERVIEW

In addition to the use of variables, another characteristic that distinguishes algebra from arithmetic is the use of negative numbers. The numbers used in algebra are the real numbers, which consist of the negative numbers, the positive numbers, and zero.

In Chapter 2, students learn to add, subtract, multiply, and divide real numbers. In order to compute with real numbers, students need to be able to compute accurately with whole numbers, fractions, and decimals. Skill in computing accurately with real numbers is essential to all further work in algebra.

In Chapter 2, students learn that the properties for addition and multiplication they learned in Chapter 1 apply to all real numbers. Students also learn addition properties that involve subtraction and division. Students learn to use these properties to simplify algebraic expressions that involve addition, subtraction, and multiplication. (Study of algebraic expressions that involve division will take place later, in Chapter 8, Algebraic Fractions and Applications.) By the end of Chapter 2, students should have learned the algebraic skills they will need for solving equations in Chapter 3.

In the final section of Chapter 2, students learn to solve problems by making a table of data. The major reason for learning mathematics is to be able to solve problems. The most frequently used strategy for solving problems in algebra is setting up equations and then solving them. However, students become much more effective problem solvers if they gain facility with a variety of problem-solving techniques. Making a table of data is an important technique for solving problems, particularly problems that are applications of mathematics.

2 Real Numbers

An object experiences the weight of the air above it as a pressure. At sea level, this pressure is 1 atmosphere (14.7 pounds per square inch). In descending below the surface of water, the pressure due to the weight of the water increases at the rate of about 1 atmosphere for every 33 feet. The total pressure at a depth of 33 feet is 2 atmospheres, one atmosphere due to the weight of the air and one atmosphere due to the weight of the water.

We can use the algebraic equation $P = \dfrac{d}{33} + 1$ to compute the total pressure P (in atmospheres) for a given depth d (in feet).

OBJECTIVE 2–1

To represent quantities using positive and negative numbers. To order real numbers using the number line. To use appropriate symbols for inequalities and absolute value.

PURPOSE

Models for real numbers should be understood before operations on real numbers are studied or their properties explored.

PREVIEW

Explore student knowledge of positive and negative numbers.

• The Preview suggests one use of positive and negative numbers. What are some other uses that you know of?

2–1 Real Numbers

Preview

Mount Everest, on the border between Nepal and Tibet in southern Asia, is the highest mountain on earth. It extends 8848 meters above sea level. The Mariana Trench, in the West Pacific, is the deepest point of the oceans. It is 11,034 meters below sea level.

Since these two measurements have opposite directions, we can use positive numbers and negative numbers to describe them.

In this lesson you will begin to study the uses of positive and negative numbers in algebra.

■ LESSON

When **opposite directions** are involved in measurements, we use **positive** and **negative numbers** to describe those measurements.

For example: 7.3 meters to the right: $^+7.3$ Earning $10: $^+10$

8 meters to the left: $^-8$ Spending $15: $^-15$

15 miles to the east: $^+15$ $50 profit: $^+50$

$9\frac{1}{2}$ miles to the west: $^-9\frac{1}{2}$ $30 loss: $^-30$

0 is neither positive nor negative

The set consisting of positive numbers, negative numbers, and zero is called the **set of real numbers.** The real numbers can be represented as points on the **number line.** The **integers** (. . ., $^-6$, $^-5$, $^-4$, $^-3$, $^-2$, $^-1$, 0, $^+1$, $^+2$, $^+3$, $^+4$, $^+5$, $^+6$, . . .) are shown on this number line.

The number line shows the **order** of the real numbers. For example, $^+6$ is to the *right* of $^+2$, so $^+6$ is *greater than* $^+2$. We write this relationship as $^+6 > {}^+2$. We can also state that $^+2$ is *less than* $^+6$. We write this relationship as $^+2 < {}^+6$.

We see by the number line that $^-2$ is to the *left* of 0, so $^-2$ is *less than* 0. That is, $^-2 < 0$. We can also write $0 > {}^-2$.

The number line below shows the order of some fractions and decimals:

We see that $^+\frac{1}{3}$ is to the *right* of $^-\frac{7}{8}$, so $^+\frac{1}{3} > {}^-\frac{7}{8}$, and that $^-0.7$ is to the *left* of $^-0.4$, so $^-0.7 < {}^-0.4$.

LESSON

As students give examples, emphasize the opposite "directions" involved.

Students have used the number line since early in elementary school. Give them an opportunity to demonstrate and expand their knowledge. Draw this picture on the board and label the points with 0 and 1.

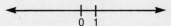

Then pick other points on the line (for example, 2, $^-1$, ½, etc.) and ask:

• What number goes with this point?
• How do you know?

When many points are labeled, continue as follows:

• If we move from left to right on the number line, do the numbers get larger or smaller? (Larger)
• Which way are we moving if the numbers get smaller? (To the left)
• Is 1 to the left or right of 2? (Left)
• Is 1 less than or greater than 2? (Less than)
• Is $^-1$ to the left or right of $^-2$? (Right)
• Is $^-1$ less than or greater than $^-2$? (Greater than)

Introduce the symbols $<$ and $>$. Continue asking questions like those above and write the results using the inequality signs. If students have trouble remembering which sign has which meaning, point out that the smaller end of the sign is always next to the smaller number.

Introduce absolute value as the distance of the number from 0 on the number line. A more formal definition is:

The absolute value of a negative number is the opposite of the number.

The absolute value of a nonnegative number is the number itself.

No formal definition of *real number* is given in this book. Students may think of real numbers as all positive numbers, their opposites (negative numbers), and zero. Until square roots are used later in the book, nearly all the real numbers appearing in examples and exercises are rational numbers. Occasionally the irrational number π is used. When the number line is used, some points between the integer points should be labeled—for example, ½, −½, 2 ¼, and, as student understanding allows, π, $\sqrt{2}$, $-\sqrt{2}$.

At first, in this section a distinction is made between ⁻5 (negative 5) and −5 (the opposite of five). Later, this distinction is dropped and only the −5 notation is used. Then, −5 is usually read "negative five." However, −*x* should be read "the opposite of *x*" because, depending on the substitutions made for *x*, −*x* may represent a positive or a negative number.

ADDITIONAL EXAMPLES

Example 1. Simplify.

   a. −⁻7   **b.** −⁺4   **c.** −|⁻2|
     7   −4   −2

Example 2. Simplify, writing without + or − signs.

   a. +9   **b.** ⁻7   **c.** −(−⁻3)
     9   −7   −3

CHECK UNDERSTANDING

- If 2 miles to the south is represented by ⁺2, what is 2 miles to the north represented by? (⁻2)
- State 3 numbers less than 0.
- State a number that has an absolute value of 5. (⁻5, ⁺5, −5, −(−5))

Note that the point ⁺3 and the point ⁻3 are the same distance from zero. This distance is called the **absolute value** of ⁺3 and ⁻3.

The absolute value of any number (except zero) is a positive number. The absolute value of zero is zero. The absolute value is indicated by the symbol, | |. For example,

   $|{}^-3| = {}^+3$ "The absolute value of negative three is positive three."

   $|{}^+1.5| = {}^+1.5$ $\left|\frac{-1}{2}\right| = \frac{+1}{2}$ $|0| = 0$

Numbers that have the same absolute value and opposite signs are called **opposites.** For example, ⁺3 and ⁻3 are opposites, and ⁺5 is the opposite of ⁻5. It is also the case that zero is the opposite of zero.

The symbol "−" is used to express opposites. For example, to write an expression for the opposite of ⁺6, write −⁺6. To write an expression for the opposite of the opposite of *y*, write −(−*y*).

> **Example 1** Simplify. **a.** −⁺5   **b.** −⁻3   **c.** −|⁻3| **d.** −0
>
>   *Solution* **a.** −⁺5 = ⁻5   **b.** −⁻3 = ⁺3
>   **c.** −|⁻3| = −(⁺3) = ⁻3   **d.** −0 = 0

To simplify notation, mathematicians do not use the raised + and − signs for positive and negative numbers. Instead, no sign is used with positive numbers and the symbol for opposites is used to indicate negative numbers.

> **Example 2** Simplify, writing without raised + and − signs.
>   **a.** ⁺8   **b.** ⁻7   **c.** −(⁺4)   **d.** −(−⁺2)
>
>   *Solution* **a.** ⁺8 = 8   **c.** ⁻7 = −7
>   **c.** −(⁺4) = −4   **d.** −(−⁺2) = −(−2) = 2

■ CLASSROOM EXERCISES

Read the symbols.

1. ⁺8 Positive eight **2.** ⁻16   **3.** < Is less than   **4.** > Is greater than **5.** |⁻3|
                         Negative sixteen   The absolute value of negative three
Read. Then state whether the sentence is true or false.

6. ⁺8 < ⁺10 T   **7.** ⁻8 > ⁻10 T   **8.** ⁻3 < 0 T   **9.** ⁻2 > ⁺1 F   **10.** ⁺7 > ⁻12 T

11. $\frac{-1}{4} < \frac{-1}{2}$ F   **12.** 0.75 > 0.39 T   **13.** |−7| = −7 F

14. |−3| = 3 T   **15.** −(−5) = −5 F   **16.** −|−2| = −2 T

CLASSROOM EXERCISES

In classroom exercises 6–16, the sentences should be read from left to right. For example, $^+8 < {^+}10$ is read "positive 8 is less than positive 10," not "positive 10 is greater than positive 8."

Go over the Strategies for Success feature so that students know what to do when they become frustrated while doing homework. Students should know whether it is acceptable to ask for help from classmates, parents, or siblings, and at what times they may approach you for extra help.

ASSIGNMENT GUIDE

Basic   1–34 all, Review Exercises
Average 1–27 odd, 29–58 all, Review Exercises
Enriched 1–45 odd, 47–64 all, Review Exercises

Write using algebraic symbols.

17. The absolute value of negative three $|^-3|$

18. The opposite of positive six $-{^+}6$

19. The opposite of negative three is equal to positive three. $-{^-}3 = {^+}3$

20. The absolute value of negative two is equal to positive two. $|^-2| = {^+}2$

■ WRITTEN EXERCISES

Use positive or negative numbers to represent each of the following:

A

1. 30 feet below sea level $^-30$

2. 520 feet above sea level $^+520$

3. 23°C above freezing $^+23$

4. 6°C below freezing $^-6$

5. A loss of $380 $^-380$

6. A profit of $870 $^+870$

7. A gain of 18 yards in football $^+18$

8. A loss of 3 yards in football $^-3$

Write each statement in algebraic symbols.

9. Positive five is greater than negative three. $^+5 > {^-}3$

10. Negative two is less than zero. $^-2 < 0$

11. One-fourth is greater than negative one. $\frac{1}{4} > {^-}1$

12. The opposite of three is less than zero. $-3 < 0$

Replace ⑦ with <, >, or = to make a true statement.

13. 2.1 ⑦ 7.3 <

14. 4.9 ⑦ 1.8 >

15. $3\frac{1}{2}$ ⑦ -1 >

16. $\frac{3}{4}$ ⑦ $6\frac{1}{4}$ <

17. 0 ⑦ -6 >

18. $-12\frac{7}{8}$ ⑦ 0 <

19. -3 ⑦ -5 >

20. -8 ⑦ -5 <

Simplify.

21. $|-8|$ 8

22. $|-6|$ 6

23. $|4|$ 4

24. $|9|$ 9

25. $|3\frac{2}{3}|$ $3\frac{2}{3}$

26. $|-5\frac{2}{5}|$ $5\frac{2}{5}$

27. $|-13.67|$ 13.67

28. $|11.24|$ 11.24

True or false?

29. $8 < 11$ T

30. $3.7 > 2.9$ T

31. $0 > -2$ T

32. $0 > -4$ T

33. $-4 < -9$ F

34. $-5.2 < -4.8$ T

B **35.** $|-8| < |3|$ F

36. $|2| > |-6|$ F

37. $|7| > |-8|$ F

38. $|-10| < |-6|$ F

39. The opposite of the opposite of y is y. T

40. The value of the opposite of x can be positive, negative, or zero depending on the value of x. T

41. The absolute value of zero is zero. T

42. The opposite of zero is zero. T

PRACTICE WORKSHEET 6

2-1 REAL NUMBERS

■ Write <, >, or = to make a true statement.

1. $^+2.3$ ⊖ $^-3.1$ 2. $^-4.1$ ⊖ $^-1.7$ 3. $^+11.7$ ⊖ $^+117$

4. $-5\frac{1}{4}$ ⊖ $-6\frac{1}{8}$ 5. $|-7.8|$ ⊖ $|7.8|$ 6. $|-10.4|$ ⊖ $|-14.3|$

7. $|^+12\frac{1}{2}|$ ⊖ $|-12\frac{1}{2}|$ 8. $\frac{1}{2}$ ⊖ $\frac{2}{3}$ 9. $\frac{1}{2}$ ⊖ $-\frac{2}{3}$

10. $-\frac{1}{2}$ ⊖ $-\frac{2}{3}$ 11. $-\frac{1}{2}$ ⊖ $\frac{2}{3}$ 12. $-1\frac{1}{4}$ ⊖ $|\frac{5}{4}|$

■ Simplify.

13. $|-8.3|$ 8.3   14. $|2.8|$ 2.8   15. $|0|$ 0

16. $-(5.7)$ -5.7 17. $-(-7.3)$ 7.3   18. $-|-3|$ -3

19. $|-0.3|$ 0.3   20. $|-(7)|$ 7   21. $-|6|$ -6

22. $-(-8.2)$ 8.2   23. $-(8.2)$ -8.2 24. $-|-8.2|$ -8.2

WRITTEN EXERCISES

Note exercises in which the opposite of a negative number is used. For example, see exercises 47, 49, and 50.

COMPUTER EXTENSION

1. Write a program with an INPUT statement that gives the absolute value of the number as the output. Do not use the ABS function in the program.

```
10 INPUT N
20 IF N < 0 THEN 50
30 PRINT N
40 GO TO 60
50 PRINT -N
60 END
```

2. Write a program using the ABS function that gives the absolute value of the number as the output.

```
10 INPUT N
20 PRINT ABS(N)
30 END
```

ENRICHMENT PROBLEMS

• The opposite of the opposite of a number is negative. What can you say about the number?

It is negative.

• $-|-|-x||$ is not negative. What can you say about x?

It is 0.

EXTRA PRACTICE, page 619
COMPUTER WORKSHEET 2

Write the numbers in order from least to greatest.

43. $0, 1, -2$ $-2, 0, 1$

44. $-10, -3, 4, -1$ $-10, -3, -1, 4$

45. $1.5, -\frac{1}{2}, 0, -1$ $-1, -\frac{1}{2}, 0, 1.5$

46. $-1.61, 1.61, -0.161, 16.1$ $-1.61, -0.161, 1.61, 16.1$

A	a	B	M	p	r
-6	-4	-2	3	5	$\frac{1}{2}$

Substitute and simplify.

47. $-B$ 2

48. $-r$ $-\frac{1}{2}$

49. $-A + p$ 11

50. $-a + M$ 7

51. $|A|$ 6

52. $|B|$ 2

53. $|M|$ 3

54. $|p|$ 5

55. $|-r|$ $\frac{1}{2}$

56. $|-a|$ 4

57. $-|r|$ $-\frac{1}{2}$

58. $-|a|$ -4

Solve.

C **59.** $|-6| = x$ (6)

60. $|x| = 6$ $(6, -6)$

61. $-a = 2$ (-2)

62. $|-a| = 2$ $(2, -2)$

63. $|x| = 0$ (0)

64. $-x = 0$ (0)

■ REVIEW EXERCISES

Simplify.

1. $3.14 + 6.7$ 9.84

2. $4.34 + 17 + 3.9$ 25.24

3. $\frac{1}{2} + \frac{1}{3}$ $\frac{5}{6}$

4. $2\frac{3}{4} + 4\frac{1}{2}$ $7\frac{1}{4}$

5. $6 - 1.27$ 4.73

6. $43.15 - 27.14$ 16.01

7. $\frac{2}{3} - \frac{1}{2}$ $\frac{1}{6}$

8. $2\frac{1}{2} - \frac{3}{4}$ $1\frac{3}{4}$

EXTENSION   Checking accounts

Some bank statements for checking accounts use positive numbers for deposits and negative numbers for withdrawals. Deposits are called credits, and withdrawals are called debits. A summary of transactions might look like that shown below. Compute the new balance (the amount currently in the account).

Previous balance:	$845.32
Credits (2):	367.26
Debits (8):	-598.52
Service charge:	$-.60$
New balance:	? $613.46

Strategy for Success   Doing assignments

Be sure to complete your assignment every day. Each idea in algebra builds on ideas that come before. If you don't understand one idea, you may have difficulty with ideas that come later.

2–2 Adding Real Numbers

Preview A model for addition

One way to think about addition of real numbers is to use the following model. There are two types of electrical charge. One type is positive and the other negative. When a positive charge and a negative charge are combined the result is a 0 charge (neutral).

Positive   Negative   Neutral

The charge on this set is 3.

Then 4 negative charges are added.

After pairing up the charges, the result is a charge of − 1.

The example above shows that $3 + (-4) = -1$.

Write addition equations for these two examples.

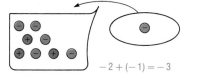
$-2 + (-1) = -3$

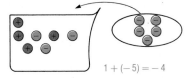
$1 + (-5) = -4$

In this lesson, you will learn the rules for adding real numbers.

■ LESSON

We can use the number line to find the sums of real numbers. Think of positive numbers as indicating "trips" to the right and negative numbers as indicating "trips" to the left. For example, consider the sum $-1 + (-2)$.

Start at 0. Go 1 unit to the left. Then go 2 more units to the left. The single equivalent "trip" is − 3.

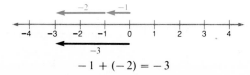

$$-1 + (-2) = -3$$

The example above illustrates that the sum of two negative numbers is a negative number. Similarly, the sum of two positive numbers is a positive number.

Replace ⑦ with $<$, $>$, or $=$ to make a true statement.

1. -7 ⑦ 5 $<$

2. $|-6|$ ⑦ 3 $>$

Use symbols to represent these expressions. Then simplify the expressions.

3. The absolute value of positive four $|4| = 4$

4. The opposite of negative three $-(-3) = 3$

5. The absolute value of the opposite of positive two $|-2| = 2$

PURPOSE

Skill in adding real numbers is a prerequisite for later work with algebraic expressions.

PREVIEW

The electrical-charge model is easily understood and is a good model for students to use to explore operations with positive and negative numbers. Use the Preview to introduce the model and its use in addition. Addition of integers is pictured as combining two sets of charges. The sum is the number of like (either positive or negative) charges that remain after all possible neutral (positive-negative) pairs have been formed.

Draw a picture like this:

- What addition equation fits the picture? $(-3 + 2 = -1)$
- Draw a picture for this equation and complete the equation. $6 + (-4) = ?$ (2)
- What is the result of adding two positive numbers? (Result is positive.)
- What is the result of adding two negative numbers? (Result is negative.)
- What is the result of adding a positive number to a negative number? (Result will be positive or negative.)

If you extended the Preview as suggested above, you may wish to go directly to the rules for adding integers given on page 45. If not, use the number-line model in the lesson to help students understand addition. Ask questions like those given for the electrical model shown above.

ADDITIONAL EXAMPLES

Use the number line to compute each sum.

Example 1. $-2 + (-4)$

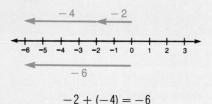

$$-2 + (-4) = -6$$

Example 2. $3 + (-4)$

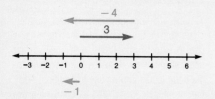

$$3 + (-4) = -1$$

Example 3. $-4 + 4$

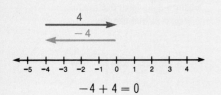

$$-4 + 4 = 0$$

$$2 + 3 = 5$$

Cases in which a positive number is added to a negative number are more complex because one trip "cancels" all or part of another.

Example 1 Use the number line to compute the sum.

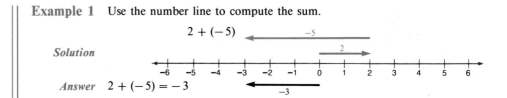

$$2 + (-5)$$

Solution

Answer $2 + (-5) = -3$

Example 1 shows that if the "negative trip" is longer than the "positive trip", then the ending point is on the negative side of 0. That is, the sum of a positive number and a negative number is negative if the negative addend has the greater absolute value.

Example 2 Use the number line to compute the sum.

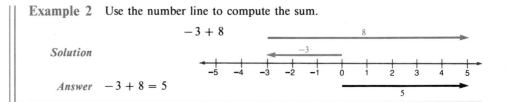

$$-3 + 8$$

Solution

Answer $-3 + 8 = 5$

Example 2 shows that the sum of a positive number and a negative number is positive, if the absolute value of the positive addend is greater.

Example 3 Use the number line to compute the sum.

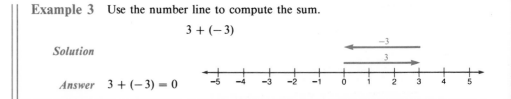

$$3 + (-3)$$

Solution

Answer $3 + (-3) = 0$

Example 3 shows that the sum of opposites is 0.

CHECK UNDERSTANDING

- What is the sum of 4 and 3? (7)
- What is the sum of -4 and -3? (-7)
- What is the sum of 4 and -3? (1)
- What can you say about the sign of the sum of two positive numbers? (Positive)
- What can you say about the sign of the sum of a positive number and a negative number? (The sum gets the sign of the number with the larger absolute value.)

Here are the rules that can be used for adding real numbers.

Rule	Examples	
1. To add real numbers with the same sign:	$3 + 2$	$-4 + (-3)$
a. Find their absolute values.	$|3| = 3$ and $|2| = 2$	$|-4| = 4$ and $|-3| = 3$
b. Add their absolute values.	$3 + 2 = 5$	$4 + 3 = 7$
c. Give the result the same sign as the addends have.	5 $3 + 2 = 5$	-7 $-4 + (-3) = -7$
2. To add real numbers with different signs:	$5 + (-2)$	$1 + (-6)$
a. Find their absolute values.	$|5| = 5$ and $|-2| = 2$	$|1| = 1$ and $|-6| = 6$
b. Subtract the smaller absolute value from the larger.	$5 - 2 = 3$	$6 - 1 = 5$
c. Give the result the sign of the addend with the larger absolute value.	3 $5 + (-2) = 3$	-5 $1 + (-6) = -5$
3. If the addends are opposites, then the sum is 0.	$4 + (-4) = 0$	
4. The sum of a real number and 0 is that same real number.	$-5 + 0 = -5$	

CLASSROOM EXERCISES

Classroom exercises 9–13 show a pattern. When the first addend is held constant and the second addend decreases by one, the sum also decreases by one. A similar pattern could be examined starting with a negative addend.

1. $-5 + 2$ **2.** $-5 + 1$ **3.** $-5 + 0$
  -3 -4 -5
4. $-5 + -1$ **5.** $-5 + -2$
  -6 -7

The sums continue a pattern.

■ CLASSROOM EXERCISES

Write an addition equation for each figure.

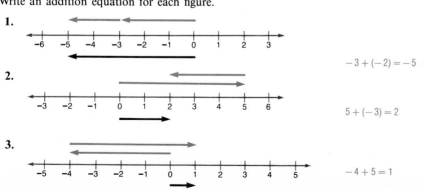

1.

$-3 + (-2) = -5$

2.

$5 + (-3) = 2$

3.

$-4 + 5 = 1$

4.

5.
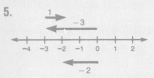

6.

7.

8.

ASSIGNMENT GUIDE

Basic   1–29 all, Review Exercises
Average   1–29 odd, 30–49 all, Review
          Exercises
Enriched   1–41 odd, 42–53 all, Review
          Exercises

PRACTICE WORKSHEET 6

2-2 ADDING REAL NUMBERS

■ Simplify.

1. $5 + (-8)$ __−3__
2. $-5 + (-8)$ __−13__
3. $-5 + 8$ __3__
4. $-2.3 + (-4.7)$ __−7.0__
5. $-2.3 + 4.7$ __2.4__
6. $2.3 + (-4.7)$ __−2.4__
7. $1\frac{2}{3} + 5\frac{1}{3}$ __7__
8. $12 + (-1)$ __11__
9. $-6 + (-6)$ __−12__
10. $-6 + 6$ __0__
11. $-5.4 + (-2.1)$ __−7.5__
12. $5.4 + (-2.1)$ __3.3__
13. $-\frac{3}{4} + \frac{3}{4}$ __0__
14. $|-8| + 3$ __11__
15. $|-8| + (-3)$ __5__
16. $-8 + (-3)$ __−11__
17. $|-8| + |-3|$ __11__
18. $|-8 + (-3)|$ __11__
19. $(-2 + 3) + 4$ __5__
20. $-2 + (3 + 4)$ __5__
21. $-1.7 + (-1.3 + 4.1)$ __1.1__
22. $(-1.7 + (-1.3)) + 4.1$ __1.1__
23. $|-1.2 + (-1.5)| + (-4.7)$ __−2.0__
24. $-1.2 + |-1.5 + (-4.7)|$ __5.0__
25. $1\frac{5}{6} + (-\frac{1}{3} + \frac{1}{2})$ __2__

EXTRA PRACTICE, page 619

Draw a number line and state each sum.

4. $2 + (-7)$ −5   **5.** $-3 + 1$ −2   **6.** $5 + (-5)$ 0   **7.** $0.2 + (-0.2)$ 0   **8.** $-\frac{3}{5} + \left(-\frac{2}{5}\right)$ −1

Simplify.

9. $4 + (-1)$ 3   **10.** $4 + (-2)$ 2   **11.** $4 + (-3)$ 1   **12.** $4 + (-4)$ 0   **13.** $4 + (-5)$ −1

14. The sum of opposites is _?_. 0

15. In which of Exercises 4–13 are opposites added? #6, 7, and 12

Simplify.

16. $(6 + (-3)) + (-5)$ −2   **17.** $-(3 + (-5))$ 2   **18.** $|-6 + 2|$ 4   **19.** $|-6| + |2|$ 8

■ WRITTEN EXERCISES

Simplify.

Ⓐ **1.** $3 + (-7)$ −4   **2.** $6 + (-11)$ −5   **3.** $-5 + (-9)$ −14   **4.** $-6 + (-8)$ −14

5. $-3 + 10$ 7   **6.** $-2 + 6$ 4   **7.** $7 + (-7)$ 0   **8.** $9 + (-3)$ 6

9. $6 + (-6)$ 0   **10.** $8 + 9$ 17   **11.** $-8 + 8$ 0   **12.** $-6 + 5$ −1

13. $9.3 + 8$ 17.3   **14.** $7.6 + 5$ 12.6   **15.** $5.31 + (-7.40)$ −2.09   **16.** $4.95 + (-6.49)$ −1.54

17. $-1.25 + 1.25$ 0   **18.** $-1.35 + (-1.35)$ −2.7   **19.** $-1.95 + 10$ 8.05   **20.** $-3.45 + 20$ 16.55

21. $-16 + 4$ −12   **22.** $5 + (-20)$ −15   **23.** $4 + (-16)$ −12   **24.** $-20 + 5$ −15

25. $(-8 + 4) + (-2)$ −6   **26.** $(-11 + 8) + (-3)$ −6   **27.** $-8 + (4 + (-2))$ −6   **28.** $-11 + (8 + (-3))$ −6

29. In which of Exercises 1–24 are opposites added? #7, 9, 11, and 17

Simplify.

Ⓑ **30.** $-(18 + (-12))$ −6   **31.** $-(26 + (-32))$ 6   **32.** $-18 + 12$ −6

33. $-26 + 32$ 6   **34.** $\left|7\frac{3}{4} + \left(-8\frac{1}{2}\right)\right|$ $\frac{3}{4}$ **35.** $\left|-2\frac{1}{2} + 3\frac{1}{4}\right|$ $\frac{3}{4}$

36. $\left|7\frac{3}{4}\right| + \left|-8\frac{1}{2}\right|$ $16\frac{1}{4}$ **37.** $\left|-2\frac{1}{2}\right| + \left|3\frac{1}{4}\right|$ $5\frac{3}{4}$ **38.** $|12.46 + (-3.51)|$ 8.95

39. $|-41.28 + 84.35|$ 43.07   **40.** $|12.46| + |-3.51|$ 15.97   **41.** $|-41.28| + |84.35|$ 125.63

a	b	c	x	y	z
-9	7	3	-2.5	3.6	-6.7

Substitute and simplify.

42. $(a + c) + y$ −2.4   **43.** $(b + x) + z$ −2.2   **44.** $a + (c + y)$ −2.4   **45.** $b + (x + z)$ −2.2

46. $|b + x|$ 4.5   **47.** $|a + y|$ 5.4   **48.** $|b| + |x|$ 9.5   **49.** $|a| + |y|$ 12.6

WRITTEN EXERCISES

In exercises 42–45, the associative property may be discussed. In exercises 46–49 point out that $|a + b| \neq |a| + |b|$.

COMPUTER EXTENSION

1. Write a computer program with INPUT statements that you could use to do exercises 1–24.

```
10 INPUT A
20 INPUT B
30 PRINT A; "+"; B; "="; A + B
40 END
```

2. Write simple computer programs using PRINT statements for exercises 25, 39, and 41.

```
25. 10 PRINT (−8 + 4) + (−2)
    20 END
39. 10 PRINT ABS(−41.28 +
       84.35)
    20 END
41. 10 PRINT ABS(−41.28) +
       ABS(84.35)
    20 END
```

ENRICHMENT PROBLEM

- Completion of the following diagram was interrupted by a telephone call. The diagram is to show the addition of four numbers. Complete the diagram and write an addition equation.

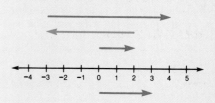

To complete the diagram, draw an arrow from 4 to 3 on the top of the diagram.

$$2 + (−5) + 7 + (−1) = 3$$

C **50.** Solvit Corporation stock was selling at $34\frac{3}{4}$ ($34.75) when trading began on Monday morning. Copy and complete the chart.

	Opening price	Net change	Closing price
Monday	$34\frac{3}{4}$	$\frac{-1}{2}$	? $34\frac{1}{4}$
Tuesday	$34\frac{1}{4}$	$+1\frac{1}{4}$	? $35\frac{1}{2}$
Wednesday	? $35\frac{1}{2}$	$\frac{-3}{4}$	? $34\frac{3}{4}$
Thursday	? $34\frac{3}{4}$	? $+2\frac{1}{4}$	37
Friday	? 37	$\frac{-1}{4}$	? $36\frac{3}{4}$

51. The Central Tigers football team took possession of the ball on their 9 yard line. They ran a series of plays that showed the following changes before calling time out.

gain of 3 yards, loss of 11 yards, gain of 17 yards, loss of 8 yards.

a. On what yard-line is the ball? 10
b. Over four plays, what was the team's net loss or gain? 1 yard gain

52. Using the numbers $-4, -3, -2, -1, 0, 1, 2, 3,$ and 4 only once, make a magic square. (Each row, column, and diagonal must add to 0.)
Answers will vary.

3	−2	−1
−4	0	4
1	2	−3

?	?	?
?	?	?
?	?	?

53. Nancy Lopez had the following rounds on a Ladies Professional Golf Association (LPGA) tour event: 2 under par, par, 3 over par, 4 under par, and 1 over par. How did she finish with respect to par? 2 under par

■ REVIEW EXERCISES

a	b	c
2	5	10

Substitute and simplify.   [1–1]

1. $\frac{b}{c}$ $\frac{1}{2}$

2. $c(b − a)$ 30

3. $3(b + 2) + b$ 26

4. $10a^2$ 40

5. $b^a − c$ 15

6. $b − \frac{c}{a}$ 0

Class Starter Quiz
on previous section

Add.

1. $-5 + 2$ -3
2. $-3 + (-4)$ -7
3. $6 + (-2)$ 4
4. $7 + (-5 + 3)$ 5
5. $(-1.3 + 0.5) + (-2.1)$ -2.9

PURPOSE

Skill in subtracting real numbers is a prerequisite for later work with algebraic expressions.

PREVIEW

The electrical-charge model is especially well suited for subtraction, since subtraction of both positive numbers and negative numbers can be visualized in terms of "taking away." Go over the Preview, asking students to follow directions. Then extend the Preview by doing exercises like the following. Draw pictures of charges if necessary.

- State two ways to change a charge from 3 to 1. (Add -2 or subtract 2.)
- State two ways to change a charge from -3 to 1. (Add 4 or subtract -4.)
- State two ways to change a charge from -2 to -6. (Add -4 or subtract 4.)
- Subtracting 3 is like adding what? (-3)
- Subtracting -2 is like adding what? (2)
- Subtracting any real number is like adding what? (The opposite of the number)

LESSON

Even though you use the discovery sequence above, go over the exposition in the text involving patterns. It is important for students to understand those patterns.

OBJECTIVE 2-3

To subtract positive and negative numbers.

2-3 Subtracting Real Numbers

Preview A model for subtraction

The electrical charge model (see Preview 2-2) can also help us understand subtraction of real numbers. To subtract a number, think about removing charges. For example, $-2 - (-3)$

Start with -2.   Remove 3 negative charges.   The result is a charge of 1.

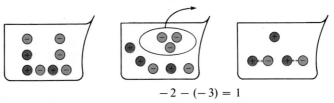

$$-2 - (-3) = 1$$

Write subtraction equations for each of the following examples.

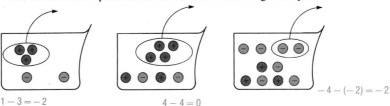

$1 - 3 = -2$ $4 - 4 = 0$ $-4 - (-2) = -2$

In this lesson you will learn how to subtract real numbers.

■ LESSON

The electrical charge model of subtraction leads to the conclusion that subtracting a real number has the same effect as adding the opposite of that real number. Number patterns such as the following support that conclusion.

A	B	C
$3 - 1 = 2$	$3 - 2 = 1$	$8 - 8 = 0$
$3 - 2 = 1$	$3 - 1 = 2$	$2 - 2 = 0$
$3 - 3 = 0$	$3 - 0 = 3$	$-3 - (-3) = ?$
$3 - 4 = ?$	$3 - (-1) = ?$	

The pattern in column A suggests that $3 - 4 = -1$. We also know that $3 + (-4) = -1$. In this case subtracting 4 and adding -4 give the same result.

   The pattern in column B suggests that $3 - (-1) = 4$. Note also that since $3 + 1 = 4$, we can conclude that subtracting -1 and adding 1 give the same result.

   Finally, the pattern in column C suggests that $-3 - (-3) = 0$. Since $-3 + 3 = 0$, we can conclude that subtracting -3 and adding 3 give the same result.

ADDITIONAL EXAMPLES

Example 1. Simplify. $-4 - 8$
Change to addition. $-4 + (-8)$
Simplify. -12

Example 2. Simplify. $-4 - (-3)$
Change to addition. $-4 + 3$
Simplify. -1

Example 3. Simplify. $(-5 - 9) - (-3)$
Change to addition. $(-5 + (-9)) + 3$
Simplify. $-14 + 3$
-11

Definition: Subtraction of Real Numbers

Subtracting any real number is the equivalent of adding the opposite of that real number.

For all real numbers a and b,
$$a - b = a + (-b).$$

According to this definition, any subtraction expression can be changed into an addition expression and then simplified by using the rules for adding real numbers.

Example 1   Simplify. $-3 - 7$

Solution
$-3 - 7$
Change to addition. $-3 + (-7)$
Simplify. -10

Answer -10

Example 2   Simplify. $-2 - (-5)$

Solution
$-2 - (-5)$
Change to addition. $-2 + 5$
Simplify. 3

Answer 3

Example 3   Simplify. $(-6 - 7) - (-8)$

Solution
$(-6 - 7) - (-8)$
Change to addition. $(-6 + (-7)) + 8$
Simplify. $-13 + 8$
-5

Answer -5

CHECK UNDERSTANDING

- Subtracting 5 is like adding what? (-5)
- Adding -4 is like subtracting what? (4)
- Subtracting any real number is the same as adding what number? (The opposite of the number)

CLASSROOM EXERCISES

Students should note that the first number remains unchanged when subtraction exercises are converted to addition exercises.

■ CLASSROOM EXERCISES

Change these subtraction expressions to addition expressions.

1. $6 - (-3)$ $6 + 3$ **2.** $-4 - 5$ $-4 + (-5)$ **3.** $-2 - (-7)$ $-2 + 7$ **4.** $3 - 5$ $3 + (-5)$

Simplify.

5. $-3 - 4$ -7 **6.** $2 - (-8)$ 10 **7.** $4 - 7$ -3 **8.** $-2 - (-8)$ 6

9. $3 - (-2)$ 5 **10.** $-5 - (-4)$ -1 **11.** $8 - (-9)$ 17 **12.** $-8 - (-10)$ 2

ASSIGNMENT GUIDE

Basic   1–20 all, Review Exercises, Self-Quiz 1
Average 1–33 odd, Review Exercises, Self-Quiz 1
Enriched 9–33 odd, 35–44 all, Review Exercises, Self-Quiz 1

PRACTICE WORKSHEET 7

2-3 SUBTRACTING REAL NUMBERS

■ Write each subtraction expression as an addition expression.
  Do not simplify.

1. $20 - 12$ $\underline{20 + (-12)}$ 2. $-20 - 12$ $\underline{-20 + (-12)}$ 3. $-20 - (-12)$ $\underline{-20 + 12}$ 4. $20 - (-12)$ $\underline{20 + 12}$

■ Simplify.

5. $-6 - 4$ $\underline{-10}$ 6. $6 - (-4)$ $\underline{10}$ 7. $-6 - (-4)$ $\underline{-2}$
8. $-12 - 8$ $\underline{-20}$ 9. $-7 - (-2)$ $\underline{-5}$ 10. $9 - 11$ $\underline{-2}$
11. $9 - (-11)$ $\underline{20}$ 12. $-9 - 11$ $\underline{-20}$ 13. $-9 - (-11)$ $\underline{2}$
14. $2.3 - 3.9$ $\underline{-1.6}$ 15. $\frac{1}{2} - (-\frac{1}{4})$ $\underline{3/4}$ 16. $-\frac{1}{2} - (-\frac{1}{4})$ $\underline{-1/4}$
17. $-5.6 - 2.4$ $\underline{-8.0}$ 18. $6.9 - 5.1$ $\underline{1.8}$ 19. $7.3 - (-10)$ $\underline{17.3}$
20. $5 - 2.3$ $\underline{2.7}$ 21. $(2 - 5) - 10$ $\underline{-13}$ 22. $2 - (5 - 10)$ $\underline{7}$
23. $7 - (9 + 3)$ $\underline{-5}$ 24. $(7 - 9) + 3$ $\underline{1}$ 25. $-7.6 - (2.4 - 1.1)$ $\underline{-8.9}$
26. $(-7.6 - 2.4) - 1.1$ $\underline{-11.1}$ 27. $\frac{5}{6} + (\frac{1}{2} - \frac{1}{3})$ $\underline{1}$ 28. $(\frac{5}{6} + \frac{1}{2}) - \frac{1}{3}$ $\underline{1}$

WRITTEN EXERCISES

Students should always change subtraction exercises to addition exercises. This may be done mentally unless the directions specify that the addition exercises be written.

These exercises should be examined in pairs after they have been answered: 35 and 36, 37 and 38. These could be added to the list of basic properties, although they will not be named and need not be memorized.

EXTRA PRACTICE, page 619

■ WRITTEN EXERCISES

Write as an addition expression. Do *not* simplify.

A 1. $11 - 3$ $11 + (-3)$ 2. $14 - 8$ $14 + (-8)$ 3. $7 - (-2)$ $7 + 2$ 4. $16 - (-5)$ $16 + 5$

5. $6 - 9$ $6 + (-9)$ 6. $4 - 7$ $4 + (-7)$ 7. $10 - (-13)$ $10 + 13$ 8. $3 - (-5)$ $3 + 5$

Simplify.

9. $42 - 21$ 21   10. $26 - 13$ 13   11. $-28 - 14$ -42 12. $-31 - 17$ -48

13. $61 - (-11)$ 72   14. $57 - (-19)$ 76   15. $-16 - (-25)$ 9   16. $-15 - (-32)$ 17

17. $(13 - (-3)) - (-6)$ 22   18. $(18 - (-4)) - (-5)$ 27

19. $13 - (-3 - (-6))$ 10   20. $18 - (-4) - (-5)$ 27

B 21. $(13 - (-12)) + (-12)$ 13   22. $(82 - (-46)) + 46$ 174

23. $(-22 - (-8)) + (-8)$ -22 24. $(-36 - (-14)) + (-14)$ -36

25. $-2\frac{1}{4} - \left(-1\frac{3}{4} + \frac{3}{4}\right)$ $-1\frac{1}{4}$ 26. $-5\frac{2}{3} - \left(-2\frac{1}{3} + 1\frac{1}{3}\right)$ $-4\frac{2}{3}$

27. $\left(2\frac{1}{4} - \left(-1\frac{3}{4}\right)\right) - \frac{3}{4}$ $3\frac{1}{4}$ 28. $\left(-5\frac{2}{3} - \left(-2\frac{1}{3}\right)\right) - 1\frac{1}{3}$ $-4\frac{2}{3}$

29. $(-6.2 - 3.5) + (8.4 - (-2.8))$ 1.5   30. $(9.7 - (-12.4)) + (-14.2 - 7)$ 0.9

31. $(-6.2 + 8.4) - (3.5 + (-2.8))$ 1.5   32. $(9.7 + (-14.2)) - (-12.4 + 7)$ 0.9

33. In a football game, a kicker punted the ball from 15 yards behind the line of scrimmage. How far would he have to kick the ball in order to have a net gain of 40 yards? (*Net gain* is the distance from the line of scrimmage forward to the point where the kick is caught.) 55 yards

34. One day the temperature in Billings, Montana, changed from $-4°C$ to $8°C$. How many degrees more or less, and in what direction was the temperature change? 12°C rise in temperature

Substitute and simplify.

a	b	m	n	x	y	z
7	-11	14	12	-13.8	26.4	0

C 35. $(m + n) - a$ 19   36. $m + (n - a)$ 19   37. $n - (m + b)$ 9

38. $(n - m) - b$ 9   39. $(y + m) - m$ 26.4   40. $x - z$ -13.8

41. $(b - x) + (z - y)$ -23.6 42. $(b + a) - (x + y)$ -16.6

43. Mr. and Mrs. Maxwell are planning to close out their checking account. Their September statement showed a balance of $200. After depositing $55, they wrote checks for $147, $23.50, $18.75, $62.25, and $15.50. The bank charges them $7.00 if their account is overdrawn, that is, if the total of the checks is more than the checking account balance. What size deposit must they make in order to show a balance of $0.00 on their closing statement? $19

44. Of the states listed, which had the greatest Fahrenheit temperature range for its record highest and lowest temperature? Which had the least range? MT, HI

CA: 134°, −45°   FL: 109°, −2°   HI: 100°, 14°   ME: 105°, −48°

TX: 120°, −23°   MT: 117°, −70°   NY: 108°, −52°   CO: 118°, −60°

■ REVIEW EXERCISES

Simplify.   [1–3]

1. $3^2 + 4^2$ 25   **2.** $(3 + 4)^2$ 49   **3.** $5^2 − 3^2$ 16   **4.** $(5 − 3)^2$ 4   **5.** $6.3 \cdot 0.4$ 2.52

6. $\frac{2}{3} \cdot \frac{4}{5}$ $\frac{8}{15}$ **7.** $3.04 \cdot 1000$ **8.** $1\frac{2}{3} \cdot \frac{3}{4}$ $1\frac{1}{4}$ **9.** $8.07 \div 100$ **10.** $\frac{2}{3} \div \frac{4}{5}$ $\frac{5}{6}$

    3040   0.0807

Simplify.

11. $6.73 − 4.8$ 1.93   **12.** $14 − 6.35$ 7.65   **13.** $\frac{1}{2} − \frac{1}{3}$ $\frac{1}{6}$

14. $3\frac{1}{2} − 1\frac{3}{4}$ $1\frac{3}{4}$ **15.** $1\frac{1}{3} − \frac{11}{12}$ $\frac{5}{12}$ **16.** $(1.6 + 3.5) + 2.2$ 7.3

Self-Quiz 1

2–1 Simplify.

1. $−(−5)$ 5   **2.** $−|−8|$ −8   **3.** The opposite of $−x$ x

Here is a number line picture.

Write the number that corresponds to each of the following points.

4. A −3   **5.** H 4   **6.** Halfway between G and H
                                                                  $3\frac{1}{2}$
Use $<$ or $>$ to make the sentence true.

7. $−6 \,?\, 0$ <   **8.** $2 \,?\, |−3|$ <   **9.** $−\frac{1}{2} \,?\, −1$ >

2–2 Simplify.

10. $8 + (−11)$ −3   **11.** $14 + (−6)$ 8   **12.** $−7 + (−2)$ −9

13. $(−12 + 17) + 9$ 14   **14.** $−20 + (3 + (−6))$ **15.** $−15 + (−4 + 18)$
                                        −23   −1

2–3

16. $7 − (−4)$ 11   **17.** $−19 − 12$ **18.** $−12 − (−14)$ 2
                              −31
19. $(14 − (−8)) − (−11)$ **20.** $16 − (9 − 15)$ 22   **21.** $−12 − (6 − 16)$ −2
        33

PROBLEM-SOLVING NOTE
Finding a pattern

Columns A, B, and C on page 48 are well worth working through to bring out the problem-solving strategy of *looking for a pattern*. You might begin by posing the question $4 − 5 = \underline{\ ?\ }$. To answer the question, you might suggest to students that one approach to a mathematical situation when they are "stuck" is to look at related problems that they can do and look for a pattern among their solutions. Similarly, work through Example 2.

ENRICHMENT PROBLEM

• State two ways to change this charge to 2.

Add 5 or subtract −5.

Simplify.

1. $3 - 5$ -2
2. $3 - (-2)$ 5
3. $-3 - 5$ -8
4. $-3 - (-2)$ -1
5. $7 - (-5 - 9)$ 21

PURPOSE

Skill in multiplying signed numbers is a prerequisite for later work with algebraic expressions.

PREVIEW

Before starting the Preview, remind students of the relationship between distance, rate, and time.

• A car travels 50 mph for 3 hours. How far does it go? (150 miles)

Then draw the Preview diagram on the board and explain the interpretations of positive and negative distance, rate, and time.

• How is each of these represented by real numbers?

  50 miles east of the house (50)
  50 miles west of the house (-50)
  traveling 40 mph west (-40)
  traveling 30 mph east (30)
  3 hours after passing the house (3)
  5 hours before passing the house (-5)
  2 hours ago (-2)
  4 hours from now (4)

Go over the situations described in the Preview, making sure that students understand how the multiplication equations fit those situations. If necessary, make up similar situations and ask students to state the multiplication equations. Finally, ask students to generalize about the product of two positive numbers, two negative numbers, and one positive and one negative number.

OBJECTIVE 2–4

To multiply positive and negative numbers.

2–4 Multiplying Real Numbers

Preview **A model for multiplication**

Think of a car traveling on an east–west road with east considered the positive direction. Traveling at a constant rate of speed, the car is *passing the house right now.* Think of time in the future as positive and time in the past as negative. Suppose that the car is traveling *east* at 50 mph. Two hours *from now* it will be 100 miles *east* of the house.

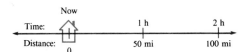

This is a distance–rate–time situation where rate × time = distance.

    Equation: $50 \cdot 2 = 100$

If the car were traveling 50 mph to the *east,* 2 hours *ago* it was 100 miles *west* of the house.

    Equation: $50 \cdot (-2) = -100$

If the car were traveling 50 mph to the *west,* 2 hours *ago* it was 100 miles *east* of the house.

    Equation: $-50 \cdot (-2) = 100$

In this lesson you will learn the rules for multiplying real numbers.

■ LESSON

The examples in the Preview suggest the following rules for multiplication of real numbers.

Rules	Examples
To multiply two real numbers:	
1. Multiply the absolute values of the factors.	
2. Use these rules to find the sign of the product.	
a. If the factors have the same sign, the product is positive.	$-2 \cdot -3 = 6$ $4 \cdot 3 = 12$
b. If the factors have different signs, the product is negative.	$3 \cdot -7 = -21$ $-5 \cdot 4 = -20$
c. If one of the factors is 0, the product is 0.	$-7 \cdot 0 = 0$ $0 \cdot 8 = 0$

We can see that these rules make sense by studying the patterns in these equations.

$$2 \cdot 3 = 6$$
$$2 \cdot 2 = 4$$
$$2 \cdot 1 = 2$$
$$2 \cdot 0 = 0$$
$$2 \cdot -1 = ?$$

As the second factor decreases by 1, the product decreases by 2. This pattern suggests that the last product should be -2.

$$2 \cdot -1 = -2$$

This result agrees with the rule that the product of a positive number and a negative number is negative.

Look at these equations and find a pattern.

$$-2 \cdot 3 = -6$$
$$-2 \cdot 2 = -4$$
$$-2 \cdot 1 = -2$$
$$-2 \cdot 0 = 0$$
$$-2 \cdot -1 = ?$$

In this case, as the second factor decreases by 1, the product increases by 2. This pattern suggests that the last product should be 2.

$$-2 \cdot -1 = 2$$

This result agrees with the rule that the product of two negative numbers is positive.

Example 1   Simplify these products.

      a. $3 \cdot 4$ **b.** $-5 \cdot -3$ **c.** $5 \cdot -7$ **d.** $-25 \cdot 0$

Solution   **a.** $3 \cdot 4 = 12$ **b.** $-5 \cdot -3 = 15$
           c. $5 \cdot -7 = -35$ **d.** $-25 \cdot 0 = 0$

Example 2   Simplify. $-3 \cdot 6 - 8 \cdot -4$

   Solution $-3 \cdot 6 - 8 \cdot -4$
          Simplify the products. $-18 - (-32)$
          Simplify the difference.   14

   Answer   14

Example 3   Simplify. $-3(12 - 17)$

   Solution $-3(12 - 17)$
          Simplify the difference. $-3(-5)$
          Simplify the product.   15

   Answer   15

CLASSROOM EXERCISES

In classroom exercise 8, note that 0 is neither positive nor negative.

ASSIGNMENT GUIDE

Basic   1–35 odd, 49–54 all, Review Exercises
Average   21–53 odd, Review Exercises
Enriched   29–53 odd, 55–65 all, Review Exercises

PRACTICE WORKSHEET 7

2-4 MULTIPLYING REAL NUMBERS

■ Simplify.

1. $3 \cdot -5$ -15 2. $-3 \cdot 5$ -15 3. $-3 \cdot -5$ 15 4. $0 \cdot -\frac{3}{4}$ 0

5. $-5.3 \cdot 0$ 0 6. $-5 \cdot -10$ 50 7. $\frac{1}{2} \cdot -\frac{2}{3}$ $-1/5$ 8. $-\frac{3}{4} \cdot -\frac{3}{4}$ $9/16$

9. $(-9 \cdot -1) \cdot 2$ 18 10. $-9 \cdot (-1 \cdot 2)$ 18 11. $-10 \cdot -10 \cdot -10$ -1000

12. $-1 \cdot -1 \cdot -1 \cdot -1$ 1 13. $-2 \cdot (-3 + 7)$ -8 14. $2 \cdot (-3 - 7)$ -20

15. $2.3 \cdot (12 - 2)$ 23.0 16. $-2.3 \cdot (12 + 2)$ -32.2 17. $7 \cdot (-2.5 \cdot 4)$ -70.0

18. $(7 \cdot -2.5) \cdot 4$ -70.0 19. $(-5 \cdot -10.8) + (-5) \cdot (0.8)$ 50.0

■ Substitute and simplify.

a	b	c	d
-2	3	$-\frac{1}{2}$	-10

20. ac 1 21. bd -30 22. cd 5

23. $(-a)b$ 6 24. $-(ab)$ 6 25. acd -10

26. $a \cdot (b + d)$ 14 27. $c \cdot (a + d)$ 6 28. $abcd$ -30

WRITTEN EXERCISES

Exercises 37–38 illustrate the commutative property of multiplication.

    Exercises 42–43 illustrate the associative property of multiplication.

    Exercises 55, 57, 62, 64, and 65 can be answered using the generalization that the product of an *even* number of negative numbers is positive.

    Exercises 58–59 can be answered using the generalization that the sum of any number of negative addends is negative.

EXTRA PRACTICE, page 620

■ CLASSROOM EXERCISES

Simplify.

1. $-4 \cdot -6$ 24 2. $(5) \cdot (3)$ 15 3. $8 \cdot -4$ -32

4. $-9 \cdot 6$ -54 5. $-10 \cdot 5$ -50 6. $-8 \cdot -5$ 40

7. $(-6)^2$ 36 8. $-12 \cdot 0$ 0 9. $(-1 \cdot -1) \cdot -2$ -2

■ WRITTEN EXERCISES

Simplify.

A

1. $8 \cdot 3$ 24 2. $7 \cdot 4$ 28 3. $9 \cdot -11$ -99

4. $10 \cdot -12$ -120 5. $25 \cdot 0$ 0 6. $0 \cdot -20$ 0

7. $0 \cdot -31$ 0 8. $0 \cdot -13$ 0 9. $-12 \cdot 4$ -48

10. $-23 \cdot 6$ -138 11. $-18 \cdot -3$ 54 12. $-21 \cdot -5$ 105

13. $4 \cdot -12$ -48 14. $6 \cdot -23$ -138 15. $-3 \cdot -18$ 54

16. $-5 \cdot -21$ 105 17. $(6 \cdot -3) \cdot -7$ 126 18. $-5(-8 \cdot 2)$ 80

19. $2(9 \cdot -4)$ -72 20. $(-7 \cdot 3) \cdot -8$ 168 21. $6 \cdot (-3 \cdot -7)$ 126

22. $-8 \cdot (2 \cdot -5)$ 80 23. $9 \cdot (-4 \cdot 2)$ -72 24. $-7 \cdot (3 \cdot -8)$ 168

25. $-8 \cdot (4 + (-6))$ 16 26. $12 \cdot (-3 + 7)$ 48 27. $(-8 \cdot 4) + (-8 \cdot -6)$ 16

28. $(12 \cdot -3) + (12 \cdot 7)$ 48 29. $9 \cdot (11 - (-4))$ 135 30. $-6 \cdot (-3 - 5)$ 48

31. $(9 \cdot 11) - (9 \cdot -4)$ 135 32. $(-6 \cdot -3) - (-6 \cdot 5)$ 48 33. $|-3| \cdot |-1|$ 3

34. $|0| \cdot |-2|$ 0 35. $|-3 \cdot -1|$ 3 36. $|0 \cdot -2|$ 0

a	b	c	d
$\frac{1}{2}$	$-\frac{1}{3}$	-7	5

Substitute and simplify.

B

37. $a \cdot b$ $-\frac{1}{6}$ 38. $b \cdot a$ $-\frac{1}{6}$ 39. $-2 \cdot b$ $\frac{2}{3}$

40. $-2 \cdot c$ 14 41. $a \cdot |b|$ $\frac{1}{6}$ 42. $a \cdot (b \cdot c)$ $1\frac{1}{6}$

43. $(a \cdot b) \cdot c$ $1\frac{1}{6}$ 44. $a \cdot (c + d)$ -1 45. $(a \cdot c) + d$ $1\frac{1}{2}$

46. $(-c + d) \cdot \frac{1}{4}$ 3 47. $(c + (-d)) \cdot \frac{1}{4}$ -3 48. b^3 $-\frac{1}{27}$

Use positive and negative numbers to write multiplication equations for these situations. Then answer each question with a real number.

49. The temperature falls 2° per hour. How many degrees more or less is the change in temperature after 3 hours? $-2 \cdot 3 = n, -6°$

50. A plane descends 100 meters per minute. How many meters more or less is the change in altitude after 5 minutes? $-100 \cdot 5 = d; -500$ m

51. Erika has been spending $5 per day of her birthday gift money. How much more money or less money did she have a week ago? $-5 \cdot -7 = m,$ $35

52. A water tank has been leaking at the rate of 3 liters per day. How much more water or less water did the tank contain 5 days ago? $-3 \cdot -5 = w;$ 15 liters

53. A water tank is being filled at the rate of 2 liters per minute. How much more water or less water did the tank contain 10 minutes ago? $2 \cdot -10 = w;$ -20 liters

54. Shawn earns $8.75 a day. How much more money or less money had Shawn earned 5 days ago? $8.75 \cdot -5 = n; -$43.75

Suppose that A, B, C, and D represent negative numbers. State whether these expressions are positive, negative, or zero.

C **55.** $A \cdot B$ Positive

56. $A \cdot B \cdot C$ Negative

57. $A \cdot B \cdot C \cdot D$ Positive

58. $A + B$ Negative

59. $A + B + C$ Negative

60. $(A \cdot B) + (C \cdot D)$ Positive

61. $A \cdot (B + C)$ Positive

62. $A^3 B$ Positive

63. $A^3 + B$ Negative

64. $A^{10} B^9 C^8 D^7$ Positive

65. $A \cdot A \cdot A \cdot A \cdot B \cdot B \cdot B \cdot C \cdot C \cdot D$ Positive

■ REVIEW EXERCISES

Simplify.

1. $1.44 \div 2.4$ 0.6

2. $1.38 \div 0.6$ 2.3

3. $\frac{1}{2} \div \frac{2}{3}$ $\frac{3}{4}$

4. $4\frac{1}{2} \div 1\frac{1}{2}$ 3

5. $1\frac{3}{4} \div 1\frac{3}{4}$ 1

6. $0 \div \frac{1}{2}$ 0

State whether the following pairs of expressions are equivalent. [1–4]

7. $5a + 6 + a$ and $6(a + 1)$ Equivalent

8. $5(a + 2) + 4$ and $3a + 6 + 2a$ Not equivalent

9. $x(x + 1)$ and $x^2 + 1$ Not equivalent

10. $(a + 1)^2$ and $a^2 + 1$ Not equivalent

Extension Stock market reports

Stock market reports show the closing price (price of the last sale of the day) and the change from the previous day's closing price in dollars. Positive numbers indicate increases and negative numbers indicate decreases in the prices. Compute the closing price of the previous day for each stock.

Company	Closing Price	Change	
Chuckies Chicken	$17\frac{1}{2}$	$+\frac{5}{8}$	$16\frac{7}{8}$
Hills Book Stores	$35\frac{7}{8}$	$-\frac{1}{2}$	$36\frac{3}{8}$

COMPUTER EXTENSION

1. Write a computer program with INPUT statements that you could use to compute exercises 1–16.

```
10 PRINT "WHAT IS THE FIRST
   NUMBER";
20 INPUT A
30 PRINT "WHAT IS THE SECOND
   NUMBER";
40 INPUT B
50 PRINT A; "X"; B; "="; A*B
60 END
```

2. Write simple programs using PRINT statements for exercises 25 and 27.

25. ```
10 PRINT -8*(4 + -6)
20 END
```

**27.** ```
10 PRINT -8*4 + -8*-6
20 END
```

ENRICHMENT PROBLEMS

- If m is an even number, then $(-1)^m = \underline{\quad ? \quad}$. 1

- If n is an odd number, then $(-1)^n = \underline{\quad ? \quad}$. -1

Simplify.

1. $-8 \cdot -2$ 16
2. $-5 \cdot 4$ -20
3. $6 \cdot -3$ -18
4. $-0.5 \cdot 6$ -3
5. $(-3 \cdot 0) \cdot -7$ 0

PURPOSE

Skill in dividing real numbers is a prerequisite for later work with algebraic expressions.

PREVIEW

The Preview can help students understand why division by zero is *undefined*. As the pattern in the Preview suggests, the quotient gets infinitely larger as the divisor approaches 0 (both dividend and divisor positive).

Here is an alternate approach to considering division by 0.

Division is defined in terms of multiplication:

We say $^{12}\!/_4 = 3$ because $4 \cdot 3 = 12$.

We say $^{18}\!/_9 = 2$ because $9 \cdot 2 = 18$.

If we were to say that $^{12}\!/_0$ were some number x, it would have to mean that $0 \cdot x = 12$. There is no number x that multiplied by 0 is 12. Therefore, we cannot assign any meaning to $^{12}\!/_0$.

OBJECTIVE 2–5

To find reciprocals of numbers, and divide positive and negative numbers.

2–5 Dividing Real Numbers

Preview **Division by zero**

Why is division by zero not permitted? It seems unusual that $\frac{12}{0}$ is undefined when 12×0, $12 + 0$, and $12 - 0$ have well-established meanings.

Look at the pattern in these division exercises:

$$\frac{12}{4} = 3 \qquad \frac{12}{2} = 6 \qquad \frac{12}{1} = 12 \qquad \frac{12}{\frac{1}{2}} = 24$$

What do these equal?

$$\frac{12}{\frac{1}{4}} \qquad \frac{12}{\frac{1}{8}} \qquad \frac{12}{\frac{1}{100}} \qquad \frac{12}{\frac{1}{100,000}}$$
$$48 \qquad 72 \qquad 1200 \qquad 1,200,000$$

Since the quotient becomes larger as the denominator gets closer to 0, does it seem likely that $\frac{12}{0}$ represents a number?

In this lesson you will learn how to divide by nonzero real numbers. Division by zero is an exception. It is *not* defined.

■ LESSON

In Section 2–3, we defined subtraction of real numbers in terms of addition of opposites. In a similar manner, we are going to define division of real numbers in terms of multiplication. Note that these expressions are equivalent.

$$4.8 \div 4 \qquad 4.8 \cdot \frac{1}{4}$$

Division by 4 is equivalent to multiplication by $\frac{1}{4}$. The numbers 4 and $\frac{1}{4}$ are **reciprocals** of one another.

Definition: Reciprocals

For all real numbers a and b (except 0),

if $ab = 1$, then a and b are reciprocals.

$\frac{1}{2} \cdot 2 = 1$ Therefore, $\frac{1}{2}$ and 2 are reciprocals.

$-\frac{1}{3} \cdot (-3) = 1$ Therefore, $-\frac{1}{3}$ is the reciprocal of -3, and -3 is the reciprocal of $-\frac{1}{3}$.

$\frac{2}{3} \cdot \frac{3}{2} = 1$ Therefore, $\frac{2}{3}$ and $\frac{3}{2}$ are reciprocals.

Since there is no number whose product with 0 is 1, 0 does not have a reciprocal.

The first example illustrated that division by 4 is equivalent to multiplication by $\frac{1}{4}$. This specific case illustrates the definition of division of real numbers.

Definition: Division of Real Numbers

Dividing by any real number (except 0) is equivalent to multiplying by the reciprocal of that real number.

For all real numbers a and b (b not equal to 0),

$$a \div b = a \cdot \frac{1}{b}$$

The reciprocal of a number a can be written $\frac{1}{a}$. Zero has no reciprocal.

Example 1   Simplify each quotient.

   a. $-49 \div 7$ **b.** $3 \div -\frac{1}{2}$ **c.** $-\frac{5}{9} \div -\frac{2}{3}$

Solution   Change divisions to multiplications. Then use the rules of multiplication.

   a. $-49 \div 7 = -49 \cdot \frac{1}{7} = -7$

   b. $3 \div -\frac{1}{2} = 3 \cdot -2 = -6$

   c. $-\frac{5}{9} \div -\frac{2}{3} = -\frac{5}{9} \cdot -\frac{3}{2} = \frac{5}{6}$

Example 2   Simplify. $0 \div -12$

   Solution $0 \div -12 = 0 \cdot -\frac{1}{12} = 0$

Note these facts about the division of real numbers.

For all real numbers a and b (b not equal to 0):
$$\left|\frac{a}{b}\right| = \frac{|a|}{|b|}.$$
The quotient of two positive numbers or two negative numbers is positive. The quotient of one positive number and one negative number is negative.

Example 3   Simplify each quotient.

   a. $\frac{12}{4}$ **b.** $\frac{-12}{4}$ **c.** $\frac{45}{-15}$ **d.** $\frac{-50}{-25}$

Solution   Use the facts about division given above.

   a. $\frac{12}{4} = 3$ **b.** $\frac{-12}{4} = -3$ **c.** $\frac{45}{-15} = -3$ **d.** $\frac{-50}{-25} = 2$

LESSON

Discuss the definitions of *reciprocal* and *division of real numbers*. Then go through examples 1 and 2. From those examples, students should discover the rules of signs for division given on page 57. Since the rules of signs for division are the same as for multiplication, students will have little difficulty remembering them.

Note that even though division may be converted to multiplication (multiplying by the reciprocal), sometimes such a conversion may be omitted.

The division $\frac{96}{-16}$ is more easily done *without* converting to the multiplication $96 \cdot \frac{1}{-16}$.

The division $-\frac{2}{3} \div -\frac{4}{5}$ is more easily done by converting to the multiplication $-\frac{2}{3} \cdot -\frac{5}{4}$.

ADDITIONAL EXAMPLES

Example 1. Simplify each quotient.

a. $-36 \div 9$ **b.** $4 \div -\frac{1}{2}$ **c.** $-\frac{4}{5} \div \frac{2}{3}$

   -4 -8 $-\frac{6}{5}$

Example 2. Simplify. $0 \div -2$
                       0

Example 3. Simplify each quotient.

a. $\frac{48}{-6}$ **b.** $\frac{-48}{6}$ **c.** $\frac{-48}{-6}$ **d.** $\frac{48}{6}$

   -8 -8 8 8

CHECK UNDERSTANDING

- Is the reciprocal of a positive number positive or negative? (Positive)
- What is the reciprocal of zero? (There is none.)
- What is the reciprocal of a fraction $\frac{n}{m}$ ($n \neq 0, m \neq 0$)? $\left(\frac{m}{n}\right)$
- What is the sign of the quotient of two negative numbers? (Positive)
- What is the sign of the quotient of two numbers with opposite signs? (Negative)

CLASSROOM EXERCISES

The fraction bar should be discussed so its meaning is clear.

Classroom exercises 16–18 should be thought of as division exercises even though they are written in fractional form.

EXTRA PRACTICE, page 620

ASSIGNMENT GUIDE

Basic   1–19 odd, 21–36 all, Review Exercises
Average 21–46 all, Review Exercises
Enriched 21–61 odd, Review Exercises

PRACTICE WORKSHEET 8

2-5 DIVIDING REAL NUMBERS

■ Write as a multiplication exercise. Do *not* simplify.

1. $-\frac{2}{3} \div \frac{3}{4}$ $-2/3 \cdot 4/3$ 2. $-\frac{7}{8} \div -\frac{1}{4}$ $-7/8 \cdot -4$

3. $\frac{5}{9} \div -2$ $5/9 \cdot -1/2$ 4. $-10 \div -3$ $-10 \cdot -1/3$

■ Write each division as a multiplication and simplify.

5. $-\frac{3}{5} \div \frac{2}{3}$ $-9/10$ 6. $-\frac{3}{5} \div -\frac{2}{3}$ $9/10$ 7. $\frac{3}{5} \div -\frac{2}{3}$ $-9/10$

8. $4 \div -1\frac{1}{3}$ -3 9. $-\frac{3}{8} \div -\frac{9}{4}$ $1/6$ 10. $0 \div 2.5$ 0

11. $-24 \div 12$ -2 12. $24 \div -3$ -8 13. $0 \div -\frac{1}{2}$ 0

14. $-100 \div 2.5$ -40 15. $100 \div -12.5$ -8 16. $-\frac{2}{5} \div -\frac{4}{15}$ $3/2$

17. $\frac{\frac{5}{6}}{-\frac{2}{3}}$ $-5/4$ 18. $\frac{-\frac{5}{6}}{\frac{2}{3}}$ $-5/4$ 19. $\frac{-\frac{5}{6}}{\frac{3}{2}}$ $-5/9$

■ CLASSROOM EXERCISES

Give the reciprocal of each number in its simplest form.

1. 8 $\frac{1}{8}$ 2. -8 $-\frac{1}{8}$ 3. $\frac{1}{2}$ 2 4. $-\frac{1}{2}$ -2

5. 0 none   6. 1 1 7. $-\frac{3}{4}$ $-\frac{4}{3}$ 8. 0.4 2.5

Complete.

9. Dividing by a real number is equivalent to multiplying by the __?__.   reciprocal

10. Dividing by 6 is equivalent to multiplying by __?__. $\frac{1}{6}$

11. Dividing by $-\frac{2}{3}$ is equivalent to multiplying by __?__. $-\frac{3}{2}$

12. The reciprocal of -1 is __?__. -1

Simplify.

13. $-12 \div -6$ 2 14. $20 \div -5$ -4 15. $-20 \div 4$ -5 16. $\frac{5}{-15}$ $-\frac{1}{3}$

17. $\frac{0}{-5}$ 0 18. $\frac{8}{-\frac{1}{2}}$ -16 19. $-16 \div \frac{1}{4}$ -64 20. $\frac{2}{3} \div -2$ $-\frac{1}{3}$

■ WRITTEN EXERCISES

Write the reciprocal of each number in its simplest form.

A   1. $-\frac{1}{6}$ -6 2. $-\frac{1}{3}$ -3 3. $\frac{2}{3}$ $\frac{3}{2}$ 4. $\frac{3}{5}$ $\frac{5}{3}$

5. -6 $-\frac{1}{6}$ 6. -8 $-\frac{1}{8}$ 7. $|-5|$ $\frac{1}{5}$ 8. $|-10|$ $\frac{1}{10}$

9. $-\frac{3}{8}$ $-\frac{8}{3}$ 10. $-\frac{5}{8}$ $-\frac{8}{5}$ 11. $-\left|-\frac{1}{5}\right|$ -5 12. $-\left|-\frac{1}{7}\right|$ -7

Write as a multiplication exercise. Do *not* simplify.

13. $\frac{2}{3} \div \frac{3}{8}$ $\frac{2}{3} \cdot \frac{8}{3}$ 14. $\frac{13}{5} \div \frac{3}{4}$ $\frac{13}{5} \cdot \frac{4}{3}$ 15. $-6 \div \frac{1}{4}$ $-6 \cdot 4$ 16. $-5 \div \frac{1}{10}$ $-5 \cdot 10$

17. $\frac{3}{8} \div -\frac{3}{5}$ $\frac{3}{8} \cdot -\frac{5}{3}$ 18. $\frac{5}{8} \div -\frac{5}{6}$ $\frac{5}{8} \cdot -\frac{6}{5}$ 19. $-\frac{3}{4} \div -\frac{2}{3}$ $-\frac{3}{4} \cdot -\frac{3}{2}$ 20. $-\frac{2}{3} \div -\frac{5}{6}$ $-\frac{2}{3} \cdot -\frac{6}{5}$

Write each division as a multiplication and simplify.

21. $-1\frac{2}{3} \div 4$ $-\frac{5}{12}$ 22. $-\frac{3}{5} \div 6$ $-\frac{1}{10}$ 23. $5 \div -3$ $-\frac{5}{3}$ 24. $6 \div -5$ $-\frac{6}{5}$

25. $3 \div -1\frac{1}{3}$ $-\frac{9}{4}$ 26. $4 \div -2\frac{1}{4}$ $-\frac{16}{9}$ 27. $-\frac{3}{8} \div -\frac{5}{8}$ $\frac{3}{5}$ 28. $-\frac{5}{6} \div -3\frac{1}{6}$ $\frac{5}{19}$

Substitute and simplify.

	a	b	c	d
	-48	12	-16	4

29. $\frac{a}{b}$ -4

30. $\frac{a}{c}$ 3

31. $\frac{b}{a}$ $-\frac{1}{4}$

32. $\frac{c}{a}$ $\frac{1}{3}$

33. $\frac{a}{d}$ -12

34. $\frac{b}{c}$ $-\frac{3}{4}$

35. $\frac{a+b}{d}$ -9

36. $\frac{b+c}{d}$ -1

Substitute and simplify.

	r	s	t	u
	5.4	-6	36	-0.3

B **37.** $\frac{r}{-3} + 0.8$ -1

38. $\frac{s}{t} + \frac{1}{3}$ $\frac{1}{6}$

39. $\frac{s}{u} + (-t)$ -16

40. $\frac{r}{-u} + \frac{t}{s}$ 12

41. $\frac{s+t}{u}$ -100

42. $\frac{s}{u} + \frac{t}{u}$ -100

43. $\frac{r+t}{s}$ -6.9

44. $\frac{r}{s} + \frac{t}{u}$ -120.9

Use positive and negative numbers to write division equations for these situations. Then answer each question with a real number.

45. Jon loses 10 pounds in 4 weeks. What is his average change in weight per week over the 4 weeks? $w = -10 \div 4; -2.5$ pounds

46. The temperature dropped 12 degrees in the past 4 hours. What was the average temperature change per hour over that time? $t = \frac{-12}{4}; -3°$

C **47.** Ten years ago, the population of Dry Gulch was 840 more than it is today. What was the average population change per month? $p = \frac{-840}{120}; -7$

48. Jan was $10\frac{1}{2}$ pounds heavier 3 weeks ago than she is today. What was her average weight change per day over the 3 weeks? $w = -10\frac{1}{2} \div 21; -\frac{1}{2}$

Suppose A, B, C, and D represent negative numbers. State whether these are expressions for positive numbers, negative numbers, or zero.

49. $\frac{A}{B}$ Positive

50. $\frac{C \times D}{A}$ Negative

51. $\frac{A+B}{C}$ Positive

52. $\frac{A \times B}{C+D}$ Negative

53. $\frac{-A}{B}$ Negative

54. $\frac{-A+A}{C}$ 0

55. $\frac{A^5 \cdot B^6}{C^7}$ Positive

56. $\frac{A^7 + B^9}{C^{16}}$ Negative

57. $\frac{-A}{-B}$ Positive

58. $\frac{A^{20}}{A^{10}}$ Positive

59. $(-A)^2$ Positive

60. $\frac{(-B)^2}{B}$ Negative

61. Describe what happens to $\frac{12}{n}$ when n is replaced with -4, -2, -1, $-\frac{1}{2}$, $-\frac{1}{4}$, $-\frac{1}{100}$, and $-\frac{1}{1,000,000}$. As the value of n increases, the value of $\frac{12}{n}$ decreases.

Exercises 29–32 show there is not a commutative property for division.

COMPUTER EXTENSION

1. Write a simple program using an INPUT statement to find the reciprocal of a number.

```
10 PRINT "WHAT IS THE NUMBER";
20 INPUT A
30 PRINT "THE RECIPROCAL OF";
   A; "IS "; 1/A
40 END
```

2. See what happens when you input 0 into the program in activity 1.

3. Modify the program in activity 1 so that it will print "ZERO HAS NO RECIPROCAL" when you input zero.

```
10 PRINT "WHAT IS THE NUMBER";
20 INPUT A
30 IF A < > 0 THEN 60
40 PRINT "ZERO HAS NO
   RECIPROCAL"
50 GO TO 70
60 PRINT "THE RECIPROCAL
   OF "; A; "IS "; 1/A
70 END
```

ENRICHMENT PROBLEMS

- What is the reciprocal of the reciprocal of the reciprocal of ½?

  2

- What is the opposite of the opposite of the opposite of ½?

  $-\frac{1}{2}$

■ REVIEW EXERCISES

State the property illustrated by each equation. [1–5]

1. $(364 + 97) + 3 = 364 + (97 + 3)$
Associative property of addition

2. $2 \cdot 5 + 8 \cdot 5 = (2 + 8)5$
Distributive property of multiplication over addition

3. $(7 + 0) + 5 = 7 + 5$ Identity property for addition

4. $(7 + 0) + 5 = 5 + (7 + 0)$
Commutative property of addition

Simplify. [1–6]

5. $3x + 5 + x$ 4x + 5

6. $10a + 3b + 5a + b$ 15a + 4b

7. $6(x + 3) + 4(2x + 1)$ 14x + 22

8. $3(a + b) + 2b + 4b$ 3a + 9b

A rectangle is 5 cm longer than it is wide. Complete each statement. [1–7]

9. If the rectangle is w cm wide, then it is ___?___ cm long. (w + 5)

10. If the rectangle is l cm long, then it is ___?___ cm wide. (l − 5)

EXTENSION   The absolute value function on a computer

Computers interpret multiple signs before a number as shown in these examples:

Computer command	Screen display
PRINT − −3	3
PRINT −5 + −6	−11

A special function programmed into the computer is the *absolute value function.* In computer terminology, ABS (-2) means $|-2|$.

EXAMPLES

Computer command	Screen display
PRINT ABS(-9)	9
PRINT ABS $\left(-\dfrac{12}{4}\right)$	3

Write the display for each command. Check on a computer if one is available.

1. PRINT −4− −10 6

2. PRINT − − −8 −8

3. PRINT −4 * −5 20

4. PRINT ABS(-6) 6

5. PRINT ABS $(-5-−3)$ 2

6. PRINT ABS(-5) − ABS(-3) 2

Write a computer command to evaluate each expression. Check on a computer if one is available.

7. $-9 - (-2)$
PRINT −9− −2

8. $(-2) \cdot (-3) \cdot (-4)$
PRINT −2 * −3 * −4

9. $8 + (-12)$
PRINT 8 + −12

10. $(-3)^2$
PRINT (−3) ↑ 2

11. $|-12|$
PRINT ABS(−12)

12. $|-7 + 4|$
PRINT ABS(−7 + 4)

OBJECTIVE 2–6

To simplify algebraic expressions involving addition and subtraction.

Class Starter Quiz
on previous section

Substitute and simplify.

A	a	b
−2	−8	16

1. $\dfrac{a}{A}$ 4

2. $\dfrac{b}{A}$ −8

3. $\dfrac{A \cdot b}{a}$ 4

4. $\dfrac{a + b}{A}$ −4

5. $\dfrac{a \cdot A}{b}$ 1

2–6 Addition and Subtraction in Expressions

Preview **Historical Note: Negative numbers**

The notation used today to represent negative numbers is a rather recent invention, coming after North America was first visited by European explorers.

Hindu writers expressed negative numbers by placing a dot or a small circle over or beside each, as in $\overset{\circ}{6}$ or $\circ 6$ for −6. The Chinese either wrote positive numbers in red or negative numbers in black or they used a diagonal stroke through the rightmost-digit figure as in $=$州 for −24.

Other early mathematicians used notations such as *m*:3, *m*.3, 0 − 3, and *m̄*3 for "negative three."

In this lesson we will make a change in the way negative numbers are written and use the new notation to simplify expressions.

PURPOSE

In this lesson, ways to simplify algebraic expressions involving negative numbers are introduced.

PREVIEW

It may be noted that many different cultures have contributed to the development of mathematics and its notation. Students should be encouraged to investigate the history of mathematics if resources are available.

Notation continues to change. Students could discuss different numerals that exist today: 7 and 7, 4 and 4, 9 and 9, for example. They could also discuss what notation they would "invent" to represent negative one if they had not already seen −1. (Possible notations suggested might include ①, *n*1, or 1.)

LESSON

Simplifying expressions involving subtraction is one of the most difficult tasks for students. This lesson should be treated very carefully. Go over the examples so that students are comfortable with the task of changing from one operation to another.

■ LESSON

Recall that "−4" can be read as "the opposite of four" or as "negative four." However, "−*x*" should be read only as "the opposite of *x*." "Negative *x*" might be misleading because it may suggest that −*x* is a negative number. The expression −*x* can be positive, negative, or zero depending on the value of *x*. For example, if *x* takes the value of −2, then −*x* = −(−2) = 2. Note that −*x* has a positive value in this case.

Because of the relationship between addition and subtraction, we can write expressions in several equivalent forms. You should be able to change one form to another. Study these examples.

> **Example 1** Rewrite $a - (-2)$ as an addition expression.
>
> *Solution*
>
> Subtracting a number is the same as adding its opposite.
>
> $$a - (-2) = a + 2$$

Example 1. Rewrite $n - (-5)$ as an addition expression.
$$n - (-5) = n + 5.$$

Example 2. Rewrite $n + (-5)$ as a subtraction expression.
$$n + (-5) = n - 5.$$

Example 3. Change so that all operations are addition. $n - 5n - 7$
$$n + (-5n) + (-7)$$

Example 4. Change so that all operations are subtraction. $5n + 3n + 6$
$$5n - (-3n) - (-6)$$

Example 5. Simplify. $x - (-y)$
$$x + y$$

Example 6. Simplify. $5y - (-3x) + (-2)$
$$5y + 3x - 2$$

CHECK UNDERSTANDING

Complete.

- Subtracting a real number is the same as adding __?__. (its opposite)
- Adding -6 is the same as subtracting __?__. (6)
- $--x$ simplifies to __?__. (x)

CLASSROOM EXERCISES

If additional classroom exercises are needed, some even-numbered written exercises selected from exercises 1–35 may be used.

It should be noted that, with the principles introduced in this lesson, two signs never need to appear side by side in a simplfied expression.

$+-$ can be replaced with $-$.
　For example, $4 + (-6) = 4 - 6$
$--$ can be replaced with $+$.
　For example, $2 - (-7) = 2 + 7$

Example 2 Rewrite $x + (-3)$ as a subtraction expression.

Solution

Adding a number is the same as subtracting its opposite.
$$x + (-3) = x - 3$$

Example 3 Rewrite $y - 2y - 3$ so that all subtractions are additions.

Solution $\quad y - 2y - 3 = y + (-2y) + (-3)$

Expressions with more than one sign between numbers or variables can also be simplified. When an expression is in simplest form, only the first term can have a negative or opposite sign.

Example 4 Simplify. $a - (-b)$

Solution $\quad a - (-b) = a + (--b) \qquad$ *The opposite of the opposite of b is b.*
$$= a + b$$

Example 5 Simplify. $2x - (-4) + (-y)$

Solution $\quad 2x - (-4) + (-y) = 2x + 4 - y$

■ CLASSROOM EXERCISES

True or false? If the statement is false, give a counterexample to show that it is false.

1. $-6 = {}^-6$

2. $-a$ is negative for all values of a. F; $a = -1$

3. $-b$ is positive for all values of b. F; $b = 1$

4. $-(-x)$ is positive for all values of x. F; $x = -1$

Change these subtractions to additions.

5. $a - 7$ $\quad a + (-7)$

6. $2x - (-8)$ $\quad 2x + 8$

7. $9 - y$ $\quad 9 + (-y)$

8. $-a - (-y)$ $\quad -a + y$

Change these additions to equivalent subtractions.

9. $b + (-3)$ $\quad b - 3$

10. $2a + (-y)$ $\quad 2a - y$

11. $2a + y$ $\quad 2a - (-y)$

12. $-x + (-2)$ $\quad -x - 2$

Simplify.

13. $a - (-4)$ $\quad a + 4$

14. $b + (-2)$ $\quad b - 2$

15. $2x - (-4)$ $\quad 2x + 4$

16. $3a + (-2b)$ $\quad 3a - 2b$

17. $c + (-5)$ $\quad c - 5$

18. $3x + (-y)$ $\quad 3x - y$

19. $2n - (-3m)$ $\quad 2n + 3m$

20. $4x + (-3)$ $\quad 4x - 3$

ASSIGNMENT GUIDE

Basic	1–35 odd, Review Exercises, Self-Quiz 2
Average	11–35 odd, 37–44 all, Review Exercises, Self-Quiz 2
Enriched	11–39 odd, 41–52 all, Review Exercises, Self-Quiz 2

■ WRITTEN EXERCISES

Write with the symbols described in this lesson.

A 1. The opposite of a $-a$

2. The opposite of b $-b$

3. The opposite of negative four $-(-4)$

4. The opposite of negative three $-(-3)$

True or false? If the statement is false, give a counterexample to show that it is false.

5. $-20 = {}^-20$ T

6. $-30 = {}^-30$ T

7. $-|-1| = -1$ T

8. $-(-a) = a$ T

9. $a > -a$ for all values of a F; $a=-1$

10. $-b < b$ for all values of b F; $b=-1$

11. $-c < 0$ for all values of c F; $c=-1$

12. $d > 0$ for all values of d F; $d=-1$

Change these subtractions to equivalent additions.

13. $h - 5$ $h+(-5)$

14. $j - 15$ $j+(-15)$

15. $k - (-3)$ $k+3$

16. $m - (-7)$ $m+7$

17. $x - y$ $x+(-y)$

18. $y - x$ $y+(-x)$

19. $-2 - p$ $-2+(-p)$

20. $-3 - q$ $-3+(-q)$

Change these additions to equivalent subtractions.

21. $r + (-9)$ $r-9$

22. $s + (-6)$ $s-6$

23. $t + (-u)$ $t-u$

24. $f + (-g)$ $f-g$

25. $k + n$ $k-(-n)$

26. $x + y$ $x-(-y)$

27. $2x + (-x)$ $2x-x$

28. $3y + (-y)$ $3y-y$

Simplify.

29. $5 - (-6)$ 11

30. $7 - (-10)$ 17

31. $-5 + (-10)$ -15

32. $-10 + (-5)$ -15

33. $x - (-2)$ $x+2$

34. $y - (-1)$ $y+1$

35. $2x + (-4)$ $2x-4$

36. $2y + (-3)$ $2y-3$

B 37. $2x - (-8) + (2y)$ $2x+8+2y$

38. $5x - (-10) + (-3w)$ $5x+10-3w$

39. $-12 + (-3w) - (-15)$ $-3w+3$

40. $-15 + (-x) - (-10)$ $-x-5$

Which is the larger number?

41. $\underline{5.6 + (-4.9) - (-3.6)}$ or $5.6 - 4.9 - 3.6$

42. $\underline{\dfrac{3}{8} - \left(-\dfrac{3}{4}\right) - \left(-\dfrac{3}{2}\right)}$ or $\dfrac{3}{8} + \left(-\dfrac{3}{4}\right) + \left(-\dfrac{3}{2}\right)$

43. $\underline{|17 + (-20) - (-1)|}$ or $17 + (-20) - (-1)$

44. The opposite of 3 or $\underline{\text{the reciprocal of } \dfrac{1}{3}}$.

a	A	n	x
-5	5	-10	$-\dfrac{1}{2}$

Substitute and simplify.

C 45. $A - (-a)$ 0

46. $A - (-n)$ -5

47. $x + (-A)$ $-5\frac{1}{2}$

48. $A + (-x)$ $5\frac{1}{2}$

49. $n + [-a + (-A)]$ -10

50. $[n + (-a)] + A$ 0

51. anx -25

52. $n \div (Ax)$ 4

PRACTICE WORKSHEET 8

2-6 ADDITION AND SUBTRACTION IN EXPRESSIONS

■ Change each subtraction to an equivalent addition.

1. $a - 5$ $a+(-5)$

2. $b - (-5)$ $b+5$

3. $5 - a$ $5+(-a)$

4. $-5 - (-b)$ $-5+b$

5. $-3 - x$ $-3+(-x)$

6. $y - (-7)$ $y+7$

7. $z - c$ $z+(-c)$

8. $-y - (-k)$ $-y+k$

9. $9 - (-t)$ $9+t$

■ Simplify.

10. $x - (-10)$ $x+10$

11. $y - (-0.3)$ $y+0.3$

12. $z + (-6)$ $z-6$

13. $r + (-1.5)$ $r-1.5$

14. $2a - (-8)$ $2a+8$

15. $3b + (-6)$ $3b-6$

16. $5 - (-10)$ 15

17. $5 + (-10)$ -5

18. $-5 - (-10)$ 5

19. $-5 + (-10)$ -15

20. $-1.3 + (-2.6)$ -3.9

21. $7.5 - (-7.5)$ 15.0

22. $-\frac{1}{2} - \left(-\frac{3}{4}\right)$ $\frac{1}{4}$

23. $\frac{1}{2} + \left(-\frac{3}{4}\right)$ $-\frac{1}{4}$

24. $5 + (-s)$ $5-s$

WRITTEN EXERCISES

Exercises 3 and 4 can be simplified:
$$-(-4) = 4 \text{ and } -(-3) = 3$$

Exercises 21–28 are intended to make students comfortable with the relationship between two signs. They are not exercises in simplifying.

- True or false?

  For all real numbers a and b,
  $$-(a - b) = b - a$$
  True

EXTRA PRACTICE, page 620
COMPUTER WORKSHEET 3

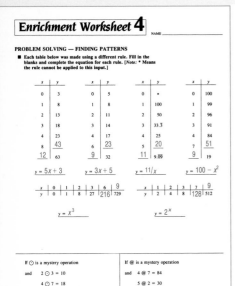

■ REVIEW EXERCISES

State the property illustrated by each equation. [1–5]

1. $(293 \cdot 25) \cdot 4 = 293 \cdot (25 \cdot 4)$
Associative property of multiplication

2. $(a + b) + 2a = 2a + (a + b)$
Commutative property of addition

3. $4x + x = 4x + 1x$ Identity property for multiplication

4. $3a + 2a = (3 + 2)a$ Distributive property

Simplify. [1–6]

5. $3a + 4b + a$ $4a + 4b$

6. $x + 3 + 6x + 5$ $7x + 8$

7. $x + 6 + 2(x + 6)$ $3x + 18$

8. $3(2a + 5b) + 2(b + 2a)$ $10a + 17b$

Use an algebraic expression to answer each question. [1–7]

Randy has $10 more than Matt.

9. How much does Matt have if Randy has R dollars? $(R - 10)$ dollars

10. How much does Randy have if Matt has M dollars? $(M + 10)$ dollars

---

Self-Quiz 2

Simplify.

2–4
1. $-6 \cdot -9$ 54

2. $-1 \cdot -2 \cdot -3$ -6

3. $(-5 \cdot 8) - (-5 \cdot 3)$ -25

2–5
4. $-84 \div 7$ -12

5. $-\dfrac{3}{8} \div -\dfrac{3}{4}$ $\dfrac{1}{2}$

6. $-12 \div |-2|$ -6

2–4,
2–5

a	b	c	d
-1	6	9	-3

Substitute and simplify.

7. $b \cdot d$ -18

8. $a \div d$ $\dfrac{1}{3}$

9. $\dfrac{b + c}{c}$ $\dfrac{5}{3}$

10. $\dfrac{a \cdot |d|}{b}$ $-\dfrac{1}{2}$

Write in symbols.

2–5 **11.** The reciprocal of negative seven $-\dfrac{1}{7}$

2–6 **12.** The opposite of negative one-half $-\left(-\dfrac{1}{2}\right)$

2–6 Rewrite the additions as equivalent subtractions and the subtractions as equivalent additions.

13. $x - 5$ $x + (-5)$

14. $b + (-3)$ $b - 3$

15. $21 - m$ $21 + (-m)$

16. $-6p + (-1)$ $-6p - 1$

The change sign key on a calculator _____

A special key on calculators is used in computations involving signed numbers. This key is called the **change sign key,** indicated on the calculator by $\boxed{\text{CHS}}$ or $\boxed{+/-}$. If we depress this key *after* entering a number, the opposite of the entered number is used by the calculator.

Examples

Compute $(-4) + (-3.2)$. $\qquad \dfrac{2-(-4)}{-3}.$

Key Sequence	Display		Key Sequence	Display
$\boxed{4}$	4		$\boxed{2}$	2
$\boxed{\text{CHS}}$	-4		$\boxed{-}$	2
$\boxed{+}$	-4		$\boxed{4}$	4
$\boxed{3}\;\boxed{.}\;\boxed{2}$	3.2		$\boxed{\text{CHS}}$	-4
$\boxed{\text{CHS}}$	-3.2		$\boxed{=}$	6
$\boxed{=}$	-7.2		$\boxed{\div}$	6
			$\boxed{3}$	3
			$\boxed{\text{CHS}}$	-3
			$\boxed{=}$	-2

Use a calculator to simplify these expressions.

1. $1 - (-3)$ 4 **2.** $(-9) + (-4.5)$ -13.5 **3.** $-[-(-6)]$ -6 **4.** $(-3.4)(-2)$ 6.8

5. $(-15) \div 3$ -5 **6.** $4(-6) + (-1)$ -25 **7.** $\dfrac{-2}{5} + \dfrac{3}{-5}$ -1 **8.** $\dfrac{14 + (-6)}{-4}$ -2

Strategy for Success **Preparing for class** _____

Learning will be easier if you read the preview and skim over the lesson before class.

Simplify.

1. $x + (-2)$ $x - 2$
2. $n - (^+3)$ $n - 3$
3. $y + (^+5)$ $y + 5$
4. $a - (-7)$ $a + 7$
5. $-8 - (-x)$ $-8 + x$

PURPOSE

The basic properties may be considered the foundations of much of mathematics. To be successful in algebra, students must be skillful in using the properties to simplify algebraic expressions. Students are expected to be familiar with the names of properties and to be able to supply them as reasons to justify steps in computations or algebraic transformations.

PREVIEW

Some students may be interested in reading about the life of Galois and other mathematicians. An excellent source book for a library guide is *The High School Mathematics Library* published by the National Council of Teachers of Mathematics, 1906 Association Drive, Reston, Virginia 22091.

LESSON

Review the list of basic properties.
One other basic property might be introduced at your discretion.

The *Closure* Property

If a and b are real numbers,
$a + b$ is a real number and
ab is a real number.

(Any system having all the basic properties of the real numbers may be called a *field*. It is not the purpose of this book to study mathematical structures as such, although some students may run across mention of various structures as they read about mathematics and its historical development.)

Go over the examples carefully so that students understand the uses of the basic properties. However, we do not consider it

To recognize the basic properties of real numbers and use the properties to simplify algebraic expressions.

2–7 Using the Basic Properties to Simplify Expressions

Preview   Biography

Major contributions to the development and understanding of the structure of modern algebra were made by the young Frenchman, Évariste Galois. At the age of 21 he spent an entire night recording his mathematical discoveries because he feared that he would be killed the following day in a duel. He did not want his findings to die with him. He was killed in that duel on May 30, 1832, but his contributions to mathematics live on.

In this lesson you will examine the fundamental principles of real numbers and use them to simplify algebraic expressions.

■ LESSON

We have discovered that the basic properties of positive numbers that we studied in Chapter 1 also apply to all numbers, including negative numbers. In this chapter we have also worked with inverse properties for addition and multiplication.

These basic properties are listed below.

Basic Properties of Real Numbers

	Addition	*Multiplication*
	For all real numbers a, b, and c	
Commutative properties	$a + b = b + a$	$ab = ba$
Associative properties	$a + (b + c) = (a + b) + c$	$a(bc) = (ab)c$
Identity properties	$a + 0 = a$	$1a = a$
Inverse properties	$a + (-a) = 0$	$a\left(\dfrac{1}{a}\right) = 1 \quad (a \neq 0)$
Distributive properties	$ab + ac = a(b + c)$ $ba + ca = (b + c)a$	

An overhead projector is especially useful for materials that can be prepared ahead of time or will be used several times, such as problem-solving check- *lists, complex diagrams, or overlays of graphs. Test transparencies for readability from all parts of the room.*

important for most students to be able to rigorously apply the properties (especially the associative properties) in simplifying expressions. The important points are (1) that once subtractions have been changed to additions, terms may be reordered and regrouped to get like terms together, and (2) that like terms may be combined into single terms.

A less rigorous process is followed in simplifying expressions by allowing the commutative and associative properties to be combined. For example, here is a complete use of the properties to simplify $3x + 5 + 4x$:

$$3x + 5 + 4x$$
$$= 3x + (5 + 4x) \quad \textit{Associative}$$
$$\qquad\qquad\qquad\qquad \textit{(addition)}$$
$$= 3x + (4x + 5) \quad \textit{Commutative}$$
$$\qquad\qquad\qquad\qquad \textit{(addition)}$$
$$= (3x + 4x) + 5 \quad \textit{Associative}$$
$$\qquad\qquad\qquad\qquad \textit{(addition)}$$
$$= (3 + 4)x + 5 \quad \textit{Distributive property}$$
$$= 7x + 5 \quad \textit{Computation}$$

But we accept a less detailed development:

$$3x + 5 + 4x$$
$$= 3x + 4x + 5 \quad \textit{Rearrange terms}$$
$$= 7x + 5 \qquad \textit{Collect like terms}$$

We can derive additional properties from the basic properties listed on page 66.

	For all real numbers a and b,
−1 property of multiplication	$(-1)a = -a$
0 property of multiplication	$0a = 0$
Multiplying opposites property	$(-a)b = a(-b) = -(ab)$ $(-a)(-b) = ab$
Dividing opposites property	$\dfrac{-a}{b} = -\dfrac{a}{b} = \dfrac{a}{-b} \ (b \neq 0)$
Opposite of an opposite property	$-(-a) = a$
Distributive property of opposites	$-(a + b) = -a + (-b)$

We can use the real number properties to explain how algebraic expressions are simplified.

Example 1   Simplify. $3x - x$

Solution

$$3x - x = 3x + (-x) \qquad \textit{Subtracting is equivalent to adding the opposite.}$$
$$= 3x + (-1)x \qquad \textit{−1 property of multiplication}$$
$$= (3 + (-1))x \qquad \textit{Distributive property}$$
$$= 2x \qquad\qquad\quad \textit{Computation}$$

Example 2   Simplify. $3b - 7 + b$

Solution

$$3b - 7 + b = 3b + (-7) + b \qquad \textit{Change to addition.}$$
$$= 3b + b + (-7) \qquad \textit{Commutative property of addition}$$
$$= 3b + 1b + (-7) \qquad \textit{Identity property for multiplication}$$
$$= (3 + 1)b + (-7) \qquad \textit{Distributive property}$$
$$= 4b + (-7) \qquad\quad \textit{Computation}$$
$$= 4b - 7 \qquad\qquad\; \textit{Change to subtraction.}$$

There are three basic steps for simplifying expressions like those in Examples 1 and 2:

1. Change all subtractions to additions.

2. Use the commutative and associative properties of addition to rearrange terms so that like terms are together.

3. Use the distributive property to replace sums of like terms by single terms.

ADDITIONAL EXAMPLES

Example 1.
Simplify. $5x + 10x$
$$5x + 10x$$
$$= (5 + 10)x \quad \textit{Distributive property}$$
$$= 15x \qquad\quad \textit{Computation}$$

Example 2.
Simplify. $5a + 6 - 2a$
$$5a + 6 - 2a$$
$$= 5a + 6 + (-2a) \quad \textit{Change to}$$
$$\qquad\qquad\qquad\qquad\;\; \textit{addition.}$$
$$= 5a + (-2a) + 6 \quad \textit{Associative and}$$
$$\qquad\qquad\qquad\qquad\;\; \textit{commutative}$$
$$\qquad\qquad\qquad\qquad\;\; \textit{properties of}$$
$$\qquad\qquad\qquad\qquad\;\; \textit{addition}$$
$$= (5 + (-2))a + 6 \quad \textit{Distributive}$$
$$\qquad\qquad\qquad\qquad\;\; \textit{property}$$
$$= 3a + 6 \qquad\qquad\;\; \textit{Computation}$$

Example 3.

Simplify. $6x - 2y - 4y - 5x$

$6x - 2y - 4y - 5x$

$= 6x + (-2y) + (-4y) + (-5x)$
Change to additions.

$= 6x + (-5x) + (-2y) + (-4y)$
Rearrange terms.

$= (6 + (-5))x + (-2 + (-4))y$
Distributive property

$= 1x + (-6)y$
Computation

$= 1x + (-6)y$
Multiplying opposites property

$= 1x - 6y$
Change to subtraction.

$= x - 6y$
Identity (multiplication)

Example 4.

Simplify. $2a - 3b + 5a + b$

$2a - 3b + 5a + b$

$= 7a - 2b$ *Collect and combine like terms.*

CHECK UNDERSTANDING

State the properties that are involved.

• $2a + 3a = 5a$
(Distributive property)

• $3x + 2 + 5x = 3x + 5x + 2$
(Commutative and associative properties of addition)

• $8c + 3 + 2c = 10c + 3$
(Commutative and associative properties of addition, and distributive property)

• $3x - 2 + 4x = 7x - 2$
(Commutative and associative properties of addition, and distributive property)

CLASSROOM EXERCISES

If greater emphasis on the basic properties is desired, students can be asked which properties were used in the simplification of classroom exercises 5–13.

Sometimes other steps are necessary.

Example 3   Simplify. $2m - 3n + 4n - 7m$

Solution $2m - 3n + 4n - 7m$
$= 2m + (-3n) + 4n + (-7m)$ *Change to additions.*

$= 2m + (-7m) + (-3n) + 4n$ *Use the commutative and associative properties of addition to collect like terms.*

$= 2m + (-7)m + (-3)n + 4n$ *Multiplying opposites property*

$= (-5)m + 1n$ *Use the distributive property to combine like terms.*

$= (-5)m + n$ *Identity property for multiplication*

$= -5m + n$ *Multiplying opposites property*

As you practice the skill of simplifying expressions, look for shortcuts and do much of the work mentally.

Example 4   Simplify. $5x + 6y - 8x + 7y$

Solution $5x + 6y - 8x + 7y = -3x + 13y$ *Collect and combine like terms.*

■ CLASSROOM EXERCISES

Give an example of each property.   Answers will vary.

1. The associative property of multiplication $(xy)z = x(yz)$

2. The distributive property $x(y + z) = xy + xz$

3. The commutative property of addition $x + y = y + x$

4. The identity properties   Add: $x + 0 = x$ Mult: $x \cdot 1 = x$

Simplify.

5. $3x + 5x$ 8x

6. $5x + 3x$ 8x

7. $-(-4a)$ 4a

8. $1b$ b

9. $-4m + m$ −3m

10. $8n - 2n$ 6n

11. $2n - 8n$ −6n

12. $2a + 5 - a$ a + 5

13. $-3c - c + 2a + a$
$-4c + 3a$

ASSIGNMENT GUIDE

Basic   1–31 odd, Review Exercises
Average   1–29 odd, 31–45 all, Review
          Exercises
Enriched 1–35 odd, 37–53 all, Review
          Exercises

EXTRA PRACTICE, page 620

■ WRITTEN EXERCISES

Change to equivalent expressions involving addition but not subtraction.

A
1. $5a - a$ $5a + (-a)$
2. $3r - r$ $3r + (-r)$
3. $5 + 10s - 8s$
   $5 + 10s + (-8s)$
4. $10 + 3b - 2b$ $10 + 3b + (-2b)$
5. $-5a - 4a + b$
   $-5a + (-4a) + b$
6. $-7x - 6x + y$
   $-7x + (-6x) + y$

Simplify.

7. $-8 + 5 + 2a$
   $-3 + 2a$
8. $-7 + 3 + 4b$
   $-4 + 4b$
9. $12a + 3a$ $15a$
10. $15b + 5b$ $20b$

11. $-7c + c$ $-6c$
12. $-9p + p$ $-8p$
13. $10q - q$ $9q$
14. $30r - r$ $29r$

15. $-6s - 5s$ $-11s$
16. $-3t - 2t$ $-5t$
17. $2a + 3b + 4a$
   $6a + 3b$
18. $7x + 3y + 2x$
   $9x + 3y$

19. $6r + 3s + 2s + 4r$ $10r + 5s$
20. $7x + 3y + 7y + 5x$ $12x + 10y$

21. $w + 3z - 5w + 2z$ $-4w + 5z$
22. $6g + 5h - 15g + h$ $-9g + 6h$

State the property illustrated in each equation.

23. $8a + 5a + 3 = (8 + 5)a + 3$ Distributive property
24. $10 + (4x + 5x) = 10 + (4 + 5)x$
   Distributive property

25. $-3x + (5y + 2x) = -3x + (2x + 5y)$
   Commutative property of addition
26. $4a + 3b + 2a = 3b + 4a + 2a$
   Commutative property of addition

27. $5c + c = 5c + 1c$ Identity property for multiplication
28. $5r + 0 = 5r$ Identity property for addition

29. $7(10a) = (7 \cdot 10)a$
   Associative property of multiplication
30. $3(a + 2b) + 4b = 3a + 6b + 4b$
   Distributive property

Write a simplified rule for each situation.

31. An orchard owner charges 15¢ per apple plus 10¢ per apple for picking, cleaning, and packaging. The cost of n apples is, therefore, $15n + 10n$. $25n$

32. The orchard owner charges 10¢ for a peach plus 8¢ per peach for picking, cleaning, and packaging. The cost of m peaches is, therefore, $10m + 8m$. $18m$

B
33. The total cost of n apples and m peaches is $15n + 10n + 10m + 8m$.
   $25n + 18m$

34. The total cost of g grapefruit and r oranges is $35g + 20r + 15g + 8r$.
   $50g + 28r$

35. After cooking, the total number of calories in a cups of asparagus and b cups of lima beans is $45a + 190b - 5a - 20b$. $40a + 170b$

36. After the waste has been removed, the total number of calories in c cantaloupes and p plums is $120c + 25p - 20c - 3p$. $100c + 22p$

Simplify these expressions.

37. $x^2 + x^2 + x$ $2x^2 + x$
38. $y^2 + y^2 + 2y$ $2y^2 + 2y$

39. $xy + 2x + x$ $xy + 3x$
40. $xy + 2x + 2xy$ $3xy + 2x$

41. $0.5x - x$ $-0.5x$
42. $-a^2 + 2b^2 + \frac{1}{4}a^2$ $-\frac{3}{4}a^2 + 2b^2$

43. $3x - x - x^2$ $2x - x^2$
44. $5x^2 - x^2 - 3x$ $4x^2 - 3x$

45. $-5 - x^2 + 6x^2$ $-5 + 5x^2$

WRITTEN EXERCISES

In exercises 37–49 note that x^2 and x are not like terms; neither are y^2 and y.

If additional experiences like those in exercises 50–51 are desired, students can be asked to write the reasons for each step in the simplifications of exercises 37–40.

In exercise 52, discuss why the perimeter is simply $4a$. (Only the area changes when you cut off a small square from a *corner* of a large square; the perimeter remains the same.)

ENRICHMENT PROBLEM

- I am thinking of a number that is its own reciprocal. I am not thinking of 1. What number am I thinking of?

$$-1$$

Simplify these expressions.

46. $-8 + 8x - 8x^2 - 8 - 8x - 8x^2$ $-16 - 16x^2$ **47.** $8 - 8x + 8x^2 - 8 - 8x - 8x^2$ $-16x$

48. $x + \dfrac{x^2}{2} + 2x^2 - x$ $2\frac{1}{2}x^2$

49. $-(a^2 - 3a + 2) + 3(-a^2 + 3a - 2)$
$-4a^2 + 12a - 8$

Write the property listed in each step of these simplifications.

50. $12 - 5x + 3x = 12 + -(5x) + 3x$ *Subtracting is equivalent to adding the opposite.*
$= 12 + (-5)x + 3x$ **a.** _____?_____ Multiplying opposites property
$= 12 + [(-5)x + 3x]$ **b.** _____?_____ Associative property of addition
$= 12 + [(-5 + 3)x]$ **c.** _____?_____ Distributive property
$= 12 + (-2)x$ *Computation*
$= 12 + -(2x)$ **d.** _____?_____ Multiplying opposites property
$= 12 - 2x$ **e.** Subtracting _?_ is equivalent to adding the opposite.

51. $5x + 2y - 10x = 2y + 5x - 10x$ **a.** _____?_____ Commutative property of addition
$= 2y + 5x + -(10x)$ **b.** Subtracting _?_ is equivalent to adding the opposite.
$= 2y + [5x + -(10x)]$ **c.** _____?_____ Associative property of addition
$= 2y + [5x + (-10)x]$ *Multiplying opposites property*
$= 2y + [(5 + (-10))x]$ *Distributive property*
$= 2y + (-5)x$ **d.** _____?_____ Computation
$= 2y + -(5x)$ *Multiplying opposites property*
$= 2y - 5x$ **e.** Subtracting _?_ is equivalent to adding the opposite.

Write an expression for each perimeter and simplify.

52.

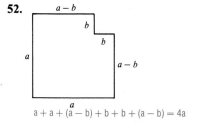

$a + a + (a - b) + b + b + (a - b) = 4a$

53.

$(a - b) + b + b + (a - b) + (a - b) + b + b + (a - b) = 4a$

■ REVIEW EXERCISES

Use an algebraic expression to complete each statement.   [1–7]

1. Carl is driving 5 miles per hour under the speed limit. Let s be the speed limit in miles per hour. Then __?__ is Carl's speed in miles per hour. $(s - 5)$

2. An airplane is flying at twice the speed of sound. If S is the speed of sound, then __?__ is the speed of the airplane. $2S$

3. A house is 10 feet longer than twice its width. If w is the width in feet, then __?__ is the length in feet. $2w + 10$

Simplify.   [2–13]

4. $-(-6)$ 6   **5.** $--(x)$ x   **6.** $|-8|$ 8   **7.** $-|9|$ -9 **8.** $-\left|-\dfrac{2}{3}\right|$ $-\frac{2}{3}$

You may wish to spend two days on this section. Refer to the Pacing Chart.

To simplify expressions containing parentheses using the basic properties.

2–8 Using the Distributive Properties to Simplify Expressions

Preview

An industrial designer submits a plan for blocks of various sizes, each depending on the lengths of a and b.

The perimeter of this figure is given by the following expression:

$$a + a + a + \frac{1}{2}(a - b) + b + b + b + \frac{1}{2}(a - b)$$

Suppose that $a = 25$ and $b = 5$. What is the perimeter?   110

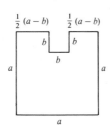

Another expression for the perimeter is $4a + 2b$. Substitute 25 for a and 5 for b in this expression to find the perimeter of the figure.   110

The two expressions for perimeter are equivalent, but the second is much simpler than the first. In this lesson we will continue to study methods of simplifying expressions.

■ LESSON

Sometimes part of an expression must be "expanded" before the whole expression can be simplified. Consider

$$2x + 3(x + 1)$$

We use the distributive property to obtain an expression without parentheses:

$$2x + 3x + 3$$

Then we simplify:

$$5x + 3$$

Study these examples.

Example 1   Simplify. $6 + 2(m - 3)$

   Solution $6 + 2(m - 3) = 6 + 2[m + (-3)]$ *Change to addition.*
                    $= 6 + [2m + 2(-3)]$ *Distributive property*
                    $= 6 + 2m + (-6)$ *Computation*
                    $= 2m + (-6 + 6)$ *Rearrange terms.*
                    $= 2m + 0$ *Inverse property of addition*
                    $= 2m$ *Identity property for addition*

Example 2.
  Simplify. $3(r - 2) - 2(3r - 5)$
    $3(r - 2) - 2(3r - 5)$
  $= 3(r + (-2)) + (-2)(3r + (-5))$
    Change to addition.
  $= 3r + (-6) + (-6)r + 10$
    Distributive property and computation
  $= 3r + (-6)r + (-6) + 10$
    Rearrange terms.
  $= -3r + 4$
    Combine like terms.

Example 3. Simplify. $4w - \frac{1}{3}(6 + 3w)$
    $4w - \frac{1}{3}(6 + 3w)$

  $= 4w + \left[-\frac{1}{3}(6 + 3w)\right]$

  $= 4w + \left(-\frac{1}{3}\right)(6) + \left(-\frac{1}{3}\right)(3w)$

  $= 4w + (-2) + (-w)$
  $= 3w + (-2)$
  $= 3w - 2$

CHECK UNDERSTANDING

Write an equivalent expression without parentheses.
$3(x + 4)$ $(3x + 12)$
$4(2a - 3)$ $(8a - 12)$

CLASSROOM EXERCISES

In classroom exercises 5 and 6, note that multiplying by -1 is the same as finding the opposite of the quantity.
  In classroom exercises 7 and 8, note that finding the opposite of the quantity is the same as multiplying the quantity by -1.

Example 2   Simplify. $2(a + 3) - 1(2a - 1)$

Solution $2(a + 3) - 1(2a - 1)$
  $= 2(a + 3) + (-1)[2a + (-1)]$ *Subtracting is equivalent to adding the opposite.*

  $= 2a + 6 + (-2)a + 1$ *Distributive property*
  $= 2a + (-2)a + 6 + 1$ *Rearrange terms.*
  $= 0 + 7$ *Computation*
  $= 7$ *Identity property for addition*

Example 3   Simplify. $5a - \frac{1}{2}(2a + 4)$

Solution $5a - \frac{1}{2}(2a + 4) = 5a + [-\frac{1}{2}(2a + 4)]$

  $= 5a + \left(-\frac{1}{2}\right)(2a) + \left(-\frac{1}{2}\right)(4)$

  $= 5a + (-a) + (-2)$
  $= 4a + (-2)$
  $= 4a - 2$

Here is a brief review of how to simplify expressions.

1. Change any subtractions to additions.

2. Use the distributive properties to expand terms.

3. Rearrange terms so that like terms are grouped, and then combine like terms.

As you practice, look for shortcuts.

■ CLASSROOM EXERCISES

Write an equivalent expression without parentheses.

1. $3(2a + 1)$ $6a + 3$ **2.** $7(a - 5)$ $7a - 35$ **3.** $-4(2y + 4)$ $-8y - 16$ **4.** $-2(7 - 3m)$ $-14 + 6m$

5. $-1(4 - 3b)$ $-4 + 3b$ **6.** $-1(-6 - 2n)$ $6 + 2n$ **7.** $-(8g + 2)$ $-8g - 2$ **8.** $-(7a - 5)$ $-7a + 5$

Simplify.

9. $3(2x + 1) - 8$ $6x - 5$ **10.** $4(3a - 2) + 5$ $12a - 3$ **11.** $2(5y - 2x) + x$ $10y - 3x$ **12.** $13 + 5(2n - 2)$ $10n + 3$

13. $3y - (4y + 6x)$ $-y - 6x$ **14.** $21 - (8 - 3c)$ $3c + 13$ **15.** $7b - (3a - 8b)$ $15b - 3a$ **16.** $5 + (4g - 7)$ $4g - 2$

17. $4(3x - 1) + 2$ $12x - 2$ **18.** $5(6x - 1) + 4$ $30x - 1$ **19.** $2(3x - 4y) - x$ $5x - 8y$ **20.** $3(2x + y) - y$ $6x + 2y$

21. $2(x + 3) - 5$ $2x + 1$ **22.** $4(x + 1) - 4$ $4x$ **23.** $4 - 3(x + 2)$ $-3x - 2$ **24.** $6 - 2(x + 3)$ $-2x$

Experienced teachers have suggested that occasionally students should be required to redo exercises until the exercises are done correctly. This is especially important for topics that are prerequisites for future work.

■ WRITTEN EXERCISES

Write an equivalent expression.

A   **1.** $3(x + 7)$ $3x + 21$ **2.** $5(x + 2)$ $5x + 10$ **3.** $7(a - 4)$ $7a - 28$ **4.** $4(a - 6)$ $4a - 24$

5. $-6(y + 2)$ $-6y - 12$ **6.** $-2(y + 10)$ $-2y - 20$ **7.** $-10(b - 8)$ $-10b + 80$ **8.** $-8(b - 2)$ $-8b + 16$

9. $5(3x - 6)$ $15x - 30$ **10.** $3(2x - 5)$ $6x - 15$ **11.** $-1(3a - 5)$ $-3a + 5$ **12.** $-1(6a - 2)$ $-6a + 2$

13. $-(3a - 5)$ $-3a + 5$ **14.** $-(6a - 2)$ $-6a + 2$ **15.** $3(2m + 4n)$ $6m + 12n$ **16.** $3(4m + 2n)$ $12m + 6n$

Simplify.

17. $8(b + 2) + 4$ $8b + 20$ **18.** $10(b + 3) + 7$ $10b + 37$ **19.** $6 + 2(x + 5)$ $2x + 16$ **20.** $2 + 6(x + 5)$ $6x + 32$

21. $3(2x - 6) + 8$ $6x - 10$ **22.** $4(5x - 2) + 3$ $20x - 5$ **23.** $3 - 2(x - 1)$ $-2x + 5$ **24.** $10 - 3(x - 4)$ $-3x + 22$

25. $5 - (x - 3)$ $-x + 8$ **26.** $6 - (x - 2)$ $-x + 8$ **27.** $5x + 2(x - 5)$ $7x - 10$ **28.** $10x + 3(x - 2)$ $13x - 6$

29. $3x - 5(x + 7)$ $-2x - 35$ **30.** $2x - 6(x + 2)$ $-4x - 12$ **31.** $2x - (x + 10)$ $x - 10$ **32.** $3x - (x + 7)$ $2x - 7$

Write a simplified rule for each situation.

33. When Tom babysits for one child, he charges $1 plus $1.50 per hour. When he babysits for three children at once, he charges twice as much. Simplify $2(1 + 1.5\,h)$. $2 + 3h$

34. When Theresa babysits for one child, she charges $2 plus $1.00 per hour. When she babysits for three children at once, she charges twice as much. Simplify $2(2 + 1h)$. $4 + 2h$

B   **35.** An amount of 1 dollar invested at $r\%$ for one year equals $(1 + 0.01r)$ dollars. A $20 investment is worth 20 times as much as one for $1. Simplify $20(1 + 0.01r)$. $20 + 0.2r$

36. An amount of 1 dollar invested at $r\%$ for one year equals $(1 + 0.01r)$ dollars. A $100 investment is worth 100 times as much as for one for $1. Simplify $100(1 + 0.01r)$. $100 + r$

37. We can write 234 as $2h + 3t + 4n$ where h, t, and n represent 100, 10, and 1, respectively. Add $2h + 3t + 4n$ and $3h + 5t + 4n$. Does the result agree with $234 + 354$? Explain. $5h + 8t + 8n$; yes

38. Add $1h + 4t + 8n$ and $5h + 3t$. Does the result agree with $148 + 53$? Explain. $6h + 7t + 8n$; no

Simplify.

39. $3(a + 2b) + 2(a + 5b)$ $5a + 16b$ **40.** $6(a + b) - 5(a - b)$ $a + 11b$

41. $-7(a - b) + 3(2a + 3b)$ $-a + 16b$ **42.** $5(2a + 6) - 2(5a - 4)$ 38

43. $4(x - 3y) - 7(2x - y)$ $-10x - 5y$ **44.** $-3(2x - 3y) + 2(3x + 5y)$ $19y$

45. $-5(x + 2y) - 6(x - 3y)$ $-11x + 8y$ **46.** $-3(3x - 5y) + 5(x + 4y)$ $-4x + 35y$

WRITTEN EXERCISES

Although the distributive property, fully stated, is "the distributive property of multiplication over addition," it is often referred to as simply "the distributive property." One should note that although it is not listed among the basic properties, multiplication is also distributive over subtraction.

$$a(b - c) = ab - ac$$
$$(b - c)a = ba - ca$$

In exercises 9 and 10, note that the multiplier is distributed over each addend, not over each factor in an addend.

$$5(3x - 6) = 5 \cdot 3x - 5 \cdot 6, \text{ or } 15x - 30$$
$$5(3x - 6) \neq 5 \cdot 3 \cdot 5x - 5 \cdot 6$$

In exercises 11 and 12, note that multiplying by -1 has the effect of changing the signs of both addends in the sum.

In exercises 13 and 14, note that finding the opposite is the same as multiplying by -1.

This is a good lesson to remind students of the helpfulness of substituting a value for the variable in the original expression and the simplified expression. If the resulting values are different, the expressions are not equivalent.

ENRICHMENT PROBLEM

• Reexamine the figures of the Preview and written exercise 53. Working backward from the answers for the perimeters, can you determine an easier way of viewing the figures to find the perimeter? [*Hint:* In exercise 53, what happens if you "unfold" the corners?]

EXTRA PRACTICE, page 621

Consider the following example of a useful shortcut.

Sample Simplify. $6(a - 2) + (a - 2) - 3(a - 2)$

Solution Note that all the terms are like terms. So, we can add the coefficients of $(a - 2)$. Since $6 + 1 - 3 = 4$, the solution is $4(a - 2)$ or $4a - 8$.

C 47. $4(2x - y) - 3(2x - y)$ $2x - y$

48. $-10(3x - 4y) + 5(3x - 4y)$ $-15x + 20y$

49. $-(a + 2b) + 3(a + 2b) - 2(a + 2b)$ 0

50. $\frac{1}{2}(3x - 2y) - 2(3x - 2y) + 3x$ $\frac{3}{2}$ $2y$
$-\frac{3}{2}x + y$

51. $-3(a^2 + a - 1) - 2(-a^2 - a + 1)$ $-a^2 - a + 1$

52. $a^2 - a + 1 - (-a^2 + a - 1)$
$2a^2 - 2a + 2$

Write an expression for the perimeter of each figure. Simplify the expression.

53.

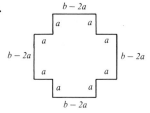

$(b - 2a) + a + a + (b - 2a) + a + a + (b - 2a)$
$+ a + a + (b - 2a) + a + a = 4b$

54.

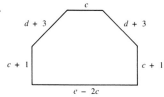

$c + (d + 3) + (c + 1) + (e - 2c) + (c + 1) + (d + 3)$
$= c + 2d + e + 8$

55.

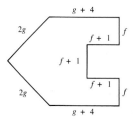

$f + (f + 1) + (f + 1) + (f + 1) + f + (g + 4) + 2g$
$+ 2g + (g + 4) = 5f + 6g + 11$

56.

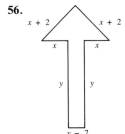

$(x + 2) + (x + 2) + x + y + (y - 7) + y + x$
$= 4x + 3y - 3$

Strategy for Success Actively questioning

Formulate questions while you are learning mathematics. Think: Is there a different way of doing this problem? What would happen if ———— were changed in the problem? What other problems can be solved using this method?

■ REVIEW EXERCISES

Use an algebraic expression to complete each statement.   [1–7]

1. A rectangle is 3 cm longer than it is wide.
   a. If its width is w cm, its length is __?__ cm. $(w + 3)$

   b. If its length is l cm, its width is __?__ cm. $(l - 3)$

2. Jean is $1\frac{1}{2}$ years older than her brother.

   a. If Jean is j years old, her brother is __?__ years old. $\left(j - 1\frac{1}{2}\right)$

   b. If her brother is b years old, Jean is __?__ years old. $\left(b + 1\frac{1}{2}\right)$

Simplify.   [2–2]

3. $7 + (-12)$ -5 **4.** $-6 + (3) + (-10)$ -13 **5.** $|-3 + 5|$ 2 **6.** $|-3| + |5|$ 8

Simplify.   [2–3]

7. $5 - 34$ -29 **8.** $-2 - (-12)$ 10 **9.** $19 - (-13)$ 32 **10.** $|-13 - (-6)|$ 7

Self-Quiz 3

2–7   Match the property name with the appropriate equation:

   1. Commutative property of addition c   **a.** $3(s + t) = 3s + 3t$

   2. Associative property of multiplication e   **b.** $5 \cdot \frac{1}{5} = 1$

   3. Identity property for multiplication f   **c.** $-4 + x = x + (-4)$

   4. Inverse property of addition d   **d.** $\frac{2}{3} + -\frac{2}{3} = 0$

   5. Inverse property of multiplication b   **e.** $8 \cdot (2x) = (8 \cdot 2)x$

   6. Distributive property a   **f.** $1 \cdot (xy) = xy$

   7. -1 property of multiplication g   **g.** $(-1)(9a) = -9a$

2–7,
2–8   Simplify.

   8. $8x - 5x$ $3x$ **9.** $-(-2y)$ $2y$ **10.** $26 + 2(3x - 9)$ $6x + 8$

   11. $3(5x - 9) - 5$ $15x - 32$ **12.** $9 - 2(x + 3)$ $-2x + 3$ **13.** $(3a + b) - (2a - 3b)$ $a + 4b$

   14. $4(2x - 1) + 3$ $8x - 1$ **15.** $3 - 2(x + 1)$ $-2x + 1$ **16.** $(2x + 3) + 4x$ $6x + 3$

   17. $5(x + 3) + 2x$ $7x + 15$ **18.** $4 - 2(x + 3)$ $-2x - 2$ **19.** $(2x + y) + (3x + 2y)$ $5x + 3y$

Simplify.

1. $9(x + 2) + 3$ $9x + 21$
2. $5 + 4(x + 1)$ $9 + 4x$
3. $8 - (x - 2)$ $10 - x$
4. $5x - 2(3 + x)$ $3x - 6$
5. $10x - 3(2x - 7)$ $4x + 21$

PURPOSE

Some problems can be solved if the pertinent data can be displayed in an appropriate way. Tables are an excellent way to show information in an organized, systematic way. Much of later problem solving depends on being able to organize the variables and given quantities in ways that help in writing the equation. To become better problem solvers, students should use tables effectively.

PREVIEW

It may be necessary to review how to find the surface area of a cube ($S = 6e^2$, where e is the length of an edge) and the volume of a cube ($V = e^3$).

If the length of an edge is measured in centimeters (cm), the surface area is measured in square centimeters (cm^2), and the volume is measured in cubic centimeters (cm^3). Regardless of the units used in the measurements, the ratio of the surface area to the volume gets smaller as the cube gets larger.

The ratios, not completely simplified, could be written in this pattern:

$$\frac{6}{1}, \frac{6}{2}, \frac{6}{3}, \frac{6}{4}, \frac{6}{5}, \frac{6}{6}, \frac{6}{7}, \frac{6}{8}, \frac{6}{9}, \frac{6}{10}$$

$$\frac{S}{V} = \frac{6e^2}{e^3} = \frac{6}{e}$$

LESSON

Go over the examples carefully. You will have best results if you "build" the table step by step on the board with students.

Note that the tables may be written horizontally or vertically. The labels on the rows (or columns) should show the units of the quantities (dollars or cents, hours or minutes, centimeters or inches, etc.) unless it is obvious from the problem what the units are.

To use tables to organize information (data) and to solve problems.

You may wish to spend two days on this section. Refer to the Pacing Chart.

2–9 Problem Solving — Using Tables

Preview **Information from tables**

When at the beach, have you ever seen a small child shivering with cold while adult swimmers seemed to be comfortably warm? The table below will help you understand why the child is cold when the adults are not.

The table shows that as a cube becomes larger, the ratio of surface area to volume becomes smaller. That is, the surface area increases at a slower rate than the volume does. Although people are not shaped like cubes, the same relationship holds: Adults have a smaller surface area relative to their volume than children do.

The amount of heat produced by a body is relative to its volume. The amount of heat lost is related to its surface area. Therefore, a small body (child) has a larger ratio of heat loss to heat produced than a large body (adult) does.

The table shows the information in an organized way so that patterns and relationships are easy to see. In this lesson you will use tables in a variety of ways to solve problems.

Edge of cube	1	2	3	4	5	6	7	8	9	10
Surface area	6	24	54	96	150	216	294	384	486	600
Volume	1	8	27	64	125	216	343	512	729	1000
Ratio of surface area to volume	$\frac{6}{1}$	$\frac{3}{1}$	$\frac{2}{1}$	$\frac{3}{2}$	$\frac{6}{5}$	$\frac{1}{1}$	$\frac{6}{7}$	$\frac{3}{4}$	$\frac{2}{3}$	$\frac{3}{5}$

■ LESSON

When solving a problem, it may be possible to make a table that shows how the quantities (numbers) are related for some cases. Then, by extending the table we can find a particular case.

Many experts believe that homework is an activity in which students should be able to make mistakes without being penalized. Therefore, they believe that if *grades are given for homework, penalties should not be assessed for errors, but rather for not doing homework or for not making required corrections.*

ADDITIONAL EXAMPLES

Example 1.
Alexander has $47 in savings and Marie has $67. Alexander saves $2 per day and Marie saves $1 per day. In how many days will Alexander's savings and Marie's savings be the same?

Start a table.

Day	Now	1	2
Alexander's savings	47	49	51
Marie's savings	67	68	69

Continue the table.

3	13	18	19	20
53	73	83	85	87
70	80	85	86	87

Their savings are the same on the 20th day.

Example 2.
The Tigers and Panthers both have 301 points. The Tigers gain 3 points each minute and the Panthers lose 2 points each minute. In how many minutes will the Tigers have 100 more points than the Panthers?

Minutes	Now	1	2	10	15	20
Tigers	301	304	307	331	346	361
Panthers	301	299	297	281	271	261

The Tigers will have 100 points more than the Panthers after 20 minutes.

Example 3.
When were the Tigers 50 points ahead of the Panthers? (See the example above.)
After 10 minutes.

Example 4.
When will the Tigers have twice as many points as the Panthers?
Continue the table.

Minutes	40	42	43
Tigers	421	427	430
Panthers	221	217	215

The Tigers will have twice as many points as the Panthers after 43 minutes.

Example 1   Two printing presses were used to print a total of 19,500 copies of a booklet. Press *A* could print 2000 copies per hour, and Press *B* could print 1500 copies per hour. Press *A* started at 8:00 A.M. Press *B* started an hour later. At what time was the job completed?

Solution   The quantities that vary are the time, the number of copies printed by each press, and the total number of copies. We can organize the information in the following table.

Time	8:00	9:00	10:00	11:00	12:00	1:00	2:00
Total number of copies printed by Press *A*	0	2,000	4,000	6,000	8,000	10,000	12,000
Press *B*	0	0	1,500	3,000	4,500	6,000	7,500
Total number of copies printed	0	2,000	5,500	9,000	12,500	16,000	19,500

Answer   The job of printing 19,500 copies was completed by 2:00 P.M.

Example 2   Terri and Kim babysit after school. Terri is paid $1 plus $1.25 per hour while Kim is paid $2 plus $1 per hour. How many hours did they work if they were paid the same amount and worked the same number of hours?

Solution

Number of hours	1	2	3	4
Terri's pay (in dollars)	2.25	3.50	4.75	6
Kim's pay (in dollars)	3	4	5	6

Answer   If they worked 4 hours, they earned the same amount.

Once we have used a table to solve a problem, we can use the same table to answer other questions.

Example 3   How many hours did Terri and Kim work if they worked the same number of hours but Kim was paid 50¢ more than Terri? (See Example 2.)

Solution   Look for the column in which Kim's pay is 50¢ more than Terri's.

Answer   They worked 2 hours.

Look at the table in Example 1.

- At approximately what time were 10,000 copies printed? (About 11:15. Don't expect much accuracy. Any time between 11:10 and 11:30 is reasonable.)
- Assume that at 2:00 P.M. Press B stopped printing. If Press A continued printing at the same rate, at what time would the total reach 20,000 copies? (2:15 P.M.)
- Assume that at 2:00 P.M., Press A stopped printing and Press B started to print at the rate of 500 copies per hour. At what time would it have printed an additional 2500 copies? (7:00 P.M.)

CLASSROOM EXERCISES

Classroom exercises 1–2 focus on understanding the problem.

Classroom exercises 3–4 focus on constructing a table to solve the problem.

ADDITIONAL ANSWERS
■ **Classroom Exercises**

3.

Time	8:00	8:30	9:00	9:30	10:00
Total miles driven by Mrs. Helper	0	25	50	75	100
Total miles driven by Mr. Helper	0	0	27.5	55	82.5

10:30	11:00	11:30	12:00	12:30	1:00	1:30
125	150	175	200	225	250	275
110	137.5	165	192.5	220	247.5	275

Example 4 How many hours did Terri and Kim work if they worked the same number of hours but Terri was paid 50¢ more than Kim? (See Example 2.)

Solution Continue adding values to the table until Terri's pay is 50¢ more than Kim's.

Number of hours	4	5	6
Terri's pay (in dollars)	6	7.25	8.50
Kim's pay (in dollars)	6	7	8

Answer They worked 6 hours.

■ CLASSROOM EXERCISES

Mr. and Mrs. Helper were moving from one city to another. At 8:00 A.M., Mrs. Helper left their old home driving a truck containing their furniture. She drove at a steady rate of 50 mph. At 8:30 A.M. Mr. Helper left the old house in the family car. He drove the same route at a steady rate of 55 mph. At what time did he catch up with his wife?

Answer these questions.

1. At 9:00 A.M., how far had each driven? How far apart were they? Mrs., 50 mi; Mr., 27.5 mi; 22.5 mi

2. Between 9:00 A.M. and 10:00 A.M. how far did each drive? How far apart were they? Mrs., 50 mi; Mr., 55 mi; 17.5 mi

3. Make a table. [*Hint:* Use 30-minute intervals in your table.]

4. Solve the problem. 1:30 P.M.

■ WRITTEN EXERCISES

Copy and complete the tables to solve the problems.

Ⓐ 1. Kim had 10 coins, consisting of dimes and quarters. How many of the coins were quarters if the total value of the coins was $2.05? 7

Number of dimes	9	8	7	· · ·
Number of quarters	1	2	3	· · ·
Value of dimes (in dollars)	0.90	0.80	0.70	· · ·
Value of quarters (in dollars)	0.25	0.50	0.75	· · ·
Total value	1.15	1.30	1.45	· · ·

ASSIGNMENT GUIDE

Basic   1–8 all, Review Exercises
Average   1–5 odd, 9–12 all, Review
          Exercises
Enriched 1–11 odd, 13–16 all, Review
          Exercises

2. Machine A can produce 50 parts per hour, whereas Machine B can produce 30 parts per hour. At what time will the job of producing 500 parts be completed if Machine A starts at 8:00 A.M. and is joined by Machine B at 10:00 A.M.? 3 P.M.

Time	8:00	9:00	10:00	11:00	· · ·
Number of parts from Machine A	0	50	100	150	· · ·
Number of parts from Machine B	0	0	0	30	· · ·
Total number of parts	0	50	100	180	· · ·

3. A painter could paint a given house by himself in 6 days. It would take his assistant 12 days to paint the same house. (This means that the painter could paint $\frac{1}{6}$ of the house each day and the assistant can paint $\frac{1}{12}$ of the house each day.) How long would it take them to paint the house if they worked together? 4 days

Day number	1	2	· · ·
Part painted by painter	$\frac{1}{6}$	$\frac{1}{6}$	· · ·
Part painted by assistant	$\frac{1}{12}$	$\frac{1}{12}$	· · ·
Part painted together in 1 day	$\frac{3}{12}$	$\frac{3}{12}$	· · ·
Total painted together	$\frac{3}{12}$	$\frac{6}{12}$	· · ·

4. One grain loader working alone can load a ship with wheat in 24 hours. A second loader working alone can load the same ship in 8 hours. (This means that the first loader can load $\frac{1}{24}$ of the ship in 1 hour and the other loader can load $\frac{1}{8}$ of the ship in 1 hour.) If both loaders are used, how long will it take to load the ship? 6 hours

Hour	1	2	3	· · ·
Part loaded by first loader	$\frac{1}{24}$	$\frac{1}{24}$	$\frac{1}{24}$	· · ·
Part loaded by second loader	$\frac{1}{8}$	$\frac{1}{8}$	$\frac{1}{8}$	· · ·
Part loaded by both in 1 hour	$\frac{4}{24}$	$\frac{4}{24}$	$\frac{4}{24}$	· · ·
Total loaded by both	$\frac{4}{24}$	$\frac{8}{24}$	$\frac{12}{24}$	· · ·

PRACTICE WORKSHEET 10

2-9 PROBLEM SOLVING — USING TABLES

■ Complete the tables to solve the problems.

1. Ashley had 10 coins, consisting of nickels and dimes. How many of the coins were nickels if the total value of the coins was 65¢? __7__

Number of nickels	1	2	3	4	5	6	7	8	9
Number of dimes	9	8	7	6	5	4	3	2	1
Value of nickels (in cents)	5	10	15	20	25	30	35	40	45
Value of dimes (in cents)	90	80	70	60	50	40	30	20	10
Total value	95	90	85	80	75	70	65	60	55

2. An old printing press produces 1000 copies per hour. A new press produces 5000 copies per hour. The old press starts printing an advertising flyer at 8 A.M. and at 11 A.M. the new press also starts printing the flyer. Both presses are kept running until 45,000 flyers are printed. At what time will the job be completed? __6:00 P.M.__

Time	8:00 A.M.	9:00	11:00	Noon	2:00	6:00
Copies from old press	0	1000	3000	4000	6,000	10,000
Copies from new press	0	0	0	5000	15,000	35,000
Total copies printed	0	1000	3000	9000	21,000	45,000

3. Working alone, Jessica can address all the invitations to a reunion in 60 min. Working alone, Benjamin can do the job in 90 min. How long will it take Jessica and Benjamin to address the invitations if they both work on the job? __36 min__

■ Make a table to solve this problem.

4. The Blue Rent-A-Car Company charges $21 per day plus $.12 per mile. The Orange Rent-A-Car Company charges $18 per day plus $.16 per mile. After how many miles of driving would the total bill for each company be the same? [Hint: Use 15-mi intervals in your table.] __75__

WRITTEN EXERCISES

Discuss how different tables may be used to solve the same problem.

PROBLEM-SOLVING NOTE
Making a table

The ability to construct and systematically fill out a table is not a well-developed skill for many students. Particular care should be taken to show students how they determine the column or row headings to be used and how to enter information in a way to permit the discovery of existing patterns among the data.

7.

Hours driven	1	2	3	4
Kilometers driven	84	168	252	336
Liters of gas	7	14	21	28

8.

Hours driven	1	2	3	4
Miles driven	56	112	168	224
Gallons of gas	1.75	3.5	5.25.	7

10.

Hours worked	1	2	3	4	5	6	7
ABC cost	$45	$65	$85	$105	$125	$145	$165
XYZ cost	$55	$70	$85	$100	$115	$130	$145

11.

Sun.	Mon.	Tues.	Wed.	Thurs.	Fri.	Sat.	Total
$400	−$300	$400	−$300	$400	−$300	$400	$700

12.

Miles	20	40	60	80	100
Red Total Cost	$17.40	$19.80	$22.20	$24.60	$27.00
Yellow Total Cost	$15.00	$18.00	$21.00	$24.00	$27.00
Green Total Cost	$27.00	$27.00	$27.00	$27.00	$27.00

13.

Day	A.M. 1	P.M. 1	A.M. 2	P.M. 2	A.M. 3	P.M. 3	A.M. 4
Position in meters	−8	−9	−7	−8	−6	−7	−5

P.M. 4	A.M. 5	P.M. 5	A.M. 6	P.M. 6	A.M. 7	P.M. 7	A.M. 8	P.M. 8	A.M. 9
−6	−4	−5	−3	−4	−2	−3	−1	−2	0

14.

Day	A.M. 1	P.M. 1	A.M. 2	P.M. 2	A.M. 3	P.M. 3	A.M. 4	P.M. 4	A.M. 5
Position (meters)	−7	−8	−5	−6	−3	−4	−1	−2	1

15.

Play	1	2	3	4	5	6	7	8	9
Points scored	+1	−2	+4	−8	+16	−32	+64	−128	+256
Total points	+1	−1	+3	−5	+11	−21	+43	−85	171

5. What number added to the numerator and to the denominator of $\frac{3}{10}$ makes a new fraction equal to $\frac{1}{2}$? 4

Numerator	3	4	5	· · ·
Denominator	10	11	12	· · ·
Fraction	$\frac{3}{10}$	$\frac{4}{11}$	$\frac{5}{12}$	· · ·

6. A rumor was spread by the following process. Each person hearing the rumor told 3 additional people each hour. How many people had heard the rumor after 6 hours? 4096

Hour	0	1	2	3	4	· · ·
Number of people who are told the rumor during the hour	0	3	12	48	192	· · ·
Total number of people who know the rumor	1	4	16	64	256	· · ·

Make a table to solve each problem.

7. Mrs. Anderson's sports car goes 12 kilometers on 1 liter of gasoline. She drives at a rate of 84 kilometers per hour. How many hours can she drive using 28 liters of gasoline? 4

8. Mr. Anderson's car goes 32 miles on 1 gallon of gasoline. He drives at a rate of 56 miles per hour. How many hours can he drive using 7 gallons of gasoline? 4

B **9.** Jack wants his diet to be low in calories in relation to protein. Which of these five foods should Jack choose on the basis of the calorie/protein ratio? Oysters

	Broiled steak (85 g)	Lamb chop (135 g)	Oysters (225 mL)	Buttermilk (225 mL)	Liver (55 g)
Food energy (in calories)	330	400	160	90	130
Protein (in grams)	20	25	20	9	15

ADDITIONAL ANSWERS

■ Written Exercises

16.

Celsius	C	0	−10	−20	−30	−40
	⁹⁄₅C	0	−18	−36	−54	−72
Fahrenheit	⁹⁄₅C + 32	32	14	−4	−22	−40

10. The ABC Electric Repair Shop charges $25 plus $20 per hour for house calls. The XYZ Fixit Service charges $40 plus $15 per hour for house calls.
   a. How many hours did a house call take if either company would have charged the same amount? 3
   b. How many hours did a house call take if the ABC shop would have charged $20 more than the XYZ service? 7

11. On the days of the week that start with the letter S or T, Pop's Grocery Store made a profit of $400 per day. On the days of the week that start with F, M, or W, it lost $300 per day.
   a. What is the total profit or loss for the store during a two-week period? $1400 profit
   b. What will be the total profit or loss in 50 weeks? $35,000

12. The Red-Rent-A-Car Company charges $15 per day plus $.12 per mile, the Yellow-Rent-A-Car Company charges $12 per day plus $.15 per mile, and the Green-Rent-A-Car Company charges $27 per day with unlimited mileage. After how many miles of driving would one day's total bill for each company be the same? [*Hint:* Use 20-mile intervals in your table.] 100

C 13. In the classic "Frog-in-the-Well" problem, a frog is at the bottom of a well 10 meters deep. In the morning the frog climbs up 2 meters. But in the afternoon the frog slips back down 1 meter. How many days does it take the frog to escape from the well? $8\frac{1}{2}$

14. In a variation of the "Frog-in-the-Well" problem (see Exercise 13), the frog climbs up 3 meters in the morning and slips back 1 meter in the afternoon. How many days does it take the frog to escape from the well? $4\frac{1}{2}$

15. Sue plays a game in which she gains 1 point on the first play, loses 2 points on the second play, gains 4 points on the third play, loses 8 points on the fourth play, and so on. She has to stop when she is either ahead or behind by 100 points. When she has to stop will she be ahead or behind? On what play? She will be ahead by 171 points and stop on the 9th play.

16. At what temperature is the Fahrenheit reading numerically equal to the Celsius reading? [*Hint:* Use the formula $F = \frac{9}{5}C + 32$; begin the table at $0°C$ and use $-10°$ intervals.] $-40°$

■ **REVIEW EXERCISES**

Simplify.

1. $6.23 + 7 + 135.1$ 148.33

2. $3.07 - 0.395$ 2.675

3. $6.3(0.007)$ 0.0441

4. $45 - 0.03$ 44.97

5. $1\frac{2}{3} + 2\frac{1}{2}$ $4\frac{1}{6}$

6. $6\frac{1}{4} - 3\frac{1}{2}$ $2\frac{3}{4}$

7. $\frac{3}{4}\left(1\frac{1}{2}\right)$ $1\frac{1}{8}$

8. $2\frac{3}{4} - \frac{1}{2}$ $2\frac{1}{4}$

COMPUTER EXTENSION

1. Use a FOR-NEXT loop to write a program that produces the table in the Preview in vertical format and extends it up to 100 for the edge of the cube.

```
10 PRINT "EDGE", "SURFACE",
   "VOLUME", "RATIO"
20 PRINT "OF CUBE", "AREA",
   " ", "A TO V"
30 FOR E = 1 TO 100
40 PRINT E, 6*E*E, E*E*E,
   6 / E
50 NEXT E
60 END
```

2. Write a program to make a table for exercise 6 in vertical format for 24 hours.

```
10 PRINT "HOUR", "NUMBER",
   "TOTAL"
20 PRINT " ", "BEING", "WHO"
30 PRINT " ", "TOLD", "KNOW"
40 N = 0
50 T = 1
60 FOR H = 0 TO 24
70 PRINT H, N, T
80 N = 3*T
90 T = T + N
100 NEXT H
110 END
```

ENRICHMENT PROBLEM
Finding a Pattern

• The following table gives the number of persons in a room and the number of handshakes required to introduce everyone. Examine the table to find patterns that predict the number of handshakes for ten people.

Persons	2	3	4	5	6	⋯	10
Handshakes	1	3	6	10	15	⋯	?

Patterns may vary. One pattern is: If *n* is the number of persons, then there are $\frac{n(n-1)}{2}$ handshakes. So, for 10 persons there are 45 handshakes.

PROBLEM SOLVING — USING LOGIC

1. Alan, Bill, and Carl have different eye colors: one has gray eyes, one has hazel eyes, and one has blue eyes. the boy with gray eyes is taller than the boy with hazel eyes. Alan is taller than the boy with gray eyes. Bill is the shortest. What color are Carl's eyes?

   gray

   Bill — hazel,
   Alan — blue

2. Tom, Dick, and Harry have some money. Tom has 6 more dollars than the oldest of the three. Dick has 3 more dollars than Harry has. The youngest of the three has one third of the money. Who is the youngest of the three?

   Dick

   Dick: $x + 3$,
   Tom: $x + 6$,
   Harry: x

3. Val, Lynn, and Chris have some money. Val has 4 times as much money as the oldest of the three. Lynn has 3 more dollars than Chris has. The youngest of the three is the only one with exactly 4 dollars. Who is the youngest of the three?

   Chris

   Chris: $4,
   Lynn: $7,
   Val: $28

4. Sue, Lois, and Carol have some quarters. Sue has 3 more quarters than the tallest of the three. Lois has 4 times as many quarters as Carol has. The shortest of the three has one third the total number of quarters. Who is the shortest of the three?

   Sue

   Carol: 2 q,
   Lois: 8 q,
   Sue: 5 q

5. Harriet had one nickel, one dime, one quarter, one half-dollar, and one silver dollar. After she lost one coin, she had 7 times as much money as her brother. Which coin did she lose?

   half-dollar

6. At first I had no money. Then I earned $4. Then I did the following things, but I can't remember in what order I did them:

   3 I earned $12 more.
   1 I earned $14 more.
   4 I spent $11.
   2 I shared equally with my two sisters all the money I had already earned, with no cents left over.

   6 + 12 = 18
   4 + 14 = 18
   18 − 11 = 7
   18 ÷ 3 = 6

   How much money did I have after doing those four things?

   $7

   Can be used after Section 2-9

© D.C. Heath & Co.

■ CHAPTER SUMMARY

Strategy for Success Using chapter summaries _____

The summary at the end of the chapter lists the new words and symbols introduced in the chapter with page references. The chapter summary also collects the major ideas presented in the chapter. Use the summary when you prepare for a test.

- **Vocabulary**

opposite directions	[page 39]
positive numbers	[page 39]
negative numbers	[page 39]
set of real numbers	[page 39]
number line	[page 39]
order (of real numbers)	[page 39]
absolute value	[page 40]
opposites	[page 40]
reciprocals	[page 56]
inverse properties	[page 66]

- *Positive* and *negative* numbers are used to measure quantities that have opposite directions. [2–1]
- The *real numbers* consist of the positive numbers, the negative numbers, and zero.
- The *absolute value* of a number is its distance from zero on the number line. The symbol "| |" is used to indicate the absolute value.
- Numbers that have the same absolute value and opposite signs are called *opposites.* Zero is the opposite of zero. The symbol "−" is used to indicate the opposite.
- Addition of Real Numbers [2–2]

   1. To add real numbers with the same sign:
      a. Add their absolute values.
      b. Give the result the same sign as the two numbers.

   2. To add real numbers with different signs:
      a. Subtract their absolute values (the smaller from the larger).
      b. Give the result the same sign as the number with the greater absolute value.

- Subtraction of Real Numbers [2–3]

   Subtracting any real number is equivalent to adding the opposite of that real number.

   For all real numbers a and b, $a - b = a + (-b)$.

- Multiplication of Real Numbers   [2–4]

  To multiply two real numbers:

  1. Multiply the absolute values of the factors.

  2. Use these rules to find the sign of the product.
     a. If the factors have the same sign, the product is positive.
     b. If the factors have different signs, the product is negative.
     c. If one of the factors is 0, the product is 0.

- Two real numbers are *reciprocals* if their product is 1.   [2–5]

  1. Dividing by any real number (except 0) is equivalent to multiplying by
  the reciprocal of that number.

  For all real numbers a and b (b not equal to 0), $a \div b = a \cdot \frac{1}{b}$.

  2. Division by 0 is not defined.

- Additional Properties of Real Numbers   [2–7]

Property	For all real numbers a and b
-1 property of multiplication	$(-1)a = -a$
0 property of multiplication	$0a = 0$
Multiplying opposites property	$(-a)b = a(-b) = -(ab)$ $(-a)(-b) = ab$
Dividing opposites property	$\dfrac{-a}{b} = \dfrac{a}{-b} = -\dfrac{a}{b}$
Opposite of an opposite property	$-(-a) = a$
Distributive property of opposites	$-(a + b) = -a + (-b)$

Rules for simplifying expressions: [2–8]

1. Change any subtractions to additions.

2. Use the distributive properties to expand terms.

3. Rearrange terms so that like terms are together, and then combine like
terms.

Strategy for Success   Using chapter reviews

The review at the end of each chapter lists the objective for each lesson
and includes several exercises for each lesson. Use the review when you
prepare for a test.

■ CHAPTER REVIEW

2–1 **Objectives:** To relate real numbers to real-life situations.

To order real numbers.

To give the absolute value of a real number.

Use real numbers to represent each of the following.

1. A temperature 10°C below freezing − 10 **2.** A $200 profit + 200

Simplify.

3. |− 2.4| 2.4 **4.** |4$\frac{2}{3}$| 4$\frac{2}{3}$

True or false?

5. − 10 < − 6 T **6.** |− 10| < |− 6| F

2–2 **Objective:** To add real numbers.

Simplify.

7. 8 + (− 12) − 4 **8.** − 7 + (− 4) − 11 **9.** − 6.5 + 4.25 − 2.25

2–3 **Objective:** To subtract real numbers.

Simplify.

10. 5 − (− 3) 8 **11.** − 6 − 4 − 10 **12.** 10 − (− 5 − 7) 22

2–4 **Objective:** To multiply real numbers.

Simplify.

13. 4 · − 5 − 20 **14.** − 2 · − 10 20 **15.** − 6 · (− 5 + 2) 18

2–5 **Objective:** To divide a real number by a nonzero real number.

Write the reciprocal.

16. − $\frac{4}{9}$ − $\frac{9}{4}$ **17.** − 5 − $\frac{1}{5}$

Write as a multiplication and simplify.

18. − 5 ÷ − 4 $\frac{5}{4}$ **19.** − $\frac{3}{5}$ ÷ $\frac{4}{5}$ − $\frac{3}{4}$

a	b	c
− 36	6	− 3

Substitute and simplify.

20. $\frac{a}{b}$ − 6 **21.** $\frac{a}{b}$ + $\frac{b}{c}$ − 8

2–6 **Objective:** To use opposites to rewrite an addition or subtraction expression.

22. Change to an equivalent addition. $2x - (-3)$ 2x + 3

23. Change to an equivalent subtraction. $a + b$ a − (−b)

Simplify.

24. $12 - (-7)$ 19

25. $-6 - (-x) - (-7)$ 1 + x

2–7 **Objective:** To simplify an expression involving addition and subtraction by using the properties of real numbers.

Simplify.

26. $7a - a$ 6a

27. $6r + 10 - 5r$ r + 10

28. $5x + y - 6x + 2y$ −x + 3y

2–8 **Objective:** To simplify an algebraic expression by using the distributive properties.

Simplify.

29. $6 + 4(x - 3)$ 4x − 6

30. $3x - (10 + 2x)$ x − 10

31. $3(x + 3y) + 5(x - y)$ 8x + 4y

2–9 **Objective:** To solve a problem by making a table.

Use a table to solve each problem.

32. What number added to the numerator and denominator of $\frac{1}{5}$ results in a new fraction equal to $\frac{1}{3}$? 1

33. A farmer has 100 feet of fencing to make a rectangular pen along the side of a barn, with the side of the barn being one side of the pen. What are the dimensions of the pen that will enclose the maximum area? Shorter length, 25 ft; longer length, 50 ft

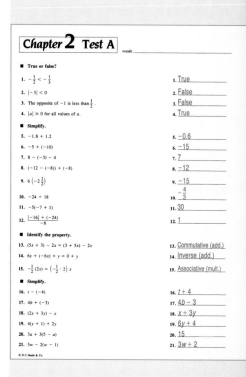

■ CHAPTER 2 SELF-TEST

Simplify.

2–1,
2–2

1. $8 + -3$ 5

2. $-9 - 26$ −35

3. $-17 + (-14)$ −31

4. $0 - (-7)$ 7

5. $-|-8|$ −8

6. $|-12 + 9|$ 3

2–4,

7. $3(-8)$ −24

8. $-49 \div 7$ −7

9. $(-5)(-12)$ 60

2–5

10. $-10 \div \frac{-2}{5}$ 25

11. $\frac{-4 + 9}{-10}$ $-\frac{1}{2}$

12. $-6 \cdot (-3 - (-1))$ 12

■ Solve.

22. What number added to the numerator and to the denominator of $\frac{4}{7}$ makes a new fraction equal to $\frac{5}{6}$?

Numerator	4	5	6	. . .
Denominator	7	8	9	. . .
Fraction	$\frac{4}{7}$	$\frac{5}{8}$	$\frac{6}{9}$	. . .

22. _11_

23. The Mobile Mechanic charges $15 plus $12 per hour for car calls. The Highway Helper charges $10 plus $13 per hour for car calls. How many hours did a car call take if both companies would have charged the same amount? [*Hint:* Make a table.]

23. _5_

★ **BONUS**

A painter can paint a house by himself in 7 days. His assistant can paint the same house by himself in $9\frac{1}{3}$ days. How long would it take them to paint the house if they worked together?

BONUS _4 days_

© D.C. Heath & Co.

Simplify.

2–6,
2–7,
2–8

13. $-(-12)$ 12

14. $x + (-3)$ $x - 3$

15. $2y - (-2)$ $2y + 2$

16. $6x - 5x$ x

17. $4r + 3r$ $7r$

18. $w + 3t - 2w$ $-w + 3t$

19. $5(a + 1) - 3$ $5a + 2$

20. $y - (3 - y)$ $2y - 3$

21. $12 + 2(a - 6)$ $2a$

22. $7(2b - 1)$ $14b - 7$

23. $(2a - 4) + (5a + 9)$ $7a + 5$

24. $(y + xy) - x$ $y + xy - x$

State the property or definition used in each equation.

2–7

25. $5(a + b) = 5a + 5b$ Distributive property

26. $-(4xy) + 4xy = 0$ Inverse property for addition

27. $3b - b = 3b + (-b)$ Subtracting is equivalent to adding the opposite.

28. $(4y + 3x) + 7x = 4y + (3x + 7x)$ Associative property of addition

29. $-(4xy) \cdot 0 = 0$ 0 property of multiplication

30. $(6x + 9) - 2x = (9 + 6x) - 2x$ Commutative property of addition

2–9 The length of a rectangle is twice its width. The width can be a whole number of centimeters from 5 to 10.

31. Make a table showing all possible whole number combinations of lengths and widths.

32. Compute the area for each case.

33. What are the dimensions of a rectangle with an area of 98 square centimeters?
7 cm by 14 cm

width	5	6	7	8	9	10
length	10	12	14	16	18	20
area	50	72	98	128	162	200

■ PRACTICE FOR COLLEGE ENTRANCE TESTS

1. If $2 \cdot 5 = x$ and $2 \cdot 3 \cdot 5 = y$, then $x - y = 10 \cdot \underline{\ ?\ }$.
A. -3 **B.** -2 C. 2   D. 3   E. 5

2. If $1, -1, 1, -1, 1, -1, \ldots$ is a sequence of numbers, what is the sum of the first 15 numbers of the sequence?
A. -7 B. -1 C. 0   **D.** 1   E. 8

3. If for all real numbers

$$<< a, b, c <> d, e, f >> = ad + be + cf,$$

then,

$$<< -1, 2, -3 <> 2, 0, -3 >> = \underline{\ ?\ }.$$

A. -11 B. -9 **C.** 7   D. 9   E. 11

4. If $y = -\frac{6}{8}$, then y is equivalent to

A. $-\frac{3}{4}$ B. $\frac{-3}{-4}$ C. $-\frac{-3}{4}$ D. $-\frac{3}{-4}$ E. $\frac{-6}{-8}$

5.

An object starts at 0 and moves 1 unit to the right, then from there it moves 2 units to the left; from there it moves 4 units to the right; from there it moves 8 units to the left; and so on. Where will the object be at the end of 6 moves?

A. −1   **B.** 3   **C.** −5   **D.** 11   **E.** −21

6. If for all numbers x, $\boxed{x}$ is defined by the equation $\boxed{x} = x(1 - x)$ then $\boxed{-4} = \underline{\ ?\ }$.

A. −20   **B.** −15   **C.** −12   **D.** 12   **E.** 20

7. If $a = -2$ and $b = -3$, then $3a - 2b - 1 = \underline{\ ?\ }$.

A. −13   **B.** −6   **C.** −4   **D.** −1   **E.** 5

8. For any number x, $[x]$ is defined as the greatest integer less than or equal to x. Then $[6.7] + [-3.3] = \underline{\ ?\ }$.

A. 2   **B.** 3   **C.** 3.4   **D.** 9   **E.** 10

9. If for all numbers a and b, $\bigotimes$ is defined by the equation $a \bigotimes b = a^2 - 2ab + b^2$, then $2 \bigotimes -3 = \underline{\ ?\ }$.

A. −17   **B.** −11   **C.** 1   **D.** 5   **E.** 25

10. If xy is negative, which of the following is possible?

A. $x < y < 0$ **B.** $0 < x < y$ **C.** $y < x$ and $x = 0$

D. $x = y$ **E.** $x < 0 < y$

11. There are 3 piles that contain 6 sticks each. What is the least number of sticks that can be moved so that the second pile contains twice as many sticks as the first pile, and the third pile contains three times as many sticks as the first pile?

A. 2   **B.** 3   **C.** 4   **D.** 5   **E.** 6

12. A wooden cube is painted on all sides and then cut into 27 smaller cubes as shown in the figure. How many of the smaller cubes will be painted on exactly two sides?

A. 3   **B.** 4   **C.** 6

D. 8   **E.** 12

Strategy for Success   Beginning a chapter

Skim over the Review at the end of the chapter to get an overview of what you will be studying in the chapter.

Chapter 2 Test B   NAME _____

■ True or false?

1. $-5 > -4$ 1. False
2. $|-7| > 0$ 2. True
3. The opposite of 6 is more than $\frac{1}{6}$.   3. False
4. $|b|$ is nonnegative for all values of b.   4. True

■ Simplify.

5. $-2.6 + 1.4$ 5. -1.2
6. $-7 + (-8)$ 6. -15
7. $13 - (-8) - 4$ 7. 17
8. $(-11 - (-3)) + (-5)$ 8. -13
9. $10 \left(-1\frac{1}{2}\right)$ 9. -15
10. $-18 \div 12$ 10. $-3/2$
11. $-2(-6 + 3)$ 11. 6
12. $\frac{|-14| + (-21)}{-7}$ 12. 1

■ Identify the property.

13. $-2\left(\frac{1}{2}x\right) = \left(-2 \cdot \frac{1}{2}\right)x$ 13. Associative (mult.)
14. $(2y + 7) + 4y = (7 + 2y) + 4y$ 14. Commutative (add.)
15. $6 + 2x + (-2x) = 6 + 0$ 15. Inverse (add.)

■ Simplify.

16. $b - (-3)$ 16. $b + 3$
17. $5a + (-7)$ 17. $5a - 7$
18. $(4x + 2y) - x$ 18. $3x + 2y$
19. $6(y + 3) + 4y$ 19. $10y + 18$
20. $8w + 8(2 - w)$ 20. 16
21. $7t - (t - 6)$ 21. $6t + 6$

© D.C. Heath & Co.

Chapter 2 Test B *(page 2)*   NAME _____

■ Solve.

22. What number added to the numerator and to the denominator of $\frac{5}{9}$ makes a new fraction equal to $\frac{3}{4}$?

Numerator	5	6	7	...
Denominator	9	10	11	...
Fraction	$\frac{5}{9}$	$\frac{6}{10}$	$\frac{7}{11}$	...

22. 7

23. The Happy Wrecker Service charges $12 plus $10 per hour for service calls. Acme Road Service charges $8 plus $11 per hour for service calls. How many hours did a service call take if both companies would have charged the same amount? [*Hint:* Make a table.]

23. 4

★ BONUS

Cold water running full force from a faucet can fill a tub in $11\frac{1}{4}$ minutes. Hot water running full force from a faucet can fill the same tub in $18\frac{3}{4}$ minutes. How long would it take both the hot and cold water running full force to fill the tub?

BONUS 7 minutes

© D.C. Heath & Co.

CHAPTER OVERVIEW

In Chapter 3, students learn basic procedures for solving simple equations. In order to solve equations, students need skill in computing with real numbers (addressed in Chapter 2) and skill in simplifying algebraic expressions (addressed in Chapters 1 and 2).

To develop an understanding of what it means to solve equations, the chapter begins with a section in which students substitute numbers in equations to determine whether the numbers are solutions of the equations. The next section develops the concept of equivalent equations, because in many cases equations are solved by writing a sequence of equivalent equations, each one simpler than the preceding one. The succeeding sections present formal procedures for solving equations using addition, subtraction, multiplication, and division.

Sections on problem solving present the strategy of writing an equation that represents the problem, solving the equation, answering the question posed in the problem, and then checking the solution in the original problem. This strategy is the most prevalent problem-solving strategy used throughout algebra.

In Section 3-8 on literal equations and formulas, students learn to solve an equation containing several variables for one of the variables, isolating that variable on one side of the equation. Skill in solving literal equations is needed for Chapters 5 and 6, which deal with equations that contain two variables.

The equations solved in this chapter are mostly linear equations in one variable. (Linear equations do not contain powers or roots of variables, nor do they contain variables in denominators.) However, the general procedures learned in this chapter will be used in solving various types of equations and inequalities in Chapters 5 through 11.

3 Solving Equations

Engineers apply the theories and principles of science and mathematics to practical technical problems. Their work is often the link between a scientific discovery and its useful application.

The engineer uses a principle such as centrifugal force in such diverse applications as the safe design of amusement rides, the separation of milk from cream, or the isolation of corpuscles from blood.

The engineer knows that, in order for a roller coaster car to complete a spiral loop, the centrifugal force must balance the weight of the car. Using this concept, the equation $v^2 = Rg$ can be obtained. In this equation, R equals the radius of the spiral loop; g equals the acceleration due to gravity; and v equals the minimum safe speed for the roller coaster to complete the loop.

To solve equations using repeated trials.

Solving equations is central to the study of algebra. Students need to understand what it means to solve an equation and how to be certain that a suspected solution is correct. Use of repeated trials teaches both concepts.

3–1 Solving Equations by Repeated Trials

Preview

This item appears on a multiple-choice test:

Choose the one best answer to each question.

If $2(x + 3) = 5x - 6$, what does x equal?

A. -4 **B.** -1 **C.** 0   **D.** 3   **E.** 4

Five possible answers are given, and one of them must be correct. One way to find the correct answer is to substitute each number for x in the equation to determine whether it makes the equation true.

For example, we can substitute -4 for x in the equation.

$$2(x + 3) = 5x - 6$$
$$2(-4 + 3) = 5(-4) - 6$$
$$2(-1) = -20 - 6$$
$$-2 = -26$$

The last equation is obviously false. Therefore, -4 is not a solution. Try to find the correct answer.   E. 4

PREVIEW

Let students test the five choices to determine which is a solution of the equation. Here is another test question:

- If $3x + 17 = 9 - x$, what does x equal?
  A. -4 **B.** -2 **C.** 0   **D.** 2   **E.** 6.5

We are not suggesting repeated trials as a technique for answering all multiple-choice questions, since test items are sometimes written so that the strategy will not work. Students might discuss this question:

- What can be done in constructing a multiple-choice test so that the repeated-trial strategy cannot be used?

(One means is to give the intervals in which the solutions occur rather than the solutions themselves.)

■ LESSON

A **solution** of an equation with one variable is a number that changes the equation into a true statement when the number is substituted for the variable. The set of numbers that may be substituted for the variable is called the domain of the variable, or the **replacement set**. To **solve an equation** means to find all solutions of the equation. The set of numbers from the domain that are solutions of the equation is called the **solution set** of the equation.

Example 1   Find the solution set of the equation $x = \dfrac{4}{x}$ for the domain $\{-2, -1, 1, 2\}$.

Solution   Substitute each member of the domain for x in the equation.

$-2 = \dfrac{4}{-2}$ True. -2 is a solution.

$-1 = \dfrac{4}{-1}$ False. -1 is not a solution.

$1 = \dfrac{4}{1}$ False.   1 is not a solution.

$2 = \dfrac{4}{2}$ True.   2 is a solution.

Answer   The solution set is $\{-2, 2\}$.

For some equations, there are no solutions in the domain. In these cases the solution set for the equation is the **empty set**. A symbol for the empty set is $\emptyset$.

LESSON

Students have almost certainly been exposed to equations and their solutions in other math courses. Go over the definitions and the examples carefully. Do not take shortcuts or try to teach equation-solving techniques.

Students have a tendency to forget that a solution of an equation is a number that makes the equation true when substituted for the variable. After learning equation-solving techniques, they begin to think of a solution as the result of manipulating both sides of the equation until a simple equation (for example, $x = 3$) is obtained. The intent of this lesson is to strongly reinforce the former idea.

ADDITIONAL EXAMPLES

Example 1.

Find the solution set of the equation $x = \dfrac{9}{x}$

for the domain $\{-3, -2, 0, 2, 3\}$.

Substitute each member of the domain for x in the equation.
The solution set is $\{-3, 3\}$.

ADDITIONAL EXAMPLES

Example 2.
Find the solution sets for these equations.
The domain is $\{-1, 0, 1, 2\}$.
a. $7x = 14$ $\quad\{2\}$
b. $a + 3 = 9$ $\quad\emptyset$
c. $x^2 = 1$ $\quad\{-1, 1\}$

CHECK UNDERSTANDING

• What is a solution of an equation? (A number from the domain that changes the equation into a true statement when the number is substituted for the variable)
• How do we determine whether a number is a solution of an equation? (Substitute the number for the variable.)
• Is 2 a solution of $6x = 12$? (Yes)

CLASSROOM EXERCISES

In classroom exercise 2, distinguish between $\emptyset$ (a set with no members that could be written { }) and {0} (a set with zero as its only member).

ASSIGNMENT GUIDE

Basic   1–35 odd, Review Exercises
Average 13–35 odd, 37–45 all, Review
         Exercises
Enriched 13–45 odd, 46–53 all, Review
         Exercises

PRACTICE WORKSHEET 11

3-1 SOLVING EQUATIONS BY REPEATED TRIALS

■ Which of the numbers $-2, -1, 0, 1, 2$ are solutions of these equations?

1. $x + 1 = -1$ $\underline{-2}$ 2. $x - 1 = -1$ $\underline{0}$ 3. $\frac{1}{2}x = 1$ $\underline{2}$
4. $\frac{x}{2} = -1$ $\underline{-2}$ 5. $\frac{-9}{x} = 9$ $\underline{-1}$ 6. $5 - x = 6$ $\underline{-1}$
7. $x^2 = x$ $\underline{0, 1}$ 8. $x^3 = x$ $\underline{-1, 0, 1}$ 9. $0 \cdot x = 0$ $\underline{-2, -1, 0, 1, 2}$
10. $2x = -2$ $\underline{-1}$ 11. $3x = 6$ $\underline{2}$ 12. $3 - x = 5$ $\underline{-2}$

■ Solve these equations for the replacement set {0, 1, 2, 3, . . . , 100}. Write $\emptyset$ if there is no solution.

13. $x - 47 = 20$ $\underline{67}$ 14. $\frac{x}{20} = 4$ $\underline{80}$ 15. $\frac{200}{x} = 5$ $\underline{40}$
16. $x + 12 = x - 12$ $\underline{\emptyset}$ 17. $x + 12 = 12 - x$ $\underline{0}$ 18. $2x = 24$ $\underline{12}$
19. $3x + x = 88$ $\underline{22}$ 20. $150 - x = 50$ $\underline{100}$ 21. $2x + x + 75$ $\underline{75}$
22. $x^2 = 0$ $\underline{0}$ 23. $-3x = -12$ $\underline{4}$ 24. $3x = -12$ $\underline{\emptyset}$

Example 2 Find the solution sets for these equations. The domain is {0, 1, 2}.

a. $x + 1 = x$ **b.** $x - 2 = 0$ **c.** $x^2 = -4$

Solution Substitute each member of the domain in the equation.

a. $x + 1 = x$ $\quad 0 + 1 = 0$ False.
$\qquad\qquad\qquad 1 + 1 = 1$ False.
$\qquad\qquad\qquad 2 + 1 = 2$ False.

Answer $\emptyset$

b. $x - 2 = 0$ $\quad 0 - 2 = 0$ False.
$\qquad\qquad\qquad 1 - 2 = 0$ False.
$\qquad\qquad\qquad 2 - 2 = 0$ True.

Answer {2}

c. $x^2 = -4$ $\quad 0^2 = -4$ False.
$\qquad\qquad\qquad 1^2 = -4$ False.
$\qquad\qquad\qquad 2^2 = -4$ False.

Answer $\emptyset$

■ CLASSROOM EXERCISES

The set of numbers from the replacement set that are solutions of the equation

1. Explain what is meant by the solution set of an equation.

2. What does the symbol $\emptyset$ represent? Empty set

Is -4 a solution for these equations?

3. $5 + x = 9$ No   4. $y - 1 = -3$ No   5. $a^2 = 16$ Yes   6. $5 \cdot |c| = 20$ Yes

Which of the numbers $\{-2, -1, 0, 1, 2\}$ are solutions of these equations?

7. $x^2 = 4$ $-2, 2$ 8. $a + 1 = 3$ 2 9. $1 - b = 2$ -1 10. $|m| = m$ $0, 1, 2$

■ WRITTEN EXERCISES

Is 6 a solution for these equations?

Ⓐ 1. $x - 3 = -3$ No   2. $x - 4 = -2$ No   3. $3x = 18$ Yes   4. $5x = 30$ Yes
5. $5x + 2 = 28$ No   6. $3x - 1 = 15$ No   7. $2x + 3 = x + 9$ Yes 8. $3x - 2 = x + 10$ Yes
9. $10 - x = x - 2$ Yes 10. $20 - x = 2x + 14$ No 11. $-3|x| = 18$ No   12. $3|x| = -18$ No

Which of the numbers $\{1, 2, 3, 4, 5\}$ are solutions of these equations?

13. $x + 2 = 5$ 3 14. $4 + x = 5$ 1 15. $-2a = -8$ 4
16. $-3x = -15$ 5 17. $0x = 0$ $1, 2, 3, 4, 5$ 18. $1 \cdot x = x$ $1, 2, 3, 4, 5$

Solve these equations for the domain $\{-2, -1, 0, 1, 2\}$.

19. $x - 2 = 0$ ⟨2⟩

20. $2 - x = 2$ ⟨0⟩

21. $\frac{1}{2}x = -1$ ⟨-2⟩

22. $\frac{1}{3}x = 0$ ⟨0⟩

23. $28 + x = 27$ ⟨-1⟩

24. $-28 + x = -27$ ⟨1⟩

25. $\frac{5}{x} = 2.5$ ⟨2⟩

26. $\frac{3}{x} = -1.5$ ⟨-2⟩

27. $\frac{x}{2} = -0.5$ ⟨-1⟩

Which of the numbers $\{0, 1, 2, 3, \ldots, 100\}$ are solutions of these equations? Write $\emptyset$ if there is no solution.

28. $x + 23 = 53$ 30

29. $x + 17 = 57$ 40

30. $x + 23 = x$ $\emptyset$

31. $x + 15 = x + 16$ $\emptyset$

32. $5x + x = 90$ 15

33. $4x + x = 55$ 11

34. $5x = x + 60$ 15

35. $6x = x + 70$ 14

36. $\frac{x}{5} = 20$ 100

Solve these equations for the domain $\{-4, -2, 0, 2, 4\}$.

B **37.** $x^2 + 2x = 8$ ⟨-4, 2⟩

38. $x^2 - 2x = 8$ ⟨-2, 4⟩

39. $5x = 3x - 8$ ⟨-4⟩

40. $5x = 3x + 8$ ⟨4⟩

41. $x + x = 2$ $\emptyset$

42. $x = x \cdot 0$ ⟨0⟩

43. $x = x + 0$ ⟨-4, -2, 0, 2, 4⟩

44. $a - a = 2$ $\emptyset$

45. $3x + 2x + x = 12$ ⟨2⟩

Find the solution sets of these equations for the indicated domains. Write $\emptyset$ if there is no solution.

C **46.** $2^x = 8$ ⟨3⟩
$\{3, 4, 6, 16\}$

47. $3x = 9$ ⟨3⟩
$\{2, 3, 6\}$

48. $x^2 = -25$ $\emptyset$
$\{-12\frac{1}{2}, -5, 5\}$

49. $x^2 + 3 = 4x$ ⟨1, 3⟩
$\{-1, 1, 3\}$

50. $x^2 + x = 6$ ⟨-3, 2⟩
$\{-3, -2, 2, 3\}$

51. $x^2 = 36$ $\emptyset$
$\{1, 2, 3, 4\}$

52. $(x + 1)^x = 64$ ⟨3⟩
$\{1, 2, 3, 4\}$

53. $(x - 1)^x = 1$ ⟨2⟩
$\{1, 2, 3, 4\}$

■ REVIEW EXERCISES

a	b	x	y
5	10	$\frac{1}{2}$	1.5

Substitute and simplify.   [1-1]

1. aby 75

2. $a - x$ $4\frac{1}{2}$

3. $\frac{y}{b}$ 0.15

Simplify.   [1-2]

4. $3 + 4 \cdot 5$ 23

5. $(10 + 1)(10 - 1)$ 99

6. $\frac{(9 + 18)}{3}$ 9

Simplify.   [1-3]

7. $3^2 + 4^2$ 25

8. $(3 + 4)^2$ 49

Indicate whether the two expressions are equivalent.   [1-4]

9. $x(x + 2) + 3(x + 2)$ and $(x + 3)x + (x + 3)2$ Yes

10. $3(x + 5)$ and $5(x + 3)$ No

WRITTEN EXERCISES

The number of solutions of an equation varies. Students should become aware that an equation may have no solution, one solution, or multiple solutions. Since this lesson is exploratory, no rules are given to determine the number of solutions.

Note that exercises 17–18 and 43 are true for all real numbers. In exercises 28–36, students may guess which of the 101 possibilities are solutions. Exercises 30–31 have no solution; each of the other exercises in this group has one solution.

PROBLEM-SOLVING NOTE
Guess and check

Numbers that prove not to be solutions of equations may still provide clues as to what the actual solutions may be. For example, in making the substitutions $x = 1$ and $x = 2$ in the equation $3x - 5 = 0$, neither proves to be a solution.

x	1	2
$3x - 5$	-2	1

The value $x = 1$ is not large enough to be a solution (that is, to make $3x - 5$ equal 0) and the value $x = 2$ is too large. However, $3(2) - 5 = 1$ is closer to zero than $3(1) - 5 = -2$. Therefore, a solution is expected to lie between 1 and 2 and to be closer to 2 than 1. The actual solution $x = \frac{5}{3}$ confirms this analysis.

ENRICHMENT PROBLEMS
Exploration

- Guess the number of solutions each equation has. Check your guesses.
  a. $|x| + 1 = 0$
  No solutions
  b. $3x - 1 = 0$
  One solution; $\{\frac{1}{3}\}$
  c. $x^2 = 1$
  Two solutions; $\{-1, 1\}$
  d. $x^2 + 2x = x(x + 2)$
  True for all real numbers
  e. $x^3 = x$
  Three solutions; $\{-1, 0, 1\}$

Solve these equations for the domain
$\{-2, -1, 0, 1, 2\}$.

1. $50 + x = 49$ $\quad\{-1\}$
2. $-2x = -2$ $\quad\{1\}$
3. $\dfrac{4}{x} = -2$ $\quad\{-2\}$
4. $3x = x + 4$ $\quad\{2\}$
5. $x + 3 = 3$ $\quad\{0\}$

PURPOSE

Students will solve equations by writing equivalent equations. The first step in this process is understanding what equivalent equations are and how they may be generated.

PREVIEW

Borrow a pan balance from the science department. Put objects on both pans until they balance. Let students suggest answers to the question in the Preview. They should suggest the following answers: *The pans will remain in balance if the objects are rearranged within a pan. The pans will remain in balance if the same thing is done to both.* For example, equal amounts could be added to both pans, equal amounts could be removed from both pans, the amounts in both pans could be halved, and so on. However, if an object is taken from one pan and placed in the other, the pans will no longer be in balance.

LESSON

Use what students learned in the Preview activity to discuss the various ways an equation can be altered to get an equivalent equation. Note that the object of this lesson is not to solve equations, but rather to become comfortable with some transformations that result in equivalent equations.

OBJECTIVE 3-2

To write equivalent equations by adding the same number to both sides of an equation or by multiplying both sides of an equation by the same number.

3-2 Equivalent Equations

Preview A model for equations

Here is a *balance* with equal weights on the two pans.

What are some ways of changing the weights on the pans and still keeping the pans in balance? For example, if the weights on the left pan are doubled, what should be done to the weights on the right pan in order to keep the pans balanced?

■ LESSON

The two equations $2x = 8$ and $2x + 1 = 9$ have the same solution sets. For this reason they are called **equivalent equations.**

Equivalent equations	*Nonequivalent equations*
$2x = 8$ $\quad\{4\}$	$3x = 12$ $\quad\{4\}$
$2x + 1 = 9$ $\quad\{4\}$	$x + 3 = 9$ $\quad\{6\}$

It is not always necessary to find the solution sets of two equations in order to determine whether they are equivalent. The balanced pans in the Preview suggest other ways of knowing that equations are equivalent. Think of an equation as being a balance with equal quantities on the two pans. Just as some changes in the weights leave the pans balanced, some changes in equations give equivalent equations. Study the following properties.

> An equivalent expression may be substituted for one side of an equation without changing the solution set of the equation.

On a balance, we can rearrange the weights on one or both pans without adding or subtracting weights. This idea is similar to using the basic properties of numbers in order to change one or both sides of an equation.

Use any "extra" minutes at the end of a period to dis-
cuss one or more of the exercises in the Practice for
College Entrance Tests at the end of the chapter.

For example, consider the equation

$$2x + 3x = 30$$

We can apply the distributive property and computation to the expression $2x + 3x$ as follows:

$$(2 + 3)x = 30$$
$$5x = 30$$

These two equations are both equivalent to the given equation $2x + 3x = 30$.

The Symmetric Property of Equations

For all real numbers a and b, if $a = b$ then $b = a$.

On a balance, the weights in the two pans can be switched. The pans will still be in balance. This is similar to interchanging the expressions on the two sides of the equation. The new equation is equivalent to the original equation. For example, these two equations are equivalent to each other:

$$7 = 9 + x$$
$$9 + x = 7$$

On a balance, the pans stay in balance if the same weight is added to both sides or if the same weight is taken from both sides. Similarly, the same quantity can be added to, or subtracted from, both sides of an equation.

An equivalent equation is obtained when the same number is added to (or subtracted from) both sides of an equation.

Start with the equation	$x - 7 = 3$
Add 7 to both sides.	$x - 7 + 7 = 3 + 7$
Simplify.	$x = 10$

All three equations are equivalent.

Start with the equation	$a + 3 = 1$
Subtract 3 from both sides.	$a + 3 - 3 = 1 - 3$
Simplify.	$a = -2$

All three equations are equivalent.

On a balance, the pans stay in balance when the weights on both pans are doubled, or when the weights on both pans are halved. Similarly, both sides of an equation can be multiplied by, or divided by, the same nonzero quantity.

ADDITIONAL EXAMPLES

Example 1.
Write an equation equivalent to $3x = 12$ by dividing both sides by 3 and simplifying.

$$\frac{3x}{3} = \frac{12}{3}$$
$$x = 4$$

Example 2.
Write two equations that are equivalent to $5x = 20$.

Some possible answers:

a. *Add 3 to both sides.*
$$5x + 3 = 20 + 3$$
Simplify.
$$5x + 3 = 23$$

b. *Multiply both sides by 2.*
$$5x \cdot 2 = 20 \cdot 2$$
Simplify.
$$10x = 40$$

c. *Divide both sides by 5.*
$$\frac{5x}{5} = \frac{20}{5}$$
Simplify.
$$x = 4$$

d. *Subtract 6 from both sides.*
$$5x - 6 = 20 - 6$$
Simplify.
$$5x - 6 = 14$$

An equivalent equation is obtained when both sides of an equation are multiplied (or divided) by the same nonzero number.

Start with the equation	$\frac{1}{2}y = 6$
Multiply both sides by 2.	$2\left(\frac{1}{2}y\right) = 2(6)$
Simplify.	$y = 12$

All three equations are equivalent.

Start with the equation	$-3m = 12$
Divide both sides by -3.	$\frac{-3m}{-3} = \frac{12}{-3}$
Simplify.	$m = -4$

All three equations are equivalent.

Example 1 Write an equation equivalent to $a - 3 = 12$ by adding 3 to both sides and simplifying.

Solution

	$a - 3 = 12$
Add 3 to both sides.	$a - 3 + 3 = 12 + 3$
Simplify.	$a = 15$

Example 2 Write two equations that are equivalent to $4x = 8$.

Solution 1

	$4x = 8$
Subtract 3 from both sides.	$4x - 3 = 8 - 3$
Simplify.	$4x - 3 = 5$

Solution 2

	$4x = 8$
Divide both sides by 4.	$\frac{4x}{4} = \frac{8}{4}$
Simplify.	$x = 2$

Answer $4x - 3 = 5$ and $x = 2$
There are many other equations equivalent to $4x = 8$.

Strategy for Success   Using examples

When you have difficulty understanding an example, read it "backward." That is, start with the answer and read back through each step to the original problem.

Equation	Directions
$3x + 3 = x + 11$	**a.** Subtract x from both sides.
	b. Subtract 3 from both sides.
	c. Divide both sides by 2.

a. *Subtract x and simplify.* $2x + 3 = 11$
b. *Subtract 3 and simplify.* $2x = 8$
c. *Divide by 2 and simplify.* $x = 4$

CHECK UNDERSTANDING

• What are equivalent equations? (Equations that have the same solution sets)
• Are $2x = 6$ and $x = 3$ equivalent? (Yes)
• Are $a + 3 = 7$ and $a - 3 = 7$ equivalent? (No)

CLASSROOM EXERCISES

In classroom exercises 7–8, a variety of possible responses should be discussed for each item. Such responses could include adding, subtracting, multiplying, and dividing both sides of the equation by some number.

Example 3   What equivalent equation results from following these directions in order? Simplify after each step.

Equation	Directions
$6x - 5 = 2x + 7$	**a.** Subtract $2x$ from each side.
	b. Add 5 to each side.
	c. Divide both sides by 4.

Solution

$6x - 5 = 2x + 7$

a. *Subtract 2x from each side.* $6x - 5 - 2x = 2x + 7 - 2x$
   Simplify. $4x - 5 = 7$
b. *Add 5 to both sides.* $4x - 5 + 5 = 7 + 5$
   Simplify. $4x = 12$
c. *Divide both sides by 4.* $\dfrac{4x}{4} = \dfrac{12}{4}$
   Simplify. $x = 3$

---

2. Add (or subtract) same number to (from) each side; interchange the expressions on each side; multiply (or divide) each side by same number; rearrange (by properties) terms of each side; simplify (by order of operations).

■ CLASSROOM EXERCISES

1. Explain what *equivalent equations* are.   Equations that have the same solution sets

2. State six ways of changing from one equation to an equivalent equation.

Write an equation equivalent to the given equation by adding 3 to both sides.

3. $2x = x + 2$ $2x + 3 = x + 5$ **4.** $2y - 3 = 17$ $2y = 20$

Write an equation equivalent to the given equation by multiplying both sides by 3.

5. $2a = 9$ $6a = 27$ **6.** $\frac{1}{3}t = 5$ $t = 15$

Write two equations that are equivalent to the given equation.   Answers will vary.

7. $3x = 12$ **8.** $\frac{1}{2}d = 4$

State whether the two equations are equivalent. Explain your answer.

9. $5x = 15$ Yes; both have (3) as its solution set.   **10.** $\frac{1}{2}c = 7$ No; each has a different solution set.

$-5x = -15$ $c = 3\frac{1}{2}$

What equations result from following these directions in order?

11. $2 - 3x = 10x + 7$
   a. Add $3x$ to both sides. $2 = 13x + 7$
   b. Add -7 to both sides. $-5 = 13x$
   c. Divide both sides by 13. $-\frac{5}{13} = x$

12. $-2x + 4 = 7 - 8x$
   a. Add $8x$ to both sides. $6x + 4 = 7$
   b. Add -4 to both sides. $6x = 3$
   c. Divide both sides by 6. $x = \frac{1}{2}$

ASSIGNMENT GUIDE

Basic   1–29 odd, Review Exercises
Average   9–29 odd, 31–39 all, Review
           Exercises
Enriched   17–29 odd, 31–42 all, Review
           Exercises

PRACTICE WORKSHEET 11

3-2 EQUIVALENT EQUATIONS

■ Write an equivalent equation by adding 5 to both sides of the
   given equation. Simplify both sides.

1. $2x + 6 = 20$ $2x + 11 = 25$ 2. $7x - 5 = 12$ $7x = 17$

3. $x - 5 = 20 - 5$ $x = 20$ 4. $4x + 5 = 14$ $4x + 10 = 19$

5. $-5x - 5 = 5$ $-5x = 10$ 6. $8x - 5 = x + 9$ $8x = x + 14$

■ Write an equivalent equation by multiplying both sides of the
   given equation by 3. Simplify both sides.

7. $2x = 5$ $6x = 15$ 8. $\frac{1}{3}x = -10$ $x = -30$ 9. $\frac{x}{3} = \frac{1}{2}$ $x = 3/2$

10. $-10x = 7$ $-30x = 21$ 11. $\frac{2}{3}x = -6$ $2x = -18$ 12. $-\frac{4x}{3} = 12$ $-4x = 36$

■ In each case, what equation results from following the given
   directions in order?

13. $\frac{1}{3}x - 5 = 6$ 14. $3a + 5 = 6$

   a. Add 5 to both sides. $1/3x = 11$ a. Add −5 to both sides. $3a = 1$

   b. Multiply both sides by 3. $x = 33$ b. Multiply both sides by $\frac{1}{3}$. $a = 1/3$

WRITTEN EXERCISES

In exercises 17–24, *without solving* the equations, students should tell whether the equations are equivalent.

In exercises 25–38, students should simplify both sides of the equations as they follow the directions.

EXTRA PRACTICE, page 622

■ WRITTEN EXERCISES

Write an equivalent equation by adding 4 to both sides of the given equation. Simplify both sides.

A   **1.** $6x - 4 = 14$ **2.** $4x + 4 = 4$ **3.** $5x + 6 = 4$ **4.** $2x - 4 = 0$
     $6x = 18$ $4x + 8 = 8$ $5x + 10 = 8$ $2x = 4$

Write an equivalent equation by subtracting n from both sides of the given equation. Simplify both sides.

5. $5n = n + 3$ $4n = 3$ **6.** $6n = n + 17$ $5n = 17$ **7.** $2 + n = 4n + 1$ **8.** $5 + n = 3n + 3$
                                                $2 = 3n + 1$ $5 = 2n + 3$

Write an equivalent equation by multiplying both sides of the given equation by 3. Simplify.

9. $\frac{1}{3}n = 6$ $n = 18$ **10.** $\frac{1}{3}n = -2$ $n = -6$ **11.** $\frac{n}{3} = -4$ $n = -12$ **12.** $\frac{n}{3} = 9$ $n = 27$

Write an equivalent equation by multiplying both sides of the given equation by $\frac{1}{2}$. Simplify.

13. $2x = -6$ $x = -3$ **14.** $2x = 20$ $x = 10$ **15.** $4x + 6 = 10$ **16.** $8x - 6 = 30$
                                             $2x + 3 = 5$ $4x - 3 = 15$

State whether the two equations are equivalent. Explain your answer.

17. $2x = 6$ **18.** $3x = 9$ **19.** $x = 7$ **20.** $x = 4$

    $6x = 18$ Yes $12x = 36$ Yes $5x = 35$ Yes $\frac{1}{2}x = 2$ Yes

21. $3x + 7 + 5x = 20$ **22.** $4x + 6 + 3x = 27$ **23.** $2x + 1 = 3$ **24.** $x - 4 = 0$

    $3x + 5x + 7 = 20$ $4x + 3x + 6 = 27$ $x + 2 = 3$ $3x = -12$
          Yes   Yes   Yes   No

What equations result from following these directions in order?

25. $4x - 5 = 15$ **26.** $7n + 14 = 35$

    a. Add 5 to both sides. $4x = 20$ **a.** Add −14 to both sides. $7n = 21$

    b. Divide both sides by 4. $x = 5$ **b.** Divide both sides by 7. $n = 3$

27. $\frac{1}{2}x - 12 = 18$ **28.** $6 + x = 3x$

                              a. Subtract x from both sides. $6 = 2x$

    a. Add 12 to both sides. $\frac{1}{2}x = 30$

    b. Multiply both sides by 2. $x = 60$ **b.** Multiply both sides by $\frac{1}{2}$. $3 = x$

29. $5x + 3x + 2 = 20$ **30.** $6y + 4y + 5 = 25$

    a. Combine the x terms. $8x + 2 = 20$ **a.** Combine the y terms. $10y + 5 = 25$

    b. Subtract 2 from both sides. $8x = 18$ **b.** Subtract 5 from both sides. $10y = 20$

    c. Divide both sides by 8. $x = \frac{9}{4}$ **c.** Divide both sides by 10. $y = 2$

B   **31.** $2(x + 3) = 25$ **32.** $\frac{1}{3}(x - 12) = 100$ $\frac{1}{3}x - 4 = 100$

    a. Use the distributive property. $2x + 6 = 25$ **a.** Use the distributive property.

    b. Subtract 6 from both sides. $2x = 19$ **b.** Add 4 to both sides. $\frac{1}{3}x = 104$

    c. Divide both sides by 2. $x = \frac{19}{2}$ **c.** Multiply both sides by 3. $x = 312$

33. $\frac{1}{4}(x - 12) = 100$ **34.** $10x + 6 - x = 8x$

    a. Use the distributive property. $\frac{1}{4}x - 3 = 100$ **a.** Simplify the left side by combining the
                                        x terms. $9x + 6 = 8x$

    b. Add 3 to both sides. $\frac{1}{4}x = 103$ **b.** Subtract $8x$ from both sides. $x + 6 = 0$

    c. Multiply both sides by 4. $x = 412$ **c.** Add −6 to both sides. $x = -6$

35. $5x + 15 = 50$
  a. Subtract 15 from both sides. $5x = 35$
  b. Divide both sides by 5. $x = 7$

36. $8x + 13 = 41$
  a. Subtract 13 from both sides. $8x = 28$
  b. Multiply both sides by $\frac{1}{8}$. $x = \frac{7}{2}$

37. $5x + 15 = 50$
  a. Divide both sides by 5. $x + 3 = 10$
  b. Subtract 3 from both sides. $x = 7$

38. $8x + 13 = 41$
  a. Multiply both sides by $\frac{1}{8}$. $x + \frac{13}{8} = \frac{41}{8}$
  b. Subtract $\frac{13}{8}$ from both sides. $x = \frac{7}{2}$

39. True or false? If all the solutions of one equation are solutions of a second equation, then the equations are equivalent. F

Fill in the missing reasons for these steps used in solving these equations.

C **40.** $3(x + 5) = 10x - 3$
  $3x + 15 = 10x - 3$ Use the distributive property.
  $15 = 7x - 3$ **a.** Subtract ___?___ from both sides and simplify. $3x$
  $18 = 7x$ **b.** Add ___?___ to both sides and simplify. 3
  $\frac{18}{7} = x$ **c.** ___?___ and simplify. Multiply by $\frac{1}{7}$

41. $3x + 5 = 10 - 2x$
  $5x + 5 = 10$ **a.** _____?_____ Add 2x to both sides.
  $5x = 5$ **b.** _____?_____ Subtract 5 from both sides.
  $x = 1$ **c.** _____?_____ Divide by 5 and simplify.

42. Puzzle. Study the two balance situations.

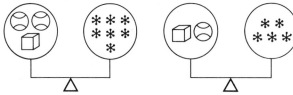

  a. How many ✳ are required to balance one ? 2
  b. How many ✳ balance one ▱ ? 3

■ REVIEW EXERCISES

r	s	t	u
3	6	12	$\frac{2}{3}$

Substitute and simplify.

1. $r + s + t$ 21

2. $\frac{u}{s}$ $\frac{1}{9}$ [1–1]

3. $r + st$ 75

4. $\frac{t}{r + s}$ $\frac{4}{3}$ [1–2]

5. rs^2 108

6. $(rs)^2$ 324

1. a.
```
10 X = 3
20 PRINT X
30 END
```
b.
```
10 3 = X
20 PRINT X
30 END
```

2. a.
```
10 X = 5
20 Y = 3*X + 2
30 PRINT Y
40 END
```
b.
```
10 X = 5
20 3*X + 2 = Y
30 PRINT Y
40 END
```

3. a.
```
10 X = 1
20 PRINT X;
30 X = X + 1
40 IF X < 101 THEN 20
50 END
```
b.
```
10 X = 1
20 PRINT X;
30 X + 1 = X
40 IF X < 101 THEN 20
50 END
```

ENRICHMENT PROBLEMS

• Why are $\frac{x}{2} = 2$ and $x^2 = 16$ not equivalent?

  —4 is a solution of the second equation but not of the first equation.

• What value must R have for $5x + R = 6x + 4$ to be equivalent to $2x + 1 = 3(x + 2)$?

  R must have the value —1.

What equations result by following these directions in order?

1. $x + 6 = 10$
  a. Add 4 to both sides. $x + 10 = 14$
  b. Subtract 3 from both sides. $x + 7 = 11$

2. $2x + 4 = 16$
  a. Subtract 4 from both sides. $2x = 12$
  b. Multiply both sides by 5. $10x = 60$

3. $2x - 6 = 7$
  a. Add 6 to both sides. $2x = 13$
  b. Divide both sides by 2. $x = 6\frac{1}{2}$

4. $2(x - 1) = 7$
  a. Use the distributive property. $2x - 2 = 7$
  b. Add 2 to both sides. $2x = 9$
  c. Divide both sides by 2. $x = 4\frac{1}{2}$

5. $\frac{1}{2}x + 5 = 3$
  a. Subtract 5 from both sides. $\frac{1}{2}x = -2$
  b. Multiply both sides by 2. $x = -4$

PURPOSE

Students need efficient methods for solving equations. Some linear equations can be solved by adding (or subtracting) the same number to (from) both sides of an equation. This method will be used later (see Section 3–5) to solve more complicated equations.

PREVIEW

Using repeated trials to solve
$$10a - 7 = 18$$
a student might proceed as follows.

Guess the solution: 3
       Test: $10(3) - 7 = 23$
   Result: 3 is too large.
Guess the solution: Try a number less than 3, say 2.
       Test: $10(2) - 7 = 13$
   Result: 2 is too small.

OBJECTIVE 3–3

To solve equations by adding (or subtracting) the same quantity to (from) both sides of an equation.

You may wish to spend two days on this section. Refer to the Pacing Chart.

3–3 Solving Equations by Addition

Preview

Try to solve this equation by making repeated trials where the domain is the set of real numbers.

$$10a - 7 = 18$$

Organize your work by making a table of values you choose for a and the corresponding values of $10a - 7$.

Did you find that the solution to the equation is 2.5?

We can use repeated trials to solve equations like this one, but it may take a lot of time and effort. There are more efficient ways to solve equations, and you will begin to study them in this lesson.

■ LESSON

In Section 3–2, we learned that an equivalent equation is obtained when the same number is added to both sides of an equation. For example, starting with

$$x - 4 = 5$$

and then adding 4 to both sides and simplifying gives:

$$x = 9$$

The fact that the second equation has the same solution as the first is a consequence of the **addition property of equations.**

Addition Property of Equations

For all real numbers a, b, and c, if $a = b$, then $a + c = b + c$.

We also learned that an equivalent equation is obtained by subtracting the same number from both sides of an equation. However, we can think of subtraction of a number as addition of the opposite of the number. Therefore, subtracting the same quantity from both sides of an equation is also described by the addition property of equations. The addition property of equations can be used to solve complex equations by changing them to simpler equations whose solutions are obvious.

Strategy for Success   Using examples

The examples in a lesson are usually related to each other. Try to spot how an example differs from the preceding one.

Learning curves show drastic drop-offs in retention without immediate review and periodic review thereafter. Therefore, it is important to use the quizzes over the preceding lessons given in the Teacher's Edition as immediate review and the Review Exercises in the student text as periodic review.

Example 1   Solve. $3x - 7 = 2x + 5$

Solution

$$3x - 7 = 2x + 5$$

Add $-2x$ to both sides. $3x - 7 + (-2x) = 2x + 5 + (-2x)$
Simplify. $x - 7 = 5$
Add 7 to both sides. $x - 7 + 7 = 5 + 7$
Simplify. $x = 12$

Answer $\{12\}$

The solution set of the last equation is $\{12\}$, so the solution set of the first equation is also $\{12\}$. Check by substitution.

Check
$$3x - 7 = 2x + 5$$
$$3 \cdot 12 - 7 \overset{?}{=} 2 \cdot 12 + 5$$
$$29 = 29 \quad \text{True!}$$

Note these things in Example 1.

1. We added $-2x$ to both sides of the equation in order to get an equivalent equation with variables on only one side.

2. We added 7 to both sides of the equation in order to get an equivalent equation in the simplest possible form: $x = 12$.

From now on, we will combine adding and simplifying into one step.

Example 2   Solve. $3 + a = -2$

Solution

$$3 + a = -2$$

Add -3 to both sides and simplify. $a = -5$

Answer $\{-5\}$

Check
$$3 + a = -2$$
$$3 + (-5) \overset{?}{=} -2$$
$$-2 = -2 \quad \text{True!}$$

Example 3   Solve. $8 - 5x = 2 - 6x$

Solution

$$8 - 5x = 2 - 6x$$

Add $6x$ to both sides and simplify. $8 + x = 2$
Subtract 8 from both sides and simplify. $x = -6$

Answer $\{-6\}$

Check
$$8 - 5x = 2 - 6x$$
$$8 - 5(-6) \overset{?}{=} 2 - 6(-6)$$
$$8 + 30 \overset{?}{=} 2 + 36$$
$$38 = 38 \quad \text{True!}$$

Preview *continued*

Guess the solution: Try a number between 2 and 3, say 2.5.
Test: $10(2.5) - 7 = 18$
Result: 2.5 is the solution.

LESSON

Students are already familiar with the fact that adding the same quantity to both sides of an equation gives an equivalent equation. Now you must point out how that fact can be used to solve some equations. Go over the examples carefully.

Students should be encouraged to use the addition property of equations, even when subtraction is possible.
For example, to solve $3x + 7 = -4$
   Add -7 to both sides: $3x = -11$
Most students find it easier to add -7 to -4 than to subtract 7 from -4.

Note in this lesson that once variables are collected on one side of the equation and like terms are combined, the coefficient of the variable is always 1.

ADDITIONAL EXAMPLES

Example 1.
Solve. $5x - 8 = 4x + 3$
Add $-4x$ to both sides.
   $5x - 8 + (-4x) = 4x + 3 + (-4x)$
Simplify.
   $x - 8 = 3$
Add 8 to both sides.
   $x - 8 + 8 = 3 + 8$
Simplify.
   $x = 11$
The solution set of each equation is $\{11\}$.

Example 2.
Solve. $5 + x = 2$
Add -5 to both sides and simplify.
   $x = -3$
The solution set is $\{-3\}$.

Example 3.
Solve. $10 - 2x = 7 - 3x$
Add $3x$ to both sides and simplify.
   $10 + x = 7$
Add -10 to both sides and simplify.
   $x = -3$
The solution set is $\{-3\}$.

Example 4   Solve. $5x + 3 = 6x + 7$

Solution

$$5x + 3 = 6x + 7$$

Subtract $5x$ from both sides and simplify. $3 = x + 7$
Subtract 7 from both sides and simplify. $-4 = x$

Some people like to end with the variable on the left side of the equation. They write the following extra step, using the symmetric property of equations to reverse the sides of the equation.

Reverse the sides of the equation. $x = -4$

Answer $\{-4\}$

Check   The check is left to the student.

■ CLASSROOM EXERCISES

1. State the addition property of equations.
For all real numbers a, b, and c, if a = b, then a + c = b + c.
2. Why is it unnecessary to write a subtraction property of equations?
Subtraction is equivalent to addition of the opposite.
State what was added to both sides of the first equation that resulted in the second equation.

3. $2x + 3 = x - 9$ $-x$
     $x + 3 = -9$

4. $2x + 3 = x - 9$ -3
     $2x = x - 12$

5. $20x - 9 = 4x + 7$ 9
     $20x = 4x + 16$

Solve by writing a series of equivalent equations.

6. $a + 3 = 9$ (6)
7. $b - 10 = 10$ (20)
8. $-3 = x - 3$ (0)

9. $x + 10 = 7$ $\{-3\}$
10. $2n + 3 = n + 16$ (13)
11. $4y - 6 = 3y + 3$ (9)

■ WRITTEN EXERCISES

State what was added to both sides of the first equation that resulted in the second equation.

A   **1.** $8a + 3 = 7a + 20$
     $a + 3 = 20$ $-7a$

2. $5a - 3 = 4a + 15$
     $a - 3 = 15$ $-4a$

3. $8x + 3 = 7x + 20$
     $8x = 7x + 17$ -3

4. $5y - 3 = 4y + 15$
     $5y = 4y + 18$ 3

5. $7a + 8 = -13$
     $7a = -21$ -8

6. $5a - 5 = -9$
     $5a = -4$ 5

Solve each equation by writing a series of equivalent equations.

7. $5t = 4t + 3$ (3)
8. $7t = 6t + 2$ (2)
9. $10x = 9x - 2$ (-2)

10. $8x = 7x - 4$ $\{-4\}$
11. $r - 6 = 10$ (16)
12. $r - 9 = 20$ (29)

13. $x + \frac{1}{2} = 2$ $\{1\frac{1}{2}\}$
14. $w + \frac{1}{4} = 3$ $\{2\frac{3}{4}\}$
15. $4a + 3 = 3a + 5$ (2)

16. $5a + 4 = 4a + 7$ (3)
17. $2x + 1 = 3x$ (1)
18. $4b + 8 = 5b$ (8)

WRITTEN EXERCISES

In exercises 15–24, note that steps may be performed in different orders, but the final solution is unique. Although there are different ways of getting there, there is only one correct answer for each exercise.

In exercise 43, note that for values of x that are 4 or less, the left side of the equation is *smaller* than the right side. For values of x that are 5 or greater, the left side of the equation is *larger* than the right side. Therefore, it should seem reasonable that for some value of x between 4 and 5 the two sides of the equation are *equal*.

CONCEPT EXTENSION

Students should note that finding solutions using repeated trials can be very cumbersome, even with the aid of a calculator. Although the use of repeated trials to solve linear equations is not an efficient technique, it is very important in developing students' thinking about equations and what a solution means. Additional examples like the one in the Preview should be explored with a table of values such as that mentioned in the Preview on page 98. At least one equation with no nonzero side and one equation with one zero side should be discussed.

EXTRA PRACTICE, page 622

19. $6x + 5 = 7x - 3$ {8}   20. $3x + 7 = 4x - 8$ {15}   21. $9x + 5\frac{2}{3} = 10x + 3\frac{2}{3}$ {2}

22. $7x + 5\frac{3}{4} = 8x + 2\frac{3}{4}$ {3}   23. $5z + 0.6 = 4z + 1$ {0.4}   24. $7z + 0.3 = 6z + 1$ {0.7}

B 25. $x + \left(-2\frac{1}{2}\right) = 3\frac{1}{2}$ {6}   26. $x + \left(-4\frac{1}{4}\right) = 8\frac{1}{4}$ {$12\frac{1}{2}$}   27. $x + 1.53 = 10.62$ {9.09}

28. $x + 4.02 = 9.48$ {5.46}   29. $1.2x = 0.2x + 3$ {3}   30. $1.7x = 0.7x + 2$ {2}

31. $5x + 1.8 = 4x - 3.2$ {−5}   32. $3x + 4.7 = 2x - 5.3$ {−10}   33. $1.6x + 4 = 2.6x$ {4}

34. $2.4x + 7 = 3.4x$ {7}   35. $2.3x - 2 = 3.3x + 2.5$ {−4.5}   36. $7.5x - 3 = 8.5x + 3.5$ {−6.5}

37. A student added $(-6x)$ to both sides of the equation $5x + 13 = 6x$. Then he became "stuck." Describe two different ways to complete the solution for him.
Add − 13; then multiply by − 1. Multiply by − 1; then add 13.

Identify the expression that can be added to both sides of each of these equations in order to solve them in one step.

Sample	$3x + 6 = 2x + 9$
Solution	$3x + 6 = 2x + 9$
Add $(-2x + -6)$ to both sides.	$3x + 6 + (-2x + -6) = 2x + 9 + (-2x + -6)$
	$x = 3$
Answer	$(-2x + -6)$

C 38. $5x + 3 = 4x + 10$ (−4x − 3)   39. $8x - 7 = 7x + 5$ (−7x + 7)   40. $2x + 8 = 3x - 5$ (−2x + 5)

Solve.

41. $5x + |-6| = 4x + |9|$ {3}   42. $3x - |-6| = 4x - |-8|$ {2}

43. This table shows the values of the left and right sides of the equation $2x - 4 = 10 - x$ for integral values of x from 0 to 8.

   a. Copy and complete the table.

   b. Whenever x increases by 1, then $2x - 4$ __?__ (increases/decreases) by __?__. increases, 2

   c. Whenever x increases by 1, then $10 - x$ __?__ (increases/decreases) by __?__. decreases, 1

   d. Between what integer values of x does the solution of $2x - 4 = 10 - x$ lie? 4 and 5

x	$2x - 4$	$10 - x$
0	−4	10
1	−2	9
2	0	8
3	? 2	? 7
4	? 4	? 6
5	? 6	? 5
6	? 8	? 4
7	? 10	? 3
8	? 12	? 2

44. Between what integer values does the solution of the equation $5x - 3 = 2x + 10$ lie? Use a method similar to that used in Exercise 43.

b. x increases by 1, $5x - 3$ increases by 5
c. x increases by 1, $2x + 10$ increases by 2
d. between 4 and 5

COMPUTER EXTENSION

Write a computer program that prints the table in exercise 43 for $x = 4.0, 4.1, 4.2, \ldots, 5$.

```
10 PRINT "X", "2 X -4",
   "10 - X"
20 FOR X = 4 TO 5 STEP 0.1
30 PRINT X, 2*X - 4, 10 - X
40 NEXT X
50 END
```

ENRICHMENT PROBLEMS

- In solving the following equation, why is the listed step usually not recommended as a beginning step?

  Solve. $8 - 4a = 4 - 3a$

  Add −4 to both sides.

  $4 - 4a = -3a$

  It does not help to isolate the variable on one side of the equation.

- Solve $-5y + 4 = 7 - 6y$ in two ways: (1) by isolating a variable term on the left side of the equation, and (2) by isolating a variable term on the right.

  (1) Add $(6y - 4)$ to both sides.

  $-5y + 4 + (6y - 4)$
  $= 7 - 6y + (6y - 4)$
  $y = 3$

  (2) Add $(5y - 7)$ to both sides.

  $-5y + 4 + (5y - 7)$
  $= 7 - 6y + (5y - 7)$
  $-3 = -y$
  $3 = y$

■ REVIEW EXERCISES

State the property illustrated by each equation. [1–5]

1. $(3x + 4) + 2x = 2x + (3x + 4)$
Commutative property of addition

2. $2x + (3x + 4) = (2x + 3x) + 4$
Associative property of addition

3. $(2x + 3x) + 4 = (2 + 3)x + 4$
Distributive property

Simplify. [1–6]

4. $5x - x$ 4x

5. $7a - 6a$ a

6. $5(2x + 3) + x + 4$
11x + 19

Use an algebraic expression to complete each statement. [1–7]

Juan has $25 more than Fernando.

7. If Fernando has f dollars, then Juan has __?__ dollars. f + 25

8. If Juan has j dollars, then Fernando has __?__ dollars. j − 25

The length of a rectangle is three times as long as the width.

9. If the width is w centimeters, then the length is __?__ centimeters. 3w

10. If the length is l centimeters, then the width is __?__ centimeters. $\frac{1}{3}l$

Self-Quiz 1

3–1 Which of the numbers $\{-3, -1, 0, 1, 3\}$ is a solution of the equation?

1. $2x + 4 = 10$ 3

2. $5 - 3x = 8$ −1

3. $6|x| = 18$ −3, 3

4. $x^2 + 2x = 5x$ 0, 3

3–2 What equivalent equation results from performing the given operation?

5. $4x + 8 = 22$ 4x = 14
Subtract 8 from each side.

6. $7x - 6 = 39 - 2x$ 9x − 6 = 39
Add $2x$ to each side.

7. $7x = -84$ x = −12
Multiply each side by $\frac{1}{7}$.

8. $4(x + 1) - 2x = -6$ 4x + 4 − 2x = −6
Apply the distributive property.

3–3 Solve by writing a series of equivalent equations.

9. $8x = 7x + 9$ (9)

10. $x + \frac{3}{4} = 2$ $\{1\frac{1}{4}\}$

11. $11x - 23 = 10x - 27$ (−4)

12. $3(x - 1) = 4x$ (−3)

Class Starter Quiz
on previous section

Solve by writing a series of equivalent equations.

1. $5 + x = -2$ $\{-7\}$
2. $x - 7 = -4$ $\{3\}$
3. $5x + 3 = 4x + 10$ $\{7\}$
4. $10x - 6 = 9x + 2$ $\{8\}$
5. $6x - 6 = 7x - 8$ $\{2\}$

3–4 Solving Equations by Multiplication

Preview

In the 1985 Boston Marathon, George Murray won the wheelchair division of the 26.2-mile race in an incredible time of 1 hour 45 minutes 34 seconds, or about 105.567 minutes. What was his average time for each mile of the race?

The answer to the question given above is the solution of this equation:

$$26.2x = 105.567$$

What operation could be used to solve the equation for x? Multiplication or division

In this lesson you will learn how to use multiplication and division to solve equations.

■ LESSON

In Section 3–2 we learned that an equivalent equation is obtained when both sides of an equation are multiplied by the same nonzero number. For example, starting with

$$3a = 15$$

and then multiplying both sides by $\frac{1}{3}$ and simplifying gives:

$$a = 5$$

The fact that the second equation has the same solutions as the first is a consequence of the **multiplication property of equations.**

Multiplication Property of Equations

For all real numbers a, b, and c, if $a = b$, then $ac = bc$.

We also learned that an equivalent equation is obtained by dividing both sides of an equation by the same nonzero number. However, we can think of division by a number as multiplication by the reciprocal of the number. Therefore, dividing both sides by the same quantity is also described by the multiplication property of equations. We will use the multiplication property of equations to solve complex equations by changing them to simpler equations whose solutions are obvious.

PURPOSE

Students need efficient methods for solving equations. Some equations can be solved by using multiplication or division. Multiplication and division will also be used later (see Section 3–5) to solve more complicated equations.

PREVIEW

Go over the Preview. Students probably know enough about averages to answer the problem by dividing the total time (in minutes) by the length of the race (in miles). His average time was about 4.03 minutes per mile. (His rate was about 14.9 mph.)

If students cannot find the average time per mile, return to the Preview after teaching the lesson. Students will then know how to solve the problem.

LESSON

Students should be familiar with the multiplication property of equations from Section 3–2. Remind them of the multiplication property. Then go over the examples carefully.

In solving equations of the form $ax = b$, students have a choice. They can either divide both sides of the equation by a, or they can multiply both sides by $\frac{1}{a}$ (the reciprocal of a). If a is an integer or written as a decimal, it may be easier to use division—for example:

- Solve. $25x = 375$
  Divide both sides by 25. $x = 15$
- Solve. $4.6x = 27.14$
  Divide both sides by 4.6. $x = 5.9$

If the coefficient of x is written as a fraction, it is probably easier to use multiplication.

CONCEPT EXTENSION

The "cover up method" is an alternative approach that can be used with some students who experience difficulty. The variable (or variable term in more complicated equations) is covered up. The student then asks what covered number satisfies the condition. That number is then set equal to the variable (or variable term). For example:

• Solve. $\dfrac{2y}{3} = 4$

Cover $2y$. $\dfrac{\blacksquare}{3} = 4$

Ask: What number divided by 3 equals 4? (12)

So, $2y = 12$.

Cover y. $2\,\blacksquare = 12$

Ask: What number multiplied by 2 equals 12? (6)

So, $y = 6$.

ADDITIONAL EXAMPLES

Example 1.

Solve. $7x = 40$

$7x = 40$

Multiply both sides by $\dfrac{1}{7}$.

$\dfrac{1}{7} \cdot 7x = \dfrac{1}{7} \cdot 40$

Simplify.

$x = {}^{40}\!/_7$

$\{{}^{40}\!/_7\}$

Example 2.

Solve. $-8a = 26$

$-8a = 26$

Divide both sides by -8.

$\dfrac{-8a}{-8} = \dfrac{26}{-8}$

Simplify.

$a = -{}^{13}\!/_4$

$\{-{}^{13}\!/_4\}$

Example 3.

Solve. $-{}^3\!/_4 t = 5$

$-\dfrac{3}{4}t = 5$

Multiply both sides by $-{}^4\!/_3$.

$-\dfrac{4}{3} \cdot -\dfrac{3}{4}t = -\dfrac{4}{3} \cdot 5$

Simplify.

$t = -{}^{20}\!/_3$

$\{-{}^{20}\!/_3\}$

Example 1   Solve. $5x = 37$

Solution

$$5x = 37$$

Multiply both sides by $\dfrac{1}{5}$. $\dfrac{1}{5} \cdot 5x = \dfrac{1}{5} \cdot 37$

Simplify. $x = \dfrac{37}{5}$ or $7\dfrac{2}{5}$

Answer $\left\{\dfrac{37}{5}\right\}$

Check $5x = 37$

$5 \cdot \dfrac{37}{5} \stackrel{?}{=} 37$

$37 = 37$ True!

Notice in Example 1 that $\dfrac{1}{5}$ was used as the multiplier in the first step since it is the reciprocal of the coefficient of x. This choice of multiplier makes the coefficient of x equal to 1 in the next step.

Example 2   Solve. $-6a = 14$

Solution

$$-6a = 14$$

Divide both sides by -6. $\dfrac{-6a}{-6} = \dfrac{14}{-6}$

Simplify. $a = -\dfrac{7}{3}$ or $-2\dfrac{1}{3}$

Answer $\left\{-\dfrac{7}{3}\right\}$

Check $-6a = 14$

$(-6)\left(-\dfrac{7}{3}\right) \stackrel{?}{=} 14$

$\dfrac{42}{3} \stackrel{?}{=} 14$

$14 = 14$ True!

Example 3   Solve. $\dfrac{2}{3}x = 16$

Solution

$$\dfrac{2}{3}x = 16$$

Multiply both sides by $\dfrac{3}{2}$. $\dfrac{3}{2} \cdot \dfrac{2}{3}x = \dfrac{3}{2} \cdot 16$

Simplify. $x = 24$

Answer $\{24\}$

Check   The check is left to the student.

Research indicates that parent support helps a student achieve. Therefore, actively work for parent involvement by sending a letter describing expectations, inviting parents to school for conferences, and phoning when students have difficulty or have made outstanding contributions in class. (See the Teacher's Resource Binder for a sample.)

Example 4   Solve. $7 = \dfrac{m}{-3}$

   Solution $7 = \dfrac{m}{-3}$

          Multiply both sides by -3. $-21 = m$

   Answer $\{-21\}$

    Check   The check is left to the student.

■ CLASSROOM EXERCISES

For all real numbers a, b, and c, if a = b, then ac = bc.
1. State the multiplication property of equations.

Dividing is multiplying by the reciprocal.
2. Why is it unnecessary to write a division property of equations?

State what both sides of the first equation were multiplied by or divided by that resulted in the second equation.

3. $2a = 7$ **4.** $\dfrac{m}{-4} = 8$ **5.** $\dfrac{2}{5}y = -8$ **6.** $0.2x = 1$

$a = \dfrac{7}{2}$ $\times \frac{1}{2}$ or $\div 2$ $m = -32$ $\times -4$ $y = -20$ $\times \frac{5}{2}$ $x = 5$
                                                            $\div 0.2$ or $\times 5$

Solve by writing simpler equivalent equations.

7. $-5n = 6$ $\left\{-\frac{6}{5}\right\}$ **8.** $4a = 9$ $\left\{\frac{9}{4}\right\}$ **9.** $\dfrac{3}{4}y = 12$ $\{16\}$

10. $\dfrac{b}{5} = 10$ $\{50\}$ **11.** $-7 = -\dfrac{1}{2}z$ $\{14\}$ **12.** $8 = 0.4y$ $\{20\}$

■ WRITTEN EXERCISES

State what both sides of the first equation were multiplied by that resulted in the second equation.

A   **1.** $-3x = 8$ **2.** $-2x = 7$ **3.** $\dfrac{3}{8}x = 24$ **4.** $\dfrac{4}{5}x = 20$

     $x = -\dfrac{8}{3}$ $-\frac{1}{3}$ $x = -\dfrac{7}{2}$ $-\frac{1}{2}$ $x = 64$ $\frac{8}{3}$ $x = 25$ $\frac{5}{4}$

5. $\dfrac{x}{7} = 2$ **6.** $\dfrac{x}{6} = 12$ **7.** $-a = 3$ **8.** $-b = -4$

$x = 14$ 7 $x = 72$ 6 $a = -3$ -1 $b = 4$ -1

State what both sides of the first equation were divided by that resulted in the second equation.

9. $7a = 18$ **10.** $9b = 16$ **11.** $-3c = 17$ **12.** $-5d = 12$

$a = 2\dfrac{4}{7}$ 7 $b = 1\dfrac{7}{9}$ 9 $c = -5\dfrac{2}{3}$ -3 $d = -2\dfrac{2}{5}$ -5

13. $-4p = -24$ **14.** $-8q = -40$ **15.** $\dfrac{1}{2}r = 3$ **16.** $\dfrac{1}{3}s = 7$

$p = 6$ -4 $q = 5$ -8 $r = 6$ $\frac{1}{2}$ $s = 21$ $\frac{1}{3}$

ADDITIONAL EXAMPLES
Example 4.

Solve. $15 = -\dfrac{n}{5}$ $15 = -\dfrac{n}{5}$

Multiply both sides by -5. $-5 \cdot 15 = -5 \cdot \dfrac{n}{-5}$

Simplify. $-75 = n$

                        $\{-75\}$

CHECK UNDERSTANDING

- What can both sides be multiplied by to get an equivalent equation with the variable alone on one side?

a. $6x = 90$ $(\frac{1}{6})$ **b.** $-\dfrac{1}{3}y = 27$ (-3)

CLASSROOM EXERCISES

In classroom exercise 3, point out that multiplying both sides of the equation by ½ will solve the equation. Division may be considered a special case of multiplication (multiplying by a reciprocal). If only one property is used, multiplication customarily is chosen, not division.

ASSIGNMENT GUIDE

Basic   1–31 odd, Review Exercises
Average   1–31 odd, 33–44 all, Review
            Exercises
Enriched 1–31 odd, 33–47 all, Review
            Exercises

PRACTICE WORKSHEET 12

3-4 SOLVING EQUATIONS BY MULTIPLICATION
■ Solve by writing a simpler equation in each case. Check your solution.

1. $3x = 5$ $\{5/3\}$ 2. $7x = 10$ $\{10/7\}$ 3. $\frac{1}{2}x = 3$ $\{6\}$

4. $\frac{1}{3}x = 10$ $\{30\}$ 5. $-\frac{1}{4}x = 8$ $\{-32\}$ 6. $\frac{1}{10}x = -20$ $\{-200\}$

7. $-2x = -15$ $\{15/2\}$ 8. $-3x = -100$ $\{100/3\}$ 9. $\frac{x}{-6} = 15$ $\{-90\}$

10. $\frac{2}{3}x = \frac{5}{6}$ $\{5/4\}$ 11. $\frac{3}{4}x = -\frac{7}{8}$ $\{-7/6\}$ 12. $-\frac{5}{6}x = -30$ $\{36\}$

13. $0.5x = 6$ $\{12\}$ 14. $-\frac{3}{8}x = -24$ $\{64\}$ 15. $0.3x = 2.7$ $\{9\}$

16. $\frac{3}{4}x = 5$ $\{20/3\}$ 17. $-\frac{2}{3}x = -\frac{3}{4}$ $\{9/8\}$ 18. $\frac{3}{8}x = 0$ $\{0\}$

19. $3x = 4\frac{1}{2}$ $\{3/2\}$ 20. $6x = 2\frac{2}{5}$ $\{2/5\}$ 21. $\frac{3}{2}x = -4\frac{4}{5}$ $\{-16/5\}$

WRITTEN EXERCISES

Exercises 17–18 illustrate common errors. Exercises 37–40 contain mixed numbers. As a first step, the mixed numbers can be changed to improper fractions. For example, rewrite $1\frac{1}{5}$ as $\frac{6}{5}$.

Exercise 47 may be too abstract for some students. Have them pick various specific values for a and b (such as 2 and 4, 2 and -4, -2 and 4, -2 and 4) and see which series of directions gives the correct solution.

COMPUTER EXTENSION

Write a program in which the input is the number of hours and minutes it takes a runner to run a marathon and the output is the number of minutes per mile that the runner averages over the course.

```
10 PRINT "HOW MANY HOURS";
20 INPUT H
30 PRINT "HOW MANY MINUTES";
40 INPUT M
50 PRINT "HOW MANY SECONDS";
60 INPUT S
70 T = (60*H + M + S/60)/26.2
80 PRINT "AVERAGE OF"; T;
   "MINUTES PER MILE"
90 END
```

ENRICHMENT PROBLEM

• The equation $\frac{14x}{-2} = 42$ can be solved many ways, but each method gives the same solution. How many different "first steps" can you find that could be used to solve this equation? Which do you prefer? Why?

Some possible ways:
Multiply both sides by -2.

Divide both sides by $\frac{1}{-2}$.

Simplify $\frac{14}{-2}$ to -7.

Divide both sides by 14.

Multiply both sides by $\frac{1}{14}$.

Multiply both sides by $\frac{-2}{14}$.

Divide both sides by -7.

Etc.

106

EXTRA PRACTICE, page 622

Check the solution listed for each equation. Write "OK" or "wrong."

17. $\frac{1}{5}x = 30$ **18.** $\frac{1}{4}x = 20$ **19.** $\frac{2}{3}x = -4$ **20.** $\frac{3}{4}x = -12$

$\{6\}$ Wrong $\{5\}$ Wrong $\{6\}$ Wrong $\{-9\}$ Wrong

Solve by writing simpler equivalent equations. Check your solutions.

21. $19 = 2x$ $\left\{\frac{19}{2}\right\}$ **22.** $13 = 2x$ $\left\{\frac{13}{2}\right\}$ **23.** $-5n = 31$ $\left\{-\frac{31}{5}\right\}$ **24.** $-6x = 33$ $\left\{-\frac{11}{2}\right\}$

25. $\frac{x}{-4} = 12$ $\{-48\}$ **26.** $\frac{n}{-7} = 14$ $\{-98\}$ **27.** $\frac{1}{6}p = -12$ $\{-72\}$ **28.** $\frac{1}{5}q = -100$ $\{-500\}$

29. $36 = \frac{3}{4}t$ $\{48\}$ **30.** $18 = \frac{2}{3}w$ $\{27\}$ **31.** $-\frac{5}{6}y = -3$ $\left\{\frac{18}{5}\right\}$ **32.** $-\frac{2}{5}z = -20$ $\{50\}$

B   **33.** $\frac{4}{3}a = \frac{2}{3}$ $\left\{\frac{1}{2}\right\}$ **34.** $\frac{5}{3}b = \frac{1}{2}$ $\left\{\frac{3}{10}\right\}$ **35.** $-\frac{7}{8}c = \frac{3}{4}$ $\left\{-\frac{6}{7}\right\}$ **36.** $-\frac{5}{8}d = -\frac{1}{3}$ $\left\{\frac{8}{15}\right\}$

37. $1\frac{1}{5} = \frac{3}{4}g$ $\left\{\frac{8}{5}\right\}$ **38.** $2\frac{1}{4} = \frac{2}{3}j$ $\left\{\frac{27}{8}\right\}$ **39.** $-\frac{5}{6}k = -1\frac{1}{3}$ $\left\{\frac{8}{5}\right\}$ **40.** $-\frac{3}{5}m = -2\frac{1}{3}$ $\left\{\frac{35}{9}\right\}$

41. $\frac{p}{1.3} = 2.1$ $\{2.73\}$ **42.** $\frac{q}{-5.2} = -7.1$ $\{36.92\}$ **43.** $-3.2r = 3.52$ $\{-1.1\}$ **44.** $7.5s = -18$ $\{-2.4\}$

C   **45.** A student tried to solve the equation $x^2 = 4x$ by dividing both sides by x. The result was $x = 4$. The solution, 4, satisfies the first equation but is not the complete solution. What is the other solution? What property of numbers did the student violate when she divided by x?
0; there is no division by 0.

46. Let k be an unknown constant. What value must k have if the equation $\frac{k}{3}x = 4$ has $\{10\}$ as its solution set?   1.2

47. Let a, b, and c be constants (b not equal to 0). Show that $\frac{bc}{a}$ is a solution of $\frac{a}{b}x - c = 0$ if a is not equal to 0.
$\frac{a}{b}x - c = 0$
$\frac{a}{b}\left(\frac{bc}{a}\right) - c = c - c = 0$

■ REVIEW EXERCISES

Simplify.   [1–6]

1. $3x + 4 + 4x + 5$ $7x + 9$ **2.** $2(x + 3) + 3x + 4$ $5x + 10$

Use a variable expression to answer each question.   [1–7]

3. What is the length (in meters) of a rectangle if the length is 4 meters greater than the width w? $w + 4$

4. What is Maria's age (in years) if she is half as old as her x-year-old brother? $\frac{1}{2}x$

5. Suppose that there are 17 dimes and nickels in a pile. How many of the coins are dimes if n of them are nickels? $17 - n$

6. The area of a rectangle is 24 cm². What is the length if the width is w? $\frac{24}{w}$

106   Chapter 3   Solving Equations

OBJECTIVE 3–5

To solve equations involving more than one operation.

3–5 Using Several Properties to Solve Equations

Preview

In business, one of the ways in which merchandise on the store shelves is managed is called the LIFO method. LIFO stands for "Last In, First Out." The merchandise last put on the shelves will be the first sold. In some stores, the packages far in the back may be quite old, while those in the front are fresh.

When you get dressed in the morning, you put on socks and then shoes. At the end of the day, you remove your shoes and then socks. The first thing done (in the morning) is the last thing undone (in the evening).

In this lesson you will learn a "last in, first out" technique for solving certain algebraic equations.

PURPOSE

Students need efficient methods for solving linear equations that involve more than one operation. It is essential that students be able to use addition, subtraction, multiplication, and division in the proper order in solving equations. Students should become highly skilled in solving equations of the form $ax + b = c$, where a, b, and c are real numbers and $a \neq 0$.

PREVIEW

Quickly go over the Preview. If you wish to expand on the ideas presented in the Preview, two suggestions are given below.

Businesses also use other methods to manage their merchandise. The LILO method —last in, last out—may be used with terms that have a short shelf-life. For example, milk is often arranged on the shelf so the oldest will be picked first.

Another example of the general notation of "putting together, taking apart" is assembling an appliance. It must be put together according to directions in a specific order (analogous to the order of operations). If the appliance needs to be repaired, it may have to be disassembled in the reverse order. The last thing done in assembling will be the first thing undone in disassembling.

■ LESSON

The addition and multiplication properties of equations can be used together to solve equations. Notice how both properties are used.

Start with the equation	$2m - 8 = 6$
Add 8 to both sides.	$2m - 8 + 8 = 6 + 8$
Simplify.	$2m = 14$
Multiply both sides by $\frac{1}{2}$.	$\frac{1}{2} \cdot 2m = \frac{1}{2} \cdot 14$
Simplify.	$m = 7$
Answer:	$\{7\}$

Notice that 8 was added to both sides, and then both sides were multiplied by $\frac{1}{2}$. That order was determined by the order of operations indicated in this expression:

$$\overset{\text{1st} \quad \text{2nd}}{2m - 8}$$

By now, students are well acquainted with the addition and multiplication properties of equations. The task now is to learn to use the properties in the proper order to solve more complex equations. Go over the examples carefully.

The equations encountered in this lesson can be solved by undoing the operations—using the order of operations in the reverse order. It may be useful to review the order of operations:

Parentheses—Work within grouping symbols first.

Exponents—Raise to powers next.

Multiplication and division—Work from left to right.

Addition and subtraction—Work from left to right.

The only grouping symbol used in this lesson is the horizontal bar (called a vinculum) used to indicate division in expressions such as $\frac{x-3}{4}$. An equivalent expression is $(x - 3) \div 4$.

The order of operations indicates that the equation could have been "built" by starting with this simple equation:

$$m = 7$$

Multiply both sides by 2. $\qquad 2m = 14$

Subtract 8 from both sides. $\qquad 2m - 8 = 6$

To solve the equation, "undo" the operations in the reverse order:

Start. $\qquad 2m - 8 = 6$

Undo the operation, subtracting 8, by adding 8 to both sides:

$$2m - 8 + 8 = 6 + 8$$

Simplify. $\qquad 2m = 14$

Undo the operation, multiplying by 2, by dividing both sides by 2:

$$\frac{2m}{2} = \frac{14}{2}$$

Simplify. $\qquad m = 7$

Think: What is the order of operations?
Then undo the operations in the reverse order.

The operation that will "undo" an operation is called the **inverse** of that operation.

Operation	*Inverse operation*
Adding 3	Subtracting 3 (or adding -3)
Adding -3	Subtracting -3 (or adding 3)
Subtracting 4.3	Adding 4.3 (or subtracting -4.3)
Subtracting -4.3	Adding -4.3 (or subtracting 4.3)
Multiplying by 5	Multiplying by $\frac{1}{5}$ (or dividing by 5)
Multiplying by -5	Multiplying by $-\frac{1}{5}$ (or dividing by -5)
Dividing by 2	Multiplying by 2 $\left(\text{or dividing by } \frac{1}{2}\right)$
Dividing by -2	Multiplying by -2 $\left(\text{or dividing by } -\frac{1}{2}\right)$

Strategy for Success **Using examples** ————

You usually have to read an example several times. On the second reading, keep thinking about how each step gets closer to the answer.

Ninth graders tend to fall into two strategy groups: those who lean toward an intuitive approach that tries to capture the numerical relationships between numbers in an equation without transforming the equation itself and those who rely on memorized or routine step-by-step procedures (algorithms) for transforming the equation and producing the answer. Students who are able to move easily between intuitive and algorithmic approaches tend to be the most successful.

Example 1.

Solve. $\frac{x}{2} - 5 = 9$

Add 5 to both sides.

$$\frac{x}{2} - 5 + 5 = 9 + 5$$

Simplify.

$$\frac{x}{2} = 14$$

Multiply both sides by 2.

$$2\left(\frac{x}{2}\right) = 2 \cdot 14$$

Simplify.

$$x = 28$$
$$\{28\}$$

Example 2.

Solve. $\frac{x + 4}{4} = 20$

Multiply both sides by 4.

$$4 \cdot \frac{x + 4}{4} = 4 \cdot 20$$

Simplify.

$$x + 4 = 80$$

Add -4 to both sides.

$$x + 4 + (-4) = 80 + (-4)$$

Simplify.

$$x = 76$$
$$\{76\}$$

Example 1 Solve. $\frac{x}{3} - 9 = 21$

Solution

Note the order of operations.

1st 2nd

$$\frac{x}{3} - 9 = 21$$

Perform the inverse operations in reverse order.

Add 9 to both sides. $\qquad \frac{x}{3} - 9 + 9 = 21 + 9$

Simplify. $\qquad\qquad\qquad \frac{x}{3} = 30$

Multiply both sides by 3. $\qquad 3\left(\frac{x}{3}\right) = 3(30)$

Simplify. $\qquad\qquad\qquad x = 90$

Answer $\{90\}$

Check $\frac{x}{3} - 9 = 21$

$$\frac{90}{3} - 9 \stackrel{?}{=} 21$$

$$30 - 9 = 21 \qquad \text{True!}$$

Example 2 Solve. $\frac{x - 9}{3} = 21$

Solution

Note the order of operations.

1st 2nd

$$\frac{x - 9}{3} = 21$$

Perform the inverse operations in reverse order.

Multiply both sides by 3. $\qquad 3\left(\frac{x - 9}{3}\right) = 3(21)$

Simplify. $\qquad\qquad\qquad x - 9 = 63$

Add 9 to both sides. $\qquad x - 9 + 9 = 63 + 9$

Simplify. $\qquad\qquad\qquad x = 72$

Answer $\{72\}$

Check The check is left to the student.

ADDITIONAL EXAMPLES

Example 3.
Solve. $-x - 7 = 2$
Add 7 to both sides and simplify.
$$-x = 9$$
Multiply both sides by -1 and simplify.
$$x = -9$$
$$\{-9\}$$

Example 4.
Solve. $8n + 3 = 3n + 12$
Add $-3n$ to both sides and simplify.
$$5n + 3 = 12$$
Add -3 to both sides and simplify.
$$5n = 9$$
Divide both sides by 5 and simplify.
$$n = \frac{9}{5}$$
$$\{\frac{9}{5}\}$$

CHECK UNDERSTANDING

- State the order of operations in this expression.

$$\overset{1}{\downarrow}\ \overset{2}{\downarrow}$$
$$\frac{2a + 1}{3}\left(\frac{2a + 1}{3} \leftarrow 3\right)$$

- What is the inverse of adding 6? (Adding -6 or subtracting 6)
- What is the inverse of multiplying by 4? (Multiplying by ¼ or dividing by 4)
- What operation should be "undone" first to solve the equation $2x - 7 = 5$? (-7)

Example 3   Solve. $-x - 6 = 5$

Solution

Add 6 to both sides and simplify. $-x - 6 = 5$
Multiply both sides by -1 and simplify. $-x = 11$
$$x = -11$$

Answer $\{-11\}$

Check   The check is left to the student.

Example 4   Solve. $3n - 2 = n + 9$

Solution

$$3n - 2 = n + 9$$
Add $-n$ to both sides and simplify. $2n - 2 = 9$
Add 2 to both sides and simplify. $2n = 11$
Divide both sides by 2 and simplify. $n = \frac{11}{2}$

Answer $\left\{\frac{11}{2}\right\}$

Check   The check is left to the student.

■ CLASSROOM EXERCISES

State the inverse operation.

1. Adding -5 Subtracting -5 **2.** Dividing by 3   Multiplying by 3   **3.** Multiplying by -2
                                                                                  Dividing by -2

4. Subtracting 5   Adding 5   **5.** Multiplying by $-\frac{1}{3}$ Dividing by $-\frac{1}{3}$

$$\overset{?1}{\downarrow}\ \overset{?2}{\downarrow}$$

6. Indicate the order of operations: $6x + 8 = -5$

7. To solve $6x + 8 = -5$:
    a. What operation should be done first to both sides of the equation?   Subtract 8.
    b. What operation should be done second to both sides of the equation?   Divide by 6.

8. To solve $\frac{3x + 1}{2} = 8$:
    a. What should be done first?   Multiply by 2.
    b. What should be done second?   Subtract 1.
    c. What should be done third?   Divide by 3.

Solve.

9. $2y + 7 = 23$ (8)   **10.** $5 + 3a = 14$ (3)   **11.** $\frac{b}{2} - 7 = 3$ (20)   **12.** $-x - 6 = 12$
                                                                                                    (−18)

Remember: When solving an equation, any operation performed on one side of the equation must be performed on the other side. Keep in mind your objectives: first to get the variable term on one side and real numbers on the other side, then to solve for the variable.

ASSIGNMENT GUIDE

Basic   1–45 odd, Review Exercises
Average 5–45 odd, 47–56 all, Review
           Exercises
Enriched 13–49 odd, 50–62 all, Review
           Exercises

Strategy for Success **Doing homework**

When you start your homework, review the examples in the lesson to re-fresh your memory. If you get "stuck" on an exercise, find an example like it and study the example.

■ WRITTEN EXERCISES

List the order in which the operations are performed.

1. $3x - 2$ **2.** $5x + 2$ **3.** $\dfrac{x+5}{3}$ **4.** $\dfrac{x-4}{5}$

State the operation to be performed first in solving the equation.

5. $5x - 2 = 10$ Add 2

6. $6x - 8 = 9$ Add 8

7. $7 + 8n = 20$ Subtract 7

8. $6 + 4n = 24$ Subtract 6

9. $\dfrac{r}{5} + 7 = 3$ Subtract 7

10. $\dfrac{s}{3} + 8 = 5$ Subtract 8

11. $\dfrac{x+5}{3} = 10$ Multiply by 3

12. $\dfrac{x+7}{4} = 5$ Multiply by 4

13. $8 - 2n = 40$ Subtract 8

14. $7 - 3n = -2$ Subtract 7

15. $3x + 8 = -10$ Subtract 8

16. $4x + 4 = -12$ Subtract 4

Solve.

17. $5 + 3x = 9$ $\left\{\dfrac{4}{3}\right\}$

18. $5 + 4x = 11$ $\left\{\dfrac{3}{2}\right\}$

19. $5x - 4 = 14$ $\left\{\dfrac{18}{5}\right\}$

20. $2x - 3 = 8$ $\left\{\dfrac{11}{2}\right\}$

21. $\dfrac{1}{2}x + 7 = 11$ (8)

22. $\dfrac{1}{3}x + 2 = 8$ (18)

23. $\dfrac{a}{3} - 5 = 11$ (48)

24. $\dfrac{a}{5} - 6 = 10$ (80)

25. $\dfrac{x-7}{5} = 6$ (37)

26. $\dfrac{x-2}{3} = 5$ (17)

27. $-2x + 7 = 15$ (−4)

28. $-3x + 2 = 11$ (−3)

29. $4a - 3 = 2a + 5$ (4)

30. $7a - 5 = 4a + 7$ (4)

31. $2a - 3 = 5a - 9$ (2)

32. $a + 7 = 3a + 1$ (3)

33. $5a + 3 = a - 9$ (−3)

34. $4a - 2 = a - 14$ (−4)

35. $7a + 8 = 3a - 6$ $\left\{-\dfrac{7}{2}\right\}$

36. $6a - 3 = 4a - 10$ $\left\{-\dfrac{7}{2}\right\}$

37. $4a + 4 = 6a - 8$ (6)

38. $2a - 6 = 3a - 4$ (−2)

39. $4a - 8 = 5a - 6$ (−2)

40. $2a - 4 = 5a + 8$ (−4)

41. $6a - 4 = 3a + 8$ (4)

42. $2a - 3 = 4a - 7$ (2)

43. $6a - 3 = 5a + 2$ (5)

44. $2a + 3 = 4a - 1$ (2)

45. $5a + 1 = 2a + 3$ $\left\{\dfrac{2}{3}\right\}$

46. $7a + 2 = 3a - 1$ $\left\{-\dfrac{3}{4}\right\}$

List the order in which the operations are performed in evaluating these expressions.

47. $3(5 \cdot 4 + 2)$ **48.** $3 + (10 - 4 \cdot 1)$ **49.** $(4 - 2 \cdot 1) \cdot 3$

PRACTICE WORKSHEET 13

3-5 USING SEVERAL PROPERTIES TO SOLVE EQUATIONS

■ State the operation to be performed first in solving the equation.

1. $10x + 2 = 15$ Add.
2. $\dfrac{x-5}{2} = 3$ Mult.
3. $\dfrac{x}{2} - 6 = 10$ Add.
4. $\dfrac{x-3}{4} = 6$ Mult.
5. $\dfrac{x}{3} + 4 = 10$ Add.
6. $-3x - 5 = 7$ Add.
7. $\dfrac{x+4}{5} = 2$ Mult.
8. $9 + 5x = 6$ Add.
9. $5x - 7 = 9$ Add.

■ Solve.

10. $4x + 2 = 14$ {3}
11. $\dfrac{x-4}{2} = 4$ {12}
12. $\dfrac{x}{3} - 5 = 15$ {60}
13. $\dfrac{x+5}{5} = 3$ {10}
14. $\dfrac{x}{3} + 6 = 18$ {36}
15. $\dfrac{x}{4} - 8 = 12$ {80}
16. $5x - 6 = 3x + 3$ {9/2}
17. $2x - 5 = 5x - 6$ {1/3}
18. $-3x + 5 = 4x + 10$ {−5/7}
19. $3x - 7 = x - 10$ {−3/2}
20. $4x + 7 = x + 6.4$ {−0.2}
21. $5x - 2 = 3x + 3.6$ {2.8}

WRITTEN EXERCISES

Exercises 1–16 could be answered orally in a group activity.

    In exercises 47–49, note how the presence of the parentheses affects the order of operations.

    If more experience writing puzzles (such as exercise 57) is desired, students could write puzzles to fit exercises 50–55.

PROBLEM-SOLVING NOTE
Working backward

Reversing the order of operations in solving a linear equation is an example of the problem-solving strategy *working backward*. This is a very important mathematical tool to empha-size. The strategy is reinforced throughout this lesson and in the following problem.

ENRICHMENT PROBLEM
Working backward

• Dorothy (of *Wizard of Oz* fame) left the Munchkin Bakery with a box of cookies. Meeting the Scarecrow, she gave him half the cookies, ate half of those left, and threw half a cookie away. Encountering the Cowardly Lion next, she shared half her cookies with him, ate half of those remaining, and discarded half a cookie. Finally she found the Tin Man, with whom she shared half her cookies, ate half of her share, and threw away the last half cookie. How many cookies did Dorothy have when she left the bakery?

42 cookies

Solve these equations by performing the inverse operations in the reverse order.

50. $3(x + 4) = 24$ {4} **51.** $5(x - 2) = 10$ {4} **52.** $18(3x + 4) = 18$ {−1}

53. $4(5 - 2x) = 44$ {−3} **54.** $5(x + 3) = 23$ $\{\frac{8}{5}\}$ **55.** $3(x - 6) = 20$ $\{\frac{38}{3}\}$

56. Let $4(b + 2) = 52$ and $4b + 8 = 52$ be equivalent equations. List the order of operations for each equation, and then solve. (11)

$$\begin{array}{cc} 2 & 1 \\ 4(b + 2) = 52; & \end{array} \quad \begin{array}{cc} 1 & 2 \\ 4b + 8 = 52 \end{array}$$

Solve these puzzles by starting with the result and performing the inverse operations in the reverse order.

C 57. Puzzle. I am thinking of a number. If I add 2 to it, multiply the result by 3, subtract 1 from the product, and divide the difference by 2, I get 10. What number am I thinking of? 5

58. Puzzle. I am thinking of a number. If I multiply it by 3, add 2 to the product, divide the sum by 2, and then subtract 1, I get 6. What number am I thinking of? 4

59. Puzzle. I am thinking of a number. If I divide it by 2, subtract 1 from the quotient, add 2 to the difference, and multiply the sum by 3, I get 12. What number am I thinking of? 6

60. Write an equation for Exercise 57. $\frac{3(n + 2) - 1}{2} = 10$

61. Write an equation for Exercise 58. $\frac{3n + 2}{2} - 1 = 6$

62. Write this equation as a puzzle similar to those in Exercises 57–59. "The number I am thinking of" is represented by n in this equation.

$$3 \cdot \left(\frac{n}{2} + 2\right) - 1 = 20$$

I am thinking of a number. If I divide it by 2, add 2 to the quotient, multiply the sum by 3, and then subtract 1, I get 20.

What number am I thinking of? 10

■ REVIEW EXERCISES

Change to expressions involving only addition. [2–6]

1. $x - 4 + y$ $x + (-4) + y$

2. $a + b - (c + d)$ $a + b + (-c) + (-d)$

3. $m - (n - 2)$ $m + (-n) + 2$

4. $3x - 5y - x$ $3x + (-5y) + (-x)$

Simplify. [2–8]

5. $4a - 3b - 8b$ $4a - 11b$

6. $12 - (2x - 4)$ $16 - 2x$

7. $2x - 8 - (3x + 5)$ $-x - 13$

8. $5m - 6 - (4 - m)$ $6m - 10$

9. $3(2x - 6) - 5(3 - 3x)$ $21x - 33$

10. $-2(x + 5) + 3(2x - 6)$ $4x - 28$

Indicate whether the two expressions are equivalent. [1–4]

11. $(a + b)^2$ and $a^2 + b^2$ No

12. $\frac{a + 1}{b + 1}$ and $\frac{a}{b}$ No

State the property illustrated by each equation. [1–5]

13. $(5 + 0) + 6 = 5 + 6$
Identity property for addition

14. $(5 + 0) + 6 = 5 + (0 + 6)$
Associative property of addition

112

3–6 A Shortcut for Solving Some Equations

Preview

Consider the order of operations in this equation:

2nd   1st
↓   ↓
$5 - 2x = 13$

The last operation is subtracting $2x$. To solve the equation, first perform the inverse operation, adding $2x$, to both sides.

$$5 - 2x + 2x = 13 + 2x$$
$$5 = 13 + 2x$$

Finish solving the equation. Can you think of a shorter way to solve the equation? (-4)

In this lesson you will learn a more efficient way of solving equations like this one.

■ LESSON

If we strictly follow the equation-solving steps given in Section 3–5, we sometimes use more steps than are necessary. For example, follow the steps in solving this equation:

$$4 - 3x = 7$$

a. *Add 3x to both sides.* $4 - 3x + 3x = 7 + 3x$
Simplify. $4 = 7 + 3x$
b. *Subtract 7 from both sides.* $4 - 7 = 7 + 3x - 7$
Simplify. $-3 = 3x$

c. *Divide both sides by 3.* $\frac{-3}{3} = \frac{3x}{3}$

Simplify. $-1 = x$

Answer: {-1}

If step (a) does not really seem like a step "forward" to you, you are correct. Here is another way of solving the equation.

$$4 - 3x = 7$$

Consider the equation to be $4 + (-3x) = 7$
a. *Subtract 4 from both sides and simplify.* $-3x = 3$
b. *Divide both sides by −3 and simplify.* $x = -1$

Answer: {-1}

Example 1.

Solve. $10 - 3x = 6$

Consider the equation to be
$$10 + (-3x) = 6$$
Add -10 to both sides and simplify.
$$-3x = -4$$
Divide both sides by -3 and simplify.
$$x = \tfrac{4}{3}$$
$$\{\tfrac{4}{3}\}$$

Example 2.

Solve. $10 - \dfrac{a}{3} = 12$

Subtract 10 from both sides and simplify.
$$-\frac{a}{3} = 2$$
Multiply both sides by -1 and simplify.
$$\frac{a}{3} = -2$$
Multiply both sides by 3 and simplify.
$$a = -6$$
$$\{-6\}$$

Example 3.

Solve. $-5 - \dfrac{b}{3} = 8$

Add 5 to both sides and simplify.
$$-\frac{b}{3} = 13$$
Multiply both sides by -3 and simplify.
$$b = -39$$
$$\{-39\}$$

Example 1 Solve. $9 - 5x = 7$

Solution

Consider the equation to be $\qquad$ $9 + (-5x) = 7$
Add -9 to both sides and simplify. $\qquad$ $-5x = -2$

Divide both sides by -5 and simplify. $\qquad$ $x = \dfrac{2}{5}$

Answer $\left\{\dfrac{2}{5}\right\}$

Check $9 - 5x = 7$

$$9 - 5\left(\frac{2}{5}\right) \overset{?}{=} 7$$

$$9 - 2 = 7 \qquad \text{True!}$$

Example 2 Solve. $7 - \dfrac{w}{2} = 10$

Solution $\qquad\qquad\qquad\qquad\qquad\qquad\qquad\qquad 7 - \dfrac{w}{2} = 10$

a. *Subtract 7 from both sides and simplify.* $\qquad -\left(\dfrac{w}{2}\right) = 3$

b. *Multiply both sides by -1 and simplify.* $\qquad \dfrac{w}{2} = -3$

c. *Multiply both sides by 2 and simplify.* $\qquad w = -6$

Answer $\{-6\}$

Check The check is left to the student.

In Example 2, if you remember that $-\left(\dfrac{w}{2}\right)$ is equivalent to $\dfrac{w}{-2}$, you can combine steps (b) and (c) into one step:

b. *Multiply both sides by -2* $\qquad -2\left[-\left(\dfrac{w}{2}\right)\right] = -2(3)$
  and simplify. $\qquad\qquad\qquad\qquad\qquad w = -6$

Example 3 Solve. $-3 - \dfrac{y}{4} = 7$

Solution $\qquad\qquad\qquad\qquad\qquad\qquad\qquad -3 - \dfrac{y}{4} = 7$

Add 3 to both sides and simplify. $\qquad -\dfrac{y}{4} = 10$

Multiply both sides by -4 and simplify. $\qquad y = -40$

Answer $\{-40\}$

Check The check is left to the student.

114

Many experts think that grading on a curve defeats the goal of having students helping students (except on tests). Grading on a curve puts students in competi- *tion with each other and penalizes them for helping one another.*

Strategy for Success   Making up work

If you have to miss algebra class, call a friend and find out what the assignment was. If possible, try to make up the assignment before you come back to class.

■ CLASSROOM EXERCISES

Rewrite each equation as an addition.

1. $2 - x = 3$
$2 + (-x) = 3$

2. $5 - 2a = 4$
$5 + (-2a) = 4$

3. $8 - \dfrac{w}{4} = 12$
$8 + \left(-\dfrac{w}{4}\right) = 12$

4. $7 - \dfrac{b}{5} = 8$
$7 + \left(-\dfrac{b}{5}\right) = 8$

State the first step in solving each equation.

5. $3 - \dfrac{1}{4}w = 9$
Add -3 to both sides.

6. $-1 - y = 5$
Add 1 to both sides.

7. $\dfrac{2}{3} - 2a = 1$
Add $-\dfrac{2}{3}$ to both sides.

8. $0.4 - 0.1x = 1.2$
Add -0.4 to both sides.

Solve.

9. $5 - 3x = 14$ (-3)

10. $-7 - 5b = 1$ $\left\{-\dfrac{8}{5}\right\}$

11. $4 - \dfrac{x}{2} = 5$ (-2)

12. $9 - \dfrac{a}{3} = 7$ (6)

■ WRITTEN EXERCISES

Solve. Check your solutions.

A

1. $2 - 3x = 8$ (-2)

2. $5 - 3x = 8$ (-1)

3. $4 - 2a = 2$ $\{1\}$

4. $6 - 2a = 2$ (2)

5. $3 - 5c = 2$ $\left\{\dfrac{1}{5}\right\}$

6. $4 - 2x = 1$ $\left\{\dfrac{3}{2}\right\}$

7. $5x - 3 = 7$ (2)

8. $4x - 2 = 5$ $\left\{\dfrac{7}{4}\right\}$

9. $3 + \dfrac{x}{2} = 4$ (2)

10. $5 - \dfrac{y}{2} = 7$ (-4)

11. $8 - \dfrac{x}{3} = 4$ (12)

12. $7 - \dfrac{x}{3} = 5$ (6)

13. $\dfrac{a}{4} - 7 = 3$ (40)

14. $\dfrac{m}{3} - 5 = 2$ (21)

15. $-8 - \dfrac{n}{2} = 5$ (-26)

16. $-3 - \dfrac{y}{3} = 5$ (-24)

17. $-3 + 2x = 8$ $\left\{\dfrac{11}{2}\right\}$

18. $-5 + 3a = 7$ (4)

19. $-4 - \dfrac{2x}{3} = -2$ (-3)

20. $5 - \dfrac{3x}{4} = -4$ (12)

Solve.

B

21. $2(3 - x) = 4$ (1)

22. $3(1 - y) = 6$ (-1)

23. $2(6 - 2x) = 4$ (2)

24. $3(6 - 2y) = 6$ (2)

25. $\dfrac{1}{2}(4 - 6a) = 6$ $\left\{-\dfrac{4}{3}\right\}$

26. $\dfrac{(8 - 2a)}{2} = 4$ (0)

27. $\dfrac{2}{3}(6 - y) = 8$ (-6)

28. $\dfrac{3}{4}(8 - 4y) = 7$ $\left\{-\dfrac{1}{3}\right\}$

29. $2x + 7 = 12$ $\left\{\dfrac{5}{2}\right\}$

30. $4a + 5 = 9$ (1)

31. $6b - 3 = 9$ (2)

32. $8b - 4 = -16$ $\left\{-\dfrac{3}{2}\right\}$

33. $-2(2x + 7) = 16$ $\left\{-\dfrac{15}{2}\right\}$

34. $3(2x + 2) = 12$ (1)

35. $5(3 - 5x) = -10$ (1)

36. $6(4 - 3y) = 18$ $\left\{\dfrac{1}{3}\right\}$

37. $5x - 2 = 4x + 5$ (7)

38. $6a - 5 = 4a + 2$ $\left\{\dfrac{7}{2}\right\}$

39. $7y + 4 = 3 - 2y$ $\left\{-\dfrac{1}{9}\right\}$

40. $4 - 8a = 9 - 3a$ (-1)

CHECK UNDERSTANDING

- Change the subtraction to addition.
  $3 - 5x = 7$ $(3 + (-5x) = 7)$
- State three different operations that *can* be done first to $4 - 2x = 7$. (Add -4 to both sides; Add $2x$; Subtract 4; Subtract $-2x$.)

CLASSROOM EXERCISES

The most efficient techniques used thus far may be used on the classroom exercises.

ASSIGNMENT GUIDE

Basic   1–20 all, Review Exercises, Self-Quiz 2

Average   1–27 odd, 29–40 all, Review Exercises, Self-Quiz 2

Enriched   1–40 odd, 41–48 all, Review Exercises, Self-Quiz 2

PRACTICE WORKSHEET 13

3-6 A SHORTCUT FOR SOLVING SOME EQUATIONS
■ Solve. Check your solutions.

1. $3 - 2x = 11$ (-4)
2. $4 - 7x = -5$ $(9/7)$
3. $6 - 3x = -12$ (6)
4. $6 - \dfrac{1}{3}x = 12$ (-18)
5. $-2 - \dfrac{x}{2} = 2$ (-8)
6. $-4 - 0.2x = 10$ (-70)
7. $7 - 5x = -8$ (3)
8. $\dfrac{1}{2} - \dfrac{1}{2}x = 3\dfrac{1}{2}$ (-6)
9. $2x - 3 = 8$ $(11/2)$
10. $\dfrac{x}{3} - 9 = 15$ (72)
11. $6 - \dfrac{2}{3}x = 18$ (-18)
12. $5 - \dfrac{5}{8}x = 10$ (-6)
13. $-5 + \dfrac{x}{4} = 6$ (44)
14. $5 - \dfrac{x}{4} = 6$ (-4)
15. $\dfrac{5 - x}{4} = 6$ (-19)
16. $\dfrac{-5 - x}{4} = 6$ (-29)
17. $\dfrac{-5 + x}{4} = 6$ (29)
18. $7 + \dfrac{x}{3} = -9$ (-48)
19. $2(x - 3) = 50$ (28)
20. $3(x + 4) = 14$ $(2/3)$
21. $2(3x - 4) = 7$ $(5/2)$

115

5.

Day	1	2	3	4	5	6	7	8	9
Blue Team	2600	2700	2800	2900	3000	3100	3200	3300	3400
Red Team	1200	1400	1600	1800	2000	2200	2400	2600	2800

Day	10	11	12	13	14	15
Blue Team	3500	3600	3700	3800	3900	4000
Red Team	3000	3200	3400	3600	3800	4000

ENRICHMENT PROBLEM

- Solve. $|a| - |2a| = 4$
  Explain your answer.

$|2a|$ is greater than $|a|$ for all a. Therefore, $|a| - |2a|$ is negative for all a. There is no solution.

Solve these absolute value equations. If there is no solution, write ∅.

Sample	Solve. $\|x\| + 2 = 12$
Solution	$\|x\| + 2 = 12$
	$\|x\| = 10$
Answer	$\{-10, 10\}$

C 41. $|x| + 4 = 7$ (−3, 3)   42. $|y| + 5 = 3$ ∅   43. $5 - |z| = 1$ (−4, 4)   44. $2|x| - 4 = 18$ (−11, 11)

45. $8 - |2a| = 3$ $\left\{-\frac{5}{2}, \frac{5}{2}\right\}$ 46. $8 - |3a| = 12$ ∅   47. $-|x| + 3 = -2$ (−5, 5)   48. $x + |x| \le 0$ (All numbers ≤ 0)

■ REVIEW EXERCISES

State the property illustrated by each equation.   [2–7]

1. $2 + (x - 3) = (x - 3) + 2$
Commutative property of addition

2. $(a + b) = 1(a + b)$
Identity property for multiplication

3. $(a - b) + -(a - b) = 0$
Inverse property for addition

4. $6(x + 3) = 6x + 18$ Distributive property

Solve by making a table.   [2–9]

5. Two teams had a contest to determine which one could collect the most newspapers in a paper drive. The Blue Team started with 2500 pounds and collected 100 pounds each day until the contest ended. The Red Team started with 1000 pounds, but they collected 200 pounds each day until the contest ended. How long did the contest last if the two teams were tied at the end? 15 days

---

Self-Quiz 2

3–4   Solve.

1. $6x = 42$ (7)   2. $-2y = 18$ (−9)

3. $\frac{d}{5} = 17$ {85}   4. $\frac{2}{3}c = 66$ (99)

3–5   Solve.

5. $3a - 4 = 17$ (7)   6. $2x + 3 = x + 12$ (9)

7. $\frac{z + 6}{3} = 5$ (9)   8. $\frac{t}{4} - 9 = 11$ (80)

3–6   Solve.

9. $12 - 3x = 8$ $\left\{\frac{4}{3}\right\}$ 10. $4 - \frac{a}{2} = 7$ (−6)

11. $-5 - \frac{2y}{3} = 1$ (−9)   12. $2(6 - t) = -10$ {11}

EXTENSION Checking the solution on a calculator

For many complicated equations, a calculator can be helpful in checking the solution. However, be careful to notice how your calculator carries out calculations.

Example 1. $\dfrac{x - 12}{3} = 16$

  Answer: {60}

  Check:

Calculator Key Steps	Display
60 − 12 =	48.
÷ 3 =	16.

The key sequence 60 − 12 ÷ 3 = may give the result 56 on some calculators. Those calculators perform the operations using the algebraic order of operations.

Example 2. $4 - 3x = -71$

  Answer {25}

  Check Rewrite the equation. $4 + (-3)x = -71$
  Enter the answer and then "build" the equation.

25 × 3 CHS =	−75.
+ 4 =	−71.

Check the answer to each equation with a calculator. If the answer is wrong, find the correct answer and check.

1. $5x + 12 = 87$; {15}

2. $4x + 19 = -17$; {−9}

3. $\dfrac{x}{3} - 12 = 16$; {81} (84)

4. $\dfrac{2x}{5} + 10 = 26$; {45} (40)

5. $7(x + 17) = 35$; {−12}

6. $\dfrac{x + 16}{-4} = -16$; {40} (48)

7. $59 - 6x = 38$; {3.5}

8. $\dfrac{35 - 2x}{3} = 7$; {7}

9. $26 - 3x = 14$; {4}

10. $\dfrac{45 - 2x}{5} = 5$; {10}

Strategy for Success Using test results

Sometimes students keep repeating an error they made earlier. To help prevent this, make notes about any errors you have made when a quiz or a test is returned to you. Keep them and review them before taking another test.

Class Starter Quiz
on previous section

Solve.

1. $2 - 4x = 8$ $\{-\frac{3}{2}\}$
2. $-3 - 5x = 10$ $\{-\frac{13}{5}\}$
3. $7 - \frac{x}{2} = 17$ $\{-20\}$
4. $7 - \frac{x}{3} = 3$ $\{12\}$
5. $6 + 7x = 26$ $\{\frac{20}{7}\}$

PURPOSE

Students should be able to solve linear equations given in different forms, including equations in which quantities are grouped by parentheses.

PREVIEW

Discuss how the problem, in spite of its awkward language, can be translated into the equation given at the end of the Preview. Some students may be able to solve the equation. (84) The Preview equation is assigned in exercise 44.

LESSON

Of the skills needed to solve equations in this lesson, correct handling of quantities grouped by parentheses will require the most attention. Go over the examples in the text and the additional examples given below. Students should become flexible in their handling of equations.

OBJECTIVE 3-7

To solve equations containing quantities grouped in parentheses.

3-7 Solving Equations

Preview History

This is the epitaph of Diophantus, one of the greatest mathematicians of the Greek civilization, who lived in Alexandria, Egypt, around the 3rd century.

This tomb holds Diophantus. Ah, what a marvel! And the tomb tells scientifically the measure of his life. God vouchsafed that he should be a boy for the sixth part of his life; when the twelfth was added, his cheeks acquired a beard; He kindled for him the light of marriage after a seventh more, and in the fifth year after his marriage He granted him a son. Alas! late begotten and miserable child, when reached the measure of half his father's life, the chill grave took him. After consoling his grief by this science of numbers for four years, he reached the end of his life.

If x is the number of years of Diophantus's age when he died, we can write the equation from the epitaph:

$$\frac{1}{6}x + \frac{1}{12}x + \frac{1}{7}x + 5 + \frac{1}{2}x + 4 = x$$

After this lesson you can solve this equation and find out how many years Diophantus lived.

■ LESSON

When confronted with a more complicated equation, we must examine its structure and plan the method to use in solving it. We usually have more than one choice of method. We base our choice on the number of steps, the difficulty of the arithmetic, and the likelihood of making errors. Consider this equation, for example.

$$2(a + 4) = -3$$

There are two methods that most people would consider. Some would first expand the left side; others would first multiply both sides by $\frac{1}{2}$.

Expand first:

$$2(a + 4) = -3$$

Expand. $2a + 8 = -3$

Add -8. $2a = -11$

Multiply by $\frac{1}{2}$. $a = -\frac{11}{2}$

Use the multiplication property of equations first:

$$2(a + 4) = -3$$

Multiply by $\frac{1}{2}$. $a + 4 = -\frac{3}{2}$

Add -4 *and simplify.* $a = -\frac{11}{2}$

Research indicates that for students to do well they must complete assignments and correct errors. Therefore, encourage such work by occasionally giving a "homework quiz." Specify a few problems (between 3 and 6) from the preceding week's assignments and have students copy from their notebooks complete solutions to be handed in and graded.

ADDITIONAL EXAMPLES

Example 1.
Solve. $3(x - 5) = x + 7$
Expand.
$$3x - 15 = x + 7$$
Add $-x$ to both sides and simplify.
$$2x - 15 = 7$$
Add 15 to both sides and simplify.
$$2x = 22$$
Divide both sides by 2.
$$x = 11$$
$\{11\}$

Example 2.
Solve. $7 - 3(x + 4) = 10 - 2(x - 5)$
Expand both sides.
$$7 - 3x - 12 = 10 - 2x + 10$$
Combine like terms on each side.
$$-3x - 5 = 20 - 2x$$
Add $3x$ to both sides and simplify.
$$-5 = 20 + x$$
Add -20 to both sides and simplify.
$$-25 = x$$
$\{-25\}$

The method of expanding has the advantage of avoiding the use of fractions until the last step. The method of immediately reversing the order of operations has the advantage of taking one fewer step. The choice one makes is a personal one. The important points are to study the equation carefully, consider various possibilities, and choose the method that is easiest.

Example 1 Solve. $4(y - 3) = 6 + y$

Solution Since there are variables in different terms and those terms must eventually be combined, it is probably easiest to expand first and then use the addition and multiplication properties of equations.

$$4(y - 3) = 6 + y$$

Expand. $\qquad\qquad\qquad\qquad\qquad 4y - 12 = 6 + y$
Add $-y$ to both sides and simplify. $\quad 3y - 12 = 6$
Add 12 to both sides and simplify. $\qquad 3y = 18$
Divide both sides by 3 and simplify. $\qquad y = 6$

Answer $\{6\}$

Check $4(y - 3) = 6 + y$
$4(6 - 3) \overset{?}{=} 6 + 6$
$4(3) = 12$ True!

Example 2 Solve. $4m - 3(m + 4) = m - 2 + 5m$

Solution Since the variable occurs in more than one term on each side, expand and simplify each side of the equation first. Then use the properties of equations to solve.

$$4m - 3(m + 4) = m - 2 + 5m$$

Expand the left side. $\qquad\qquad\qquad 4m - 3m - 12 = m - 2 + 5m$
Combine like terms on each side. $\qquad m - 12 = 6m - 2$
Add $-6m$ to each side and simplify. $\quad -5m - 12 = -2$
Add 12 to each side and simplify. $\qquad -5m = 10$
Divide each side by -5 and simplify. $\qquad m = -2$

Answer $\{-2\}$

Check $4m - 3(m + 4) = m - 2 + 5m$
$4(-2) - 3(-2 + 4) \overset{?}{=} -2 - 2 + 5(-2)$
$-8 - 3(2) \overset{?}{=} -4 - 10$
$-8 - 6 \overset{?}{=} -4 - 10$
$-14 = -14$ True!

CHECK UNDERSTANDING

• Describe two different first steps for solving these equations.

$2(x + 1) = 8$ (Expand $2(x + 1)$; Divide both sides by 2.)

$\frac{6x + 3}{3} = 5$ (Multiply both sides by 3; Write $6x + 3$ as $3(2x + 1)$.)

CLASSROOM EXERCISES

Students should discuss each step in the solutions. If additional classroom exercises are needed, exercises 14–15 can be discussed.

ASSIGNMENT GUIDE

Basic   1–20 all, Review Exercises
Average   9–31 all, Review Exercises
Enriched   16–44 all, Review Exercises

PRACTICE WORKSHEET 14

120

EXTRA PRACTICE, page 623

Some people want to avoid having to divide by a negative number in solving equations. They would prefer this alternative solution of Example 2:

$$4m - 3(m + 4) = m - 2 + 5m$$

Expand the left side. $4m - 3m - 12 = m - 2 + 5m$
Combine like terms on each side. $m - 12 = 6m - 2$
Add $-m$ to each side and simplify. $-12 = 5m - 2$
Add 2 to each side and simplify. $-10 = 5m$
Divide both sides by 5 and simplify. $-2 = m$

Answer: {−2}

■ CLASSROOM EXERCISES

Describe the first step you would use in solving each equation. State the reason for your choice. Do not solve.

1. $5(x - 6) = 40$
Multiply both sides by $\frac{1}{5}$.

2. $5(x - 6) = 41$
Expand the left side.

3. $2y + 6y = 15 - 2y + 8$
Simplify each side.

Solve.

4. $3(x + 1) = 36$ {11}

5. $5(a - 4) = 39$ $\left\{\frac{59}{5}\right\}$

6. $3x - 3(5 - x) = 40$ $\left\{\frac{55}{6}\right\}$

7. $2y + 8 - 3y = 24$ {−16}

8. $5b = 2(3b - 8)$ {16}

9. $2(4x + 1) = 3(4 + 2x)$ {5}

■ WRITTEN EXERCISES

Solve.

A   **1.** $5(a - 3) = 20$ {7}

2. $3(a - 6) = 15$ {11}

3. $2(b + 4) = 20$ {6}

4. $4(b + 7) = 12$ {−4}

5. $3(c - 6) = 8$ $\left\{\frac{26}{3}\right\}$

6. $5(c - 4) = 12$ $\left\{\frac{32}{5}\right\}$

7. $6d + 3(d + 2) = 30$ $\left\{\frac{8}{3}\right\}$

8. $3d + 6(d + 2) = 30$ {2}

9. $5(k + 3) = 2(k + 10)$ $\left\{\frac{5}{3}\right\}$

10. $6(k + 3) = 4(k + 7)$ {5}

11. $6(n - 4) = 3n$ {8}

12. $5(n - 3) = 2n$ {5} $\left\{\frac{5}{3}\right\}$

13. $5(2p + 3) = 50$ $\left\{\frac{7}{2}\right\}$

14. $2(5p + 3) = 50$ $\left\{\frac{22}{5}\right\}$

15. $2 - 3(x + 4) = 8$ {−6}

16. $3 - 2(x + 4) = 8$ $\left\{-\frac{13}{2}\right\}$

17. $10 = 3(5 - x)$ $\left\{\frac{5}{3}\right\}$

18. $20 = 5(3 - x)$ {−1}

19. $2(3 - 2x) = 3(4 - x)$ {−6}

20. $3(2 - 3x) = 4(3 - x)$ $\left\{-\frac{6}{5}\right\}$

B   **21.** $2x + 3x + 5x - 4x - x = 2x + 10$ $\left\{\frac{10}{3}\right\}$

22. $6x + 3x - 7x + 5x - 4x = x + 10$ {5}

23. $5x + \frac{1}{2}(x - 4) = 3(x + 2) - 6x + 3$ $\left\{\frac{22}{17}\right\}$

24. $7x + 4(x - 5) + 2(x + 5) = 10x + 1$ $\left\{\frac{11}{3}\right\}$

25. $x + 2(x - 1) = 3x$ ∅

26. $5x - x + 2(3 + x) = 0$ {−1}

27. $(x - 2) - 2(x - 3) = 2x - 5$ {3}

28. $6x - 3(2 - x) = -6 + x$ {0}

29. $\frac{1}{2}(a + 4) = 5$ {6}

30. $\frac{1}{3}(a + 12) = 8$ {12}

31. Solve $2(1 - t) = 3$ two ways: (a) by first expanding the left side of the equation; (b) by first using the multiplication property of equations. Which method do you prefer and why? $\left\{-\frac{1}{2}\right\}$; Answers will vary.

Solve.

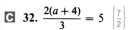 32. $\dfrac{2(a + 4)}{3} = 5$ $\left\{\frac{7}{2}\right\}$

33. $\dfrac{3(x + 2)}{4} = 4$ $\left\{\frac{10}{3}\right\}$

34. $\left(x - \dfrac{2}{3}\right)6 = \left(x - \dfrac{3}{4}\right)8$ (1)

35. $\left(x + \dfrac{2}{3}\right)6 = \left(x + \dfrac{3}{4}\right)8$ (−1)

36. $2[3 + 4(x + 5)] = 5[4 + 3(x + 2)]$ $\left\{-\frac{4}{7}\right\}$

37. $4[3 - 2(x + 5)] = 5[2 + 4(x - 3)]$ $\left\{\frac{11}{14}\right\}$

38. $\dfrac{1}{3}(6 - 3a) = -12$ (14)

39. $2x = -\dfrac{1}{2}(4x - 8)$ (1)

40. $4(n - 7) - 2(1 - 3n) = 6n$ $\left\{\frac{15}{2}\right\}$

41. $\dfrac{1}{2}(4b + 1) + \dfrac{1}{4}(6b - 2) = 7$ (2)

42. $x - 5(x + 2) = x + 3(3 - 2x)$ (19)

43. $2(5a - 4) - 3(a - 5) = 8(2a - 7)$ (7)

44. Solve the equation in the Preview to determine how old Diophantus was at his death. 84

■ REVIEW EXERCISES

Write each of the following in algebraic symbols. [2–1]

1. The absolute value of negative three equals the absolute value of three.

2. The opposite of negative five equals the absolute value of negative five. $-(-5) = |-5|$ $|-3| = |3|$.

Simplify. [2–2]

3. $-3\dfrac{1}{2} + \left(-4\dfrac{1}{2}\right)$ −8

4. $-4.1 + 5.7$ 1.6

Simplify. [2–3]

5. $-12 - (-10)$ −2

6. $45 - 63$ −18

Simplify. [2–4]

7. $-5(25)$ −125

8. $-12\left(-\dfrac{3}{4}\right)$ 9

Simplify. [2–5]

9. $-27 \div 3$ −9

10. $-18 \div -\dfrac{2}{3}$ 27

Strategy for Success   Doing homework

Make a note in the margin of your homework paper of anything that you don't understand or cannot do. Then you can ask these questions during your next class.

WRITTEN EXERCISES

Exercises 36 and 37 have grouping symbols within grouping symbols. Explain that expanding is used to remove the innermost grouping symbols first. For example:

$$5 + 4[x + 3(x + 2)] = 17$$
$$5 + 4(x + 3x + 6) = 17$$
$$5 + 4x + 12x + 24 = 17$$
$$16x + 29 = 17$$
$$16x = -12$$
$$x = \frac{-12}{16} = -\frac{3}{4}$$
$$\{-¾\}$$

ENRICHMENT PROBLEM

• Write and simplify an algebraic expression to show how this puzzle works.

Pick any number. Multiply by 12. Subtract 18. Take ⅙ of this number. Add 3. Divide by 2. The result is the original number.

Let $x =$ the number.

$12x \rightarrow 12x - 18 \rightarrow \dfrac{1}{6}(12x - 18)$

or $2x - 3 \rightarrow 2x - 3 + 3$ or $2x \rightarrow$

$\dfrac{2x}{2}$ or x.

Solve.

1. $3(x + 4) = 14$ $\{2/3\}$
2. $5(a - 4) = 3a$ $\{10\}$
3. $5 + 3(n - 7) = 10$ $\{82/3\}$
4. $7(c + 2) = 3(c - 3)$ $\{-23/4\}$
5. $5 - 2(y - 4) = 19$ $\{-3\}$

PURPOSE

Solving equations can be extended to formulas in which coefficients and other quantities are represented by letters. Generalizing equation-solving techniques to these applications shows greater command of these techniques. This skill is especially useful in rewriting formulas in desired forms.

PREVIEW

The learning of *some* facts is necessary. The saying "It's wise to memorize" has its value. However, it's impossible to memorize everything. A more efficient and practical use of time and effort is to learn how a few facts can be used to generate others. By the use of only a few basic principles, algebra has been developed into an extensive body of knowledge.

LESSON

As you explain how to solve literal equations, emphasize that exactly the same techniques are used as in solving other equations. The only difference is that it is usually not possible to simplify the resulting expression in literal equations. Therefore, the work is somewhat "messier."

Note the use of subscripts on variables such as b_1 and b_2. With subscripts, the same letter can be used for many variables; the alphabet no longer limits us to just 26 variables.

We assume that no denominator is ever zero. For example, in Example 1 we assume that $l \neq 0$ and $h \neq 0$. In Example 2 we assume that $h \neq 0$.

OBJECTIVE 3–8

To solve literal equations for a given variable.   You may wish to spend two days on this section. Refer to the Pacing Chart.

3–8 Solving Literal Equations

Preview

The human brain has a remarkable capacity to store and recall information. For example, the average person uses approximately 25,000 words. However, most people prefer to memorize as few facts as necessary. Why try to remember two facts if one will do!

In this lesson we will see how one formula can be used to generate other formulas. Then, for example, you can memorize just one of the three equivalent distance-rate-time formulas and derive the other two whenever you need them: $d = rt \quad r = \dfrac{d}{t} \quad t = \dfrac{d}{r}$

■ LESSON

This formula relates temperature measurements on the Fahrenheit *(F)* scale to those on the Celsius *(C)* scale:

$$F = \frac{9}{5}C + 32$$

We can use the formula to change measurements from Celsius to Fahrenheit. For example, to change 10°C to Fahrenheit, substitute 10 for *C:*

$$F = \frac{9}{5}(10) + 32$$

$$F = 18 + 32$$
$$F = 50 \qquad \text{Thus, 10°C is equivalent to 50°F.}$$

The same formula can be used to change 23°F to Celsius.

$$23 = \frac{9}{5}C + 32$$

$$-9 = \frac{9}{5}C$$

$$-5 = C \qquad \text{Thus, 23°F is equivalent to } -5°C.$$

Notice that it is easier to use the formula $F = \dfrac{9}{5}C + 32$ to change from degrees Celsius to degrees Fahrenheit than to change from degrees Fahrenheit to degrees Celsius. That is because the formula is in the form "$F = \underline{\ ?\ }$." If we had many Fahrenheit temperatures to change to Celsius temperatures, we would want to have a formula in the form "$C = \underline{\ ?\ }$." We can change from one form to the other by using equation-solving skills.

Start with the equation	$F = \dfrac{9}{5}C + 32$
Add -32 *to both sides and simplify.*	$F - 32 = \dfrac{9}{5}C$
Multiply both sides by $\dfrac{5}{9}$ *and simplify.*	$\dfrac{5}{9}(F - 32) = C$
Use the symmetric property of equations.	$C = \dfrac{5}{9}(F - 32)$

Some experts suggest that teachers should use mathematical language precisely, but that in order to encourage open communication, they should not expect the same precision from students. For example, they suggest that teachers refer to 3.14 as an approximation for π. However, once that is understood, students can be allowed to speak as though 3.14 is equal to π.

Formulas and other equations containing more than one variable are called **literal equations.**

$$i = prt \qquad ab = c + d \qquad A = bh \qquad A = \frac{1}{2}h(b_1 + b_2)$$

A literal equation can be solved for any of its variables. For example, when the equation $i = prt$ is written in the form $p = \dfrac{i}{rt}$, it has been solved for p. Literal equations are solved using the sames properties that were used to solve other equations.

Example 1   Solve $V = lwh$ for w.

Solution	
	$V = lwh$
Multiply both sides by $\dfrac{1}{lh}$.	$\dfrac{V}{lh} = \dfrac{lwh}{lh}$
Simplify.	$\dfrac{V}{lh} = w$
Use the symmetric property of equations.	$w = \dfrac{V}{lh}$

Example 2

The formula for the area of a trapezoid is given below:

$$A = \frac{1}{2}h(b_1 + b_2)$$

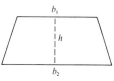

In this formula, h is the length of the altitude and b_1 and b_2 are the lengths of the two bases. The 1 and 2 in b_1 and b_2 are **subscripts** that indicate that b_1 and b_2 are related to each other (they are both lengths of bases) but are different variables. Subscripts should not be confused with exponents: b_2 means the length of the lower base of the trapezoid shown above, while b^2 means $b \cdot b$.

Solve the formula for b_1.

Solution	
	$A = \dfrac{1}{2}h(b_1 + b_2)$
Multiply both sides by $\dfrac{2}{h}$.	$\dfrac{2}{h} \cdot A = \dfrac{2}{h} \cdot \dfrac{1}{2}h(b_1 + b_2)$
Simplify the right side.	$\dfrac{2}{h} \cdot A = b_1 + b_2$
Simplify the left side.	$\dfrac{2A}{h} = b_1 + b_2$
Add $-b_2$ to both sides.	$\dfrac{2A}{h} - b_2 = b_1$
Use the symmetric property of equations.	$b_1 = \dfrac{2A}{h} - b_2$

ADDITIONAL EXAMPLES

Example 1.

Solve. $A = \dfrac{3}{4}B - 24$ for B.

Add 24 to both sides.

$$A + 24 = \frac{3}{4}B$$

Multiply both sides by $\dfrac{4}{3}$.

$$\frac{4}{3}(A + 24) = B$$

Simplify.

$$\frac{4}{3}A + 32 = B$$

Use the symmetric property of equations.

$$B = \frac{4}{3}A + 32$$

Example 2.

Solve for c. $ac + bc = d$

Use the distributive property.

$$(a + b)c = d$$

Divide both sides by $(a + b)$.

[Note: $(a + b) \neq 0$]

$$\frac{(a + b)c}{a + b} = \frac{d}{a + b}$$

Simplify. $c = \dfrac{d}{a + b}$

CHECK UNDERSTANDING

• What is the first operation to be done to both sides in solving for x?

$ax + b = c$ (Add $-b$.)
$a(x + b) = c$ (Divide by a.)
$abx = c$ (Divide by ab.)

PROBLEM-SOLVING NOTE
Checking answers

Solving a literal equation for a different variable means to find an equivalent equation in the desired form. How can we be sure the new equation is equivalent to the original?

For example, is $h = \dfrac{A}{2b} - b^2$ equivalent to the original equation $A = 2bh + b^2$? (No)

Remind students that substituting simple values for variables is a quick check to show when equations are *not* equivalent (in the example above, let b and h equal 1 and solve for A in each equation).

CLASSROOM EXERCISES

In classroom exercise 1, any one of the formulas *could* be considered basic, with the remaining three developed from it. In practice, $i = prt$ (interest = principal × rate × time) is the formula usually learned.

EXTRA PRACTICE, page 623
COMPUTER WORKSHEET 5

■ CLASSROOM EXERCISES

1. Explain why it is necessary to memorize only one of these four formulas.
The four formulas are equivalent.
$$i = prt \qquad p = \frac{i}{rt} \qquad r = \frac{i}{pt} \qquad t = \frac{i}{pr}$$

2. Solve for h. $A = bh$ $h = \frac{A}{b}$ **3.** Solve for b. $A = \frac{1}{2}bh$ $b = \frac{2A}{h}$ **4.** Solve for n. $C = 2n + 5$
$n = \frac{C-5}{2}$

■ WRITTEN EXERCISES

Solve the literal equation for n.

A
1. $an = 7$ $\frac{7}{a}$
2. $pn = -2$ $\frac{-2}{p}$
3. $\frac{n}{r} = 0.2$ $0.2r$
4. $\frac{n}{x} = \frac{3}{4}$ $\frac{3}{4}x$

5. $a + n = 15$ $15 - a$
6. $c - n = 45$ $c - 45$
7. $2n - j = 10$ $\frac{j+10}{2}$
8. $10n - t = 5$ $\frac{t+5}{10}$

Solve the literal equation for the indicated variable.

9. $ab + 2 = c,$
  for a $a = \frac{c-2}{b}$
10. $ab - 5 = c,$
  for b $b = \frac{c+5}{a}$
11. $pq = r + 3,$
  for p $p = \frac{r+3}{q}$
12. $pq = 8 - s,$
  for q $q = \frac{8-s}{p}$

13. $3q = r + s,$
  for r $r = 3q - s$
14. $3q = r + s,$
  for s $s = 3q - r$
15. $3x + 4y = 12,$
  for y $y = \frac{12-3x}{4}$
16. $3x + 4y = 12,$
  for x $x = \frac{12-4y}{3}$

17. $5x + 10 = 10y + 20$, for x $x = 2y + 2$
18. $5x + 10 = 10y + 20$, for y $y = \frac{x-2}{2}$

19. $y = \frac{1}{2}x + 3$, for x $x = 2y - 6$
20. $y = \frac{1}{3}x + 4$, for x $x = 3y - 12$

21. $2x - 3y = 18,$
  for y $y = \frac{2x-18}{3}$
22. $3x - 2y = 18,$
  for y $y = \frac{3x-18}{2}$
23. $3x_1 + 4x_2 = 24,$
  for x_2 $x_2 = \frac{24-3x_1}{4}$
24. $3x_1 + 4x_2 = 24,$
  for x_1 $x_1 = \frac{24-4x_2}{3}$

B
25. $rs + t = w,$
  for r $r = \frac{w-t}{s}$
26. $a(b + c) = d,$
  for c $c = \frac{d}{a} - b$
27. $ax + by = z,$
  for x $x = \frac{z-by}{a}$
28. $x_1x_2 = x_3x_4,$
  for x_3 $x_3 = \frac{x_1x_2}{x_4}$

29. A formula for the area of a trapezoid is A $= \frac{1}{2}h(b_1 + b_2)$.
  a. Solve for h. $h = \frac{2A}{b_1 + b_2}$
  b. Find h when $A = 240$, $b_1 = 11$, and $b_2 = 21$. $h = 15$

30. A formula for the expansion of a steel rod is $l = l_o(1 + at)$.
  a. Solve for t. $t = \left(\frac{l}{l_o} - 1\right) \div a$
  b. Find t when $l = 11$, $l_o = 10$, and $a = 2$. $t = \frac{1}{20}$

Solve each formula for x_1 and x_2.

C
31. $x_1x_3 + x_2 = 10$
$x_1 = \frac{10 - x_2}{x_3}$, $x_2 = 10 - x_1x_3$
32. $x_1(x_2 - x_3) = 10$
$x_1 = \frac{10}{x_2 - x_3}$, $x_2 = \frac{10}{x_1} + x_3$
33. $x_1x_3 = 10x_2$
$x_1 = \frac{10x_2}{x_3}$, $x_2 = \frac{x_1x_3}{10}$

34. $\frac{x_1}{x_3} = x_2 + 10$
$x_1 = x_3(x_2 + 10)$, $x_2 = \frac{x_1}{x_3} - 10$
35. $x_1 - x_2x_3 = 10$
$x_1 = 10 + x_2x_3$, $x_2 = \frac{x_1 - 10}{x_3}$
36. $\frac{x_1x_3}{12} + \frac{x_2}{6} = 1$
$x_1 = \frac{12 - 2x_2}{x_3}$, $x_2 = 6 - \frac{x_1x_3}{2}$

■ REVIEW EXERCISES

Simplify.

1. $5x + (-10) - (-3x)$ $8x - 10$
2. $-3a + (-4b) - (-5a)$ $2a - 4b$ [2-6]

3. $7x + 5y - 6x - y$ $x + 4y$
4. $4r - 5s - 6r + 12s$ $-2r + 7s$ [2-7]

ASSIGNMENT GUIDE

Basic   1–23 odd, Review Exercises
Average   1–15 odd, 25–30 all, Review
          Exercises
Enriched 9–29 odd, 31–36 all, Review
          Exercises

PRACTICE WORKSHEET 14

3-8 SOLVING LITERAL EQUATIONS

■ Solve the literal equation for the variable indicated.

1. $ab = c$, for b $b = \frac{c}{a}$
2. $a + b = c$, for a $a = c - b$
3. $\frac{c}{a} = b$, for c $c = ab$
4. $5 + a = c$, for a $a = c - 5$
5. $x - 5 = y$, for x $x = y + 5$
6. $m + n = 100$, for n $n = 100 - m$
7. $2x + 6a = 8$, for x $x = \frac{4 - 3a}{}$
8. $\frac{1}{2}x - 8 = y$, for x $x = 2y + 16$
9. $ax + by = c$, for y $y = \frac{c - ax}{b}$
10. $5rs = 15$, for r $r = 3/s$
11. $5(r + s) = 15$, for r $r = 3 - s$
12. $\frac{5r}{x} = 15$, for r $r = 3s$
13. $\frac{5s}{r} = 15$, for r $r = s/3$
14. $(5 - r)s = 15$, for r $r = 5 - 15/s$
15. $s - (5 - r) = 15$, for r $r = 20 - s$
16. $\frac{r + s}{5} = 15$, for r $r = 75 - s$
17. $6j + 7 = 4j + k$, for j $j = \frac{k - 7}{2}$
18. $5 - k = n - 2k$, for k $k = n - 5$

WRITTEN EXERCISES

The situation in which the formulas are used need not be discussed.

ENRICHMENT PROBLEM

• These equations express common formulas in unfamiliar forms. Rewrite the equations in their more familiar forms.

$\frac{bh}{A} = 2$ (triangle) $A = \frac{1}{2}bh$

$\frac{A}{\pi} - r^2 = 0$ (circle) $A = \pi r^2$

$w = \frac{P}{2} - l$ (rectangle) $P = 2l + 2w$

OBJECTIVE 3–9

To write equations to represent relationships given in word problems.

Class Starter Quiz
on previous section

Solve the literal equation for the indicated variable.

1. $rs + t = w$, for s $s = \dfrac{w - t}{r}$

2. $n_1 n_2 = n_3 n_4$, for n_1 $n_1 = \dfrac{n_3 n_4}{n_2}$

3. $p(q + r) = s$, for q $q = \dfrac{s - pr}{p}$

4. $ab - cd = e$, for d $d = \dfrac{ab - e}{c}$

5. $5xy = w$, for x $x = \dfrac{w}{5y}$

3–9 Problem Solving—Writing Equations

Preview

Puzzle

I am thinking of a number. If 8 is multiplied by twice the number decreased by 4, the result is 16. What number am I thinking about?   3

You may find the number by solving the equation $8(2x - 4) = 16$. In this lesson you will write equations that fit word problems.

■ LESSON

Here is a "common sense" model for problem solving. The model has just three steps, but each step is very important.

1. *Study the problem until you understand it.*

   Upon first reading a problem, you may not understand it. Reread it—perhaps several times. Sometimes reading softly aloud helps. You may have to find the meaning of key words that are unfamiliar to you. Perhaps the relationships in the problem may not be clear. Drawing pictures, diagrams, and figures can often help you organize your thoughts and understand what is being asked and what information is given.

2. *Decide what to do and then do it.*

   You may decide to write and solve an equation. Perhaps the problem simply requires choosing the correct operation. Systematic trials can be used to solve some problems. Sometimes lists, tables, or examples from the text can be helpful. If the first method you try does not work, then try something else.

3. *Answer the question and check your answer.*

   Think about your understanding of the problem, the method you used to solve it, and the calculations you made. Ask yourself, "How sure am I that my answer is correct?" Estimate to determine whether your answer is reasonable. If your answer seems wrong solve the problem in a different way. Check your arithmetic. Don't be satisfied with your first answer.

   Thomas Edison once said: "Genius is 10% inspiration and 90% perspiration." The same can be said of problem solving. Hard work is required to solve real problems.

   You may be able to solve some word problems without writing equations. However, it is important to develop the skill to translate word problems into algebraic equations. This skill is essential when you encounter problems that cannot be solved in any other way.

PURPOSE

Using equations to solve word problems is a useful problem-solving strategy. Writing equations is an important step in the process.

PREVIEW

Have students solve the equation and check that solution in the problem.

LESSON

Emphasize that solving problems involves much thought and effort. Students should not expect to immediately write an equation as they are reading a problem for the first time. Emphasize that variables always represent numbers. In Example 1, "*a*" represents the number of years in Aretha's age. It does not represent Aretha. In another problem, "*a*" might represent the number of centimeters in Aretha's height, the number of kilograms in her mass, the number of records in her collection, the number of hours she worked, and so on. It is important that the variable be clearly defined.

   Some of the problems presented in the lesson could easily be solved using repeated trials or other methods. The goal for students should not be to simply solve the problem, but rather to develop translation skills.

   To sharpen the focus on translation skills, several exercises ask the students to write an equation that fits the problem, but not to solve the equation or answer the question that appears in the problem.

ADDITIONAL EXAMPLES

Example 1.
Doris has four times as much money as Kenneth. If Doris has 60 dollars, how much money does Kenneth have?

Let k = the number of dollars Kenneth has.
Then $4k$ = the number of dollars Doris has.

$$4k = 60$$

The solution of the equation is 15.
Kenneth has $15.

Example 2.
Together Sarah and Emily have 80 dollars. If Sarah has 30 dollars more than Emily, how much does each have?

Solution 1.
Let s = the number of dollars Sarah has.
Then $s - 30$ = the number of dollars Emily has.

$$s + (s - 30) = 80$$

The solution of the equation is 55. Therefore, Sarah has $55 and Emily has $25.

Solution 2.
Let e = the number of dollars Emily has.
Then $e + 30$ = the number of dollars Sarah has.

$$e + (e + 30) = 80$$

The solution of the equation is 25. Therefore, Emily has $25 and Sarah has $55.

Example 1 Write an equation and solve the problem.
Eric is 1.5 times as old as Aretha.
If Eric is 21 years old, how old is Aretha?

Solution Since you want Aretha's age, it makes sense to do this:

Let a = Aretha's age in years.

Then $1.5a$ = Eric's age in years.

The problem indicates that Eric is 21 years old. There are two ways to write Eric's age in years:

$$1.5a \text{ and } 21$$

This gives the equation:

$$1.5a = 21$$
$$a = 14$$

Answer Aretha is 14 years old.

Example 2 Write an equation and solve the problem.
Nancy and Carmen are saving money to buy a motorcycle. Their combined savings is $180. Carmen has saved $10 more than Nancy. How much has each saved?

Solution 1 Let n = Nancy's savings in dollars.
Then $n + 10$ = Carmen's savings in dollars.

Nancy's savings	plus	Carmen's savings	is	180
n	$+$	$(n + 10)$	$=$	180
		$2n + 10$	$=$	180
		$2n$	$=$	170
		n	$=$	85

Answer Nancy saved $85 and Carmen saved $95.

Check Have they saved $180?
$95 + $85 = $180. Yes.
Did Carmen save $10 more than Nancy?
$95 = $10 + $85. Yes.

Solution 2 Let c = Carmen's savings in dollars.
Then $c - 10$ = Nancy's savings in dollars.

$$c + (c - 10) = 180$$
$$2c - 10 = 180$$
$$2c = 190$$
$$c = 95$$

Answer Carmen saved $95 and Nancy saved $85.

Encourage a systematic procedure for solving word problems by discussing the Problem-Solving flow chart from the Teacher's Resource Binder.

James has $8 more than Chuck. Together they have $50.

- Let J be the number of dollars James has. How much does Chuck have? ($J - 8$)
- Let C be the number of dollars Chuck has. How much does James have? ($C + 8$)
- Use J and $J - 8$ to write an equation. ($J + (J - 8) = 50$)
- Solve and state how much money each boy has. (James has $29. Chuck has $21.)

Note that the answers are checked by referring to the problem itself not just to the equation. The equation may have been solved correctly, but it may be the wrong equation.

CLASSROOM EXERCISES

Answer each part (a, b, c, . . . , f) for each exercise. Some of the exercises should be worked two ways. If students are having difficulty at the end of the classroom exercises, some of the regular exercises can be worked together as a class.

Example 3 A rectangle is 2 times as long as it is wide. Its perimeter is 24 cm. What are the two dimensions?

Solution 1

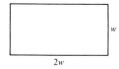

Let w = width in centimeters.
Then $2w$ = length in centimeters.
Perimeter: 24 cm and $(w + 2w + w + 2w)$cm
Equation: $w + 2w + w + 2w = 24$
$$6w = 24$$
$$w = 4$$

Answer The width is 4 cm and the length is 8 cm.

Solution 2

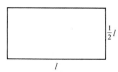

Let l = length in centimeters.

Then $\frac{1}{2}l$ = width in centimeters.

Perimeter: 24 and $l + \frac{1}{2}l + l + \frac{1}{2}l$

Equation: $l + \frac{1}{2}l + l + \frac{1}{2}l = 24$

$$3l = 24$$
$$l = 8$$

Answer The length is 8 cm and the width is 4 cm.

Note in both Example 2 and Example 3 that the two solutions use different variables and different equations, and that the equations have different solutions. However, the answers to the original problems are the same.

■ CLASSROOM EXERCISES

Carry out these directions for each problem.

   a. Represent one number by a variable.
   b. Write expressions for other numbers using the variable.
   c. Give an equation.
   d. Solve the equation.
   e. Answer the question.
   f. Check the solution.

1. Sidney is 4 years younger than Marcia. Sidney is 17 years old. How old is Marcia? $m - 4 = 17$; 21

2. Tracy scored 30 points. That was twice as many points as Kevin scored. How many points did Kevin score? $2k = 30$; 15

ASSIGNMENT GUIDE

Basic   1–13 odd, 15–18 all, Review Exercises, Self-Quiz 3
Average   1–17 odd, 19–23 all, Review Exercises, Self-Quiz 3
Enriched   9–23 odd, 24–27 all, Review Exercises, Self-Quiz 3

PRACTICE WORKSHEET 15

3-9 PROBLEM SOLVING: WRITING EQUATIONS

■ For each problem, write four things: (a) what the variable represents (always a *number* of something); (b) an equation that fits the problem; (c) the solution to the equation; and (d) the answer to the question (with proper units).

1. The width of a rectangle is 3 cm less than the length. What is the length if the width is 11 cm?
   a. Length
   b. $l - 3 = 11$
   c. {14}
   d. 14 cm

2. Lori has 37 more dimes than nickels in her collection. How many dimes does she have if she has 100 nickels?
   a. Number of dimes
   b. $x = 100 + 37$
   c. {137}
   d. 137

3. The length of a rectangle is 3 times its width. What is the width if the length is 36 cm?
   a. Width
   b. $3w = 36$
   c. {12}
   d. 12 cm

4. The diameter of Callisto (a satellite of Jupiter) is 30 times the diameter of Amalthea. What is the diameter of Amalthea if the diameter of Callisto is 3000 mi?
   a. Amalthea's diameter
   b. $30\,A = 3000$
   c. {100}
   d. 100 mi

5. The diameter of Iapetus (a satellite of Saturn) is 3.25 times the diameter of Hyperion. What is the diameter of Iapetus if the diameter of Hyperion is 220 mi?
   a. Iapetus' diameter
   b. $I = 3.25\,(220)$
   c. {715}
   d. 715 mi

6. Lawrence has saved one-third of the cost of a radio he wants. How much does the radio cost if he has saved $18?
   a. Radio's cost
   b. $1/3\,c = 18$
   c. {54}
   d. $54

WRITTEN EXERCISES

Note that in exercises 1–14 the task is to write equations, *not* to solve the equations.

Pairs of students or groups of four students might work cooperatively on the exercises. Such an arrangement often increases class productivity and better addresses individual student needs.

EXTRA PRACTICE, page 623

3. A rectangle is 4 times as long as it is wide. Its perimeter is 50 cm. What are the dimensions? $4w + w + 4w + w = 50$; width is 5 cm, length is 20 cm

4. Joan and Carrie together scored 26 points. Joan scored 6 points more than Carrie. How many points did each score? $c + c + 6 = 26$; Carrie: 10, Joan: 16

Strategy for Success **Doing assignments**

Do as much of your assignment as you can before leaving school for the day. Then if you have trouble with any of the problems, you can seek help at school.

■ WRITTEN EXERCISES

Let w = width of the rectangle in centimeters. Write an equation that fits each problem. Do *not* solve the equation.

A 1. Half the width of a rectangle is 30 cm. What is the width? $\frac{1}{2}w = 30$

2. One third the width of a rectangle is 30 cm. What is the width? $\frac{1}{3}w = 30$

3. If the width of a rectangle is increased by 5 cm, it will be 12.3 cm wide. What is the width? $w + 5 = 12.3$

4. If the width of a rectangle is decreased by 5 cm, it will be 12.3 cm wide. What is the width? $w - 5 = 12.3$

5. The length of a rectangle is 1.3 times the width. The sum of the length and width is 10.35 cm. What is the width? $1.3w + w = 10.35$

6. The length of a rectangle is 2.8 times the width. The sum of the length and width is 133 cm. What is the width? $2.8w + w = 133$

7. The length of a rectangle is 5 cm more than the width. If the perimeter is 78 cm, what is the width of the rectangle? $(w + 5) + w + (w + 5) + w = 78$

8. The length of a rectangle is 3 cm more than the width. If the perimeter is 96 cm, what is the width of the rectangle? $(w + 3) + w + (w + 3) + w = 96$

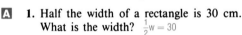

Let x = the number of dimes in Kari's collection. Write an equation that fits each problem. Do *not* solve.

9. Brad has 15 more dimes in his collection than Kari. Together they have 237 dimes. How many dimes does Kari have? $x + (x + 15) = 237$

10. Kevin has 15 fewer dimes in his collection than Kari. Together they have 237 dimes. How many dimes does Kari have? $x + (x - 15) = 237$

11. The value of the dimes in Kari's collection is $11.20. How many dimes does Kari have? $0.10x = 11.20$

12. The value of the dimes in Kari's collection is $8.70. How many dimes does Kari have? $0.10x = 8.70$

13. If Kari added 12 more dimes to her collection, she would have 200 dimes. How many dimes are in Kari's collection? $x + 12 = 200$

14. If Kari added 39 more dimes to her collection, she would have 400 dimes. How many dimes are in Kari's collection? $x + 39 = 400$

For each problem, write four things.

    a. What the variable represents (always a *number* of something).
    b. An equation that fits the problem.
    c. The solution to the equation.
    d. The answer to the question (with proper units).

15. James is 8 cm taller than Tom. James is 150 cm tall. How tall is Tom?
$t + 8 = 150$; 142 cm

16. Sue is 3 cm shorter than Heidi who is 158 cm tall. How tall is Sue?
$s = 158 - 3$; 155 cm

17. James is 32 pounds lighter than Carla. James weighs 111 pounds. How much does Carla weigh? $c - 32 = 111$; 143 pounds

18. Lana is 25 pounds heavier than her brother. Her brother weighs 89 pounds. How much does Lana weigh?
$L = 89 + 25$; 114 pounds

B **19.** Mrs. Wilson has saved one-third the cost of the car she plans to buy. How much does the car cost if she saved $2715?
$\frac{1}{3}c = 2715$; $8145

20. The combined weight of Terri and Keith is 230 pounds. Keith weighs 20 pounds more than Terri. How much does Terri weigh? $t + (t + 20) = 230$; 105 pounds

21. Gerry and Sandy bought a bicycle for $110. Sandy paid $10 more of the cost than Gerry. How much did each pay?
$g + (g + 10) = 110$; Gerry: $50, Sandy: $60

22. A rectangle is 3 m longer than it is wide. The perimeter is 34 m. What are the dimensions of the rectangle?
$w + (w + 3) + w + (w + 3) = 34$; width: 7 m, length: 10 m

23. A rectangle is 3 times as long as it is wide. The perimeter is 48 m. $w + 3w + w + 3w = 48$; width: 6 m, length: 18 m
What are the dimensions of the rectangle?

C **24.** Lyle bowled two games. His score in the first game was 18 higher than his second game score. The total was 226. What were his scores in the two games?
$n + (n + 18) = 226$; 122 and 104

25. Connie has a record collection. Joel has half as many records as Connie. Together they have 54 records. How many records does Connie have? $c + \frac{1}{2}c = 54$; 36

26. Greg has some money in a savings account. After the bank added interest to his account equal to 0.05 times the amount he had in savings, he had $126. How much was in his account before the interest was added? $x + 0.05x = 126$; $120

27. A rectangle is 1.4 times as long as it is wide. Its area is 315 cm². What is the width of the rectangle? $w(1.4w) = 315$; 15 cm

■ REVIEW EXERCISES

Simplify.   [2-8]

1. $15 - 2(2a - 4)$ $23 - 4a$

2. $3(x - 5) - 2(2x + 5)$ $-x - 25$

3. $2x - (5 - 2x) + (3 + 3x)$ $7x - 2$

Solve.   [3-7]

4. $2m - 4 = 5m + 12$ $\left\{-\frac{16}{3}\right\}$

5. $2(3n - 5) = 14$ {4}

6. $2(3x - 1) = 4(2 - x)$ {1}

PROBLEM-SOLVING NOTE
Writing equations

One way to help students write equations is to reverse the process: Give students an equation and have them make up a story about it. For example, ask the students to write a story about each of these equations:

1. $5x = 49$
2. $x + (x + 30) = 200$
3. $w + 4w + w + 4w = 150$
4. $n + (n + 1) = 67$
5. $a + (a - 5) = 23$

ENRICHMENT PROBLEM

• Five members of a bowling team scored a team total of 980. Each individual score was 10 pins different from some other score on the team and no two scores were alike. Find the individual scores.

176, 186, 196, 206, 216

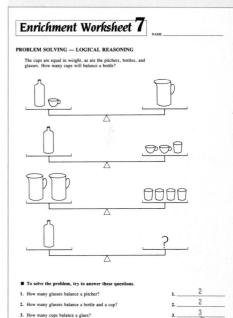

Enrichment Worksheet 7   NAME _____

PROBLEM SOLVING — LOGICAL REASONING

The cups are equal in weight, as are the pitchers, bottles, and glasses. How many cups will balance a bottle?

■ To solve the problem, try to answer these questions.

1. How many glasses balance a pitcher?	1. _2_
2. How many glasses balance a bottle and a cup?	2. _2_
3. How many cups balance a glass?	3. _3_
4. How many cups balance a bottle?	4. _5_

Can be used after Section 3-9

© D.C. Heath & Co.

Self-Quiz 3

3-7 Solve.

1. $4(n - 2) = 2n$ (4)
2. $32 - 3a = 17$ (5)
3. $3(x - 1) + 2x = 12$ (3)
4. $3n - 31 = 7 - n$ $\left[\frac{19}{2}\right]$
5. $9 - 2(x + 1) = 0$ $\left[\frac{7}{2}\right]$
6. $5(6 - x) = 2(7 - 2x)$ (16)

3-8 Solve the equation for the indicated variable.

7. $E = IR$, (Ohm's Law) for I $\quad I = \frac{E}{R}$
8. $A = 7 + 8t$, for t $\quad t = \frac{A - 7}{8}$

3-9 Using the given variable, write an equation and solve.

9. The perimeter of a square is 84 cm. Find the length (l) of one side.
$4l = 84$; 21 cm
10. Drew is four years older than Mike (M). Their ages total 24 years. How old is each? $M + (M + 4) = 24$; Mike: 10, Drew: 14

EXTENSION   Evaluating formulas on a computer

An equation in a computer program is a definition of a variable. For example, this equation

```
P = 2 * L + 2 * W
```

defines P in terms of L and W. Given values of L and W **(inputs),** the computer will compute corresponding values of P **(output).** If values of P and W are inputs, the computer cannot compute values of L using the above equation. The computer needs an equation such as:

```
L = P/2 - W
```

in order to find values of L.

   When you write equations in a computer program, you should always be sure that the equation is solved for the desired output variable in terms of the given input variables.

Write equations for a computer to use given the following inputs and outputs.

1. Inputs: the length and width of a rectangle
   Output: the area of the rectangle $\quad$ A = L · W

2. Inputs: A, B, C, and D for the equation $AX + B = CX + D$
   Output: X $\quad$ X = (D - B)/(A - C)

3. Is there a Symmetric Property of Equations for equations in a computer program? (See page 93). No

You may wish to spend two days on this section. Refer to the Pacing Chart.

To use drawings to help solve word problems.

3–10 Problem Solving—Drawing Figures

Preview   History

Archimedes (287 ?–212 B.C.) is considered one of the greatest mathematicians who ever lived. He lived in Syracuse, Sicily at the time the city was captured by the Romans. Archimedes was intently studying a geometric figure drawn in the sand when he was killed by a Roman soldier.

Mathematicians and mathematics students long ago discovered the value of pictures and diagrams in solving problems. This lesson will help you develop skill in using figures to solve problems.

Let x represent the number of pine trees in the park. Solve each problem by writing an equation.

1. There are 4 times as many trees of other types in the park as there are pines. How many pine trees are in the park if there are 155 trees in all?
   $x + 4x = 155$; 31 pine trees

2. There are 7 more oak trees than pine trees in the park. How many pine trees are in the park if 69 of the trees are either pines or oaks?
   $x + (x + 7) = 69$; 31 pine trees

3. There are 10 fewer maple trees than pine trees in the park. How many pine trees are in the park if 52 of the trees are either pines or maples?
   $x + (x - 10) = 52$; 31 pine trees

4. If the number of pine trees were doubled, there would be 62 pine trees. How many pine trees are in the park?
   $2x = 62$; 31 pine trees

5. There are twice as many elm trees as pine trees in the park. How many pine trees are in the park if 93 of the trees are either pines or elms?
   $x + 2x = 93$; 31 pine trees

PURPOSE

To solve problems, it is necessary to keep information organized and to clearly understand the relationships involved. The ability to use drawings is a skill that helps problem solvers represent information and discover relationships in a problem.

LESSON

Ask students if they used any drawings, figures, or sketches in the previous lesson. Have class members share these examples with the entire class.

■ LESSON

A good way to help yourself understand a problem, assign variables, and write equations is to draw pictures of the situation described in the problem. The pictures don't need to be "artistic." They merely should show the important relationships.

Example 1   A rectangle is 30 cm longer than it is wide. What are its dimensions if its perimeter is 88 cm?

Solution   A picture for this problem can help you set up an equation.

width $= w$

w length $= w + 30$

(... "30 cm longer than it is wide")

$w + 30$

The perimeter is 88 cm. The sum of the lengths of the sides (2 lengths plus 2 widths) also represents the perimeter. Therefore,

$$88 = l + w + l + w$$
$$= (w + 30) + w + (w + 30) + w$$
$$88 = 4w + 60$$
$$28 = 4w$$
$$7 = w$$

Answer   The width of the rectangle is 7 cm and the length is 37 cm.

Check   The check is left to the student.

ADDITIONAL EXAMPLES

Example 1.
The length of a rectangle is 20 cm more than the width. What are the dimensions of the rectangle if its perimeter is 100 cm?

Let w = the number of centimeters in the width.
This drawing helps.

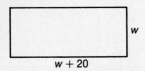

$$w + (w + 20) + w + (w + 20) = 100$$
$$w = 15$$

The width of the rectangle is 15 cm and the length is 35 cm.

Example 2.
Susan and Diane earned a total of $200. Diane earned ¼ as much as Susan. How much did each earn?

This drawing helps.

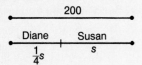

If s = the number of dollars Susan earned, then $\frac{1}{4}s$ = the number of dollars Diane earned.

$$s + \frac{1}{4}s = 200$$

The solution of the equation is 160. Susan earned $160 and Diane earned $40.

CHECK UNDERSTANDING

Elaine and Maria scored a total of 18 points in a basketball game. Maria scored twice as many points as Elaine.

- Draw a diagram using a segment to represent the total number of points scored.
- Separate the segment into two parts to represent the points scored by each girl.
- Use a variable to represent the number of points scored by one girl.
- Write an expression for the number of points scored by the other girl.
- Write an equation, solve it, and answer the question.

  Elaine = 6 points; Maria = 12 points.

132

Example 2   Harry and Juan bought a hang glider for $900. Harry paid one half as much as Juan. How much did each pay?

Solution   You can represent the amount they each spent by segments.

Juan |————————————————|
Harry |——————————|

The amount they spent *together* can be represented by joining segments end-to-end.

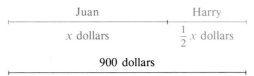

Now pick a variable for one dollar amount. Write a variable expression for the other dollar amount.

Two ways of writing the total length gives an equation.

$$x + \frac{1}{2}\,x = 900$$

$$\frac{3}{2}\,x = 900$$

$$x = 600$$

Answer   Juan spent $600, and Harry spent $300.

Check   The check is left to the student.

■ CLASSROOM EXERCISES

1. Draw a picture for this situation.
   You can drive straight from Cedar City to Nestone, a distance of 10 miles, or you can drive straight east for 8 miles and then straight north for 6 miles.

2. Draw a picture for this problem.
   James scored 4 points fewer than Wes. Together they scored 40 points. How many did each score?

Students should realize that everyone errs sometimes —students, teachers, textbook authors, and publishers. They should report any apparent errors, even though they may find instead that they misunderstood

the material. Feeling free to challenge whether materials and ideas are correct, students will be more critical learners and sometimes uncover genuine errors.

■ WRITTEN EXERCISES

Draw and label a figure to organize the information in these problems. Do *not* solve the problems.

A

1. A rectangle is 20 cm longer than it is wide. What is its length if its perimeter is 92 cm?

2. The width of a rectangle is 10 cm less than its length. What is its width if its perimeter is 52 cm?

3. A recipe calls for 50 grams more flour than sugar. How much of each are in 380 grams of a flour-sugar mixture?

4. A recipe calls for 500 mL (milliliters) more apple juice than cranberry juice. How much of each are in 1000 mL of the apple-cranberry juice mixture?

5. Ted is 23 years older than Theresa. Vin is 2 years younger than Theresa. How old is Theresa if the sum of their ages is 60 years?

6. Heather is 3 years older than Steve. Vickie is 20 years older than Steve. How old is Steve if the sum of their three ages is 68 years?

7. One side of a triangle is 10 cm longer than another side. The third side is 12 cm longer than the shortest side. How long is the shortest side if the perimeter is 67 cm? (Draw a triangle. Label one side x cm. Label the other two sides in terms of x.)

8. One side of a triangle is 1.2 times as long as another side. The third side is 1.5 times as long as the shortest side. How long is the shortest side if the perimeter is 74 cm? (Draw a triangle. Label the shortest side x cm. Label the other two sides in terms of x.)

For each problem, write five things.

    a. What the variable represents (always a *number* of something).
    b. A figure that helps organize the information.
    c. An equation that fits the problem.
    d. The solution to the equation.
    e. The answer to the question.

9. The length of a rectangular cutting board is 7 cm more than its width. What is the width of the board if its perimeter is 94 cm?
$w + (w + 7) + w + (w + 7) = 94$; 20 cm

10. The width of a rectangular desk is 8 cm less than its length. What is the length of the desk if its perimeter is 176 cm? $l + (l - 8) + l + (l - 8) = 176$; 48 cm

11. Robert and Jonathan bought a band saw for $250. Jonathan paid $80 more than Robert. How much did Robert pay? $x + (x + 80) = 250$; $85

12. Melanie and Shawn bought a chain saw for $420. Melanie paid $120 less than Shawn. How much did Melanie pay? $x + (x + 120) = 420$; $150

ADDITIONAL ANSWERS
■ **Classroom Exercises**

1.

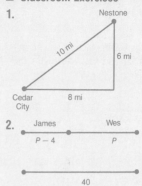

2.
  James   Wes
     $P - 4$ P

         40

ASSIGNMENT GUIDE

Basic   1–8 all, 9–13 odd, Review Exercises
Average 1–17 odd, Review Exercises
Enriched 15–22 all, Review Exercises

Note: Additional Answers (drawings) for Written Exercises 1–22 are on pages 134, 135, and 136.

PRACTICE WORKSHEET 16

3-10 PROBLEM SOLVING — DRAWING FIGURES

■ For each problem, write five things: (a) what the variable represents (always a *number* of something); (b) a figure that helps organize the information; (c) an equation that fits the problem; (d) the solution to the equation; and (e) the answer to the question (with proper units).

1. A sheet of paper is 6 cm longer than it is wide. The perimeter of the paper is 98 cm. What is the width of the paper?
    a. Width
    c. $2w + 2(w + 6) = 98$
    d. [21.5]
    e. 21.5 cm

2. A rectangular flower garden is twice as long as it is wide. What is the width of the garden if its perimeter is 12 m?
    a. Width
    c. $2w + 2(2w) = 12$
    d. [2]
    e. 2 m

3. One side of a triangle is 2 m longer than the shortest side. The longest side is 4 m longer than the shortest side. How long is the shortest side if the perimeter of the triangle is 36 m?
    a. Length of shortest side
    c. $s + (s + 2) + (s + 4) = 36$
    d. [10]
    e. 10 m

4. A wire 10 cm long is cut so that one piece is 2 cm longer than the other piece. How long is the shorter piece of wire?
    a. Length of shorter piece
    c. $s + (s + 2) = 10$
    d. [4]
    e. 4 cm

5. A 12-ft board is cut once. One piece is twice as long as the other. How long is the shorter piece?
    a. Length of shorter piece
    c. $s + 2s = 12$
    d. [4]
    e. 4 ft

ENRICHMENT PROBLEMS

- Try to draw a triangle with sides 8 cm, 4 cm, and 14 cm.

  Can't be done.

- Two sides of a triangle are x cm and $2x$ cm. What can you say about the length of the third side?

  $x <$ third side $< 3x$

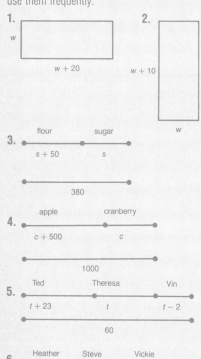
134

EXTRA PRACTICE, page 624

13. The Wildcat football team scored 7 more points in the second half of the game than it did in the first half. How many points did the Wildcats score in the second half if they scored 27 points in the game? $x + (x - 7) = 27$; 17

14. The Lynx football team scored 4 more points in the first half of the game than it did in the second half. How many points did the Lynx score in the first half if they scored 24 points in the game? $x + (x - 4) = 24$; 14

Ⓑ 15. One side of a quadrilateral is 4 cm longer than the shortest side. Another side is 5 cm longer than the shortest side. The longest side is 10 cm longer than the shortest side. How long is the shortest side if the perimeter of the quadrilateral is 139 cm? (A quadrilateral is a 4-sided polygon.)
$x + (x + 4) + (x + 5) + (x + 10) = 139$; 30 cm

16. One side of a quadrilateral is 10 cm longer than the shortest side. Another side is 20 cm longer than the shortest side. The longest side is 30 cm longer than the shortest side. How long is the shortest side if the perimeter of the quadrilateral is 820 cm? $x + (x + 10) + (x + 20) + (x + 30) = 820$; 190 cm

17. Cliff drove on a straight road from Town A to Town B, a distance of 35 miles. Darlene drove a route which was 7 miles longer. If one leg of her trip was 16 miles long, how long was the rest of her trip? $16 + x = 35 + 7$; 26 miles

18. When Julius had driven from home to Town A, and then halfway back home he had covered 126 miles. How far did he live from Town A?
$x + \frac{1}{2}x = 126$; 84 miles

Ⓒ 19. A carpenter cut a 12-foot board into three unequal lengths. Each of the shorter lengths was $\frac{1}{2}$ foot less than the next larger length. Find the three lengths. $x + (x + \frac{1}{2}) + (x + 1) = 12$; $3\frac{1}{2}$ ft, 4 ft, $4\frac{1}{2}$ ft

20. Crystal, Sabrina, and Felipe divided $9 unevenly. Crystal received 50¢ less than the greatest amount, and Felipe received 25¢ more than the least amount. How much money did each receive?
$x + (x - 50) + (x - 50 + 25) = 900$; Crystal: $2.75, Sabrina: $3.25, Felipe, $3.00

21. The length of the sides of a triangle, in centimeters, are consecutive whole numbers. What is the length of the shortest side if the perimeter of the triangle is 96 cm? $x + (x + 1) + (x + 2) = 96$; 31 cm

22. The lengths of the sides of a quadrilateral, in centimeters, are consecutive whole numbers. What is the length of the longest side if the perimeter of the quadrilateral is 162 cm? $x + (x - 1) + (x - 2) + (x - 3) = 162$; 42 cm

■ **REVIEW EXERCISES**

Complete.

1. 1 kilogram = __?__ grams 1000
2. 1 liter = __?__ milliliters 1000
3. 1.5 liters = __?__ milliliters 1500
4. 27.3 centimeters = __?__ meters 0.273

Simplify.

[1–2]

5. $\dfrac{5 \cdot 2 - 1}{3}$ 3
6. $8 - 4 \cdot 2 + 3$ 3

7.

8.

9. 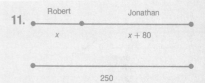 10.

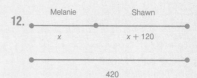

11.

12.

13.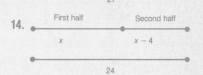

14.

15.

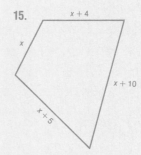

■ CHAPTER SUMMARY

• Vocabulary

• The symmetric property of equations   [3-2]
  For all numbers a and b,
    if $a = b$ then $b = a$.

• Properties of equations
    For all real numbers a, b, and c:
  Addition: If $a = b$, then $a + c = b + c$.   [3-3]
  Multiplication: If $a = b$, then $ac = bc$.   [3-4]

• Steps in solving linear equations   [3-6]
  1. Simplify the expressions on both sides.
  2. Collect the variables on one side.
  3. Use the addition and multiplication properties of equations.

• To *solve* a literal equation for one of its variables, find an   [3-9]
  equivalent equation that has the variable on one side of the
  equation and does not contain the variable on the other side.

■ CHAPTER REVIEW

3-1   **Objective** To solve an equation by repeated trials.

For each equation below, state which of the numbers $\{-2, -1, 0, 1, 2\}$
are solutions. Write "none" if there is no solution in the domain.

1. $x + 18 = 17$ -1 **2.** $\dfrac{x}{-2} = -1$ 2 **3.** $x^2 + 2 = 3x$ $1, 2$

3-2   **Objective** To write equations that are equivalent to a given equation.

State whether the two equations are equivalent.

4. $3x + 2 = 20$ **5.** $x = 6$

    $3x = 22$ Not equivalent $\dfrac{x}{6} = 36$ Not equivalent

16.

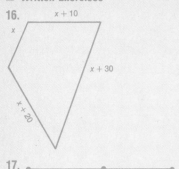

17.

18.

19.

20.

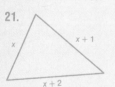

21.

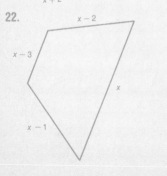

22.

136

3–3 **Objective** To solve equations by adding (or subtracting) the same quantity to (from) both sides.

Solve by writing a series of equivalent equations.

6. $7x = 6x - 5$ $\{-5\}$ **7.** $6x + 5 = 5x + 10$ $\{5\}$ **8.** $3x - 2\frac{1}{2} = 4x + 3\frac{1}{2}$ $\{-6\}$

3–4 **Objective** To solve equations by multiplying (or dividing) both sides by the same number.

Solve by writing simpler equivalent equations.

9. $3x = -10$ $\left\{-\frac{10}{3}\right\}$ **10.** $\frac{3}{4}r = \frac{1}{2}$ $\left\{\frac{2}{3}\right\}$ **11.** $-4y = 13$ $\left\{-\frac{13}{4}\right\}$

3–5 **Objective** To use several properties of equations to solve equations.

Solve.

12. $6z + 7 = 17$ $\left\{\frac{5}{3}\right\}$ **13.** $\frac{x}{4} - 10 = 8$ $\{72\}$

14. $\frac{x + 8}{3} = 12$ $\{28\}$ **15.** $6x - 3 = 2x + 11$ $\left\{\frac{7}{2}\right\}$

3–6 **Objective** To solve equations of the form $a - bx = c$.

Solve.

16. $7 - 2x = -3$ $\{5\}$ **17.** $5 - \frac{y}{3} = 8$ $\{-9\}$ **18.** $-12 - 3x = 5$ $\left\{-\frac{17}{3}\right\}$

3–7 **Objective** To solve linear equations in one variable.

Solve.

19. $6(a - 2) = 24$ $\{6\}$ **20.** $5y + 3(y - 4) = 20$ $\{4\}$

21. $5(x - 3) = 2(3 - x)$ $\{3\}$ **22.** $10 - 2(4 - x) = 15$ $\left\{\frac{13}{2}\right\}$

3–8 **Objective** To solve a literal equation for any one of its variables.

Solve each literal equation for the variable indicated.

23. $d = rt$, **24.** $P = 2l + 2w$, **25.** $y = 3x - 7$,
for r $r = \frac{d}{t}$ for w $w = \frac{P - 2l}{2}$ for x $x = \frac{y + 7}{3}$

3–9 **Objective** To solve problems by writing equations.

For each problem define a variable and write an equation. Then solve the equation, and answer the question.

26. A rectangle is 3 times as long as it is wide. The perimeter of the rectangle is 52 m. What are the length and width?
$w + 3w + w + 3w = 52$; width: 6.5 m, length: 19.5 m

27. Mark is 23 pounds heavier than Joseph. If Mark weighs 151 pounds, how much does Joseph weigh? $j + 23 = 151$; 128 pounds

3–10 **Objective** To use drawings to help solve problems.

Draw a figure. Then solve the problem by using an equation.

28. One side of a parallelogram is 5 cm longer than another. If the perimeter of the parallelogram is 70 cm, what are the lengths of the sides? $s + (s + 5) + s + (s + 5) = 70$; 15 cm and 20 cm

■ CHAPTER 3 SELF-TEST

Which of the numbers $\{-3, -2, -1, 0, 1\}$ are solutions of these equations?

3–1 **1.** $\dfrac{4.5}{x} - 5 = -50$ None   **2.** $x^2 = x$ 0, 1

Write the equation that results from following these directions.

3–2 **3.** $5x - 4 = x - 7$ **4.** $-6 - \dfrac{2}{3}y = 4$

    a. Subtract x from both sides.   **a.** Add 6 to both sides.
    b. Add 4 to both sides.   **b.** Multiply both sides by $-\dfrac{3}{2}$.
    c. Divide both sides by 4. $x = -\dfrac{3}{4}$
                                                  $y = -15$

Solve.

3–3 **5.** $12x - 7 = 13x + 4$ $\{-11\}$ **6.** $4t - 2\dfrac{1}{3} = 1\dfrac{2}{3} + 3t$ $\{4\}$

3–4 **7.** $-9a = 12$ $\left\{-\dfrac{4}{3}\right\}$ **8.** $\dfrac{b}{-4} = -8$ $\{32\}$

3–5 **9.** $2x + 15 = 19$ $\{2\}$ **10.** $\dfrac{1}{2}y - 3 = 1$ $\{8\}$

    11. $\dfrac{w + 4}{2} = 3.3$ $\{2.6\}$ **12.** $6(r - 1) = 36$ $\{7\}$

State what is done to the sides of the equation at each step.

3–6 **13.** Solve. $\dfrac{6 - 2s}{3} = 4$

           $6 - 2s = 12$ **a.** _____?_____ Multiply by 3.
             $-2s = 6$ **b.** _____?_____ Add -6.
               $s = -3$ **c.** _____?_____ Multiply by $-\dfrac{1}{2}$.

Solve.

3–6 **14.** $4 - \dfrac{x}{7} = 8$ $\{-28\}$ **15.** $\dfrac{1}{4}(3 - 2w) = 5$ $\left\{-\dfrac{17}{2}\right\}$

3–7 **16.** $2(p + 12) + p - 14 = 4$ $\{-2\}$ **17.** $2(k - 2) = 4 - 2k$ $\{2\}$

3–8 Solve the equation for the indicated variable.

    18. $A = 2\pi rh$, for r $r = \dfrac{A}{2\pi h}$ **19.** $y = 3 + 5x$, for x $x = \dfrac{y - 3}{5}$

Chapter 3 Test A   NAME _____

■ **Which of these numbers**
   $-3, -2, -1, 0, 1, 2, 3,$
   are solutions of the equation?

1. $3x + x = 0$ 1. 0
2. $\dfrac{9}{x} = x$ 2. −3, 3
3. $x^2 + 6 = 5x$ 3. 2, 3

■ **Write the equation that results from following the directions in order.**

4. $-x + 3 = 4x + 7$
   Add x to both sides.
   Subtract 7 from both sides.   4. −4 = 5x

■ **Solve.**

5. $9x + 2 = 10x - 4$ 5. {6}
6. $y - 3 = 2 + 2y$ 6. {−5}
7. $\dfrac{3}{5}w = 15$ 7. {25}
8. $12 = \dfrac{b}{6}$ 8. {72}
9. $\dfrac{r}{3} - 4 = 1$ 9. {15}
10. $\dfrac{x + 6}{2} = 3$ 10. {0}
11. $-5t + 0.2 = 3.2$ 11. {−0.6}
12. $5(y - 1) = 20$ 12. {5}
13. $2 - 4c = 10$ 13. {−2}
14. $7(2 - m) = 21$ 14. {−1}
15. $4d + 2(d - 1) = 22$ 15. {4}
16. $5(x - 4) = 4(x + 5)$ 16. {40}

© D.C. Heath & Co.

Chapter 3 Test A *(page 2)*   NAME _____

■ **Solve.**

17. $A = \dfrac{1}{2}bh$, for h 17. $h = \dfrac{2A}{b}$
18. $v = 5 + 32t$, for t 18. $t = \dfrac{v - 5}{32}$

■ **Write equations for these problems and solve.**

19. Jennifer is 7 cm taller than Carol. Jennifer is 148 cm tall. How tall is Carol?   19. 141 cm
20. A camera and a radio cost $80. The camera costs $14 less than the radio. How much does the radio cost?   20. $47
21. Arthur is 24 years older than Nicole. The sum of their ages is 52. How old is Arthur?   21. 38
22. The length of a rectangle is 4 times the width. The perimeter of the rectangle is 60 cm. What are the length and width?   22. 6 cm × 24 cm

★ **BONUS**

The area of a square is $16x^4y^2$ square units. What is the length of a side?   BONUS $4x^2y$

© D.C. Heath & Co.

■ Which of these numbers
    $-3, -2, -1, 0, 1, 2, 3,$
    are solutions of the equation?

1. $-2x + 2 = 0$
                                          1. 1

2. $\frac{1}{x} = x$
                                          2. $-1, 1$

3. $x^2 + 3 = 4x$
                                          3. $1, 3$

■ Write the equation that results from following the directions
    in order.

4. $-2y + 4 = -7y - 6$
    Add $7y$ to both sides.
    Subtract 4 from both sides.   4. $5y = -10$

■ Solve.

5. $8t - 2 = 9t - 6$
                                          5. $\{4\}$

6. $x - 20 = 27 + 2x$
                                          6. $\{-47\}$

7. $\frac{4}{3}a = 12$
                                          7. $\{9\}$

8. $15 = \frac{v}{5}$
                                          8. $\{75\}$

9. $\frac{w}{4} - 3 = 1$
                                          9. $\{16\}$

10. $\frac{x + 14}{7} = 6$
                                          10. $\{28\}$

11. $-4b + 0.5 = 3.5$
                                          11. $\{-0.75\}$

12. $9(r - 6) = 45$
                                          12. $\{11\}$

13. $2 - 4m = 10$
                                          13. $\{-2\}$

14. $8(5 - d) = 32$
                                          14. $\{1\}$

15. $x + 5(x - 1) = 61$
                                          15. $\{11\}$

16. $7(c - 4) = 8(c + 3)$
                                          16. $\{-52\}$

© D.C. Heath & Co.

■ Solve.

17. $i = prt$, for p
                                          17. $p = \frac{i}{rt}$

18. $a = \frac{d}{22} + 1$, for d
                                          18. $d = 22(a - 1)$

■ Write equations for these problems and solve.

19. Loren is 7 cm taller than Jonah. Loren is 151 cm tall.
    How tall is Jonah?   19. 144 cm

20. A TV set and a stereo set cost $580. The TV set costs $28 more
    than the stereo set. How much does the stereo set cost?
                                          20. $\$276$

21. Chris is 22 years older than Dory. The sum of their ages is 52.
    How old is Dory?   21. 15

22. The length of a rectangle is 3 times the width. The perimeter of the
    rectangle is 56 cm. What are the length and width?
                                          22. 7 cm × 21 cm

★ BONUS

    The area of a rectangle is $12x^2y^3$ square units. The width is $2xy$
    units. What is the length?   BONUS $6xy^2$

© D.C. Heath & Co.

3–9,   Solve by writing and solving an equation.

3–10   20. One side of a triangle is 3 cm longer than the shortest side. The
                third side is 8 cm longer than the shortest side. What is the length
                of the shortest side if the perimeter of the triangle is 59 cm?
                $x + (x + 3) + (x + 8) = 59$; 16 cm
            21. Kim and Karen bought a record for $5.50. Kim paid $5 more than
                Karen. How much did each girl pay?
                $x + (x + 5) = 5.50$; Kim: $5.25, Karen: $.25

■ PRACTICE FOR COLLEGE ENTRANCE TESTS

Choose the one best answer to each question.

1. If $2 \cdot x \cdot 3 = 9$, then $x = \underline{\ ?\ }$.

   A. $\frac{2}{27}$ **B.** 3   **C.** $1\frac{1}{2}$ **D.** 6   **E.** $\frac{2}{3}$

2. What is the sum of five consecutive integers if the middle integer is 40?

   A. 8   **B.** 40   **C.** 160   **D.** 200   **E.** 220

3. In a sequence of numbers, each number after the first is four more than
three times the previous number. If the third number is 7, what is the first
number?

   A. -1 **B.** $\frac{-1}{3}$ **C.** 0   **D.** $\frac{1}{3}$ **E.** 1

4. If $4x - 2 = 10$, then $8x = \underline{\ ?\ }$.

   A. 8   **B.** 16   **C.** 24   **D.** 32   **E.** 40

5. The operation $\boxed{\times}$ is defined for all numbers a and b as $a \boxed{\times} b = a^2 + ab$. If
$3 \boxed{\times} n = 3$, then $n = \underline{\ ?\ }$.

   A. -3 **B.** -2 **C.** -1 **D.** 1   **E.** 2

6. If $x - 3 = x + k$, then $k = \underline{\ ?\ }$.

   A. $2x - 3$ **B.** $-2x + 3$ **C.** $-2x - 3$ **D.** -3 **E.** 3

7. Erik is two years older than Juanita, and Juanita is twice as old as Zelda. If
Zelda is z years old, then an expression for Erik's age in terms of z is $\underline{\ ?\ }$.

   A. $\frac{z + 2}{2}$ **B.** $2(z + 2)$ **C.** $\frac{z - 2}{2}$ **D.** $2(z + 2)$ **E.** $2z + 2$

8. If $a - b = 5$, then $a - b - 3 = \underline{\ ?\ }$.

   A. -8 **B.** 1   **C.** 2   **D.** 4   **E.** 8

9. If a, b, and c are consecutive odd integers and $a < b < c$, then, in terms of c,
$a = \underline{\ ?\ }$.

   A. $c - 2$ **B.** $c - 3$ **C.** $c - 4$ **D.** $c + 2$ **E.** $c + 4$

10. If $1 - k^2 = m$ and $k = -2$, then $m = \underline{\ ?\ }$.

   A. -3 **B.** -1 **C.** 1   **D.** 3   **E.** 5

11. The square piece of paper shown below is folded along the diagonal with point B placed on top of point D to form a triangle. Then the triangle is folded again along the dashed line shown with point C placed on top of point A to form a smaller triangle.

The shaded portion shown in the small section is cut from all four layers of the folded paper. When the paper is unfolded, which of the following diagrams would it look like?

A.

B.

C.

D.

E.

12. If $a + b = 0$, then which of the following must be true?

   A. $a^2 = ab$ **B.** $ab = 1$ **C.** $ab = b^2$ **D.** $a - b > 0$ **E.** $a^2 = b^2$

■ CUMULATIVE REVIEW (Chapters 1–3)

1–1

a	B	r	t	y
3	0	9	18	$\frac{2}{3}$

Substitute and simplify.

   1. $t - r$ 9   **2.** $y \times r + a$ 9   **3.** $B \div t$ 0   **4.** $\frac{r}{t} + a \times y$ $2\frac{1}{2}$

1–2   Simplify.

   5. $4 \times 9 + 8$ 44   **6.** $18 - 12 \div 2$ 12   **7.** $9 \times (8 - 2)$ 54   **8.** $\frac{30 - 6}{10 + 2}$ 2

1–3   Evaluate for $x = 5$.

   9. $6x$ 30   **10.** $3x^2$ 75   **11.** $x - 2^2$ 1

1–4   State whether the expressions in each pair are equivalent.

   12. $\frac{x+2}{x+4}, \frac{x+1}{x+2}$ No   **13.** $9a - a$, $8a$ Yes

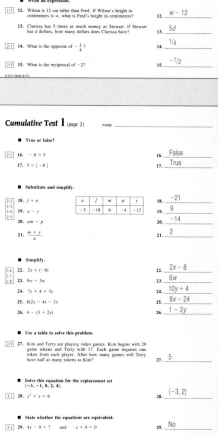

■ Solve.

3-3 3-4 3-5 3-6 3-7	**30.** $4x + 6 = 5x$	**30.** {6}
	31. $\frac{t}{-5} = 7$	**31.** {−35}
	32. $7(y + 1) = 28$	**32.** {3}
	33. $12w − 1 = 8w + 5$	**33.** {3/2}
	34. $\frac{k-1}{4} = 2$	**34.** {9}
	35. $6(1 − 2x) = 30$	**35.** {−2}

3-9 **36.** Judy and Vince paid $84 for a birthday present for their mother. Vince paid $13 less for the present than Judy paid. How much did Judy pay?

36. $48.50

© D.C. Heath & Co.

ADDITIONAL ANSWERS

■ **Cumulative Review**

48.   +1+2+3+4+5+6+7+8

Numerator	1	2	3	4	5	6	7	8	9
Denominator	4	5	6	7	8	9	10	11	12
Fraction	$\frac{1}{4}$	$\frac{2}{5}$	$\frac{3}{6}$	$\frac{4}{7}$	$\frac{5}{8}$	$\frac{6}{9}$	$\frac{7}{10}$	$\frac{8}{11}$	$\frac{9}{12}$

49.

Time	8:30	9:00	9:30	10:00	10:30	11:00	11:30
Taxi (miles)	30	60	90	120	150	180	210
Bus (miles)		25	50	75	100	125	150
Difference	30	35	40	45	50	55	60

1–5 Identify the property illustrated in each equation.

14. $2x \cdot 1 = 2x$ Identity (mult)

15. $(36 + 4y) + 5 = (4y + 36) + 5$ Commutative (add)

16. $9 + 0 = 9$ Identity (add)

17. $4 \cdot 20 + 4 \cdot x = 4 \cdot (20 + x)$ Distributive

1–6 Simplify.

18. $12a + 6b − 3a$ 9a + 6b

19. $\frac{1}{2}(8x)$ 4x

20. $8(y + 2) − 7$ 8y + 9

1–7 Let B be Bill's age in years. Write an expression for:

21. twice Bill's age   2B

22. Bill's age in 3 years   B + 3

23. Bill's age 4 years ago   B − 4

24. one-fourth Bill's age 1 year from now $\frac{1}{4}(B + 1)$

2–1 True or false?

25. $−14 < −13$ T

26. $|−9.2| = |9.2|$ T

27. No number is its own opposite.   F (0 is)

2–2, 2–3, 2–4 Simplify.

28. $−14 + 8$ −6

29. $−7 \cdot −5$ 35

30. $9 − (−3\frac{1}{2})$ $12\frac{1}{2}$

31. $5.6 + (−3.1)$ 2.5

32. $−13 − (−7)$ −6

33. $16 \cdot −4$ −64

34. $(−9 + 14) + (−6)$ −1

35. $−12 \cdot (−5 + 7)$ −24

2–5 **36.** What is the reciprocal of $−6$? $−\frac{1}{6}$

a	b	c
−48	4	−16

Substitute and simplify.

37. $a \div b$ −12

38. $\frac{b + c}{a}$ $\frac{1}{4}$

39. $\frac{c}{b} − \frac{a}{c}$ −7

2–6, 2–7, 2–8 Simplify.

40. $4y − (−7)$ 4y + 7

41. $13 + (−x) − 8.5$ 4.5 − x

42. $8b − 4b$ 4b

43. $9t + 3 − 8t$ t + 3

44. $7x + y − 8x + 3y$ −x + 4y

45. $5(a − 2) − 6$ 5a − 16

46. $4y − (3 − 2y)$ 6y − 3

47. $8(x − y) + 9(y + 2x)$ 26x + y

2–9 Use a table to solve.

48. What number added to the numerator and denominator of $\frac{1}{4}$ results in a new fraction equal to $\frac{3}{4}$?   8

Use a table to solve.

49. A bus and taxi leave Gotham City Airport traveling in the same direction. The taxi leaves at 8:00 A.M. traveling at 60 mph. The bus leaves at 8:30 A.M. traveling at 50 mph. At what time will the bus and taxi be 60 miles apart? 11:30 A.M.

3-1 Solve the equation for the replacement set $\{-4, -2, -1, 2, 4\}$.

50. $2|x| = 4$ (-2, 2) 51. $\dfrac{4}{x} = -2$ (-2) 52. $x^2 - 3x = 4$ (-1, 4)

3-2 What equation results from following these directions in order?

53. Original equation: $3y + 5 + 4y = 23$
   a. Combine the y-terms. $7y + 5 = 23$
   b. Subtract 5 from both sides. $7y = 18$

State whether each pair of equations is equivalent.

54. $x + 6 = 0, -4x = 24$ Yes   55. $2x + 3 = 4, x + 2 = 3$ No

3-3, Solve.
3-4,
3-5, 56. $7x - 3 = 8x$ (-3)   57. $\dfrac{n}{5} = -7$ (-35)   58. $\dfrac{3}{8}p = 24$ (64)
3-6,
3-7 59. $\dfrac{y}{2} + 4 = 9$ (10)   60. $11x + 8 = 10x + 14$ (6)

61. $2w - 5 = 21$ (13)   62. $\dfrac{a - 2}{3} = 6$ (20)

63. $4m - 10 = 2m - 16$ (-3)   64. $1 - 2x = 7$ (-3)
65. $-2 - \dfrac{t}{3} = 4$ (-18)   66. $2(1 - 4y) = 10$ (-1)
67. $2b + 4(b - 1) = 32$ (6)   68. $5 - 2(x - 1) = 7$ (0)

3-8 Solve the equations for the indicated variables.

69. $6n - t = 1$, for n $n = \dfrac{t+1}{6}$ 70. $A = \dfrac{1}{2}bh$, for b $b = \dfrac{2A}{h}$

3-9 For each problem, write these four things:

   a. What the variable represents (always a *number* of something).
   b. An equation that fits the problem.
   c. The solution to the equation.
   d. The answer to the question (with proper units).

71. The length of a rectangle is 8 cm more than its width. What is the width if the perimeter of the rectangle is 40 cm?
   b. $2(w + 8) + 2w = 40$; **c.** $w = 6$; **d.** 6 cm
72. The combined weight of the Simpson twins is 235 pounds. If Wyomia Simpson weighs 25 pounds less than Ralph Simpson, how much does each weigh?
   b. $R + (R - 25) = 235$; **c.** $R = 130$; **d.** Ralph: 130 pounds; Wyomia: 105 pounds

CHAPTER OVERVIEW

In this chapter, students begin their study of polynomials, which are algebraic expressions that can be generated from numbers and variables using the operations of addition, subtraction, and multiplication. Polynomials are similar to integers in that both are closed under the three operations named above and neither is closed under division. In order to perform operations with polynomials, students will need skill in simplifying algebraic expressions (addressed in Chapters 1 and 2).

In Chapter 4, students learn to add and subtract polynomials and to do some multiplication and division of polynomials. More will be learned about multiplying polynomials in Chapter 7 and about dividing polynomials in Chapter 8.

Scientific notation is an application of polynomials that is addressed in this chapter. Problems involving uniform motion, money, and integers are also addressed.

The skills that students acquire in this chapter will be needed in Chapters 7, 8, 10, and 11.

4 Polynomials

The prefix poly- from the Greek word "polys" means much or many. Several mathematical terms contain this prefix — polygon, polyhedron, and polynomial.

A famous sculpture created by Ron Resch, a computer scientist and artist, is the Vegreville Alberta Easter Egg. This polyhedral egg is 31 feet high, 18 feet wide, and weighs 5000 pounds. Its 3512 facets are made from 524 star-shaped and 2208 triangular pieces of aluminum.

OBJECTIVE 4–1

To add and subtract polynomials.

PURPOSE

To write algebraic expressions in simplest form and to solve equations efficiently, it is necessary to compute with polynomials. Adding and subtracting polynomials is a skill students should master.

PREVIEW

Students may not know how to write the answers to the more difficult questions as polynomials, but they should be able to compute the answers. Those met by the person going to St. Ives were

the man
7 wives
$7 \cdot 7$ or 49 sacks
$7 \cdot 7 \cdot 7$ or 343 cats
$7 \cdot 7 \cdot 7 \cdot 7$ or 2401 kites

The total number of kits, cats, sacks, wives, and man could be written

$7^4 + 7^3 + 7^2 + 7 + 1$, or 2801

4–1 Adding and Subtracting Polynomials

Preview

A child's nursery rhyme goes like this:

As I was going to St. Ives,
I met a man with seven wives;
Each wife had seven sacks,
Each sack had seven cats,
Each cat had seven kits:
Kits, cats, sacks, and wives,
How many were going to St. Ives?

The answer is one.

A more difficult question is, "Man, kits, cats, sacks, and wives: How many were met by the person going to St. Ives?"

In this lesson, you will learn how to represent expressions such as the one for the nursery rhyme.

■ LESSON

A **monomial** is a number, a variable, or the product of numbers, and/or variables. In a monomial, only 0 and the positive integers can be used as exponents. The following expressions are examples of monomials:

$$y \qquad -x \qquad ab \qquad \frac{1}{3}z \qquad x^2 \qquad 8 \qquad xy^2 \qquad cd^2 \qquad (abcd^2)^3$$

No monomial has a variable as an exponent, nor does it have a variable in the denominator of a fraction. The following expressions are not monomials, because the numbers and variables are involved in operations other than multiplication and because the variables appear as powers and as denominators of fractions:

$$t + 2 \qquad bc - 8 \qquad x^2 + 1 \qquad a + b \qquad \frac{7}{y} \qquad 4^x$$

A **polynomial** is the sum (or difference) of monomials. Monomials are also polynomials. These expressions are examples of polynomials:

$$a + b \qquad 7 - x \qquad -2x^2 + yx - 3 \qquad a^2b^3 - \frac{1}{7}a \qquad r + 9$$

Monomials joined by addition (or subtraction) are called the **terms** of the resulting polynomial. The following polynomial has 6 terms:

$$\overset{\text{terms}}{5x^2 + 7x + 9 - 6x^2 + 2x - 5}$$

We have used the word "term" before when referring to like and unlike terms. Remember that like terms have identical variable parts.

Like terms	*Unlike terms*
$5x^2$ and $-6x^2$	$5x$ and $7x^2$
$7a$ and a	$3x$ and $3y$
9 and 4	$2x$ and -5

LESSON

Be sure that students realize that a monomial is a polynomial. In discussing like and unlike terms, note that x and x^2 are *unlike* terms even though they have the same variable. Therefore, the sum $x + x^2$ cannot be simplified.

After subtractions have been changed to additions, the addends can be arranged in order by using the commutative and associative properties of addition.

When a quantity is subtracted, each term of the quantity is subtracted. For example,

$5 - (x + y) = 5 - x - y$
(Both x and y are subtracted.)
$10 - (a - b) = 10 - a - (-b)$
(Both a and $-b$ are subtracted.)
$= 10 - a + b$

Students may use either the vertical or the horizontal form when adding or subtracting polynomials. Exercises in more advanced work are usually given in the horizontal form.

We added and subtracted polynomials in Chapter 2. Study these examples as a review.

Example 1 Add $5x + 7$ and $8 - 2x$.

Solution $(5x + 7) + (8 - 2x)$

$= (5x + 7) + [8 + (-2)x]$ *Change subtraction to addition.*

$= [5x + (-2)x] + (7 + 8)$ *Commutative and associative properties of addition*

$= 3x + 15$ *Distributive property and computation*

Note that when two polynomials are added, the parentheses around the polynomials can be omitted.

$$(5x + 7) + (8 - 2x) = 5x + 7 + 8 - 2x$$
$$(3a - 5) + (-4 + 2a) = 3a - 5 + (-4) + 2a$$

Example 2 Subtract $3a + b$ from $7a + 5b$.

Solution $(7a + 5b) - (3a + b)$

$= (7a + 5b) + [-(3a + b)]$ *Change subtraction to addition.*

$= (7a + 5b + (-1)(3a + b)$ *-1 property of multiplication*

$= (7a + 5b) + [(-3)a + (-1)b]$ *Distributive property*

$= [7a + (-3)a] + [5b + (-1)b]$ *Commutative and associative properties of addition*

$= 4a + 4b$ *Distributive property and computation*

In Examples 3 and 4, note that we add and subtract polynomials in much the same way that we add and subtract numbers.

Example 3 Add $3x + 5y - 8$ and $4x - 2y - 5$.

Solution Arrange like terms in columns and add.

$$\begin{array}{r} 3x + 5y - 8 \\ 4x - 2y - 5 \\ \hline 7x + 3y - 13 \end{array}$$

Answer $7x + 3y - 13$

Student attention-spans seldom permit the same activity to last more than 15–20 minutes. Therefore, divide the class period into time blocks and use a different type of activity in each block.

ADDITIONAL EXAMPLES

Example 4.

Subtract $4r + 3s - 7$ from $5r + 2s + 6$.

Arrange like terms in columns.

$$5r + 2s + 6$$
$$4r + 3s - 7$$

Change the bottom polynomial to its opposite and add.

$$5r + 2s + 6$$
$$\underline{-4r - 3s + 7}$$
$$r - s + 13$$

Example 4   Subtract $5c + 6d - 7$ from $2c - 3d + 1$.

Solution   Arrange like terms in columns.

$$2c - 3d + 1$$
$$5c + 6d - 7$$

Change the signs of the polynomial to be subtracted in order to get its opposite. Then *add* like terms in columns.

$$2c - 3d + 1$$
$$\underline{-5c - 6d + 7}$$
$$-3c - 9d + 8$$

Answer $-3c - 9d + 8$

CHECK UNDERSTANDING

- Give an example of a polynomial. A monomial.
- Is 7 a polynomial? (Yes)
- Are 12*ab* and 3*b* like terms? (No)
- Are 7*xy* and *yx* like terms? (Yes)

■ CLASSROOM EXERCISES

Which of these expressions are monomials? $x^2y^2, \frac{1}{7}$

1. x^2y^2 2. $\dfrac{x^2}{y^2}$ 3. $\dfrac{1}{7}$ 4. $ax^2 + bx + c$ 5. $\dfrac{1}{x} + y$

Which of these expressions are polynomials?   All except $\frac{1}{x} + y$

6. $x^2 + y^2$ 7. x^3 8. $x^2 - \dfrac{1}{3}$ 9. $ax^2 + bx + c$ 10. $\dfrac{1}{x} + y$

Add.

11. $(x + y)$ and $(y + x)$ $2x + 2y$ 12. $(2x + 7)$ and $(3x - 4)$ $5x + 3$

Subtract.

13. $(x + y)$ from $(x - y)$ $-2y$ 14. $(4c - 1)$ from $(2c - 8)$ $-2c - 7$

CLASSROOM EXERCISES

In classroom exercises 1–10, adhere strictly to the definitions of monomials and polynomials.

In classroom exercises 13–14, the polynomial that is subtracted *from* another must be written *after* the other.

■ WRITTEN EXERCISES

Ⓐ 1. Which of these expressions are monomials?

$$2a \qquad 5b^2 \qquad \dfrac{3}{c} \qquad \dfrac{8}{9}d \qquad e + f \quad 2a, 5b^2, \tfrac{8}{9}d$$

2. Which of these expressions are polynomials?

$$p \qquad \dfrac{q}{2} \qquad r^3 \qquad -5s \qquad t - u \quad \text{All}$$

How many terms does each polynomial contain?

3. $7xyz + 8x$ 2   4. $5abc + 3ab$ 2   5. $2x + 5y - 8z$ 3

6. $7a + 5b + 2c$ 3   7. $5x^3 + 4x^2 - 9x - 2$ 4   8. $8a^3 + a^2 - 9a + 18$ 4

Add these polynomials.

9. $5x^2 + 3x + 8$ 10. $2b^2 + 3b + 4$ 11. $2a + 3b - c$ 12. $8x - y$
   $\underline{2x^2 - 7x + 3}$ $\underline{3b^2 + 7b - 6}$ $\underline{6a \qquad - 4c}$ $\underline{x - 5y - z}$
   $7x^2 - 4x + 11$ $5b^2 + 10b - 2$ $8a + 3b - 5c$ $9x - 6y - z$

ASSIGNMENT GUIDE

Basic   1–28 all, Review Exercises
Average 1–19 odd, 21–38 all, Review
              Exercises
Enriched 3–38 odd, 39–46 all, Review
              Exercises

EXTRA PRACTICE, page 624

Simplify each sum.

13. $(x^2 + 5x - 3) + (3x^2 + 2x + 4)$ $\quad 4x^2 + 7x + 1$ 14. $(7a^2 + 4a + 8) + (2a^2 + a - 9)$
$\qquad\qquad\qquad\qquad\qquad\qquad\qquad\qquad\qquad\qquad\qquad\qquad 9a^2 + 5a - 1$

15. $(2a + 3b) + (4b + c)$ $\quad 2a + 7b + c$ 16. $(4x + 2y) + (3x + 5w)$ $\quad 7x + 2y + 5w$

Write and simplify an expression for the *perimeter* of each of the following figures.

17.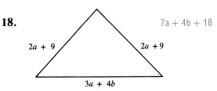
     $2x + 3$ (top), $2x + 3$ (left), $2x + 3$ (right), $2x + 3$ (bottom) $8x + 12$

18.
     $2a + 9$ (left), $2a + 9$ (right), $3a + 4b$ (bottom) $7a + 4b + 18$

19.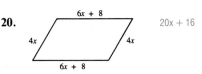
     $5n$ (top), $2n + 3$ (left), $2n + 3$ (right), $5n + 6m$ (bottom) $14n + 6m + 6$

20.
     $6x + 8$ (top), $4x$ (left), $4x$ (right), $6x + 8$ (bottom) $20x + 16$

Subtract these polynomials.

21. $8a^2 + 7a + 6$ 22. $10x^2 + 8x + 6$ 23. $5x - 6y + 3z$ 24. $7a \qquad - 3c$
    $6a^2 + 6a + 1$ $9x^2 + 3x + 2$ $3y - 3z$ $2a - 2b + 2c$
   $2a^2 + a + 5$ $x^2 + 5x + 4$ $5x - 9y + 6z$ $5a + 2b - 5c$

Simplify each difference.

25. $(5x^2 + 2x + 7) - (x^2 - 5x - 9)$ $\quad 4x^2 + 7x + 16$ 26. $(7a^2 + 3a + 5) - (a^2 - 4a + 9)$
$\qquad\qquad\qquad\qquad\qquad\qquad\qquad\qquad\qquad\qquad\qquad\qquad\qquad\qquad\qquad 6a^2 + 7a - 4$

27. $(3a + 4b) - (b + 2c)$ $\quad 3a + 3b - 2c$ 28. $(5x + 3y) - (y + 3z)$ $\quad 5x + 2y - 3z$

Simplify.

B   29. $(2x^2 - 3x + 5) + (5x^2 + 8x - 5) - (x^2 + 5x + 6)$ $\quad 6x^2 - 6$

30. $(8a^3 + 6a - 5) - (8a^3 + 5a^2 + 6a + 5) + (6a^2 + 3)$ $\quad a^2 - 7$

31. $(7a^2 - 6ab + 5b^2 - 4a + 3b - 2) - (7a^2 - 6ab + 5b^2) - (4a + 3b)$
$\qquad\qquad\qquad\qquad\qquad\qquad\qquad\qquad\qquad\qquad\qquad\qquad\qquad\qquad -8a - 2$

32. $(5x^2 + 5xy + 5y^2 - 5x - 5y - 5) - (5x^2 - 5xy + 5y^2) - (5x + 5y)$
$\qquad\qquad\qquad\qquad\qquad\qquad\qquad\qquad\qquad\qquad\qquad\qquad -10x + 10xy - 10y - 5$

33. $(4t^3 + 2t^2 + 7t + 4) + (9t^3 + 6t^2 + 2)$ $\quad 13t^3 + 8t^2 + 7t + 6$

34. $(8t^4 + 5t^2 + 7) + (3t^3 + 3t^2 + 3t)$ $\quad 8t^4 + 3t^3 + 8t^2 + 3t + 7$

35. $(5t^3 + 6t^2 + 7t + 8) - (5t^2 + 6t + 8)$ $\quad 5t^3 + t^2 + t$

36. $(8t^4 + 7t^3 + 6t^2) - (7t^3 + 6t^2 + 1)$ $\quad 8t^4 - 1$

37. $(8t^3 + 5t^2 + 9t + 5) + (7t^2 + 9) - (8t^2 + 8)$ $\quad 8t^3 + 4t^2 + 9t + 6$

38. $(3t^3 + 2t^2 + 7t + 8) - (5t^2 + 9t + 3) + (4t^2 + 8t)$ $\quad 3t^3 + t^2 + 6t + 5$

39. If *n* is an integer, write and simplify an expression for the sum of *n* and the next 4 consecutive integers. $n + (n + 1) + (n + 2) + (n + 3) + (n + 4) = 5n + 10$

40. If *n* is an even integer, write and simplify an expression for the sum of *n*, the preceding smaller integer, and the next larger integer.
$n + (n - 1) + (n + 1) = 3n$

41. If *n* is an odd integer, write and simplify an expression for the sum of *n* and the next 5 consecutive odd integers.
$n + (n + 2) + (n + 4) + (n + 6) + (n + 8) + (n + 10) = 6n + 30$

Write and simplify an expression for the total *surface area* of each of the following solid figures.

42. Cube $6e^2$

43. Rectangular solid $2wl + 2wh + 2lh$

44. Triangular prism $ab + cd + ad + bd$
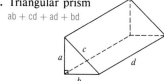

45. Cylinder $2\pi r^2 + 2\pi rh$

46. Write and simplify an expression for "everything" on the St. Ives road. [See the Preview on page 143.] $1 + 1 + 7 + 7^2 + 7^3 + 7^4 = 2802$

■ REVIEW EXERCISES

Simplify.   [1–2, 1–3]

1. $8 + 6 \div 2$ 11

2. $\dfrac{6 + 15}{3}$ 7

3. $8 + \dfrac{24}{4} - 2$ 12

4. $2 \cdot 5^2$ 50

5. $(2 + 5)^2$ 49

6. $(7 + 3)^2 - (7^2 + 3^2)$ 42

a	b	c	d
2	5	10	20

Substitute and simplify.

7. $a + bc - d$ 32

8. $(a + b)c + ad$ 110   [1–2]

9. $(ab)^2$ 100

10. $(c + d)^2 - (c^2 + d^2)$ 400   [1–3]

List the order in which the operations are performed in evaluating this expression.

11. $40 - 3^2 \cdot 4 + 2$ [1–3]
  ↑ ↑↑ ↑
  3 12 4

WRITTEN EXERCISES

In exercises 42–45, students may find the total surface area by adding the areas of all of the faces.

ENRICHMENT PROBLEM

Have a student write a small number on the board. Next, have another student write a second number (greater than or equal to the first) below it. Have a third student write eight more numbers below the first two according to this rule:

  Rule: Each succeeding number in the list is the sum of the preceding two.

  Now announce the sum as the student writes the last number by mentally multiplying the 7th number in the list by 11.

  Tell students that the trick involves addition of polynomials. Help them get started on discovering the trick by considering the first few addends; then have them work on the problem overnight.

  If *a* is the first number and *b* is the second, then the list is

          a
              b
      a + *b*
      a + 2*b*
     2*a* + 3*b*
     3*a* + 5*b*
     5*a* + 8*b* ← 7th number
     8*a* + 13*b*
    13*a* + 21*b*
    21*a* + 34*b*
    ─────────────
    55*a* + 88*b* ← sum

Add and subtract the polynomials as indicated.

1. $(5a + 6b + 3) + (4b + 2)$
$5a + 10b + 5$

2. $(7r + 3s + 4t) - (3r + s)$
$4r + 2s + 4t$

3. $(5c - 3d + 6e) + (2c - 7d - 7e)$
$7c - 10d - e$

4. $(3x^2 + 9x - 8) - (x^2 + 10x - 10)$
$2x^2 - x + 2$

5. $(7t^3 + 3t^2) + 6t^2 - (t^3 + t - 5)$
$6t^3 + 9t^2 - t + 5$

PURPOSE

To discuss polynomials, students need to learn the standard terminology associated with polynomials.

PREVIEW

Various classification schemes of polynomials are possible, but the students' vocabulary to describe them may be undeveloped. (1) The polynomials may be classified by the number of terms: 1 term; 2 terms; 3 terms. (2) The polynomials may be classified according to their powers of x: x^2 term; x term but no x^2 term; no x^2 and no x term. (3) The eight polynomials may be classified according to the number of negative coefficients.

Students may find other, nonstandard classification schemes.

OBJECTIVE 4–2

To identify polynomials by number of terms and by degree.

4–2 Types of Polynomials

Preview

Consider these polynomials. Find two different ways to group them into three distinct categories. By number of terms, by degree of variable

$7x^2 + 4x - 5$ $\qquad$ $8x^2$ $\qquad\qquad$ 6 $\qquad\qquad$ $5x + 3$

$5x^2 + 3$ $\qquad$ $-3 + 4x - x^2$ $\qquad$ $6x^2 - 4x$ $\qquad$ $7x$

In this lesson you will learn some ways to classify polynomials.

■ LESSON

Polynomials can have one or more terms. One way to classify polynomials is according to the number of terms they have.

Monomials have one term.	*Binomials* have two terms.	*Trinomials* have three terms.
6	$5x + 3$	$3x^2 + 5x - 6$
$7a$	$6y^2 - 2$	$3b^2 + 2a - 2ab$
$5x^2$	$a - b$	$-3m + m^3 - 2$
$-4m^3n^2$	$2x^2y + 3xy^2$	$4x^2 - 4xy + 3y^2$

Polynomials with more than three terms are simply called *polynomials.*

A polynomial can also be classified according to the powers of its variables. The **degree of a monomial** is the sum of the exponents of the variables. Monomials that are numbers are called **constants.** The degree of a constant is 0.

Monomial	*Degree*	
x^3	3	
x^3y^2	5	
$3x^3y^2$	5	
$3^2x^3y^2$	5	
9	0	
x	1	[Remember that $x = x^1$.]
$5xy$	2	

Strategy for Success Finding information

> At the back of the book is a glossary that gives definitions of the mathematical terms and symbols used in the book. For example, look up the term *variable* in the glossary.

When giving an assignment to read all or part of the next lesson, encourage students to read by assigning a few beginning exercises too. For example, if students are to read the Preview, they should also answer any questions that are part of the Preview. If students are to read the Lesson, they should also answer some of the Classroom Exercises.

The **degree of a polynomial** is the highest degree of any of its terms *after* the polynomial has been simplified.

Polynomial	Degree
$3x^2 + 5x + 7$	2
highest-degree term	
$3x^2 - 9xyz + y + z$	3
highest degree term	
$x + y + 7$	1
highest degree terms	
$2x^2 + 7x - 3 - 2x^2$	1

The polynomial $2x^2 + 7x - 3 - 2x^2$ has second-degree terms, but it can be simplified to $7x - 3$. The polynomial $7x - 3$ is a first-degree polynomial.

Terms of a polynomial in one variable are usually written in order of their degrees, as follows.

Ascending order (from lowest to highest degree):

$$3 + 4x - x^2 \qquad 4y - 4y^2 + 2y^3 \qquad 7 - 3a + 2a^2 - 5a^6$$

Descending order (from highest to lowest degree):

$$-x^2 + 4x + 3 \qquad 2y^3 - 4y^2 + 4y \qquad -5a^6 + 2a^2 - 3a + 7$$

If the terms of a polynomial have more than one variable, the terms are arranged in ascending or descending order for one of the variables.

$3x^2 + 3xy^2 - 2y \leftarrow$ descending order in x
$3xy^2 - 2y + 3x \leftarrow$ descending order in y
$2a^2 - 3ab + 2b^2 \leftarrow$ descending order in a and ascending order in b

■ CLASSROOM EXERCISES

1. Which of these expressions are monomials? 6a, x²y

$$6a \qquad 3a + 1 \qquad x^2y \qquad \frac{3}{x}$$

2. Which of these expressions are binomials? 5a + 2b

$$3x \qquad 5a + 2b \qquad 6x^2y \qquad 8x^2 + x + 1$$

3. Which of these expressions are trinomials? 5 + 3x + 2x², 7x − 3y − z

$$5 + 3x + 2x^2 \qquad 5ab \qquad 7x - 3y - z \qquad a^3 + 3$$

State the degree of each monomial.

4. $5x^3$ 3 **5.** 6 0 **6.** $3a$ 1 **7.** $2mn$ 2 **8.** $3a^2b^3$ 5

Attention should be given to prefixes *mono-*, *bi-*, and *tri-*, which mean 1, 2, and 3 respectively. The prefixes are used in many words, such as *monorail* (single rail serving as a track), *monotone* (repetition of the same tone), *biannual* (coming twice a year), *bicycle* (vehicle mounted on two wheels), *triangle* (figure with three angles and three sides), *trichotomy* (division into three parts), *tricycle* (three-wheeled vehicle).

In determining the degree of a monomial, it is important to remember that exponents of the variables are added. If no exponent is written with a variable, the exponent is 1. For example,

$$xy^2 = x^1y^2 \quad \text{The degree is 3.}$$

CHECK UNDERSTANDING

- How many terms does a monomial have? (1) A binomial? (2) A trinomial? (3) A polynomial? (One or more)
- Write an example of a binomial. Of a trinomial.
- What is the degree of $3x^2$? (2)
- What is the degree of 3^2? (0)
- What is the degree of $abcd$? (4)
- What is the degree of $5abcd$? (4)

ASSIGNMENT GUIDE

Basic 1–32 all, Review Exercises
Average 1–31 odd, 33–44 all, Review
Exercises
Enriched 1–35 odd, 37–48 all, Review
Exercises

PRACTICE WORKSHEET 17

4-2 TYPES OF POLYNOMIALS

■ State whether each polynomial is a monomial, binomial, or trinomial.

1. $a^2 + 2a + 1$ Tri   2. $x + y$ Bi   3. $x^3 - 4$ Bi   4. $5ab$ Mono
5. $\frac{1}{2}x^2y$ Mono   6. $x^2 - x + 1$ Tri   7. $r^2 - 2s$ Bi   8. $t^3 + 2t^2 - 4t$ Tri

■ State the degree of each polynomial.

9. $2 + 3t + 4t^2$ 2   10. $2c^6$ 6   11. $5x^2y$ 3   12. $\frac{2}{3}a^2 + \frac{3}{4}a - \frac{4}{5}$ 2
13. $xy + 2xy^2$ 3   14. $5x^2y^2 - 2x^2$ 4   15. 8 0   16. $p + q + r - s$ 1

■ Write each polynomial in descending order.

17. $2x + x^3 - 4x$ 18. $-2x^4 + 8 + 6x^2$ 19. $7y + 8y^2$ 20. $2 - 5y$
$x^3 - 2x$ $-2x^4 + 6x^2 + 8$ $8y^2 + 7y$ $-5y + 2$

■ Write each polynomial in descending order of x.

21. $5xy + 3y^2 + x^2$ 22. $5 - 2x^2$ 23. $y^3 - 2xy + 7x^2y$ 24. $x^4 + 3y^4 - 2x^2y^2$
$x^2 + 5xy + 3y^2$ $-2x^2 + 5$ $7x^2y - 2xy + y^3$ $x^4 - 2x^2y^2 + 3y^4$

EXTRA PRACTICE, page 624

State the degree of each polynomial.

9. $4x^2 + 3x - 8$ 2   10. $3a^2b - 2a^2b^2 + 4b$ 4   11. $3x^2 + 5 - 3x^2 + 2$ 0

12. Arrange the terms in ascending order: $5x + 3 - 2x^2$.
$3 + 5x - 2x^2$

13. Arrange the terms in descending order: $5a - 3a^2 + 2a^3 - 5$.
$2a^3 - 3a^2 + 5a - 5$

14. Arrange the terms in descending order in x: $4x^2y + 3x^3 - 2xy + y$.
$3x^3 + 4x^2y - 2xy + y$

Strategy for Success Doing assignments

Set aside a time and a place to do your mathematics each day. Choose a time and a place free of distractions so that you can have the best conditions for concentrating.

■ WRITTEN EXERCISES

Ⓐ 1. Which of these expressions are monomials? $5x, xy, -6, 6^2$

$5x$ $5 + x$ xy $\dfrac{x}{y}$ -6 6^2

2. Which of these expressions are binomials? $2 + y, z - x$

wx $2 + y$ $z - x$ $2xy + 3w - z$

3. Which of these expressions are trinomials? All but $3xy^3$

$3xy^3$ $2x + 2y + 2z$ $x^7 - 2x^6 - x^5$

4. Which of these expressions are polynomials? All but $\frac{1}{y}$

x $3a^2b + 1$ 5 $a + 2b - c$ $\dfrac{1}{y}$

State the degree of each term.

5. $3x^2$ 2   6. $7x^3$ 3   7. 8 0   8. 2 0   9. $2r^2s^3$ 5

10. $5a^3b^2$ 5   11. $\frac{1}{2}xyz$ 3   12. $\frac{1}{3}abc$ 3   13. $-2x^2y$ 3   14. $-4xy^2$ 3

State the degree of each polynomial.

15. $3x^2 + 4x + 5$ 2   16. $6a^2 + 5a - 4$ 2

17. $a + b + c + d$ 1   18. $w + x - y - z$ 1

19. $5 + 9$ 0   20. $2 + 3$ 0

21. $2a^2 + abc - 5d^2$ 3   22. $8x + 7xy - 5y$ 2

23. $-5xy^3 + 7$ 4   24. $\frac{2}{3}a^2b - 4b^2$ 3

In exercises 33–36, the expression should be simplified before determining the degree.

In exercises 45–48, note that the degree of the sum is *never greater* than the degree of the polynomials that are added. The degree of the sum may be equal to or less than the degree of the polynomials that are added. Similar statements can be made about the degree of the differences when one polynomial is subtracted from another.

Write each polynomial in ascending order.

25. $5x + 9x^2 + 4$ $4 + 5x + 9x^2$

26. $3a^2 + 8 - 7a$ $8 - 7a + 3a^2$

27. $9b^3 - 3b + 5$ $5 - 3b + 9b^3$

28. $4v^4 + 3v^2 + 8 - v$ $8 - v + 3v^2 + 4v^4$

Write each polynomial in descending order.

29. $2x + 5 + 8x^2$ $8x^2 + 2x + 5$

30. $5a^2 - 7 - 9a$ $5a^2 - 9a - 7$

31. $-7y^2 + 5y^3 + 4y$ $5y^3 - 7y^2 + 4y$

32. $3w^4 + 4w - 7 - 2w^2$ $3w^4 - 2w^2 + 4w - 7$

State the degree of each polynomial.

B   **33.** $2x^2 - 3x + 5 - 2x^2$ 1

34. $3b - 7 + 5 + 3b^3 - 3b + 2$ 3

35. $2ab - 3b^2 + 2ab + 5$ 2

36. $5mn + 3m^2 - 2m - 3m^2$ 2

Write each polynomial in ascending order in x.

37. $3xy - 5y^2 + 7x^2$ $-5y^2 + 3xy + 7x^2$

38. $2x^3 - 3xy^2 + 5y^3 + 6x^2y$ $5y^3 - 3xy^2 + 6x^2y + 2x^3$

39. $6x^2y^2 - 7xy + 8$ $8 - 7xy + 6x^2y^2$

40. $9 + 5x^2y^2 - 4xy$ $9 - 4xy + 5x^2y^2$

41.–44. Write each polynomial in Exercises 37–40 in descending order in y.
  41. See 37.   42. See 38.   43. $6x^2y^2 - 7xy + 8$ 44. $5x^2y^2 - 4xy + 9$

C   **45. a.** What is the degree of $(3x^2 + 2x - 7)$?   2

     b. What is the degree of $(5x - x^2 + 2)$?   2

     c. Add the polynomials from parts (a) and (b). What is the degree of the sum?   2

46. a. What is the degree of $(2x - 3x^2 + 4)$?   2

     b. What is the degree of $(x^3 - 2x + 1)$?   3

     c. What is the degree of the sum of the polynomials from parts (a) and (b)?   3

47. a. What is the degree of $(4x^2 - 7x + 2)$?   2

     b. What is the degree of $(x - 4x^2 + 1)$?   2

     c. What is the degree of the sum of the polynomials from parts (a) and (b)?   1

48. How are the degrees of two polynomials related to the degree of their sum?
  Degree of sum ≤ degree of higher degree polynomial

ENRICHMENT PROBLEMS

- Two 3rd-degree polynomials were added and the sum was only of 1st-degree. What do you conclude?

  The 3rd-degree terms (and 2nd-degree, if any) were opposites.

- Can a 4th-degree polynomial be subtracted from a 3rd-degree polynomial? If so, what is the degree of the difference?

  Yes; 4.

■ REVIEW EXERCISES

Indicate whether the expressions are equivalent.   [1–4]

   1. $3(x + 2)$ and $3x + 6$ Yes   **2.** $3x^2$ and $6x$ No   **3.** $4(a + 8)$ and $4a + 8$ No

   4. $a^2 + b^2$ and $(a + b)^2$ No   **5.** $a^2 - b^2$ and $(a - b)^2$ No   **6.** $\dfrac{a + 1}{b + 1}$ and $\dfrac{a}{b}$ No

Indicate the property that is illustrated by each equation.   [1–5]

   7. $2a + a = 2a + 1a$ Identity property for multiplication   **8.** $2a + 1a = (2 + 1)a$ Distributive property

   9. $10 + (3a + 7a) = (3a + 7a) + 10$
     Commutative property of addition

   10. $a \cdot 0 = 0 \cdot a$
     Commutative property of multiplication

   11. $6a + (3a + 5) = (6a + 3a) + 5$
     Associative property of addition

   12. $8a(3a \cdot 6) = (3a \cdot 6)8a$
     Commutative property of multiplication

If you need to evaluate the trinomial

$$4x^2 - 10xy + 3y^2$$

for a number of different values of x and y, you might use the following BASIC program. The statements could be numbered from 1–6, but it is customary to use multiples of ten so that additional statements can be inserted without renumbering the entire program.

```
10  PRINT "WHAT VALUE FOR X";
20  INPUT X
30  PRINT "WHAT VALUE FOR Y";
40  INPUT Y
50  PRINT 4 * X ↑ 2 — 10 * X * Y + 3 * Y ↑ 2
60  END            [The last line in a BASIC program is always END.]
```

The quotation marks in lines 10 and 30 indicate to the computer to print the text between them exactly as it is typed. The computer on reading the command INPUT in lines 20 and 40 will type a ?, then wait for you to enter values for X and Y. The semicolons at the end of lines 10 and 30 indicate to the computer to type the ? from the INPUT statements on the same line as the PRINT statements.

1. Type the program and run it to evaluate the polynomial for the following values of x and y. (Type RUN each time you want to enter a pair of values.)

x	10	-10	10	1	1	1
y	10	10	-10	1	2	3
$4x^2 - 10xy + 3y^2$	?	?	?	?	?	?

$$-300 \quad 1700 \quad 1700 \quad -3 \quad -4 \quad 1$$

2. If x has the value 1, what value of y (to the nearest tenth) results in the smallest value for the polynomial? 1.7

3. Change line 50 so that the program can be used to evaluate the polynomial $x^2 + 7xy - y^2$. 50 PRINT X ↑ 2 + 7 * X * Y − Y ↑ 2

4. Change line 50 so that the program can be used to evaluate the polynomial $x^4 + 3x^2y - y^2$. 50 PRINT X ↑ 4 + 3 * X ↑ 2 * Y − Y ↑ 2

You may wish to spend two days on this section. Refer to the Pacing Chart.

To multiply monomials.

1. Which of these polynomials are binomials?
$xy, 2x^2, x + 3, x - y, x^2 + 3x - 2$
$x + 3$ and $x - y$

2. What is the degree of $5x^2y$?
3

3. What is the degree of the polynomial $3x^4 - x^2y^3 + xyz$?
5

4. Write the polynomial in ascending order in x. $5x^2 + 2y^4 + 3x^3$
$2y^4 + 5x^2 + 3x^3$

5. Write the polynomial in descending order in x. $2xy - 5y^3 + x^2$
$x^2 + 2xy - 5y^3$

4–3 Multiplying Monomials

Preview Discovery

Complete these multiplication equations. Then use the table to write the equations using powers of 2. Look for a pattern.

$4 \cdot 8 = \underline{\ ?\ }$ 32 $16 \cdot 16 = \underline{\ ?\ }$ 256
$2^2 \cdot 2^3 = 2^?$ 5 $2^4 \cdot 2^4 = 2^?$ 8

$256 \cdot 8 = \underline{\ ?\ }$ 2048 $8 \cdot 16 = \underline{\ ?\ }$ 128
$2^? \cdot 2^? = 2^?$ 8, 3, 11 $2^? \cdot 2^? = 2^?$ 3, 4, 7

Guess; then check your guess.

$3^2 \cdot 3^3 = 3^?$ 5 $10^3 \cdot 10^5 = 10^?$ 8 $10^7 \cdot 10^4 = 10^?$ 11

Guess.

$a^3 \cdot a^5 = a^?$ 8 $b^7 \cdot b^2 = b^?$ 9 $x^3 \cdot x^9 = x^?$ 12

$2^1 = 2$
$2^2 = 4$
$2^3 = 8$
$2^4 = 16$
$2^5 = 32$
$2^6 = 64$
$2^7 = 128$
$2^8 = 256$
$2^9 = 512$
$2^{10} = 1024$
$2^{11} = 2048$
$2^{12} = 4096$

■ LESSON

The exercises in the Preview illustrate the **addition property of exponents.**

The Addition Property of Exponents

For all real numbers a, and all positive numbers m and n,
$$a^m \cdot a^n = a^{m+n}.$$

For example,

$$2^3 \cdot 2^4 = \overbrace{(2 \cdot 2 \cdot 2)}^{3 \text{ factors}} \overbrace{(2 \cdot 2 \cdot 2 \cdot 2)}^{4 \text{ factors}}$$

$$= \overbrace{2 \cdot 2 \cdot 2 \cdot 2 \cdot 2 \cdot 2 \cdot 2}^{3 + 4 \text{ factors}}$$
$$= 2^7$$

In general, we have

$$x^m \cdot x^n = \overbrace{(x \cdot x \cdot \ldots)}^{m \text{ factors}} \overbrace{(x \cdot x \cdot \ldots)}^{n \text{ factors}}$$

$$= \overbrace{x \cdot x \cdot x \cdot \ldots}^{m + n \text{ factors}}$$
$$= x^{m+n}$$

In order to multiply algebraic expressions, a student must be able to multiply monomials.

Use the Preview as an opportunity for student discovery. Students can find the products by using their arithmetic skills. Then they can complete the "exponent" equations by using the results of their computation and the information in the table. It is expected that students will guess that exponents are added when the powers of the same base are multiplied. Check guesses by computation.

Emphasize that exponents may be added only if the factors have the same base. Review the fact that the exponent indicates the number of times the base is used as a factor. $2^3 \cdot 2^5$ may be simplified to 2^8 using this rule. However, $2^5 \cdot 3^4$ *cannot* be simplified by combining exponents. A common student error is multiplying bases and adding exponents.

$$2^5 \cdot 3^4 \neq 6^9$$

Students must remember that the exponent is 1 in expressions such as x, y, a, $3b$, $-5c$. Therefore, in simplifying $(5x)(2x^3)$, think $(5x^1)(2x^3) = (10x^4)$.

The addition property of exponents and the commutative and associative properties of multiplication can be used to simplify the product of two monomials.

Example 1 Multiply. $3x^2$ and $-5x^4$

Solution $(3x^2)(-5x^4) = 3(-5)(x^2 \cdot x^4)$ *Commutative and associative properties*

$= -15(x^2 \cdot x^4)$ *Computation*

$= -15x^6$ *Addition property of exponents*

To simplify the product of monomials, first multiply the numerical factors and then find the product of variable factors with like bases by using the addition property of exponents.

Example 2 Simplify. $(4ab)\left(\frac{1}{3}a^2b\right)$

Solution $4ab\left(\frac{1}{3}a^2b\right) = \left(4 \cdot \frac{1}{3}\right)(a \cdot a^2)(b \cdot b)$

$= \frac{4}{3}a^3b^2$

Example 3 Simplify. $(-2m^3n)(-8m^2n^2)(3mn)$

Solution $(-2m^3n)(-8m^2n^2)(3mn) = (-2)(-8)(3)(m^3 \cdot m^2 \cdot m)(n \cdot n^2 \cdot n)$

$= 48m^6n^4$

■ CLASSROOM EXERCISES

Complete.

1. $3^2 \cdot 3^4 = 3^?$ 6

2. $3^{10} \cdot 3^2 = ?$ 3^{12}

3. $4 \cdot 4^6 = ?$ 4^7

4. $x^3 \cdot x^5 = x^?$ 8

5. $y^? \cdot y^3 = y^{12}$ 9

6. $r^a \cdot r^b = ?$ r^{a+b}

Simplify.

7. $y^7 \cdot y^4$ y^{11}

8. $(3x^2)(4x^3)$ $12x^5$

9. $(5x^2y)(-2xy^2)$ $-10x^3y^3$

■ WRITTEN EXERCISES

Complete.

A **1.** $2^3 \cdot 2^4 = 2^?$ 7

2. $2^5 \cdot 2^2 = 2^?$ 7

3. $5^4 \cdot 5^4 = 5^?$ 8

4. $5^3 \cdot 5^6 = 5^?$ 9

5. $3 \cdot 3^4 = 3^?$ 5

6. $3^5 \cdot 3 = 3^?$ 6

7. $4^? \cdot 4^2 = 4^8$ 6

8. $4^3 \cdot 4^? = 4^{12}$ 9

9. $2 \cdot 2^3 \cdot 2^6 = 2^?$ 10

10. $2^8 \cdot 2^4 \cdot 2 = 2^?$ 13

11. $\left(\frac{2}{3}\right)^2 \cdot \left(\frac{2}{3}\right)^2 = \left(\frac{2}{3}\right)^?$ 4

12. $\left(\frac{3}{4}\right)^4 \cdot \left(\frac{3}{4}\right)^3 = \left(\frac{3}{4}\right)^?$ 7

Immediately after the starting bell rings, have students write an objective of the previous day's lesson and an example of that objective.

ASSIGNMENT GUIDE

Basic   1–11 odd, 13–34 all, Review Exercises, Self-Quiz 1

Average   1–31 odd, 33–46 all, Review Exercises, Self-Quiz 1

Enriched   1–45 odd, 47–56 all, Review Exercises, Self-Quiz 1

Simplify.

13. $a^5 \cdot a^{15}$ a^{20}

14. $a^4 \cdot a^{12}$ a^{16}

15. $(2b^3)(3b^2)$ $6b^5$

16. $(4c^4)(3c^3)$ $12c^7$

17. $(-2q^{10})(-6q^{10})$ $12q^{20}$

18. $(-8q^9)(-3q^9)$ $24q^{18}$

19. $(5r)(20r^{100})$ $100r^{101}$

20. $(25s)(4s^{50})$ $100s^{51}$

21. $\left(\frac{1}{2}t^2\right)\left(\frac{1}{4}t^4\right)$ $\frac{1}{8}t^6$

22. $\left(\frac{1}{3}t^3\right)\left(\frac{1}{6}t^6\right)$ $\frac{1}{18}t^9$

23. $(5ab^2)(3a^2b^3)$ $15a^3b^5$

24. $(2xy^3)(6x^4y^6)$ $12x^5y^9$

Write the degree of each product.

25. $(5a^2)(10a^8)$ 10

26. $(7a^4)(3a^5)$ 9

27. $(4y^3)(2y^{20})$ 23

28. $(5y^{30})(6y^5)$ 35

29. $(4xy)(2x^2y)$ 5

30. $(5ab)(2ab^2c)$ 6

31. $(-2x^2y)(-3xy^2)(2x)$ 7

32. $(4mn)(-3m^2n)(-2mn)$ 7

Use the table in the Preview to answer these questions.

33. In the quiz show "Double or Nothing," a contestant won $2 for answering a question correctly, $4 for answering 2 questions correctly, $8 for answering 3 questions correctly, and so on, doubling the winnings for each correct answer. How many questions did the contestant answer correctly to win $64? 6

34. Under the right conditions the mass of a bacteria culture doubles every hour. After 10 hours, what will be the mass of a culture that began with a mass of 1 gram? 1024 g

B **35.** An investment of $100 doubles in value every decade. What is the value of an investment after 8 decades? $25,600

36. A rumor was spread by one person telling two others. An hour later each of the new people told two others. In another hour each of those four told two others; and each hour thereafter, the process continued. If one person started the rumor at noon, how many would have heard the rumor by 6 P.M.? 254 plus the person who started the rumor

37. One bean is placed on the lower lefthand square of a checkerboard. On the square to its right are placed two beans, to their right four beans, and to their right eight beans. If the process of doubling continues, how would you represent the number of beans piled on the final (64th) square? 2^{63}

Simplify.

38. $(2a^2b)(3ab^2)(2a)$ $12a^4b^3$

39. $(-5xy^3)(-3x^2)(-24)$ $-360\,x^3y^3$

40. $(3m^2n)(-2mn)(-2n^2)$ $12m^3n^4$

41. $a^3 + a^3$ $2a^3$

42. $a^3 \cdot a^3$ a^6

43. $-2a^4 \cdot \frac{a^2}{2}$ $-a^6$

44. $\left(-\frac{1}{2}a^6\right)(8a^3)$ $-4a^9$

45. $(x^2)^4$ x^8

46. $(x^3)^2$ x^6

PRACTICE WORKSHEET 18

4-3 MULTIPLYING MONOMIALS

■ Complete.

1. $3^3 \cdot 3^4 = 3^?$ 9   2. $4^{50} \cdot 4^{20} = 4^?$ 70   3. $2^? \cdot 2^3 = 2^9$ 6

4. $7 \cdot 7 = 7^?$ 2   5. $5 \cdot 5^{20} = 5^?$ 21   6. $8^3 \cdot 8^? = 8^6$ 3

7. $3^2 \cdot 3^? = 3^3$ 1   8. $6^5 \cdot 6^? = 6^{25}$ 20

9. $\left(\frac{1}{2}\right)^4 \cdot \left(\frac{1}{2}\right)^? = \left(\frac{1}{2}\right)^?$ 9   10. $(-2)^? \cdot (-2)^4 = (-2)^?$ 1

11. $(0.3) \cdot (0.3) = (0.3)^?$ 2   12. $7^5 \cdot 7^? = 7^{12}$ 9

■ Simplify.

13. $a^3 \cdot a^4$ a^7 14. $a^{10} \cdot a^{10}$ a^{20} 15. $b \cdot b^2$ b^3

16. $(2a^2)(3a^3)$ $6a^5$ 17. $(2b^6)\left(\frac{1}{2}b^4\right)$ b^{10} 18. $(4b^3)(b^5)$ $4b^8$

19. $a^{100} \cdot a$ a^{101} 20. $(3b)(b^8)$ $3b^9$ 21. $\left(\frac{1}{4}a^4\right)(8a^2)$ $4a^6$

22. $(x^2y)(xy)$ x^3y^2 23. $(x^3)(xy^2)$ x^3y^2 24. $(xy)(y^3)$ xy^4

WRITTEN EXERCISES

Exercises 11–12 are intended to remind students that the addition property of exponents is true for any real number *a* (including fractions).

Exercise 34 could be extended further, noting that the "right conditions" for doubling are not likely to continue. Food, water, space, temperature, and other factors are likely to change as the mass increases. After 10 hours, 1 gram supposedly grows to 1024 grams (which is little more than 1 kilogram). After 20 hours, the mass would be 2^{20} g, or 1,048,576 g (which is 1048.576 kilograms—more than a ton).

Exercise 35 is not farfetched at all. The annual rate of an investment that doubles in 10 years is a little more than 7%.

COMPUTER EXTENSION

1. Write a computer program to complete this table for 24 hours for exercise 36.

Hour	New People	Total
0	1	1
1	2	3
2	4	7
3	8	15

```
10 PRINT "HOUR", "NEW",
   "TOTAL"
20 PRINT " ", "PEOPLE"
30 P = 1
40 T = 0
50 FOR H = 0 TO 24
60 T = T + P
70 PRINT H, P, T
80 P = 2*P
90 NEXT H
100 END
```

2. Write a computer program to provide the following output for exercise 37.

Square	Number of Beans
1	1
2	2
3	4
4	8
. . .	. . .
64	

```
10 PRINT "SQUARE", "NUM.OF"
20 PRINT " ", "BEANS"
30 B = 1
40 FOR S = 1 TO 64
50 PRINT S, B
60 B = 2*B
70 NEXT S
80 END
```

ENRICHMENT PROBLEMS

• Correct any mistakes in these statements.

a. $2x^3 + x^3 = 2x^7$ $3x^3$
b. $(3y^2)(4y^5) = 7y^7$ $12y^7$
c. $2^5 \cdot 2^4 = 4^9$ 2^9
d. $(2x)^3(2x)^7 = 2x^{10}$ $(2x)^{10}$
e. $a^{12} \cdot 3a^4 \cdot 6a = 18a^{16}$ $18a^{17}$
f. $3y^2 \cdot 3y^2 = (3y)^4$ $9y^4$ or $(3y^2)^2$

156

EXTRA PRACTICE, page 625

Are these like terms? (Answer yes or no.)

47. $(3xy^2)(x)$ and $(4x^2y)(y)$ Yes

48. $(5ab^2)(-3a^2b)$ and $(11ab)(ab^2)$ No

49. $(2x^2)^3$ and $(5x^3)^2$ Yes

50. $(3x^3)^4$ and $(4x^4)^3$ Yes

Write an expression for the area of each figure.

51.
6ab

52.
$3x^2$

53.
$6k^2$
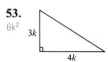

Write an expression for the volume of each figure.

54.
$2a^2b$
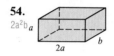

55.
$\frac{1}{2}abc$
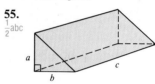

56.
$\pi r^2 h$
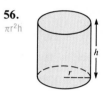

■ REVIEW EXERCISES

Simplify.

1. $6x - x$ 5x

2. $4x - 5 + x$ 5x − 5   [1–6]

3. $x + 7 + x$ 2x + 7

4. $3(x + 4) + 4x$ 7x + 12

Self-Quiz 1

4–1 Identify each of the following polynomials as a monomial, binomial, or trinomial.

1. $3x^2 + 5$ Binomial

2. $4xy^3$ Monomial

3. $8x^2y + 5xy - 3xy^2$ Trinomial

4–2 Simplify.

4. $(3x^2 + 5x - 8) + (8x^2 - 2x + 3)$ $11x^2 + 3x - 5$

5. $(a^2 + 2ab + b^2) + (3a^2 - ab - b^2)$ $4a^2 + ab$

6. $(5x^2 + 6x + 7) - (2x^2 + 4x - 3)$ $3x^2 + 2x + 10$

7. $(7x^2 - 3x - 5) - (2x^2 - 4x - 7)$ $5x^2 + x + 2$

4–3 Simplify.

8. $x^2 \cdot x^4 \cdot x^3$ x^9

9. $(-4y^2)\left(\frac{1}{2}y^3\right)$ $-2y^5$

10. $(3a^2b)(5ab^3)$ $15a^3b^4$

11. $(-8x^2y^3)\left(\frac{3}{4}x^4y^2\right)$ $-6x^6y^5$

Class Starter Quiz
on previous section

Simplify.

1. $n^4 \cdot n^3$ n^7
2. $(2n^5) \cdot (3n^4)$ $6n^9$
3. $(-6n^2) \cdot (n)$ $-6n^3$
4. $(ab^5) \cdot \left(\frac{1}{2}ab^2\right)$ $\frac{1}{2}a^2b^7$
5. $(-a^2b) \cdot (-5a^3c) \cdot (2bc)$ $10a^5b^2c^2$

4–4 Scientific Notation

Preview Application

The closest star to the earth is the sun, at a distance of about 149 million kilometers. The next closest star is Alpha Centauri, a distance of about 4.3 light years from earth. A *light year* is a unit for measuring astronomical distances. It represents the distance light travels in one year at a speed of about 300,000 kilometers per second (km/s).

To determine the distance in kilometers from the earth to Alpha Centauri, we must first compute the number of kilometers in a light year.

$$\begin{array}{cccccc} 300,000 & \times & 60 & \times & 60 & \times & 24 & \times 365.25 \\ \text{km/s} & & \text{s/min} & & \text{min/h} & & \text{h/day} & \text{day/yr} \end{array}$$

$$\approx 9,467,280,000,000 \text{ km}$$

If we used a computer or calculator to perform the above computation, the calculator or computer would print the result as follows:

9.46728 E+12   or   9.46728   12

Alpha Centauri, a double-star system, appear as a single star when viewed with the naked eye.

Both of the expressions are ways of writing the product:

$$9.46728 \times 10^{12}$$

This last expression is written in *scientific notation,* a simple way of writing very large or very small numbers. In this lesson you will learn to use scientific notation.

■ LESSON

Scientific notation is a way of writing a number as the product of two factors. One factor is a number greater than or equal to 1 and less than 10. The other factor is a power of 10 written in exponential form. For example,

The speed of light is about 300,000 km/s.

$$300,000 = 3 \times 10^5$$

between   power
1 and 10   of 10

The earth is about 93,000,000 miles from the sun.

$$93,000,000 = 9.3 \times 10^7$$

between   power
1 and 10   of 10

PURPOSE

An efficient means to communicate very large and very small numbers is desirable. Scientific notation provides a suitable convention. Similar notation is used with computers and calculators.

PREVIEW

To find the numbers of kilometers from Earth to Alpha Centauri, multiply 4.3 and (9.46728×10^{12}). The product, expressed in scientific notation, is approximately 4.07093×10^{13}. Calculators or computers might display the product as 4.07093 13 or 4.07093 E+13.

LESSON

Although scientific notation may be used to express any rational number, it will be used here to express only numbers whose absolute value is greater than 10. Numbers whose absolute value is less than 1 require the use of negative exponents in scientific notation. Similarly, numbers between 1 and 10 will not be written in scientific notation, because 0 is the required exponent of 10. (For example, $5.2 = 5.2 \times 10^0$.)

Example 1.
Change to scientific notation. 38,000
$$38,000 = 3.8 \times 10,000 = 3.8 \times 10^4$$

Example 2.
Change to scientific notation. 80,300,000
$$80,300,000 = 8.03 \times 10,000,000$$
$$= 8.03 \times 10^7$$

Example 3.
Change 2.17×10^6 to standard decimal notation.
$$2.17 \times 10^6 = 2.17 \times 1,000,000$$
$$= 2,170,000$$

Example 4.
Simplify. $(2.5 \times 10^8)(3.8 \times 10^9)$
$(2.5 \times 10^8)(3.8 \times 10^9)$
$= (2.5 \times 3.8)(10^8 \times 10^9)$ *Commutative and associative properties*
$= (2.5)(3.8)(10^{17})$ *Addition property of exponents*
$= 9.5 \times 10^{17}$ *Computation*

Example 5.
Simplify. $(4 \times 10^6)(8.1 \times 10^{12})$
$(4 \times 10^6)(8.1 \times 10^{12})$
$= (4 \times 8.1)(10^6 \times 10^{12})$
$= 32.4 \times 10^{18}$
$= (3.24 \times 10^1) \times 10^{18}$
$= 3.24 \times 10^{19}$

CHECK UNDERSTANDING

- A number in scientific notation is written as a product. How many factors are written? (Two)
- What number is the first factor? (A number between 1 and 10 written as a decimal)
- What number is the second factor? (A power of 10)
- Are these numbers written in scientific notation?
  $1.34 \cdot 10^3$ (Yes) $5 \cdot 10^1$ (Yes)
  7.2 (No) 10^1 (No)

To change from standard decimal notation to scientific notation, factor the number so that one factor is a number between 1 and 10 and the other is a power of 10. Then write the power of 10 using exponents.

> **Example 1**   Change to scientific notation. 5400
> *Solution* $5400 = 5.4 \times 1000 = 5.4 \times 10^3$

> **Example 2**   Change to scientific notation. 765,000,000
> *Solution* $765,000,000 = 7.65 \times 100,000,000 = 7.65 \times 10^8$

To change from scientific notation to standard decimal notation, write the power of 10 in standard form. Then simplify the remaining product.

> **Example 3**   Change to standard decimal notation. 4.53×10^5
> *Solution* $4.53 \times 10^5 = 4.53 \times 100,000 = 453,000$

Look for shortcuts. Note the relationship between the exponent and the number of places that the decimal point is moved.

$$4.53 \times 10^5 = \underset{\text{5 places}}{453,000} \longrightarrow$$

The basic number properties as well as the addition property of exponents can be used to simplify the product of two numbers that are expressed in scientific notation.

> **Example 4**   Write the product in scientific notation. $(3.4 \times 10^2)(2.8 \times 10^3)$
> *Solution* $(3.4 \times 10^2)(2.8 \times 10^3)$
> $= (3.4 \times 2.8)(10^2 \times 10^3)$ *Commutative and associative properties of multiplication*
> $= (3.4 \times 2.8)(10^5)$ *Addition property of exponents*
> $= 9.52 \times 10^5$ *Computation*

Note in Example 4 that the product of 3.4 and 2.8 was between 1 and 10. Therefore, the simplified product was already in scientific notation. Now consider $(5 \times 10^3)(4 \times 10^5)$. The product simplifies to 20×10^8, which is not in scientific notation. Therefore, two more steps are required to write the product in scientific notation.

Example 5   Write the product in scientific notation. $(5 \times 10^3)(4 \times 10^5)$

Solution $(5 \times 10^3)(4 \times 10^5)$
$= (5 \times 4)(10^3 \times 10^5)$
$= 20 \times 10^8$
$= (2 \times 10^1) \times 10^8$
$= 2 \times 10^9$

■ CLASSROOM EXERCISES

State whether the number is expressed in scientific notation.

1. 2.3×10^7 Yes   **2.** 34×10^1 No   **3.** 0.55×10^4 No   **4.** 6007×10^1 No

Change to scientific notation.

5. 6000 6×10^3 **6.** 468,000 4.68×10^5 **7.** 567.5×10^5 5.675×10^7 **8.** 26,000,000 2.6×10^7

Change to standard decimal notation.

9. 3×10^4 30,000   **10.** 8.9×10^5 890,000   **11.** 7.07×10^1 70.7   **12.** 4.505×10^9 4,505,000,000

Write the product in scientific notation.

13. $(4 \times 10^3)(2 \times 10^5)$ 8×10^8 **14.** $(3.3 \times 10^4)(8.1 \times 10^3)$ 2.673×10^8

■ WRITTEN EXERCISES

State whether the number is expressed in scientific notation.

A **1.** 56×10^5 No   **2.** 742×10^4 No   **3.** 8.6×10^8 Yes   **4.** 7.5×10^3 Yes

5. 0.368×10^3 No   **6.** 0.42×10^7 No   **7.** 6.2×2^8 No   **8.** 1.6×2^6 No

Write the number in scientific notation.

9. 530,000 5.3×10^5 **10.** 1,200,000,000,000 1.2×10^{12}

11. 328×10^6 3.28×10^8 **12.** 662×10^{12} 6.62×10^{14}

13. 0.25×10^8 2.5×10^7 **14.** 0.97×10^6 9.7×10^5

15. 217,000,000,000,000 2.17×10^{14} **16.** 82,800,000,000,000,000 8.28×10^{16}

Write in standard decimal notation.

17. 5×10^6 5,000,000   **18.** 8×10^9 8,000,000,000 **19.** 6.503×10^2 650.3   **20.** 9.027×10^1 90.27

21. 8.123×10^1 81.23   **22.** 1×10^{12} 1,000,000,000,000   **23.** 4.00×10^9 4,000,000,000   **24.** 7.3×10^6 7,300,000

Express these quantities using scientific notation.

B **25.** Maximum distance of the earth from the sun: 152,000,000 km
1.52×10^8 km
26. Maximum distance of Pluto from the sun: 7,323,000,000 km
7.323×10^9 km
27. Distance of the star Alpha Centauri from the earth: 40,710,000,000,000 km 4.071×10^{13} km

CLASSROOM EXERCISES

A classroom discussion might bring out "rules of thumb" or shortcuts for changing numbers to scientific notation. For example, in classroom exercises 5–8, a decimal point can be inserted after the left-hand digit and the power of 10 determined by the number of digits to the right of the decimal point. In classroom exercise 8, there are 7 digits to the right of 2.

$$26,000,000 = 2.6 \times 10^7$$

In classroom exercises 9–12, a possible shortcut is to "move" the decimal point to the right as many places as the exponent of 10. For example, $3 \times 10^4 = 30,000$.

In classroom exercise 14, note that 3.3×8.1 is greater than 10. Therefore, the power of 10 must be adjusted appropriately.

$$(3.3 \times 10^4)(8.1 \times 10^3)$$
$$= (3.3 \times 8.1)(10^4 \times 10^3)$$
$$= 26.73 \times 10^7$$
$$= 2.673 \times 10 \times 10^7$$
$$= 2.673 \times 10^8$$

ASSIGNMENT GUIDE

Basic   1–24 all, Review Exercises
Average   9–41 odd, Review Exercises
Enriched 9–41 odd, 43–46 all, Review
              Exercises

PRACTICE WORKSHEET 18

4-4 SCIENTIFIC NOTATION

■ Write the number in scientific notation.

1. 200 $\underline{2 \times 10^2}$ 2. 230 $\underline{2.3 \times 10^2}$ 3. 234 $\underline{2.34 \times 10^2}$

4. 58,000,000 $\underline{5.8 \times 10^7}$ 5. 7,000,000,000 $\underline{7 \times 10^9}$ 6. 990,000,000,000 $\underline{9.9 \times 10^{11}}$

7. 20×10^5 $\underline{2 \times 10^6}$ 8. 0.53×10^8 $\underline{5.3 \times 10^7}$ 9. 873×10 $\underline{8.73 \times 10^3}$

■ Write in standard decimal notation.

10. 7×10^3 $\underline{7000}$ 11. 8×10^6 $\underline{8,000,000}$ 12. 5.43×10^5 $\underline{543,000}$

13. 8.47×10^1 $\underline{84.7}$ 14. 5×10^1 $\underline{50}$ 15. 1×10^3 $\underline{1000}$

16. 1.01×10^9 $\underline{1,010,000,000}$ 17. 9.99×10^8 $\underline{999,000,000}$ 18. 5.060×10^7 $\underline{50,600,000}$

■ Write the product in scientific notation.

19. $(2 \times 10^4)(3 \times 10^3)$ $\underline{6 \times 10^7}$ 20. $(5 \times 10^6)(4 \times 10^8)$ $\underline{2 \times 10^{15}}$

21. $(3 \times 10^{15})(7 \times 10^3)$ $\underline{2.1 \times 10^{19}}$ 22. $(2.5 \times 10^4)(2 \times 10)$ $\underline{5.0 \times 10^5}$

23. $(2.25 \times 10^{12})(6 \times 10^7)$ $\underline{1.35 \times 10^{20}}$ 24. $(8)(9 \times 10^7)$ $\underline{7.2 \times 10^8}$

25. $(3 \times 10^4)^2$ $\underline{9 \times 10^8}$ 26. $(2 \times 10^5)^3$ $\underline{8 \times 10^{15}}$ 27. $(4 \times 10^6)^3$ $\underline{6.4 \times 10^{19}}$

WRITTEN EXERCISES

In exercises 31–32, 35–36, and 38–42, the students may have to be reminded not to stop before their answer is written in proper scientific notation. For example, in exercise 32, 40×10^8 is not standard form; 4×10^9 is the correct expression.

EXTRA PRACTICE, page 625
COMPUTER WORKSHEET 6

Express these quantities using scientific notation.

28. Distance of the star Capella from the earth: 425,000,000,000,000 km 4.25×10^{14} km

29. Area of the Pacific Ocean: 166,000,000 km² 1.66×10^8 km²

30. Area of the Atlantic Ocean: 86,520,000 km² 8.652×10^7 km²

Write the product in scientific notation.

31. $(5 \times 10^4)(4 \times 10^5)$ 2×10^{10} **32.** $(8 \times 10^5)(5 \times 10^3)$ 4×10^9

33. $(1.1 \times 10^{20})(1.1 \times 10^{30})$ 1.21×10^{50} **34.** $(2.3 \times 10^{15})(1.2 \times 10^{10})$ 2.76×10^{25}

35. $(9 \times 10^3)(9 \times 10^6)(9 \times 10^9)$ 7.29×10^{20} **36.** $(3 \times 10^4)(7 \times 10^6)(8 \times 10^8)$ 1.68×10^{20}

37. $(2 \times 10^4)^3$ 8×10^{12} **38.** $(3 \times 10^5)^4$ 8.1×10^{21}

39. $400,000 \times 5,000,000$ 2×10^{12} **40.** $60,000 \times 45,000 \times 700,000$ 1.89×10^{15}

41. $6,200,000 \times 3,100,000$ 1.922×10^{13} **42.** $5,000 \times 75,000 \times 80,000$ 3×10^{13}

Ⓒ The volume of a sea can be estimated by multiplying its area (in square meters) by its average depth (in meters). Write the volume (in cubic meters) of these seas using scientific notation.

Sea	Area (m^2)	Average depth (m)	
43. Mediterranean	2.5×10^{12}	1500	3.75×10^{15} cubic meters
44. Red	4.5×10^{11}	580	2.61×10^{14} cubic meters
45. Yellow	2.9×10^{11}	37	1.073×10^{13} cubic meters
46. Bering	2.25×10^{12}	1500	3.375×10^{15} cubic meters

■ REVIEW EXERCISES

Simplify these absolute value expressions.   [2–1]

1. $\left| -3\frac{1}{2} \right|$ $3\frac{1}{2}$ **2.** $|-1.5| + |1.5|$ 3

Simplify.   [2–2, 2–3]

3. $4 + (-7)$ -3 **4.** $(-8 + (-5)) + 7$ -6 **5.** $|-3 + 5| + |-3| + |5|$ 10

6. $-6 - (-5)$ -1 **7.** $-7.5 - 6.25$ -13.75 **8.** $|-4 - 10|$ 14

r	s	t
-3	4	-12

Substitute and simplify.

9. $|r| + |s|$ 7 [2–1]

10. $(r + s) + t$ -11 [2–2]

11. $s - t$ 16 [2–3]

EXTENSION Scientific notation on a calculator

The numbers displayed on most calculators are limited to 8 or 10 digits. However, you can compute with numbers that have more digits by using scientific notation on a calculator that has a key labeled $\boxed{\text{EXP}}$ or $\boxed{\text{EE}}$.

Example 1   Enter 4,764,000,000,000 on a calculator.

Solution   Express the number using scientific notation.

$$4{,}764{,}000{,}000{,}000 = 4.764 \cdot 10^{12}$$

Key Sequence	Display
4.764 $\boxed{\text{EXP}}$ 12	4.764 12

Example 2   Simplify. $1{,}725{,}900{,}000{,}000 \times 3{,}940{,}000$

Express the product using scientific notation.

Solution

Key Sequence	Display
1.7259 $\boxed{\text{EXP}}$ 12 $\times$ 3.94 $\boxed{\text{EXP}}$ 6 =	6.800046 18

Write the number using standard decimal notation.

1. 5.218   07   *52,180,000*   **2.** 3.946281   09   *3,946,281,000*

3. 4.6   05   *460,000*   **4.** 9.57   02   *957*

5. 4.87   01   *48.7*   **6.** 3.001   05   *300,100*

Simplify. Express the answer using scientific notation.

7. $482{,}000 \times 3000$ *$1.446 \cdot 10^9$*

8. $485{,}000 \times 36{,}170{,}000$ *$1.754245 \cdot 10^{13}$*

9. $2{,}198{,}073 \times 328{,}651$ *$7.223988895 \cdot 10^{11}$*

10. $685{,}000 \div 50{,}000$ *$1.37 \cdot 10$*

11. $729{,}800{,}000{,}000 \div 89{,}000{,}000$ *$8.2 \cdot 10^3$*

12. $23{,}278{,}000{,}000{,}000{,}000 \div 565{,}000{,}000{,}000$ *$4.12 \cdot 10^4$*

Answers will vary according to the number of digits in the calculator display.

Class Starter Quiz
on previous section

Write the number in scientific notation.

1. 320,000,000 3.2×10^8
2. 500×10^7 5×10^9

Write the number in standard decimal notation.

3. 4.23×10^5 423,000
4. 8.08×10^1 80.8

Simplify. Write the product in scientific notation.

5. $(7 \times 10^5)(8 \times 10^4)$ 5.6×10^{10}

PURPOSE

Properties of exponents must be applied to efficiently compute and simplify algebraic expressions. Knowledge of the properties of exponents also provides a foundation for the study of exponential and logarithmic functions in advanced algebra.

PREVIEW

Use the Preview as a discovery experience. Encourage students to try to develop and state generalizations or general principles as a result of the exercises in the Preview.

LESSON

The principles stated in the lesson are based on experiences the students received in the Preview. Additional numerical examples might be worthwhile—for example, $(2^2)^3$ or $(2^2 \cdot 3)^5$. Students should, of course, use the properties of exponents directly in doing exercises such as simplifying $(2^2)^3$. However, they should also understand exponents well enough to use the definition of exponent to do the simplifying. For example, if a student makes an error in simplifying $(2^2)^3$, the student should be able to go back to the definition of exponents.

$$(2^2)^3 = (2 \cdot 2)(2 \cdot 2)(2 \cdot 2) = 2^6$$

OBJECTIVE 4–5

To find powers of monomials.

4–5 Powers of Monomials

Preview Discovery

Use your knowledge of exponents to complete these equations.

$(a^3)^2 = (a^3)(a^3) = a^?$ 6

$(b^4)^3 = (b^?)(b^?)(b^?) = b^?$ 4, 4, 4, 12

$(y^2)^4 = y^?$ 8

$(a^2)^3 = (a^2)(a^2)(a^2) = a^?$ 6

$(x^5)^2 = (x^?)(x^?) = x^?$ 5, 5, 10

$(a^m)^2 = a^?$ 2m

The following expressions consist of two factors raised to a power. Write each expression without using parentheses.

$(2x)^3 = (2x)(2x)(2x) = ?$ $8x^3$

$(ab^2)^3 = a^?b^?$ 3, 6

$(a^5b^m)^2 = a^{10}b^?$ 2m

$(3a^2)^2 = ?a^4$ 9

$(x^2y^3)^4 = ?$ x^8y^{12}

$(x^my^n)^2 = ?$ $x^{2m}y^{2n}$

■ LESSON

The first group of problems in the Preview illustrates this property of exponents.

> ## The Multiplication Property of Exponents
> For all numbers a, and all positive integers m and n,
> $$(a^m)^n = a^{mn}.$$

The multiplication property of exponents is a consequence of the definition of an exponent and the basic number properties.

$$(4^3)^2 = (4^3)(4^3) = 4^{3+3} = 4^6$$

$$(a^m)^n = \overbrace{a^m \cdot a^m \cdot \ \cdots \ \cdot a^m}^{n \text{ factors}} = \overbrace{a^{m+m+\cdots+m}}^{n \text{ addends}} = a^{mn}$$

If a number with an exponent is raised to a power, multiply the exponents.

> **Example 1** Simplify. **a.** $(x^2)^4$ **b.** $(y^3)^n$
> *Solution* **a.** $(x^2)^4 = x^{2 \cdot 4} = x^8$ **b.** $(y^3)^n = y^{3n}$

Students should not be given homework they cannot do. Therefore, if the end of the planned lesson is not reached with time to check for understanding, either adjust the homework to fit the part of the lesson you know is understood or do not give any homework.

Example 1.
Simplify. **a.** $(a^4)^3$ **b.** $(x^m)^2$
a. $(a^4)^3 = a^{4 \cdot 3}$ **b.** $(x^m)^2 = x^{m \cdot 2}$
$= a^{12}$ $= x^{2m}$

Example 2.
Simplify. $(2x^3y^2)^5$
$(2x^3y^2)^5 = 2^5(x^3)^5(y^2)^5$
$= 32x^{15}y^{10}$

The second group of problems in the Preview illustrates this property of exponents.

The Distributive Property of Exponents over Multiplication

For all numbers a and b, and all positive integers n,
$$(ab)^n = a^n b^n.$$

The distributive property of exponents over multiplication is also a consequence of the definition of an exponent and basic number properties.

$$(2x)^3 = (2x)(2x)(2x) = (2 \cdot 2 \cdot 2)(xxx) = 2^3 x^3$$

$$(a^m b^n)^p = \overbrace{(a^m b^n) \cdot \ \cdots \ \cdot (a^m b^n)}^{p \text{ factors of } a^m b^n}$$

$$= \overbrace{(a^m \cdot a^m \cdot \ \cdots \ \cdot a^m)}^{p \text{ factors of } a^m} \overbrace{(b^n \cdot b^n \cdot \ \cdots \ \cdot b^n)}^{p \text{ factors of } b^n}$$

$$= a^{mp} b^{np}$$

If the product of two factors is raised to a power, *each* factor is raised to that power.

Example 2 Simplify. $(3a^2b^3)^4$
Solution $(3a^2b^3)^4 = 3^4(a^2)^4(b^3)^4$
$= 81a^8 b^{12}$

Some students confuse these two expressions:
$$a^2 \cdot a^3 \quad \text{and} \quad (a^2)^3$$

Remember! If you are not sure how to simplify an expression involving exponents, think about what the exponent means.
$$a^2 \cdot a^3 = (aa)(aaa) = a^5 \qquad (a^2)^3 = (aa)(aa)(aa) = a^6$$

CHECK UNDERSTANDING

- Are the expressions $2^2 \cdot 2^4$ and $(2^2)^4$ equivalent? (No)
- Which number is larger, $(3^4 \cdot 3^6)$ or $(3 \cdot 3^2)^3$? $(3^4 \cdot 3^6)$
- Use the definition of exponents to express $(3a^2)^5$. Then simplify.
$((3a^2)^5 = (3a^2)(3a^2)(3a^2)(3a^2)(3a^2)$
$= 3^5 a^{10} = 243a^{10})$

ASSIGNMENT GUIDE

Basic 1–24 all, Review Exercises
Average 1–23 odd, 25–40 all, Review Exercises
Enriched 1–23 odd, 25–44 all, Review Exercises

PRACTICE WORKSHEET 19

4-5 POWERS OF MONOMIALS
■ Simplify.
1. $(a^{10})^2$ a^{20} 2. $(a^{100})^1$ a^{100} 3. $(a^3)^9$ a^{27} 4. $(b^{10})^{100}$ b^{1000}
5. $(2b^3)^4$ $16b^{12}$ 6. $2(b^3)^4$ $2b^{12}$ 7. $(3b^2)^4$ $81b^8$ 8. $3(b^2)^4$ $3b^8$
9. $(0.1c^2)^3$ $0.001c^6$ 10. $(c^2d^3)^4$ c^8d^{12} 11. $(2c^2d^4)^3$ $8c^6d^{12}$ 12. $(3c^3d^4)^2$ $9c^6d^8$
13. $(\frac{1}{2}x)^3$ $\frac{1}{8}x^3$ 14. $(\frac{2}{3}x^3)^2$ $\frac{4}{9}x^6$ 15. $\frac{2}{3}(3a)^2$ $6a^2$ 16. $\frac{1}{4}(2y)^2$ y^2
■ Write the larger number.
17. $(2^3)^4$ or $(2^3)(2^4)$ $(2^3)^4$ 18. 3^2 or 2^3 3^2
19. $(2 \cdot 3)^5$ or $2 \cdot 3^5$ $(2 \cdot 3)^5$ 20. $[(\frac{1}{2})^3]^4$ or $(\frac{1}{2})^3(\frac{1}{2})^4$ $(1/2)^3(1/2)^4$
21. $(2 \cdot 4)^3$ or $2 \cdot 4^3$ $(2 \cdot 4)^3$ 22. $(\frac{1}{2} \cdot 3)^4$ or $\frac{1}{2} \cdot 3^4$ $1/2 \cdot 3^4$

■ CLASSROOM EXERCISES

Simplify.
1. $a^2 \cdot a^4$ a^6 2. $(a^2)^4$ a^8 3. $(m^3)^3$ m^9 4. $m^3 \cdot m^3$ m^6
5. $(x^3)^5$ x^{15} 6. $(3x)^2$ $9x^2$ 7. $(2x)^3$ $8x^3$ 8. $(2x^2y)^4$ $16x^8y^4$

In exercises 21–24, encourage students to determine which number is larger by doing a minimum amount of computation. For example, in exercise 21,

$(5 \cdot 7)^3 = 5^3 \cdot 7^3$

$5^3 \cdot 7^3$ is greater than $5 \cdot 7^3$, since it has 2 more factors of 5.

ENRICHMENT PROBLEMS

- True or false?
  a. $(3^2)^2 = 3^{(2^2)}$ T
  b. $(3^2)^3 = 3^{(2^3)}$ F
  c. For all positive integers m and n,
  $(3^m)^n = 3^{(m^n)}$ F
- a^{bc} is defined to mean $a^{(b^c)}$.
  Simplify. 10^{3^4} 10^{81}

EXTRA PRACTICE, page 625

■ WRITTEN EXERCISES

Simplify.

A   **1.** $(x^4)^5$ x^{20} **2.** $(y^3)^4$ y^{12} **3.** $(a^3)^7$ a^{21} **4.** $(b^5)^6$ b^{30}

5. $(2c)^4$ $16c^4$ **6.** $(3d)^3$ $27d^3$ **7.** $(4y^2)^3$ $64y^6$ **8.** $(2x^3)^5$ $32x^{15}$

9. $\left(\frac{1}{2}b^3\right)^3$ $\frac{1}{8}b^9$ **10.** $\left(\frac{1}{3}c\right)^3$ $\frac{1}{27}c^3$ **11.** $(0.1r^4)^2$ $0.01r^8$ **12.** $(0.01s^3)^2$ $0.0001s^6$

13. $(-2x^3)^2$ $4x^6$ **14.** $(-3y^2)^4$ $81y^8$ **15.** $(-w^5)^3$ $-w^{15}$ **16.** $(-t^4)^5$ $-t^{20}$

17. $(x^2y)^4$ x^8y^4 **18.** $(a^3b^2)^3$ a^9b^6 **19.** $(2c^3d)^5$ $32c^{15}d^5$ **20.** $(3rs^4)^4$ $81r^4s^{16}$

Which number is larger? Why?

21. $\underline{(5 \cdot 7)^3}$ or $5 \cdot 7^3$ 5^2 times as large   **22.** $5^4 \cdot 2^5$ or $\underline{(5 \cdot 2)^5}$ 5 times as large

23. $\underline{(4^5 \cdot 4^{10})}$ or 4^{50} 4^{35} times as large   **24.** $(4^{10} \cdot 4^{20})$ or $(4^{10})^3$ Neither

Simplify.

B   **25.** $2x^3 \cdot (3x)^2$ $18x^5$ **26.** $3y^2 \cdot (2y)^3$ $24y^5$

27. $(-ab)(a^2b)^2$ $-a^5b^3$ **28.** $(-rs)(rs^3)^2$ $-r^3s^7$

29. $(-2xy)^3(-x^2)$ $8x^5y^3$ **30.** $(-3cd)^3(-d^2)$ $27c^3d^5$

31. $(4a^2)^3\left(\frac{1}{2}a^3\right)^2$ $16a^{12}$ **32.** $(8b^3)^2\left(\frac{1}{4}b^2\right)^2$ $4b^{10}$

33. $(-x)^5(-x)^2(-x)^3$ x^{10} **34.** $(-y)^4(-y)^3(-y)^2$ $-y^9$

35. $(2t)^3(-t^2)$ $-8t^5$ **36.** $(-w^3)(3w^2)^2$ $-9w^7$

37. $(abc^2)^3(a^2b)^2$ $a^7b^5c^6$ **38.** $(r^2st^3)^2(s^4t)^3$ $r^4s^{14}t^9$

39. $(-3xy^2)^3(-2x^2y)^2$ $-108x^7y^8$ **40.** $(-5c^2d)^2(-2cd^2)^3$ $-200c^7d^8$

Rewrite as a single number with an exponent.

Sample $8 \cdot 6^3 = 2^3 \cdot 6^3 = (2 \cdot 6)^3 = 12^3$

C   **41.** $16 \cdot 5^4$ 10^4 **42.** $64 \cdot 27$ 12^3 **43.** $25 \cdot 2^5 \cdot 5^3$ 10^5 **44.** $3^2 \cdot 18 \cdot 2^3$ 6^4

■ REVIEW EXERCISES

Simplify.   [2–4, 2–5, 2–6]

1. $(-5)(-6)$ 30   **2.** $(-3)(-6) + (-2)(-8)$ 34   **3.** $(3)(-4) + (-3)(-4)$ 0

4. $\frac{-24}{-8}$ 3   **5.** $-\frac{12}{3} + -\frac{12}{4}$ -7 **6.** $-\frac{2}{3} \div \frac{3}{4}$ $-\frac{8}{9}$

7. $-5 - (-3x) - (-x)$ $-5 + 4x$ **8.** $3x - (-7) - (-x)$ $4x + 7$

r	s	t
-3	4	-12

Substitute and simplify.   [2–4, 2–5, 2–6]

9. $rs + rt$ 24   **10.** $\frac{t}{r} + \frac{t}{s}$ 1   **11.** $r - s - t$ 5

To multiply a monomial and a polynomial.

Class Starter Quiz
on previous section

Simplify.

1. $(x^5)^4$ x^{20}
2. $(a^2b^3)^4$ a^8b^{12}
3. $(2x^5y)^3$ $8x^{15}y^3$

Simplify by writing in standard decimal notation.

4. $(10^3)^4$ 1,000,000,000,000
5. $(3^2)^3$ 729

4–6 Multiplying a Polynomial by a Monomial

Preview

The multiplication algorithm is based on the distributive property.

$$\begin{array}{r} 231 \\ \times\ 3 \\ \hline 693 \end{array}$$

By writing the numbers in expanded form, we can see how the distributive property is applied.

$$\begin{aligned} 3(231) &= 3(200 + 30 + 1) \\ &= 3 \cdot 200 + 3 \cdot 30 + 3 \cdot 1 \\ &= 600 + 90 + 3 \\ &= 693 \end{aligned}$$

Note that the equation shows the product of a monomial and a polynomial. In this lesson, you will use the same skills with polynomials that have variables in them.

■ LESSON

To find the product of a monomial and a polynomial, use the distributive property to multiply each term of the polynomial by the monomial. Then simplify.

Example 1 Simplify. $7(3x - 2y)$

Solution $7(3x - 2y) = (7 \cdot 3x) - (7 \cdot 2y)$ *Distributive property*

$= 21x - 14y$ *Computation*

Example 2 Simplify. $4a(2a + 8)$

Solution $4a(2a + 8) = (4a \cdot 2a) + (4a \cdot 8)$

$= 8a^2 + 32a$

When using the distributive properties to expand expressions, be careful when multiplying negative factors.

Example 3 Simplify. $-2x(-3x + 5y)$

Solution $-2x(-3x + 5y) = (-2x)(-3x) + (-2x)(5y)$

$= (6)x^2 + (-10)xy$

$= 6x^2 - 10xy$

PURPOSE

Many applications in algebra necessitate multiplying polynomials. In order to multiply two polynomials, a student must first be able to multiply a polynomial by a monomial.

PREVIEW

Use the Preview to demonstrate how the multiplication algorithm utilizes the distributive property. You may wish to show in the multiplication of 2 two-digit numbers.

$$\begin{array}{r} 23 \\ \times\ 54 \\ \hline 92 \\ 1150 \\ \hline 1242 \end{array}$$

$23 \cdot 54$
$= (20 + 3)(50 + 4)$
$= (20 + 3)50 + (20 + 3)4$
$= 20 \cdot 50 + 3 \cdot 50 + 20 \cdot 4 + 3 \cdot 4$
$= 1000 + 150 + 80 + 12$
$= 1150 + 92$
$= 1242$

ADDITIONAL EXAMPLES

Example 1. Simplify. $10(2x + 5y)$

$10(2x + 5y)$
$= (10 \cdot 2x) + (10 \cdot 5y)$ *Distributive property*
$= 20x + 50y$ *Computation*

Example 2. Simplify. $3a(5a - 6)$

$3a(5a - 6)$
$= (3a \cdot 5a) - (3a \cdot 6)$
$= 15a^2 - 18a$

Example 3. Simplify. $-3n(-2n + m)$

$-3n(-2n + m)$
$= (-3n)(-2n) + (-3n)(m)$
$= 6n^2 + (-3nm)$
$= 6n^2 - 3nm$

Example 4. Simplify. $3x^2(4x^2 + 5x - 6)$

$$3x^2(4x^2 + 5x - 6)$$
$$= 3x^2 \cdot 4x^2 + 3x^2 \cdot 5x - 3x^2 \cdot 6$$
$$= 12x^4 + 15x^3 - 18x^2$$

Example 5.

Simplify. $-4b^2(5a^2 - 2ab - 3b^2)$

$$-4b^2(5a^2 - 2ab - 3b^2)$$
$$= (-4b^2)(5a^2) + (-4b^2)(-2ab) +$$
$$(-4b^2)(-3b^2)$$
$$= -20b^2a^2 + 8b^3a + 12b^4$$

As you go over the above examples, emphasize these points.

- Each term inside the grouping symbols is multiplied by the term outside the grouping symbols.
- Care must be taken to get the proper signs for the terms of the product.
- Care must be taken to get the proper powers in the terms of the product.

CHECK UNDERSTANDING

Simplify.

a. $2(a + b)$ $(2a + 2b)$
b. $2(a - b)$ $(2a - 2b)$
c. $-2(a + b)$ $(-2a - 2b)$
d. $-2(a - b)$ $(-2a + 2b)$
e. $-2(x - y + z)$ $(-2x + 2y - 2z)$

CLASSROOM EXERCISES

In classroom exercises 3, 7, 8, and 11, note that signs are changed when multiplying by a negative number (or opposite).

Example 4 Simplify. $2x^2(3x^2 - x + 7)$

Solution $2x^2(3x^2 - x + 7) = (2x^2 \cdot 3x^2) - (2x^2 \cdot x) + (2x^2 \cdot 7)$
$$= 6x^4 - 2x^3 + 14x^2$$

Example 5 Simplify. $-3a(5a - b + 2)$

Solution $-3a(5a - b + 2) = -3a[5a + (-b) + 2]$
$$= (-3a) \cdot (5a) + (-3a) \cdot (-b) + (-3a) \cdot 2$$
$$= -15a^2 + 3ab + (-6a)$$
$$= -15a^2 + 3ab - 6a$$

By substituting simple values for variables, we can check to determine whether the polynomial product is equivalent to the original expression.

Check Let $a = 1$ and $b = 2$. Then
$$-3a(5a - b + 2) = -3(5 - 2 + 2) = -15$$
$$-15a^2 + 3ab - 6a = -15 + 6 - 6 = -15 \qquad \text{It checks.}$$

■ CLASSROOM EXERCISES

Simplify.

1. $3(4x + 2y)$ $12x + 6y$ **2.** $2(3a - 5b)$ $6a - 10b$ **3.** $-5(3x - 4)$ $-15x + 20$ **4.** $x(3x + 4)$ $3x^2 + 4x$

5. $3a(2a + 1)$ $6a^2 + 3a$ **6.** $3c^2(-9c - 4c^2)$ $-27c^3 - 12c^4$ **7.** $-3ab(a^2 + b^2)$ $-3a^3b - 3ab^3$ **8.** $-y(7 - 3y)$ $-7y + 3y^2$

9. $4a^2(2a - 3)$ $8a^3 - 12a^2$ **10.** $7(6a + 2b - c)$ $42a + 14b - 7c$ **11.** $-2a(-5b + 3c + 2d)$ $10ab - 6ac - 4ad$

■ WRITTEN EXERCISES

Simplify.

A   **1.** $4(a + 3)$ $4a + 12$ **2.** $3(b + 5)$ $3b + 15$ **3.** $5(2d + 4)$ $10d + 20$ **4.** $5(2d - 4)$ $10d - 20$

5. $-5(n - 2m)$ $-5n + 10m$ **6.** $-4(a - 2b)$ $-4a + 8b$ **7.** $-5d(3d - 2)$ $-15d^2 + 10d$ **8.** $-2x(8x - 10)$ $-16x^2 + 20x$

Multiply the monomial and the polynomial. Check.

9. $3(100 + 30 + 2)$ *Check:* $3 \cdot 132$ 396   **10.** $2(400 + 20 + 3)$ *Check:* $2 \cdot 423$ 846

11. $5(300 - 1)$ *Check:* $5 \cdot 299$ 1495   **12.** $6(200 - 1)$ *Check:* $6 \cdot 199$ 1194

13. $\frac{1}{2}(200 + 80 + 6)$ *Check:* $\frac{1}{2} \cdot 286$ 143   **14.** $\frac{1}{3}(600 + 90 + 3)$ *Check:* $\frac{1}{3} \cdot 693$ 231

15. $0.1(5 + 0.2)$ *Check:* $0.1 \cdot 5.2$ 0.52   **16.** $0.6(4 + 0.5)$ *Check:* $0.6 \cdot 4.5$ 2.70

Check students' ability to translate algebraic symbols into words by having them read expressions such as $(a + b) - (a + b)$ aloud.

ASSIGNMENT GUIDE

Basic   1–16 all, Review Exercises, Self-Quiz 2

Average   1–23 odd, 25–34 all, Review Exercises, Self-Quiz 2

Enriched   1–33 odd, 35–39 all, Review Exercises, Self-Quiz 2

PRACTICE WORKSHEET 19

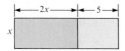

Simplify.

17. $-5r(3r^2 - 2r - 8)$
$-15r^3 + 10r^2 + 40r$

18. $-4s(2s^2 - 3s - 4)$
$-8s^3 + 12s^2 + 16s$

19. $10t^2(3t^2 + 6t + 5)$
$30t^4 + 60t^3 + 50t^2$

20. $3t^2(10t^2 + 20t + 30)$
$30t^4 + 60t^3 + 90t^2$

21. $a^2(a + b)$ $a^3 + a^2b$

22. $y^2(x + y)$ $xy^2 + y^3$

23. $2y^3(2x + y)$ $4xy^3 + 2y^4$

24. $3a^3(2a + b)$ $6a^4 + 3a^3b$

25. $-ab(a + b)$ $-a^2b - ab^2$

26. $-xy(x + y)$ $-x^2y - xy^2$

27. $-st(2s - t)$ $-2s^2t + st^2$

28. $-mn(m - 2n)$
$-m^2n + 2mn^2$

29. $x^2y(x + y)$ $x^3y + x^2y^2$

30. $ab^2(a + b)$ $a^2b^2 + ab^3$

31. $x^2y(x + xy + y)$
$x^3y + x^3y^2 + x^2y^2$

32. $-ab^2(a - ab + b)$
$-a^2b^2 + a^2b^3 - ab^3$

33. $-ab^2(a - 2ab + b)$
$-a^2b^2 + 2a^2b^3 - ab^3$

34. $3x^2y(2x + xy - y)$
$6x^3y + 3x^3y^2 - 3x^2y^2$

For each figure below:

a. Express the area of the shaded region as a product of a monomial and a polynomial.

b. Simplify the product.

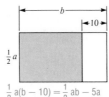

Sample

Solution   **a.** $x(2x + 5)$
b. $2x^2 + 5x$

WRITTEN EXERCISES

In exercises 17–34, students should carry out the multiplication of the polynomial by the monomial mentally if possible.

For additional exercises similar to exercises 35–37, ask students to express the total surface area of the solids in exercises 38 and 39 and simplify the expressions for the area.

35.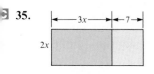

$2x(3x + 7) = 6x^2 + 14x$

36.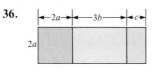

$2a(2a + 3b + c) = 4a^2 + 6ab + 2ac$

37.

$\frac{1}{2}a(b - 10) = \frac{1}{2}ab - 5a$

For each solid pictured below:

a. Express the volume of the solid as a product.

b. Simplify the product.

38. Triangular prism

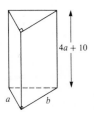

$\frac{1}{2}ab(4a + 10) = 2a^2b + 5ab$

39. Cylinder

$\pi r^2(2r + 5) = 2\pi r^3 + 5\pi r^2$

[*Hint:* The volume equals the area of the base times the height.]

CONCEPT EXTENSION

A valuable algebraic skill is the ability to perceive the relationship of one number or expression to another. In the following two examples, we take advantage of a given number being close to "a nice number."

Compute. $999 \cdot 23 = (1000 - 1) \cdot 23$
$= 23{,}000 - 23$
$= 22{,}977$

Compute. $\dfrac{176}{18} = \dfrac{180 - 4}{18}$

$= \dfrac{1}{18}(180) - \dfrac{1}{18}(4)$

$= 10 - \dfrac{4}{18}$

$= 9\dfrac{7}{9}$

- Simplify mentally.

a. $39 \cdot 90$

$40(90) - 90 = 3600 - 90 = 3510$

b. $18 \cdot 73$

$20(73) - 2(73) = 1460 - 146 \cdot$
$= 1314$

c. $99 \cdot 99$

$100(99) - 99 = 9900 - 99 = 9801$

d. $337 \div 17$

$\dfrac{340}{17} - \dfrac{3}{17} = 20 - \dfrac{3}{17} = 19\dfrac{14}{17}$

e. $10035 \div 99$

$\dfrac{9999}{99} + \dfrac{36}{99} = 101 + \dfrac{4}{11} = 101\dfrac{4}{11}$

f. $\frac{1}{2}$ of $59\frac{3}{8}$

$\dfrac{1}{2}\left(60 - \dfrac{5}{8}\right) = 30 - \dfrac{5}{16} = 29\dfrac{11}{16}$

Enrichment Worksheet 8

NAME _____

INTERPRETING ALGEBRAIC EXPRESSIONS

■ Match each expression with a picture.

1. $2n$ D   2. $n + 2$ L   3. n^2 A

4. $n(n + 2)$ B   5. $2n^2$ I   6. $2n + 2$ E

7. $(n + 2)^2$ J   8. $2(n + 2)$ C   9. $n^2 + 2$ G

10. $2 - n^2$ K   11. $2n - 2$ H   12. $n^2 - 2$ F

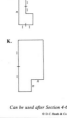

Can be used after Section 4-6
© D.C. Heath & Co.

EXTRA PRACTICE, page 625

Strategy for Success   Using review exercises

The review exercises after each lesson help you review mathematics from previous lessons and previous courses. Lesson numbers are given along with the review exercises so that if you have difficulty with an exercise, you can review the related lesson itself.

■ REVIEW EXERCISES

Simplify.

1. $5x - x$ 4x

2. $7x - x - 7$ 6x − 7   [2–7]

3. $3x + 6y - 2x - 6$ x + 6y − 6

4. $4x + 3y - 3x - 2y$ x + y

5. $7(x - 2)$ 7x − 14

6. $3(x + 5) - (x - 6)$ 2x + 21   [2–8]

7. $2(3a - 5) - 3(2a - 6)$ 8

8. $4(a - b) - (a + 4b)$ 3a − 8b

9. $3(5a - 1) - 2(a - 3)$ 13a + 3

10. $2(a - b) - (a - b)$ a − b

11. $2(a + b) - 3(b - 1)$ 2a − b + 3

12. $3(a + b) + (a + b)$ 4a + 4b

Solve this problem by making a table of data.   [2–9]

13. Michelle deposits $1 in the bank on the first day, $2 on the second day, $4 on the third day. On which day will she have a total of $1023 in the bank?   Tenth

---

Self-Quiz 2

4–4   **1.** Express 2,890,000 in scientific notation. 2.89×10^6

2. Express 5.7×10^4 in standard decimal notation.   57,000

3. Find the product $2400 \times 190,000$. Express the answer in scientific notation. 4.56×10^8

4–5   Simplify.

4. $(y^4)^3$ y^{12} **5.** $(2a^2)^4$ $16a^8$ **6.** $(a^2b^3)^5$ $a^{10}b^{15}$ **7.** $(-3b^3)^3$
  $-27b^9$

4–6   Simplify.

8. $4(2x + 5y)$ 8x + 20y   **9.** $3(8a - 6b)$ 24a − 18b

10. $-2r(3r - 8)$ $-6r^2 + 16r$ **11.** $3c^2(2a - 3b + c)$
  $6ac^2 - 9bc^2 + 3c^3$

You may wish to spend two days on this section. Refer to the Pacing Chart.

4-7 Problem Solving — Uniform Motion

Preview

The distance between town A and town B is 160 kilometers. Mrs. Carter and Mrs. Brown left town A in separate cars at 8:00 A.M. Mrs. Carter drove at a very steady rate and arrived in town B at 10:00 A.M. Mrs. Brown did not drive steadily. She sometimes drove 100 kilometers per hour (km/h) and sometimes 30 kilometers per hour. She even stopped once for 5 minutes to watch a hot-air balloon. However, Mrs. Brown also arrived in town B at 10:00 A.M.

- How many kilometers did each person drive?   160
- How much time did each trip require?   2 h
- What was each driver's average rate in kilometers per hour?   80
- Where was each driver at 9:00 A.M.?   Mrs. Carter: halfway, Mrs. Brown: can't say
- Did Mrs. Brown ever pass Mrs. Carter?   Can't say

In this lesson you will learn to solve problems involving uniform motion.

■ LESSON

In the Preview, Mrs. Carter's motion is an example of **uniform motion.** That is, her speed was constant. When motion is uniform, the relationship among distance traveled (d), rate of speed (r), and time traveled (t) is given by this formula:

$$d = rt$$

The units used for the time and the "time element" of the rate must be the same. For example, if the rate is given in miles per hour and the time is given in minutes, then the time units are not the same. At least one of the units *must* be changed.

Example 1   Mrs. Green drove at a rate of 80 km/h for 30 min. How far did she drive?

Solution 1   Change 30 min to 0.5 h.
$$d = rt$$
$$d = 80(0.5)$$
$$d = 40$$

Answer   Mrs. Green drove 40 km.

Solution 2   Change 80 km/h to km/min.
$$80 \text{ km/h} = \frac{80}{60} \text{ km/min} = \frac{4}{3} \text{ km/min}$$
$$d = rt$$
$$d = \frac{4}{3}(30)$$
$$d = 40$$

Answer   Mrs. Green drove 40 km.

Lesson *continued*

An alternate solution to Example 2 on page 170 is as follows:

Let x = the number of hours flown by the UFO. Then $x - 0.25$ = the number of hours flown by the INT.

$$800x + 1200(x - 0.25) = 5000$$
$$800x + 1200x - 300 = 5000$$
$$2000x - 300 = 5000$$
$$2000x = 5300$$
$$x = 2.65$$

It took the INT $2.65 - 0.25 = 2.4$ h to reach the UFO.
The UFO traveled $800 \cdot 2.65 = 2120$ km.
The INT traveled $5000 - 2120 = 2880$ km.

ADDITIONAL EXAMPLES

Example 1.
Mr. Reed drove at a rate of 75 km/h for 1 hour 20 minutes. How far did he drive?

Solution 1: Change 20 min to $\frac{1}{3}$ h.
$$d = rt$$
$$d = 75(1\tfrac{1}{3})$$
$$d = 100$$
Mr. Reed drove 100 km.

Solution 2: Change 75 km/h to $\frac{75}{60}$ or $\frac{5}{4}$ km/min.

Change 1 h 20 min to 80 min.
$$d = rt$$
$$d = \frac{5}{4} \cdot 80$$
$$d = 100$$
Mr. Reed drove 100 km.

Example 2.
Radar spotted a UFO 10,000 kilometers away approaching at a rate of 1500 km/h. In 10 minutes a plane left, flying at 1800 km/h, to intercept the UFO. How long did it take the plane to reach the UFO?

First draw a figure.

1500 km/h (UFO)

(Plane) 1800 km/h

10,000 km

The figure shows that the sum of the distances flown by the UFO and the plane is 10,000 kilometers

170

As motion problems become more complex, a drawing and/or table can make the problems easier to solve.

Example 2   Radar picked up an unidentified flying object (UFO) 5000 miles away approaching at a rate of 800 miles per hour (mph). In 15 minutes an intercepter plane (INT) was on its way to meet the UFO at a rate of 1200 mph. How long did it take the INT to reach the UFO? How far away did they meet?

Solution   First draw a figure.

UFO

INT

$\text{rate}_{\text{UFO}} = 800$ mph

$\text{rate}_{\text{INT}} = 1200$ mph

5000 miles

The figure shows that the sum of the distances flown by the UFO and the INT is 5000 miles.

Let x = the number of hours flown by the INT.
Then $x + 0.25$ = the number of hours flown by the UFO after radar sighting. [*Remember:* 15 min = 0.25 h.]

	Rate (mph)	Time (h)	Distance (mi)
UFO	800	$x + 0.25$	$800(x + 0.25)$
INT	1200	x	$1200x$

Total: 5000

$$1200x + 800(x + 0.25) = 5000$$
$$1200x + 800x + 200 = 5000$$
$$2000x + 200 = 5000$$
$$2000x = 4800$$
$$x = 2.4$$

Answer   It took the INT 2.4 h to reach the UFO.

Now find the distance traveled by the INT.

$$d = rt$$
$$d = 1200 \cdot 2.4$$
$$d = 2880$$

Answer   The INT traveled 2880 mi before it reached the UFO.

Do not label a question in advance as "hard" or "easy." The hard questions might be ignored by insecure students, and the easy questions would present all students with a no-win situation: it would be no accomplishment to know the answer, and it would be embarrassing not to know the answer.

Example 3   Mr. and Mrs. Kamm were moving from Houston to Toledo. Mr. Kamm left Houston driving one car, pulling a trailer filled with their belongings. He drove at a steady 50 mph. One-half hour later, Mrs. Kamm left, driving the other car. They both agreed that she could drive 55 mph because she was not pulling the trailer. After three hours Mr. Kamm became worried because his wife had not yet caught up with him. Should he have been worried?

Solution   One way to solve this problem is to find out how long it should take Mrs. Kamm (MRS) to catch Mr. Kamm (MR).

MR 50 mph →

MRS 55 mph →

When MRS catches up with MR, they will have driven the same distance.

Let x = the number of hours driven by MRS.

Then $x + 0.5$ = the number of hours driven by MR.

	Rate (mph)	Time (h)	Distance (mi)	
MR	50	$x + 0.5$	$50(x + 0.5)$	} Distances
MRS	55	x	$55x$	} are equal

$$55x = 50(x + 0.5)$$
$$55x = 50x + 25$$
$$5x = 25$$
$$x = 5$$

Answer   It will take Mrs. Kamm 5 hours to catch up with Mr. Kamm. Mr. Kamm should not have worried after only 3 hours.

Mathematics and Your Future

Some students are tempted to take easier courses in high school in order to earn a higher grade-point average. Using that reasoning to avoid mathematics courses is counterproductive. People responsible for college admissions and scholarships are interested in the courses you have taken as well as your average grade. They also look at scores on college entrance tests, all of which have major mathematics components. If you are interested in obtaining a scholarship or entering a selective college, you should take plenty of mathematics.

ADDITIONAL EXAMPLES

Let x = the number of hours flown by the plane.
The $x + \frac{1}{6}$ = the number of hours flown by the UFO after the radar sighting.

	Rate (km/h)	Time (h)	Distance (km)
UFO	1500	$x + \frac{1}{6}$	$1500(x + \frac{1}{6})$
Plane	1800	x	$1800x$

$$1500(x + \tfrac{1}{6}) + 1800x = 10{,}000$$
$$1500x + 250 + 1800x = 10{,}000$$
$$3300x + 250 = 10{,}000$$
$$3300x = 9750$$
$$x = \frac{9750}{3300}$$
$$x \approx 2.95$$

The plane took about 2.95 hours (or 2 hours 57 minutes) to reach the UFO.

Example 3.
William started walking at 3 mph. A half hour later, Tami followed the same route walking at 4 mph. How long will it take Tami to catch William?

Let $x + 0.5$ = the number of hours William walks.

	Rate (mph)	Time (h)	Distance (mi)
Tami	4	x	$4x$
William	3	$x + 0.5$	$3(x + 0.5)$

$$4x = 3(x + 0.5)$$
$$4x = 3x + 1.5$$
$$x = 1.5$$

Tami will catch William in 1.5 hours.

CHECK UNDERSTANDING

- If you drive 50 mph, how far do you travel in 2 hours? (100 mi)
  In ½ hour? (25 mi)
- If you ride a bicycle 20 km in 0.5 h, what is your rate in km/h? (40 km/h)
- If you walk 1 mi in 12 min, what is your rate in mph? (5 mph)

CLASSROOM EXERCISES

Note the symbols used for miles per hour (mph) and kilometers per hour (km/h).

ASSIGNMENT GUIDE

Basic   1–25 odd, Review Exercises
Average 1, 3, 11–25 odd, 27–32 all, Review Exercises
Enriched 1, 3, 11–29 odd, 30–33 all, Review Exercises

PRACTICE WORKSHEET 20

4-7 PROBLEM SOLVING — UNIFORM MOTION

■ The distances for A and B are equal. Write an equation for each problem and solve for x.

1. A: Rate is x km/h and time is 5 h.
   B: Rate is $(x + 10)$ km/h and time is 3 h. $5x = 3(x + 10)$, {15}

2. A: Rate is 200 km/h and time is x h.
   B: Rate is 240 km/h and time is $(x - 1)$ h. $200x = 240(x - 1)$, {6}

3. A: Rate is 4 mph and time is x h.
   B: Rate is 3 mph and time is $(x + 2)$ h. $4x = 3(x + 2)$, {6}

4. A: Rate is x mph and time is 10 h.
   B: Rate is $(x - 5)$ mph and time is 11 h. $10x = 11(x - 5)$, {55}

■ The sum of the distances for A and B is 480 mi. Write an equation for each problem and solve for x.

5. A: Rate is 50 mph and time is x h.
   B: Rate is 10 mph and time is x h. $50x + 10x = 480$, {8}

6. A: Rate is x mph and time is 4 h.
   B: Rate is $(x - 3)$ mph and time is 5 h. $4x + 5(x - 3) = 480$, {55}

7. A: Rate is 40 mph and time is x h.
   B: Rate is 43 mph and time is $8x$ h. $40x + (8x)43 = 480$, {5/4}

WRITTEN EXERCISES

In exercises 11–14, the formula $d = rt$ may be considered a literal equation that can be solved for r and t. $\left(r = \dfrac{d}{t}; t = \dfrac{d}{r} \right)$

   In exercises 25–33, a figure and a table are useful in understanding the relationships and in organizing the information.

EXTRA PRACTICE, page 626

■ CLASSROOM EXERCISES

1. State a formula that relates distance, rate, and time. $d = rt$

Copy and complete the table.

	Distance	Rate	Time
2.	? 30 km	60 km/h	$\frac{1}{2}$ h
3.	3.5x ? mi	x mph	3.5 h
4.	100 km	50 ? km/h	2 h
5.	y km	$\frac{y}{5}$? km/min	5 min
6.	5 mi	40 mph	? $\frac{1}{8}$ h
7.	? (55x + 27.5) mi	55 mph	$(x + 0.5)$ h

Solve.

8. Two airplanes left the same airport at the same time. One flew east at 150 mph. The other flew west at 250 mph. They are able to maintain radio contact until they are 1000 miles apart. For how many hours can they maintain radio contact? 2.5

■ WRITTEN EXERCISES

Complete these sentences.

A **1.** 300 km/h = __?__ km/min 5   **2.** 240 km/h = __?__ km/min 4

3. 300 m/min = __?__ m/s 5   **4.** 240 m/min = __?__ m/h 14,400

Copy and complete the tables.

	Distance	Rate	Time	
5.	?	50 mph	3 h	150 mi
6.	?	55 mph	2 h	110 mi
7.	?	30 m/s	1.5 s	45 m
8.	?	20 m/s	2.5 s	50 m
9.	?	600 mph	x h	600x mi
10.	?	350 mph	t h	350t mi

	Distance	Rate	Time	
11.	280 km	70 km/h	?	4 h
12.	400 km	80 km/h	?	5 h
13.	100 m	?	2 s	50 m/s
14.	200 m	?	10 s	20 m/s
15.	?	x mph	10 h	10x mi
16.	?	$(x + 10)$ mph	8 h	(8x + 80) mi

The distances for A and B are equal. Write an equation for each problem and solve for x.

17. **A:** Rate is x mph and time is 10 h
    B: Rate is $(x + 10)$ mph and time is 8 h 40

18. **A:** Rate is x km/h and time is 4 h
    B: Rate is $(x - 20)$ km/h and time is 5 h 100

19. **A:** Rate is 60 km/h and time is x h
    B: Rate is 80 km/h and time is $(x - 1)$ h 4

20. **A:** Rate is 80 mph and time is x h
    B: Rate is 50 mph and time is $(x + 3)$ h 5

The sum of the distances for A and B is 1000 km. Write an equation for each problem and solve for x.

21. **A:** Rate is 40 km/h and time is x h
    B: Rate is 60 km/h and time is x h 10

22. **A:** Rate is x km/h and time is 12 h
    B: Rate is x km/h and time is 13 h 40

23. **A:** Rate is 40 km/h and time is x hours
    B: Rate is 60 km/h and time is $(x + 5)$ hours 7

24. **A:** Rate is x km/h and time is 2 hours
    B: Rate is $(x + 60)$ km/h and time is 5 hours 100

Solve.

25. Two planes left O'Hare International Airport in Chicago at 2:00 P.M. One was flying east at 300 mph and the other was flying west at 350 mph. How many miles apart are they at 4 P.M.? 1300

26. Two planes left Will Rogers World Airport in Oklahoma City at 3:00 P.M. One was flying south at 150 mph and the other was flying south at 250 mph. How many miles apart are they at 5 P.M.? 200

27. A car left the Mile High Stadium in Denver driving north at 70 km/h. One hour later a second car left the Mile High Stadium driving south at 80 km/h. How long had the second car been driving when the two cars were 520 km apart? 3 h

28. A bus left the Astrodome in Houston driving west at 60 km/h. Two hours later another bus left the Astrodome driving east at 80 km/h. How long had the second bus been driving when the two buses were 820 km apart? 5 h

29. A zebra leaves a water hole running at 60 km/h. After the zebra has been running for 1.5 min, a wild dog leaves the water hole and chases after the zebra at 70 km/h. If both animals maintain their speed, how long would it take the hunting dog to catch the zebra? 9 min

Although the goal of this lesson is to help students develop their algebraic skills to solve uniform-motion problems, students should be encouraged to use common sense as well as problem-solving skills to check their answers. Consider Example 3. Mr. Kamm leaves a half hour before Mrs. Kamm, traveling at 50 mph. He therefore has a 25-mile head start. The difference in their speeds once she starts is 5 mph. She will gain 5 miles each hour and consequently take 5 hours to catch him.

ENRICHMENT PROBLEM

Solve by writing an equation. Check by "common sense."

• Two friends reside in towns 200 miles apart. They agree to meet for lunch at a restaurant between the two towns. Both travel at 40 mph, but the first friend leaves an hour before the second. How far is the restaurant from the first friend's town?

When the second friend leaves home, the first has traveled 40 miles. Therefore, they are 160 miles apart and each will now travel 80 miles. The restaurant is 120 miles from the first friend's home.

30. A zebra who is running at 60 km/h passes a resting cheetah. After the zebra has been running for 1 minute, the cheetah chases after the zebra at 100 km/h. If both animals maintain their speed, in how many minutes will the cheetah catch the zebra? $1\frac{1}{2}$

31. A garden snail, crawling at 60 cm/min, goes through a chicken coop. After the snail has been crawling for 299 min, a chicken leaves the coop and chases after the snail at 18,000 cm/min. If both animals maintain their speed, in how many minutes will the chicken catch the snail? 1

32. A tortoise, moving at a rate of 4 m/min, passes a rabbit. The rabbit plans to catch the tortoise after 100 m by running 800 m/min. How many minutes head start can the rabbit give the tortoise? $24\frac{7}{8}$

C **33.** Mr. Douglas and Mrs. Douglas left their home in New Orleans at the same time. Mrs. Douglas drove her car at 95 km/h and Mr. Douglas drove his car at 90 km/h. Mrs. Douglas stopped in Jackson. Mr. Douglas drove 4 hours longer and stopped in Memphis. They drove 915 km in all.
  a. How many hours did each drive? Mrs. Douglas: 3, Mr. Douglas: 7
  b. How many kilometers is Jackson from New Orleans? 285
  c. How many kilometers is Memphis from New Orleans? 630

■ REVIEW EXERCISES

State which of the numbers $\{-2, -1, 0, 1, 2\}$ are solutions to the following equations.   [3–1]

  1. $|x| + 1 = 2$ −1, 1   **2.** $x^2 = x$ 0, 1   **3.** $x^2 + x = 2$ −2, 1

What equations do you get by following these directions in order?   [3–2]

  4. $4x + 5 = 25$ x = 5   **a.** Subtract 5 from both sides.
                                   b. Divide both sides by 4.

  5. $\frac{1}{2}x - 5 = 20$ x = 50   **a.** Add 5 to both sides.
                                   b. Multiply both sides by 2.

  6. $\frac{1}{3}(x - 12) = 6$ x = 30   **a.** Use the distributive property.
                                   b. Add 4 to both sides.
                                   c. Multiply both sides by 3.

Solve.   [3–3]

  7. $5x = 4x + 7$ {7}   **8.** $6x + 7 = 7x + 6$ {1}   **9.** $7x + 5.5 = 6x - 3$
                                                                         {−8.5}

Class Starter Quiz
on previous section

A car traveled east at 70 km/h, and a truck traveled west from the same starting place at 86 km/h. The truck left a half hour before the car. Suppose x represents the number of hours the car traveled.

1. What expression represents the number of hours the truck traveled?

$x + 0.5$

2. What expression represents the number of kilometers the car traveled?

$70x$

3. What expression represents the number of kilometers the truck traveled?

$86(x + 0.5)$ or $86x + 43$

4. Write and solve an equation to find how many hours the car had traveled when the car and truck were 277 km apart.

$70x + 86(x + 0.5) = 277$
or $70x + 86x + 43 = 277$ \{1.5\}

5. How many km had the car traveled when the car and truck were 277 km apart?

105 km

4–8 Dividing Monomials

Preview Discovery

In Section 4–3, we multiplied numbers with like bases by adding exponents. Determine a rule for *dividing* numbers with like bases. You should discover the rule after solving the following equations.

$\dfrac{64}{16} = \underline{\ ?\ }$ 4

$\dfrac{128}{4} = \underline{\ ?\ }$ 32

$\dfrac{2^6}{2^4} = 2^?$ 2

$\dfrac{2^7}{2^2} = 2^?$ 5

$\dfrac{1024}{128} = \underline{\ ?\ }$ 8

$\dfrac{64}{64} = \underline{\ ?\ }$ 1

$\dfrac{2^{10}}{2^7} = 2^?$ 3

$\dfrac{2^6}{2^6} = 2^?$ 1

Does your rule seem to work?

$\dfrac{4}{8} = \underline{\ ?\ }$ $\frac{1}{2}$ $\dfrac{32}{128} = \underline{\ ?\ }$ $\frac{1}{4}$ $\dfrac{64}{1024} = \underline{\ ?\ }$ $\frac{1}{16}$

$\dfrac{2^2}{2^3} = \dfrac{1}{2^?}$ 1 $\dfrac{2^5}{2^7} = \dfrac{1}{2^?}$ 2 $\dfrac{2^6}{2^{10}} = \dfrac{1}{2^?}$ 4

$2^1 = 2$
$2^2 = 4$
$2^3 = 8$
$2^4 = 16$
$2^5 = 32$
$2^6 = 64$
$2^7 = 128$
$2^8 = 256$
$2^9 = 512$
$2^{10} = 1024$

In this lesson you will learn how to divide numbers with like bases.

PURPOSE

Simplifying algebraic expressions sometimes requires the ability to divide monomials. The property for subtracting exponents may also be applied to numerical expressions.

PREVIEW

Use the Preview to allow students to discover the subtraction property of exponents and the definition of the zero power of a number. The usual sequence of events in such a discovery lesson is as follows:

- Using computation and the table of values
- Making a conjecture about a shortcut
- Testing the conjecture by using it and then checking the results by computation
- Accepting or rejecting the conjecture

If the conjecture is accepted, it is used with a high degree of confidence. If it is rejected, a new conjecture is made and tested.

■ LESSON

The exercises in the Preview illustrate the subtraction property of exponents.

$$\frac{2^7}{2^4} = \frac{\overbrace{2 \cdot 2 \cdot 2 \cdot 2 \cdot 2 \cdot 2 \cdot 2}^{7 \text{ factors}}}{\underbrace{2 \cdot 2 \cdot 2 \cdot 2}_{4 \text{ factors}}} = \frac{2 \cdot 2 \cdot 2 \cdot 2}{2 \cdot 2 \cdot 2 \cdot 2} \cdot 2 \cdot 2 \cdot 2 = 1 \cdot 2^3 = 2^3 \text{ or } 2^{7-4}$$

$$\frac{2^5}{2^9} = \frac{2 \cdot 2 \cdot 2 \cdot 2 \cdot 2}{2 \cdot 2 \cdot 2 \cdot 2 \cdot 2 \cdot 2 \cdot 2 \cdot 2 \cdot 2} = \frac{2 \cdot 2 \cdot 2 \cdot 2 \cdot 2}{2 \cdot 2 \cdot 2 \cdot 2 \cdot 2} = \frac{1}{2 \cdot 2 \cdot 2 \cdot 2} = 1 \cdot \frac{1}{2^4} = \frac{1}{2^4} \text{ or } \frac{1}{2^{9-5}}$$

The Subtraction Property of Exponents

For all numbers a (except 0) and for all positive integers m and n,

$$\text{if } m > n, \text{ then } \frac{a^m}{a^n} = a^{m-n}$$

$$\text{if } m < n, \text{ then } \frac{a^m}{a^n} = \frac{1}{a^{n-m}}.$$

As with other properties of exponents, students should use the subtraction property of exponents directly in doing exercises such as simplifying $\frac{2^7}{2^4}$. However, they should also understand exponents well enough to use the definition of exponent to do the simplifying. For example, if a student is confused when simplifying $\frac{2^7}{2^4}$, the student should be able to go back to the definition of exponent.

Note that the property for subtracting exponents excludes division by zero. Division by 0 is not defined.

Remember that x^1 is written simply as x.

ADDITIONAL EXAMPLES

Example 1. Simplify. $\frac{x^5}{x^2}, x \neq 0$

$\frac{x^5}{x^2} = x^{5-2} = x^3$

Example 2.

Simplify. $\frac{-10a^5b^{12}}{12a^{15}b^4}, a \neq 0, b \neq 0$

$\frac{-10a^5b^{12}}{12a^{15}b^4} = \left(\frac{-10}{12}\right)\left(\frac{a^5}{a^{15}}\right)\left(\frac{b^{12}}{b^4}\right)$

$= \left(\frac{-5}{6}\right)\left(\frac{1}{a^{10}}\right)(b^8)$

$= -\frac{5b^8}{6a^{10}}$

Example 3. Simplify. $-\frac{rs^6}{r^5s}$, $r \neq 0$, $s \neq 0$

$-\frac{rs^6}{r^5s} = (-1)\left(\frac{r}{r^5}\right)\left(\frac{s^6}{s}\right)$

$= (-1)\left(\frac{1}{r^4}\right)(s^5)$

$= -\frac{s^5}{r^4}$

Example 4. Simplify. $\frac{4x^5}{8x^5}, x \neq 0$

$\frac{4x^5}{8x^5} = \left(\frac{4}{8}\right)\left(\frac{x^5}{x^5}\right) = \frac{1}{2}x^0 = \frac{1}{2} \cdot 1 = \frac{1}{2}$

Example 5.

Write the quotient using scientific notation.

$\frac{5.4 \times 10^{15}}{6.6 \times 10^6}$

$\frac{5.4 \times 10^{15}}{6.6 \times 10^6} = \left(\frac{5.4}{6.6}\right)\left(\frac{10^{15}}{10^6}\right)$

$\approx (0.82)(10^9)$

$= (0.82)(10)(10^8)$

$= 8.2 \times 10^8$

The subtraction property of exponents helps us to simplify the quotient $\frac{a^m}{a^n}$ $(a \neq 0))$ when m and n are *not* equal. We already know that when m and n are equal, the quotient is 1 (that is, any number (except 0) divided by itself is equal to 1). Note what happens if we subtract equal exponents.

$$\text{If } m = n, \frac{a^m}{a^n} = \frac{a^m}{a^m} = a^{m-m} = a^0.$$

The example given above suggests this definition.

Definition: Zero Exponents

For all numbers a (except 0),

$$a^0 = 1.$$

For example,

$$\frac{2^5}{2^5} = 2^{5-5} = 2^0 = 1$$

$$\frac{x^3}{x^3} = x^{3-3} = x^0 = 1 \quad (x \neq 0)$$

Study these examples to see how you can use the subtraction property of exponents to simplify the quotient of two monomials.

Example 1 Simplify. $\frac{x^4}{x^3}$ $(x \neq 0)$

Solution $\frac{x^4}{x^3} = x^{4-3} = x^1 = x$

Example 2 Simplify. $\frac{-12m^3n^2}{-9mn^4}$ $(m \neq 0, n \neq 0)$

Solution $\frac{-12m^3n^2}{-9mn^4} = \left(\frac{-12}{-9}\right)\left(\frac{m^3}{m^1}\right)\left(\frac{n^2}{n^4}\right) = \frac{4}{3}(m^2)\left(\frac{1}{n^2}\right) = \frac{4m^2}{3n^2}$

Example 3 Simplify. $\frac{-x^2y^3}{xy}$ $(x \neq 0, y \neq 0)$

Solution $\frac{-x^2y^3}{xy} = (-1)\left(\frac{x^2}{x}\right)\left(\frac{y^3}{y}\right) = (-1)(x)(y^2) = -xy^2$

Example 4 Simplify. $\frac{2x^7}{5x^7}$ $(x \neq 0)$

Solution $\frac{2x^7}{5x^7} = \left(\frac{2}{5}\right)\left(\frac{x^7}{x^7}\right) = \frac{2}{5}x^0 = \frac{2}{5} \cdot 1 = \frac{2}{5}$

It is generally agreed that the same assignment is not always appropriate for all students. Assignments can be informally differentiated by first giving a core assignment to everyone. Then in passing through the class assisting students, you can adjust the assignments, telling some students to concentrate on the A-level exercises and other students to skip to the end of the A-level exercises, doing the B-level and some C-level exercises.

Example 5   Write the quotient using scientific notation.

$$\frac{3.7 \times 10^8}{5.4 \times 10^5}$$

Solution $\frac{3.7 \times 10^8}{5.4 \times 10^5} = \left(\frac{3.7}{5.4}\right)\left(\frac{10^8}{10^5}\right) \approx (0.69)(10^3)$

$$= (0.69)(10)(10^2)$$

$$= 6.9 \times 10^2$$

■ CLASSROOM EXERCISES

Simplify. Assume that no variable is equal to 0.

1. $\frac{x^5}{x^3}$ x^2

2. $\frac{x^3}{x^5}$ $\frac{1}{x^2}$

3. $\frac{2y^4}{8y^2}$ $\frac{y^2}{4}$

4. $\frac{3^2 y^5}{3y}$ $3y^4$

5. $\frac{8a^2}{12a^4}$ $\frac{2}{3a^2}$

6. $\frac{6a^3 b}{9ab^2}$ $\frac{2a^2}{3b}$

7. $\frac{-15x^3 y^3}{6x^4 y}$ $\frac{-5y^2}{2x}$

8. $\frac{-8m^3 n^5}{-6m^2 n^7}$ $\frac{4m}{3n^2}$

9. x^0 1

10. $\frac{x^7}{x^7}$ 1

Write the quotient using scientific notation.

11. $\frac{6 \times 10^5}{3 \times 10^2}$ 2×10^3

12. $\frac{3.2 \times 10^4}{8 \times 10^1}$ 4×10^2

■ WRITTEN EXERCISES

Simplify. Assume that no variable is equal to 0.

1. $\frac{c^8}{c^2}$ c^6

2. $\frac{a^{12}}{a^4}$ a^8

3. $\frac{b^3}{b^{12}}$ $\frac{1}{b^9}$

4. $\frac{x^2}{x^{10}}$ $\frac{1}{x^8}$

5. $\frac{15a^8}{10a^6}$ $\frac{3a^2}{2}$

6. $\frac{18b^{10}}{12b^6}$ $\frac{3b^4}{2}$

7. $\frac{24c^3}{18c^9}$ $\frac{4}{3c^6}$

8. $\frac{24d^4}{15d^8}$ $\frac{8}{5d^4}$

9. $\frac{8j^5}{8j^4}$ j

10. $\frac{6k^7}{6k^6}$ k

11. $\frac{10p^5}{2p^5}$ 5

12. $\frac{9q^6}{3q^6}$ 3

13. $\frac{-15r^2 s^3}{10rs}$ $\frac{-3rs^2}{2}$

14. $\frac{-12x^4 y^6}{8xy}$ $\frac{-3x^3 y^5}{2}$

15. $\frac{x^3 y^6}{x^3 y^7}$ $\frac{1}{y}$

16. $\frac{a^2 y^4}{a^3 y^4}$ $\frac{1}{a}$

17. $\frac{-bc}{b^2 c}$ $\frac{-1}{b}$

18. $\frac{-rs}{rs^2}$ $\frac{-1}{s}$

19. $\frac{5x^4}{5x^4}$ 1

20. $\frac{3y^3}{3y^3}$ 1

Solve.

21. $\frac{2^{12}}{2^4} = 2^x$ {8}

22. $\frac{2^{10}}{2^2} = 2^x$ {8}

23. $\frac{3^4}{3^3} = 3^x$ {1}

24. $\frac{3^5}{3^4} = 3^x$ {1}

25. $\frac{4^5}{4^6} = x$ $\left\{\frac{1}{4}\right\}$

26. $\frac{5^3}{5^4} = x$ $\left\{\frac{1}{5}\right\}$

27. $\frac{2^{10}}{2^7} = x$ {8}

28. $\frac{2^8}{2^6} = x$ {4}

CHECK UNDERSTANDING

Simplify.

- 2^0 (1)
- 0^0 (undefined)
- $\frac{10^6}{10^2}$ (10^4)
- $\frac{10^2}{10^6}$ $\left(\frac{1}{10^4}\right)$

CLASSROOM EXERCISES

No variable is 0, thus eliminating any possibility of division by zero. In classroom exercises 6–8, students should first simplify the numerical coefficients, then simplify the first variable, and finally simplify the last variable. For example, in classroom exercise 6, think in these steps:

$$\frac{6a^3 b}{9ab^2} = \frac{2a^3 b}{3ab^2} = \frac{2a^2 b}{3b^2} = \frac{2a^2}{3b}$$

However, the students may simply write the final answer:

$$\frac{6a^3 b}{9ab^2} = \frac{2a^2}{3b}$$

ASSIGNMENT GUIDE

Basic	1–20 all, 21–27 odd, Review Exercises
Average	13–35 odd, 37–44 all, Review Exercises
Enriched	21–35 odd, 37–48 all, Review Exercises

PRACTICE WORKSHEET 20

4-8 DIVIDING MONOMIALS

■ Simplify. Assume that no denominator is equal to zero.

1. $\frac{r^{12}}{r^3}$ r^9

2. $\frac{s^{50}}{s^{10}}$ s^{40}

3. $\frac{4t^{16}}{4t^2}$ t^{14}

4. $\frac{24w^8}{3w^{10}}$ $8/w^2$

5. $\frac{20x}{20x^3}$ $1/x^2$

6. $\frac{12a^3}{18a}$ $2a^4/3$

7. $\frac{c^3 d^5}{cd}$ cd^0

8. $\frac{x^2 y}{xy^3}$ x/y

■ Solve.

9. $\frac{3^{12}}{3^3} = 3^x$ {10}

10. $\frac{3^{15}}{3^3} = 3^x$ {12}

11. $\frac{5^6}{5^1} = 5^x$ {1}

12. $\frac{5^3}{5} = 5^x$ {2}

13. $\frac{2^9}{2^7} = x$ {2^6}

14. $\frac{4^3}{4^4} = x$ {1/4}

15. $\frac{3^7}{3^9} = x$ {1/3^2}

16. $\frac{5^{10}}{5^8} = x$ {5^2}

■ Write the quotient in scientific notation.

17. $\frac{8 \times 10^{12}}{2 \times 10^3}$ 4×10^9

18. $\frac{2.8 \times 10^{10}}{4 \times 10^3}$ 7×10^6

19. $\frac{9.6 \times 10^7}{4}$ 2.4×10^7

20. $\frac{8.6 \times 10^9}{10}$ 8.6×10^8

177

WRITTEN EXERCISES

In exercises such as 21–28, students may need to be reminded that the answer is the replacement for x that makes the sentence true. The solution of $\frac{2^{12}}{2^4} = 2^x$ is 8; it is not 2^8. The solution of $\frac{2^{10} \cdot 2^4}{2^7} = x$ is 2^3; it is not 3.

In exercises 34–36, the expressions must first be simplified for factors in which the variable does not appear. Then the other side of the equation may be rewritten as an appropriate power. In exercise 34,

	Alternate solution:
$\frac{3^x \cdot 2^5}{3^7 \cdot 2^4} = 6$	$\frac{3^x \cdot 2^5}{3^7 \cdot 2^4} = 6$
$3^{x-7} \cdot 2 = 6$	$\frac{3^x}{3^7} \cdot 2 = 6$
$3^{x-7} = 3$	$\frac{3^x}{3^7} = 3^1$
$x - 7 = 1$	$x = 8$
$x = 8$	

Remember that an answer expressed in proper scientific notation should be written as the product of a number between 1 and 10 and a power of 10.

ENRICHMENT PROBLEMS

• Correct the errors that were made in simplifying these expressions.

a. $3^3 - 3^2 = 3$ $27 - 9 = 18$

b. $\frac{8x^4}{2x} = 6x^3$ $4x^3$

c. $\frac{10^6}{10^3} = 10^2$ 10^3

d. $\frac{12y^3}{3y} = 4y^3$ $4y^2$

e. $\frac{(2x)^4}{2x} = x^3$ $(2x)^3$ or $8x^3$

f. $\frac{b^4}{2b^2} = \frac{b^2}{2} = b$ $\frac{b^2}{2}$ cannot be simplified.

178

EXTRA PRACTICE, page 626

Solve.

B 29. $\frac{3 \cdot 2^5}{6 \cdot 2^3} = x$ (2)   30. $\frac{5 \cdot 2^7}{3 \cdot 2^9} = x$ $\left\{\frac{5}{12}\right\}$ 31. $\frac{9 \cdot 2^8}{3 \cdot 2^9} = x$ $\left\{\frac{3}{2}\right\}$ 32. $\frac{15 \cdot 2^8}{5 \cdot 2^{10}} = x$ $\left\{\frac{3}{4}\right\}$

33. $\frac{3^8 \cdot 2^{100}}{3^9 \cdot 2^{100}} = x$ $\left\{\frac{1}{3}\right\}$ 34. $\frac{3^x \cdot 2^5}{3^7 \cdot 2^4} = 6$ (8)   35. $\frac{5^4 \cdot 2^6}{5^5 \cdot 2^x} = 0.1$ (7)   36. $\frac{2^5 x}{2^3} = -12$ $\{-3\}$

Write the quotient using scientific notation.

37. $\frac{7.5 \times 10^7}{2.5 \times 10^2}$ 3×10^5 38. $\frac{5.3 \times 10^8}{4.6 \times 10^5}$ $\approx 1.2 \times 10^3$ 39. $\frac{7.1 \times 10^5}{8.8 \times 10^2}$ $\approx 8.1 \times 10^2$ 40. $\frac{8.7 \times 10^9}{9.2 \times 10^7}$ $\approx 9.5 \times 10$

Each number in a box is the product of the numbers in the two boxes directly below it. Copy the figures and use the pattern to fill in the blank boxes.

41.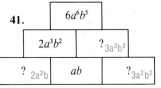

42.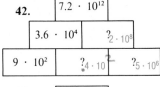

43.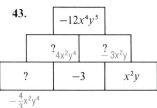

$-\frac{4}{3}x^2y^4$

44.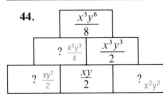

C The average depth of these bodies of water may be estimated by dividing the volume by the area. Write the average depth (in meters) using scientific notation.

	Body of water	Volume (m^3)	Area (m^2)
45.	Persian Gulf	2.3×10^{13}	2.3×10^{11}
46.	Pacific Ocean	6.8×10^{17}	1.7×10^{14}
47.	Gulf of California	10.5×10^{14}	1.5×10^{11}
48.	Caribbean Sea	6.5×10^{15}	2.5×10^{12}

45. 1×10^2 46. 4×10^3 47. 7×10^3 48. 2.6×10^3

■ REVIEW EXERCISES

Solve each equation.

1. $4x = -7$ $\left\{-\frac{7}{4}\right\}$ 2. $\frac{1}{3}x = 15$ (45)   3. $\frac{3}{4}x = 24$ (32) [3–4]

4. $5x + 7 = 7x$ $\left\{\frac{7}{2}\right\}$ 5. $\frac{x+4}{5} = 6$ (26)   6. $\frac{x-5}{2} = 10$ (25) [3–5]

7. $3x + 4 = 5(4 - x) + 8$ (3)   8. $5x - 10 = 3(x + 5)$ $\left\{\frac{25}{2}\right\}$ 9. $6(x - 4) = 4x$ (12) [3–6]

You may wish to spend two days on this section. Refer to the Pacing Chart.

To solve problems involving numbers of items and their values.

Class Starter Quiz
on previous section

Simplify.

1. $\dfrac{x^{10}}{x^2}$ x^8

2. $\dfrac{12a^6}{3a^3}$ $4a^3$

3. $\dfrac{n^3}{n^{12}}$ $\dfrac{1}{n^9}$

4. $\dfrac{15a^2b}{10ab^3}$ $\dfrac{3a}{2b^2}$

5. $\dfrac{6 \times 10^{20}}{2 \times 10^5}$ 3×10^{15}

4–9 Problem Solving — Money Problems

Preview

Many practical problems encountered every day involve money. Some puzzles involve money, too. Try solving this one:

A student had 14 coins — some dimes and some nickels. Their value was 90 cents. How many of the coins were nickels?   10

The puzzle can be solved by systematic trials. But in this lesson you will learn another method. Using equations is a powerful problem-solving approach that has many applications.

PURPOSE

It is important in many problems for students to be able to distinguish between (a) how many there are of an item, (b) how much the item is worth, and (c) what the value is of all the items. For example, a quarter is worth 25 cents, and 3 quarters have a total value of 75 cents. Students must distinguish between the number of quarters (3), the value in cents of a quarter (25), and the value in cents of all the quarters (75).

PREVIEW

Let students try to solve the problem by systematic trials—make a guess, test the guess, adjust the guess according to what was learned from the test, test the new guess, etc.

■ LESSON

In most money problems, you are given two kinds of quantities: *numbers* of items and *values* of items.

Items	Number of items	Value in cents	Value in dollars
Dimes	5	10×5	0.1×5
Nickels	n	$5n$	$0.05n$
$35 auto tires	m	$3500m$	$35m$
25¢ pens	$x + 2$	$25(x + 2)$	$0.25(x + 2)$

A table can help organize information in money problems. It can also make it easier to recognize expressions that must be equivalent. These equivalent expressions can then be used to write an equation for the problem.

LESSON

Call student attention to the similarity between these problems about money and the uniform-motion problems.

distance = rate × time
   $d = rt$
value (v) = value per item (i)
      × number of items (n)
   $v = in$

The problems in this lesson are rate problems.

  Emphasize the importance of tables for organizing the data and finding the equal quantities necessary for writing equations.

Example 1   Mrs. Cooper bought four tires for her car. The cost, including $11.04 in taxes, was $194.96. What was the price for one tire before taxes?

Solution   Let x = the cost of one tire in dollars.

Cost of 1 tire in dollars	Cost of 4 tires in dollars	Total cost in dollars
x	$4x$	$4x + 11.04$ or 194.96

Example 1
Mr. Pickens bought 3 cans of oil. The cost, including 21 cents in sales tax, was $3.39. What was the price of 1 can of oil before taxes?

Let c = the cost in cents of 1 can of oil.

Cost of 1 can in cents	Cost of 3 cans in cents	Total cost in cents
c	$3c$	$3c + 21$ or 339

$$3c + 21 = 339$$
$$3c = 318$$
$$c = 106$$

The cost of one can is $1.06.

Example 2.
Eighteen coins (dimes and quarters) are worth $3.45. How many coins of each kind are there?

Let d = the number of dimes.

	Number	Value in cents
Dimes	d	$10d$
Quarters	$18 - d$	$25(18 - d)$

Total value: 345

$$10d + 25(18 - d) = 345$$
$$10d + 450 - 25d = 345$$
$$-15d = -105$$
$$d = 7$$

There are 7 dimes and $18 - 7$, or 11, quarters.

Example 1   (continued)

Since the cost of the tires plus tax equals $194.96, we have:

$$4x + 11.04 = 194.96$$
$$4x = 183.92$$
$$x = 45.98$$

Answer   The cost of 1 tire before taxes is $45.98.

Check   Cost of 4 tires = 4 × $45.98 = $183.92
(before taxes)
Tax = $11.04
Total cost = $183.92 + $11.04 = $194.96   It checks.

Recall these two important points for solving written problems.

1. When solving a written problem using an equation, you are not finished when you have solved the equation. The solution of an equation is a number. You must interpret the number in terms of the question asked. The problem in Example 1 did not ask for a number but an amount of money.

2. When checking a written problem, go back to the problem itself instead of just substituting the answer into the equation. You may have solved the equation correctly, but it could have been the wrong equation.

Example 2   Twenty-five coins (dimes and nickels) are worth $1.80. How many coins of each kind are there?

Solution 1   Let d = the number of dimes.

	Number	Value in cents
Dimes	d	$10d$
Nickels	$25 - d$	$5(25 - d)$

Total value: 180

The sum of the values of the dimes and nickels must equal 180 cents. The table gives the following equation:

$$10d + 5(25 - d) = 180$$
$$10d + 125 - 5d = 180$$
$$5d = 55$$
$$d = 11 \qquad 25 - 11 = 14$$

Answer   There are 11 dimes and 14 nickels.

Check   Value of dimes = 11 × $0.10 = $1.10

Value of nickels = 14 × $0.05 = $0.70

Total value = $1.10 + $0.70 = $1.80   It checks.

Research indicates that students respond best when the classroom atmosphere is positive. Therefore, provide positive reinforcement when students achieve objectives—praise success, praise effort, praise participation.

CHECK UNDERSTANDING

- What is the value in cents of 3 nickels? (15) 5 dimes? (50) 4 quarters? (100)
- What is the value in dollars of 12 nickels? (0.60) 13 dimes? (1.30) 4 quarters? (1)
- Apple juice costs 40 cents per can. What is the cost of 2 cans? (80 cents) g cans? ($40g$ cents)
- In a pile, there are 4 dimes and twice as many quarters. How many quarters are there? (8)
- In a pile, there are n nickels and 5 more dimes. How many dimes are there? ($n + 5$)

Example 2 (continued)

Solution 2 Let n = the number of nickels.

	Number	Value in cents
Nickels	n	$5n$
Dimes	$25 - n$	$10(25 - n)$

Total value: 180

The table gives the following equation:

$$5n + 10(25 - n) = 180$$
$$5n + 250 - 10n = 180$$
$$-5n = -70$$
$$n = 14$$
$$25 - n = 11 \qquad 25 - 14 = 11$$

Answer There are 14 nickels and 11 dimes.

CLASSROOM EXERCISES

By the time students have completed the Classroom Exercises, they should be quite good at representing both numbers of objects and values of objects using variables.

■ CLASSROOM EXERCISES

1. What is the value in cents of x quarters? $25x$

2. What is the value in dollars of y dimes? $0.1y$

3. Soup costs 39 cents per can. What is the cost in cents of g cans of soup? $39g$

4. Soup costs c cents per can. What is the cost in cents of 5 cans of soup? $5c$

5. If 4 apples cost 64¢, what does 1 apple cost? 16 cents

6. If b apples cost 68¢, what does 1 apple cost? $\frac{68}{b}$ cents

7. If c apples cost d¢, what does 1 apple cost? $\frac{d}{c}$ cents

8. There are twice as many dimes as quarters. If there are q quarters, then:
   a. How many dimes are there? $2q$
   b. What is the value of the dimes in cents? $20q$
   c. What is the value of the quarters in cents? $25q$

Define the variables, write the equations, and then solve.

9. There are 2 times as many quarters as dimes in a stack worth $4.20. How many coins of each type are there? 7 dimes, 14 quarters

10. There are 4 more nickels than dimes in a stack worth $1.55. How many coins of each type are there? 9 dimes, 13 nickels

ASSIGNMENT GUIDE

Basic   1–15 odd, 17–22 all, Review Exercises, Self-Quiz 3
Average 1–21 odd, 23–28 all, Review Exercises, Self-Quiz 3
Enriched 7–27 odd, 29–31 all, Review Exercises, Self-Quiz 3

PRACTICE WORKSHEET 21

4-9 PROBLEM SOLVING — MONEY PROBLEMS

■ Solve.

1. The cost of 4 tires is $210. What is the cost of one tire?	$52.50	
2. The cost of 3 boxes of Crunchy Corn Flakes is $3.57. What is the cost of 1 box?	$1.19	
3. A typewriter repair shop charges $22 per hour plus parts. How long did a repair take if the bill was $39.50 including $6.50 for parts?	1 1/2 hours	
4. Ace Fixit charges $15 per hour for bicycle repairs plus parts. How long did a repair take if the bill was $42 including $12 for parts?	2 hours	
5. Mr. Washington paid $7.53, including 36 cents tax, for 3 boxes of detergent. What was the cost of one box of detergent before the tax?	$2.39	
6. Mrs. Monroe paid $3.79, including 28 cents tax, for 3 rolls of aluminum foil. What was the cost of one roll of foil before the tax?	$1.17	

WRITTEN EXERCISES

Exercises 17–22 can be easily done by most students without writing equations. Students will realize this, too. Be sure that students understand that the reason for writing equations for such simple problems is to increase their skill in writing and solving equations.

EXTRA PRACTICE, page 626

■ WRITTEN EXERCISES

A 1. What is the value in cents of h half dollars? 50h

2. What is the value in cents of d dimes? 10d

3. What is the value in dollars of d dimes? 0.1d

4. What is the value in dollars of q quarters? 0.25q

5. Stamps cost 30¢ each. What is the cost in cents of s stamps? 30s

6. Frozen vegetables cost 79¢ per package. What is the cost in cents of p packages? 79p

7. If 6 cans of juice cost j dollars, what does 1 can of juice cost? $\frac{j}{6}$ dollars

8. If 12 rolls cost r cents, what does 1 roll cost? $\frac{r}{12}$ cents

9. There are 4 more nickels than dimes. If there are d dimes, then:
   a. How many nickels are there? d + 4
   b. What is the value of the nickels in cents? 5(d + 4)
   c. What is the value of the dimes in cents? 10d

10. There is a total of 25 dimes and quarters. If there are d dimes, then:
   a. How many quarters are there? 25 − d
   b. What is the value of the dimes in cents? 10d
   c. What is the value of the quarters in cents? 25(25 − d)

Write an expression for each situation. Let x represent the cost in dollars for 1 tire.

11. The cost of 2 tires 2x

12. The cost of 4 tires 4x

13. Half the cost of a tire $\frac{1}{2}x$

14. $\frac{3}{4}$ the cost of a tire $\frac{3}{4}x$

15. The cost of a tire and $4.20 tax x + 4.20

16. The cost of a tire and $5.00 for mounting and balancing x + 5

Solve.

17. The cost of 3 bottles of milk is $6.15. What is the cost of 1 bottle of milk? $2.05

18. The cost of 4 notebooks is $9.00. What is the cost of 1 notebook? $2.25

19. The cost of 5 cans of oil, including 26¢ tax, is $4.51. What is the cost of 1 can of oil before taxes? $0.85

20. The cost of 2 boxes of laundry detergent, including $0.63 tax, is $11.13. What is the cost of 1 box of detergent before taxes? $5.25

21. An electrician charges $25, plus $20 per hour, for making a service call. How many hours were charged if the total bill was $75? 2.5

22. An auto mechanic charges $20, plus $25 per hour. How many hours were charged if the total bill was $57.50? 1.5

B 23. There are 2 times as many dimes as nickels in a stack of coins worth $1.50. How many nickels are in the stack? 6

24. There are 2 times as many nickels as dimes in a stack of coins worth $1.60. How many dimes are in the stack? 8

25. A stack of coins is worth $3.25. There are 5 more nickels than quarters. How many quarters are in the stack? 10

26. A stack of coins is worth $2.75. There are 5 more quarters than nickels. How may nickels are in the stack? 5

27. A stack of 30 coins consists of dimes and quarters. How many of the coins are dimes if the stack is worth $4.65? 19

28. A stack of 30 coins consists of dimes and quarters. How many of the coins are dimes if the stack is worth $5.10? 16

C 29. A shopper bought some cans of soup at 39¢ per can and some packages of frozen vegetables at 59¢ per package. Twice as many packages of vegetables were purchased as cans of soup. How many packages of vegetables were purchased if the total bill was $9.42? 12

30. A club sold student tickets for $3.25 and full-price tickets for $5.25, and 16 more student tickets were sold than full-price tickets. How many student tickets were sold if the total sales were $2559.50? 311

31. Solve this problem in two ways: First, let x represent the number of dimes; then let x represent the number of quarters. Explain which of the five steps in the two solutions are different and which are alike.

A stack of dimes and quarters is worth $7.60. It has 6 more dimes than quarters. How many coins of each type are in the stack? 20 quarters, 26 dimes
Only the answer to the problem and the check are the same.

■ REVIEW EXERCISES

Solve.

1. $5(x - 2) = 40$ (10)

2. $6a + 2(a + 3) = 10$ $\left\{\frac{1}{2}\right\}$ [3–7]

3. $5(y - 6) = 30$ (12)

4. $3(x - 5) = 2(5 - x)$ (5)

Solve for the indicated variable. [3–8]

5. $A = \frac{1}{2}bh$, for h $h = \frac{2A}{b}$

6. $V = lwh$, for w $w = \frac{V}{lh}$

7. $A = \frac{1}{2}h(b_1 + b_2)$, for h $h = \frac{2A}{b_1 + b_2}$

8. $A = \frac{1}{2}h(b_1 + b_2)$, for b_1 $b_1 = \frac{2A}{h} - b_2$

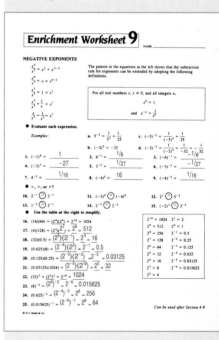

ENRICHMENT PROBLEM

• There are twice as many dimes as quarters in a bank. If the number of dimes and quarters is reversed, by what fraction does the bank's value increase?

Let n = original number of quarters and

$2n$ = original number of dimes.

Then $10(2n) + 25n$ = original value.

If the number of dimes and quarters is reversed,

$2n$ = new number of quarters and

n = new number of dimes.

Then $10n + 25(2n)$ = new value.

new value − original value = $\dfrac{\text{increase}}{\text{in value}}$

$60n \quad - \quad 45n \quad = \quad 15n$

This represents a fractional increase of $\dfrac{15n}{45n}$ or $\dfrac{1}{3}$.

Self-Quiz 3

4-7 Copy and complete the chart.

	r (rate)	t (time)	d (distance)
1.	42 mph	1.5 h	? 63 mi
2.	1.6 m/s	? 9s	14.4 m
3.	? 84 km/h	2 h 15 min $\left(2\frac{1}{4}\text{ h}\right)$	189 km

Solve.

4. A bicyclist riding at 30 mph leaves Metro City at 10 A.M. One hour later, a second cyclist riding at 25 mph travels in the opposite direction. At what time will the cyclists be 250 miles apart? 3 P.M.

4-8 Simplify.

5. $\dfrac{x^3}{x^4}$ $\frac{1}{x}$

6. $\dfrac{2z^{10}}{6z^2}$ $\frac{z^8}{3}$,

7. $\dfrac{14p^4q^7}{7p^4q^5}$ $2q^2$

8. $\dfrac{-ab^2}{a^2b}$ $\frac{-b}{a}$

4-9 Complete.

4-1 **9.** Write an expression for the value in cents of $(n + 1)$ quarters. $25(n + 1)$

10. A stack of dimes and quarters is worth $2.85. If there are 4 more dimes than quarters, how many of each kind of coin are there? 7 quarters, 11 dimes

EXTENSION Fuel economy

The fuel economy of an automobile depends on many factors, including air resistance, the gear being used, and the rate of acceleration. Air resistance depends on the speed and shape of the automobile. Air resistance increases by a factor that is the square of the factor by which the speed is increased. For example, if the speed is tripled, the air resistance is multiplied by 9. If the speed is increased by a factor of $\frac{5}{4}$, the air resistance is increased by a factor of $\frac{25}{16}$.

By what factor is the air resistance increased when the speed is increased from 50 mph to 55 mph? $\frac{121}{100}$

The best fuel economy is achieved when the automobile is driven at the lowest constant speed possible in the highest gear possible.

OBJECTIVE 4–10

To solve integer problems by writing and solving equations.

Class Starter Quiz
on previous section

Write an algebraic expression.

1. There is a total of 15 dimes and quarters. If there are *q* quarters, how many dimes are there?

    $15 - q$

2. If 2 cans of juice cost *j* cents, how much will 6 cans cost?

    $3j$ cents

3. There are two times as many pennies as nickels. How many nickels are there if there are *p* pennies?

    $\frac{p}{2}$

Write an equation and solve.

4. The cost of 4 pounds of apples is \$3.96. What is the cost of 1 pound of apples?

    $4a = 3.96$

    \$.99

5. Twenty-seven nickels and dimes are worth \$1.75. How many dimes are there?

    $10d + 5(27 - d) = 175$

    8

4–10 Problem Solving — Integer Problems

Preview

In cross-country running, the number of points a runner earns for the team is equal to the number of the runner's finishing position. For example, the 3rd-place finisher earns 3 points and the 27th-place finisher earns 27 points. The team score is the sum of the scores of its top five finishers and the team with the lowest score wins. In one meet, five runners for one team finished one right after another. Their team's score was 55. In what places did the runners finish? 9th, 10th, 11th, 12th, and 13th

In this lesson you will learn to solve problems like this one by writing equations.

■ LESSON

Tuesday, Wednesday, and Thursday are *consecutive* days. October, November, and December are *consecutive* months. Integers that "follow" one after another are called **consecutive integers.** In a sequence of consecutive integers, each is one greater than the integer that precedes it.

7, 8, 9, 10	are consecutive integers
$-4, -3, -2, -1, 0$	are consecutive integers

If *n* is an integer, then:

$n, n + 1, n + 2, n + 3$	are consecutive integers
$n - 3, n - 2, n - 1, n, n + 1$	are consecutive integers

The difference between two consecutive *even* integers *or* two consecutive *odd* integers is *always* two.

$-4, -2, 0, 2, 4, 6, 8, \ldots,$	are *consecutive even* integers, and
$-3, -1, 1, 3, 5, 7, 9, \ldots,$	are *consecutive odd* integers

If *n* is an *even* integer, then $n - 4, n - 2, n, n + 2, n + 4, n + 6, \ldots,$ are consecutive *even* integers.

However, if *n* is an *odd* integer, then $n - 4, n - 2, n, n + 2, n + 4, n + 6, \ldots,$ are consecutive *odd* integers.

PURPOSE

Integer problems, while not practical per se, help students develop facility in selecting variables, writing and solving equations, and using the solution of the equation in writing the answer of a problem.

PREVIEW

Let students solve the problem by systematic trials (guess and check).

LESSON

As you teach the material in the exposition and do the examples, concentrate on these points:

1. Students must read carefully to determine what numbers are used—consecutive integers, consecutive odd integers, consecutive multiples of 5, etc.

Lesson *continued*

2. If consecutive integers are involved, any one of them can be represented by a variable, say n. Then the smaller ones are represented by $n - 1$, $n - 2$, etc. Larger ones are represented by $n + 1$, $n + 2$, etc. Similarly, since consecutive odd integers differ by 2 as do consecutive even integers, if one of them is n, then the smaller ones are $n - 2$, $n - 4$, etc., and the larger ones are $n + 2$, $n + 4$, etc.

3. Care must be taken in using the solution of the equation to determine the answer to the problem. The solution of the equation will be one number, while there may be several numbers required to answer the problem. Also, students should pay careful attention to answer the question asked rather than some other question. For example, if the question asks for the largest of three integers, the student should not answer by writing all three integers.

ADDITIONAL EXAMPLES

Example 1.
The sum of four consecutive integers is 82. What are the integers?

Let n = the second integer. Then the first integer is $n - 1$, the third is $n + 1$, and the fourth is $n + 2$.

$$(n - 1) + n + (n + 1) + (n + 2) = 82$$
$$4n + 2 = 82$$
$$4n = 80$$
$$n = 20$$

The integers are 19, 20, 21, and 22.

Example 2.
The sum of two consecutive even numbers is 290. What is the smaller integer?

Let n = the smaller number. Then $n + 2$ is the larger.

$$n + (n + 2) = 290$$
$$2n + 2 = 290$$
$$2n = 288$$
$$n = 144$$

The smaller integer is 144.

Example 1 The sum of three consecutive integers is 132. What are the integers?

Here are three solutions based on three different ways to define variables. Study each of these solutions.

Solution 1 Let n = the smallest integer. Then $n + 1$ = the next larger integer, and $n + 2$ = the largest integer.

$$n + (n + 1) + (n + 2) = 132$$
$$3n + 3 = 132$$
$$3n = 129$$
$$n = 43 \leftarrow \text{the smallest integer}$$

Answer The integers are 43, 44, 45.

Solution 2 Let n = the middle integer. Then $n - 1$ = the smallest integer, and $n + 1$ = the largest integer.

$$n + (n - 1) + (n + 1) = 132$$
$$3n = 132$$
$$n = 44 \leftarrow \text{the middle integer}$$

Answer The integers are 43, 44, 45.

Solution 3 Let n = the largest integer. Then $n - 1$ = the middle integer, and $n - 2$ = the smallest integer.

$$n + (n - 1) + (n - 2) = 132$$
$$3n - 3 = 132$$
$$3n = 135$$
$$n = 45 \leftarrow \text{the largest integer}$$

Answer The integers are 43, 44, 45.

Example 2 Find two consecutive odd integers whose sum is -36.

Solution Let n = the smaller integer. Then $n + 2$ = the larger integer.

$$n + (n + 2) = -36$$
$$2n + 2 = -36$$
$$2n = -38$$
$$n = -19 \leftarrow \text{the smaller integer}$$
$$n + 2 = -17 \leftarrow \text{the larger integer}$$

Answer The integers are -19 and -17.

Always be aware that the solution of the equation may be one number, but the answer to the problem may be more than one number. In Example 1, the solution to the problem is 43, 44, and 45, not just 43.

Ideas learned through discovery tend to be integrated more quickly with existing knowledge. Therefore, from time to time, use exploratory activities such as the discovery-oriented Previews in the student text.

■ CLASSROOM EXERCISES

1. State four consecutive positive integers.   Answers will vary.

2. State four consecutive negative integers.   Answers will vary.

3. State three consecutive integers, the largest of which is 0. $-2, -1, 0$

4. State three consecutive odd integers, the smallest of which is -7. $-7, -5, -3$

5. State three consecutive even integers, the largest of which is 20.   16, 18, 20

6. Suppose x is an integer. State the preceding smaller integer and the following larger integer. $x - 1, x + 1$

7. Suppose that y is an even integer. State the next two larger even integers. $y + 2, y + 4$

8. Suppose that z is an odd integer. State the next two smaller odd integers. $z - 2, z - 4$

Define the variables, give an equation, solve the equation, and answer the question.

9. Find two consecutive integers whose sum is 31.   15 and 16

10. Find two consecutive even integers whose sum is 174.   86 and 88

■ WRITTEN EXERCISES

A **1.** List four consecutive integers starting with 17.   17, 18, 19, 20

2. List four consecutive integers starting with 12.   12, 13, 14, 15

3. List three consecutive even integers starting with 30.   30, 32, 34

4. List three consecutive even integers starting with 98.   98, 100, 102

5. List three consecutive odd integers starting with -17. $-17, -15, -13$

6. List three consecutive odd integers starting with -3. $-3, -1, 1$

Suppose n represents an integer. Express these numbers.

7. The next two consecutive integers. $n + 1, n + 2$

8. The two preceding integers. $n - 1, n - 2$

9. The next two consecutive even integers if n is an even number. $n + 2, n + 4$

10. The next two consecutive odd integers if n is an odd number. $n + 2, n + 4$

For each problem, define the variables, write an equation that fits the problem, solve the equation, and answer the question.

11. The sum of two consecutive integers is 75. What is the smaller integer?   37

12. The sum of two consecutive integers is 59. What is the smaller integer?   29

CHECK UNDERSTANDING

- State three consecutive integers; three consecutive negative integers; three consecutive odd integers.
- State three consecutive integers the smallest of which is 14. (14, 15, 16)
- State four consecutive even integers the largest of which is 20. (14, 16, 18, 20)
- State five consecutive integers if the middle integers is n. ($n - 2$, $n - 1$, n, $n + 1$, $n + 2$)
- State two consecutive odd integers if the larger one is 27. (25, 27)

CLASSROOM EXERCISES

In listing consecutive integers, as in classroom exercises 1–2, it is customary to list the smallest first.

ASSIGNMENT GUIDE

Basic   1–22 all, Review Exercises
Average   1–9 odd, 11–28 all, Review Exercises
Enriched 1–21 odd, 23–33 all, Review Exercises

PRACTICE WORKSHEET 21

4-10 PROBLEM SOLVING: INTEGER PROBLEMS

■ Let k represent an integer. Express these numbers.

1. The next three consecutive integers.	$k + 1, k + 2, k + 3$
2. The three preceding integers.	$k - 1, k - 2, k - 3$
3. The next odd number if k is odd.	$k + 2$
4. The preceding even number if k is even.	$k - 2$

■ Solve.

5. The sum of two consecutive integers is 117. What is the smaller integer?	58
6. The sum of three consecutive integers is 342. What is the smallest of the integers?	113
7. The sum of two consecutive odd integers is 428. What is the smaller integer?	213
8. The sum of three consecutive integers is -240. What is the smallest of the integers?	-81
9. The sum of five consecutive integers is -185. What is the middle integer?	-37
10. The sum of four consecutive odd integers is 272. What is the largest of the integers?	71

COMPUTER EXTENSION

Write a program that for any positive integer N will give the sum of the first N positive integers.

```
10 PRINT "WHAT IS YOUR NUMBER";
20 INPUT N
30 S = 0
40 FOR I = 1 to N
50 S = S + I
60 NEXT I
70 PRINT "THE SUM OF 1 + 2 +
   . . . + "; N; " IS "; S
80 END
```

Alternate program

```
10 PRINT "WHAT IS YOUR NUMBER";
20 INPUT N
30 S = (N*(N + 1))/2
40 PRINT "THE SUM OF 1 + 2 +
   . . . + "; N; " IS "; S
50 END
```

ENRICHMENT PROBLEM

- The numbers 13 and 14 can be expressed as the sum of consecutive positive integers as follows:

$$13 = 6 + 7$$
$$14 = 2 + 3 + 4 + 5$$

Which positive whole numbers cannot be expressed as the sum of consecutive integers?

All powers of 2

EXTRA PRACTICE, page 626

For each problem, define the variables, write an equation that fits the problem, solve the equation, and answer the question.

13. The sum of three consecutive integers is 171. What are the integers? 56, 57, 58

14. The sum of three consecutive integers is 216. What are the integers? 71, 72, 73

15. The sum of three consecutive integers is 0. What is the smallest integer? −1

16. The sum of three consecutive integers is −336. What is the smallest integer? −113

17. The sum of three consecutive even integers is 390. What are the integers? 128, 130, 132

18. The sum of three consecutive odd integers is 447. What are the integers? 147, 149, 151

Solve each problem in two different ways. First, let x equal the smallest integer in the sequence and solve. Then let x equal the middle integer in the sequence and solve.

19. The sum of five consecutive integers is 165. What are the integers? 31, 32, 33, 34, 35

20. The sum of five consecutive integers is 275. What are the integers? 53, 54, 55, 56, 57

21. The sum of five consecutive even integers is 440. What are the integers? 84, 86, 88, 90, 92

22. The sum of five consecutive even integers is 370. What are the integers? 70, 72, 74, 76, 78

B 23. The sum of nine consecutive integers is odd. Is the smallest integer even or odd? Explain your answer. Odd

24. The sum of nine consecutive integers is even. Is the largest integer even or odd? Explain your answer. Even

25. The sum of 11 consecutive odd integers is 891. What is the largest integer in the sequence? [*Hint:* Let the sixth number be n.] 91

26. The sum of 11 consecutive integers is −946. What is the middle integer in the sequence? −86

Solve these problems.

27. The sum of three numbers is 150. The smallest number is 1 less than the middle number. The largest number is 1 more than the middle number. What are the three numbers? 49, 50, 51

28. In a cross-country meet (see the Preview), the first runner to finish for the Cougars was followed by two opponents, then a teammate, two opponents, another teammate, two opponents, a teammate, and so on. The five-runner Cougar team scored 70 points. In what place did the first runner for the Cougars finish? 8th

C **29.** The sum of 1001 consecutive integers is 0. What is the middle integer in the sequence? 0

30. The sum of 1001 consecutive integers is 1001. What is the middle integer in the sequence? 1

31. One number is 1 larger than another. Their sum is 2. What are the two numbers? $\frac{1}{2}$ and $1\frac{1}{2}$

32. The 30 lockers on the south hallway at Wilson School have consecutive even integers. The sum of the locker numbers is 6990. What are the smallest and largest numbers on the lockers? 204 and 262

33. "The 30 lockers on the east hallway at Wilson School have consecutive odd numbers and their sum is 2401," said Carol. "That's not right," said Ken. Find who was correct and why. Ken: sum should be even.

■ **REVIEW EXERCISES**

Solve each formula for the indicated variable.   [3–9]

1. $d = rt$, for r $r = \frac{d}{t}$
2. $i = prt$, for p $p = \frac{i}{rt}$

3. $ax + b = 0$, for x $x = \frac{-b}{a}$
4. $p = 2(l + w)$, for l $l = \frac{p}{2} - w$

Simplify.   [2–8]

5. $-(a + b) - (a - b)$ $-2a$
6. $3 - (2x + 7)$ $-4 - 2x$
7. $4x - 2(x - 5) - (x + 3)$ $x + 7$

Strategy for Success **Preparing for a test** —————

Start reviewing early enough so that you will be able to seek help if you need it.

■ CHAPTER SUMMARY

- **Vocabulary**

monomial	[page 143]	constant	[page 148]
polynomial	[page 143]	degree of a polynomial	[page 149]
term	[page 143]	ascending order	[page 149]
like terms	[page 143]	descending order	[page 149]
unlike terms	[page 143]	scientific notation	[page 157]
binomial	[page 148]	uniform motion	[page 169]
trinomial	[page 148]	zero exponent	[page 176]
degree of a monomial	[page 148]	consecutive integers	[page 185]

- The Addition Property of Exponents   [4–3]
  For all numbers a, and all positive numbers m and n,

$$a^m \cdot a^n = a^{m+n}.$$

- *Scientific notation* is a way of writing a number as the product of two factors.   [4–4]
  One factor is a number between 1 and 10, and the other factor is a power of
  10. For example, $43{,}000 = 4.3 \times 10^4$.

- The Multiplication Property of Exponents   [4–5]
  For all numbers a, and all positive integers m and n,

$$(a^m)^n = a^{mn}.$$

- The Distributive Property of Exponents over Multiplication   [4–6]
  For all numbers a and b, and all positive integers n,

$$(ab)^n = a^n b^n.$$

- The formula $d = rt$ gives the relationship between distance, rate, and time   [4–7]
  when the units are comparable.

- The Subtraction Property of Exponents   [4–8]
  For all numbers a (except 0) and for all positive integers m and n,

$$\text{If } m > n, \text{ then } \frac{a^m}{a^n} = a^{m-n};$$

$$\text{If } m < n, \text{ then } \frac{a^m}{a^n} = \frac{1}{a^{n-m}};$$

$$\text{If } m = n, \text{ then } \frac{a^m}{a^n} = a^0 = 1.$$

■ CHAPTER REVIEW

4–1   **Objective** To add and subtract polynomials.

Add.

1. $(3x^2 - 2x + 5) + (x^2 + x)$ $4x^2 - x + 5$

Subtract.

2. $4r + 3s$
        $\underline{-6r \qquad - t}$ $10r + 3s + t$

Simplify.

3. $(6x^3 - x^2 + 2) - (4x^2 + 3x) + (x^3 - 3)$ $7x^3 - 5x^2 - 3x - 1$

4–2   **Objective** To identify polynomials by number of terms and by degree.

Answer the following.

4. a. Which of these polynomials is a binomial?

$$2x^2 + y \quad \text{or} \quad 2x^2y \quad {\scriptstyle 2x^2 + y}$$

b. Which of these polynomials is a trinomial?

$$2xy + 3x^2 + 4y^2 + 7 \quad \text{or} \quad 4x + 2y + 3z \quad {\scriptstyle 4x + 2y + 3z}$$

State the degree of each polynomial.

5. $3x^2 + 2x + 1$ 2   **6.** $2abc + b^2$ 3   **7.** $2x^3 + 3x - 2x^3 + 4x^2$ 2

4–3   **Objective** To multiply monomials.

Simplify.

8. $a^3 \cdot a^4$ a^7 **9.** $(3xy^2)(-2xy)$ $-6x^2y^3$

4–4   **Objective** To write numbers using scientific notation and standard decimal notation.

10. Write 9,620,000 using scientific notation. 9.62×10^6

11. Write $3.64 \cdot 10^7$ using standard decimal notation.   36,400,000

Objective To multiply numbers expressed in scientific notation.

Multiply. Write the product using scientific notation.

12. $(3 \cdot 10^4) \cdot (5 \cdot 10^3)$ $1.5 \cdot 10^8$

4–5   **Objective** To find powers of monomials.

Simplify.

13. $(x^3)^4$ x^{12} **14.** $(3y^2)^3$ $27y^6$ **15.** $(5ab^3)^2$ $25a^2b^6$

4–6 **Objective** To multiply a monomial and a polynomial.

Simplify.

16. $-3(4a - b)$
$-12a + 3b$

17. $5y(2y - x)$
$10y^2 - 5xy$

18. $5x^2(x^2 - 3x + 4)$
$5x^4 - 15x^3 + 20x^2$

4–7 **Objective** To solve uniform-motion problems.

Solve.

19. Truck terminals A and B are 200 miles apart. At noon a truck leaves terminal A heading for terminal B at a speed of 55 mph, and a truck leaves terminal B heading for terminal A at a speed of 45 mph. At what time will they meet each other? How far will they be from terminal A when they meet? 2 P.M., 110 miles

20. A ship leaves port traveling east at 17 knots (nautical miles per hour). Two hours later another ship leaves port, heading east at 22 knots. How long will it take for the second ship to overtake the first? How many nautical miles will they be from home port? 6.8 hours, 149.6 nautical miles

4–8 **Objective** To divide monomials.

Simplify. (Assume that none of the variables equals zero.)

21. $\dfrac{2x^2}{6x^4}$ $\frac{1}{3x^2}$

22. $\dfrac{-12ab^3}{6a^2b}$ $\frac{-2b^2}{a}$

Objective To divide numbers expressed in scientific notation.

Simplify. Write the quotient using scientific notation.

23. $\dfrac{4.9 \cdot 10^8}{7 \cdot 10^5}$ $7 \cdot 10^2$

4–9 **Objective** To solve money problems by writing and solving equations.

Solve by using an equation.

24. If 21 nickels and quarters are worth $2.45, how many coins are nickels? 14

25. A plumber charges $16 for a service call plus $24 per hour. How many hours did he work if he charged $76? 2.5

4–10 **Objective** To use equations to solve problems about consecutive integers.

Solve by using an equation.

26. The sum of three consecutive integers is 174. What is the middle integer? 58

27. The sum of two consecutive odd numbers is 188. What are the numbers? 93 and 95

■ CHAPTER 4 SELF-TEST

Simplify.

4-1 **1.** $(3x^2 + 4xy) - (x^2 + 2xy)$ $\quad$ **2.** $(4a^2 - 2bc) + (6a^2 + 3bc)$
$\qquad\qquad\qquad\qquad\qquad\qquad$ $2x^2 + 2xy$ $\qquad\qquad\qquad\qquad$ $10a^2 + bc$

3. $(2x^2 + 3x - 8) + (3x^2 - 4x - 11)$ $\;5x^2 - x - 19$

Here are four expressions.

4-2 **A.** $5x^2$ $\qquad$ **B.** $4y - 2$ $\qquad$ **C.** $\dfrac{7}{x}$ $\qquad$ **D.** $3x^2y + 8x - 5$

4. Which expressions above are monomials? $\;$ A

5. Which expressions are binomials? $\;$ B

6. What is the degree of the polynomial in (D)? $\;$ 3

Simplify.

4-3 **7.** $(2a^3)(3a^2)$ $\;6a^5$ $\qquad$ **8.** $(-3x^4)(5x^3)$ $\;-15x^7$ $\quad$ **9.** $(4x^3y^2)(-6x^5y^3)$
$\qquad\qquad\qquad\qquad\qquad\qquad\qquad\qquad\qquad\qquad\qquad\qquad\qquad$ $-24x^8y^5$

Write in scientific notation.

4-4 **10.** $820,000,000$ $\qquad$ **11.** $2.8 \cdot 300$ $\;8.4 \cdot 10^2$ $\quad$ **12.** $(3.4 \cdot 10^5) \cdot (7 \cdot 10^2)$
$\qquad\qquad$ 8.2×10^8 $\qquad\qquad\qquad\qquad\qquad\qquad\qquad\qquad\qquad$ $2.38 \cdot 10^8$

Simplify.

4-5 **13.** $(x^2)^5$ $\;x^{10}$ $\qquad$ **14.** $(2y^3)^4$ $\;16y^{12}$ $\qquad$ **15.** $\left(\dfrac{1}{2}a^2b^3\right)^2$ $\;\dfrac{1}{4}a^4b^6$

Multiply.

4-6 **16.** $2x(3x - 5)$ $\qquad$ **17.** $\dfrac{2}{3}(9y^2 - 12x^2)$ $\qquad$ **18.** $3a^2(a + 2b)$
$\qquad\quad$ $6x^2 - 10x$ $\qquad\qquad\qquad$ $6y^2 - 8x^2$ $\qquad\qquad\qquad$ $3a^3 + 6a^2b$

Solve.

4-7 **19.** Two cars start from the same place and travel in opposite directions, one at 75 km/h and the other at 85 km/h. How far apart are they after 3 hours? $\;$ 480 km

Simplify.

4-8 **20.** $\dfrac{3x^2y}{6xy^2}$ $\;\dfrac{x}{2y}$ $\qquad$ **21.** $\dfrac{-18x^4y^3}{-6x^2y}$ $\;3x^2y^2$ $\qquad$ **22.** $\dfrac{9a^3b^2}{3a^2b^3}$ $\;\dfrac{3a}{b}$

23. Simplify. Write the quotient in scientific notation.

$$\dfrac{8.8 \cdot 10^8}{3.6 \cdot 10^5} \approx 2.4 \cdot 10^3$$

Solve by using an equation.

4-9 **24.** If 33 nickels and quarters are worth $5.05, how many of the coins are nickels? $\;$ 16

4-10 **25.** The sum of three consecutive even integers is 180. What are the numbers? $\;$ 58, 60, 62

---

1. Add. $\quad \begin{array}{r} x - 2y + 3z \\ -2x + 5y - z \end{array}$ $\qquad$ 1. $-x + 3y + 2z$

■ **Simplify.**

2. $(2x^2 + 3x - 5) - (x^2 + x + 1)$ $\qquad$ 2. $x^2 + 2x - 6$

3. $(3a^2 - 6b^2) - (a^2 - ab) + (3ab - b^2)$ $\qquad$ 3. $2a^2 + 4ab - 7b^2$

4. State the degree of $4a^2b$. $\qquad$ 4. 3

5. State the degree of the polynomial $5x - x^2 + 4$. $\qquad$ 5. 2

6. Write the polynomial $1 + 8b^2 - b + 2b^3$ in descending order. $\qquad$ 6. $2b^3 + 8b^2 - b + 1$

■ **Simplify.**

7. $(x^2)(x^7)$ $\qquad$ 7. x^9

8. $(3a^2)(2a^2)$ $\qquad$ 8. $6a^4$

9. $(-4y^3)\left(\frac{1}{2}y\right)$ $\qquad$ 9. $-2y^4$

10. $(b^3)^5$ $\qquad$ 10. b^{15}

11. $(-2x)^3$ $\qquad$ 11. $-8x^3$

12. $(4x^2)(4x)^2$ $\qquad$ 12. $64x^4$

13. $-5(2x - 6)$ $\qquad$ 13. $-10x + 30$

14. $6xy(2x^2 - xy + y^2)$ $\qquad$ 14. $12x^3y - 6x^2y^2 + 6xy^3$

15. $\dfrac{y^7}{y^9}$ $\qquad$ 15. $\dfrac{1}{y^2}$

16. $\dfrac{24x^5}{15x^3}$ $\qquad$ 16. $\dfrac{8}{5}x^2$

17. $14x^3y^3 \div 7x^2y$ $\qquad$ 17. $2y^2$

© D.C. Heath & Co.

■ **Express in scientific notation.**

18. The distance covered by Apollo XI is approximately 480,000 miles. $\qquad$ 18. $4.8 \cdot 10^5$

19. $(2.4 \cdot 10^5)(3 \cdot 10^4)$ $\qquad$ 19. $7.2 \cdot 10^9$

■ **Solve.**

20. A train left Boston traveling south at 80 km/h. Three hours later another train left Boston traveling north at 60 km/h. How long had the second train been traveling when the two trains were 520 km apart? $\qquad$ 20. 2 h

21. A set of dimes and quarters has a value of $4.25. There are 4 more dimes than quarters. How many coins are there in all? $\qquad$ 21. 26

22. The sum of three consecutive integers is 144. Find the greatest integer. $\qquad$ 22. 49

★ **BONUS**

The alternating sum and difference of six consecutive odd integers is 20. Find the smallest integer. $\qquad$ BONUS 7

© D.C. Heath & Co.

Chapter 4 Test B

NAME _____

1. Add. $2x - 2y - 2z$
$\underline{-3x - y + 5z}$

1. $-x - 3y + 3z$

■ Simplify.

2. $(3x^2 - 5x + 6) - (2x^2 + x + 3)$
2. $x^2 - 6x + 3$

3. $(4a^2 - 5b^2) - (2a^2 - 2ab) + (3ab + b^2)$
3. $2a^2 + 5ab - 4b^2$

4. State the degree of $5xy^3$.
4. 4

5. State the degree of the polynomial $4y - 2y^2 + 6$.
5. 2

6. Write the polynomial $2 - 5a^2 + 3a + 4a^3$ in descending order.
6. $4a^3 - 5a^2 + 3a + 2$

■ Simplify.

7. $(y^3)(y^5)$
7. y^8

8. $(2b^3)(3b^2)$
8. $6b^5$

9. $(-8x)(\frac{1}{4}x^4)$
9. $-2x^5$

10. $(y^2)^4$
10. y^8

11. $(-3x)^3$
11. $-27x^3$

12. $(2a^2)(2a)^2$
12. $8a^4$

13. $-4(3y - 2)$
13. $-12y + 8$

14. $4xy(3x^2 - xy + y^2)$
14. $12x^3y - 4x^2y^2 + 4xy^3$

15. $\frac{a^5}{a^7}$
15. $\frac{1}{a^2}$

16. $\frac{18x^6}{12y^3}$
16. $\frac{3}{2}y^3$

17. $48x^3y^2 \div 12xy^2$
17. $4x^2$

© D.C. Heath & Co.

Chapter 4 Test B (page 2)   NAME _____

■ Express in scientific notation.

18. The number of times the average human heart beats in a lifetime is approximately 2,850,000,000 beats.
18. $2.85 \cdot 10^9$

19. $(3.7 \cdot 10^4)(2 \cdot 10^5)$
19. $7.4 \cdot 10^9$

■ Solve.

20. A train left Philadelphia traveling south at 70 km/h. Two hours later another train left Philadelphia traveling north at 50 km/h. How long had the second train been traveling when the two trains were 620 km apart?
20. 4 h

21. A set of dimes and quarters has a value of $5.20. There are 3 more dimes than quarters. How many coins are there in all?
21. 31

22. The sum of three consecutive integers is 267. Find the middle integer.
22. 89

★ **BONUS**

The alternating sum and difference of six consecutive even integers is 30. Find the smallest integer.
BONUS 12

© D.C. Heath & Co.

194

■ PRACTICE FOR COLLEGE ENTRANCE TESTS

Strategy for Success   Taking tests ————

If you have any extra time when taking a multiple-choice test, go back to the questions you have not answered. Sometimes you can find the right answer by checking each of the choices in the problem.

Choose the best answer for each problem.

1. A number n is doubled, the result is decreased by 5, and this result is multiplied by 3. Which of the expressions below represents the final result?

A. $2(3n - 5)$ **B.** $\frac{3}{2}(n - 5)$ **C.** $3(2n - 5)$

D. $6n - 5$ **E.** $3(5 - 2n)$

2. Which of the following is (are) true?

I. $3^2 \cdot 4^2 = 3^2 \cdot 2^4$ II. $2^3 \cdot 4^2 = 3^2 \cdot 4^2$ III. $2^3 \cdot 3^5 = 6^3 \cdot 3$

A. I only   **B.** II only   **C.** III only

D. I and II only   **E.** I and III only

3. If a, b, and c are whole numbers, then the expression $a(b + c)$ will represent an odd number if:

A. The numbers a, b, and c are all odd.   **B.** The number a is odd.

C. The number a is even and the numbers b and c are odd.

D. The numbers a and b are even and the number c is odd.

E. The numbers a and b are odd and the number c is even.

4. If $x \neq 0$, then $\frac{(-3x)^2}{-3x^2} = $ ___?___ .

A. -3 **B.** -1 **C.** 1 **D.** 3 **E.** 6

5. If for all numbers x and y, $x \diamondplus y$ is defined by the equation $x \diamondplus y = x^2 + xy$, then $a \diamondplus (b \diamondplus c) = $ ___?___ .

A. $a^2 + b^2 + abc$ **B.** $a^2 + ab^2 + abc$ **C.** $a^2 + ab^2 + bc$

D. $(a^2 + ab)^2 + a^2 + abc$ **E.** $a^2 + a^2b^2 + abc$

6. $5 \cdot 10^2 + 3 \cdot 10^4 = $ ___?___

A. 5030   **B.** 50,300   **C.** 3500   **D.** 3050   **E.** 30,500

194   Chapter 4   Polynomials

7. If x and y are positive integers and $a \neq 0$, then $\dfrac{(a^x)^y}{a^x} = \underline{\ ?\ }$.

   A. $a^{x(y-1)}$ **B.** a^y **C.** $a^{xy} - a^x$

   D. $a^{x+y/x}$ **E.** $a^{x(y-x)}$

8. If $(2^5)(3^4) = 2(6^n)$, then $n = \underline{\ ?\ }$.

   A. 2   **B.** 3   **C.** 4   **D.** 5   **E.** 8

9. $xy = x + \underline{\ ?\ }$

   A. $x(y-1)$ **B.** $x(1-y)$ **C.** $(x-1)y$ **D.** $(1-x)y$ **E.** $y-x$

10. For all numbers m and all numbers $n \neq 0$, $\left\{\begin{matrix} m \\ n \end{matrix}\right\}$ is defined as $\dfrac{m^2}{n}$.
Then $\left\{\begin{matrix} 2 \\ 3 \end{matrix}\right\} \cdot \left\{\begin{matrix} 3 \\ 4 \end{matrix}\right\} = \underline{\ ?\ }$.

   A. $\dfrac{1}{4}$ **B.** $\dfrac{4}{3}$ **C.** $\dfrac{3}{2}$ **D.** 3   **E.** $\dfrac{9}{4}$

11. The first number of a sequence is $1^2 + 1$. The second number is $2^2 + 1$, the third number is $3^2 + 1$, and so on. Which of the following numbers in the sequence will be odd?

   I. The 99th number   II. The 100th number   III. The 101st number

   A. I only   **B.** II only   **C.** III only

   D. I and III only   **E.** I, II, and III

12. How many different four-digit numbers can be formed using the digits 1, 2, 3, and 4 one time each? [*Example:* 1234, 1243.]

   A. 4   **B.** 6   **C.** 8   **D.** 16   **E.** 24

13. $\dfrac{\frac{2}{3} + \frac{2}{3} + \frac{2}{3}}{\frac{3}{2} + \frac{3}{2} + \frac{3}{2} + \frac{3}{2}} = ?$

   A. $\dfrac{1}{3}$ **B.** $\dfrac{4}{9}$ **C.** $\dfrac{2}{3}$ **D.** 1   **E.** $\dfrac{9}{4}$

Strategy for Success   Beginning a chapter ————

Think about the "major plot" that is being developed in the chapter. Turn to the table of contents, read the chapter title, and read each section title. Think about how one section leads to the next, and how this chapter relates to the other chapters.

CHAPTER 5

CHAPTER OVERVIEW

Relations are sets of ordered pairs; functions are relations in which every first component has a unique second component. In this chapter students learn to graph functions and relations on the coordinate plane. To graph functions and relations, students need skills acquired in Chapters 1, 2, and 3 in evaluating expressions, computing with real numbers, and solving equations.

The slope of a line is a measure of its steepness; in this chapter, students will learn to determine slopes of lines. An understanding of the concept of slope is essential for later work in algebra, coordinate geometry, physics, and calculus. Slope has many important applications; for example, in a motion problem where time is plotted along the horizontal axis and distance along the vertical axis, the slope of the graph represents the rate at which the object is moving.

The graph of an equation in x and y of the form $y = mx + b$ is a straight line whose slope is the number m. Such an equation is called a linear equation, and the function it defines is called a linear function. In this chapter, students learn about linear equations and linear functions. Students will need this knowledge for studying systems of linear equations in Chapter 6, studying ratio, proportion, and variation in Chapter 8, and studying inequalities and their graphs in Chapter 9.

5 Graphing Linear Equations and Functions

The slope is the ratio of the change in height (rise or decline) for a given distance (run). It is used in many descriptions of steepness.

$$\text{slope} = \frac{\text{rise (or decline)}}{\text{run}}$$

The rate of change in the height of a riverbed is used to divide the course of a river into three parts—upper, middle, and lower. In the upper course of a river, the slope of the channel, called the gradient, is steep (usually more than 50 feet per mile) and the current is swift.

PURPOSE

A visual representation of a relationship helps many students understand that relationship better.

5–1 Graphing Ordered Pairs

Preview

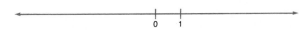

What do these three statements have in common?

- My address is 1234 W. 25th Street.
- Our ship is located at 48° N latitude and 30° W longitude.
- A theater ticket is for row 10 seat 15.

Each statement is an example of locating a position by giving a *pair* of quantities: 1234 and W. 25th St., 48° N latitude and 30° W longitude, and 10th row, 15th seat.

In this lesson you will study a system for locating points by using pairs of numbers.

PREVIEW

Use the Preview to introduce students to the use of pairs of numbers to give locations on a two-dimensional surface.

- How many numbers are needed to locate a point on a line? (1)
- Give an example. (A house number locates a house on a given street.)
- How many numbers are needed to locate a point in three-dimensional space? (3)
- Give an example. (To locate an airplane flying over an ocean requires latitude, longitude, and altitude.)

■ LESSON

A number line is constructed by drawing a line, picking a point for 0, and then picking a point for 1.

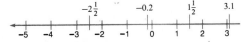

Once that is done, the unit distance between 0 and 1 determines the location of other numbers. Each point on the line has a number associated with it, and every number has a point associated with it. The number is the **coordinate** of the point and the point is the **graph** of the number. The coordinate is the "address" of the point.

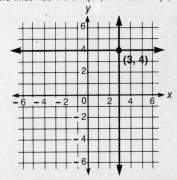

If we wish to assign "addresses" to points in a plane, we must use pairs of numbers. To assign a pair of numbers to each point, select two perpendicular number lines, called **axes**. The horizontal axis is usually called the **x-axis,** and the vertical axis is usually called the **y-axis.** The point of intersection of the two axes is called the **origin.** The axes divide the plane into four regions called **quadrants.** The axes are not a part of any quadrant; they are boundaries of the quadrants.

Point *A* is 3 units to the left of the *y*-axis and 4 units above the *x*-axis. The "address" of point *A* is $(-3, 4)$. Note the order of the two numbers in the number pair. The first component of the pair gives the direction and distance to move from the *y*-axis, and the second component gives the direction and distance to move from the *x*-axis. The number pair $(-3, 4)$ is called an **ordered pair** since the order of the numbers is important.

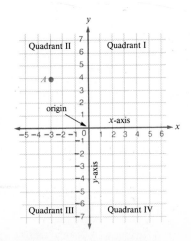

LESSON

Carefully define all terms introduced in this lesson (with the possible exceptions of ordinate and abscissa). Students should quickly become comfortable with the terms.

An alternate way of locating an ordered pair such as (3, 4) is to think of the coordinates as an *address*. The first coordinate, 3, is part of the address. Visualize all those points in the coordinate plane that have this part of their address the same.

The second coordinate, 4, is also part of the address. The points having this part of their address the same are viewed as a horizontal line.

But only the point of intersection of these two lines has the unique, full address (3, 4).

The numbering of the quadrants is done in a counterclockwise manner starting in the upper right fourth of the plane.

Example 1. Graph. (−3, −2)

Start at the origin, (0, 0). Move left 3 units. Move down 2 units.

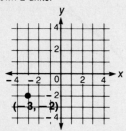

Example 2. Graph. (1, −3)

Start at the origin. Move 1 unit to the right, then 3 units down.

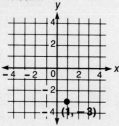

CHECK UNDERSTANDING

On a large pair of axes, point to points with integer coordinates and ask students to state the coordinates. Also give pairs of integer coordinates and ask students to locate their graphs.

CLASSROOM EXERCISES

For classroom exercises 9 and 10, students should look for pairs of points that are on vertical or horizontal lines.

For classroom exercises 12–16, remind the students that the horizontal axis is the x-axis (and the vertical axis is the y-axis).

Point B is the graph of (4, −1) and the numbers 4 and −1 are the coordinates of point B. The first coordinate, 4, is called the **x-coordinate**. The second coordinate, −1, is called the **y-coordinate**. (The x-coordinate is also called the **abscissa** of the point, and the y-coordinate the **ordinate** of the point.)

The coordinates of point C are (2, 5) and of point D are (5, 2). Note that points C and D are different points and that (2, 5) and (5, 2) are different ordered pairs. Ordered pairs are equal only if they have both the same **first components** and the same **second components**.

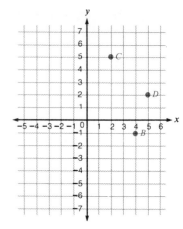

Definition: Equal Ordered Pairs

For all real numbers a, b, c, and d,

$$(a, b) = (c, d) \text{ if and only if } a = c \text{ and } b = d.$$

Example 1   Graph (−2, −3).

Solution

Draw a pair of axes. Start at the origin (0, 0). The x-coordinate indicates the direction and distance to move horizontally (move *left* 2 units). The y-coordinate indicates the direction and distance to move vertically (move *down* 3 units).

Make a dot and label it (−2, −3).

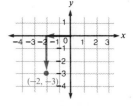

Example 2   Graph $\left(3, 1\frac{1}{2}\right)$.

Solution

Start at the origin. Move 3 units to the right, then $1\frac{1}{2}$ units up.

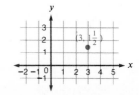

Having students work together in small mixed-ability groups provides many more opportunities for students to get help with their specific problems than can be achieved in a whole-class organization.

ASSIGNMENT GUIDE

Basic   1–35 odd, Review Exercises
Average 1–31 odd, 33–44 all, Review Exercises
Enriched 1–41 odd, 43–49 all, Review Exercises

PRACTICE WORKSHEET 22

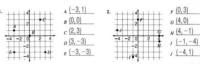

■ CLASSROOM EXERCISES

State the coordinates of each point.

1. *A* (2, 4)
2. *B* (−1, 4)
3. *C* (−2, 0)
4. *D* (0, 1)
5. *E* (−2, −3)
6. *F* (0, −4)
7. *G* (2, −5)
8. *H* (4, 0)

9. Name the points that have the same *x*-coordinate.
   A and G, C and E, D and F
10. Name the points that have the same *y*-coordinate.
    A and B, C and H
11. What are the coordinates of the origin?   (0, 0)

Identify the quadrant in which the graph of each ordered pair is found. If the graph is on an axis, state which one.

12. (5, 3) I
13. (5, −3) IV
14. $\left(-2, 1\frac{1}{2}\right)$ II
15. (0, −2) y-axis
16. (−3, −2) III

■ WRITTEN EXERCISES

State the coordinates of each point.

1. *A* (−5, 3)
2. *B* (−2, 4)
3. *C* (0, 3)
4. *D* (2, 4)
5. *E* (4, 1)
6. *F* (1, 0)
7. *G* (2, −1)
8. *H* (2, −4)
9. *I* (0, −5)
10. *J* (−2, −4)
11. *K* (−5, −2)
12. *L* (−2, 0)

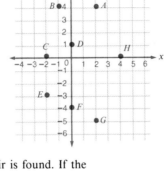

Identify the quadrant each point is in or the axis it is on.

13. *A* II
14. *B* II
15. *C* y-axis
16. *D* I
17. *E* I
18. *F* x-axis
19. *G* IV
20. *H* IV
21. *I* y-axis
22. *J* III
23. *K* III
24. *L* x-axis

Name the point having these coordinates.

25. (5, 2) Q
26. (2, 5) P
27. (−5, 2) M
28. (−2, 5) N
29. (3, 0) R
30. (0, −3) U
31. (−5, −2) W
32. (−2, −5) V

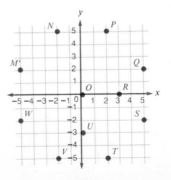

ENRICHMENT PROBLEMS

- Two numbers are used to locate a point in the plane. What happens if you try to specify a point using just one number? Describe the graph of points satisfying these one-number conditions.

  a. point(s) 4 units from the *x*-axis
  The horizontal line $y = 4$

  b. point(s) −2 units from the *y*-axis
  The vertical line $x = -2$

  c. point(s) 5 units from the origin
  A circle whose center is (0, 0) with a radius 5

- The location of a forest fire is determined by sightings given from two fire towers. What two numbers locate points in the forest? Describe a coordinate system that could be used.
  The two numbers could be angle measures or compass directions.

33.

34.

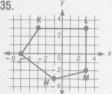

35.

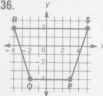

36.

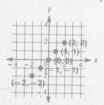

47. Answers will vary.

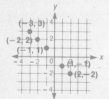

48. Answers will vary.

49. Answers will vary.

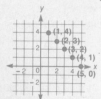

200

EXTRA PRACTICE, page 627

33. Graph these points: $A(-3, 4)$, $B(2, 4)$, $C(-5, -2)$, and $D(4, -2)$. Draw line segments from A to B, B to C, C to D, and D to A.

34. Graph these points: $E(-2, 4)$, $F(0, 8)$, $G(4, 8)$, and $H(0, 0)$. Draw line segments from E to F, F to G, G to H, and H to E.

35. Graph these points: $J(-5, 0)$, $K(-3, 3)$, $L(3, 3)$, $M(3, -2)$, and $N(-1, -3)$. Draw line segments from J to K, K to L, L to M, M to N, and N to J.

36. Graph these points: $P(3, -4)$, $Q(-2, -4)$, $R(-4, 2)$, and $S(5, 2)$. Draw line segments from P to Q, Q to R, R to S, and S to P.

Identify the quadrant in which each point is located.

B **37.** The x-coordinate is positive and the y-coordinate is negative. IV

38. The x-coordinate is negative and the y-coordinate is positive. II

39. The x-coordinate is positive and the y-coordinate is greater than the x-coordinate. I

40. The x-coordinate is negative and the y-coordinate is less than its x-coordinate. III

41. The sum of the coordinates is positive and the product of the coordinates is positive. I

42. The x-coordinate is negative and the y-coordinate is -5 times the x-coordinate. II

Coordinates are given for three vertices of a square. Give the coordinates of the fourth vertex.

43. $(0, 4)$, $(0, 0)$, $(4, 0)$ (4, 4)

44. $(2, 3)$, $(-3, 3)$, $(-3, -2)$ (2, -2)

C **45.** $(2, 3)$, $(0, 0)$, $(3, -2)$ (5, 1)

46. $(2, -3)$, $(-3, -2)$, $(-2, 3)$ (3, 2)

Graph and label five points that meet the given condition(s).

47. The x-coordinate and the y-coordinate are equal.

48. The x-coordinate and the y-coordinate are opposites.

49. The sum of the coordinates is 5.

■ REVIEW EXERCISES

a	b	x	y
3	-4	12	-6

Substitute and simplify.

1. $ax + by$ 60

2. $x - 3y$ 30

3. $a^2 + b^2$ 25

4. $(a + b)^2$ 1   [2-4]

5. $\dfrac{x}{b} + \dfrac{y}{a}$ -5

6. $\dfrac{(-ax + b)}{y}$ $6\frac{2}{3}$

7. $\dfrac{x}{a} + \dfrac{y}{b}$ $5\frac{1}{2}$

8. $\dfrac{(x + y)}{(a + b)}$ -6 [2-5]

5–2 Graphing Relations

Preview History

The principles of coordinate geometry based on ordered pairs of numbers were developed by René Descartes in 1637 while he was still in his teens. A popular, but possibly fictional, version of his discovery is told as follows. Because of poor health, he had to spend much of his time in bed. One day while lying on his back he watched a fly crawling around on the ceiling. He discovered that the fly's position on the ceiling could be determined by an ordered pair of numbers, the first number being the distance of the fly from one wall and the second number being the fly's distance from a wall perpendicular to the first wall. Extending this idea, he saw that all points in a plane could be represented as ordered pairs of real numbers. This invention by Descartes was called by one English writer "the greatest single step ever made in the progress of exact science."

■ LESSON

A **relation** is a set of ordered pairs. Three common ways of describing a relation are as follows.

1. Listing the pairs.

$$\left\{(2,\ 3),\ (-1,\ 4),\ (0,\ 1),\ \left(5,\ \tfrac{1}{4}\right)\right\}$$

2. Making a table.

x	y
2	3
-1	4
0	1
5	$\tfrac{1}{4}$

3. Making a graph.

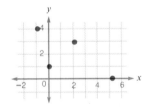

For the relation described above, the first components of the ordered pairs are 2, -1, 0, and 5. The set of first components of a relation is called the **domain of the relation.** The second components of the above relation are 3, 4, 1, and $\tfrac{1}{4}$. The set of second components of a relation is called the **range of the relation.**

Example 1 Given the following table, list the ordered pairs in the relation. State the domain and the range. Then graph the relation.

x	-2	0	1	3	$\tfrac{1}{2}$
y	-1	-3	3	0	$1\tfrac{1}{2}$

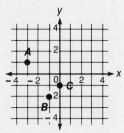

State the coordinates of each point.

1. A $(-3, 1)$ **2.** C $(0, -1)$

Identify the quadrant each point is in or the axis it is on.

3. B III **4.** C y-axis

5. Graph these points: $D(1, 3)$ and $E(3, -1)$. Draw the line segment from D to E.

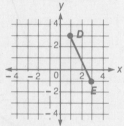

PURPOSE

To picture numerical relationships, it is helpful to graph sets of ordered pairs on the same coordinate system. Identifying the set of first coordinates (domain) and second coordinates (range) of the relation lays the groundwork for writing the equation or inequality that relates these sets of values.

PREVIEW

Descartes' contribution to coordinate geometry is immortalized by naming the coordinate system "the Cartesian plane" and the (x, y) number pairs "the Cartesian coordinates."

LESSON

The relations in this lesson contain only a small number of ordered pairs. It is important for students to master the graphing of finite relations before going on to infinite relations, since there is a tendency for some students to overgeneralize about graphs.

ADDITIONAL EXAMPLES

Example 1.

Given the following table, list the ordered pairs in the relation. State the domain and range. Then graph the relation.

x	-1	$-\frac{1}{2}$	0	$\frac{1}{2}$	1
y	1	$1\frac{1}{2}$	2	$2\frac{1}{2}$	3

The relation is $\{(-1, 1), (-\frac{1}{2}, 1\frac{1}{2}), (0, 2), (\frac{1}{2}, 2\frac{1}{2}), (1, 3)\}$. The domain is $\{-1, -\frac{1}{2}, 0, \frac{1}{2}, 1\}$. The range is $\{1, 1\frac{1}{2}, 2, 2\frac{1}{2}, 3\}$.

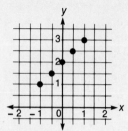

Example 2.

List the ordered pairs in the relation shown. State the domain and the range.

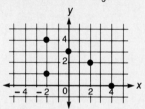

The relation is $\{(-2, 1), (-2, 4), (0, 3), (2, 2), (4, 0)\}$. The domain is $\{-2, 0, 2, 4\}$. The range is $\{0, 1, 2, 3, 4\}$.

Example 3.

List and graph five ordered pairs in the relation: The set of all ordered pairs in which the first and second components are reciprocals, $x \neq 0$.

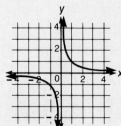

Example 1 (continued)

Solution The relation is $\left\{(-2, -1), (0, -3), (1, 3), (3, 0), \left(\frac{1}{2}, 1\frac{1}{2}\right)\right\}$.

The domain is $\left\{-2, 0, 1, 3, \frac{1}{2}\right\}$.

The range is $\left\{-1, -3, 3, 0, 1\frac{1}{2}\right\}$.

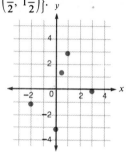

Example 2 List the ordered pairs in the relation shown on the graph. State the domain and the range.

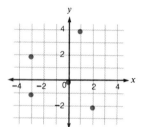

Solution The relation is $\{(-3, -1), (-3, 2), (0, 0), (2, -2), (1, 4)\}$.
The domain is $\{-3, 0, 2, 1\}$.
The range is $\{-1, 2, 0, -2, 4\}$.

Relations are sometimes described in words.

Example 3 List and graph five ordered pairs in the relation.

Relation: The set of all ordered pairs with first and second components equal.

Solution

x	y
1	1
-3	-3
2	2
$\frac{1}{2}$	$\frac{1}{2}$
0	0

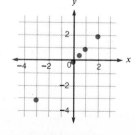

Immediately after the starting bell rings, have students do one or more problems from the Practice for College Entrance Tests given at the end of the chapter. This activity is suitable for groups of two or three students.

In Example 3 only five ordered pairs were listed and graphed. The graph of the whole relation is a straight line since the domain and the range is the set of real numbers.

■ CLASSROOM EXERCISES

1. Define "relation."   A set of ordered pairs

2. Is the set $\{-2, 0, 2, 4, 6\}$ a relation? Why or why not?   No

3. Is the set $\{(2, 1), (3, 2)\}$ a relation? Why or why not?   Yes

4. State the domain of the relation $\{(3, 1)\}$.   {3}

List the ordered pairs in each relation. State the domain and the range.

5.
x	y
−1	4
−2	2
−2	3
2	4

{(−1, 4), (−2, 2), (−2, 3), (2, 4)}
Domain: {−1, −2, 2};
range: {4, 2, 3}

6.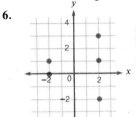

{(2, 3), (2, 1), (2, −2), (−2, 0), (−2, 1)}
Domain: {2, −2};
range: {3, 1, −2, 0, 1}

7. Graph the relation $\{(1, -1), (3, 2), (5, -1), (-3, 0)\}$.

8. Relation *T* is the set of all ordered pairs in which the first and second components are opposites.
   Answers will vary.
   a. List 6 ordered pairs in Relation *T*.
   b. Graph the ordered pairs that you listed.
   c. Guess what the graph of the whole relation would be.   A line
   Answers will vary.
   d. Test your guess by listing more ordered pairs in the relation and graphing them.
   e. What are the domain and range of Relation *T*?   Real numbers

■ WRITTEN EXERCISES

State whether the set is a relation.

A

1. $\{(1, 2), (1, 3), (1, 4)\}$ Yes

2. $\{(1, 4), (2, 3), (3, 2), (4, 1)\}$ Yes

3. $\left\{0, \frac{1}{2}, 1, 1\frac{1}{2}\right\}$ No

4. $\{-3, -2, -1\}$ No

5. $\{(1, 2, 3), (4, 5, 6)\}$ No

6. $\{(1, 3, 5), (2, 4, 6)\}$ No

List the ordered pairs in the relation shown by the table.
((2, −2), (−3, 3), (0.5, −0.5), (−100, 100))

7.
x	y
2	−2
−3	3
0.5	−0.5
−100	100

8.
x	y
−1	1
−10	10
5	−5
−0.8	0.8

((−1, 1), (−10, 10), (5, −5), (−0.8, 0.8))

((6, 6), (−6, 6), (8, 8), (−8, 8))

9.
x	y
6	6
−6	6
8	8
−8	8

10.
x	y
−3	3
−1	1
1	1
3	3

((−3, 3), (−1, 1), (1, 1), (3, 3))

ADDITIONAL EXAMPLES

Sample ordered pairs.

x	3	−3	2	$\frac{1}{4}$	−1
y	$\frac{1}{3}$	$-\frac{1}{3}$	$\frac{1}{2}$	4	−1

CHECK UNDERSTANDING

• Are these sets relations? Explain your answers.
   a. $\{(1, 2), (-2, 4)\}$ (Yes. It is a set of ordered pairs.)
   b. $\{1, 2, -2, 4\}$ (No. The elements of the set are not ordered pairs.)
• State the domain and range of this relation.

x	3	2	−1	7	−5
y	0	8	4	−3	−1

(Domain: $\{3, 2, -1, 7, -5\}$
Range: $\{0, 8, 4, -3, -1\}$)
• List the ordered pairs of a relation such that the domain has four numbers and the range has one number. (One possible answer: $\{(1, 2), (3, 2), (0, 2), (-7, 2)\}$)

ADDITIONAL ANSWERS

■ Classroom Exercises

7.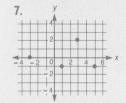

8. Answers will vary.
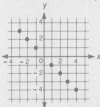

ASSIGNMENT GUIDE

Basic   1–23 odd, Review Exercises
Average 1–23 odd, 25–30 all, Review Exercises
Enriched 1–29 odd, 31–35 all, Review Exercises

203

5-2 GRAPHING RELATIONS

■ Each exercise describes a relation.
  a. List the ordered pairs in the relation.
  b. List the domain.
  c. List the range.

1.

x	0	1	2	3	4
y	0	3	6	9	12

a. {(0,0),(1,3),(2,6),(3,9),(4,12)}
b. {0,1,2,3,4}
c. {0,3,6,9,12}

2.

x	-2	-1	0	1	2
y	4	2	0	-2	-4

a. {(-2,4),(-1,2),(0,0),(1,-2),(2,-4)}
b. {-2,-1,0,1,2}
c. {-4,-2,0,2,4}

3. The set of ordered pairs in which both components are positive integers having a sum of 5.

a. {(1,4),(2,3),(3,2),(4,1)}
b. {1,2,3,4}
c. {1,2,3,4}

4. The set of ordered pairs in which both components are negative integers having a product of 15.

a. {(-1,-15),(-3,-5),(-5,-3),(-15,-1)}
b. {-15,-5,-3,-1}
c. {-15,-5,-3,-1}

5. The set of ordered pairs in which the first components are positive integers, the second components are negative integers, and the product of the components is −12.

a. {(1,-12),(2,-6),(3,-4),(4,-3),(6,-2),(12,-1)}
b. {1,2,3,4,6,12}
c. {-12,-6,-4,-3,-2,-1}

6. The set of ordered pairs in which both components are negative integers having a sum of −4.

a. {(-1,-3),(-2,-2),(-3,-1)}
b. {-3,-2,-1}
c. {-3,-2,-1}

7.

a. {(0,2),(1,1),(2,0),(3,-1)}
b. {0,1,2,3}
c. {-1,0,1,2}

8.

a. {(-2,-3),(-1,-1),(0,1),(1,3)}
b. {-2,-1,0,1}
c. {-3,-1,1,3}

PROBLEM-SOLVING NOTES
Understanding a problem

Much of algebra consists of a study of relationships between two variable quantities that can be expressed with an equation or inequality. When given sets of data without this relationship's being explicitly stated, we ask several questions, often in order.

1. What are the kinds of values each variable assumes?
2. What are the ranges for these sets of values?
3. Do the values for each variable vary in some regular fashion? Is a pattern evident?

Each of these *organizing actions* in comprehending data pairs involves separating the information into distinct sets—domains and ranges. The next step is to relate the sets with an equation or inequality.

List the domain and range of each relation.

11. {(1, 2), (3, 4), (5, 6)}
Domain: {1, 3, 5}; range: {2, 4, 6}

12. {(10, 9), (8, 7)} Domain: {10, 8}; range: {9, 7}

13. $\left\{\left(\frac{1}{2}, \frac{1}{3}\right)\right\}$ Domain: $\left\{\frac{1}{2}\right\}$; range: $\left\{\frac{1}{3}\right\}$

14. {(0, 100)} Domain: {0}; range: {100}

15.

x	5	−1	−4
y	6	0	−3

Domain: {5, −1, −4}; range: {6, 0, −3}

16.

x	3	−4	0
y	−1	6	2

Domain: {3, −4, 0}; range: {−1, 6, 2}

17. Relation P is the set of ordered pairs in which both components are positive integers having a sum of 4. Domain and range: {1, 2, 3}

18. Relation Q is the set of ordered number pairs in which the first component is a positive integer less than 5 and the second component is twice as large as the first component. Domain: {1, 2, 3, 4}; range: {2, 4, 6, 8}

19. The graph of Relation A is shown.
  a. List the ordered pairs in Relation A.
    {(1, 1), (−1, 3), (−3, 2), (3, −2)}
  b. List the domain.
    {1, −1, −3, 3}
  c. List the range.
    {1, 3, 2, −2}

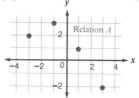

20. The graph of Relation B is shown.
  a. List the ordered pairs in Relation B.
    {(2, 1), (−2, −1), (−2, −2), (2, 0)}
  b. List the domain.
    {2, −2}
  c. List the range.
    {1, −1, −2, 0}

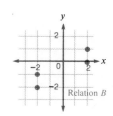

Graph the following relations.

21. {(−3, 3), (−1, 1), (0, −2), (0, 4)}

22. {(−3, −3), (−1, −1), (0, 2), (2, 4)}

23.

x	4	3	2	1
y	0	−1	−2	−3

24.

x	−4	−2	0	2
y	0	2	4	6

The following exercises describe a relation.

  a. List the ordered pairs in the relation.
  b. Graph the relation.
  c. List the domain.
  d. List the range.

B **25.** The components are integers having a product of 10.
  {(1, 10), (10, 1), (−1, −10), (−10, −1), (2, 5), (5, 2), (−2, −5), (−5, −2)}

26. The components are integers having a product of 6.
  {(1, 6), (6, 1), (2, 3), (3, 2), (−1, −6), (−6, −1), (−2, −3), (−3, −2)}

27. The first component is a negative integer greater than −6 and the second component is the absolute value of the first component.
  {(−5, 5), (−4, 4), (−3, 3), (−2, 2), (−1, 1)}

28. The first component is a positive integer less than 6 and the second component is the opposite of the first component.
⟨(5, − 5), (4, − 4), (3, − 3), (2, − 2), (1, − 1)⟩

29. The first component is a negative integer greater than − 5 and the second component is the square of the first component.
⟨(− 4, 16), (− 3, 9), (− 2, 4), (− 1, 1)⟩

30. The first component is a negative integer greater than − 5 and the second component is the cube of the first component.
⟨(− 4, − 64), (− 3, − 27), (− 2, − 8), (− 1, − 1)⟩

31. The first and second components of a relation are positive integers less than 6 and the second component is less than the first component.
⟨(5, 4), (5, 3), (5, 2), (5, 1), (4, 3), (4, 2), (4, 1), (3, 2), (3, 1), (2, 1)⟩

32. The first and second components of a relation are positive integers less than 6 and the second component is equal to the first component.
⟨(5, 5), (4, 4), (3, 3), (2, 2), (1, 1)⟩

33. The first component x and the second component y of a relation are integers such that $|x|$ and $|y| = 3$. ⟨(3, 3), (− 3, 3), (3, − 3), (− 3, − 3)⟩

34. The first component x and the second component y of a relation are integers such that $x^2 + y^2 = 5$.
⟨(1, 2), (− 1, 2), (1, − 2), (− 1, − 2), (2, 1), (2, − 1), (− 2, 1), (− 2, − 1)⟩

35. The first component x and the second component y of a relation are integers such that $x^2 + y^2 = 25$.
⟨(3, 4), (− 3, 4), (3, − 4), (− 3, − 4), (0, 5), (0, − 5), (4, 3), (4, − 3), (− 4, 3), (− 4, − 3), (5, 0), (− 5, 0)⟩

▓ REVIEW EXERCISES

w	x	y	z
− 2	8	− 6	− 12

Substitute and simplify.

1. $3x - 2y$ 36

2. $x - y - 2z$ 38 [2–4]

3. $2w - 3x + 4y$ − 52

4. $\frac{1}{2}x - \frac{2}{3}y$ 8

5. $\frac{w}{x} + \frac{y}{z}$ $\frac{1}{4}$

6. $\frac{w + x}{y - z}$ 1 [2–5]

7. $\frac{x - y}{w - z}$ $1\frac{2}{5}$

8. $\frac{1}{x} + \frac{1}{y}$ $-\frac{1}{24}$

Solve by making and using a table of data.

9. Andrea earns $1 the first day, $3 the second day, $5 the third day, and so on, earning $2 more each day. How many days will it take her to earn a total of $100? 10 [2–9]

10. Jane starts with $60 and earns $5 a day. Sue starts with $25 and earns $10 a day. In how many days will Sue have as much money as Jane? 7 [2–9]

ENRICHMENT PROBLEMS

• Although *relation* is a mathematical term, the word is also used in much the same way in families. Identify with ordered pairs these *relations* from your own family.
  a. "is the nephew of" (For example, (*a, b*) means *b* is the nephew of *a*.)
  b. "is the daughter of"
  c. "is the cousin of"

• Reverse the pairs in the problem above and write a new relation to describe the pairs.

ADDITIONAL ANSWERS
■ Written Exercises

21.

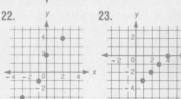

22.

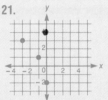

23.

24.

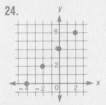

Graphs for Written Exercises 25–35 are on page 649.

Use this table.

x	−2	−1	0	1	2
y	1	2	3	4	5

1. List the number pairs in the relation.
{(−2, 1), (−1, 2), (0, 3), (1, 4), (2, 5)}

2. State the domain of the relation.
{−2, −1, 0, 1, 2}

3. State the range of the relation.
{1, 2, 3, 4, 5}

4. Graph the relation.

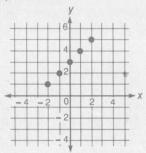

5. Is the graph a set of individual points, a straight line, or a curve?
A set of five points

PURPOSE

Many problems involve relationships between two variable quantities. The relationship may be expressed in equations. It is important to be able to find the value of one quantity when the value of the other quantity is known.

PREVIEW

Use the Preview to show that the solution of an open sentence with two variables is an ordered pair.

LESSON

Emphasize that the solutions of equations in two variables are ordered pairs. Also emphasize that we determine whether an ordered pair is a solution of an equation by substituting the components of the pair for the variables in the equation and then simplifying to find out whether the equation is true.

206

To find solutions to equations in two variables.

You may wish to spend two days on this section. Refer to the Pacing Chart.

5–3 Solving Equations in Two Variables

Preview

This question was on a history exam.

> The European explorer __?__ came to North
>   (name)
> America in the ship __?__.
>   (name)

Which of these answers could be correct? a, c
a. Christopher Columbus, Santa Maria
b. Santa Maria, Christopher Columbus
c. Henry Hudson, Half Moon
d. Half Moon, Henry Hudson

■ LESSON

The solutions of equations containing two variables, x and y, are ordered pairs of numbers. We can determine whether an ordered pair is a solution by substituting the first component for x and the second component for y. If the resulting equation is true, then the ordered pair is a solution. If the resulting equation is false, then the ordered pair is not a solution.

   Given the equation $x + 2y = 5$:

The ordered pair $(1, 2)$ is a solution since $1 + 2 \cdot 2 = 5$ is true.
The ordered pair $(2, 1)$ is not a solution since $2 + 2 \cdot 1 = 5$ is false.
The ordered pair $(5, 0)$ is a solution since $5 + 2 \cdot 0 = 5$ is true.
The ordered pair $(7, -1)$ is a solution since $7 + 2 \cdot (-1) = 5$ is true.

   To find solutions of equations in two variables, pick a number and substitute it for one of the variables. Then solve the equation for the other variable.

Example 1   Make a table of some solutions of this equation.

$$3x - 2y = 6$$

Solution   **1.** Pick a value, say 4, and substitute for x.

$$
\begin{aligned}
3(4) - 2y &= 6 \\
12 - 2y &= 6 \\
-2y &= -6 \\
y &= 3
\end{aligned}
$$

Now solve for y.

This gives one solution of the original equation:

x	y
4	3

Experienced teachers state that students are more likely to volunteer when they know that their responses and questions can truly affect the direction in which the lesson will flow. Therefore, if student participation is one of your goals, be flexible enough in your lesson plan to entertain questions at any time. Let the questions and answers direct the flow of the lesson, so long as the general direction of that flow is toward accomplishing the objectives of the day.

At first some students may have trouble making tables of solutions of equations in two variables. Be sure that students understand that they are to *select* a value for one of the variables and then compute the corresponding value(s) for the other variable. Students may simplify their computations by selecting numbers to avoid fractions. However, negative numbers should be included, and fractions should not be avoided completely.

Example 1 (continued)

2. Pick another value for x, say -2, and substitute.

$$3(-2) - 2y = 6$$

Solve for y.
$$-6 - 2y = 6$$
$$-2y = 12$$
$$y = -6$$

This gives a second solution.

x	y
4	3
-2	-6

3. Pick a value for y, say $\frac{1}{2}$, and substitute.

$$3x - 2\left(\frac{1}{2}\right) = 6$$

Solve for x.
$$3x - 1 = 6$$
$$3x = 7$$
$$x = \frac{7}{3}$$

Answer

x	y
4	3
-2	-6
$\frac{7}{3}$	$\frac{1}{2}$

ADDITIONAL EXAMPLES

Example 1.
Make a table of some solutions of this equation:

$$2x + 5y = 20$$

Answers may vary.

x	0	5	-2
y	4	2	4.8

Example 2.
Make a table of some solutions of this equation:

$$y = |x - 3|$$

Answers may vary.

x	5	0	-5
y	2	3	8

Example 3.
Make a table of solutions (p, q) for the equation $p + 2q = 8$ for the domain $\{-4, -2, 0, 2, 4\}$.

$$p + 2q = 8$$

p	-4	-2	0	2	4
q	6	5	4	3	2

Example 2 Make a table of some solutions of this equation.

$$y = |x|$$

Solution **1.** Pick 5 for x.
$$y = |5|$$
$$y = 5$$

One solution is (5, 5).

2. Pick -3 for x.
$$y = |-3|$$
$$y = 3$$

Another solution is $(-3, 3)$.

3. Pick 0 for y.
$$0 = |x|$$
$$0 = x$$

Another solution is (0, 0).

Answer

x	y
5	5
-3	3
0	0

CHECK UNDERSTANDING

Given the equation $2x + y = 9$.

- Is (1, 4) a solution? (No)
- Is (4, 1) a solution? (Yes)
- Find the second component so that $(-3, y)$ is a solution. (15)
- Find the first component so that $(x, -3)$ is a solution. (6)
- Find two other solutions.

CLASSROOM EXERCISES

In classroom exercise 4, it is assumed the domain of the variable is the set of real numbers. Only one number (namely, 4) is a solution.

In classroom exercise 5, infinitely many number pairs of real numbers are possible solutions.

ASSIGNMENT GUIDE

Basic   1–21 odd, Review Exercises, Self-Quiz 1

Average   1–29 odd, Review Exercises, Self-Quiz 1

Enriched 19–29 odd, 30–35 all, Review Exercises, Self-Quiz 1

PRACTICE WORKSHEET 24

5-3 SOLVING EQUATIONS IN TWO VARIABLES

■ Find the missing number for each solution. Complete each table.

1. $y = 3x - 4$

x	2	1	0	-1
y	2	-1	-4	-7

2. $y = 7x + 3$

x	-1	0	1	2
y	-4	3	10	17

3. $y = \frac{1}{2}x + 2$

x	-2	0	2	4
y	1	2	3	4

4. $y = -2x + 3$

x	2	0	3	3/2
y	-1	3	-3	0

5. $y = -\frac{1}{2}x - 3$

x	-4	0	-6	14
y	-1	-3	0	4

6. $y = -3x - 4$

x	0	1	-4/3	-2
y	-4	-7	0	2

7. $3x + 4y = 12$

x	4	0	8	-4
y	0	3	-3	6

8. $4x + 3y = 12$

x	3	0	3/2	2
y	0	4	2	4/3

9. $5x - 2y = 8$

x	2	4	0	2
y	1	6	-4	1

COMPUTER EXTENSION

1. Write a computer program that produces a table of values of x and y for the equation $3x + 4y = 12$. Use integral values of x from −5 to 5.

```
10 PRINT "3X + 4Y = 12"
20 PRINT "X", "Y"
30 FOR X = -5 TO 5
40 Y = (12 - 3 * X)/4
50 PRINT X, Y
60 NEXT X
70 END
```

EXTRA PRACTICE, page 627
COMPUTER WORKSHEET 7

If the variables are not x and y, then the problem will usually indicate which variable is associated with the first component of the ordered pairs, and which variable is associated with the second component. In the following example, (m, n) indicates that m is the variable for the first component and n is the variable for the second component. In word problems, you may have to make your own decision about the order of the variables.

Example 3   Make a table of solutions (m, n) of the equation $5m - 7n = 70$ for the domain $\{-14, -7, 0, 7, 14\}$.

Solution   Remember that the numbers in the domain are first-component values to be substituted for m.

m	−14	−7	0	7	14
n					

Answer   The table of solutions is:

m	−14	−7	0	7	14
n	−20	−15	−10	−5	0

■ CLASSROOM EXERCISES

State whether the ordered pairs are solutions of the equation.

1. $x + y = 7$
  a. (4, 3) Yes
  b. (3, 4) Yes
  c. (−2, 9) Yes

2. $x = |y|$
  a. (−3, 3) No
  b. (3, −3) Yes
  c. $\left(\frac{1}{2}, \frac{1}{2}\right)$ Yes

3. $y = x^2$
  a. (2, 4) Yes
  b. (3, 6) No
  c. (16, 4) No

4. How many numbers are solutions of the equation $2x + 3 = 11$? 1

5. How many ordered pairs are solutions of the equation $2x + 3y = 11$? Infinitely many

Find the missing number of each solution pair.

6. $2x - 2y = 12$

x	4	? (10)	−3	? (3)
y	? (−2)	4	? (−9)	−3

7. $q - p = -3$

p	7	? (10)	−2	? (1)
q	? (4)	7	? (−5)	−2

■ WRITTEN EXERCISES

State whether the ordered pairs are solutions of the equation.

Ⓐ **1.** $3x + y = 6$
  a. (0, 3) No
  b. (2, 0) Yes
  c. (4, −6) Yes

2. $x + 3y = 6$
  a. (0, 2) Yes
  b. (3, 0) No
  c. (9, −1) Yes

3. $x - y = 4$
  a. (4, 0) Yes
  b. (6, −2) No
  c. (8, 4) Yes

4. $x - y = 6$
  a. (10, 4) Yes
  b. (0, 6) No
  c. (6, 0) Yes

Write the set of solutions (x, y) of each equation for the domain $\{-2, 0, 2\}$.

5. $x = y$ $\{(-2, -2), (0, 0), (2, 2)\}$ **6.** $x = 2y$ $\{(-2, -1), (0, 0), (2, 1)\}$ **7.** $y = 2x$
$\{(-2, -4), (0, 0), (2, 4)\}$

Write the set of solutions (x, y) of each equation for the domain $\{-4, 0, 4\}$.

8. $x + y = 4$ $\{(-4, 8), (0, 4), (4, 0)\}$ **9.** $y = 4x$ $\{(-4, -16), (0, 0), (4, 16)\}$ **10.** $y = \dfrac{1}{4}x$
$\{(-4, -1), (0, 0), (4, 1)\}$

Find the missing number for each solution.

11. $x - 2y = 6$

x	y	
12	?	3
6	?	0
8	?	1
16	?	5

12. $x - 3y = 6$

x	y	
12	?	2
6	?	0
9	?	1
21	?	5

13. $2x - y = 8$

x	y	
6	?	4
4	?	0
5	?	2
9	?	10

14. $3a - b = 8$

a	b	
6	?	10
4	?	4
3	?	1
5	?	7

15. $2a + 3b = 12$

a	b	
0	?	4
6	?	0
1	?	$3\frac{1}{3}$
$4\frac{1}{2}$	?	1

16. $3a + 2b = 12$

a	b	
0	?	6
4	?	0
1	?	$4\frac{1}{2}$
$3\frac{1}{3}$	?	1

17. $2a - 3b = 12$

a	b	
0	?	-4
6	?	0
1	?	$-3\frac{1}{3}$
$7\frac{1}{2}$	?	1

18. $3a - 2b = 12$

a	b	
0	?	-6
4	?	0
1	?	$-4\frac{1}{2}$
$4\frac{2}{3}$	?	1

Copy and complete each table.

19. $5x + 2y = 10$

x	0	2	4	-2
y	?	?	?	?
	5	0	-5	10

20. $3x + 2y = 6$

x	0	1	3	-1
y	?	?	?	?
	3	$1\frac{1}{2}$	$-1\frac{1}{2}$	$4\frac{1}{2}$

21. $3y = x + 6$

x	0	3	-3	1
y	?	?	?	?
	2	3	1	$2\frac{1}{3}$

22. $3y = x + 9$

x	0	3	-3	1
y	?	?	?	?
	3	4	2	$3\frac{1}{3}$

23. $y = 3x^2$

x	0	-4	4	$\frac{1}{3}$
y	?	?	?	?
	0	48	48	$\frac{1}{3}$

24. $y = (3x)^2$

x	0	-4	4	$\frac{1}{3}$
y	?	?	?	?
	0	144	144	1

25. $\dfrac{x}{y} = 6$

x	12	6	-6	3
y	?	?	?	?
	2	1	-1	$\frac{1}{2}$

26. $\dfrac{1}{2}x - \dfrac{1}{3}y = 2$

x	4	6	-4	0
y	?	?	?	?
	0	3	-12	-6

2. Use input statements to write a computer program that produces a table of x and y for the equation $Ax + By = C$. The program should allow the operator to input any values for A, B, and C provided $B \neq 0$. The operator should be able to state the smallest and largest values of x for the table.

```
10  PRINT "AN EQUATION HAS
    THE FORM"
20  PRINT "AX + BY = C."
30  PRINT "WHAT IS THE
    VALUE OF A";
40  INPUT A
50  PRINT "WHAT IS THE
    VALUE OF B";
60  INPUT B
70  IF B <> 0 THEN 100
80  PRINT "B = 0 IS NOT
    ALLOWED."
90  GO TO 50
100 PRINT "WHAT IS THE
    VALUE OF C";
110 INPUT C
120 PRINT "WHAT IS THE
    LEAST VALUE OF X";
130 INPUT L
140 PRINT "WHAT IS THE
    GREATEST VALUE OF X";
150 INPUT G
160 PRINT A; "X + "; B;
    "Y = "; C
170 PRINT "X", "Y"
180 FOR X = L TO G
190 Y = (C - A * X)/B
200 PRINT X, Y
210 NEXT X
220 END
```

PROBLEM-SOLVING NOTE
Making a table

A table containing ordered pairs is more than just an organized place to store the pairs as they are generated. It can also list pairs of values in such a way that relationships between the values become apparent. For this to occur, it is important to list the values for

Problem-Solving Note *continued*

one variable (usually *x*) in increasing or decreasing order. For example, the first table is much more informative than the second.

x	y
2	4
1	1
0	-2
$-\frac{4}{3}$	-6

x	y
0	-2
1	1
$-\frac{4}{3}$	-6
2	4

You can observe a trend among *y*-values for the first table *because* the *x*-values are in order. You can surmise that the *y*-coordinate is zero for an *x*-value between 1 and 0.

Moreover, the pattern of values that develops as you fill in a table in this manner may influence the next *x*-value to be selected. Or it may cause you to detect an incorrect entry because it violates the trend of values.

ENRICHMENT PROBLEM

- Sometimes the form of an equation restricts certain values from being in the domain. What *x*-values are excluded by these equations?

  a. $\frac{1}{x} + \frac{1}{y} = 0$ *x cannot be 0.*

  b. $x^2 + y^2 = 0$ *x cannot be negative or positive.*

  c. $x = |y|$ *x cannot be negative.*

ADDITIONAL ANSWERS

■ Self-Quiz 1

1.

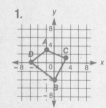

3a.

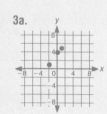

4a.

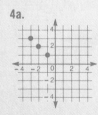

Equivalent equations have the same solutions. Find the solution set of each equation using the given domain. State whether the two equations are equivalent.

27. Domain: {0, 1, 2}   No
$y = x + 3$ {(0, 3), (1, 4), (2, 5)}
$x = y + 3$ {(0, −3), (1, −2), (2, −1)}

28. Domain: {−2, 0, 2}   No
$y = x^2$ {(−2, 4), (0, 0), (2, 4)}
$y = −x^2$ {(−2, −4), (0, 0), (2, −4)}

29. Domain: {−3, 0, 3}   Yes
$y = |x|$ {(−3, 3), (0, 0), (3, 3)}
$y = |−x|$ {(−3, 3), (0, 0), (3, 3)}

C **30.** Domain: {6, 0, −6}   Yes
$y = 3 − x$ {(6, −3), (0, 3), (−6, 9)}
$x = 3 − y$ {(6, −3), (0, 3), (−6, 9)}

31. Domain: {0, 3, 5}   Yes
$y = (2x)^2$ {(0, 0), (3, 36), (5, 100)}
$y = 4x^2$ {(0, 0), (3, 36), (5, 100)}

32. Domain: {−3, 0, 3}   Yes
$y = −|x^2|$ {(−3, −9), (0, 0),
$y = −x^2$ (3, −9)}
{(−3,−9),(0,0),(3,−9)}

Find three solutions of each equation. State whether you think the two equations are equivalent.

33. $y = \frac{1}{2}x + 6$

$y = \frac{x + 3}{2}$ No

34. $y = (x + 3)^2$
$y = x^2 + 9$ No

35. $y = (x − 2)(x + 2)$
$y = x^2 − 4$ Yes

■ REVIEW EXERCISES

Simplify.

1. $a − (−5)$ $a + 5$

2. $5x − (−8) + (−y)$ $5x + 8 − y$ [2–6]

3. $6a − 3 − 5a + 3b$ $a − 3 + 3b$

4. $3x − 4y − 4x − 3y$ $−x − 7y$ [2–7]

5. $4a + 4b − 3a − b$ $a + 3b$

6. $−(a − b) + 4(2a + b)$ $7a + 5b$ [2–8]

Self-Quiz 1

5–1 **1.** Graph these points: $A(−2, 3)$, $B(0, −4)$, $C(3, 1)$, $D(−6, 0)$.
Draw line segments from A to C, C to B, B to D, and D to A.

2. Identify the quadrant each point is in or the axis it is on.
  a. $P(−4, −2)$ III   **b.** $Q(0, −5)$ y-axis   **c.** $R(−9, 6)$ II

5–2 The following exercises describe a relation.

  a. Graph the relation.   **b.** List the domain.   **c.** List the range.

  3. {(1, 5), (−2, 1), (0, 4)}   Domain: {1, −2, 0}; range: {5, 1, 4}

  4. The first component is a negative integer greater than −4 and the second component is the absolute value of the first component.
  Domain: {−3, −2, −1}; range: {1, 2, 3}

5–3 Copy and complete the table of solutions.

  5. $2x − y = 1$ 1

x	−2	?	0.5	3
y	?	1	?	?
	−5		0	5

  6. $4a + 3b = 12$ $1\frac{1}{2}$; 3

a	0	?	?	−3
b	?	2	0	?
	4			8

210

210   Chapter 5   Graphing Linear Equations and Functions

You may wish to spend two days on this section. Refer to the Pacing Chart.

Class Starter Quiz
on previous section

1. Is (5, 10) a solution of $3x - 2y = 5$? No
2. Is (8, 2) a solution of $y - x = 6$? No
3. Find the missing number of each solution pair for the equation. $4x + y = 12$.

x	y	
4	?	−4
2	?	4
?	8	1

5–4 Graphing Equations

Preview

Two students went for a bike ride. This table shows how far they had traveled from home at the end of each 10-minute interval during the first hour.

Time from home, in minutes	0	10	20	30	40	50	60
Distance from home, in miles	0	2	4	6	6	8	10

Here is the same information plotted on a graph. From this information we know exactly where they were only at the start and the end of each 10-minute interval. However, we can use our imagination to fill in the spaces between the dots. If we assume that they traveled at a steady rate for the first half hour, rested for 10 minutes, and then traveled at a steady rate for the last 20 minutes, we can connect the dots and use this graph to represent their trip.

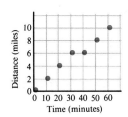

In this lesson you will learn to graph equations by plotting points and then connecting the points.

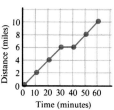

PURPOSE

To better understand the relationship between two variable-quantities, it is important to be able to graph the equations that describe the relationship.

PREVIEW

Use the Preview to teach students that we make certain assumptions when we join individual points of a graph.

If points of a graph are connected by line segments, the cyclists rode at a constant rate or were stopped. It is assumed that the cyclists rode in a straight line away from home. You may discuss other interpretations of the graphs. The most obvious interpretation of the horizontal segment of the graph is that the bicycles were stopped. However, it could be that the cyclists changed direction, taking a circular path.

(The distance from home remains constant.)

Home

If two points of the graph (within a 10-minute interval) are joined by this curve,

the cyclists rode at a faster rate during the first minutes and at a slower rate toward the end of the time interval.

■ LESSON

The equations in one variable that we have solved usually have had just one solution. For example,

the equation $2x + 3 = 8$ has only one solution, $\frac{5}{2}$.

However, equations in two variables usually have infinitely many solutions. For example,

the equation $2x + y = 8$ has infinitely many solutions

including $(-3, 14)$, $(-2, 12)$, $(0, 8)$, $\left(\frac{1}{2}, 7\right)$, $(10, -12)$, and $(4, 0)$.

Since the solutions of the equations in two variables are ordered pairs, they can be graphed in the coordinate plane. The graph can show the patterns of the solution set and make the equations easier to understand. The graph of the set of all solutions of an equation is called the **graph of the equation.**

If two points of the graph (within a 10-minute interval) are joined by this broken segment,

the cyclist rode toward home for a while before changing direction and riding away from home. These other interpretations illustrate that certain *assumptions* are made whenever two points are connected. We usually make the most simple assumption and join the points with a line segment or smooth curve.

LESSON

The concept of infinity is difficult to understand. One misconception common to beginning students is that if an equation has infinitely many ordered-pair solutions, every ordered pair is a solution. This is not true. For example, $2x + 3y = 6$ has infinitely many solutions, but (1, 2) is not a solution. On the other hand, $2x + 3y = 3y + 2x$ has infinitely many solutions and, in fact, every number pair is a solution. (The equation is an identity.)

In this lesson the graphs may be lines, broken lines, or curves.

If students see only straight-line graphs at first, they overgeneralize and assume the graphs of all equations are straight lines. Some students often develop the habit of finding two points of a graph and joining those points by a straight line. In order to "head off" the formation of this habit, this lesson includes graphs that are not straight lines. Not knowing the nature of the graph ahead of time, students are required to plot several points before the pattern develops.

Example 1   Graph this equation. $x + y = 4$

Solution

Here is a table of some solutions and a graph of those solutions.

x	y
1	3
3	1
-2	6
6	-2
0	4
4	0

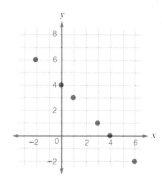

The graph of the six number pairs shows six points. Since the equation has infinitely many solutions, its graph has infinitely many points. We make an educated guess about the complete graph. The graph looks like a straight line. We test that guess by finding more solutions and checking whether their graphs are on the same straight line.

x	y
2	2
$3\frac{1}{2}$	$\frac{1}{2}$
-3	7

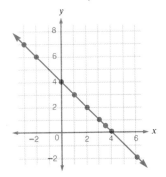

The graphs of these three points are on the line, so the guess seems correct.

Example 2   Graph. $y = |x|$

Solution

Here are some solutions and their graph.

x	1	0	3	4	5
y	1	0	3	4	5

It looks as if the graph of all the solutions may again be a straight line. This guess can be tested by finding more solutions. It is always wise to try some negative numbers. Since none have been used yet, they should be used to test the guess.

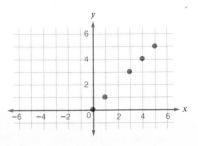

CLASSROOM STRATEGY *Effective questioning*

Avoid asking the whole class to give an oral response. When the whole class responds, it is difficult to determine which students are giving the response because they know the answer and which students are giving the response they hear others give.

ADDITIONAL EXAMPLES

Example 1. Graph this equation.
$$y - x = 3$$
Although y is written first in the equation, it is the second component in the number pairs.

x	-3	-2	0	½	2
y	0	1	3	3½	5

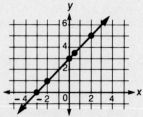

Example 2. Graph. $y = |x - 3|$

x	-3	-1	0	3	3½	5
y	6	4	3	0	½	2

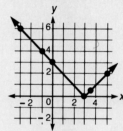

Example 3. Graph. $y = -\dfrac{x^2}{4}$

X	-4	-2	0	½	2	4
y	-4	-1	0	$-\frac{1}{16}$	-1	-4

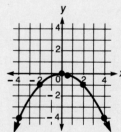

Example 2 (continued)

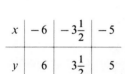

x	-1	-3	$-\frac{1}{2}$
y	1	3	$\frac{1}{2}$

The guess that the graph was a straight line was not correct. Now it seems that the graph is shaped like a "v" with the tip of the v at (0, 0). This guess should be tested.

x	-6	$-3\frac{1}{2}$	-5
y	6	$3\frac{1}{2}$	5

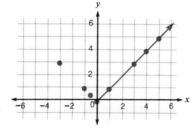

The solutions support the second guess. The graph is two rays that have (0, 0) as a common endpoint.

Example 3 Graph. $y = \dfrac{x^2}{4}$

Solution

Here are some solutions and their graph.

x	0	2	4
y	0	1	4

These three points are certainly not on a straight line, and it is a little difficult to visualize the whole graph.

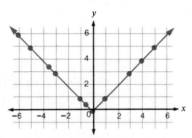

Here are five more solutions and their graph.

x	-2	-4	1	-1	6
y	1	4	$\frac{1}{4}$	$\frac{1}{4}$	9

These extra points make the graph clearer, and a guess about the whole graph can be made. The graph appears to be a curve with the origin at its bottom.

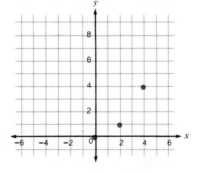

In graphing an equation, these solutions were found and plotted.

x	3	7	10
y	1	9	15

- What should be done next?
  (Select more values of x, including negative numbers and fractions, compute the corresponding values of y, and graph.)

CLASSROOM EXERCISES

In classroom exercise 6, include values for x between -1 and 1. Note that $x \neq 0$. For example, include (½, 2), (⅕, 5), $(-\frac{1}{3}, -3)$, $(-\frac{1}{8}, -8)$.

Additional Answers for the Classroom Exercises are on page 649.

ASSIGNMENT GUIDE

Basic   1–13 odd, Review Exercises
Average   15–28 all, Review Exercises
Enriched 15–23 odd, 25–30 all, Review Exercises

PRACTICE WORKSHEET 24

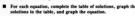
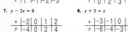

WRITTEN EXERCISES

In exercises 23–30, the horizontal axis must be associated with the *first* components of the number pairs.

Additional Answers for the Written Exercises are on pages 650 and 651.

EXTRA PRACTICE, page 628

Example 3 (continued)

Check the guess with these three solutions.

x	$-\frac{1}{2}$	-6	3
y	$\frac{1}{16}$	9	$\frac{9}{4}$

The new solutions support the guess. The graph is a curve known as a *parabola*.

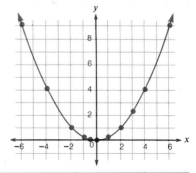

> **Summary:** Follow these steps to graph an equation in two variables.
>
> 1. Find at least three solutions of the equation.
>
> 2. Graph these solutions.
>
> 3. Guess the pattern for the graph of all the solutions.
>
> 4. Sketch a graph of all solutions.
>
> 5. Check by finding and plotting at least two additional solutions.
>
> In Steps 1 and 5 be sure to use fractions, zero, and negative numbers.

■ CLASSROOM EXERCISES

Graph these equations.

1. $y = 3x$
2. $y = 3x + 1$
3. $x + 2y = 5$
4. $y = x$
5. $y = x^2$
6. $y = \frac{1}{x}$

■ WRITTEN EXERCISES

For each equation, copy and complete the table of solutions, graph the solutions in the table, and graph the equation.

A **1.** $y = 2x + 3$

x	-2	0	2
y	?	?	?
	-1	3	7

2. $y = 2x + 5$

x	-3	0	1
y	?	?	?
	-1	5	7

3. $y = \frac{1}{4}x + 3$

x	-8	0	8
y	?	?	?
	1	3	5

4. $y = \frac{1}{3}x + 5$

x	-6	0	3
y	?	?	?
	3	5	6

5. $2x + 3y = 6$

x	0	3	6
y	?	?	?
	2	0	-2

6. $3x + 2y = 12$

x	0	2	4
y	?	?	?
	6	3	0

Graph each equation.

7. $y = 3x - 3$ **8.** $y = 3x - 5$ **9.** $y = \frac{1}{2}x^2$ **10.** $y = 2x^2$

11. $y = -2x^2$ **12.** $y = -\frac{1}{2}x^2$ **13.** $xy = 6$ **14.** $xy = 12$

$y = -x + 6$ $y = -x + 12$

15. $3y - 2x = -6$ **16.** $4y - 2x = -8$ **17.** $y = \frac{1}{2}x^3$ **18.** $y = \frac{1}{2}x^4$

$y = \frac{2}{3}x - 2$ $y = \frac{1}{2}x - 2$

19. $y = (x + 1)^2$ **20.** $y = 2(x - 1)$ **21.** $y = x^2 + 1$ **22.** $y = 2x - 1$

Graph the formula or equation that describes each situation.

23. Tom charges $1 plus $1.50 per hour when he babysits for a child. He uses the formula $C = 1 + 1.5h$ to find the total charge C, where h represents the number of hours he babysits. Graph the pairs (h, C).

24. Tom charges $2 plus $3.00 per hour when he babysits for three children at once. He uses the formula $C = 2 + 3h$ to find the total charge C, where h represents the number of hours he babysits. Graph the pairs (h, C).

25. The formula $A = 6e^2$ shows the relationship between the length of an edge of a cube (e cm) and the area of the surface of the cube (A cm^2). Graph the pairs (e, A).

26. The formula $V = e^3$ shows the relationship between the length of an edge of a cube (e cm) and the volume of the cube (V cm^3). Graph the pairs (e, V).

27. The formula $2l + 2w = 12$ shows the relationship between the length (l cm) and the width (w cm) of a rectangle that has a perimeter of 12 cm. Graph the pairs (l, w).

28. The formula $lw = 12$ shows the relationship between the length (l cm) and the width (w cm) of a rectangle that has an area of 12 cm^2. Graph the pairs (l, w).

29. Barbara and Ed were 10 miles from home and started walking home at the rate of 3 miles per hour. The formula $d = -3t + 10$ gives their distance d from home at any time t. Draw a graph with t as the first component. Start at $t = 0$ and end the graph when they reach home.

30. Peggy and Sally were 2 miles from home when they began hiking toward a nature preserve at 4 miles per hour. The nature preserve is 12 miles from home. The formula $d = 4t + 2$ indicates their distance d from home at any time t. Draw the graph with t as the first component. Start at $t = 0$ and end the graph when they reach the nature preserve.

■ REVIEW EXERCISES

Solve.

1. $4x + 3.75 = x - 6$ (-3.25)

2. $7x + 4\frac{1}{4} = 6x - 3\frac{1}{2}$ $\left\{-7\frac{3}{4}\right\}$ [3-3]

3. $\frac{2}{3}x = -18$ (-27)

4. $0.06x = 7.20$ (120) [3-4]

Making a table
The orientation of a table sometimes affects the ability of students to perceive relationships among table values. For example, to detect and use the pattern from this vertical set of values,

x	y	
1	1	> 2
2	3	> 3
3	6	> 4
4	10	> 5
5	15	

you might more readily discern that successive differences in y-values are increasing by 1 each time. However, expressing the same values in a horizontal table

x	1	2	3	4	5
y	1	3	6	10	15

helps some people to detect that any y-value is half the product of the x-value and the next larger x-value. Generally, it is good practice to give students some experience with both horizontal and vertical tables.

ENRICHMENT PROBLEM
Analyzing a table

• You can think of an equation as stating the relationship between first and second components of ordered pairs. Find the equations that describe the relationship for these ordered pairs.

a.

x	3	1	0	$-\frac{1}{2}$	-2	-4
y	-3	-1	0	$\frac{1}{2}$	2	4

$y = -x$

b.

m	4	1	0	$-\frac{2}{3}$	-3	-5
n	3	0	-1	$-1\frac{2}{3}$	-4	-6

$n = m - 1$

c.

R	Q
5	25
2	4
$\frac{1}{2}$	$\frac{1}{4}$
0	0
-1	1
-3	9

$Q = R^2$

215

$y = 2x - 1$

x	y
2	?
1	?
-1	?

x	y
2	3
1	1
-1	-3

2. Graph. $y = 2x - 1$
(Use the table above.)

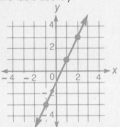

3. Graph. $x - 2y = -2$
(First, make a table of solutions.)

PURPOSE

To describe how one line compares to another, identifying characteristics need to be developed. The slope of a line is one of its principal characteristics.

PREVIEW

It is not necessary to use *numbers* to describe the slopes pictures in the Preview, but students should agree that the slopes on the right are steeper than on the left. Later, when numbers are used to describe the slopes, steeper slopes will be associated with numbers having greater absolute values.

Other examples of slope might include the "grade" of a mountain road or the incline of a treadmill used in a stress test.

OBJECTIVE 5–5

To find the slope of a line given the graph of the line or given the coordinates of two points on the line.

You may wish to spend two days on this section. Refer to the Pacing Chart.

5–5 Slopes of Lines

Preview

Whether a climber climbs a gentle slope or a steep slope, the motion has two components, a vertical component and a horizontal component. The climber moves both up and forward at the same time.

Explain in terms of the upward and forward movement how a steep slope differs from a gentle slope.

Explain in terms of a downward component and a forward component how these two ski slopes differ.

■ LESSON

In moving from one point to another on a line, there is a vertical component and a horizontal component to the motion. For example, in going from point A to point B, the vertical change is $5 - 1$, or 4, while the horizontal change is $4 - 2$, or 2. The ratio of the vertical change to the horizontal change is called the **slope** of the line.

$$\text{slope of } \overleftrightarrow{AB} \text{ (line } AB) = \frac{5 - 1}{4 - 2} = 2$$

The slope indicates that in moving from point to point on the line (in either direction), the vertical change is 2 times as great as the horizontal change.

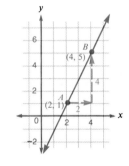

Definition: Slope of a Line

The slope of a line is the ratio of the change in y to the corresponding change in x between two points on the line.

$$\text{slope of } \overleftrightarrow{MN} = \frac{y_2 - y_1}{x_2 - x_1}$$

or

$$\text{slope of } \overleftrightarrow{MN} = \frac{y_1 - y_2}{x_1 - x_2}$$

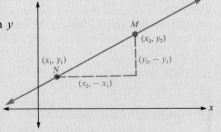

Use the full chalkboard. Do not erase too quickly. If the chalkboard space is ample, write on two or three panels before erasing.

Treat this lesson very carefully so that students develop both an intuitive "feel" relating slopes to lines and the ability to compute slopes.

In picturing the slope, the vertical change may be drawn first and the horizontal change next.

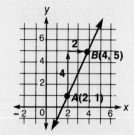

The slope of a line is the difference in two *y*-values divided by the difference in the two *corresponding x*-values.

[**Remember:** In y_1 and y_2 the numbers 1 and 2 are *subscripts* that show that y_1 and y_2 are different components. Be sure not to confuse subscripts with exponents.]

$$\frac{y_2 - y_1}{x_2 - x_1}$$

This represents one ordered pair. ⟶ ⟵ This represents another ordered pair.

Lines that *rise* as you move from left to right along the *x*-axis have positive slopes.

But customarily, the horizontal change is drawn first and the vertical change next.

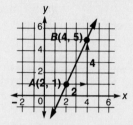

Example 1 Find the slope of $\overleftrightarrow{CD}$.

Solution Substitute the coordinates of points C and D in the formula.

$$\text{slope} = \frac{y_2 - y_1}{x_2 - x_1}$$

$$= \frac{-1 - 2}{2 - 5} = \frac{-3}{-3} = 1$$

or

$$\text{slope} = \frac{2 - (-1)}{5 - 2} = \frac{3}{3} = 1$$

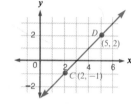

Regardless of the order of the changes, slope is defined as the ratio of the vertical change (numerator) to the horizontal change (denominator).

In using two points to calculate the slope, either point may be considered as the "first" point. For example, either of these calculations can be used to find the slope of the line containing (3, 6) and (5, 1).

$$\text{slope} = \frac{6 - 1}{3 - 5} = \frac{5}{-2} = -\frac{5}{2}$$

$$\text{slope} = \frac{1 - 6}{5 - 3} = \frac{-5}{2} = -\frac{5}{2}$$

Horizontal lines, lines parallel to the *x*-axis, have 0 slope.

Example 2 Find the slope of $\overleftrightarrow{GH}$.

Solution $\text{slope} = \dfrac{1 - 1}{3 - (-2)} = 0$

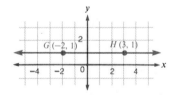

However, emphasize this point to students: The *x*-coordinate and *y*-coordinate from the *same pair* must be substituted for (x_1, y_1).

Vertical lines, lines parallel to the *y*-axis, have no slope.

Example 3 Find the slope of $\overleftrightarrow{MN}$.

Solution $\text{slope} = \dfrac{2 - (-3)}{2 - 2} = \dfrac{5}{0} \leftarrow$ not defined

Since division by 0 is not defined, $\overleftrightarrow{MN}$ has no slope.

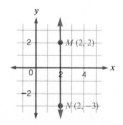

ADDITIONAL EXAMPLES

Find the slope of these lines.

Example 1. $\overrightarrow{AB}$ ½

Example 2. $\overrightarrow{CD}$ 0

Example 3. $\overrightarrow{EF}$ −2

Example 4. $\overrightarrow{GH}$ undefined

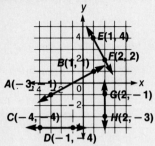

Example 5. Draw a line through point $K(2, 1)$ with slope $= -\frac{1}{2}$.

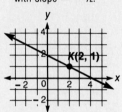

CHECK UNDERSTANDING

Graph I

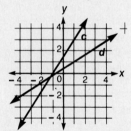

Graph II

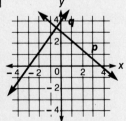

218

Lines that descend as you move from left to right along the x-axis have negative slopes.

Example 4   Find the slope of $\overrightarrow{AB}$.

Solution   slope $= \dfrac{-1-1}{2-1} = \dfrac{-2}{1} = -2$

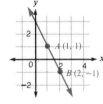

Example 5   Draw a line through point $A(1, -2)$ with slope 3.

Solution   Since the slope of the line is 3, the change in y is 3 times the change in x between any two points on the line.

1. Start at point A.

2. Go up 3 units.

3. Move 1 unit to the right to get a second point, B.

4. Draw a line through the two points.

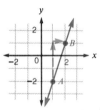

■ CLASSROOM EXERCISES

1. Explain the difference between "no slope" and "0 slope."
   Vertical lines have no slope, horizontal lines have 0 slope.

2. In moving from left to right on a line, state whether the line rises, falls, or is horizontal in these situations.
   a. Negative slope   Falls   **b.** 0 slope   Horizontal   **c.** Positive slope   Rises

Use the labeled points to find the slopes of these lines.

3.

2

4.
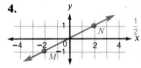
$\frac{1}{2}$

5.
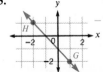
−1

6.
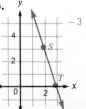
−3

7. Draw a line through point $(1, -8)$ with slope $\frac{1}{2}$.

8. Draw a line through point $(-1, 2)$ with slope -1.

EXTRA PRACTICE, page 628

- For the same change in *x*, which line in Graph I has the greater change in *y*? (Line *c*)
- Which line in Graph I has the greater slope? (Line *c*)
- Which line in Graph II has negative slope? (Line *p*)

■ WRITTEN EXERCISES

In moving from one point on a line to another, follow the given directions. State whether the slope is positive, negative, or zero.

A 1. Go up 5 and go right 3. Positive
  2. Go up 3 and go right 5. Positive
  3. Go down 5 and go right 3. Negative
  4. Go down 3 and go right 5. Negative
  5. Go up 5 and go left 3. Negative
  6. Go up 3 and go left 5. Negative

Find the slopes of these lines.

  7. $\overleftrightarrow{AB}$ $\frac{1}{3}$
  8. $\overleftrightarrow{CD}$ 2
  9. $\overleftrightarrow{EF}$ 3
  10. $\overleftrightarrow{GH}$ 1
  11. *x*-axis 0

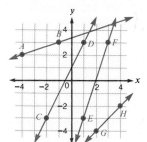

Find the slopes of these lines.

  12. $\overleftrightarrow{PQ}$ $-\frac{1}{2}$
  13. $\overleftrightarrow{RS}$ -2
  14. $\overleftrightarrow{TU}$ $-\frac{1}{4}$
  15. $\overleftrightarrow{VW}$ -3
  16. *y*-axis None

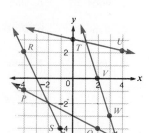

  17. Find the slope of each side of square *JKLM*.
    a. $\overline{JK}$ 5
    b. $\overline{KL}$ $-\frac{1}{5}$
    c. $\overline{LM}$ 5
    d. $\overline{MJ}$ $-\frac{1}{5}$

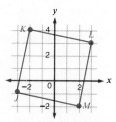

  18. Find the slope of each side of rectangle *ABCD*.
    a. $\overline{AB}$ 3
    b. $\overline{BC}$ $-\frac{1}{3}$
    c. $\overline{CD}$ 3
    d. $\overline{DA}$ $-\frac{1}{3}$

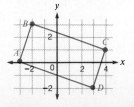

CLASSROOM EXERCISES

In classroom exercise 1, slopes of horizontal lines (0 slope) and vertical lines (no slope or undefined slope) may be considered special cases that deserve special attention.

ADDITIONAL ANSWERS
■ Classroom Exercises

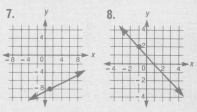

7.

8.

ASSIGNMENT GUIDE

Basic   1–23 odd, Review Exercises, Self-Quiz 2
Average   17–35 odd, Review Exercises, Self-Quiz 2
Enriched   17, 18, 25, 26, 31–38 all, Review Exercises, Self-Quiz 2

5-5 SLOPES OF LINES

■ Write the slope of each line.

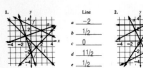

Line
a ___-2___
b ___1/2___
c ___0___
d ___11/2___
e ___1/2___

Line
f ___-1/2___
g ___1/3___
h ___1___
i ___-1___
j ___-3___

■ Draw and label.

3. Line *k* through point (2, 0) with slope $\frac{1}{2}$.

4. Line *l* through point (−1, 0) with slope −1.

5. Line *m* through point (0, 2) with slope 1.

6. Line *n* through point (2, 3) with slope 0.

7. Line *p* through point (0, 0) with slope 4.

8. Line *q* through point (−4, −2) with slope $\frac{2}{3}$.

9. Line *r* through point (−4, 4) with slope −$\frac{1}{2}$.

10. Line *s* through point (2, 3) with no slope.

WRITTEN EXERCISES

Discuss exercises 36–38. Point out that (1) if lines are parallel, their slopes are equal; (2) if lines are perpendicular, the product of their slopes is −1; and (3) if distance is plotted against time, the slope of the line represents the rate.

In exercise 38, point out that the scales on the axes are different. The slope is calculated using the definition. With these scales, a slope of 8 appears to be a slope of 1 (using equal scales on the axes).

ADDITIONAL ANSWERS

■ **Written Exercises**

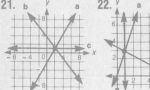

21. 22.

---

19. Find the slope of each side of right triangle *EFG*.
   a. $\overline{EF}$ $-\frac{2}{3}$
   b. $\overline{FG}$ 0
   c. $\overline{GE}$ None

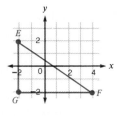

20. Find the slope of each side of right triangle *HIJ*.
   a. $\overline{HI}$ 0
   b. $\overline{IJ}$ None
   c. $\overline{JH}$ −1

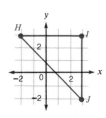

Graph the point, and then draw lines with the stated slopes through the point. Label the lines *a*, *b*, and *c*.

21. Point (2, 1)   a. slope 2   b. slope −1   c. slope 0

22. Point (1, 3)   a. slope 3   b. slope −$\frac{1}{2}$ c. no slope

23. Point (−4, 0)   a. slope −$\frac{1}{2}$ b. slope $\frac{1}{4}$ c. no slope

24. Point (0, −3)   a. slope −3   b. slope $\frac{1}{2}$ c. slope 0

▣ 25. Point (0, 2)   a. slope $\frac{2}{5}$ b. slope −$\frac{5}{2}$ c. slope $2\frac{1}{2}$

26. Point (4, 0)   a. slope $\frac{2}{7}$ b. slope −$\frac{2}{7}$ c. slope $3\frac{1}{2}$

Find the slope of the line that goes through the two points.

27. *A*(0, 0) $\frac{2}{3}$ 28. *C*(0, 0) 4   29. *E*(1, 2) 3   30. *G*(2, 1) 9
   B(3, 2)   *D*(2, 8)   *F*(2, 5)   *H*(3, 10)

31. *K*(−2, 2) $\frac{1}{2}$ 32. *P*(3, −2) −$\frac{5}{4}$ 33. *R*(5, 7) None   34. *T*(−5, 7) None
   L(−4, 1)   *Q*(−1, 3)   *S*(5, −7)   *U*(−5, −7)

35. Draw a line with slope 2 that passes through the given point.
   a. (−1, 2)   b. (1, 2)   c. (3, 2)

▣ 36. a. What is the relationship between the slopes of the opposite sides of square *JKLM* in Exercise 17? Equal
   b. What is the relationship between the slopes of the *opposite* sides of rectangle *ABCD* in Exercise 18? Equal
   c. What is the relationship between the slopes of *parallel* lines? Equal

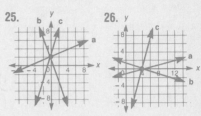

37. **a.** For each pair of *adjacent* sides of square *JKLM* in Exercise 17, find the product of their slopes (that is, find the product of the slopes of $\overline{JK}$ and $\overline{KL}$, etc.). $-1, -1, -1, -1$

b. For each pair of adjacent sides of rectangle *ABCD* in Exercise 18, find the product of their slopes. $-1, -1, -1, -1$

c. What is the relationship between the slopes of *perpendicular* lines that are neither vertical nor horizontal? Product is -1.

38. On a set of axes like this, draw graphs for the following:

a. A person crawling at 1 mph
b. A person walking at 4 mph
c. A person running at 8 mph
d. Describe the relationship between the slopes of the lines and the rates.
The greater the rate, the greater the slope.

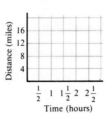

■ REVIEW EXERCISES

Solve.

1. $8 - 3x = 20$ $\{-4\}$

2. $6 + \dfrac{x}{2} = 10$ $\{8\}$

3. $\dfrac{a}{3} + 4 = 8$ $\{12\}$ [3–6]

4. $12 - 3(2 - x) = x$ $\{-3\}$

5. $6x - (5 - x) = 5(x + 3)$ $\{10\}$ **6.** $\dfrac{1}{2}(x - 8) = 20$ $\{48\}$ [3–7]

Self-Quiz 2

5–4 Copy and complete the table of solutions. Then graph the equation.

1. $x + 2y = 6$

x	-1	0	2
y	? $3\frac{1}{2}$	? 3	? 2

2. $y = x^3$

x	-2	-1	0	1	2
y	? -8	? -1	? 0	? 1	? 8

3. A babysitter charges \$3 plus \$2 per hour. The formula $C = 3 + 2h$ is used to find the total charge C, where h represents the number of hours spent babysitting. Graph the equation.

5–5 Determine the slopes of the lines.

4. $\overleftrightarrow{AB}$ $-\dfrac{1}{2}$

5. $\overleftrightarrow{CD}$ $\dfrac{3}{5}$

6. Draw lines through the point $(3, 2)$ with the stated slopes. Label the lines a, b, and c.

a. $m = \dfrac{1}{3}$

b. $m = -2$

c. $m = 0$

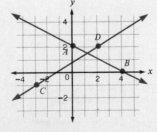

23.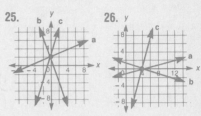

24.

25.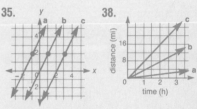

26.

35.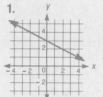

38.

ADDITIONAL ANSWERS

■ Self-Quiz 2

1.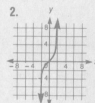

2.

3.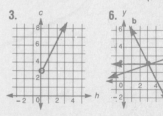

6.

COMPUTER EXTENSION

Write a program that gives the slope of a line passing through two points.

```
10 PRINT "FOR THE FIRST
   POINT, ENTER"
20 PRINT "THE FIRST
   COORDINATE, A COMMA"
30 PRINT "AND THE SECOND
   COORDINATE."
40 INPUT X1, Y1
50 PRINT "FOR THE SECOND
   POINT, ENTER"
60 PRINT "THE FIRST
   COORDINATE, A COMMA"
70 PRINT "AND THE SECOND
   COORDINATE."
80 INPUT X2, Y2
90 IF X1 <> X2 THEN 120
100 PRINT "THE LINE HAS NO
    SLOPE"
110 GO TO 140
120 M = (Y2 - Y1)/(X2 - X1)
130 PRINT "THE SLOPE OF THE
    LINE IS "; M
140 END
```

ENRICHMENT PROBLEM

- Let $P_0(0, 0)$, $P_1(1, 1)$, $P_2(2, 2)$, $P_3(3, 3)$ be points on the line $y = x$. Let $Q_0(0, 0)$, $Q_1(1, 1)$, $Q_2(2, 4)$, $Q_3(3, 9)$ be points on the graph of $y = x^2$.

  a. Find the slopes m_1, m_2, and m_3 for the segments $\overline{P_0P_1}$, $\overline{P_1P_2}$, and $\overline{P_2P_3}$.

  $m_1 = 1, m_2 = 1, m_3 = 1$

  b. Find the slopes s_1, s_2, s_3 for the segments $\overline{Q_0Q_1}$, $\overline{Q_1Q_2}$, and $\overline{Q_2Q_3}$.

  $s_1 = 1, s_2 = 3, s_3 = 5$

  c. What happens to the slope ratio for these two equations as different points are used?

  For the equation $y = x$, the slope stays constant.

  For the equation $y = x^2$, the slope changes.

  d. Graph these two equations and explain why this happens.

  The graph of $y = x$ is a straight line with a constant slope. The graph of $y = x^2$ is a parabola and does not have a constant slope.

EXTENSION   Finding slopes on a calculator

The expression for slope

$$m = \frac{y_2 - y_1}{x_2 - x_1}$$

can be evaluated easily on a calculator that has memory keys.

- The keys labeled $\boxed{\text{STO}}$ or $\boxed{\text{M+}}$ or $\boxed{\text{MIN}}$ store a number in memory.
- The keys labeled $\boxed{\text{RCL}}$ or $\boxed{\text{MR}}$ or $\boxed{\text{RM}}$ recall a number from memory.

Example 1   Find the slope of the line passing through (2, 8) and (6, 20).

Solution   To evaluate the slope, first compute the difference of the x-values and store the result in memory.

ENTER: 6 − 2 $\boxed{\text{STO}}$

The difference 4 is stored in memory.

Next, compute the difference in the y-values (in the same order) and divide by the number recalled from memory.
The complete calculation is:

Key Sequence	Display
6 − 2 $\boxed{\text{STO}}$	4
20 − 8 =	12
÷ $\boxed{\text{RCL}}$ =	3

The slope of the line is 3.

Use a calculator to find the slope of the line passing through the two points.

1. (5, 1) and (9, 3)   0.5

2. (4, 0) and (6, −8)   −4

3. (1, 2) and (4, 17)   5

4. (−6, 2) and (−2, 4)   0.5

5. (14, −9) and (12, 6)   −7.5

6. (89, −11) and (84, −13)   0.4

7. (−21, 7) and (21, −7) $-0.\overline{3}$

8. (14.5, 3.5) and (2, 9)   −0.44

Strategy for Success   **Learning from mistakes**

Whenever you make a mistake, be sure to find out why you made it. Otherwise you may continue to make mistakes on other problems that use the same skill or concept.

OBJECTIVE 5–6

To determine the slope and y-intercept of a line given an equation or graph.

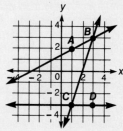

4. Draw a line through the point $(-2, 3)$ having slope $= -2$. Label the line "*a*."
5. Draw a line through the point $(-2, 3)$ having slope $= \frac{1}{3}$. Label the line "*b*."

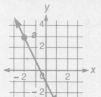

5–6 Slope-Intercept Form

Preview

Even though the axes below do not show a scale, can you match these lines with their slopes?

Line	Slope
a	− 1
b	− 4
c	3
d	$\frac{1}{4}$

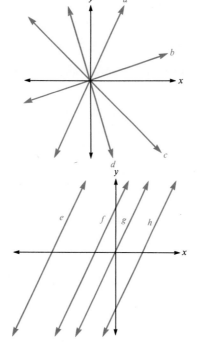

These lines all have the same slope. Can you describe how the lines differ from one another?

In this lesson you will learn to describe how lines *e*, *f*, *g*, and *h* differ.

PURPOSE

To identify the slope and *y*-intercept of a line, it is helpful to write the equation of the line in the form $y = mx + b$.

PREVIEW

Unless scales are given, it is not possible to determine slopes. It is possible, however, to determine whether one slope is greater than another. In describing lines *e*, *f*, *g*, and *h*, it is incorrect to say that line *e* is to the left of line *f*; some points of line *e* are to the right of line *f*. The choice of the *y*-intercept as a second condition to describe a line is a consequence of choosing $y = mx + b$ as the form used to write the equation of the line (when $x = 0$, $y = b$). Other forms could have been chosen instead. In the form $\frac{x}{a} + \frac{y}{b} = 1$, *a* is the *x*-intercept and *b* is the *y*-intercept.

■ LESSON

This figure shows the graph of the equation $y = 2x + 3$. The line crosses the *y*-axis at the point $(0, 3)$. The *y*-value of the point at which a graph crosses the *y*-axis is called the **y-intercept**. The *y*-intercept of this graph is 3. The slope of the line can be computed using the coordinates of points *A* and *B*:

$$\frac{7 - 3}{2 - 0} = 2$$

Note that for the equation $y = 2x + 3$, the value of the slope (2) is the coefficient of the *x*-term and that the value of the *y*-intercept (3) is the constant term in the equation. In general, when the equation of a line is written in the form $y = mx + b$, where *m* is the slope of the line and *b* is the *y*-intercept, the equation is said to be written in **slope–intercept form**.

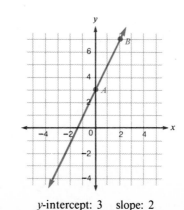

y-intercept: 3   slope: 2

Be sure that students understand the differences between *y-intercept* and the *point* where the line crosses the *y*-axis. By definition, the *y*-intercept is a *number*. When the point where a line crosses the *y*-axis is referred to, a number *pair* should be used. For example, if the *y*-intercept is 12, the point is (0, 12).

CONCEPT EXTENSION

It is important in this lesson to develop a broader notion of slope than the number resulting from substitution in the formula

$$m = \frac{y_2 - y_1}{x_2 - x_1}.$$

One means to do this is to illustrate the constant nature of the slope ratio for table values satisfying a linear equation.

For the equation $y = 3x + 4$,

	x	y	
	0	4	
x-changes	1	7	*y*-changes
of 1	2	10	of 3
	3	13	

ratio: $\dfrac{y\text{-changes}}{x\text{-changes}} = \dfrac{3}{1} = 3$

	x	y	
	−2	−2	
x-changes	0	4	*y*-changes
of 2	2	10	of 6
	4	16	

ratio: $\dfrac{6}{2} = 3$

Students will now be able to think of slope as a definition involving two points, as a constant ratio associated with table values of the equation of a straight line, and as a coefficient of an equation written in the form $y = mx + b$. Multiple representations of an idea or ways of applying an idea enhance the ability of students to apply that concept. Many of the problems of this and subsequent sections should periodically be solved in more than one way to provide a deeper understanding of the ideas involved and their relationships.

Definition: Slope–Intercept Form of a Linear Equation

The equation $y = mx + b$ is called the slope–intercept form of a linear equation. The graph of the equation is a straight line with slope m and *y*-intercept b.

If an equation is written in slope–intercept form, the form clearly displays the slope and *y*-intercept. If the equation is not already in slope–intercept form, it can be transformed into an equivalent equation in slope–intercept form in order to find the slope and *y*-intercept.

Example 1   Find the slope and *y*-intercept of the line with equation $2y + x = 6$.

   Solution   Transform $2y + x = 6$ to an equivalent equation in the form $y = mx + b$.

$$2y + x = 6$$
$$2y = -x + 6$$
$$y = -\frac{1}{2}x + 3$$

   Answer   The slope is $-\frac{1}{2}$ and the *y*-intercept is 3.

Example 2   Write the equation of the line with slope -3 and *y*-intercept 1.

   Solution   Substitute -3 for m and 1 for b in $y = mx + b$.

   Answer $y = -3x + 1$

This figure shows the graphs of three lines. The lines appear to be parallel. Note that their slopes are equal, but that their *y*-intercepts are different.

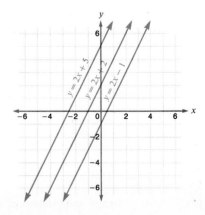

Routine tasks such as returning papers may effectively be done in the same manner each day, but other tasks, such as providing instruction, require variety from day to day.

Example 1.
Find the slope and y-intercept of the line with equation $y = 5x - 8$.
$$5; -8$$

Example 2.
Write the equation of the line with slope $-\frac{1}{3}$ and y-intercept 5.
$$y = -\tfrac{1}{3}x + 5$$

Example 3.
Show that $y = 3x + 2$ and $2y - 6x = 14$ are equations of parallel lines.
$$y = 3x + 2 \qquad 2y - 6x = 14$$
$$\text{slope: } 3 \qquad\quad 2y = 6x + 14$$
$$y = 3x + 7$$
$$\text{slope: } 3$$

The slopes are equal and their y-intercepts are unequal, so the lines are parallel.

Example 4.
Write the equation of the line parallel to the graph of $y - 4x + 2 = 0$ that has a y-intercept of 3.
$$y = 4x + 3$$

This figure shows the graphs of four vertical lines. These lines have undefined slopes.

The graphs on these two pages illustrate an important relationship between lines and their slopes:

Parallel lines have the same slope, or they are vertical lines and have undefined slopes.

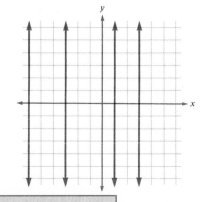

Property: Slopes of Parallel Lines

Two lines are parallel if and only if they have the same slope or they have no slope.

Example 3   Show that $y = 2x - 1$ and $4x = 2y - 1$ are equations of parallel lines.

Solution   The lines are parallel if they both have the same slope.

$$y = 2x - 1 \qquad\qquad 4x = 2y - 1$$
$$\text{slope: } 2 \qquad\qquad 4x + 1 = 2y$$
$$2x + \frac{1}{2} = y$$
$$y = 2x + \frac{1}{2}$$
$$\text{slope: } 2$$

Answer   Since their slopes are equal, the lines are parallel.

Example 4   Write the equation of the line that is parallel to the graph of $y - 5 + 3x = 0$ and that has a y-intercept of -5.

Solution   Transform the equation $y - 5 + 3x = 0$ to slope–intercept form.
$$y - 5 + 3x = 0$$
$$y = -3x + 5$$

The slope of the given line is -3.
The desired line has slope -3 and y-intercept -5.

Answer   The equation of the line is $y = -3x - 5$.

Example 5.
Show that $y = 2x - 3$ and $x + 2y = 4$ are equations of perpendicular lines.

$$y = 2x - 3 \qquad x + 2y = 4$$
$$\text{slope: } 2 \qquad 2y = -x + 4$$
$$y = -\frac{1}{2}x + 2$$
$$\text{slope: } -\frac{1}{2}$$

The product of the slopes is $2\left(-\frac{1}{2}\right) = -1$.
Therefore, the lines are perpendicular.

CHECK UNDERSTANDING

- Is each equation in slope-intercept form?
  a. $x = 2y + 3$ (No)
  b. $y = 2x + 3$ (Yes)
  c. $y = 0x - 2$ (Yes)
- State the slope and y-intercept of $y = -3x + 1$. (Slope: -3; y-intercept: 1)
- Line AB has slope 3. What is the slope of a line parallel to line AB? (3) Perpendicular to line AB? ($-\frac{1}{3}$)

Enrichment Worksheet 10   NAME _____

APPLICATION — GEOMETRY

1. A parallelogram is a four-sided figure with opposite sides parallel. Show that the figure below is a parallelogram.

If the slopes are equal, the sides are parallel.
Slope of $\overline{AB}$ = slope of $\overline{CD}$ = $-4/9$
Slope of $\overline{BC}$ = slope of $\overline{AD}$ = $5/4$
Therefore, $\overline{AB}$ is parallel to $\overline{CD}$ and $\overline{BC}$ is parallel to $\overline{AD}$.

2. A rectangle is a parallelogram with adjacent sides perpendicular. Show that the figure below is a rectangle.

Slope of $\overline{PQ}$ = slope of $\overline{RS}$ = $-1/2$
Slope of $\overline{PS}$ = slope of $\overline{QR}$ = 2
Therefore, the opposite sides are parallel.
Since $-1/2 \cdot 2 = -1$, the adjacent sides are perpendicular.

3. Show that the diagonals of this figure are perpendicular.

Slope of $\overline{XZ}$: 1
Slope of $\overline{WY}$: -1
Since $1 \cdot -1 = -1$, the diagonals are perpendicular.

Can be used after Section 5-6
© D.C. Heath & Co.

Consider the graphs of these two equations.

$$y = \frac{3}{4}x - 1 \quad \text{and} \quad y = -\frac{4}{3}x + 2$$

The lines appear to be perpendicular. The slopes of the given lines are $\frac{3}{4}$ and $-\frac{4}{3}$. The product of the slopes is -1. The graphs illustrate another important relationship between lines and their slopes: Two lines are perpendicular if the product of their slopes is -1.

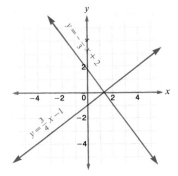

Horizontal lines, which have 0 slope, are perpendicular to vertical lines, which have undefined slopes.

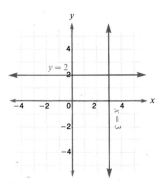

Property: Slopes of Perpendicular Lines

Two lines are perpendicular if and only if the product of their slopes is -1, or if one slope is zero and the other is undefined.

Example 5   Show that $y = 3x - 2$ and $3y + x = 4$ are equations of perpendicular lines.

Solution   Write both equations in slope–intercept form and find the slopes.

$$y = 3x - 2 \qquad 3y + x = 4$$
$$\text{slope: } 3 \qquad 3y = -x + 4$$
$$y = -\frac{1}{3}x + \frac{4}{3}$$
$$\text{slope: } -\frac{1}{3}$$

The product of the slopes is $3\left(-\frac{1}{3}\right) = -1$.

Answer   The lines are perpendicular since the product of their slopes is -1.

EXTRA PRACTICE, page 628
COMPUTER WORKSHEET 8

CLASSROOM EXERCISES

In classroom exercise 2 (or in any equation), the y-intercept can be found by replacing x with 0 and solving for y.

■ CLASSROOM EXERCISES

1. Write the equation $6 - 2y = 5x$ in slope–intercept form. $y = -\frac{5}{2}x + 3$

State the slope and y-intercept of the line with the given equation.

2. $y = -0.5x + 7$ Slope: -0.5, y-intercept: 7   **3.** $3y - 5x = 2$ Slope: $\frac{5}{3}$, y-intercept: $\frac{2}{3}$

4. Write an equation of the line with slope -5 and y-intercept 0. $y = -5x$

5. Are the graphs of the equations $y = -2x$ and $y = -2x + 1$ parallel? Yes

6. Are the graphs of the equations $y = 3x$ and $y = \frac{1}{3}x + 1$ perpendicular? No

7. Are the graphs of the equations $y = 3x$ and $y = -3x + 1$ perpendicular?
No

■ WRITTEN EXERCISES

State the slope and y-intercept of the line with the given equation.

A
1. $y = 5x + 3$ 5, 3   **2.** $y = -3x + 4$ $-3, 4$ **3.** $y = -\frac{1}{2}x - 6$ $-\frac{1}{2}, -6$

4. $y = \frac{1}{3}x - 5$ $\frac{1}{3}, -5$ **5.** $y = \frac{1}{2}x$ $\frac{1}{2}, 0$ **6.** $y = -8x$ $-8, 0$

State the slope and y-intercept of the line.

7. line a 2, 2   **8.** line e 0, 3

9. line b 1, 0   **10.** line f $-\frac{1}{2}, -1$

11. line c $\frac{1}{2}, -1$ **12.** line g $-1, 0$

13. line d 0, -2 **14.** line h $-2, 2$

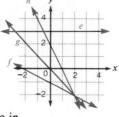

Use the given slope and y-intercept to write an equation of the line in slope–intercept form.

15. Slope 3; y-intercept 10 $y = 3x + 10$ **16.** Slope 2; y-intercept 7 $y = 2x + 7$

17. Slope -6; y-intercept 0.75 $y = -6x + 0.75$ **18.** Slope -5; y-intercept 2.25
$y = -5x + 2.25$

19. Slope 0; y-intercept -3 $y = 0x - 3$ **20.** Slope 0; y-intercept -10 $y = 0x - 10$

21. Slope $\frac{2}{3}$; y-intercept -2 $y = \frac{2}{3}x - 2$ **22.** Slope $\frac{3}{4}$; y-intercept -3 $y = \frac{3}{4}x - 3$

State whether the graphs of these pairs of equations are parallel, perpendicular, or neither.

23. $y = 2x + 3$
$y = -2x - 3$ neither

24. $y = 2x + 3$
$y = -2x + 3$ neither

25. $y = -2x + 3$
$y = 2x - 3$ neither

26. $y = \frac{1}{2}x + 5$

$y = -2x - 5$ perpendicular

27. $y = -\frac{1}{2}x + 5$

$y = -2x + 5$ neither

28. $y = 3x + 5$

$y = 3x - 5$ parallel

ASSIGNMENT GUIDE

Basic   1–39 odd, Review Exercises
Average   15–39 multiples of 3, 41–59 odd,
          Review Exercises
Enriched 35–59 odd, 61–66 all, Review
          Exercises

PRACTICE WORKSHEET 26

5-6 SLOPE–INTERCEPT FORM

■ Use the given slope and y-intercept to write an equation of the line in slope–intercept form.

1. Slope, 3; y–intercept, -2
$y = 3x - 2$

2. Slope, -2; y-intercept, 3
$y = -2x + 3$

3. Slope, $-\frac{1}{2}$; y-intercept, -4
$y = -1/2x - 4$

4. Slope, $\frac{2}{3}$; y-intercept, 10
$y = 2/5x + 10$

5. Slope, 0.53; y-intercept, 50
$y = 0.53x + 50$

6. Slope, -0.006; y-intercept, -10
$y = -0.006x - 10$

■ Write an equivalent equation in slope-intercept form.

7. $y = 10 - 3x$
$y = -3x + 10$

8. $y = \frac{4x + 5}{2}$
$y = 2x + 5/2$

9. $2x - 5y = 20$
$y = 2/5x - 4$

10. $4y - 3x = 36$
$y = 3/4x + 9$

11. $2x + y = -6$
$y = -2x - 6$

12. $2x - 3y - 6 = 0$
$y = 2/3x - 2$

13. $\frac{1}{2}y = 2x - 4$
$y = 4x - 8$

14. $-\frac{2}{3}y = 6x - 18$
$y = -9x + 27$

15. $7x - 5y = 11$
$y = 7/5x - 11/5$

16. $2(x - 3y) = 5$
$y = 1/3x - 5/6$

COMPUTER EXTENSION

1. Write a program that gives the equation in slope-intercept form of a line that has slope m and passes through point (x_1, y_1).

```
10 PRINT "GIVE THE SLOPE OF
   THE LINE"
20 INPUT M
30 PRINT "GIVE THE FIRST
   COORDINATE "
40 PRINT "OF THE POINT,
   FOLLOWED BY "
50 PRINT "A COMMA, FOLLOWED
   BY "
60 PRINT "THE SECOND
   COORDINATE."
70 INPUT X1, Y1
80 B = Y1 - M * X1
90 PRINT "THE EQUATION OF
   THE LINE IS"
100 PRINT "Y = "; M; "X + "; B
110 END
```

2. Write a program that gives the equation in slope-intercept form of a line that passes through points (x_1, y_1) and (x_2, y_2).

```
10 PRINT "GIVE THE FIRST
   COORDINATE OF THE "
20 PRINT "FIRST POINT,
   FOLLOWED BY A COMMA, "
30 PRINT "FOLLOWED BY THE
   SECOND COORDINATE "
40 PRINT "OF THE FIRST POINT."
50 INPUT X1, Y1
60 PRINT "GIVE THE FIRST
   COORDINATE OF THE "
70 PRINT "SECOND POINT,
   FOLLOWED BY A COMMA, "
80 PRINT "FOLLOWED BY THE
   SECOND COORDINATE "
90 PRINT "OF THE SECOND
   POINT."
100 INPUT X2, Y2
110 IF X1 <> X2 THEN 150
120 PRINT "THE LINE IS
   VERTICAL."
130 PRINT "ITS EQUATION IS: X
   = "; X1
140 GO TO 190
150 M = (Y2 - Y1)/(X2 - X1)
160 B = Y1 - M * X1
170 PRINT "THE EQUATION OF
   THE LINE IS "
180 PRINT "Y = "; M; "X + "; B
190 END
```

Write an equivalent equation in slope–intercept form. State the slope and y-intercept of the line.

29. $2x + 3y = 6$ $\quad -\frac{2}{3}, 2$ **30.** $3x + 2y = 6$ $\quad -\frac{3}{2}, 3$ **31.** $4y - 6x = 12$ $\quad \frac{3}{2}, 3$

32. $6y - 4x = 12$ $\quad \frac{2}{3}, 2$ **33.** $2y + 3 = 4x$ $\quad 2, -\frac{3}{2}$ **34.** $3y + 4 = 15x$ $\quad 5, -\frac{4}{3}$

State whether the graphs of these pairs of equations are parallel, perpendicular, or neither.

35. $2x + 3y = 6$
$-3x + 2y = 6$ $\quad$ perpendicular

36. $2x + 3y = 6$
$-2x + 3y = 6$ $\quad$ neither

37. $2x - 3y = 6$
$-2x + 3y = 6$ $\quad$ parallel

38. $2x - 3y = 6$
$3x + 2y = 6$ $\quad$ perpendicular

39. $y = \frac{1}{2}x + 3$
$2y = -2x + 4$ $\quad$ neither

40. $y = \frac{2}{5}x + 3$
$5y - 2x = 10$ $\quad$ parallel

Write an equivalent equation in slope–intercept form. State the slope and y-intercept of the line.

B **41.** $5x - 3y = 9$ $\quad \frac{5}{3}, -3$ **42.** $7x - 2y = 8$ $\quad \frac{7}{2}, -4$ **43.** $2(x + 3y) = 7$ $\quad -\frac{1}{3}, \frac{7}{6}$

44. $4(2x + y) = 6$ $\quad -2, \frac{3}{2}$ **45.** $3x + \frac{1}{2}y = 4$ $\quad -6, 8$ **46.** $7x + \frac{1}{3}y = 6$ $\quad -21, 18$

47. $3(x + 2y) = 8$ $\quad -\frac{1}{2}, \frac{4}{3}$ **48.** $2x + 3y = 5y + x + 1$ $\quad \frac{1}{2}, -\frac{1}{2}$ **49.** $2(y + 3) = 3(2y + x)$ $\quad -\frac{3}{4}, \frac{3}{2}$

Match the graphs with the given descriptions.

50. $m = \frac{2}{3}$; $b = 2$ $\quad$ r

51. $m = -\frac{2}{3}$; $b = 2$ $\quad$ q

52. $m = -\frac{3}{2}$; $b = -2$ $\quad$ p

53. $m = \frac{2}{3}$; $b = -2$ $\quad$ s

54. Slope undefined $\quad$ u

55. $m = 0$; $b = 0$ $\quad$ t

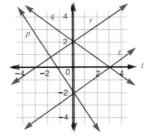

Write an equation in slope–intercept form for each line.

56. A line parallel to the graph of $y = 3x + 4$ and with y-intercept 5. $\quad y = 3x + 5$

57. A line parallel to the graph of $y = -2x + 8$ and passing through the origin. $\quad y = -2x$

58. A line perpendicular to the graph of $y = 3x + 4$ and with y-intercept 5. $\quad y = -\frac{1}{3}x + 5$

59. A line perpendicular to the graph of $y = -2x + 8$ and passing through the origin. $\quad y = \frac{1}{2}x$

60. A line perpendicular to the graph of $x = 5$ and with y-intercept 3. $\quad y = 3$

The **x-intercept** of a line is the *x*-coordinate of the point at which the line crosses the *x*-axis. State the *x*-intercept of the line with the given equation.

C **61.** $2x + 3y = 6$ 3

62. $y = \frac{1}{2}x - 5$ 10

63. $7x - 5y = 14$ 2

64. If an equation is written in the form $x = ny + c$, where n and c are real numbers, what does the value c represent?   x-intercept

65. Find the slope of the line with *y*-intercept 2 that passes through the point (5, 5). Write the equation of the line in slope–intercept form. $y = \frac{3}{5}x + 2$

66. Find the *y*-intercept of the line with slope $-\frac{1}{2}$ that passes through the point (4, −1). Write the equation of the line in slope–intercept form. $y = -\frac{1}{2}x + 1$

■ REVIEW EXERCISES

Simplify.

1. $\frac{3}{4} + \frac{5}{6}$ $1\frac{7}{12}$

2. $\frac{3}{4} - \frac{5}{6}$ $-\frac{1}{12}$

3. $\frac{3}{4} \cdot \frac{5}{6}$ $\frac{5}{8}$

4. $\frac{3}{4} \div \frac{5}{6}$ $\frac{9}{10}$

Draw a figure and write an equation to help you solve this problem.   [3–10]

5. The two congruent sides of an isosceles triangle are each 10 cm longer than the base. What are the lengths of the congruent sides and the base if the perimeter of the triangle is 125 cm?
$b + (b + 10) + (b + 10) = 125$
45 cm, 45 cm, 35 cm

EXTENSION   Unit pricing

Consumers are often confronted by questions like the following:

> The same brand of mustard comes in two sizes, 9 oz for 47 cents and 6.5 oz for 35 cents. Which is the better buy?

The question can be answered by computing a "unit price" for each size. In this case we compute the cost per ounce.

$$\frac{47}{9} \approx 5.2 \qquad \frac{35}{6.5} \approx 5.4$$

The larger size costs about 5.2 cents per ounce. The smaller size costs about 5.4 cents per ounce. The larger size is the better buy.

1. Graph the two ordered pairs (9, 47) and (6.5, 35). Draw a line from each point through the origin.

2. Find the slope of each line. $\approx 5.2, \approx 5.4$

3. How can graphs be used to determine the better buy?   The graph with the smaller slope produces the better buy.

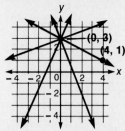

ENRICHMENT PROBLEMS

All of the lines crossing the *y*-axis at (0, 3) can be written in the form $y = mx + 3$. Find *two ways* to determine the equation of the line that also passes through (4, 1).

Substitute the point (4, 1) in the equation $y = mx + 3$; or use the two points (0, 3) and (4, 1) to determine the slope.
$y = -\frac{1}{2}x + 3$

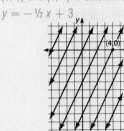

All of the lines with slope $m = 2$ can be written $y = 2x + b$. Find *two ways* to determine the equation of the line with *x*-intercept of 4.

Substitute the point (4, 0) in the equation $y = 2x + b$; or read the *y*-intercept from the graph; or solve $y = mx + b$ for *x*, then substitute.
$y = 2x - 8$

ADDITIONAL ANSWER   ■ **Extension**

1.

1. State the y-intercept of the line $y = 5x + 3$.   3
2. State the y-intercept of line a.   2

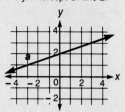

Write an equation in slope-intercept form for the following lines.

3. The line with slope 5 and y-intercept 2 $y = 5x + 2$.
4. The line parallel to $y = \frac{1}{2}x + 5$ and with a y-intercept of $\frac{1}{3}$ $y = \frac{1}{2}x + \frac{1}{3}$
5. The line perpendicular to $y = \frac{4}{3}x - 5$ and with a y-intercept of 6 $y = -\frac{3}{4}x + 6$

PURPOSE

Students should be able to write the slope-intercept equation of any line, given any two determining facts about the line.

PREVIEW

Pose the question in the Preview. Some answers are:

1. slope and intercept
2. slope and a point of the line
3. a point and the angle the line makes with some reference line

LESSON

Be sure that students understand these important points.

1. We can write the equation of a line if we know the slope and y-intercept.
2. The slope of a line can be found if we are given an equation of the line, a line parallel to the desired line, a line perpendicular to the desired line, or any two points on the line.

To write an equation of a line given (a) the slope and a point or (b) two points of the line.

5–7 Writing Equations for Lines

Preview

The line shown at the right is clearly identified by the name "line AB" because there is only one line that contains both point A and point B. What other ways can be used to identify a particular line?

In this lesson you will learn ways of writing equations to identify lines.

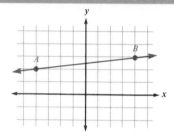

■ LESSON

There are two basic ways to identify a line: (1) by stating the slope of the line and the coordinates of a point on the line, or (2) by stating the coordinates of two points on the line. In both cases, an equation can be written for the line by determining the slope and y-intercept.

Example 1   Write an equation of the line that has slope 2 and that passes through point $(3, 4)$.

Solution   Since the slope of the line is 2, the equation of the line is in the form

$$y = 2x + b$$

Next, determine the value of b. Since the line contains the point $(3, 4)$, the values 3 for x and 4 for y satisfy the equation. Substitute those values into the equation $y = 2x + b$ and solve for b.

$$4 = 2(3) + b$$
$$4 = 6 + b$$
$$b = -2$$

The y-intercept is -2.

Answer   An equation of the line is $y = 2x - 2$.

Example 2   Write an equation of the line that has x-intercept 6 and that is parallel to the graph of $y = -\frac{1}{2}x + 3$.

Solution   Determine the slope of the line. The line is parallel to the graph of $y = -\frac{1}{2}x + 3$, which has slope $-\frac{1}{2}$. Therefore, the slope of the desired line is $-\frac{1}{2}$. The equation of the line has the form $y = -\frac{1}{2}x + b$.

Participation by each student is important. Therefore, attempts to answer questions, even if incorrect, should be positively reinforced.

3. The coordinates of every point on a line satisfy the equation of the line. Therefore, given the slope and one point on the line, we know three of the four variables in the general equation $y = mx + b$. This means that we can substitute for m, x, and y and solve for b.

Example 2 (continued)

Next determine the y-intercept. Since the x-intercept is 6, the coordinates $(6, 0)$ satisfy the equation. Substitute those values in the equation $y = -\frac{1}{2}x + b$ and solve for b.

$$0 = -\frac{1}{2}(6) + b$$

$$0 = -3 + b$$
$$b = 3$$

Answer An equation of the line is $y = -\frac{1}{2}x + 3$.

Note the steps in determining an equation of a line.

1. Determine the slope of the line and write the slope–intercept form of the equation, using the value for m.

2. Substitute the coordinates of a point on the line into the equation and solve for b, the y-intercept.

3. Write the slope–intercept form of the equation using the slope for m and the y-intercept for b.

Example 3

Write an equation of the line that passes through the points $(-2, 3)$ and $(4, 1)$.

Solution Determine the slope by substituting in the formula.

$$m = \frac{y_2 - y_1}{x_2 - x_1}$$

$$m = \frac{3 - 1}{-2 - 4}$$

$$= \frac{2}{-6}$$

$$= -\frac{1}{3}$$

The equation is of the form $y = -\frac{1}{3}x + b$.

Substitute -2 for x and 3 for y, and solve for b.

$$3 = -\frac{1}{3}(-2) + b$$

$$b = \frac{7}{3}$$

Substitute $-\frac{1}{3}$ for m and $\frac{7}{3}$ for b.

Answer $y = -\frac{1}{3}x + \frac{7}{3}$

ADDITIONAL EXAMPLES

Example 1. Write the equation of a line with slope -2 that passes through point $(-1, 3)$.
$$y = -2x + 1$$

Example 2. Write an equation of the line that passes through $(3, -2)$ and that is parallel to the graph of $y = 5x - 2$.
$$y = 5x - 17$$

Example 3. Write the equation of the line that passes through the points $(-3, -2)$ and $(-5, 1)$.
$$y = -\frac{3}{2}x - \frac{13}{2}$$

CHECK UNDERSTANDING

- What two facts do you have to know to immediately write the slope-intercept form of the equation of a line?
  (Slope and y-intercept)
- Give the slope of the line having the given properties:
  a. Parallel to the graph of $y = -4x - 7$. (-4)
  b. Perpendicular to the graph of $y = 0.5x - 4$. (-2)
  c. Passes through $(2, 3)$ and $(6, 5)$. (½)
- How do you find the y-intercept of the line with slope 3 and passing through the point $(4, 0)$? (Substitute 3 for m, 4 for x, and 0 for y in the equation $y = mx + b$. Then solve for b.)

EXTRA PRACTICE, page 628
COMPUTER WORKSHEET 9

PRACTICE WORKSHEET 27

5-7 WRITING EQUATIONS FOR LINES

■ Write an equation in the form $y = mx + b$ for the line that has the given slope, m, and that passes through the point (6, 2).

1. $m = 1$ $y = 1x - 4$
2. $m = -1$ $y = -1x + 8$
3. $m = -2$ $y = -2x + 14$
4. $m = \frac{1}{3}$ $y = 1/3x$
5. $m = -\frac{1}{3}$ $y = -1/3x + 4$
6. $m = 0$ $y = 2$
7. $m = \frac{2}{3}$ $y = 2/3x - 2$
8. $m = -\frac{1}{2}$ $y = -1/2x + 5$

■ Write an equation in slope-intercept form for the line that passes through the two points.

9. (0, 0), (7, 2) $y = 2/7x$
10. (4, −2), (0, 0) $y = -1/2x$
11. (1, 3), (5, 7) $y = 1x + 2$
12. (2, 3), (4, 4) $y = 1/2x + 2$
13. (3, −3), (5, −7) $y = -2x + 3$
14. (6, 6), (3, 4) $y = 2/3x + 2$
15. (−2, 3), (2, 1) $y = -1/2x + 2$
16. (4, 1), (8, 4) $y = 3/4x - 2$

■ CLASSROOM EXERCISES

Write an equation for the line with the given characteristics.

1. Has slope 4 and passes through (3, 1). $y = 4x - 11$

2. Passes through (−1, 2) and (1, −2). $y = -2x$

■ WRITTEN EXERCISES

Write an equation in slope–intercept form for the line that has the given slope and that passes through the point (4, 2).

A **1.** $m = 1$ $y = x - 2$ **2.** $m = 2$ $y = 2x - 6$ **3.** $m = \frac{1}{4}$ $y = \frac{1}{4}x + 1$ **4.** $m = \frac{1}{2}$ $y = \frac{1}{2}x$

5. $m = -2$ $y = -2x + 10$ **6.** $m = -1$ $y = -x + 6$ **7.** $m = -\frac{1}{2}$ $y = -\frac{1}{2}x + 4$ **8.** $m = -\frac{1}{4}$ $y = -\frac{1}{4}x + 3$

Write an equation in slope–intercept form for the line that has slope 2 and that passes through the given point.

9. (1, 4) $y = 2x + 2$ **10.** (1, 6) $y = 2x + 4$ **11.** (3, 10) $y = 2x + 4$ **12.** (3, 8) $y = 2x + 2$

13. (−3, 2) $y = 2x + 8$ **14.** (−5, 0) $y = 2x + 10$ **15.** (−1, −2) $y = 2x$ **16.** (−3, −10) $y = 2x - 4$

Write an equation in the form $y = mx + b$ for the line with the given characteristics.

17. Has slope 3 and passes through (4, 6). $y = 3x - 6$

18. Has slope 0 and passes through (2, 4). $y = 4$

19. Has slope $\frac{1}{2}$ and passes through (4, 6). $y = \frac{1}{2}x + 4$

20. Has no slope and passes through (2, 4). $x = 2$

21. Has slope $-\frac{2}{3}$ and passes through (−3, 6). $y = -\frac{2}{3}x + 4$

22. Has slope $-\frac{3}{2}$ and passes through (−6, 6). $y = -\frac{3}{2}x - 3$

23. Is parallel to the graph of $y = -2x + 5$ and passes through (−3, 10). $y = -3x + 21$

24. Is parallel to the graph of $y = -3x - 10$ and passes through (−4, 0). $y = 4x - 5$

25. Is perpendicular to the graph of $y = \frac{1}{3}x + 2$ and passes through (5, 6). $y = -3x + 21$

26. Is perpendicular to the graph of $y = -\frac{1}{4}x + 8$ and passes through (2, 3). $y = 4x - 5$

Find the slope of the line that passes through the two points.

27. (5, 6), (6, 9)   3   **28.** (3, 1), (4, 8)   7

29. (8, 2), (11, 8)   2   **30.** (2, 6), (5, 15)   3

31. (4, −2), (6, −6)   −2   **32.** (−4, 3), (−2, 5)   1

33. (−3, 2), (−5, 3) $-\frac{1}{2}$ **34.** (1, −5), (−1, −4) $-\frac{1}{2}$

Write an equation in the form $y = mx + b$ for the line that passes through the two points.

35. (2, 3), (3, 1) $y = -2x + 7$ **36.** (3, 5), (4, 2) $y = -3x + 14$

37. (5, 0), (8, 6) $y = 2x - 10$ **38.** (2, 0), (4, 6) $y = 3x - 6$

In exercises 43–46, the questions are equivalent to asking for the slope-intercept equation of a line given two points on the line. For example, in exercise 43 we know that two ordered pairs that satisfy the desired equation are (3, 95) and (5, 145).

ENRICHMENT PROBLEMS

- Write the equation of the line through (8, 1) and perpendicular to the line $x = 2$.

$$y = 1$$

- Write the equation of the line that is parallel to the line $y = 4$ and passes through $(-1, 5)$.

$$y = 5$$

- Find the slope of the line that is perpendicular to the line $y = 2x + 3$ and parallel to the line $y = -x + 3$.

There is no such line.

---

39. $(0, 5)$, $(8, 6)$ $y = \frac{1}{8}x + 5$

40. $(0, 2)$, $(4, 6)$ $y = x + 2$

41. $(-3, 5)$, $(-1, 8)$ $y = \frac{3}{2}x + \frac{19}{2}$

42. $(-2, 1)$, $(1, 5)$ $y = \frac{4}{3}x + \frac{11}{3}$

Write an equation in the form $y = mx + b$ for each situation.

B **43.** The U-Smash-M repair service charges \$95 for a job that takes 3 hours. It charges \$145 for a 5-hour job. Write an equation that shows how the charge (y) is related to the number of hours (x). $y = 25x + 20$

44. The I-Fix-M garage charges \$95 for a 3-hour job and \$135 for a 5-hour job. Write an equation that shows how the amount charged (y) is related to the number of hours worked (x). $y = 20x + 35$

45. When the temperature is 32° Fahrenheit, it is 0° Celsius. When it is 212°Fahrenheit, it is 100° Celsius. Write an equation that shows how degrees Fahrenheit (x) are related to degrees Celsius (y). $y = \frac{5}{9}x - \frac{160}{9}$

46. When the temprature is 37° Celsius, it is 98.6° Fahrenheit. When it is -40° Celsius, it is -40° Fahrenheit. Write an equation that shows how degrees Celsius (x) are related to degrees Fahrenheit (y). $y = \frac{9}{5}x + 32$

Point A has coordinates (x_1, y_1) and point B has coordinates (x_2, y_2).

C **47.** What is the slope of the line that passes through points A and B? $\frac{y_2 - y_1}{x_2 - x_1}$

48. What is the y-intercept of the line that passes through points A and B? $y_2 - \left(\frac{y_2 - y_1}{x_2 - x_1}\right)x_2$ or $y_1 - \left(\frac{y_2 - y_1}{x_2 - x_1}\right)x_1$

49. What is the y-intercept of the line with slope m that passes through point A? $y_1 - mx_1$

◼ REVIEW EXERCISES

1. State the degree of the polynomial $4x - 3x^2 - 7$.   2   [4–2]

2. Which of these expressions are binomials? $x - 3, a^2 + b^2$ [4–2]

$$2xy \qquad 3\frac{a}{b} \qquad x^2 + 3x + 2 \qquad x - 3 \qquad a^2 + b^2$$

3. Write the polynomial $4 - 3x^2 + 5x$ in descending order. $-3x^2 + 5x + 4$ [4–2]

4. Solve: $2 \cdot 2^3 \cdot 2^x = 2^{10}$ (6)   [4–3]

Simplify.

5. $a^2 \cdot a^4$ a^6

6. $(3ab^2) \cdot (-4ab)$ $-12a^2b^3$ [4–3]

Complete.

7. 3 km/min = ___?___ km/h   180   [4–7]

Solve.

8. Two planes left Denver at the same time, one flying east at 560 mph and one flying west at 500 mph. How many miles apart will they be after an hour and a half?   1590   [4–7]

1. Write the equation of the line that is parallel to the graph of $y = 3x + 4$ and that has y-intercept -5.

    $y = 3x - 5$

2. Write the equation of the line that is perpendicular to the graph of $y = -0.25x - 7$ and that has y-intercept 3.

    $y = 4x + 3$

3. Write the equation of the line that has slope 4 and that passes through the point $(2, 1)$.

    $y = 4x - 7$

4. Write the equation of the line that passes through $(4, 2)$ and $(3, 5)$.

    $y = -3x + 14$

PURPOSE

The function concept is considered by some mathematicians to be the most important idea studied in algebra.

PREVIEW

The function described in the table could be graphed with the amount of the order (x) paired with the postage/handling fee (y). The stair-step appearance is unusual.

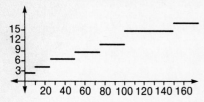

OBJECTIVE 5–8

To determine whether a relation is a function and whether a function is a linear function.

You may wish to spend two days on this section. Refer to the Pacing Chart.

5–8 Linear Functions

Preview

The Classic Gift Company charges its customers a postage and handling fee based on the amount of the order.

Amount of order	Postage and handling fee
Up to $10.00	$2.75
10.01 to 25.00	4.25
25.01 to 50.00	6.95
50.01 to 75.00	8.95
75.01 to 100.00	10.95
100.01 to 150.00	14.95
Over $150.00	16.95

It would be poor public relations for a company to charge two customers different amounts for the same purchases. In this lesson you will learn that the relationship shown in the table above is an example of a *function*.

What is the total bill for each amount of order?

- $9.00 $11.75
- $10.05 $14.30
- $101.00 $115.95
- $10.00 $12.75
- $100.00 $110.95
- $110.00 $124.95

True or false?

- Two orders for the *same* amount could have *different* total bills. False
- Two orders for *different* amounts could have the *same* total bills. True

■ LESSON

Any set of ordered pairs is a relation, but the relations $\{(0, 0), (1, 3), (4, 6)\}$ and $\left\{(1, 1), \left(2, \frac{1}{2}\right), \left(3, \frac{1}{3}\right)\right\}$ have an important property that the relation $\left\{(1, 3), \left(1, \frac{1}{3}\right), (2, 4), \left(2, \frac{1}{2}\right)\right\}$ does not have. No two ordered pairs have the same first component. The relations $\{(0, 0), (1, 3), (4, 6)\}$ and $\left\{(1, 1), \left(2, \frac{1}{2}\right), \left(3, \frac{1}{3}\right)\right\}$ are examples of a kind of relation called a **function.**

Definition: Function

A relation is a function if and only if each first component in the relation is paired with exactly one second component.

LESSON

Functions may be described in a variety of ways including tables, graphs, and equations. In every case, a function is a set of ordered pairs.

Although the graph of every linear function is a straight line, it is not true that every straight line is the graph of a linear function. The exceptions are vertical lines that are not the graphs of functions.

Students should clearly understand that the vertical-line test detects whether a relation violates the definition of function.

Functions and relations can be described by graphs. The relation shown in this figure is not a function, because the ordered pairs (4, 2) and (4, − 2) are both members of the relation. Note that some vertical lines of the grid cross the graph twice since there are first components that are matched with two second components.

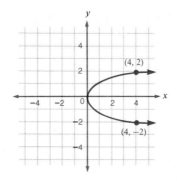

The relation shown in this figure is a function. No vertical line crosses the graph of the relation more than once. A vertical line can never cross the graph of a function more than once since there are no two ordered pairs with the same first component. This method of using vertical lines to determine whether a relation is a function is called the **vertical-line test.**

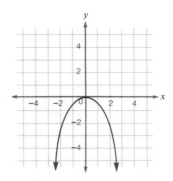

Functions and relations can also be described by equations. The relation defined by the equation $y = 2x$ is a function since each real number x is matched with its double, $2x$, and no real number has more than one double.

The relation defined by the equation $x = |y|$ is not a function since two ordered pairs (4, 4) and (4, − 4) with the same first component are in the relation. The graph of the relation fails the vertical-line test.

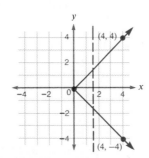

A function whose graph is a straight line is called a **linear function.** Each linear function can be defined by an equation in the slope–intercept form:

$$y = mx + b$$

Equations that define linear functions are called **linear equations in two variables.** In a linear equation the degree of both variables is 1.

$$y = 5x + 13$$
first degree

ADDITIONAL EXAMPLES

Example 1.
State whether $5x - 2y + 4 = 0$ is the equation of a linear function.

Yes, the equation can be transformed to $y = \frac{5}{2}x + 2$, which is in the form $y = mx + b$.

Example 2.
State whether $y = 2x^2$ is the equation of a linear function.

No. It is the equation of a function, but it is not and cannot be written in the form $y = mx + b$.

Example 3.
State whether $0x - y = 4$ is the equation of a linear function.

Yes. It can be transformed to $y = 0x - 4$, which is in the form $y = mx + b$.

CHECK UNDERSTANDING

- Which of the following graphs represents a function? (a) Does it represent a linear function? (No)

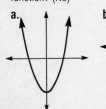

- Which of the following relations defines a function? (a)

a.

x	-3	-2	0	2	3
y	3	2	0	2	3

b. $\{(0, 0), (1, -1), (1, 1), (4, -2), (4, 2)\}$

CLASSROOM EXERCISES

In classroom exercises 8–15, the domain of the function (or relation) is assumed to be the set of real numbers unless stated otherwise.

In classroom exercise 11, the function $y = |x|$ is not linear, even though its graph contains parts of lines.

Example 1 State whether $2y - 3x = 4$ is the equation of a linear function.

Solution The equation $2y - 3x = 4$ can be transformed to the equivalent equation in slope–intercept form $y = \frac{3}{2}x + 2$. Therefore, it is an equation of a linear function.

Example 2 State whether $y = x^2$ is the equation of a linear function.

Solution The equation $y = x^2$ is the equation of a function since each number has exactly one square. However, the function is not a linear function since the degree of the x-term is 2, not 1.

Example 3 State whether $x = 0y + 2$ is the equation of a linear function.

Solution These are some solutions of the equation $x = 0y + 2$:

$$\{(2, 8), (2, 3), (2, -5)\}$$

Therefore, the relation defined by $x = 0y + 2$ is not a function. Its graph is a vertical line.

■ CLASSROOM EXERCISES

1. State the definition of a function. See page 234.

State whether these relations are functions. Give a reason for your answer.

2. $\{(2, 3), (4, 5), (-2, 5), (0, 4)\}$ Yes

3. $\{(1, 5), (-1, 4), (1, 3), (5, -2)\}$ No

4. $\{(2, 6), (3, 6), (4, 6), (5, 6)\}$ Yes

5. $\{(3, 0), (0, 3), (4, 8), (8, 4)\}$ Yes

6. Yes

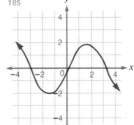

7. No

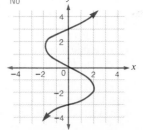

State whether the equation represents a function. Give a reason for your answer.

8. $y = -2x$ Yes **9.** $y = x^2$ Yes **10.** $x = y^2$ No **11.** $y = |x|$ Yes

State whether the equation represents a linear function.

12. $y = -3x$ Yes **13.** $y = 2x - 6$ Yes **14.** $y + x = -2$ Yes **15.** $y = |x|$ No

236

EXTRA PRACTICE, page 629

ASSIGNMENT GUIDE

Basic   1–16 all, Review Exercises, Self-
          Quiz 3
Average   1–42 all, Review Exercises, Self-
          Quiz 3
Enriched 17–41 odd, 49–51 all, Review Ex-
          ercises, Self-Quiz 3

■ WRITTEN EXERCISES

State whether the relation is a function.

1. {(1, 2), (2, 3), (3, 4)} Yes

2. {(4, 3), (3, 2), (2, 1)} Yes

3. {(3, 5), (−3, 5)} Yes

4. {(−7, 8), (7, 8)} Yes

5. {(16, 4), (16, −4)} No

6. {(25, −5), (25, 5)} No

State whether the graph represents a function.

7. Yes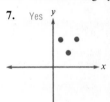

8. No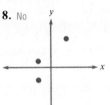

9. Yes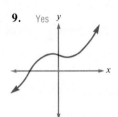

10. Yes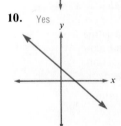

11. No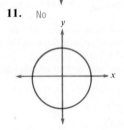

12. Yes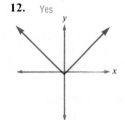

State whether the relation defined by the table is a function.

13.

x	−4	−1	2
y	3	5	3

Yes

14.

x	−3	1	5
y	−2	−2	3

Yes

15.

x	0.25	$\frac{1}{4}$	1
y	0.5	$\frac{1}{2}$	1

Yes

16.

x	$\frac{4}{6}$	$\frac{2}{3}$	$-\frac{1}{2}$
y	4	4	4

Yes

State whether the equation defines a function.

17. $y = 10x + 9$ Yes

18. $y = 7x + 2$ Yes

19. $y = |x + 2|$ Yes

20. $y = |x − 3|$ Yes

21. $y = (x + 1)^2$ Yes

22. $y = (5 − x)^2$ Yes

23. $x^2 = y^2$ No

24. $y^3 = x^3$ Yes

State whether the equation defines a *linear* function.

25. $2x − 3y = 5$ Yes

26. $3y − 5x = 8$ Yes

27. $y = \frac{1}{2}x + 4$ Yes

28. $y = \frac{1}{3}x + 2$ Yes

29. $y = x^4$ No

30. $y = x^2 + 2$ No

CONCEPT EXTENSION

Having more than one way to think about an idea increases the depth of a student's understanding. Moreover, it is practical; one way of applying an idea may fit a given situation when another may not.

A student may be said to possess a full understanding of an idea when that student can produce not only examples of that concept, but also nonexamples—that is the student can describe and give examples of functions and also give examples of relations that are not functions.

COMPUTER EXTENSION

In computer language, the greatest integer function is named by INT( ). Write a computer program that will give the greatest integer that is less than or equal to any number that is entered.

```
10 PRINT "WHAT IS THE NUMBER";
20 INPUT X
30 Y = INT(X)
40 PRINT "THE GREATEST
   INTEGER LESS THAN"
50 PRINT "OR EQUAL TO
   "; X; " IS "; Y
60 END
```

ENRICHMENT PROBLEM

- For each *relation* below, write ordered pairs using members of your family. Indicate whether the relation is a function or not.
  a. "is the niece of"
  b. "is the brother of"
  c. "is the spouse of"
  d. "is at least two years older than"

 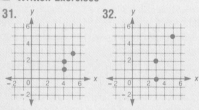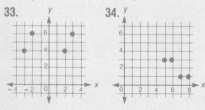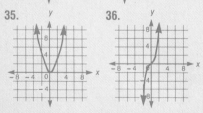
Graph each relation and state whether it is a function.

31. {(5, 3), (4, 2), (4, 1)}   No

32. {(3, 0), (3, 2), (5, 5)}   No

33.

x	2	-2	3	-3
y	4	6	6	4

Yes

34.

x	5	6	7	8
y	3	3	1	1

Yes

Graph these equations and state whether the relation is a function. If it is a function, state whether it is a linear function.

35. $y = x^2$ Yes, no

36. $y = x^3$ Yes, no

37. $x + y = 4$ Yes, yes

38. $x + y = 8$ Yes, yes

39. $y = x + 2$ Yes, yes

40. $y = x - 4$ Yes, yes

41. $2x + 4y = 8$ Yes, yes

42. $3x + 6y = 18$ Yes, yes

State whether the equation defines a function. If it does, state whether it is a linear function.

Ⓒ 43. $x + y = 4$ Yes, yes

44. $x - y = 4$ Yes, yes

45. $xy = 4$ Yes, no

46. $\dfrac{y}{x} = 4$ Yes, no

47. $\dfrac{1}{x} + \dfrac{1}{y} = 4$ Yes, no

48. $\dfrac{1}{x + y} = 4$ Yes, yes

49. The table in the Preview describes a function whose first component is the amount of the order and whose second component is the postage and handling fee. This function is a special kind of function called a step function. Graph the number pairs (amount of the order, postage and handling fee).

A phone call costs 50¢ for the first minute and 25¢ for each additional minute or part of a minute.

50. Calculate the cost for a phone call that lasts:

a. $2\frac{1}{2}$ min $1

b. 3 min 1 s $1.25

c. 6 min 59 s $2

51. Draw a graph of the phone-call costs for calls lasting up to 10 min.

■ REVIEW EXERCISES

1. Write 30,000,000,000 in scientific notation. $3 \cdot 10^{10}$ [4–4]

2. Write $3.45 \cdot 10^5$ in standard decimal notation.   345,000   [4–4]

3. Simplify. Write the product in scientific notation.   [4–4]

$$(4 \cdot 10^4) \cdot (6 \cdot 10^3)   2.4 \cdot 10^8$$

Simplify.   [4–5]

4. $(a^2)^4$ a^8

5. $(2x^3)^2$ $4x^6$

6. $(10a^2b^3)^4$ $10,000a^8b^{12}$

7. What is the value in cents of q quarters?   25q   [4–9]

Solve.

8. There are three times as many dimes as quarters in a pile worth $3.30. How many dimes and how many quarters are in the pile?   18 dimes, 6 quarters   [4–9]

37.

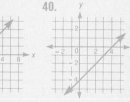

38.

Self-Quiz 3

5–6 **1.** State the slope and y-intercept of the line whose equation is $3y - 2x = 12$. $\frac{2}{3}, 4$

2. Write the equation of the line that is parallel to the graph of $y = 2x - 5$ and passes through $(0, 5)$. $y = 2x + 5$

3. Show that the lines whose equations are $5x - 2y = 10$ and $y = -\frac{2}{5}x + 1$ are perpendicular by finding their slopes. $\frac{5}{2} \cdot -\frac{2}{5} = -1$

39.

40.

5–7 Find the equation of the line meeting these conditions. Write the equation in slope-intercept form.

4. Has slope $\frac{2}{3}$ and passes through $(3, 6)$. $y = \frac{2}{3}x + 4$

5. Is perpendicular to $y = -\frac{1}{2}x + 5$ and has y-intercept -3. $y = 2x - 3$

6. Passes through $(1, 2)$ and $(4, -4)$. $y = -2x + 4$

41.

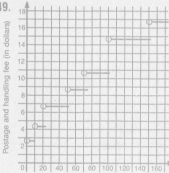

42.

5–8 State whether each of the following represents a function.

7. No

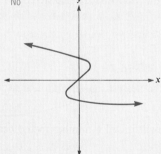

8.

x	y
-3	5
-1	3
0	2
-1	1

No

9. State whether the equation $2(x - y) = 5$ defines a linear function. Yes

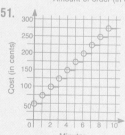

49.

51.

Strategy for Success **Taking tests** _____

Write your solutions in a neat, orderly fashion so your teacher can help you diagnose the kinds of errors you are making, and also perhaps award partial credit.

EXTENSION Rounding numbers on a computer

There is no BASIC command to round a number, but a number can be rounded by using the greatest integer function. The function is written in BASIC as INT(X).

Examples

```
PRINT INT (3.67)       PRINT INT (4.38)       PRINT INT (5)
3                      4                      5
```

For positive numbers, INT deletes the digits to the right of the decimal point. To use INT to round a number to the nearest integer, add 0.5 to the number and find the greatest integer of the sum.

Examples

```
PRINT INT (3.67 + 0.5)  PRINT INT (4.38 + 0.5)  PRINT INT (5 + 0.5)
4                       4                       5
```

The following program rounds numbers to the nearest integer.

```
10  PRINT "WHAT IS THE NUMBER";
20  INPUT X
30  Y = INT (X + 0.5)
40  PRINT X; " ROUNDED TO THE NEAREST INTEGER IS "; Y
50  END
```

To round a number to the nearest tenth, lines 30 and 40 can be changed to

```
30  Y = INT (10 * X + 0.5)/10
40  PRINT X; " ROUNDED TO THE NEAREST TENTH IS "; Y
```

Run each program to round these numbers to the nearest integer and nearest tenth.

1. 7.283 7,7.3   **2.** 4.609 5,4.6   **3.** 0.514 1,0.5

4. Rewrite lines 30 and 40 so that the program will round a number to the nearest hundredth. Check your program. `30  Y = INT (100 * X + 0.05)/100`
`40  PRINT X; " ROUNDED TO THE NEAREST HUNDREDTH IS "; Y`

Strategy for Success Believing in yourself

The chances are great that if you believe that you can learn algebra and you work at it, then you will learn algebra. Everyone has difficulty in mathematics at one time or another. However, those who believe they can learn mathematics and persevere usually do succeed.

OBJECTIVE 5–9

To determine whether a set of ordered number pairs belongs to a linear function.

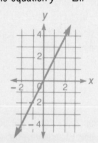
5–9 Problem Solving with Linear Functions

Preview   Charles's Law

Gases expand when heated and contract when cooled. This fact can be tested by blowing up a balloon, putting it in a very warm place (in bright sunlight) or a very cold place (a freezer), and noting how the diameter of the balloon changes. The law that relates the volume of a gas to its temperature was first stated by scientist Jacques Charles in 1787.

Charles measured the volumes of a quantity of gas at various temperatures. These data can be graphed.

Temperature (°C)	15	30	45	60	75
Volume (cm³)	480	505	530	555	580

Charles noted that the data appeared to be linear and wrote a linear formula relating the temperature and volume of the gas. After this lesson you will be able to write Charles's formula.

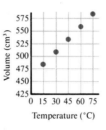

PURPOSE

To apply mathematics to practical problems, it is important to be able to determine whether number pairs belong to a linear set, another type of function, or a relation that is not a function.

■ LESSON

A naturalist noted that a certain species of crickets chirps faster as the temperature rises. Here are some data about the number of chirps.

	20	20	20	
Chirps per minute	40	60	80	100
Temperature (°F)	47	52	57	62
	5	5	5	

   For equal increases in the number of chirps per minute, there are equal increases in the temperature. This means that the formula relating the two quantities is linear. The ratio of the increase in temperature to the increase in chirps is the slope of the graph of the formula.

$$\text{slope} = \frac{\text{change in temperature}}{\text{change in chirps}} = \frac{5}{20} = \frac{1}{4}$$

If T represents the number of degrees Fahrenheit and c represents the number of chirps per minute, the set of number pairs (c, T) is a linear function. The equation of the function is of the form

$$T = \frac{1}{4} c + b$$

PREVIEW

Charles's law relates the temperature of gas and its volume. It assumes that other factors, such as pressure, remain constant. In the graph, notice that only part of the vertical scale is shown. The intercept on the horizontal axis (where the volume is 0) is −273. This point is of special importance. −273°C is the lowest theoretical temperature and is referred to as absolute zero. On the Kelvin scale, this temperature is designated 0°K.

LESSON

A camper may use the number of cricket chirps to estimate the temperature. Although the chirps do not *cause* the temperature (the opposite is more likely), the number of chirps is treated as the independent variable. The number of chirps (c) is used to find the temperature (T).

ADDITIONAL EXAMPLES

Example 1.
Determine whether the (x, y) number pairs are a linear function.

x	-3	-1	1	3	5
y	7	4	1	-2	-5

Yes

Example 2.
Show that these pairs belong to a linear function. $(-1, -6)$, $(0, -4)$, $(2, 0)$, $(5, 6)$

Find the slopes of the lines joining successive pairs of points.

$$(-1, -6) \quad (0, -4) \quad (2, 0) \quad (5, 6)$$

$$m: \quad \frac{2}{1} \quad \frac{4}{2} \quad \frac{6}{3}$$

Since the slopes are equal, the points are on the same line. Therefore, the function is linear.

To determine the value of b, that is, the T-intercept, substitute one of the (c, T) number pairs from the table in the formula and then solve for b.

$$T = \frac{1}{4}c + b$$

Substitute (40, 47). $\qquad 47 = \frac{1}{4} \cdot 40 + b$

Solve for b. $\qquad\qquad 47 = 10 + b$
$$37 = b$$

Here is a graph of the formula $T = \frac{1}{4}c + 37$.

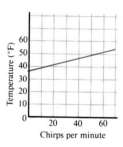

Example 1 Determine whether the (x, y) number pairs are a linear function.

x	-2	-1	0	1	2	3
y	1	$-\frac{1}{2}$	-1	$-\frac{1}{2}$	1	$3\frac{1}{2}$

Solution First find the successive differences of the x-values and of the y-values.

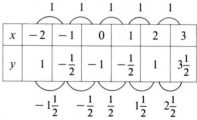

The successive differences in x-values are constant, but the successive differences in y-values are not constant. The ordered pairs are not part of a linear function. The graph shows that the points do not lie on a straight line.

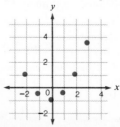

242   Chapter 5   Graphing Linear Equations and Functions

Example 2   Show that the pairs in the table belong to a linear function.

x	y
-1	-8
0	-5
2	1
5	10
20	55

Solution   Find the slopes of the lines joining successive pairs of points.

$$m = \frac{y_2 - y_1}{x_2 - x_1}$$

x	y
-1	-8
0	-5
2	1
5	10

$m_1 = \dfrac{3}{1} = 3$

$m_2 = \dfrac{6}{2} = 3$

$m_3 = \dfrac{9}{3} = 3$

Since the slopes are equal, the points are on the same line. Therefore, the function is linear.

Example 3   Write a linear equation in the form $y = mx + b$ that relates x and y.

x	2	0	-1	3	4	1
y	1	3	4	0	-1	2

Solution   Arrange the data so that the x-values are in order. Then find successive differences.

1   1   1   1   1

x	-1	0	1	2	3	4
y	4	3	2	1	0	-1

-1 -1 -1 -1 -1

The ordered pairs belong to a linear function. Selecting the fourth and fifth number pairs we have:

slope: $m = \dfrac{y_2 - y_1}{x_2 - x_1} = \dfrac{1 - 0}{2 - 3} = \dfrac{1}{-1} = -1$

y-intercept: $b = 3$

Answer $y = -1x + 3$

ADDITIONAL EXAMPLES

Example 3.
Write a linear equation that relates x and y.

x	4	1	-3
y	10	1	-11

$y = 3x - 2$

CHECK UNDERSTANDING

- Do these three pairs belong to a linear function? (Yes)

x	1	3	5
y	4	8	12

- If the second component of the last ordered pair above is changed to 13, do the three ordered pairs belong to a linear function? (No)

Enrichment Worksheet 11

NAME _____

USING POLYNOMIALS

■ Complete each chart.

	Write any number here.	Write n here.
1.	_____	n
Add the number of sides of a rectangle.	_____	$n + 4$
Multiply by the number of sides of a hexagon.	_____	$6n + 24$
Subtract the number of vertices of a cube.	_____	$6n + 16$
Divide by the number of bases of a trapezoid.	_____	$3n + 8$
Subtract the number of angles of a pentagon.	_____	$3n + 3$
Divide by the number of ways to get a sum of 4 with two dice.	_____	$n + 1$
Subtract the number you began with.	_____	1

	Write any number here.	Write n here.
2.	_____	n
Subtract the number of faces of a cube.	_____	$n - 6$
Multiply by the number of ways to get a sum of 3 with two dice.	_____	$2n - 12$
Add the number of edges of a cube.	_____	$2n$
Multiply by the number of sides of a quadrilateral.	_____	$8n$
Add the number of ounces in a pound.	_____	$8n + 16$
Divide by the number of angles in an octagon.	_____	$n + 2$
Subtract the number you began with.	_____	2

© D.C. Heath & Co.

Can be used after Section 5-9

243

CLASSROOM EXERCISES

Point out that the slope of a line segment joining any pair of points must be constant if the function is linear. Only one exception is needed to show that a function is not linear.

ASSIGNMENT GUIDE

Basic   1–19 odd, Review Exercises
Average 9–27 odd, 29–35 all, Review Exercises
Enriched 9–27 odd, 33–39 all, Review Exercises

PRACTICE WORKSHEET 28

5-9 PROBLEM SOLVING WITH LINEAR FUNCTIONS

■ For these linear functions, determine the slope, y-intercept, and equation in slope–intercept form.

1.

x	2	1	0	−1
y	9	7	5	3

slope 2
y-intercept 5
equation $y = 2x + 5$

2.

x	1	2	3	4
y	1	−2	−5	−8

slope −3
y-intercept 4
equation $y = -3x + 4$

3.

x	8	6	4	2
y	1	0	−1	−2

slope 1/2
y-intercept −3
equation $y = 1/2x - 3$

4.

x	3	4	5	6
y	−1	−4/3	−5/3	−2

slope −1/3
y-intercept 0
equation $y = -1/3x$

5.

x	−4	−2	2	4
y	−10	−7	−1	2

slope 3/2
y-intercept −4
equation $y = 3/2x - 4$

6.

x	−3	−1	1	3
y	3	2	1	0

slope −1/2
y-intercept 3/2
equation $y = -1/2x + 3/2$

■ The tables show the number of handbooks printed and the cost of printing the handbooks. State whether the number pairs belong to a linear function.

7.

Handbooks printed	100	150	200	250
Total cost in dollars	60	85	110	135

Yes

8.

Handbooks printed	100	200	300	400
Total cost in dollars	65	110	145	180

No

EXTRA PRACTICE, page 629

■ CLASSROOM EXERCISES

State whether the ordered pairs belong to a *linear* function.

1.

x	y
−2	−3
0	1
4	9
6	13

Yes

2.

x	y
−2	−10
−1	−3
0	−2
1	−1
2	6

No

3.

x	y
2	−3
5	−1.5
−2	−5
4	−2
0	−4

Yes

4. In Exercises 1–3, if the function is linear, determine its slope, y-intercept, and equation in slope–intercept form. $y = 2x + 1, y = \frac{1}{2}x - 4$

■ WRITTEN EXERCISES

State whether the ordered pairs belong to a *linear* function.

Ⓐ 1.

x	−2	−1	0	1	2
y	−8	−6	−4	−2	0

Yes

2.

x	−2	−1	0	1	2
y	−8	−5	−2	1	4

Yes

3.

x	−2	−1	0	1	2
y	5	2	−1	−4	−7

Yes

4.

x	−2	−1	0	1	2
y	10	8	6	4	2

Yes

5.

x	−2	−1	0	1	2
y	4	1	0	1	4

No

6.

x	−2	−1	0	1	2
y	6	8	10	10	12

No

7.

x	3	4	1	2	5
y	10	13	4	7	16

Yes

8.

x	3	4	2	5	1
y	11	15	7	19	3

Yes

For these linear functions, determine the slope, y-intercept, and equation in slope–intercept form.

9.

x	4	2	0
y	11	7	3

Slope: 2; y-intercept: 3; $y = 2x + 3$

10.

x	6	3	0
y	19	10	1

Slope: 3; y-intercept: 1; $y = 3x + 1$

11.

x	3	2	1
y	13	8	3

Slope: 5; y-intercept: −2; $y = 5x - 2$

12.

x	6	4	2
y	21	13	5

Slope: 4; y-intercept: −3; $y = 4x - 3$

13.

x	5	3	1
y	14	8	2

Slope: 3; y-intercept: −1; $y = 3x - 1$

14.

x	5	3	1
y	9	5	1

Slope: 2; y-intercept: −1; $y = 2x - 1$

15.

x	−6	−4	1
y	15	11	1

Slope: −2; y-intercept: 3; $y = -2x + 3$

16.

x	−5	−1	2
y	23	11	2

Slope: −3; y-intercept: 8; $y = -3x + 8$

The tables show the amount of weight attached to a spring and the length of the extended spring. Show whether the number pairs belong to a linear function.

17.

weight (in grams)	0	100	200	300
length (in centimeters)	50	55	60	65

Yes

18.

weight (in grams)	0	1000	2000
length (in centimeters)	40	80	100

No

The tables show the number of books printed and the total cost of printing the books. Show whether the number pairs belong to a linear function.

19.

books printed	1000	2000	3000
total cost	2075	4075	6075

Yes

20.

books printed	1000	2000	3000
total cost	1600	3100	4600

Yes

The tables show the number of miles driven in a month and the cost of owning a car for the month. Show whether the number pairs belong to a linear function.

21.

miles	100	200	300	400
cost (in dollars)	125	145	162	170

No

22.

miles	100	200	300	400
cost (in dollars)	150	175	200	225

Yes

Show whether the number pairs belong to a linear function.

23.

x	-2	0	5	10
y	-8	-2	13	28

Yes

24.

x	-5	-1	0	4
y	-5	3	5	12

No

25.

x	-3	1	6	-2
y	10	-6	-26	6

Yes

26.

x	-2	-1	1	2
y	4	2	2	4

No

27. In the Preview, the number pairs (15, 480) and (30, 505) were found to be members of a linear function. Write an equation in slope–intercept form for the volume V in terms of the temperature T. $V = \frac{5}{3}T + 455$

ENRICHMENT PROBLEM

- The equations $y = 3x - 6$ and $x = \frac{1}{3}y + 2$ are different forms of the same equation.

a. Complete this table using the first equation.

x	y	
-2	?	-12
0	?	-6
1	?	-3
3	?	3
6	?	12

b. Complete this table using the second equation.

	x	y
-2	?	-12
0	?	-6
1	?	-3
3	?	3
6	?	12

c. What do you conclude?

The completed tables are the same.

d. Which equation represents a linear function?

Both equations do.

e. How could you use the form of each equation to graph the equation?

Use $y = 3x - 6$ to obtain the y-intercept and $x = \frac{1}{3}y + 2$ to obtain the x-intercept.

28. Two temperature pairs that show how the Celsius and Kelvin temperature scales are related are shown in the table.

	Oxygen boils	Aspirin melts
Degrees Celsius, C	− 183	135
Degrees Kelvin, K	90	408

Write an equation in slope–intercept form for the Kelvin temperature K in terms of the Celsius temperature C.   K = C + 273

29.–32. Write equations of the form $y = mx + b$ for the data tables in Exercises 17, 19, 20, and 22. $I = \frac{1}{20}w + 50$, t = 2b + 75, t = $\frac{3}{2}$b + 100, c = $\frac{1}{4}$m + 125

These results were obtained in an experiment investigating the effect of temperature on the resistance of a copper wire.

Temperature (°C)	15	30	45	100
Resistance (ohms)	23.5	25	26.5	32

33. Do the number pairs appear to belong to a *linear* function? Explain.   Yes
34. Estimate the resistance of the wire at 0°C.   22 ohms
35. Estimate the resistance of the wire at − 10°C.   21 ohms

C Here is a table of first, second, and third successive differences for the function $y = x^2$.

x	$y = x^2$	First differences	Second differences	Third differences
0	0			
1	1	1	2	0
2	4	3	2	0
3	9	5	2	0
4	16	7	2	
5	25	9		

36. Complete this table of first and second successive differences for the function $y = 2x + 3$.

x	$y = 2x + 3$	First differences	Second differences
0	? 3		
		? 2	
1	? 5		? 0
		? 2	
2	? 7		? 0
		? 2	
3	? 9		? 0
		? 2	
4	? 11		? 0
		? 2	
5	? 13		

37. How can successive differences be used to determine whether a table of values represents a linear function? Pick a linear function and check your guess. For a linear function, the second differences are all zero.

38. Complete this table of first, second, and third successive differences for the function $y = x^2 + x - 4$.

x	$y = x^2 + x - 4$	First differences	Second differences	Third differences
0	? −4			
		? 2		
1	? −2		? 2	
		? 4		? 0
2	? 2		? 2	
		? 6		? 0
3	? 8		? 2	
		? 8		? 0
4	? 16		? 2	
		? 10		
5	? 26			

39. How can successive differences be used to determine whether a table of values represents a second-degree function? Pick a second-degree function and check your guess. For a second-degree function, the third differences are all zero.

■ REVIEW EXERCISES

Simplify. Assume that no denominator equals zero.   [4–6]

1. $6x(x - 3)$ $6x^2 - 18x$

2. $(x^2 - 4x + 3) \cdot 2x$
$2x^3 - 8x^2 + 6x$

3. $3a(2a - b + c)$
$6a^2 - 3ab + 3ac$

4. $\dfrac{8a^6}{2a^2}$ $4a^4$

5. $\dfrac{-16xy^3}{4x^2y^2}$ $\dfrac{-4y}{x}$ [4–8]

6. Write the quotient in scientific notation. $\dfrac{6.4 \cdot 10^6}{8 \cdot 10^2}$ $8 \cdot 10^3$ [4–8]

7. The sum of five consecutive integers is 100. What are the integers?   [4–10]
18, 19, 20, 21, 22

8. The sum of three consecutive even integers is -72. What are the integers? $-26, -24, -22$ [4–10]

Write an equation that fits the problem. Do not solve the equation.   [3–9]

9. John worked two weeks during winter holidays, earning a total of $100. If he earned $10 more the second week than he did the first week, how much did he earn each week? $x + (x + 10) = 100$

Write an equation that fits the problem and solve it.   [3–9]

10. If a rectangle is 3 times as long as it is wide, and the perimeter is 40 cm, what are the length and width? $w + 3w + w + 3w = 40$; length: 15 cm, width: 5 cm

EXTENSION A computer program for finding the equation of a line

If the coordinates of two points are known, an equation of the line that passes through them can be determined. When the coordinates of the two points are entered into the program below,

first, the slope M is determined;
next, the slope is used to determine the y-intercept B;
finally, the equation of the line is determined.

```
10   PRINT "WHAT ARE THE X- AND Y-COORDINATES OF THE FIRST
     POINT";
20   INPUT X1, Y1
30   PRINT "WHAT ARE THE X- AND Y-COORDINATES OF THE SECOND
     POINT";
40   INPUT X2, Y2
50   M = (Y1 - Y2)/(X1 - X2)
60   PRINT "M =   "; M
70   B = Y1 - M * X1
80   PRINT "B =   "; B
90   PRINT "THE EQUATION OF THE LINE IS Y =   "; M; "X +   ";
     B
100  END
```

Run the program for each pair of points.

1. (2, 6), (7, −4) Y = −2X + 10

2. (0, −1), (−4, 3) Y = −1X − 1

3. (−2, 1), (−1, 5) Y = 4X + 9

4. (4, −3), (6, 0) Y = 1.5X − 9

5. What happens when you enter two points, such as (−1, 2) and (4, 2), that lie on a horizontal line? Y = 0X + 2

6. What happens when you enter two points, such as (3, 7) and (3, 1), that lie on a vertical line? Division by zero error in 50.

Strategy for Success Preparing for a test

Review with a friend can be helpful. You can quiz each other on the meanings of mathematical symbols and words. You can give each other the kinds of questions you expect on a test.

■ CHAPTER SUMMARY

• **Vocabulary**

• To graph the equation of a line, graph three ordered pairs that satisfy the equation and then draw the line through them. (Two ordered pairs are enough. The third pair is used as a check.) [5–4]

• To graph an equation in two variables, find as many ordered pairs as necessary to determine the pattern of the graph. Use positive integers, zero, negative integers, and possibly fractions as first components. Graph them and connect the points according to an observed pattern. (More points may be needed in places where the graph turns sharply.) [5–4]

• The *slope m* of the line through points $A(x_1, y_1)$ and $B(x_2, y_2)$ is equal to [5–5]

$$\frac{y_2 - y_1}{x_2 - x_1} \quad \text{or} \quad \frac{y_1 - y_2}{x_1 - x_2}.$$

• An equation in the form $y = mx + b$ is in *slope–intercept form*. The value of m is the slope of the line and the value of b is the y-intercept. [5–6]

• A relation of ordered pairs is a *function* if and only if each first component in the relation is paired with exactly one second component. [5–8]

• A function can be described by:
  Listing the ordered pairs.
  Using a table of solutions.
  A graph.
  An equation.
  A worded description.

3.

4.

7.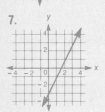

8.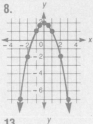

10.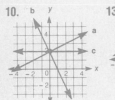

13.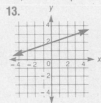

■ CHAPTER REVIEW

5–1 **Objective:** To graph ordered pairs of real numbers.

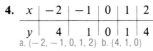

1. Identify the coordinates of each point.
  a. A $(2, -3)$
  b. B $(-2, -1)$
  c. C $(-3, 0)$
  d. D $(2, 2)$

2. Identify the quadrant the point is in or the axis it is on.
  a. A IV   **b.** B III   **c.** C x-axis   **d.** D I

5–2 **Objective:** To graph relations.

The following exercises describe a relation.
  a. List the domain.   **b.** List the range.   **c.** Graph the relation.

3. $\{(1, 2), (2, 2), (3, 6)\}$
  a. {1, 2, 3} b. {2, 6}

4.

x	-2	-1	0	1	2
y	4	1	0	1	4

  a. {−2, −1, 0, 1, 2} b. {4, 1, 0}

5–3 **Objective:** To identify solutions to equations in two variables.

5. State whether the ordered pair is a solution of the equation $2x + y = 8$.
  a. $(1, 6)$ Yes   **b.** $(0, 4)$ No   **c.** $(-2, 12)$ Yes

6. Copy and complete the solution table for the equation $3a - b = 9$.

a	0	?	1	?
b	?	0	?	3

  3   4
  -9 -6

5–4 **Objective:** To graph equations.

7. Select three values of x, copy and complete the table, plot the points, and then graph the equation. Answers will vary.

$y = 2x - 3$

x	?	?	?
y	?	?	?

  0 1 2
  -3 -1 1

8. Copy and complete the table. Then use the ordered pairs to graph the equation.

$y = 2 - x^2$

x	-3	-2	-1	$-\frac{1}{2}$	0	$\frac{1}{2}$	1	2	3
y	?	?	?	?	?	?	?	?	?

  -7 -2 1 $1\frac{3}{4}$ 2 $1\frac{3}{4}$ 1 -2 -7

5–5   **Objective:** To find the slope of a line.

9. State the slope of each line.

   a. $\overleftrightarrow{AB}$ $\frac{1}{2}$ b. $\overleftrightarrow{BC}$ -3

   c. $\overleftrightarrow{EF}$ 0   d. $\overleftrightarrow{GE}$ no slope

10. Draw lines with the given slopes through the point (0, 2). Label the lines *a*, *b*, and *c*.

   a. Slope $\frac{1}{2}$ b. Slope -2 c. Slope 0

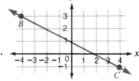

5–6   **Objective:** To determine the slope and *y*-intercept of a line.

11. State the slope and *y*-intercept of the line with equation $y = \frac{1}{2}x - 3$. $\frac{1}{2}, -3$

12. State the slope and the *y*-intercept of line *BC*. $-\frac{1}{2}, 1$

13. Graph the line with slope $\frac{1}{3}$ and *y*-intercept 2.

14. Write the equation $2x + 3y = 12$ in slope–intercept form.
   $y = -\frac{2}{3}x + 4$

   Objective: To use slopes to determine whether two lines are parallel, perpendicular, or neither.

15. State whether the lines with these equations are parallel.
   $y = 3x - 7$, $2y - 6x = 4$ Yes

16. State the slope of a line perpendicular to the graph of $y = 4x - 2$. $-\frac{1}{4}$

5–7   **Objective:** To write the equation, in slope–intercept form, of a line given two characteristics of the line. $y = \frac{5}{2}x - 2$

17. Write an equation of the line that passes through (2, 3) and $(-2, -7)$.

18. Write an equation of the line through $(-1, 2)$ that is parallel to the graph of $y = -x - 5$. $y = -x + 1$

5–8   **Objective:** To identify functions. To identify linear functions.

19. State whether the relation {(2, 3), (1, 0), (2, 4)} is a function. Explain. No

20. How can you show that the graph represents a function? Use the vertical-line test.

21. State whether the equation $x^2 + y^2 = 4$ represents a function. No

22. State whether the equation $4x - 3y = 12$ represents a linear function. Yes

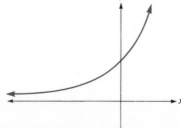

■ Questions 1 and 2 refer to the diagram in Question 3.

1. State the coordinates of point *A*. 1. (1, −1)

2. State the slope of $\overleftrightarrow{BC}$. 2. −1/2

3. Graph the point *D*(0, 2), and label it on the diagram. 3.

4. Identify the quadrant in which the point is located. Its first coordinate is negative, and the product of its coordinates is negative. 4. II

■ Questions 5 and 6 refer to the relation graphed.

5. State the domain. 5. {−2, 0, 3}

6. State the range. 6. {−1, 2}

■ State whether the ordered pair is a solution of the equation.

7. $2x + 5y = 12$; (1, 2) 7. Yes

8. $y = 3x^2$; (−1, 6) 8. No

9. Graph the equation.
$y = \frac{1}{2}x^2$ 9.

© D.C. Heath & Co.

■ Draw a line through the given point with the stated slope.

10. $m = \frac{1}{3}$ 10.

11. $m = -2$ 11.

■ Find the slope of each side of triangle *ABC*.

12. $\overline{AB}$ 12. 0

13. $\overline{BC}$ 13. 2

14. $\overline{CA}$ 14. −1

15. Find the slope of the line through the points *P*(2, −1) and *Q*(4, 5). 15. 3

16. Write the equation $2y + 3x = -6$ in slope–intercept form. 16. $y = -\frac{3}{2}x - 3$

© D.C. Heath & Co.

5–9 **Objective:** To determine whether a set of ordered pairs belongs to a linear function.

23. State whether these ordered pairs belong to a linear function. No

x	−2	0	2	4
y	9	5	9	13

24. State the slope, *y*-intercept, and equation in slope–intercept form of this linear function.
Slope: −2;
y-intercept: 5;
$y = -2x + 5$

x	2	4	−1
y	1	−3	7

■ CHAPTER 5 SELF-TEST

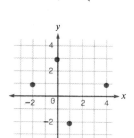

5–1 1. State the coordinates of point *A*. (−3, 2)

5–5 2. State the slope of $\overleftrightarrow{AB}$. $-\frac{5}{4}$

5–1 3. In what quadrant are the points whose *x*-coordinates are negative and *y*-coordinates are −3 times their *x*-coordinates? II

5–2 Exercises 4 and 5 refer to the graph of the relation at the right.

4. List the ordered pairs in the relation. {(4, 1), (1, −2), (0, 3), (−2, 1)}

5. State the domain and range of the relation. {4, 1, 0, −2}, {1, −2, 3}

6. Write the ordered pairs of the relation whose components are positive integers with a product of 12. {(1, 12), (2, 6), (3, 4), (4, 3), (6, 2), (12, 1)}

5–3 7. Find the missing numbers in the table of solutions for the equation $2x + y = 4$.

x	6	−3	2
y	−8	10	0

State whether the ordered pair is a solution of the equation.

8. $y = 3x + 2$, No
   (−2, 3)

9. $y = (3x)^2$, Yes
   (−1, 9)

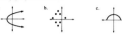
5–4 Graph each equation.

10. $3y = 2(x - 1)$ 11. $y = |2x|$

5–5 12. Find the slope of $\overleftrightarrow{MN}$. $\frac{1}{3}$

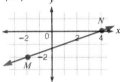

13. Draw a line with slope 2 through the point $(-1, 4)$.

5–6 14. What is the slope of any line perpendicular to $2x + 3y = 5$? $\frac{3}{2}$

Write the slope–intercept form of the equation of the line determined by these conditions.

15. Has slope $-\frac{1}{4}$ and y-intercept 3. $y = -\frac{1}{4}x + 3$

16. Is parallel to the graph of $y = 3x$ and crosses the y-axis at $(0, -1)$.
$y = 3x - 1$

5–7 17. Passes through $(1, 4)$ and $(2, 0)$. $y = -4x + 8$

18. Is perpendicular to the graph of $y = 2x + 4$ and passes through $(-2, 5)$. $y = -\frac{1}{2}x + 4$

5–8 19. Which of these graphs represent functions?

a. No   b. Yes   c. No   d. Yes   e. No

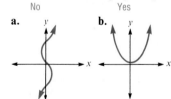

20. Do the ordered pairs determine a linear function?

x	−2	−1	0	1
y	−10	−7	−3	−1

No

5–9 21. Two temperature pairs that show how the Celsius and Fahrenheit scales are related are shown in the table. Write an equation in slope–intercept form for the Celsius temperature in terms of the Fahrenheit temperature. $C = \frac{5}{9}F - \frac{160}{9}$

	Only temperature where °C = °F	Water boils
Celsius, °C	−40	100
Fahrenheit, °F	−40	212

ADDITIONAL ANSWERS

■ **Chapter 5 Self-Test**

10. 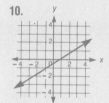   11.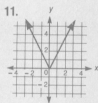

13.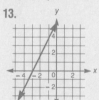

■ Questions 1 and 2 refer to the diagram in Question 3.

1. State the coordinates of point *P*.   1. (2, −1)

2. State the slope of $\overleftrightarrow{QR}$.   2. 1/4

3. Graph the point *S*(3, 1) and label it on the diagram.   3.

4. Identify the quadrant in which the point is located.   4. III
   Its first coordinate is negative, and the product of its coordinates is positive.

■ Questions 5 and 6 refer to the relation graphed.

5. State the domain.   5. {−1, 2}

6. State the range.   6. {−2, −1, 1}

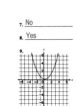

■ State whether the ordered pair is a solution of the equation.

7. $3x − 4y = 2$; (2, −1).   7. No

8. $y = \frac{1}{4}x^2$; (−4, 4)   8. Yes

9. Graph the equation.   9.
   $y = \frac{x^2}{2}$

© D.C. Heath & Co.

■ Draw a line through the given point with the stated slope.

10. $m = \frac{1}{2}$ 10.

11. $m = −3$ 11.

■ Find the slope of each side of triangle *ABC*.

12. $\overline{AB}$ 12. 3/2

13. $\overline{BC}$ 13. −1

14. $\overline{CA}$ 14. 0

15. Find the slope of the line through the points *P*(−1, 3) and *Q*(3, 5).   15. 1/2

16. Write the equation $3y − 2x = 12$ in slope-intercept form.   16. $y = \frac{2}{3}x + 4$

© D.C. Heath & Co.

■ PRACTICE FOR COLLEGE ENTRANCE TESTS

1. In the figure, the coordinates of point *A* are (3, −2). If $\overline{AB}$ is the diameter of the circle with center *O*, what are the coordinates of point *B*?

A. (−2, 3)   **B.** (2, −3)   **C.** (−3, 2)

D. (−3, −2)   **E.** (−2, −3)

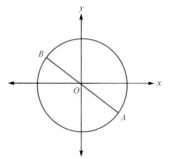

2. The coordinates of points *A* and *B* are shown in the figure. If $\overline{AB}$ and $\overline{BC}$ are the same length and $\overline{AB}$ is perpendicular to $\overline{BC}$, what are the coordinates of point *C*?

A. (2, −2)   **B.** (3, −2)   **C.** (2, −3)

D. (3, −3)   **E.** (−3, 3)

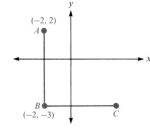

3. If the area of triangle *OPQ* is 24 square units, what is the value of *x*? (The figure is not drawn to scale.)

A. 3   **B.** 4   **C.** 6

D. 8   **E.** 12

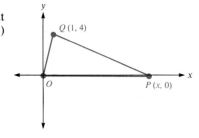

4. What is the length of $\overline{PQ}$?

A. 0.08 unit   **B.** 0.5 unit   **C.** 0.8 unit

D. 7 units   **E.** 8 units

5. Which quadrants contain pairs (*x*, *y*) that satisfy the condition $y = −x$?

A. III only   **B.** II and III only   **C.** III and IV only

D. II and IV only   **E.** I and III only

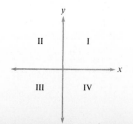

■ **Write the equation in the form y = mx + b for the line with the given characteristics.**

17. Has slope $\frac{3}{2}$ and passes through (2, 8).   17. $y = \frac{3}{2}x + 5$

18. Is parallel to the graph of $y = 3x - 4$ and passes through (1, 5).   18. $y = 3x + 2$

19. Is perpendicular to the graph of $y = \frac{1}{4}x - 3$ and passes through (0, 5).   19. $y = -4x + 5$

20. Which graph represents a function?   20. _a_

a.   b.   c.

21. State whether the ordered pairs belong to a linear function.   21. _Yes_

x	-1	0	1	2	3
y	5	3	1	-1	-3

★ **BONUS**

Write the equation of the line that is perpendicular to the line $y = -3$ and that passes through the point (1, 6).   BONUS _x = 1_

© D.C. Heath & Co.

6. The coordinates of points B and C are shown. What is the value of x?

   A. -2 B. $-2\frac{1}{2}$ C. -4

   D. $-4\frac{1}{2}$ E. -5

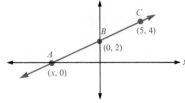

7. A line containing the points (0, 0) and (2, 3) will also contain which of the following points?

   A. (3, 2)   B. (6, 4)   C. (10, 15)   D. (12, 16)   E. (15, 20)

8. Let the symbol $\overline{X}$ represent one more than the number of digits in an integer X. If $X = 1{,}234{,}567{,}890$, then $(\overline{\overline{X}}) = \underline{\quad ? \quad}$.

   A. 0   B. 1   C. 2   D. 3   E. 4

9. If Heidi is x years old and Anita is 4 years younger, what will Anita's age be 6 years from now?

   A. $x + 2$ B. $x - 2$ C. $x - 4$ D. $x + 6$ E. $x + 10$

10. The perimeter of a 5-sided figure is 11 units. If the length of each side of the figure is increased by 3 units, what is the perimeter of the new figure?

    A. 16 units   B. 19 units   C. 26 units   D. 33 units   E. 70 units

11.

Which of the following values is the closest approximation to the product of the four numbers indicated by the arrows?

A. 1   B. $\frac{1}{2}$ C. 2   D. $\frac{1}{4}$ E. 4

12. If the odometer of an automobile reads 7777.7, what is the least number of miles the automobile must travel before all the digits will again be the same?

    A. 1000.0   B. 1111.1   C. 8888.8   D. 9999.9   E. 111.1

Strategy for Success Taking tests

On multiple-choice tests, find out whether points are deducted for wrong answers. If not, answer every question even though you are not sure which answer is right. You can pick up some extra points that way.

CHAPTER 6

CHAPTER OVERVIEW

When the graphs of two linear equations intersect in a point, the coordinates of the point are called the solution of the system. These coordinates satisfy each of the two equations. In this chapter, students learn to solve systems of two linear equations in two variables by graphing and by algebraic methods. Students learn to solve problems by setting up systems of linear equations and then solving the systems. To solve these systems, students will need algebraic skills learned in Chapters 1, 2, and 3 and graphing skills learned in Chapter 5.

Knowledge of systems of linear equations will be used in working with compound inequalities and their graphs in Chapter 9. In advanced algebra, students will study systems that contain nonlinear equations, and they will study systems that contain more than two equations and more than two variables.

6 Systems of Linear Equations

The Golden Gate Bridge is considered to be one of the most beautiful suspension bridges in the world. The main cable is in the shape of a parabola. The supporting towers are 1280 meters apart and rise 166 meters above the roadway. The lowest point of the main cable is 2 meters above the roadway. Suspension cables hang from the main cable and support the roadway.

The mathematical problems faced in the design of the bridge involved the stresses and forces that would act on the towers. The solution of the problem required a system of 33 linear equations in as many variables.

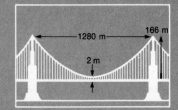

You may wish to spend two days on this section. Refer to the Pacing Chart.

PURPOSE

Many practical problems can be solved using two equations in two variables. Visualizing this process aids understanding. Therefore, solving systems of equations is first approached graphically. Other methods are introduced later in this chapter.

6–1 Solving Systems by Graphing

Preview

The Federal Communications Commission used a mobile direction finder to locate an illegal radio transmitter. The direction finder was positioned near the point where the FCC thought the transmitter was located. The antenna was then turned until it pointed in the direction from which the illegal signal was strongest. This position and direction were marked on a map. The FCC now knew that the transmitter was located somewhere along the line drawn on the map, but they could not tell at which point.

The direction finder was moved to another position and the process was repeated. The FCC knew that the illegal transmitter was located along the second direction line, too. Where do you think that the transmitter was located? Why do you think that?

Where the two lines intersected

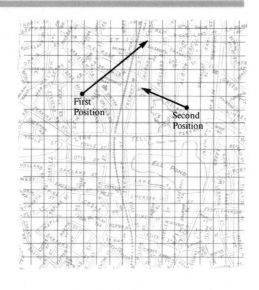

PREVIEW

Use the Preview to introduce the idea that two intersecting lines determine a single point.

The direction finder indicates the illegal transmitter is on a particular *ray*. The two rays drawn on the map meet in exactly one point although the picture of the rays must be extended before the point is located. Discuss why the direction finder was not moved in the direction of the illegal transmitter in selecting its second position.

LESSON

Emphasize that all solutions of one equation lie on one line and all solutions of the second equation lie on the second line. The one point that is a solution of the system (both equations) is the intersection of the lines.

A system of equations may consist of more than two equations. A solution must satisfy all conditions. In this lesson (and throughout the book) systems will consist of two equations.

■ LESSON

In Chapter 3 you solved problems by writing an equation in one variable. Many problems can be solved more easily by using two equations in two variables. For example, let's look at the following problem.

A rectangle is 2 times as long as it is wide. Its perimeter is 30 cm. What are the dimensions of the rectangle?

Let x = the width in centimeters.
Let y = the length in centimeters.

The first condition can be written: $y = 2x$ ("... is 2 times as long as it is wide").
The second condition can be written: $2x + 2y = 30$ ("Its perimeter is 30 cm").

There are infinitely many ordered pairs that are solutions of the first equation. These solutions lie on the graph of $y = 2x$.

There are also infinitely many ordered pairs that are solutions of the second equation, and they lie on the graph of the second equation, $2x + 2y = 30$.

Example 1. Solve this system by graphing.

$$x + y = 5$$
$$y = x + 1$$

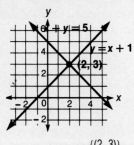

$$\{(2, 3)\}$$

Example 2. Solve this system by graphing.

$$x - y = 4$$
$$y = x - 4$$

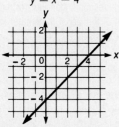

The graphs coincide. All solutions of one equation are solutions of both.

The graphs intersect at point (5, 10). The point where the two graphs intersect is a solution of both equations. Therefore, the rectangle is 5 cm wide and 10 cm long.

The pair of equations

$$y = 2x$$
$$2x + 2y = 30$$

is called a **system of equations**. The system above is a system with two equations in two variables. The **solution of the system** is an ordered pair that is a solution of each of the two equations. We have illustrated that one way of finding the solution of a system with two equations is to graph the two equations and find the points of intersection.

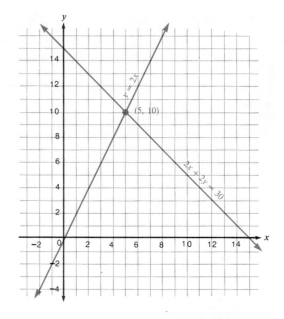

Example 1 Solve this system by graphing. $x + y = 7$
$y = 2x - 5$

Solution Graph the equations using the same pair of axes.

The point of intersection appears to be (4, 3).

Answer $\{(4, 3)\}$

Check Substitute 4 for x and 3 for y in both equations.

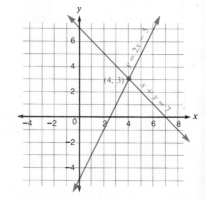

$x + y = 7$	$y = 2x - 5$
$4 + 3 \overset{?}{=} 7$	$3 \overset{?}{=} 2(4) - 5$
$7 = 7$	$3 = 3$

The answer checks in both equations.

Example 2   Solve this system by graphing. $y = 3x$
$y = 3x + 2$

Solution   Graph the equations using the same axes.

The two lines are parallel. They have no points in common. This indicates that there are no solutions of the system.

Answer $\emptyset$

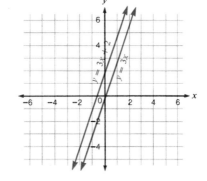

■ CLASSROOM EXERCISES

State whether the number pair is a solution of the system of equations.

1. (4, 2)   Yes
$y = x - 2$
$y = \frac{1}{2}x$

2. (−4, −8)   No
$x + y = -12$
$y = 3x$

Use the graphs to solve each of these systems.

3. $y = \frac{1}{3}x$
$x + y = 4$ {(3, 1)}

4. $x + y = 4$
$y = x$ {(2, 2)}

5. $y = \frac{1}{3}x$
$y = x$ {(0, 0)}

Solve these systems by graphing.

6. $y = -2x$
$x - y = 9$ {(3, −6)}

7. $y = x^2$
$y = x$ {(0, 0), (1, 1)}

• This is the graph of a system.

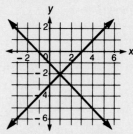

What is the solution of the system?
{(1, −2)}

• Write a system of equations that has {(3, 1)} as its solution.
(One possible answer is
$2x + y = 7$
$x - y = 2$)

CLASSROOM EXERCISES

Always check the solution in *both* equations.

ADDITIONAL ANSWERS
■ Classroom Exercises

6.
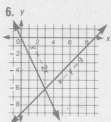

7.
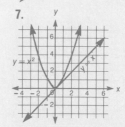

ASSIGNMENT GUIDE

Basic   1–29 odd, Review Exercises
Average   3–30 multiples of 3, 31–36 all, Review Exercises
Enriched   3–36 multiples of 3, 37–39 all, Review Exercises

6-1 SOLVING SYSTEMS BY GRAPHING

■ Solve each system of equations by graphing.

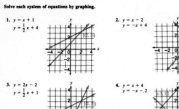

1. $y = x + 1$
   $y = \frac{1}{2}x + 4$

2. $y = x - 2$
   $y = -x + 4$

3. $y = 2x - 2$
   $y = \frac{1}{2}x + 1$

4. $y = x + 4$
   $y = -x - 2$

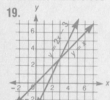

5. $y = -2x + 2$
   $y = \frac{1}{2}x - 3$

6. $y = 2x$
   $y = -x - 3$

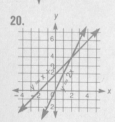

7. $y - x = 0$
   $2y - x = -4$

8. $y + 2x = 2$
   $2y + x = -2$

ADDITIONAL ANSWERS
■ Written Exercises
19.

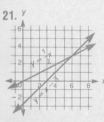

20.

21.

EXTRA PRACTICE, page 629

■ WRITTEN EXERCISES

Use the graphs at the right to solve these systems of equations.

A

1. $y = -x + 1$
   $y = \frac{1}{2}x + 4$ ⟨(−2, 3)⟩

2. $y = -x + 1$
   $y = x + 3$ ⟨(−1, 2)⟩

3. $y = \frac{1}{2}x + 4$
   $y = x + 3$ ⟨(2, 5)⟩

4. $y = -x + 1$
   $y = \frac{1}{2}x - 2$ ⟨(2, −1)⟩

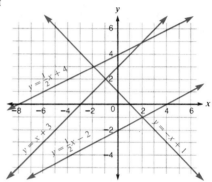

Use the graphs at the right to solve these systems of equations.

5. $y = -\frac{1}{2}x - 3$
   $y = 2x + 2$ ⟨(−2, −2)⟩

6. $y = -\frac{1}{2}x + 2$
   $y = 2x - 3$ ⟨(2, 1)⟩

7. $y = -\frac{1}{2}x + 2$
   $y = 2x + 2$ ⟨(0, 2)⟩

8. $y = -\frac{1}{2}x - 3$
   $y = 2x - 3$ ⟨(0, −3)⟩

9. $y = 2x + 2$
   $y = 2x - 3$ ∅

10. $y = -\frac{1}{2}x + 2$
    $y = -\frac{1}{2}x - 3$ ∅

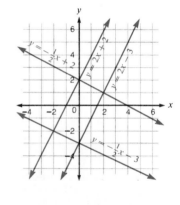

State whether the number pair is a solution of the system of equations.

11. (3, 11)
    $y = 3x + 2$
    $y = 2x + 5$ Yes

12. (2, 9)
    $y = 4x + 1$
    $y = 3x + 3$ Yes

13. (5, 3)
    $y = 2x - 7$
    $y = x - 2$ Yes

14. (12, 2)
    $y = x - 10$
    $y = 3x - 34$ Yes

15. (2, 6)
    $y = 5x - 4$
    $y = 2x - 2$ No

16. (4, 8)
    $y = 3x - 4$
    $y = x - 4$ No

17. (4, 2)
    $y + x = 6$
    $y + x = 0$ No

18. (1, 2)
    $x + 2y = 5$
    $x - 2y = 3$ No

Solve these systems of equations by graphing.

19. $y = 2x - 3$
    $y = x$ ⟨(3, 3)⟩

20. $y = x + 2$
    $y = 2x$ ⟨(2, 4)⟩

21. $y = \frac{1}{2}x$
    $y = x - 3$ ⟨(6, 3)⟩

22. $y = \frac{1}{3}x$
    $y = x - 2$ ⟨(3, 1)⟩

23. $x + y = 5$
    $x - y = 3$ ⟨(4, 1)⟩

24. $x + y = 6$
    $x - y = 4$ ⟨(5, 1)⟩

25. $2x + y = 7$
    $x + y = 3$ ⟨(4, −1)⟩

26. $x + 2y = 7$
    $x + y = 1$
    ⟨(−5, 6)⟩

260

A system of equations is given for each problem. Solve the system by graphing and then solve the problem.

27. The length of a rectangle is 3 times the width. Find the dimensions of the rectangle if its perimeter is 16 cm.

Let x = the number of centimeters in the width.
Let y = the number of centimeters in the length.

$$y = 3x$$
$$2x + 2y = 16$$

$((2, 6))$; width: 2 cm, length: 6 cm

28. Crystal is two years older than Sabrina. The sum of their ages is 10. Find their ages.

Let x = the number of years in Sabrina's age.
Let y = the number of years in Crystal's age.

$$y = x + 2$$
$$x + y = 10$$

$((4, 6))$; Sabrina's age: 4, Crystal's age: 6

29. Brian has a total of 8 nickels and dimes. Their total value is 70 cents. How many coins of each type does he have?

Let x = the number of nickels.   Let y = the number of dimes.

$$x + y = 8$$
$$5x + 10y = 70$$

$((2, 6))$; 2 nickels, 6 dimes

30. The sum of two consecutive integers is 5. What are the numbers?

Let x = the first integer.   Let y = the next integer.

$$y = x + 1$$
$$x + y = 5$$

$((2, 3))$; 2, 3

One equation is given for each problem. Write a second equation that describes the situation. Solve the system by graphing and then answer the question.

B 31. Vince charges $1 plus $3 per hour for babysitting with the Young Mother's Club. Shelley charges $3 plus $2 per hour for the same job. For how many hours worked would Vince and Shelly receive the same pay?

Let x = the number of hours each worked.
Let y = the number of dollars paid.

Vince: $y = 3x + 1$
Shelley: ?

$y = 2x + 3$; 2

32. The length of a rectangle is twice the width. Find the dimensions of the rectangle if its perimeter is 15 cm.

Let x = the number of centimeters in the width.
Let y = the number of centimeters in the length.

Length: $y = 2x$
Perimeter: ?

$2x + 2y = 15$; width: 2.5 cm, length: 5 cm

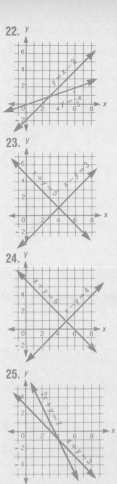

22.

23.

24.

25.

Graphs for exercises 26–39 are on pages 651 and 652.

PROBLEM–SOLVING NOTE
Checking solutions

Checking is an integral part of the problem-solving process. When applied to systems of equations, checking emphasizes that the solution must satisfy conditions stated by both equations.

Students need to be reminded that for real problems, the solutions must *also* be checked against the original conditions posed by the problem.

A *mathematical* solution may not solve the real-world situation. The student may solve correctly a wrong system for the given problem, perhaps using an equation that does not correctly represent a condition of that problem. Or a correct solution to a valid system may have to be *interpreted* to make sense for the real-world situation. For example, see the Enrichment Problems below.

ENRICHMENT PROBLEMS

- A supply of 75 legs to make 3-legged stools and 4-legged chairs is available. Suppose a woodworker wishes to make twice as many chairs as stools. How many stools and chairs could be made?
  a. Write two equations that must be satisfied in order to solve the problem.
  $3S + 4C = 75$ and $C = 2S$
  b. Find a graphical solution.
  S is between 6 and 7; C is between 13 and 14. Actually, $S = 6\frac{9}{11}$ and $C = 13\frac{7}{11}$.
  c. How is the graphical solution related to the practical solution?
  The solution to the real problem must be a whole number regardless of what the mathematical solution indicates.
  The woodworker could make 6 stools and 12 chairs with 9 legs left over, from which he could make additional stools or chairs.

- Find a graphical solution to this problem and then select an answer to fit the actual situation.
  A machine can make either of two kinds of parts. Part A requires 2 hours to make and part B 4 hours. An order for a display sample requests a total of 15 parts with as many of part B as possible. There are 39 hours available to operate the machine. How many parts of each type should be made?
  11 of part A and 4 of part B
  (The actual solution is 10.5 of part A and 4.5 of part B.)

Solve these systems of equations by graphing. There may be more than one solution.

33. $y = |x|$
$y = -\frac{1}{2}x + 3$ $\{(2, 2), (-6, 6)\}$

34. $y = x^2$
$y = x + 2$ $\{(2, 4), (-1, 1)\}$

35. $y = x^2$
$y = 2x + 3$ $\{(3, 9), (-1, 1)\}$

36. $y = (x + 2)^2$
$y = x + 8$ $\{(-4, 4), (1, 9)\}$

The following systems of equations each have one solution but the solution is difficult to find by graphing. Try to solve each system by graphing and explain what makes finding the solution difficult.

37. $2x + 3y = 8$
$6x - 3y = 4$ $\left\{\left(1\frac{1}{2}, 1\frac{2}{3}\right)\right\};$
graphs don't intersect at a grid point.

38. $y = \frac{1}{5}x - 12$
$y = \frac{1}{10}x - 2$ $\{(100, 8)\};$
graphs intersect at a point far from the origin.

39. $y = \frac{1}{9}x - \frac{1}{3}$
$y = \frac{1}{8}x - \frac{1}{2}$ $\{(12, 1)\};$
graphs are almost, but not, identical.

■ REVIEW EXERCISES

Substitute and simplify.

a	b	c	d
−2	3	−6	12

1. $(a + b) + (c + d)$ 7

2. $a - b - c$ 1 [2–2]

3. $ad \div bc + ac$ $13\frac{1}{3}$

4. $\frac{c}{a} + \frac{d}{c}$ 1 [2–5]

Solve. [3–6]

5. $3x + 2(2x - 4) = 7$ $\{2\frac{1}{7}\}$

6. $2(x + 3) + 3x = 26$ (4)

Solve each equation for the indicated variable. [3–8]

7. $3x + 4y = 24$, for x $x = \frac{24 - 4y}{3}$

8. $3x - 4y = 12$, for y $y = \frac{12 - 3x}{-4}$

Mathematics and Your Future

Teaching is an example of a field in which there are more employment opportunities for people with a background in mathematics. Teachers tend to enter the field because they like to work with people and because they wish to make a significant contribution to society. Many school systems have difficulty finding and hiring mathematics teachers; those same systems may have surpluses of teachers in other disciplines. You will find that as you increase your knowledge of mathematics, you will increase your opportunities.

OBJECTIVE 6–2

To solve systems of equations by substitution.

Class Starter Quiz
on previous section

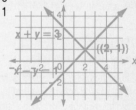

Use the graph to solve the system of equations.

1. $y = \frac{1}{2}x + \frac{5}{2}$ $\{(1, 3)\}$
 $y = 2x + 1$

2. $y = -x - 2$ $\{(-3, 1)\}$
 $y = \frac{1}{2}x + \frac{5}{2}$

State whether the number pair is a solution of the equations.

3. $\{(2, 3)\}$ No
 $x + y = 5$
 $x - y = 1$

4. $\{(-2, -7)\}$ Yes
 $y = 2x - 3$
 $y = -x - 9$

Solve this system by graphing.

5. $x + y = 3$
 $x - y = 1$

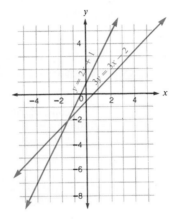

6–2 Solving Systems by Substitution

Preview

The graph of the system

$$y = 2x + 1$$
$$3y = 3x - 2$$

is shown at the right.

- What point appears to be the solution of the system?
- Does that apparent solution satisfy the system? Answers will vary.

In this lesson, you will learn a method for solving systems that does not depend on graphing.

■ LESSON

If the solutions of a system are not pairs of integers, it is often difficult to find exact answers by graphing. However, we can find exact answers by working with the equations directly.

$$y = 3x$$
$$2y = x - 5$$

The first equation indicates that the values of the expressions y and $3x$ are equal. This means that y and $3x$ can be used interchangeably. Therefore, we can substitute $3x$ for y in the second equation and get an equation in one variable that we can solve.

$$2(3x) = x - 5$$
$$6x = x - 5$$
$$5x = -5$$
$$x = -1$$

The final equation, $x = -1$, indicates that -1 is the x-coordinate of the point of intersection of the graphs of the original equations. To find the y-coordinate, substitute -1 for x in either equation of the system. For example, substituting -1 for x in the first equation gives

$$y = 3x$$
$$y = 3(-1)$$
$$y = -3$$

Therefore the solution of the system is $\{(-1, -3)\}$.

PURPOSE

Some systems of equations are solved more easily by using the substitution method.

PREVIEW

Although graphing systems of equations helps us "visualize" the solution, it may be cumbersome and inexact. This is especially apparent when solutions are fractions. Because graphing may yield only approximate solutions, an alternative method is needed. This section introduces an algebraic process for finding exact solutions.

LESSON

A basic principle of equality is used repeatedly in this lesson: If $a = b$, then a can replace b in any sentence without changing the truth value of the sentence. This replacement (or substitution) principle allows us to replace any quantity or expression with its equal.

There are shortcuts that good students may learn to use with more complex systems of equations. For example, to solve the system

$$2x + 6y = 18$$
$$2x - 4y = 13$$

first solve the second equation for $2x$ and then substitute into the first equation.

$$2x = 4y + 13$$

$$4y + 13 + 6y = 18$$

Solve for y. $10y = 5$

$$y = 0.5$$

Substitute 0.5 for y and solve for x.

$$2x = 4y + 13$$
$$= 4(0.5) + 13$$
$$= 15$$
$$x = 7.5$$

The solution is $\{(7.5, 0.5)\}$.

PROBLEM–SOLVING NOTE
Selecting a method

The substitution method of solving a system may appear particularly attractive to students after the graphical method. They may question the value of the graphical approach.

Emphasize to them the value of each method for particular circumstances (see the second Enrichment Problem on page 268). When the system has no solution or infinitely many solutions (see the next section), the graph of the system helps us understand why this occurs, whereas the substitution result is not so illuminating.

Example. Solve the system by substitution.
$$4x + 2y = 5$$
$$4x + 2y = 8$$
Substituting in the first equation.
$$4x + (8 - 4x) = 5$$
$$8 = 5$$

We already know that this solution checks in the first equation of the system. Now we must check it in the second equation.

$$2y = x - 5$$
$$2(-3) \overset{?}{=} -1 - 5$$
$$-6 = -6 \quad \text{It checks!}$$

This method of finding the solutions of systems of equations is called the **substitution method.**

Example 1   Solve the system by substitution.
$$2x + 3y = 7$$
$$y + 1 = x$$

Solution   The second equation indicates that x is equal to $y + 1$. Therefore, we substitute $y + 1$ for x in the first equation.

$$2x + 3y = 7$$
$$2(y + 1) + 3y = 7$$
$$2y + 2 + 3y = 7$$
$$5y + 2 = 7$$
$$5y = 5$$
$$y = 1$$

Now substitute 1 for y in the second equation to find the value for x.

$$y + 1 = x$$
$$1 + 1 = x$$
$$2 = x$$
$$x = 2$$

Answer $\{(2, 1)\}$

Check   We use the first equation to check the solution.

$$2x + 3y = 7$$
$$2(2) + 3(1) \overset{?}{=} 7$$
$$4 + 3 = 7 \quad \text{It checks!}$$

Mathematics and Your Future

Mathematics has been described as the "critical filter" that determines one's opportunities for the future. A sound knowledge of mathematics is necessary to succeed in the information society of the future. Those with a limited background in mathematics are more likely to have limited opportunities. The choice you make today about how much mathematics you will take in high school is very important for your future.

Problem-Solving Note *continued*

The graph shows that the lines are parallel. Therefore, they will not intersect.

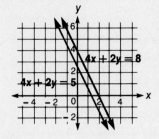

Example 2   Solve the system by substitution.

$$2x - y = 4$$
$$3x + 2y = 7$$

Solution   Solve the first equation for y.

$$2x = y + 4$$
$$2x - 4 = y$$

Substitute $2x - 4$ for y in the second equation and solve for x.

$$3x + 2y = 7$$
$$3x + 2(2x - 4) = 7$$
$$3x + 4x - 8 = 7$$
$$7x = 15$$
$$x = \frac{15}{7}$$

Substitute $\frac{15}{7}$ for x in one of the equations (the first) and solve for y.

$$2x - y = 4$$

$$2\left(\frac{15}{7}\right) - y = 4$$

$$\frac{30}{7} - y = 4$$

$$-y = 4 - \frac{30}{7}$$

$$-y = \frac{28}{7} - \frac{30}{7}$$

$$-y = -\frac{2}{7}$$

$$y = \frac{2}{7}$$

Answer $\left\{\left(\frac{15}{7}, \frac{2}{7}\right)\right\}$

Check   Use one of the equations (the second) to check.

$$3x + 2y = 7$$

$$3\left(\frac{15}{7}\right) + 2\left(\frac{2}{7}\right) \overset{?}{=} 7$$

$$\frac{45}{7} + \frac{4}{7} \overset{?}{=} 7$$

$$\frac{49}{7} = 7 \quad \text{It checks!}$$

ADDITIONAL EXAMPLES

Solve each system by substitution.

Example 1. $5x + y = 32$
$y = 3x$

Solve for x.
$5x + 3x = 32$
$8x = 32$
$x = 4$

Solve for y.
$y = 3(4) = 12$
$\{(4, 12)\}$

Example 2. $y - 3x = 7$
$y = 5x + 3$

Solve for x.
$5x + 3 - 3x = 7$
$2x = 4$
$x = 2$

Solve for y.
$y = 5(2) + 3 = 13$
$\{(2, 13)\}$

Example 3.　$3x + 4y = 23$
　　　　　　$6x - 4y = 22$

Solve for 4y.
$6x - 4y = 22$
$6x - 22 = 4y$

Solve for x.
$3x + 6x - 22 = 23$
　　　　$9x = 45$
　　　　　$x = 5$

Solve for y.
$3(5) + 4y = 23$
　　　　　$y = 2$
　　　　$\{(5, 2)\}$

CHECK UNDERSTANDING

• Solve $2x + y = 7$ for y. ($y = 7 - 2x$)
• Solve $x - 3y = 5$ for x. ($x = 3y + 5$)
• Solve the system by substitution.
　　$y = 3x + 1$　　$(\{(3, 10)\})$
　　$y = 2x + 4$

ASSIGNMENT GUIDE

Basic　　1–23 odd, Review Exercises
Average　3–36 multiples of 3, 37–41 odd,
　　　　　Review Exercises
Enriched　25–42 odd, 43–47 all, Review
　　　　　Exercises

PRACTICE WORKSHEET 30

6-2 SOLVING SYSTEMS BY SUBSTITUTION

■ Solve by substitution.

1. $y = 3x + 1$　$\{(3, 10)\}$
$x + y = 13$

2. $y = x - 10$　$\{(4, -6)\}$
$2x + y = 2$

3. $y = 6x$　$\{(1/2, 3)\}$
$4x + y = 5$

4. $x = y + 2$　$\{(-2, -4)\}$
$x - 2y = 6$

5. $y = -3x$　$\{(-1/3, 1)\}$
$y - 3x = 2$

6. $y = 3x$　$\{(1/6, 1/2)\}$
$y = 9x - 1$

7. $x = y - 20$　$\{(10, 30)\}$
$x = \frac{1}{3}y$

8. $y = 5x$　$\{(11/5, 11)\}$
$10x - y = 11$

9. $x + y = -8$　$\{(-10, 2)\}$
$x - y = -12$

10. $5x = 4y$　$\{(4/3, 5/3)\}$
$5x - y = 5$

11. $x = 4y$　$\{(100, 25)\}$
$2x - 7y = 25$

12. $x - 6y = 3$　$\{(-6, -3/2)\}$
$2x - 2y = 9$

Example 3　Solve the system by substitution.

$$2x + 3y = 7$$
$$2x - 2y = 2$$

Solution　There are several ways of doing substitution. You should look ahead to see if you can save yourself some work. For example, study the system. Note that $2x$ occurs in both equations. An easy way to proceed is to solve the first (or the second) equation for $2x$ and then substitute for $2x$ in the other equation.

First equation:　　$2x + 3y = 7$
Solve for $2x$.　　 $2x = 7 - 3y$

Substitute $(7 - 3y)$ for $2x$ in the second equation.

Second equation:　　　$2x - 2y = 2$
　　　　　　　　　$(7 - 3y) - 2y = 2$
　　　　　　　　　　　$7 - 5y = 2$
　　　　　　　　　　　　$-5y = -5$
　　　　　　　　　　　　　$y = 1$

Substitute 1 for y in the first equation and solve for x.

First equation:　　　$2x + 3y = 7$
　　　　　　　　$2x + 3(1) = 7$
　　　　　　　　　　$2x = 4$
　　　　　　　　　　　$x = 2$

Answer　$\{(2, 1)\}$

Check　The check is left to the student.

■ CLASSROOM EXERCISES

Use the first equation to make a substitution in the second equation.

1. $y = 3x + 1$
$2x + 3y = 4$
$2x + 3(3x + 1) = 4$
Solve for y.

2. $y = \frac{1}{2}x - 2$
$y - 3 = x + 2$
$\left(\frac{1}{2}x - 2\right) - 3 = x + 2$

3. $y + 6 = x$
$y + 7 = 2x$
$y + 7 = 2(y + 6)$

4. $y = \frac{x}{2}$
$2y - x = 0$
$2\left(\frac{x}{2}\right) - x = 0$

5. $x + y = 5$　$y = 5 - x$
Solve for x.

6. $x - y = -3$
$y = x + 3$

7. $3x - 2y = 6$
$y = \frac{3}{2}x - 3$

8. $3y + x = 1$
$y = \frac{1}{3} - \frac{1}{3}x$

9. $3x + 5y = 9$
$x = 3 - \frac{5}{3}y$
Solve by substitution.

10. $2x - y = 6$
$x = \frac{1}{2}y + 3$

11. $2y - 3x = 6$
$x = \frac{2}{3}y - 2$

12. $y + 2x = 1$
$x = \frac{1}{2} - \frac{1}{2}y$

13. $y = 2x$
$2x + y = 7$　$\left\{\left(\frac{7}{4}, \frac{7}{2}\right)\right\}$

14. $x = y + 2$
$3x - 2y = 8$　$\{(4, 2)\}$

15. $3x + y = -3$
$6x - 2y = 2$
$\left\{\left(-\frac{1}{3}, -2\right)\right\}$

16. $2x - y = -4$
$x + 3y = 12$
$\{(0, 4)\}$

Write a computer program using INPUT statements to solve a system of equations given in the form

$$y = m_1x + b_1$$
$$y = m_2x + b_2, \text{ where } m_1 \neq m_2$$

and where the values of m_1, b_1, m_2, and b_2 are integers or decimal fractions.

Then use the program to solve systems such as

$$y = 3x + 5$$
$$y = -0.5x - 2$$

```
10 PRINT "THIS PROGRAM
   SOLVES TWO EQUATIONS"
20 PRINT "IN THE FORM"
30 PRINT "Y = (M1)X + B1"
40 PRINT "Y = (M2)X + B2"
50 PRINT "WHAT IS THE VALUE
   OF M1";
60 INPUT M1
70 PRINT "WHAT IS THE VALUE
   OF B1";
80 INPUT B1
90 PRINT "WHAT IS THE VALUE
   OF M2";
100 INPUT M2
110 PRINT "WHAT IS THE VALUE
    OF B2";
120 INPUT B2
130 X = (B2 - B1)/(M1 - M2)
140 Y = M1 * X + B1
150 PRINT "THE SOLUTION IS
    (";X;",",";Y;")."
160 END
```

■ WRITTEN EXERCISES

Use the first equation to make a substitution in the second equation. Solve the system of equations.

A

1. $y = 3x$ $\{(4, 12)\}$
$y + 4x = 28$

2. $y = 4x$ $\{(2, 8)\}$
$y + 5x = 18$

3. $y = 2x + 3$ $\{(4, 11)\}$
$y + 3x = 23$

4. $y = 3x - 2$ $\{(5, 13)\}$
$y + x = 18$

5. $x = 2y - 4$
$x + 3y = 11$ $\{(2, 3)\}$

6. $x = 4y + 2$
$x + 2y = 14$ $\{(10, 2)\}$

7. $3x = y - 5$
$3x + 2y = 7$ $\left\{\left(-\frac{1}{3}, 4\right)\right\}$

8. $2x = y - 2$
$2x + 3y = 10$ $\left\{\left(\frac{1}{2}, 3\right)\right\}$

Solve for y.

9. $2x + 4y = 8$
$y = 2 - \frac{1}{2}x$

10. $2x + 3y = 18$
$y = 6 - \frac{2}{3}x$

11. $6x - 3y = 15$
$y = -5 + 2x$

12. $7x - 2y = 28$
$y = -14 + \frac{7}{2}x$

Solve for x.

13. $2x + 4y = 8$
$x = 4 - 2y$

14. $6x + 3y = 18$
$x = 3 - \frac{1}{2}y$

15. $3y - 6x = 15$
$x = -\frac{5}{2} + \frac{1}{2}y$

16. $2y - 7x = 28$
$x = -4 + \frac{2}{7}y$

Solve by substitution.

17. $2x + 4y = 8$
$3x + 5y = 14$
$\{(8, -2)\}$

18. $6x + 3y = 18$
$5x + 2y = 16$
$\{(4, -2)\}$

19. $6x - 3y = 15$
$4x + 5y = 3$ $\{(2, -1)\}$

20. $7x - 2y = 28$
$3x + 2y = 2$
$\left\{\left(3, -\frac{7}{2}\right)\right\}$

21. $y = 3x$
$2y + 5x = 33$ $\{(3, 9)\}$

22. $y = 5x$
$3y + x = 32$ $\{(2, 10)\}$

23. $y = x + 3$
$2y + 3x = 26$ $\{(4, 7)\}$

24. $y = x + 4$
$3y + 2x = 32$
$\{(4, 8)\}$

B

25. $x + y = 8$
$2x + 3y = 15$ $\{(9, -1)\}$

26. $y - 2x = 12$
$2y + 3x = 10$ $\{(-2, 8)\}$

27. $2x + 3y = 10$
$3x + 3y = 13$ $\left\{\left(3, \frac{4}{3}\right)\right\}$

28. $2x + 3y = 10$
$2x + 5y = 16$ $\left\{\left(\frac{1}{2}, 3\right)\right\}$

29. $y = 2x + 1$
$3y = 3x - 2$ $\left\{\left(-\frac{5}{3}, -\frac{7}{3}\right)\right\}$

30. $y = 3x - 36$
$y = 2x + 64$ $\{(100, 264)\}$

31. $x = 50 - 4y$
$5y - 2x = 1200$ $\{(-350, 100)\}$

32. $50x + 10y = 0$
$50x - 10y = 1$ $\left\{\left(\frac{1}{100}, -\frac{1}{20}\right)\right\}$

33. $y = 2 - x$
$2y + x = 5$ $\{(-1, 3)\}$

34. $x = 5 - 2y$
$3x + 10y = 11$ $\{(7, -1)\}$

35. $y = \frac{1}{2}x$
$4y + 3x = 15$ $\left\{\left(3, \frac{3}{2}\right)\right\}$

36. $2y = 3x$
$6y - 5x = 2$ $\left\{\left(\frac{1}{2}, \frac{3}{4}\right)\right\}$

Write two equations in two variables that fit the problem. Solve the system by substitution and then solve the problem.

37. The length of a rectangle is 3 times the width. Find the dimensions if the perimeter is 20 cm.   Width: 2.5 cm, length: 7.5 cm

Let $w =$ the number of centimeters in the width.
Let $l =$ the number of centimeters in the length.

38. Hal is 10 years younger than Colleen. In 4 years he will be half her age. Find their ages now.   Hal is 6, Colleen is 16

Let $h =$ the number of years in Hal's age now.
Let $c =$ the number of years in Colleen's age now.

• Solve the following system two ways.

$$4x + y = 5$$
$$x - 2y = 2$$
$$\{(\tfrac{4}{3}, -\tfrac{1}{3})\}$$

a. Substitute for x in the first equation using the second equation and solve for the y-coordinate. Then substitute the y-coordinate of the solution into the second equation to determine the x-coordinate of the solution.

b. Substitute for x in the first equation using the second equation and solve for the y-coordinate. Substitute for y in the second equation using the first equation and solve for the x-coordinate.

c. Which method seemed easier? Why? Under what conditions would one method be preferred over the other?

• Try to solve this system first by substitution and then by graphing.

$$y = x^2$$
$$y = 3x + 4$$
$$\{(-1, 1)\} \text{ and } \{(4, 16)\}$$

Graphing, though not always quick, provides a reliable method for determining approximate solutions of systems of equations as the equations become more complex.

Write two equations in two variables that fit the problem. Solve the system by substitution and then solve the problem.

39. Greg has 4 more nickels than dimes. The total value of his nickels and dimes is \$4.10. How many coins of each type does he have?

Let n = the number of nickels.   Let d = the number dimes.   26 dimes, 30 nickels

40. Tami said, "I am thinking of two numbers. The second number is 4 times the first number. If I multiply the first number by 4 and subtract that product from the product of 4 and the second number, I get 6." What two numbers was Tami thinking of?

Let x = the first number.   Let y = the second number.   First number: $\tfrac{1}{2}$,   second number: 2

41. The sum of two numbers is 80. The first number is 10 more than the second. What are the numbers?   First number: 45, second number: 35

42. Bob has a total of 30 coins, all dimes and quarters. How may coins of each type does he have if their total value is \$6.00?   10 dimes, 20 quarters

The solutions of these systems of equations are number triples, that is, a value of x, a value of y, and a value of z. Solve each system by substitution.

43. $y = z$
$y = x + z$
$x + y = 12$ $\{(0, 12, 12)\}$

44. $x = y + 2$
$x + y + z = 8$
$z = 4y$ $\{(3, 1, 4)\}$

45. $x = 6$
$y = x + z$
$2y = 4z + 9$ $\left\{\left(6, \tfrac{15}{2}, \tfrac{3}{2}\right)\right\}$

Write two equations in two variables for each of the following problems. Solve the system of equations by substitution, and then answer the question.

46. Geraldine is 3 times as old as Kate. In 10 years she will be twice as old as Kate. What are their ages today?   Kate is 10, Geraldine is 30

47. An automobile starts out on a trip at an average speed of 50 mph. A half hour later a second automobile follows the first at 55 mph. How long will it take the second automobile to catch up to the first?   5 hours

■ REVIEW EXERCISES

1. Write 37% as a decimal.   0.37

2. Write $\dfrac{7}{20}$ as a percent.   35%

3. Write 0.4 as a percent.   40%

4. What is 40% of 80?   32

5. State which of these numbers $\{-2, -1, 0, 1, 2\}$ are solutions of the equation $x^2 = x$.   0, 1   [3–1]

Solve.

6. $3x - 7 = 14$ (7)

7. $\dfrac{x + 4}{5} = 20$ (96)   [3–5]

8. $3(x - 4) = 2(4 - x)$ (4)

9. $3(2a + 1) = \dfrac{3}{2}(a - 2)$ $\left\{-\tfrac{4}{3}\right\}$ [3–6]

Class Starter Quiz
on previous section

Solve each system by substitution.

1. $y = 3x$ $\{(2, 6)\}$
$5x + y = 16$

2. $x = 2y$ $\{(4, 2)\}$
$2x + 3y = 14$

3. $y = x - 4$ $\{(7, 3)\}$
$5x + y = 38$

4. $y - x = 4$ $\{(-1, 3)\}$
$3x + 2y = 3$

5. $y = 2x - 3$ $\{(4, 5)\}$
$2x + y = 13$

6–3 Systems with No Solutions or Infinitely Many Solutions

Preview

In solving first-degree equations in one variable, we usually obtained exactly one solution. Sometimes, however, we encountered an equation that had no solution, or an equation that had many solutions.

Which of these equations have no solutions, which have one solution, and which have many solutions?

- $3x + 5 = 2x + 10$ One
- $4x + 3 = 4x + 3$ Many
- $x + 6 = x$ None
- $2(x + 3) = 2x + 6$ Many

In this lesson we will study a similar situation for systems of first-degree equations in two variables.

■ LESSON

If we attempt to solve this system by substitution, something unusual happens.

$$y = 2x$$
$$y = 2x + 3$$

First, substitute from the first equation into the second equation. $2x = 2x + 3$

Next, subtract $2x$ from both sides. $0 = 3$

The variables drop out and the resulting sentence is false. The fact that the substitution method resulted in the false sentence $0 = 3$ suggests that there is no solution to the system.

Here are the graphs of the equations.

Note that the lines have the same slope, 2. Therefore, the lines are parallel. Parallel lines have no points in common, so there are no solutions to the system of equations.

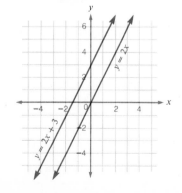

PURPOSE

The graphs of two lines may intersect in one point, no points, or an infinite number of points. Students should recognize this situation graphically and understand its implications for solving a system algebraically.

PREVIEW

The Preview exercises can serve as a brief review of solving first-degree equations in one variable. However, their principal purpose is to remind students that equations may have one solution, more than one solution (even infinitely many), or no solutions at all.

LESSON

Precise vocabulary may be introduced at the teacher's discretion. Systems of linear equations having no solutions are called *inconsistent*. For example, $y = 2x$ and $y = 2x + 1$ are inconsistent equations. It is inconsistent for y to equal both $2x$ and $2x + 1$.

Systems of linear equations that are equivalent (and whose graphs coincide) are called *dependent*. For example, $y = x + 5$ and $y - x = 5$ are dependent equations.

In this section, it is appropriate to review *equivalent expressions*. The equations of a dependent system are *equivalent*. In making an algebraic substitution, the new equation that results is *equivalent* to the original. Any solution of the new equation must be a solution of the original, and vice versa.

Example 1.

How many solutions does this system have?

$$y = 3x + 2 \qquad \text{None}$$
$$y - 3x = 6$$

The graphs are two parallel lines.

Example 2.

How many solutions does this system have?

$$y = 3x - 2 \qquad \text{One}$$
$$y - 2x = 3$$

The graphs are two lines crossing at one point (5,13).

Example 3.

How many solutions does this system have?

$$y = 5x - 10 \qquad \text{Infinitely}$$
$$\text{many}$$
$$10x - 2y = 20$$

The graphs are the same line.

Note what happens when we try to solve this system by substitution.

$$y = 2x + 3$$
$$2y - 4x = 6$$

Substitute from the first equation into the second equation.

$$2(2x + 3) - 4x = 6$$

Simplify. $\qquad 4x + 6 - 4x = 6$
$$6 = 6$$

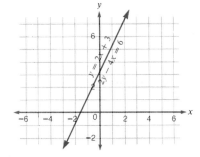

The variables again dropped out. However, this time the resulting sentence is true. The graphs of the equations show why this happened.

The graphs of the two equations are the same line. The equations are equivalent and have the same set of solutions. A system of the two equivalent equations has infinitely many solutions because the ordered pair for any point on the line is a solution for both equations.

Example 1 How many solutions does this system have?

$$y - x = 3$$
$$6 + 2x = 2y$$

Solution Solve the first equation for y. $\qquad y - x = 3$
$$y = 3 + x$$

Substitute in the second equation. $\qquad 6 + 2x = 2(3 + x)$
Solve. $\qquad 6 + 2x = 6 + 2x$
$$6 = 6$$

The variables drop out and the resulting sentence is true.

Answer The equations are equivalent and the system has infinitely many solutions.

Example 2 How many solutions does this system have?

$$y = 3x + 5$$
$$4y - 12x = 5$$

Solution Substitute in the second equation. $\qquad 4(3x + 5) - 12x = 5$
Solve. $\qquad 12x + 20 - 12x = 5$
$$20 = 5$$

The variables drop out and the resulting sentence is false.

Answer The system has no solution.

When students seek assistance, pay close attention first to their incorrect procedures. Show students why those procedures do not work. This "unlearning" helps the student to accept correct procedures.

Example 3   How many solutions does this system have?

$$y = 2x - 5$$
$$3x - y = 9$$

Solution   Substitute in the second equation.

$$3x - (2x - 5) = 9$$
$$3x - 2x + 5 = 9$$
$$x + 5 = 9$$
$$x = 4$$

Substitute 4 for x in the first equation.

$$y = 2(4) - 5$$
$$y = 3$$

The solution is $\{(4, 3)\}$.

Answer   The system has one solution.

CHECK UNDERSTANDING

Describe the graphs of the equations of a system that has
- one solution
  (The graphs are two lines crossing at one point.)
- no solutions.
  (The graphs are two parallel lines.)
- infinitely many solutions.
  (The graphs are the same line.)

CLASSROOM EXERCISES

Point out that a system consisting of two equations with different slopes must have exactly one solution. The graphs of the equation intersect in one point.

■ CLASSROOM EXERCISES

A system of equations and the graphs of the equations are given. How many solutions does each system have?

1. $x + y = 6$ 1
$y = 2x + 1$

2. $2(x - 1) = y$ Many
$2x - 2 = y$

3. $y = 2x + 1$ None
$y = 2x - 1$

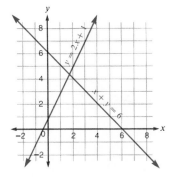
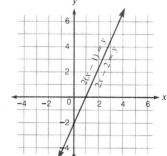
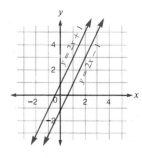

How many solutions does each system of equations have?

4. $y + x = 3$ Many
$y = 3 - x$

5. $x + y = 5$ 1
$x - y = 5$

6. $y + x = 5$ None
$y + x = 3$

7. $y - x = 3$ Many
$4y = 12 + 4x$

8. $2x + y = 10$ 1
$x + y = 8$

9. $y = 2x + 3$ None
$y = 2x - 3$

ASSIGNMENT GUIDE

Basic   1–23 odd, Review Exercises, Self–
          Quiz 1
Average   3–24 multiples of 3, 25–34 all,
          Review Exercises, Self–Quiz 1
Enriched   9–27 multiples of 3, 29–42 all,
          Review Exercises, Self–Quiz 1

PRACTICE WORKSHEET 30

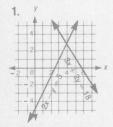

6-3 SYSTEMS WITH NO SOLUTIONS OR INFINITELY MANY SOLUTIONS

■ If possible, solve the system by substituting from the first
equation into the second equation. State the number of solutions
each system has.

1. $y = 2x - 1$ $\{(2, 3)\}$, one
   $3x - y = 3$

2. $y = 3x + 4$ None
   $6x - 2y = 7$

3. $y = 3x$ Many
   $y - 3x = 0$

4. $y = -2x + 3$ Many
   $2y + 4x = 6$

5. $y = -5x$ None
   $5x + y = 5$

6. $x = y + 8$ $\{(2, -6)\}$, one
   $4x + y = 2$

7. $2y = 5x$ None
   $4y - 10x = 3$

8. $y = 4x$ $\{(1/2, 2)\}$, one
   $2y + 8x = 8$

9. $y = 5x - 3$ None
   $5x - y = -3$

10. $2y = x + 5$ Many
   $x - 2y = -5$

11. $2x = 3y + 4$ Many
   $2x - 3y = 4$

12. $3x = 4y - 5$ None
   $2(3x) = 8y - 5$

ADDITIONAL ANSWERS

Additional Answers for the Written Exercises are on page 652.

■ **Self-Quiz 1**

1.
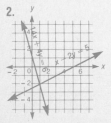

2.

■ WRITTEN EXERCISES

The graphs of equations a, b, c, d, and e are shown at the right. How many solutions does each system of equations have?

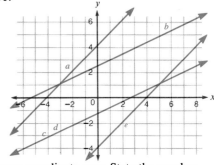

A 1. Equations a and b   1

2. Equations d and e   1

3. Equations a and e   None

4. Equations b and c   None

5. Equations c and d   Many

6. Equations d and b   None

7. Equations b and e   1

8. Equations a and c   1

Graph each pair of equations using the same coordinate axes. State the number of solutions each system has.

9. $y = 2x + 3$ None
   $y = 2x + 1$

10. $y = x + 1$ None
    $y = x - 1$

11. $x + y = 4$ 1
    $x - y = -4$

12. $x - y = 5$ 1
    $x + y = -5$

13. $y = 2x - 3$ One
    $y + 3 = 3x$

14. $y = x - 4$ Many
    $y + 4 = x$

15. $x + y = 6$ Many
    $2x + 2y = 12$

16. $y = 3x - 3$ Many
    $3y = 9x - 9$

If possible, solve the system by substituting from the first equation into the second equation. State the number of solutions each system has.

17. $y = 2x$ Many
    $2y = 4x$

18. $y = 3x$ Many
    $8y = 24x$

19. $y = 2x - 3$ Many
    $3y + 9 = 6x$

20. $y = 2x + 1$ None
    $2y - 4x + 5 = 6$

21. $y = 3x - 2$ None
    $3y + 2 = 9x$

22. $y = 2x - 3$ Many
    $2y + 6 = 4x$

23. $2y = 5x$ $\{(2, 5)\}$; 1
    $2y + 3x = 16$

24. $3y = 12x$ $\{(2, 8)\}$; 1
    $3y - 2x = 20$

B 25. $y = \frac{1}{2}x + 1$ $\left\{\left(\frac{1}{2}, \frac{5}{4}\right)\right\}$; 1
    $2y - 3x = 1$

26. $y = \frac{1}{4}x + 3$ $\{(12, 6)\}$; 1
    $8y - 3x = 12$

27. $y = 3x - 5$ Many
    $6x - 2y = 10$

28. $y = 5x - 3$ Many
    $15x - 3y = 9$

Four babysitters gave these rules for setting their fees, F.

Kari charges 3 dollars plus 2 dollars per hour. $F = 3 + 2h$

Justin charges 2 dollars plus 2 dollars per hour. $F = 2 + 2h$

Lana charges 2 dollars for every hour worked and for 1 hour of traveling. $F = 2(h + 1)$

Mike charges 2 dollars plus 3 dollars per hour. $F = 2 + 3h$

State the number of solutions each system of rules has.

29. Kari's and Justin's rules   None

30. Kari's and Lana's rules   None

31. Kari's and Mike's rules   1

32. Justin's and Lana's rules   Many

33. Justin's and Mike's rules   1

34. Lana's and Mike's rules   1

For each system described below, list all the possibilities for the number of solutions. [*Hint:* Make a sketch.]

Sample Both equations have the same y-intercept.
Answer One solution or infinitely many solutions.

35. Both equations have the same slope.
None or many

36. The equations have different slopes. 1

37. The y-intercepts are different. None or 1

38. The x-intercepts are the same. Many or 1

39. The x-intercepts are different. None or 1

40. The slopes and y-intercepts are the same.
Many

41. The slopes are different and the y-intercepts are the same. 1

42. The slopes are the same and the y-intercepts are different. None

▤ REVIEW EXERCISES

Simplify.

1. $3 + 4 \cdot 5 - 2$ 21

2. $3^2 + 4^2 + (3 + 4)^2$ 74   [1–2, 1–3]

3. $6x - 5x + 7y - y$ $x + 6y$

4. $2(a - 3) - (3a + 4)$ $-a - 10$ [2–7, 2–8]

Solve the problem by making and using a table of data.

5. What number can be added to the numerator and denominator of $\frac{1}{5}$ so that   [2–9]
the resulting fraction will be equivalent to $\frac{1}{3}$? 1

Self-Quiz 1

6-1 Solve by graphing.

1. $2x - y = 5$ $\{(4, 3)\}$
$3x + 2y = 18$

2. $x - 2y = 5$ $\{(1, -2)\}$
$14x + 4y = 6$

6-2 Solve by substitution.

3. $x = 3y$ $\{(3, 1)\}$
$2x - y = 5$

4. $y = 2x - 5$ $\{(3, 1)\}$
$3x + 2y = 11$

6-3 State whether the graphs of these systems of equations have 0, 1, or infinitely many points of intersection.

5. $3x - 2y = -1$ 1
$2x + y = 11$

6. $4x + 2y = 18$ 1
$-12x - 9y = 54$

How many solutions do these systems of equations have?

7. $8x - 4y = -32$ Many
$-2x + y = 8$

8. $3x + 2y = -5$ None
$-9x - 6y = -15$

ENRICHMENT PROBLEMS

• Graph the following systems and describe the solutions.

a. $y = |x|$
$y = x$

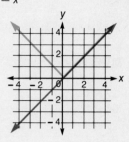

If $x > 0$, $y = |x|$ is equivalent to $y = x$, so there are infinitely many solutions of the form $\{(x, y)\}$ where $y = x$ and $x \geq 0$. If $x < 0$, there are no solutions.

b. $\dfrac{1}{x} - \dfrac{1}{y} = 0$
$y = x$

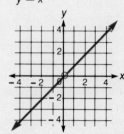

The graphs coincide except for $(0, 0)$, which is not a solution of the first equation.

• $x^2 + y^2 = 0$
$y = x^2$

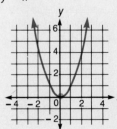

One solution, $\{(0, 0)\}$

State the number of solutions for each system of equations.

1. $y = 2x + 3$ One
    $y = -2x - 3$

2. $x + y = 5$ Infinitely many
    $y = 5 - x$

3. $y = 3x + 4$ None
    $y = 3x - 4$

4. $2x + 3y = 4$ Infinitely many
    $6x + 9y = 12$

5. $3x - 2y = 5$ None
    $2y - 3x = 6$

PURPOSE

Many problems can be solved using systems of equations. Therefore, students need to acquire skills in translating word problems into systems of equations.

PREVIEW

Students may need to review using language involving digits—tens digit, sum of digits, and so on. Students should be able to give at least two numbers that satisfy each of the clues separately. By using any *two clues together* and systematic trials, students may find that the only number that satisfies all the clues is 41.

LESSON

The word problems in this section can be solved by using only one variable. However, encourage students to use two variables and to write two equations.

OBJECTIVE 6–4

To use systems of equations to solve word problems.

You may wish to spend two days on this section. Refer to the Pacing Chart.

6–4 Problem Solving with Systems of Equations

Preview

Mr. Williams said, "I am thinking of a two-digit positive integer." Which one of these clues is sufficient to allow you to figure out Mr. Williams's number? None

Clue 1: The tens digit is 3 more than the units digit.
Clue 2: The tens digit is 4 times the units digit.
Clue 3: If the tens digit and the units digit are reversed, the new number is 27 less than the original number.
Clue 4: The sum of the digits is 5.

In this lesson we will learn how to use systems of equations to solve problems, including puzzles about digits.

■ LESSON

To solve a word problem, we must note the conditions stated in the problem. If we express these conditions as an equation containing only *one* variable, that equation can be solved and the problem answered. But if we use *two* variables, then we must write a system of two equations. Each of the equations must express a different condition stated in the problem.

Example 1   Solve the following problem.

Kent and Carol started at the same place and rode their bicycles in opposite directions. Carol rode 5 km/h faster than Kent. After 2 h they were 94 km apart. How fast did each ride?

Solution

One equation	**Two equations**
Let x = Kent's rate (km/h).	Let x = Kent's rate (km/h).
Then $x + 5$ = Carol's rate (km/h).	Let y = Carol's rate (km/h).

Diagram

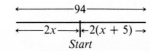

Diagram

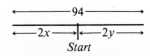

CLASSROOM STRATEGY   *Using the chalkboard*

It is essential that material written on the chalkboard be legible and illustrate the organization expected of students in their work. Therefore, periodically inspect *the work you put on the board to be sure that it meets your own standards.*

ADDITIONAL EXAMPLES

Example 1. Solve.
Troy rode his bicycle west. One hour later, Jennifer rode her bicycle in the same direction at a speed 2 miles per hour faster than Troy's. After 4 hours, Jennifer caught up to Troy. What was the speed of each cyclist? How far had each traveled?

Let x = Troy's rate in miles per hour
Let y = Jennifer's rate in miles per hour
Equations: $y = x + 2$
$4y = 5x$

Troy rode at 8 miles per hour and Jennifer rode at 10 miles per hour. Each had traveled 40 miles.

Example 2. Solve.
The digit in the tens place of a two-digit number is 3 less than twice the ones digit. If the two digits are reversed, the new number is 18 less than the original number. What is the original number?

Let t = the tens digit
Let u = the ones digit
Equations:
$$t = 2u - 3$$
$$(10t + u) - (10u + t) = 18$$
$$9t - 9u = 18$$
$$t - u = 2$$
$$(2u - 3) - u = 2$$
$$u = 5$$
$$t = 2u - 3$$
$$t = 2(5) - 3$$
$$t = 7$$

The number is 75.

Example 1   (continued)

Table

	Rate (km/h)	Time (h)	Distance (km)
Kent	x	2	$2x$
Carol	$x + 5$	2	$2(x + 5)$

Equation

$2x + 2(x + 5) = 94$
$2x + 2x + 10 = 94$
$4x + 10 = 94$
$4x = 84$
$x = 21$

$x + 5 = 26$

Table

	Rate (km/h)	Time (h)	Distance (km)
Kent	x	2	$2x$
Carol	y	2	$2y$

Equations

$y = x + 5$
$2x + 2y = 94$

Solve for x by substitution.

$2x + 2(x + 5) = 94$
$2x + 2x + 10 = 94$
$4x + 10 = 94$
$4x = 84$
$x = 21$

$y = x + 5$
$y = 21 + 5$
$y = 26$

The solution of the system is $\{(21, 26)\}$.

Answer   Kent rode 21 km/h and Carol rode 26 km/h.

There are some problems for which it is easier to use two equations than one. In this lesson we will practice using systems of equations to solve problems.

Example 2   Solve this "puzzle" problem.

The digit in the ones place of a two-digit number is 2 times the digit in the tens place. If the two digits are reversed, the new number is 27 more than the original number. What is the original number?

Solution

Let t = the tens digit and u = the ones digit. (For example, if the number were 64, t would equal 6 and u would equal 4.)

	Tens digit	Ones digit	Value
First number	t	u	$10t + u$
Second number	u	t	$10u + t$

CHECK UNDERSTANDING

• In the number 648,
what is the tens digit? (4)
what is the ones digit? (8)
what value does 4 represent?   ($4 \cdot 10$, or 40)
what value does 6 represent?   ($6 \cdot 10^2$, or 600)
what value does 8 represent?   (8)
• What number results from reversing the digits of 57? (75)
• If h represents the hundreds digit, t the tens digit, and u the ones digit, write an expression for a three-digit number.
($100h + 10t + u$)

PROBLEM–SOLVING NOTE
Understanding a problem

A difficulty many students have in solving a word problem is finding an appropriate place to start. They mistakenly believe they should be able to write equations for the problems after one or two readings.

This section emphasizes intermediate action: *making a sketch, choosing variables to represent unknowns,* and *arranging given and wanted information in a table.* A point to stress is how these actions arrange problem information in a way that makes it easier to understand that information and to see other relationships. Out of these organizing and representing steps, relationships should become apparent that can then be expressed with equations.

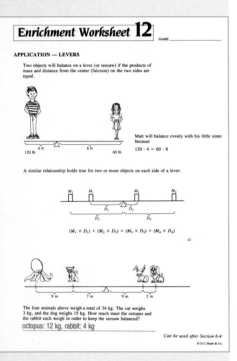

Example 2 (continued)

The two conditions given in the statement of the problem can be expressed as this system of equations.

$$u = 2t$$
$$(10u + t) = (10t + u) + 27$$

Substitute $2t$ for u in the second equation and solve for t.

$$[10(2t) + t] = (10t + 2t) + 27$$
$$21t = 12t + 27$$
$$9t = 27$$
$$t = 3$$

Solve for u.
$$u = 2t$$
$$u = 2(3)$$
$$u = 6$$

The solution of the system is $\{(3, 6)\}$.

Answer The number is 36.

Check The ones digit is 2 times the tens digit.
$63 - 36 = 27$ It checks!

■ CLASSROOM EXERCISES

Let $t =$ the tens digit and $u =$ the ones digit of a two-digit number.

1. Write an expression for the value of the number. $10t + u$

2. Write an expression for the value of the number formed by reversing the digits.
$10u + t$

Write an equation for each statement.

3. The sum of the digits of the two-digit number is 7. $t + u = 7$

4. The tens digit is 3 greater than the ones digit. $t = u + 3$

5. The sum of the number and the number formed by reversing the digits is 85.
$(10t + u) + (10u + t) = 85$

Write two equations. Solve the system and answer the questions.

6. One number is 15 greater than another. The sum of the numbers is 123. What are the numbers? $y = x + 15; x + y = 123; ((54, 69)); 54$ and 69

7. There are 8 more nickels than dimes in a stack of coins worth $4.00. How many nickels and how many dimes are there?
$n = d + 8; 10d + 5n = 400; ((24, 32)); 32$ nickels, 24 dimes

■ WRITTEN EXERCISES

Write an equation for each statement. Let t represent the tens digit and let u represent the ones digit of a two-digit number.

A **1.** The tens digit is 3 times the ones digit. $t = 3u$

ASSIGNMENT GUIDE

Basic	1–19 odd, Review Exercises
Average	3–18 multiples of 3, 21–26 all, Review Exercises
Enriched	11–23 odd, 25–29 all, Review Exercises

EXTRA PRACTICE, page 630

2. The ones digit is 3 times the tens digit. $u = 3t$

3. The ones digit is 4 more than the tens digit. $u = t + 4$

4. The tens digit is 4 more than the ones digit. $t = u + 4$

5. The two-digit number is 58. $10t + u = 58$

6. The two-digit number is 97. $10t + u = 97$

7. If the digits are reversed, the new number is 31. $10u + t = 31$

8. If the digits are reversed, the new number is 19. $10u + t = 19$

9. If the digits are reversed, the new number is 9 more than the original number. $10u + t = (10t + u) + 9$

10. If the digits are reversed, the new number is 72 more than the original number. $10u + t = (10t + u) + 72$

For each problem, let t represent the tens digit and u represent the ones digit of a two-digit number. Write two equations. Solve the system and answer the question.

11. The tens digit is 3 more than the ones digit. The sum of the digits is 5. What is the number? 41

12. The ones digit is 4 less than the tens digit. The sum of the digits is 10. What is the number? 73

13. The tens digit is three times the ones digit. The sum of the digits is 12. What is the number? 93

14. The tens digit is three times the ones digit. The sum of the digits is 8. What is the number? 62

15. The tens digit is 2 more than the ones digit. If the digits are reversed and the new number is doubled, the result is 17 more than the original number. What is the original number? 53

16. The ones digit is 3 less than the tens digit. If the digits are reversed and the new number is doubled, the result is 20 more than the original number. What is the original number? 74

Solve.

17. One number is 3 times as large as another. If their difference is 42, what are the numbers? [*Hint:* Let x and y represent the numbers.] 21 and 63

18. One number is 4 times as large as another. If their difference is 105, what are the numbers? [*Hint:* Let x and y represent the numbers.] 35 and 140

19. The length of a rectangle is 25 cm greater than its width. If the perimeter of the rectangle is 250 cm, what are the length and width?
Width: 50 cm, length: 75 cm

20. The length of a rectangle is 30 cm greater than its width. If the perimeter of the rectangle is 300 cm, what are the length and width?
Width: 60 cm, length: 90 cm

PRACTICE WORKSHEET 31

6-4 PROBLEM SOLVING WITH SYSTEMS OF EQUATIONS

■ Write an equation for each statement. Let t represent the tens digit and u the ones digit of a two-digit number.

1. The tens digit is 4 times the ones digit. $t = 4u$

2. The tens digit is 5 more than the ones digit. $t = u + 5$

3. The two-digit number is 47. $10t + u = 47$

4. If the digits are reversed, the new number is 38. $10u + t = 38$

5. If the digits are reversed, the new number is 18 more than the original number. $10u + t + 18 = 10t + u$ or $t = u + 2$

■ For each problem, let t represent the tens digit and u the ones digit of a two-digit number. Write two equations. Solve the system and answer the question.

6. The tens digit is 5 more than the ones digit. The sum of the digits is 11. What is the number? $t = u + 5, t + u = 11; 83$

7. The tens digit is 3 times the ones digit. The sum of the digits is 12. What is the number? $t = 3u, t + u = 12; 93$

8. The tens digit is 3 more than the ones digit. If the digits are reversed and the new number is doubled, the result is 13 less than the original number. What is the original number? $t = u + 3, 2(10u + t) = (10t + u) - 13; 41$

COMPUTER EXTENSION

Write a program that will give the hundreds digit, the tens digit, and the ones digit of a three-digit number that is entered into the program.

```
 10 PRINT "ENTER A THREE-DIGIT
    WHOLE NUMBER."
 20 INPUT N
 30 N1 = N/100
 40 H = INT(N1)
 50 N2 = N - 100 * H
 60 N3 = N2/10
 70 T = INT(N3)
 80 U = N2 - 10 * T
 90 PRINT "THE HUNDREDS DIGIT
    IS "; H
100 PRINT "THE TENS DIGIT
    IS "; T
110 PRINT "THE ONES DIGIT
    IS "; U
120 END
```

ENRICHMENT PROBLEMS

- A formula for converting Celsius to Fahrenheit is $F = \frac{9}{5}C + 32$. When are the two temperature scales numerically equal?

$$C = F$$
$$\text{So, } C = \frac{9}{5}C + 32$$
$$-40°F = -40°C$$

- What point on the line $y = 3x + 5$ has coordinates that are opposites? [*Hint:* What do you know about x and y at this point?]

$$y = -x$$
$$\text{So, } -x = 3x + 5$$
$$(-\tfrac{5}{4}, \tfrac{5}{4})$$

- If the tens digit and the ones digit of a two-digit number are reversed, the difference in the numbers is 63. Find all numbers for which this is true.

  70 and 7, 81 and 18, 92 and 29.

B **21.** In a two-digit number, the tens digit is 2 more than twice the ones digit. If the digits are reversed and the new number is doubled, the result is 7 less than the original number. What was the original number?   83

22. In a two-digit number, the ones digit is 3 more than twice the tens digit. If the digits are reversed, the result is 9 less than the original number tripled. What was the original number?   27

23. In a three-digit number, the hundreds digit is 1 more than the tens digit and the ones digit is 5. If the digits are reversed, the new number is 198 greater than the original number. What was the original number?   325

24. In a three-digit number, the hundreds digit is 3 more than the tens digit and the ones digit is 8. If the digits are reversed, the new number is 99 greater than the original number. What was the original number?   748

For each problem, let b represent Barbara's rate in kilometers per hour and let c represent Carl's rate in kilometers per hour. Write two equations. Solve the system and answer the question.

25. Carl jogs 4 km/h faster than Barbara walks. At noon, Carl jogged straight west and Barbara walked straight east from the same point. Two hours later they were 32 km apart. What were Carl's and Barbara's rates?
Carl's: 10 km/h, Barbara's: 6 km/h

26. Barbara runs 3 times as fast as Carl walks. At 10 A.M. Carl walked straight north and Barbara ran straight south from the same point. Two hours later they were 32 km apart. What were Barbara's and Carl's rates?
Carl's: 4 km/h, Barbara's: 12 km/h

C **27.** At noon Carl drove east at a constant rate. One hour later Barbara left from the same point following the same route as Carl and driving at a constant rate 11 km/h faster than Carl. She drove for 7 hours before she caught up to him. What were Carl's and Barbara's rates?   Carl's: 77 km/h, Barbara's: 88 km/h

28. Carl finished an auto race in 4 h. Barbara finished 10 min later with a 5 km/h slower rate. What were Carl's and Barbara's rates and what distance did each of them drive?   Carl's: 125 km/h, Barbara's: 120 km/h; 500 km

Solve.

29. Pat earns 25¢ per hour more than Carol. One weekend Carol worked 14 hours and earned $10 more than Pat who worked 11 hours. What were Pat's and Carol's hourly pay rates?   Pat's: $4.50, Carol's: $4.25

■ REVIEW EXERCISES

1. Write 125% as a decimal.   1.25

2. Write $\frac{3}{100}$ as a percent.   3%

3. Write 0.08 as a percent.   8%

4. What is 4% of 520?   20.8

Simplify.

5. $x^2 \cdot x^3$ x^5

6. $(2xy^2)(-3x^3)$ $-6x^4y^2$

7. $(x^2)^4$ x^8

[4-3, 4-5]

6–5 Solving Systems by Addition

Preview

Graph this system of linear equations.

$$y = 2x$$
$$y = x + 3$$

Now form a new equation by adding the left sides and the right sides of these equations.
It intersects the other two lines at the same point, (3, 6).

$$\begin{array}{r} y = 2x \\ y = x + 3 \\ \hline 2y = 3x + 3 \end{array}$$

Graph the new equation on the same axes that you used to graph the system. What happened?

■ LESSON

The Preview indicates that the solution of a system of equations is also a solution of the equation formed by adding the left sides and the right sides of the equations of the system. This fact is a consequence of the following property of equality.

The Addition Property of Equality

For all numbers *a*, *b*, *c*, and *d*,

$$\text{if } a = b \text{ and } c = d, \text{ then } a + c = b + d.$$

The addition property of equality provides a method of solving some systems of equations. For example, consider this system:

$$2x + y = -4$$
$$-2x + 3y = 12$$

Note that the coefficients of the *x*-terms are opposites. When the left sides and the right sides are added, the result is an equation in one variable.

$$\begin{array}{r} 2x + y = -4 \\ -2x + 3y = 12 \\ \hline 4y = 8 \end{array}$$

Solving the equation $4y = 8$ gives $y = 2$.

The second component of the ordered-pair solution of the system is 2. Substituting 2 for *y* in the first equation and solving for *x* gives the first component of that solution.

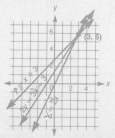

Point out that not all systems of equations can be solved by the addition method—only those in which one of the variables is eliminated by the addition.

ADDITIONAL EXAMPLES

Example 1. Solve.

$$4x - 3y = 15$$
$$-4x + 2y = -14$$

$\{(3, -1)\}$

Solve for y first.

$$-y = 1$$
$$y = -1$$
$$4x - 3(-1) = 15$$
$$4x + 3 = 15$$
$$4x = 12$$
$$x = 3$$

Example 2. Solve.

$$4a = 3b - 7$$
$$2a + 3b = 1$$

$\{(-1, 1)\}$

Rewrite the second equation.

$$4a = 3b - 7$$
$$2a = -3b + 1$$
$$6a = -6$$
$$a = -1$$
$$4(-1) = 3b - 7$$
$$-4 = 3b - 7$$
$$3 = 3b$$
$$1 = b$$

CHECK UNDERSTANDING

- Which variable is being solved for when the sides of these equations are added? (*y*)

$$3x - 2y = 14$$
$$-3x - 4y = 18$$

- What must be the value of *a* so that this system can be solved by adding? (5)

$$2x - 5y = -4$$
$$3x + ay = 19$$

$$2x + y = -4$$
$$2x + 2 = -4$$
$$2x = -6$$
$$x = -3$$

The solution of the system is $\{(-3, 2)\}$. We can check the solution by substituting in the second equation.

$$-2x + 3y = 12$$
$$-2(-3) + 3(2) \stackrel{?}{=} 12$$
$$6 + 6 = 12 \qquad \text{Check.}$$

Whenever the coefficients of one of the variables in the equations of a system are opposites, the system can be solved easily by addition.

Example 1 Solve. $2x + 3y = 7$
$\qquad\qquad\qquad x - 3y = 8$

Solution Since the coefficients of *y* are opposites, add the equations and solve for *x*.

$$2x + 3y = 7$$
$$x - 3y = 8$$
$$\overline{3x = 15}$$
$$x = 5$$

Now substitute 5 for *x* in the first equation and solve for *y*.

$$2x + 3y = 7$$
$$2(5) + 3y = 7$$
$$3y = -3$$
$$y = -1$$

Answer $\{(5, -1)\}$

Example 2 Solve. $3a = 2b + 7$
$\qquad\qquad\qquad 2b = 9 - a$

Solution *Rearrange terms and add.*

$$3a - 2b = 7$$
$$a + 2b = 9$$
$$\overline{4a = 16}$$

Solve for a. $\qquad\qquad a = 4$
Solve for b. $\qquad\qquad 3a = 2b + 7$
$$3(4) = 2b + 7$$
$$12 = 2b + 7$$
$$5 = 2b$$
$$\frac{5}{2} = b$$

Answer $\left\{\left(4, \frac{5}{2}\right)\right\}$

When beginning a new topic that depends on ideas from previous study, be sure that students recall those prerequisite ideas. Therefore, such ideas should be re-viewed immediately before they are used. That review is included in the Review Exercises in the student text.

ASSIGNMENT GUIDE

Basic   1–23 odd, 25–26, Review Exercises

Average   3–24 multiples of 3, 27–34 all, Review Exercises

Enriched   3–33 multiples of 3, 35–37 all, Review Exercises

■ CLASSROOM EXERCISES

Solve by addition.

1. $c + 2d = 6$
$-c + 3d = -1$ $\{(4, 1)\}$

2. $a + b = 7$
$a - b = 9$ $\{(8, -1)\}$

3. $5x + y = 17$
$-y = x - 1$ $\{(4, -3)\}$

■ WRITTEN EXERCISES

Solve by addition.

A

1. $-x + 2y = 1$
$x + 3y = 14$ $\{(5, 3)\}$

2. $x + 3y = 19$
$-x + 4y = 16$ $\{(4, 5)\}$

3. $x + y = 8$
$-x + y = 4$ $\{(2, 6)\}$

4. $-x + y = 5$
$x + y = 11$ $\{(3, 8)\}$

5. $x + y = 8$
$x - y = 6$ $\{(7, 1)\}$

6. $x - y = 3$
$x + y = 13$ $\{(8, 5)\}$

7. $2x - 3y = 4$
$8x + 3y = 46$ $\{(5, 2)\}$

8. $3x - 2y = 7$
$5x + 2y = 33$ $\{(5, 4)\}$

9. $2x + y = 5$
$3x - y = 15$ $\{(4, -3)\}$

10. $3x + y = 5$
$2x - y = 10$ $\{(3, -4)\}$

11. $4x + y = -6$
$3x - y = -1$ $\{(-1, -2)\}$

12. $12x + y = 6$
$9x - y = 1$ $\left\{\left(\frac{1}{3}, 2\right)\right\}$

13. $x - 2y = 7$
$-x - 3y = 18$ $\{(-3, -5)\}$

14. $-x + 3y = 3$
$x - 8y = 2$ $\{(-6, -1)\}$

15. $4x - y = 5$
$y = 3x - 3$ $\{(2, 3)\}$

16. $5x - y = 5$
$y = 2x + 1$ $\{(2, 5)\}$

17. $3x - 2y = 1$
$2y = x + 5$ $\{(3, 4)\}$

18. $4x - 3y = 6$
$3y = x + 3$ $\{(3, 2)\}$

19. $2y + x = 17$
$3y = x + 8$ $\{(7, 5)\}$

20. $2y + x = 4$
$5y = x + 14$ $\left\{\left(-\frac{8}{7}, \frac{18}{7}\right)\right\}$

21. $3y + 2x = 5$
$5x = 3y - 19$ $\{(-2, 3)\}$

22. $3y + x = 7$
$2x = 3y - 31$ $\{(-8, 5)\}$

23. $5x + 3y = 15$
$7x - 3y = -15$ $\{(0, 5)\}$

24. $3x - 4y = 9$
$2x + 4y = 6$ $\{(3, 0)\}$

For each puzzle, let x represent the first number and let y represent the second number. Write two equations and solve the puzzle.

25. I am thinking of two numbers whose sum is 11. If I subtract the second number from the first, I get 7. What are the numbers? 9 and 2

26. I am thinking of two numbers whose sum is 11. If I double the first number and then subtract the second number, I get 10. What are the numbers?
7 and 4

B

27. I am thinking of two numbers. If I double the first number and add the second number, I get 1. If I add 7 to the first number, I get the second number. What are the numbers? −2 and 5

28. I am thinking of two numbers. If I double the second number and subtract the product from the first number, I get 10. Doubling the second number gives the same result as subtracting the first number from 2. What are the numbers? 6 and −2

29. I am thinking of two numbers. If I multiply the first number by 3 and subtract twice the second number, I get 1. If I multiply the first number by 3 and add twice the second number, I get 3. What are the numbers? $\frac{2}{3}$ and $\frac{1}{2}$

PRACTICE WORKSHEET 32

6-5 SOLVING SYSTEMS

■ Solve

1. $x + 3y = 1$
$-x + 2y = 4$ $\{(-2, 1)\}$

2. $x + y = -1$
$x - y = 7$ $\{(3, -4)\}$

3. $x - 2y = 10$
$3x + 2y = -18$ $\{(-2, -6)\}$

4. $2x + 3y = 7$
$-2x + 3y = 5$ $\{(1/2, 2)\}$

5. $3x - y = 0$
$2x + y = 25$ $\{(5, 15)\}$

6. $2x - 3y = 1$
$5x + 3y = 6$ $\{(1, 1/3)\}$

7. $3x - 6y = 3$
$6x + 6y = 15$ $\{(2, 1/2)\}$

8. $x - 2y = 22$
$-x - y = 8$ $\{(2, -10)\}$

9. $x = y - 25$
$2x + y = 250$ $\{(75, 100)\}$

10. $8x + y = 11$
$y - 8x = 19$ $\{(-1/2, 15)\}$

11. $3x - y = 1$
$y = 2x$ $\{(1, 2)\}$

12. $3x = 2y + 9$
$5y = 3x + 9$ $\{(7, 6)\}$

CONCEPT EXTENSION

In adding two linear equations, the graph of the result passes through the point of intersection of the original system. In adding

$$x + 2y = 5$$
$$x - 2y = 1$$

the y-term is eliminated and you can easily solve for x. However, the y-term merely has a zero coefficient $2x + 0y = 6$. The graph of this vertical line passes through the point of intersection (3, 1) of the original system. Similarly, subtracting the second equation from the first results in $0x + 4y = 4$. This horizontal line also passes through (3, 1). This lesson provides an excellent opportunity to link the algebraic solution of a system to the graphical representation of those steps.

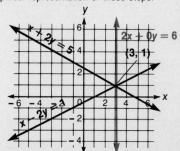

35.

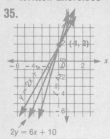

$2y = 6x + 10$

36.

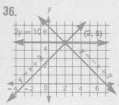

ENRICHMENT PROBLEMS

• Graph the system. $x + 3y = 5$
$x - y = 1$

a. Add the two equations.
Graph the resulting equation on the same coordinate system.

$2x + 2y = 6$

b. Add *twice* the second equation to the first.
Graph on the same coordinate system.

$3x + y = 7$

c. Add *three* times the second equation to the first and graph.

$4x = 8$

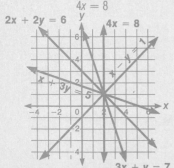

d. Explain what has happened.

All of the graphs pass through the solution of the system (2, 1). The vertical line ($4x = 8$) through that point indicates the x-value of the solution (2).

282

---

30. I am thinking of two numbers. If I multiply the first number by 2 and subtract 3 times the second number, I get 2. If I multiply the first number by 4 and add 3 times the second number, I get 1. What are the numbers? $\frac{1}{2}$ and $-\frac{1}{3}$

For each problem, write two equations, solve the equations by addition, and use the result to solve the problem.

31. John is 5 years older than Mary, and the sum of their ages is 45. How old is each? John is 25, Mary is 20

32. Bill weighs 20 pounds more than Suzanne, and the sum of their weights is 230 pounds. How much does each weigh? Bill: 125 lb, Suzanne: 105 lb

33. Sally earns $20 more per week than John, and her earnings equal $100 minus John's earnings. How much does each earn? Sally: $60, John: $40

34. The sum of the temperatures at noon for yesterday and today in Frozen Falls, Minnesota, is $-18°F$. If it was 8° warmer yesterday than today, what were the noon temperatures on the two days? Yesterday: $-5°F$, today: $-13°F$

Graph the two given equations. Then graph the equation formed by adding the left sides and right sides of the given equations. Graph all three equations on the same coordinate system.

C **35.** $y = 4x + 6$
$y = 2x + 4$

36. $y = x + 3$
$y = -x + 7$

37. a. Add the equations $y = m_1 x + b_1$ and $y = m_2 x + b_2$ and then rewrite the new equation in slope–intercept form. $y = (\frac{m_1 + m_2}{2})x + \frac{b_1 + b_2}{2}$
b. If equations with slopes 1 and 2 are added, what is the slope of the new equation? $\frac{3}{2}$
c. If equations with y-intercepts 2 and -4 are added, what is the y-intercept of the new equation? -1

■ REVIEW EXERCISES

1. Write 256,000 in scientific notation. $2.56 \cdot 10^5$ [4–4]

2. Write $2.5 \cdot 10^6$ in standard decimal notation. 2,500,000 [4–4]

Simplify.

3. $(3 \cdot 10^2) \cdot (4 \cdot 10^4)$ (Express the answer in scientific notation.) 1.2×10^7 [4–4]

4. $3a(a^2 - 2ab + b^2)$ $3a^3 - 6a^2b + 3ab^2$ [4–6]

5. $-2x(x^2 - 4x + 5)$ $-2x^3 + 8x^2 - 10x$ [4–6]

6. $\frac{6x^2}{8x^3}$ $(x \neq 0)$ $\frac{3}{4x}$ [4–8]

7. $\frac{a^2b^4}{a^5b^2}$ $(a \neq 0, b \neq 0)$ $\frac{b^2}{a^3}$ [4–8]

8. A long-distance phone call costs $.25 for the first minute plus $.15 for each additional minute. How long can you talk for $2.50? 16 minutes [4–9]

You may wish to spend two days on this section. Refer to the Pacing Chart.

To solve systems of equations by multiplication and addition.

Class Starter Quiz
on previous section

Solve by addition.

1. $x + y = 4$ $\{(-2, 6)\}$
$x - y = -8$

2. $-2x + 3y = 3$ $\{(-3, -1)\}$
$2x - 8y = 2$

3. $2x - 4y = 10$ $\{(3, -1)\}$
$3x + 4y = 5$

4. $x - y = 3$ $\{(5, 2)\}$
$-x + 4y = 3$

5. $x = 5y + 2$ $\{(7, 1)\}$
$3x + 5y = 26$

6–6 Solving Systems by Multiplication and Addition

Preview

This system of equations was in a homework assignment. It was supposed to be solved by addition.

$$4x - y = 13$$
$$x + 2y = 1$$

At first, one student thought that the textbook was wrong. When the equations were added, the new equation still had two variables.

$$4x - y = 13$$
$$\underline{x + 2y = 1}$$
$$5x + y = 14$$

Suddenly the student had an idea. What would happen if the first equation is added again? Yes

$$5x + y = 14$$
$$\underline{4x - y = 13}$$
$$9x = 27$$

Complete the work and then check the answer in the original system. Did the idea work?

■ LESSON

Suppose that we wish to solve this system by addition.

$$x + y = 9$$
$$3x - 2y = 32$$

When we add, we get this equation, which still has two variables.

$$4x - y = 41$$

None of the variables drops out because neither the coefficients of the x-terms nor the coefficients of the y-terms are opposites. However, we can use the multiplication property of equations to transform one of the equations so that some pair of coefficients are opposites. For example, if we multiply both sides of the first equation by 2, the coefficients of y in the equations become opposites.

Adding results in one equation in one variable.

$$2x + 2y = 18$$
$$\underline{3x - 2y = 32}$$
$$5x = 50$$
$$x = 10$$

Substituting 10 for x in the first equation and solving for y gives:

$$x + y = 9$$
$$10 + y = 9$$
$$y = -1$$

The solution of the system is $\{(10, -1)\}$.

PURPOSE

Multiplication and addition is an efficient method to solve any system of linear equations.

PREVIEW

Have students work through the solution. Let them explain why the method works.

The key to understanding the student's solution is the generalization that the graph of the sum of two equations passes through their point of intersection. This generalization is used twice.

LESSON

Multiplication can be considered as repeated addition. Therefore, the "multiplication and addition" method is simply an extension of the addition method for solving systems of equations.

Students should be encouraged to avoid fractional coefficients by choosing appropriate numbers to multiply by.

Solve each system.

Example 1. $x - y = 5$ $\{(8, 3)\}$
         $3x + 5y = 39$

First solve for x.

$5x - 5y = 25$
$3x + 5y = 39$
$8x = 64$
$x = 8$

Solve for y.

$8 - y = 5$
$-y = -3$
$y = 3$

Example 2. $3x - y = 2$ $\{(-1, -5)\}$
         $4x - 2y = 6$

Example 3. $4x + 3y = 6$ $\{(3, -2)\}$
         $3x - 2y = 13$

CHECK UNDERSTANDING

Here is a system of equations.

$$2x - y = 5$$
$$4x + 3y = 25$$

- How can the variable y be eliminated?
  (Multiply the first equation by 3 and add.)
- How can the variable x be eliminated?
  (Multiply the first equation by -2 and add.)
- What is the solution of the system?
  $$\{(4, 3)\}$$

Example 1   Solve. $5x - 2y = 45$
                  $3x + y = 5$

Solution   Multiply both sides of the second equation by 2.

          $5x - 2y = 45$
          $6x + 2y = 10$

       Add. $11x = 55$
       Solve for x. $x = 5$
       Substitute 5 for x in the second equation and solve for y. $3x + y = 5$
                  $3(5) + y = 5$
                  $y = -10$

Answer $\{(5, -10)\}$

Check   The check is left to the student.

Example 2   Solve. $x + y = 8$
                  $x + 2y = 13$

Solution   Multiply both sides of the first equation by -1.

          $-x - y = -8$
          $x + 2y = 13$

       Add. $y = 5$
       Substitute 5 for y in the first equation and solve for x. $x + y = 8$
                  $x + 5 = 8$
                  $x = 3$

Answer $\{(3, 5)\}$

Check   The check is left to the student.

Note, in Example 2, that multiplying both sides of the first equation by -1 and then adding the sides of the first equation to the sides of the second equation is the same as subtracting the sides of the first equation from the sides of the second equation. Just as we can solve systems by adding, we can also solve them by subtracting. Sometimes it is necessary to use the multiplication property of equations on both equations in order to make pairs of coefficients into opposites.

Example 3   Solve. $2x + 3y = -1$
                  $3x + 5y = -1$

Solution 1   Multiply both sides of the first equation by -3.
          Multiply both sides of the second equation by 2.

          $-6x + (-9y) = 3$
          $6x + 10y = -2$

       Add. $y = 1$
       Substitute 1 for y and solve for x. $2x + 3y = -1$
                  $2x + 3(1) = -1$
                  $2x = -4$
                  $x = -2$

Answer $\{(-2, 1)\}$

Check   The check is left to the student.

Pause after asking a question, giving the whole class time to get the answer. Then call on the student from whom you want the answer.

There are several ways of solving a system of equations by multiplication and addition. Here are two other solutions of the system in Example 3.

$$2x + 3y = -1$$
$$3x + 5y = -1$$

Solution 2

Multiply both sides of the first equation by 3 and the second equation by −2.

$$
\begin{array}{r}
6x + \quad 9y = -3 \\
-6x + (-10y) = \quad 2 \\
\hline
-y = -1 \\
y = 1
\end{array}
$$

Solution 3

Multiply both sides of the first equation by 5 and the second equation by −3.

$$
\begin{array}{r}
10x + \quad 15y = -5 \\
-9x + (-15y) = \quad 3 \\
\hline
x \quad\quad = -2
\end{array}
$$

Solve for x.

$$3x + 5y = -1$$
$$3x + 5(1) = -1$$
$$3x = -6$$
$$x = -2$$

Solve for y.

$$3x + 5y = -1$$
$$3(-2) + 5y = -1$$
$$5y = 5$$
$$y = 1$$

Answer $\{(-2, 1)\}$

Answer $\{(-2, 1)\}$

Here is a summary of the steps for solving a system of equations by multiplication and addition:

1. Apply the multiplication property of equations to one or both equations of the system to obtain a new system in which the coefficients of one variable are opposites.

2. Add the sides of one equation to the sides of the other equation to obtain one equation in one variable.

3. Solve for the variable.

4. Substitute the value found in step 3 for the appropriate variable in one of the original equations.

5. Solve for the other variable.

6. Check your answer in the original system.

■ CLASSROOM EXERCISES

Explain how to eliminate the *x*-terms by multiplication and addition.

Sample $3x + \ y = 5$
$6x - 4y = 7$

Answer   Multiply the first equation by −2 and add.

Multiply 1st by	−3	3
Multiply 2nd by	2	−2
and add.		

1. $x + \ y = 11$ Multiply either   2. $3x - \ y = -5$ Multiply 2nd   3. $2x + \ y = 7$
   $x + 2y = 13$ −1 and add. $x + 2y = -5$ −3 and add. $3x - 2y = 7$

In exercises 7–8, point out that either variable may be eliminated first. In exercise 7, it is easier to eliminate *c* first; in exercise 8, there is little difference in the difficulty regardless of which variable is eliminated first.

ASSIGNMENT GUIDE

Basic   1–25 odd, Review Exercises, Self-Quiz 2

Average   3–27 multiples of 3, 29–35 odd, Review Exercises, Self-Quiz 2

Enriched   3, 7, 21–36 multiples of 3, 37–42 all, Review Exercises, Self-Quiz 2

PRACTICE WORKSHEET 32

6-6 SOLVING SYSTEMS BY MULTIPLICATION AND ADDITION

■ Solve these systems by multiplication and addition.

1. $2x - y = 2$
   $2x - 2y = 3$ $\{(1/2, -1)\}$

2. $3x - 2y = 7$
   $2x - 2y = 5$ $\{(2, -1/2)\}$

3. $x + 2y = 1$
   $2x + 5y = 4$ $\{(-3, 2)\}$

4. $2x - y = 12$
   $x - 2y = 3$ $\{(7, 2)\}$

5. $x - 2y = 10$
   $3x + 4y = 10$ $\{(6, -2)\}$

6. $2x - 5y = 5$
   $4x - 5y = -5$ $\{(-5, -3)\}$

7. $3x + 4y = 6$
   $5x + 8y = 11$ $\{(1, 3/4)\}$

8. $3x - 2y = 6$
   $9x + y = 4$ $\{(2/3, -2)\}$

9. $2x + 3y = 6$
   $3x + 4y = 7$ $\{(-3, 4)\}$

10. $3x - 4y = 5$
    $12x + 12y = -1$ $\{(2/3, -3/4)\}$

11. $3x - 4y = -1$
    $2x + 3y = 22$ $\{(5, 4)\}$

12. $5x - 2y = 6$
    $7x - 5y = 15$ $\{(0, -3)\}$

285

COMPUTER EXTENSION

Write a program to solve a system of equations given in the form

$$a_1x + b_1y = c_1$$
$$a_2x + b_2y = c_2$$

where a_1, b_1, c_1 and a_2, b_2, and c_2 are integer or decimal values.

```
10 PRINT "THIS PROGRAM
   SOLVES TWO EQUATIONS"
20 PRINT "IN THE FORM"
30 PRINT "(A1)X + (B1)Y = C1"
40 PRINT "(A2)X + (B2)Y = C2"
50 PRINT "ENTER THE VALUES
   OF A1, B1, AND C1"
60 PRINT "SEPARATED BY
   COMMAS."
70 INPUT A1, B1, C1
80 PRINT "ENTER THE VALUES
   OF A2, B2, AND C2"
90 PRINT "SEPARATED BY
   COMMAS."
100 INPUT A2, B2, C2
110 IF A1 * B2<>A2 * B1 THEN 200
120 IF B1 * C2<>B2 * C1 THEN 170
130 PRINT "THE GRAPHS OF BOTH
    EQUATIONS"
140 PRINT "ARE THE SAME LINE.
    THERE ARE"
150 PRINT "INFINITELY MANY
    SOLUTIONS."
160 GO TO 230
170 PRINT "THE GRAPHS ARE
    PARALLEL LINES."
180 PRINT "THERE ARE NO
    SOLUTIONS."
190 GO TO 230
200 X = (B2 * C1 − B1 *
    C2)/(A1 * B2 − A2 * B1)
210 Y = (A1 * C2 − A2 *
    C1)/(A1 * B2 − A2 * B1)
220 PRINT "THE SOLUTION IS
    (";X;",";Y;")."
230 END
```

EXTRA PRACTICE, page 630

Explain how to eliminate the y-terms by multiplication and addition.

4. $3x + 2y = 4$ Multiply 2nd by 2
$2x − y = 3$ and add.

5. $3x − 2y = 7$ Multiply either by
$2x − 2y = 4$ -1 and add.

6. $3x + 5y = 4$
$3x + 3y = 12$

Multiply 1st by	-3	3
Multiply 2nd by	5	-5	and add

Solve by using multiplication and addition.

7. $c − 5d = 0$
$2c − 3d = 7$ $\{(5, 1)\}$

8. $3x + 5y = -1$
$2x − 6y = -10$ $\{(-2, 1)\}$

■ WRITTEN EXERCISES

Explain how to eliminate the x-terms by multiplication and addition.

A

1. $2x − y = 8$ Multiply 1st by
$6x − 5y = 12$ -3 and add.

2. $x + 2y = 18$ Multiply 1st by
$3x − 4y = 4$ -3 and add.

3. $-4x + 3y = 7$ Multiply 2nd by
$x + 2y = 12$ 4 and add.

4. $-8x + 11y = 1$ Multiply 2nd by
$4x − 3y = 7$ 2 and add.

Explain how to eliminate the y-terms by multiplication and addition.

5. $x + 2y = 18$ Multiply 1st by
$3x − 4y = 4$ 2 and add.

6. $3x − 4y = 1$ Multiply 1st by
$5x + 8y = 31$ 2 and add.

7. $3x − 5y = 15$ Multiply 1st by $\begin{array}{c|c} 3 & -3 \end{array}$
$2x − 3y = 9$ Multiply 2nd by $\begin{array}{c|c} -5 & 5 \end{array}$
and add.

8. $3x − 2y = 17$ Multiply 1st by $\begin{array}{c|c} 3 & -3 \end{array}$
$4x − 3y = 26$ Multiply 2nd by $\begin{array}{c|c} -2 & 2 \end{array}$
and add.

Solve these systems by multiplication and addition.

9. $3x + 2y = 13$
$5x + 2y = 19$ $\{(3, 2)\}$

10. $3x + 4y = 19$
$3x + 2y = 11$ $\{(1, 4)\}$

11. $3x + 3y = 3$
$4x + 2y = 18$ $\{(8, -7)\}$

12. $3x + 2y = 4$
$2x + 4y = 16$ $\{(-2, 5)\}$

13. $3x − 2y = 6$
$5x − 6y = 26$ $\{(-2, -6)\}$

14. $x − 3y = 2$
$3x − 8y = 3$ $\{(-7, -3)\}$

15. $2x − y = 3$
$6x + y = 1$ $\left\{\left(\frac{1}{2}, -2\right)\right\}$

16. $x + 10y = 1$
$-x + 2y = 5$ $\left\{\left(-4, \frac{1}{2}\right)\right\}$

17. $6x + 4y = 7$
$3x + 8y = 5$ $\left\{\left(1, \frac{1}{4}\right)\right\}$

18. $3x − 4y = 1$
$6x + 16y = 11$ $\left\{\left(\frac{5}{6}, \frac{3}{8}\right)\right\}$

19. $2x + 3y = 28$
$3x + 2y = 27$ $\{(5, 6)\}$

20. $4x + 3y = 29$
$3x + 4y = 34$ $\{(2, 7)\}$

21. $3x + 8y = 1$
$2x + 7y = 4$ $\{(-5, 2)\}$

22. $5x + 11y = 3$
$3x + 7y = 3$ $\{(-6, 3)\}$

23. $7x − 2y = 4$
$9x − 3y = 3$ $\{(2, 5)\}$

24. $8x − 5y = 4$
$5x + 3y = 27$ $\{(3, 4)\}$

25. $2x − 7y = 21$
$3x + 5y = 16$ $\{(7, -1)\}$

26. $3x + 2y = 6$
$4x − 3y = 25$ $\{(4, -3)\}$

Write each equation in the form $ax + by = c$. Then solve the system of equations.

B

27. $x + 2(x − y) = 2$
$5x = 3x + y + 3$ $\{(4, 5)\}$

28. $8x − y = 6x − 2$
$4x + y = 2x + 4$ $\left\{\left(\frac{1}{2}, 3\right)\right\}$

29. $2x − 6y = 4y + 5$
$4(x − 2y) = 3x + 1$ $\left\{\left(5, \frac{1}{2}\right)\right\}$

30. $3(x − 2y) = x + y$
$3(x − 5) = 2(y + 1)$ $\{(7, 2)\}$

Solve these systems of equations. If the system does not have exactly one solution, state whether there are no solutions or infinitely many solutions.

31. $2x + 3y = 6$
$4x + 5y = 3$ $\left\{\left(-10\frac{1}{2}, 9\right)\right\}$

32. $5x - y = 8$
$10x - 2y = 16$ Many

33. $-x + y = 7$
$x - y = 7$ None

34. $3x + 7y = 50$
$7x + 3y = 50$ $\{(5, 5)\}$

35. $y = 3$
$y = -3$ None

36. $-2x - 3y = 12$
$2x + 3y = -12$ Many

Solve.

C

37. Twice a first number plus 3 times a second number equals 87. Three times the first number minus twice the second number equals -6. What are the numbers? 12 and 21

38. Five years ago John was 3 times as old as Carla. Five years from now John will be twice as old as Carla. How old is each now? John is 35, Carla is 15

39. For a school play student tickets cost $2.00 and adult tickets cost $5.00. If ticket sales amounted to $1480 and 500 tickets were sold, how many were adult tickets and how many were student tickets? 160 adult and 340 student

40. When Judy worked 8 hours and Ben worked 10 hours, their combined pay was $80. When Judy worked 9 hours and Ben worked 6, their combined pay was $69. What was the hourly rate of pay for each? Judy's: $5, Ben's: $4

41. Solve for x and y in terms of a_1, b_1, c_1, a_2, b_2, c_2.

$x = \dfrac{b_2c_1 - b_1c_2}{b_2a_1 - b_1a_2}$ or $\dfrac{b_1c_2 - b_2c_1}{b_1a_2 - b_2a_1}$ $\quad a_1x + b_1y = c_1$
$a_2x + b_2y = c_2$ $\quad y = \dfrac{a_2c_1 - a_1c_2}{a_2b_1 - a_1b_2}$ or $\dfrac{a_1c_2 - a_2c_1}{a_1b_2 - a_2b_1}$

42. Use the results from Exercise 41 to show the computations needed to solve this system. Do not carry out the calculations.

$x = \dfrac{(-4.3) \cdot 4.68 - 5.7 \cdot 1.97}{(-4.3) \cdot 0.26 - 5.7 \cdot 2.95}$ $\quad 0.26x + 5.7y = 4.68$
$2.95x - 4.3y = 1.97$ $\quad y = \dfrac{2.95 \cdot 4.68 - 0.26 \cdot 1.97}{2.95 \cdot 5.7 - 0.26 \cdot (-4.3)}$

■ REVIEW EXERCISES

1. Identify the quadrant each point is in or the axis it is on. [5–1]

a. A II

b. B y-axis

c. C IV

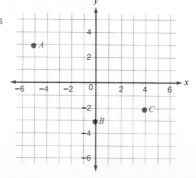

Choosing a method
Students have three distinct means to solve systems of linear equations: graphing, substitution, and multiplication/addition. At this point, it is appropriate to review and contrast these methods, listing advantages and disadvantages of each. You might write systems on the board and ask students which method they would use and why. You might pose questions such as "What method is easiest? most efficient? most reliable? Under what conditions might you solve a system by graphing? substitution? multiplication/addition?"

ENRICHMENT PROBLEM

- If k is an unknown constant, solve these systems in terms of k.

a. $x + 3y = k$
$2x - 4y = 8$ $\quad \left\{\left(\dfrac{2(k + 6)}{5}, \dfrac{k - 4}{5}\right)\right\}$

b. $kx + 2y = 3$
$x - y = 4$ $\quad \left\{\left(\dfrac{11}{k + 2}, \dfrac{3 - 4k}{k + 2}\right)\right\}$,
$k \neq -2$

2b.

4.

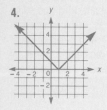

5.

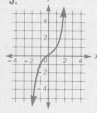

---

2. a. List the domain and range of this relation.   [5–2]

x	-2	-1	0	1	2
y	0	1	2	1	0

Domain: $\{-2, -1, 0, 1, 2\}$; range: $\{0, 1, 2\}$

b. Graph the relation.

3. Find the missing number for each solution pair.   [5–3]

$4c - d = 10$

c	0	$\overset{2.5}{?}$	2	$\overset{3}{?}$
d	$\underset{-10}{?}$	0	$\underset{-2}{?}$	2

Copy and complete the table. Then use the ordered pairs to graph the equation.   [5–4]

4. $y = |x - 1|$

x	-3	-2	-1	0	1	2	3
y	$\underset{4}{?}$	$\underset{3}{?}$	$\underset{2}{?}$	$\underset{1}{?}$	$\underset{0}{?}$	$\underset{1}{?}$	$\underset{2}{?}$

5. $y = x^3$

x	-2	-1	$-\frac{1}{2}$	0	$\frac{1}{2}$	1	2
y	$\underset{-8}{?}$	$\underset{-1}{?}$	$\underset{-\frac{1}{8}}{?}$	$\underset{0}{?}$	$\underset{\frac{1}{8}}{?}$	$\underset{1}{?}$	$\underset{8}{?}$

Self-Quiz 2

6–4   Write an equation for each statement, letting t represent the tens digit and letting u represent the ones digit of a two-digit number.

    1. The ones digit of a two-digit number is 6 more than the tens digit. $u = t + 6$

    2. A two-digit number is equal to 47. $10t + u = 47$

Solve.

    3. The ones digit of a two-digit number is 3 times the tens digit. If the digits are reversed and the new number is added to the original number, the sum is 132. Find the original number.   39

6–5   Solve by addition.

    4. $x - 3y = 5$
          $2x + 3y = 1$ $\{(2, -1)\}$

    5. $-5x + 4y = 12$
          $5x - 8y = -14$ $\left\{\left(-2, \frac{1}{2}\right)\right\}$

6–6   Solve by multiplication and addition.

    6. $-3x + 8y = 34$
          $5x - 2y = 0$ $\{(2, 5)\}$

    7. $4x + 6y = 12$
          $6x - 4y = -21$ $\left\{\left(-\frac{3}{2}, 3\right)\right\}$

You may wish to spend two days on this section. Refer to the Pacing Chart.

To use systems of equations to solve mixture problems.

Class Starter Quiz
on previous section

Solve these systems of equations.

1. $3x + 2y = 2$ $\{(-2, 4)\}$
$x + y = 2$

2. $x - 2y = 7$ $\{(3, -2)\}$
$2x + y = 4$

3. $2x - 2y = 5$ $\{(3, \frac{1}{2})\}$
$x + 4y = 5$

4. $3x - 7y = 1$ $\{(-2, -1)\}$
$2x - 9y = 5$

5. $6x - 5y = 12$ $\{(\frac{1}{3}, -2)\}$
$9x - 3y = 9$

6-7 Problem Solving — Mixture Problems

Preview

Select the most reasonable choice in each mixture situation.

- One pound of $1.34 candy is mixed with one pound of $2.50 candy. What is a reasonable price per pound for the mixture?

  $3.84   or $1.92 $1.92

- A quiz contestant is asked to select 30 coins totaling $6.00 in value from a pile of dimes and a pile of quarters. Should more dimes or quarters be selected?

  dimes   or   quarters   quarters

- Two acid solutions are to be mixed to produce a 35% acid mixture. Which choice of acid solutions could be used to make the mixture?

  90% solution and   or   10% solution and   or   20% solution and
  50% solution   25% solution   40% solution
  20% solution and 40% solution

In this lesson, you will use algebra to investigate mixture problems.

■ LESSON

Mixture problems can be solved by using two equations in two variables. However, we must be careful to distinguish among quantities, price per unit, and values of quantities. Example 1 shows how to set up a table of values that will be used to write the equations.

> **Example 1**   Solve using a system of equations.
>
> Dee paid $6.00 for 5 pounds of candy. She bought two kinds of candy, one that cost $1.10 per pound and one that cost $1.50 per pound. How many pounds of each kind did she buy?
>
> *Solution*   Let x = the number of pounds of $1.10 candy.
> Let y = the number of pounds of $1.50 candy.
>
> **Table**
>
> | | Number of pounds | Cost per pound | Value in dollars |
> |---|---|---|---|
> | $1.10 candy | x | 1.10 | $1.1x$ |
> | $1.50 candy | y | 1.50 | $1.5y$ |
> | Mixture | 5 | 1.20 | 6.00 |

PURPOSE

Mixture problems provide an opportunity to apply algebraic skills to practical situations. Systems of equations are useful in a variety of problem situations, including those involving mixture.

PREVIEW

Students should be able to answer the first question by realizing that the cost per pound of the mixture must be between the costs per pound of the candies that were mixed. ($1.92)

In the second question, students may test extremes. For example, 30 dimes are worth $3, while 30 quarters are worth $7.50. Since $7.50 is closer to $6 than $3 is, more quarters than dimes are needed to make $6.

In the third question, they should realize that the percent of acid in a mixture is between the percents of the solutions that were mixed. This fact eliminates the first two choices from consideration.

LESSON

Emphasize using a table to organize information in solving problems. Point out that the value (V) of a product equals the cost per pound (c) times the number of pounds (p).

$$V = cp$$

This is the same basic structure as other problems involving rates. For example, distance-rate-time problems use the formula

$$d = rt$$

Example 1. Solve using a system of equations. A fancy mix of nuts costing $4.59 per pound is mixed with peanuts costing $1.25 per pound to make a 10-pound mixture costing $3.99 per pound. How many pounds of each kind of nut are needed?

Let x = the number of pounds of fancy mix.
Let y = the number of pounds of peanuts.

	Number of pounds	Cost per pound	Value in dollars
Fancy mix	x	4.59	$4.59x$
Peanuts	y	1.25	$1.25y$
Mixture	10 ,	3.99	39.90

System of equations:

$$x + y = 10$$
$$4.59x + 1.25y = 39.90$$

Solve the system.

$$-1.25x - 1.25y = -12.5$$
$$\underline{4.59x + 1.25y = 39.90}$$
$$3.34x \qquad = 27.4$$
$$x \approx 8.2$$
$$y \approx 1.8$$

Use 8.2 pounds of the fancy mix and 1.8 pounds of peanuts.

Example 1 (continued)

System of equations
$$x + y = 5$$
$$1.1x + 1.5y = 6$$

Solve the system.

Multiply the first equation by 1.5.	$1.5x + 1.5y = \quad 7.50$
Multiply the second equation by -1.	$\underline{-1.1x - 1.5y = -6.00}$
Add.	$0.4x \qquad = \quad 1.50$
Solve for x.	$x = \quad 3.75$
Substitute in the first equation.	$3.75 + y = \quad 5$
Solve for y.	$y = \quad 1.25$

The solution of the system is $\{(3.75, 1.25)\}$.

Answer Dee bought 1.25 pounds of the $1.50 per pound candy and 3.75 pounds of the $1.10 per pound candy.

Check $1.25 + 3.75 = 5$

1.25 pounds of the $1.50 per pound candy is worth $1.875 and 3.75 pounds of the $1.10 per pound candy is worth $4.125. Together they are worth $1.875 + $4.125, or $6.00. The answer checks.

Example 2 Solve using a system of equations.

Tom wanted to mix antifreeze that was 60% alcohol with antifreeze that was 40% alcohol to make a solution that was 52% alcohol. How much of the alcohol solution was needed to make 5 liters of the new solution?

Solution Let x = the number of liters of the 60% solution.
Let y = the number of liters of the 40% solution.

Table

	Number of liters of solution	Number of liters of alcohol
60% solution	x	$0.6x$
40% solution	y	$0.4y$
52% solution	5	$0.52(5)$

System of equations
$$x + y = 5$$
$$0.6x + 0.4y = 0.52(5)$$

Solve the system.

Multiply the first equation by -0.4.	$-0.4x + 0.4y = -2$
Add the second equation.	$\underline{0.6x + 0.4y = \quad 2.6}$
	$0.2x \qquad = \quad 0.6$
Solve for x.	$x = \quad 3$

Example 2   (continued)

$$x + y = 5$$

Substitute in the first equation. $3 + y = 5$

Solve for y. $y = 2$

The solution of the system is $\{(3, 2)\}$.

Answer   Tom must mix 2 liters of the 40% solution with 3 liters of the 60% solution.

Check   The final solution will have $2 + 3 = 5$ liters. There are $0.4(2) = 0.8$ liters of alcohol in the 2 liters of the 40% solution, and $0.6(3) = 1.8$ liters of alcohol in 3 liters of the 60% solution. There are $0.8 + 1.8 = 2.6$ liters of alcohol in the final solution and $2.6 \div 5 = 0.52 = 52\%$. It checks.

■ CLASSROOM EXERCISES

Suppose that solution A is 55% alcohol in water and solution B is 70% alcohol in water. Answer these questions.

1. **a.** How many milliliters of alcohol are in 100 milliliters of solution A? 55
   b. How many milliliters of alcohol are in 40 milliliters of solution B? 28

2. **a.** If 40 milliliters of solution A are mixed with 60 milliliters of solution B, how many milliliters of alcohol are in the new solution? 64
   b. What percent of the new solution is alcohol? 64%

3. How many liters of alcohol are in x liters of solution A? 0.55x

4. How many liters of alcohol are in y liters of solution B? 0.7y

5. **a.** How many liters of alcohol are in a mixture of x liters of solution A and y liters of solution B? 0.55x + 0.7y
   b. How many liters of the new solution are there? $x + y$

6. Write a system of equations for this problem: How many liters of solutions A and B are needed to make 10 liters of a solution that is 60% alcohol?
   $x + y = 10$ $0.55x + 0.7y = 0.6(10)$

■ WRITTEN EXERCISES

1. A birdseed mixture contains two kinds of seeds. Type A costs 20¢ per pound and type B costs 40¢ per pound.
   a. How much would x pounds of type A seed cost? 20x cents
   b. How much would x pounds of type A seed and y pounds of type B seed cost? (20x + 40y) cents
   c. How many pounds of seed are in a mixture of x pounds of type A seed and y pounds of type B seed? $x + y$
   d. Write an equation for this condition: A 10-pound mixture contains x pounds of type A seed and y pounds of type B seed. $x + y = 10$
   e. Write an equation for this condition: The cost of a mixture of x pounds of type A seed and y pounds of type B seed is $3.50. 20x + 40y = 350

ADDITIONAL EXAMPLES

Example 2. Solve using a system of equations. An alloy that is 30% copper is mixed with an alloy that is 70% copper to produce 50 kilograms of an alloy that is 60% copper. How many kilograms of each type of alloy were used?

Let x represent the number of kilograms of the first alloy.

Let y represent the number of kilograms of the second alloy.

	Percent copper	Kilograms of alloy	Kilograms of copper
First alloy	30%	x	0.30x
Second alloy	70%	y	0.70y
New alloy	60%	50	(0.60)(50)

System of equations:

$$x + y = 50$$
$$0.30x + 0.70y = (0.60)(50)$$

Solve the system.

$$-0.30x - 0.30y = -15$$
$$\underline{0.30x + 0.70y = 30}$$
$$0.40y = 15$$
$$y = 37.5$$
$$x = 12.5$$

Use 12.5 kg of the alloy that is 30% copper and 37.5 kg of the alloy that is 70% copper.

CHECK UNDERSTANDING

- 10 liters of a 16%-acid solution are mixed with 6 liters of a 20%-acid solution. Estimate the percent of acid in the mixture.

(All students should be able to state that the percent of acid is between 16% and 20%. Most students should also be able to determine that the percent is nearer to 16% than to 20%, since there is more of the 16% solution.)

ASSIGNMENT GUIDE

Basic   1–13 odd, Review Exercises
Average   3–19 odd, Review Exercises
Enriched   3–18 multiples of 3, 20–23 all,
            Review Exercises

PRACTICE WORKSHEET 33

6-7 PROBLEM SOLVING — MIXTURE PROBLEMS

■ Write two equations. Solve the system and answer the question.

1. Some $1.00-per-ounce spice and some $2.00-per-ounce spice are to be mixed to produce 12 ounces of a mixture worth $1.25 per ounce. How many ounces of each spice should be used?

9 oz of $1.00/oz
3 oz of $2.00/oz

	Number of ounces	Value in dollars
$1.00/oz spice	x	1x
$2.00/oz spice	y	2y
$1.25/oz mixture	12	1.25(12)

2. Some 40¢-per-pound bird feed is mixed with 60¢-per-pound bird feed to produce 100 pounds of a mixture worth 53¢ per pound. How many pounds of each type of bird feed are used?

35 lb of 40¢/lb
65 lb of 60¢/lb

	Number of pounds	Value in cents
40¢/lb feed	x	40x
60¢/lb feed	y	60y
53¢/lb mixture	100	53(100)

3. Cheeses costing $2.50 per pound and $3.00 per pound are mixed to produce a 25-pound cheese tray that sells for $2.76 per pound. How many pounds of each type of cheese are used?

12 lb of $2.50/lb
13 lb of $3.00/lb

4. Milk that is 6% butterfat is mixed with milk that is 1% butterfat to produce 100 gallons of milk that is 2% butterfat. How many gallons of each type of milk are used?

20 gal of 6%
80 gal of 1%

5. Sandwich meats costing $2.75 per pound and $3.50 per pound are mixed to produce 50 pounds of mixed packages that sell for $3.32 per pound. How many pounds of each type of sandwich meat are used?

12 lb of $2.75/lb
38 lb of $3.50/lb

2. A pet food contains two ingredients, cereal and meat. The cereal costs 25¢ per pound and the meat costs 75¢ per pound.
   a. How much would x pounds of cereal cost?   25x cents
   b. What is the total cost of x pounds of cereal and y pounds of meat?   (25x + 75y) cents
   c. How many pounds of ingredients are in a mixture of x pounds of cereal and y pounds of meat?   x + y
   d. Write an equation for this condition: A 20-pound bag of pet food contains x pounds of cereal and y pounds of meat.   x + y = 20
   e. Write an equation for this condition: The cost of a mixture of x pounds of cereal and y pounds of meat is $7.00.   25x + 75y = 700

Write two equations. Solve the system and answer the question.

3. Some $4.00-per-pound candy and some $1.00-per-pound candy are to be mixed to produce 5 pounds of a mixture that sells for $2.20 per pound. How many pounds of each type of candy should be used?

	Number of pounds	Value in dollars
$4.00/lb candy	x	4x
$1.00/lb candy	y	1y
$2.20/lb candy	5	(2.2)5

2 lb of $4/lb, 3 lb of $1/lb

4. Some $4.00-per-pound candy and some $1.00-per-pound candy are to be mixed to produce 5 pounds of a mixture that sells for $2.80 per pound. How many pounds of each type of candy should be used?

	Number of pounds	Value in dollars
$4.00/lb candy	x	4x
$1.00/lb candy	y	1y
$2.80/lb candy	5	(2.8)5

3 lb of $4/lb, 2 lb of $1/lb

5. A shopowner plans to mix $2.00-per-pound nuts and $3.00-per-pound nuts to produce 10 pounds of a mixture that sells for $2.30 per pound. How many pounds of each type of nuts are required?   7 lb of $2/lb, 3 lb of $3/lb

6. A social club mixed some $3.00-per-pound tea and some $4.00-per-pound tea to produce a 2-pound package of a mixture valued at $6.25. How many pounds of each type of tea were used?   1.75 lb of $3/lb, 0.25 lb of $4/lb

7. Some $1.75-per-pound coffee and some $2.25-per-pound coffee are mixed to produce 100 pounds of a coffee mixture valued at $1.98 per pound. How many pounds of each type of coffee were used?   54 lb of $1.75/lb, 46 lb of $2.25/lb

8. Cheeses costing $2.75 per pound and $3.50 per pound are mixed to produce a 50-pound cheese tray that sells for $2.96 per pound. How many pounds of each type of cheese are used?   36 lb of $2.75/lb, 14 lb of $3.50/lb

In mixture and rate problems, students must realize that some quantities are not additive.

Volume: x mL $+ y$ mL $= (x + y)$ mL
Distance: x mi $- 2y$ mi $= (x - 2y)$ mi

BUT

Rates: Speeds of 40 mph and 60 mph usually result in a combined speed of neither 100 mph nor 50 mph.

Percents: A 40% solution added to a 60% solution usually results in neither a 100% solution nor a 50% solution.

You might emphasize this point with the following problem:

If a race car is driven at 30 mph around a 1-mile track for one lap, how fast must the car go on a second lap to average 60 mph for the two laps? (There is no solution. $\frac{d}{r} = t$, so $\frac{1\text{ mi}}{30\text{ mph}} =$ 2 min; but so does $\frac{2\text{ mi}}{60\text{ mph}} = 2$ min. There is no possible rate x for the second lap such that $\frac{1\text{ mi}}{x} = 0$ min.)

To help students write a correct algebraic equation for any situation, you might encourage them to first write a concept equation using a quantity that must be preserved throughout the problem. The following concept equations can be written for Example 1.

Pounds of $1.10 candy $+$ Pounds of $1.50 candy $=$ Pounds of mixture

Value of x pounds of $1.10 candy $+$ Value of y pounds of $1.50 candy $=$ Value of mixture

9. Sandwich meats costing $3.25 per pound and $2.25 per pound are mixed to produce 100 pounds of party platters that sell for $2.69 per pound. How many pounds of each type of sandwich meat are used?
44 lb of $3.25/lb, 56 lb of $2.25/lb

10. Ground beef costing $2.40 per pound is mixed with ground pork costing $1.80 per pound to produce 60 pounds of a meatloaf mixture that sells for $1.99 per pound. How many pounds of each type of meat are used?
19 lb of beef, 41 lb of pork

11. Grass seed valued at $3.00-per-pound is mixed with $2.20-per-pound grass seed to produce 25 pounds of a mixture that sells for $2.40 per pound. How many pounds of each type of grass seed are used?
6.25 lb of $3/lb, 18.75 lb of $2.20/lb

12. Milk that is 9% butterfat is mixed with milk that is 1.5% butterfat to produce 100 liters of milk that is 3% butterfat. How much milk of each type is used?

	Liters of milk	Liters of butterfat
Milk with 9% butterfat	x	$0.09x$
Milk with 1.5% butterfat	y	$0.015y$
Milk with 3% butterfat	100	$(0.03)100$

20 L of 9%, 80 L of 1.5%

13. An alloy that is 40% copper is mixed with an alloy that is 60% copper to produce 80 kilograms of an alloy that is 56% copper. How many kilograms of each type of alloy are used? 16 kg of 40%, 64 kg of 60%

B 14. Liquid that is 80% antifreeze is mixed with a liquid that is 40% antifreeze to produce 10 L of a liquid that is 76% antifreeze. How many liters of each liquid are used? 9 L of 80%, 1 L of 40%

15. Liquid that is 80% antifreeze is mixed with a liquid that is 40% antifreeze to produce 10 L of a liquid that is 50% antifreeze. How many liters of each liquid are used? $2\frac{1}{2}$ L of 80%, $7\frac{1}{2}$ L of 40%

16. An investor put a total of $10,000 in stocks and bonds for one year. The stocks paid $9\frac{1}{2}$% and the bonds paid 6%. The earnings for the year were $824. How much was invested in stocks and how much in bonds?
$6400 in stocks, $3600 in bonds

17. A chemist mixed a solution that was 25% acid with a solution that was 40% acid and got 50 mL of a solution that was 37% acid. How many milliliters of each solution were used? 10 mL of 25%, 40 mL of 40%

18. A 10-L container is filled with an alcohol–water solution that is 40% alcohol. How much of the solution should be poured out and replaced with pure water in order to have a container filled with a solution that is 35% alcohol? 1.25 L

19. A 100-L container is filled with a solution that is 20% acid. How much of the solution should be poured out and replaced with pure acid in order for the container to have a solution that is 25% acid? 6.25 L

ENRICHMENT PROBLEM

- An unknown quantity of 44% sulfuric acid solution is mixed with an unknown quantity of 72% sulfuric acid solution. What can you say about the sulfuric acid concentration of the mixture?

  The concentration is between 44% and 72%.

- Two jars of equal volume are half full of water and vinegar respectively. A test tube full of water is removed from the water jar and mixed with the vinegar. A test tube full of this mixture is transferred back to the water jar. The original volumes have been restored. Is there more water in the vinegar than vinegar in the water?

  No; they are the same.

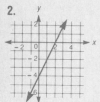
C 20. A 12-L gasoline–alcohol solution is 10% alcohol. How many liters of gasoline must be added to the solution to make it 8% alcohol? 3

21. A butcher had 100 lb of ground beef that was 85% lean (15% fat). How many pounds of fat must be added to the ground beef so that the mixture can be sold as 70% lean (30% fat)? (Round your answer to the nearest pound.) 21

22. How many pounds of nuts that cost $2.25/lb must be added to 100 lb of nuts that cost $4.75/lb to make a mixture that costs $3.25/lb? 150

23. How many liters of a 90%-alcohol solution must be added to 3 L of a 60%-alcohol solution to obtain a 72%-alcohol solution? 2

■ REVIEW EXERCISES

1. Give the slopes of the lines. Write "none" if the line has no slope. [5–6]

    a. $\overleftrightarrow{AB}$ 1
    b. $\overleftrightarrow{BC}$ $-\frac{1}{3}$
    c. $\overleftrightarrow{AC}$ None

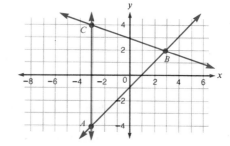

2. Graph the line with slope 2 and y-intercept -4. [5–6]

3. State the slope and y-intercept of the line for the equation $y = \frac{2}{3}x - 6$. $\frac{2}{3}, -6$ [5–6]

4. Write the equation in slope–intercept form of the line with slope 2 that passes through (2, 3). $y = 2x - 1$ [5–7]

5. State whether the relation {(2, 3), (3, 4), (4, 4)} is a function. Yes [5–8]

6. State whether the ordered pairs belong to a linear function. [5–8]

x	-3	-1	0	1
y	2	1	0	1

    No

7. Cities A and B are 380 mi apart. At noon, a train leaves city A heading for city B at 50 mph. An hour later, another train leaves city B heading for city A at 60 mph. When will the trains meet each other? How far from city A will they be? 4 P.M., 200 mi [4–7]

EXTENSION   Systematic trials on a computer

The program below illustrates how a computer can be used to solve a problem using systematic trials in BASIC. It uses the greatest integer function to round the cost to the nearest cent.

A 10-lb mixture of nuts is to consist of nuts that sell for $4.59 per lb and peanuts that sell for $1.25 per lb. If the mixture is to be sold for $3.99 per lb, how many pounds of nuts and how many pounds of peanuts should be in the mixture?

```
10  PRINT "LB AT", "LB AT", "MIX"

20  PRINT "$4.59", "$1.25", "COST"

30  FOR X = 0 TO 10

40  Y = 10 - X

50  Z = (4.59 * X + 1.25 * Y)/10

60  Z = (INT(100 * Z + 0.5))/100

70  PRINT X, Y, Z

80  NEXT X

90  END
```

[Commas in PRINT statements separate the output into columns, so line 10 prints the table headings.]

[Lines 30 and 80 set up a ''FOR-NEXT'' loop in which X is successively given the values 0, 1, 2, . . . , 10. The computations in lines 40 through 70 are made on these successive values of X.]

[Line 50 computes the price per pound of the mixture.]

[Line 60 rounds the price per pound to the nearest cent.]

[Line 70 prints the table.]

Run the program.

Notice that the cost of the mixture is below $3.99 when there are 8 lb of $4.59 nuts and above $3.99 when there are 9 lb of $4.59 nuts. Therefore, the correct answer is between 8 and 9 lb of $4.59 nuts.

To get an approximation to the answer between successive tenths of a pound, change line 30 to the following and run the program again.

```
30 FOR X = 8 TO 9 STEP 0.1
```

What do you get for an answer?   8.2 lb at $4.59, 1.8 lb at $1.25

■ CHAPTER SUMMARY

- **Vocabulary**

system of equations	[page 258]
solution of a system of equations	[page 258]
substitution method of solving systems	[page 264]

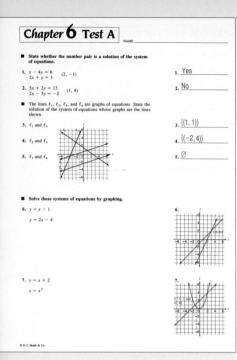

Chapter 6 Test A

NAME _____

■ State whether the number pair is a solution of the system of equations.

1. $x - 4y = 6$
   $2x + y = 3$ $(2, -1)$

   1. Yes

2. $5x + 2y = 13$
   $2x - 3y = -2$ $(1, 4)$

   2. No

■ The lines ℓ_1, ℓ_2, ℓ_3, and ℓ_4 are graphs of equations. State the solution of the system of equations whose graphs are the lines shown.

3. ℓ_1 and ℓ_3

   3. $\{(1, 1)\}$

4. ℓ_2 and ℓ_3

   4. $\{(-2, 4)\}$

5. ℓ_1 and ℓ_4

   5. $\varnothing$

■ Solve these systems of equations by graphing.

6. $y = x - 1$
   $y = 2x - 4$

   6.

7. $y = x + 2$
   $y = x^2$

   7.

© D.C. Heath & Co.

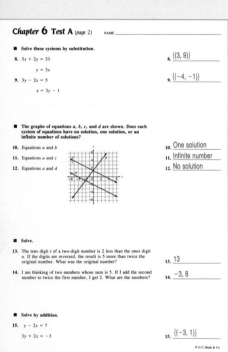

Chapter 6 Test A (page 2)

NAME _____

■ Solve these systems by substitution.

8. $5x + 2y = 33$
   $y = 3x$

   8. $\{(3, 9)\}$

9. $3y - 2x = 5$
   $x = 3y - 1$

   9. $\{(-4, -1)\}$

■ The graphs of equations a, b, c, and d are shown. Does each system of equations have no solution, one solution, or an infinite number of solutions?

10. Equations a and b

    10. One solution

11. Equations a and c

    11. Infinite number

12. Equations a and d

    12. No solution

■ Solve.

13. The tens digit t of a two-digit number is 2 less than the ones digit u. If the digits are reversed, the result is 5 more than twice the original number. What was the original number?

    13. 13

14. I am thinking of two numbers whose sum is 5. If I add the second number to twice the first number, I get 2. What are the numbers?

    14. $-3, 8$

■ Solve by addition.

15. $y - 2x = 7$
    $3y + 2x = -3$

    15. $\{(-3, 1)\}$

© D.C. Heath & Co.

- To solve a system of linear equations in two variables by graphing, graph each of the equations. If the graphs intersect, the point of intersection is the solution of the system. [6–1]

- To solve a system of equations by substitution: [6–2]

  1. Using whichever equation is more convenient, express one variable in terms of the other.

  2. Substitute this expression for the variable in the other equation to obtain a simpler equation in one variable that can be solved.

  3. Substitute this value in either equation to solve for the other variable.

  4. Check the solution pair in both equations of the original system.

- A system of two linear equations can have 0, 1, or infinitely many solutions. [6–3]

  1. Solve the system by using substitution or graphing. If the system has one solution, it can be determined.

  2. If, after substitution, the variables drop out and the resulting sentence is false, the system has no solutions. The graph of the equations is parallel lines with the same slope and different y-intercepts.

  3. If, after substitution, the variables drop out and the resulting sentence is true, the system has an infinite number of solutions. The equations are equivalent and have the same slope and the same y-intercept. The graphs of the equations are the same line.

- The Addition Property of Equations [6–5]

  For all numbers a, b, c, and d,
  if $a = b$ and $c = d$, then $a + c = b + d$.

- Wherever the coefficients of one of the variables in the equations of a system are opposites, the system can be solved by using the addition property of equality and substitution. [6–5]

- To solve a system of equations by multiplication and addition: [6–6]

  1. Apply the multiplication property of equations to one or both equations of the system to obtain a new system in which the coefficients of one variable are opposites.

  2. Add the sides of one equation to the sides of the other equation to obtain one equation in one variable.

  3. Solve for the variable.

  4. Substitute the value found in step 3 for the appropriate variable in one of the original equations.

  5. Solve for the other variable.

  6. Check your answer in the original system.

Chapter 6 Test A (page 3)   NAME _____

■ Assume that you are going to use addition to
 eliminate terms in this system:

$$2x - 5y = 7$$
$$6x + y = 5$$

16. To eliminate the x-terms, multiply the first equation
 by what number?   16. -3

17. To eliminate the y-terms, multiply the second equation
 by what number?   17. 5

■ Pecans at $1.75 per pound and cashews at $2.50
 per pound are combined to make a 5-pound
 mixture worth $2.02 per pound.

18. Complete the table for the situation given above.

	Number of pounds	Price per pound	Value in dollars
Pecans	x	1.75	$1.75x$
Cashews	y	2.50	$2.50y$
Mixture	5	2.02	$2.02 \cdot 5$

18.

19. How many pounds of pecans were used?   19. 3.2

★ BONUS

The length of a rectangular prism is 3 times the width.
The height of the prism is 2 cm more than the width.
The sum of the three dimensions is 12 cm. What is the
volume of the prism?   BONUS 48 cm^3

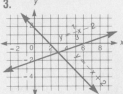

© D.C. Heath & Co.

■ CHAPTER REVIEW

6–1 **Objective:** To solve systems of equations by graphing.

Use the graphs to solve each of these systems.

1. $y = x + 2$
 $x + y = 2$ $\{(0, 2)\}$

2. $x + y = 2$
 $x - 3y = 6$ $\{(3, -1)\}$

3. Solve this system by graphing.
 $y = -x + 2$

 $y = \frac{1}{3}x - 2$ $\{(3, -1)\}$

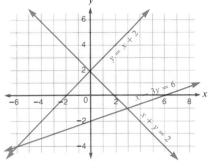

6–2 **Objective:** To solve systems of equations by substitution.

Solve by substitution.

4. $y = 2x - 5$
 $x + 3y = 20$ $\{(5, 5)\}$

5. $3x = y$
 $3x - 4y = 9$ $\{(-1, -3)\}$

6–3 **Objective:** To determine the number of solutions for a system of
   equations.

State whether each of the following systems has 0, 1, or infinitely many
solutions.

6. $x + y = 4$
 $x + y = 5$ 0

7. $y = 3x + 2$
 $2y = 6x + 4$ Many

8. $y = 2x + 4$
 $y = 3x + 4$ 1

6–4 **Objective:** To use systems of equations to solve problems.

For each problem below, write two equations, solve the system, and
solve the problem.

9. The tens digit of a two-digit number is 3 less than twice the ones
 digit. The difference between the number and the number formed
 by reversing the digits is 18. What is the number?   75

10. One number is 4 times another. If the sum of the two numbers is
 1000, what are the numbers?   800 and 200

11. The width of a rectangle is 20 cm less than its length. The perimeter
 is 68 cm. Find the length and width.   Length: 27 cm, width: 7 cm

ADDITIONAL ANSWER

■ **Chapter Review**

3.

6–5 **Objective:** To solve systems of equations by addition.

Solve by addition.

12. $x + y = 14$
$x - y = 6$ $\{(10, 4)\}$

13. $2y + 3x = 14$
$2y = 3x + 10$ $\left\{\left(\frac{2}{3}, 6\right)\right\}$

14. I am thinking of two numbers. If I double the second number and subtract the product from the first, the difference is 5. If I double the second number and add the product to the first, the sum is 65. What are the two numbers? First: 35, second: 15

6–6 **Objective:** To solve systems of equations by multiplication and addition.

15. $3a + b = 5$
$2a + 3b = 1$ $\{(2, -1)\}$

16. $3x + 4y = -8$
$5x - 3y = 35$ $\{(4, -5)\}$

6–7 **Objective:** To solve mixture problems.

17. Some \$3.75-per-pound candy is mixed with \$5.00-per-pound candy to obtain 10 pounds of \$4.25-per-pound candy. How many pounds of each kind of candy are used? 6 lb of \$3.75/lb, 4 lb of \$5.00/lb

■ CHAPTER 6 SELF-TEST

6–1 **1.** State whether the ordered pair $\left(2, \frac{1}{2}\right)$ is a solution of the system.

$$3x + 4y = 8$$
$$x - 6y = 5$$

Refer to the graphs to solve each system of equations.

2. $5x + 2y = 25$
$3x - 3y = -6$ $\{(3, 5)\}$

3. $5x + 2y = 25$
$y = x - 5$ $\{(5, 0)\}$

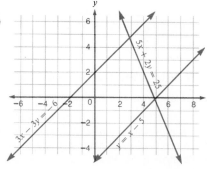

6–2 **4.** Solve the equation $2y + 4x = 12$ for y. $y = -2x + 6$

5. Solve by substitution.

$$y = x - 5$$
$$2x + 3y = 0$$ $\{(3, -2)\}$

6-3 State whether each system has 0, 1, or infinitely many solutions.

6. $x + y = 5$
$x + y = 10$ 0

7. $2x - 3y = 6$
$-4x + 6y = 3$ 0

6-5 Solve by addition.

8. $2x + 3y = 0$
$3x - 3y = -6$ $\left\{\left(-\frac{6}{5}, \frac{4}{5}\right)\right\}$

6-6 Solve by multiplication and addition.

9. $7x + 3y = 0$
$5x + 2y = 25$ $\{(75, -175)\}$

6-4,
6-7 Solve.

10. A solution is 45% alcohol in water. How much alcohol is in x milliliters of the solution? 0.45x

11. Two numbers have a sum of 84. One number is 8 less than 3 times the other. Find the numbers. 61 and 23

12. For a given two-digit number, the ones digit is 4 less than the tens digit. If the digits are reversed and the new number is doubled, the result is 1 more than the original number. Find the original number. 73

13. Ms. Macaw, who works for Sunset Birdseed Corporation, must mix first-quality seed worth 60¢ per pound with filler seed worth 35¢ per pound. How much of each type must she mix to produce 100 pounds of a mixture worth 50¢ per pound? 60 lb of 60¢/lb, 40 lb of 35¢/lb

■ PRACTICE FOR COLLEGE ENTRANCE TESTS

Choose the best answer for each question.

1. If the sum of two numbers is 21 and the difference between the two numbers is 11, then the average of the two numbers is ___?___.

A. 9   B. $10\frac{1}{2}$ C. 12   D. 21   E. $40\frac{1}{2}$

2. The cost C in dollars of producing n units of a product is given by the formula $C = kn + 1000$. If it costs $3000 to produce 10 units, what does it cost to produce 20 units?

A. $4000   B. $4500   C. $5000   D. $5500   E. $6000

3. If $2x - 1 = 7$ and $x + y = 12$, then $y = $ ___?___.

A. 3   B. 4   C. 6   D. 8   E. 9

■ Assume that you are going to use addition to eliminate terms in this system:

$x + 8y = -6$
$3x - 2y = 8$

16. To eliminate the x-terms, multiply the first equation by what number?
16. -3

17. To eliminate the y-terms, multiply the second equation by what number?
17. 4

■ Walnuts at $2.30 per pound and pecans at $1.70 per pound are combined to make a 10-pound mixture worth $1.91 per pound.

18. Complete the table for the situation given above.

18.

	Number of pounds	Price per pound	Value in dollars
Walnuts	x	2.30	$2.30x$
Pecans	y	1.70	$1.70y$
Mixture	10	1.91	$10 \cdot 1.91$

19. How many pounds of pecans were used?
19. 6.5

★ BONUS

Jessica is 4 years older than Alexander, and Dan is 5 times as old as Alexander. The sum of all their ages is 25. How many years older is Jessica than Dan?
BONUS 8

Cumulative Test **2**   NAME _____

PART 1   CHAPTERS 1–3

■ Substitute and simplify.

1. $A - s$

r	s	A	B
5	4	20	8

1. 16

2. $\frac{A}{r} + B$ 2. 12

3. $3z^2$ 3. 48

■ Simplify.

4. $(7 + 4) \times 2$ 4. 22

5. $16 - 8 \div 4$ 5. 14

■ Write an expression.

6. Clyde weighs 23 pounds more than Elaine. If E is Elaine's weight in pounds, what is Clyde's weight in pounds?   6. $E + 23$

■ True or false.

7. $15 < -18$ 7. False

8. $|-6| > |-4|$ 8. True

9. The opposite of $\frac{1}{4}$ is 4.   9. False

■ Substitute and simplify.

10. $n + t$ 10. -15

11. $c - b$

b	c	n	t
-6	4	-12	-3

11. 10

12. $\frac{n}{t} \cdot b$ 12. -24

■ Simplify.

13. $3y - (-4)$ 13. $3y + 4$

14. $4(2w - 3) - 6w$ 14. $2w - 12$

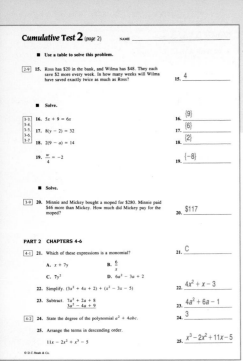

■ Use a table to solve this problem.

2-9 **15.** Ross has $20 in the bank, and Wilma has $48. They each save $2 more every week. In how many weeks will Wilma have saved exactly twice as much as Ross?

15. 4

■ Solve.

3-3 **16.** $5x + 9 = 6x$ 16. {9}
3-4
3-5 **17.** $8(y - 2) = 32$ 17. {6}
3-6
3-7 **18.** $2(9 - a) = 14$ 18. {2}

19. $\frac{w}{4} = -2$ 19. {−8}

■ Solve.

3-9 **20.** Minnie and Mickey bought a moped for $280. Minnie paid $46 more than Mickey. How much did Mickey pay for the moped?

20. $117

PART 2 CHAPTERS 4-6

4-1 **21.** Which of these expressions is a monomial?   21. C

A. $x + 7y$ B. $\frac{6}{x}$

C. $7y^2$ D. $6a^2 - 3a + 2$

22. Simplify. $(3x^2 + 4x + 2) + (x^2 - 3x - 5)$ 22. $4x^2 + x - 3$

23. Subtract. $\begin{array}{c} 7a^2 + 2a + 8 \\ 3a^2 - 4a + 9 \end{array}$ 23. $4a^2 + 6a - 1$

4-2 **24.** State the degree of the polynomial $a^2 + 4abc$.   24. 3

25. Arrange the terms in descending order.

$11x - 2x^2 + x^3 - 5$ 25. $x^3 - 2x^2 + 11x - 5$

© D.C. Heath & Co.

■ Simplify.

4-3 **26.** $b^3 \cdot b^8$ 26. b^{11}

27. $(2c^4)(5c^2)$ 27. $10c^6$

4-4 **28.** Write the number 21,000,000 in scientific notation.   28. $2.1 \cdot 10^7$

29. Write the product $(3 \cdot 10^4)(4.1 \cdot 10^7)$ in scientific notation.   29. $1.23 \cdot 10^{12}$

■ Simplify.

4-5 **30.** $(y^3)^4$ 30. y^{12}

31. $(3c)^2$ 31. $9c^2$

32. $(a^2b)^3$ 32. a^6b^3

4-6 **33.** $6r(2r - 3)$ 33. $12r^2 - 18r$

34. $xy(x - y)$ 34. $x^2y - xy^2$

■ Simplify. Assume that no variable is zero.

4-8 **35.** $\frac{y^8}{y^2}$ 35. y^6

36. $\frac{28s^2}{4s^7}$ 36. $\frac{7}{s^5}$

■ Solve.

4-7 **37.** Tom and Jean drive the same distance. Tom drives at 60 km/h for x hours. Jean drives at 80 km/h for $(x - 1)$ hours. Solve for x.   37. 4

4-10 **38.** The sum of three consecutive integers is 174. What is the smallest integer?   38. 57

© D.C. Heath & Co.

---

4. Carla had 3 times as much money as Emily. After Carla gave Emily $10, Carla still had $4 more than Emily. How much money did Emily have originally?

A. $6   B. $8   C. $9   D. $10   E. $12

5. If $x + y + z = 14$ and $x + y - z = 10$, then $x + y = \underline{\ ?\ }$.

A. 4   B. 10   C. 12   D. 14   E. 24

6. If $xy = 24$ and $y = 3$, then $x - y = \underline{\ ?\ }$.

A. 5   B. 8   C. 11   D. 18   E. 21

7. The sum of two numbers is 14. The difference of the two numbers is 6. The product of the two numbers is $\underline{\ ?\ }$.

A. 21   B. 28   C. 30   D. 32   E. 40

8. If $a = 12b$ and $b = 3c$, then what is a in terms of c?

A. $\frac{1}{4}c$ B. $4c$ C. $9c$ D. $15c$ E. $36c$

9. Each term of a sequence is obtained by doubling the preceding term and adding 1. If the third term is 15, what is the first term?

A. 2   B. 3   C. 4   D. 5   E. 7

■ CUMULATIVE REVIEW (Chapters 1–6)

a	B	f	H	m
14	3	9	7	4

1-1, 1-3 Substitute and simplify.

1. $H + a$ 21   **2.** $a - \frac{f}{B}$ 11   **3.** $m \cdot B^2$ 36

1-2 Simplify.

4. $19 - (14 - 2)$ 7   **5.** $8 + 4 \cdot 2$ 16   **6.** $16 \div 4 \cdot 2$ 8

1-5, 1-6 **7.** Which of these expressions is equivalent to $7a + a$? d

a. $6a$ b. 7   c. $7a^2$ d. $8a$ e. $14a$

1-7 Write an expression.

8. Luana has 43 cents less than Trini. If Trini has T cents, how many cents does Luana have? $T - 43$

2-1 True or false?

9. $24 > -25$ True   **10.** $|-4| + |-8| < 0$ False

2-2,
2-3,
2-4, Substitute and simplify.
2-5

c	d	r	s
−4	8	−20	−2

11. $s - c$ 2   **12.** $d + r$ −12   **13.** $c \cdot s$ 8   **14.** $\dfrac{c + r}{d}$ −3

2-6, Simplify.
2-7,
2-8 **15.** $4a + (2 - 3a)$ $a + 2$ **16.** $5(x + 2) - (x + 6)$ $4x + 4$

2-9 Make a table to solve this problem.

17. Robert has $40 and earns $3 each day. Chico has $32 and earns $5 each day. In how many days will they have the same amount of money?   4 days

17.	Start	1	2	3	4
Robert	40	43	46	49	52
Chico	32	37	42	47	52

Day

3-3, Solve.
3-4,
3-5, **18.** $8y = 7y - 4$ (−4)   **19.** $\dfrac{2w}{3} = -4$ (−6)
3-6,
3-7 **20.** $5(x + 3) = 15$ 0   **21.** $3(2x + 1) = 8x - 7$ (5)

3-9 **22.** Gloria made twice as many gizmos for a Junior Achievement project as Rob. Together, they made 48 gizmos. How many did Gloria make?   32

4-1 **23.** Simplify. $(9x^2 + 3x - 6) + (4x^2 - x + 1)$ $13x^2 + 2x - 5$ **24.** Subtract. $\begin{array}{r} 5b^2 - 6b + 7 \\ 2b^2 + 3b + 1 \\ \hline 3b^2 - 9b + 6 \end{array}$

4-2 **25.** Which of these expressions is a binomial? d

    a. 7   **b.** $4x^2$ **c.** $1 - 6y^2 + 8y$ **d.** $11s^2 - 25$ **e.** $\dfrac{3}{x^2}$

26. What is the degree of $a^2b - 7b^2 + 4a$? 3

27. Arrange the terms in descending order. $12x^2 + 6 + 9x^3 - x$ $9x^3 + 12x^2 - x + 6$

4-3 Simplify.

28. $x^5 \cdot x^4$ x^9 **29.** $(-4y^2)(3y)$ $-12y^3$ **30.** $(m^2n)(m^3n^2)$ m^5n^3

4-4 **31.** Write in scientific notation. 573,000 $5.73 \cdot 10^5$

32. Write the product in scientific notation. $(3 \cdot 10^4)(5 \cdot 10^3)$ $1.5 \cdot 10^8$

4-5, Simplify.
4-6,
4-8 **33.** $(a^2)^5$ a^{10} **34.** $(5x^3)^2$ $25x^6$ **35.** $(xy^4)^3$ x^3y^{12}

36. $2r(r + 6)$ $2r^2 + 12r$ **37.** $b^2(1 - 5b^2)$ $b^2 - 5b^4$ **38.** $xy(x^2 + y)$ $x^3y + xy^2$

39. $\dfrac{x^{10}}{x^5}$ x^5 **40.** $\dfrac{32y^2}{4y^5}$ $\dfrac{8}{y^3}$ **41.** $-\dfrac{ab}{ab^2}$ $-\dfrac{1}{b}$ **42.** $\dfrac{8t^3}{2t^3}$ 4

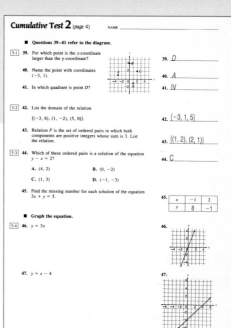

Cumulative Test 2 (page 4)   NAME _____

■ Questions 39–41 refer to the diagram.

5-1 **39.** For which point is the x-coordinate larger than the y-coordinate?   **39.** D

40. Name the point with coordinates $(-3, 1)$.   **40.** A

41. In which quadrant is point D?   **41.** IV

5-2 **42.** List the domain of the relation $\{(-3, 6), (1, -2), (5, 0)\}$.   **42.** {−3, 1, 5}

43. Relation P is the set of ordered pairs in which both components are positive integers whose sum is 3. List the relation.   **43.** {(1, 2), (2, 1)}

5-3 **44.** Which of these ordered pairs is a solution of the equation $y - x = 2$?   **44.** C

   A. (4, 2)   **B.** (0, −2)

   C. (1, 3)   **D.** (−1, −3)

45. Find the missing number for each solution of the equation $3x + y = 5$.

x	−1	2
y	8	−1

■ Graph the equation.

5-4 **46.** $y = 3x$ **46.**

47. $y = x - 4$ **47.**

© D.C. Heath & Co.

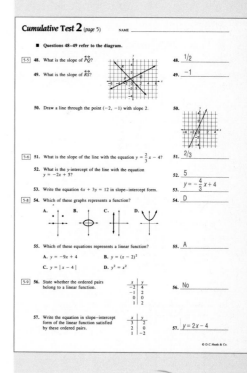

Cumulative Test 2 (page 5)   NAME _____

■ Questions 48–49 refer to the diagram.

5-5 **48.** What is the slope of $\overleftrightarrow{PQ}$?   **48.** 1/2

49. What is the slope of $\overleftrightarrow{RS}$?   **49.** −1

50. Draw a line through the point $(-2, -1)$ with slope 2.   **50.**

5-6 **51.** What is the slope of the line with the equation $y = \frac{2}{3}x - 4$?   **51.** 2/3

52. What is the y-intercept of the line with the equation $y = -2x + 5$?   **52.** 5

53. Write the equation $4x + 3y = 12$ in slope–intercept form.   **53.** $y = -\frac{4}{3}x + 4$

5-8 **54.** Which of these graphs represents a function?   **54.** D

   A.   **B.**   **C.**   **D.**

55. Which of these equations represents a linear function?   **55.** A

   A. $y = -9x + 4$ **B.** $y = (x - 2)^2$

   C. $y = |x - 4|$ **D.** $y^2 = x^2$

5-9 **56.** State whether the ordered pairs belong to a linear function.   **56.** No

x	y
−2	4
−1	2
0	0
1	2

57. Write the equation in slope–intercept form of the linear function satisfied by these ordered pairs.   **57.** $y = 2x - 4$

x	y
3	2
2	0
1	−2

© D.C. Heath & Co.

301

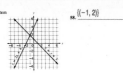

6-1 58. What is the solution of the system graphed in the diagram?

58. $\{(-1, 2)\}$

59. State whether the ordered pair (3, 1) is a solution of this system of equations.
$y = 2x - 5$
$y = -x + 4$

59. Yes

■ Solve the systems by substitution.

6-2 60. $y = 2x$
$y = 3x - 4$

60. $\{(4, 8)\}$

61. $x + 2y = 8$
$y = x + 1$

61. $\{(2, 3)\}$

■ How many solutions do the following systems have?
A. none   B. one   C. two   D. infinitely many

6-3 62. $y = 3x$
$y = 3x - 4$

62. A

63. $y = 2x - 4$
$2y = 4x - 8$

63. D

6-5 64. Solve this system for x only.
$2x + y = 10$
$x - y = 8$

64. $x = 6$

65. Solve this system for y only.
$-2x + 3y = -7$
$2x - 2y = 6$

65. $y = -1$

© D.C. Heath & Co.

ADDITIONAL ANSWERS

■ **Cumulative Review**

45.
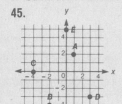

51.
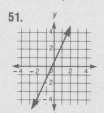

52.
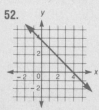

302

4-7 Solve.

43. Mr. Elmo drove at x miles per hour for 5 hours. Mrs. Elmo drove at $(x - 9)$ miles per hour for 6 hours. If they drove the same distance, what was Mr. Elmo's rate of driving? 54 mph

4-10 44. The sum of three consecutive integers is 105. What is the smallest integer? 34

5-1 45. Graph the points $A(1, 2)$, $B(-2, -4)$, $C(-4, 0)$, $D(3, -3)$, and $E(0, 5)$.

46. Which point in Exercise 45 is on the y-axis? E

47. Which point in Exercise 45 is in quadrant IV? D

5-2 48. List the domain and range of the relation shown here. Domain: $\{-3, 2\}$
Range: $\{2, -1, 1\}$

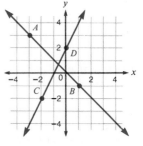

5-3 49. Is the ordered pair (2, 3) a solution of the equation $y = 3x - 7$? No

50. Find the missing number for each solution.   3

$4x - y = 7$

x	?	2
y	5	?

1

5-4 Graph the equation.

51. $y = 2x + 1$ 52. $y + x = 4$

5-5 53. What is the slope of $\overleftrightarrow{AB}$? -1

54. What is the slope of $\overleftrightarrow{CD}$? 2

55. Draw a line through the origin with slope $\frac{1}{2}$.

5-6 56. What are the slope and y-intercept of the line with the equation

$y = -\frac{2}{3}x + 4$? Slope: $-\frac{2}{3}$; y-intercept: 4

57. Write the equation $4x - 2y = 5$ in slope–intercept form. $y = 2x - \frac{5}{2}$

5-8 58. Which graph represents a function? b

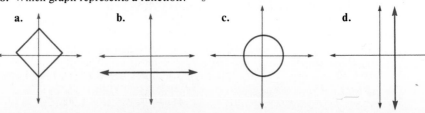

a.   b.   c.   d.

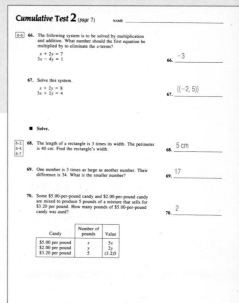
59. Does $5x - 4y = 6$ represent a linear function? yes

60. Ordered pairs of a linear function are shown. Find the missing number.

x	3	2	1	-1
y	1	3	5	?

9

61. Write the equation of the linear function satisfied by these ordered pairs. $y = 3x$

x	1	0	-1
y	3	0	-3

6–1

62. State whether the number pair (1, 5) is a solution of the system. no

$y = 2x + 3$
$y = -3x + 2$

63. Solve the system by graphing. $\{(2, 3)\}$

$y = 2x - 1$
$y = -x + 5$

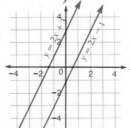

6–2 Solve by substitution.

64. $y = -x$ $\{(1, -1)\}$
$\quad y = 3x - 4$

65. $x + y = 8$ $\{(3, 5)\}$
$\quad y = x + 2$

6–3 **66.** How many solutions does the graphed system have? none

67. How many solutions does this system have? infinitely many

$y = 3x + 4$
$2y = 6x + 8$

6–5 Solve the system by addition.

68. $x + y = 3$ $\{(2, 1)\}$
$\quad 3x - y = 5$

69. $4x - y = 2$ $\{(1, 2)\}$
$\quad -4x + 3y = 2$

6–6 **70.** Tell how to eliminate the x-terms by multiplication and addition.

$x + 2y = 4$
$3x - y = -9$ Multiply first equation by -3 and add.

Solve.

71. Solve this system by multiplication and addition.

$4x - y = 6$
$2x + 3y = 10$ $\{(2, 2)\}$

6–1 **72.** Marcia is 3 years older than Donna. The sum of their ages is 21. Find Marcia's age. 12

6–4, 6–7 **73.** The ones digit of a two-digit number is 3 times the tens digit. The difference of the digits is 6. Find the number. 39

74. Some $5.00-per-lb candy is mixed with $3.00-per-lb candy to make a mixture that sells for $3.40 per lb. How many pounds of each type of candy are used? 8 lb of $3, 2 lb of $5

55.

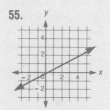

63.

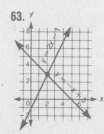

CHAPTER OVERVIEW

In this chapter, students extend the knowledge of polynomials they gained in Chapter 4. Just as factoring numbers can be considered as "undoing" multiplication of numbers, factoring polynomials can be considered as "undoing" multiplication of polynomials. Students proceed from factoring numbers to factoring polynomials. They learn to factor monomials from polynomials. They learn to find the product of two binomials and to factor polynomials that are products of two binomials. They learn how this type of factoring is used to solve quadratic equations (equations that contain second-degree polynomials).

The knowledge about polynomials learned in this chapter will be needed for work in Chapter 8, Algebraic Fractions and Applications, in Chapter 10, Rational and Irrational Numbers, and in Chapter 11, Solving Quadratic Equations. In addition, knowledge of polynomials is an essential prerequisite for later work in advanced algebra, statistics, and calculus.

7 Multiplying and Factoring Polynomials

When the water in a fountain is projected upward with an initial velocity v, it rises more and more slowly until it reaches a maximum height of h meters. Then it falls back to the ground, picking up speed as it falls. The formula $h = vt - 5t^2$ (where t is the time in seconds) and techniques learned in this chapter can be used to help determine when the water will hit the ground.

7–1 Prime Factorization

Preview

Imagine a row of wall lockers numbered from 1 to 1000 in a school with 1000 students. The locker doors are all closed. Student number 1 walks by the row of lockers, opening each one of them. Student number 2 walks by the lockers and closes every second locker beginning with locker 2. Student number 3 changes the state of the doors (opening closed doors and closing open doors) of every third locker beginning with locker 3. Student number 4 changes the state of the doors of every fourth locker beginning with locker 4. In general, student number n changes the state of every nth door beginning with locker n.

The lockers with numbers that have exactly two factors
- Which lockers will be touched exactly twice?
- After the 1000th student has passed by the row of lockers, which locker doors will be closed?

The lockers with numbers that have an even number of factors
The numbers that answer the first question will be used extensively in this lesson.

■ LESSON

You have probably used the word "factor" to refer to "numbers that are multiplied."

4 is a **factor** of 12 since there is a positive integer n such that $4n = 12$.
5 is not a factor of 12 since there is no positive integer n such that $5n = 12$.
The positive factors of 12 are 1, 2, 3, 4, 6, and 12.

Here is a table of the first ten positive integers and their positive factors.

Positive Integer	Factors
1	1
2	1, 2
3	1, 3
4	1, 2, 4
5	1, 5
6	1, 2, 3, 6
7	1, 7
8	1, 2, 4, 8
9	1, 3, 9
10	1, 2, 5, 10

Some numbers have exactly two factors. They are called **prime numbers**. The prime numbers listed in the table above are 2, 3, 5, and 7.

Positive numbers with more than two factors are called **composite numbers**. Composite numbers listed in the table above are 4, 6, 8, 9, and 10.

The number 1 is special. It is the only positive integer with just one factor and it is neither prime nor composite.

PURPOSE

Common factors and multiples are used to simplify, factor, and compute with rational expressions. Basic to understanding the process for finding greatest common factors and least common multiples is the concept of prime factorization.

PREVIEW

Start the solution by writing the first seven locker numbers, and indicate they are all closed (C). Show what happens to the lockers as the student walks by.

Locker Number

		1	2	3	4	5	6	7
		C	C	C	C	C	C	C
S	1	O	O	O	O	O	O	O
t	2		C		C		C	
u	3			C			O	
d	4				O			
e	5					C		
n	6						C	
t	7							C

Considering only 7 lockers rather than all 1000 lockers is an example of a problem-solving strategy sometimes called *making a simpler problem*.

The lockers that are changed twice (2, 3, 5, 7, 11, 13, . . .) have exactly two factors; that is, they are prime numbers. The number 1 is not prime. The lockers that are closed at the end of the process have been changed an even number of times; they have an even number of factors.

Go over the new terms carefully. Be sure students can use the word *factor* both as a noun and as a verb.

If the prime factors are written in numerical order, any prime factorization of a number will produce the same result. Therefore, the prime factorization of a number is unique. This important idea is called the *fundamental theorem of arithmetic.*

ADDITIONAL EXAMPLES

Example 1. Factor 10.
Some answers are: $1 \cdot 10$, $10 \cdot 1$, $2 \cdot 5$, $5 \cdot 2$.
Example 2. Factor 18.
Some answers are: $1 \cdot 18$, $18 \cdot 1$, $2 \cdot 9$, $9 \cdot 2$, $3 \cdot 6$, $6 \cdot 3$, $2 \cdot 3 \cdot 3$, $3 \cdot 2 \cdot 3$, $3 \cdot 3 \cdot 2$.
Example 3. Factor 10 over the set of integers.
Some answers are: $1 \cdot 10$, $-1 \cdot -10$, $2 \cdot 5$, $-2 \cdot -5$.
Example 4. Factor -15 over the set of integers.
Some answers are: $-1 \cdot 15$, $-1 \cdot 3 \cdot 5$, $-3 \cdot 5$, $3 \cdot -5$.

CHECK UNDERSTANDING

- Is 3 a factor of 15? (Yes) Why? ($3 \cdot 5 = 15$)
- Is 4 a factor of 15? (No) Why not? (There is no integer solution of $4x = 15$.)
- State all positive integer factors of 16. (1, 2, 4, 8, 16)
- Is 13 a prime number? (Yes)
- Is 15 a prime number? (No)

CLASSROOM EXERCISES

In classroom exercises 1 and 2, point out that an even number can be expressed as $2n$, where n is an integer. An odd number can be expressed as $2n + 1$. Therefore, an odd number is *not* evenly divisible by 2.

In classroom exercises 3 and 4, emphasize that a number is always a factor of itself and that 1 is a factor of every number.

The word "factor" is also used as a verb. To **factor a number** is to write the number and the product of two or more of its factors.

Example 1	Factor 6.

Solution To factor 6, we can write:
$$1 \cdot 6 \qquad 6 \cdot 1 \qquad 2 \cdot 3 \quad \text{or} \quad 3 \cdot 2$$

Example 2	Factor 12.

Solution Some answers are:
$$3 \cdot 4 \qquad 12 \cdot 1 \qquad 2 \cdot 6 \qquad 2 \cdot 2 \cdot 3 \qquad 3 \cdot 2 \cdot 2 \quad \text{and} \quad 2 \cdot 3 \cdot 2$$

For the factorization $2 \cdot 2 \cdot 3$, each of the factors is prime. Such a factorization is called a **prime factorization.**

Positive integer	Prime factorization
6	$2 \cdot 3$
9	$3 \cdot 3$, or 3^2
24	$2 \cdot 2 \cdot 2 \cdot 3$, or $2^3 \cdot 3$
36	$2 \cdot 2 \cdot 3 \cdot 3$, or $2^2 \cdot 3^2$

Factoring is often assumed to involve only positive integers. This is called factoring **over the set of positive integers.** We can also factor over the set of *all* integers.

Example 3	Factor 6 over the set of integers.

Solution Some answers are:
$$1 \cdot 6 \qquad -1 \cdot -6 \qquad 2 \cdot 3 \quad \text{and} \quad -2 \cdot -3$$

Example 4	Factor -8 over the set of integers.

Solution Some answers are:
$$-1 \cdot 2 \cdot 2 \cdot 2 \qquad -2 \cdot -2 \cdot -2 \quad \text{and} \quad -4 \cdot 2$$

■ CLASSROOM EXERCISES

True or false? Explain your answer.

1. 2 is a factor of 18.   T
2. 2 is a factor of 17.   F
3. 38 is a factor of 38.   T
4. 1 is a factor of 209.   T
5. 5 is a prime number.   T
6. 7 is a composite number.   F
7. 1 is a prime number.   F
8. 1 is a composite number.   F

ASSIGNMENT GUIDE

Basic	1–65 multiples of 3, Review Exercises
Average	15–66 multiples of 3, 67–74 all, Review Exercises
Enriched	15–72 multiples of 3, 75–82 all, Review Exercises

State the prime factorization of each number.

9. 12 $2^2 \cdot 3$ **10.** 15 $3 \cdot 5$ **11.** 2 2 **12.** 27 3^3

State three factorizations over the set of integers.

$5 \cdot 2, -5 \cdot -2, -10 \cdot -1, 1 \cdot 10$

13. 4 $1 \cdot 4, -1 \cdot -4, -2 \cdot -2, 2 \cdot 2$ **14.** -8 $1 \cdot -8, -1 \cdot 8, -2 \cdot 4, -4 \cdot 2, -2 \cdot 2 \cdot 2, -2 \cdot -2 \cdot -2$ **15.** -6 $-3 \cdot 2, -2 \cdot 3, -1 \cdot 6, 6 \cdot -1$ **16.** 10

■ WRITTEN EXERCISES

A List the numbers from the given set that are factors of the given number.

1. 45; {1, 2, 3, 4, 5} $(1, 3, 5)$ **2.** 28; {1, 2, 3, 4, 5} $(1, 2, 4)$

3. 52; {4, 13, 14, 21} $(4, 13)$ **4.** 33; {3, 11, 13, 33} $(3, 11, 33)$

5. 49; {2, 7, 14} (7) **6.** 34; {1, 17, 19} $(1, 17)$

List all positive integer factors of the given number.

7. 18 $(1, 2, 3, 6, 9, 18)$ **8.** 20 $(1, 2, 4, 5, 10, 20)$ **9.** 49 $(1, 7, 49)$ **10.** 25 $(1, 5, 25)$

11. 35 $(1, 5, 7, 35)$ **12.** 39 $(1, 3, 13, 39)$ **13.** 42 $(1, 2, 3, 6, 7, 14, 21, 42)$ **14.** 70 $(1, 2, 5, 7, 10, 14, 35, 70)$

15. 84 $(1, 2, 3, 4, 6, 7, 12, 14, 21, 28, 42, 84)$ **16.** 31 $(1, 31)$ **17.** 47 $(1, 47)$ **18.** 28 $(1, 2, 4, 7, 14, 28)$

State whether the number is prime or composite.

19. 99   composite   **20.** 50   composite   **21.** 97   prime   **22.** 53   prime

23. 57   composite   **24.** 93   composite   **25.** 43   prime   **26.** 59   prime

27. 17   prime   **28.** 29   prime   **29.** 34   composite   **30.** 41   prime

31. 101   prime   **32.** 51   composite   **33.** 61   prime   **34.** 39   composite

Write each number as the product of two factors in three different ways.

35. 44 $1 \cdot 44, 2 \cdot 22, 4 \cdot 11$ **36.** 68 $1 \cdot 68, 2 \cdot 34, 4 \cdot 17$ **37.** 63 $1 \cdot 63, 3 \cdot 21, 7 \cdot 9$ **38.** 12 $1 \cdot 12, 2 \cdot 6, 3 \cdot 4$

39. 75 $1 \cdot 75, 3 \cdot 25, 5 \cdot 15$ **40.** 98 $1 \cdot 98, 2 \cdot 49, 7 \cdot 14$ **41.** 76 $1 \cdot 76, 2 \cdot 38, 4 \cdot 19$ **42.** 242 $1 \cdot 242, 2 \cdot 121, 11 \cdot 22$

Write the prime factorization of each number. List the factors in increasing order.

43. 30 $2 \cdot 3 \cdot 5$ **44.** 66 $2 \cdot 3 \cdot 11$ **45.** 24 $2^3 \cdot 3$ **46.** 40 $2^3 \cdot 5$

47. 54 $2 \cdot 3^3$ **48.** 88 $2^3 \cdot 11$ **49.** 91 $7 \cdot 13$ **50.** 86 $2 \cdot 43$

51. 50 $2 \cdot 5^2$ **52.** 100 $2^2 \cdot 5^2$ **53.** 72 $2^3 \cdot 3^2$ **54.** 28 $2^2 \cdot 7$

55. 56 $2^3 \cdot 7$ **56.** 49 7^2 **57.** 81 3^4 **58.** 42 $2 \cdot 3 \cdot 7$

Write three factorizations over the set of integers.

59. -15 $1 \cdot -15, -1 \cdot 15, -3 \cdot 5, -5 \cdot 3$ **60.** -14 $1 \cdot -14, -1 \cdot 14, -2 \cdot 7, -7 \cdot 2$ **61.** 10 $1 \cdot 10, -1 \cdot -10, 2 \cdot 5, -2 \cdot -5$ **62.** 6 $1 \cdot 6, -1 \cdot -6, 2 \cdot 3, -2 \cdot -3$

63. -77 $1 \cdot -77, -1 \cdot 77, -7 \cdot 11, -11 \cdot 7$ **64.** -74 $1 \cdot -74, -1 \cdot 74, -2 \cdot 37, -37 \cdot 2$ **65.** 69 $1 \cdot 69, -1 \cdot -69, 3 \cdot 23, -3 \cdot -23$ **66.** 65 $1 \cdot 65, -1 \cdot -65, 5 \cdot 13, -5 \cdot -13$

COMPUTER EXTENSION

Write a program that lists the prime numbers less than 1000.

```
10 PRINT "2",
20 FOR N = 3 TO 1000
30 FOR K = 2 TO N/2
40 IF INT(N/K) < > N/K THEN 60
50 GO TO 80
60 NEXT K
70 PRINT N,
80 NEXT N
90 END
```

Time the program. Then change line 30 to
```
30 FOR K = 2 TO SQR(N)
```
Run and time the program again.

PROBLEM–SOLVING NOTE
Solving simpler but similar problems

When stymied by a problem, it is frequently helpful to consider a simpler situation. That situation might consist of parts of the given problem, or it might represent specific examples of a more general case. It is important for the situation to be simple enough to work with, to permit the discovery of important relationships, and to enable the solver to relate those discoveries back to the more difficult problem.

ENRICHMENT PROBLEMS

• A dart board consists of two areas—7 points and 3 points. Given an unlimited supply of darts, what positive score totals are *not* possible?

1, 2, 4, 5, 8, and 11

• A given number has 2, 3, and 5 as factors. Which of the following numbers are also factors? 1, 4, 6, 8, 10, 12, 15, 18, 20, 30

1, 6, 10, 15, 30

• List the numbers 1 to 100 in six columns. Circle each prime number. What can you say about all primes except 2 and 3? Explain.

They are in the first and fifth columns, since every number in the second, fourth, and sixth columns is even and every number in the third column is an odd multiple of 3.

EXTRA PRACTICE, page 631

A "factor tree" can be used to determine the prime factorization of a composite number. First, write the number as the product of two factors. Next, write each composite factor as the product of two factors. Continue the process until only prime factors are used. In the example, the prime factors are circled.

Sample Find the prime factorization of 48.

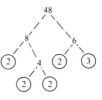

Solution The prime factorization of 48 is $2^4 \cdot 3$.

Use a factor tree to determine the prime factorization of each number.

B
67. 60 $2^2 \cdot 3 \cdot 5$ **68.** 80 $2^4 \cdot 5$ **69.** 84 $2^2 \cdot 3 \cdot 7$ **70.** 72 $2^3 \cdot 3^2$

71. 81 3^4 **72.** 32 2^5 **73.** 90 $2 \cdot 3^2 \cdot 5$ **74.** 92 $2^2 \cdot 23$

C **75.** How many different factors does each number have?

    a. 2^1 2   **b.** 2^2 3   **c.** 2^3 4   **d.** 2^4 5   **e.** 2^5 6

76. Complete this rule for the number of different factors of a power of 2.

    For all positive integers n, 2^n has __?__ different factors. $n + 1$

77. How many factors does each number have?

    a. 5^1 2   **b.** 5^2 3   **c.** 5^3 4   **d.** 5^4 5   **e.** 5^5 6

78. Complete this rule for the number of different factors of a power of 5.

    For all positive integers n, 5^n has __?__ different factors. $n + 1$

79. Complete this rule.

    For each prime number p and each positive integer n, p^n has __?__ different factors. $n + 1$

80. How many factors does each number have?

    a. $2^1 \cdot 5^1$ 4   **b.** $2^2 \cdot 5^1$ 6   **c.** $2^3 \cdot 5^1$ 8   **d.** $2^2 \cdot 5^2$ 9

81. Complete this rule for the number of different factors for a product of powers of 2 and powers of 5.

    For all positive integers m and n, $2^m \cdot 5^n$ has __?__ different factors.
$(m + 1)(n + 1)$ or $1 + m + n + mn$

82. Complete this rule.

    For all prime numbers p_1 and p_2 ($p_1 \neq p_2$) and for all positive integers m and n, $p_1{}^m \cdot p_2{}^n$ has __?__ different factors.
$(m + 1)(n + 1)$ or $1 + m + n + mn$

■ REVIEW EXERCISES

State the property illustrated in each equation.

1. $3x + (4x + 2) = (3x + 4x) + 2$ Assoc. (add)   **2.** $4a + 5a = (4 + 5)a$ Dist. over add.   [1–5]

Which of the numbers $-2, -1, 0, 1,$ and 2 are solutions of the following equations?

3. $x^3 = x$ $\{-1, 0, 1\}$ **4.** $\dfrac{1}{x} = \dfrac{x}{4}$ $\{-2, 2\}$ [3–1]

Simplify.

5. $2a^2(-2ab)$ $-4a^3b$ **6.** $(3xy)(3xy)$ $9x^2y^2$ [4–3]

7. $\dfrac{12x^2y^3}{4xy}$ $(x \neq 0,\ y \neq 0)$ $3xy^2$ **8.** $\dfrac{-18a^2b}{6ab}$ $(a \neq 0,\ b \neq 0)$ $-3a$ [4–8]

EXTENSION   Determining prime numbers on a computer

Recall that the greatest integer function INT(X) finds the greatest integer that is less than or equal to X. We can use this function to determine whether a whole number A is divisible by a whole number B. If B does not divide A evenly, then A/B and INT(A/B) are not equal. If A/B = INT(A/B), then B is a factor of A. This fact is used in the following program to determine whether a whole number greater than 1 is prime.

```
10  PRINT "WHAT IS THE WHOLE NUMBER";
20  INPUT X
30  FOR Y = 2 TO X - 1
40  IF X/Y = INT(X/Y) THEN 80
50  NEXT Y
60  PRINT X; "   IS A PRIME NUMBER."
70  GOTO 90
80  PRINT X; "   IS NOT A PRIME NUMBER."
90  END
```

[If the statement in line 40 is true, the computer skips lines 50, 60, and 70 in the program. If the statement is false, the computer reads lines 50, 60, and 70.]

Use the program to determine whether the whole number is prime.

1. 103 Yes   **2.** 203 No   **3.** 403 No   **4.** 503 Yes

Although the program tells you when a number is not prime, it does not help you find the prime factors of that number. You can have the program print the smallest prime factor of the number just by adding this line:

    85 PRINT "A PRIME FACTOR IS   "; Y

If the number is not prime, find its prime factors.

5. 127 Prime   **6.** 129 3,43   **7.** 131 Prime   **8.** 133 7,19

PROBLEM SOLVING — FINDING PATTERNS

1. Find factors that will give the products in the following multiplication table.

Cover three *products* in the table so there is only one product covered in any row or column. Multiply the three products. Repeat this procedure with other products. Record your results.

×	3	-4	-5
3	9	-12	-15
2	6	8	-10
1	3	-4	-5

	Covered Products	Final Product
Trial 1		360
Trial 2		360
Trial 3		360

*What final product will this procedure generate for any multiplication table of this form?

abcdef

×	d	e	f
a			
b			
c			

2. Pick three consecutive integers. Square the middle integer. Multiply the first and last integers.

	Consecutive Integers	(Middle Integer)²	First Integer × Third Integer
Trial 1	-10, -9, -8	$(-9)^2 = 81$	$(-10)(-8) = 80$
Trial 2			
Trial 3			
Trial 4			

* What pattern holds for your answers in the last two columns?
The square of the middle integer is always 1 more than the product of the first and third.

Why does this pattern exist? Let $(n - 1), n, (n + 1)$ be the integers, then $n^2 - (n - 1)(n + 1) = n^2 - (n^2 - 1) = 1$.

Can be used after Section 7-1

© D.C. Heath & Co.

1. List *all* positive integer factors of 21.   1, 3, 7, 21

2. List *all* positive integer factors of 25.   1, 5, 25

3. State whether 39 is prime or composite.   Composite

4. Write the prime factorization of 42, listing the factors in increasing order. $2 \cdot 3 \cdot 7$

5. Write the prime factorization of 90, listing the factors in increasing order. $2 \cdot 3 \cdot 3 \cdot 5$, or $2 \cdot 3^2 \cdot 5$

PURPOSE

The greatest common factor of two monomials is used to simplify rational expressions, factor polynomials, and solve equations.

PREVIEW

The Euclidean algorithm can be used to find the greatest common factor (GCF) of two *numbers*. However, it cannot be used to find the GCF of two *algebraic* expressions.

Here are the steps for using the Euclidean algorithm to find the GCF of 330 and 1260.

$$
\begin{array}{ll}
\textbf{1.} \ 330\overline{)1260} & \textbf{2.} \ 270\overline{)330} \\
\quad\ \ \underline{990} & \quad\ \ \underline{270} \\
\quad\ \ 270 & \quad\ \ \ 60
\end{array}
$$

$$
\begin{array}{ll}
\textbf{3.} \ 60\overline{)270} & \textbf{4.} \ 30\overline{)60} \\
\quad\ \underline{240} & \quad\ \underline{60} \\
\quad\ \ 30 & \quad\ \ \ 0
\end{array}
$$

The GCF of 330 and 1260 is 30.

LESSON

To find the GCF of two (or more) monomials, students should first find the GCF of the numerical coefficients. Next, determine the GCF of the first variable, then the GCF of the second variable, and so on. For example, here's how to find the GCF of $24a^2bc^4$ and $21a^3c^3d$: The GCF of 24 and 21 is 3, the GCF of the "a" factors is a^2, the GCF of the "b" factors is 1, the GCF of the "c" factors is c^3, and the GCF of the "d" factors is 1. The GCF is $3 \cdot a^2 \cdot 1 \cdot c^3 \cdot 1$, or simply $3a^2c^3$.

310

OBJECTIVE 7–2

To find the greatest common factor of a pair of monomials.

7–2 Greatest Common Factor

Preview   Euclidean algorithm

In the branch of mathematics known as number theory, a step-by-step process has been developed to find the largest number that divides two given numbers exactly. Suppose we wish to find the largest number that exactly divides 495 and 572.

Follow this process.

1. Divide the larger number by the smaller.

$$
\begin{array}{r}
1 \\
495\overline{)572} \\
\underline{495} \\
77
\end{array}
$$

2. Divide the previous divisor by the remainder.

$$
\begin{array}{r}
6 \\
77\overline{)495} \\
\underline{462} \\
33
\end{array}
$$

3. Repeat step 2 until the remainder is 0.

$$
\begin{array}{r}
2 \\
33\overline{)77} \\
\underline{66} \\
11
\end{array}
$$

4. The divisor that produces the 0 is the answer.

$$
\begin{array}{r}
3 \\
11\overline{)33} \\
\underline{33} \\
0
\end{array}
$$

The largest number that exactly divides 495 and 572 is 11. This step-by-step process is called the **Euclidean algorithm.** This method was included in the writings of Euclid (about 300 B.C.), but most likely was invented even earlier than that. Use the Euclidean algorithm to find the largest number that exactly divides 330 and 1260.   30

In this lesson you will study a similar process in algebra.

■ LESSON

These are the factors of 12: 1, 2, 3, 4, 6, 12.
These are the factors of 16: 1, 2, 4, 8, 16.
Some numbers are factors of both 12 and 16. They are called **common factors** of 12 and 16.

Common factors of 12 and 16:   1, 2, 4.

The greatest of the common factors is called the **greatest common factor (GCF).**

The greatest common factor of 12 and 16 is 4.

Use any "extra" minutes at the end of a period to re-view the overall objectives of the chapter, the lessons in the chapter that have been studied, and the lessons that remain.

Find the greatest common factor of the two expressions.
Example 1. 30 and 75
   The GCF of 30 and 75 is $3 \cdot 5$, or 15.
Example 2. $8a^2b^3$ and $12ab^4$
   The GCF of $8a^2b^3$ and $12ab^4$ is $4ab^3$.
Example 3. $7rs^2t^3$, $21s^2t$, and $14r^2s^2t^2$
   The GCF of $7rs^2t^3$, $21s^2t$, and $14r^2s^2t^2$ is $7 \cdot s \cdot s \cdot t$, or $7s^2t$.

CHECK UNDERSTANDING

- Is 5 a common factor of 20 and 32? (No) Why not? (5 is not a factor of 32.)
- Is 4 a common factor of 20 and 32? (Yes) Why? ($4 \cdot 5 = 20$ and $4 \cdot 8 = 32$.)
- Is 3 the greatest common factor of 18 and 27? (No) Why not? (9 is a factor of 18 and 27, and 9 is greater than 3.)
- Is x^2 a common factor of $3x^3$ and $4x$? (No) Why not? (x^2 is not a factor of $4x$.)

Definition: The Greatest Common Factor (of Integers)

The greatest common factor of two or more integers is the greatest integer that is a factor of each given integer.

Example 1   Find the greatest common factor of 36 and 48.

Solution   Find the prime factorization of each number and identify common prime factors.

   Prime factorization of 36: $2 \cdot 2 \cdot \qquad 3 \cdot 3$
   Prime factorization of 48: $2 \cdot 2 \cdot 2 \cdot 2 \cdot 3$

Answer   The greatest common factor of 36 and 48 is $2 \cdot 2 \cdot 3$, or 12.

We can use a similar method to find the greatest common factor of expressions that contain variables.

Definition: The Greatest Common Factor (of Monomials)

The greatest common factor of two or more monomials is a monomial whose coefficient is the greatest common factor of the coefficients of the given monomials and whose variables have the greatest common degree of each variable in the given monomials.

Example 2   Find the GCF of $9x^2y$ and $12xy^2$.

Solution   *Prime factorization of $9x^2y$:* $\qquad 3 \cdot 3 \cdot x \cdot x \cdot y$
   Prime factorization of $12xy^2$: $2 \cdot 2 \cdot 3 \cdot x \cdot \quad y \cdot y$

Answer   The GCF of $9x^2y$ and $12xy^2$ is $3xy$.

Example 3   Find the GCF of $15a^3b^2$, $30a^2b^2c$, and $10a^2b^3$.

Solution $15a^3b^2$: $\quad 3 \cdot 5 \cdot a \cdot a \cdot a \cdot b \cdot b$
   $30a^2b^2c$: $2 \cdot 3 \cdot 5 \cdot a \cdot a \cdot \quad b \cdot b \cdot c$
   $10a^2b^3$: $2 \cdot \quad 5 \cdot a \cdot a \cdot \quad b \cdot b \cdot b$

Answer   The GCF of $15a^3b^2$, $30a^2b^2c$, and $10a^2b^3$ is $5 \cdot a \cdot a \cdot b \cdot b$, or $5a^2b^2$.

CLASSROOM EXERCISES

In classroom exercises 5 and 6, use prime factorization to solve at least one of the exercises. For example, in exercise 6, $24 = 2^3 \cdot 3$ and $56 = 2^3 \cdot 7$, so the GCF is 2^3 or 8.

ASSIGNMENT GUIDE

Basic   1–39 odd, Review Exercises
Average   3–45 multiples of 3, 46–56 all, Review Exercises
Enriched 3–39 multiples of 3, 41–49 odd, 51–64 all, Review Exercises

PRACTICE WORKSHEET 34

7-2 GREATEST COMMON FACTOR

■ List the common factors of each pair of monomials.

1. $2x^2$, $6x$ 2, x, 2x
2. a^2b, ab^2 a, b, ab
3. abc^2, ac^2 a, c, c², ac, ac²
4. $10xy$, $15y^2$ 5, y, 5y
5. $12rs$, $20st$ 2, 4, s, 2s, 4s
6. c^3d, c^2d^2 c, c², d, cd, c²d
7. w^2y^2, $3w^2z^3$ w, w²
8. $5r^2s^2$, $8rs^2$ r, s, s², rs, rs²

■ List the greatest common factor of each pair of monomials.

9. $2ab^2$, $3ab$ ab
10. $4x^2y^2$, $6x^2$ 2x²
11. $16x$, $24x^2$ 8x
12. rst, rt rt
13. r^3s^2t, r^2s^3 r²s²
14. $15ab^2$, $10a$ 5a
15. $24jk^3$, $18j^2k$ 6jk
16. r^3s^4, r^2s^2 r²s²
17. $7ab$, $5ac$ a
18. $6xyz$, $9z^2$ 3z
19. $18rs^2t^3$, $27r^2s^2$ 9rs²
20. $36j^2k$, $54j^3$ 18j²

WRITTEN EXERCISES

In exercises 59–60, students may use the Euclidean algorithm described in the Preview. Some students may remember that a six-digit number composed of three digits that are repeated is the product of 1001 and the three-digit number.

For example, $123{,}123 = 1001 \cdot 123$
$543{,}543 = 1001 \cdot 543$

The prime factors of 1001 are 7, 11, and 13. Additional common factors in the example can be found by examining 123 and 543. The prime factors of 123 are 3 and 41; the prime factors of 543 are 3 and 181. Therefore, the GCF of 123,123 and 543,543 is $3 \cdot 7 \cdot 11 \cdot 13$, or 3003.

EXTRA PRACTICE, page 631
COMPUTER WORKSHEET 12

■ CLASSROOM EXERCISES

List the factors of each number (over the set of positive integers).

1. 14 1, 2, 7, 14   2. 17 1, 17

List the common factors of each pair of numbers.

3. 12, 18 1, 2, 3, 6   4. 45, 46 1

Find the greatest common factor of each pair of numbers.

5. 15, 21 3   6. 24, 56 8

List the six factors of each monomial.

7. $25x$ 1, 5, 25, x, 5x, 25x   8. $7x^2$ 1, 7, x, x², 7x, 7x²

List the common factors of each pair of monomials.

9. x^2y, xy^3 x, y, xy   10. $4xy$, $6x^2$ 2, x, 2x

Find the greatest common factor of each pair of monomials.

11. $3a^2b$, $6a^2b$ 3a²b   12. $12m^2n^3$, $16mn^4$ 4mn³

■ WRITTEN EXERCISES

List the factors of each number (over the set of positive integers).

A 1. 58 1, 2, 29, 58   2. 55 1, 5, 11, 55   3. 31 1, 31   4. 41 1, 41

List the common factors of each pair of numbers.

5. 48, 60 1, 2, 3, 4, 6, 12   6. 30, 45 1, 3, 5, 15   7. 39, 65 1, 13   8. 66, 55 1, 11

9. 26, 33 1   10. 51, 38 1   11. 20, 30 1, 2, 5, 10   12. 30, 40 1, 2, 5, 10

Find the greatest common factor of each pair of numbers.

13. 8, 12 4   14. 9, 12 3   15. 65, 68 1   16. 33, 38 1

17. 50, 150 50   18. 20, 120 20   19. 46, 62 2   20. 38, 26 2

List the six different factors of each monomial.

21. 12 1, 2, 3, 4, 6, 12   22. 18 1, 2, 3, 6, 9, 18   23. $2x^2$ 1, 2, x, x², 2x, 2x²   24. $3y^2$ 1, 3, y, y², 3y, 3y²

25. $9a$ 1, 3, 9, a, 3a, 9a   26. $4b$ 1, 2, 4, b, 2b, 4b   27. ab^2 1, a, b, b², ab, ab²   28. a^2b 1, a, b, a², ab, a²b

List the common factors of each pair of monomials.

29. $3x^2$, $2xy$ 1, x   30. $4ab$, $5ab^2$ 1, a, b, ab   31. $6a^2b^2$, $3ab$ 1, 3, a, b, 3a, 3b, ab, 3ab   32. $2xy^2$, $4x^2y$ 1, 2, x, y, 2x, 2y, xy, 2xy

Find the greatest common factor of each pair of monomials.

33. $2x^3y$, $3x^3$ x³   34. $5xy^3$, $7y^3$ y³   35. $6x^2y$, $8xy^2$ 2xy   36. $6xy^2$, $9x^2y$ 3xy

37. $10abc$, $15ad$ 5a   38. $25abc$, $20cd$ 5c   39. $18a^2bc^2$, $45abc^2$ 9abc²   40. $35ab^2c^2$, $21ab^2c$ 7ab²c

Find the greatest common factor of the three monomials.

41. 10, 16, 20 2

42. 8, 12, 14 2

43. 24, 18, 30 6

44. 16, 20, 40 4

45. $2x^2y$, $3xy$, $4xy^2$ xy

46. $3a^2b^2$, $5ab^2$, $6a^2b$ ab

47. $6x^2y^2$, $8xy^2$, $12x^3y^2$ $2xy^2$

48. $4a^3b$, $8a^2b$, $12a^2$ $4a^2$

49. $4xy$, $8x^2y$, $12xy^2$ 4xy

50. $5a^2b^3$, $2ab^2$, $8a^3b^3$ ab^2

True or false? If the answer is false, provide a specific example to illustrate your answer.

51. Two is a factor of every even number. T

52. If two numbers are even, their greatest common factor is 2. F

53. If two numbers are prime, their greatest common factor is 1. T

54. If the greatest common factor of two numbers is 1, the two numbers are prime. F

55. One is a factor of every number. T

56. Zero is a factor of every positive number. F

Find the greatest common factor of each pair of monomials.

57. $x^{50}y^{50}$ and $x^{37}y^{87}$ $x^{37}y^{50}$

58. $a^{10}b^{20}c^{30}$ and $a^{20}b^{10}c$ $a^{10}b^{10}c$

59. 132,132 and 543,543 3003

60. 132,132 and 234,234 6006

The symbol $n!$, "n factorial," is defined to be

$$n \cdot (n - 1) \cdot (n - 2) \cdot \cdots \cdot 1$$

where n is any positive integer. For example,

$$6! \text{ is } 6 \cdot 5 \cdot 4 \cdot 3 \cdot 2 \cdot 1, \text{ or } 720$$

Find the greatest common factor of each pair of factorials.

61. 6! and 7! 6!

62. 10! and 5! 5!

63. 4! and 8! 4!

64. 100! and 6! 6!

◼ REVIEW EXERCISES

Solve.

1. $4x + 12 = 0$ $\{-3\}$

2. $2x - 5 = 0$ $\left\{2\frac{1}{2}\right\}$ [3–5]

3. $6(x - 4) = 30$ $\{9\}$

4. $\dfrac{x + 4}{3} = 12$ $\{32\}$ [3–6]

5. Solve for I: $E = IR$. $I = \dfrac{E}{R}$

6. Solve for y: $ax + by = c$. $y = \dfrac{c - ax}{b}$ [3–8]

ENRICHMENT PROBLEMS
Interpreting a table

- A list of the prime numbers less than 1000 is needed to solve the following problems. Such a list may be found in a book of mathematical tables, or the list may be generated by running the computer program given in the Section 7–1, Computer Extension.

- In sets of 100 numbers, what do you notice about the number of primes in each set?

  The sequence of the numbers of primes by sets 1–100, 101–200, etc., is 25, 21, 16, 16, 17, 14, 16, 14, 15, 14. The largest number of primes occurs in the numbers 1–200. As the sets increase to 1000, the number of primes decreases.

- One measure of the frequency of primes is the number of composites between consecutive primes. What is the largest number of consecutive composite numbers in the first 500 numbers? The first 1000 numbers?

  13 (114–126, 294–306, 318–330)
  19 (888–906)

- 3 and 5 are called *twin primes,* because they differ by only two. What happens to the number of twin primes as numbers get larger?

  The sequence of the number of twin primes by sets 1–100, 101–200, etc., is 8, 7, 4, 2, 3, 2, 3, 0, 3, 0. The largest number of twin primes occurs in the numbers 1–200. As the numbers increase to 1000, the number of twin primes decreases.

1. List all the positive integer factors of 18. 1, 2, 3, 6, 9, 18

List the greatest common factor of each pair of numbers.

2. 21 and 28 7
3. 12 and 15 3

List the greatest common factor of each pair of monomials.

4. a^2b^3c and $a^3b^2c^2$ a^2b^2c
5. $6xyz^2$ and $9x^2z^2$ $3xz^2$

PURPOSE

Equations written as a product of factors equaling zero can be easily solved by setting each factor equal to zero.

PREVIEW

The Preview explores the zero-product property.

If the product of several factors is 0, at least one of the factors is 0. If the product is *not* 0, then none of the factors is 0. For example, if $ab = 12$, a could be any number except 0. The first generalization (the zero-product property) is useful in solving equations; the second generalization is not.

LESSON

Emphasize that two conditions must be met for using the zero-product property to solve equations: (1) One side of the equation is the product of at least two factors; (2) The other side of the equation is 0.

ADDITIONAL EXAMPLES

Example 1. Solve. $x(x - 15) = 0$
$$x = 0 \text{ or } x - 15 = 0$$
$$x = 15$$
$$\{0, 15\}$$

OBJECTIVE 7–3

To solve equations using the zero-product property.

You may wish to spend two days on this section. Refer to the Pacing Chart.

7–3 The Zero-Product Property

Preview

Which of these number pairs (a, b) are solutions of the equation $ab = 0$?

$(5, 0)$ Yes $(5, -5)$ No $(0, -5)$ Yes $(0, 0)$ Yes
$(0.5, 0)$ Yes $(0, 0.5)$ Yes $(-0.5, 0.5)$ No $(0, 5000)$ Yes

Can you list additional solutions?
At least one factor is 0.

Although there are infinitely many solutions of the equation $ab = 0$ and you could not possibly list them all, can you describe what all solutions have in common?

In this lesson you will solve equations that are similar to $ab = 0$.

■ LESSON

For the product of two numbers to be zero, one or both numbers must be zero. This property is called the **zero-product property.**

> ### The Zero-Product Property
> For all numbers a and b,
> $$\text{if } ab = 0, \text{ then } a = 0 \text{ or } b = 0.$$

Mathematicians use the word "or" to mean "and/or." Therefore, in the zero-product property, if $ab = 0$, then both a and b can be 0.

The zero-product property permits us to solve some equations.

Example 1 Solve. $x(x + 1) = 0$

Solution The product of the two factors x and $x + 1$ is 0. Therefore, one or both factors is equal to 0. This means that the following sentence is equivalent to $x(x + 1) = 0$:

$$x = 0 \quad \text{or} \quad x + 1 = 0.$$

Therefore 0 is a solution of the first equation, and -1 is a solution of the second equation.

Answer $\{0, -1\}$

Check
$$x(x + 1) = 0 \qquad\qquad x(x + 1) = 0$$
$$0(0 + 1) \overset{?}{=} 0 \qquad\qquad -1(-1 + 1) \overset{?}{=} 0$$
$$0(1) = 0 \quad \text{It checks.} \qquad\qquad -1(0) = 0 \quad \text{It checks.}$$

ADDITIONAL EXAMPLES

Example 2. Solve. $(2a + 5)(3a - 1) = 0$

$$2a + 5 = 0 \quad \text{or} \quad 3a - 1 = 0$$
$$2a = -5 \qquad\qquad 3a = 1$$
$$a = -\tfrac{5}{2} \qquad\qquad a = \tfrac{1}{3}$$
$$\{-\tfrac{5}{2}, \tfrac{1}{3}\}$$

Example 2   Solve. $(2a - 1)(a + 3) = 0$

Solution

$$(2a - 1)(a + 3) = 0$$

Use the zero-product property. $2a - 1 = 0 \quad \text{or} \quad a + 3 = 0$
Solve both equations.

$$2a - 1 = 0 \qquad a + 3 = 0$$
$$2a = 1 \qquad a = -3$$
$$a = \frac{1}{2}$$

Answer $\left\{\dfrac{1}{2}, -3\right\}$

Check $(2a - 1)(a + 3) = 0$

$$\left(2\left(\frac{1}{2}\right) - 1\right)\left(\frac{1}{2} + 3\right) \stackrel{?}{=} 0$$

$$(1 - 1)\left(\frac{1}{2} + 3\right) \stackrel{?}{=} 0$$

$$0\left(3\frac{1}{2}\right) = 0 \qquad \text{It checks.}$$

$(2a - 1)(a + 3) = 0$
$(2(-3) - 1)(-3 + 3) \stackrel{?}{=} 0$
$(-6 - 1)(0) = 0$
It checks.

■ CLASSROOM EXERCISES

Solve.

1. $x(x - 2) = 0$ $\{0, 2\}$
2. $a(a + 3) = 0$ $\{0, -3\}$
3. $y(2y - 1) = 0$ $\left\{0, \frac{1}{2}\right\}$
4. $b(3b + 1) = 0$ $\left\{0, -\frac{1}{3}\right\}$
5. $(x - 1)(x - 2) = 0$ $\{1, 2\}$
6. $(a - 5)(a - 2) = 0$ $\{5, 2\}$
7. $(2a + 1)(a - 3) = 0$ $\left\{-\frac{1}{2}, 3\right\}$
8. $(3x + 2)(2x + 1) = 0$ $\left\{-\frac{2}{3}, -\frac{1}{2}\right\}$

■ WRITTEN EXERCISES

Solve.

1. $(x - 3)x = 0$ $\{3, 0\}$
2. $(x - 5)x = 0$ $\{5, 0\}$
3. $a(a + 4) = 0$ $\{0, -4\}$
4. $a(a + 7) = 0$ $\{0, -7\}$
5. $(y - 3)(y - 8) = 0$ $\{3, 8\}$
6. $(y - 6)(y - 2) = 0$ $\{6, 2\}$
7. $(x + 5)(x + 5) = 0$ $\{-5\}$
8. $(x - 6)(x - 6) = 0$ $\{6\}$
9. $(x - 5)(x + 5) = 0$ $\{5, -5\}$
10. $(x + 9)(x - 9) = 0$ $\{-9, 9\}$
11. $(3n + 1)(2n - 1) = 0$ $\left\{-\frac{1}{3}, \frac{1}{2}\right\}$
12. $(2n + 1)(3n - 1) = 0$ $\left\{-\frac{1}{2}, \frac{1}{3}\right\}$
13. $(3x + 5)(4x - 3) = 0$ $\left\{-\frac{5}{3}, \frac{3}{4}\right\}$
14. $(5x - 3)(3x + 4) = 0$ $\left\{\frac{3}{5}, -\frac{4}{3}\right\}$
15. $5(2x - 3)(3x + 2) = 0$ $\left\{\frac{3}{2}, -\frac{2}{3}\right\}$
16. $6(5x - 8)(x + 7) = 0$ $\left\{\frac{8}{5}, -7\right\}$
17. $x(2x - 8)(3x - 9) = 0$ $\{0, 3, 4\}$
18. $6x(x - 4)(x - 3) = 0$ $\{0, 3, 4\}$

CHECK UNDERSTANDING

• Is 0 a solution of $(x - 2)(x + 3) = 0$? (No) Why not? (When 0 is substituted for x, the equation simplifies to $-6 = 0$, a false sentence.)
• Is 2 a solution of $(x - 2)(x + 3) = 0$? (Yes) Why? (When 2 is substituted for x, the resulting equation is true.)

CLASSROOM EXERCISES

Emphasize that solving equations written in factored form and equaling zero becomes a search for replacements for the variable that will make a factor equal zero. In classroom exercise 8, it should be apparent that the solutions are both negative and that neither is an integer.

ASSIGNMENT GUIDE

Basic   1–17 odd, Review Exercises, Self-Quiz 1
Average   1–25 odd, Review Exercises, Self-Quiz 1
Enriched 3–27 multiples of 3, 28–39 odd, Review Exercises, Self-Quiz 1

PRACTICE WORKSHEET 35

7-3 THE ZERO-PRODUCT PROPERTY
■ Solve.
1. $x(x - 2) = 0$ $\{0, 2\}$
2. $(x - 4)x = 0$ $\{0, 4\}$
3. $n(n + 3) = 0$ $\{-3, 0\}$
4. $(p + 5)p = 0$ $\{-5, 0\}$
5. $(t - 7)(t - 9) = 0$ $\{7, 9\}$
6. $(r - 12)(r + 4) = 0$ $\{-4, 12\}$
7. $(q + 0.5)(q - 0.25) = 0$ $\{-0.5, 0.25\}$
8. $(y + 1.7)(y - 2.3) = 0$ $\{-1.7, 2.3\}$
9. $(3m + 5)(2m - 7) = 0$ $\{-5/3, 7/2\}$
10. $(c - 9)(4c - 3) = 0$ $\{3/4, 9\}$
11. $(3b - 8)(3b + 8) + 0$ $\{-8/3, 8/3\}$
12. $(h - 6)(h - 6) = 0$ $\{6\}$
13. $(6z - 9)(9z - 6) = 0$ $\{2/3, 3/2\}$
14. $(d - 3)(2d - 3) = 0$ $\{3/2, 3\}$
15. $10(k + 2)(k + 5) = 0$ $\{-5, -2\}$
16. $9(6w - 50)(3w - 5) = 0$ $\{5/3, 25/3\}$
17. $t(t - 1)(t - 2) = 0$ $\{0, 1, 2\}$
18. $2t(t + 2)(t + 4) = 0$ $\{-4, -2, 0\}$
19. $(2t - 1)(3t - 1)(4t - 1) = 0$ $\{1/4, 1/3, 1/2\}$
20. $(7t - 2)(7t - 4)(7t - 6) = 0$ $\{2/7, 4/7, 6/7\}$

Give your students this equation to solve:

$$(x + 2)(x + 5) = 4$$

Two benefits derive from this problem.
(1) The meaning of the zero-product property is emphasized. When teaching a generalization, it is important to show students examples that almost satisfy, but do not completely satisfy, the conditions of the generalization. The above equation cannot be solved by the zero-product property, since one side of the equation is not 0. If it is transformed to $(x + 2)(x + 5) - 4 = 0$, then the left side is not a product.
(2) "Going back to fundamentals" is emphasized as a problem-solving strategy. Students do not have mechanical methods for solving the given equation. Therefore, they must use "common sense." They can think as follows:

> What two numbers have 4 as a product? (1 and 4, −1 and −4, 2 and 2, −2 and −2, ½ and 8, etc.) The possibilities involving a fraction and an integer can be discarded since the sums $(x + 2)$ and $(x + 5)$ must be both fractions or both integers for any values of x. Is there a number x such that $x + 2$ is 1 and $x + 5$ is 4? Systematic trials can be used to find the solution $x = -1$, and the solution $x = -6$.

EXTRA PRACTICE, page 631

For each of the following problems:

   a. Write an equation that fits the problem, letting x represent the missing number.
   b. Solve the equation and answer the question.
   c. Check your answer in the original problem.

B **19.** The product of a number decreased by 5 and the number increased by 7 is zero. What is the number? $(x - 5)(x + 7) = 0$; 5 or −7

20. The product of a number increased by 10 and the number decreased by 10 is zero. What is the number? $(x + 10)(x - 10) = 0$; −10 or 10

21. The product of a number decreased by 7 and the number increased by 3 is zero. What is the number? $(x - 7)(x + 3) = 0$; 7 or −3

22. The product of a number increased by 6 and the number decreased by 2 is zero. What is the number? $(x - 6)(x - 2) = 0$; −6 or 2

23. The product of twice a number and the number increased by 2 is zero. What is the number? $2x(x + 2) = 0$; 0 or −2

24. The product of a number and twice the number is zero. What is the number? $x(2x) = 0$; 0

25. The product of 3 less than a number and 5 less than twice the number is zero. What is the number? $(x - 3)(2x - 5) = 0$; 3 or $2\frac{1}{2}$

26. The square of 5 more than a number is zero. What is the number? $(x + 5)^2 = 0$; −5

C **27.** In the coming 162-game baseball season, Sarah is willing to bet that the *sum* of the runs scored per game by the St. Louis Cardinals for the season will be greater than the *product* of the runs scored per game by the Chicago Cubs for the season. Explain why Sarah is willing to make this bet. Chances are good the Cubs won't score any runs in at least 1 game. So, product will be 0.

How many different solutions does each of the following equations have?

28. $x(x - 1)(x - 2)(x - 3) = 0$ 4

29. $(x - 1)(x - 1) = 0$ 1

30. $(x + 2)(x - 2) = 0$ 2

31. $x \cdot x \cdot x \cdot x = 0$ 1

32. $(2x - 1)(2x + 1) = 0$ 2

33. $(x + 3)^2(x - 4)^5 = 0$ 2

34. $(x - 1)(x - 2)(x - 1)(x - 2) = 0$ 2

35. $(x + 3)^2(x - 4) = 0$ 2

36. $5(x + 5)(x - 5)(5x)\left(\frac{x}{5}\right) = 0$ 3

37. $\dfrac{(x - 5)(x - 4)(x - 3)}{(x - 2)(x - 1)} = 0$ 3

38. $\dfrac{(x - 5)(x - 4)}{(x - 3)(x - 2)(x - 1)} = 0$ 2

39. $\dfrac{x - 5}{(x - 4)(x - 3)(x - 2)(x - 1)} = 0$ 1

- Three factors contain the variable x. Their product is zero, but there are only two distinct solutions. What do you know about the factors?

  Two of the variable factors are identical. Therefore, there can be one or two zero-factors.

- The quotient of two consecutive integers is zero. What are the integers?

  -1 and 0 or 0 and 1

- For what value(s) of x is $\dfrac{x-3}{x+4} = 0$?

  Check your answer.

  $x = 3$. If $x = -4$, the expression is undefined.

- Define your own zero-quotient property.

  a. For all numbers a and b, if $\dfrac{a}{b} = 0$, then __?__.

  $a = 0$

  b. Do you need any other restrictions in your statement?

  Yes: "and $b \neq 0$."

- For each of these equations, write a word problem similar to exercises 19–26.

  a. $(x - 3)(x + 4) = 0$
  b. $3x(x + 5) = 0$
  c. $(x - 10)^2 = 0$

■ REVIEW EXERCISES

Simplify.

1. $4 + 6 \cdot 2 - 2$ 14   2. $4 \cdot 5 - 3 \cdot 2$ 14   [1–2]

3. $5 \cdot 2^3$ 40   4. $(3 \cdot 2)^2$ 36   [1–3]

Simpify.

5. $2x(x + 2)$ $2x^2 + 4x$ 6. $a(3bc - 2 + 3b)$ $3abc - 2a + 3ab$ [4–6]

7. $6mn(2m - 3n)$ $12m^2n - 18mn^2$ 8. $10(2x - 1)$ $20x - 10$ [4–6]

The formula for the area of a circle is $A = \pi r^2$.

9. Write an equation for the area of a circle with radius 10 units. $A = \pi 10^2$ [3–9]

10. Write an equation for the area of a semicircle with radius x units. $A = \frac{1}{2}\pi x^2$ [3–9]

Self-Quiz 1

7–1   List all positive integer factors of the given number.

    1. 45   1, 3, 5, 9, 15, 45   **2.** 52   1, 2, 4, 13, 26, 52

    Write the prime factorization of each number.

    3. 120 $2^3 \cdot 3 \cdot 5$ **4.** 126 $2 \cdot 3^2 \cdot 7$

7–2   Find the greatest common factor.

    5. 45, 75   15   **6.** 70, 105, 350   35   **7.** $8x^2y$, $18xy^3$ $2xy$

7–3   Use the zero-product property to solve each equation. $\left\{\frac{3}{2}, -\frac{2}{5}\right\}$

    8. $5a(a - 4) = 0$ (0, 4)   **9.** $(n - 7)(n + 2) = 0$ $\{7, -2\}$ **10.** $(2x - 3)(5x + 2) = 0$

Mathematics and Your Future

In recent years the fields that require more preparation in mathematics have also been those paying higher salaries. For example, surveys of recent college graduates indicate that engineering and science majors receive higher salaries than do business and economics majors, who in turn receive higher salaries than do social science and humanities majors. This trend is likely to continue as the information society generates greater needs for people with strong backgrounds in mathematics. You can keep your options open for higher-paying careers by continuing to take mathematics in high school.

Solve.

1. $x(x - 4) = 0$ {0, 4}
2. $(y - 2)(y - 3) = 0$ {2, 3}
3. $(b + 4)(b - 7) = 0$ {−4, 7}
4. $2x(3x - 7) = 0$ {0, 7/3}
5. $(2x + 9)(2x - 7) = 0$ {−9/2, 7/2}

PURPOSE

Factoring polynomials is useful in simplifying rational expressions and solving equations.

PREVIEW

Point out that the height of the object is equal to zero at two times—at the time it is projected upward and again when it returns to the ground. Halfway between these times, the object should reach its maximum height.

ADDITIONAL ANSWER

■ Preview

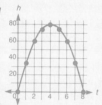

LESSON

Two special cases may be discussed. Some expressions with integer coefficients cannot be factored. If the greatest common factor of the terms is 1, the expression is said to be *irreducible* over the set of integers, as, for example, $6x^2 + 35y$. Writing the expression $1(6x^2 + 35y)$ is trivial and of little use.

Example 3 should be discussed to explain how 1 should be introduced as a factor in some exercises to show the term remaining when the monomial factor is removed.

ADDITIONAL EXAMPLES

Example 1. Factor. $6x^2 + 9x$

$3x(2x + 3)$

318

OBJECTIVE 7–4

To factor a polynomial as the product of a monomial and a polynomial.

7–4   Factoring Monomials from Polynomials

Preview   Application: Projectiles

Imagine an object projected upward from the ground. As it rises its speed gets less and less, until it stops rising at its peak. Then it falls back toward the ground, with its speed increasing until it strikes the ground.

If the object is projected at an initial velocity of 40 meters per second, its height h, in meters, after t seconds is given by the formula

$$h = t(40 - 5t)$$

• Complete this table.

t	0	1	2	3	4	5	6	7	8
h	0	35	?	?	?	?	?	?	?
			60	75	80	75	60	35	0

• Graph the ordered pairs (t, h).
• Solve the equation: $t(40 - 5t) = 0$.   {0, 8}
• What do the table, the graph, and the equation indicate about how long it will take the object to fall back to Earth?
   8 seconds

In this lesson you will learn to write polynomials in factored form and solve some second-degree equations like the one above.

■ LESSON

In earlier lessons we used the distributive properties to change products from factored form to expanded form. The process of changing from factored form to polynomial form is called **expanding**.

Factored form	*Polynomial form*
$2(3x + 7)$	$6x + 14$
$5a(2a - 4 + b)$	$10a^2 - 20a + 5ab$
$2x^2y(3x + 2y)$	$6x^3y + 4x^2y^2$

We can also use the distributive properties to accomplish the opposite result—changing from polynomial form to factored form. This process is called **factoring**. The following examples show how to factor a monomial term from a polynomial.

Example 1   Factor. $2x^2 + 4x$

Solution   Find the greatest common factor of the terms of the polynomial.

     $2x^2$: $2 \cdot x \cdot x$
     $4x$: $2 \cdot 2 \cdot x$
     GCF: $2x$

Write each term as the product of the GCF and another factor.
Use the distributive property to factor out the GCF.

     $2x^2 + 4x = 2x(x) + 2x(2)$
            $= 2x(x + 2)$

Answer   The factored form is $2x(x + 2)$.

Check   Check by expanding.

Example 2 Factor. $3abc - 2a + 3ab$

Solution *Find the GCF of the terms.*

$3abc$: $3 \cdot a \cdot b \cdot c$
$2a$: $2 \cdot a$
$3ab$: $3 \cdot a \cdot b$
GCF: a

Write each term as the product of the GCF and another factor.

$3abc - 2a + 3ab = a(3bc) - a(2) + a(3b)$

Use the distributive property to factor out the GCF.

$= a(3bc - 2 + 3b)$

Answer $a(3bc - 2 + 3b)$

Check Check by expanding.

Example 3 Factor. $20x - 10$

Solution *Find the GCF of the terms.*

$20x$: $2 \cdot 2 \cdot 5 \cdot x$
10: $2 \cdot 5$
GCF: $2 \cdot 5 = 10$

Write each term as the product of the GCF and another factor.
[*Note:* Use 1 as the other factor if the term is equal to the GCF.]

$20x - 10 = 10(2x) - 10(1)$

Factor out the GCF.

$= 10(2x - 1)$

Answer $10(2x - 1)$

Check Check by expanding.

Factoring can be used with the zero-product property to solve some polynomial equations. If the polynomial can be expressed as two or more factors whose product is zero, the zero-product property indicates that one or more of these factors must be zero.

Example 4 Solve. $x^2 - 3x = 0$

Solution *Factor out the greatest common monomial factor.*

$x^2 - 3x = 0$
$x(x - 3) = 0$

Use the zero-product property.
Solve each equation.

$x = 0$ or $x - 3 = 0$
$x = 0$ or $x = 3$

Answer $\{0, 3\}$

Check

$x^2 - 3x = 0$ $x^2 - 3x = 0$
$0^2 - 3(0) \stackrel{?}{=} 0$ $3^2 - 3(3) = 0$
$0 - 0 = 0$ It checks. $9 - (9) \stackrel{?}{=} 0$
$0 = 0$ It checks.

In classroom exercise 5, emphasize that 1 is introduced into the expression as the coefficient of x to make factoring possible.

In exercises 3–8, point out that factoring can be checked by expanding and comparing the expanded result to the original expression. They should be the same.

Also stress that factoring is not complete or correct until the *greatest* common factor of the terms has been used. For example, in classroom exercise 7, the expression can be written in factored form in several ways, including these:

$$7(3b^2c - 2bc)$$
$$bc(21b - 14)$$
$$7b(3bc - 2c)$$
$$7bc(3b - 2)$$

Only in the last expression has the greatest common factor been removed.

ASSIGNMENT GUIDE

Basic   1–31 odd, Review Exercises
Average 3–30 multiples of 3, 33–43 odd, Review Exercises
Enriched 3–42 multiples of 3, 43–49 all, Review Exercises

PRACTICE WORKSHEET 35

7-4 FACTORING MONOMIALS FROM POLYNOMIALS

■ Factor. If the expression cannot be factored, write "prime."

1. $9x + 27y$ $9(x + 3y)$
2. $14a - 21b$ $7(2a - 3b)$
3. $2c^2 + 3c$ $c(2c + 3)$
4. $4t^2 - 6t$ $2t(2t - 3)$
5. $3r^2 + r$ $r(3r + 1)$
6. $15n + 20n^2$ $5n(3 + 4n)$
7. $ab^2 + a^2b$ $ab(b + a)$
8. $12a + 5b$ Simplest form
9. $k^2 + 4$ Simplest form
10. $4r^2s^2t^2 + 6r^2st^2 - 8r^2s^2t$ $2r^2st(2st + 3t - 4s)$

■ Solve.

11. $t^2 - t = 0$ $\{0, 1\}$
12. $w^2 + 2w = 0$ $\{-2, 0\}$
13. $2k - 6 = 0$ $\{3\}$
14. $2c^2 - 5c = 0$ $\{0, 5/2\}$
15. $q^2 = 7q$ $\{0, 7\}$
16. $d^2 = -3d$ $\{-3, 0\}$
17. $5m^2 + 2m = 0$ $\{-2/5, 0\}$
18. $1.3m^2 - 6.5m = 0$ $\{0, 5\}$

320

EXTRA PRACTICE, page 632

■ CLASSROOM EXERCISES

Expand.

1. $2x(3x + 4)$ $6x^2 + 8x$
2. $3a(a - 2ab + b)$ $3a^2 - 6a^2b + 3ab$

Factor.

3. $3x + 3b$ $3(x + b)$
4. $6x + 3y$ $3(2x + y)$
5. $4x^2 + x$ $x(4x + 1)$
6. $7a^2 - 3a$ $a(7a - 3)$
7. $21b^2c - 14bc$ $7bc(3b - 2)$
8. $6a^3b + 4a^2bc - 8abc$ $2ab(3a^2 + 2ac - 4c)$

Solve.

9. $x^2 + 4x = 0$ $(0, -4)$
10. $2y - y^2 = 0$ $(0, 2)$
11. $5a^2 = 10a$ $(0, 2)$

■ WRITTEN EXERCISES

Find the greatest common factor of the terms of the polynomial.

A
1. $5x + 15y$ 5
2. $3x + 21y$ 3
3. $14x^2 - 3x$ x
4. $10x^3 - 7x^2$ x^2
5. $12x^2 + 6x$ $6x$
6. $15x^2 + 5x$ $5x$
7. $6a^2b + 10ab$ $2ab$
8. $21ab^2 + 18ab$ $3ab$

Factor. If the expression cannot be factored, write "not factorable."

9. $2x + 10b$ $2(x + 5b)$
10. $5a + 25b$ $5(a + 5b)$
11. $21a^2 - 7a$ $7a(3a - 1)$
12. $15a^2 - 3a$ $3a(5a - 1)$
13. $3x + 4y$ Not factorable
14. $5x + 6y$ Not factorable
15. $ab + a$ $a(b + 1)$
16. $ab + b$ $b(a + 1)$
17. $2xy + 4x^2y + 6xy^2$ $2xy(1 + 2x + 3y)$
18. $3x^2y + 6xy^2 + 9xy$ $3xy(x + 2y + 3)$
19. $4x^2 + 9$ Not factorable
20. $9x^2 + 16$ Not factorable

Solve.

21. $a^2 - 3a = 0$ $(0, 3)$
22. $x^2 - 5x = 0$ $(0, 5)$
23. $x^2 + 4x = 0$ $(0, -4)$
24. $a^2 + 9a = 0$ $\{0, -9\}$
25. $y^2 = 6y$ $(0, 6)$
26. $p^2 = 10p$ $(0, 10)$
27. $2x^2 - 3x = 0$ $\left\{0, \frac{3}{2}\right\}$
28. $3x^2 - 5x = 0$ $\left\{0, \frac{5}{3}\right\}$

Write an equation that fits the problem, letting x represent the number. Solve the equation and answer the question.

29. The square of a number is 10 times the number. What is the number?
$x^2 = 10x$; 0 or 10
30. The square of a number is 20 times the number. What is the number?
$x^2 = 20x$; 0 or 20
31. A number squared plus twice the number is zero. What is the number?
$x^2 + 2x = 0$; 0 or -2
32. A number squared plus three times the number is zero. What is the number?
$x^2 + 3x = 0$; 0 or -3

The following computations can be done mentally by first factoring the expressions. Write only the simplified answer.

B
33. $7 \cdot 49 + 7 \cdot 51$ 700
34. $19 \cdot 89 + 19 \cdot 11$ 1900
35. $8 \cdot 6.53 + 8 \cdot 3.47$ 80
36. $43 \cdot 124 - 43 \cdot 24$ 4300
37. $43 \cdot 6.7 - 33 \cdot 6.7$ 67
38. $113 \cdot 417 - 13 \cdot 417$ $41,700$

For each shaded region:

a. Write an expression for the area in polynomial form.
b. Write an expression for the area in factored form.

[*Remember:* The formula for the area of a circle is $A = \pi r^2$.]

39.

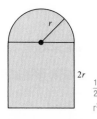

$\frac{1}{2}\pi r^2 + 4r^2$

$r^2\left(\frac{\pi}{2} + 4\right)$

40.

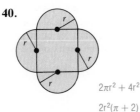

$2\pi r^2 + 4r^2$

$2r^2(\pi + 2)$

41.

$4r^2 - \pi r^2$

$r^2(4 - \pi)$

42.

$wl_1 + wl_2$

$w(l_1 + l_2)$

43.

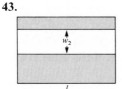

$w_1 l - w_2 l$

$l(w_1 - w_2)$

44.

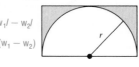

$2r^2 - \frac{1}{2}\pi r^2$

$r^2\left(2 - \frac{\pi}{2}\right)$

C 45.

$\frac{1}{2}\pi r^2 + r^2$

$r^2\left(\frac{\pi}{2} + 1\right)$

46.

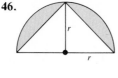

$\frac{1}{2}\pi r^2 - r^2$

$r^2\left(\frac{\pi}{2} - 1\right)$

47.

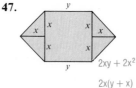

$2xy + 2x^2$

$2x(y + x)$

48.

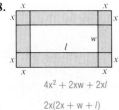

$4x^2 + 2xw + 2xl$

$2x(2x + w + l)$

49.

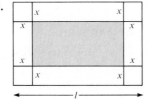

$lw - 2xw - 2xl + 4x^2$

$(l - 2x)(w - 2x)$

■ REVIEW EXERCISES

Simplify.

1. $5x - x$ 4x

2. $4a - 3a$ a [2–7]

3. $4(a - b) - (a - b)$ 3a − 3b

4. $x^2 + (-3)x + 4x + (-3)4$
 $x^2 + x - 12$

5. $x^2 + 5x - 5x - 25$ x² − 25

6. $(x^2 + 3x - 2) + (2x^2 + 5)$ [2–8, 4–1]
 $3x^2 + 3x + 3$

PROBLEM–SOLVING NOTES
Interpreting data

Exploring the formula $h = vt - 5t^2$ can develop a better understanding of the relationship between mathematics and the real world. A mathematical formula is frequently used to describe real-world phenomena. However, the use and interpretation are usually restricted by practical considerations or conditions.

Discuss the meaning of negative t-values. Have students extend the graph of the Preview data to include negative t-values and values greater than 8.

ENRICHMENT PROBLEMS

- For each of the following equations, write a word problem similar to exercises 29–32.
   a. $x^2 = 7x$
   b. $x^2 - 4x = 0$

Class Starter Quiz
on previous section

Factor.

1. $4a^2 + 40a$ $\quad 4a(a + 10)$
2. $6x^2y + 9xy^2$ $\quad 3xy(2x + 3y)$
3. $5s^2 + 5s$ $\quad 5s(s + 1)$

Solve.

4. $x^2 + 5x = 0$ $\quad \{0, -5\}$
5. $50t - 5t^2 = 0$ $\quad \{0, 10\}$

PURPOSE

It is necessary to expand the product of two binomials in simplifying expressions and in solving some equations. Understanding how to expand products is also a required skill in factoring trinomials.

PREVIEW

For each pizza (especially the last), ask students to state the dimensions of the four parts and the whole pizza. Have an equation written for each figure. For example:
$8 \cdot 8 + 8 \cdot 12 + 7 \cdot 8 + 7 \cdot 12 = 20 \cdot 15$.
The equation for the last figure is an example of expanding a binomial.

LESSON

The vertical form for multiplying binomials can be introduced and comparisons made between it and the conventional algorithm for multiplying two-digit numbers.

$3x + 2$	32
$4x + 1$	41
$\overline{3x + 2}$ *Multiply by 1.*	$\overline{32}$
$12x^2 + 8x$ *Multiply by 4x*	1280
$\overline{12x^2 + 11x + 2}$ *(or by 40).*	$\overline{1312}$

Examples in the student text will use the horizontal form. Students should be encouraged to use the FOIL method.

OBJECTIVE 7–5

To expand the product of two binomials.

You may wish to spend two days on this section. Refer to the Pacing Chart.

7–5 Expanding Products of Binomials

Preview **A model for multiplying binomials**

A rectangular pizza is to be shared by four people. They will divide it into four sections by making two cuts, one parallel to the long side and one parallel to the short side. To determine how much is to be paid for each section, it is necessary to find the area of the four sections. Find the areas of the four pieces for each pair of cuts.

  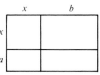

100, 100, 50, and 50 square in.; 64, 96, 56, and 84 square in.; x^2, xb, xa, and ab

In this lesson we will use areas of regions of rectangles as a model for multiplying binomials.

■ LESSON

We have used the distributive properties of multiplication over addition and over subtraction to expand the product of a monomial and a binomial.

$$x(a + b) = xa + xb \quad \text{and} \quad x(a - b) = xa - xb$$

We can also use the distributive properties to expand the product of two binomials.

$$(a + b)(c + d)$$

Distribute (c + d) over the $(a + b)(c + d) = a(c + d) + b(c + d)$
other sum.
Distribute a over the sum (c + d). $= ac + ad + b(c + d)$
Distribute b over the sum (c + d). $= ac + ad + bc + bd$

Therefore, $(a + b)(c + d) = ac + ad + bc + bd$.

We can think of the binomials $(a + b)$ and $(c + d)$ as the sides of a rectangle. The product $(a + b)(c + d)$ represents the area of the rectangle.

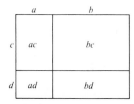

The sum $ac + bc + ad + bd$ is the sum of the areas of the smaller regions that make up the large figure.

Area of a large rectangle $=$ Sum of areas of small rectangles
$(a + b)(c + d)$ $=$ $ac + ad + bc + bd$

322

A good way for students to review for a test is to write their own representative test questions and answer those questions. To teach students the value of this activity, have them write sample test questions from which you construct a practice or real test.

Example 1. Expand. $(x + 2)(y + 3)$

$(x + 2)(y + 3) = xy + 3x + 2y + 6$

Example 2. Expand. $(x + 5)^2$

$(x + 5)^2 = x^2 + 10x + 25$

Example 3. Expand. $(x - 6)(x + 2)$

$(x - 6)(x + 2) = x^2 - 4x - 12$

Example 4. Expand. $(2x - 3)(3x - 4)$

$(2x - 3)(3x - 4) = 6x^2 - 17x + 12$

Here is a way to help you remember how to expand the product of binomials. This procedure is sometimes called the **FOIL method.**

The FOIL method

F   *Multiply FIRST terms of the binomials.* $(a + b)(c + d)$ ac

O   *Multiply OUTER terms of the binomials.* $(a + b)(c + d)$ $+ ad$

I   *Multiply INNER terms of the binomials.* $(a + b)(c + d)$ $+ bc$

L   *Multiply LAST terms of the binomials.* $(a + b)(c + d)$ $+ bd$

The sum of these products gives us the expanded form of $(a + b)(c + d)$.

$(a + b)(c + d) = ac + ad + bc + bd$

CHECK UNDERSTANDING

In the product $(3a + b)(a + 2c)$,
- what are the first terms? ($3a$ and a)
  the outer terms? ($3a$ and $2c$)
  the inner terms? (b and a)
  the last terms? (b and $2c$)
- what is the product of the first terms? ($3a^2$)
  the outer terms? ($6ac$)
  the inner terms? (ab)
  the last terms? ($2bc$)
- what is the expanded form? ($3a^2 + ab + 6ac + 2bc$)

Example 1   Expand. $(2x + 3)(y + 5)$

Solution $(2x + 3)(y + 5)$

Multiply first terms. $(2x + 3)(y + 5)$ $2xy$
Multiply outer terms. $(2x + 3)(y + 5)$ $10x$
Multiply inner terms. $(2x + 3)(y + 5)$ $3y$
Multiply last terms. $(2x + 3)(y + 5)$ 15
Add products. $2xy + 10x + 3y + 15$

Answer $(2x + 3)(y + 5) = 2xy + 10x + 3y + 15$

Example 2   Expand and simplify. $(x + 3)^2$

Solution $(x + 3)^2 = (x + 3)(x + 3)$
$= x^2 + 3x + 3x + 9$
$= x^2 + 6x + 9$

Answer $(x + 3)^2 = x^2 + 6x + 9$

Binomials involving subtraction can be rewritten as sums before expanding.

Example 3   Expand. $(x + 4)(x - 3)$

Solution   *Change subtraction to addition.* $(x + 4)(x - 3) = (x + 4)(x + (-3))$
Expand. $= x^2 + (-3)x + 4x + 4(-3)$
Simplify. $= x^2 + x - 12$

Answer $(x + 4)(x - 3) = x^2 + x - 12$

CLASSROOM EXERCISES

Point out that the simplified expanded product of two binomials has *at most* four terms (exercise 1). It may have three terms (exercise 2), or it may have two terms (exercise 5).

ASSIGNMENT GUIDE

Basic   1–27 odd, Review Exercises
Average   3–27 multiples of 3, 29–43 odd,
           Review Exercises
Enriched   3–42 multiples of 3, 44–51 all,
           Review Exercises

PRACTICE WORKSHEET 36

7-5 EXPANDING PRODUCTS OF BINOMIALS

■ **Expand and simplify.**

1. $(a + 2)(a + 10)$ $a^2 + 12a + 20$
2. $(b - 3)(b - 8)$ $b^2 - 11b + 24$
3. $(c - 4)(c - 8)$ $c^2 - 12c + 32$
4. $(d - 10)(d + 1)$ $d^2 - 9d - 10$
5. $(h - 2)(h + 9)$ $h^2 + 7h - 18$
6. $(j - 7)(j + 7)$ $j^2 - 49$
7. $(k + 12)(k - 12)$ $k^2 - 144$
8. $(m + 6)^2$ $m^2 + 12m + 36$
9. $(n - 7)^2$ $n^2 - 14n + 49$
10. $(p + \frac{1}{2})^2$ $p^2 + p + 1/4$
11. $(q + \frac{1}{3})(q - \frac{1}{3})$ $q^2 - 1/9$
12. $(r + 12)(r - 6)$ $r^2 + 6r - 72$
13. $(2s + 5)(3s + 4)$ $6s^2 + 23s + 20$
14. $(4t - 1)(t + 3)$ $4t^2 + 11t - 3$
15. $(5w - 4)(4w + 5)$ $20w^2 + 9w - 20$
16. $(y - 0)(y + 0)$ y^2
17. $(2z - 3)^2$ $4z^2 - 12z + 9$
18. $(\frac{1}{2}x - 1)(2x + 4)$ $x^2 - 4$

PROBLEM–SOLVING NOTES
Drawing a figure

The use of a geometric model to illustrate an algebraic procedure is very powerful. It gives the student something concrete to associate with the algebraic steps. It underscores the value of the diagram in understanding a problem. And it gives the student practice in representing dimensions with algebraic terms.

324

EXTRA PRACTICE, page 632

It is not necessary to change subtractions to additions in the written work. That change can be made mentally. Then the expansion is written with addition and subtraction signs.

Example 4   Expand and simplify. $(x - 2)(x - 3)$

    Solution   *Expand.* $(x - 2)(x - 3) = x^2 - 3x - 2x + 6$
             Simplify. $= x^2 - 5x + 6$

    Answer $(x - 2)(x - 3) = x^2 - 5x + 6$

■ CLASSROOM EXERCISES

Expand.

1. $(m + n)(p + q)$ **2.** $(m + 3)(m + 2)$ $m^2 + 5m + 6$ **3.** $(x - y)(x - y)$
    $mp + mq + np + nq$ $x^2 - 2xy + y^2$
4. $(a - 2)(a + 1)$ $a^2 - a - 2$ **5.** $(s - 3)(s + 3)$ $s^2 - 9$ **6.** $(2t + 1)(t - 3)$
                                                                $2t^2 - 5t - 3$

■ WRITTEN EXERCISES

For each pair of binomials, list the product of (a) the first terms, (b) the outer terms, (c) the inner terms, and (d) the last terms.

A   **1.** $(2x + 3y)(3x + 2y)$ **2.** $(2x + 5y)(5x + 2y)$ **3.** $(3a + 4b)(a - 2b)$
       $6x^2, 4xy, 9xy, 6y^2$ $10x^2, 4xy, 25xy, 10y^2$ $3a^2, - 6ab, 4ab, - 8b^2$
4. $(a + 3b)(2a - 5b)$ **5.** $(p - q)(p - 6q)$ **6.** $(p - q)(5p - q)$
    $2a^2, - 5ab, 6ab, - 15b^2$ $p^2, - 6pq, - pq, 6q^2$ $5p^2, - pq, - 5pq, q^2$
Expand the product.

7. $(a + b)(c + d)$ **8.** $(a + c)(b + d)$ **9.** $(a - c)(b + d)$
    $ac + ad + bc + bd$ $ab + ad + bc + cd$ $ab + ad - bc - cd$
10. $(a - b)(c + d)$ **11.** $(a - d)(b - c)$ **12.** $(a - d)(c - b)$
    $ac + ad - bc - bd$ $ab - ac - bd + cd$ $ac - ab - cd + bd$
Expand and simplify.

13. $(a + 3)(a + 7)$ $a^2 + 10a + 21$ **14.** $(a + 5)(a + 4)$ $a^2 + 9a + 20$ **15.** $(b - 2)(b - 3)$
                                                                   $b^2 - 5b + 6$
16. $(b - 4)(b - 5)$ $b^2 - 9b + 20$ **17.** $(c - 8)(c + 8)$ $c^2 - 64$ **18.** $(c - 7)(c + 7)$ $c^2 - 49$

19. $(d + 3)(d - 3)$ $d^2 - 9$ **20.** $(d + 6)(d - 6)$ $d^2 - 36$ **21.** $(x + 3)^2$ $x^2 + 6x + 9$

22. $(x + 5)^2$ $x^2 + 10x + 25$ **23.** $(y - 5)^2$ $y^2 - 10y + 25$ **24.** $(y - 3)^2$ $y^2 - 6y + 9$

To express the area of each large rectangle:

    a. Write an expression for the area of each of the smaller rectangles.
    b. Add the areas of the smaller rectangles and simplify.

25.   **26.**   **27.**   **28.**

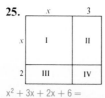

$x^2 + 3x + 2x + 6 =$
$x^2 + 5x + 6$

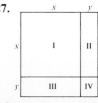

$x^2 + 2x + 2x + 4 =$
$x^2 + 4x + 4$

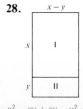

$x^2 + xy + xy + y^2 =$
$x^2 + 2xy + y^2$

$x^2 - xy + xy - y^2 =$
$x^2 - y^2$

Write the letter of the area that matches each region.

Region	Area
29. I e	**a.** $x^2 - xz - yx + yz$
30. II a	**b.** $x^2 - xy$
31. III f	**c.** $xz - yz$
32. IV c	**d.** $x^2 - xz$
33. II and IV combined b	**e.** $xy - zy$
34. I and II combined d	**f.** yz

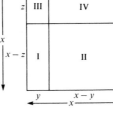

Expand and simplify.

35. $(2n + 5)(3n + 2)$ **36.** $(5n + 2)(2n + 3)$ **37.** $(3n - 7)(n + 3)$
$6n^2 + 19n + 10$ $10n^2 + 19n + 6$ $3n^2 + 2n - 21$
38. $(2a - 3b)(2a + 3b)$ $4a^2 - 9b^2$ **39.** $(5a - b)(a + 5b)$ **40.** $(x + y)(2x + y)$
$5a^2 + 24ab - 5b^2$ $2x^2 + 3xy + y^2$
41. $(2x - 3)^2$ $4x^2 - 12x + 9$ **42.** $(x + 0.5)^2$ $x^2 + x + 0.25$ **43.** $(x - 0.5)(x + 0.5)$
$x^2 - 0.25$

These two-digit numbers can be multiplied mentally by thinking of them as binomials. Find the products.

44. $88 \cdot 92 = (90 - 2)(90 + 2)$ 8096   **45.** $42 \cdot 42 = (40 + 2)(40 + 2)$ 1764

46. $71 \cdot 71 = (70 + 1)(70 + 1)$ 5041   **47.** $8.1 \cdot 7.9 = (8 + 0.1)(8 - 0.1)$ 63.99

Solve. [*Hint:* Expand each side and collect like terms on one side of the equation.]

48. $(x + 2)(x + 6) = (x + 3)^2$ $\left[-\frac{3}{2}\right]$ **49.** $(x + 3)(x + 4) = (x + 1)(x + 2)$ $\left[-\frac{5}{2}\right]$

50. $(x - 3)(x + 3) = (x - 1)(x - 4)$ $\left[\frac{13}{5}\right]$ **51.** $(x + 5)^2 = (x + 1)(x + 7)$ (-9)

■ REVIEW EXERCISES

Solve Exercises 1 and 2 by making and using a table.   [2–9]

1. What is the number n for which the sum of the whole numbers from 1 to n equals 105?   14

2. What is the number n for which 2^n equals 1024?   10

3. Write $3.14 \cdot 10^6$ in standard decimal notation.   3,140,000   [4–4]

4. Write 463,000 in scientific notation. $4.63 \cdot 10^5$ [4–4]

Solve.   [4–7]

5. How long will it take a cyclist traveling at 20 km/h to travel 25 km? $1\frac{1}{4}$ h

6. An automobile begins a trip traveling at 40 mph. A half hour later a second automobile leaves the same point traveling at 50 mph. How long will it take the second automobile to overtake the first?   2 h

ENRICHMENT PROBLEMS

• Fill in the missing parts of these diagrams. Then show the product and expansion of the binomials represented in each figure.

a.

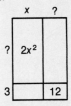

$(x + 4)(2x + 3)$
$= 2x^2 + 3x + 8x + 12$
$= 2x^2 + 11x + 12$

b.

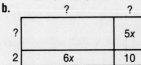

$(3x + 5)(x + 2)$
$= 3x^2 + 6x + 5x + 10$
$= 3x^2 + 11x + 10$

c.

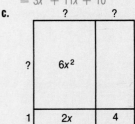

$(2x + 4)(3x + 1)$
$= 6x^2 + 2x + 12x + 4$
$= 6x^2 + 14x + 4$

d.

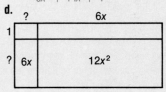

$(3 + 6x)(1 + 2x)$
$= 3 + 6x + 6x + 12x^2$
$= 3 + 12x + 12x^2$

Expand and simplify.

1. $(x + 5)(x + 10)$ $x^2 + 15x + 50$
2. $(x - 2)(x - 6)$ $x^2 - 8x + 12$
3. $(x - 8)(x + 1)$ $x^2 - 7x - 8$
4. $(x + 4)^2$ $x^2 + 8x + 16$
5. $(2x + 1)(x + 3)$ $2x^2 + 7x + 3$

PURPOSE

Factoring is useful in simplifying expressions and in solving equations. The difference of two squares is a special case in which factoring may be applied.

PREVIEW

The problem presented in the Preview may be solved in a developmental manner using an overhead projector.

Have a square sheet of paper (approximately 15 cm by 15 cm) marked as follows:

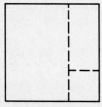

Display the square on the screen.

• What is the area of the large square if the length of one side is x cm? (x^2 cm²)

Cut off the small square in the lower right corner.

• What is the area of the small square if the length of one of its sides is y cm? (y^2 cm²)
• What is the area of the figure with the part removed? (($x^2 - y^2$)cm²)

Cut off the smaller rectangle, and arrange the pieces as pictured in the Preview.

• What are the dimensions of the composite rectangle? (They are $(x - y)$ cm and $(x + y)$ cm.)
• What is the area of the composite rectangle? (The area is (($x - y)(x + y)$)cm².)

Point out that the area has been expressed two ways. Apparently $x^2 - y^2$ equals $(x - y)(x + y)$.

326

OBJECTIVE 7–6

To factor the difference of two squares.

You may wish to spend two days on this section. Refer to the Pacing Chart.

7–6 The Difference of Two Squares

Preview

The shaded region in the figure below represents the area of the square with side x *minus* the area of the square with side y. The area of the shaded region is $x^2 - y^2$.

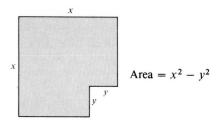

Area $= x^2 - y^2$

The area of the shaded region can be computed in another way. First divide the region into two rectangles.

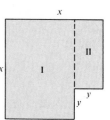

Then rearrange the two rectangles to form one rectangle.

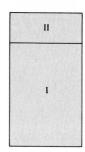

• How long is the vertical side of the rectangle? $x + y$
• How long is the horizontal side of the rectangle? $x - y$
• Express the area of the rectangle as the product of its length and width.
  $(x + y)(x - y)$

In this lesson you will use the relationship that you discovered to factor expressions.

■ LESSON

The product of the sum of two terms and the difference of those terms is a simple binomial.

$$(x + 3)(x - 3) = x^2 - 3x + 3x - 3^2$$
$$= x^2 - 3^2$$

The middle terms "drop out" (add to zero). The product is the *difference* of the squares of those two numbers.

Students are more likely to achieve the objectives of a lesson if they clearly understand what those objectives are. Before assigning the homework, review the title of the lesson and discuss how the examples in the lesson exemplify the objectives.

The Difference of Squares Property

For all numbers a and b,

$$(a + b)(a - b) = a^2 - b^2$$

The left side of this equation is the factored form and the right is the expanded form.

> **Factored form**   **Expanded form**
> $(x - 4)(x + 4)$ $=$ $x^2 - 16$

It is important to recognize both forms and to be able to change from either form to the other.

Example 1   Expand. $(2x + 3)(2x - 3)$

Solution $(2x + 3)(2x - 3) = (2x)^2 - 3^2$
$= 4x^2 - 9$

Answer $4x^2 - 9$

Example 2   Factor. $m^2 - 49$

Solution   *Write as the difference of squares.* $m^2 - 49 = m^2 - 7^2$
Factor. $= (m + 7)(m - 7)$

Answer $(m + 7)(m - 7)$

Example 3   Factor. $9p^2 - 1$

Solution $9p^2 - 1 = (3p)^2 - (1)^2$
$= (3p + 1)(3p - 1)$

Answer $(3p + 1)(3p - 1)$

Example 4   Factor. $2x^2 - 50$

Solution   *Factor out the monomial factor 2.* $2x^2 - 50 = 2(x^2 - 25)$
Factor the difference of the two squares. $= 2(x + 5)(x - 5)$

Answer $2(x + 5)(x - 5)$

In earlier lessons, students multiplied the sum and difference of two quantities and found the expanded product consisted of just two terms. For example, in multiplying the sum $(x + 3)$ and difference $(x - 3)$, the product $(x^2 - 9)$ has just two terms. This lesson builds on those previous experiences.

To support the fact that the generalization

$$x^2 - y^2 = (x + y)(x - y)$$

holds for *all* numbers, including negative numbers, have students complete this table:

$x^2 - y^2$	$x + y$	$x - y$	$(x + y)(x - y)$

using these values of x and y.

x	y
2	3
2	-3
-2	3
-2	-3

ADDITIONAL EXAMPLES

Example 1. Expand. $(a - 2b)(a + 2b)$
$a^2 - 4b^2$
Example 2. Factor. $9c^2 - d^2$
$(3c + d)(3c - d)$
Example 3. Factor. $x^2 - 25y^2$
$(x + 5y)(x - 5y)$
Example 4. Factor. $3r^2 - 48$
$3(r + 4)(r - 4)$

Example 5. Factor. $x^4 - 16y^4$

$(x^2 + 4y^2)(x + 2y)(x - 2y)$

Example 6. Solve. $2x^2 = 50$

$\{-5, 5\}$

CHECK UNDERSTANDING

- Write $4x^2$ as the square of a quantity. $(2x)^2$
- Write $36y^4$ as the square of a quantity. $(6y^2)^2$
- Factor $a^2 - b^2$. $((a + b)(a - b))$
- Factor $4x^2 - 9y^2$. $((2x - 3y)(2x + 3y))$

CLASSROOM EXERCISES

In exercise 3, point out that a similar exercise may be written $\dfrac{4x^4}{9}$. It is written as a square $\left(\dfrac{2x^2}{3}\right)^2$ instead of $\left(\dfrac{2}{3}x^2\right)^2$.

The difference of squares sometimes can be used more than once to factor an expression.

Example 5   Factor. $x^4 - 81$

> *Solution* $x^4 - 81 = (x^2)^2 - 9^2$
> $= (x^2 + 9)(x^2 - 9)$
> $= (x^2 + 9)(x + 3)(x - 3)$
>
> *Answer* $(x^2 + 9)(x + 3)(x - 3)$

The sum of two perfect squares cannot be factored as the product of two binomials. For example, the binomials $x^2 + 9$, $a^2 + b^2$, and $p^2 + 5^2$ cannot be factored.

Factoring and the zero-product property can be used to solve some equations.

Example 6   Solve. $3x^2 = 300$

> *Solution*
>
> | | |
> |---|---|
> | Divide both sides by 3. | $x^2 = 100$ |
> | Subtract 100 from both sides. | $x^2 - 100 = 0$ |
> | Factor. | $(x - 10)(x + 10) = 0$ |
> | Use the zero-product property. | $x - 10 = 0$ or $x + 10 = 0$ |
> | Solve. | $x = 10$ or $x = -10$ |
>
> *Answer* $\{10, -10\}$
>
> *Check* $3x^2 = 300$ $3x^2 = 300$
> $3 \cdot 10^2 \stackrel{?}{=} 300$ $3(-10)^2 \stackrel{?}{=} 300$
> $3 \cdot 100 = 300$ It checks. $3 \cdot 100 = 300$ It checks.

■ CLASSROOM EXERCISES

Write as squares.

1. $9x^2$ $(3x)^2$ **2.** $16a^2$ $(4a)^2$ **3.** $\dfrac{4}{9}x^4$ $\left(\dfrac{2}{3}x^2\right)^2$

4. $16a^2b^2$ $(4ab)^2$ **5.** $25m^4n^2$ $(5m^2n)^2$ **6.** $\dfrac{1}{9}a^2$ $\left(\dfrac{1}{3}a\right)^2$

Expand.

7. $(x - 4)(x + 4)$ $x^2 - 16$ **8.** $(2a + 5)(2a - 5)$ $4a^2 - 25$ **9.** $(2x + 1)(2x - 1)$ $4x^2 - 1$

10. $(2a + 6)(2a - 6)$ $4a^2 - 36$ **11.** $(4a - 3)(4a + 3)$ $16a^2 - 9$ **12.** $(a - 1)(a + 1)$ $a^2 - 1$

Factor.

13. $9a^2 - 25$ $(3a + 5)(3a - 5)$ **14.** $16x^2 - 1$ $(4x + 1)(4x - 1)$ **15.** $4y^2 - z^2$ $(2y + z)(2y - z)$

Solve.

16. $x^2 - 9 = 0$ $\{-3, 3\}$ **17.** $a^2 - 16 = 0$ $\{-4, 4\}$ **18.** $4x^2 = 100$ $\{-5, 5\}$

ASSIGNMENT GUIDE

Basic   3–45 multiples of 3, 46, Review
         Exercises, Self–Quiz 2
Average 3–48 multiples of 3, 49–59 odd,
         Review Exercises, Self–Quiz 2
Enriched 4–60 multiples of 4, 61–64 all,
         Review Exercises, Self–Quiz 2

EXTRA PRACTICE, page 632

■ WRITTEN EXERCISES

Write as squares.

A
1. $25a^2$ (5a)²
2. $36b^2$ (6b)²
3. $9c^2d^2$ (3cd)²
4. $4r^2s^2$ (2rs)²

5. p^4 (p²)²
6. q^6 (q³)²
7. $\frac{9}{25}s^{12}t^8$ $\left(\frac{3}{5}s^6t^4\right)^2$
8. $\frac{16}{49}g^{10}h^6$
$\left(\frac{4}{7}g^5h^3\right)^2$

Expand and simplify.

9. $(x+5)(x-5)$ x² – 25
10. $(x+3)(x-3)$ x² – 9
11. $(x-6)(x+6)$ x² – 36

12. $(x-10)(x+10)$ x² – 100
13. $(6+x)(6-x)$ 36 – x²
14. $(10+x)(10-x)$ 100 – x²

15. $(2x+5)(2x-5)$ 4x² – 25
16. $(3x+4)(3x-4)$ 9x² – 16
17. $(x-a)(x+a)$ x² – a²

18. $(x-r)(x+r)$ x² – r²
19. $(x+5y)(x-5y)$ x² – 25y²
20. $(5x+y)(5x-y)$ 25x² – y²

Factor.

21. x^2-4 (x+2)(x–2)
22. x^2-1 (x+1)(x–1)
23. $9x^2-1$ (3x+1)(3x–1)
24. $25x^2-1$ (5x+1)(5x–1)

25. x^2-100 (x+10)(x–10)
26. x^2-64 (x+8)(x–8)
27. $9x^2-16$ (3x+4)(3x–4)
28. $16x^2-9$ (4x+3)(4x–3)

29. $2x^2-18$ 2(x+3)(x–3)
30. $3x^2-12$ 3(x+2)(x–2)
31. c^2d^2-49 (cd+7)(cd–7)
32. r^2s^2-36 (rs+6)(rs–6)

Solve.

33. $x^2-49=0$ {7, –7}
34. $x^2-25=0$ {5, –5}
35. $x^2=64$ {8, –8}

36. $x^2=36$ {6, –6}
37. $9x^2-16=0$ $\left\{\frac{4}{3}, -\frac{4}{3}\right\}$
38. $4x^2-25=0$ $\left\{\frac{5}{2}, -\frac{5}{2}\right\}$

39. $16x^2=25$ $\left\{\frac{5}{4}, -\frac{5}{4}\right\}$
40. $100x^2=1$ $\left\{\frac{1}{10}, -\frac{1}{10}\right\}$
41. $2x^2=50$ {5, –5}

42. $3x^2=48$ {4, –4}
43. $2x^2-18=0$ {3, –3}
44. $3x^2-12=0$ {2, –2}

Write an equation that fits the problem. Solve the equation.

45. Five times the square of a number is 80. What is the number? 4 or –4
46. Seven times the square of a number is 63. What is the number? 3 or –3

Write the area of the shaded region in factored form.

(a + b)(a − b)
B **47.**
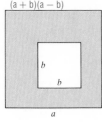

(p + q)(p − q)
48.
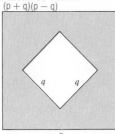

π(R + r)(R − r)
49.
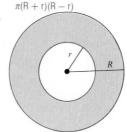

Factor.

50. $x^2-\frac{1}{16}$ $\left(x+\frac{1}{4}\right)\left(x-\frac{1}{4}\right)$
51. $x^2-0.25$ (x + 0.5)(x − 0.5)
52. $x^2-1.44$ (x + 1.2)(x − 1.2)
53. $x^2-\frac{4}{9}$ $\left(x+\frac{2}{3}\right)\left(x-\frac{2}{3}\right)$

Write as the product of three binomial factors.

54. x^4-16 (x² + 4)(x + 2)(x − 2)
55. x^4-1 (x² + 1)(x + 1)(x − 1)
56. $81x^4-1$ (9x² + 1)(3x + 1)(3x − 1)
57. $16x^4-81$ (4x² + 9)(2x + 3)(2x − 3)

PRACTICE WORKSHEET 36

7-6 THE DIFFERENCE OF TWO SQUARES

■ Expand and simplify.

1. $(a + 6)(a - 6)$ a² – 36
2. $(b - 8)(b + 8)$ b² – 64
3. $(3c - 2)(3c + 2)$ 9c² – 4
4. $(2d + 7)(2d - 7)$ 4d² – 49
5. $(h + \frac{1}{2})(h - \frac{1}{2})$ h² – 1/4
6. $(2j + 0.1)(2j - 0.1)$ 4j² – 0.01

■ Factor.

7. $k^2 - 16$ (k + 4)(k – 4)
8. $m^2 - 1$ (m + 1)(m – 1)
9. $p^2 - 100$ (p + 10)(p – 10)
10. $q^2 - 400$ (q + 20)(q – 20)
11. $9r^2 - 25$ (3r + 5)(3r – 5)
12. $16t^2 - 81$ (4t + 9)(4t – 9)

■ Solve.

13. $w^2 - 4 = 0$ {–2,2}
14. $y^2 - 49 = 0$ {–7,7}
15. $2z^2 - 50 = 0$ {–5,5}
16. $3a^2 - 27 = 0$ {–3,3}
17. $4b^2 - 49 = 0$ {–7/2,7/2}
18. $100c^2 = 9$ {–3/10,3/10}

CONCEPT EXTENSION

In solving equations such as in Example 6 ($3x^2 = 300$), students may know the solutions as soon as the equation is written in the form $x^2 = a$, $a \geq 0$. The solutions are $\sqrt{a}$ and $-\sqrt{a}$. Students should solve the equations by factoring, because this provides an explanation (by the zero-product property) of why the process works. Factoring also emphasizes that there are two solutions to the equation.

ENRICHMENT PROBLEM

Finding patterns

$$48 \cdot 52 = (50 - 2)(50 + 2)$$
$$= 50^2 - 2^2$$
$$= 2500 - 4$$
$$= 2496$$

- Find an easy way to make these calculations.

a. $103 \cdot 97$ **b.** $56 \cdot 64$
c. $31 \cdot 29$ **d.** $48^2 - 28^2$
e. $37^2 - 13^2$ **f.** $999^2 - 1$

a. $103 \cdot 97 = (100 + 3)(100 - 3)$
$$= 10,000 - 9 = 9991$$
b. $56 \cdot 64 = (60 - 4)(60 + 4)$
$$= 3600 - 16 = 3584$$
c. $31 \cdot 29 = (30 + 1)(30 - 1)$
$$= 900 - 1 = 899$$
d. $48^2 - 28^2 = (48 + 28)(48 - 28)$
$$= (76)(20) = 1520$$
e. $37^2 - 13^2 = (37 + 13)(37 - 13)$
$$= (50)(24) = 1200$$
f. $999^2 - 1 = (999 + 1)(999 - 1)$
$$= (1000)(998) = 998,000$$

The formula $d = 5t^2$ shows the distance d in meters that an object will fall in t seconds. Find the number of seconds it takes for an object to fall these distances.

58. 80 meters   4   **59.** 500 meters   10   **60.** 18,000 meters   60

Expand, simplify, and then factor these expressions.

61. $(x + 2)(x - 5) + (3x + 1)$ $(x + 3)(x - 3)$ **62.** $(x + 7)(x - 2) - (5x + 2)$ $(x + 4)(x - 4)$

63. $(x + 5)^2 - 10(x + 5)$ $(x + 5)(x - 5)$ **64.** $(x - 5)^2 + 2(5x - 17)$ $(x + 3)(x - 3)$

■ REVIEW EXERCISES

Simplify.

1. $(a^3)^2$ a^6 **2.** $\left[\left(\dfrac{2}{3}\right)x^2 y\right]^2$ $\frac{4}{9}x^4y^2$ **3.** $(2x^2)^3$ $8x^6$ **4.** $(3xy^2)^3$ $27x^3y^6$ [4–5]

5. $(x + 3)^2$ $x^2 + 6x + 9$ **6.** $(y - 5)^2$ $y^2 - 10y + 25$ **7.** $(a + b)^2$ $a^2 + 2ab + b^2$ **8.** $(a - b)^2$ [7–5]
                                                                                            $a^2 - 2ab + b^2$
9. Draw and label a figure to illustrate this problem. Then solve the problem.   [3–10]

    The length of a rectangle is 4 in. more than the width, and the perimeter is 48 in. What are the length and width?   Length: 14 in., width: 10 in.

Self-Quiz 2

7–4   Factor. If the expression cannot be factored, write "not factorable."

     1. $25x^2 + 5x$ $5x(5x + 1)$ **2.** $21b - 14ab$ $7b(3 - 2a)$ **3.** $9y^2 + 4$ Not factorable

     4. Write an expression for the area in factored form. $x(x + y)$

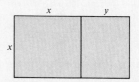

7–5   Expand and simplify.

     5. $(c + 7)(c + 3)$ $c^2 + 10c + 21$ **6.** $(2r + 5)(r - 8)$ $2r^2 - 11r - 40$

7–6   Factor.

     7. $x^2 - 49$ $(x + 7)(x - 7)$ **8.** $4y^2 - 81$ $(2y + 9)(2y - 9)$ **9.** $2b^2 - 50$ $2(b + 5)(b - 5)$

7–4, 7–6   Solve.

     10. $x^2 + 7x = 0$ $\{0, -7\}$ **11.** $4a^2 = 64$ $\{4, -4\}$ **12.** $9x^2 - 100 = 0$ $\left\{\dfrac{10}{3}, -\dfrac{10}{3}\right\}$

OBJECTIVE 7–7

To factor perfect square trinomials.

7–7 Perfect Trinomial Squares

Preview

Show how these four rectangles can be arranged to form a square. What are the dimensions of the square? What is the area of the square?

7 units by 7 units   49 square units

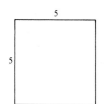  

Let x and y be any positive numbers. Show how these four rectangles can be arranged to form a square. What are the dimensions of the square? $(x + y)$ units by $(x + y)$ units; $(x + y)^2$ square units

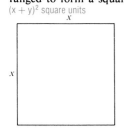  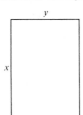 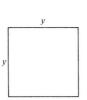

In this lesson you will study patterns that always produce squares.

■ LESSON

To find the square of a binomial, the FOIL method of expansion can be simplified.

F: *Multiply first terms.* $(3b + 5)^2 = (3b + 5)(3b + 5)$ $9b^2$

(The product of the first terms is the *square* of the binomial's first term.)

O: *Multiply outer terms.* $(3b + 5)^2 = (3b + 5)(3b + 5)$ $15b$

I: *Multiply inner terms.* $(3b + 5)^2 = (3b + 5)(3b + 5)$ $15b$

(The products of the inner and outer terms are the same. Each product is the product of the first and second terms of the binomial.)

PURPOSE

Factoring perfect-square trinomials is the basis for techniques that are studied later in Algebra 1 and in advanced work. These techniques include completing the square and developing the quadratic formula.

PREVIEW

The squares and rectangles pictured in the Preview may be shown on the overhead projector as cutouts. The cutouts can then be rearranged to form a square.

Point out that *perfect-square* trinomials are a special type of trinomial and that they have special importance. Students are expected to look for relationships between the coefficients *(a, b, c, d, e)* in

$$(ax + by)^2 = cx^2 + dxy + ey^2$$

for several specific examples.

The skill of factoring perfect-square trinomials is used in solving an equation. Perfect square trinomials are a special case. They yield only one solution.

ADDITIONAL EXAMPLES

Example 1. Expand. $(2x - 5y)^2$

$$4x^2 - 20xy + 25y^2$$

L: *Multiply last terms.* $\qquad (3b + 5)^2 = (3b + 5)(3b + 5) \qquad 25$

(The product of the last terms is the square of the binomial's last term.)

Add the products. $\qquad (3b + 5)^2 = 9b^2 + 30b + 25$

To square a binomial such as $(3b + 5)^2$

1. Square its first term. $\qquad\qquad (3b)^2 = 9b^2$

2. Double the product of its terms. $\quad 2(3b)(5) = 30b$

3. Square its last term. $\qquad\qquad 5^2 = 25$

4. Add the products. $\qquad\qquad (3b + 5)^2 = 9b^2 + 30b + 25$

This property can be stated for any binomial.

The Perfect Square Property

For all numbers a and b,

$$(a + b)^2 = a^2 + 2ab + b^2$$
$$\text{and}$$
$$(a - b)^2 = a^2 - 2ab + b^2$$

Knowing this property, you can expand or factor some expressions quickly and easily. Study these examples.

> **Example 1** Expand. $(3x + 2)^2$
>
> *Solution* $(3x + 2)^2 = (3x)^2 + 2(3x)(2) + 2^2$
> $\qquad\qquad\qquad = 9x^2 + 12x + 4$
>
> *Answer* $9x^2 + 12x + 4$

Mathematics and Your Future

As you learn algebra today, you are preparing to live and work in what has been called "the information society of tomorrow." To succeed in that society, you will need skills in the areas of mathematics and communication (speaking, listening, reading, and writing). Take enough mathematics in high school to prepare yourself for the future.

Create a classroom environment in which it is acceptable for students to take risks and make mistakes, provided that they work to correct the mistakes. Students should be willing to guess or make conjectures.

ADDITIONAL EXAMPLES

Example 2. Is $16x^2 + 24x + 9$ a perfect square?

Yes: $(4x + 3)^2$

Example 3. Factor. $x^2 + 6xy^2 + 9y^4$

$(x + 3y^2)^2$

Example 4. Factor. $3x^2 - 24x + 48$

$3(x - 4)^2$

Example 2   Is the following trinomial a perfect square? That is, can we write it as the square of a binomial?

$$4x^2 + 12x + 9$$

Solution   Factor the first and last terms of the trinomial into squares. $4x^2 = (2x)^2$
$9 = 3^2$

If the trinomial is a perfect square then the factored form must be

$$(2x + 3)^2$$

[The binomial is a *sum* since all coefficients of the trinomial are positive.]

Expand this expression to see whether the $(2x + 3)^2 = 4x^2 + 12x + 9$
"middle" term is 12x.

Answer   The trinomial *is* a perfect square.

Example 3   Factor. $9x^2 - 6x + 1$

Solution   Factor the first and last terms of the trinomial into squares. $9x^2 = (3x)^2$
$1 = 1^2$

The coefficient of the middle term, -6, is negative, so the coefficient of the last term of the binomial must be negative. The factored form is

$$(3x - 1)^2$$

Expand to check the middle term. $(3x - 1)^2 = 9x^2 - 6x + 1$
It checks.

Answer $(3x - 1)^2$

Inspect the trinomial for common monomial factors before attempting other factoring.

Example 4   Factor. $2x^2 + 8x + 8$

Solution   *First factor out the GCF of the terms.* $2x^2 + 8x + 8 = 2(x^2 + 4x + 4)$
Factor the trinomial. $= 2(x + 2)^2$
Expand to check, squaring first. $2(x + 2)^2 = 2(x^2 + 4x + 4)$
$= 2x^2 + 8x + 8$
It checks.

Answer $2x^2 + 8x + 8 = 2(x + 2)^2$

Example 5. Solve. $x^2 + 12x + 36 = 0$

$\{-6\}$

CHECK UNDERSTANDING

- Expand.
  $(x + y)^2$ $\quad$ $(x^2 + 2xy + y^2)$
  $(2a - 3b)^2$ $\quad$ $(4a^2 - 12ab + 9b^2)$
- Factor.
  $m^2 - 2mn + n^2$ $\quad$ $((m - n)^2)$
  $m^2 - n^2$ $\quad$ $((m - n)(m + n))$

CLASSROOM EXERCISES

In exercise 6, point out that *three* factors are to be multiplied and that they can be multiplied in any order. It is customary (and probably easier) to multiply the binomials first.

ASSIGNMENT GUIDE

Basic $\quad$ 1–49 odd, Review Exercises
Average $\quad$ 3–54 multiples of 3, 55–62 all,
$\qquad$ Review Exercises
Enriched $\quad$ 3–60 multiples of 3, 63–70 all,
$\qquad$ Review Exercises

PRACTICE WORKSHEET 37

7-7 PERFECT TRINOMIAL SQUARES

■ Expand and simplify.
1. $(a + 10)^2$ $a^2 + 20a + 100$ $\quad$ 2. $(b - 11)^2$ $b^2 - 22b + 121$
3. $(c + \frac{1}{2})^2$ $c^2 + c + 1/4$ $\quad$ 4. $(2d - 7)^2$ $4d^2 - 28d + 49$
5. $(4d - 3)^2$ $16d^2 - 24d + 9$ $\quad$ 6. $3(5h + 1)^2$ $75h^2 + 30h + 3$

■ Factor. If the trinomial cannot be factored, write "simplest form."
7. $k^2 - 8k + 16$ $(k - 4)^2$ $\quad$ 8. $m^2 + 10m - 25$ Simplest form
9. $p^2 + 16p + 64$ $(p + 8)^2$ $\quad$ 10. $9r^2 + 18r + 9$ $9(r + 1)^2$
11. $4s^3 - 24s + 36$ $4(s - 3)^2$ $\quad$ 12. $9t^2 + 42t + 49$ $(3t + 7)^2$

■ Solve.
13. $w^2 - 4w + 4 = 0$ $\{2\}$ $\quad$ 14. $z^2 + 26z + 169 = 0$ $\{-13\}$
15. $c^3 + 40c + 400 = 0$ $\{-20\}$ $\quad$ 16. $9n^2 - 6n + 1 = 0$ $\{1/3\}$
17. $q^2 - 100 = 0$ $\{-10, 10\}$ $\quad$ 18. $(q - 100)^2 = 0$ $\{100\}$

EXTRA PRACTICE, page 632

Factoring and the zero-product property can be used to solve some equations.

Example 5 $\quad$ Solve. $x^2 - 10x + 25 = 0$

Solution $\quad$ *Factor the trinomial.* $\qquad$ $(x - 5)(x - 5) = 0$
$\qquad$ *Use the zero-product property.* $\qquad$ $x - 5 = 0$
$\qquad$ *Solve.* $\qquad$ $x = 5$

Answer $\quad$ $\{5\}$

■ CLASSROOM EXERCISES

Write as squares.

1. $4x^2$ $(2x)^2$ $\qquad$ **2.** $9a^2b^2$ $(3ab)^2$ $\qquad$ **3.** x^4 $(x^2)^2$ $\qquad$ **4.** $\frac{9}{16}a^2b^4$ $\left(\frac{3}{4}ab^2\right)^2$

Expand and simplify.

5. $(x - 3)^2$ $x^2 - 6x + 9$ $\qquad\qquad$ **6.** $2(x + 5)^2$ $2x^2 + 20x + 50$

Is the trinomial a perfect square?

7. $-9x^2 - 6xy + y^2$ No $\qquad$ **8.** $9a^2 + 18ab + 9b^2$ Yes $\qquad$ **9.** $4x^2 - 4xy + y^2$ Yes

Factor.

10. $x^2 + 2xy + y^2$ $(x + y)^2$ $\qquad$ **11.** $m^2 - 2mn + n^2$ $(m - n)^2$ $\qquad$ **12.** $9a^2 + 12ab + 4b^2$ $(3a + 2b)^2$

13. $x^4 - 4x^2y + 4y^2$ $(x^2 - 2y)^2$ $\qquad$ **14.** $9a^2 - 4b^2$ $(3a + 2b)(3a - 2b)$ $\qquad$ **15.** $3x^2 + 6x + 3$ $3(x + 1)^2$

Solve.

16. $x^2 + 14x + 49 = 0$ $\{-7\}$ $\qquad\qquad$ **17.** $x^2 - 81 = 0$ $\{9, -9\}$

■ WRITTEN EXERCISES

Write as squares.

A $\quad$ **1.** $9a^2$ $(3a)^2$ $\qquad$ **2.** $49b^2$ $(7b)^2$ $\qquad$ **3.** $16c^2d^2$ $(4cd)^2$ $\qquad$ **4.** $64r^2s^2$ $(8rs)^2$

5. p^6 $(p^3)^2$ $\qquad$ **6.** q^4 $(q^2)^2$ $\qquad$ **7.** $\frac{16}{81}s^8t^{10}$ $\left(\frac{4}{9}s^4t^5\right)^2$ $\qquad$ **8.** $\frac{9}{100}x^4y^6$ $\left(\frac{3}{10}x^2y^3\right)^2$

Is the trinomial a perfect square?

9. $x^2 + 4x - 4$ No $\qquad$ **10.** $y^2 - 6x - 9$ No $\qquad$ **11.** $4x^2 - 8xy + y^2$ No

12. $x^2 - 12xy + 36y^2$ Yes $\qquad$ **13.** $a^2 - a + \frac{1}{4}$ Yes $\qquad$ **14.** $a^2 + \frac{2}{3}a + \frac{1}{9}$ Yes

Expand and simplify.

15. $(x + 5)^2$ $x^2 + 10x + 25$ $\qquad$ **16.** $(y + 4)^2$ $y^2 + 8y + 16$ $\qquad$ **17.** $(a - 6)^2$ $a^2 - 12a + 36$

18. $(b - 3)^2$ $b^2 - 6b + 9$ $\qquad$ **19.** $(3y + 2)^2$ $9y^2 + 12y + 4$ $\qquad$ **20.** $(4x + 3)^2$ $16x^2 + 24x + 9$

21. $(3b - 4)^2$ $\quad 9b^2 - 24b + 16$ **22.** $(2a - 3)^2$ $\quad 4a^2 - 12a + 9$ **23.** $(5c - d)^2$
                                                                             $25c^2 - 10cd + d^2$

24. $(8p - q)^2$ $\quad 64p^2 - 16pq + q^2$ **25.** $2(x + 10)^2$ $\quad 2x^2 + 40x + 200$ **26.** $3(x + 1)^2$ $\quad 3x^2 + 6x + 3$

Factor.

27. $x^2 + 6x + 9$ $\quad (x + 3)^2$ **28.** $x^2 + 12x + 36$ $\quad (x + 6)^2$ **29.** $x^2 - 8xz + 16z^2$
                                                                                  $(x - 4z)^2$

30. $x^2 - 10xy + 25y^2$ $\quad (x - 5y)^2$ **31.** $2x^2 + 8xy + 8y^2$ $\quad 2(x + 2y)^2$ **32.** $3x^2 + 6xz + 3z^2$
                                                                                        $3(x + z)^2$

33. $x^2 - 16$ $\quad (x + 4)(x - 4)$ **34.** $x^2 - 25$ $\quad (x + 5)(x - 5)$ **35.** $5x^2 - 45$ $\quad 5(x + 3)(x - 3)$

36. $3x^2 - 12$ $\quad 3(x + 2)(x - 2)$ **37.** $4x^2 - 12x + 9$ $\quad (2x - 3)^2$ **38.** $9x^2 - 24x + 16$
                                                                                             $(3x - 4)^2$

Solve.

39. $x^2 - 10x + 25 = 0$ $\quad \{5\}$ **40.** $x^2 - 8x + 16 = 0$ $\quad \{4\}$ **41.** $x^2 + 12x + 36 = 0$
                                                                                             $\{-6\}$

42. $x^2 + 6x + 9 = 0$ $\quad \{-3\}$ **43.** $(x - 0.5)^2 = 0$ $\quad \{0.5\}$ **44.** $(x - 2.5)^2 = 0$ $\quad \{2.5\}$

45. $2x^2 - 4x + 2 = 0$ $\quad \{1\}$ **46.** $3x^2 - 12x + 12 = 0$ $\quad \{2\}$ **47.** $(x + 1.5)^2 = 0$ $\quad \{-1.5\}$

48. $(x + 3.5)^2 = 0$ $\quad \{-3.5\}$ **49.** $x^2 - 100 = 0$ $\quad \{10, -10\}$ **50.** $x^2 - 64 = 0$ $\quad \{8, -8\}$

Write the area of each square as a binomial squared. Then expand and simplify.
Copy and subdivide each square into rectangles and write the area of each rectangle on your diagram.

51. 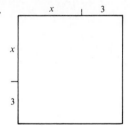 $\quad x^2 + 6x + 9$ **52.** 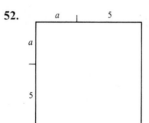 $\quad a^2 + 10a + 25$

53. 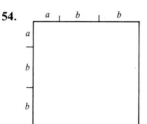 $\quad 4a^2 + 4ab + b^2$ **54.** $\quad a^2 + 4ab + 4b^2$

Write as the product of three factors.

55. $x^3 - 6x^2 + 9x$ $\quad x(x - 3)^2$ **56.** $x^3 + 22x^2 + 121x$ $\quad x(x + 11)^2$ **57.** $x^3 - 9x$ $\quad x(x + 3)(x - 3)$

Write as the product of four factors.

58. $x^4 - 2x^2 + 1$ $\quad (x + 1)^2(x - 1)^2$ **59.** $x^4 - 8x^2 + 16$ $\quad (x + 2)^2(x - 2)^2$ **60.** $x^4 - 18x^2 + 81$
                                                                                              $(x + 3)^2(x - 3)^2$

CONCEPT EXTENSION

The models representing perfect square trinomials in the Preview have two important characteristics: They move from specific examples to the general abstract case, and they are intended to be manipulated. Though students at this level may be somewhat reluctant, it is important to have them cut out these rectangular regions and actually construct the squares. Actually going through the physical movements, as compared to mentally moving the pieces, has a decidedly stronger and longer-lasting learning effect.

Moreover, you may wish to have students show the areas of each rectangle on the region and compare the sum of these areas to the area of the binomial squared. As another test of the understanding of the model, you might give students these two squares and ask them to construct two other pieces that can be arranged to form a square with area $(x + 4)^2$.

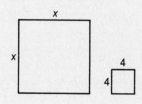

ENRICHMENT PROBLEMS
Interpreting diagrams

• Sketch a diagram to show the expansion of each expression. Show the area of each region of your diagram.

a. $(x - y)^2$

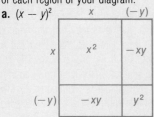

$$(x - y)^2 = x^2 - 2xy + y^2$$

b. $(x + y + 5)^2$

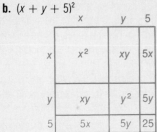

$$(x + y + 5)^2$$
$$= x^2 + 2xy + 10x + 10y + y^2 + 25$$

• If $(x + 2)^2$ expanded can be associated with regions of a square with sides $(x + 2)$, what kind of figure would you expect for $(x + 2)^3$? Can you sketch the figure with its various parts?

A cube with sides $x + 2$.

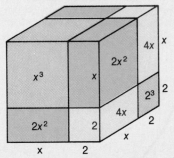

$$(x + 2)^3 = x^3 + 3(x^2)(2) + 3(x)(4) + 2^3$$
$$= x^3 + 6x^2 + 12x + 8$$

ADDITIONAL ANSWER

■ **Review**
Exercises 5.

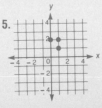

61. General Jones said, "$(x + y)^2 = x^2 + y^2$." Show that he is wrong.
$(x + y)^2 = x^2 + 2xy + y^2$

62. Admiral Thompson said, "$(x - y)^2 = x^2 - y^2$." Show that she is wrong.
$(x - y)^2 = x^2 - 2xy + y^2$

C 63. Copy and complete the table.

n	15	25	35	45	55	65
n^2	225	625	?	?	?	?
			1225	2025	3025	4225

If t represents the tens digit and u represents the ones digit, a two-digit number can be written as $10t + u$.

64. Expand and simplify $(10t + u)^2$. $100t^2 + 20tu + u^2$

65. Expand and simplify $(10t + 5)^2$. $100t^2 + 100t + 25$

66. Expand and simplify $100t(t + 1) + 25$. $100t^2 + 100t + 25$

67. Use the results of Exercise 65 to explain why the square of a whole number ending in 5 ends in 25. $(10t + 5)^2 = 100(t^2 + t) + 25$

68. Use the results of Exercises 65 and 66 to explain why the square of a whole number ending in 5 has digits to the left of the tens place that are the product of a number and its successor. $(10t + 5)^2 = 100(t)(t + 1) + 25$

69. Expand and simplify $(10t + 2)^2$. Use the results to explain why the squares of two-digit numbers ending in 2 are divisible by 4.
$100t^2 + 40t + 4 = 4(25t^2 + 10t + 1)$

70. Expand and simplify $(10t + 6)^2$. Use the results to explain why the squares of two-digit numbers ending in 6 are divisible by 4.
$100t^2 + 120t + 36 = 4(25t^2 + 30t + 9)$

■ REVIEW EXERCISES

Expand and simplify.

1. $(x + 2)(x + 6)$ $x^2 + 8x + 12$ **2.** $(x - 3)(x - 5)$ $x^2 - 8x + 15$ [7–5]

3. State the quadrant each point is on or the axis it is on.   [5–1]

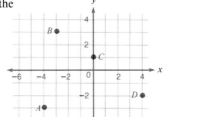

a. A III

b. B II

c. C y-axis

d. D IV

4. List the domain and range of the relation $\{(1, 4), (2, 4), (3, 5), (4, 5)\}$.   [5–2]
$(1, 2, 3, 4), \{4, 5\}$

5. Graph the relation $\{(1, 2), (0, 2), (1, 1)\}$.   [5–2]

6. State whether the ordered pair is a solution of the equation $3x + y = 12$.   [5–3]

  a. $(2, 6)$ Yes   **b.** $(-4, 0)$ No   **c.** $(6, -2)$ No

336

You may wish to spend two days on this section. Refer to the Pacing Chart.

7–8 Factoring $x^2 + bxy + cy^2$ with c Positive

PURPOSE

Quadratic equations may be solved by several different methods, including factoring. Equations studied in this section and the next section are especially well suited for solving by factoring.

Preview

Here is a list of all pairs of integers having the product 12.

| 1 and 12 | 2 and 6 | 3 and 4 |
| -1 and -12 | -2 and -6 | -3 and -4 |

- Which of these pairs has the sum 7? 3 and 4
- Which of these pairs has the sum 13? 1 and 12
- Find a pair of integers that has the product 6 and the sum 5. 2 and 3

- List all pairs of integers having the product 15. 1 and 15, -1 and -15, 3 and 5, -3 and -5
  a. Which pair has the sum 16? 1 and 15
  b. Which pair has the sum -8? -3 and -5

In this lesson you will use the skill of finding a pair of numbers that has a given product and a given sum to factor trinomials.

PREVIEW

Discuss the meaning of *sum* and *product*. In the fourth question, point out that two conditions must be satisfied at the same time.

■ LESSON

In factoring the difference of two squares (such as $x^2 - 9$) or in factoring perfect squares (such as $x^2 + 6x + 9$), there is a step-by-step procedure to find the factors. For other polynomials, however, you will have to check several choices to find the pair that works. For example, consider factoring $x^2 + 8x + 12$.

We know that the first term of each binomial is x: $(x\quad)(x\quad)$.

We also know that the product of the last terms of the binomials is 12. Therefore, the second terms of the binomials are 3 and 4, 2 and 6, 1 and 12, -3 and -4, -2 and -6, or -1 and -12.

These are the possible factors.

$$(x + 3)(x + 4)$$
$$(x + 2)(x + 6)$$
$$(x + 1)(x + 12)$$
$$(x - 3)(x - 4)$$
$$(x - 2)(x - 6)$$
$$(x - 1)(x - 12)$$

Now we mentally expand each choice to determine whether any of them produces the middle term, $8x$.

$$(x + 3)(x + 4) = x^2 + 7x + 12$$
$$(x + 2)(x + 6) = x^2 + 8x + 12 \quad \leftarrow$$
$$(x + 1)(x + 12) = x^2 + 13x + 12$$
$$(x - 3)(x - 4) = x^2 - 7x + 12$$
$$(x - 2)(x - 6) = x^2 - 8x + 12$$
$$(x - 1)(x - 12) = x^2 - 13x + 12$$

Only $(x + 2)(x + 6)$ correctly factors the polynomial. Note that $2 \cdot 6 = 12$ (last term) and $2 + 6 = 8$ (middle-term coefficient.)

LESSON

Discuss the importance of checking factored answers by multiplying the factors and comparing the results to the original trinomial. In multiplying the two binomial factors, students should think through all four steps using the FOIL method. This method of checking will continue to be used in more complicated examples, such as those studied in Section 7-10.

In solving equations such as $7y = y^2 + 6$, point out that the equation can be written

$$0 = y^2 - 7y + 6$$
$$0 = (y - 6)(y - 1)$$

The trinomial and the factors can be written on the right side of the equation. Although students may *always* write the zero on the right side of the equation, there is no advantage in doing so.

Write a computer program that will factor expressions of the form $x^2 + bx + c$, where b is any integer and c is a positive integer.

```
10 PRINT "THIS PROGRAM
   FACTORS EXPRESSIONS"
20 PRINT "OF THE FORM X ↑ 2
   + BX + C WHERE"
30 PRINT "B IS ANY INTEGER
   AND C IS"
40 PRINT "A POSITIVE INTEGER."
50 PRINT "ENTER B, FOLLOWED
   BY A COMMA"
60 PRINT "THEN ENTER C"
70 INPUT B, C
80 IF C < 1 THEN 10
90 FOR K = 1 TO C
100 IF INT(C/K) <> C/K THEN 180
110 IF B <> 0 THEN 150
120 IF B <> - (C/K + K) THEN 180
130 PRINT "X ↑ 2 - ";-B;" X
    + ";C;" = (X - ";K;")
    (X - ";C/K;")"
140 GO TO 200
150 IF B <> C/K + K THEN 180
160 PRINT "X ↑ 2 + ";B;" X
    + ";C;" = (X + ";K;")(X
    + ";C/K;")"
170 GO TO 200
180 NEXT K
190 PRINT "X ↑ 2 + ";B;" X
    + ";C;" IS IN SIMPLEST
    FORM."
200 END
```

We can usually eliminate some of the possibilities by noting the signs of the coefficients.

Example 1   Factor. $a^2 - 5a + 6$

Solution   The first terms of the binomials are a.

$$(a \qquad)(a \qquad)$$

The last term of the trinomial (6) is positive, so the last terms of the binomials are both positive or both negative. Write the pairs of numbers whose product is 6.

$$\begin{array}{cc} 1 \text{ and } 6 & 2 \text{ and } 3 \\ -1 \text{ and } -6 & -2 \text{ and } -3 \end{array}$$

The coefficient of the middle term of the trinomial (-5) indicates that both signs are negative, so the possible factors are

$$(a - 1)(a - 6)$$
$$(a - 2)(a - 3)$$

Mentally expand each choice to determine the one that gives the correct middle term.

$$(a - 1)(a - 6) = a^2 - 7a + 6$$
$$(a - 2)(a - 3) = a^2 - 5a + 6 \quad \leftarrow$$

Note that $-2 \cdot -3 = 6$ (last term) and $-2 + (-3) = -5$ (middle-term coefficient).

Answer $(a - 2)(a - 3)$

At first, this process of "guess and check" can seem very tedious. With practice, most of the work can be done quickly "in your head."

Example 2   Factor. $y^2 + 8yz + 16z^2$

Solution   The first terms of the binomials are both y. The last terms of the binomials must contain the variable z.

$$(y \qquad z)(y \qquad z)$$

The coefficient of the middle term (8) and the last term (16) of the trinomial are both positive, so the coefficients of both terms of the binomials are positive. Write the pairs of positive numbers whose product is 16.

$$1 \text{ and } 16 \quad 2 \text{ and } 8 \quad 4 \text{ and } 4$$

The coefficient of the middle term of the trinomial indicates that the sum of the coefficients of the last terms of the binomials is 8. So choose the pair whose sum is 8.

$$4 \text{ and } 4$$

Example 2   (continued)

Write the binomial factors.

$$(y + 4z)(y + 4z)$$

Answer $(y + 4z)(y + 4z)$

Check $(y + 4z)(y + 4z) = y^2 + 8yz + 16z^2$ It checks.

Always remember to remove a common monomial factor before attempting other factoring.

Example 3   Factor. $5x^2 - 35x + 60$

Solution   *Factor out the GCF of the terms.* $5(x^2 - 7x + 12)$
   Factor the trinomial. $5(x - 3)(x - 4)$

Answer $5(x - 3)(x - 4)$

Factoring and the zero-product property can be used to solve some equations.

Example 4   Solve. $y^2 + 15 = 8y$

Solution $y^2 + 15 = 8y$

   Collect all terms on one side of the equation and arrange the terms in descending order. $y^2 - 8y + 15 = 0$
   Factor. $(y - 3)(y - 5) = 0$
   Apply the zero-product property. $y = 3$ or $y = 5$

Answer   {3, 5}

Check

$y^2 + 15 = 8y$	$y^2 + 15 = 8y$
$3^2 + 15 \stackrel{?}{=} 8 \cdot 3$	$5^2 + 15 \stackrel{?}{=} 8 \cdot 5$
$9 + 15 \stackrel{?}{=} 24$	$25 + 15 \stackrel{?}{=} 40$
$24 = 24$ It checks.	$40 = 40$ It checks.

■ CLASSROOM EXERCISES

Factor.

1. $x^2 + 5x + 6$ $(x + 3)(x + 2)$ **2.** $x^2 - 5x + 6$ $(x - 3)(x - 2)$ **3.** $a^2 + 7a + 6$
$(a + 6)(a + 1)$

4. $b^2 - 7b + 6$ $(b - 6)(b - 1)$ **5.** $c^2 + 4c + 4$ $(c + 2)^2$ **6.** $a^2 - b^2$ $(a + b)(a - b)$

7. $x^2 + 6xy + 9y^2$ $(x + 3y)^2$ **8.** $3a^2 - 18a + 15$ $3(a - 5)(a - 1)$ **9.** $y^2 - 8yz + 7z^2$
$(y - 7z)(y - z)$

Solve.

10. $x^2 + 7x + 12 = 0$ $\{-4, -3\}$ **11.** $x^2 + 5 = 6x$ $\{1, 5\}$ **12.** $t^2 - 5t + 4 = 0$ $\{1, 4\}$

Example 1. Factor. $x^2 + 7x + 12$
$(x + 3)(x + 4)$

Example 2. Factor. $a^2 + 11ab + 24b^2$
$(a + 3b)(a + 8b)$

Example 3. Factor. $3x^2 - 24x + 36$
$3(x - 2)(x - 6)$

Example 4. Solve. $9y = y^2 + 14$
$\{2, 7\}$

CHECK UNDERSTANDING

• List positive-integer factor pairs of 12. (3 and 4, 2 and 6, 1 and 12)
• State the sum of the integers in each pair. (7, 8, 13)
• State a factor pair of 18 with sum 11. (2 and 9)
• Factor. $a^2 + 11a + 18$ $((a + 2)(a + 9))$
• Factor. $a^2 - 11a + 18$ $((a - 2)(a - 9))$

CLASSROOM EXERCISES

Exercise 6 is a review of the factoring studied in Section 7-6. Exercise 7 reviews the factoring studied in Section 7-7.

ASSIGNMENT GUIDE

Basic   1–35 odd, Review Exercises
Average   3–57 multiples of 3, 58–63 all,
           Review Exercises
Enriched   9–57 multiples of 3, 58, 59, 61–
           73 odd, Review Exercises

EXTRA PRACTICE, page 633

PRACTICE WORKSHEET 37

7-8 FACTORING $x^2 + bxy + cy^2$ WITH c POSITIVE

■ **Factor.**

1. $x^2 - 5x + 6$ $(y-3)(y-2)$
2. $y^2 - 7y + 10$ $(y-5)(y-2)$
3. $z^2 + 13z + 42$ $(z+7)(z+6)$
4. $a^2 - 13a + 36$ $(a-9)(a-4)$
5. $b^2 + 8b + 15$ $(b+5)(b+3)$
6. $c^2 + 11c + 10$ $(c+10)(c+1)$
7. $r^2 + 9rs + 18s^2$ $(r+6s)(r+3s)$
8. $a^2 + 13ab + 40b^2$ $(a+8b)(a+5b)$
9. $3x^2 + 21xy + 18y^2$ $3(x+y)(x+6y)$
10. $2m^2 - 12m + 18$ $2(m-3)^2$

■ **Solve.**

11. $a^2 - 11a + 18 = 0$ $\{2, 9\}$
12. $b^2 - 4b + 4 = 0$ $\{2\}$
13. $c^2 + 11c + 28 = 0$ $\{-7, -4\}$
14. $d^2 + 14d + 40 = 0$ $\{-10, -4\}$
15. $h^2 - 19h + 90 = 0$ $\{9, 10\}$
16. $k^2 - 4k + 3 = 0$ $\{1, 3\}$
17. $m^2 - 9m + 20 = 0$ $\{4, 5\}$
18. $p^2 + 14p + 49 = 0$ $\{-7\}$
19. $r^2 + 10r + 16 = 0$ $\{-8, -2\}$
20. $s^2 - 12s + 20 = 0$ $\{2, 10\}$

■ WRITTEN EXERCISES

Factor.

A   1. $a^2 + 4a + 3$ $(a+3)(a+1)$ 2. $p^2 + 6p + 5$ $(p+5)(p+1)$ 3. $x^2 + 6x + 8$ $(x+4)(x+2)$

4. $x^2 + 7x + 10$ $(x+5)(x+2)$ 5. $a^2 - 8a + 12$ $(a-6)(a-2)$ 6. $a^2 - 7a + 12$ $(a-4)(a-3)$

7. $x^2 + 9x + 20$ $(x+5)(x+4)$ 8. $x^2 + 12x + 20$ $(x+10)(x+2)$ 9. $a^2 - 9a + 18$ $(a-6)(a-3)$

10. $a^2 - 11a + 18$ $(a-9)(a-2)$ 11. $c^2 + 19c + 18$ $(c+18)(c+1)$ 12. $b^2 + 9b + 18$ $(b+6)(b+3)$

13. $b^2 - 10b + 21$ $(b-7)(b-3)$ 14. $c^2 - 8c + 15$ $(c-5)(c-3)$ 15. $a^2 - 8a + 16$ $(a-4)^2$

16. $a^2 - 10a + 25$ $(a-5)^2$ 17. $a^2 + 26a + 25$ $(a+25)(a+1)$ 18. $a^2 + 17a + 16$ $(a+16)(a+1)$

19. $x^2 + 5x + 4$ $(x+4)(x+1)$ 20. $x^2 + 8x + 7$ $(x+7)(x+1)$ 21. $x^2 + 5xy + 6y^2$ $(x+3y)(x+2y)$

22. $x^2 + 7xy + 6y^2$ $(x+6y)(x+y)$ 23. $x^2 - 9xy + 8y^2$ $(x-8y)(x-y)$ 24. $x^2 - 6xy + 8y^2$ $(x-4y)(x-2y)$

Solve.

25. $(2t - 3)(t - 4) = 0$ $\left\{\frac{3}{2}, 4\right\}$ 26. $(3x - 5)(x - 1) = 0$ $\left\{\frac{5}{3}, 1\right\}$ 27. $x^2 - 4x + 3 = 0$ $\{3, 1\}$

28. $y^2 - 6y + 5 = 0$ $\{5, 1\}$ 29. $x^2 + 7x + 6 = 0$ $\{-6, -1\}$ 30. $x^2 + 5x + 6 = 0$ $\{-3, -2\}$

31. $x^2 + 6x + 9 = 0$ $\{-3\}$ 32. $x^2 + 4x + 4 = 0$ $\{-2\}$ 33. $v^2 - 9v + 14 = 0$ $\{7, 2\}$

34. $w^2 - 10w + 16 = 0$ $\{8, 2\}$ 35. $x^2 - 11x + 24 = 0$ $\{8, 3\}$ 36. $x^2 - 10x + 24 = 0$ $\{6, 4\}$

B   37. $y^2 + 8 = 6y$ $\{4, 2\}$ 38. $2y^2 + 14 = 16y$ $\{7, 1\}$ 39. $2x^2 + 12 = 10x$ $\{3, 2\}$

40. $5x^2 + 15x + 10 = 0$ $\{-2, -1\}$ 41. $3x^2 + 15x + 12 = 0$ $\{-4, -1\}$ 42. $2x^2 + 10 = 12x$ $\{5, 1\}$

43. $35 = 40t - 5t^2$ $\{7, 1\}$ 44. $40 = 30t - 5t^2$ $\{4, 2\}$ 45. $36 = 30x - 6x^2$ $\{3, 2\}$

List all integer values for k for which these polynomials can be factored.

46. $x^2 + kx + 7$ $8, -8$ 47. $x^2 + kx + 3$ $4, -4$ 48. $x^2 + kx + 4$ $5, -5, 4, -4$

49. $x^2 + kx + 9$ $10, -10, 6, -6$ 50. $x^2 + kx + 12$ $13, -13, 8, -8, 7, -7$ 51. $x^2 + kx + 18$ $19, -19, 11, -11, 9, -9$

List all positive integer values of k for which these polynomials can be factored.

52. $x^2 + 3x + k$ 2 53. $x^2 + 4x + k$ $4, 3$ 54. $x^2 - 4x + k$ $4, 3$

55. $x^2 - 5x + k$ $6, 4$ 56. $x^2 - 7xy + ky^2$ $12, 10, 6$ 57. $x^2 + 7xy + ky^2$ $12, 10, 6$

Suppose the equation $x^2 + bx + c = 0$ has two solutions, r and s.

58. What does rs equal? c 59. What does $r + s$ equal? $-b$

Solve.

60. If 9 more than the square of a number equals 10 times the number, what values could the number have? $9, 1$

61. If 12 more than the square of a number equals 7 times the number, what values could the number have? $4, 3$

62. The area of a rectangular dog pen is 600 ft^2 and the pen is enclosed with 100 ft of fencing. What are the length and width of the pen?   Length: 30 ft, width: 20 ft

63. The area of a rectangle is 180 m^2 and the perimeter is 56 m. What are the length and width of the rectangle?
   Length: 18 m, width: 10 m

Expand, simplify, and then factor the expressions.

C **64.** $(x + 3)^2 + (x + 1)$ (x + 5)(x + 2)

65. $(x + 3)(x + 4) + x$ (x + 6)(x + 2)

66. $(x - 2)(x - 3) - 2x$ (x − 6)(x − 1)

67. $(x - 2)^2 - 1$ (x − 3)(x − 1)

68. $(2x + 3)(x + 4) - (x^2 + 3x)$ (x + 6)(x + 2)

69. $(2x - 3)(3x - 2) - (5x^2 - 6x)$
   (x − 6)(x − 1)

Solve.

70. $(x - 4)^2 - 2x = 0$ {8, 2}

71. $(x - 4)(x - 1) + x = 0$ {2}

72. $(x + 2)(x + 3) - 2 = 0$ {−4, −1}

73. $(x - 5)(x - 2) + 2 = 0$ {4, 3}

■ REVIEW EXERCISES

Expand and simplify.

1. $(x - 3)(x + 5)$ x² + 2x − 15

2. $(x + y)(x - 4y)$ x² − 3xy − 4y²   [7–5]

3. Select three values of x. Then copy and complete the table, plot the points, and graph the equation $y = \frac{1}{2}x - 2$.   [5–4]

x	?	?	?
y	?	?	?

4. Copy and complete the table and then use the ordered pairs to graph the equation $y = x^2 - 2$.   [5–4]

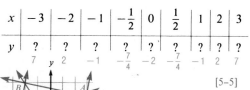

x	−3	−2	−1	−$\frac{1}{2}$	0	$\frac{1}{2}$	1	2	3
y	?	?	?	?	?	?	?	?	?
	7	2	−1	−$\frac{7}{4}$	−2	−$\frac{7}{4}$	−1	2	7

5. State the slopes of the lines.   [5–5]

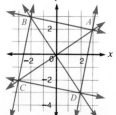

a. $\overrightarrow{AC}$ $\frac{2}{3}$

b. $\overrightarrow{BD}$ $-\frac{3}{2}$

c. $\overrightarrow{AB}$ $-\frac{1}{5}$

d. $\overrightarrow{BC}$ 5

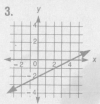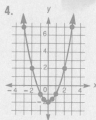

Class Starter Quiz
on previous section

Factor.

1. $x^2 + 9x + 8$ $(x + 1)(x + 8)$
2. $x^2 - 7x + 10$ $(x - 2)(x - 5)$
Solve.
3. $x^2 - 8x + 12 = 0$ $\{2, 6\}$
4. $x^2 + 6x + 5 = 0$ $\{-5, -1\}$
5. $x^2 + 7 = 8x$ $\{1, 7\}$

PURPOSE

The equations solved in this section are especially well suited for solution by factoring.

PREVIEW

The problem presented in the Preview affords an opportunity to review the use of equations in solving problems. Solving the equation may be postponed until after the lesson has been presented.

OBJECTIVE 7–9

To factor trinomials of the form $x^2 + bxy + cy^2$ with c negative.

You may wish to spend two days on this section. Refer to the Pacing Chart.

7–9 Factoring $x^2 + bxy + cy^2$ with c Negative

Preview

A large department store wants a display window installed. The Louden Glass Company installs a rectangular window with 96 ft² of viewing area and a length 4 ft more than the width. What are the length and width of the window?

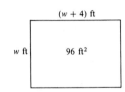

To solve this problem, we could write this equation

$$w(w + 4) = 96$$

Expanding and collecting terms on one side, we have

$$w^2 + 4w - 96 = 0$$

We can solve this equation if we can factor the polynomial:

$$w^2 + 4w - 96$$

In this lesson you will learn to factor trinomials in which the last term is negative.

■ LESSON

Consider this equation:

> ***Expanded form***   ***Factored form***
> $$x^2 + (p + q)x + pq = (x + p)(x + q)$$

In Section 7–8, it was stated that when the *product pq* is positive, the values of *p* and *q* have the same sign. Thus with *pq* positive:

If the value of $(p + q)$ is positive, then *p* and *q* are both positive.

$$x^2 + 18x + 77 = (x + 7)(x + 11)$$

↑ *positive*   ↑ *positive*   ↑ *both positive*

If the value of $(p + q)$ is negative, then *p* and *q* are both negative.

$$y^2 - 10y + 9 = y^2 + (-10)y + 9 = (y + (-1))(y + (-9))$$

↑ *negative* ↑ *positive*   ↑ *both negative*

LESSON

Students should check their factoring by multiplying the binomial factors and comparing the result to the original trinomial. They should think through all four steps in the FOIL method.

ADDITIONAL EXAMPLES

Example 1. Factor. $a^2 - 6a - 7$

$$(a - 7)(a + 1)$$

Now consider the case in which the product pq is negative. This means that p and q differ in sign.

$$x^2 + 2x - 15 = (x - 3)(x + 5) \qquad y^2 - 2y - 24 = (y + 4)(y - 6)$$

$\uparrow$ $\qquad$ $\uparrow$ $\quad$ $\uparrow$ $\qquad\qquad$ $\uparrow$ $\qquad$ $\uparrow$ $\quad$ $\uparrow$

negative $\qquad$ *different* $\qquad$ *negative* $\qquad$ *different*
$\qquad\qquad\quad$ *signs* $\qquad\qquad\qquad\qquad\qquad$ *signs*

The above information helps us factor trinomials such as

$$a^2 + 2a - 15$$

We know that the first term of each binomial is a.

$$(a \quad)(a \quad)$$

The last term of the trinomial indicates that the *product* of the last terms of the binomials is -15. The factors of -15 have opposite signs. The possibilities are

$$-1 \text{ and } 15 \qquad 1 \text{ and } -15$$
$$3 \text{ and } -5 \qquad -3 \text{ and } 5$$

The coefficient of the middle term of the trinomial indicates that the *sum* of the last terms of the binomials must be 2. Therefore, the last terms are -3 and 5, and the correct factorization is

$$(a - 3)(a + 5)$$

Check by expanding: $\quad (a - 3)(a + 5) = a^2 + 5a - 3a - 15$
$$= a^2 + 2a - 15$$

Example 1 Factor. $x^2 + 4x - 5$

Solution *The first term of each binomial is x.* $\qquad (x \quad)(x \quad)$
The product of the last terms is -5.
Write pairs of numbers whose product is -5. $\quad$ 1 and -5, -1 and 5

The middle term of the trinomial indicates that the sum of the last terms of the binomials is 4. So, choose the pair whose sum is 4.

$$-1 \text{ and } 5$$

Write the binomial factors. $\qquad\qquad (x - 1)(x + 5)$

Answer $(x - 1)(x + 5)$

Check $(x - 1)(x + 5) = x^2 + 5x - x - 5$
$$= x^2 + 4x - 5 \quad \text{It checks.}$$

Example 2   Factor. $a^2 + a - 6$

Solution $a^2 + a - 6$

The first term of each binomial is a. $(a \quad)(a \quad)$
The product of the last terms of the bi-   1 and -6, 2 and -3,
nomials is -6. Write the pairs of numbers whose
product is -6. -1 and 6, 3 and -2

The middle term of the trinomial indicates that the sum of the last terms of the binomials is 1. So, choose the pair whose sum is 1.

$$3 \text{ and } -2$$

Write the binomial factors. $(a + 3)(a - 2)$

Answer $(a + 3)(a - 2)$

Check $(a + 3)(a - 2) = a^2 - 2a + 3a - 6$
$= a^2 + a - 6$ It checks.

Example 3   Factor. $2x^2 - 22x - 24$

Solution   Factor out the GCF. $2x^2 - 22x - 24 = 2(x^2 - 11x - 12)$
Factor the trinomial. $= 2(x - 12)(x + 1)$

Answer $2(x - 12)(x + 1)$

Check   The check is left to the student.

Example 4   Factor. $x^2 + 8x + 6$

Solution   Since the middle and last terms of the trinomial are positive, the last terms of the binomials are positive. The choices are 1 and 6 or 2 and 3. The possible factorizations are

$$(x + 1)(x + 6)$$
$$(x + 2)(x + 3)$$

Mentally expand each possible factorization to see which one produces the middle term $8x$.

	Middle term
$(x + 1)(x + 6)$	$+ 7x$
$(x + 2)(x + 3)$	$+ 5x$

In no case is there a middle term of $8x$. Thus, $x^2 + 8x + 6$ cannot be factored into the product of two binomials.

Answer $x^2 + 8x + 6$ is not factorable over the set of integers.

CLASSROOM EXERCISES

In exercise 6, indicate that the first step in solving an equation by factoring is to rewrite the equation with all terms on one side of the equation.

EXTRA PRACTICE, page 633

Example 5   Solve. $x^2 + 4x = 12$

     Solution   *Collect terms so that the right side is 0.* $x^2 + 4x - 12 = 0$
           Factor. $(x + 6)(x - 2) = 0$
           Use the zero-product property. $x + 6 = 0$ or $x - 2 = 0$
                                                 $x = -6$ or $x = 2$

     Answer $\{-6, 2\}$

      Check   The check is left to the student.

ASSIGNMENT GUIDE

Basic	3–39 odd, Review Exercises, Self-Quiz 3
Average	15–39 multiples of 3, 41–52 all, Review Exercises, Self-Quiz 3
Enriched	15–51 multiples of 3, 53–61 odd, Review Exercises, Self-Quiz 3

PRACTICE WORKSHEET 38

7-9 FACTORING $x^2 + bxy + cy^2$ **WITH** c **NEGATIVE**

■ Factor.

1. $a^2 + 2a - 8$ $(a + 4)(a - 2)$ 2. $b^2 - 2b - 24$ $(b - 6)(b + 4)$
3. $c^2 - 2c - 80$ $(c - 10)(c + 8)$ 4. $d^2 + d - 12$ $(d + 4)(d - 3)$
5. $h^2 + 5h - 14$ $(h + 7)(h - 2)$ 6. $k^2 - 7k - 30$ $(k - 10)(k + 3)$
7. $r^2 + 6rs - 27s^2$ $(r + 9s)(r - 3s)$ 8. $a^2 + ab - 72b^2$ $(a + 9b)(a - 8b)$
9. $p^2 + 8pq - 9q^2$ $(p + 9q)(p - q)$ 10. $x^2 + 3xy - 70y^2$ $(x + 10y)(x - 7y)$

■ Solve.

11. $x^2 - x - 2 = 0$ $\{-1, 2\}$ 12. $w^2 + 4w - 12 = 0$ $\{-6, 2\}$
13. $t^2 + 4t - 21 = 0$ $\{-7, 3\}$ 14. $q^2 - 4s - 32 = 0$ $\{-4, 8\}$
15. $r^2 + r - 30 = 0$ $\{-6, 5\}$ 16. $q^2 - 3q - 4 = 0$ $\{-1, 4\}$
17. $p^2 - 2p - 35 = 0$ $\{-5, 7\}$ 18. $n^2 + 5n - 50 = 0$ $\{-10, 5\}$
19. $m^2 + 3m - 54 = 0$ $\{-9, 6\}$ 20. $k^2 - 6k - 7 = 0$ $\{-1, 7\}$

■ CLASSROOM EXERCISES

Factor.

1. $x^2 + 2x - 8$ **2.** $y^2 - y - 6$ **3.** $b^2 + b - 6$ **4.** $a^2 - 7ab - 18b^2$
$(x + 4)(x - 2)$ $(y - 3)(y + 2)$ $(b + 3)(b - 2)$ $(a - 9b)(a + 2b)$

Solve.

5. $x^2 - 3x - 4 = 0$ **6.** $x^2 = 2x + 15$ **7.** $x^2 + x = 12$ $\{3, -4\}$ **8.** $-11x - 28 = x^2$
$\{4, -1\}$ $\{5, -3\}$ $\{-7, -4\}$

■ WRITTEN EXERCISES

Ⓐ Factor.

1. $a^2 - 5a - 6$ $(a - 6)(a + 1)$ **2.** $a^2 - a - 6$ $(a - 3)(a + 2)$ **3.** $b^2 + b - 6$ $(b + 3)(b - 2)$

4. $b^2 + 5b - 6$ $(b + 6)(b - 1)$ **5.** $c^2 + c - 12$ $(c + 4)(c - 3)$ **6.** $c^2 + 4c - 12$
                                                                       $(c + 6)(c - 2)$

7. $a^2 - 11a - 12$ $(a - 12)(a + 1)$ **8.** $a^2 - a - 12$ $(a - 4)(a + 3)$ **9.** $b^2 - 8b - 9$
                                                                      $(b - 9)(b + 1)$

10. $b^2 - 9$ $(b + 3)(b - 3)$ **11.** $c^2 - 16$ $(c + 4)(c - 4)$ **12.** $c^2 - 6c - 16$
                                                                      $(c - 8)(c + 2)$

13. $2x^2 + 12x - 14$ **14.** $3x^2 + 3x - 6$ $3(x + 2)(x - 1)$ **15.** $y^2 - 5y - 36$
$2(x + 7)(x - 1)$ $(y - 9)(y + 4)$

16. $y^2 - 9y - 36$ $(y - 12)(y + 3)$ **17.** $z^2 + 16z - 36$ $(z + 18)(z - 2)$ **18.** $z^2 + 23z - 24$
                                                                      $(z + 24)(z - 1)$

19. $x^2 + 5x - 24$ $(x + 8)(x - 3)$ **20.** $x^2 + 2x - 24$ $(x + 6)(x - 4)$ **21.** $x^2 + 2xy - 3y^2$
                                                                      $(x + 3y)(x - y)$

22. $x^2 - 10xy - 11y^2$ **23.** $x^2 + xy - 2y^2$ $(x + 2y)(x - y)$ **24.** $x^2 + 3xy - 4y^2$
$(x - 11y)(x + y)$ $(x + 4y)(x - y)$

Solve.

25. $x^2 - 3x - 4 = 0$ $\{4, -1\}$ **26.** $x^2 - 4x - 5 = 0$ $\{5, -1\}$ **27.** $y^2 - 6y - 7 = 0$ $\{7, -1\}$

28. $y^2 - 2y - 8 = 0$ $\{4, -2\}$ **29.** $a^2 + 3a - 10 = 0$ $\{2, -5\}$ **30.** $a^2 + 3a - 18 = 0$
                                                                      $\{3, -6\}$

31. $b^2 + 4b = 12$ $\{2, -6\}$ **32.** $b^2 + b = 12$ $\{3, -4\}$ **33.** $t^2 = 11t + 12$ $\{12, -1\}$

34. $t^2 = 5t + 6$ $\{6, -1\}$ **35.** $v^2 + 9v + 18 = 0$ $\{-6, -3\}$ **36.** $v^2 + 17v - 18 = 0$
                                                                      $\{1, -18\}$

COMPUTER EXTENSION

Write a computer program that will factor expressions of the form $x^2 + bx + c$ where b is any integer and c is negative.

```
10 PRINT "THIS PROGRAM
   FACTORS EXPRESSIONS"
20 PRINT "OF THE FORM X ↑ 2
   + BX + C WHERE"
30 PRINT "B IS ANY INTEGER
   AND C IS"
40 PRINT "A NEGATIVE INTEGER."
50 PRINT "ENTER B"
60 INPUT B
70 PRINT "ENTER C"
80 INPUT C
90 IF C > -1 THEN 70
100 IF B > 0 THEN PRINT "X ∧
    2 + ";B;" X - ";-C;
110 IF B < 0 THEN PRINT "X ∧
    2 - ";-B;" X - ";-C;
120 FOR K = 1 TO -C
130 IF INT(-C/K) < > -C/K
    THEN 150
140 IF B = C/K + K THEN 180
150 NEXT K
160 PRINT " IS NOT FACTORABLE"
170 GO TO 190
180 PRINT " = (X + ";K;")(X
    - ";-C/K;")"
190 END
```

For each problem, let n represent the missing number, and write an equation that fits the problem. Then solve.

37. The square of a number increased by the number equals 20. What is the number? 4 or −5

38. The square of a number increased by the number equals 30. What is the number? 5 or −6

39. Twice a number subtracted from the square of the number equals 35. What is the number? 7 or −5

40. Twice a number subtracted from the square of the number equals 48. What is the number? 8 or −6

B List all integer values of k for which these polynomials can be factored.

41. $x^2 + kx - 7$ 6, −6 **42.** $x^2 + kx - 3$ 2, −2 **43.** $x^2 + kx - 4$ 3, −3, 0

44. $x^2 + kx - 9$ 8, −8, 0 **45.** $x^2 + kx - 12$ 11, −11, 4, −4, 1, −1 **46.** $x^2 + kx - 18$ 17, −17, 7, −7, 3, −3

Suppose the equation $x^2 + bx - 24 = 0$ has two solutions, r and s, with $r > s$.

47. Which of these expressions must represent positive numbers?

$$r \qquad s \qquad rs \qquad r + s \qquad \text{r}$$

48. Which of these expressions must represent negative numbers?

$$r \qquad s \qquad rs \qquad r + s \qquad \text{s, rs}$$

Write an equation that fits the problem. Then solve.

49. The area of a rectangular lawn is 54 m². The lawn is 3 m longer than it is wide. What is the width of the lawn? 6 m

50. The area of a rectangular court is 140 m². The court is 4 m longer than it is wide. What is the width of the court? 10 m

51. The product of two consecutive negative integers is 272. What are the integers? −17, −16

52. The product of two consecutive negative odd integers is 143. What are the integers? −13, −11

C **53.** One number is 3 larger than another and the sum of their squares is 269. What are the numbers? 10 and 13, or −13 and −10

54. The difference between two numbers is 5 and the sum of the squares of the numbers is 193. What are the numbers? 7 and 12, or −12 and −7

55. The sum of two numbers is 15 and the sum of their squares is 117. What are the numbers? 6, 9

56. An 8-in. by 10-in. picture has a border of uniform width. The total area of the border and picture is 224 in.^{2} What is the width of the border? _3 in._

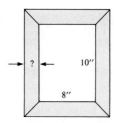

Solve.

57. $(x + 4)(x - 3) = 5x$ _(6, −2)_

58. $(x + 4)(x - 3) = 12x$ _(12, −1)_

59. $(2x + 1)(x - 3) = x^2 + 11$ _(7, −2)_

60. $(2x + 3)(3x - 2) = 5x^2 + 9x + 6$ _(6, −2)_

61. $(x + 1)(x + 3) = x + 13$ _(2, −5)_

62. $(2x - 3)(x - 4) = (x - 4)^2$ _(4, −1)_

■ REVIEW EXERCISES

Expand and simplify.

1. $(2x + 3)(3x + 1)$ _$6x^2 + 11x + 3$_

2. $2(3a + b)(a - 2b)$ _$6a^2 - 10ab - 4b^2$_ [7–5]

3. State the slope and the y-intercept of the line for the equation $y = \frac{2}{3}x + 4$. [5–6]
$\frac{2}{3}$, 4

4. Graph the line with slope $-\frac{1}{2}$ and y-intercept 1. [5–6]

5. State whether the relation is a function. [5–8]

$$\{(1, 4), (2, 5), (1, 10)\}$$ _No_

6. State whether the equation represents a function. [5–8]

$$y^2 = x$$ _No_

Self-Quiz 3

Factor.

7–7	**1.** $x^2 + 8x + 16$	**2.** $y^2 - 14y + 49$	**3.** $3w^2 - 6w + 3$
	$(x + 4)^2$	$(y - 7)^2$	$3(w - 1)^2$
7–8	**4.** $a^2 + 5a + 6$	**5.** $t^2 - 11t + 28$	**6.** $r^2 - 10r + 16$
	$(a + 3)(a + 2)$	$(t - 7)(t - 4)$	$(r - 8)(r - 2)$
7–9	**7.** $x^2 - 5x - 6$	**8.** $b^2 + 12b - 28$	**9.** $y^2 + 15y - 16$
	$(x - 6)(x + 1)$	$(b + 14)(b - 2)$	$(y + 16)(y - 1)$

Solve.

7–8,
7–9   **10.** $x^2 - 16x + 63 = 0$ _(7, 9)_   **11.** $y^2 + y = 20$ _(4, −5)_

- The length of a rectangle is decreased by 3 and the width increased by 1. The resulting figure is a square with an area of 16 units. What are the dimensions of the original rectangle?

  7 units by 3 units
  $(x - 3)(y + 1) = 4 \cdot 4$
  $x - 3 = 4$ and $y + 1 = 4$
  $x = 7$ and $y = 3$

- Twice a number minus 8, squared, is equal to the number squared times 2 plus 8. Find the number(s).

  2 and 14
  $(2x - 8)^2 = 2x^2 + 8$
  $4x^2 - 32x + 64 = 2x^2 + 8$
  $2x^2 - 32x + 56 = 0$
  $(x^2 - 16x + 28) = 0$
  $(x - 14)(x - 2) = 0$
  $x = 14$ or $x = 2$

ADDITIONAL ANSWER

■ Review Exercises

4.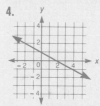

Factor.

1. $a^2 - 3a - 18$ $(a - 6)(a + 3)$
2. $x^2 + 3xy - 10y^2$ $(x + 5y)(x - 2y)$

Solve.

3. $y^2 + y - 20 = 0$ $\{-5, 4\}$
4. $c^2 - 2c - 35 = 0$ $\{-5, 7\}$
5. The square of a number decreased by the number equals 12. Find the number(s). -3 and 4

PURPOSE

This topic completes the sequence of sections on factoring trinomials with integer coefficients.

PREVIEW

The puzzle in the Preview will very likely seem difficult to students. However, they should realize that the algebra learned in this section can make such problems solvable and within their abilities.

Indicate that the integers in the Preview are just the coefficients of two binomials: $(ax + b)(cx + d) = 12x^2 + 5x - 2$. An alternative puzzle is the following:

I am thinking of four integers. The product of the first and third is 6. The product of the second and fourth is -35. The product of the first and fourth added to the product of the second and third is 1. What are the integers?
$(2, 5, 3, -7; (2x + 5)(3x - 7)$
$= 6x^2 + x - 35)$

OBJECTIVE 7–10

To factor any trinomial of the form $ax^2 + bxy + cy^2$.

You may wish to spend two days on this section. Refer to the Pacing Chart.

7–10 Factoring $ax^2 + bxy + cy^2$

Preview

The Great Gustav posed this puzzle.

I am thinking of four integers. The product of the first and third is 12. The product of the second and fourth is -2. The product of the first and fourth added to the product of the second and third is 5. What are the integers?

This puzzle is quite difficult. There are many possibilities to check. In this lesson you will learn a method of factoring trinomials that could be used to solve the puzzle.

1st	2nd	3rd	4th
4	-1	3	2
3	2	4	-1
-4	1	-3	-2
-3	-2	-4	1

■ LESSON

The technique for factoring a trinomial whose first coefficient is different from 1 is the same as the technique that we used in earlier lessons. But there are more choices. Consider the expression

$$6x^2 + 11x + 3$$

The possible first terms of the binomials are

$$(1x \qquad)(6x \qquad)$$
$$(2x \qquad)(3x \qquad)$$

Since the middle and last terms of the trinomials are positive, the signs of the last terms of the binomial factors must be positive.

$$(1x + \quad)(6x + \quad)$$
$$(2x + \quad)(3x + \quad)$$

The factors of the last term of the trinomial are 1 and 3. These are all of the possible factorizations.

$$(1x + 1)(6x + 3)$$
$$(1x + 3)(6x + 1)$$
$$(2x + 1)(3x + 3)$$
$$(2x + 3)(3x + 1)$$

Next find the middle terms of the expansions.

$$9x \qquad 19x \qquad 9x \qquad 11x$$

The last expression is the correct middle term. Therefore,
$6x^2 + 11x + 3 = (2x + 3)(3x + 1)$.

Research indicates that a review, consisting of a practice test followed by explanations, helps students succeed. The explanations are an important factor.

Example 1   Factor. $6a^2 - 10ab - 4b^2$

Solution   *Factor out the GCF of the three terms.* $2(3a^2 - 5ab - 2b^2)$
List possible first terms of the binomials. $(3a \quad)(a \quad)$
List possible second terms of the binomials. b and $-2b$ or $-b$ and $2b$

These are all the possible factorizations and their expansions.

$(3a + 2b)(a - b) = 3a^2 - ab - 2b^2$ Wrong middle term
$(3a - 2b)(a + b) = 3a^2 + ab - 2b^2$ Wrong middle term
$(3a - b)(a + 2b) = 3a^2 + 5ab - 2b^2$ Wrong middle term
$(3a + b)(a - 2b) = 3a^2 - 5ab - 2b^2$ Correct middle term!

Answer $2(3a + b)(a - 2b)$

If the first and last terms of the trinomial have several factors, the number of combinations to check may be great. However, the general technique is the same.

To factor trinomials of the form $ax^2 + bxy + cy^2$

1. Factor out the GCF of the terms.

2. List the possible first terms of the binomials.

3. List the possible last terms of the binomials.

4. Expand the possible products until the one that produces the correct middle term is found.

Example 2   Solve. $2x^2 + 7x = -3$

Solution $2x^2 + 7x = -3$

Collect terms on the left side of the equation. $2x^2 + 7x + 3 = 0$
Factor the trinomial. $(2x + 1)(x + 3) = 0$
Use the zero-product property. $2x + 1 = 0$ or $x + 3 = 0$
                                          $2x = -1$ or $x = -3$

                                          $x = -\dfrac{1}{2}$ or $x = -3$

Answer $\left\{-\dfrac{1}{2}, -3\right\}$

Check   The check is left to the student.

LESSON

As in previous lessons, it is important that students routinely check their factoring by multiplying the binomial factors and comparing the result to the original trinomial. All four steps in the FOIL method should be used.

Many factoring attempts may be needed on some exercises. But as students gain experience, they will become more efficient and quickly eliminate some of the possibilities.

In factoring $6x^2 + 25x + 24$, point out that the terms in a binomial factor cannot both have *even* coefficients (because in that case 2 would be a factor of the original trinomial). Therefore, these factors can be eliminated from consideration:

$(2x + 2)$, $(2x + 4)$, $(2x + 6)$, $(2x + 8)$, $(2x + 12)$, $(2x + 24)$, $(6x + 4)$, $(6x + 8)$, $(6x + 12)$, and $(6x + 24)$.

Using similar reasoning, 3 cannot be a factor of both terms of a binomial factor because 3 is not a factor of the original trinomial. Therefore, these factors are eliminated from consideration:

$(3x + 3)$, $(3x + 6)$, $(3x + 12)$, $(3x + 24)$, $(6x + 3)$, $(6x + 6)$, $(6x + 12)$, and $(6x + 24)$.

ADDITIONAL EXAMPLES

Example 1. Factor. $6x^2 + 9xy - 6y^2$
$3(2x - y)(x + 2y)$
Example 2. Solve. $12x^2 + 11x - 15 = 0$
$12x^2 + 11x - 15 = 0$
$(3x + 5)(4x - 3) = 0$
$3x + 5 = 0$ or $4x - 3 = 0$
$x = -\frac{5}{3}$ or $x = \frac{3}{4}$
$\{-\frac{5}{3}, \frac{3}{4}\}$

CHECK UNDERSTANDING

- List all possible factors of $2x^2 - 7x - 15$.
  $((2x - 3)(x + 5), (2x + 3)(x - 5),$
  $(2x - 5)(x + 3),$ and $(2x + 5)(x - 3))$
- Which factor pair is correct?
  $((2x + 3)(x - 5))$

Indicate that not all trinomials can be factored over the rational numbers—for example, the trinomial $2x^2 + 3x + 2$. However,
students should assume that they will con-
front very few, if any, trinomials that cannot
be factored in this lesson.

ASSIGNMENT GUIDE

Basic   3–39 multiples of 3, Review
         Exercises
Average 9–39 multiples of 3, 41–51 odd,
         Review Exercises
Enriched 15–51 multiples of 3, 52–58 all,
         Review Exercises

PRACTICE WORKSHEET 38

7-10 FACTORING $ax^2 + bxy + cy^2$

■ Factor.

1. $2a^2 + 13a + 15$ $(2a + 3)(a + 5)$ 2. $6b^2 - 31b + 5$ $(6b - 1)(b - 5)$
3. $3c^2 + 13c + 4$ $(3c + 1)(c + 4)$ 4. $2k^2 + 9k + 10$ $(2k + 5)(k + 2)$
5. $3m^2 - 19m - 14$ $(3m + 2)(m - 7)$ 6. $5r^2 - 53r - 22$ $(5r + 2)(r - 11)$
7. $7s^2 + 48st - 7t^2$ $(7s - t)(s + 7t)$ 8. $6x^2 - 19x + 15$ $(3x - 5)(2x - 3)$
9. $15p^2 - 26pq + 8q^2$ $(5p - 2q)(3p - 4q)$ 10. $9a^2 - 18ab - 7b^2$ $(3a + b)(3a - 7b)$

■ Solve.

11. $7d^2 - 12d + 5 = 0$ $\{5/7, 1\}$ 12. $3h^2 + 37h + 44 = 0$ $\{-11, -4/3\}$
13. $4k^2 + 15k + 9 = 0$ $\{-3, -3/4\}$ 14. $2n^2 - n - 3 = 0$ $\{-1, 3/2\}$
15. $4w^2 - 12w + 9 = 0$ $\{3/2\}$ 16. $5y^2 - 9y - 2 = 0$ $\{-1/5, 2\}$
17. $9z^2 + 6z - 8 = 0$ $\{-4/3, 2/3\}$ 18. $6a^2 + a - 12 = 0$ $\{-3/2, 4/3\}$
19. $4c^2 - 19c + 12 = 0$ $\{3/4, 4\}$ 20. $9t^2 + 18t - 7 = 0$ $\{-7/3, 1/3\}$

EXTRA PRACTICE, page 633

■ CLASSROOM EXERCISES

Given the trinomial $4x^2 - 4x - 3$, answer the following questions.

1. What are the possible first terms of the binomial factors?   4x and x, 2x and 2x
2. What are the possible second terms of the binomial factors?
   — 3 and 1, 3 and — 1
3. What do you know about the signs of the last terms of the binomial factors?
   One is positive, one is negative.
4. Factor the trinomial. $(2x - 3)(2x + 1)$

Factor.

5. $6a^2 + 7a + 2$ $(3a + 2)(2a + 1)$ 6. $2x^2 - 5x + 3$ $(2x - 3)(x - 1)$ 7. $10m^2 + 13mn - 3n^2$
$(5m - n)(2m + 3n)$

Solve.

8. $2x^2 - 3x - 2 = 0$ $\left\{2, -\dfrac{1}{2}\right\}$ 9. $2x^2 = x + 3$ $\left\{\dfrac{3}{2}, -1\right\}$ 10. $6x^2 - 22x - 8 = 0$
$\left\{4, -\dfrac{1}{3}\right\}$

■ WRITTEN EXERCISES

Factor.

A 1. $2x^2 + 5x + 3$ $(2x + 3)(x + 1)$ 2. $2x^2 + 7x + 3$ $(2x + 1)(x + 3)$ 3. $3x^2 - 7x + 2$
$(3x - 1)(x - 2)$
4. $3x^2 - 5x + 2$ $(3x - 2)(x - 1)$ 5. $5a^2 - 13a - 6$ $(5a + 2)(a - 3)$ 6. $5a^2 - 7a - 6$
$(5a + 3)(a - 2)$
7. $5a^2 + 7a - 6$ $(5a - 3)(a + 2)$ 8. $5a^2 + 13a - 6$ $(5a - 2)(a + 3)$ 9. $5n^2 - 29n - 6$
$(5n + 1)(n - 6)$
10. $5n^2 + 29n - 6$ $(5n - 1)(n + 6)$ 11. $6n^2 - 13n - 5$ $(3n + 1)(2n - 5)$ 12. $6n^2 - 7n - 5$
$(3n - 5)(2n + 1)$
13. $7y^2 + 30y + 8$ $(7y + 2)(y + 4)$ 14. $7y^2 + 18y + 8$ $(7y + 4)(y + 2)$ 15. $7y^2 - 57y + 8$
$(7y - 1)(y - 8)$
16. $7y^2 - 15y + 8$ $(7y - 8)(y - 1)$ 17. $14a^2 - 20a + 6$ 18. $14a^2 - 8a - 6$
$2(7a - 3)(a - 1)$ $2(7a + 3)(a - 1)$
19. $8x^2 + 23xy - 3y^2$ 20. $8x^2 - 5xy - 3y^2$ 21. $4a^2 + ab - 5b^2$
$(8x - y)(x + 3y)$ $(8x + 3y)(x - y)$ $(4a + 5b)(a - b)$
22. $4a^2 - 19ab - 5b^2$ 23. $6x^2 - 11xy - 10y^2$ 24. $6x^2 + 11xy - 10y^2$
$(4a + b)(a - 5b)$ $(3x + 2y)(2x - 5y)$ $(3x - 2y)(2x + 5y)$

Solve.

25. $2a^2 - 7a + 5 = 0$ $\left\{1, \dfrac{5}{2}\right\}$ 26. $2a^2 - 5a + 3 = 0$ $\left\{1, \dfrac{3}{2}\right\}$
27. $3a^2 + 2a - 8 = 0$ $\left\{\dfrac{4}{3}, -2\right\}$ 28. $3a^2 - 10a - 8 = 0$ $\left\{4, -\dfrac{2}{3}\right\}$
29. $4a^2 - 4a - 15 = 0$ $\left\{\dfrac{5}{2}, -\dfrac{3}{2}\right\}$ 30. $4a^2 - 8a - 21 = 0$ $\left\{\dfrac{7}{2}, -\dfrac{3}{2}\right\}$
31. $6x^2 + 23x + 7 = 0$ $\left\{-\dfrac{1}{3}, -\dfrac{7}{2}\right\}$ 32. $6x^2 - 17x + 7 = 0$ $\left\{\dfrac{1}{2}, \dfrac{7}{3}\right\}$
33. $12x^2 - 28x + 11 = 0$ $\left\{\dfrac{11}{6}, \dfrac{1}{2}\right\}$ 34. $12x^2 + 68x + 11 = 0$ $\left\{-\dfrac{1}{6}, -\dfrac{11}{2}\right\}$
35. $12x^2 + x = 20$ $\left\{\dfrac{5}{4}, -\dfrac{4}{3}\right\}$ 36. $12x^2 - x = 20$ $\left\{\dfrac{4}{3}, -\dfrac{5}{4}\right\}$

- Why is $-x^2 + 4x + 32$ more difficult to factor than $x^2 - 4x - 32$?

  In $-x^2 + 4x + 32$, the leading coefficient is negative, so the rules for factoring do not apply.

- How are the trinomials related?
  $-x^2 + 4x + 32$ and $x^2 - 4x - 32$

  They are opposites.

- Which equation is easier to solve,
  $x^2 + \frac{7}{2}x - 2 = 0$ or
  $2x^2 + 7x - 4 = 0$?

  $2x^2 + 7x - 4 = 0$

- How are these two equations related?

  They are equivalent.

- In solving the following equation, what should you do first?
  $-x^2 + \frac{1}{2}x - \frac{15}{2} = 0$

  Multiply both sides by -2 to clear of fractions and make the leading coefficient positive.

For each problem, let n represent the missing number, and write an equation that fits the problem. Then solve.

37. The sum of twice the square of a number and 7 times the number equals 15. What is the number? $1\frac{1}{2}$ or -5

38. Twice the square of a number added to the number equals 15. What is the number? $2\frac{1}{2}$ or -3

39. Twice the square of a number equals 3 more than the number. What is the number? $1\frac{1}{2}$ or -1

40. Twice the square of a number equals the sum of 5 times the number and 7. What is the number? $3\frac{1}{2}$ or -1

List all integer values of k for which these trinomials can be factored.

B **41.** $2x^2 + kx + 3$ $5, -5, 7, -7$

42. $4x^2 + kx + 3$ $7, -7, 8, -8, 13, -13$

43. $6x^2 + kx + 3$ $9, -9, 11, -11, 19, -19$

44. $2x^2 + kx - 3$ $1, -1, 5, -5$

45. $4x^2 + kx - 3$ $1, -1, 4, -4, 11, -11$

46. $6x^2 + kx - 3$ $3, -3, 7, -7, 17, -17$

For each problem, write an equation that fits the problem. Then solve the equation and answer the question.

47. The length of a rectangle is 3 m more than twice the width. What is the width of the rectangle if its area is 9 m²? 1.5 m

48. A rectangular garden has a length that is 6 m greater than 4 times its width. What are the dimensions of the garden if its area is 40 m²? Width: 2.5 m, length: 16 m

49. The height of a triangle is 4 m less than the base. If the area of the triangle is 6 m², what is the height? 2 m

50. The length of a rectangular garden is 2 times the width. There is a cement walk around the garden that is 1 m wide. The area of the walk and the garden is 544 m². What are the dimensions of the garden? Width: 15 m, length: 30 m

51. Solve the problem in the Preview. See Preview.

For how many different integer values of k are these trinomials factorable?

C **52.** $10x^2 + kx + 21$ 16

53. $15x^2 + kx - 22$ 16

54. $4x^2 + kx + 9$ 10

Solve.

55. $(x + 2)(x + 3) + (x + 5)(x - 3) = 0$ $\left\{1, -\frac{9}{2}\right\}$

56. $(x + 1)^2 + (x + 1)(x + 2) = 0$ $\left\{-1, -\frac{3}{2}\right\}$

57. The shorter base of a trapezoid is 1 m longer than the altitude, and the longer base is 5 m longer than the altitude. Find the altitude of the trapezoid if its area is 40 m². $\left[\text{Remember: } A = \dfrac{h(a + b)}{2}.\right]$ 5 m

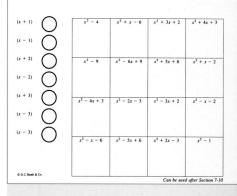

58. The height h, in feet, of an object projected upward with an initial velocity of v feet per second is given by the formula $h = vt - 16t^2$, where t represents the number of seconds. After how many seconds will an object projected vertically at 88 ft/s reach a height of 120 ft? $2\frac{1}{2}$ and 3

■ REVIEW EXERCISES

1. Use the graph to find the solution to this system.   [6–1]

$$x - y = 2$$
$$x + y = 0 \quad \{(1, -1)\}$$

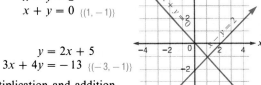

2. Solve by substitution.   [6–2]

$$y = 2x + 5$$
$$3x + 4y = -13 \quad \{(-3, -1)\}$$

3. Solve this system by multiplication and addition.   [6–6]

$$3a + 2b = 5$$
$$5a + b = 27 \quad \{(7, -8)\}$$

4. Solve by using a system of equations.   [6–7]

The Drama Society sold 200 tickets and raised a total of $650. If student tickets cost $1.00 and adult tickets cost $4.00, how many of each kind of ticket were sold? Adult: 150, student: 50

EXTENSION Compound interest

If $1000 is invested at a simple-interest rate of 6% per year, the value of the investment after 5 years is

$$1000 + 1000(0.06)5 = 1000(1 + (0.06)5).$$

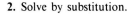

principal   rate time

If the same principal is invested at 6% per year compounded annually, the value of the investment after 5 years is

$$1000(1.06)^5.$$

1. Use a calculator to compute each amount.

a. $1000[1 + (0.06)5]$ 1300
b. $1000(1.06)^5$ [*Hint:* Use the power key if your calculator has one, or use the key sequence $1.06 \times = = = =$ to evaluate $(1.06)^5$.]
   1338.23
2. Which investment is worth more? b
3. How much more is it worth? $38.23

■ CHAPTER SUMMARY

- **Vocabulary**

factor	[page 305]	greatest common factor of two	[page 310]
prime number	[page 305]	or more integers [GCF]	
composite number	[page 305]	greatest common factor of two	[page 311]
to factor a number	[page 306]	or more monomials	
prime factorization	[page 306]	expanding	[page 318]
common factors	[page 310]	factoring	[page 318]

- *Factoring over a set of numbers* means that the factors must belong to the set. [7–1]

- The Zero-Product Property [7–3]

$$\text{For all numbers } a \text{ and } b,$$
$$\text{if } ab = 0, \text{ then } a = 0 \text{ or } b = 0.$$

- The FOIL method of expanding binomials [7–5]

  F Multiply FIRST terms of the binomials.
  O Multiply OUTER terms of the binomials.
  I Multiply INNER terms of the binomials.
  L Multiply LAST terms of the binomials.

- The sum of these products gives the expanded form of $(a + b)(c + d)$.

$$(a + b)(c + d) = ac + ad + bc + bd$$

  first   outer   inner   last
  terms   terms   terms   terms

- Factoring a difference of squares [7–6]

$$\text{For all numbers } a \text{ and } b,$$
$$a^2 - b^2 = (a + b)(a - b).$$

- Factoring a perfect square trinomial [7–7]

$$a^2 + 2ab + b^2 = (a + b)^2$$
$$\text{and}$$
$$a^2 - 2ab + b^2 = (a - b)^2$$

- To factor trinomials of the form $ax^2 + bxy + cy^2$ [7–10]

  1. Factor out the GCF of the terms.

  2. List the possible first terms of the binomials.

  3. List the possible last terms of the binomials.

  4. Expand the possible products until the one that produces the correct middle term is found.

■ CHAPTER REVIEW

7–1 **Objective:** To write the prime factorization of an integer.

1. List the prime numbers between 1 and 10. 2, 3, 5, 7

2. a. Which of the following are composite numbers?

$$11,\ 12,\ 13,\ 14,\ 15 \quad \text{12, 14, 15}$$

b. Write a prime factorization of each composite number found in part (a), listing the factors in increasing order. $2^2 \cdot 3, 2 \cdot 7, 3 \cdot 5$

List all the positive integer factors.

3. 30 1, 2, 3, 5, 6, 10, 15, 30   **4.** 100 1, 2, 4, 5, 10, 20, 25, 50, 100

7–2 **Objective:** To find the greatest common factor of a pair of monomials.

5. List the common factors of 20 and 30. 1, 2, 5, 10

6. List the greatest common factor of 18 and 27. 9

7. List the common factors of $3a^2$ and $6ab$. 1, 3, a, 3a

8. List the greatest common factor of $6xy$ and $8y^2$. 2y

7–3 **Objective:** To solve equations using the zero-product property.

Solve.

9. $(x - 4)x = 0$ $\{0, 4\}$ **10.** $(x + 3)(x - 7) = 0$ $\{7, -3\}$ **11.** $6(2x - 1)(2x + 3) = 0$ $\left\{\frac{1}{2}, -\frac{3}{2}\right\}$

7–4 **Objective:** To factor a monomial from a polynomial.

Factor completely.

12. $3x + 6y$ $3(x + 2y)$ **13.** $2x^2 - 10x$ $2x(x - 5)$

Solve.

14. $x^2 + 5x = 0$ $\{0, -5\}$

15. The square of a number is 3 times the number. What is the number? 0 or 3

7–5 **Objective:** To expand the product of two binomials.

Expand and simplify.

16. $(x + 2)(x + 5)$ $x^2 + 7x + 10$ **17.** $(a + 10)(a - 10)$ $a^2 - 100$

18. $(y - 4)^2$ $y^2 - 8y + 16$ **19.** $(2x + 3)(x - 4)$ $2x^2 - 5x - 12$

7-6 Objective: To factor the difference of two squares.

Factor.

20. $x^2 - 25$ $(x + 5)(x - 5)$ **21.** $9x^2 - 1$ $(3x + 1)(3x - 1)$

Solve.

22. $x^2 - 100 = 0$ $\{10, -10\}$ **23.** $2x^2 = 32$ $\{4, -4\}$

7-7 Objective: To factor perfect square trinomials.

Factor.

24. $x^2 + 14x + 49$ $(x + 7)^2$ **25.** $2x^2 - 12x + 18$ $2(x - 3)^2$

26. Solve $x^2 - 12x + 36 = 0.$ $\{6\}$

7-8 Objective: To factor trinomials of the form $x^2 - bxy + cy^2$ with
c positive.

Factor.

27. $x^2 + 5x + 6$ $(x + 3)(x + 2)$ **28.** $x^2 - 7xy + 12y^2$ $(x - 4y)(x - 3y)$

29. Solve $x^2 - 12x + 20 = 0.$ $\{10, 2\}$

7-9 Objective: To factor trinomials of the form $x^2 + bxy + cy^2$ with
c negative.

Factor.

30. $b^2 - 2b - 8$ $(b - 4)(b + 2)$ **31.** $a^2 + 7a - 8$ $(a + 8)(a - 1)$

Solve.

32. $x^2 - 5x - 6 = 0$ $\{6, -1\}$ **33.** $x^2 + x = 20$ $\{4, -5\}$

7-10 Objective: To factor trinomials of the form $ax^2 + bxy + cy^2$.

Factor.

34. $2x^2 + 11x + 5$ $(2x + 1)(x + 5)$ **35.** $3x^2 + xy - 2y^2$ $(3x - 2y)(x + y)$

Solve.

36. $2x^2 - 3x + 1 = 0$ $\left\{1, \frac{1}{2}\right\}$ **37.** $2x^2 = 3x + 5$ $\left\{\frac{5}{2}, -1\right\}$

Mathematics and Your Future

Strong preparation in mathematics is important for both boys and girls.
Nine out of ten females will work fulltime at some point in their lives.
Many will become heads of households or be major contributors in two-
earner families. By continuing to study mathematics you will improve
your earning capacity.

1. Write the prime factorization of 60.   **1.** $2^2 \cdot 3 \cdot 5$

■ **Find the greatest common factor.**

2. 42 and 70   **2.** 14

3. $8mn^2$ and $12mn^3$ **3.** $4mn^2$

■ **Factor. If the expression cannot be factored, write "not factorable."**

4. $8ab - 12a$ **4.** $4a(2b - 3)$

5. $45r - 42r^2$ **5.** $3r(15 - 14r)$

6. $x^2 + 7x + 12$ **6.** $(x + 4)(x + 3)$

7. $n^2 - 4n + 1$ **7.** Not factorable

8. $y^2 - 16$ **8.** $(y - 4)(y + 4)$

9. $c^2 - 14c + 45$ **9.** $(c - 9)(c - 5)$

10. $w^2 + 6w + 9$ **10.** $(w + 3)^2$

11. $4d^2 + 4d - 3$ **11.** $(2d + 3)(2d - 1)$

12. $3t^2 - 3t - 6$ **12.** $3(t - 2)(t + 1)$

■ **Expand and simplify.**

13. $(3a - 1)(a + 4)$ **13.** $3a^2 + 11a - 4$

14. $(5t - 3)(5t + 3)$ **14.** $25t^2 - 9$

15. $(x - 7)^2$ **15.** $x^2 - 14x + 49$

16. $(w + 6)(w + 8)$ **16.** $w^2 + 14w + 48$

© D.C. Heath & Co.

■ **Solve.**

17. $(2t - 17)(t + 4) = 0$ **17.** $\{17/2, -4\}$

18. $2x^2 + 6x = 0$ **18.** $\{0, -3\}$

19. $5w^2 = 180$ **19.** $\{6, -6\}$

20. $y^2 - 2y - 48 = 0$ **20.** $\{8, -6\}$

21. Twice a number is 8 less than its square. What is the number?   **21.** 4 or −2

22. The length of a rectangle is 5 m more than its width. What is the width of the rectangle if its area is 84 m²?   **22.** 7 m

★ **BONUS**

Write an expression in factored form for the shaded region. [*Hint:* The area of a circle is πr^2.]   **BONUS** $2r^2(4 - \pi)$

© D.C. Heath & Co.

■ CHAPTER 7 SELF-TEST

7-1   State the prime factorization.

   1. 252 $2^2 \cdot 3^2 \cdot 7$ **2.** 600 $2^3 \cdot 3 \cdot 5^2$

7-2   Find the GCF.

   3. 252 and 600   12   **4.** $36a^2b^3c$ and $84ab^2c^2$ $12ab^2c$

7-3   Solve.

   5. $y(y + 3) = 0$ $(0, -3)$ **6.** $(2x - 1)(x + 5) = 0$ $\left\{\frac{1}{2}, -5\right\}$

7-5,
7-6   Expand and simplify.

   7. $3x(5x - 9)$ $15x^2 - 27x$ **8.** $(2x + 7y)(2x - 7y)$ $4x^2 - 49y^2$

   9. $(3a - 11)(2a + 9)$ $6a^2 + 5a - 99$ **10.** $(t - 9)^2$ $t^2 - 18t + 81$

7-4–
7-6   Factor completely.

   11. $5x^2 - 35x$ $5x(x - 7)$ **12.** $9a^2 - 4$ $(3a + 2)(3a - 2)$

   13. $y^2 + 10y + 25$ $(y + 5)^2$ **14.** $2w^2 - 12w + 18$ $2(w - 3)^2$

7-7–
7-10   **15.** $x^2 + 9x + 20$ $(x + 5)(x + 4)$ **16.** $c^2 + 5c - 24$ $(c + 8)(c - 3)$

   17. $a^2 - ab - 6b^2$ $(a - 3b)(a + 2b)$ **18.** $r^2 - 5r + 6$ $(r - 3)(r - 2)$

   19. $2x^2 - 3x - 54$ $(2x + 9)(x - 6)$

7-4–
7-9   Solve.

   20. $5a^2 = 125$ $(5, -5)$ **21.** $b^2 - 14b + 49 = 0$ (7)

   22. $x^2 - 7x + 10 = 0$ $(2, 5)$ **23.** $w^2 + 7w = 78$ $(6, -13)$

   24. The square of a number added to its double is 143. Find the number.   11 or −13

   25. A 5-inch by 8-inch picture has a border of uniform width. The total area of the border and picture is 130 in². What is the width of the border? $2\frac{1}{2}$ in.

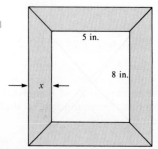

■ PRACTICE FOR COLLEGE ENTRANCE TESTS

1.

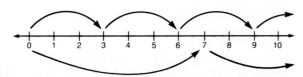

In the figure above, arcs are drawn above the number line every 3 units starting at 0 and arcs are drawn below the number line every 7 units starting at 0. At which of the following points on the number line will the arcs meet?

   A. 101   **B.** 102   **C.** 103   **D** 104   **E.** 105

2. If $a = 5 - t$, $b = 5 + t$, and $t^2 = 9$, then $ab = $ ___?___ .

   A. 4   **B.** 7   **C.** 16   **D.** 34   **E.** 64

3. The number n is a positive whole number whose only positive whole number factors are 1 and n. If $15n$ is divisible by 10, then $n = $ ___?___ .

   A. 2   **B.** 3   **C.** 9   **D.** 10   **E.** 13

4. If $xy = 3$ and $(x + y)^2 = 16$, then $x^2 + y^2 = $ ___?___ .

   A. 6   **B.** 7   **C.** 9   **D.** 10   **E.** 13

5. If $x - 2 = 5$, then $(x - 1)^2 = $ ___?___ .

   A. 4   **B.** 9   **C.** 16   **D.** 25   **E.** 36

6. If x is an even integer and n is the number of distinct prime factors of x, then the number of distinct prime factors of $2x$ is ___?___ .

   A. $n - 1$ **B.** n **C.** $n + 1$ **D.** x **E.** $2x$

7. If n is a positive integer and $n^2 - n = k$, then which of the following could be the value of k?

   A. 42   **B.** 43   **C.** 44   **D.** 45   **E.** 46

8. $35^2 - 2(35)(15) + 15^2 = $ ___?___ .

   A. 225   **B.** 400   **C.** 625   **D.** 1225   **E.** 2500

9. If $a + b = 4$ and $a - b = 2$, then $a^2 - b^2 = $ ___?___ .

   A. 4   **B.** 8   **C.** 12   **D.** 16   **E.** 20

10. If $r = 3t + 2$ and $s = 9t^2$, then what is s in terms of r?

   A. $(r - 2)^2$ **B.** $(4 + 2)^2$ **C.** $3(r - 2)^2$ **D.** $(r + 2)^2$ **E.** $9(r - 2)^2$

11. What fraction of the number of integer multiples of 5 between 1 and 49 are also multiples of 3?

   A. $\dfrac{3}{49}$ **B.** $\dfrac{5}{49}$ **C.** $\dfrac{1}{3}$ **D.** $\dfrac{5}{9}$ **E.** $\dfrac{3}{5}$

Chapter 7 Test B NAME _____

1. Write the prime factorization of 90.   1. $\underline{2 \cdot 3^2 \cdot 5}$

■ **Find the greatest common factor.**

2. 45 and 105   2. $\underline{15}$

3. $9a^3b^2$ and $24a^3b$ 3. $\underline{3a^3b}$

■ **Factor. If the expression cannot be factored, write "not factorable."**

4. $6xy - 9y$ 4. $\underline{3y(2x - 3)}$

5. $26w - 30w^2$ 5. $\underline{2w(13 - 15w)}$

6. $a^2 + 10a + 24$ 6. $\underline{(a + 6)(a + 4)}$

7. $n^2 - 25$ 7. $\underline{(n + 5)(n - 5)}$

8. $r^2 + 3r - 1$ 8. $\underline{\text{Not factorable}}$

9. $b^2 - 10b + 16$ 9. $\underline{(b - 8)(b - 2)}$

10. $c^2 + 4c + 4$ 10. $\underline{(c + 2)^2}$

11. $2d^2 + 4d - 6$ 11. $\underline{2(d + 3)(d - 1)}$

12. $6t^2 - 7t + 2$ 12. $\underline{(3t - 2)(2t - 1)}$

■ **Expand and simplify.**

13. $(4y - 1)(y + 3)$ 13. $\underline{4y^2 + 11y - 3}$

14. $(2x - 5)(2x + 5)$ 14. $\underline{4x^2 - 25}$

15. $(w - 8)^2$ 15. $\underline{w^2 - 16w + 64}$

16. $(a + 5)(a + 7)$ 16. $\underline{a^2 + 12a + 35}$

© D.C. Heath & Co.

Chapter 7 Test B (page 2) NAME

■ **Solve.**

17. $(x + 1)(2x - 13) = 0$ 17. $\underline{\{-1, 13/2\}}$

18. $4t^2 + 8t = 0$ 18. $\underline{\{0, -2\}}$

19. $9y^2 = 144$ 19. $\underline{\{4, -4\}}$

20. $w^2 - 9w - 36 = 0$ 20. $\underline{\{-3, 12\}}$

21. The sum of 3 times a number and the square of the number is 54. What is the number?   21. $\underline{-9 \text{ or } 6}$

22. The length of a rectangle is 7 m more than its width. What is the width of the rectangle if its area is 120 m²?   22. $\underline{8 \text{ m}}$

★ **BONUS**

Write an expression in factored form for the shaded region. [*Hint:* The area of a circle is πr^2.]

BONUS $\underline{r^2(6 - \pi)}$

© D.C. Heath & Co.

357

CHAPTER 8

CHAPTER OVERVIEW

Algebraic fractions are formed when one polynomial is divided by another. In this chapter, students learn to simplify algebraic fractions and to add, subtract, multiply, and divide algebraic fractions. Students find that the rules for operating with algebraic fractions are the same as the rules for computing with numerical fractions. In this chapter, students will need their knowledge of computation with numerical fractions as well as the knowledge they gained about polynomials in Chapter 7.

Students learn to solve applied problems involving parallel electrical circuits. Students also learn about applications of algebraic fractions in ratio and proportion, percent, direct variation, and inverse variation.

Algebraic fractions will be used in the remaining chapters of the book. In addition, algebraic fractions have many important applications in mathematics, science, business, and other fields.

8 Algebraic Fractions and Applications

By the late 1700s, French paper makers and scientists began experimenting with hot air balloons. The Montgolfier brothers discovered that hot air can cause a paper bag to rise. They were successful in launching the first hot air balloon on June 4, 1783.

Later that year, a French chemist, Jacques Charles, began experimenting with hydrogen and launched the first hydrogen balloon on August 27, 1783. Charles went on to discover nearly every essential of modern balloon design.

His work with balloons led to the discovery of the law that bears his name, the Charles Law, as follows:

The volume V of a gas under constant pressure is directly related to its temperature T in degrees Kelvin:

$$V = kT \quad \text{or} \quad \frac{V_1}{V_2} = \frac{T_1}{T_2}$$

Algebraic fractions (and numerical fractions) should be written in simplest form. Such expressions can be written and compared more easily.

8–1 Simplifying Algebraic Fractions

Preview

The Wizard of Odds performed number feats. In one trick the Wizard would ask a volunteer to do the following:

- Think of a number other than 1.

- Square the number and subtract 1.

- Divide this difference by 1 less than the original number.

When told the result, the Wizard could immediately give the original number. Copy and complete this table to determine how the Wizard was so quick with the answer.

Number	2	3	4	5	6	7	8	9	10
Result	?	?	?	?	?	?	?	?	?

$n+1$: 3 4 5 6 7 8 9 10 11

The trick used by the Wizard can be explained by simplifying an algebraic fraction.

PREVIEW

Have students determine whether the Wizard's trick is equally apparent with large numbers, negative numbers, and fractions. For example, find the result for 100, -3, and ½. (The results are 101, -2, and 1½ respectively.)

Express the three steps in the trick using algebraic notation.

1. $x; x \neq 1$

2. $x^2 - 1$

3. $\dfrac{x^2 - 1}{x - 1}$

The result is $x + 1$ (because $\dfrac{x^2 - 1}{x - 1} = \dfrac{(x - 1)(x + 1)}{x - 1} = x + 1$, provided $x \neq 1$).

■ LESSON

Fractions that contain variables are called **algebraic fractions**. These are examples of algebraic fractions.

$$\frac{x}{5} \qquad \frac{7}{y} \qquad \frac{3+a}{2+a} \qquad \frac{6n}{7n}$$

Recall that division by 0 is not defined. Therefore, the values of the variables in algebraic fractions must be restricted so that the denominators of the fractions do not equal 0. Consider, for example, this fraction:

$$\frac{3}{x^2 + 2x}$$

To determine the restrictions on the value of x:

Solve the equation. $x^2 + 2x = 0$
Factor and use the $x(x + 2) = 0$
zero-product property. $x = 0$ or $x + 2 = 0$
                       $x = 0$ or $x = -2$

In order for the denominator not to be 0, these restrictions must be placed on the values of x:

$$x \neq 0, \qquad x \neq -2$$

Values of the variables for which a fraction is defined are called **admissible values**. In the example above, the set of admissible values is the set of all real numbers x, except $x = 0$ and $x = -2$.

LESSON

Students may wonder if there are examples of undefined expressions other than those resulting in division by zero. Although radicals are not used in this lesson, it may be pointed out that $\sqrt{x}$ is undefined (that is, not a real number) when x is negative.

Point out that $\dfrac{2}{x}$ and $\dfrac{2(x - 1)}{x(x - 1)}$ are equivalent expressions *only if* $x \neq 1$. $\dfrac{2}{x}$ is defined for $x = 1$, but $\dfrac{2(x - 1)}{x(x - 1)}$ is not. Therefore, the expressions will result in the same number only if $x = 1$ is *not* included in the replacement set. (Note that zero is not a permissible value for either expression.)

Emphasize to students that it is correct to simplify an algebraic fraction by removing common *factors*. However, it is incorrect to eliminate common *terms*. Use numerical examples to illustrate this point.

$$\frac{5 \cdot \cancel{2}}{7 \cdot \cancel{2}} = \frac{5}{7} \text{ but } \frac{5 + \cancel{2}}{7 + \cancel{2}} \neq \frac{6}{8} \text{ and } \frac{5 + \cancel{2}}{7 + \cancel{2}} \neq \frac{5}{7}$$

Example 1.
State restrictions on the values of the variable x for the fraction.

$$\frac{5}{x^2 - 5x + 6}$$

Find the values of x that make the denominator 0.

$$x^2 - 5x + 6 = 0$$
$$(x - 2)(x - 3) = 0$$
$$x = 3 \text{ or } x = 2$$

Restrictions: $x \neq 2$ and $x \neq 3$

Example 2.

Show that $\frac{x + 4}{2x + 4}$ and $\frac{x}{2x}$ are not equivalent.

Substitute 3 for x and simplify.

$$\frac{3 + 4}{2(3) + 4} \overset{?}{=} \frac{3}{2(3)}$$

$$\frac{7}{10} \neq \frac{3}{6}$$

Example 1 State the restrictions on the variables in this algebraic fraction.

$$\frac{b}{a^2 - ab}$$

Solution Find the values of a and b that make the denominator 0.

$$a^2 - ab = 0$$
$$a(a - b) = 0$$
$$a = 0 \quad \text{or} \quad a = b$$

Answer These restrictions must be placed on a and b: $a \neq 0$, $a \neq b$.

If two fractions are not equivalent, we can show that fact by finding admissible values that give the fractions different values.

Example 2 Show that $\frac{x + 1}{3x + 1}$ and $\frac{x}{3x}$ are not equivalent.

Solution Substitute 2 for x and simplify.

$$\frac{x + 1}{3x + 1} \qquad\qquad \frac{x}{3x}$$

$$\frac{2 + 1}{3(2) + 1} \qquad\qquad \frac{2}{3 \cdot 2}$$

$$\frac{3}{7} \qquad\qquad \frac{2}{6} \text{ or } \frac{1}{3}$$

Answer Since $\frac{3}{7} \neq \frac{1}{3}$, $\frac{x + 1}{3x + 1}$ and $\frac{x}{3x}$ are not equivalent.

If two fractions are **equivalent fractions,** we can show that fact by transforming one fraction into the other, using the properties given below.

Multiplicaton and Division Properties for Equivalent Fractions

For all admissible values of a, b, and c,

$$\frac{a}{b} = \frac{ac}{bc} \quad \text{and} \quad \frac{a}{b} = \frac{a \div c}{b \div c}$$

These same properties can also be used to simplify algebraic fractions.

Research clearly shows that student achievement is enhanced when students know their progress in achieving what is expected of them.

ADDITIONAL EXAMPLES

ADDITIONAL EXAMPLES

Example 3. Simplify. $\dfrac{10a - 15b}{20}$

$= \dfrac{2a - 3b}{4}$

Example 4. Simplify. $\dfrac{x^2 - x}{x^2 + x}$

$= \dfrac{x - 1}{x + 1}, x \neq 0, x \neq -1$

Example 5. Simplify. $\dfrac{a - b}{b - a}$

$= -1, a \neq b$

CHECK UNDERSTANDING

- Are $\dfrac{1}{2}$ and $\dfrac{1 \cdot 3}{2 \cdot 3}$ equivalent? (Yes)

- Are $\dfrac{1}{2}$ and $\dfrac{1 + 3}{2 + 3}$ equivalent? (No)

- What restrictions are there on the value of the variable for the fraction $\dfrac{3}{x - 5}$? $(x \neq 5)$

Example 3   Simplify. $\dfrac{3x + 6y}{21}$

Solution   Factor the numerator and denominator.

$$\dfrac{3x + 6y}{21} = \dfrac{3(x + 2y)}{3 \cdot 7}$$

Divide both numerator and denominator by the common factor 3.

$$= \dfrac{\overset{1}{3}(x + 2y)}{\underset{1}{3} \cdot 7}$$

Answer $\dfrac{x + 2y}{7}$

$$= \dfrac{x + 2y}{7}$$

Example 4   Simplify. $\dfrac{2a - 2b}{6a^2 - 6b^2}$

Solution   Factor the numerator and denominator.

$$\dfrac{2a - 2b}{6a^2 - 6b^2} = \dfrac{2(a - b)}{2 \cdot 3(a - b)(a + b)}$$

Use the factored forms to determine the necessary restrictions on the values of the variables:

$$a \neq b, a \neq -b$$

Eliminate the common factors.

$$= \dfrac{2(\overset{1}{a - b})}{\underset{1}{2} \cdot 3(\underset{1}{a - b})(a + b)}$$

$$= \dfrac{1}{3(a + b)}$$

Answer $\dfrac{1}{3(a + b)}, a \neq b, a \neq -b$

Note that factors that restrict the values of variables may be removed in the simplifying process. (For example, in Example 4, $a - b$ was removed from both numerator and denominator.) Therefore, restrictions on variables must be determined from the original factored expression, *not* the simplified result.

Example 5   Simplify. $\dfrac{x - 1}{1 - x}$

Solution   Note that the denominator is the opposite of the numerator.

Factor. List the necessary restrictions on the value of x.

$$\dfrac{x - 1}{1 - x} = \dfrac{(x - 1)}{-1(x - 1)}, x \neq 1$$

Eliminate the common factor.

$$= \dfrac{\overset{1}{(x - 1)}}{-1\underset{1}{(x - 1)}}$$

$$= -1$$

Answer $-1, x \neq 1$

In exercises 1–6 point out that one or two values are *not* admissible, but infinitely many other values *are* admissible. Sometimes it is important to focus on the exceptions, as we do here, but we should not lose track of the admissible values in the process.

In exercise 9, emphasize that we cannot add (or subtract) a number to both numerator and denominator of a fraction without changing the value of the fraction (except for the trivial case in which the numerator and denominator are equal).

In exercise 15, discuss two ways of simplifying the fraction:

First method—Read the numerator as "the opposite of *a* minus *b*."

Write $-(a - b) = -a + b = b - a$

Then simplify $\dfrac{-(a - b)}{b - a} = \dfrac{b - a}{b - a} = 1$

Second method—Multiply by one in the form $\dfrac{-1}{-1}$.

$$\dfrac{-(a - b)}{b - a} \cdot \dfrac{(-1)}{(-1)} = \dfrac{a - b}{-b + a} = \dfrac{a - b}{a - b} = 1$$

■ CLASSROOM EXERCISES

List any necessary restrictions on the value of the variable.

1. $\dfrac{7}{x}$ $x \neq 0$

2. $\dfrac{3}{x + 1}$ $x \neq -1$

3. $\dfrac{5}{x(x - 1)}$ $x \neq 0, 1$

4. $\dfrac{19 + y}{x^2 - 4}$ $x \neq 2, -2$

5. $\dfrac{2a}{a - b}$ $a \neq b$

6. $\dfrac{17}{a^2 + 6a}$ $a \neq 0, -6$

7. $\dfrac{7b}{a^2 + 4}$ None

8. $\dfrac{2a - 3}{5}$ None

State whether the following pairs of fractions are equivalent.

9. $\dfrac{x + 1}{x + 2}$ and $\dfrac{1}{2}$ No

10. $\dfrac{x}{2x}$ and $\dfrac{1}{2}$ Yes

11. $\dfrac{3x + 2}{5x + 2}$ and $\dfrac{3x}{5x}$ No

12. $\dfrac{3(x + 2)}{5(x + 2)}$ and $\dfrac{3}{5}$ Yes

Simplify. List any necessary restrictions on the variables.

13. $\dfrac{(a + b)(a - b)}{(a - b)(a - b)}$ $\dfrac{a + b}{a - b}, a \neq b$

14. $\dfrac{2c + 2d}{5c + 5d}$ $\dfrac{2}{5}, c \neq -d$

15. $\dfrac{-(a - b)}{b - a}$ $1, a \neq b$

16. $\dfrac{x^2 + 2x + 1}{2x + 2}$ $\dfrac{x + 1}{2}, x \neq -1$

■ WRITTEN EXERCISES

List the values of x that are not admissible.

A

1. $\dfrac{x - 1}{x - 3}$ 3

2. $\dfrac{x - 2}{x - 4}$ 4

3. $\dfrac{5}{2x - 3}$ $\dfrac{3}{2}$

4. $\dfrac{4}{3x - 5}$ $\dfrac{5}{3}$

5. $\dfrac{5x}{(x - 2)(x - 4)}$ 2, 4

6. $\dfrac{3x}{(x - 1)(x + 2)}$ $-2, 1$

7. $\dfrac{10}{x^2 - 5x + 6}$ 2, 3

8. $\dfrac{8}{x^2 - 6x + 8}$ 2, 4

List any necessary restrictions for the fractions to be defined.

9. $\dfrac{5}{a - 5}$ $a \neq 5$

10. $\dfrac{7}{7 - a}$ $a \neq 7$

11. $\dfrac{b}{b + 3}$ $b \neq -3$

12. $\dfrac{b}{b + 4}$ $b \neq -4$

13. $\dfrac{4}{a(b - 2)}$ $a \neq 0, b \neq 2$

14. $\dfrac{8}{b(a - 3)}$ $b \neq 0, a \neq 3$

15. $\dfrac{b}{a^2 + 3a}$ $a \neq 0, -3$

16. $\dfrac{a}{b^2 + 4b}$ $b \neq 0, -4$

State whether these pairs of fractions are equivalent for admissible values of x.

17. $\dfrac{3x}{4x}$ and $\dfrac{3}{4}$ Yes

18. $\dfrac{3x}{8x}$ and $\dfrac{3}{8}$ Yes

19. $\dfrac{5 + x}{8 + x}$ and $\dfrac{5}{8}$ No

20. $\dfrac{5 + x}{6 + x}$ and $\dfrac{5}{6}$ No

21. $\dfrac{1}{x - 2}$ and $\dfrac{2}{2x - 4}$ Yes

22. $\dfrac{1}{x - 3}$ and $\dfrac{2}{2x - 6}$ Yes

23. $\dfrac{1}{x + 5}$ and $\dfrac{2}{x + 10}$ No

24. $\dfrac{1}{x + 4}$ and $\dfrac{3}{x + 12}$ No

Simplify. List any necessary restrictions on the variables.

25. $\dfrac{5x}{15x}$ $\dfrac{1}{3}, x \neq 0$

26. $\dfrac{6x}{16x}$ $\dfrac{3}{8}, x \neq 0$

27. $\dfrac{4x^2}{15x^3}$ $\dfrac{4}{15x}, x \neq 0$

28. $\dfrac{12x}{15x^2}$ $\dfrac{4}{5x}, x \neq 0$

29. $\dfrac{(b + 2)(b + 3)}{(b + 3)(b + 4)}$ $\dfrac{b + 2}{b + 4}, b \neq -3, -4$

30. $\dfrac{(c + 3)(c + 4)}{(c + 2)(c + 3)}$ $\dfrac{c + 4}{c + 2}, c \neq -3, -2$

31. $\dfrac{2x + 4}{5x + 10}$ $\dfrac{2}{5}, x \neq -2$

32. $\dfrac{6x + 9}{9x + 12}$ $\dfrac{2x + 3}{3x + 4}, x \neq -\dfrac{4}{3}$

ASSIGNMENT GUIDE

Basic 3–51 multiples of 3, Review Exercises

Average 9–51 multiples of 3, 53–63 odd, Review Exercises

Enriched 21–63 multiples of 3, 64–69 all, Review Exercises

33. $\dfrac{x^2+5x}{2x^2-7x}$ $\dfrac{x+5}{2x-7}$, $x \neq 0, \dfrac{7}{2}$

34. $\dfrac{x^2-8x}{3x^2+5x}$ $\dfrac{x-8}{3x+5}$, $x \neq 0, -\dfrac{5}{3}$

35. $\dfrac{5a^2}{a^3+2a^2+a}$ $\dfrac{5a}{(a+1)^2}$, $a \neq 0, -1$

36. $\dfrac{7a^2}{a^3-5a^2+6a}$ $\dfrac{7a}{(a-3)(a-2)}$, $a \neq 0, 2, 3$

37. $\dfrac{c+3}{c^2+5c+6}$ $\dfrac{1}{c+2}$, $c \neq -3, -2$

38. $\dfrac{c-2}{c^2-5c+6}$ $\dfrac{1}{c-3}$, $c \neq 2, 3$

39. $\dfrac{3t-12}{t^2+t-20}$ $\dfrac{3}{t+5}$, $t \neq -5, 4$

40. $\dfrac{2t+10}{t^2+t-20}$ $\dfrac{2}{t-4}$, $t \neq -5, 4$

41. $\dfrac{a^2+a-2}{a^2+3a+2}$ $\dfrac{a-1}{a+1}$, $a \neq -2, -1$

42. $\dfrac{a^2-a-2}{a^2+3a+2}$ $\dfrac{a-2}{a+2}$, $a \neq -2, -1$

43. $\dfrac{2x^2+3x}{2x^2+5x+3}$ $\dfrac{x}{x+1}$, $x \neq -\dfrac{3}{2}, -1$

44. $\dfrac{12x-4}{3x^2+5x-2}$ $\dfrac{4}{x+2}$, $x \neq -2, \dfrac{1}{3}$

The values of the area and width of a rectangle are given. Express the value of the length of the rectangle in simplest form.

45. area: $x^2 + 3x$;
    width: x $x+3$

46. area: $5y + 20$;
    width: 5 $y+4$

47. area: $a^2 - 4$;
    width: $a - 2$ $a+2$

48. area: $b^2 - 9$;
    width: $b - 3$ $b+3$

49. area: $a^2 + 4a - 12$;
    width: $a - 2$ $a+6$

50. area: $a^2 + 3a - 18$;
    width: $a - 3$ $a+6$

51. area: $a^2 + 8a + 16$;
    width: $a + 4$ $a+4$

52. area: $a^2 + 6a + 9$;
    width: $a + 3$ $a+3$

Evaluate the fractions for the given values of x and state whether the fractions are equivalent.

B 53.

x	$\dfrac{2+x}{6+x}$	$\dfrac{1+x}{3+x}$	No
2	? $\frac{1}{2}$	? $\frac{3}{5}$	
1	? $\frac{3}{7}$	? $\frac{1}{2}$	
0	? $\frac{1}{3}$	? $\frac{1}{3}$	
-1	? $\frac{1}{5}$	? 0	

54.

x	$\dfrac{x-3}{x^2-9}$	$\dfrac{1}{x+3}$	Yes
2	? $\frac{1}{5}$	? $\frac{1}{5}$	
1	? $\frac{1}{4}$	? $\frac{1}{4}$	
0	? $\frac{1}{3}$	? $\frac{1}{3}$	
-1	? $\frac{1}{2}$	? $\frac{1}{2}$	

55.

x	$\dfrac{x+3}{x^2+x-6}$	$\dfrac{x}{x^2-2x}$	Yes
-2	? $-\frac{1}{4}$	? $-\frac{1}{4}$	
-1	? $-\frac{1}{3}$	? $-\frac{1}{3}$	
1	? -1	? -1	
3	? 1	? 1	

56.

x	$\dfrac{x+4}{x^2+2x-8}$	$\dfrac{x}{x^2-2x}$	Yes
-3	? $-\frac{1}{5}$	? $-\frac{1}{5}$	
-1	? $-\frac{1}{3}$	? $-\frac{1}{3}$	
1	? -1	? -1	
3	? 1	? 1	

The use of a table to examine how an expression varies with different replacements for the variable is a powerful problem-solving tool. The value of this technique becomes more apparent as the complexity of the expression increases. If students develop the habit of examining or comparing expressions through a table of values, they will be able to draw on this technique for more difficult expressions in the future. For example, they may test conjectures about the appropriateness of a particular procedure.

To check	use a table:		
$\dfrac{x+1}{2x} = \dfrac{2}{2} = 1$		x	$\dfrac{x+1}{2x}$
		1	$\dfrac{2}{2}=1$
		2	$\dfrac{3}{4}$ No!

Only one counterexample is required to show that two expressions are not equivalent.

ENRICHMENT PROBLEMS

- Determine whether the following expressions are equivalent. Support your conclusion.

  a. $\dfrac{2x}{3|x|}$ and $\dfrac{2x}{3x}$

  No; if $x < 0$, $\dfrac{2x}{3|x|} \neq \dfrac{2x}{3x}$

  b. $\sqrt{x^2}$ and $|x|$

  Yes; the symbol $\sqrt{\ }$ indicates the principal or positive square root.

  c. $\dfrac{4x^3 + 4x}{x^2 + 1}$ and $4x$

  Yes; there are no restrictions needed for the variable x.

The following exercises list the formulas for the volume and surface area of some solids.

a. Write a fraction for the ratio of the volume to the total surface area of each solid.
b. Simplify the fractions.

57. Cube $\dfrac{s}{6}$
$V = s^3$
$S = 6s^2$

58. Square pyramid
$V = \dfrac{1}{3}b^2h$ $\dfrac{bh}{3(b+2a)}$
$S = b^2 + 2ab$

59. Square prism
$V = hs^2$
$S = 2s^2 + 4hs$ $\dfrac{hs}{2(s+2h)}$

60. Cylinder
$V = \pi r^2 h$
$S = 2\pi r^2 + 2\pi rh$
$\dfrac{rh}{2(r+h)}$

61. Sphere
$V = \dfrac{4}{3}\pi r^3$
$S = 4\pi r^2$ $\dfrac{r}{3}$

62. Circular torus
$V = 2\pi^2 Rr^2$
$S = 4\pi^2 Rr$ $\dfrac{r}{2}$

63. Write an algebraic fraction to explain the number trick presented in the Preview. Then write the fraction in simplest form. $\dfrac{n^2 - 1}{n - 1} = n + 1$

For each of the following fractions, (a) state the values of the variable for which the fraction is undefined, (b) state the values of the variable that make the fraction equal to zero, and (c) simplify the fraction.

64. $\dfrac{a^2 - a - 2}{a^2 + 3a + 2}$
a. $-2, -1$ b. 2 c. $\dfrac{a-2}{a+2}$

65. $\dfrac{a^2 + 3a}{3a + 9}$
a. -3 b. 0 c. $\dfrac{a}{3}$

66. $\dfrac{b^2 + b - 6}{b^2 - b - 6}$
a. $-2, 3$ b. $-3, 2$ c. As is

67. $\dfrac{a^2 - 16}{a^2 + 8a + 16}$
a. -4 b. 4 c. $\dfrac{a-4}{a+4}$

68. $\dfrac{3b^2 - 14b + 8}{3b^2 + 14b + 8}$
a. $-4, -\dfrac{2}{3}$ b. $\dfrac{2}{3}, 4$ c. As is

69. $\dfrac{2b^2 + 7b - 15}{2b^2 - b - 6}$
a. $-\dfrac{3}{2}, 2$ b. $-5, \dfrac{3}{2}$ c. As is

■ REVIEW EXERCISES

Substitute and simplify.

a	b	c	d
12	18	2	3

[1–2]

1. $\dfrac{a}{b} \cdot \dfrac{c}{d}$ $\dfrac{4}{9}$

2. $\dfrac{a}{b} \div \dfrac{c}{d}$ 1

3. $\dfrac{a}{c} + \dfrac{b}{c}$ 15

4. $\dfrac{a+b}{c}$ 15

5. $\dfrac{a}{d} - \dfrac{b}{d}$ -2

6. $\dfrac{a-b}{d}$ -2

To multiply and divide algebraic fractions.

Simplify. Assume no denominators are zero.

1. $\dfrac{6x}{3x^2}$ $\dfrac{2}{x}$

2. $\dfrac{2(x+1)}{3(x+1)}$ $\dfrac{2}{3}$

3. $\dfrac{9x(x-1)}{12x(x+1)}$ $\dfrac{3(x-1)}{4(x+1)}$

4. $\dfrac{a+2}{a^2+4a+4}$ $\dfrac{1}{a+2}$

5. $\dfrac{a^2+5a+6}{a^2+7a+12}$ $\dfrac{a+2}{a+4}$

8–2 Multiplying and Dividing Fractions

Preview

Simplify this product:

$$\frac{21}{22}\cdot\frac{33}{35}$$

In simplifying did you multiply first then re-move the common facors? Or did you re-move the common factors first and then multiply?

a. $\dfrac{21}{22}\cdot\dfrac{33}{35}=\dfrac{693}{770}=\dfrac{9\cdot\overset{1}{\cancel{77}}}{10\cdot\cancel{77}}=\dfrac{9}{10}$

b. $\dfrac{\overset{3}{\cancel{21}}}{\underset{2}{\cancel{22}}}\cdot\dfrac{\overset{3}{\cancel{33}}}{\underset{5}{\cancel{35}}}=\dfrac{9}{10}$

c. $\dfrac{21}{22}\cdot\dfrac{33}{35}=\dfrac{3\cdot\overset{1}{\cancel{7}}\cdot 3\cdot\overset{1}{\cancel{11}}}{2\cdot\underset{1}{\cancel{11}}\cdot 5\cdot\underset{1}{\cancel{7}}}=\dfrac{9}{10}$

In this lesson you will multiply fractions using these methods.

PURPOSE

Products and quotients of algebraic fractions occur in the solution of fractional equations and the simplification of other expressions. Students should be able to write such ex-pressions in simplest form.

PREVIEW

Although both methods used in the Preview are acceptable, the second method should seem simpler and, therefore, be used most of the time. Another method includes ideas from both of the other methods.

Multiply. Leave the product in factored form.

$$\frac{21}{22}\cdot\frac{33}{35}=\frac{21\cdot 33}{22\cdot 35}$$

Divide the numerator and the denominator by common factors.

$$=\frac{\overset{3}{\cancel{21}}\cdot\overset{3}{\cancel{33}}}{\underset{2}{\cancel{22}}\cdot\underset{5}{\cancel{35}}}$$

Simplify the fraction.

$$=\frac{9}{10}$$

■ LESSON

Algebraic fractions are multiplied in the same way as arithmetic fractions.

Definition: Multiplication of Fractions

For all real numbers a and c, and all nonzero real numbers b and d,

$$\frac{a}{b}\cdot\frac{c}{d}=\frac{ac}{bd},\ b\neq 0,\ d\neq 0$$

Suppose that we wish to simplify the product

$$\frac{5ab^2}{3}\cdot\frac{6}{a^2b}$$

Here are two methods of doing so.

Method 1. Multiply first and then eliminate common factors.

Multiply. State restrictions. $\dfrac{5ab^2}{3}\cdot\dfrac{6}{a^2b}=\dfrac{30ab^2}{3a^2b},\ a\neq 0,\ b\neq 0$

Factor the numerator and denominator and eliminate common factors. $=\dfrac{2\cdot\overset{1}{\cancel{3}}\cdot 5\cdot\overset{1}{\cancel{a}}\cdot\overset{1}{\cancel{b}}\cdot b}{\cancel{3}\cdot a\cdot a\cdot\cancel{b}}$

The simplified product is as follows: $=\dfrac{10b}{a},\ a\neq 0,\ b\neq 0$

Briefly review how numerical fractions are multiplied and divided. Examples such as these should be discussed.

$$\frac{14}{15} \cdot \frac{10}{7} \qquad\qquad \frac{20}{27} \div \frac{5}{9}$$

$$= \frac{\overset{2}{\cancel{14}}}{\underset{3}{\cancel{15}}} \cdot \frac{\overset{2}{\cancel{10}}}{\underset{1}{\cancel{7}}} \qquad = \frac{\overset{4}{\cancel{20}}}{\underset{3}{\cancel{27}}} \cdot \frac{\overset{1}{\cancel{9}}}{\underset{1}{\cancel{5}}}$$

$$= \frac{4}{3} \qquad\qquad = \frac{4}{3}$$

In multiplying and dividing algebraic fractions, point out that expressions should be written in factored form so that common factors may be identified and eliminated. Algebraic expressions in the numerator and denominator of the product may be left in factored form.

ADDITIONAL EXAMPLES

Example 1. Simplify. $\dfrac{a}{b^2}(ab^3 + a^2b^2)$

$$= a^2b + a^3$$

Example 2. Simplify. $\dfrac{3x}{2y} \cdot \dfrac{x^2 + x}{xy + y}$

$$= \frac{3x^2}{2y^2}$$

Method 2. Eliminate common factors first and then multiply.

Factor the numerators and denominators. $\quad \dfrac{5ab^2}{3} \cdot \dfrac{6}{a^2b} = \dfrac{5 \cdot a \cdot b \cdot b}{3} \cdot \dfrac{2 \cdot 3}{a \cdot a \cdot b}$

State restrictions. $\qquad a \neq 0, \quad b \neq 0$

Eliminate common factors. $\qquad = \dfrac{5 \cdot \overset{1}{\cancel{a}} \cdot b \cdot \overset{1}{\cancel{b}}}{\underset{1}{\cancel{3}}} \cdot \dfrac{2 \cdot \overset{1}{\cancel{3}}}{\overset{}{\underset{1}{\cancel{a}} \cdot a \cdot \underset{1}{\cancel{b}}}}$

Multiply. $\qquad = \dfrac{10b}{a}, \quad a \neq 0, \quad b \neq 0$

Either of these methods can be used to simplify products.

> **Note:** From this point on in the text, you can assume that unless otherwise stated, the variables are restricted so that no denominator of an algebraic fraction equals zero.

Example 1 Simplify. $\dfrac{x^2}{y}(3y^2 + 2y)$

Solution Use the distributive property to expand.

$$\frac{x^2}{y}(3y^2 + 2y) = \frac{x^2}{y}(3y^2) + \frac{x^2}{y}(2y)$$

Factor each term and eliminate common factors.

$$= \frac{x \cdot x}{\underset{1}{\cancel{y}}} \cdot \frac{3 \cdot y \cdot \overset{1}{\cancel{y}}}{1} + \frac{x \cdot x}{\underset{1}{\cancel{y}}} \cdot \frac{2 \cdot \overset{1}{\cancel{y}}}{1}$$

Answer $3x^2y + 2x^2$

$$= 3x^2y + 2x^2$$

Example 2 Simplify. $\dfrac{x}{4y} \cdot \dfrac{y^2 - y}{xy - x}$

Solution Factor.

$$\frac{x}{4y} \cdot \frac{y^2 - y}{xy - x} = \frac{x}{4y} \cdot \frac{y(y - 1)}{x(y - 1)}$$

Eliminate common factors.

$$= \frac{\overset{1}{\cancel{x}}}{4y} \cdot \frac{\overset{1}{\cancel{y}}\overset{1}{\cancel{(y-1)}}}{\underset{1}{\cancel{x}}\underset{1}{\cancel{(y-1)}}} = \frac{1}{4}$$

Answer $\dfrac{1}{4}$

ADDITIONAL EXAMPLES

Example 3. Simplify. $\dfrac{x^2 - 4x + 4}{x + 2} \cdot \dfrac{1}{x - 2}$

$= \dfrac{x - 2}{x + 2}$

Example 4. Simplify. $\dfrac{7a}{5b} \div \dfrac{a}{10}$

$= \dfrac{14}{b}$

Example 5. Simplify. $\dfrac{3x + 6y}{x^2 + 2xy} \div \dfrac{3}{x}$

$= 1$

CHECK UNDERSTANDING

- Simplify. $\dfrac{2x}{3y} \cdot \dfrac{2y}{3x}$ ($\frac{4}{9}$)

- Simplify. $\dfrac{4a}{3b} \div \dfrac{3a}{4b}$ ($\frac{16}{9}$)

Example 3   Simplify. $\dfrac{x^2 - 1}{x^2 + 1} \cdot \dfrac{1}{x - 1}$

Solution $\dfrac{x^2 - 1}{x^2 + 1} \cdot \dfrac{1}{x - 1} = \dfrac{\overset{1}{\cancel{(x - 1)}}(x + 1)}{x^2 + 1} \cdot \dfrac{1}{\underset{1}{\cancel{x - 1}}}$

$= \dfrac{x + 1}{x^2 + 1}$

Note that the expressions $x + 1$ and $x^2 + 1$ have no common factors other than 1. Therefore, $\dfrac{x + 1}{x^2 + 1}$ cannot be simplified further.

Answer $\dfrac{x + 1}{x^2 + 1}$

Dividing by a real number is equivalent to multiplying by its reciprocal. So we can write the following definition of division of fractions.

Definition: Division of Fractions

For all real numbers a, and all nonzero real numbers b, c, and d,

$$\dfrac{a}{b} \div \dfrac{c}{d} = \dfrac{a}{b} \cdot \dfrac{d}{c}, \quad b \neq 0, \quad c \neq 0, \quad d \neq 0$$

Any division expression can be transformed into an equivalent multiplication expression. Then that product can be simplified by the previous methods.

Example 4   Simplify. $\dfrac{3x}{5y} \div \dfrac{y}{15x}$

Solution   *Rewrite as a multiplication expression.* $\dfrac{3x}{5y} \div \dfrac{y}{15x} = \dfrac{3x}{5y} \cdot \dfrac{15x}{y}$

Eliminate common factors and simplify. $= \dfrac{3x}{\underset{1}{\cancel{5}}y} \cdot \dfrac{\overset{3}{\cancel{15}}x}{y} = \dfrac{9x^2}{y^2}$

Answer $\dfrac{9x^2}{y^2}$

Example 5   Simplify. $\dfrac{2a + 2b}{a^2 + ab} \div \dfrac{4}{a}$

Solution   *Rewrite as a multiplication expression.* $\dfrac{2a + 2b}{a^2 + ab} \div \dfrac{4}{a} = \dfrac{2a + 2b}{a^2 + ab} \cdot \dfrac{a}{4}$

Factor and eliminate common factors. $= \dfrac{\overset{1}{\cancel{2}}\overset{1}{\cancel{(a + b)}}}{\underset{1}{\cancel{a}}\underset{1}{\cancel{(a + b)}}} \cdot \dfrac{\overset{1}{\cancel{a}}}{2 \cdot 2} = \dfrac{1}{2}$

Answer $\dfrac{1}{2}$

CLASSROOM EXERCISES

In exercise 2, be sure that students distribute $2x$ over the sum before simplifying.

ASSIGNMENT GUIDE

Basic   1–39 odd, Review Exercises
Average   3–48 multiples of 3, 49–55 odd,
       Review Exercises
Enriched   9–54 multiples of 3, 57–63 odd,
       Review Exercises

PRACTICE WORKSHEET 39

8-2 MULTIPLYING AND DIVIDING FRACTIONS

■ Write each product in simplest form. Assume that no denominator is equal to zero.

1. $\frac{t^2}{s}\cdot\frac{t}{s}$ t^3/s^2 2. $\frac{t^3}{s}\cdot\frac{s^2}{t^6}$ s/t^3 3. $\frac{a^2}{6}\cdot\frac{3}{a}$ $a/2$

4. $\frac{12a}{b^2}\cdot\frac{b^3}{8a}$ $3b/2$ 5. $8\left(\frac{a}{2}+\frac{b}{4}\right)$ $4a+2b$ 6. $a^2\left(\frac{3}{a}+\frac{4}{a}\right)$ $3a+4$

7. $\frac{d(r+3)}{4}\cdot\frac{c}{d^2(r+3)}$ $c/4d$ 8. $\frac{3(p+2q)}{2}\cdot\frac{8(p-4)}{9(p+2q)}$ $\frac{4(p-4)}{3}$

■ Write each quotient in simplest form. Assume that no denominator is equal to zero.

9. $\frac{x^2}{y}\div\frac{x}{y^3}$ xy 10. $\frac{t^2}{3}\div\frac{t^4}{6}$ $2/t^2$

11. $\frac{p^2q^2}{4}\div\frac{pq^3}{5}$ $5p/4q$ 12. $\frac{k^2}{k+1}\div\frac{2k}{(k+1)^2}$ $\frac{k(k+1)}{2}$

13. $\frac{x+y}{2}\div\frac{x-y}{8}$ $\frac{4(x+y)}{x-y}$ 14. $\frac{x-3}{7}\div\frac{x-3}{14}$ 2

15. $\frac{2(c+6)}{5(c+3)}\div\frac{6(c+6)}{10(c+3)}$ $2/3$ 16. $\frac{5}{(x-4)^2}\div\frac{5}{x-4}$ $\frac{1}{x-4}$

EXTRA PRACTICE, page 634

■ CLASSROOM EXERCISES

Simplify.

1. $\frac{x}{y}\cdot\frac{y}{x}$ 1

2. $2x\left(\frac{3}{x}+\frac{5}{2x}\right)$ 11

3. $\frac{3(x-2)}{4}\cdot\frac{2}{5(x-2)}$ $\frac{3}{10}$

4. $\frac{c+3d}{4}\cdot\frac{12}{2c+6d}$ $\frac{3}{2}$

5. $\frac{6x^2}{y}\div\frac{2y}{3x}$ $\frac{9x^3}{y^2}$

6. $\frac{ab+b^2}{4a+4b}\div\frac{b}{4}$ 1

■ WRITTEN EXERCISES

Write each product in simplest form.

A   1. $\frac{a}{b}\cdot\frac{b}{a^2}$ $\frac{1}{a}$

2. $\frac{a}{b^2}\cdot\frac{b}{a}$ $\frac{1}{b}$

3. $\frac{x}{3}\cdot\frac{6}{x^2}$ $\frac{2}{x}$

4. $\frac{y}{2}\cdot\frac{8}{y^3}$ $\frac{4}{y^2}$

5. $\frac{a^2}{3}\cdot\frac{9}{a}$ $3a$

6. $\frac{s^3}{2}\cdot\frac{4}{s}$ $2s^2$

7. $\frac{2x}{5}\cdot\frac{3}{x}$ $\frac{6}{5}$

8. $\frac{4a}{3}\cdot\frac{2}{3a}$ $\frac{8}{9}$

9. $\frac{5x}{y^2}\cdot xy$ $\frac{5x^2}{y}$

10. $\frac{3x^2}{y^2}\cdot xy$ $\frac{3x^3}{y}$

11. $12\left(\frac{a}{3}+\frac{b}{4}\right)$ $4a+3b$

12. $16\left(\frac{x}{4}-\frac{y}{8}\right)$ $4x-2y$

13. $2x\left(\frac{3}{x}+\frac{5}{2}\right)$ $6+5x$

14. $4a\left(\frac{3}{4a}+\frac{4}{a}\right)$ 19

15. $\frac{x}{y}(3y^2+y)$ $3xy+x$

16. $\frac{2x}{y}(y^2+3y)$ $2xy+6x$

17. $\frac{x}{3}\left(\frac{2}{x}+\frac{6}{x^2}\right)$ $\frac{2}{3}+\frac{2}{x}$

18. $\frac{a^2}{4}\left(\frac{2}{a}+\frac{8}{a^3}\right)$ $\frac{a}{2}+\frac{2}{a}$

19. $\frac{a(a-b)}{b}\cdot\frac{b}{2(a-b)}$ $\frac{a}{2}$

20. $\frac{a}{b(a+b)}\cdot\frac{3(a+b)}{a}$ $\frac{3}{b}$

Write each quotient in simplest form.

21. $\frac{3a}{5b}\div\frac{9a}{10a}$ $\frac{2a}{3b}$

22. $\frac{3a}{4b}\div\frac{12a}{5b}$ $\frac{5}{16}$

23. $\frac{a^2}{2b}\div\frac{a}{b}$ $\frac{a}{2}$

24. $\frac{x^3}{3y}\div\frac{x^2}{y}$ $\frac{x}{3}$

25. $\frac{2x^2}{3y}\div\frac{2y}{3x^2}$ $\frac{x^4}{y^2}$

26. $\frac{3a^2}{2b}\div\frac{\cdot 3b}{2a^2}$ $\frac{a^4}{b^2}$

27. $\frac{5c^2d}{2d^2}\div\frac{3cd}{c}$ $\frac{5c^2}{6d^2}$

28. $\frac{4a^2b}{3a}\div\frac{2a}{3b}$ $2b^2$

29. $\frac{a(a-b)}{b(a+b)}\div\frac{a-b}{ab}$ $\frac{a^2}{a+b}$

30. $\frac{a(a+b)}{a-b}\div\frac{ab}{b(a-b)}$ $a+b$

31. $\frac{2(x+3)}{(x-4)^2}\div\frac{4}{x-4}$ $\frac{x+3}{2(x-4)}$

32. $\frac{2(x+3)^2}{x-4}\div\frac{4(x+3)}{(x-4)^2}$ $\frac{(x+3)(x-4)}{2}$

The values of the length and width of a rectangle are given. Find the area of each rectangle.

33. length: $\frac{2a}{b}$ $\frac{2}{a}$

width: $\frac{b}{a^2}$

34. length: $\frac{b}{3a}$ $\frac{a}{3b}$

width: $\frac{a^2}{b^2}$

35. length: $\frac{2x^2}{y}$ $6xy$

width: $\frac{3y^2}{x}$

36. length: $\frac{a^2b}{3}$ $\frac{5a}{3}$

width: $\frac{5}{ab}$

The values of the area and width of a rectangle are given. Find the length of each rectangle.

37. area: $\dfrac{2x}{y}$ $\;{}^{\frac{6}{y^2}}$

38. area: $\dfrac{3}{2}$ $\;{}^{\frac{y}{2x}}$

39. area: $\dfrac{x}{2}$ $\;{}^{\frac{y}{4}}$

40. area: $\dfrac{5ab^2}{2}$ $\;{}^{\frac{3b}{4}}$

width: $\dfrac{xy}{3}$

width: $\dfrac{3x}{y}$

width: $\dfrac{2x}{y}$

width: $\dfrac{10ab}{3}$

An object's average speed (in meters per second) and the time (in seconds) it travels are given. Find the distance traveled.

B 41. speed: $\dfrac{t^2-4}{4}$ $\;{}^{3(t+2)}$

time: $\dfrac{12}{t-2}$

42. speed: $(t+3)(t+4)$ $\;{}^{7t+23}$

time: $\dfrac{2}{t+3}+\dfrac{5}{t+4}$

An object's average speed (in meters per second) and the distance (in meters) it travels are given. Find the time traveled.

43. speed: $\dfrac{x+5}{x+3}$ $\;{}^{\frac{x+3}{x+4}}$

distance: $\dfrac{x+5}{x+4}$

44. speed: $\dfrac{x+2}{x-3}$ $\;{}^{\frac{x-3}{x+1}}$

distance: $\dfrac{x^2-x-6}{x^2-2x-3}$

Find the area of each triangle. Assume that the dimensions are given in centimeters.

45. base: $\dfrac{4a+12}{a-2}$ $\;{}^{a+4}$

altitude: $\dfrac{a^2+2a-8}{2a+6}$

46. base: $\dfrac{x+2}{x+1}$ $\;{}^{\frac{x-3}{2(x+3)}}$

altitude: $\dfrac{x^2-2x-3}{x^2+5x+6}$

47. base: $\dfrac{2x^2+7x+6}{x+6}$ $\;{}^{\frac{3(x+2)}{x+6}}$

altitude: $\dfrac{6x-24}{2x^2-5x-12}$

48. base: $\dfrac{2a+2b}{a-b}$ $\;{}^{\frac{1}{a+2b}}$

altitude: $\dfrac{a-b}{a^2+3ab+2b^2}$

Write each expression in simplest form.

49. $\dfrac{x^2-3x-4}{4}\cdot\dfrac{8x-16}{x^2-x-2}$ $\;{}^{2(x-4)}$

50. $\dfrac{y^2-4}{9}\div\dfrac{y^2+2y}{3y}$ $\;{}^{\frac{y-2}{3}}$

51. $\dfrac{5r+5}{r+3}\cdot\dfrac{2r+6}{r^2+2r+1}$ $\;{}^{\frac{10}{r+1}}$

52. $\dfrac{1}{x^2+2x-3}\div\dfrac{x+3}{2x-2}$ $\;{}^{\frac{2}{(x+3)^2}}$

53. $\dfrac{10}{a^2+2ab+b^2}\div\dfrac{5}{a^2-b^2}$ $\;{}^{\frac{2(a-b)}{a+b}}$

54. $\dfrac{p^2+2p}{p^2+5p+6}\cdot\dfrac{p^2+3p}{4}$ $\;{}^{\frac{p^2}{4}}$

55. $\dfrac{s}{s-3}\cdot\dfrac{s^2-9}{3s^2+9s}$ $\;{}^{\frac{1}{3}}$

56. $\dfrac{2x^2y-8xy}{y-2}\div\dfrac{xy-4y}{2y-4}$ $\;{}^{4x}$

COMPUTER EXTENSION

Write a computer program that finds the product of two fractions and prints the answer in simplest form.

```
10 PRINT "THIS PROGRAM
   MULTIPLIES"
20 PRINT "TWO FRACTIONS."
30 PRINT "FOR THE FIRST
   FRACTION:"
40 PRINT "ENTER THE
   NUMERATOR.";
50 INPUT P
60 PRINT "ENTER THE
   DENOMINATOR.";
70 INPUT Q
80 PRINT "FOR THE SECOND
   FRACTION:"
90 PRINT "ENTER THE
   NUMERATOR.";
100 INPUT R
110 PRINT "ENTER THE
    DENOMINATOR.";
120 INPUT S
130 PRINT "("; P; "/"; Q;
    ") ("; R; "/"; S;") = ";
140 N = P * R
150 D = Q * S
160 FOR K = 2 TO N
170 IF INT(N / K) <> N / K
    THEN 220
180 IF INT(D / K) <> D / K
    THEN 220
190 N = N / K
200 D = D / K
210 GO TO 160
220 NEXT K
230 PRINT N; "/"; D
240 END
```

How can you change the program to find the quotient of two fractions?

You would change the following lines:
```
10 PRINT "THIS PROGRAM
   DIVIDES"
130 PRINT "("; P; "/";
    Q;")/ ("; R; "/" S; ")
    = ";
140 N = P * S
150 D = Q * R
```

ENRICHMENT PROBLEM

- The Wizard of Odds has another number trick:

  i. Think of any number. Subtract the number from its square.

  ii. Divide this result by one less than your number.

  a. What is the number?

  The quotient is the number you started with.

  b. Show algebraically why the Wizard's trick works.

  If n is the number you started with, then you get the expression

  $$\frac{n^2 - n}{n - 1} = \frac{n(n - 1)}{(n - 1)} = n$$

  c. For what number will the Wizard's trick *not* work?

  If $n = 1$, the trick will not work.

Find the volume of each prism. Assume that the dimensions are given in centimeters.

57.

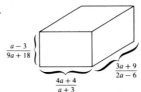

$\frac{2(a + 1)}{3(a + 2)}$

58.

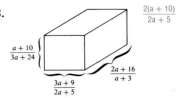

$\frac{2(a + 10)}{2a + 5}$

59.

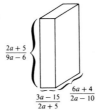

$\frac{3a + 2}{3a - 2}$

60.

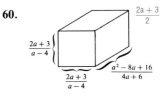

$\frac{2a + 3}{2}$

The values of the volume, width, and height of a prism are given. Find the length of each prism.

61. volume: $\frac{2a + 3}{a - 4}$ $\frac{a - 4}{2a + 3}$

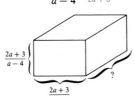

62. volume: $\frac{a}{a + 5}$ $\frac{a}{a + 6}$

63. volume: $\frac{x^2 + 7x + 10}{x^2 - 2x}$ $\frac{x + 2}{x - 3}$

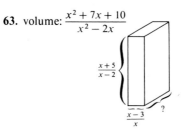

64. volume: $\frac{x + 1}{x^2 - 7x + 6}$ $\frac{(x + 1)(x + 6)}{(x - 6)(x - 1)}$

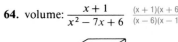

■ REVIEW EXERCISES

Compute.

1. $\frac{3}{4} \cdot \frac{4}{5}$ $\frac{3}{5}$

2. $\frac{3}{4} \div \frac{4}{5}$ $\frac{15}{16}$

3. $\frac{3}{4} + \frac{4}{5}$ $\frac{31}{20}$

4. $\frac{3}{4} - \frac{4}{5}$ $-\frac{1}{20}$

5. $4\left(\frac{1}{3}\right) + 5\left(\frac{1}{3}\right)$ 3

6. $\frac{4 + 5}{\frac{1}{3}}$ 27

You may wish to spend two days on this section. Refer to the Pacing Chart.

To add and subtract algebraic fractions with like denominators.

Class Starter Quiz
on previous section

Simplify. Write each answer as a fraction in simplest form.

1. $\dfrac{a^2}{b} \cdot \dfrac{b}{a}$ $\quad\quad\quad a$

2. $\dfrac{2x + 2y}{x^2 - xy} \cdot \dfrac{x}{2}$ $\quad \dfrac{x + y}{x - y}$

3. $\dfrac{x + 2)(x + 3)}{x + 4} \cdot \dfrac{x + 4}{(x + 2)^2}$ $\quad \dfrac{x + 3}{x + 2}$

4. $\dfrac{2a + 4b}{3ab} \div \dfrac{b}{a}$ $\quad \dfrac{2(a + 2b)}{3b^2}$

5. $\dfrac{x^2 - y^2}{x + y} \div \dfrac{x - y}{2x - y}$ $\quad 2x - y$

8-3 Adding and Subtracting Fractions with Like Denominators

Preview Fractional notation

The evolution of terms and symbols for fractions is an interesting account of how such numbers were considered by early mathematicians. The Arabic word for fraction, "al-kasr," comes from the verb "to break." Early English writers referred to fractions as "broken numbers." Authors of eighteenth-century American arithmetics called fractions "vulgar" or "common."

In the sixth century A.D., fractions were written with the numerator above the denominator but without a dividing bar. The vinculum (or fraction bar) was used by the Arab writers as early as the year 1000 in the forms

$$a/b \text{ and } \frac{a}{b}$$

but the modern notation was not commonly accepted until the thirteenth century.

PURPOSE

Adding and subtracting algebraic fractions are used in solving fractional equations and in simplifying two fractional expressions.

PREVIEW

Have students read the Preview. The historical Previews are intended to help students see that mathematical notation and ideas grew slowly over many years and that many people and cultures contributed to the growth.

◼ LESSON

Algebraic fractions are added or subtracted in the same way as arithmetic fractions. If the fractions have the same denominators, the following definition is used.

Definition: Addition and Subtraction of Fractions with Like Denominators

For all real numbers a, b, and c ($c \neq 0$)

$$\frac{a}{c} + \frac{b}{c} = \frac{a + b}{c} \quad \text{and} \quad \frac{a}{c} - \frac{b}{c} = \frac{a - b}{c}$$

For example, consider adding $\dfrac{x}{10}$ and $\dfrac{3x}{10}$.

Write the sum as a single fraction. $\quad \dfrac{x}{10} + \dfrac{3x}{10} = \dfrac{x + 3x}{10}$

Simplify. $\quad\quad\quad\quad\quad\quad\quad = \dfrac{\overset{2}{\cancel{4}x}}{\underset{5}{\cancel{10}}} = \dfrac{2x}{5}$

The simplified sum is $\dfrac{2x}{5}$.

Example 1 Simplify. $\dfrac{a}{6} - \dfrac{b}{6}$

Solution Use the definition of subtraction to write the difference as a single fraction.

$$\frac{a}{6} - \frac{b}{6} = \frac{a - b}{6}$$

Answer $\dfrac{a - b}{6}$

LESSON

Bring out that algebraic fractions are added or subtracted in the same manner as numerical fractions—you rewrite them as fractions with a common denominator, then add or subtract the numerators and keep the same denominator. Remind students that the least common denominator of two fractions is the least common multiple (LCM) of the two denominators.

ADDITIONAL EXAMPLES

Example 1. Simplify. $\dfrac{6}{a} + \dfrac{4}{a}$

$$= \frac{10}{a}$$

Example 2. Simplify. $\dfrac{a}{a+b} + \dfrac{b}{a+b}$

$= 1$

Example 3. Simplify. $\dfrac{x(x-3)}{x+2} - \dfrac{2x}{x+2}$

$\dfrac{x(x-3)}{x+2} - \dfrac{2x}{x+2}$

$= \dfrac{x^2 - 3x - 2x}{x+2}$

$= \dfrac{x^2 - 5x}{x+2}$

$= \dfrac{x(x-5)}{x+2}$

CHECK UNDERSTANDING

- Simplify. $\dfrac{3}{4} + \dfrac{3}{4}$ $\left(\dfrac{3}{2}\right)$

- Simplify. $\dfrac{5}{a} - \dfrac{2}{a}$ $\left(\dfrac{3}{a}\right)$

- Simplify. $\dfrac{3}{x-1} - \dfrac{x}{x-1}$ $\left(\dfrac{3-x}{x-1}\right)$

CLASSROOM EXERCISES

In exercises 5 and 6, be sure that students factor and then simplify.

ASSIGNMENT GUIDE

Basic	1–23 odd, Review Exercises, Self-Quiz 1
Average	3–24 multiples of 3, 25–35 odd, Review Exercises, Self-Quiz 1
Enriched	3–36 multiples of 3, 37–41 odd, Review Exercises, Self-Quiz 1

PRACTICE WORKSHEET 40

8-3 ADDING AND SUBTRACTING FRACTIONS WITH LIKE DENOMINATORS

■ Simplify. Assume that no denominator is equal to zero.

1. $\dfrac{k}{5} + \dfrac{2k}{5}$ $3k/5$

2. $\dfrac{m}{4} - \dfrac{3}{4}$ $\dfrac{m-3}{4}$

3. $\dfrac{5}{r} - \dfrac{1}{r}$ $4/r$

4. $\dfrac{2s+1}{7} + \dfrac{5s+6}{7}$ $s+1$

5. $\dfrac{2}{t+8} + \dfrac{3}{t+8}$ $\dfrac{5}{t+8}$

6. $\dfrac{y+10}{2v+4} - \dfrac{8}{2v+4}$ $1/2$

7. $\dfrac{a}{(a-3)^2} - \dfrac{3}{(a-3)^2}$ $\dfrac{1}{a-3}$

8. $\dfrac{2t^2}{3r} + \dfrac{5r}{3r}$ $\dfrac{2r+5}{3}$

9. $\dfrac{2b-19}{b-7} + \dfrac{5}{b-7}$ 2

10. $\dfrac{c^2}{c+2} - \dfrac{4}{c+2}$ $c-2$

11. $\dfrac{c^2+c}{c+4} - \dfrac{12}{c+4}$ $c-3$

12. $\dfrac{d^2+3}{d^2} + \dfrac{d^2-3}{d^2}$ $\dfrac{d^2+1}{d}$

EXTRA PRACTICE, page 634

Example 2 Simplify. $\dfrac{x^2}{x-1} - \dfrac{x}{x-1}$

Solution Write the difference as a single fraction.

$\dfrac{x^2}{x-1} - \dfrac{x}{x-1} = \dfrac{x^2 - x}{x-1}$

Simplify.

$= \dfrac{x(\cancel{x-1})}{\cancel{x-1}}$

$= x$

Answer x

Example 3 Simplify. $\dfrac{a(a+4)}{a+2} + \dfrac{4}{a+2}$

Solution $\dfrac{a(a+4)}{a+2} + \dfrac{4}{a+2} = \dfrac{a^2 + 4a + 4}{a+2}$

$= \dfrac{\cancel{(a+2)}^2}{\cancel{a+2}}$

$= a + 2$

Answer $a + 2$

■ CLASSROOM EXERCISES

Simplify.

1. $\dfrac{7}{8}b + \dfrac{1}{8}b$ b

2. $\dfrac{5x}{9} - \dfrac{2x}{9}$ $\dfrac{x}{3}$

3. $\dfrac{4}{a} + \dfrac{1}{a}$ $\dfrac{5}{a}$

4. $\dfrac{2c}{2c+4} + \dfrac{4}{2c+4}$ 1

5. $\dfrac{x}{x^2-1} - \dfrac{1}{x^2-1}$ $\dfrac{1}{x+1}$

6. $\dfrac{a}{a^2-1} + \dfrac{1}{a^2-1}$ $\dfrac{1}{a-1}$

■ WRITTEN EXERCISES

Simplify.

A

1. $\dfrac{3x}{2} + \dfrac{9x}{2}$ $6x$

2. $\dfrac{x}{2} + \dfrac{5x}{2}$ $3x$

3. $\dfrac{5}{a} + \dfrac{1}{a}$ $\dfrac{6}{a}$

4. $\dfrac{2}{a} + \dfrac{3}{a}$ $\dfrac{5}{a}$

5. $\dfrac{11x}{3} - \dfrac{2x}{3}$ $3x$

6. $\dfrac{10x}{3} - \dfrac{4x}{3}$ $2x$

7. $\dfrac{7}{2y} - \dfrac{4}{2y}$ $\dfrac{3}{2y}$

8. $\dfrac{10}{2y} - \dfrac{3}{2y}$ $\dfrac{7}{2y}$

9. $\dfrac{b}{b+2} + \dfrac{1}{b+2}$ $\dfrac{b+1}{b+2}$

10. $\dfrac{b}{b-2} + \dfrac{2}{b-2}$ $\dfrac{b+2}{b-2}$

11. $\dfrac{c}{c-7} - \dfrac{3}{c-7}$ $\dfrac{c-3}{c-7}$

12. $\dfrac{c}{c-5} - \dfrac{8}{c-5}$ $\dfrac{c-8}{c-5}$

13. $\dfrac{2s}{s-1} - \dfrac{2}{s-1}$ 2

14. $\dfrac{3s}{s-4} - \dfrac{12}{s-4}$ 3

15. $\dfrac{4x}{x+1} + \dfrac{4}{x+1}$ 4

After discussing a problem that was missed by many students, have them immediately work a similar problem.

16. $\dfrac{5x}{x+2} + \dfrac{10}{x+2}$ 5

17. $\dfrac{a+1}{2a+6} + \dfrac{a+7}{2a+6}$ $\frac{a+4}{a+3}$

18. $\dfrac{2a+1}{3a+6} + \dfrac{a+8}{3a+6}$ $\frac{a+3}{a+2}$

19. $\dfrac{5a+11}{3a+6} - \dfrac{a+3}{3a+6}$ $\frac{4}{3}$

20. $\dfrac{6a+13}{2a+6} - \dfrac{3a+4}{2a+6}$ $\frac{3}{2}$

21. $\dfrac{c^2+7c}{c^2-4c} - \dfrac{c^2+2c}{c^2-4c}$ $\frac{5}{c-4}$

22. $\dfrac{r^2+5r}{r^2-3r} - \dfrac{r^2+r}{r^2-3r}$ $\frac{4}{r-3}$

23. $\dfrac{s^2+2s}{s^2-9} + \dfrac{2s+3}{s^2-9}$ $\frac{s+1}{s-3}$

24. $\dfrac{s^2+s}{s^2-4} + \dfrac{2s+2}{s^2-4}$ $\frac{s+1}{s-2}$

Simplify. State the values of the variables that are not admissible.

25. $\dfrac{2c}{c+3} + \dfrac{6}{c+3}$ $2; -3$

26. $\dfrac{3h}{h-4} - \dfrac{12}{h-4}$ $3; 4$

27. $\dfrac{6h}{h^2-1} - \dfrac{6}{h^2-1}$ $\frac{6}{h+1}; -1, 1$

28. $\dfrac{2k+3}{k^2-k} + \dfrac{5k-3}{k^2-k}$ $\frac{7}{k-1}; 0, 1$

29. $\dfrac{3d+7}{d-4} - \dfrac{3d+7}{d-4}$ $0; 4$

30. $\dfrac{7p+5}{(p+2)^2} + \dfrac{p+11}{(p+2)^2}$ $\frac{8}{p+2}; -2$

31. $\dfrac{q^2-3q}{4q} + \dfrac{q^2+6q}{4q}$ $\frac{2q+3}{4}; 0$

32. $\dfrac{v^2-6}{3v^2} - \dfrac{2v^2-6}{3v^2}$ $\frac{-1}{3}; 0$

33. $\dfrac{x^2}{x^2-4} - \dfrac{x}{x^2-4} - \dfrac{6}{x^2-4}$ $\frac{x-3}{x-2}; -2, 2$

34. $\dfrac{x(x-4)}{x-2} + \dfrac{4}{x-2}$ $x-2; 2$

35. $\dfrac{a(a+3)}{a+1} + \dfrac{2}{a+1}$ $a+2; -1$

36. $\dfrac{x}{x-1} + \dfrac{1}{1-x}$ $1; 1$

37. $\dfrac{x+8}{x^2-5x+6} + \dfrac{x^2-7x}{x^2-5x+6}$ $\frac{x-4}{x-3}; 2, 3$

38. $\dfrac{x^2-3}{x^2+2x-8} + \dfrac{x-9}{x^2+2x-8}$ $\frac{x-3}{x-2}; -4, 2$

39. $\dfrac{a^2+8a+5}{2a^2+5a-12} - \dfrac{4a+1}{2a^2+5a-12}$ $\frac{(a+2)^2}{(2a-3)(a+4)}; \frac{3}{2}, -4$

40. $\dfrac{8a^2+3a+3}{6a^2+a-2} - \dfrac{2a^2-4a+1}{6a^2+a-2}$ $\frac{2a+1}{2a-1}; -\frac{2}{3}, \frac{1}{2}$

41. $\dfrac{6}{2a-3} - \dfrac{4a}{3-2a}$ $\frac{2(2a+3)}{2a-3}; \frac{3}{2}$

42. $\dfrac{b^2}{2-b} + \dfrac{2b}{b-2}$ $-b; 2$

■ REVIEW EXERCISES

Compute.

1. $12\left(\dfrac{1}{4} + \dfrac{1}{3}\right)$ 7

2. $10\left(\dfrac{3}{5} - \dfrac{1}{2}\right)$ 1

3. What is the least common denominator of $\dfrac{7}{8}$ and $\dfrac{5}{12}$?   24

Solve.

4. $\dfrac{1}{3}x - 5 = \dfrac{3}{4}$ $\left\{17\frac{1}{4}\right\}$

5. $\dfrac{x}{100} = \dfrac{4}{5}$ (80)

[3–7]

ENRICHMENT PROBLEM
Egyptian Fractions

• With only a few exceptions, ancient Egyptians expressed all fractional amounts as sums of unit fractions (fractions with unit numerators). For example, they expressed $\dfrac{3}{4}$ as $\dfrac{1}{2} + \dfrac{1}{4}$. However, any single expression could only contain the same unit fraction once. Therefore, $\dfrac{2}{5}$ had to be written as $\dfrac{1}{5} + \dfrac{1}{6} + \dfrac{1}{30}$ or as $\dfrac{1}{3} + \dfrac{1}{15}$, not as $\dfrac{1}{5} + \dfrac{1}{5}$.

Find a combination of unit fractions for these values.

a. $\dfrac{3}{8}$ **b.** $\dfrac{2}{3}$ **c.** $\dfrac{4}{5}$ **d.** $\dfrac{2}{7}$

Some possible answers:

a. $\dfrac{3}{8} = \dfrac{1}{4} + \dfrac{1}{8}$, or $\dfrac{3}{8} = \dfrac{1}{3} + \dfrac{1}{24}$

b. $\dfrac{2}{3} = \dfrac{1}{2} + \dfrac{1}{6}$, or $\dfrac{2}{3} = \dfrac{1}{3} + \dfrac{1}{4} + \dfrac{1}{12}$

c. $\dfrac{4}{5} = \dfrac{1}{2} + \dfrac{1}{5} + \dfrac{1}{10}$, or $\dfrac{4}{5} = \dfrac{1}{3} + \dfrac{1}{4} + \dfrac{1}{6} + \dfrac{1}{20}$

d. $\dfrac{2}{7} = \dfrac{1}{7} + \dfrac{1}{8} + \dfrac{1}{56}$, or $\dfrac{2}{7} = \dfrac{1}{5} + \dfrac{1}{14} + \dfrac{1}{70}$

Substitute and simplify.

a	b	c	d
100	-50	-5	10

6. $\dfrac{a}{b}$ -2

7. $\dfrac{ac}{bc}$ -2

8. $\dfrac{(a+c)}{(b+c)}$ $-1\frac{8}{11}$ [2–5]

Self-Quiz 1

8–1   List any restrictions on the variables.

1. $\dfrac{2}{ab}$ $a \neq 0, b \neq 0$

2. $\dfrac{x(x-4)}{(x-2)(x+2)}$ $x \neq -2, 2$

Simplify. Assume that no denominators are equal to zero.

3. $\dfrac{3xy}{12x^2y}$ $\frac{1}{4x}$

4. $\dfrac{5(a+2b)}{(a+2b)^2}$ $\frac{5}{a+2b}$

8–2   **5.** $\dfrac{12a^2b}{5} \cdot \dfrac{25}{3ab^2}$ $\frac{20a}{b}$

6. $\dfrac{x(y-1)}{xy} \cdot \dfrac{y^2}{y(y-1)}$ 1

7. $\dfrac{2m}{7n^2} \div \dfrac{4m^2}{21n}$ $\frac{3}{2mn}$

8. $\dfrac{9(r+2)}{2} \div \dfrac{3(r+2)}{8r}$ 12r

8–3   **9.** $\dfrac{6}{x} - \dfrac{3}{x} + \dfrac{2}{x}$ $\frac{5}{x}$

10. $\dfrac{c}{c-2} - \dfrac{2}{c-2}$ 1

11. $\dfrac{2b}{b+4} + \dfrac{2-b}{b+4}$ $\frac{b+2}{b+4}$

12. $\dfrac{x+7}{2x+6} - \dfrac{x+1}{2x+6}$ $\frac{3}{x+3}$

EXTENSION   Using a calculator to determine equivalent fractions

You can use a calculator to determine whether two fractions $\dfrac{a}{b}$ and $\dfrac{c}{d}$ are equivalent by following these steps.

1. Use the key sequence a ⊠ d ÷ b =

2. Look at the display. If the display shows the value of c, then the fractions are equivalent.

Use the steps above to decide whether these fractions are equivalent.

1. $\dfrac{117}{149}, \dfrac{585}{755}$ No

2. $\dfrac{221}{718}, \dfrac{884}{2872}$ Yes

3. $\dfrac{118}{127}, \dfrac{2714}{2921}$ Yes

Suppose the fractions in each pair are equivalent. Find the value of x.

4. $\dfrac{97}{107}, \dfrac{x}{3103}$ 2813

5. $\dfrac{37}{83}, \dfrac{x}{18426}$ 8214

6. $\dfrac{53530}{67670}, \dfrac{x}{67}$ 53

OBJECTIVE 8–4

To add and subtract algebraic fractions with unlike denominators.

Class Starter Quiz
on previous section

Simplify.

1. $\dfrac{3}{x} + \dfrac{4}{x}$ $\quad\dfrac{7}{x}$

2. $\dfrac{3}{2y} - \dfrac{5}{2y}$ $\quad\dfrac{-1}{y}$

3. $\dfrac{a}{b} + \dfrac{c}{b}$ $\quad\dfrac{a+c}{b}$

4. $\dfrac{a}{a+2} + \dfrac{4}{a+2}$ $\quad\dfrac{a+4}{a+2}$

5. $\dfrac{6x}{x+2} + \dfrac{12}{x+2}$ $\quad 6$

8–4 Adding and Subtracting Fractions with Unlike Denominators

Preview

How would you simplify the following expression?

$$\frac{7}{12} + \frac{4}{15}$$

Most students use one of these methods to simplify this sum.

Use $12 \cdot 15$ as the common denominator.

$$\frac{7}{12} + \frac{4}{15} = \frac{7 \cdot 15 + 4 \cdot 12}{12 \cdot 15}$$

$$= \frac{105 + 48}{180}$$

$$= \frac{153}{180}$$

$$= \frac{17}{20}$$

Use 60 as the common denominator.

$$\frac{7}{12} + \frac{4}{15} = \frac{7}{12} \cdot \frac{5}{5} + \frac{4}{15} \cdot \frac{4}{4}$$

$$= \frac{35}{60} + \frac{16}{60}$$

$$= \frac{35 + 16}{60}$$

$$= \frac{51}{60}$$

$$= \frac{17}{20}$$

Which method would you use? Which method is simpler?

In this lesson you will use one of the above methods to add or subtract algebraic fractions.

■ LESSON

If fractions to be added or subtracted do not have common denominators, the following definition can be used.

Definition: Addition and Subtraction of Fractions with Unlike Denominators

For all real numbers a, b, c, and d ($b \neq 0$ and $d \neq 0$),

$$\frac{a}{b} + \frac{c}{d} = \frac{ad + bc}{bd} \quad \text{and} \quad \frac{a}{b} - \frac{c}{d} = \frac{ad - bc}{bd}, \ b \neq 0, \text{ and } d \neq 0$$

PURPOSE

Most algebraic fractions students will encounter will have unlike denominators. Students need to know techniques for adding and subtracting such fractions.

PREVIEW

Go over the two techniques given. This activity will give another review of adding arithmetic fractions with unlike denominators and point out the two common ways of adding such fractions.

LESSON

The definition of addition and subtraction corresponds to the first addition technique given in the Preview. Students should become very familiar with this technique. It will work with all fractions, even though it is not the most efficient method.

Compare the method for finding the least common multiple of two expressions to that for finding the greatest common factor. Both methods begin with finding the prime factorization of the expressions. In finding the GCF, the greatest power of a variable *common to the prime factorizations* is selected. In finding the LCM, the greatest power of each variable is used.

Some students become confused in working with algebraic fractions. They may treat an addition problem as a multiplication problem or vice versa. Show students how to relate their given problem to the simpler situation of a numerical example. The key to stress is writing the numerical example in the same form as the algebraic problem. Work through the numerical situation step-by-step, carrying out the identical procedure on the algebraic example.

Given $\dfrac{5}{a^2} - \dfrac{3}{2a}$, write $\dfrac{5}{7^2} - \dfrac{3}{2 \cdot 7}$

1. Determine the common denominators.

$$2a^2 \qquad\qquad 2 \cdot 7^2$$

2. Rewrite each fraction with the common denominator.

$$\dfrac{5}{a^2} \cdot \dfrac{2}{2} - \dfrac{3}{2a} \cdot \dfrac{a}{a} \qquad \dfrac{5}{7^2} \cdot \dfrac{2}{2} - \dfrac{3}{2 \cdot 7} \cdot \dfrac{7}{7}$$

$$\dfrac{10}{2a^2} - \dfrac{3a}{2a^2} \qquad\qquad \dfrac{10}{98} - \dfrac{21}{98}$$

3. Combine fractions.

$$\dfrac{10 - 3a}{2a^2} \qquad\qquad \dfrac{10 - 21}{98} = \dfrac{-11}{98}$$

ADDITIONAL EXAMPLES

Example 1.

Write the least common denominator of $\dfrac{5}{6}$ and $\dfrac{3}{10}$

$$30$$

For example, consider this difference:

$$\frac{2x}{3y} - \frac{5}{3}$$

Write the difference as a single fraction.

$$\frac{2x}{3y} - \frac{5}{3} = \frac{2x(3) - 5(3y)}{3y(3)}$$

Simplify the numerator and denominator.

$$= \frac{6x - 15y}{9y}$$

Factor the numerator and denominator and simplify.

$$= \frac{\overset{1}{3}(2x - 5y)}{\underset{1}{3} \cdot 3y} = \frac{2x - 5y}{3y}$$

The difference is $\dfrac{2x - 5y}{3y}$.

The definition for adding or subtracting fractions with unlike denominators works for all fractions. However, the work can be done more efficiently if the **least common denominator,** rather than the product of the denominators, is used.

Definition: Least Common Denominator

The least common denominator of two or more algebraic fractions is the least common multiple of the denominators of the fractions.

To find the least common multiple of the denominators of two algebraic fractions, write the prime factorization of each denominator. Then identify the highest power of each prime factor and write the product of the highest powers.

Example 1 Write the least common denominator of $\dfrac{3}{8}$ and $\dfrac{5}{12}$.

Solution   *Write the prime factorization of the denominators.*   8: 2^3
   12: $2^2 \cdot 3$

Identify the highest power of each prime factor.   8: 2^3
   12: $2^2 \cdot 3$

Write the product of these highest powers. $2^3 \cdot 3 = 24$

Answer   24

The same process can be used with algebraic fractions.

Students are often reluctant to give indications that they do not understand. Therefore, instead of asking "Do you understand?" it is better to ask questions that the students must understand in order to give correct answers. For example, students must under-

stand the ideas being discussed in order to correctly answer questions like What step would you do next in solving this equation? What purpose does that step serve?

Example 2.

Write the least common denominator of $\frac{7}{4a^2}$ and $\frac{5}{6a}$.

$$12a^2$$

Example 3. Simplify. $\frac{7}{4a^2} - \frac{5}{6a}$

$$= \frac{21 - 10a}{12a^2}$$

Example 4. Simplify. $2a + \frac{4a}{3b}$

$$= \frac{6ab + 4a}{3b}$$

Example 2   Write the least common denominator of $\frac{5}{6x^2}$ and $\frac{2}{9x}$.

Solution

$$6x^2 = 2 \cdot 3 \cdot x^2$$
$$9x = 3^2 \cdot x$$

Write the product of the highest powers of the prime factors.

$$2 \cdot 3^2 x^2 = 18x^2$$

Answer $18x^2$

Fractions with unlike denominators can be added or subtracted by changing them to equivalent fractions that have the least common denominator as their denominators.

Example 3   Simplify. $\frac{5}{6x^2} - \frac{2}{9x}$

Solution   *Find the least common denominator.*   The least common denominator of $6x^2$ and $9x$ is $18x^2$.

Write equivalent fractions with $18x^2$ as a common denominator.

$$\frac{5}{6x^2} = \frac{5}{6x^2} \cdot \frac{3}{3} = \frac{15}{18x^2}$$

$$\frac{2}{9x} = \frac{2}{9x} \cdot \frac{2x}{2x} = \frac{4x}{18x^2}$$

Substitute and simplify.

$$\frac{5}{6x^2} - \frac{2}{9x} = \frac{15}{18x^2} - \frac{4x}{18x^2}$$

$$= \frac{15 - 4x}{18x^2}$$

Answer $\dfrac{15 - 4x}{18x^2}$

Example 4   Simplify. $x + \frac{5x}{3y}$

Solution $x + \dfrac{5x}{3y} = \dfrac{x}{1} + \dfrac{5x}{3y}$

$$= \frac{x(3y)}{3y} + \frac{5x}{3y}$$

$$= \frac{3xy + 5x}{3y}$$

Answer $\dfrac{3xy + 5x}{3y}$

Example 5. Simplify. $\dfrac{5}{x+y} - \dfrac{6}{x+2y}$

$$= \dfrac{4y-x}{(x+y)(x+2y)}$$

CHECK UNDERSTANDING

- What is the least common denominator of $\dfrac{1}{9a}$ and $\dfrac{4}{3ab}$? (9*ab*)

- Simplify. $\dfrac{4}{5x} - \dfrac{2}{3x}$ $\left(\dfrac{2}{15x}\right)$

CLASSROOM EXERCISES

In exercises 1–5, be sure that students state the *least* common denominator rather than some other common denominator.

ASSIGNMENT GUIDE

Basic   1–33 odd, Review Exercises
Average   3–48 multiples of 3, Review Exercises
Enriched   9–60 multiples of 3, Review Exercises

PRACTICE WORKSHEET 40

8-3 ADDING AND SUBTRACTING FRACTIONS WITH UNLIKE DENOMINATORS

■ Simplify. Assume that no denominator is equal to zero.

1. $\frac{7}{r} + \frac{4}{3r}$ 25/3r

2. $\frac{5}{6s} - \frac{2}{s}$ −7/6s

3. $\frac{4t}{3} - \frac{t}{2}$ 5t/6

4. $\frac{u}{2} + \frac{v}{4}$ $\frac{2u+v}{4}$

5. $\frac{2}{w} + \frac{3}{w^2}$ $\frac{2w+3}{w^2}$

6. $\frac{5}{x} - \frac{1}{x^2}$ $\frac{5x-1}{x^2}$

7. $\frac{y}{y+1} - \frac{y+1}{y}$ $\frac{-2y-1}{y(y+1)}$

8. $\frac{4}{z+3} + \frac{5}{z}$ $\frac{z^2+5z}{z(z+3)}$

9. $\frac{4}{a+2} + \frac{2}{a-1}$ $\frac{6a}{(a+2)(a-1)}$

10. $\frac{5}{2b} - \frac{1}{b-3}$ $\frac{3b-15}{2b(b-3)}$

11. $\frac{5}{c+4} + \frac{2}{c+6}$ $\frac{7c+38}{(c+4)(c+6)}$

12. $\frac{k}{k-1} - \frac{2}{k+2}$ $\frac{k^2+2}{(k-1)(k+2)}$

378

EXTRA PRACTICE, page 634

Example 5   Simplify. $\dfrac{3}{a+b} + \dfrac{4}{a-b}$

Solution   The least common denominator is $(a+b)(a-b)$.

$$\frac{3}{a+b} + \frac{4}{a-b} = \frac{3}{a+b}\cdot\frac{a-b}{a-b} + \frac{4}{a-b}\cdot\frac{a+b}{a+b}$$

$$= \frac{3(a-b) + 4(a+b)}{(a+b)(a-b)}$$

$$= \frac{3a - 3b + 4a + 4b}{(a+b)(a-b)}$$

$$= \frac{7a+b}{(a^2-b^2)}$$

Answer $\dfrac{7a+b}{a^2-b^2}$

■ CLASSROOM EXERCISES

State the least common denominator of the fractions.

1. $\dfrac{1}{x}, \dfrac{1}{2x}$ 2x

2. $\dfrac{3}{2a^2}, \dfrac{5}{6a}$ 6a²

3. $\dfrac{1}{4b}, \dfrac{1}{6ab}$ 12ab

4. $\dfrac{2}{2x^2y}, \dfrac{4}{2xy^2}$ 2x²y²

5. $\dfrac{2}{x+1}, \dfrac{3}{x^2-1}$ (x + 1)(x − 1)

Simplify.

6. $\dfrac{3}{2x} + \dfrac{2y}{x}$ $\frac{3+4y}{2x}$

7. $\dfrac{3}{x} + \dfrac{2}{x^2}$ $\frac{3x+2}{x^2}$

8. $\dfrac{2x}{y} + \dfrac{2y}{x}$ $\frac{2x^2+2y^2}{xy}$

9. $\dfrac{9}{5xy^2} - \dfrac{3}{2x^2y}$ $\frac{18x-15y}{10x^2y^2}$

10. $\dfrac{4}{a+3} - \dfrac{12}{(a+3)^2}$ $\frac{4a}{(a+3)^2}$

■ WRITTEN EXERCISES

State the least common denominator of the fractions.

A

1. $\dfrac{5}{6}, \dfrac{2}{9}$ 18

2. $\dfrac{1}{4}, \dfrac{5}{6}$ 12

3. $\dfrac{2}{3}, \dfrac{1}{3x}$ 3x

4. $\dfrac{4}{5}, \dfrac{3}{5x}$ 5x

5. $\dfrac{3}{a}, \dfrac{2}{b}$ ab

6. $\dfrac{4}{x}, \dfrac{1}{y}$ xy

7. $\dfrac{1}{a^2}, \dfrac{2}{a}$ a²

8. $\dfrac{3}{b^2}, \dfrac{5}{b}$ b²

9. $\dfrac{x}{a^2b}, \dfrac{x}{ab^2}$ a²b²

10. $\dfrac{a}{x^2y}, \dfrac{b}{xy^2}$ x²y²

11. $\dfrac{5}{2a^3b}, \dfrac{7}{6ab^2}$ 6a³b²

12. $\dfrac{6}{5a^2b^2}, \dfrac{1}{15a^2b}$ 15a²b²

13. $\dfrac{x}{x+2}, \dfrac{x}{x^2-4}$ (x + 2)(x − 2)

14. $\dfrac{5}{x-5}, \dfrac{5}{x^2-25}$ (x + 5)(x − 5)

15. $\dfrac{3}{x^2+3x}, \dfrac{4}{2x}$ 2x(x + 3)

16. $\dfrac{5}{x^2-4x}, \dfrac{2}{3x}$ 3x(x − 4)

Simplify.

17. $\dfrac{5}{6} + \dfrac{2}{9}$ $\;\;\dfrac{19}{18}$

18. $\dfrac{1}{6} + \dfrac{3}{8}$ $\;\;\dfrac{13}{24}$

19. $\dfrac{5}{a} - \dfrac{2}{3a}$ $\;\;\dfrac{13}{3a}$

20. $\dfrac{4}{a} - \dfrac{1}{2a}$ $\;\;\dfrac{7}{2a}$

21. $\dfrac{5}{a} + \dfrac{2}{3}$ $\;\;\dfrac{15 + 2a}{3a}$

22. $\dfrac{4}{a} + \dfrac{1}{2}$ $\;\;\dfrac{8 + a}{2a}$

23. $\dfrac{4}{x} - \dfrac{3}{x^2}$ $\;\;\dfrac{4x - 3}{x^2}$

24. $\dfrac{7}{x^2} - \dfrac{5}{x}$ $\;\;\dfrac{7 - 5x}{x^2}$

25. $\dfrac{x}{3} + \dfrac{x}{2}$ $\;\;\dfrac{5x}{6}$

26. $\dfrac{x}{4} + \dfrac{x}{8}$ $\;\;\dfrac{3x}{8}$

27. $\dfrac{x}{y} - \dfrac{y}{x}$ $\;\;\dfrac{x^2 - y^2}{xy}$

28. $\dfrac{a}{b} - \dfrac{b}{a}$ $\;\;\dfrac{a^2 - b^2}{ab}$

29. $\dfrac{3b}{a^2} - \dfrac{2b}{a}$ $\;\;\dfrac{3b - 2ab}{a^2}$

30. $\dfrac{2y}{x^2} - \dfrac{3y}{x}$ $\;\;\dfrac{2y - 3xy}{x^2}$

31. $\dfrac{6y}{5x} + \dfrac{7y}{10x^2}$ $\;\;\dfrac{12xy + 7y}{10x^2}$

32. $\dfrac{3z}{7y^2} - \dfrac{2z}{y}$ $\;\;\dfrac{3z - 14yz}{7y^2}$

Find the perimeter of each figure. Assume that the dimensions are given in centimeters.

33.

$\dfrac{5}{x}$ $\dfrac{1}{2x}$ $\dfrac{2}{x}$

34.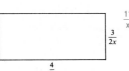

$\dfrac{11}{x}$ $\dfrac{3}{2x}$ $\dfrac{4}{x}$

35.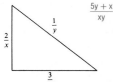

$\dfrac{5y + x}{xy}$ $\dfrac{1}{y}$ $\dfrac{2}{x}$ $\dfrac{3}{x}$

36.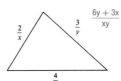

$\dfrac{6y + 3x}{xy}$ $\dfrac{2}{x}$ $\dfrac{3}{y}$ $\dfrac{4}{x}$

37.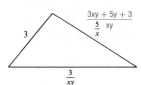

$\dfrac{3xy + 5y + 3}{xy}$ 3 $\dfrac{5}{x}$ $\dfrac{3}{xy}$

38.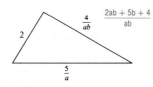

$\dfrac{2ab + 5b + 4}{ab}$ $\dfrac{4}{ab}$ 2 $\dfrac{5}{a}$

Simplify. State the values of the variable that are not admissible.

39. $\dfrac{3}{x + 2} + \dfrac{2}{x}$ $\;\;\dfrac{5x + 4}{x(x + 2)}; 0, -2$

40. $\dfrac{3}{x - 2} + \dfrac{3}{x + 2}$ $\;\;\dfrac{6x}{(x - 2)(x + 2)}; 2, -2$

41. $\dfrac{x}{x + 2} + \dfrac{3}{x + 3}$ $\;\;\dfrac{x^2 + 6x + 6}{(x + 2)(x + 3)}; -2, -3$

42. $\dfrac{3x + 2}{x} + \dfrac{2x + 4}{x + 2}$ $\;\;\dfrac{5x + 2}{x}; 0, -2$

43. $\dfrac{5}{x} - \dfrac{3}{x + 6}$ $\;\;\dfrac{2x + 30}{x(x + 6)}; 0, -6$

44. $\dfrac{2x}{x - 2} - \dfrac{3}{x - 3}$ $\;\;\dfrac{2x^2 - 9x + 6}{(x - 2)(x - 3)}; 2, 3$

45. $\dfrac{7}{x - 5} - \dfrac{3}{x - 2}$ $\;\;\dfrac{4x + 1}{(x - 5)(x - 2)}; 2, 5$

46. $\dfrac{2x}{x + 5} - \dfrac{2x}{x + 4}$ $\;\;\dfrac{-2x}{(x + 5)(x + 4)}; -5, -4$

47. $\dfrac{3}{2x} + \dfrac{2}{x + 1}$ $\;\;\dfrac{7x + 3}{2x(x + 1)}; 0, -1$

48. $\dfrac{5}{1 - x} - \dfrac{4}{x}$ $\;\;\dfrac{9x - 4}{x(1 - x)}; 0, 1$

49. $\dfrac{x}{2x - 1} + \dfrac{3}{x}$ $\;\;\dfrac{x^2 + 6x - 3}{x(2x - 1)}; 0, \dfrac{1}{2}$

50. $\dfrac{x}{x + 1} - \dfrac{x + 1}{x}$ $\;\;\dfrac{-2x - 1}{x(x + 1)}; 0, -1$

COMPUTER EXTENSION

Write a computer program that finds the sum of two fractions and write the answer in simplest form.

```
10 PRINT "THIS PROGRAM ADDS"
20 PRINT "TWO FRACTIONS."
30 PRINT "FOR THE FIRST
   FRACTION:"
40 PRINT "ENTER THE
   NUMERATOR,";
50 INPUT P
60 PRINT "ENTER THE
   DENOMINATOR.";
70 INPUT Q
80 PRINT "FOR THE SECOND
   FRACTION:"
90 PRINT "ENTER THE
   NUMERATOR,";
100 INPUT R
110 PRINT "ENTER THE
    DENOMINATOR.";
120 INPUT S
130 PRINT "(";P; "/";Q;")
    + (";R; "/";S;") = ";
140 N = P * S + R * Q
150 D = Q * S
160 FOR K = 2 TO N
170 IF INT(N / K) < > N / K
    THEN 220
180 IF INT(D / K) < > D / K
    THEN 220
190 N = N / K
200 D = D / K
210 GO TO 160
220 NEXT K
230 PRINT N;"/"; D
240 END
```

ENRICHMENT PROBLEM

- Write a general rule for adding three fractions.

$$\frac{a}{b} + \frac{c}{d} + \frac{e}{f} = \frac{adf + cbf + ebd}{bdf},$$

$$b \neq 0, d \neq 0, f \neq 0$$

- Find two fractions whose sum is the given fraction and such that all three fractions have different denominators. For example,

$$\frac{2}{3} = \frac{8}{12} = \frac{6}{12} + \frac{2}{12} = \frac{1}{2} + \frac{1}{6}.$$

a. $\frac{3}{4}$ **b.** $\frac{5}{8}$

Answers will vary.

$$\frac{3}{4} = \frac{2}{3} + \frac{1}{12} \qquad \frac{5}{8} = \frac{1}{3} + \frac{7}{24}$$

- Find two fractions whose difference is the given fraction and such that all three fractions have different denominators.

a. $\frac{1}{4}$ **b.** $\frac{2}{3}$

Answers will vary.

$$\frac{1}{4} = \frac{1}{3} - \frac{1}{12} \qquad \frac{2}{3} = \frac{3}{4} - \frac{1}{12}$$

C **51.** $\dfrac{3}{x^2 - 4} + \dfrac{4}{x + 2}$ $\dfrac{4x - 5}{(x + 2)(x - 2)}$; 2, −2

52. $\dfrac{x}{x + 3} + \dfrac{x}{x^2 + x - 6}$ $\dfrac{x^2 - x}{(x + 3)(x - 2)}$; 2, −3

53. $\dfrac{1}{x^2 + 5x + 6} + \dfrac{1}{x^2 + 3x + 2}$ $\dfrac{2}{(x + 3)(x + 1)}$; −3, −2, −1

54. $\dfrac{2}{x^2 + 2x - 8} - \dfrac{1}{x^2 - x - 2}$ $\dfrac{1}{(x + 4)(x + 1)}$; −4, −1, 2

55. $\dfrac{1}{x^2 + 7x + 12} - \dfrac{2}{x^2 + 6x + 8}$ $\dfrac{-1}{(x + 3)(x + 2)}$; −4, −3, −2

56. $\dfrac{3}{x^2 - x - 2} + \dfrac{1}{x^2 - 5x + 6}$ $\dfrac{4}{(x + 1)(x - 3)}$; −1, 2, 3

Find the perimeter of each polygon. Assume that the dimensions are given in centimeters.

57.

58.

59.

60.

■ REVIEW EXERCISES

1. State which of the numbers −2, −1, 0, 1, and 2 are solutions to the equation.   [3–1]

$$x^2 = \frac{1}{x^2} \quad 1, -1$$

Solve.   [3–6]

2. $3(x - 2) = 2 - x$ (2)

3. $\dfrac{2(x + 4)}{3} = 12$ (14)

4. Solve $P = 2l + 2w$, for w. $w = \dfrac{p - 2l}{2}$

5. Solve $A = \dfrac{1}{2}bh$, for h. $h = \dfrac{2A}{b}$ [3–8]

Solve by writing an equation.

6. There are 20 bills in a stack of five and ten dollar bills worth $140. How many of each kind are there?   12 $5, 8 $10   [3–9]

7. A class of 30 students went on a field trip and stopped at a refreshment stand. Each of the boys had a regular ice cream cone that cost 60 cents and each of the girls had a large ice cream cone that cost 90 cents. If the total bill (not including sales tax) was $21, then how many of these students were boys and how many were girls?   20 boys, 10 girls

OBJECTIVE 8–5

To solve equations containing fractions.

Class Starter Quiz
on previous section

State the least common denominator.

1. $\dfrac{2}{b^2}$ and $\dfrac{5}{2b}$ $2b^2$

2. $\dfrac{3}{b^2 + 2b}$ and $\dfrac{4}{2b}$ $2b(b^2 + 2b)$

Simplify.

3. $\dfrac{x}{3} + \dfrac{x}{6}$ $\dfrac{x}{2}$

4. $\dfrac{x}{y} - \dfrac{y}{x}$ $\dfrac{x^2 - y^2}{xy}$

5. $\dfrac{a}{a + 2} + \dfrac{3}{a + 3}$ $\dfrac{a^2 + 6a + 6}{a^2 + 5a + 6}$

8–5 Solving Fractional Equations

Preview

Tom Sawyer can whitewash the back fence in 6 h, while Ben Rogers can whitewash it in only 4 h. How long would it take them to whitewash it if they work together?

- Make a rough estimate of the answer. Will it take them longer than 6 h, between 4 and 6, or less than 4 h? Less than 4 h
- What fraction of the fence can Tom whitewash in 1 h? $\frac{1}{6}$
- What fraction of the fence can Ben whitewash in 1 h? $\frac{1}{4}$
- Together what fraction of the fence can they whitewash in 1 h? $\frac{5}{12}$
- If t is the number of hours required to whitewash the fence together, what fraction of the fence can they whitewash in 1 h? $\frac{1}{t}$

One equation that can be used to solve this problem is:

$$\frac{1}{6} + \frac{1}{4} = \frac{1}{t}$$

In this lesson you will learn to solve equations that contain fractions.

■ LESSON

Equations with fractions are usually more complicated than equations without fractions. Therefore, the first step in solving the equation is to rid the equation of fractions by multiplying both sides of the equation by the least common denominator of the fractions. For example, to solve the problem given in the Preview we must solve the equation:

$$\frac{1}{6} + \frac{1}{4} = \frac{1}{t}$$

Find the least common denominator of the fractions.	The least common denominator is $12t$.
Eliminate the fractions by multiplying both sides of the equation by the least common denominator. Simplify.	$12t\left(\dfrac{1}{6} + \dfrac{1}{4}\right) = 12t\left(\dfrac{1}{t}\right)$ $2t + 3t = 12$ $5t = 12$
Solve the new equation.	$t = \dfrac{12}{5}$

The solution of the equation is $\left\{\dfrac{12}{5}\right\}$.

Since $t = \dfrac{12}{5} = 2\dfrac{2}{5}$, Tom and Ben working together can whitewash the fence in $2\dfrac{2}{5}$ h (2 h and 24 min).

PURPOSE

Equations that arise in problems in the real world may contain fractions. Students need to develop techniques to solve such equations.

PREVIEW

Emphasize the importance of making an estimate (as in the first question). After a problem has been solved, the solution and the estimate should be compared. See if the solution makes sense in relation to the estimate. This also improves students' abilities to make better estimates.

   The equation given in the Preview is solved in the Lesson.

To solve equations containing fractions, any previous equation-solving skill may be used. One additional skill is introduced in this lesson—eliminating fractions from the equation. Eliminating fractions involves the principle that

$$\text{if } a = b, \text{ then } ac = bc$$

where c is the least common denominator of the fractions.

ADDITIONAL EXAMPLES

Example 1. Solve.

$$\frac{1}{2} + \frac{1}{4} = \frac{1}{x} \qquad \left\{\frac{4}{3}\right\}$$

Example 2. Solve.

$$5 + \frac{3}{x} = \frac{6}{2x} \qquad \varnothing$$

Example 1   Solve. $\frac{1}{x} + 3 = \frac{2}{x}$

Solution

$$\frac{1}{x} + 3 = \frac{2}{x}$$

Multiply both sides by the least common denominator x.

$$x\left(\frac{1}{x} + 3\right) = x\left(\frac{2}{x}\right)$$

$$1 + 3x = 2$$

$$3x = 1$$

$$x = \frac{1}{3}$$

Note that multiplying both sides of an equation by the same number and then applying the distributive property has the effect of multiplying each term on both sides by that number.

Answer $\left\{\frac{1}{3}\right\}$

Check $\frac{1}{x} + 3 = \frac{2}{x}$

$$\frac{1}{\frac{1}{3}} + 3 \stackrel{?}{=} \frac{2}{\frac{1}{3}}$$

$$3 + 3 = 6 \qquad \text{It checks.}$$

Remember that division by 0 is not allowed. When there are variables in the denominators of fractions, the variables must be restricted to admissible values so that the denominators do not equal 0.

Example 2   Solve. $1 + \frac{5}{2x} = \frac{2.5}{x}$

Solution

$$1 + \frac{5}{2x} = \frac{2.5}{x}$$

First, list any restrictions.   Restriction: $x \neq 0$

Multiply both sides by 2x. $2x\left(1 + \frac{5}{2x}\right) = 2x\left(\frac{2.5}{x}\right)$

$$2x + 5 = 5$$

$$2x = 0$$

$$x = 0$$

We know that x cannot equal 0 in the original equation. Therefore, even though 0 is a solution of the last equation, it is not a solution of the original equation.

Answer $\varnothing$ (The equation has *no* solution.)

Promote student-student as well as student-teacher interactions during class discussions. For example, encourage students to listen to each other by not repeating student responses to questions.

Example 3. Solve.

$$3x - \frac{4}{x} = 4 \qquad \left\{ -\frac{2}{3}, 2 \right\}$$

Example 4. Solve.

$$0.3n + 1.7 = 0.05n \qquad \{-6.8\}$$

CHECK UNDERSTANDING

What should both sides be multiplied by to clear the equation of fractions?

- $\dfrac{x}{2} + \dfrac{1}{3} = 7$ (6)

- $\dfrac{3}{x} - \dfrac{1}{4} = 6$ (4x)

- $\dfrac{1}{x} - \dfrac{2}{x^2} = -1$ (x²)

Example 2   (continued)

Check Note what happens if we check whether 0 is a solution.

$$1 + \frac{5}{2x} = \frac{2.5}{x}$$

$$1 + \frac{5}{0} \overset{?}{=} \frac{2.5}{0}$$

Since $\dfrac{5}{0}$ and $\dfrac{2.5}{0}$ are not real numbers, 0 is not a solution.

Example 3   Solve. $x - \dfrac{6}{x} = 1$

Solution

$$x - \frac{6}{x} = 1$$

Restriction: $x \neq 0$

Multiply both sides by x.

$$x\left(x - \frac{6}{x}\right) = x \cdot 1$$

$$x^2 - 6 = x$$

$$x^2 - x - 6 = 0$$

Factor and solve.

$$x + 2 = 0 \quad \text{or} \quad x - 3 = 0$$

$$x = -2 \quad \text{or} \qquad x = 3$$

Answer $\{-2, 3\}$

Check Check *each* solution in the original equation.

$$x - \frac{6}{x} = 1 \qquad\qquad x - \frac{6}{x} = 1$$

$$3 - \frac{6}{3} \overset{?}{=} 1 \qquad\qquad -2 - \frac{6}{-2} \overset{?}{=} 1$$

$$3 - 2 \overset{?}{=} 1 \qquad\qquad -2 - (-3) \overset{?}{=} 1$$

$$1 = 1 \qquad\qquad\qquad 1 = 1 \qquad \text{The answer checks.}$$

Equations that contain decimal fractions are sometimes difficult to solve. One way to eliminate decimal fractions is to multiply both sides of an equation by the power of 10 that makes each term in the equation a whole number.

Example 4   Solve. $0.5x = 5 + 0.25x$

Solution

$$0.5x = 5 + 0.25x$$

Multiply both sides by 100.

$$100(0.5x) = 100(5 + 0.25x)$$

Simplify and solve.

$$50x = 500 + 25x$$

$$25x = 500$$

$$x = 20$$

Answer $\{20\}$

Check The check is left to the student.

In exercise 5 a quadratic equation is the result of clearing the equation of fractions. Therefore, techniques such as factoring may be required in finding the solutions.

Be sure the students check the solutions to all equations.

ASSIGNMENT GUIDE

Basic   1–32 odd, Review Exercises
Average   3–48 multiples of 3, Review Exercises
Enriched 21–59 odd, Review Exercises

PRACTICE WORKSHEET 41

8-5 SOLVING FRACTIONAL EQUATIONS

■ Solve. Write Ø if there is no solution.

1. $\frac{4}{c} = \frac{6}{21}$ {14}

2. $\frac{6}{16} = \frac{d}{24}$ {9}

3. $\frac{g}{6} + \frac{1}{3} = 2$ {10}

4. $\frac{7}{12} - \frac{m}{24} = 3$ {−58}

5. $\frac{5}{12} - \frac{2}{y} = 6$ {−24/67}

6. $\frac{4}{5} - \frac{z}{15} = 3$ {−33}

7. $\frac{1}{a} + \frac{1}{2} = \frac{11}{a}$ {20}

8. $6 + \frac{3}{b} = \frac{9}{2b}$ {1/4}

9. $\frac{1}{h} - 2 = \frac{3}{5h}$ {1/5}

10. $\frac{7}{x} - \frac{1}{3x} = 2$ {10/3}

11. $\frac{3}{21} + \frac{1}{7} = 10$ {207/2}

12. $\frac{1}{k} + \frac{13}{2k} = 4$ {15/8}

EXTRA PRACTICE, page 635

■ CLASSROOM EXERCISES

Solve.

1. $\frac{2x}{3} + \frac{5}{3} = 8$ $\left\{\frac{19}{2}\right\}$

2. $\frac{3}{5} = \frac{x}{100}$ { 60 }

3. $\frac{8}{x} + 1 = \frac{1}{x}$ { −7 }

4. $\frac{45}{x} = \frac{60}{100}$ { 75 }

5. $x - \frac{4}{x} = 3$ { −1, 4 }

6. $0.5x = 7 - 0.2x$ { 10 }

7. $0.87x - 0.41(x - 1) = 1.79$ { 3 }

■ WRITTEN EXERCISES

State the least common denominator of each of these pairs of fractions.

A 1. $\frac{5}{6}, \frac{3}{4}$ 12

2. $\frac{1}{6}, \frac{7}{8}$ 24

3. $\frac{2}{3}, \frac{5}{x}$ 3x

4. $\frac{3}{4}, \frac{2}{2}$ 4

5. $\frac{x}{7}, \frac{5}{14x}$ 14x

6. $\frac{3}{4x}, \frac{x}{6}$ 12x

7. $\frac{8}{3x}, \frac{7}{2x}$ 6x

8. $\frac{5}{4x}, \frac{8}{3x}$ 12x

Solve. Write Ø if there is no solution.

9. $\frac{2}{3} = \frac{x}{24}$ { 16 }

10. $\frac{x}{12} = \frac{3}{4}$ { 9 }

11. $\frac{a}{30} = \frac{5}{6}$ { 25 }

12. $\frac{9}{6} = \frac{a}{12}$ { 18 }

13. $\frac{12}{b} = \frac{3}{2}$ { 8 }

14. $\frac{24}{b} = \frac{4}{3}$ { 18 }

15. $\frac{x}{3} + \frac{1}{2} = 10$ $\left\{\frac{57}{2}\right\}$

16. $\frac{x}{4} + \frac{1}{3} = 3$ $\left\{\frac{32}{3}\right\}$

17. $\frac{x}{5} - 4 = \frac{9}{2}$ $\left\{\frac{85}{2}\right\}$

18. $\frac{x}{4} - 3 = \frac{8}{5}$ $\left\{\frac{92}{5}\right\}$

19. $\frac{1}{2}x + \frac{3}{4}x = 10$ { 8 }

20. $\frac{1}{3}x + \frac{3}{4}x = 13$ { 12 }

21. $\frac{1}{5}x - \frac{7}{10}x = 5$ { −10 }

22. $\frac{5}{12}x - \frac{7}{12}x = 1$ { −6 }

23. $\frac{2}{3}x - \frac{1}{6}x = 9$ { 18 }

24. $\frac{4}{5}x - \frac{1}{5}x = 9$ { 15 }

25. $\frac{1}{3}x - \frac{3}{4}x = 10$ { −24 }

26. $\frac{2}{3}x - \frac{8}{9}x = 2$ { −9 }

27. $\frac{3}{x} + \frac{1}{2} = \frac{5}{x}$ { 4 }

28. $\frac{3}{x} + \frac{5}{2} = \frac{8}{x}$ { 2 }

29. $\frac{3}{2x} + \frac{1}{x} = 5$ $\left\{\frac{1}{2}\right\}$

30. $\frac{2}{x} + \frac{1}{x} = 9$ $\left\{\frac{1}{3}\right\}$

31. $\frac{6}{x} - \frac{16}{x} = 5$ { −2 }

32. $\frac{6}{x} - \frac{20}{2x} = 1$ { −4 }

B 33. $2.4x - 0.8 = 0.4$ { 0.5 }

34. $0.3x - 0.12 = 0.06$ { 0.6 }

35. $0.05x + 0.73 = 0.8$ { 1.4 }

36. $0.05x + 0.84 = 1$ { 3.2 }

37. $x + \frac{6}{x} = 5$ { 2, 3 }

38. $x + \frac{4}{x} = 5$ { 1, 4 }

39. $x + 2 = \frac{8}{x}$ { −4, 2 }

40. $x + 1 = \frac{6}{x}$ { −3, 2 }

41. $x + 3 = \frac{10}{x}$ { −5, 2 }

42. $x + 4 = \frac{5}{x}$ { −5, 1 }

43. $4 + \frac{3}{x} = \frac{6}{2x}$ Ø

44. $5 + \frac{2}{x} = \frac{6}{3x}$ Ø

45. $x = 10 - \dfrac{24}{x}$ $\{4, 6\}$ **46.** $x = 12 - \dfrac{27}{x}$ $\{3, 9\}$ **47.** $1 = \dfrac{2}{x} + \dfrac{3}{x^2}$ $\{-1, 3\}$

48. $1 = \dfrac{1}{x} + \dfrac{12}{x^2}$ $\{-3, 4\}$ **49.** $\dfrac{5}{x^2} + 1 = \dfrac{6}{x}$ $\{1, 5\}$ **50.** $\dfrac{x}{4} + \dfrac{1}{x} = 1$ $\{2\}$

C   **51.** $2x = 1 + \dfrac{3}{x}$ $\left\{-1, \dfrac{3}{2}\right\}$ **52.** $3x + \dfrac{4}{x} = 8$ $\left\{\dfrac{2}{3}, 2\right\}$ **53.** $6x + \dfrac{3}{x} = 11$ $\left\{\dfrac{1}{3}, \dfrac{3}{2}\right\}$

54. $7 = \dfrac{4}{x} - 2x$ $\left\{-4, \dfrac{1}{2}\right\}$ **55.** $\dfrac{12}{x} = 23 - 5x$ $\left\{\dfrac{3}{5}, 4\right\}$ **56.** $\dfrac{3x}{2} + \dfrac{4}{x} = 5$ $\left\{\dfrac{4}{3}, 2\right\}$

57. $3x = \dfrac{1}{2} + \dfrac{1}{x}$ $\left\{-\dfrac{1}{2}, \dfrac{2}{3}\right\}$ **58.** $1 = \dfrac{3}{2x} - 4x$ $\left\{-\dfrac{3}{4}, \dfrac{1}{2}\right\}$ **59.** $\dfrac{5}{x} = 7 - \dfrac{6x}{5}$ $\left\{\dfrac{5}{6}, 5\right\}$

■ REVIEW EXERCISES

Simplify.

1. $(x^2 + 4x - 3) + (x^2 - 2x) - (3x + 5)$ $2x^2 - x - 8$ [4-1]

2. $(2ab^2) \cdot (-3ab)$ $-6a^2b^3$ **3.** $(-2xy)(-3y^2)$ $6xy^3$ [4-3]

4. $(3x^3)^2$ $9x^6$ **5.** $(-2ab^2)^3$ $-8a^3b^6$ [4-5]

6. $\dfrac{3x^2}{9x^4}$ $(x \neq 0)$ $\dfrac{1}{3x^2}$ **7.** $\dfrac{8x^4}{4x^3}$ $(x \neq 0)$ $2x$ [4-8]

8. Write $4.32 \cdot 10^6$ in standard decimal notation.   4,320,000   [4-4]

9. Simplify and write the quotient in scientific notation.   [4-8]

$\dfrac{6.4 \cdot 10^7}{1.6 \cdot 10^3}$ $4 \cdot 10^4$

Solve.

10. Genevieve and Helen like to run on a path around a lake with a circumfer-   [4-7]
ence of 5 km. Genevieve runs at a rate of 12 km/h and Helen runs at a rate
of 8 km/h. If they start at the same point and run in opposite directions,
how long will it take until they meet? When they meet, how far will each
have run?

$\dfrac{1}{4}$ h; Genevieve: 3 km, Helen: 2 km

Mathematics and Your Future

Today in many colleges and universities, at least three years of precollege
high school mathematics, including algebra, geometry, and advanced algebra is required for many majors. Four years of mathematics, including
trigonometry, is necessary for majors in mathematics, science, computer
science, or engineering. Take all the mathematics in high school that you
will need to prepare you for college. Do not limit your options or delay
your college education while you take enough mathematics courses to
catch up.

Developing estimation skills is not a task that
is learned quickly. The most effective means
of developing such skills is to make estimation a routine part of lessons throughout the
year, practiced by teacher and students. All
students should be able to approximate the
solution to an equation—even ones they cannot solve exactly. If students have difficulty in
making a reasonable estimate, have them use
a table of values to "home in" on a satisfac-
tory value. For example:

Estimate the solution of $3 - \dfrac{1}{x} = \dfrac{5}{2x}$.

x	$3 - \dfrac{1}{x}$	$\dfrac{5}{2x}$
4	$2\dfrac{3}{4}$	$\dfrac{5}{8}$
2	$2\dfrac{1}{2}$	$1\dfrac{1}{4}$
1	2	$2\dfrac{1}{2}$

Answer: About 1 (between 1 and 2).

ENRICHMENT PROBLEM

• Estimate the solutions of these equations. Do not solve.

a. $\dfrac{6}{x} - 2 = \dfrac{1}{x}$

b. $\dfrac{x}{4} + 3 = \dfrac{2x}{3}$

c. $\dfrac{2}{x - 1} - 1 = \dfrac{3}{2}$

d. $x + \dfrac{3}{x} = \dfrac{7}{2}$ (2 values)

Actual answers are given:

a. $2\dfrac{1}{2}$ **b.** $7\dfrac{1}{5}$

c. $1\dfrac{4}{5}$ **d.** $1\dfrac{1}{2}$ and 2

Solve.

1. $\dfrac{3}{4} = \dfrac{x}{24}$ {18}

2. $\dfrac{x}{6} + \dfrac{1}{2} = \dfrac{2}{3}$ {1}

3. $\dfrac{5}{x} + \dfrac{3}{2} = \dfrac{7}{x}$ $\left\{\dfrac{4}{3}\right\}$

4. $\dfrac{7}{x} + \dfrac{4}{3x} = \dfrac{5}{3}$ {5}

5. $2.3x - 2.8 = 0.3x$ {1.4}

PURPOSE

One of the principal reasons for learning mathematical skills is to apply them in solving real-world problems.

PREVIEW

In the diagram the symbol ∧∧∧ represents a resistance such as a light bulb. Point out that a string of decorative lights is sometimes in a *series* circuit. When one light is out, the circuit is broken and the entire string is out. If a string of lines is in a parallel circuit, the others will remain lit when one light is out.

LESSON

Students should be asked to estimate the answer of the problem in Example 1 before looking at the solution. All students should understand that the two painters together can paint the house in a time between 6 and 8 hours. Two painters working as fast as the master painter can paint the house in 6 hours, while two painters working as fast as the assistant can paint the house in 8 hours. Therefore, one slower and one faster painter can paint the house in between 6 and 8 hours. This kind of estimating is important for students to learn and practice.

OBJECTIVE 8–6

To use fractional equations to solve problems.

You may wish to spend two days on this section. Refer to the Pacing Chart.

8–6 Problem Solving—Fractional Equations

Preview **Applications: Electrical circuits**

All electrical circuits have parts that resist the flow of electricity. The filament of a lightbulb and the heating element of a toaster are examples of resistors. The ohm (Ω) is a unit of electrical resistance.

Two resistors may be connected in a series so that all of the current must pass through each one. The total resistance (R) of the two resistors in series is the sum of the individual resistances, r_1 and r_2.

$$R = r_1 + r_2$$

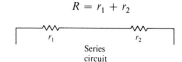

Series
circuit

For two resistors connected in a parallel circuit, the current "splits up," with part of it going through one resistor and part going through the other. The total resistance R is given by the formula

$$\frac{1}{R} = \frac{1}{r_1} + \frac{1}{r_2}$$

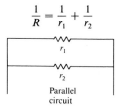

Parallel
circuit

In this lesson you will use this formula and other formulas that contain algebraic fractions.

■ LESSON

The formula

$$\frac{1}{R} = \frac{1}{r_1} + \frac{1}{r_2}$$

can be used to solve problems about resistances in parallel circuits. For example, suppose that we wish to know the total resistance of a 3-ohm (3Ω) resistance and a 4-ohm (4Ω) resistance connected in parallel.

Substitute 3 for r_1 and 4 for r_2 in the formula.

$$\frac{1}{R} = \frac{1}{r_1} + \frac{1}{r_2}$$

$$\frac{1}{R} = \frac{1}{3} + \frac{1}{4}$$

Multiply both sides by the least common denominator, 12R.
Simplify and solve.

$$12R\left(\frac{1}{R}\right) = 12R\left(\frac{1}{3} + \frac{1}{4}\right)$$

$$12 = 4R + 3R$$

$$12 = 7R$$

$$R = \frac{12}{7}$$

The total resistance of the circuit is $\dfrac{12}{7}$ ohms. Note that the resistance of the parallel circuit is less than either of the individual resistances.

Often give students helpful hints as part of the home-work assignment—for example: "On exercise _____ you may need to refer back to Example _____ in the

lesson." Or "Problem _____ refers to scoring in foot-ball. Recall that touchdowns are worth 6 points."

Fractional equations are also used in problems involving work rates, since fractions are used to express the rate of work. For example, if a farmer can mow a hay field in 5 h, the farmer's rate of work is $\frac{1}{5}$ of a field per hour. In general, if a job can be done in n hours, the rate is $\frac{1}{n}$ of the job per hour.

The relationship between the amount (w) of work, the rate (r) of work, and the time (t) worked is

$$w = rt$$

If the farmer mows at the rate of $\frac{1}{5}$ of a field per hour, then in 3 h he can mow $3\left(\frac{1}{5}\right)$ of the field.

Example 1   A master painter can paint a house in 12 h. An assistant can paint the house in 16 h. How long will it take the two painters working together to paint the house?

Solution   Let t = the number of hours for the painters to paint the house together.

We know three pieces of information for each painter and for the two painters together: (1) the rate worked, (2) the time worked, and (3) the amount of work done. A table can be used to organize the information.

	Rate (houses per hour)	Time (hours)	Amount of work (houses painted)
Painter	$\frac{1}{12}$	t	$\left(\frac{1}{12}\right)t$
Assistant	$\frac{1}{16}$	t	$\left(\frac{1}{16}\right)t$
Together	$\frac{1}{t}$	t	$\left(\frac{1}{t}\right)t$ or 1

Word equation:	Amount of work done by master painter	plus	Amount of work done by assistant	equals	Amount of work done by pair
Equation:	$\frac{1}{12}t$	$+$	$\frac{1}{16}t$	$=$	1

Multiply both sides by 48.

$$48\left(\frac{1}{12}t + \frac{1}{16}t\right) = 48(1)$$

$$4t + 3t = 48$$

$$7t = 48$$

$$t = \frac{48}{7}$$

Answer   The two painters can paint the house in $6\frac{6}{7}$ h (about 6 h and 51 min).

Lesson *continued*

In Example 2, point out to students that the "word equation" could be used to help understand the problem. The table in the example shows how to find expressions to represent the amounts mowed by Mark and his sister. The total amount is 1 (1 lawn).

Example 2 is sometimes called a "work problem." A variety of work problems are presented in the exercises. Emphasize that work problems may be considered a type of rate problem, similar to uniform-motion problems.

In uniform-motion problems,
   (rate) · (time) = (distance)
In work problems,
   (rate) · (time) = (work done)

ADDITIONAL EXAMPLES

Example 1.

Anne could type a manuscript in 6 hours. Ken could type the same manuscript in 8 hours. How long would it take them to type the manuscript together?

	Rate (manuscripts per hour)	Time (hours)	Work (manuscripts typed)
Anne	$\frac{1}{6}$	t	$\left(\frac{1}{6}\right)t$
Ken	$\frac{1}{8}$	t	$\left(\frac{1}{8}\right)t$
Together	$\frac{1}{t}$	t	$\left(\frac{1}{t}\right)t$ or 1

$$\frac{t}{6} + \frac{t}{8} = 1$$
$$4t + 3t = 24$$
$$7t = 24$$
$$t = \frac{24}{7}$$

Together it would take them $3\frac{3}{7}$ hours to type the manuscript.

ADDITIONAL EXAMPLES

Example 2.

Pump A can fill a storage tank in 6 hours. After pump A had been working ¾ of an hour, pump B began filling the tank. Together, they finished filling the tank in 3 hours. How long would it have taken pump B to fill the tank alone?

	Rate (tanks per hour)	Time (hours)	Work (tanks filled)
Pump A	$\frac{1}{6}$	$3\frac{3}{4}$ or $\frac{15}{4}$	$\left(\frac{1}{6}\right)\left(\frac{15}{4}\right)$
Pump B	$\frac{1}{x}$	3	$\left(\frac{1}{x}\right)(3)$

$$\left(\frac{1}{6}\right)\left(\frac{15}{4}\right) + \left(\frac{1}{x}\right)(3) = 1$$

$$\frac{5}{8} + \frac{3}{x} = 1$$

$$5x + 24 = 8x$$

$$24 = 3x$$

$$8 = x$$

Pump B could fill the tank alone in 8 hours.

Example 1   (continued)

Check   (Check by estimating.) Two fast painters working at the rate of the master painter (one house in 12 h) could paint the house in 6 h. Two slower painters working at the rate of the assistant (one house in 16 h) could paint the house in 8 h. Therefore, it will take the painter and his assistant between 6 and 8 h to paint the house. The answer ($6\frac{6}{7}$ h) is reasonable.

Example 2   Mark uses his tractor mower to mow his neighbor's 2-acre lawn. He can mow the lawn by himself in 3 h. One day, after Mark had mowed for a half hour, his younger sister began helping him with a small mower. Together they finished the job in 2 more hours. How long would it have taken Mark's sister to have done the job alone using the small mower?

Solution   Let x = the number of hours it would take Mark's sister to mow the lawn alone.

	Rate (lawns per hour)	Time worked (hours)	Amount of work (lawns mowed)
Mark	$\frac{1}{3}$	$\frac{5}{2}$	$\left(\frac{1}{3}\right)\left(\frac{5}{2}\right)$
Sister	$\frac{1}{x}$	2	$\left(\frac{1}{x}\right)(2)$
			Total: 1 lawn

Word equation: Amount of work done by Mark plus Amount of work done by sister equals Total amount of work

Equation: $\left(\frac{1}{3}\right)\left(\frac{5}{2}\right) + \left(\frac{1}{x}\right)(2) = 1$

Multiply both sides by 6x. $6x\left[\left(\frac{1}{3}\right)\left(\frac{5}{2}\right) + \left(\frac{1}{x}\right)(2)\right] = 6x(1)$

$$5x + 12 = 6x$$

$$x = 12$$

Answer   Mark's sister could mow the lawn in 12 h.

Check   Mark's sister mowed $\frac{1}{12}$ of the lawn per hour. In the 2 hours she worked, she mowed $2\left(\frac{1}{12}\right)$, or $\frac{1}{6}$ of the lawn. Mark mowed $\left(\frac{1}{3}\right)\left(\frac{5}{2}\right)$, or $\frac{5}{6}$ of the lawn in the $2\frac{1}{2}$ hours he worked. Since $\frac{1}{6} + \frac{5}{6} = 1$, the answer checks.

Example 3.
Solve this literal equation for a.

$$\frac{a}{n} + \frac{b}{m} = 1$$

$$mn\left(\frac{a}{n} + \frac{b}{m}\right) = mn(1)$$

$$am + bn = mn$$

$$am = mn - bn$$

$$a = \frac{mn - bn}{m}$$

CHECK UNDERSTANDING

- If a painter can paint a room in 35 minutes, what is the rate of work? ($\frac{1}{35}$ room per minute)
- If a printing press can print 3000 pages in 2 hours, what is its work rate? (1500 pages per hour)
- Two people deliver a truckload of pamphlets in 3 days. What is the total amount of work done? (1 truckload of pamphlets delivered)

CLASSROOM EXERCISES

In exercise 2, have the students write an equation letting x equal the rate for Cindy's brother. This table could be used:

	Rate	Time	Work
Cindy	$2x$	4	$8x$
Brother	x	4	$4x$

An alternative solution is to let x represent the time it takes Cindy's brother to clean the house by himself. This table could be used:

	Rate	Time	Work
Cindy	$\frac{2}{x}$	4	$\frac{8}{x}$
Brother	$\frac{1}{x}$	4	$\frac{4}{x}$

Example 3 Solve this literal equation for b. $\dfrac{1}{a} + \dfrac{1}{2a} = \dfrac{1}{b}$

Solution

The least common denominator is 2ab.

$$\frac{1}{a} + \frac{1}{2a} = \frac{1}{b}$$

Multiply both sides by 2ab.

$$2ab\left(\frac{1}{a} + \frac{1}{2a}\right) = 2ab\left(\frac{1}{b}\right)$$

Simplify.

$$2b + b = 2a$$

$$3b = 2a$$

Divide both sides by 3.

$$b = \frac{2a}{3}$$

Answer $b = \dfrac{2a}{3}$

Check   The check is left to the student.

■ CLASSROOM EXERCISES

1. If two 10-ohm resistors are connected in parallel, what is the total resistance of the circuit? $5\,\Omega$

2. Cindy works 2 times as fast as her brother. Together they cleaned the house in 4 h. How long would it take each of them alone to clean the house?
Cindy: 6 h, her brother: 12 h

3. Find the total resistance of a circuit made up of a 5-ohm resistor and a 10-ohm resistor connected in parallel. $3\frac{1}{3}\,\Omega$

4. If the total resistance of a circuit with two parallel resistances is 100 ohms and one resistance is 300 ohms, then what is the other resistance? $150\,\Omega$

5. If $\dfrac{1}{a} = \dfrac{1}{b} - \dfrac{1}{c}$, solve for b in terms of a and c. $b = \frac{ac}{a+c}$

■ WRITTEN EXERCISES

Find the total resistance of a circuit if the two given resistors are connected in parallel. Use the formula $\dfrac{1}{R} = \dfrac{1}{r_1} + \dfrac{1}{r_2}$.

A
1. 6 ohms and 6 ohms $3\,\Omega$ 2. 4 ohms and 4 ohms $2\,\Omega$ 3. 2 ohms and 4 ohms $1\frac{1}{3}\,\Omega$

4. 3 ohms and 6 ohms $2\,\Omega$ 5. 12 ohms and 6 ohms $4\,\Omega$ 6. 12 ohms and 4 ohms $3\,\Omega$

ASSIGNMENT GUIDE

Basic   1–19 odd, Review Exercises, Self-
          Quiz 2
Average   3–24 multiples of 3, 25–31 odd,
          Review Exercises, Self-Quiz 2
Enriched 6–24 multiples of 3, 25–35 odd,
          Review Exercises, Self-Quiz 2

PRACTICE WORKSHEET 41

8-6 PROBLEM SOLVING — FRACTIONAL EQUATIONS

■ Solve these work problems. Write an equation that fits the
problem. Solve the equation and answer the question.

1. Working alone, Kim takes 5 h to paint a room. Lynn can do the
same job in 4 h. How long does it take Kim and Lynn to paint the
room working together?   22/9 h

2. A large pump can drain a pond in 20 h. A smaller pump takes 50 h
to drain the pond. How long does it take to drain the pond if both
pumps are used?   142/7 h

3. Franklin takes 3 h to complete a delivery route. When his brother
helps with the deliveries, they take 2 h. How long does it take
Franklin's brother to make the deliveries by himself?   6 h

4. Machine A can polish 20 products in 1 h. Machine B polishes
25 products per hour. At 8:00 A.M. machine A starts polishing
products and at 9:00 A.M. machine B starts polishing. Both
machines continue polishing until a total of 128 products are
polished. At what time is the job finished?   11:24 A.M.

5. Mr. Baker can polish a waxed hallway in 20 min. Mr. Cook takes
25 min to polish the hallway. How long does it take them to polish
the hallway if they work together?   11 1/9 min

EXTRA PRACTICE, page 635

Two resistors are connected in parallel. The total resistance of the circuit and the resistance of one of the resistors is given. Find the resistance of the other resistor. Use the formula $\frac{1}{R} = \frac{1}{r_1} + \frac{1}{r_2}$.

7. $R = 4$ ohms $5\,\Omega$
   $r_1 = 20$ ohms

8. $R = 8$ ohms $12\,\Omega$
   $r_1 = 24$ ohms

9. $R = 6$ ohms $18\,\Omega$
   $r_1 = 9$ ohms

10. $R = 12$ ohms $36\,\Omega$
    $r_1 = 18$ ohms

11. $R = 14$ ohms $21\,\Omega$
    $r_1 = 42$ ohms

12. $R = 1$ ohm $2\,\Omega$
    $r_1 = 2$ ohms

Solve these work problems. Write an equation that fits the problem. Solve the equation and answer the question.

13. Kim can paint a room in 4 h. Kristen can paint the same room in 6 h. How long does it take Kim and Kristen to paint the room if they work together? $\frac{1}{4}t + \frac{1}{6}t = 1$, $2\frac{2}{5}$ h

14. Chris can address all the envelopes for a publicity mailing in 8 h. Mike can address all the envelopes in 7 h. How long does it take Chris and Mike to address the envelopes if they work together? $\frac{1}{8}t + \frac{1}{7}t = 1$, $3\frac{11}{15}$ h

15. Amy delivered an advertisement to the residents in her section of town in 6 h. Last week, when Amy and Adam worked together, they completed the deliveries in 4 h. How long would it take Adam working alone to make the deliveries? $\frac{1}{6}(4) + \frac{1}{x}(4) = 1$, 12 h

16. Jon can mow a lawn in 4 h. When Jon and Alexander work together, they mow the same lawn in 1 h. How long does it take Alexander to mow the lawn alone? $\frac{1}{4} + \frac{1}{t} = 1$, $1\frac{1}{3}$ h

17. An old machine and a new machine produce the same item. The new machine produces twice as many items as the old machine in the same time. When both machines work, they produce the day's quota in 3 h. How long would it take the old machine alone to produce the quota? How long would it take the new machine alone to produce the quota? $\frac{3}{t} + \frac{6}{t} = 1$, 9 h, $4\frac{1}{2}$ h

18. A small pipe and a large pipe both carry water to a storage tank. The large pipe fills the tank twice as fast as the small pipe. When both pipes are used, the tank is filled in 8 h. How long would it take the small pipe to fill the tank by itself? How long would it take the large pipe to fill the tank by itself? $\frac{8}{t} + \frac{16}{t} = 1$, 24 h, 12 h

Solve.

19. Solve for r_1. $r_1 = \frac{r_2 R}{r_2 - R}$

$$\frac{1}{R} = \frac{1}{r_1} + \frac{1}{r_2}$$

20. Solve for r_2. $r_2 = \frac{r_1 R}{r_1 - R}$

$$\frac{1}{R} = \frac{1}{r_1} + \frac{1}{r_2}$$

The total resistance R of a circuit made up of three resistors, r_1, r_2, and r_3, connected in parallel is given by the formula

$$\frac{1}{R} = \frac{1}{r_1} + \frac{1}{r_2} + \frac{1}{r_3}$$

B 21. Individual resistors of 2 ohms, 3 ohms, and 6 ohms are connected in parallel. What is the total resistance? 1 Ω

22. Find the total resistance when individual resistors of 2 ohms, 5 ohms, and 10 ohms are connected in parallel. What is the total resistance? $1\frac{1}{4}$ Ω

23. Three identical resistors connected in parallel have a total resistance of 6 ohms. What is the resistance of each resistor? 18 Ω

24. Three resistors are connected in parallel. The resistance of the second is twice the first and the resistance of the third is twice the second. The total resistance is 4 ohms. What is the resistance of each resistor? [*Hint:* The three resistances could be called x, $2x$, and $4x$.] 7 Ω, 14 Ω, 28 Ω

Solve.

25. A large water tank has a leak that completely drained the tank in 20 hours. It takes 4 hours to fill the tank when there is no leak. How long will it take to fill the leaking tank? 5 h

26. Three machines working alone can produce a day's quota in 2 h, 3h, and 6 h, respectively. How long does it take to produce the quota when all three machines work together? 1 h

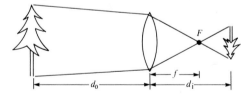

When parallel light rays pass through a convex lens, they converge at a point beyond the lens. The distance from the center of the lens to this focal point F is called the focal length f. An object at distance d_o from the lens projects an image on the other side of the lens at distance d_i from the lens. The relationship between d_o, d_i, and f is given by this formula:

$$\frac{1}{d_o} + \frac{1}{d_i} = \frac{1}{f}.$$

27. An object is 30 cm from a lens that has a focal length of 10 cm. How far is the image from the lens? 15 cm

28. An object is 24 cm from a lens that has a focal length of 6 cm. How far is the image from the lens? 8 cm

Write a computer program that tells how long it will take two people (or machines) to complete a job working together if the first can complete the job in F hours and the second can complete the job in S hours.

```
10 PRINT "THIS PROGRAM
   DETERMINES HOW LONG"
20 PRINT "IT WILL TAKE TWO
   PERSONS"
30 PRINT "(OR MACHINES)
   WORKING TOGETHER"
40 PRINT "TO COMPLETE A JOB."
50 PRINT
60 PRINT "ENTER TIME FOR THE
   FIRST.";
70 INPUT F
80 PRINT "ENTER TIME FOR THE
   SECOND.";
90 INPUT S
100 T = F * S / (F + S)
110 PRINT "IT TAKES ";T;"
    HOURS FOR BOTH"
120 PRINT "WORKING TOGETHER
    TO COMPLETE THE JOB."
130 END
```

In striving for success in solving word problems, students frequently look for "the method" that will solve each problem. Initially, this student inclination can be used to advantage to teach students an organized format to follow in setting up problems such as the work of this lesson. However, it is also important to help students avoid a rotelike application of any format. The use of questions to determine reasonable estimates of answers before solution and the application of word equations can be helpful in assisting students to *think through* the procedures they are applying. As students develop confidence in solving particular types of problems, variations of the problems should be given to students to assess their understanding of the algebraic methods and their ability to extend these ideas.

ENRICHMENT PROBLEMS

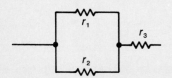

- Three resistances are used in an electrical circuit, two in parallel and a third in series. If the parallel resistances are 2 ohms each and the third resistance is 5 ohms, find the total resistance of the circuit.

  6 ohms

- A bucket is being filled by the dripping from two pipes. One pipe can fill the bucket in 8 hours. The other pipe can fill the bucket in 12 hours. If the bucket is presently half full, when will it be full?

  $2\frac{2}{5}$ hours

- Write a word problem for each equation.

  a. $\dfrac{1}{x} = \dfrac{1}{3} + \dfrac{1}{5}$ **b.** $\dfrac{1}{4} = \dfrac{1}{x} + \dfrac{1}{10}$

29. An object is 12 cm from a lens and its image is 4 cm from the lens. What is the focal length of the lens? 3 cm

30. Solve the formula for f. (Express f in terms of d_o and d_i.) $f = \dfrac{d_i d_o}{d_i + d_o}$

31. Solve the formula for d_i. (Express d_i in terms of f and d_o.) $d_i = \dfrac{d_o f}{d_o - f}$

The *harmonic mean h* of two numbers a and b is given by the formula

$$\frac{1}{h} = \frac{\dfrac{1}{a} + \dfrac{1}{b}}{2}$$

If a and b are rates, then h is the average rate.

32. Solve the formula for h. $h = \dfrac{2ab}{a+b}$

33. A salesperson drives to an office at 60 km/h and returns home by the same route at 40 km/h. What was the average speed for the total trip? (If $a = 60$ and $b = 40$, find h.) 48 km/h

34. A passenger plane flies into the wind to its destination and flies with the wind on the return trip. The ground speed is 450 mph going and 550 mph returning. What is the average speed for the round trip? 495 mph

35. Lori paddled a canoe from the dock to an island at 4 km/h going with the current. On her return trip, against the current, Lori averaged 1 km/h. What was her average speed for the round trip? 1.6 km/h

■ REVIEW EXERCISES

1. For each point below, either state the quadrant the point is in or the axis it is on. [5–1]

   a. $(0, -5)$ y-axis   **b.** $(4, -3)$ IV   **c.** $(-3, 4)$ II   **d.** $(1, 7)$ I

2. The table defines a relation. [5–2]

x	0	1	1	2	2
y	0	1	-1	2	-2

   a. List the domain of the relation. $\{0, 1, 2\}$

   b. List the range of the relation. $\{-2, -1, 0, 1, 2\}$

   c. Graph the relation.

3. Indicate whether the ordered pair is a solution of the equation $3x + y = 12$. [5–3]

   a. $(0, 4)$ No   **b.** $(2, 6)$ Yes   **c.** $(-2, 18)$ Yes

4. Find the missing number for each solution pair of the equation
$2a - b = 10$. [5-3]

a	0	? (5)	2	? (7)
b	? (−10)	0	? (−6)	4

5. Select three values of x, complete the table, plot the points, and then graph
the equation $y = \frac{1}{2}x - 2$. [5-4]

x	?	?	?
y	?	?	?

6. Complete the table and then use the ordered pairs to graph the equation
$y = x^2 - 4$. [5-4]

x	−3	−2	−1	$-\frac{1}{2}$	0	$\frac{1}{2}$	1	2	3
y	? (5)	? (0)	? (−3)	? ($-\frac{15}{4}$)	? (−4)	? ($-\frac{15}{4}$)	? (−3)	? (0)	? (5)

Self-Quiz 2

8-4 Simplify.

1. $\dfrac{2}{x} - \dfrac{5}{3x}$ $\dfrac{1}{3x}$

2. $\dfrac{8}{y} - \dfrac{y}{4}$ $\dfrac{32 - y^2}{4y}$

3. $\dfrac{6}{x^2} + \dfrac{7}{x}$ $\dfrac{6 + 7x}{x^2}$

4. $\dfrac{3}{x - 2} + \dfrac{1}{x}$ $\dfrac{4x - 2}{x(x - 2)}$

8-5 Solve.

5. $\dfrac{s}{4} - 1 = \dfrac{3}{2}$ $\{10\}$

6. $x - 3 = \dfrac{18}{x}$ $\{-3, 6\}$

7. $\dfrac{1}{3x} + \dfrac{1}{2x} = \dfrac{5}{6}$ $\{1\}$

8-6 Solve.

8. Using the formula $\dfrac{1}{R} = \dfrac{1}{r_1} + \dfrac{1}{r_2}$, find the resistance r_1 when $r_2 = 3$ ohms and
the total resistance $R = 2$ ohms. $6\,\Omega$

9. A new letter-sorting machine A can complete a task in $3\frac{1}{2}$ h. An older machine
can do the same job in 5 h. How long will it take both machines to do the
task together? $2\frac{1}{17}$ h

2c.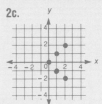

5.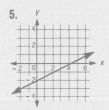

6.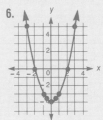

Solve. Use the formula $\frac{1}{R} = \frac{1}{r_1} + \frac{1}{r_2}$.

1. Find R if $r_1 = 3$ ohms and $r_2 = 6$ ohms.

> 2 ohms

2. Find r_2 if $R = 3$ ohms and $r_1 = 4$ ohms.

> 12 ohms

Working alone, Erynn could stuff advertising flyers in all the envelopes in 45 minutes. Working alone, Laura can complete the same job in 30 minutes.

3. What fraction of the job could Erynn do in one minute?

> $\frac{1}{45}$

4. Let x represent the number of minutes it takes Erynn and Laura to finish the job if they both work on it. Write an equation that fits the problem.

> $\frac{1}{45}x + \frac{1}{30}x = 1$

5. How many minutes does it take Erynn and Laura working together to complete the job?

> 18 minutes

PURPOSE

Problems involving proportions are among the most common situations encountered in everyday living. A high level of skill in solving such problems should be reached by all students.

PREVIEW

The ratios in the Preview exercises should be written in their simplest form:

a. 2 to 1   **b.** 3 to 2   **c.** 4 to 3
d. 23 to 13   **e.** 3 to 2   **f.** 23 to 13

OBJECTIVE 8–7

To simplify ratios and solve proportions.

8–7 Ratio and Proportion

Preview   **Historical note: Agreeable sounds**

In experimenting with the relative lengths of strings needed to produce musical notes, Pythagoras (pih-THAG-oh-ras), a Greek mathematician who lived more than 2500 years ago, found that string lengths in ratios of small integers, such as 2 to 1, 3 to 2, and 4 to 3, produced especially agreeable sounds. Two strings of a more complicated ratio of length, such as 23 to 13, produced an unpleasant sound combination.

Determine whether Pythagoras would have thought the sound pleasant if the string-lengths were in these ratios:

a. 24 to 12   Yes   **b.** 24 to 16   Yes

c. 24 to 18   Yes   **d.** $11\frac{1}{2}$ to $6\frac{1}{2}$ No

e. 1.5 to 1   Yes   **f.** 2.3 to 1.3   No

In this lesson you will work with ratios. Many people consider the ability to use ratios as the most practical problem-solving skill studied in school.

■ LESSON

The **ratio** of a number a to a number b ($b \neq 0$) is the quotient of a divided by b. The ratio can be written in several ways.

$$a \text{ to } b \qquad a{:}b \qquad \frac{a}{b}$$

For example, the ratio of the number of inches in a foot to the number of inches in a yard can be expressed as 12 to 36 or 12:36 or $\frac{12}{36}$.

In this text, ratios will most often be written using fraction notation.

Ratios are simplified in the same way that fractions are simplified. For example, the above ratio of the number of inches in a foot to the number of inches in a yard $\left(\frac{12}{36}\right)$ can be simplified to $\frac{1}{3}$.

An equation that states that two ratios are equal is called a **proportion**.

For example, $\frac{12}{36} = \frac{1}{3}$.

Consider how fractions can be eliminated from a proportion. Let a, b, c, and d be real numbers ($b \neq 0$ and $d \neq 0$).

$$\frac{a}{b} = \frac{c}{d}$$

Multiply both sides by bd.

$$bd \cdot \frac{a}{b} = bd \cdot \frac{c}{d}$$

Simplify.

$$ad = bc$$

We have just proved the **cross-multiplication** property.

Cross-Multiplication Property

For all numbers a, b, c, and d ($b \neq 0$, $d = 0$),

$$\text{if } \frac{a}{b} = \frac{c}{d}, \text{ then } ad = bc.$$

The operation is called *cross multiplying* because the numbers that are multiplied (a and d, b and c) are related by a cross.

$$\frac{a}{b} \diagdown\!\!\!\!\diagup \frac{c}{d}$$

The cross-multiplication property can be used to determine whether a proportion is true or false. For example, consider the proportions

$$\frac{57}{38} = \frac{3}{2} \quad \text{and} \quad \frac{27}{81} = \frac{1}{4}.$$

$$\frac{57}{38} = \frac{3}{2} \qquad\qquad \frac{27}{81} = \frac{1}{4}$$

$$57(2) = 38(3) \qquad\qquad 27(4) = 81(1)$$

$$114 = 114 \quad \text{True.} \qquad 108 = 81 \quad \text{False.}$$

The first proportion is true because the cross products are equal. The second proportion is false because the cross products are not equal.

The cross-multiplication property can also be used to solve proportions.

Mathematics and Your Future

As the use of technology in vocational fields increases, so too do the mathematics requirements for vocational and technical programs. Most of these programs require a knowledge of algebra and geometry. Many programs in the agricultural, business, health, trade, and industrial areas also require advanced algebra, while some specialized fields require trigonometry. If you want to keep your options open for enrolling in various vocational programs, be sure to take enough mathematics.

The converse of the cross-multiplying property may be stated and proved. If $ad = bc$, then $\frac{a}{b} = \frac{c}{d}$, $b \neq 0$ and $d \neq 0$.

Proof: $ad = bc$

Multiply both sides by $\frac{1}{bd}$.

$$\left(\frac{1}{bd}\right)ad = \left(\frac{1}{bd}\right)bc$$

Simplify. $\frac{a}{b} = \frac{c}{d}$

Example 1. Solve. $\dfrac{x}{5} = \dfrac{9}{4}$

$$4 \cdot x = 5 \cdot 9$$
$$x = \dfrac{45}{4}$$
$$\left\{ \dfrac{45}{4} \right\}$$

Example 2. Solve. $\dfrac{3}{4} = \dfrac{x+8}{x+13}$

$$3(x+13) = 4(x+8)$$
$$3x + 39 = 4x + 32$$
$$x = 7$$
$$\{7\}$$

Example 3.

In a collection of 112 coins, the ratio of the number of nickels to the number of dimes is 3 to 4. Find the number of each type of coin.

Let $3x$ = the number of nickels.
Let $4x$ = the number of dimes.

$$3x + 4x = 112$$
$$7x = 112$$
$$x = 16$$
$$(3x = 48 \text{ and } 4x = 64)$$

48 nickels and 64 dimes

CHECK UNDERSTANDING

- Is this a true statement? $\dfrac{17}{53} = \dfrac{136}{424}$ (Yes)
- In simplest form, what is the ratio of the number of feet in 440 yards to the number of feet in a mile? (¼)
- Solve. $\dfrac{x}{3} = \dfrac{2}{7}$ ({6/7})

Example 1   Solve. $\dfrac{x}{6} = \dfrac{5}{8}$

Solution

$$\dfrac{x}{6} = \dfrac{5}{8}$$

Cross multiply.

$$8x = 6 \cdot 5$$
$$x = \dfrac{30}{8}$$
$$= \dfrac{15}{4}$$

Answer $\left\{ \dfrac{15}{4} \right\}$

Check   The check is left to the student.

Example 2   Solve. $\dfrac{2}{3} = \dfrac{x+4}{x+13}$

Solution

$$\dfrac{2}{3} = \dfrac{x+4}{x+13}$$

Cross multiply.

$$2(x+13) = 3(x+4)$$
$$2x + 26 = 3x + 12$$
$$-x = -14$$
$$x = 14$$

Answer $\{14\}$

Check   The check is left to the student.

Example 3   The ratio of the length of a rectangle to the width is 5 to 2. Find the dimensions of the rectangle if its perimeter is 70 cm.

Solution   Let $5x$ = the length and $2x$ = the width.
(Note that $5x$ and $2x$ are in the ratio 5 to 2.)

$$5x + 2x + 5x + 2x = 70$$
$$14x = 70$$
$$x = 5$$

Answer   The length is $5 \cdot 5$ cm, or 25 cm. The width is $2 \cdot 5$ cm, or 10 cm.

Check $\dfrac{25}{10} = \dfrac{5}{2}$ The perimeter is 25 cm + 10 cm + 25 cm + 10 cm = 70 cm. It checks.

■ CLASSROOM EXERCISES

First write the two measurements using the same unit. Then write the ratio in simplest form.

1. 1 in. to 1 ft $\frac{1}{12}$

2. 1 year to 5 weeks $\frac{52}{5}$

3. 1 cm to 1 m $\frac{1}{100}$

True or false?

4. $\frac{3}{4} = \frac{15}{20}$ T

5. $\frac{5}{8} = \frac{35}{54}$ F

6. $\frac{7}{4} = \frac{3.5}{2}$ T

Solve.

7. $\frac{x}{5} = \frac{12}{15}$ {4}

8. $\frac{12}{a} = 6$ {2}

9. $\frac{3}{4} = \frac{y}{27}$ $\left\{20\frac{1}{4}\right\}$

10. If there are 10 boys and 20 girls in an algebra class, simplify the ratio of the number of boys to the number of girls. $\frac{1}{2}$

11. In Exercise 10, simplify the ratio of the number of students to the number of girls. $\frac{3}{2}$

■ WRITTEN EXERCISES

Write the two measurements using the same units. Then write the ratio in simplest form.

1. 2 feet to 1 yard $\frac{2}{3}$

2. 1 yard to 2 feet $\frac{3}{2}$

3. 1 kilometer to 1 meter $\frac{1000}{1}$

4. 1 meter to 1 kilometer $\frac{1}{1000}$

5. 10 seconds to 1 minute $\frac{1}{6}$

6. 1 day to 32 hours $\frac{3}{4}$

7. 8 ounces to 2 pounds $\frac{1}{4}$

8. 1 pound to 12 ounces $\frac{4}{3}$

A bicycle shop has 20 five-speeds, 34 ten-speeds, and 45 twelve-speeds. Simplify the ratio of bikes for the given speeds.

9. five-speeds to ten-speeds $\frac{10}{17}$

10. ten-speeds to twelve-speeds $\frac{34}{45}$

11. ten-speeds to total $\frac{34}{99}$

12. twelve-speeds to total $\frac{5}{11}$

Simplify these ratios.

13. $\frac{36}{48}$ $\frac{3}{4}$

14. $\frac{40}{48}$ $\frac{5}{6}$

15. $\frac{28}{32}$ $\frac{7}{8}$

16. $\frac{20}{32}$ $\frac{5}{8}$

17. $\frac{80}{100}$ $\frac{4}{5}$

18. $\frac{75}{100}$ $\frac{3}{4}$

19. $\frac{34}{51}$ $\frac{2}{3}$

20. $\frac{38}{57}$ $\frac{2}{3}$

True or false?

21. $\frac{30}{80} = \frac{12}{32}$ T

22. $\frac{50}{70} = \frac{15}{21}$ T

23. $\frac{12}{15} = \frac{20}{25}$ T

24. $\frac{6}{15} = \frac{8}{20}$ T

25. $\frac{18}{30} = \frac{14}{20}$ F

26. $\frac{9}{12} = \frac{18}{21}$ F

27. $\frac{26}{34} = \frac{38}{52}$ F

28. $\frac{46}{38} = \frac{68}{59}$ F

CLASSROOM EXERCISES

In exercises 1–3, emphasize that a common unit must be used for the two quantities comprising the ratio—both inches, both weeks, both centimeters, and so on.

In exercises 4–6, point out that the cross-products test can be employed but that other methods are easier to use in some situations. For example, in exercise 4, both quantities in the first ratio can be multiplied by 5 and the resulting ratio compared to the second ratio. (They are identical.) Another acceptable method is to simplify both ratios. If the simplified ratios are identical, the proportion is true.

In exercise 8, point out that 6 could be written as the ratio $^6/_1$.

ASSIGNMENT GUIDE

Basic   1–41 odd, Review Exercises
Average 3–51 multiples of 3, 53–59 odd,
            Review Exercises
Enriched 3–60 multiples of 3, 61–63 all,
            Review Exercises

PRACTICE WORKSHEET 42

8-7 RATIO AND PROPORTION

■ Write the two measurements using the same units. Then write the ratio in simplest form.

1. 30 min to 2 h $\frac{1}{4}$
2. 20 h to 1 day $\frac{5}{6}$
3. 12 oz to 3 lb $\frac{1}{4}$
4. 1 T to 1500 lb $\frac{4}{3}$
5. 1 yd to 8 in. $\frac{9}{2}$
6. 440 yd to 1 mi $\frac{1}{4}$
7. 2 kg to 50 g $\frac{40}{1}$
8. 100 in.² to 1 ft² $\frac{25}{36}$
9. 1 cm² to 1 m² $\frac{1}{10,000}$
10. 5 ft³ to 1 yd³ $\frac{5}{27}$

■ Simplify these ratios.

11. $\frac{35}{100}$ $\frac{7}{20}$
12. $\frac{39}{52}$ $\frac{3}{4}$
13. $\frac{12}{15}$ $\frac{4}{5}$
14. $\frac{40}{48}$ $\frac{5}{6}$
15. $\frac{12}{180}$ $\frac{1}{15}$
16. $\frac{38}{80}$ $\frac{19}{40}$

■ Solve these proportions.

17. $\frac{5}{6} = \frac{n}{18}$ {15}
18. $\frac{7}{8} = \frac{56}{x}$ {64}
19. $\frac{1}{2.5} = \frac{a}{20}$ {8}
20. $\frac{4}{c} = \frac{24}{9}$ {3/2}
21. $\frac{d}{7.5} = \frac{40}{25}$ {12}
22. $\frac{10}{h} = \frac{15}{36}$ {24}
23. $\frac{6}{3.5} = \frac{b}{84}$ {144}
24. $\frac{3}{x} = \frac{9}{x+2}$ {13}
25. $\frac{p+4}{8} = \frac{9}{16}$ {1/2}
26. $\frac{5}{7} = \frac{m+1}{m}$ {-7/2}
27. $\frac{i-2}{3} = \frac{i}{10}$ {20/7}
28. $\frac{3q+1}{q} = \frac{22}{7}$ {7}

397

This lesson concerns equality of ratios in which the quantities being compared are of the same type. When we are concerned only with whether two such ratios are equal, the cross-multiplying principle is very useful. However, in real-life situations we are frequently confronted with comparing two ratios in which the quantities being compared are different—for example, price comparisons. For such comparisons, we usually convert the given ratios to a unit amount:

$$\frac{\$4.50}{3\text{ golf balls}} = \frac{\$1.50}{1\text{ ball}}$$

Or we convert each of two ratios to the same amount:

$$\frac{2\text{ pencils}}{15\cent} = \frac{6\text{ pencils}}{45\cent} \qquad \frac{3\text{ pencils}}{20\cent} = \frac{6\text{ pencils}}{40\cent}$$

Sometimes it is necessary to be careful in choosing just what we wish to compare. Which is the better buy, a 6-inch pizza at $1.50 or a 12-inch pizza at $3.60?

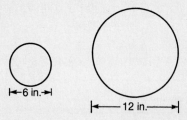

|←6 in.→| |←— 12 in.—→|

(The areas are 9π square inches and 36π square inches. The larger pizza is actually *4 times* the size of the smaller pizza.)

Discuss some of these ideas with your students to improve their ability to apply ratios to real-world problems.

Solve these proportions.

29. $\frac{2}{3} = \frac{x}{54}$ { 36 }

30. $\frac{3}{4} = \frac{x}{68}$ { 51 }

31. $\frac{48}{42} = \frac{56}{x}$ { 49 }

32. $\frac{63}{56} = \frac{36}{x}$ { 32 }

33. $\frac{5}{8} = \frac{7.5}{x}$ { 12 }

34. $\frac{5}{6} = \frac{7.5}{x}$ { 9 }

35. $\frac{x}{6} = \frac{9}{4}$ $\left\{13\frac{1}{2}\right\}$

36. $\frac{x}{10} = \frac{11}{4}$ $\left\{27\frac{1}{2}\right\}$

Solve.

37. If 60 of the 300 students at Grant School are left-handed, what is the ratio of left-handed students to right-handed students? $\frac{1}{4}$

38. The ratio of the sides of two squares is 3 to 1. What is the ratio of their perimeters? $\frac{3}{1}$

39. The ratio of the length to the width of a rectangle is 4 to 3. What are the dimensions of the rectangle if its perimeter is 84 cm? Length: 24 cm, width: 18 cm

40. An 81-cm cable is cut into two pieces whose lengths are in the ratio 4 to 5. How long are the pieces? 36 cm, 45 cm

41. An inheritance of $50,000 is divided between two people in the ratio 7 to 3. How much does each person get? $35,000; $15,000

Solve these proportions.

B **42.** $\frac{3}{4} = \frac{x+5}{x+10}$ { 10 }

43. $\frac{2}{3} = \frac{x+4}{x+10}$ { 8 }

44. $\frac{5}{2} = \frac{x+6}{x-6}$ { 14 }

45. $\frac{7}{3} = \frac{x+6}{x-6}$ { 15 }

46. $\frac{5}{7} = \frac{3x+6}{5x+2}$ { 8 }

47. $\frac{4}{9} = \frac{3x-1}{6x+3}$ { 7 }

48. $\frac{1}{x-3} = \frac{x-2}{2}$ { 1, 4 }

49. $\frac{x-2}{5x-16} = \frac{1}{x-2}$ { 4, 5 }

50. $\frac{2x-1}{x+1} = \frac{x-2}{x-3}$ { 1, 5 }

51. The ratio of the sides of two squares is 3 to 1. What is the ratio of their areas? $\frac{9}{1}$

52. The ratio of the radii of two circles is 4 to 1. What is the ratio of their circumferences? $\frac{4}{1}$

53. The radii of two circles are in the ratio 10 to 1. What is the ratio of their areas? $\frac{100}{1}$

54. The edges of two cubes are in the ratio $\frac{1}{2}$. What is the ratio of their surface areas? $\frac{1}{4}$

55. What is the ratio of the volumes of two cubes if their edges are in the ratio $\frac{2}{3}$? $\frac{8}{27}$

398

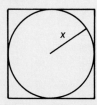

a. Determine the ratio of the area of the square to the area of the circle.

$$\frac{(2x)^2}{\pi x^2} = \frac{4}{\pi}$$

b. Determine the ratio of the perimeter of the square to the circumference of the circle.

$$\frac{4(2x)}{\pi(2x)} = \frac{4}{\pi}$$

• If 5 girls can complete 5 equal projects in 5 weeks, and 3 boys can complete 3 of the same projects in 3 weeks, how many projects can a class of 15 girls and 15 boys complete in 15 weeks?

$$\frac{\frac{5 \text{ girls}}{5 \text{ projects}}}{5 \text{ weeks}} = \frac{\frac{15 \text{ girls}}{x \text{ projects}}}{15 \text{ weeks}} \text{ and}$$

$$\frac{\frac{3 \text{ boys}}{3 \text{ projects}}}{3 \text{ weeks}} = \frac{\frac{15 \text{ boys}}{y \text{ projects}}}{15 \text{ weeks}}$$

$$x = 45 \text{ projects}$$
$$y = 75 \text{ projects}$$

Total: 120 projects

---

56. The ratio of the lengths, of the widths, and of the heights of two rectangular prisms is $\frac{3}{4}$. Is the volume of the smaller prism more than half, half, or less than half the volume of the larger prism? Explain. Less than half, $\frac{3^3}{4^3} = \frac{27}{64}$

57. The ratio of adult to student tickets for a concert is $\frac{3}{2}$. How many of each kind were sold if 300 tickets were sold in all? Adult: 180, student: 120

58. Three numbers are in the ratio 2:3:4. What are the numbers if their sum is 30? [*Hint:* Let $2x$, $3x$, and $4x$ represent the numbers.] $6\frac{2}{3}$, 10, $13\frac{1}{3}$

59. Three numbers are in the ratio 3:4:5. What are the numbers if their sum is 240? 60, 80, 100

60. Three numbers are in the ratio 5:7:9. What are the numbers if their sum is 105? 25, 35, 45

Suppose that $\frac{a}{b} = \frac{c}{d}$ and $a \neq 0$, $b \neq 0$, $c \neq 0$, and $d \neq 0$. Show that these statements are true.

61. $\frac{a}{c} = \frac{b}{d}$ $ad = bc$

62. $\frac{a}{b} = \frac{a+c}{b+d}$ $ad = bc$

63. $\frac{a}{b} = \frac{a+2c}{b+2d}$ $ad = bc$

■ REVIEW EXERCISES

1. Draw these three lines through the point $(2, 0)$. Label the lines a, b, and c. [5–5]

   a. Line with slope 2

   b. Line with slope $-\frac{2}{3}$

   c. Line with no slope

2. State the slopes of the lines. [5–5]

   a. $\overleftrightarrow{AB}$ 0

   b. $\overleftrightarrow{AC}$ $-\frac{1}{2}$

   c. $\overleftrightarrow{BD}$ 2

   d. $\overleftrightarrow{BC}$ No slope

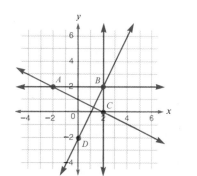

3. State the slope and y-intercept of the line whose equation is $y = 2x - 5$. [5–6]
   2, −5

4. Write this equation in slope–intercept form. [5–6]

   $$3x + 5y = 15 \quad y = -\frac{3}{5}x + 3$$

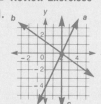

Simplify these ratios.

1. $^{30}/_{75}$ $^2/_5$

2. $^{36}/_{48}$ $^3/_4$

Solve these proportions.

3. $\dfrac{5}{6} = \dfrac{35}{x}$ {42}

4. $\dfrac{x}{3} = \dfrac{36}{27}$ {4}

5. The ratio of the length to the width of a rectangle is 5 to 2. What are the dimensions of the rectangle if its perimeter is 70 centimeters?

length: 25 cm; width: 10 cm

PURPOSE

Percent is a special type of ratio that is widely used and frequently encountered in everyday problems. The ability to do simple interest problems is important for many applications that involve money.

PREVIEW

Although several countries have "dollar and cent" monetary units, this does not mean the dollars have the same value. For example, a Canadian dollar and a U.S. dollar have different values. The relationship between the two currencies fluctuates from week to week.

Additional Preview questions that could be asked include these:

• If "double" means multiply by 2, "triple" means multiply by 3, and "quadruple" means multiply by 4, what does "centuple" mean? (Multiply by 100)

• How many centiliters are in one liter? (100)

OBJECTIVE 8–8

To solve percent problems and simple interest problems.

You may wish to spend two days on this section. Refer to the Pacing Chart.

8–8 Percent

Preview

A student noticed that some words containing "cent" have similar meanings. For example,

cent: A monetary unit equal to $\dfrac{1}{100}$ of the dollar of the United States, Australia, Canada, Ethiopia, Guyana, Liberia, Malaysia, New Zealand, Hong Kong, and Singapore.

centenary: Pertaining to a 100-year period.

centigram: $\dfrac{1}{100}$ of a gram.

centuplicate: To multiply by 100.

century: 100 years.

Can you guess the meaning of the following words that contain "cent"?

• A souvenir in Mexico City costs 37 pesos and 50 centavos. What is one centavo worth? $\dfrac{1}{100}$ of a peso

• Payette, Idaho, had a centennial celebration. How old is the town? 100 years

• The Roman centurion led his soldiers in battle. How many soldiers did he command? 100

In this lesson, you will learn to use an important ratio called percent.

■ LESSON

The ratio of one quantity to another is sometimes written as a percent. **Percent** means "hundredth" and is usually denoted by the symbol %. For example,

$$5\% = \frac{5}{100} = 0.05 \qquad 100\% = \frac{100}{100} = 1$$

$$6.7\% = \frac{6.7}{100} = 0.067 \qquad 143\% = \frac{143}{100} = 1.43$$

If the ratio is given as a fraction, it can be changed to a percent by

1. changing to an equivalent fraction with denominator of 100 and then writing the numerator of the fraction followed by a percent symbol, or

2. changing the fraction to a decimal, multiplying the decimal by 100, and writing that number followed by a percent symbol.

For example, to change $\dfrac{3}{20}$ to a percent notation:

Method 1

Change the fraction to an equivalent fraction with a denominator of 100.

$$\frac{3}{20} = \frac{15}{100} = 15\%$$

Method 2

Divide the numerator by the denominator to change the fraction to a decimal.

$$\frac{3}{20} = 0.15 = 15\%$$

LESSON

Point out that $x\%$ can be interpreted as $0.01x$. For example, $13.5\% = (0.01)(13.5) = 0.135$. This interpretation avoids the use of complex fractions such as $\frac{13.5}{100}$.

In the simple interest formula $i = prt$, point out that i and p are measured in the same monetary units (usually both are numbers of dollars), r is the annual interest rate (usually a percent written as a decimal), and t is the time measured in years.

Proportions can be used to solve percent problems.

Example 1   About 17% of the 30 students in an algebra class earned an A during the second quarter. About how many students earned an A?

Solution   Let P = the number of students who earned an A. Then the ratio of P to 30 must be equal to the ratio of 17 to 100.

$$\frac{P}{30} = \frac{17}{100}$$

$$100P = 510$$

$$P = 5.1$$

Answer   About 5 students earned an A.

Example 2   In one high school about 53% of the students are girls. If there are 332 girls in the school, how many students are there in all?

Solution   Let n = the number of students in the school. Then the ratio of 332 to n must equal the ratio of 53 to 100.

$$\frac{332}{n} = \frac{53}{100}$$

$$53n = 33{,}200$$

$$n \approx 626.42$$

Answer   There are about 626 students in the school.

In general, if $a\%$ of b equals c, then $\frac{a}{100} \cdot b = c$ or $\frac{a}{100} = \frac{c}{b}$.

Example 3   A few years ago, the best time for the women's marathon was about 111% of the best time for the men's marathon. If the women's best time was about 2 h 22 min, approximately what was the men's best time?

Solution   We know that 2h 22 min = 142 min. Let m = the men's best time.

$$111\% \text{ of } m = 142$$

$$\frac{111}{100} \cdot m = 142$$

$$\frac{111}{100} = \frac{142}{m}$$

$$111m = 14{,}200$$

$$m \approx 127.93$$

Answer   The men's best time was about 128 min, or 2h 8 min.

ADDITIONAL EXAMPLES

Example 1.
  Jill made 80% of her 15 free throws in a basketball game. How many free throws did she make?

12

Example 2.
  In a recent election, 40% of the voters voted for Mayor Crews, who got 1016 votes. How many people voted in the election?

2540

Example 3.
  The night shift produced 264 parts, which was 110% of its goal. What was its goal?

240 parts

ADDITIONAL EXAMPLES

Example 4.
Jeff Wilson invested $500 at 9.5% for 2 years. How much simple interest did he receive?

$95

CHECK UNDERSTANDING

- Write each percent as a common fraction.
  a. 9% (^{9}/$_{100}$) **b.** 50% (^{50}/$_{100}$ or ½)
  c. 110% (^{110}/$_{100}$ or 1^1/$_{10}$)
- Write each percent as a decimal.
  a. 3% (0.03) **b.** 25% (0.25)
  c. 210% (2.1)
- Write each number as a percent.
  a. ¾ (75%) **b.** 0.43 (43%)
  c. 3 (300%)
- What is 12% of 50? (6)
- What percent is 15 of 12? (125%)

CLASSROOM EXERCISES

In exercises 6–8, emphasize that numbers of a simplified ratio should contain no common factors.

In exercises 9–14, use questions to help students determine reasonable estimates for answers before solving algebraically. Relating the given expression to one involving 100% is usually helpful.

Examples.   15% of 95 = x
100% of 95 = ? (95)
How does x compare to 95?
x% of 20 = 15
100% of 20 = ? (20)
How does x compare to 100?

Another important use of percents is in interest problems. The relationship between **interest** i (in dollars), **principal** p (in dollars), **rate** r (percent per year), and time t (in years) is given by the formula $i = prt$.

Example 4 Barbara Lynch borrowed $5200 for 2 years to pay for her new car. The interest rate was 9.9% per year. How much did she pay each month for the two years?

Solution She paid interest on the entire $5200 even though she paid some of the principal each month.

p	r	t
5200	9.9%, or 0.099	2

$$i = prt$$
$$i = 5200 \cdot 0.099 \cdot 2$$
$$i = 1029.6$$

She paid $1029.60 in interest and $5200 in principal for a period of 24 months.

Answer The monthly payment was
$$\frac{\$5200 + \$1029.60}{24}, \quad \text{or} \quad \$259.57.$$

■ CLASSROOM EXERCISES

Write these ratios as percents.

1. $\frac{1}{2}$ 50%   **2.** $\frac{7}{10}$ 70%   **3.** $\frac{5}{8}$ $62\frac{1}{2}$%   **4.** $\frac{1}{3}$ $33\frac{1}{3}$%   **5.** $\frac{5}{4}$ 125%

Write these percents as simplified ratios.

6. 45% $\frac{9}{20}$ **7.** 5.5% $\frac{11}{200}$ **8.** 150% $\frac{3}{2}$

Solve.

9. 15% of 95 = x { 14.25 }   **10.** 130% of 45 = n { 58.5 }   **11.** 25% of y = 40 { 160 }

12. 1.4% of m = 0.7 { 50 }   **13.** x% of 20 = 15 { 75 }   **14.** z% of 60 = 70 { $116\frac{2}{3}$ }

Solve.

15. Ms. Carson requires students to score at least 92% on a test in order to get an A. Carolyn scored 43 out of 46 possible points. Did she get an A on the test? Yes

16. Mr. Crandal borrowed $2500 for 6 months. He paid interest at the rate of 11.5% per year. How much did he have to repay at the end of 6 months? $2643.75

EXTRA PRACTICE, page 636

ASSIGNMENT GUIDE

Basic   1–41 odd, Review Exercises
Average 3–42 multiples of 3, 43–52 all,
           Review Exercises
Enriched 1–51 odd, 53–58 all, Review
           Exercises

■ WRITTEN EXERCISES

Write these ratios as percents.

1. $\frac{3}{8}$ $37\frac{1}{2}\%$

2. $\frac{7}{8}$ $87\frac{1}{2}\%$

3. $\frac{6}{5}$ 120%

4. $\frac{3}{2}$ 150%

5. $\frac{1}{400}$ $\frac{1}{4}\%$

6. $\frac{1}{200}$ $\frac{1}{2}\%$

7. $\frac{2.5}{50}$ 5%

8. $\frac{3.5}{25}$ 14%

Write these percents as simplified ratios.

9. 32% $\frac{8}{25}$

10. 44% $\frac{11}{25}$

11. 125% $\frac{5}{4}$

12. 175% $\frac{7}{4}$

13. 0.5% $\frac{1}{200}$

14. 0.4% $\frac{1}{250}$

15. $1\frac{1}{2}\%$ $\frac{3}{200}$

16. $2\frac{1}{2}\%$ $\frac{1}{40}$

Solve these proportions.

17. $25\% = \frac{x}{12}$ $\{3\}$

18. $20\% = \frac{x}{40}$ $\{8\}$

19. $30\% = \frac{60}{x}$ $\{200\}$

20. $10\% = \frac{30}{x}$ $\{300\}$

21. $x\% = \frac{12}{15}$ $\{80\}$

22. $x\% = \frac{9}{15}$ $\{60\}$

Solve.

23. 5% of $80 = x$ $\{4\}$

24. 8% of $50 = x$ $\{4\}$

25. 150% of $x = 9$ $\{6\}$

26. 140% of $x = 7$ $\{5\}$

27. $x\%$ of $500 = 40$ $\{8\}$

28. $x\%$ of $400 = 60$ $\{15\}$

29. 150% of $50 = x$ $\{75\}$

30. 125% of $40 = x$ $\{50\}$

31. 12% of $x = 9.6$ $\{80\}$

32. 15% of $x = 7.2$ $\{48\}$

33. $x\%$ of $250 = 35$ $\{14\}$

34. $x\%$ of $180 = 27$ $\{15\}$

Solve. Use the formula $i = prt$, where i = interest in dollars, p = principal in dollars, r = annual rate as a percent, and t = time in years.

35. Mr. Banks invested $4000 for 2 years at an annual rate of 9.5%. How much interest did he earn? $760

36. Ms. Cash invested $800 for 5 years at an annual rate of 7.5%. How much interest did she earn? $300

37. Sarah Blank borrowed $6000 for 3 years at an annual rate of 12%. How much interest did she pay on her loan? $2160

38. Bud Nichols borrowed $1500 for 2 years at an annual rate of 18%. How much interest did he pay on his loan? $540

PROBLEM-SOLVING NOTES
Drawing a figure

Though exposed to percent ideas in earlier courses, some students will have poorly formed notions of percent. They may have developed a mechanical approach to problems that is ill suited to algebra applications. It is important to reemphasize the notion of 100% and to use models or pictures to help students visualize the problem posed. Such diagrams will not help students set up or solve an equation. However, these techniques will establish a reasonable reference to help students avoid making absurd mistakes.

Example. 25% of $x = 40$

100% of x

25% of x

ENRICHMENT PROBLEMS

- Which of the amounts is greatest, a, b, or c?

  a. A quantity x is increased by 20% and then the increased amount decreased by 20%.

  b. A quantity x is decreased by 20% and then the decreased amount increased by 20%.

  c. The original amount x.

  Amount a
  $= (x + 0.2x) - 0.2(x + 0.2x)$
  $= 0.96x$
  Amount b
  $= (x - 0.2x) + 0.2(x - 0.2x)$
  $= 0.96x$
  Amount c $= x \leftarrow$ greatest

- Write a word problem for each equation.

  a. $i = (1000)(0.08)(3)$
  b. $0.75x = 30$
  c. $\dfrac{x}{100} = \dfrac{36}{40}$

Solve.

39. In a basketball game, the Lakers made 36 out of 45 free throws. What percent of their free throws were made?   80%

40. A record store reported that only 18 out of 90 records sold were instrumentals. What percent of the records sold were instrumentals?   20%

41. A newspaper reported that 30% of the registered voters questioned in a telephone poll favored candidate Robertson. If 66 voters questioned favored Robertson, how many voters were questioned in all?   220

42. The Rattlers' leadoff batter got on base 40% of the time in the month of July. If the batter was on base 38 times, how many times was the batter at bat during July?   95

Solve these proportions.

B **43.** $\dfrac{1}{2}\% = \dfrac{x}{300}$ { 1.5 }   **44.** $\dfrac{3}{4}\% = \dfrac{x}{200}$ { 1.5 }   **45.** $\dfrac{117}{60} = x\%$ { 195 }

46. $\dfrac{126}{90} = x\%$ { 140 }   **47.** $0.35\% = \dfrac{28}{x}$ { 8000 }   **48.** $0.18\% = \dfrac{9}{x}$ { 5000 }

Solve.

49. Burt Corning borrowed $300 for 6 months and was charged $30 interest. What was the annual interest rate of the loan?   20%

50. Carole Ziegler invested $15,000 for 6 months and earned $900 interest. What was the annual interest rate?   12%

51. The Bailey family budgets 30% of its income for food. If they spent $5700 on food in one year, what was their family income? $19,000

52. The annual budget of a large city department was $1,200,000. The next year the budget was 5% greater and the following year it was decreased by 5%. What was the budget after the decrease? $1,197,000

Solve.

C **53.** $\dfrac{x+2}{x+4} = 20\%$ $\left\{-1\dfrac{1}{2}\right\}$ **54.** $\dfrac{x-2}{x-4} = 20\%$ $\left\{1\dfrac{1}{2}\right\}$

55. $\dfrac{x-2}{80} = (x+4)\%$ (26)   **56.** $\dfrac{2x-3}{x+6} = 40\%$ $\left\{3\dfrac{3}{8}\right\}$

57. $\dfrac{2x-3}{20} = (3x-10)\%$ $\left\{\dfrac{5}{7}\right\}$ **58.** $\dfrac{3x+4}{40} = (5x-3)\%$ $\left\{-5\dfrac{1}{5}\right\}$

■ REVIEW EXERCISES

1. Use the graph to find the solution
of this system.

$$x - 3y = 1 \quad \{-2, -1\}$$
$$2x + y = -5$$

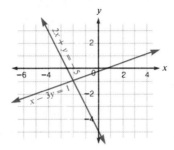

[6–1]

Solve each system by substitution.

[6–2]

2. $y = 2x - 2$ $\{2, 2\}$

$2x + 3y = 10$

3. $y = 2x + 2$ $\{4, 10\}$

$3x + 2y = 32$

State whether the system has one solution, no solution, or infinitely many
solutions.

[6–3]

4. $x + y = 2$ Many solutions

$3x + 3y = 6$

5. $2x + y = 3$ No solution

$2x + y = 4$

Solve each problem by writing a system of equations.

[6–4]

6. One number is 4 more than 3 times another. If the sum of the two numbers
is 100, what are the numbers? $y = 3x + 4, x + y = 100$, 24 and 76

7. A pile of 50 coins consists of nickels and dimes. If its total value is four
dollars, how many coins are nickels and how many are dimes?
$n + d = 50, 5n + 10d = 400$, 20 nickels, 30 dimes

EXTENSION   The "waste factor" in computing prices

Some products that appear to be similar have different prices. One reason for
the difference in price is the varying amount of "waste" included in the product. For example, a ham with the bone in costs less *per pound* than boned ham,
because the bone is waste and because extra labor is needed to remove the bone.
The following problem involves differences in the amounts of a "waste"
element.

Solve.

Regular ground beef that contains 28% fat sells for $1.29 per lb. Lean
ground beef that contains 24% fat sells for $1.89 per lb. Extra-lean ground
beef that contains 20% fat sells for $2.19 per lb. Diet ground beef that
contains 15% fat sells for $2.49 per lb. For which type is the cost per
pound of the nonfat beef the least? For which type is it the greatest?

regular; diet

1. Write 80% as a simplified ratio. $\frac{4}{5}$

2. Solve. $10\% = \frac{30}{x}$ {300}

3. Solve. 5% of 50 = x $\left\{2\frac{1}{2}\right\}$

4. Erasmo invested $200 for 2 years at an annual rate of 8%. How much interest did he earn?

   $32

5. In free-throw practice, Gretchen sank the ball 90% of the time. If she was successful 27 times, how many free throws did she attempt?

   30

PURPOSE

Applying the skills of writing and solving proportions to real-world problems will help students appreciate the usefulness of algebra. Students should see that many very common problems may be solved using the same basic mathematical principles.

PREVIEW

Discuss some of the assumptions that are made. For example, we usually assume that the 30 tagged fish are still living in the pond, that they are scattered about the pond, and that all the fish in the pond have the same chance of being caught in the sample. With these assumptions met, the ratio of the tagged fish to the total number of fish will be constant; that is, $\frac{2}{40} = \frac{30}{?}$.

   Since it is likely that some of the assumptions are *not* met, the answer (600 fish) should be interpreted as an *estimate* of the total number of fish.

LESSON

In discussion, point out that proportions can be used to solve a wide variety of problems. The use of proportions assumes that two ratios are constant and may be set equal.

OBJECTIVE 8–9

To solve problems using proportions.

You may wish to spend two days on this section. Refer to the Pacing Chart.

8–9 Problem Solving—Using Proportions

Preview **A sampling technique**

The Department of Natural Resources wanted to estimate the number of fish in a pond. They caught and tagged 30 fish and returned them to the pond. Several days later, they caught a sample of 40 fish and found that 2 of them had tags. They organized the information in a table.

	In the sample	In the pond
Number of fish with tags	2	30
Total number of fish	40	?

Can you find an estimate of the total number of fish in the pond? 600

In this lesson you will learn how to solve problems using proportions.

■ LESSON

There are many practical situations in which the ratio of two quantities remains constant or is assumed to remain constant. For example, suppose that a school cafeteria serves 9 students in 2 minutes. It is reasonable to assume that all students will be served at the same rate. That is, the ratio of the number of students served to the number of minutes it takes to serve them is $\frac{9}{2}$. If we wish to determine how long it will take to serve 225 students, we set up and solve this proportion.

$$\frac{9}{2} = \frac{225}{x}$$

$$9x = 450$$

$$x = 50$$

It will take 50 minutes to serve 225 students.

If a question requires more than simple recall of a fact, students should be given ample time to generate an answer. A good rule of thumb is to wait until you think students have had enough time, and then wait twice as long.

Example 1 Solve.

Cathy scored 115 points on a 130-point test. What percent of the possible points did she score?

Solution A table can help you write the proportion.

Let x be the percent of points scored by Cathy.

	Ratios	
Number scored	115	x
Number possible	130	100

$$\frac{115}{130} = \frac{x}{100}$$

$$130x = (115)(100)$$

$$x \approx 88.46$$

Answer Cathy scored about 88%.

Example 2 Mary and Cherie shared the costs of buying a car. The ratio of the amount Mary paid to the amount Cherie paid was $\frac{4}{3}$. If the car cost $8400, how much did each pay?

Solution Let $m =$ the amount Mary paid. Then $(8400 - m)$ is the amount Cherie paid.

$$\frac{m}{8400 - m} = \frac{4}{3}$$

$$3m = 33,600 - 4m$$

$$7m = 33,600$$

$$m = 4800$$

Answer Mary paid $4800 and Cherie paid $3600.

Check $4800 + $3600 = $8400; \quad \frac{4800}{3600} = \frac{4 \cdot 1200}{3 \cdot 1200} = \frac{4}{3}$ The answer checks.

■ CLASSROOM EXERCISES

State a proportion for the problem. Solve the proportion and answer the question.

1. If 8 cm on a map represents 96 km, how many kilometers are represented by 12 cm on the map? $\frac{8}{96} = \frac{12}{x}$, 144

2. Human hair grows about 1.95 in. in 2 mo. How long will it take hair to grow 8 in.? $\frac{1.95}{2} = \frac{8}{x}$, about 8 mo

ADDITIONAL EXAMPLES

Example 1.
You notice that a leaking faucet drips 6 times in 10 seconds. Estimate how many times it drips in an hour.

Number of drips	6	x
Number of seconds	10	3600

(One hour = 3600 seconds)

$$\frac{6}{10} = \frac{x}{3600}$$

$$x = 2160$$

2160 drips

Example 2.
The total cost of a tape and a record was $12.60. If the ratio of the cost of the tape to the cost of the record was $\frac{5}{4}$, how much did the record cost?

$$\frac{12.6 - x}{x} = \frac{5}{4}$$

$5.60

CHECK UNDERSTANDING
State a proportion.

• If 25 people were served in the cafeteria in 10 minutes, about how long will it take to serve 110 people? $\left(\frac{25}{10} = \frac{110}{x}\right)$

• A jogger ran 12 miles in 90 minutes. How far did she run in an hour? $\left(\frac{12}{90} = \frac{x}{60}\right)$

CLASSROOM EXERCISES

In exercise 2, indicate that the answer can be quickly estimated. Since the growth is about one inch per month, it takes a little more than 8 months to grow 8 inches. The calculated answer (8.205128 months) and the estimate agree. "About 8 months" is an acceptable answer.

ASSIGNMENT GUIDE

Basic   1–25 odd, Review Exercises
Average   3–27 multiples of 3, 28–36 all,
             Review Exercises
Enriched   3–27 multiples of 3, 29–35 odd,
             37–41 all, Review Exercises

PRACTICE WORKSHEET 44

8-9 PROBLEM SOLVING — USING PROPORTIONS

■ Write a proportion for each problem. Solve the proportion and answer the question.

1. At a checkpoint on Hudson Road, a survey crew found that 1140 cars went by between 3:00 P.M. and 4:00 P.M. How many cars passed the checkpoint each minute?   19

2. A grocery store finds that salt free margarine is preferred by 1 out of 8 customers. If the store orders 200 cases of margarine, how many should be salt free?   25

3. Cynthia Amhof walked 14 mi in 4 h. What was her average speed in miles per hour? At that rate, how long would she take to walk to the post office 0.7 mi away?   3.5 mph; 12 min

4. How much will 12 ounces of cheese cost if it sells for $3.20 per pound? $2.40

5. Joseph Washington got 9 hits in his last 20 times at bat in a baseball game. What was his batting average during that time? (Batting average is number of hits per 1000 times at bat.)   0.450

6. On a map of Florida, 1 in. represents 23 mi. How far is Fort Myers from West Palm Beach if the distance is 5.5 in. on the map?   126.5 mi

■ WRITTEN EXERCISES

Write a proportion that fits the problem. Do not solve.

A 1. The cashier at a supermarket checked out 3 customers every 10 minutes. At that rate, how many customers would be checked out in one hour? $\frac{3}{10} = \frac{n}{60}$

2. Twenty-four persons go on one of the rides at an amusement park every 3 minutes. At that rate, how long would it take 120 people to go on the ride? $\frac{24}{3} = \frac{120}{n}$

3. Cheese is selling for $3.20 per lb. What does 6 oz of cheese cost at that rate? $\frac{3.20}{16} = \frac{n}{6}$

4. A 3-oz package of oriental noodle soup mix costs 36¢. What does 1 lb of mix cost at that rate? $\frac{3}{36} = \frac{16}{n}$

5. Ms. Reed drove at a constant rate of 54 mph. How far did she go in 20 min? $\frac{54}{60} = \frac{n}{20}$

6. Mr. Wright drove at a constant rate of 52 mph. How long did it take him to go 65 mi? $\frac{52}{1} = \frac{65}{n}$

7. Mr. Jefferson received 45% of the votes in a recent election. If 1460 persons voted, how many votes did he get? $\frac{45}{100} = \frac{n}{1460}$

8. Ms. Monroe received 40% of the votes in a recent election. If she got 672 votes, how many people voted in the election? $\frac{40}{100} = \frac{672}{n}$

9. Kathy made 12 of 16 free throws in a basketball game. What percent of her free throws did she make? $\frac{12}{16} = \frac{n}{100}$

10. Brad made 8 of 12 field goal attempts in a basketball game. What percent of his field goal attempts did he make? $\frac{8}{12} = \frac{n}{100}$

Write a proportion for each problem. Solve the proportion and answer the question.

11. On the map of Antarctica, 1 in. represents 1200 mi. How far is Palmer from the South Pole if the distance is $1\frac{1}{2}$ in. on the map?   1800 mi

12. On the map of Colorado, 1.5 cm represents 40 km. How many kilometers is Cortez from Pueblo if the distance is 14.1 cm on the map?   376

13. Ms. Maple drove 756 km and used 56 L of gasoline. What was her average fuel consumption (km/L)?   13.5 km/L

14. Mr. Pine drove 588 mi and used 21 gal of gasoline. What was his average fuel consumption (mi/gal)?   28 mi/gal

15. The sales tax in Davis City is 5%. What is the tax on a purchase that cost $22.84? (Round your answer to the nearest cent.) $1.14

16. The hotel tax in Benton is 8%. What is the tax on a hotel bill of $55.50? $4.44

17. The Mustangs' quarterback completed 80% of his passes. How many passes did he throw if he completed 12?   15

18. The catcher on the Panthers softball team was hitting .350 (350 hits per 1000 at bat). If she had 56 hits, how many times was she at bat? 160

19. Three of the 25 students in a class were absent on Monday. What percent of the students were absent? 12%

20. Tony scored 38 out of a possible 40 points on a test. What percent did he get wrong? 5%

21. Marie is paid $6.25 per hour. How much is she paid for working 4 h, 15 min? $26.56

22. Crystal is paid $6.30 per hour. How many minutes did she work if she was paid $8.19? 78

23. Bars of soap are selling at the price of 3 for $1.17. What will 5 bars of soap cost? $1.95

24. Cans of soup are selling at the price of 2 for 65¢. What will 10 cans of soup cost? $3.25

25. At a constant speed of 55 mph, how many minutes will it take to drive 20 mi? About 22

26. At a constant rate of 4 mph, how many minutes will it take to walk $\frac{2}{3}$ mi? 10

B 27. The width and length of a rectangle are in the ratio $\frac{5}{7}$. How wide is the rectangle if the length is 34 cm more than the width? 85 cm

28. Approximately 9,912,500 people live in Belgium, which has an area of 30,500 km². If Iceland, with an area of approximately 100,000 km², had the same population density (population per square kilometer) as Belgium, what would Iceland's population be? (Iceland's actual population is approximately 230,000.) 32,500,000

29. Alberts topped Barlow in a recent election by a 6-to-5 margin. (The ratio was $\frac{6}{5}$.) How many votes did each get if a total of 4191 votes were cast for the two candidates? Alberts: 2286, Barlow: 1905

30. Approximately 127,500,000 people live in Brazil, which has an area of 8,500,000 km². India has an area of about 3,187,500 km². If India had the same population density as Brazil, what would India's population be? (The actual population of India is more than 670,000,000.) 47,812,500

31. The Ace Financial Company charges 18% on loans for one year. If $2000 is borrowed, how much must be repaid, including the interest charges? $2360

32. If an investment earns $9\frac{1}{2}$% interest for one year, what is the value of a $500 investment after one year, including the interest earned? $547.50

PROBLEM-SOLVING NOTES
Making a table

A table is used in the examples of this lesson to organize the information of each problem. Each table presents the information in a way that makes evident the proportion required to solve the problem. Assist students in learning how to set up such a table, particularly stressing appropriate labels for columns and rows. The choice of a good heading can help students avoid some errors. For example, consider Written Exercise 1.

Poor Choice

Customers checked	3	x
Time	10	1

Better Choice

Customers checked	3	x
Time (in minutes)	10	60

ENRICHMENT PROBLEMS

- Write a word problem for each proportion.

  a. $\frac{40}{100} = \frac{x}{600}$

  b. $\frac{5}{8} = \frac{x}{x + 12}$

33. During their careers in the National Football League, which of these quarterbacks completed the greatest percent of his passes? Bart Starr

Player	Passes attempted	Passes completed	
Sonny Jurgenson	4262	2433	57.1%
Bart Starr	3149	1808	57.4%
Roger Staubach	2958	1685	57.0%
Fran Tarkenton	6467	3686	57.0%
Johnny Unitas	5186	2830	54.6%

34. A $32 sweater is marked "20% off." What is the sale price? $25.60

35. A clerk earns $90 a week plus a commission of 10% on sales. What were the clerk's sales if her total wage for a week was $202.55? $1125.50

36. The Tylers drove 341 mi, getting 27.5-mi/gal fuel consumption. Then they drove 315 mi, getting 25-mi/gal fuel consumption. What was their average fuel consumption for the entire trip? 26.24 mi/gal

C **37.** An investment of $1280 was worth $1382.40 at the end of one year. What was the annual interest rate? 8%

38. A jacket marked $48.50 was on sale for $39.77. What percent was the discount? 18%

39. On a map of Switzerland, 4 cm represents 50 km. How many miles is it from Zurich to Berne if it is 7.4 cm on the map? (1 mi = 1.6 km) Round your answer to the nearest mile. 58

40. In Germany the price of beef is given in marks per kilogram. Suppose that the monetary exchange rate is 2.5 marks per dollar. What is the cost in marks per kilogram of beef that costs $2.40 per pound? (1 kg = 2.2 lb) 13.2 marks per kilogram

41. A jogging suit was on sale for 25% off. When it didn't sell, the price was reduced an additional 20% and marked $19.20. What was the original price? $32

▪ REVIEW EXERCISES

Solve each system by multiplication and addition.

1. $2x - 3y = -7$ {(1, 3)} 　　　　　　**2.** $2x + 3y = 4$ {(−10, 8)} 　　　[6–6]

　$4x + 2y = 10$ 　　　　　　　　　　$3x + 5y = 10$

Solve.

3. We want to create a 10-lb assortment of nuts costing $4.25/lb. In order to do this, we mix nuts worth $4.00/lb with nuts worth $5.00/lb. How many pounds of each will we use? $4/lb: 7.5, $5/lb: 2.5 　　　[6–7]

4. List all of the positive integer factors of 18. 1, 2, 3, 6, 9, 18 　　　[7–1]

5. Write the prime factorization of 60. $2^2 \cdot 3 \cdot 5$ 　　　[7–1]

6. State the greatest common factor of 40 and 60. 20 　　　[7–2]

OBJECTIVE 8–10

You may wish to spend two days on this section. Refer to the Pacing Chart.

To solve direct variation problems.

On a map of the western United States, 1 inch represents 370 miles. Denver is approximately 2.5 inches from San Francisco on the map.

1. Write a proportion that can be solved to find the number of miles from Denver to San Francisco.

$$\frac{1}{370} = \frac{2.5}{x}$$

2. Approximately how far is Denver from San Francisco?

925 miles

Tajma scored 32 out of a possible 40 points on a test.

3. Write a proportion that can be solved to find the percent of possible points that Tajma scored.

$$\frac{32}{40} = \frac{x}{100}$$

4. What percent of the possible points did Tajma score?

80%

5. Driving at a constant speed of 50 miles per hour, how many minutes does it take to drive 15 miles?

18 minutes

8–10 Problem Solving—Direct Variation

Preview

The distance traveled by a person walking at a rate of 5 km/h is shown in the equation, table, and graph.

$$d = 5t$$

Time (h)	0	0.5	1	2	3
Distance (km)	0	2.5	5	10	15

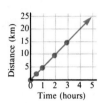

- If the time is doubled, what happens to the distance? It doubles.
- If the time is tripled, what happens to the distance? It triples.
- If the time is halved, what happens to the distance? It is halved.

In the above example one quantity varies proportionately as another. In this lesson you will study this type of function.

■ LESSON

Suppose that someone is paid $4 per hour. If x is the number of hours worked and y is the total wage paid, then these formulas show the relationship between x and y:

$$y = 4x \quad \text{and} \quad \frac{y}{x} = 4$$

This relationship is called **direct variation,** and 4 is called the **constant of variation.** We say that y varies directly as x. That is, the wage paid varies directly as the number of hours worked. Here are some values of x and y.

x	1	2	3	4	5	6
y	4	8	12	16	20	24

Note that if the number of hours is doubled, the wage is doubled, and if the number of hours is divided by three, the total wage is also divided by three. That is what is meant by direct variation—if one value increases or decreases, the other value increases or decreases proportionately.

Both the equation $y = 4x$ and the graph show that when two quantities vary directly, they are components of a linear function in which the y-intercept is 0.

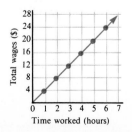

PURPOSE

Many physical problems are examples of direct variation. It is important to be able to recognize and solve such problems.

PREVIEW

The domain of the function is limited to nonnegative numbers. That is, the time must be zero or a positive number of hours; it cannot be negative. In a practical situation, there are upper limits on the domain as well. A person could not walk for 1000 hours, for example. Perhaps the function makes sense only for values of t from 0 to 5.

Point out that the graph is part of a straight line and that it contains the point (0, 0). Both characteristics are important.

LESSON

Although the graph of a direct variation is linear, restrictions on the domain usually prevent the graph from being a complete line. Negative numbers are frequently excluded from the domain. Sometimes the domain is limited to whole numbers, and occasionally there is an upper limit on the set of domain values.

The y-intercept of the line is always 0. The slope is positive for all examples and exercises in this lesson. However, there are examples of direct variation with negative slope.

The equation for direct variation $y = kx$ can be written in the form $\frac{y}{x} = k$. Therefore, direct variation can also be described in terms of constant ratio.

ADDITIONAL EXAMPLES

Example 1.
A car goes 33 miles for each gallon of gasoline used. Does distance traveled vary directly as the fuel consumed?
$$\text{Yes } (d = 33g)$$

Example 2.
If y varies directly as x, and $x = 4$ when $y = 3$, then what is the value of x when $y = 18$?

24

Definition: Direct Variation

A direct variation is a function defined by an equation of the form

$$y = kx \quad \text{or} \quad \frac{y}{x} = k$$

where k is a constant not equal to zero. y is said to *vary directly* as x, and k is called the *constant of variation*.

In this text, we will consider only direct variation in which k is positive.

Example 1 A certain brand of taco sauce costs $.99 per bottle. Does the total cost vary directly as the number of bottles purchased?

Solution If b is the number of bottles purchased and C is the total cost, then this equation shows the relationship:

$$C = 0.99b \quad (b \text{ is a positive integer})$$

Answer The equation is in the form $y = kx$ ($k \neq 0$). Therefore, the total cost varies directly as the number of bottles purchased.

Example 2 A class made arrangements to go on a field trip by having some parents drive their cars. One car would be needed for every 5 students. Does the number of cars vary directly as the number of students?

Solution Here are some values of the numbers of cars and students.

Number of students	1	2	5	6	7	11	16	20
Number of cars	1	1	1	2	2	3	4	4

The number of cars does not increase in the same way that the number of students increases.

Answer The number of cars needed does not vary directly as the number of students.

This graph shows that the relationship between the number of students and the number of cars needed is not linear.

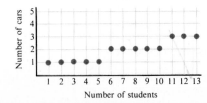

If (x_1, y_1) and (x_2, y_2) are ordered pairs of a direct variation, there is a number k such that

$$y_1 = kx_1 \quad \text{and} \quad y_2 = kx_2,$$

$$\frac{y_1}{x_1} = k \quad \text{and} \quad \frac{y_2}{x_2} = k.$$

So,

$$\frac{y_1}{x_1} = \frac{y_2}{x_2} \quad \text{and} \quad \frac{x_1}{y_1} = \frac{x_2}{x_2}.$$

The following example shows how to use proportions to solve direct variation problems.

Example 3   If y varies directly as x, and $x = 2$ when $y = 7$, then what is the value of x when $y = 16$?

Solution   Since y varies directly as x, we can write this proportion:

$$\frac{2}{7} = \frac{x}{16}$$

$$7x = 32$$

$$x = \frac{32}{7}$$

Answer   When $y = 16$, $x = \frac{32}{7}$.

■ CLASSROOM EXERCISES

Does y vary directly as x?

1. $y = 7x$ Yes

2. $y = 3x + 1$ No

3. $y = x^2$ No

4. $\frac{y}{x} = 10$ Yes

5.
x	1	2	3	4	5
y	1.5	3	4.5	6	7.5

Yes

6.
x	1	2	3	4	5
y	3	6	7	8	9

No

7.   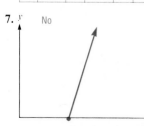   No

8.   Yes

9. Suppose that x and y vary directly. If x is 5 when y is 3, what is the value of x when y is 15?   25

10. A bicyclist rides at the constant rate of 25 km/h. Do the distance ridden and the time ridden vary directly?   Yes

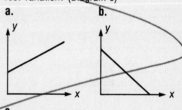
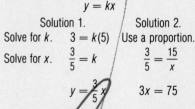

ASSIGNMENT GUIDE

Basic 3–39 multiples of 3, Review Exer-
cises, Self-Quiz 3
Average 3–45 multiples of 3, 46–48 all,
Review Exercises, Self-Quiz 3
Enriched 3–48 multiples of 3, 49–52 all,
Review Exercises, Self-Quiz 3

PRACTICE WORKSHEET 45

8-10 PROBLEM SOLVING: DIRECT VARIATION

■ Suppose y varies directly as x.

1. $y = 7$ when $x = 8$. Find y when $x = 12$. __10.5__

2. $y = 12$ when $x = 5$. Find y when $x = 60$. __144__

3. $y = 15$ when $x = 4$. Find x when $y = 120$. __32__

4. $y = 100$ when $x = 96$. Find x when $y = 25$. __24__

5. $y = 2$ when $x = 300$. Find y when $x = 50$. __1/3__

6. $y = 10$ when $x = 2$. Find y when $x = 120$. __600__

■ Suppose the quantities in the following exercises vary directly.
Write an equation that fits the problem. Solve the equation and
answer the question.

7. Rebecca Frank worked 3 h babysitting and was paid $6.75. How much is she paid for babysitting 2 h? __$4.50__

8. Three of every 48 Glitch Radios are defective. How many defective radios are expected in a shipment of 32 Glitch Radios? __2__

9. A recipe that serves 12 takes $\frac{3}{4}$ cup of milk to prepare. To make the recipe to serve 18, how much milk should be used? __1 1/8 cup__

10. Thirty marbles weigh 200 g. How many marbles weigh 1 kg? __150__

EXTRA PRACTICE, page 636

■ WRITTEN EXERCISES

Determine whether y varies directly as x.

A

1. $y = 3x + 2$ No

2. $y = \frac{1}{3}x + 6$ No

3. $y = \frac{1}{2}x$ Yes

4. $y = 4x$ Yes

5. $\frac{y}{x} = 6$ Yes

6. $\frac{y}{x} = 5$ Yes

7.

x	2	4	6	8
y	1	2	3	4

Yes

8.

x	3	6	9	12
y	3	6	7	8

No

9.

x	4	8	12	16
y	2	6	10	14

No

10.

x	1	2	3	4
y	12	6	4	3

No

11. No
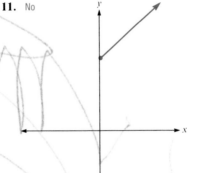

12. No
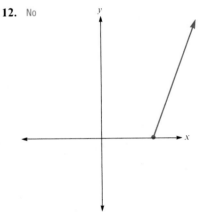

13. Yes
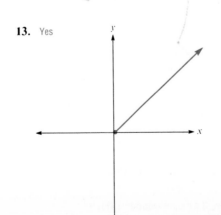

14. Yes
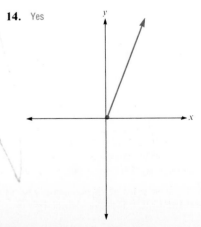

15. First-class stamps cost 22¢. Let x = the number of stamps purchased and y = the total cost of the stamps. Yes

16. Shawn charges $1 plus $1.50 per hour for babysitting. Let x = the number of hours babysitting and y = Shawn's total charge. No

17. The width of a rectangle is 5 cm. Let x = the length in centimeters and y = the area in square centimeters. Yes

18. The base of a triangle is 10 cm. Let x = the altitude in centimeters and y = the area in square centimeters. Yes

19. The area of a rectangle is 24 cm². Let x = the length in centimeters and y = the width in centimeters. No

20. A walker traveled 6 miles. Let x = the walker's rate (in miles per hour) and y = the time (in hours). No

Suppose y varies directly as x. Find the constant of variation, k.

21. $y = 8$ when $x = 2$ 4   22. $y = 8$ when $x = 4$ 2   23. $y = 2$ when $x = 8$ $\frac{1}{4}$

24. $y = 4$ when $x = 8$ $\frac{1}{2}$ 25. $y = 13$ when $x = 7$ $\frac{13}{7}$ 26. $y = 17$ when $x = 11$ $\frac{17}{11}$

Suppose y varies directly as x in the following exercises.

27. $y = 2$ when $x = 3$. Find y when $x = 24$.   16

28. $y = 2$ when $x = 3$. Find y when $x = 18$.   12

29. $y = 2$ when $x = 3$. Find x when $y = 24$.   36

30. $y = 2$ when $x = 3$. Find x when $y = 18$.   27

31. $y = 15$ when $x = 12$. Find y when $x = 40$.   50

32. $y = 15$ when $x = 12$. Find y when $x = 100$.   125

33. $y = 15$ when $x = 12$. Find x when $y = 40$.   32

34. $y = 15$ when $x = 12$. Find x when $y = 100$.   80

Suppose the quantities in the following exercises vary directly. Write an equation that fits the problem. Solve the equation and answer the question.

35. Jenny worked 5 h and was paid $18.75. How much is she paid for working 8 h? $\frac{5}{18.75} = \frac{8}{x}$, $30

36. A 10-m length of string weighs 350 g. How long is a string that weighs 875 g? $\frac{10}{350} = \frac{x}{875}$, 25 m

37. When the population of Falls City was 25,000, the residents used 40,000,000 gal of water in one year. Estimate the amount of water which will be used by the residents of Falls City when the population grows to 35,000. $\frac{25,000}{40,000,000} = \frac{35,000}{x}$, 56,000,000 gal

38. Eight slices of white enriched bread yield 18 g of protein. How many grams of protein are in 3 slices of white enriched bread? $\frac{8}{18} = \frac{3}{x}$, 6.75

CONCEPT EXTENSION

The equation for a direct variation is linear and of the form $y = kx$. The constant of proportionality, k, is also the slope of the function. Since $k = \frac{y}{x}$, the ratio of y to x is constant. Slope is a measure of the change in y for a unit change in x. The following relationships are well worth pointing out for direct-variation relationships or linear relationships in general.

Suppose $y = 3x$ is the equation for a direct variation. Then the following tables of values could be written:

x	y
0	0
1	3
2	6
3	9
4	12

For unit changes in x, the change in y-values is the constant of proportionality (or slope).

x	y
0	$(3 \cdot 0)$
1	$(3 \cdot 1)$
2	$(3 \cdot 2)$
3	$(3 \cdot 3)$
·	·
·	·
·	·
x	$3x$

ENRICHMENT PROBLEM

- Suppose y varies directly as x and the constant of proportionality is 5. Let (x, y) be a pair of values that satisfies the variation.
  - **a.** If x increases by 1, how is y changed?

    Increases by 5
  - **b.** If y decreases by 2, how is x changed?

    Decreases by ⅖
  - **c.** If the x value is doubled, how is y changed?

    Doubled
  - **d.** By what amount must y change to cause x to increase by 10?

    Increase by 50

39. A gallon of paint will cover 450 ft^2 of a previously painted smooth surface. How many gallons of paint are needed to cover 2000 ft^2? (Round your answer to the nearest whole number of gallons.) $\frac{1}{450} = \frac{x}{2000}$; 4

40. A gallon of paint will cover 300 ft^2 of an unpainted rough surface. How many gallons of paint are needed to cover 2000 ft^2? (Round your answer to the nearest whole number of gallons.) $\frac{1}{300} = \frac{x}{2000}$; 7

Which of the following relations are examples of direct variation?

B 41. $y - 2x = 0$ Yes   42. $y - 8 = x + 8$ No   43. $\dfrac{y + 14}{2} = x + 7$ Yes

44. The amount of gasoline purchased and its cost. (Number of gallons, number of dollars.) Yes

45. The weight of an object in grams and its weight in kilograms. (Number of grams, number of kilograms.) Yes

46. A student's age and the student's grade level. (Number of years, number of the grade level.) No

The formula $V = kT$ (Charles' Law) expresses the relationship between the volume of a gas V under constant pressure and its temperature T measured in degrees Kelvin. Use the formula to solve these problems.

47. Nine cubic meters of oxygen are kept under constant pressure while the oxygen's temperature is raised from 300° Kelvin to 350° Kelvin. What is the new volume? 10.5 m^3

48. Forty liters of helium, kept under constant pressure, are cooled from 373° Kelvin (the boiling point of water) to 273° Kelvin (the freezing point of water). What is the new volume? (Round your answer to the nearest whole number of liters.) 29 L

If there is a constant k such that $y = kx^2$ (or $y = kx^3$), then we say that y varies directly as the square (or cube) of x. Write an equation that fits the problem. Solve the equation and answer the question.

C 49. The surface area of a cube varies directly as the square of the length of an edge. If the edge is 3 cm and the surface area is 54 cm^2, what is the surface area of a cube when the edge is 6 cm? [*Hint:* To find k, solve $54 = k(3^2)$.]
216 cm^2

50. The area of a circle varies directly as the square of its diameter. If the diameter is 100 m, the area is 7854 m^2. What is the area of a circle when the diameter is 1000 m? 785,400 m^2

51. The volume of a tetrahedron varies directly as the cube of the length of one of its edges. The volume is 117.85 cm^3 when the edge is 10 cm. What is the volume when the edge is 100 cm? 117,850 cm^3

52. The surface area of a sphere varies directly as the square of its diameter. The surface area is 28.278 cm^2 when the diameter is 3 cm. What is the radius of a sphere if its surface area is 113.112 cm^2?
3 cm

■ REVIEW EXERCISES

Expand and simplify.

1. $(x + 3)(x - 5)$ $x^2 - 2x - 15$ **2.** $(2x + 3)(x + 4)$ $2x^2 + 11x + 12$ [7–5]

Factor completely.

3. $2a^2 - 6a$ $2a(a - 3)$ [7–4]

4. $x^2 - 49$ $(x + 7)(x - 7)$ [7–6]

5. $x^2 + 10x + 25$ $(x + 5)^2$ [7–7]

6. $x^2 - 7x + 12$ $(x - 4)(x - 3)$ [7–8]

7. $x^2 + 2x - 8$ $(x + 4)(x - 2)$ [7–9]

8. $2x^2 + 5x + 3$ $(2x + 3)(x + 1)$ [7–10]

a	b	c	d
−6	12	−4	3

Substitute and simplify.

9. $\dfrac{a}{b} + \dfrac{c}{d}$ $-\dfrac{11}{6}$ **10.** $\dfrac{(a + c)}{(b + d)}$ $-\dfrac{2}{3}$ **11.** $\dfrac{a}{b} \cdot \dfrac{c}{d}$ $\dfrac{2}{3}$ **12.** $\dfrac{ac}{bd}$ $\dfrac{2}{3}$ [2–5]

Self-Quiz 3

8–7,
8–8 Solve.

1. $\dfrac{16}{x} = \dfrac{4}{3}$ { 12 }   **2.** $\dfrac{y - 1}{y + 2} = \dfrac{2}{5}$ { 3 }

3. $15\% = \dfrac{45}{x}$ { 300 }   **4.** $\dfrac{w}{w + 17} = 32\%$ { 8 }

8–8,
8–9

5. The interest charged on a \$4500 loan over a period of 30 months was \$1575. What was the annual interest rate? 14%

6. The width and height of a rectangular window are in the ratio $\dfrac{5}{9}$. What is the height if it is 36 cm more than the width? 81 cm

7. The Rowdies basketball team was successful on 45% of their shots in one game. How many shots did they shoot if they made 36 baskets? 80

8–10

8. Suppose that y varies directly as x. If $y = 48$ when $x = 15$, find y when $x = 35$. 112

Determine whether *y* varies directly as *x*.

1. $y = 3x + 10$ No

2.

x	1	2	3	4
y	5	10	15	20

Yes

3. The length of a side of a square is *x* cm and the perimeter of the square is *y* cm.   Yes

Suppose *b* varies directly as *a* in these exercises.

4. $b = 15$ when $a = 5$. Find *b* when $a = 10$.   30

5. $b = 8$ when $a = 16$. Find *a* when $b = 10$.   20

PURPOSE

It is important to be able to recognize examples of inverse variation and to solve inverse-variation problems.

PREVIEW
Additional Preview questions:

- Which function could be described as follows? *x* and *y* are the width and length of a rectangle that has an area of 16 cm². (E)
- Which function is an example of none of these: constant product, constant quotient, constant sum, constant difference? (C)

Point out that constant-quotient functions (for example, A) are examples of direct variation, studied in the previous lesson.

OBJECTIVE 8–11

To solve inverse variation problems.

You may wish to spend two days on this section. Refer to the Pacing Chart.

8–11 Problem Solving—Inverse Variation

Preview

Compare the *x*- and *y*-values in these functions. In which functions is the product of the *x*- and *y*-values constant?   B, E

In which ones is the difference or quotient constant?   A, D

A:

x	30	60	45	15	900
y	1	2	1.5	0.5	30

B:

x	30	15	10	7.5	6
y	1	2	3	4	5

C:

x	10	12	14	16	18
y	14	15	16	17	18

D:

x	10	12	14	16	18
y	12	14	16	18	20

E:

x	0.5	1	2	4	8
y	32	16	8	4	2

F:

x	6	10	14	18	22
y	24	20	16	12	8

Did you find that two functions have constant products?

For each statement below, identify the function above (A, B, C, D, E, or F) that is being described.

- *x* and *y* are the length and width of a rectangle that has an area of 30 cm².   B
- *x* and *y* are the area and width of a rectangle that is 30 cm long.   A
- *x* and *y* are the width and length of a rectangle in which the length is 2 cm more than the width.   D

In this lesson you will study functions involving constant products.

■ LESSON

Suppose that you have to drive 100 mi. This table shows the time that would be required to complete the trip at various speeds.

Rate (mph)	2	5	10	20	25	50
Time (h)	50	20	10	5	4	2

Note that as one quantity gets larger, the other gets proportionately smaller. For example, if the speed is doubled from 5 mph to 10 mph, the time is halved from 20 h to 10 h. If the speed is quartered from 20 mph to 5 mph, the time is quadrupled from 5 h to 20 h. The product of the rate *r* and the time *t* is always equal to the constant distance 100.

$$rt = 100$$

Various learning activities are best supported by different seating arrangements. For example, lecture-demonstration is most efficient in a conventional system of seating students in rows. Discussions in-volving student-student interaction are best carried out with students facing each other in a U-shape. When students work together in small groups on problems or projects, desks should be clustered in groups.

LESSON

In discussion, bring out the point that inverse variation is an example of a constant product, $xy = k$. Ask students whether it is sufficient in describing an inverse variation to simply state that y gets larger as x gets smaller and vice versa. Use $y = 10 - x$ as an example to illustrate that other functions (not necessarily inverse variations) could fit the description.

The graph of the equation shows that as r gets larger, t gets smaller, and as r gets smaller, t gets larger. The graph is not a straight line, so clearly this is not a linear function. The equation is a second-degree equation and its graph is part of a curve called a **hyperbola.**

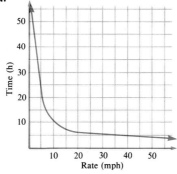

We say that time **varies inversely** as the rate.

ADDITIONAL EXAMPLES

Example 1.
   Consider all triangles with area equal to 15 cm². Do their bases and heights vary inversely?

Yes ($bh = 30$)

Definition: Inverse Variation

An inverse variation is a function defined by an equation of the form

$$xy = k \quad \text{or} \quad y = \frac{k}{x},$$

where k is a constant greater than 0. y is said to *vary inversely* as x, and k is called the *constant of variation*.

Example 1   Consider all rectangles with area equal to 12 cm². Do their lengths and widths vary inversely?

Solution   The formula for the area of a rectangle is $lw = A$. In his case the area is 12.

$$lw = 12$$

This equation has the required form, $xy = k$ where $k = 12$.

Answer   The length and width of rectangles with areas equal to 12 cm² vary inversely.

420

ADDITIONAL EXAMPLES

Example 2.

Draw a graph of the equation $bh = 30$.

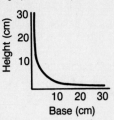

Example 3.

Suppose that y varies inversely as x, and that $y = 6$ when $x = 4$. What is the value of y when $x = 3$?

$$x_1 y_1 = x_2 y_2$$
$$4(6) = 3(y_2)$$
$$8 = y_2$$

CHECK UNDERSTANDING

- Which of these diagrams is a graph of an inverse variation? (Diagram b)

a.

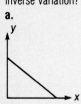

b.

c.

- If x and y vary inversely, and $y = 4$ when $x = 5$, what is the constant of variation? (20)

Example 2 Draw the graph of the equation $lw = 12$.

Solution Since it would not make sense to have negative values for the length and width, $l > 0$ and $w > 0$.

Make a table of some values of l and w.

Length (cm)	$\frac{1}{2}$	1	2	3	4	6	12	24
Width (cm)	24	12	6	4	3	2	1	$\frac{1}{2}$

Answer

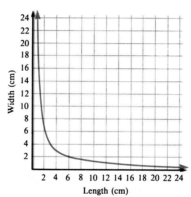

Example 3 Suppose that y varies inversely as x. If $x = 3$ when $y = 12$, what is the value of y when $x = 9$?

Solution Since y varies inversely as x, there is a k such that

$$x_1 y_1 = k \quad \text{and} \quad x_2 y_2 = k$$

so

$$x_1 y_1 = x_2 y_2.$$

Substitute 3 for x_1, 12 for y_1, and 9 for x_2.

$$3(12) = 9y_2$$

Solve for y_2. $$36 = 9y_2$$

$$4 = y_2$$

Answer When $x = 9$, $y = 4$.

■ CLASSROOM EXERCISES

Does y vary inversely as x? If it does, state the value of the constant of variation.

1. $xy = 4$ Yes, 4

2. $2xy = 8$ Yes, 4

3. $xy - 1 = 9$ Yes, 10

4. $3x = y$ No

5. $\dfrac{xy}{2} = 3$ Yes, 6

6. $y = \dfrac{2}{x}$ Yes, 2

7.

x	1	2	3	6	9	18
y	18	9	6	3	2	1

Yes, 18

8.

x	1	2	3	4	5	6	7	8	9
y	9	8	7	6	5	4	3	2	1

No

9. 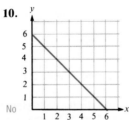   Yes, 6

10. No

11. Suppose that y varies inversely as x. If $x = 5$ when $y = 10$, what is the value of x when $y = 4$? $12\frac{1}{2}$

12. Graph $xy = 6$ for $x > 0$.   See Classroom Exercise 9.

■ WRITTEN EXERCISES

Indicate how x and y vary—inversely, directly, or "other."

A

1. $xy = 18$ Inversely

2. $xy = 24$ Inversely

3. $y = \dfrac{2}{3}x$ Directly

4. $y = \dfrac{3}{4}x$ Directly

5. $xy = \dfrac{4}{3}$ Inversely

6. $xy = \dfrac{6}{5}$ Inversely

7. $x + y = 24$ Other

8. $x + y = 18$ Other

9. $y = \dfrac{5}{x}$ Inversely

10. $y = \dfrac{8}{x}$ Inversely

11. $xy + 2 = 2xy - 2$ Inversely

12. $xy - 3 = 3xy - 30$ Inversely

Find the constant of variation, k.

13. $xy = 20$ 20

14. $xy = \dfrac{1}{20}$ $\dfrac{1}{20}$

15. $y = \dfrac{0.5}{x}$ 0.5

16. $y = \dfrac{10}{x}$ 10

17. $3xy - 6 = 15$ 7

18. $2xy - 4 = 16$ 10

WRITTEN EXERCISES

ASSIGNMENT GUIDE

PRACTICE WORKSHEET 46

8-11 PROBLEM SOLVING — INVERSE VARIATION

■ Suppose that x and y vary inversely.

1. $y = 12$ when $x = 50$. Find y when $x = 60$.   10

2. $y = 1.5$ when $x = 4$. Find x when $y = 12$.   0.5

3. $y = 6$ when $x = 5$. Find y when $x = 15$.   2

4. $y = 0.2$ when $x = 5$. Find x when $y = 20$.   0.05

5. $y = 12$ when $x = 3$. Find y when $x = \frac{1}{2}$.   72

6. $y = 500$ when $x = 3$. Find x when $y = 100$.   15

■ Suppose the quantities in the following exercises vary inversely. Write an equation that fits the problem. Solve the equation and answer the question.

7. A class of 25 contributed $3 per student to pay for the rental of a bus. If only 15 students agree to share the rental charge next time, how much will each have to pay? $5

8. Averaging 80 km/h, a sales representative covered her route in 5 h. The return trip took 8 h. What was the sales representative's average speed on the return trip?   50 km/h

9. A can of paint will cover a strip 5 in. wide and 720 ft long. If the strip is 6 in. wide, how long is the strip that can be painted?   600 ft

10. A square and a regular hexagon have the same perimeter. How long is each side of the hexagon if each side of the square is 1 ft?   2/3 ft

19.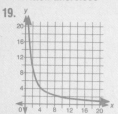

20.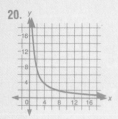

21.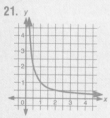

22.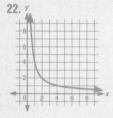

23.

24.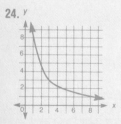

Graph each equation for $x > 0$.

19. $xy = 18$ **20.** $xy = 15$ **21.** $y = \dfrac{1}{x}$

22. $y = \dfrac{4}{x}$ **23.** $xy + 2 = 8$ **24.** $xy - 3 = 6$

Assume that x and y vary inversely in the following exercises.

25. $y = 5$ when $x = 6$. Find y when $x = 12$. $2\frac{1}{2}$

26. $y = 8$ when $x = 5$. Find y when $x = 2.5$.   16

27. $y = 5$ when $x = 6$. Find x when $y = 10$.   3

28. $y = 8$ when $x = 5$. Find x when $y = 4$.   10

29. $y = \dfrac{1}{2}$ when $x = 40$. Find y when $x = 20$.   1

30. $y = \dfrac{1}{3}$ when $x = 30$. Find y when $x = 10$.   1

Assume that the quantities in the following exercises vary inversely. Write an equation that fits the problem. Solve the equation and answer the question.

31. A distance was traveled in 4 h at an average speed of 50 mph. The return trip was made in 5 h. What was the average speed on the return trip?
(50)(4) = (x)(5); 40 mph

32. A trip was made in 4 h at an average speed of 55 mph. The return trip was made in 5 h. What was the average speed on the return trip?
(55)(4) = (x)(5); 44 mph

33. A canoeist paddled downstream for 5 h, averaging 6 mph. On the return trip the average speed against the current was 3 mph. How long did it take the canoeist to make the return trip?   (6)(5) = 3x; 10 h

34. Flying into a headwind, a light plane, averaging 180 mph, took 2 h 20 min to reach its destination. The return trip, flying with a tailwind, took only 2 h. What was the average speed on the return trip?
(180)(140) = (x)(120); 210 mph

35. The average score for the starting five players on a basketball team was 12 points each. If one of the players made no points, how many points would each of the other 4 players have to average in order for the starting team to maintain its average score?   4x = (5)(12); 15

36. Twenty-five students were asked to contribute $4 each for a class project. If 5 of the students did not contribute, how much must each of the other students contribute to achieve the same total?   (25)(4) = 20x; $5

37. A gallon of paint will cover a length of 50 ft of a wall that is 9 ft high. What length of a 10-ft high wall would be covered by this gallon of paint?
(9)(50) = 10x; 45 ft

38. A bag of lawn food covers a rectangular lawn that is 40 ft wide and 125 ft long. A golf course has a strip of lawn that is 8 ft wide along a path. How long a strip could be covered by a bag of lawn food?   40(125) = 8x; 625 ft

$y = \dfrac{4}{x}$		$y = 4x$	
x	y	x	y
¼	16	¼	1
½	8	½	2
1	4	1	4
2	2	2	8
4	1	4	16

39. A regular hexagon and a regular octagon have the same perimeter. The hexagon's sides are 12 cm long. How long is each of the octagon's sides?   (6)(12) = 8x; 9 cm

40. An equilateral triangle and a square have the same perimeter. How long is a side of the square if each side of the triangle is 90 cm?   (3)(90) = 4x; 67.5 cm

If two objects on a lever are balanced, their mass and their distance from the *fulcrum* (point of balance) vary inversely. For example, a 60-g object that is 8 cm from the fulcrum balances a 40-g object that is 12 cm from the fulcrum (since $60 \cdot 8 = 40 \cdot 12$).

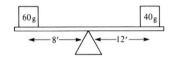

B **41.** If a 50-kg object 2 m from a fulcrum balances a 40-kg object, how far is the 40-kg object from the fulcrum?   (50)(2) = 40x; 2.5 m

42. A 100-kg object 1.8 m from a fulcrum balances an object that is 1.2 m from the fulcrum. What is the mass of the other object?   (1.8)(100) = 1.2x; 150 kg

43. How much mass must be placed 2 m from the fulcrum to balance a 74-kg object that is 2.2 m from the fulcrum?   2x = (2.2)(74); 81.4 kg

44. A 40-kg object and a 60-kg object are placed on opposite ends of a board that is 3 m long. How far from the 40-kg object is the fulcrum if the objects are balanced?   40x = 60(3 − x); 1.8 m

45. A 174-lb person and 114-lb person sitting on opposite ends of a 12-ft seesaw are in balance. How far is the fulcrum from the 174-lb person?
174x = (114)(12 − x); $4\frac{3}{4}$ ft

The formula $PV = k$ (Boyle's Law) expresses the relationship between the volume of a gas V at a constant temperature and its pressure P. Use the formula to solve these problems.

46. The pressure acting on 10 m³ of air is raised from 1 atmosphere to 2 atmospheres. The temperature is kept constant. What is the volume of the air after the pressure is applied?   5 m³

47. A helium-filled balloon has a volume of 20 m³ at sea level (where the pressure is 1 atmosphere). What is the volume of the balloon after it rises to an altitude where the pressure is 0.8 atmosphere? (Assume its temperature is kept constant.)   25 m³

ENRICHMENT PROBLEM

- Classify these real-world situations as approximately the behavior of direct variation, inverse variation, or neither.
  - **a.** light intensity versus distance from a light source
  - **b.** hunger versus elapsed time from eating a meal
  - **c.** your height versus your age
  - **d.** sound intensity versus distance from a speaker
  - **e.** level of drowsiness versus number of hours from awaking
  - **f.** sales tax rate versus cost of an item

  Direct variation: b, e
  Inverse variation: a, d
  Neither: c, f

- State some other examples of behaviors that could be classified as direct or inverse variation.

  Direct variation:
  a. Height of a balloon versus temperature of gas in it.
  b. Distance traveled versus time traveled (constant rate).
  c. Pressure versus distance below sea level.
  d. Salary earned versus years of education completed.

  Inverse variation:
  a. Gravitational attraction versus distance from Earth.
  b. Rate versus time traveled (constant distance).
  c. Temperature versus distance above sea level.
  d. Test scores versus hours of television watched.

48. At a depth of 21 m under water, the pressure is 3 atmospheres. At the surface the pressure is 1 atmosphere. A bubble of air with a volume of 6 cm³ escapes from the mouthpiece of a diver working 21 m below the surface. What is the volume of the bubble as it reaches the surface? 18 cm³

Solve.

C **49.** In ellipses that have an area of 100 cm², the values of a and b vary inversely. If $a = 3$ cm when $b = 10.61$ cm, what does b equal when $a = 1.5$ cm? 21.22 cm

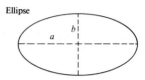
Ellipse

50. In pyramids that have a volume of 720 cm³, the altitude (in centimeters) and the area of the base (in square centimeters) vary inversely. When the altitude is 30 cm, the area of the base is 72 cm². What is the area of the base if the altitude is 20 cm? 108 cm²

51. In pyramids with square bases that have a volume of 540 cm³, the altitude (in centimeters) and the square of the length of a side of the square vary inversely. When the altitude is 20 cm, the side of the square is 9 cm. What is the side of the square when the altitude is 5 cm? 18 cm

■ REVIEW EXERCISES

Solve.

1. $x(x + 5) = 0$ $\{0, -5\}$ **2.** $(x + 4)(2x - 1) = 0$ $\left\{-4, \frac{1}{2}\right\}$ [7-3]

3. $x^2 + 3x = 0$ $\{0, -3\}$ **4.** $2x^2 = -6x$ $\{0, -3\}$ [7-4]

5. $x^2 + 12x + 36 = 0$ $\{-6\}$ **6.** $x^2 + 16x + 64 = 0$ $\{-8\}$ [7-7]

7. $2x^2 + 7x - 4 = 0$ $\left\{-4, \frac{1}{2}\right\}$ **8.** $3x^2 + 4x - 4 = 0$ $\left\{-2, \frac{2}{3}\right\}$ [7-10]

■ CHAPTER SUMMARY

- **Vocabulary**

algebraic fractions	[page 359]	rate	[page 402]
admissible value	[page 359]	principal	[page 402]
equivalent fractions	[page 360]	interest	[page 402]
least common denominator	[page 376]	direct variation	[page 411]
ratio	[page 394]	constant of variation	[page 411]
proportion	[page 394]	hyperbola	[page 419]
cross multiply	[page 395]	inverse variation	[page 419]
percent	[page 400]		

- Two fractions are equivalent if one of them can be transformed into the other by multiplication or division.

  For all numbers a, b, and c ($b \neq 0$ and $c \neq 0$),

  $$\frac{a}{b} = \frac{ac}{bc} \quad \text{and} \quad \frac{a}{b} = \frac{a \div c}{b \div c}$$

  [8–1]

- Multiplying fractions

  For all numbers a, b, c, and d ($b \neq 0$ and $d \neq 0$),

  $$\frac{a}{b} \cdot \frac{c}{d} = \frac{ac}{bd}$$

  [8–2]

- Dividing fractions

  For all numbers a, b, c, and d ($b \neq 0$, $c \neq 0$, and $d \neq 0$),

  $$\frac{a}{b} \div \frac{c}{d} = \frac{a}{b} \cdot \frac{d}{c}$$

  [8–2]

- Adding or subtracting fractions with like denominators

  For all numbers a, b, and c ($c \neq 0$),

  $$\frac{a}{c} + \frac{b}{c} = \frac{a+b}{c} \quad \text{and} \quad \frac{a}{c} - \frac{b}{c} = \frac{a-b}{c}$$

  [8–3]

- To add or subtract fractions with unlike denominators, transform the fractions into equivalent fractions with a common denominator.

  [8–4]

- Adding or subtracting fractions with unlike denominators

  For all numbers a, b, c, and d ($c \neq 0$ and $d \neq 0$),

  $$\frac{a}{c} + \frac{b}{d} = \frac{ad+bc}{cd} \quad \text{and} \quad \frac{a}{c} - \frac{b}{d} = \frac{ad-bc}{cd}$$

- To find the least common multiple of the denominators of two algebraic fractions, write the prime factorization of each denominator. Then identify the highest power of each prime factor and write the product of the highest powers.

  [8–5]

- To solve an equation containing fractions, multiply both sides of the equation by the least common denominator of the fractions to clear the equation of fractions.

- Cross-multiplication property

  For all real numbers a, b, c, and d ($b \neq 0$ and $d \neq 0$),

  $$\text{if } \frac{a}{b} = \frac{c}{d}, \text{ then } ad = bc.$$

  [8–7]

- A ratio written as a fraction can be changed to a percent by:

  [8–8]

  1. changing to an equivalent fraction with a denominator of 100 and then writing the numerator of that fraction followed by a percent symbol, or

  2. changing the fraction to a decimal, multiplying the decimal by 100, and writing that number followed by a percent symbol.

- If $a\%$ of $b = c$, then

  $$\frac{a}{100} \cdot b = c \quad \text{and} \quad \frac{a}{100} = \frac{c}{b}$$

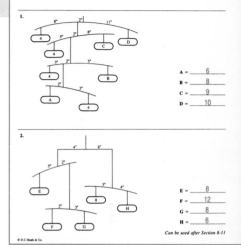

- The relationship between interest (i), principal (p), rate (r), and time (t) is given by the formula $i = prt$. [8–10]

- A direct variation is a function defined by an equation of the form [8–11]

$$y = kx \quad \text{or} \quad \frac{y}{x} = k, \ k \neq 0$$

- An indirect variation is a function defined by an equation of the form [8–11]

$$xy = k \quad \text{or} \quad y = \frac{k}{x}, \ k > 0$$

■ CHAPTER REVIEW

8–1 Objectives: To determine admissible values of variables in algebraic fractions.
To simplify algebraic fractions.

1. Which values of x are not admissible for the fraction $\dfrac{x}{x - 1}$ to be defined? $x = 1$

2. State whether the fractions $\dfrac{2x + 1}{3x + 1}$ and $\dfrac{2x}{3x}$ are equivalent. No

Simplify. List any necessary restrictions on the variables.

3. $\dfrac{2x^2y}{4xy}$ $\frac{x}{2}; x \neq 0, y \neq 0$

4. $\dfrac{(x + 2)(x - 1)}{(x - 1)(x - 2)}$ $\frac{x+2}{x-2}; x \neq 1, 2$

8–2 Objective: To multiply and divide algebraic fractions.

Simplify. Assume that no denominator is zero.

5. $\dfrac{6x}{y} \cdot \dfrac{2y}{3x^2}$ $\frac{4}{x}$

6. $\dfrac{(a + b)^2}{(a + b)(a - b)} \cdot \dfrac{a - b}{a + b}$ 1

7. $\dfrac{16a^2}{9b} \div \dfrac{4a}{3b}$ $\frac{4a}{3}$

8. $\dfrac{x(x - y)}{xy} \div \dfrac{x - y}{y(x - y)}$ $x - y$

8–3 Objective: To add and subtract fractions with like denominators.

Simplify. Assume that no denominator is zero.

9. $\dfrac{2c}{c + 4} + \dfrac{8}{c + 4}$ 2

10. $\dfrac{4h}{h^2 - 16} - \dfrac{16}{h^2 - 16}$ $\frac{4}{h+4}$

Simplify. List any necessary restrictions on the variables.

11. $\dfrac{b}{b + 2} - \dfrac{4}{b + 2}$ $\frac{b-4}{b+2}; b \neq -2$

12. $\dfrac{2a + 4}{a - 1} + \dfrac{a - 7}{a - 1}$ $3; a \neq 1$

8–4 Objective: To add and subtract fractions with unlike denominators.

13. State the least common denominator for $\dfrac{3}{2ab^2}$ and $\dfrac{5}{12a^2}$. $12a^2b^2$

Simplify. Assume that no denominator is zero.

14. $\dfrac{3}{x} - \dfrac{2}{3x}$ $\dfrac{7}{3x}$

15. $\dfrac{1}{mn} + \dfrac{3}{n^2}$ $\dfrac{n+3m}{mn^2}$

16. $\dfrac{6}{y^2+2} - \dfrac{4}{y}$ $\dfrac{-4y^2+6y-8}{y(y^2+2)}$

8–5 Objective: To solve equations that contain algebraic fractions.

Solve.

17. $\dfrac{x}{36} = \dfrac{4}{9}$ $\{\,16\,\}$

18. $\dfrac{3}{y} = \dfrac{2}{3} - \dfrac{5}{y}$ $\{\,12\,\}$

19. $x + \dfrac{5}{x} = 6$ $\{\,1,5\,\}$

8–6 Objective: To use fractional equations to solve problems.

Solve.

20. A circuit is made up of two resistors in parallel. The total resistance is 4 ohms. If one of the resistors has a resistance of 12 ohms, what is the resistance of the other resistor? (Use the equation $\dfrac{1}{R} = \dfrac{1}{r_1} + \dfrac{1}{r_2}$). 6Ω

21. If one printing press can complete a job in a 4 h and another press can complete the job in 6 h, how long will it take both machines working together to complete the job? $2\frac{2}{5}$ h

8–7 Objective: To simplify ratios and to solve proportions.

22. For the ratio 14 in. to 2 ft, write the measurements using the same units. Then simplify the ratio. $\frac{7}{12}$

23. Simplify this ratio. $\dfrac{45}{100}$ $\frac{9}{20}$

24. Solve this proportion. $\dfrac{2}{3} = \dfrac{x+4}{x+9}$ $\{\,6\,\}$

25. The ratio of the adjacent sides of a rectangle is 5 to 2. What are the length and width if the perimeter is 21 cm? Length: 7.5 cm, width: 3cm

8–8 Objective: To solve percent and simple interest problems.

26. Write $\dfrac{2}{5}$ as a percent. 40%

27. Write 65% as a simplified ratio. $\frac{13}{20}$

Solve.

28. $75\% = \dfrac{300}{x}$ $\{\,400\,\}$

29. 6% of $x = 15$ $\{\,250\,\}$

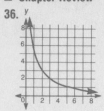

Chapter **8** Test A

NAME

■ List any necessary restrictions on the variable for the fraction to be defined.

1. $\frac{x-1}{2x+8}$ 1. $x \neq -4$

2. $\frac{x(x+2)}{(x-3)(x+5)}$ 2. $x \neq 3, x \neq -5$

■ Simplify. Assume that no denominators are zero.

3. $\frac{20r^2}{12r}$ 3. $\frac{5}{3}r$

4. $\frac{2a+8}{a^2+2a-8}$ 4. $\frac{2}{a-2}$

■ Write as one fraction and simplify.

5. $\frac{4x}{3} \cdot \frac{9y}{2x}$ 5. $6y$

6. $\frac{2r^2}{15s} \cdot \frac{10s^2}{4r}$ 6. $\frac{rs}{3}$

7. $\frac{5a+5}{3} \div \frac{a+1}{a}$ 7. $\frac{5a}{3}$

8. $\frac{10x^2}{6y} \div \frac{25x}{30y}$ 8. $2x$

9. $\frac{a^2-b^2}{49} \cdot \frac{7}{a+b}$ 9. $\frac{a-b}{7}$

10. $\frac{18}{t} - \frac{12}{t}$ 10. $\frac{6}{t}$

11. $\frac{4t}{t+1} + \frac{4}{t+1}$ 11. 4

12. $\frac{7}{w^2} + \frac{3}{w}$ 12. $\frac{7+3w}{w^2}$

13. $\frac{5}{x} - \frac{3}{x+2}$ 13. $\frac{2(x+5)}{x(x+2)}$

© D.C. Heath & Co.

428

---

30. Ms. Salgado invested $2000 for 3 years at an annual rate of 9%. How much interest did she earn? $540

8–9 Objective: To solve problems using proportions.

Solve.

31. John rode his bicycle at the rate of 24 km/h. How far did he go in 25 min? 10 km

32. When Mr. Kozlak's home room raised $200 in a student fundraising drive, he told them that they had achieved 80% of their goal. What was their goal? $250

8–10 Objective: To solve direct variation problems.

33. Does y vary directly as x when $y = \frac{2}{3}(x+6)$? No

34. If y varies directly as x and $y = 15$ when $x = 10$, find y when $x = 24$. 36

35. If Suzanne earns $7.00 in 2 h, how much will she earn at the same rate in 5 h?
$17.50

8–11 Objective: To solve inverse variation problems.

36. Graph the equation $xy = 6$ for $x > 0$.

37. Suppose that x and y vary inversely and that $y = 8$ when $x = 3$. Find y when $x = 6$. 4

38. Averaging 15 km/h, June and Sue took 2 h to ride their bikes to Long Lake. If their return trip along the same route took an hour and a half, what was their average speed returning? 20 km/h

■ CHAPTER 8 SELF-TEST

Simplify. List any restrictions on the variables.

8–1 1. $\frac{6x^2y}{3xy^2}$ $\frac{2x}{y}$; $x, y \neq 0$

2. $\frac{(y-2)(y+3)}{5(y-2)}$ $\frac{y+3}{5}$; $y \neq 2$

Simplify. Assume that no divisor is zero.

8–2,
8–3,
8–4

3. $\frac{9a}{7b^2} \cdot \frac{14b}{3a}$ $\frac{6}{b}$

4. $\frac{6x}{25y} \div \frac{2}{5xy}$ $\frac{3x^2}{5}$

5. $\frac{5m}{m+2n} \cdot \frac{6(m+2n)}{10m^2}$ $\frac{3}{m}$

6. $\frac{(x-y)(x+y)}{3(x+2y)} \div \frac{x-y}{9}$ $\frac{3(x+y)}{x+2y}$

7. $\frac{2w}{w-5} - \frac{10}{w-5}$ 2

8. $\frac{12}{a^2} - \frac{3}{a^2}$ $\frac{9}{a^2}$

9. $\frac{1}{y} + \frac{3}{4}$ $\frac{4+3y}{4y}$

10. $\frac{1}{x^2} - \frac{2}{xy}$ $\frac{y-2x}{x^2y}$

11. $\frac{5}{x-2} - \frac{4}{x}$ $\frac{x+8}{x(x-2)}$

Solve.

8–5   **12.** $\dfrac{y}{32} = \dfrac{3}{4}$ $\{24\}$ **13.** $\dfrac{5}{x} + \dfrac{4}{3} = \dfrac{9}{x}$ $\{3\}$ **14.** $t + 1 = \dfrac{2}{t}$ $\{-2, 1\}$

8–7,
8–8   **15.** $\dfrac{2}{5} = \dfrac{x+1}{x-2}$ $\{-3\}$ **16.** 125% of $x = 15$ $\{12\}$ **17.** $\dfrac{35}{125} = y\,\%$ $\{28\}$

8–6   **18.** Use the formula $\dfrac{1}{R} = \dfrac{1}{r_1} + \dfrac{1}{r_2}$ to find r_2 when $R = 3\ \Omega$ and $r_1 = 12\ \Omega$. $4\ \Omega$

8–7   **19.** The ratio of the sides of two squares is 2 to 5. What is the ratio of their areas? $\dfrac{4}{25}$

8–10   **20.** Suppose y varies directly as x. If $y = 48$ when $x = 30$, find y when $x = 105$.   168

8–11   **21.** Suppose y varies inversely as x. If $y = 15$ when $x = 56$, find x when $y = 35$.   24

8–8   **22.** In a six-month period, Mr. Q earned $450 interest on $15,000. What annual rate of interest did Mr. Q earn?   6%

8–9   **23.** If one side of a square is decreased by 2 m and another side increased by 2 m, the sides will be in the ratio 5 to 7. Find the original length of a side of the square.   12 m

8–10   **24.** Ms. Melville drove 288 mi on 14 gal of gasoline. How far can she drive on 35 gal of gasoline?   720 mi

8–11   **25.** Twelve boxes of oranges contain 8 oranges each. Hoping to boost sales, the grocer re-packages the oranges 6 to a package. How many smaller packages can he make?   16

■ PRACTICE FOR COLLEGE ENTRANCE TESTS

Each question consists of two quantities, one in column A and one in column B. Compare the two quantities and select one of the following answers.

A if the quantity in column A is greater;
B if the quantity in column B is greater;
C if the two quantities are equal;
D if the relationship cannot be determined from the information given.

Comments:

- Letters such as a, b, x, and y are variables that can be replaced by real numbers.
- A symbol that appears in both columns in a question stands for the same thing in column A as in column B.
- In some questions information that applies to quantities in both columns is centered above the two columns.

■ Solve. Write ∅ if there is no solution.

14. $\dfrac{12}{y} = \dfrac{4}{3}$ 14. $\{9\}$

15. $4 + \dfrac{3}{a} = \dfrac{6}{2a}$ 15. $\varnothing$

16. $x - 9 = \dfrac{22}{x}$ 16. $\{11, -2\}$

17. $\dfrac{3}{4} = \dfrac{7.5}{n}$ 17. $\{10\}$

18. $\dfrac{t+2}{t-5} = \dfrac{3}{4}$ 18. $\{-23\}$

19. 30% $= \dfrac{18}{x}$ 19. $\{60\}$

20. 15% of $x = 9.6$ 20. $\{64\}$

21. Use the formula $\dfrac{1}{R} = \dfrac{1}{r_1} = \dfrac{1}{r_2}$ to find the resistance r_2 when $R = 3$ ohms and $r_1 = 9$ ohms.   21. 4.5 ohms

22. An older addressing machine can finish a mailing in 9 hours. A newer addressing machine can finish the mailing in 3 hours. How long does it take to do the mailing if both machines are used?   22. 2 1/4 h

23. The width and length of a rectangle are in the ratio 5 to 8. Find the width if the length is 18 cm more than the width.   23. 30 cm

24. In the last 30 minutes, 4 patients have gone in to see the doctor. There are still 6 patients ahead of you. In how many minutes can you expect to see the doctor?   24. 45

25. Suppose y varies directly as x. If $x = 45$ when $y = 16$, find x when $y = 24$.   25. 67.5

26. Suppose y varies indirectly as x. If $x = 45$ when $y = 16$, find x when $y = 24$.   26. 30

★ **BONUS**

Write and simplify an expression for the ratio of the volume to the surface area of this solid.   BONUS $\dfrac{sh}{2(s + 2h)}$

■ List any necessary restrictions on the variable for the fraction to be defined.

1. $\dfrac{y+1}{3y-6}$ 1. $y \neq 2$

2. $\dfrac{y(y-6)}{(y+4)(y-3)}$ 2. $y \neq -4, y \neq 3$

■ Simplify. Assume that no denominators are zero.

3. $\dfrac{18a^2}{12a}$ 3. $\dfrac{3a}{2}$

4. $\dfrac{3t+6}{t^2 - 2t - 8}$ 4. $\dfrac{3}{t-4}$

■ Write as one fraction and simplify.

5. $\dfrac{8c}{5} \cdot \dfrac{30d}{4c}$ 5. $\dfrac{12d}{}$

6. $\dfrac{4y^2}{21z} \cdot \dfrac{14z^3}{2y}$ 6. $\dfrac{4yz}{3}$

7. $\dfrac{6t+6}{4} \div \dfrac{t+1}{2t}$ 7. $3t$

8. $\dfrac{6a^2}{15b} \div \dfrac{8a}{35b}$ 8. $\dfrac{7a}{4}$

9. $\dfrac{40}{a^2 - b^2} \cdot \dfrac{a-b}{8}$ 9. $\dfrac{5}{a+b}$

10. $\dfrac{15}{x} - \dfrac{9}{x}$ 10. $\dfrac{6}{x}$

11. $\dfrac{3x}{x+4} + \dfrac{12}{x+4}$ 11. 3

12. $\dfrac{2}{y} + \dfrac{5}{y^3}$ 12. $\dfrac{2y+5}{y^2}$

13. $\dfrac{5}{y} - \dfrac{4}{y+1}$ 13. $\dfrac{y+5}{y(y+1)}$

■ **Solve. Write ∅ if there is no solution.**

14. $\dfrac{18}{y} = \dfrac{6}{5}$ 14. $\{15\}$

15. $x + 5 = \dfrac{24}{x}$ 15. $\{-8, 3\}$

16. $3 + \dfrac{4}{a} = \dfrac{8}{2a}$ 16. $\varnothing$

17. $\dfrac{5}{8} = \dfrac{7.5}{n}$ 17. $\{12\}$

18. $\dfrac{t + 3}{t - 7} = \dfrac{4}{5}$ 18. $\{-43\}$

19. $40\% = \dfrac{12}{x}$ 19. $\{30\}$

20. 45% of $x = 6.3$ 20. $\{14\}$

21. Use the formula $\dfrac{1}{R} = \dfrac{1}{r_1} = \dfrac{1}{r_2}$ to find the resistance r_2 when $R = 2$ ohms and $r_1 = 10$ ohms.   21. 2.5 ohms

22. An older tractor can plow a field in 10 hours. A newer tractor can plow the field in 6 hours. How long does it take to plow the field if both tractors are used?   22. $3\frac{3}{4}$ h

23. The length and width of a rectangle are in the ratio 7 to 4. Find the length if the width is 12 cm less than the length.   23. 28 cm

24. In the last 40 minutes, 6 people have gone in to see the veterinarian. There are still 9 people ahead of you. In how many minutes can you expect to see the veterinarian?   24. 60

25. Suppose y varies directly as x. If $x = 15$ when $y = 36$, find y when $x = 35$.   25. 84

26. Suppose y varies indirectly as x. If $x = 54$ when $y = 36$, find x when $y = 81$.   26. 24

★ **BONUS**

Write and simplify an expression for the ratio of the perimeter to the area of this triangle.   BONUS $\dfrac{2(2 + y)}{3x}$

7-1 1. List the prime factorization of 56.   1. $2^3 \cdot 7$

7-2 2. What is the greatest common factor of 24 and 32?   2. 8

■ **Expand and simplify.**

7-5 3. $(x + 4)(x + 5)$ 3. $x^2 + 9x + 20$

4. $(y - 8)(y + 3)$ 4. $y^2 - 5y - 24$

■ **Factor.**

7-4 5. $12a + 16b$ 5. $4(3a + 4b)$

7-6 6. $y^2 - 36$ 6. $(y - 6)(y + 6)$

7-7 7. $x^2 + 10x + 25$ 7. $(x + 5)^2$

7-8 8. $b^2 - 3b + 2$ 8. $(b - 1)(b - 2)$

7-10 9. $2y^2 + 11y + 5$ 9. $(2y + 1)(y + 5)$

■ **Solve.**

7-3 10. $(x - 4)(x + 2) = 0$ 10. $\{4, -2\}$

7-4 11. $x^2 - 8x = 0$ 11. $\{0, 8\}$

7-6 12. $2a^2 = 32$ 12. $\{4, -4\}$

7-9 13. $x^2 - 5x - 6 = 0$ 13. $\{6, -1\}$

8-1 14. For what value(s) is the fraction $\dfrac{6}{x - 4}$ not defined?   14. $x = 4$

EXAMPLES

Column A	Column B	Answers
$3 + 4$	$3 \cdot 4$	B
$a = 5$		
$a + b$	$b + 5$	C
$2x + y$	$x + 2y$	D

	Column A	Column B	
1.	20% of 300	300% of 20	C
2.	x is 50% of y		
	The percent that y is of x	500%	B
3.	$\dfrac{1}{2} + \dfrac{1}{4} + \dfrac{1}{8}$	$\dfrac{1}{16} + \dfrac{1}{8} + \dfrac{1}{4}$	A
4.	$2a - 4$	$\dfrac{6a - 12}{3}$	C
5.	$x \neq 2$		
	0	$\dfrac{1}{(x - 2)^2}$	B
6.	The ratio of $\dfrac{2}{3}$ to $\dfrac{1}{4}$	The ratio of $\dfrac{3}{4}$ to $\dfrac{1}{3}$	A
7.	a and b are positive and $\dfrac{a}{b} = 3$		
	$a + b$	4	D
8.	The price of a stereo increases by 20% and then decreases by 20%.		
	The original price of the stereo	The final price of the stereo	A
9.	a and b are positive integers		
	40% of a + 20% of b	30% of $(a + b)$	D
10.	12% of $3x = 45$		
	12% of x	15	C
11.	$\dfrac{0.2}{0.5} = \dfrac{0.5}{x}$		
	x	1	A

■ CUMULATIVE REVIEW (*Chapters 7–8*)

7–1 List all positive-integer factors of the given number.

1. 39 1, 3, 13, 39   **2.** 92 1, 2, 4, 23, 46, 92

Write the prime factorization of each number.

3. 48 $2^4 \cdot 3$ **4.** 60 $2^2 \cdot 3 \cdot 5$

7–2 State the greatest common factor of each pair of numbers or monomials.

5. 24, 56 8   **6.** 45, 72 9

7. $9xy^2, 12x^2y$ 3xy   **8.** $6a^2b, 4a^2b^3$ $2a^2b$

7–3 Solve.

9. $x(x - 2) = 0$ (0, 2)   **10.** $(a - 7)(a + 7) = 0$ {7, −7}   **11.** $(2y - 1)(3y + 1) = 0$ $\left\{\frac{1}{2}, -\frac{1}{3}\right\}$

7–4 **12.** Find the greatest common factor of the terms of the polynomial $8x + 10y$. 2

Factor.

13. $14y - 7x$ 7(2y − x)   **14.** $ab - b^2$ b(a − b)

Solve.

15. $x^2 + 4x = 0$ (0, −4)   **16.** $y^2 = 5y$ (0, 5)

7–5 Expand and simplify.

17. $(a + 2)(a + 7)$ $a^2 + 9a + 14$ **18.** $(c - 5)(c + 5)$ $c^2 - 25$

19. $(2n + 4)(n - 3)$ $2n^2 - 2n - 12$ **20.** $(x - 8)^2$ $x^2 - 16x + 64$

7–6 **21.** Write $49b^2$ as a square. $(7b)^2$

Factor.

22. $x^2 - 9$ (x + 3)(x − 3)   **23.** $4x^2 - 1$ (2x + 1)(2x − 1)

Solve.

24. $x^2 - 49 = 0$ {−7, 7}   **25.** $x^2 = 81$ {−9, 9}

7–7 Expand and simplify.

26. $(x + 10)^2$ $x^2 + 20x + 100$ **27.** $(2b - 1)^2$ $4b^2 - 4b + 1$

7–7, 7–8 Factor.

28. $a^2 + 12a + 36$ $(a + 6)^2$ **29.** $x^2 - 10x + 25$ $(x - 5)^2$

30. $p^2 - 6p + 5$ (p − 1)(p − 5)   **31.** $a^2 + 7a + 12$ (a + 4)(a + 3)

7-8 Solve.

32. $x^2 - 3x + 2 = 0$ (1, 2) **33.** $y^2 + 6y + 9 = 0$ (−3)

7-9, Factor.
7-10

34. $a^2 - 11a - 12$ (a − 12)(a + 1) **35.** $y^2 + 3y - 18$ (y + 6)(y − 3)

36. $2x^2 + 7x + 3$ (2x + 1)(x + 3) **37.** $6n^2 - n - 1$ (3n + 1)(2n − 1)

Solve.

38. $x^2 - x - 30 = 0$ (−5, 6) **39.** $b^2 - b = 6$ (−2, 3)

40. Twice the square of a number minus 3 times the number equals 2. What is the number? $-\frac{1}{2}$ or 2

8-1 **41.** State whether this pair of fractions is equivalent for admissible values of x.

$$\frac{1}{x-4} \quad \text{and} \quad \frac{3}{x-12} \quad \text{No}$$

42. What value(s) of b are not admissible for the fraction to be defined?

$$\frac{b}{b+2} \quad -2$$

8-1, Simplify. Assume that no denominators are zero.
8-2

43. $\frac{6x}{18x}$ $\frac{1}{3}$ **44.** $\frac{2x-4}{5x-10}$ $\frac{2}{5}$ **45.** $\frac{b+2}{b^2+5b+6}$ $\frac{1}{b+3}$

46. $\frac{a}{b^2} \cdot \frac{b}{a}$ $\frac{1}{b}$ **47.** $\frac{16x}{y} \cdot \frac{3y}{4x}$ 12 **48.** $\frac{2a}{b} \cdot (b^2 + 4b)$ 2ab + 8a

49. $\frac{6x}{y} \div \frac{2x}{y}$ 3 **50.** $\frac{5a}{c^2} \div \frac{10a}{c}$ $\frac{1}{2c}$ **51.** $\frac{12}{a-2} \div \frac{a}{a^2-4}$ $\frac{12(a+2)}{a}$

8-3, Simplify. Assume that no denominators are zero.
8-4

52. $\frac{4b}{3} + \frac{2b}{3}$ 2b **53.** $\frac{3}{a-2} + \frac{4}{a-2}$ $\frac{7}{a-2}$ **54.** $\frac{c}{c-6} - \frac{6}{c-6}$ 1

55. $\frac{x}{4} + \frac{x}{3}$ $\frac{7x}{12}$ **56.** $\frac{3}{4y} - \frac{1}{2y}$ $\frac{1}{4y}$ **57.** $\frac{5}{x-1} - \frac{1}{x}$ $\frac{4x+1}{x(x-1)}$

8-5 Solve.

58. $\frac{16}{12} = \frac{2a}{3}$ (2) **59.** $\frac{x}{3} - \frac{1}{2} = \frac{7}{6}$ (5)

60. $\frac{4}{y} + \frac{5}{3} = \frac{9}{y}$ (3) **61.** $\frac{5}{x} - \frac{1}{2x} = 3$ $\left\{\frac{3}{2}\right\}$

8-6 **62.** Use the formula $\frac{1}{R} = \frac{1}{r_1} + \frac{1}{r_2}$ to find the total resistance R when $r_1 = 4$ ohms and $r_2 = 6$ ohms. $\frac{12}{5}$ ohms

8–6 Write an equation to solve this problem.

63. Lucinda can make the pep-rally posters in 5 h. Gary can make the same number of posters in 6 h. How long does it take Lucinda and Gary to make posters for the pep rally if they work together? $\frac{x}{5} + \frac{x}{6} = 1$; $\frac{30}{11}$ hours

8–7 64. Write the measurement in the same units, and then write the ratio in simplest form. 50 minutes to 2 hours $\frac{5}{12}$

65. Simplify the ratio. $\frac{26}{39}$ $\frac{2}{3}$

8–8 66. Write $\frac{7}{20}$ as a percent. 35%

67. Write 48% as a simplified ratio. $\frac{12}{25}$

Solve.

68. x% of $40 = 32$ (80)

69. 16% of $x = 9.6$ (60)

70. Claude Rich invested $2000 at 8% for 3 years. How much did he earn in interest? (Use $i = prt$.) $480

8–9 71. Mattie stocked four shelves at Foodland in 30 minutes. At that rate, how long would it take her to stock 14 shelves? 105 min or 1 h 45 min

72. Jerry drove 135 mi on 6 gal of gasoline. How far can he drive on a full tank of 15 gal? 337.5

73. The ratio of ninth-grade students who can curl their tongues to those who cannot is 4 to 3. How many students have this genetic trait if there are 56 ninth-grade students? 32

8–10 74. Suppose y varies directly as x. If $y = 24$ when $x = 15$, find y when $x = 40$. 64

75. Does y vary directly as x if $y = 4x + 2$? No

76. Suppose y varies directly as x. If $y = 16$ when $x = 12$, find the constant of variation and write the direct-variation equation. $y = \frac{4}{3}x$

8–11 77. Suppose y varies inversely as x. If $y = 12$ when $x = 3$, find x when $y = 2$. 18

78. If y varies inversely as x and k is the constant of variation, which of these equations is true? b

    a. $x + y = k$ **b.** $xy = k$ **c.** $\frac{y}{x} = k$

    d. $y = x - k$ **e.** $y = x^k$

79. A trucker can drive from Baltimore to Indianapolis in 11 h at 50 mph. How fast must he drive in order to complete the return trip in 10 h? 55 mph

CHAPTER OVERVIEW

In this chapter, students extend their knowledge of equations to solving and graphing inequalities. Inequalities studied in this chapter include the following relations:

> greater than
< less than
≥ greater than or equal to
≤ less than or equal to
≠ not equal to

Students learn to solve inequalities in one variable and graph them on the number line. In the process, they build on their knowledge of real numbers, equations, and absolute value from Chapters 2 and 3. Students learn to graph inequalities in two variables on the coordinate plane, building on the ability to graph linear equations that they acquired in Chapter 5. Students will also learn to graph compound inequalities (containing "and" or "or") on the coordinate plane, using the knowledge of systems of equations that they acquired in Chapter 6.

Knowledge of inequalities is necessary for later study in geometry, advanced algebra, and calculus. In addition, there are many practical applications of inequalities in science, business, and other fields.

9 Inequalities and Their Graphs

A manufacturer makes a cattle feed from various grains. Rather than requiring exact amounts of the grains, the recipe for the feed specifies ranges of the amounts to be used. The amount of each grain used also depends on the amounts of the other grains used. As costs of the various grains fluctuate, the manufacturer can vary the amount of each grain in order to minimize the cost of the feed and maximize the profits.

The relative amounts of the grains and their ranges are stated as inequalities. The graphs of the inequalities help to determine the optimal amount of each grain to use for maximum profit.

$$c + t \geq 60$$
$$c + t \leq 100$$
$$c \geq 2t$$
$$c \leq 5t$$

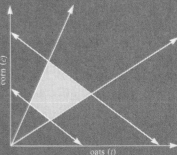

To determine inequalities as true or false and to graph them on the number line.

Many practical problems involve inequalities rather than equations. It is important to be able to solve and rewrite equivalent expressions involving "greater than" or "less than."

9–1 Graphing Inequalities

Preview

The qualifying standards for the 1984 Olympic trials were as follows.

Running Events	Time (min:s)	Field Events	Distance
100 meters	10.35	High jump	2.24 m
200 meters	20.74	Long jump	7.85 m
400 meters	46.00	Triple jump	16.20 m
800 meters	1:47.44	Shot put	19.81 m
1,500 meters	3:42.20	Discus	61.26 m
5,000 meters	13:49.00	Pole vault	5.40 m
10,000 meters	28:46.00	Javelin	78.80 m
		Hammer throw	63.00 m

In order to compete for a berth on the 1984 U.S. Olympic track and field team, an athlete must have had a performance in 1982–83 that equaled or bettered the qualifying standards. To qualify for a running event, the athlete's time must have been equal to or less than these standards. To compete in a field event, the athlete's performance must have been equal to or greater than the standard height or distance.

■ LESSON

Mathematical sentences that state that two quantities are not equal are called **inequalities.** These symbols are used in inequalities:

$$<\quad \text{is less than}$$
$$>\quad \text{is greater than}$$
$$\neq\quad \text{is not equal to}$$

Here are some examples of inequalities. These inequalities are true.

$6 < 8$	6 is less than 8
$8 > 6$	8 is greater than 6
$6 \neq 8$	6 is not equal to 8

The two other inequality symbols are $\leq$ and $\geq$.

$$\leq\quad \text{is less than or equal to}$$
$$\geq\quad \text{is greater than or equal to}$$

Inequalities using the $\leq$ or $\geq$ symbols are **compound inequalities.** The sentence

$$6 \leq 8$$

is a short way of writing

$$6 < 8 \quad \text{or} \quad 6 = 8$$

Students should notice that in some contests, success comes with smaller numbers—faster times in track and swimming, lower scores in golf. In other contests the object is to get larger numbers—greater distances in throwing, jumping, and vaulting; greater weights in weight lifting; larger scores in basketball, soccer, and figure skating. Ties (equality of scores) are never the objective.

Point out that the symbols for "is less than" and "is greater than," $<$ and $>$ respectively, both point to the smaller quantity. Another way to remember the meaning of the symbol is to notice that the wider part of the symbol is next to the larger quantity. Thus, if $x > 3$, x is greater than 3. If $-8 < y$, -8 is less than y (and y is greater than -8).

In graphing inequalities on the number line, emphasize that sometimes there is a largest (or smallest) solution and sometimes there is not. For example, the largest solution for $5 \geq x$ is 5. However, the inequality $5 > x$ has no largest solution. To distinguish between these two situations, a solid or an open circle is used in the graph at 5.

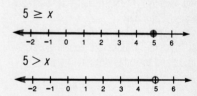

Example 1. True or false? $12 \leq 11$

   False

Example 2. True or false? $6 + 5 \leq 11$

   True

Example 3. Graph on the number line.

   $y > 6$

Example 4. Graph on the number line.
$y \leq -2$

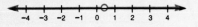

Example 5. Graph on the number line. $a \neq \frac{1}{2}$

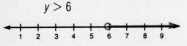

CHECK UNDERSTANDING

- Is 5 a solution of $x < 5$? (No)
- Is 5 a solution of $x \leq 5$? (Yes)
- Is 7 a solution of $x \geq 7$? (Yes)
- Is 8 a solution of $x \geq 7$? (Yes)
- Is 13 a solution of $x \neq 13$? (No)

CLASSROOM EXERCISES

In exercise 10, point out that $x > 15$ is preferred to $15 < x$, although the two inequalities are equivalent. It is conventional in inequalities, as in equations, to have the variable on the left. Furthermore, "$x > 15$" is a more literal translation of the word sentence. "$15 < x$" would be a translation of "15 is less than the number."

   In exercise 11, note that "at least 20" means "20 or more."

   Contrast exercises 12 and 13 by pointing out that one includes the equals possibility ($\geq$) and the other does not ($<$).

A compound sentence using "or" is true if at least one of the two conditions is true. It is false if both of the conditions are false.

Example 1   True or false? $12 \leq 13$

Solution $12 \leq 13$ says that "$12 < 13$ or $12 = 13$." Since $12 < 13$ is true, the compound inequality is true.

Example 2   True or false? $12 \leq 12$

Solution $12 \leq$ says that "$12 < 12$ or $12 = 12$." Since $12 = 12$ is true, the compound inequality is true.

Inequalities with variables are open sentences just as equations with variables are open sentences. Open sentences are neither true nor false. The **solutions of an inequality** are those numbers that make the inequality true when they are substituted for the variable. Inequalities in one variable usually have infinitely many numbers as solutions. Number-line graphs make the solutions easier to understand.

Example 3   Graph on a number line. $x < 4$

Solution   Any number less than 4 is a solution. This is shown by coloring red points on the number line that have coordinates less than 4. The red arrowhead indicates that the graph extends infinitely far to the left. The open circle indicates that the graph begins at 4 but does not include 4.

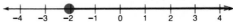

Example 4   Graph on a number line. $y \geq -2$

Solution -2 and any number that is greater than -2 is a solution. The solid circle indicates that the graph starts at -2 and includes -2. The red arrowhead indicates that the graph extends infinitely far to the right.

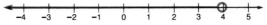

Example 5   Graph on a number line. $b \neq 2.5$

Solution   Every number except 2.5 makes the inequality true. The red arrowheads indicate that the graph extends infinitely far in both directions.

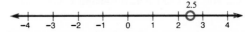

CLASSROOM STRATEGY   *Correcting errors*

Students often enter algebra classes with serious mis-conceptions and with their own incorrect rules. It is, therefore, necessary to constantly be on the lookout for error patterns in the process being used by the student, and then correct the misconceptions.

■ CLASSROOM EXERCISES

True or false?

1. $5 < 12$ T

2. $5 < -12$ F

3. $5 \leq 12$ T

4. $5 \leq -12$ F

5. $5 \leq 5$ T

6. $-3 > -6$ T

7. $-2 \geq 0$ F

8. $7 \geq -13$ T

9. $3.5 \neq -3.5$ T

Let x represent the number. Write an inequality that fits the situation.

10. The number is greater than 15. $x > 15$

11. The number is at least 20. $x \geq 20$

12. 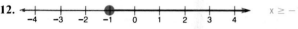 $x \geq -1$

13.  $x < 0$

Graph on a number line.

14. $x < 5$

15. $y \geq -3$

16. $a \neq 0$

■ WRITTEN EXERCISES

True or false?

1. $3 < 5$ T

2. $4 < -6$ F

3. $2 > -7$ T

4. $0.3 > 0.5$ F

5. $-8 > 1$ F

6. $9 > -3$ T

7. $0.5 < -0.3$ F

8. $-500 < 300$ T

9. $-\frac{1}{5} \leq -\frac{1}{5}$ T

10. $-\frac{1}{3} \leq -\frac{1}{3}$ T

11. $-3\frac{1}{2} \geq -5\frac{1}{2}$ T

12. $-\frac{81}{2} \geq 10$ F

13. $-2\frac{1}{2} > -2\frac{1}{4}$ F

14. $2\frac{1}{2} > 2\frac{1}{4}$ T

15. $3\frac{1}{5} < 3\frac{1}{10}$ F

16. $-3\frac{1}{5} < -3\frac{1}{10}$ T

Let x represent the number. Write an inequality that fits the description.

17. The number is less than 100. $x < 100$

18. The number is greater than 500. $x > 500$

19. The number is at least 70. $x \geq 70$

20. The number is not more than 30. $x \leq 30$

21. The number is greater than -90. $x > -90$

22. The number is less than -10. $x < -10$

23. The number is not 2. $x \neq 2$

24. The number is not 0. $x \neq 0$

Graph on a number line.

25. $x > 3$

26. $x > 5$

27. $x < 5$

28. $x < 3$

29. $x \neq 2$

30. $x \neq -2$

31. $x \geq -3$

32. $x \geq -5$

33. $x \leq -5$

34. $x \leq -3$

35. $x < \frac{1}{2}$

36. $x > -\frac{1}{2}$

 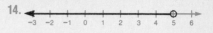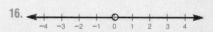

ADDITIONAL ANSWERS

■ Written Exercises

30.
(number line: −6 to 2, open circle at −2, arrow left)

31.
(number line: −6 to 2, closed dot at −3, arrow left)

32.
(number line: −6 to 2, closed dot at −5, arrow right)

33.
(number line: −6 to 2, closed dot at −5, arrow left)

34.
(number line: −6 to 2, closed dot at −3, arrow left)

35.
(number line: −4 to 5, open circle at $\frac{1}{2}$, arrow left)

36.
(number line: −5 to 4, open circle at $-\frac{1}{2}$, arrow right)

61.
(number line: 0 to 80, closed dots at 0 and 80)

62.
(number line: 0 to 90, closed dots at 0 and 70)

63.
(number line: 0 to 18, closed dot at 10, arrow left)

64.
(number line: 0 to 60, closed dot at 40, arrow right)

65.
(number line: 0 to 9, closed dot at 7, arrow right)

66.
(number line: 0 to 9, open circle at 5, arrow right)

67.
(number line: 0 to 70, open circle at 50, arrow right)

68.
(number line: 0 to 2.25, closed dot at 2.25, arrow right)

79.
(number line: −4 to 4, open circles at −1 and 1)

80.
(number line: −4 to 5, closed dots at −2 and 1)

81.
(number line: −4 to 5, open circles at 0 and 1)

82.
(number line: −4 to 5, open circles at 1 and 2)

438

Write an inequality using x for each graph.

37.
(number line: 1 to 7, open circle at 4, arrow right) $x > 4$

38.
(number line: −5 to 1, open circle at −3, arrow right) $x > -3$

39.
(number line: −5 to 2, open circle at −2, arrow left) $x < -2$

40.
(number line: −2 to 4, open circle at 1, arrow left) $x < 1$

41.
(number line: −3 to 3, open circle at 0) $x \neq 0$

42.
(number line: 67 to 73, open circle at 70) $x \neq 70$

43.
(number line: −2 to 2, closed dot at $\frac{1}{2}$, arrow right) $x \geq \frac{1}{2}$

44.
(number line: −4 to 0, closed dot at $-2\frac{1}{2}$, arrow left) $x \leq -2\frac{1}{2}$

List all the numbers in $\{-100, -20, 0, 20, 100\}$ that are solutions of the inequality.

45. $x < 35$
20, 0, −20, −100
46. $x < -35$ −100
47. $x \neq -20$
100, 20, 0, −100
48. $x \neq 100$
20, 0, −20, −100

49. $x \geq 0$ 100, 20, 0
50. $x \geq -15$ 100, 20, 0
51. $x \leq 15$ 0, −20, −100
52. $x \leq 20$
20, 0, −20, −100

List all the numbers in $\{-5, -0.55, 0.505, 0.55, 5.5\}$ that are solutions of the inequality.

53. $x \geq 0.5$
5.5, 0.55, 0.505
54. $x \geq -0.5$
5.5, 0.55, 0.505
55. $x \leq -0.5$
−0.55, −5
56. $x \leq -0.55$
−0.55, −5

57. $x \neq 5$ All
58. $x \neq -5$
5.5, 0.55, 0.505, −0.55
59. $x < 5(0.11)$
0.505, −0.55, −5
60. $x < \dfrac{1.01}{2}$
−0.55, −5

Write an inequality for each situation. Then graph the inequality on a number line.

B **61.** To fit in the trash can, the sticks cannot be more than 90 cm long. (Let l represent the length in centimeters.) $l \leq 90$

62. A delivery service will accept packages up to and including 70 lb. (Let w represent the weight in pounds.) $w \leq 70$

63. The tomato plants were at least 10 cm tall before they were put on sale. $t \geq 10$

64. The diameter of each tree in the park was at least 40 cm. $d \geq 40$

65. Each coin in the collection was at least 7 years old. $c \geq 7$

66. No one had a score of 5 on the test. $s \neq 5$

67. The value of the purchase was under 50¢. $v < 50$

68. The purchase was at least $2.25. $p \geq 2.25$

438   Chapter 9   Inequalities and Their Graphs

In exercise 75, point out that with the exception of 1, the sum of any positive number and its reciprocal is greater than 2. Have students verify this by evaluating $b + \dfrac{1}{b}$ for $b = \frac{1}{10}$ and for $b = \frac{11}{10}$.

List the numbers in $\{-3, -2, -1, 0, 1, 2, 3\}$ that satisfy the inequality.

C **69.** $5x + 2 < -6$ $-2, -3$ **70.** $4x - 3 \le -7$ $-1, -2, -3$ **71.** $x + x + x \ge 2$ $3, 2, 1$

72. $2 + x > 0$ $3, 2, 1, 0, -1$ **73.** $1 - x > 0$ $0, -1, -2, -3$ **74.** $-2x \ge -1$ $0, -1, -2, -3$

75. For what values of b is it true that $b + \dfrac{1}{b} > 2$? $b > 1$ or b is between 0 and 1

76. For what values of a is it true that $a - \dfrac{2}{a} > 1$?

[*Hint:* Some values may be negative.]
$a > 2$ or a is between 0 and -1

77. For what values of x is $x^2 > x$? $x > 1$ or $x < 0$

78. For what values of y is $y \le \sqrt{y}$? $y \ge 0$ and $y \le 1$

Graph.

79. $x^2 > 1$ **80.** $x^2 \le 4$ **81.** $x^2 > x$ **82.** $x^2 \ne x$

■ REVIEW EXERCISES

Substitute and simplify.

a	b	x	y
-3	2	-5	-4

1. $(a - b) - (x - y)$ -4

2. $x - (a + y)$ 2 [2–3]

3. $|ax| + |by|$ 23

4. $|ab + xy|$ 14 [2–4]

Solve.

5. $3x + 8 = 5 - 2x$ $\left\{-\dfrac{3}{5}\right\}$

6. $2x - 5 = 4(x + 3)$ $\left\{-\dfrac{17}{2}\right\}$ [3–6]

7. Solve $P = 2\pi r$ for r. $r = \dfrac{P}{2\pi}$

8. Solve $ax + by = c$ for y. $y = \dfrac{c - ax}{b}$ [3–8]

EXTENSION Extra costs _____

Increasing the number of steps used in producing an item usually increases the cost of the product. For example, a frozen TV dinner costs more than the same items of food purchased fresh and cooked at home. The extra costs reflect the labor, equipment, and packaging materials needed to prepare and package the dinner.

Solve the following problem to find the additional cost of extra steps in production.

Thrift-T mending tape in a dispenser costs $.82 for 950 ft of tape. The same kind of tape without the dispenser costs $.82 for 1020 feet. How much does the dispenser cost? 6¢

PROBLEM SOLVING NOTES
Understanding a problem

The B exercises 61–68 ask students to write an inequality to describe each situation. Through discussion, bring out the meaning of phrases such as "not more than" and "at least." Direct students' attention to whether equality is permitted. Also point out how a *negative* phrase, such as "not" or "nobody," affects the inequality statement. Emphasize to students how much more precise the mathematical statement is than the English expression.

Checking the inequality statement against the original situation should be emphasized through specific cases. For example, if "$x > \$1.19$" is written for "no item purchased cost less than $1.19," students should ask whether the statement is true for a representative value for x such as $1.25 and also for the boundary value of $1.19. Since the original statement is true if the purchase price is $1.19, the inequality needs to be corrected to $x \ge \$1.19$.

ENRICHMENT PROBLEM

- Charles thinks that he knows the largest number that is a solution of $x < 2.5$. How can you prove that his answer (whatever it is) is wrong?

  If n_1 and n_2 are two rational numbers such that $n_1 < n_2$, then the rational number $\dfrac{n_1 + n_2}{2}$ is between n_1 and n_2. If Charles's number c is less than 2.5, then $\dfrac{c + 2.5}{2}$ is larger than c and less than 2.5.

Graph on the number line.

1. $x < 3$

2. $x \geq -2$

3. $x \neq 1$

List all the numbers in $\{-4, -2, 0, 2, 4\}$ that satisfy the inequality.

4. $x > 1$ 2, 4

5. $x \leq 2$ $-4, -2, 0, 2$

PURPOSE

A clear understanding of the meaning of "and" and "or" in compound sentences is necessary for the application of logic in mathematics, computer science, and other fields.

PREVIEW

Be sure students note that in the first game, 64 is both a square of an integer and a cube of an integer. It is a winning number. There may be some disagreement about this point, since in ordinary conversation the word "or" is used ambiguously. For example, the sentence "After dinner I am going roller skating or to a movie" would usually be interpreted to mean that the speaker will do one but not both of the activities. The word "or" is being used in the **exclusive** sense. However, the sentence "Bob or Mary will go to the movie with me" would usually be interpreted to mean that one or both people will go to the movie with the speaker. In this case, the word "or" is being used in the **inclusive** sense. In mathematics, the word "or" is always used in the inclusive sense.

440

OBJECTIVE 9–2

To graph compound inequalities on the number line.

You may wish to spend two days on this section. Refer to the Pacing Chart.

9–2 Compound Inequalities and Graphs

Preview **Discovery**

The Wizard of Odds operates two games of skill at the amusement park.

DART THROW

1	19	6	25	84
27	55	48	3	16
0	72	8	30	24
13	42	27	69	36
64	20	15	81	7

WHEEL OF FORTUNE

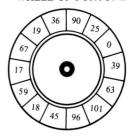

To win on the dart throw, a player has to hit a number that is a square *or* a cube. On which of these numbers does the Wizard have to award a prize?

69   36   15   27   64   36, 27, 64

In order for a player to win on the wheel of fortune, a number has to be odd *and* a multiple of 9. On which of these numbers does the Wizard award a prize?

25   36   96   18   45   45

In this lesson you will find numbers that satisfy two conditions joined by the word *or* or *and*.

■ LESSON

In the preceding lesson we saw that the symbols $\geq$ and $\leq$ are short ways to state that two conditions are joined by the word *or*. For example, $x \leq 4$ means "$x < 4$ or $x = 4$." Sentences that state two or more conditions are called compound sentences.

Consider this compound sentence in which the two conditions are joined by the word *or*.

$$a < -1 \quad \text{or} \quad a > 2$$

To be a solution of the sentence, a number must satisfy one condition or the other, but not necessarily both conditions. To determine whether a number is a solution, substitute it into each part of the sentence.

There are advantages to having students work to-gether occasionally. Studies consistently show that peer tutoring is the most cost-efficient means to improve achievement.

$$a < -1 \quad \text{or} \quad a > 2$$

Substitute -4: $\quad -4 < -1 \quad \text{or} \quad -4 > 2$

$\qquad\qquad\qquad$ True $\qquad\qquad$ False

-4 is a solution since it satisfies one of the conditions.

$$a < -1 \quad \text{or} \quad a > 2$$

Substitute 0: $\quad 0 < -1 \quad \text{or} \quad 0 > 2$

$\qquad\qquad\quad$ False $\qquad\qquad$ False

0 is not a solution since it does *not* satisfy *either* condition.

$$a < -1 \quad \text{or} \quad a > 2$$

Substitute 5: $\quad 5 < -1 \quad \text{or} \quad 5 > 2$

$\qquad\qquad\quad$ False $\qquad\qquad$ True

5 is a solution since it satisfies one of the conditions.

Numbers less than -1 are solutions of the compound sentence since they satisfy the first condition. Numbers between -1 and 2 and the numbers -1 and 2 are not solutions since they do not satisfy either condition. Numbers greater than 2 are solutions since they satisfy the second condition. The solution sets of compound sentences can be described using graphs. The following graph shows all the solutions of the compound sentence $a < -1$ or $a > 2$.

Note that -1 and 2 are key numbers. They are the boundaries of the parts of the number line that are solutions.

Some compound sentences contain the word *and*. When two conditions of a compound sentence are joined by "and," *both* conditions must be satisfied to make the sentence true.

Example 1   Graph on a number line. $x > -1$ and $x \le 2$

Solution $x > -1$ and $x \le 2$

The numbers -1 and 2 are key numbers. They divide the number line into three parts. It is important to test numbers in each of the three parts to determine whether they satisfy both conditions of the inequality.

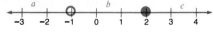

Test part a.

-1 and each number less than -1 make the compound inequality false because those numbers do not satisfy the first condition.

$$-1 > -1 \quad \text{and} \quad -1 \le 2$$

$\qquad$ False $\qquad\qquad\quad$ True

For students familiar with the language of sets, indicate that "or" is often used in describing the union of sets.

If x is in the union of set $A = \{1, 2, 3\}$ and set $B = \{2, 3, 4\}$, x is in set A or in set B (possibly in both). That is, $A \cup B = \{1, 2, 3, 4\}$.

The word "and" is used in describing the intersection of sets.

If x is in the intersection of set $A = \{1, 2, 3\}$ and set $B = \{2, 3, 4\}$, x is in both sets. That is, $A \cap B = \{2, 3\}$.

Here is a geometric example. If a point P is on line a *and* line b, then it must be located where the two lines cross.

If point P is on line a *or* line b, then it could be located anywhere on either line.

Point out that in graphing on the number line, a quick sketch will do. The endpoints must be clearly marked with an open or solid dot and labeled with the proper numbers. It is not necessary, however, to label the points that are not boundaries of the region. Solutions are graphed with a heavy dark line or by using color.

Example 1. Graph on the number line.

$$x \geq -4 \text{ and } x \leq -2$$

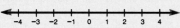

Example 2. Graph. $x < -2$ and $x > 2$

There is no solution.

Example 3. Graph. $x > -3$ or $x < 2$

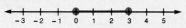

Since every number is either greater than -3 or less than 2, every number is a solution. The graph is the entire number line.

Example 4. Graph. $a \geq 0$ and $a \leq 3$

Numbers between, and including, 0 and 3 are solutions since they satisfy both conditions. Numbers greater than 3 or less than 0 are not.

CHECK UNDERSTANDING

- State a number that is less than 4 and less than -1. (Any number less than -1)
- State a number that is less than 5 and greater than 4. (Any number between 4 and 5)
- State a number that is less than 5 and greater than 6. (There is no such number.)
- State a number that is less than 5 or greater than 6. (Any number less than 5 is an answer. So is any number greater than 6.)

442

Example 1 (continued)

Test part b.

Numbers between -1 and 2, and 2, satisfy both conditions and are, therefore, solutions of the inequality.

$$1 > -1 \quad \text{and} \quad 1 \leq 2$$
True   True

Test part c.

Numbers greater than 2 are not solutions of the inequality because those numbers do not satisfy the second condition.

$$5 > -1 \quad \text{and} \quad 5 \leq 2$$
True   False

Answer

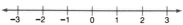

Example 2   Graph. $x < 2$ and $x > 3$

Solution   There are no numbers that are both less than 2 and greater than 3. Therefore, there are no solutions to the compound sentence, and the graph contains no points.

Example 3   Graph. $a \geq 3$ or $a > 4$

Solution   Numbers less than 3 are not solutions since they do not satisfy either condition.

$$1 \geq 3 \quad \text{or} \quad 1 > 4$$
False   False

The numbers 3 and 4, and numbers between 3 and 4 are solutions since they satisfy the first condition

$$3.5 \geq 3 \quad \text{or} \quad 3.5 > 4$$
True   False

Numbers greater than 4 are solutions since they satisfy both conditions.

$$6 \geq 3 \quad \text{or} \quad 6 > 4$$
True   True

Answer

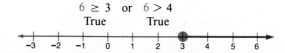

EXTRA PRACTICE, page 637
COMPUTER WORKSHEET 13

Example 4 Graph. $b \le 0$ and $b \le 3$

Solution Numbers less than or equal to 0 are solutions since they satisfy both conditions.

$$-1 \le 0 \quad \text{and} \quad -1 \le 3$$
$$\text{True} \qquad\qquad \text{True}$$

Numbers between 0 and 3, and 3, are not solutions since they do not satisfy the first condition.

$$2 \le 0 \quad \text{and} \quad 2 \le 3$$
$$\text{False} \qquad\qquad \text{True}$$

Numbers greater than 3 are not solutions since they do not satisfy either condition.

$$5 \le 0 \quad \text{and} \quad 5 \le 3$$
$$\text{False} \qquad\qquad \text{False}$$

Answer

■ CLASSROOM EXERCISES

True or false?

1. $2 < 4$ and $2 < 6$ T
2. $2 < 4$ or $2 < 6$ T
3. $6 < 8$ and $6 < -4$ F
4. $9 < 12$ or $9 < -4$ T
5. $6 < 5$ or $6 < 1$ F
6. $8 \le 8$ or $8 > 8$ T

Graph.

7. $a < -1$ or $a > 3$
8. $x \le -1$ and $x > 3$
9. $y > -2$ or $y > 0$
10. $y \ge -2$ and $y \ge 0$
11. $-2 < x$ and $x \le 2$
12. $-2 < x$ or $x \le 2$

Write a compound inequality for the graph.

13.

$x > -2$ and $x \le 3$

■ WRITTEN EXERCISES

True or false?

A
1. $10 < 20$ or $10 < 30$ T
2. $10 < 15$ or $10 < 25$ T
3. $10 < 20$ and $10 < 30$ T
4. $10 < 15$ and $10 < 25$ T
5. $5 < 8$ or $5 < 0$ T
6. $5 < 8$ or $5 < 3$ T
7. $5 < 8$ and $5 < 0$ F
8. $5 < 8$ and $5 < 3$ F
9. $2 < -20$ or $2 < -30$ F

CLASSROOM EXERCISES

In exercise 5, the compound statement is false because *both* simple statements are false. Exercise 6 is a specific example of a general property called the trichotomy property:

For all real numbers x and y, exactly one of these conditions exists:

$$x < y, \ x = y, \ \text{or} \ x > y$$

The general property could be stated as $x \le y$ or $x > y$. It could also be stated as $x < y$ or $x \ge y$.

ADDITIONAL ANSWERS

■ **Classroom Exercises**

7.
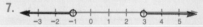

8.

9.

10.

11.

12.

ASSIGNMENT GUIDE

Basic	1–43 odd, Review Exercises, Self-Quiz 1
Average	3–42 multiples of 3, 45–61 odd, Review Exercises, Self-Quiz 1
Enriched	3–61 odd, 62–69 all, Review Exercises, Self-Quiz 1

PRACTICE WORKSHEET 47

ADDITIONAL ANSWERS

■ **Written Exercises**

19.

20.

21.

22.

23.

24.

25.

26.

27.

28.

29.

30.

31.

444

True or false?

10. $3 < -15$ or $3 < -25$ F

11. $6 < -12$ and $6 < -18$ F

12. $7 < -5$ and $7 < -15$ F

13. $5 \geq 5$ or $5 \geq 3$ T

14. $3 \geq 2$ or $3 \geq 3$ T

15. $4 > 2$ or $3 < 1$ T

16. $6 \geq 5$ and $5 \leq 6$ T

17. $7 \leq 8$ and $8 > -10$ T

18. $7 < 10$ or $7 > 10$ T

Graph on a number line.

19. $a < 2$ or $a > 3$

20. $a > 4$ or $a < 1$

21. $b \geq 4$ or $b \leq 0$

22. $b \leq 3$ or $b \geq 5$

23. $x < -2$ or $x \geq -1$

24. $x \leq -3$ or $x > 0$

25. $y > 2$ and $y < 5$

26. $y < 10$ and $y > 7$

27. $f < 5$ and $f > -2$

28. $f > -3$ and $f < 4$

29. $q < 3$ or $q > 2$

30. $q < 4$ or $q > 1$

31. $n < 3$ and $n > 2$

32. $n < 4$ and $n > 1$

33. $r = 2$ or $r < 1$

34. $r = 3$ or $r < -1$

35. $s \neq 3$ and $s > 0$

36. $s \neq 2$ and $s > 0$

Write a compound sentence for each graph.

37. $x < 0$ or $x > 2$

38. $x < -1$ or $x > 2$

39. $x \leq -8$ or $x \geq -5$

40. $x \leq -3$ or $x \geq -1$

41. $x > 33$ and $x < 37$

42. $x > 52$ and $x < 53$

43. $x \geq 0$ and $x \neq 2$

44. $x \leq 3$ and $x \neq 0$

List all the numbers in $\left\{2, 2\frac{1}{2}, 3, 3\frac{1}{2}, 4\right\}$ that are solutions of the compound sentence.

B 45. $x < 3\frac{7}{8}$ and $x > 2\frac{1}{2}$ $3, 3\frac{1}{2}$

46. $x > 2$ and $x \leq 3\frac{1}{4}$ $2\frac{1}{2}, 3$

444   Chapter 9   Inequalities and Their Graphs

32.

33.

34.

35.

36.

53.

54.

55.

56.

57.

58.

59.

60.

61.

47. $x < 2\frac{3}{4}$ or $x > 3\frac{3}{4}$ $2, 2\frac{1}{2}, 4$

48. $x > 3\frac{1}{4}$ or $x < 2\frac{1}{4}$ $2, 3\frac{1}{2}, 4$

49. $x \neq 3\frac{1}{2}$ and $x \geq 3$ $3, 4$

50. $x \neq 3$ and $x < 3\frac{1}{2}$ $2, 2\frac{1}{2}$

51. $x > 3$ and $x > 2\frac{1}{2}$ $3\frac{1}{2}, 4$

52. $x < 3$ and $x < 3\frac{1}{2}$ $2, 2\frac{1}{2}$

Write a compound sentence for each situation. Then graph the sentence on a number line.

53. An applicant's height must be between 157 cm and 173 cm. (Let h represent the height in centimeters.) $h > 157$ and $h < 173$

54. An applicant's mass must be between 45 kg and 79 kg. (Let m represent the mass in kilograms.) $m > 45$ and $m < 79$

55. The rod must be at least 6.5 cm long but it cannot be more than 6.7 cm long. $l \geq 6.5$ and $l \leq 6.7$

56. The food should be heated at 325°, plus or minus 10°. ("Plus or minus" 10° means the temperature could be as great as 10° more than 325° or as little as 10° less than 325°.) $t \geq 315$ and $t \leq 335$

57. The food should be heated for 12 min, plus or minus 2 min.
$m \geq 10$ and $m \leq 14$
58. The denominator could be any number greater than -2 but it cannot be 0.
$d > -2$ and $d \neq 0$
59. The numerator is either less than -5 or greater than 5. $n < -5$ or $n > 5$

60. The absolute value of a number is greater than 4. $|v| > 4$

61. The absolute value of a number is less than 4. $|v| < 4$

List all the numbers in $\{-2, -1, 0, 1, 2\}$ that are solutions of the compound sentence.

C **62.** $x + 2 > 1$ and $2x < 3$ $0, 1$

63. $2x > 1$ or $x + 3 < 1\frac{1}{2}$ $-2, 1, 2$

64. $3x + 1 \leq 5$ and $3x - 1 \geq 1$ 1

65. $x^2 > 0.5$ and $x \neq -1$ $-2, 1, 2$

66. $|x| > 1.5$ and $x \leq 1.5$ -2

67. $|x + 1| > 1.5$ or $x < -1.5$ $-2, 1, 2$

68. $x^2 + 3 > 5$ or $(x + 3)^2 < 5$ $-2, -1, 2$

69. $x^2 - 2x < 0$ or $x^2 + 2x < 0$ $-1, 1$

■ REVIEW EXERCISES

Simplify.

1. $(x^2 + 3x - 4) + (x - 5) - (x^2 - 2)$ $4x - 7$

2. $2x^2 \cdot xy^2$ $2x^3y^2$ [4–1, 4–3]

3. $(2x^2)^3$ $8x^6$

4. $2x \cdot (x^2 - 3x + 4)$ $2x^3 - 6x^2 + 8x$

5. $\dfrac{10^3}{10^5}$ $\dfrac{1}{10^2}$ [4–5, 4–6, 4–8]

CONCEPT EXTENSION

The role of the boundary value is an important concept in using "key numbers" to solve compound inequalities. Be sure that students understand that in graphing an inequality such as $x > 4$, the value 4 "divides" the number line (or set of numbers) into three groups—those on each side of 4 and 4 itself. All the numbers "to one side of 4" behave in the same fashion; either *all* satisfy the inequality or *none* satisfy the inequality. Therefore, only one representative number from that group needs to be tested to determine whether the group is part of the graph. Then the boundary value (or key number) needs to be checked.

Once this concept is in place, union and intersection ideas can be effectively used with key numbers to divide the number line into subsets for testing.

ENRICHMENT PROBLEMS

• Write a simple inequality that is equivalent to the compound inequality.

   a. $x < 3$ and $x < 6$ **b.** $x < 3$ or $x < 6$
   $x < 3$ $x < 6$

• What is the difference, if any, between these compound inequalities?

   a. $x > 2$ or $(x < 3$ and $x > 1)$
   b. $(x > 2$ or $x < 3)$ and $x > 1$
   There is no difference.

ADDITIONAL ANSWERS

■ Self-Quiz 1

3.

4.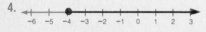

8.

9.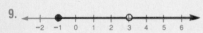

---

6. Change 463,000 to scientific notation. $4.63 \cdot 10^5$ [4–4]

7. Change $4.65 \cdot 10^6$ to standard decimal notation. 4,650,000   [4–4]

Solve.

8. Ms. Jones can grade 25 mathematics tests per hour and Ms. Smith can grade 20 mathematics tests per hour. If Ms. Smith starts at 3:00 P.M. and Ms. Jones starts at 3:30 P.M., at what time will they finish grading a total of 100 tests? 5:30 P.M.   [4–10]

Self-Quiz 1

9–1 True or false?

   1. $6 < -4$ F   **2.** $5 \geq 5$ T

   Graph on a number line.

   3. $x < 2\frac{1}{2}$ **4.** $x \geq -4$

   Write an inequality using x for this graph.

   5. $x \geq 6$

9–2 True or false?

   6. $-7 < -8$ and $5 > 4\frac{1}{2}$ False   **7.** $15 \geq 18$ or $-3 < 0$ True

   Graph on a number line.

   8. $x > 5$ or $x < 1$ **9.** $x \neq 3$ and $x \geq -1$

   Write a compound inequality using x for this graph.

   10. $x \geq -5$ and $x < -2$

9–1, Write an inequality or compound inequality for each situation.
9–2

   11. No student in the class is taller than 135 cm. (Let h represent the height in centimeters.) $h \leq 135$

   12. The cooking time should be between 3 and 5 min. (Let t represent the cooking time in minutes.) $t > 3$ and $t < 5$

   List the numbers in $\left\{ 3, 3\frac{1}{2}, 4, 4\frac{1}{2}, 5 \right\}$ that are solutions of the inequality.

   13. $x > 3\frac{1}{2}$ $4, 4\frac{1}{2}, 5$ **14.** $x < 4$ or $x \geq 4\frac{1}{2}$ $3, 3\frac{1}{2}, 4\frac{1}{2}, 5$

Graph on a number line.

1. $x > 2$ and $x < 5$

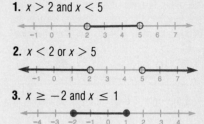

2. $x < 2$ or $x > 5$

3. $x \geq -2$ and $x \leq 1$

Write a compound sentence for each graph.

4.

$x \leq 20$ or $x \geq 25$

5.

$x > 50$ and $x < 60$

9–3 Solving Inequalities by Addition

Preview A puzzle

Graybeard the pirate and his 13 crew members captured 975 gold pieces and a solid gold box. Graybeard wanted the gold box for himself, but promised to buy it by putting an equal weight of gold pieces into the pile of loot. He said that the bag of gold pieces on this balance matched the box in weight. Was Graybeard lying or telling the truth? How do you know? Graybeard was lying.

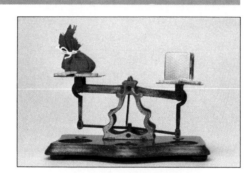

In this lesson you will learn a property that can be used to solve some inequalities.

■ LESSON

The basic strategy used to solve equations is to change them to simpler equivalent equations until the variable is alone on one side. We use the same technique to solve an inequality — changing to simpler equivalent inequalities until the variable is alone on one side. The addition property of inequalities permits us to change from one inequality to an equivalent inequality (one with the same set of solutions).

The Addition Property of Inequalities

For all numbers a, b, and c,

$$\text{if } a < b, \text{ then } a + c < b + c$$
$$\text{and}$$
$$\text{if } a > b, \text{ then } a + c > b + c.$$

For example, the inequality $x - 5 < 2$ can be solved as follows.

$$x - 5 < 2$$
Add 5 to both sides. $\quad x - 5 + 5 < 2 + 5$
Simplify. $\qquad\qquad\qquad x < 7$

PURPOSE

Just as equations may be solved by writing simpler equivalent equations, inequalities may be solved by writing simpler equivalent inequalities. Solving inequalities is useful in dealing with many practical problems.

PREVIEW

Point out that the right side of the balance is lower than the left. Therefore, the objects on the right side weigh more than those on the left. Assuming the gold pieces all weigh the same, three pieces could be removed from each side, preserving the relationship, and leaving only the bag of gold pieces and the gold box on the balance. The imbalance remains and the gold box is clearly heavier.

This relationship may be stated, "If $a + 3 < b + 3$, then $a < b$" (where a represents the weight of the bag of gold pieces, b represents the weight of the gold box, and each gold piece is a unit weight).

LESSON

The balance scale illustrated in the Preview or a seesaw can serve as a physical model for inequalities. Imagine two persons sitting at the opposite ends of a seesaw with the left end touching the ground. If equal weights are handed to each person, will they balance?

Will the right end go down? The answer to both questions is no; the left end will remain touching the ground. Similarly, if equal weights are removed from both ends, the seesaw will remain imbalanced in the same manner as it was originally. This situation is formally stated in the *addition property of inequalities*.

Removing a weight can be thought of as either subtracting a (positive) number or adding a negative number. Handing both persons identical helium-filled balloons can represent adding negative weights to both sides in the seesaw model.

ADDITIONAL EXAMPLES

Example 1. Solve. $c + 4 \leq 5.3$

The set of all numbers less than or equal to 1.3

Example 2. Solve. $2r - 6 \leq 3r + 4$

The set of all numbers greater than or equal to -10

Example 3. Solve and graph. $a + 5 \neq 1$

The set of all numbers except -6

The solution set is the set of real numbers less than 7. The graph is as shown here.

Example 1   Solve. $y + 4 \geq 3.2$

Solution
$$y + 4 \geq 3.2$$
Add -4 to both sides. $y \geq -0.8$

Answer   The set of all numbers greater than or equal to -0.8

Example 2   Solve. $3x - 6 < 2x + 3$

Solution
$$3x - 6 < 2x + 3$$
Add $-2x$ to both sides. $x - 6 < 3$
Add 6 to both sides. $x < 9$

Answer   The set of all numbers less than 9

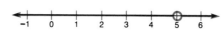

Example 3   Solve and graph. $x - 3 \neq 2$

Solution
$$x - 3 \neq 2$$
Add 3 to both sides. $x \neq 5$

Answer   The set of all numbers except 5

Example 4   Solve by writing and solving an inequality: After finding a quarter, Beverly knew that she had at least $2.15. How much did she have before she found the quarter?

Solution   "At least" means the amount of money is greater than or equal to $2.15. Let $x =$ the amount of money (in dollars) that Beverly started with.

$$x + 0.25 \geq 2.15$$
$$x \geq 1.90$$

Answer   Beverly started with at least $1.90.

CLASSROOM STRATEGY   Reinforcement

Research indicates that students are more likely to remember what they have learned if (1) the teacher describes what has been learned and (2) the teacher asks students to describe what they have learned.

■ CLASSROOM EXERCISES

Solve.

1. $a + 6 > -2$ $a > -8$
2. $x - 2 \le -3$ $x \le -1$
3. $5 + x < 3$ $x < -2$

4. $4x + 3 \ge 3x + 1$ $x \ge -2$
5. $4 - 3x < 6 - 4x$ $x < 2$
6. $2x + 5 \ne x - 3$ $x \ne -8$

■ WRITTEN EXERCISES

Solve.

A

1. $a + 5 > -1$ $a > -6$
2. $x + 4 > -3$ $x > -7$
3. $x - 3 \ge 6$ $x \ge 9$

4. $x - 2 \ge 5$ $x \ge 7$
5. $3x \le 2x + 4$ $x \le 4$
6. $4x \le 3x + 2$ $x \le 2$

7. $x - 6 < -2$ $x < 4$
8. $x - 4 < -3$ $x < 1$
9. $5x + 2 \ge 4x + 3$ $x \ge 1$

10. $3x + 6 \ge 2x + 10$ $x \ge 4$
11. $2x + 6 < x - 4$ $x < -10$
12. $3x + 2 < 2x - 5$ $x < -7$

Solve. Graph the solutions on a number line.

13. $6x \le 5x - 2$ $x \le -2$
14. $5x \le 4x - 3$ $x \le -3$
15. $2x + 3 > 3x + 2$ $x < 1$

16. $4x + 5 < 5x + 3$ $x > 2$
17. $x + 2 > 2x + 5$ $x < -3$
18. $3x + 4 > 4x + 1$ $x < 3$

Solve the compound sentence. Graph the solutions on a number line.

19. $x + 2 < 5$ or $x + 1 > 6$ $x < 3$ or $x > 5$
20. $x + 1 < 3$ or $x + 2 > 6$ $x < 2$ or $x > 4$

21. $x + 2 > 5$ and $x + 1 < 6$ $x > 3$ and $x < 5$
22. $x + 1 > 3$ and $x + 2 < 6$ $x > 2$ and $x < 4$

23. $2x \ge x + 5$ or $x + 6 < 7$ $x \ge 5$ or $x < 1$
24. $2x < x + 2$ or $x + 2 \ge 6$ $x < 2$ or $x \ge 4$

25. $2x \ge 3x + 5$ and $3x + 2 \ge 2x - 4$ $x \le -5$ and $x \ge -6$
26. $3x + 5 \ge 2x$ and $2x \ge 3x + 2$ $x \ge -5$ and $x \le -2$

Write an inequality for each situation. Then solve the inequality.

27. If Dustin grew 2 cm, he would be at least 172 cm tall. How tall is Dustin now? $d \ge 170$

28. If Nicole gained 3 kg, she would weigh at least 45 kg. What is Nicole's present weight? $n \ge 42$

29. After Kara spent $2.50 she had less than $5.50 left. How much money did Kara have originally? $k < 8$

30. Jeremy had less than $2.50 left after paying a $4 bill. How much money did Jeremy have before he paid the bill? $j < 6.5$

31. If the music shop sold 25 records it would still have more than 850 records. How many records does it have now? $m > 875$

32. The video store had more than 635 tapes left after selling 35 tapes. How many tapes did the store have originally? $v > 670$

ADDITIONAL EXAMPLES

Example 4. Solve.

If Todd scored 15 points on the next test, he would have more than 200 total points. How many points does Todd have now?

Let x = the number of points Todd has now.

$$x + 15 > 200$$
$$x > 185$$

Todd has more than 185 points now.

CHECK UNDERSTANDING

Solve.

• $x - 5 < 9$ (The set of all numbers less than 14)
• $a + 3 \ge 2$ (The set of all numbers greater than or equal to -1)

CLASSROOM EXERCISES

Contrast exercises 1 and 2. Exercise 1 is a strict inequality (greater than). Exercise 2 is a compound sentence permitting equality or inequality. Also note that in solving exercise 1, a negative number is added to both sides; in solving exercise 2, a positive number is added to both sides.

ADDITIONAL ANSWERS

■ Written Exercises

13.
14.
15.
16.
17.
18.
19.

ASSIGNMENT GUIDE

Basic   1–35 odd, Review Exercises
Average   1–45 odd, Review Exercises
Enriched   3–45 multiples of 3, 46–53 all,
            Review Exercises

PRACTICE WORKSHEET 48

9-3 SOLVING INEQUALITIES BY ADDITION

■ Solve.

1. $p + 3 \geq 7$ $p \geq 4$ 2. $n - 5 < 2\frac{1}{2}$ $n < 7\frac{1}{2}$
3. $c - 6 > -2$ $c > 4$ 4. $4q \leq 3q - 5$ $q \leq -5$
5. $r + 3 \leq 2r - 8$ $r \geq 11$ 6. $3a + 7 > 2a - 2$ $a > -9$
7. $5s - 1 < 6s - 5$ $s > 4$ 8. $z + 4 \geq 2z + 4$ $z \leq 0$

■ Solve the compound sentence. Graph the solution on the number line.

9. $a + 4 < 5$ or $a - 2 > 2$ $a > 4$ or $a < 1$ 10. $q + 2 \leq 3$ and $q + 3 \geq -1$ $-4 \leq q \leq 1$

11. $3v - 1 \geq 2v + 1$ and $2v + 3 \geq 3v - 2$ 12. $z - 2 \leq 2z - 6$ or $4z + 1 \leq 3z + 1$
     $2 \leq v \leq 5$ $z \leq 0$ or $z \geq 4$

ADDITIONAL ANSWERS

■ **Written Exercises**

20.
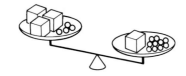

21.

22.

23.

24.

25.

26.

From these unbalanced situations, find the number of unit weights (○) that would balance a block (⬠). Assume that each block weighs the same and each rod (⬭) weighs the same.

33. Less than 3

34. More than 10

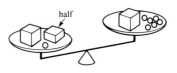

35. Less than 5

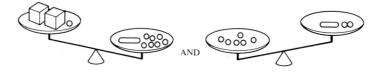

AND

Solve.

B **36.** $3(x - 3) > 2x + 1$ $x > 10$ **37.** $2(x - 3) > 3x + 1$ $x < -7$
38. $2(x + 4) < 3x + 4$ $x > 4$ **39.** $4(x + 3) < 3x - 4$ $x < -16$
40. $2(x + 3) + 5 \geq x + 8$ $x \geq -3$ **41.** $5x - 3 \geq 6(x - 1) + 2$ $x \leq 1$
42. $x^2 + 3x + 4 \leq x^2 + 4x$ $x \geq 4$ **43.** $x^2 + 3x + 4 \leq x^2 + 2x$ $x \leq -4$
44. $x(x + 6) + 1 > x(x + 5) + 3$ $x > 2$ **45.** $x(x + 6) + 5 > x(x + 7) + 8$ $x < -3$

Solve. Graph the solutions on a number line.

C **46.** $x + 5 < 2(x + 4)$ and $x + 5 > 2(x - 4)$ $x > -3$ and $x < 13$
47. $x + 5 > 2(x + 4)$ or $x + 5 < 2(x - 4)$ $x < -3$ or $x > 13$
48. $4.5x + 3.2 \geq 3.5x + 5.7$ and $2.3x - 1.7 \leq 1.3x + 1.8$ $x \geq 2.5$ and $x \leq 3.5$
49. $4.5x + 3.2 \leq 3.5x + 5.7$ or $2.3x - 1.7 \geq 1.3x + 1.8$ $x \leq 2.5$ or $x \geq 3.5$

List all the numbers in $\{-2, -1, 0, 1, 2\}$ that are solutions of these compound sentences.

50. $x^2 + 2x < x^2 + x$ and $5x + 2 > 4x$ -1
51. $x^2 + 3x < x^2 + 2x$ or $3x - 1 > 2x$ $-2, -1, 2$

52. $2(x - 1) \le 3x - 1$ and $3(x - 1) \le 2x - 2$ $_{-1, 0, 1}$

53. $x(x + 1) \ge x^2 + 1$ or $3(x + 2) \le 2x + 4$ $_{-2, 1, 2}$

■ REVIEW EXERCISES

1. In which quadrant or on which axis do the following points lie? [5-1]

  a. $(3, 0)$ x-axis   **b.** $(4, -3)$ IV   **c.** $(-1, 5)$ II

2. The set $\{(0, 4), (1, 4), (1, 5), (2, 5)\}$ describes a relation. [5-2]

  a. List the domain. $_{(0, 1, 2)}$ **b.** List the range. $_{(4, 5)}$ **c.** Graph the relation.

3. Select three values of x, complete the table, plot the points, and then graph [5-4]
the equation $3x + 3y = 12$.

x	?	?	?
y	?	?	?

4. Copy and complete the table. Then graph the equation $y = (x - 1)^2$. [5-4]

x	-3	-2	-1	0	1	2	3
y	?	?	?	?	?	?	?
	16	9	4	1	0	1	4

5. Draw these three lines through the point $(0, -2)$ labeling the lines a, b, and c. [5-5]

  a. line with slope $\dfrac{2}{3}$ **b.** line with slope -1 **c.** line with slope 0

6. State the slopes of lines a, b, and c. [5-5]

  a: $-\dfrac{1}{2}$ b: 2   c: 0

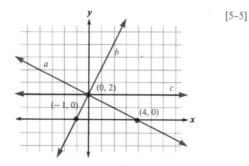

7. State the slope and y-intercept of the equation $2x - 3y = 6$. $\frac{2}{3}, -2$ [5-6]

In exercises 33–35, let a variable (for example, x) represent the weight of a box. The solutions may be found algebraically by solving these inequalities:

  33. $3x + 4 < x + 10$

  34. $1.5x + 1 > x + 6$

  35. $2x + 1 < y + 7$ and $6 > y + 2$

Exercise 35 is most easily solved by thinking of substituting 4 unit weights for a rod on the right side of the first scale.

ADDITIONAL ANSWERS

■ Written Exercises

46.

47.

48.

49.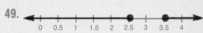

Additional answers for the Review Exercises are on page 652.

CONCEPT EXTENSION

The use of an actual balance to provide a physical model of inequality operations should be considered in developing this and subsequent lessons. Using a balance not only helps students visualize the algebraic steps; it also aids in retention. (A balance problem is much easier to recall than a chalkboard example.) Moreover, you may use the balance to pose some challenge problems that preview some ideas that will be introduced in the next two lessons.

ENRICHMENT PROBLEM

• Knowing the weights of four astronauts is critical for space missions. The following information is known:

    Dimitri weighs less than Carlos.

    Carlos weighs less than Brian.

    Alex and Brian weigh less together than do Carlos and Dimitri.

Rank the astronauts by weight.

  Alex < Dimitri < Carlos < Brian

Solve. Graph the solutions on a number line.

1. $5x \le 4x + 3$ $\qquad$ $x \le 3$

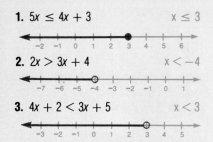

2. $2x > 3x + 4$ $\qquad$ $x < -4$

3. $4x + 2 < 3x + 5$ $\qquad$ $x < 3$

Solve the compound sentence. Graph the solutions on a number line.

4. $x + 3 < 2$ or $2x + 1 > x + 2$ $\qquad$ $x < -1$ or $x > 1$

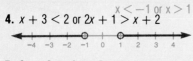

5. $3x - 2 \ge 2x + 5$ and
$4x - 3 \le 3x + 5$ $\qquad$ $7 \le x \le 8$

PURPOSE

The multiplication property of inequalities is sometimes needed to write a simpler, equivalent expression in the solution of a linear inequality.

PREVIEW

Let students complete the exercises so that they discover the multiplication property of inequalities. In each exercise, both sides of the original inequality have been multiplied by the same number. To determine whether the statement is true, simplify both sides of the inequality. Multiplying by zero makes both sides zero. Therefore $0(3) < 0(7)$ is false, since 0 is not less than 0. But $0(4) \ge 0(-2)$ is true because the equality part of the compound sentence is satisfied. Emphasize that multiplying both sides of an inequality by a negative number produces an equivalent statement *only if* the sense of the inequality is reversed—for example, $3 < 7$ so $-2(3) > -2(7)$.

OBJECTIVE 9–4

To solve inequalities by using the multiplication property of inequalities.

9–4 Solving Inequalities by Multiplication

Preview

The multiplication property of equality states that multiplying both sides of an equation by a nonzero number results in an equivalent equation. What can you discover about multiplication of inequalities from these examples?

True or false?

1. a. $\quad 3 < 7$ $\quad$ T
b. $6(3) < 6(7)$ $\quad$ T
c. $0.2(3) < 0.2(7)$ $\quad$ T
d. $0(3) < 0(7)$ $\quad$ F
e. $-2(3) < -2(7)$ $\quad$ F
f. $-2(3) > -2(7)$ $\quad$ T

2. a. $\quad 4 \ge -2$ $\quad$ T
b. $3(4) \ge 3(-2)$ $\quad$ T
c. $0.5(4) \ge 0.5(-2)$ $\quad$ T
d. $0(4) \ge 0(-2)$ $\quad$ T
e. $-1(4) \ge -1(-2)$ $\quad$ F
f. $-3(4) \le -3(-2)$ $\quad$ T

3. a. $\quad -5 < -2$ $\quad$ T
b. $2(-5) < 2(-2)$ $\quad$ T
c. $0.1(-5) < 0.1(-2)$ $\quad$ T
d. $0(-5) < 0(-2)$ $\quad$ F
e. $-10(-5) < -10(-2)$ $\quad$ F
f. $-2(-5) > -2(-2)$ $\quad$ T

The multiplication property of inequalities has two cases, one for positive multipliers and one for negative multipliers. Try to state both cases.

In this lesson you will use the multiplication property of inequalities to solve inequalities.

■ LESSON

The inequalities $a > b$ and $c > d$ are said to be inequalities in the **same sense,** whereas $a < b$ and $c > d$ are said to be inequalities in the **opposite sense** (that is, the inequality signs are reversed).

Multiplying both sides of an inequality by a positive number results in an equivalent inequality in the same sense. Multiplying both sides of an inequality by a negative number results in an equivalent inequality in the opposite sense.

The Multiplication Property of Inequalities

For all numbers a, b, and c, $c > 0$,

$$\text{if } a < b, \text{ then } ca < cb$$

$$\text{and}$$

$$\text{if } a > b, \text{ then } ca > cb.$$

For all numbers a, b, and c, $c < 0$,

$$\text{if } a < b, \text{ then } ca > cb$$

$$\text{and}$$

$$\text{if } a > b, \text{ then } ca < cb.$$

These examples show how to use the multiplication property to solve inequalities.

Example 1   Solve and graph on a number line. $4x > 9$

Solution
$$4x > 9$$

Multiply both sides by $\frac{1}{4}$. $\frac{1}{4}(4x) > \frac{1}{4}(9)$ (The sense of the inequality is maintained.)

$$x > \frac{9}{4}$$

Answer   The set of all numbers greater than $\frac{9}{4}$

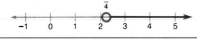

Example 2   Solve and graph on a number line. $-2x \geq 5$

Solution
$$-2x \geq 5$$

Multiply both sides by $-\frac{1}{2}$. $-\frac{1}{2}(-2x) \leq -\frac{1}{2}(5)$ (The sense of the inequality is reversed.)

$$x \leq -\frac{5}{2}$$

Answer   The set of all numbers less than or equal to $-\frac{5}{2}$

Example 3   Solve and graph. $-\frac{3x}{8} \leq 24$

Solution
$$-\frac{3x}{8} \leq 24$$

Multiply both sides by 8 and simplify. $8\left(-\frac{3x}{8}\right) \leq 8(24)$

$$-3x \leq 192$$

Multiply both sides by $-\frac{1}{3}$ and simplify. $-\frac{1}{3}(-3x) \geq -\frac{1}{3}(192)$

$$x \geq -64$$

Answer   The set of all numbers greater than or equal to -64

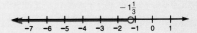

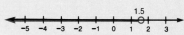
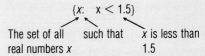
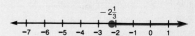

Example 4. During the first three months of the year the Zorkel Corporation made a profit of at least $1.5 million. What was the average profit per month?

$$3x \geq 1,500,000$$
$$x \geq 500,000$$

The average monthly profit was at least $.5 million (that is, at least $500,000).

CHECK UNDERSTANDING

Write an equivalent inequality by multiplying both sides by the given number.

- $4x < 12$ by ¼ $(x < 3)$
- $-2a < 6$ by $-½$ $(a > -3)$
- $\frac{y}{2} > 14$ by 2 $(y > 28)$
- $\frac{b}{-5} > -15$ by -5 $(b < 75)$

CLASSROOM EXERCISES

Contrast exercises 1 and 2 by bringing out that the sense of an inequality is reversed when both sides are multiplied by a negative number.

Contrast exercises 5 and 7 by bringing out that in one case the boundary point is included and in the other it is not. Consequently, an open circle is used for the boundary point in the first case and a darkened circle is used in the second case.

ADDITIONAL ANSWERS
■ **Classroom Exercises**

5.

6.

7.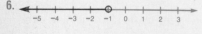

8.

Example 4   A 12-oz bottle of liquid soap sells for $0.82. At what price is a 15-oz bottle more economical?

Solution   One bottle is more economical than another if its unit price is less. The unit price can be expressed as the ratio of cost to weight. Let c be the cost of the 15-oz bottle. The unit price of the 12-oz bottle is $\frac{0.82}{12}$ and the unit price of the 15-oz bottle is $\frac{c}{15}$.

$$\frac{0.82}{12} > \frac{c}{15}$$

Multiply by 60 to eliminate fractions. $60\left(\frac{0.82}{12}\right) > 60\left(\frac{c}{15}\right)$

$$4.1 > 4c$$

$$\frac{1}{4}(4.1) > \frac{1}{4}(4c)$$

$$1.025 > c$$

Answer   The cost of a 15-oz bottle must be less than $1.025. That means that the cost must be $1.02 or less.

■ CLASSROOM EXERCISES

What is the missing inequality sign: $<$, $>$, $\leq$, or $\geq$?

1. If $x < 9$, then $2x$ Ⓐ $2(9)$. $<$ **2.** If $y < 4$, then $-3y$ Ⓐ $-3(4)$. $>$

3. If $a > 2$, then $-0.2a$ Ⓐ $-0.2(2)$. $<$ **4.** If $b > 5$, then $4b$ Ⓐ $4(5)$. $>$

Solve and graph.

5. $\frac{x}{3} < 6$ < 18 **6.** $-5y > 5$ $y < -1$ **7.** $-2a \leq -4$ $a \geq 2$ **8.** $\frac{3x}{4} \geq -2$

                                                                              $x \geq -\frac{8}{3}$

■ WRITTEN EXERCISES

What is the missing inequality sign, $<$ or $>$?

Ⓐ **1.** If $x < 3$, then $4x$ Ⓐ $4(3)$. $<$ **2.** If $x < 2$, then $3x$ Ⓐ $3(2)$. $<$

3. If $x > 5$, then $4x$ Ⓐ $4(5)$. $>$ **4.** If $x > 12$, then $3x$ Ⓐ $3(12)$. $>$

5. If $x < 8$, then $-5x$ Ⓐ $-5(8)$. $>$ **6.** If $x < 4$, then $-6x$ Ⓐ $-6(4)$. $>$

7. If $x > 7$, then $-10x$ Ⓐ $-10(7)$. $<$ **8.** If $x > 6$, then $-8x$ Ⓐ $-8(6)$. $<$

True or false?

9. If $x \geq -2$, then $5x \geq 5(-2)$. T   **10.** If $x \geq -5$, then $3x \geq 3(-5)$. T

ASSIGNMENT GUIDE

Basic   1–33 odd, Review Exercises
Average 3–33 multiples of 3, 35–49 odd,
           Review Exercises
Enriched 15–54 multiples of 3, 57–60 all,
           Review Exercises

PRACTICE WORKSHEET 48

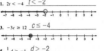

True or false?

11. If $x \le -6$, then $\frac{1}{2}x \ge \frac{1}{2}(-6)$. F
           12. If $x \le -6$, then $\frac{1}{3}x \ge \frac{1}{3}(-6)$. F

13. If $2x \ge 10$, then $\frac{1}{2}(2x) \ge \frac{1}{2}(10)$. T
           14. If $3x \le 12$, then $\frac{1}{3}(3x) \le \frac{1}{3}(12)$. T

15. If $-2x \le 10$, then $-\frac{1}{2}(-2x) \le -\frac{1}{2}(10)$. F **16.** If $-3x \ge 12$, then $-\frac{1}{3}(-3x) \ge -\frac{1}{3}(12)$. F

Solve and graph on a number line.

17. $3a < 6$ $a < 2$ **18.** $2a < 6$ $a < 3$ **19.** $\frac{1}{2}b > 6$ $b > 12$ **20.** $\frac{1}{3}b > 6$ $b > 18$

21. $-4c < 12$ $c > -3$ **22.** $-6c < 12$ $c > -2$ **23.** $-\frac{1}{6}d > 12$ $d < -72$ **24.** $-\frac{1}{4}d > 12$ $d < -48$

25. $2r \ge -5$ $r \ge -\frac{5}{2}$ **26.** $2r \ge -3$ $r \ge -\frac{3}{2}$ **27.** $-\frac{1}{2}s \le -9$ $s \ge 18$ **28.** $-\frac{1}{2}s \le -7$ $s \ge 14$

Write an inequality for each situation. Then solve the inequality and answer the question.

29. Mr. Bradley paid more than \$7.20 for 3 lb of meat. What was the cost per pound? (Let c represent the cost per pound.) $c > \frac{7.20}{3}$; cost > \$2.40/lb

30. Two pounds of cheese cost Mrs. Corning more than \$5.50. What was the cost per pound? $c > \frac{5.50}{2}$; cost > \$2.75/lb

31. Denise Dravell bought $\frac{1}{2}$ lb of spices and paid less than \$4.00. What was the cost per pound? $c < 2(4.00)$; cost < \$8/lb

32. Ernie Ersland bought $\frac{1}{4}$ lb of chemicals and paid less than \$2.00. What was the cost per pound? $c < 4(2.00)$; cost < \$8/lb

33. The Zelco Corporation made a profit of less than $-\$10,000$ (actually a loss) during the first 5 months of the year. What was their average monthly profit? $p < \frac{-10,000}{5}$; profit < $-\$2000$/mo

34. The Velnor Company made a profit of less than $-\$1800$ (actually a loss) during the first 3 months of the year. What was their average monthly profit? $p < \frac{-1800}{3}$; profit < $-\$600$/mo

B **35.** A 6-pack of juice costs \$1.00. At what price is an 8-pack of juice more economical? $\frac{p}{8} < \frac{1.00}{6}$; price < \$1.34

36. A $2\frac{1}{2}$-oz jar of onion salt sells for 75¢. The $9\frac{1}{4}$-oz jar has a smaller unit selling price. What is the selling price of the $9\frac{1}{4}$-oz jar? $\frac{p}{9.25} < \frac{.75}{2.5}$; price < \$2.78

37. The Wildcats basketball team made 12 field goals in 25 attempts in the first half of a game. In the second half of the game they took only 20 shots but had a higher shooting percentage than in the first half. How many field goals did the Wildcats make in the second half? $\frac{n}{20} > \frac{12}{25}$; number of field goals > 9

ADDITIONAL ANSWERS

■ **Written Exercises**

25.

26.

27.

28.

39.

40.

41.

42.

43.

44.

45.

46.

47.

48.

49.

50.

51.

52.

53.

54.

Graphs for Written Exercises 55–60, and Review Exercise 1 are on page 652.

38. Denise Waller used 16 gal of gasoline driving 480 mi on the first day of a trip. On the second day she drove 500 mi and had a better fuel consumption rate. How many gallons of gasoline did Denise use on the second day? $\frac{480}{16} < \frac{500}{n}$; number of gallons $< 16\frac{2}{3}$

Solve and graph on a number line.

39. $\frac{2}{3}x \le -12$ $x \le -18$

40. $-\frac{2}{3}x \le -12$ $x \ge 18$

41. $\frac{5}{8}x \le 40$ $x \le 64$

42. $-\frac{5}{4}x \le 20$ $x \ge -16$

43. $-\frac{3}{4}y \ge -12$ $y \le 16$

44. $\frac{3}{4}y \ge -12$ $y \ge -16$

45. $\frac{9}{4}y \ge 72$ $y \ge 32$

46. $-\frac{2}{9}y \ge 90$ $y \le -405$

47. $\frac{x}{5} > 10$ $x > 50$

48. $\frac{x}{5} > -10$ $x > -50$

49. $-\frac{x}{3} > -60$ $x < 180$

50. $-\frac{x}{4} > 20$ $x < -80$

Solve and graph these compound inequalities.

C **51.** $-2x \le -6$ and $x - 2 \le 4$ $x \ge 3$ and $x \le 6$

52. $-2x \ge -6$ or $x - 2 \ge 4$ $x \le 3$ or $x \ge 6$

53. $-\frac{1}{2}x \ge 4$ or $x + 2 \ge 12$ $x \le -8$ or $x \ge 10$

54. $\frac{1}{2}x \le -4$ and $x + 12 \ge 2$
   $x \le -8$ and $x \ge -10$

55. $\frac{3}{8}x \ge 24$ or $x + 8 \le 24$ $x \ge 64$ or $x \le 16$

56. $-\frac{3}{8}x \ge -24$ and $x - 8 \ge 24$
   $x \le 64$ and $x \ge 32$

Solve and graph on a number line. [*Remember:* The values for a variable may be positive or negative.]

57. $\frac{1}{y} \le 3$
   $y \ge \frac{1}{3}$ or $y < 0$

58. $\frac{1}{2y} \le 10$
   $y \ge \frac{1}{20}$ or $y < 0$

59. $\frac{4}{x} > \frac{1}{2}$ $x < 8$ and $x > 0$

60. $-\frac{6}{x} < 3$
   $x > 0$ or $x < -2$

■ **REVIEW EXERCISES**

1. Solve this system by graphing.   [6–1]
   $\begin{aligned} x + y &= 6 \\ x - 2y &= -6 \end{aligned}$ $\{(2, 4)\}$

2. Solve this system by substitution.   [6–2]
   $\begin{aligned} x + 2y &= 12 \\ x &= 2y \end{aligned}$ $\{(6, 3)\}$

3. State whether the following system has zero, one, or infinitely many   [6–3]
   solutions.
   $\begin{aligned} 2x + y &= 4 \\ 6x + 3y &= 12 \end{aligned}$ Many

4. Solve this system by multiplication and addition.   [6–6]
   $\begin{aligned} 3x + y &= 5 \\ x - 2y &= 4 \end{aligned}$ $\{(2, -1)\}$

Solve.

5. One number is 10 more than twice another. If the sum of the two numbers is 100, what are the numbers? 30, 70   [6–4]

6. We need to make 20 L of a solution that is 50% alcohol. If we mix a solution of 40% alcohol with a solution of 80% alcohol, how many liters of each solution should we use? 40%: 15L, 80%: 5L   [6–7]

EXTENSION   Solving direct variation problems on a computer

The electrical resistance of a wire is directly proportional to the length of the wire. If 200 m (X1) of an 18-gauge wire has a resistance of 4.3 ohms (Y1), we can compute the length (X2) of this wire for a given resistance (Y2). We can also compute its resistance (Y2) for any length (X2). The following program can be used to solve problems like this that involve direct variation.

```
10   PRINT "WHAT ARE THE VALUES OF X1 AND Y1";
20   INPUT X1, Y1
30   PRINT "IS THE VALUE OF X2 KNOWN (Y OR N)";
40   INPUT A$
50   IF A$ = "Y" THEN 110
60   PRINT "WHAT IS THE VALUE OF Y2";
70   INPUT Y2
80   X2 = X1 * Y2/Y1
90   PRINT "X2 =    "; X2
100  GOTO 150
110  PRINT "WHAT IS THE VALUE OF X2";
120  INPUT X2
130  Y2 = Y1 * X2/X1
140  PRINT "Y2 =    "; Y2
150  END
```

[The dollar sign indicates to the computer that the input is a letter (or any other symbol) rather than a number.]

What is the resistance of the following lengths of the wire described above?

1. 500 m   **2.** 10 m   **3.** 1 m   **4.** 2 km
    10.75 ohms   0.215 ohm   0.0215 ohm   43 ohms

What length of this wire can be used if its resistance can be no more than the following?

5. 10 ohms   **6.** 450 ohms   **7.** 1 ohm   **8.** 0.3 ohm
    465.1 m   20.93 km   46.51 m   13.95 m

CONCEPT EXTENSION

The key idea behind the multiplication property of inequalities is the notion that an equivalent expression results; that is, any value that makes the first inequality true (or false) will also make the second inequality true (or false). For a given inequality, a comparison of table values might bring this point out:

	$x > 2$		$2x > 4$
x	$x > 2$	$2x$	$2x > 4$
3	true	6	true
2.01	true	4.02	true
1.98	false	3.96	false
−1	false	−2	false

$$-\frac{1}{2}x < -1$$

x	$-\frac{1}{2}x$	$-\frac{1}{2}x < -1$
3	−1.5	true
2.01	−1.005	true
1.98	−0.99	false
−1	0.5	false

Note that all three inequalities are true when x is replaced with 3 or 2.01. All three are false when x is replaced with 1.98 or −1.

ENRICHMENT PROBLEMS

- Solve the inequality $-3 < -x$ in two ways:
  a. Multiply both sides by −1.
  b. Add $x + 3$ to both sides.
  The set of all numbers less than 3

- Two numbers a and b are related in this way:
$$a < b.$$
If $ca + d > cb + d$, what can you say about the numbers c and d?
d could be any real number; c must be negative.

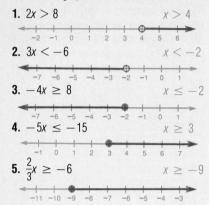

1. $2x > 8$ $\qquad x > 4$

2. $3x < -6$ $\qquad x < -2$

3. $-4x \geq 8$ $\qquad x \leq -2$

4. $-5x \leq -15$ $\qquad x \geq 3$

5. $\frac{2}{3}x \geq -6$ $\qquad x \geq -9$

PURPOSE

Inequalities may be written to describe many problems that arise in the real world. Solving the inequalities may require the use of addition and multiplication properties.

PREVIEW

It is not necessary for students to know a great deal about probability in order to appreciate the situation. However, you may wish to explain briefly what a probability of 0.06 means. Out of each 100 possible outcomes of the game, 6 of those outcomes are favorable to the player. For example, a dart board may have the numbers from 1 to 100. If the numbers 30, 40, 50, 60, 70, and 80 are winning numbers and the others are losing numbers, the probability of winning is 0.06.

LESSON

Emphasize that inequalities are solved by using the same basic properties used in solving equations; that is, the distributive, associative, and commutative properties for combining like terms by adding the same quantity to both sides of the sentence, and so on. One difference in the technique occurs, however, when both sides of an inequality are multiplied by a negative number; then the sense of the inequality must be reversed.

OBJECTIVE 9–5

To solve inequalities by using the addition and multiplication properties of inequalities.

You may wish to spend two days on this section. Refer to the Pacing Chart.

9–5 Solving Inequalities by Addition and Multiplication

Preview **Average gain**

Ms. Armand's students are running a carnival booth as a money-raising project. The class developed a game in which the probability of winning for each play is 0.06. The average amount a player can expect to gain per play is given by this formula:

$$\begin{array}{ccccc} \text{Player's average gain} \\ \text{in one play} \end{array} = \begin{array}{c} \text{Probability} \\ \text{of winning} \end{array} \times \begin{array}{c} \text{Value} \\ \text{of prize} \end{array} - \begin{array}{c} \text{Cost of} \\ \text{one play} \end{array}$$

A positive average gain means that the player can expect to win and the class can expect to lose. A negative average gain means that the player can expect to lose and the class can expect to win.

What should be the value of each prize if the class charges $0.25 for each play and wants its profit to be at least $0.13 on each play? $2

In this lesson you will learn to solve inequalities such as the following to help you solve problems like the one above.

$$0.06x - 0.25 \leq -0.13$$

■ LESSON

The addition and multiplication properties of inequalities can be used together to solve inequalities. The general approach to solving inequalities is the same as that for solving equations. However, care must be taken to reverse the sense of the inequality when multiplying or dividing by a negative number.

Example 1	Solve and graph. $4x - 2 > x + 1$

Solution

$$4x - 2 > x + 1$$
Add $-x$ *to both sides.* $\qquad 3x - 2 > 1$
Add 2 *to both sides.* $\qquad 3x > 3$

Multiply both sides by $\frac{1}{3}$. $\qquad x > 1$

Answer The set of all numbers greater than 1

Example 2 Solve and graph. $2(x - 3) \leq 5x - 12$

Solution

$$2(x - 3) \leq 5x - 12$$

Expand. $\qquad\qquad\qquad\qquad 2x - 6 \leq 5x - 12$

Add $-5x$ to both sides. $\qquad -3x - 6 \leq -12$

Add 6 to both sides. $\qquad\quad -3x \leq -6$

Divide both sides by -3. $\qquad x \geq 2$ (The sense of the inequality is reversed.)

Answer The set of all numbers greater than or equal to 2

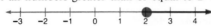

Example 3 In one city a taxi ride costs \$0.50 for the first quarter-mile and \$0.20 for each additional quarter-mile or part of a quarter-mile. How far can you ride at a cost of \$5.00 or less?

Solution Setting up a table can make the problem easier to understand. Let q be the number of quarter-miles ridden.

Number of quarter-miles ridden		Cost in dollars
More than	Less than or equal to	
0	1	0.50
1	2	0.50 + 0.20(1)
2	3	0.50 + 0.20(2)
3	4	0.50 + 0.20(3)
.	.	.
.	.	.
.	.	.
$q - 1$	q	0.50 + 0.20($q - 1$)

Inequality: $\qquad\qquad\qquad\qquad 0.50 + 0.20(q - 1) \leq 5.00$

Multiply both sides by 10 to eliminate decimals. $\qquad 5 + 2(q - 1) \leq 50$

$\qquad\qquad\qquad\qquad\qquad\qquad\qquad 5 + 2q - 2 \leq 50$

$\qquad\qquad\qquad\qquad\qquad\qquad\qquad 2q + 3 \leq 50$

$\qquad\qquad\qquad\qquad\qquad\qquad\qquad\qquad 2q \leq 47$

$\qquad\qquad\qquad\qquad\qquad\qquad\qquad\qquad q \leq 23.5$

Answer The number of quarter-miles that can be ridden for \$5.00 or less is less than or equal to 23.5. However, the inequality indicates that the cost increases smoothly rather than jumping \$.20 for each additional quarter-mile. Therefore, the number of quarter-miles must be less than or equal to 23, and the number of miles is less than or equal to $5\frac{3}{4}$.

Lesson continued

Students should be reminded of the importance of checking their solution of an inequality. As inequalities increase in complexity, particularly with the possibility of a change in the sense of the inequality, a check is most advisable. Caution students to substitute their solution in the *original* inequality or, if given a word problem, in the word problem itself. Bring out the point that the original inequality expression for a word problem could itself be incorrect, thereby invalidating the check at a later point.

ADDITIONAL EXAMPLES

Example 1. Solve and graph.
$$3x + 4 < x + 3$$

The set of all numbers less than $-\frac{1}{2}$

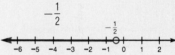

Example 2. Solve and graph.
$$4x + 5 \geq 2(x - 3)$$

The set of all numbers greater than or equal to $-5\frac{1}{2}$

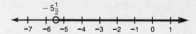

Example 3.
The length of a rectangle is 3 times the width. What is the width of the rectangle if the perimeter is at least 60 cm?

$$w + w + 3w + 3w \geq 60$$
$$w \geq 7.5$$

The width is at least 7.5 cm.

CHECK UNDERSTANDING

Given the inequality $2x - 5 < 7$:

- What should be done first to solve this inequality? (Add 5 to both sides.)
- What is the resulting equivalent inequality? ($2x < 12$)
- What should be done next to solve the inequality? (Divide both sides by 2.)
- What is the resulting inequality? ($x < 6$)

CLASSROOM EXERCISES

In exercise 6, discuss two ways of solving the inequality.

Method 1.
$$5a - 7 > 2a + 8$$
$$3a > 15$$
$$a > 5$$

Method 2.
$$5a - 7 > 2a + 8$$
$$-15 > -3a$$
$$5 < a$$

EXTRA PRACTICE, page 637

Example 3 (continued)

Check A trip of exactly 23 quarter-miles will cost $.50 + $.20(22) = $4.90. A trip of a little more than 23 quarter-miles will cost $.50 + $.20(23) = $5.10. The answer checks.

ASSIGNMENT GUIDE

Basic 1–27 odd, Review Exercises, Self-Quiz 2

Average 1–41 odd, Review Exercises, Self-Quiz 2

Enriched 3–18 multiples of 3, 19–41 odd, 43–46 all, Review Exercises, Self-Quiz 2

PRACTICE WORKSHEET 49

9-5 SOLVING INEQUALITIES BY MULTIPLICATION AND ADDITION

■ Solve and graph on the number line.

1. $3a + 2 \geq 8$ $a \geq 2$

2. $7b - 10 \leq 11$ $b \leq 3$

3. $3c + 8 > c$ $c > -4$
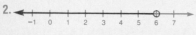
4. $4d + 5 < d - 1$ $d < -2$

5. $5h + 3 \geq 3h + 6$ $h \geq 3/2$
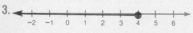
6. $j + 2 \geq 3j + 7$ $j \leq -5/2$

7. $2(k + 3) \geq 6k - 8$ $k \leq 7/2$

8. $m - 15 \leq 3(m - 2)$ $m \geq -9/2$

ADDITIONAL ANSWERS

■ Classroom Exercises

1.
-1 0 1 2 3 4 5 6 7

2.
-1 0 1 2 3 4 5 6 7

3.
-2 -1 0 1 2 3 4 5 6

4.
-4 -3 -2 -1 0 1 2 3 4

5.
-6 -5 -4 -3 -2 -1 0 1 2

6.
0 1 2 3 4 5 6 7 8

■ Written Exercises

1.
0 1 2 3 4 5 6 7 8

■ CLASSROOM EXERCISES

Solve and graph on a number line.

1. $5x + 5 > 15$ $x > 2$
2. $9m - 9 < 45$ $m < 6$
3. $6z - 4 \leq 20$ $z \leq 4$
4. $5y + 16 \geq 11$ $y \geq -1$
5. $3 - 2x < 11$ $x > -4$
6. $5a - 7 > 2a + 8$ $a > 5$

■ WRITTEN EXERCISES

Solve and graph on a number line.

A
1. $4x + 8 > 20$ $x > 3$
2. $3x + 6 > 15$ $x > 3$
3. $5y - 10 < 20$ $y < 6$
4. $2y - 6 < 10$ $y < 8$
5. $3n - 6 \leq 0$ $n \leq 2$
6. $4n - 8 \leq 12$ $n \leq 5$
7. $3a + 2 \geq a + 6$ $a \geq 2$
8. $4a + 6 \geq 2a + 14$ $a \geq 4$
9. $4(t - 1) > 3t + 5$ $t > 9$
10. $3(t - 2) > 2t + 1$ $t > 7$
11. $2(x + 3) < 5x - 3$ $x > 3$
12. $4(x + 2) < 6x - 2$ $x > 5$
13. $-2a + 3 \leq 8$ $a \geq -\frac{5}{2}$
14. $-3a + 3 \leq 7$ $a \geq -\frac{4}{3}$
15. $-\frac{1}{2}c + 5 > 7$ $c < -4$
16. $-\frac{1}{3}c + 1 > 4$ $c < -9$
17. $\frac{1}{2}x + 5 \geq x - 1$ $x \leq 12$
18. $\frac{1}{2}x + 3 \geq x - 2$ $x \leq 10$

Write an inequality. Solve the inequality and answer the question.

19. The length of a rectangular lot is 2 m more than the width. What is the width of the lot if the perimeter is less than 28 m? (Let w be the width in meters and $(w + 2)$ be the length in meters.) $2w + 2(w + 2) < 28$; width < 6 m

20. The length of a rectangle is 3 cm more than the width. What is the width of the rectangle if the perimeter is less than 52 cm? (Let w be the width in centimeters and $(w + 3)$ be the length in centimeters.) $2w + 2(w + 3) < 52$; width < 11.5 cm

21. Tina is half as old as her uncle. The sum of their ages is at least 45 years old. How old is Tina? (Let t represent Tina's age.) $t + 2t \geq 45$; Tina's age ≥ 15

22. Tim is one third as old as his aunt. The sum of their ages is at least 64 years. How old is Tim? (Let t represent Tim's age.) $t + 3t \geq 64$; Tim's age ≥ 16

23. The lengths of the sides of a triangle are in the ratio 5:6:7. What is the length of the longest side if the perimeter is not more than 54 cm? (Let the sides be $5x$, $6x$, and $7x$.) $5x + 6x + 7x \leq 54$; length ≤ 21 cm

460

Create a mathematics learning environment for indirect instruction. For example, have famous quotations of mathematicians prominently displayed and changed periodically. Display posters and student projects.

Prepare transparencies with historical tidbits or anecdotes involving mathematics. "Squeeze" those in during spare minutes at the end of a period.

24. The lengths of the sides of a triangle are in the ratio 4:5:6. What is the length of the shortest side if the perimeter is not more than 60 cm? (Let the sides be $4x$, $5x$, and $6x$.) $4x + 5x + 6x \le 60$; length ≤ 16 cm

25. The sum of two consecutive integers is greater than 16. What is the smaller integer? $x + (x + 1) > 16$; integer $> 7\frac{1}{2}$

26. The sum of two consecutive integers is greater than 22. What is the smaller integer? $x + (x + 1) > 22$; integer $> 10\frac{1}{2}$

27. The sum of two consecutive even integers is less than -13. What is the smaller integer? $x + (x + 2) < -13$; even integer $< -7\frac{1}{2}$

28. The sum of two consecutive odd integers is less than -13. What is the smaller integer? $x + (x + 2) < -13$; odd integer $< -7\frac{1}{2}$

Solve and graph on a number line.

B 29. $5(x + 3) \le 2(x - 6)$ $x \le -9$

30. $3x + 2 \ge 2\frac{1}{2}x - 6$ $x \ge -16$

31. $3(x + 2) \ge 2\frac{1}{2}(x - 6)$ $x \ge -42$

32. $\frac{1}{2}(x + 2) > \frac{1}{3}(x + 6)$ $x > 6$

33. $x(x + 3) < x\left(x - 2 + \frac{10}{x}\right)$ $x < 2$ and $x \ne 0$

34. $0.2x + 1.3 < x - 0.3$ $x > 2$

35. $0.5(x + 3) > 0.6 - 0.7x$ $x > -0.75$

36. $0.25x - 0.2 > 0.15(x + 2)$ $x > 5$

Write an inequality. Solve the inequality and answer the question.

37. A salesperson earns a salary of $500 per month plus 2% of the sales. What must the sales be if the salesperson is to have a monthly income of at least $1600? $500 + 0.02s \ge 1600$; sales $\ge \$55,000$

38. The owner of an apartment house must get at least $100,000 in rent each year to meet expenses and make a reasonable profit. On the average, 80% of the 25 apartments are occupied. What should the monthly rent be for one of the apartments if the same rent is charged for all the occupied apartments? $0.8(25)r \ge \frac{100,000}{12}$; rent $\ge \$416.67$

39. A manufacturer of components for motorcycles estimates that 1% of the parts are defective. How many parts must be made in order to have at least 4500 nondefective parts? $p - 0.01\,p \ge 4500$; number of parts ≥ 4546

40. A worker is paid $9.00 an hour but 30% of the earnings is deducted for taxes, social security, and insurance. What whole number of hours must be worked to have at least $250 take-home pay (after deductions)? $9h - 0.3(9h) \ge 250$; number of hours ≥ 40

41. A band agrees to play for $200 plus 25% of the ticket sales. How much must the ticket sales be if the band is to make at least $500? $200 + 0.25s \ge 500$; sales $\ge \$1200$

42. A car repair costs $20 for the replacement part plus $25 per hour for labor. The owner has $100. How many hours of labor can she afford before she needs additional money? $20 + 25h \le 100$; number of hours $\le 3\frac{1}{5}$

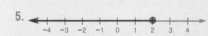

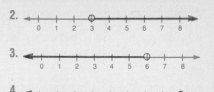

Graphs for Written Exercises 32–36, 43–46 are on page 653.

Solve and graph these compound sentences on a number line.

C 43. $2x + 3 < 6x - 1$ and $3(x + 2) < x + 10$
  x > 1 and x < 2

44. $2(x + 3) \le 5x - 6$ or $3x + 2 \ge 5x + 6$
  x ≥ 4 or x ≤ −2

45. $-\frac{1}{2}x + 2 > 5$ or $-\frac{2}{3}x + 2 < -4$
  x < −6 or x > 9

46. $\frac{3}{4}x \ge x + 2$ and $\frac{1}{4}x \le x + 12$
  x ≤ −8 and x ≥ −16

■ REVIEW EXERCISES

1. Write the prime factorization of 28. $2^2 \cdot 7$ [7–1]

2. Give the greatest common factor of 12 and 18. 6   [7–2]

3. Write the greatest common factor of $3ab$ and $6b^2$. 3b   [7–2]

4. Expand and simplify $(2x + 1)(x - 2)$. $2x^2 - 3x - 2$ [7–5]

Self-Quiz 2

True or false?

9–3   **1.** If $x \le -2$, then $3(x) \le 3(-2)$. T   **2.** If $-\frac{1}{2}x > 5$, then $-2\left(-\frac{1}{2}x\right) < -2(5)$. T

Solve the compound inequality and graph the solution on a number line.

3. $x - 1 < 3$ or $x + 3 > 8$ x < 4 or x > 5   **4.** $2x > x + 6$ and $x - 7 < 2$
  x > 6 and x < 9

Graph on a number line.

9–4   **5.** $-\frac{1}{3}x > 2$ **6.** $2x + 3 \le -1$

Solve.

9–4,   **7.** $3x + 1 \le 2x + 4$ x ≤ 3   **8.** $4(x - 2) > 3(2x - 1)$ x < −$\frac{5}{2}$
9–5

Write and solve an inequality for the situation.

9. In 3 min, there will be less than 1 h left. How much time is left now? (Let t represent the time left in minutes.) Time < 63 minutes

10. A buyer's share of $\frac{1}{4}$ of the boat's price was more than $1200. What was the boat's price? (Let b represent the boat's price.) Price > $4800

11. The width of a rectangle is half its length. The perimeter must be no more than 60 cm. What is the rectangle's length? (Let l be the rectangle's length in centimeters.) Length ≤ 20 cm

To solve inequalities that contain absolute values.

You may wish to spend two days on this section. Refer to the Pacing Chart.

Solve and graph on a number line.

1. $5x - 2 < x + 10$ $x < 3$

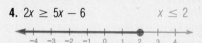

2. $5x + 2 > x + 10$ $x > 2$

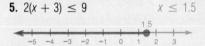

3. $-3x + 3 \le 9$ $x \ge -2$

4. $2x \ge 5x - 6$ $x \le 2$

5. $2(x + 3) \le 9$ $x \le 1.5$

9–6 Absolute Values and Inequalities

Preview

The absolute value of a number can be defined as the distance of that number from 0. Therefore, the solution of the inequality

$$|x| < 2$$

is the set of all numbers that are less than 2 units from 0.

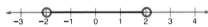

Here is another inequality involving absolute value, a table of some values, and a graph of all solutions.

$$|x - 1| < 2$$

solutions

x	-3	-2	-1	-0.9	0	0.5	1	2	2.9	3	4
$|x - 1|$	4	3	2	1.9	1	0.5	0	1	1.9	2	3

less than 2

- The solutions of $|x - 1| < 2$ are all numbers that are less than 2 units from ___?___ . 1
- Can you write a similar sentence for this inequality? $|x - 3| \le 2$

In this lesson you will learn to solve inequalities that involve absolute values.

PURPOSE

In many problems (especially distance problems) the required answer is a magnitude without regard to direction (or sign). In such problems, absolute values may be used. Solving and graphing inequalities that involve absolute value are therefore important in problem solving.

PREVIEW

Have students state some solutions greater than 2.9 and some less than −0.9. What are the boundaries between solutions and nonsolutions? In the Preview, the solutions are all the numbers between −1 and 3. Discuss why boundary points are important.

■ LESSON

Inequalities that contain absolute values are equivalent to compound inequalities. For example, we saw in the Preview that the solutions of $|x| < 2$ are numbers between -2 and 2. These numbers can also be described by this compound inequality:

$$-2 < x \quad \text{and} \quad x < 2$$

A short way of writing this compound inequality is $-2 < x < 2$.

LESSON

A special case of an inequality containing absolute values is $|x| < 0$. There is no solution.

The inequality $|x| > 0$, on the other hand, has infinitely many solutions—all real numbers except 0.

For the inequality $|x| < a$, where a is a positive number, notice that all solutions are between a and the opposite of a. For the inequality $|x| \geq a$, where a is a positive number, the solutions are all the real numbers except those between a and the opposite of a.

CONCEPT EXTENSION

Classroom exercises 13–14 and written exercises 25–32 require the student to write an inequality for a given graph using absolute value. An effective model that can be used draws upon the symmetry of such graphs relative to a particular point.

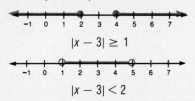

Note that 3 is the point about which each graph is symmetric. This is also the value that appears within absolute-value bars. If we interpret $|x - 3|$ as representing the distance between the points with coordinates 3 and x, the inequality states a condition concerning the location of these points:

$|x - 3| \geq 1$ The distance between 3 and any point x on the graph is at least 1.

$|x - 3| < 2$ The distance between 3 and any point on the graph is less than 2.

ADDITIONAL EXAMPLES

Example 1. Graph on the number line.
$|x| \leq 2$

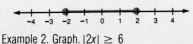

Example 2. Graph. $|2x| \geq 6$

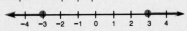

464

The Absolute Value Property of Inequalities

For all real numbers x and a,

if a is 0 or positive
$|x| < a$ is equivalent to $-a < x$ and $x < a$
which is equivalent to $-a < x < a$.

Now consider this inequality:

$$|x| > 3$$

Solutions of this inequality are numbers that are greater than 3 and numbers that are less than -3. Therefore, the inequality $|x| > 3$ is equivalent to the compound inequality

$$x < -3 \quad \text{or} \quad x > 3.$$

The Absolute Value Property of Inequalities

For all real numbers x and a,

if a is 0 or positive,
$|x| > a$ is equivalent to $x < -a$ or $x > a$.

Study these examples to see how to solve inequalities that involve absolute values.

Example 1 Graph on a number line. $|x| < 3$

Solution $|x| < 3$
$-3 < x < 3$

Answer

Example 2 Graph. $|2r| \geq 6$

Solution $|2r| \geq 6$
$2r \leq -6 \quad \text{or} \quad 2r \geq 6$
$r \leq -3 \quad \text{or} \quad r \geq 3$

Use less formal language to introduce new concepts and gradually move toward the more precise and rigorous terminology that clarifies communication and sharpens understanding.

Example 2 (continued)

Answer

Example 3   Graph. $|x + 1| > 2$

Solution $|x + 1| > 2$
$x + 1 < -2$ or $x + 1 > 2$
$x < -3$ or $x > 1$

Answer

Example 4   Graph. $|y - 3| \leq 1$

Solution $|y - 3| \leq 1$
$y - 3 \geq -1$ and $y - 3 \leq 1$
$y \geq 2$ and $y \leq 4$
$2 \leq y \leq 4$

Answer

We can think of $|y - 3|$ on the number line as the distance between a number y and the number 3. Then the inequality in Example 4 describes all numbers y that are no more than 1 unit away from 3.

Example 5   Write an inequality involving absolute value that describes this graph.

Solution   Note that the graph includes all numbers that are 1 unit or more from 3. An inequality that describes those numbers is:

$$|x - 3| \geq 1$$

Example 3. Graph. $|x + 2| > 1$

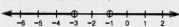

Example 4. Graph. $|a - 5| \leq 2$

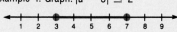

Example 5. Write an inequality involving absolute value that describes the graph.

$|x + 1| < 2$

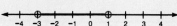

CHECK UNDERSTANDING

- What are the solutions of $|x| = 3$?
  $(\{-3, 3\})$
- What are the boundary points of $|x| < 3$?
  $(-3$ and $3)$
- What are the boundary points of $|x| > 3$?
  $(-3$ and $3)$
- Which inequality is satisfied by the numbers between -3 and 3? $(|x| < 3)$

Enrichment Worksheet 18   NAME _____

PROBLEM SOLVING — FINDING PATTERNS

If you had been a student of mathematics in ancient Egypt (2000–1800 B.C.) you would have used only unit fractions $\left(\frac{1}{n}\right)$ to express fractional quantities. You would have used $\frac{1}{10} + \frac{1}{5}$ instead of $\frac{3}{10}$.

■ Express each of these fractions as the sum of unlike unit fractions.   Answers may vary.

1. $\frac{7}{12} =$ $1/2 + 1/12$
2. $\frac{11}{15} =$ $1/2 + 1/5 + 1/30$
3. $\frac{4}{5} =$ $1/2 + 1/4 + 1/20$
4. $\frac{9}{10} =$ $1/2 + 1/4 + 1/10 + 1/20$

■ Unit fractions themselves can be expressed as the sum of other unlike unit fractions. Look for patterns that will help you write formulas.

5. $\frac{1}{2} = \frac{1}{3} + \frac{1}{6}$
   $\frac{1}{3} = \frac{1}{4} + \frac{1}{12}$
   $\frac{1}{4} =$ $1/5 + 1/20$
   $\frac{1}{5} =$ $1/6 + 1/30$
   $\frac{1}{n} =$ $\frac{1}{n+1} + \frac{1}{n(n+1)}$

6. $\frac{1}{4} = \frac{1}{12} + \frac{1}{6}$
   $\frac{1}{6} = \frac{1}{18} + \frac{1}{9}$
   $\frac{1}{8} =$ $1/24 + 1/12$
   $\frac{1}{10} =$ $1/30 + 1/15$
   $\frac{1}{2n} =$ $\frac{1}{6n} + \frac{1}{3n}$

7. $\frac{1}{6} = \frac{1}{24} + \frac{1}{8}$
   $\frac{1}{9} = \frac{1}{36} + \frac{1}{12}$
   $\frac{1}{12} =$ $1/48 + 1/16$
   $\frac{1}{15} =$ $1/60 + 1/20$
   $\frac{1}{3n} =$ $\frac{1}{12n} + \frac{1}{4n}$

8. Use the patterns you found to express $\frac{1}{24}$ as the sum of two unit fractions in three ways.
   $1/24 = 1/25 + 1/600 = 1/72 + 1/36 = 1/96 + 1/32$

Can be used after Section 9-6
© D.C. Heath & Co.

CLASSROOM EXERCISES

Contrast exercises 1 and 2 by pointing out that the conjunction "and" is used in compound sentences for < inequalities; the conjunction "or" is used with > inequalities.

5.

6.

7.

8.
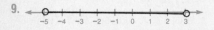

9.

10.

11.
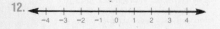

12.
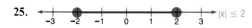

ASSIGNMENT GUIDE

Basic   1–37 odd, Review Exercises
Average   1–47 odd, Review Exercises
Enriched   3–45 multiples of 3, 48–56 all,
          Review Exercises

PRACTICE WORKSHEET 49

9-6 ABSOLUTE VALUES AND INEQUALITIES

■ Graph on the number line.

1. |x| ≥ 3   2. |x| ≤ 4

3. |x + 2| < 1   4. |x - 1| > 2

5. |3x| ≤ 9   6. |½x| ≥ 2

7. |-4x| > 8   8. |-x/3| < 1

466

■ CLASSROOM EXERCISES

Write as compound sentences without absolute values.

1. $|x| < 5$ $\quad -5 < x < 5$ **2.** $|x| > 3$ **3.** $|d - 4| \le 7$ **4.** $|b + 3| \ge 1$
$\quad\quad\quad\quad\quad\quad\quad\quad\quad\quad\quad x > 3 \text{ or } x < -3 \quad\quad -3 \le d \le 11 \quad\quad b \ge -2 \text{ or } b \le -4$

Graph.

5. $|x| < 1$ **6.** $|y| > 1$ **7.** $|c| \ge 4$ **8.** $|b| \le 0$

9. $|x + 1| < 4$ **10.** $|t - 2| > 2$ **11.** $|3x| < 6$ **12.** $|y - 3| \ge 0$

Use absolute value to write an inequality that describes the graph.

13.
$|x + 1| > 2$

14.
$|x - 3| \le 2$

■ WRITTEN EXERCISES

Write as compound sentences without absolute values.

Ⓐ **1.** $|x| < 10$ $\,-10 < x < 10$ **2.** $|x| < 20$ $\,-20 < x < 20$ **3.** $|x| > 15$ **4.** $|x| > 5$
$\quad\quad\quad\quad\quad\quad\quad\quad\quad\quad\quad\quad\quad\quad\quad\quad\quad\quad\quad x > 15 \text{ or } x < -15 \quad x > 5 \text{ or } x < -5$
5. $|b + 3| \le 8$ **6.** $|b + 5| \le 12$ **7.** $|a - 6| \ge 8$ **8.** $|a - 4| \ge 7$
$\quad -11 \le b \le 5 \quad\quad\quad -17 \le b \le 7 \quad\quad a \ge 14 \text{ or } a \le -2 \quad a \ge 11 \text{ or } a \le -3$
Graph on a number line.

9. $|x| < 4$ **10.** $|x| < 6$ **11.** $|x| > 7$ **12.** $|x| > 5$

13. $|x + 4| \le 6$ **14.** $|x + 2| \le 4$ **15.** $|x - 1| \ge 3$ **16.** $|x - 5| \ge 2$

17. $|2x| \ge 5$ **18.** $|4x| \ge 6$ **19.** $|-3x| < 12$ **20.** $|-5x| < 15$

21. $\left|\dfrac{x}{3}\right| > 6$ **22.** $\left|\dfrac{x}{2}\right| > 8$ **23.** $\left|-\dfrac{x}{4}\right| \le 1$ **24.** $\left|-\dfrac{x}{5}\right| \le 2$

Use absolute value to write an inequality that describes the graph.

25.
$|x| \le 2$

26.
$|x| < 2$

27.
$|x| > 1$

28.
$|x| \ge 1$

29.
$|x - 1| \ge 1$

30.
$|x - 2| > 1$

EXTRA PRACTICE, page 637

31. 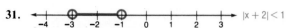 $|x + 2| < 1$

32.  $|x + 1| \leq 2$

Use absolute value to write an inequality for each problem. Then graph the inequality. (Use x for the variable.)

33. The temperature was within 5 degrees of 0. $|x| < 5$

34. The temperature was within 10 degrees of 0. $|x| < 10$

35. The production goal for the week was 2500 cars. The number of cars produced was within 100 of the goal. $|x - 2500| < 100$

36. The charity campaign goal was $50,000. The fund raisers came within $3000 of their goal. $|x - 50,000| < 3000$

37. The rod was supposed to be 25 cm long, plus or minus 0.5 cm. $|x - 25| \leq 0.5$

38. The temperature of the oven was supposed to be $160°C$, plus or minus $10°C$. $|x - 160| \leq 10$

Solve.

B **39.** $|2x + 1| > 4$ $x > \frac{3}{2}$ or $x < -\frac{5}{2}$ **40.** $|2x - 1| < 4$ $-\frac{3}{2} < x < \frac{5}{2}$ **41.** $|3x + 2| \leq 5$ $-\frac{7}{3} \leq x \leq 1$

42. $3|x + 2| \geq 6$ $x \geq 0$ or $x \leq -4$ **43.** $|-2x + 3| \geq 11$ $x \leq -4$ or $x \geq 7$ **44.** $|-3x + 6| \leq 9$ $-1 \leq x \leq 5$

45. $|4x - 2| \leq 10$ $-2 \leq x \leq 3$ **46.** $2|3x - 9| \geq 12$ $x \geq 5$ or $x \leq 1$ **47.** $-2|x - 3| \leq 8$ x is any real number

Graph.

C **48.** $|x| \geq 5$ and $|x| \leq 6$ **49.** $|x| \geq 6$ or $|x| < 5$ **50.** $|x - 5| \leq 3$ or $|x + 5| \leq 3$

51. $|x - 5| \leq x$ **52.** $|x| \leq x + 5$ **53.** $|x + 10| \leq |x|$

54. $|x - 3| \neq |3 - x|$ **55.** $|x| \cdot |x| \leq |x|$ **56.** $|x| \cdot |x| \geq |x|$

■ REVIEW EXERCISES

Solve.

1. $(x + 3) \cdot x = 0$ $(-3, 0)$ **2.** $(x + 2)(x - 5) = 0$ $(-2, 5)$ [7–3]

3. $x^2 - 4x = 0$ $(0, 4)$ **4.** $2x^2 - 5x = 0$ $\left\{0, \frac{5}{2}\right\}$ [7–4]

5. $x^2 - 81 = 0$ $(-9, 9)$ **6.** $16x^2 - 25 = 0$ $\left\{-\frac{5}{4}, \frac{5}{4}\right\}$ [7–6]

Factor.

7. $x^2 + 10x + 25$ $(x + 5)^2$ **8.** $x^2 - 9x + 18$ $(x - 6)(x - 3)$ [7–7, 7–8]

9. $x^2 + 4x - 5$ $(x + 6)(x - 1)$ **10.** $2x^2 + x - 1$ $(2x - 1)(x + 1)$ [7–9, 7–10]

WRITTEN EXERCISES

In exercise 53, point out that two cases should be considered:

Case I. $x \geq 0$ Case II. $x < 0$
$|x| = x$ and $|x| = -x$ and
$-|x| = -x$ $-|x| = x$

ADDITIONAL ANSWERS
■ Written Exercises

9.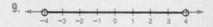

10.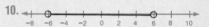

11.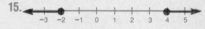

12.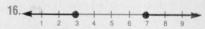

13.

14.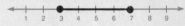

15.

16.

Graphs for Written Exercises 17–24, 33–38, 48–56 are on page 653.

ENRICHMENT PROBLEMS

• Graph the set of all points that are at least 3 units from the graph of -2.

• Graph the set of all points that are at most 2 units from the graph of 5.

• Is there a difference between $|x - 3|$ and $|3 - x|$? Support your answer. [*Hint:* Substitute values for x and check.]

$|x - 3| = |3 - x|$ for all values of x, since $x - 3$ and $3 - x$ are opposites and $|-x| = |x|$.

Graph on a number line.

1. $|x| \leq 4$

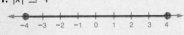

2. $|x| \geq 5$

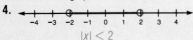

3. $|x - 2| \leq 6$

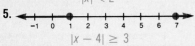

Use absolute value to write an inequality that describes each graph.

4.

$|x| < 2$

5.

$|x - 4| \geq 3$

PURPOSE

Many practical problems involve two related quantities that vary within certain constraints. Writing inequalities, finding solutions for inequalities, and graphing inequalities are important techniques required to apply mathematics to such problems.

PREVIEW

Expansion joints are needed to prevent structural damage to highways. However, too many expansion joints cause the highway to be a little rougher than is otherwise necessary and increase the cost of construction. Therefore, a construction engineer is interested in knowing the maximum temperature range in the area where the highway is to be located.

Students can substitute 80 for *T* in the formula and find that $E = 15$. However, they should realize that 15 inches is the minimum total length of the expansion joints. Therefore, 20 inches and 25 inches are also enough.

LESSON

Graphing *inequalities* in two variables is similar to graphing *equations* in two variables, with two additional considerations. First, the boundary must be considered. If the boundary is to be included in the graph, it will be

OBJECTIVE 9–7

To graph inequalities in two variables.

You may wish to spend two days on this section. Refer to the Pacing Chart.

9–7 Inequalities in Two Variables

Preview **Application: Highway expansion**

Highways sometimes buckle on very hot days. Construction engineers know they must provide expansion joints between sections of the highway to allow for the expansion. The following formula can be used to determine the expansion *E* (in inches) of one mile of a two-lane highway that was built when the temperature was 60°F, where *T* is the present temperature in degrees Fahrenheit.

$$E = 0.75T - 45$$

To prevent buckling, the total length of the expansion joints in each mile of highway must be greater than or equal to *E*.

- If the temperature reaches 80°F, which of these total lengths for the joints will be enough? b, c, d

  a. 10 in.   **b.** 15 in.
  c. 20 in.   **d.** 25 in.

- If the temperature reaches 100° F, which of these total lengths for the expansion joints will be enough? c, d

  a. 15 in.   **b.** 25 in.
  c. 35 in.   **d.** 45 in.

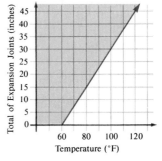

In this lesson you will make graphs of inequalities like the one above.

■ LESSON

Since the solutions of inequalities in two variables are ordered pairs of numbers, the solutions of the inequalities can be graphed in the coordinate plane. For example, suppose we wish to graph the solutions of this inequality:

$$y \geq x$$

This sentence is equivalent to:

$$y = x \quad \text{or} \quad y > x$$

Solutions of the compound sentence must satisfy one condition or the other.

drawn with a solid line. If the boundary is not to be included in the graph, it will be drawn with a dashed line. Second, the region included in the graph must be determined. The line divides the plane into two regions, only one of which consists of points satisfying the inequality. A point clearly on one side of the boundary line is tested. If the coordinates of the point are a solution, then all the points on that side of the boundary line are also in the graph. If the tested point is not a solution, then the points on the other side of the boundary line are in the graph.

CONCEPT EXTENSION

Determining the half-plane that satisfies a given linear inequality is a good opportunity to stress the relationship between the x- and y-coordinates expressed by the linear equation. For example, consider the inequality $y > x + 3$ and the equation for any vertical line, say $x = 2$.

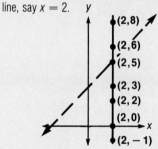

First, graph the ordered pairs that satisfy the equation $y = x$.

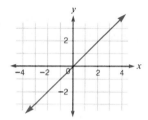

Next, find some ordered pairs that satisfy the condition $y > x$ and graph them.

x	2	1	1	0	-1	-3	-3
y	3	1.5	3	1	-0.5	-2	3

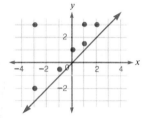

It seems that every point "above" the line is in the graph. To test that guess, find more solutions.

x	2	0	-2	-2
y	2.5	3	0	-1.5

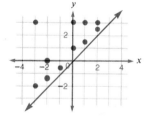

Then, test some points "below" the line.

(1, 0) is not a solution, because $0 > 1$ is false.
$(-1, -3)$ is not a solution, because $-3 > -1$ is false.

x	y	$x + 3$	Points (x, y) are
2	8	5	in upper half-plane;
2	6	5	
2	5	5	←on line $y = x + 3$;
2	3	5	
2	2	5	in lower half-plane.
2	0	5	
2	-1	5	

Examining the coordinates of points on the vertical line that are above the line $y = x + 3$, we observe that the y-coordinate is more than the x-coordinate plus three ($y > x + 3$). Below the skew line, the y-coordinate is less than the x-coordinate plus three ($y < x + 3$). At the point of intersection, the y-coordinate equals the x-coordinate plus three ($y = x + 3$).

It seems that no point below the line is a solution. The graph includes the line $y = x$ and all points above it.

We shade the region above the line and use a solid line to show that the boundary is part of the graph. If the boundary is not part of the graph, a dashed line is used.

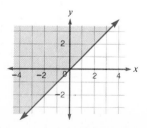

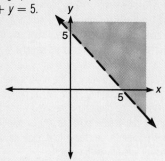
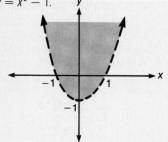
Example 1   Graph. $x + y < 3$

Solution   First, graph the line $x + y = 3$. Use a dashed line because none of those points is a solution of the inequality.

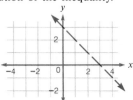

Next, find some solutions of the inequality $x + y < 3$ and graph them.

x	y
1	1
4	-2
2	-2
0	2
-1	3

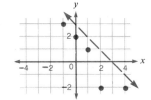

Answer   The graph includes all points below the line $x + y = 3$.

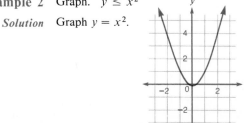

Example 2   Graph. $y \leq x^2$

Solution   Graph $y = x^2$.

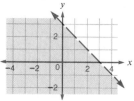

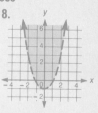
EXTRA PRACTICE, page 637

Example 2 (continued)

Find some solutions of the inequality $y < x^2$.

x	y
3	4
0	-2
-2	3
-1	-3

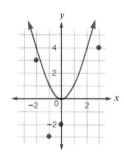

Answer   The graph includes all points on the curve and below it.

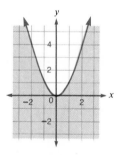

These steps should be used to graph an inequality in two variables.

1. Graph the corresponding equation to get the boundary of the graph. The boundary should be a dashed line if the boundary points are not included in the graph. The boundary should be a solid line if the boundary points are included in the graph.
2. The boundary divides the plane into regions. Test points in all regions to find which regions are to be included in the graph.
3. Shade the points that are included in the graph.

■ CLASSROOM EXERCISES

State whether the boundary should be dashed or solid for these graphs.

1. $y \geq 2x + 1$ Solid

2. $y < 3x - 5$ Dashed

ASSIGNMENT GUIDE

Basic   1–27 odd, Review Exercises, Self-Quiz 3

Average   3–30 multiples of 3, 31–37 odd, Review Exercises, Self-Quiz 3

Enriched   3–36 multiples of 3, 39–44 all, Review Exercises, Self-Quiz 3

PRACTICE WORKSHEET 50

9-7 INEQUALITIES IN TWO VARIABLES

■ Graph.

1. $x + y \leq 3$

2. $y \geq x - 2$

3. $y \leq \frac{1}{2}x + 2$

4. $y > -x + 3$

5. $y \geq \frac{1}{2}x^2$

6. $y \leq 2x + 1$

15.

16.

17.

18.

19.

20.

21.

State whether the given point is in the graph of the inequality.

3. $(0, 0)$; $y > x - 1$ Yes

4. $(1, 10)$; $y \geq 2x + 5$ Yes

Graph.

5. $y < x$

6. $y \geq 2x$

7. $y > 2x + 1$

8. $y > x^2 - 1$

9. Write an inequality for this graph. $y < \frac{1}{2}x$

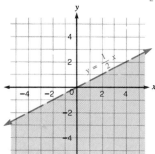

■ WRITTEN EXERCISES

State whether the boundary should be dashed or solid for these graphs.

A   **1.** $y \leq 3x - 1$ Solid   **2.** $y \geq 2x + 3$ Solid   **3.** $y > \frac{1}{2}x + 4$ Dashed   **4.** $y < \frac{1}{3}x + 2$

Dashed

State whether the given point is in the graph of the inequality.

5. $(0, 0)$; $y < x + 3$ Yes

6. $(0, 0)$; $y < x + 5$ Yes

7. $(0, 0)$; $y \leq x - 4$ No

8. $(0, 0)$; $y \leq x - 1$ No

9. $(1, 10)$; $y \geq 2x - 3$ Yes

10. $(10, 1)$; $y \geq 3x - 2$ No

11. $(100, 1)$; $y > \frac{1}{2}x + 5$ No

12. $(1, 100)$; $y > \frac{1}{3}x + 1$ Yes

13. $(0, 1)$; $y > \frac{1}{2}x - 2$ Yes

14. $(2, 0)$; $y \geq \frac{1}{2}x - 3$ Yes

Graph.

15. $y \geq 2x - 3$

16. $y \geq \frac{1}{2}x + 2$

17. $y > \frac{1}{3}x$

18. $y > 3x$

19. $y < x + 3$

20. $y < x - 3$

21. $y \leq -2x + 2$

22. $y \leq -3x + 3$

23. $y \leq \frac{1}{2}x^2$

24. $y \leq \frac{1}{4}x^2$

25. $x + y \geq 6$

26. $x + y \geq 3$

Write an inequality for each graph.

27. 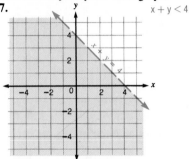 $x + y < 4$

28. 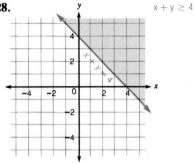 $x + y \geq 4$

 29. 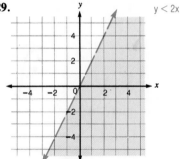 $y < 2x$

30. 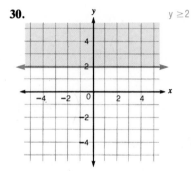 $y \geq 2$

Graph.

31. $2x + 3y \leq 6$ **32.** $2x - 3y \leq 6$ **33.** $-2x + 3y \leq 6$ **34.** $-2x - 3y \leq 6$

35. $y \geq 2$ **36.** $x \leq 5$ **37.** $xy > 12$ **38.** $xy > -12$

39. $x \geq 2$ and $y \geq 3$ **40.** $x \geq 2$ or $y \leq 3$

41. $|x| + |y| \leq 5$ **42.** $|x + y| < 5$

43. $|y| < |x|$ [*Hint:* What are the boundaries?]   **44.** $|y| > x^2$ [*Hint:* What are the boundaries?]

22.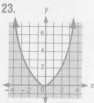

23.

24.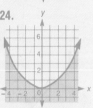

25.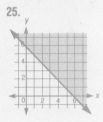

26.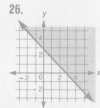

Graphs for Written Exercises 31–44 are on pages 653–654.

■ REVIEW EXERCISES

1. Which values of x are not admissible?   [8–1]

$$\frac{3}{x^2 - 5x}$$ 0, 5

Simplify.

2. $\dfrac{6x}{9x}$ $\dfrac{2}{3}$

3. $\dfrac{6x^2}{5} \cdot \dfrac{3}{4x}$ $\dfrac{9x}{10}$

4. $\dfrac{1}{x} + \dfrac{1}{2x}$ $\dfrac{3}{2x}$ [8–2, 8–3, 8–4]

ENRICHMENT PROBLEM

- Suppose that a railroad rail is firmly anchored at both ends and has no expansion joints. Suppose also that the rail is 4000 feet long, expands 1 foot on a hot day, and buckles upward as shown.

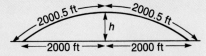

a. Guess the height h.
b. This picture is an approximation of the situation. Use the Pythagorean theorem to find h.

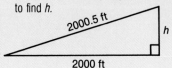

44.7 feet

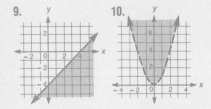
Solve.

5. $\dfrac{3}{x} = \dfrac{60}{80}$ {4}

6. $\dfrac{1}{x} = \dfrac{1}{3} + \dfrac{1}{5}$ $\left\{1\dfrac{7}{8}\right\}$ [8–5]

7. $24 = x\%$ of 80   {30}

8. $80\% = \dfrac{48}{x}$ {60}   [8–8]

9. George can stock the grocery shelves in 8 h and Bill can stock them in 10 h. How long does it take George and Bill working together to stock the shelves? $4\dfrac{4}{9}$ h   [8–6]

10. A resistance of 10 ohms is placed in parallel with a resistance of 20 ohms. What is the total resistance of the circuit?
$\left(\text{Use the formula } \dfrac{1}{R} = \dfrac{1}{r_1} + \dfrac{1}{r_2}.\right)$ $6\dfrac{2}{3}\,\Omega$

Self-Quiz 3

9–6 Graph on a number line.

1. $|x| \geq 3$ **2.** $|x + 4| < 2$ **3.** $|2x + 1| \leq 5$

Use absolute value to write an inequality to describe the graph.

4. $|x| < 1$

5. $|x + 1| \geq 1$

9–7 State whether the given number pair is a solution of the inequality $y \leq x + 3$.

6. $(-2, 4)$ No   **7.** $(-3, 0)$ Yes   **8.** $(-1, -5)$ Yes

Graph.

9. $y \leq x - 4$ **10.** $y > x^2$

Write an inequality for each condition.

11. Maureen decided to add a minimum of $5 each week to her existing savings account of $315. (Let x represent the number of weeks later and y the amount of money in Maureen's account.) $y \geq 315 + 5x$

12. A carpenter must construct this month's quantity of 3-legged stools and 4-legged stools. His supply of wooden legs for the month will be no more than 196 legs. (Let x represent the number of 3-legged stools and y the number of 4-legged stools.) $3x + 4y \leq 196$

OBJECTIVE 9–8

To graph compound inequalities in two variables.

Class Starter Quiz
on previous section

Graph.

1. $y \leq x + 2$

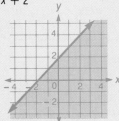

2. $x + y \geq 4$

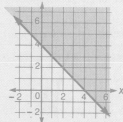

3. $y < x^2$

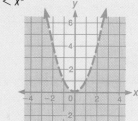

4. $y \geq 4x + 2$

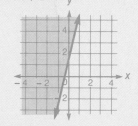

9–8 Compound Inequalities in Two Variables

Preview

The April Frost Show is a 30-minute television show that divides its time among three types of activity: (1) April Frost sings, dances, and tells jokes, (2) guest stars perform, and (3) sponsors of the show have commercial messages. If e represents the number of minutes April entertains and c represents the number of minutes for commercials, match an inequality to each of these conditions.

1. The sponsors insist on at least 3 min of commercials. d
2. The network limits the total commercial time to 6 min. c
3. April's agent insists that she perform at least 10 min. f
4. April's writer says that she cannot perform more than 25 min. e
5. It is a half-hour show. b
6. Guest stars cannot perform more than 16 minutes. a

a. $e + c \geq 14$ **b.** $e + c \leq 30$
c. $c \leq 6$ **d.** $c \geq 3$
e. $e \leq 25$ **f.** $e \geq 10$

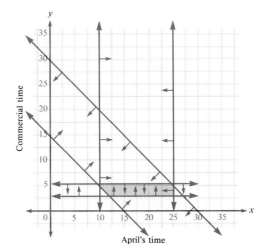

April's time

The graph shows all the conditions at once. The shaded region is where all six conditions are satisfied.

The graph helps answer such questions as, "What combination of times is most pleasing to viewers?"

In this lesson you will study systems of linear inequalities and their applications to problems such as the one above.

PURPOSE

Solving systems of linear inequalities by graphing is a powerful technique in many practical problems.

■ LESSON

Solutions to compound sentences involving "and" must satisfy all the conditions. Solutions to compound sentences involving "or" must satisfy at least one of the conditions. Consider the following compound inequality in two variables.

$$x + y \leq 6 \quad \text{and} \quad x > 3$$

To graph this compound inequality, we first graph the condition $x + y \leq 6$.

PREVIEW

Show an enlarged picture of the shaded region where all six conditions are satisfied. Have the students find the corner points of the shaded region.

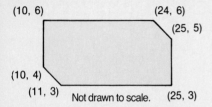

(10, 6)   (24, 6)
                (25, 5)
(10, 4)
  (11, 3)   Not drawn to scale.   (25, 3)

The coordinates of the corner points can be used to answer additional questions such as:

The number of products sold (S) can be predicted using the formula

$$S = 1000e + 5000c,$$

where e represents the number of minutes April entertains and c represents the number of minutes of commercials. What combination of times would sell the most products? (24 minutes of April and 6 minutes of commercials; 54,000 products)

LESSON

In graphing compound inequalities, students should first indicate the graph of each inequality by using arrows on the boundary pointed toward the appropriate region. After all the inequalities have been graphed separately, the appropriate region should be shaded.

Draw the boundary with a solid line and use arrows to show which side of the boundary is included in the graph.

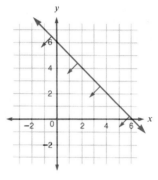

Next, graph the second condition, $x > 3$. Draw the boundary with a dashed line, and use arrows to show which side of the boundary is included in the graph.

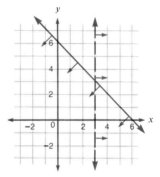

Finally, shade the region that lies within the graphs of *both* conditions. This is the graph of the compound inequality.

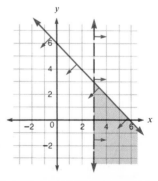

Problem-solving experts suggest that occasionally teachers should actively engage in problem solving as part of their instruction. This means allowing students to "look over your shoulder" as you solve a problem, perhaps for the first time. Such modeling should include looking at various ways the problem might be solved and finally coming up with a way that works.

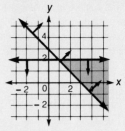
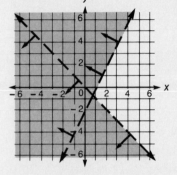
Example 1   Graph. $y \leq x + 2$ and $x \leq 3$ and $y \geq -1$

Solution   First graph $y \leq x + 2$.

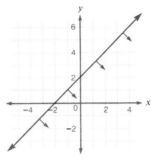

Then graph $x \leq 3$.

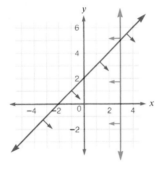

Finally, graph $y \geq -1$.

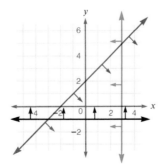

CLASSROOM EXERCISES

Contrast exercises 5 and 6 and exercises 7 and 8. The compound sentences use "and" and "or" respectively. The graphs of each pair of exercises have the same boundaries, but different regions are shaded.

 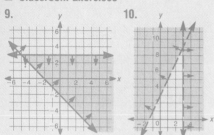
ASSIGNMENT GUIDE

Basic   1–25 odd, Review Exercises
Average   3–24 multiples of 3, 27–36 all,
           Review Exercises
Enriched 9–24 multiples of 3, 27–43 all,
           Review Exercises

PRACTICE WORKSHEET 51

9-8 COMPOUND INEQUALITIES IN TWO VARIABLES

■ Graph.

1. $y \geq 3x - 4$ and $y \leq \frac{1}{2}x$

2. $y \geq x$ or $y \geq 2x$

3. $y \geq -2$ and $x \leq 3$

4. $y \geq 2$ or $y \leq -3$

5. $y \geq 2x$ and $y \leq -x + 3$

6. $y \leq x - 2$ or $y \geq 2x + 3$

EXTRA PRACTICE, page 637

Example 1 (continued)

Shade the region that satisfies all three conditions.

Answer   The graph is a triangle and its interior.

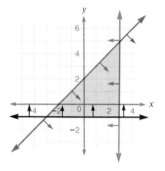

Example 2   Graph. $y \leq x - 2$ or $y < -x + 1$

Solution   Note that the compound sentence joins the conditions with "or." The graph will consist of points that satisfy either condition.

First, graph $y \leq x - 2$.   Then graph $y < -x + 1$.

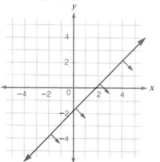

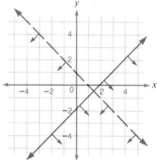

Shade the region that satisfies either condition.

Answer

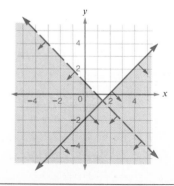

These steps should be used to graph compound inequalities in two variables.

1. Graph each of the conditions, using arrows to indicate which side of the boundary is included.
2. If the compound sentence involves "and," shade the region that satisfies all the conditions.
3. If the compound sentence involves "or," shade the region that satisfies one or more of the conditions.

■ CLASSROOM EXERCISES

State whether the boundaries of these graphs will be solid lines or dashed lines.

1. $x + y < 5$ and $x - y < 6$ Dashed

2. $x - 2y \leq 6$ and $y \leq 2x - 6$ Solid

3. $y \geq 3$ or $x \geq 4$ Solid

4. $y > \frac{1}{2}x - 2$ or $y > 2x + 2$ Dashed

Match the graphs in Exercises 5–8 with these compound inequalities.

a. $y \leq 2$ or $x \leq 4$

b. $x + y \leq 4$ and $y \geq -x$

c. $y \leq 2$ and $x \leq 4$

d. $x + y \geq 4$ or $y \leq -x$

5.   d

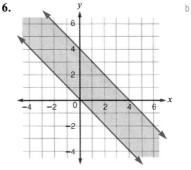

6.   b

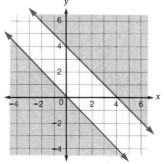

7.   c

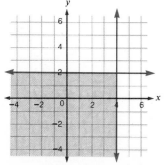

8.   a

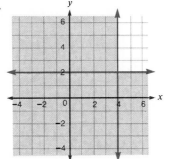

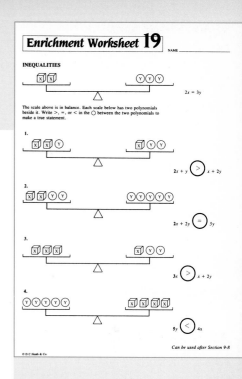

9.

10.

11.

12.

13.
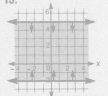

14.

15.
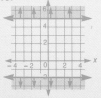

480

Graph.

9. $x + y \geq -2$ and $y \leq 3$

10. $y > 2x + 3$ or $x > 3$

■ WRITTEN EXERCISES

Match the graphs in Exercises 1–8 with the compound inequalities.

A
a. $x \leq -2$ and $y \leq 3$

b. $x \leq -2$ or $y \leq 3$

c. $x \leq -2$ and $y \geq 3$

d. $x \leq -2$ or $y \geq 3$

e. $x \geq -2$ and $y \leq 3$

f. $x \geq -2$ or $y \leq 3$

g. $x \geq -2$ and $y \geq 3$

h. $x \geq -2$ or $y \geq 3$

1.   d
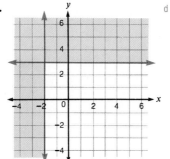

2.   b
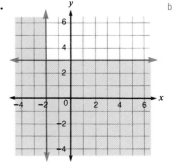

3.   a
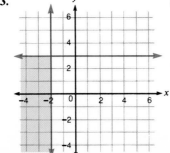

4.   e
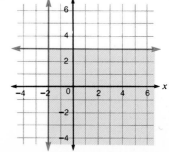

5. 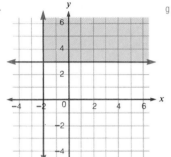 g

6. 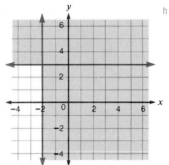 h

7. 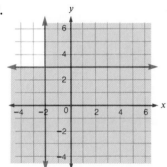 f

8. 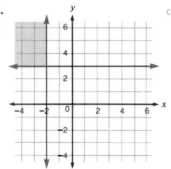 c

Graph.

9. $y \geq 2x$ and $x < 0$

10. $y \geq \frac{1}{2}x$ and $x < 2$

11. $y < 3$ or $y > x$

12. $y < 4$ or $y < x$

13. $y \leq 5$ and $y \geq -2$

14. $x \geq -2$ and $x \leq 3$

15. $y \geq 5$ or $y \leq -2$

16. $x \leq -2$ or $x \geq 3$

17. $y \geq x + 2$ and $y \leq 2x$

18. $y \leq x + 2$ and $y \geq 2x$

19. $y < 2x - 3$ and $y > x - 3$

20. $y > 2x - 3$ and $y < x - 3$

In each situation, let x represent the mass in kilograms of the flour and y the mass in kilograms of the sugar. Write an inequality for each condition. Graph both conditions.

21. The total mass of a flour–sugar mixture is less than 5 kg. There is at least 1 more kg of flour than sugar. $x + y < 5, x \geq y + 1$

22. The total mass of a flour–sugar mixture is at least 5 kg. There is more flour than sugar. $x + y \geq 5, x > y$

23. There is at least twice as much flour as sugar. There are less than 3 kilograms of sugar. $x \geq 2y, y < 3$

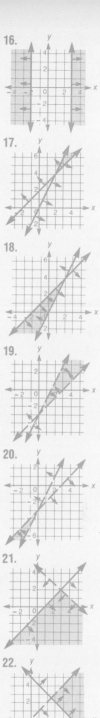

23.

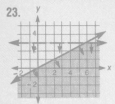

24.

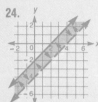

25.

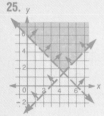

26.

32.

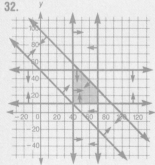

38.

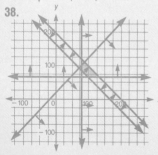

482

---

24. There are at least 2 more kg of flour than sugar. The amount of flour exceeds the amount of sugar by less than 4 kg. $x \geq y + 2, x - y < 4$

25. The total mass of the flour–sugar mixture is more than 6 kg. The mass of the flour exceeds the mass of the sugar by less than 3 kg. $x + y > 6, x - y < 3$

26. The mass of the sugar is at least half the mass of the flour. There are at least 3 kg of flour. $y \geq \frac{1}{2}x, x \geq 3$

State whether the point of intersection of the two boundaries is part of the graph.

B **27.** $y > x$ and $x \leq 4$ No   **28.** $y \leq 2x$ or $y > 5$ No

29. $y > \frac{1}{2}x$ or $y < 4x$ No   **30.** $x \leq 5$ and $y \geq -3$ Yes

A farmer wants to mix corn and oats for feed. Let x represent the number of pounds of corn and y the number of pounds of oats.

a. The total mixture should not exceed 100 lb. $x + y \leq 100$
b. There should be at least 50 lb of the mixture. $x + y \geq 50$
c. There should be at least 40 lb of corn. $x \geq 40$
d. There should be no more than 70 lb of corn. $x \leq 70$
e. There should be no more than 50 lb of oats. $y \leq 50$
f. There should be at least 10 lb of oats. $y \geq 10$

31. Write an inequality for each condition. See above.

32. Graph the six inequalities from Exercise 31.

33. Which of the six conditions is not needed because it is covered by the other conditions? b

34. Which of these (corn, oats) combinations satisfy all the conditions?
a, c, d, e, f, g
a. (40, 10)   **b.** (30, 20)   **c.** (40, 50)   **d.** (50, 50)   **e.** (70, 30)
f. (70, 10)   **g.** (60, 30)   **h.** (80, 20)   **i.** (40, 60)

35. Which of the acceptable (corn, oats) combinations has the largest corn/oats ratio? f

36. Which of the acceptable (corn, oats) combinations has the largest oats/corn ratio? c

Two classes decide to raise money by running a chili supper.

a. They have 200 tickets to sell. $x + y \leq 200$
b. Class A agrees to sell at least 80 tickets. $x \geq 80$
c. Class B agrees to sell at least 60 tickets. $y \geq 60$
d. They must sell at least 160 tickets. $x + y \geq 160$
e. Class B will sell no more than 20 more tickets than class A. $y \leq x + 20$

C **37.** Let x represent the number of tickets sold by class A and y the number of tickets sold by class B. Write an inequality for each condition. See above.

38. Graph the five inequalities.

39. Which of these (class A, class B) combinations satisfy all the conditions?
b, c, e, f, g, h, i
   a. (80, 120)   **b.** (120, 80)   **c.** (140, 60)   **d.** (60, 140)   **e.** (100, 60)
   f. (80, 80)   **g.** (80, 100)   **h.** (90 110)   **i.** (100, 80)

40. In which of the acceptable combinations does class A sell the greatest number of tickets? c

41. In which of the acceptable combinations does class B sell the greatest number of tickets? h

42. If 160 tickets were sold and class A sold as many as possible, how many tickets did each class sell? A: 100, B: 60

43. If class A made a profit of 50¢ on each ticket it sold and class B made a 40¢ profit on each ticket it sold, what is the maximum profit possible? $94

■ REVIEW EXERCISES

1. What is the ratio of the width to the length of a 60-ft by 150-ft rectangular lot? $\frac{2}{5}$ [8–7]

2. What is the interest on $300 invested for three years at an annual rate of 10%? [8–8]
$90

3. If Caryl's car travels 300 mi on 12 gal of gasoline, how far should it be able to travel on 10 gal? 250 mi [8–9]

4. A recipe for 8 people calls for a half-dozen eggs. How many eggs should be used if 12 people are to be served? 9 [8–9]

5. Heidi's mother earns three times as much as Heidi does. How much does her mother earn if Heidi earns $150.00? $450 [8–10]

6. If y varies directly as x, and $y = 12$ when $x = 5$, find y when $x = 100$. 240 [8–10]

7. Suppose x and y vary inversely and $y = 10$ when $x = 2$. Find y when $x = 5$. [8–11]
4

8. Graph the equation $xy = 12$ for $x > 0$. [8–11]

■ CHAPTER SUMMARY

• **Vocabulary**

inequality	[page 435]	equivalent inequalities	[page 447]
compound inequality	[page 435]	solve an inequality	[page 447]
$<, >, \neq, \leq, \geq$	[page 435]	sense of an inequality	[page 452]
solutions of inequalities	[page 436]		

• The Addition Property of Inequalities   [9–3]

For all numbers a, b, and c,
$$\text{if } a < b, \text{ then } a + c < b + c$$
$$\text{and}$$
$$\text{if } a > b, \text{ then } a + c > b + c.$$

ENRICHMENT PROBLEMS

• Write a compound inequality for these graphs.

a.
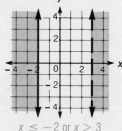
$x \leq -2$ or $x > 3$

b.
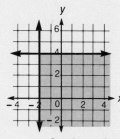
$x \geq -2$ and $y \leq 4$

c.
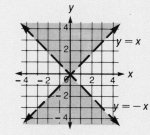
$y > |x|$ or $y < -|x|$

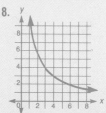

2.

4.

5.

6.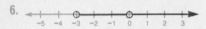

9.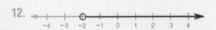

11.

12.

13.

14.

17.

19.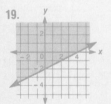

20.

21.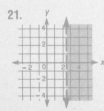

- The Multiplication Property of Inequalities   [9–4]

  For all numbers a, b, and c, $c > 0$,

  $$\text{if } a < b, \text{ then } ca < cb$$
  $$\text{and}$$
  $$\text{if } a > b, \text{ then } ca > cb.$$

  For all numbers a, b, and c, $c < 0$,

  $$\text{if } a < b, \text{ then } ca > cb$$
  $$\text{and}$$
  $$\text{if } a > b, \text{ then } ca < cb.$$

- The Absolute Value Property of Inequalities   [9–6]

  If $a \geq 0$, then

  $$|x| < a \text{ is equivalent to } -a < x \text{ and } x < a,$$
  $$\text{which is equivalent to } -a < x < a;$$
  $$|x| > a \text{ is equivalent to } x < -a \text{ or } x > a.$$

- Solutions to compound sentences involving "and" must satisfy all the conditions.   [9–8]

- Solutions to compound sentences involving "or" must satisfy at least one of the conditions.   [9–8]

■ CHAPTER REVIEW

9–1 Objective: To determine whether inequalities are true or false, and to graph inequalities on a number line.

    1. Letting x be a number, write an inequality that states that the number is not less than 21. $x \geq 21$

    2. Graph on a number line $x > -2$.

    3. Write the inequality that is graphed on this number line. $x \leq 1$

9–2 Objective: To graph compound inequalities on a number line.

    Graph on a number line.

    4. $x \geq -2$ and $x \leq 1$ **5.** $x < -2$ or $x > 2$ **6.** $x > -3$ and $x \neq 0$

9–3 Objective: To solve inequalities by using the addition property of inequalities.

    Solve.

    7. $x + 5 < 12$ $x < 7$ **8.** $3x - 5 \geq 2x + 3$ $x \geq 8$

    Graph the solution on a number line.

    9. $2x + 4 < 3x + 2$

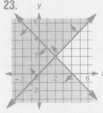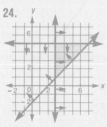
9–4 Objective: To solve inequalities by using the multiplication property of inequalities.

10. What is the missing inequality sign, $<$ or $>$?
If $x < 5$, then $-2x$ Ⓞ $-2 \cdot 5$. $>$

Graph on a number line.

11. $4x \geq -12$

12. $-3x < 6$

9–5 Objective: To solve inequalities by using both the addition and multiplication properties of inequalities.

Solve and graph on a number line.

13. $3x + 5 > 17$ $x > 4$

14. $3 - x \leq 2(x - 3)$ $x \geq 3$

Write an inequality. Solve the inequality and answer the question.

15. If Sally begins with $50, what is the least amount she must save per week to buy a $199 stereo in 10 weeks? $14.90

9–6 Objective: To solve inequalities that contain absolute values.

16. Write $|x - 3| > 5$ as a compound sentence without absolute values. $x > 8$ or $x < -2$

17. Graph on a number line $|x + 3| \leq 2$.

18. Use absolute values to write an inequality that describes this graph. $|x| \geq 2$

9–7 Objective: To graph inequalities in two variables.

Graph.

19. $y \geq \frac{1}{2}x - 2$

20. $x + y < 4$

21. $2x > 5$

9–8 Objective: To graph compound inequalities in two variables.

Graph.

22. $y > x + 1$ and $x > 0$

23. $x + y \leq 4$ or $y \geq x$

24. $y \leq 5$ and $x \geq 3$ and $y \geq x - 2$

■ CHAPTER 9 SELF-TEST

9–1 Write an inequality for the expression. Let n represent the number.

1. The number is at least -8. $n \geq -8$

2. One-fourth the number is less than 17. $\frac{1}{4}n < 17$

9–2 Graph on a number line.

3. $x \geq \frac{7}{2}$

4. $y < 1$ or $y > 4$

5. $w \geq -\frac{1}{2}$ and $w \leq \frac{5}{2}$

Chapter Review   **485**

■ Write an inequality for the number. Let x represent the number.

1. The number is not more than 14. 1. $x \le 14$

2. Half the number is more than -3. 2. $\frac{1}{2}x > -3$

■ Graph the inequality on the number line.

3. $x \ne -1$ 3.

4. $x \ge 5$ 4.

■ Indicate whether the given statement is true or false.

5. $-3 < 2$ or $12 > 15$ 5. True

6. $6 \ge 5$ and $-3 \le -3$ 6. True

■ Graph each compound sentence on the number line.

7. $x < \frac{5}{2}$ and $x > -1$ 7.

8. $x \le -2$ or $x \ge 4$ 8.

■ Solve.

9. $a < 2a - 4$ 9. $a > 4$

10. $-2n > 8$ 10. $n < -4$

11. $-\frac{1}{3}d \le 6$ 11. $d \ge -18$

12. $5(t - 1) < 15$ 12. $t < 4$

13. $4(b - 2) \ge 6 + 6b$ 13. $b \le -7$

14. $5 \le \frac{1}{4}r + 3$ 14. $t \ge 8$

15. $\frac{1}{2}x + 3 > x + 7$ 15. $x < -8$

■ Write as a compound inequality without absolute value.

16. $|w| > 4$ 16. $w < -4$ or $w > 4$

17. $|y + 2| < 7$ 17. $-9 < y < 5$

© D.C. Heath & Co.

■ State whether the given point is in the graph of the inequality.

18. $(-1, 4)$ $y < x + 4$ 18. No

19. $(7, -2)$ $x + y \ge 5$ 19. Yes

■ Graph the inequalities in the plane.

20. $y \ge x - 4$ 20.

21. $y < 2x$ and $y > 1$ 21.

■ Solve.

22. Kay had less than $1.50 left after she spent $3.00 for a book. How much did Kay have before she bought the book? 22. < $4.50

23. A 6-pack of juice costs $1.40. At what price is an 8-pack of juice more economical? 23. < $1.87

★ BONUS

The sum of two integers is more than -12. One integer is 3 more than the other. What is the smaller integer? BONUS -7

© D.C. Heath & Co.

Write a compound inequality for these graphs.

6.  $x \le -4$ or $x \ge -1$

7.  $3 < x < 8$

9-3 Solve.

8. $2w - 3 > w + 5$ $w > 8$

9. $4(x - 5) \le 5(x + 3)$ $x \ge -35$

9-4, 9-5 Graph the solution of the inequality.

10. $\frac{5}{4}t - 1 \ne 4$

11. $-6s < 15$

12. $3(3 - x) \ge 2x + 14$

13. $\frac{1}{4}y + 8 < \frac{1}{2}y + 6$

9-5 Write and solve an inequality for each situation.

14. The area of a rectangular flower bed must be at least 42 ft². The width must be 3 ft. (Use x to express possible lengths.) $3x \ge 42; x \ge 14$

15. The perimeter of an isosceles triangle can be no more than 25 cm. The length of an equal side is twice the base. (Use x to express possible lengths for the base.) $2x + 2x + x \le 25; x \le 5$

9-2, 9-5 True or false?

16. $-13 < -11$ or $4 \ge 5$ T

17. $|-3| > 2$ and $-3 < -5$ F

9-6 Write as a compound inequality.

18. $|s - 1| > 3$ $s > 4$ or $s < -2$

19. $|2w| < 6$ $-3 < w < 3$

9-7 State whether the given point is part of the graph of the inequality.

20. $(3, -1); 2x - y < 6$ No

21. $(2, 5); x \ge y - 4$ Yes

9-7, 9-8 Graph.

22. $y > 2x - 6$

23. $x + y \ge 4$ and $x - y \le 1$

■ PRACTICE FOR COLLEGE ENTRANCE TESTS

Each question consists of two quantities, one in column A and one in column B. Compare the two quantities and select one of the following answers.

A   if the quantity in column A is greater
B   if the quantity in column B is greater
C   if the two quantities are equal
D   if the relationship cannot be determined from the information given

Comments

- Letters such as a, b, x, and y are variables that can be replaced by real numbers.
- A symbol that appears in both columns in a question stands for the same thing in column A as in column B.
- In some questions information that applies to quantities in both columns is centered above the two columns.

EXAMPLES

Column A		Column B	Answers
$3 + 4$		$3 \cdot 4$	B
$a + b$	$a = 5$	$b + 5$	C
$2x + y$		$x + 2y$	D

	Column A		Column B	
1.	$\dfrac{a}{b}$	$a > 1$ $b < -1$	-1	D
2.	y	y and $\dfrac{49}{y}$ are both prime numbers.	49	B
3.	$a - b$	$a < b$	$b - a$	B
4.	$\boxed{2}$	$\boxed{x} = \lvert x - 6 \rvert$	$\boxed{10}$	C
5.	$a^2 + b^2$	$a < 0 < b$	$(a + b)^2$	A
6.	x	$4x^2 > y^2$	y	D
7.	Margaret's age now	In 30 years Margaret will be 3 times as old as she is now. Seven years ago Louis was half as old as he is now.	Louis' age now	A
8.	x	$3x + 5 < 2$	0	B
9.	x	$2x > y > 0$	y	D
10.	$\dfrac{1}{a}$	$a < b < 0$	$\dfrac{1}{b}$	A

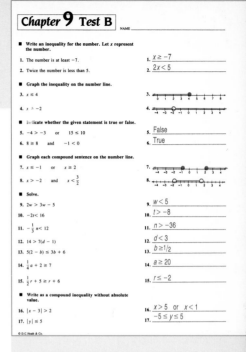

Chapter 9 Test B   NAME

■ Write an inequality for the number. Let x represent the number.

1. The number is at least -7.   1. $x \geq -7$

2. Twice the number is less than 5.   2. $2x < 5$

■ Graph the inequality on the number line.

3. $x \leq 4$ 3.

4. $x \geq -2$ 4.

■ Indicate whether the given statement is true or false.

5. $-4 > -3$ or $15 \leq 10$ 5. False

6. $8 \geq 8$ and $-1 < 0$ 6. True

■ Graph each compound sentence on the number line.

7. $x \leq -1$ or $x \geq 2$ 7.

8. $x > -2$ and $x < \frac{3}{2}$ 8.

■ Solve.

9. $2w > 3w - 5$ 9. $w < 5$

10. $-2t < 16$ 10. $t > -8$

11. $-\frac{1}{3}n < 12$ 11. $n > -36$

12. $14 > 7(d - 1)$ 12. $d < 3$

13. $5(2 - b) \leq 3b + 6$ 13. $b \geq 1/2$

14. $\frac{1}{4}a + 2 \geq 7$ 14. $a \geq 20$

15. $\frac{1}{2}r + 5 \geq r + 6$ 15. $r \leq -2$

■ Write as a compound inequality without absolute value.

16. $\lvert x - 3 \rvert > 2$ 16. $x > 5$ or $x < 1$

17. $\lvert y \rvert \leq 5$ 17. $-5 \leq y \leq 5$

© D.C. Heath & Co.

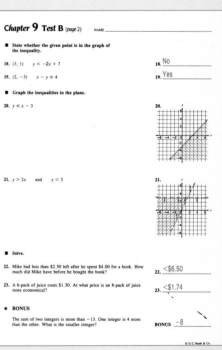

Chapter 9 Test B (page 2)   NAME

■ State whether the given point is in the graph of the inequality.

18. $(3, 1)$ $y < -2x + 7$ 18. No

19. $(2, -3)$ $x - y \geq 4$ 19. Yes

■ Graph the inequalities in the plane.

20. $y \leq x - 3$ 20.

21. $y > 2x$ and $y < 3$ 21.

■ Solve.

22. Mike had less than $2.50 left after he spent $4.00 for a book. How much did Mike have before he bought the book?   22. $< 6.50

23. A 6-pack of juice costs $1.30. At what price is an 8-pack of juice more economical?   23. $< 1.74

★ BONUS

The sum of two integers is more than -13. One integer is 4 more than the other. What is the smaller integer?   BONUS -8

© D.C. Heath & Co.

CHAPTER 10

CHAPTER OVERVIEW

This chapter focuses on square roots. First, students learn the meaning of square root and of the radical sign ($\sqrt{}$) and learn how to find approximations of square roots of numbers using a table. Students learn to manipulate and simplify expressions containing radicals, and to solve equations that contain radicals. Students learn to use the Pythagorean theorem and to use the distance formula, which is based on the Pythagorean theorem. In this chapter, students draw on their knowledge of real numbers and equations from Chapters 2 and 3 and on their knowledge of polynomials and algebraic fractions from Chapters 4, 7, and 8.

Knowledge of square roots and radicals is a prerequisite for the solving of quadratic equations using the quadratic formula in Chapter 11. This knowledge is also a prerequisite for the study of geometry, advanced algebra, trigonometry, statistics, and calculus. For example, in advanced algebra the idea of square roots will be extended to cube roots, fourth roots, and higher-order roots.

10 Rational and Irrational Numbers

If a point C divides a line segment AB into two parts so that $\dfrac{AC}{CB} = \dfrac{AB}{AC}$, each fraction is equal to the Golden Ratio, $\dfrac{1 + \sqrt{5}}{2}$.

In architecture and nature, rectangles in which the ratio of length to width equals the Golden Ratio are considered most pleasing to the eye. Many blossoms have the shape of a pentagon, which also illustrates the Golden Ratio.

$$\frac{PR}{PQ} = \frac{1 + \sqrt{5}}{2}$$

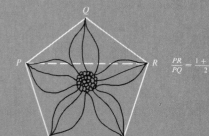

$$\frac{PR}{PQ} = \frac{1 + \sqrt{5}}{2}$$

OBJECTIVE 10–1

To simplify expressions involving square roots of perfect squares.

PURPOSE

Many commonly used formulas involve squares and square roots. It is important to be able to express quantities in the simplest way, using radicals only when necessary.

10–1 Square Roots

Preview

A manufacturer of card tables makes one model that is 3 ft long on each side. A new model is to have a playing surface that is $\frac{1}{3}$ greater than the 3-ft model.

- What is the surface area of the top of the new model? 12 ft²
- How long must each side of the new model be? $\sqrt{12}$ ft

■ LESSON

The number 25 is called the **square** of 5 because $5^2 = 25$. The number 25 is also the square of -5 because $(-5)^2 = 25$.

For the same reason, we say that 5 and -5 are **square roots** of 25.

> ### Definition: Square Root
>
> If $x^2 = y$, then x is a *square root* of y.

The positive square root of 25 is written $\sqrt{25}$.

$$\sqrt{25} = 5$$

The negative square root of 25 is written $-\sqrt{25}$.

$$-\sqrt{25} = -5$$

For example,

$$\sqrt{16} = 4 \qquad -\sqrt{16} = -4$$
$$\sqrt{49} = 7 \qquad -\sqrt{49} = -7$$
$$\sqrt{144} = 12 \qquad -\sqrt{144} = -12$$

The symbol $\sqrt{}$ is called a **radical sign**. The expression under the radical sign is the **radicand**. The entire expression is called a **radical**.

$$\sqrt{25} \text{ is a radical} \qquad 25 \text{ is the radicand}$$

Note that $\sqrt{16}$, $\sqrt{49}$, $\sqrt{144}$, and $\sqrt{0}$ are positive numbers or zero. The radical sign is used to indicate the **principal square root** of a number. The principal square root is never negative.

For the set of real numbers, a radicand cannot be a negative number. No real number squared is equal to a negative number. In the expression $\sqrt{x}$, x represents a number greater than or equal to 0.

If x is positive, then $\sqrt{x}$ is positive.
If x is positive, then $-\sqrt{x}$ is negative.
If x is 0, then $\sqrt{x}$ is 0.

Example 1.
Simplify. $\sqrt{400}$ 20

Example 2.
Simplify. $-\sqrt{81}$ -9

Example 3.
Simplify. $\sqrt{324}$ 18

Example 4.
Simplify. $\sqrt{\frac{25}{64}}$ $\frac{5}{8}$

Example 5.
Simplify. $\pm\sqrt{49}$ ±7

Example 6.
Simplify. $(\sqrt{100})^2$ 100

CHECK UNDERSTANDING

Consider the numbers $\sqrt{36}$, $-\sqrt{36}$, and $\sqrt{-36}$.

• Which are real numbers? ($\sqrt{36}$ and $-\sqrt{36}$)
• Which is positive? ($\sqrt{36}$)
• Which is negative? ($-\sqrt{36}$)
• Simplify the real numbers. ($\sqrt{36} = 6$, $-\sqrt{36} = -6$)

The expression $\sqrt{25}$ can be read "the principal square root of 25," "the square root of 25," or "radical 25." The expression $-\sqrt{25}$ is read "the negative square root of 25" or "negative radical 25."

Example 1 Simplify. $\sqrt{100}$

Solution The radical sign identifies the principal square root, a positive number.

Answer $\sqrt{100} = 10$, because $10^2 = 100$.

Example 2 Simplify. $-\sqrt{64}$

Solution The expression $-\sqrt{64}$ identifies the opposite of the principal square root, a negative number.

Answer $-\sqrt{64} = -8$

Example 3 Simplify. $\sqrt{225}$

Solution *Find the prime factorization of the radicand.* $\sqrt{225} = \sqrt{3^2 \cdot 5^2}$
Write the radicand as a square. $= \sqrt{(3 \cdot 5)^2}$
Simplify. $= 3 \cdot 5 = 15$

Answer $\sqrt{225} = 15$

Example 4 Simplify. $\sqrt{\frac{4}{9}}$

Solution *Factor the numerator and denominator.* $\sqrt{\frac{4}{9}} = \sqrt{\frac{2^2}{3^2}}$

Write the radicand as a square. $= \sqrt{\left(\frac{2}{3}\right)^2}$

Simplify. $= \frac{2}{3}$

Answer $\sqrt{\frac{4}{9}} = \frac{2}{3}$

Sometimes we wish to refer to both the positive square root and the negative square root in the same equation. We can write this as follows:

$$\pm\sqrt{25} = \pm 5$$

The sentence above is a short way of writing

$$+\sqrt{25} = +5 \quad \text{and} \quad -\sqrt{25} = -5$$

The symbol $\pm$ is read "positive or negative."

Many teachers claim that they have developed a much better understanding of mathematics as a result of teaching it. This suggests that students can also gain in understanding when they are given opportunities in peer tutoring.

Example 5   Simplify. $\pm\sqrt{81}$

  Solution $\pm\sqrt{81} = \pm 9$ because $+\sqrt{81} = +9$ and $-\sqrt{81} = -9$.

Example 6   Simplify. $(\sqrt{36})^2$

  Solution $\sqrt{36}$ is the principal square root of 36. That is, $\sqrt{36}$ is the nonnegative number whose square is 36.

  Answer $(\sqrt{36})^2 = 36$

  Check $(\sqrt{36})^2 = 6^2 = 36$

■ CLASSROOM EXERCISES

Complete by choosing the correct word.

1. $\sqrt{49}$ is ___?___ (positive/negative).   **2.** $-\sqrt{36}$ is ___?___ (positive/negative).
Positive   Negative
3. For all positive values of a, $\sqrt{a}$ is ___?___ (positive/negative).   Positive

Simplify.

4. $\sqrt{4}$ 2   **5.** $-\sqrt{9}$ -3 **6.** $\sqrt{1}$ 1   **7.** $\sqrt{0}$ 0

8. $\sqrt{196}$ 14   **9.** $\sqrt{1.96}$ 1.4   **10.** $-\sqrt{441}$ -21 **11.** $-\sqrt{4.41}$ -2.1

12. $\sqrt{\dfrac{16}{25}}$ $\frac{4}{5}$ **13.** $\dfrac{\sqrt{16}}{\sqrt{25}}$ $\frac{4}{5}$ **14.** $\sqrt{\dfrac{49}{36}}$ $\frac{7}{6}$ **15.** $\dfrac{\sqrt{49}}{\sqrt{36}}$ $\frac{7}{6}$

16. Answer both questions and state how the answers differ.

 a. What does $\sqrt{100}$ equal? 10   **b.** What are the square roots of 100? 10 and -10

17. How are the solutions to these equations different?
 a. $x^2 = 64$ **b.** $x = \sqrt{64}$ (8)
 $(8, -8)$ Equation a has two solutions, equation b has only one solution.

■ WRITTEN EXERCISES

Identify whether the expression represents a positive number, a negative number, or zero, or does not represent a real number.

1. $-\sqrt{49}$ Negative   **2.** $-\sqrt{16}$ Negative   **3.** $\sqrt{81}$ Positive   **4.** $\sqrt{121}$ Positive

5. $\sqrt{-25}$ Not a real   **6.** $\sqrt{-36}$ Not a real   **7.** $\sqrt{2.56}$ Positive   **8.** $\sqrt{1.96}$ Positive

9. $\sqrt{0.64}$ Positive   **10.** $\sqrt{0.49}$ Positive   **11.** $-\sqrt{1.21}$ Negative   **12.** $-\sqrt{1.69}$ Negative

Simplify.

13. $\sqrt{10,000}$ 100   **14.** $\sqrt{400}$ 20   **15.** $\sqrt{2500}$ 50   **16.** $\sqrt{1600}$ 40

17. $-\sqrt{40,000}$ -200 **18.** $-\sqrt{100}$ -10 **19.** $-\sqrt{1.44}$ -1.2 **20.** $-\sqrt{2.25}$ -1.5

CLASSROOM EXERCISES

In exercise 3, discuss how the answer changes if the sentence begins, "For all *negative* values . . ." (Answer is undefined.) Ask students how the sentence must be changed to give *negative* as the correct answer. (Replace $\sqrt{a}$ by $-\sqrt{a}$.)

Contrast exercises 8 and 9 by pointing out that the answers have the same digits but with different place value. Note that
$$\sqrt{1.96} = \sqrt{\frac{196}{100}} = \frac{14}{10} = 1.4.$$

Discuss exercises 12 and 13, bringing out that although the answers are the same, the process for finding the answers differs.

In exercise 17 point out that part a has two solutions, 8 and -8, but part b has one solution, 8. Also note that although $(-8)^2 = 64$, $-8 \neq \sqrt{64}$. The generalization "If $x^2 = a$, then $x = \sqrt{a}$" is true only when $x \geq 0$.

ASSIGNMENT GUIDE

Basic   1–43 odd, Review Exercises
Average   13–61 odd, Review Exercises
Enriched   25–79 odd, Review Exercises

PRACTICE WORKSHEET 52

10-1 SQUARE ROOTS

■ Simplify.

1. $\sqrt{49}$ 7   2. $-\sqrt{36}$ -6 3. $\sqrt{0.16}$ 0.4

4. $\sqrt{25}$ 5   5. $\sqrt{900}$ 30   6. $-\sqrt{144}$ -12

■ Solve. The equation may have two solutions, one solution, or no solution. Write Ø if the equation has no solution.

7. $x^2 = 4$ $\{-2, 2\}$ 8. $x = \sqrt{4}$ $\{2\}$ 9. $x = -\sqrt{4}$ $\{-2\}$

10. $x = \sqrt{-4}$ Ø   11. $\sqrt{x} = 4$ $\{16\}$ 12. $x^2 = -4$ Ø

13. $\sqrt{x} = -4$ Ø   14. $x^2 = \frac{1}{4}$ $\left\{-\frac{1}{2}, \frac{1}{2}\right\}$ 15. $x = \sqrt{\frac{1}{4}}$ $\{1/2\}$

16. $x = -\sqrt{0.04}$ $\{-0.2\}$ 17. $x = \sqrt{40,000}$ $\{200\}$ 18. $x = \sqrt{0.0004}$ $\{0.02\}$

Students frequently confuse the process of finding a square root with the symbol for the principal square root of a number. An important idea to emphasize is that $\sqrt{25}$ represents a number, and like the symbol for any number, it should unambiguously represent a *single* number. On the other hand, in solving an equation such as $x^2 = 25$, we are seeking each number whose square is 25. Therefore, the proper sequence of steps is as follows:

$$x^2 = 25 \qquad\qquad x^2 = 25$$
$$x = \pm\sqrt{25} \quad \text{and } not \quad x = \sqrt{25}$$
$$x = \pm 5 \qquad\qquad x = \pm 5$$

ENRICHMENT PROBLEM

• True or false? Explain your answer.
$$\sqrt{12^2} = \sqrt{(-12)^2}$$

True. Since the $\sqrt{}$ symbol indicates the principal square root, $\sqrt{12^2} = 12$ and $\sqrt{(-12)^2} = \sqrt{144} = 12$.

EXTRA PRACTICE, page 638

Simplify.

21. $\dfrac{\sqrt{9}}{\sqrt{16}}$ $\frac{3}{4}$
22. $\dfrac{\sqrt{4}}{\sqrt{25}}$ $\frac{2}{5}$
23. $\sqrt{\dfrac{9}{16}}$ $\frac{3}{4}$
24. $\sqrt{\dfrac{4}{25}}$ $\frac{2}{5}$

Find the square roots of these numbers.

25. 400 $20, -20$
26. 2500 $50, -50$
27. 1600 $40, -40$
28. 100 $10, -10$

Solve these equations. The equations may have two solutions, one solution, or no solution. Write ∅ if the equation has no solution.

29. $x^2 = 16$ $\{4, -4\}$
30. $x^2 = 36$ $\{6, -6\}$
31. $x = \sqrt{25}$ $\{5\}$
32. $x = \sqrt{16}$ $\{4\}$

33. $x = -\sqrt{64}$ $\{-8\}$
34. $x = -\sqrt{25}$ $\{-5\}$
35. $x^2 = 64$ $\{8, -8\}$
36. $x^2 = 25$ $\{5, -5\}$

37. $x = \sqrt{-36}$ ∅
38. $x = \sqrt{-64}$ ∅
39. $\sqrt{x} = 4$ $\{16\}$
40. $\sqrt{x} = 9$ $\{81\}$

The area A of a square with side s is given by the formula $A = s^2$. The formula $s = \sqrt{A}$ expresses the length of the side of a square when its area is known. Find the length of the side of the square with the given area.

41. 100 cm² 10 cm
42. 64 km² 8 km
43. 36 km² 6 km
44. 49 m² 7 m

Solve.

B **45.** Jacksonville, Florida, is one of the largest cities in the United States. Its area is approximately 2025 km². The area of Los Angeles, California is approximately 1225 km². If both cities were in the shape of squares, how much longer would a side of the Jacksonville square be? 10 km

46. The area of Oklahoma City is approximately 1681 km². The area of San Francisco is approximately 121 km². If both cities were in the shape of squares, how much longer would a side of the Oklahoma City square be? 30 km

Simplify.

47. $(\sqrt{0.36})^2$ 0.36
48. $(\sqrt{0.49})^2$ 0.49
49. $\sqrt{1.6^2}$ 1.6
50. $\sqrt{2.5^2}$ 2.5

51. $\sqrt{3^2 \cdot 4^2}$ 12
52. $3^2 \cdot \sqrt{4^2}$ 36
53. $3 \cdot \sqrt{4}$ 6
54. $3 \cdot (\sqrt{4})^2$ 12

55. $\sqrt{\dfrac{0}{9}}$ 0
56. $\sqrt{\dfrac{81}{100}}$ $\frac{9}{10}$
57. $\dfrac{\sqrt{81}}{100}$ $\frac{9}{100}$
58. $\dfrac{81}{\sqrt{100}}$ $\frac{81}{10}$

59. $(\sqrt{0.64})^2$ 0.64
60. $\sqrt{0.64^2}$ 0.64
61. $(\sqrt{0.0001})^2$ 0.0001
62. $\sqrt{0.01^2}$ 0.01

C An old "rule of thumb" for sailors is that the maximum speed of a sailboat in knots (nautical miles per hour) is 1.35 times the square root of the length (in feet) of the waterline ($K = 1.35\sqrt{l}$). Find the maximum speed of a sailboat with each of these waterline lengths.

63. 25 ft 6.75 knots
64. 36 ft 8.1 knots

65. 49 ft 9.45 knots
66. 64 ft 10.8 knots

492   Chapter 10 Rational and Irrational Numbers

The time in seconds for an object h meters above the ground to fall to the ground is given by the formula $t = \sqrt{\dfrac{h}{5}}$. How long will it take an object to fall to the ground from each of these heights?

67. 5 m 1 s   **68.** 20 m 2 s   **69.** 80 m 4 s   **70.** 500 m 10 s

The time in seconds for a pendulum to swing back and forth is given by the formula $t = 2\pi\sqrt{\dfrac{l}{10}}$, where l is the length of the pendulum in meters. (Use 3.14 as an approximation for π.) For pendulums of the following lengths, find the time for a full swing.

71. 10 m 6.28 s   **72.** 2.5 m 3.14 s   **73.** 40 m 12.56 s   **74.** 0.1 m 0.628 s

A *geometric mean* of two numbers a and b is a number x such that $\dfrac{a}{x} = \dfrac{x}{b}$. Find the positive geometric mean for each pair of numbers.

75. 12; 48 24   **76.** 75; 12 30   **77.** 45; 20 30   **78.** 7; 0.28 1.4

79. A square swimming pool is bounded by a concrete walk that is 3 ft wide. The area of the pool plus the walk is 2304 ft². Find the dimensions of the pool. 42 ft by 42 ft

■ REVIEW EXERCISES

State the property that is illustrated in each equation.   [1–5]

1. $4x + 5x = (4 + 5)x$ Dist. Mult. over Add.   **2.** $(37 \cdot 25)4 = 37(25 \cdot 4)$ Assoc. Mult.

Solve.   [3–7]

3. $3x = 4(x - 3)$ (12)   **4.** $3(x - 2) = 5x + 4$ (−5)

Solve each equation for r.   [3–8]

5. $L = 2\pi rh$ $r = \dfrac{L}{2\pi h}$ **6.** $A = p + prt$ $r = \dfrac{A - p}{pt}$

7. Write 93,000,000 in scientific notation. $9.3 \cdot 10^7$ [4–4]

EXTENSION Evaluating square roots on a calculator _____

You can use the square root key ($\sqrt{\ }$) on a calculator to compute the square root of a number. For example, if you enter 9 and then press the square root key, you should see a calculator display of 3, the principal square root of 9.
 Follow these steps.

1. Enter any number greater than 1.
2. Press $\sqrt{\ }$ $\sqrt{\ }$ $\sqrt{\ }$ $\sqrt{\ }$ $\sqrt{\ }$, noting the display after each time you press the key.
3. Repeat with other numbers greater than 1.
4. Repeat with numbers between 0 and 1.

Can you explain why, in all cases, the sequence of displayed numbers approaches 1? If $x = 1$, $\sqrt{x} = 1$.   If $x > 1$, $\sqrt{x} < x$.   If $x > 0$ and $x < 1$, $\sqrt{x} > x$.

Class Starter Quiz
on previous section

Simplify.
1. $-\sqrt{64}$ -8

2. $\sqrt{900}$ 30

3. $\sqrt{0.36}$ 0.6

Solve these equations.

4. $x^2 = 25$ $\{-5, 5\}$

5. $x = -\sqrt{25}$ $\{-5\}$

PURPOSE

Radicals such as $\sqrt{5}$ symbolize irrational numbers exactly. However, for many practical applications, decimal approximations are needed. Therefore, it is important for students to be able to determine decimal approximations for square roots of numbers.

PREVIEW

Students can gain an appreciation for the intellectual development of the mathematicians in ancient Babylon and Greece by noting their understanding of the square root of 2. The understanding of mathematicians 2500 years ago was not surpassed until relatively recently. As in any field, advances in mathematics today have been built upon the work of many others over the centuries.

LESSON

We recommend that students use the $\sqrt{}$ function on a calculator or a table to compute approximations of square roots in most situations. However, it is worthwhile for a guess-and-check method to be used a few times in order to reinforce an understanding of the concept of square root.

Students should clearly understand that, for example, $\sqrt{12}$ is an exact way of writing the positive solution of $x^2 = 12$ and that while 3.4, 3.46, 3.464, . . . are successively better approximations of $\sqrt{12}$, there is no *exact* decimal or fraction representation.

10–2 Approximations of Square Roots

Preview   Historical note—Square roots

The ancient Mesopotamians were skilled at finding square roots. They used the symbol  to represent the square root of a number. Using a base-60 numeration system, they achieved amazing accuracy in determining approximations of common square roots. An ancient Babylonian tablet lists the square root of 2 as ⟨cuneiform⟩ or 1.414222, a result that was not exceeded in accuracy until the Renaissance.

Babylonian table of squares and square roots

The Mesopotamians, however, believed that all square roots could be expressed as rational numbers, the quotient of two whole numbers. It was not until about 450 B.C. that the Pythagorean Society of Greece discovered that $\sqrt{2}$ is not a rational number, and that some square roots can only be approximated by a decimal representation.

In this lesson you will learn how to find approximations of square roots.

■ LESSON

If you wish to build a square storage-shed floor with an area of 70 ft², the length of each side must be $\sqrt{70}$ ft. However, since measuring tapes are not marked with symbols such as $\sqrt{70}$, we must find another way of writing that number.

We know that $\sqrt{70}$ is not an integer or even a **rational number.** This means that it cannot be expressed exactly as a common fraction or as a decimal. Thus, $\sqrt{70}$ is an example of an **irrational number.**

> ### Definitions: Rational and Irrational Numbers
>
> A *rational number* is a number that can be expressed as the quotient of two integers.
>
> An *irrational number* is a real number that cannot be expressed as the quotient of two integers.

ADDITIONAL EXAMPLES

Example 1.

Use the table on page 495 to find a decimal approximation of $\sqrt{19}$ to the nearest hundredth.

$$\sqrt{19} \approx 4.36$$

Although we cannot express $\sqrt{70}$ as an exact decimal fraction, we can find a decimal approximation to any degree of accuracy required by using systematic trials. For example, consider finding a decimal approximation of $\sqrt{70}$ accurate to the nearest hundredth.

First, determine which consecutive integers $\sqrt{70}$ lies between.

$$8^2 = 64$$
$$(\sqrt{70})^2 = 70$$
$$9^2 = 81$$

So, $8 < \sqrt{70} < 9$.

Next, improve the approximation to tenths.

$$8.3^2 = 68.89$$
$$(\sqrt{70})^2 = 70$$
$$8.4^2 = 70.56$$

Thus, $8.3 < \sqrt{70} < 8.4$.

Continue to hundredths.

$8.36^2 \approx 69.89$ [*Remember:* $\approx$ means "is approximately equal to."]
$(\sqrt{70})^2 = 70$
$8.37^2 \approx 70.06$

So, $8.36 < \sqrt{70} < 8.37$ ($\sqrt{70}$ is between 8.36 and 8.37, but it is closer to 8.37). Thus, the decimal approximation of $\sqrt{70}$ to the nearest hundredth is 8.37.

The decimal approximations of square roots of numbers can be determined by using a calculator or by using the table on page 641.

Example 1   Use this table to find a decimal approximation of $\sqrt{20}$ to the nearest hundredth.

Number	Square of number	Square root of number
n	n^2	$\sqrt{n}$
18	324	4.243
19	361	4.359
20	400	4.472
21	441	4.583

Solution   Find 20 in the n-column. Then find a decimal approximation of $\sqrt{20}$ in the $\sqrt{n}$-column.

Answer $\sqrt{20} \approx 4.47$

The same table can be used to find the squares of integers.

Example 2.

Use the table on page 496 to simplify 51^2.

$$51^2 = 2601$$

Example 3.

Solve $x^2 = 54$, and then give a decimal approximation of the solution to the nearest hundredth.

The exact solution is $\{\sqrt{54}, -\sqrt{54}\}$.
The approximate solution is $\{7.35, -7.35\}$.

CHECK UNDERSTANDING

Consider the equation $x^2 = 20$.

- Find the exact solutions. ($\sqrt{20}$ and $-\sqrt{20}$)
- Is 4.5 a solution? (No. $4.5^2 = 20.25$.)
- Is 4.47 a solution? (No. $4.47^2 = 19.98$.)
- Is 4.5 an approximation of a solution to the nearest tenth? (Yes)

CLASSROOM EXERCISES

In exercises 7–9 remind students that the equations have two solutions. Ask students to state the exact solutions as well as the approximations. For example, the exact solutions of exercise 7 are $\sqrt{45}$ and $-\sqrt{45}$.

ASSIGNMENT GUIDE

Basic   1–33 odd, Review Exercises
Average 3–45 multiples of 3, Review
         Exercises
Enriched 9–51 multiples of 3, 54–57 all,
         Review Exercises

PRACTICE WORKSHEET 52

10-2 APPROXIMATIONS FOR SQUARE ROOTS

■ State the consecutive integers between which the given number lies.

1. $\sqrt{7.3}$ _2,3_   2. $\sqrt{19}$ _4,5_   3. $\sqrt{89}$ _9,10_

4. $\sqrt{0.2025}$ _0,1_   5. $\sqrt{63.2}$ _7,8_   6. $\sqrt{130}$ _11,12_

■ Use the table on page 641 to find a decimal approximation to the nearest hundredth.

7. $\sqrt{6}$ _2.45_   8. $-\sqrt{8}$ _−2.83_   9. $\sqrt{60}$ _7.75_

10. $-\sqrt{80}$ _−8.94_   11. $\sqrt{89}$ _9.43_   12. $\sqrt{17}$ _4.12_

■ Use the table on page 641 to simplify.

13. 65^2 _4225_   14. 24^2 _576_   15. 48^2 _2304_

16. $\sqrt{9025}$ _95_   17. $\sqrt{729}$ _27_   18. $\sqrt{3136}$ _56_

EXTRA PRACTICE, page 638

Example 2   Use this table to simplify 53^2.

n	n^2	$\sqrt{n}$
51	2601	7.141
52	2704	7.211
53	2809	7.280
54	2916	7.348

Solution   Find 53 in the n-column. Then find 53^2 in the n^2-column.

Answer $53^2 = 2809$

The solutions of some equations are square roots. We can use a table or a calculator to find decimal approximations for irrational numbers.

Example 3   Solve $x^2 = 37$, giving a decimal approximation of the solution to the nearest hundredth.

Solution
$$x^2 = 37$$
$$x = \pm\sqrt{37}$$

The exact solution is $\{\sqrt{37}, -\sqrt{37}\}$.

Answer   The approximate solution is $\{6.08, -6.08\}$.

■ CLASSROOM EXERCISES

State the consecutive integers between which the given number lies.

1. $\sqrt{39}$ 6, 7   **2.** $\sqrt{75}$ 8, 9   **3.** $\sqrt{14.4}$ 3, 4

Use the table on page 641 to find an approximation to the nearest hundredth.

4. $\sqrt{23}$ 4.80   **5.** $\sqrt{68}$ 8.25   **6.** $\sqrt{85}$ 9.22

Solve, giving approximations of the solutions to the nearest hundredth.

7. $x^2 = 45$ $\{6.71, -6.71\}$ **8.** $x^2 = 59$ $\{7.68, -7.68\}$ **9.** $x^2 = 76$ $\{8.72, -8.72\}$

■ WRITTEN EXERCISES

State the consecutive integers between which the given number lies.

A   **1.** $\sqrt{57}$ 7, 8   **2.** $\sqrt{95}$ 9, 10   **3.** $\sqrt{20.3}$ 4, 5   **4.** $\sqrt{27.9}$ 5, 6

Use the table on page 641 to find a decimal approximation to the nearest hundredth.

5. $\sqrt{2}$ 1.41   **6.** $\sqrt{3}$ 1.73   **7.** $\sqrt{30}$ 5.4⟍ 5.48   **8.** $\sqrt{20}$ 4.47

9. $-\sqrt{18}$ −4.24   **10.** $-\sqrt{43}$ −6.56   **11.** $-\sqrt{72}$ −8.49   **12.** $-\sqrt{92}$ −9.59

Write a computer program that lists the square root of each integer from 1 to 100.

```
10 PRINT "NUMBER", "SQUARE
   ROOT"
20 FOR N = 1 TO 100
30 PRINT N, SQR (N)
40 NEXT N
50 END
```

The number given is the square root of an integer accurate to the nearest tenth. What is the integer?

13. 3.6 13
14. 6.4 41
15. 7.8 61
16. 7.2 52

Use the table on page 641 to simplify.

17. 75^2 5625
18. 88^2 7744
19. 44^2 1936
20. 76^2 5776

21. $\sqrt{8281}$ 91
22. $\sqrt{6889}$ 83
23. $\sqrt{1444}$ 38
24. $\sqrt{3844}$ 62

Solve. List the solutions exactly, using radicals, not decimals.

25. $x^2 = 10$ $(\sqrt{10}, -\sqrt{10})$
26. $x^2 = 21$ $(\sqrt{21}, -\sqrt{21})$
27. $x^2 = 19$ $(\sqrt{19}, -\sqrt{19})$
28. $x^2 = 91$ $(\sqrt{91}, -\sqrt{91})$

Solve. List approximations for the solutions to the nearest hundredth.

29. $x^2 = 10$ $(3.16, -3.16)$
30. $x^2 = 21$ $(4.58, -4.58)$
31. $x^2 = 19$ $(4.36, -4.36)$
32. $x^2 = 91$ $(9.54, -9.54)$

33. The area of a square is 57cm^2. What is the length of each side of the square to the nearest hundredth of a centimeter? 7.55 cm

34. The area of a square is 95 cm^2. What is the length of each side of the square to the nearest hundredth of a centimeter? 9.75 cm

B The time in seconds for an object to fall h meters is given by the formula $t = \sqrt{\dfrac{h}{5}}$.

Find to the nearest tenth of a second the time for an object to fall to the ground from these heights.

35. 25 m 2.2 s
36. 50 m 3.2 s
37. 100 m 4.5 s
38. 200 m 6.3 s

The electrical current in amperes (I) that flows through an appliance is given by the formula $I = \sqrt{\dfrac{W}{R}}$, where W is the power of the appliance in watts and R is the resistance of the appliance in ohms. Find the current through these appliances.

39. A 50-watt lightbulb with a resistance of 200 ohms 0.5 amperes
40. A 500-watt iron with a resistance of 20 ohms 5 amperes

41. The surface area of a cube is 240 cm^2. Find the length of an edge to the nearest thousandth of a centimeter. (The six faces of a cube are squares.) 6.325 cm

Use systematic trials to calculate the principal square root to the nearest tenth. Show your work.

42. $\sqrt{22}$ 4.7
43. $\sqrt{45}$ 6.7
44. $\sqrt{92}$ 9.6
45. $\sqrt{13}$ 3.6
46. $\sqrt{231}$ 15.2
47. $\sqrt{185}$ 13.6

Use systematic trials to calculate the principal square root to the nearest hundredth. Show your work.

48. $\sqrt{300}$ 17.32
49. $\sqrt{417}$ 20.42
50. $\sqrt{631}$ 25.12
51. $\sqrt{722}$ 26.87
52. $\sqrt{200}$ 14.14
53. $\sqrt{156}$ 12.49

CONCEPT EXTENSION

Careful attention should be given to helping students read and interpret tables of squares and square roots such as those in Examples 1 and 2. The ability to read tables may not be a well-developed skill. Therefore, some questions to introduce students to these skills are advised before seeking particular square roots. Here are some questions to ask about the table in Example 1.

- Numbers in the n^2 column are not consecutive whole numbers. What information about square roots of numbers between 324 and 361 does the table provide? (The square roots of numbers between 324 and 361 are between 18 and 19.)
- Find an approximation for the square of 4.5. (4.5^2 is between 20 and 21. It is closer to 20. It is exactly 20.25.)
- Find an approximation for the square root of 380. ($\sqrt{380}$ is between 19 and 20. It is about 19.494.)
- Find an approximation for the square root of 18.5. ($\sqrt{18.5}$ is about halfway between 4.243 and 4.359. It is about 4.301.)
- Find an approximation for the square of 20.75. (20.75^2 is about three fourths of the way between 400 and 441. It is about 430.75. It is exactly 430.5625.)

ENRICHMENT PROBLEMS

- Solve.
  a. The sum of the squares of two consecutive integers is less than 300. What are the two largest integers for which this is true?

  11 and 12

  b. The square root of a number is between m and n. Between what two numbers will the square of the number be?

  m^4 and n^4

2.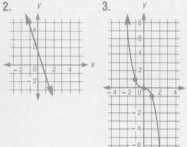

3.

4.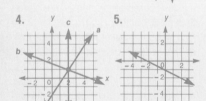

5.

---

54. True or false?

$\sqrt{9 + 16} = \sqrt{9} + \sqrt{16}$ False

What do you conclude from your answer?

$\sqrt{a + b} \neq \sqrt{a} + \sqrt{b}$

55. True or false?

$\sqrt{100 - 36} = \sqrt{100} - \sqrt{36}$ False

What do you conclude from your answer?

$\sqrt{a - b} \neq \sqrt{a} - \sqrt{b}$

56. True or false?

$\sqrt{4 \cdot 49} = \sqrt{4} \cdot \sqrt{49}$ True

What do you conclude from your answer?

$\sqrt{ab} = \sqrt{a} \cdot \sqrt{b}$

57. True or false?

$\sqrt{\dfrac{25}{9}} = \dfrac{\sqrt{25}}{\sqrt{9}}$ True

What do you conclude from your answer?

$\sqrt{\dfrac{a}{b}} = \dfrac{\sqrt{a}}{\sqrt{b}}$

■ REVIEW EXERCISES

1. Find the missing number for each solution pair of the equation $d = 10t + 40$. [5–3]

t	0	2	?	?	?	0.2
d	?	?	50	100	20	?

(answers: 1, 6, −2 / 40, 60, 42)

2. Select three values of x, complete the table, plot the points, and then graph the equation $3x + y = 2$. [5–4]

x	?	?	?
y	?	?	?

3. Copy and complete the table and then use the ordered pairs to graph the equation $y = -x^3$. [5–4]

x	−3	−2	−1	$-\dfrac{1}{2}$	0	$\dfrac{1}{2}$	1	2	3
y	?	?	?	?	?	?	?	?	?

(answers: 27, 8, 1, $\dfrac{1}{8}$, 0, $-\dfrac{1}{8}$, −1, −8, −27)

4. Draw these three lines through point $(2, 1)$. Label the lines a, b, and c. [5–5]

a. line with slope $\dfrac{3}{2}$

b. line with slope $-\dfrac{1}{3}$

c. line with no slope

5. Graph the line with a slope of $-\dfrac{1}{2}$ and y-intercept of -1. [5–6]

6. Write the equation $3x - 2y = 6$ in slope–intercept form. $y = \dfrac{3}{2}x - 3$ [5–6]

7. State whether the relation $\{(1, 2), (1, 3), (2, 4)\}$ represents a function. No [5–8]

8. State whether the equation $y = \dfrac{4}{x}$ represents a linear function. No [5–8]

EXTENSION   A computer program for square root

The computer program below takes any positive number and any estimate of its square root to compute better and better approximations of the principal square root of the number. Lines 70 and 80 compute these approximations. A new value of the estimate (E) is computed by averaging the old estimate and the quotient of the number divided by the old estimate (A). The new estimate becomes the old estimate for the next approximation. Lines 60 and 90 count the number of times that lines 70 and 80 are used. Line 120 rounds the answer to the nearest tenth.

```
10   PRINT "ENTER A POSITIVE NUMBER."
20   INPUT P
30   IF P < = 0 THEN 10
40   PRINT "TYPE ANY POSITIVE ESTIMATE OF THE
     SQUARE ROOT OF YOUR NUMBER."
50   INPUT E
60   X = 0
70   A = P/E
80   E = (A + E)/2
90   X = X + 1
100  PRINT X
110  IF ABS(A - E) > = .1 THEN 70
120  E = INT(10 * E + .5)/10
130  PRINT "SQUARE ROOT OF    "; P; "    =    "; E
140  PRINT "ANY MORE SQUARE ROOTS? (Y/N)"
150  INPUT Q$
160  IF Q$ = "N" THEN 180
170  GOTO 10
180  END
```

Use the program to find the principal square root of each number to the nearest tenth.

1. 29 5.4   **2.** 53 7.3   **3.** 82 9.1   **4.** 14 3.7

Change .1 to .01 in line 110 and change (10 * E + .5)/10 to (100 * E + .5)/100 in line 120 to find the principal square root of each number to the nearest hundredth.

5. 29 5.39   **6.** 53 7.28   **7.** 82 9.06   **8.** 14 3.74

How many times are steps 70 and 80 used (with new line 110) if P is 200 and E is each of the following?

9. 10 4   **10.** 50 5   **11.** 14 2   **12.** 15 3

Class Starter Quiz
on previous section

Use the table on page 641 to find the decimal approximations to the nearest hundredth.

1. $\sqrt{5}$ 2.24
2. $-\sqrt{50}$ -7.07
3. $\sqrt{34}$ 5.83

The number given is the square root of an integer to the nearest tenth. What is the integer?

4. 4.7   22   **5.** 6.7   45

PURPOSE

Numerous practical problems involve situations where right triangles are used. The ability to use the Pythagorean theorem is a powerful problem-solving tool.

PREVIEW

The triangle shown in the Preview happens to be a special triangle—an isosceles, right triangle. Point out that it is not necessary that the right triangle be isosceles for the relationship (later called the Pythagorean theorem) to hold.

LESSON

Remind students that it is customary to denote the right angle of a geometric figure with the symbol ⌐

Although the Pythagorean theorem is applied to triangles, other figures such as squares and rectangles can be subdivided into right triangles by drawing a diagonal.

Students may not recognize the difference between a theorem and its converse. If p and q represent statements, then *If p, then q* and *If q, then p* are converses. The truth values of the two sentences are not related. Both may be true, both may be false, or one of the statements may be true while the other is false.

Discuss these converses considering the first to be true. The converse is not necessarily true.

If John is sick, then John is absent.
If John is absent, then John is sick.

OBJECTIVE 10–3

To use the Pythagorean theorem to find missing lengths of sides of right triangles.

You may wish to spend two days on this section. Refer to the Pacing Chart.

10–3 The Pythagorean Theorem

Preview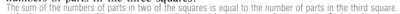

More than 2500 years ago Egyptian and Greek mathematicians made an interesting and useful discovery about the sides of a right triangle. It is possible that the relationship among the sides was discovered while the mathematicians were studying patterns in floor tiles.

Triangle *ABC* is a right triangle. Each floor tile consists of four triangular parts.

- How many triangular parts cover the square on side *AB*?   4
- How many triangular parts cover the square on side *AC*?   8
- How many triangular parts cover the square on side *BC*?   4
- What relationship do you see among the numbers of parts in the three squares?

The sum of the numbers of parts in two of the squares is equal to the number of parts in the third square.

In this lesson you will study the relationship among the areas of the three squares. This relationship, named for the Greek mathematician Pythagoras, has many uses.

■ LESSON

Ancient mathematicians discovered that the area of the square on the longest side (**hypotenuse**) of a right triangle is equal to the sum of the areas of the squares on the two shorter sides (**legs**).

That property can be stated in algebraic terms as follows.

The Pythagorean Theorem

For a right triangle, the square of the hypotenuse is equal to the sum of the squares of the legs.

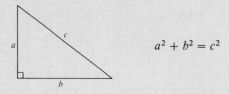

$$a^2 + b^2 = c^2$$

Right triangles are the only triangles for which this special relationship is true.

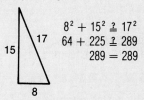
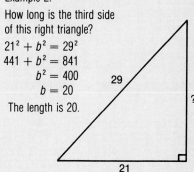
Converse of the Pythagorean Theorem

If sides a, b, and c of a triangle are such that $a^2 + b^2 = c^2$, then the triangle is a right triangle. The right angle is opposite the longest side.

These examples show some uses of the Pythagorean theorem and its converse.

Example 1   Are these triangles right triangles?

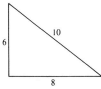 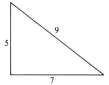

Solutions   Let $a = 6$, $b = 8$, and $c = 10$.   Let $a = 5$, $b = 7$, and $c = 9$.
Then $a^2 + b^2 = 36 + 64 = 100$ Then $a^2 + b^2 = 25 + 49 = 74$
$$c^2 = 100$$ $$c^2 = 81$$
$$a^2 + b^2 = c^2$$ $$a^2 + b^2 \neq c^2$$

Answer   The triangle is a right triangle.   The triangle is not a right triangle.

Example 2   How long is the third side of this right triangle?

Solution $a^2 + b^2 = c^2$
$$7^2 + b^2 = 12^2$$
$$49 + b^2 = 144$$
$$b^2 = 95$$
$$b = \pm \sqrt{95} \approx \pm 9.75$$

There are two solutions of the algebraic equation. However, only the positive solution makes sense as an answer to the problem. The length of the third side is $\sqrt{95}$.

Answer   The length is 9.75 to the nearest hundredth. (See the table on page 641.)

CHECK UNDERSTANDING

• For this right triangle, state the relationship given by the Pythagorean theorem. ($x^2 + y^2 = z^2$)

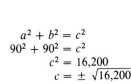

• Convince me that this is a right triangle. ($6^2 + 8^2 = 100 = 10^2$)

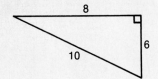

CLASSROOM EXERCISES

Point out that the hypotenuse is always the longest side on a right triangle and that it is opposite the right angle.

Example 3 A baseball diamond is a square 90 ft long on each side. How far is home plate from second base?

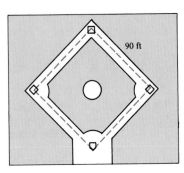

Solution
$$a^2 + b^2 = c^2$$
$$90^2 + 90^2 = c^2$$
$$c^2 = 16{,}200$$
$$c = \pm \sqrt{16{,}200}$$

The negative solution of the equation is not an answer to the problem. The distance from home plate to second base is exactly $\sqrt{16{,}200}$. Using a calculator, we find an approximation to the nearest tenth:

$$c \approx 127.3$$

Answer The length is 127.3 ft to the nearest tenth.

■ CLASSROOM EXERCISES

State whether the triangle is a right angle.

1. Yes

2. No

3. Yes
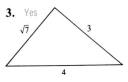

Find the missing lengths.

4.
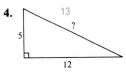

5. $\sqrt{5}$

6. 6
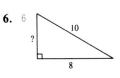

■ WRITTEN EXERCISES

State whether a triangle with these sides is a right triangle.

A **1.** 20 cm, 21 cm, 29 cm Yes

2. 7 cm, 24 cm, 25 cm Yes

3. 42 m, 40 m, 52 m No

4. 28 m, 45 m, 63 m No

5. 16 m, 30 m, 34 m Yes

6. 12 m, 35 m, 37 m Yes

7. 28 km, 96 km, 100 km Yes

8. 32 m, 32 m, 40 m No

Find the missing lengths.

9.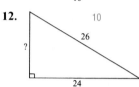

10.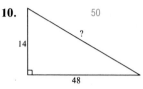

11.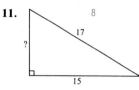

12.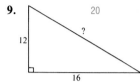

13.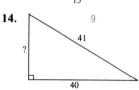

14.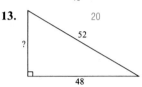

15. 60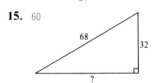

16. 40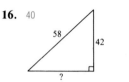

17. 80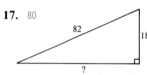

18. 80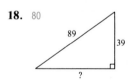

19. 80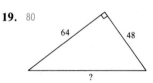

20. 40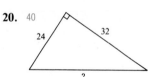

Find the missing lengths. Use the table on page 641 to approximate to the nearest tenth.

21. 2.2

22. 3.2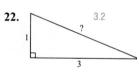

23. 3.6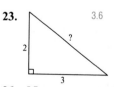

24. 4.5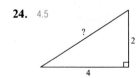

25. 7.1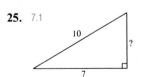

26. 5.7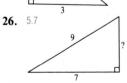

Find the length of the diagonal of a rectangle with the given length and width. Use the table on page 641 to approximate to the nearest tenth.

27. length: 8 cm
width: 2 cm   8.2 cm

28. length: 6 cm
width: 2 cm   6.3 cm

29. length: 30 km
width: 20 km   36.1 km

30. length: 35 km
width: 27 km   44.2 km

31. length: 48 mm
width: 36 mm   60 mm

32. length: 62 mm
width: 43 mm   75.5 mm

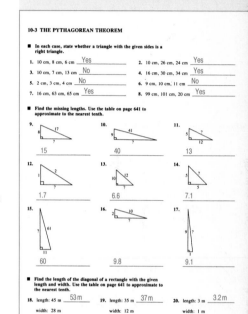

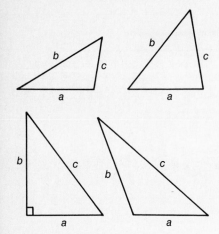
Solve.

33. The highway route from Cedar Falls to Cedar Rapids is 40 mi east, then 30 mi south. What is the airline distance from Cedar Falls to Cedar Rapids? 50 mi

34. Pearl City is approximately 8 mi west and 6 mi north of Honolulu. What is the straight-line distance between the two cities? 10 mi

B 35. A vacant lot is 36 m long and 27 m wide. How many meters shorter is the direct (diagonal) route from one corner to the opposite corner than the route that follows the boundary of the lot? 18

36. Cities A and B are joined by a direct highway. They are also connected by a highway that runs 24 km east from city A and then 70 km north to city B. How much shorter is the direct route than the east–north route? 20 km

37. An antenna is 60 m tall. A supporting cable is attached to the top of the antenna and to an anchor 11 m from the foot of the antenna. How long is the cable? 61 m

38. What is the longest line segment that can be drawn on a rectangular sheet of wrapping paper that is 28 in. wide and 45 in. long? 53 in.

39. The diagonals of two different rectangles are 85 cm long. The length of one rectangle is 77 cm and the length of the other rectangle is 84 cm. How much wider is one rectangle than the other rectangle? 23 cm

40. The diagonal brace of a rectangular door is 106 in. long. If the width of the door is 56 in., how high is the door? 90 in.

41. A square field is 1 km long on each side. How many meters shorter is the diagonal distance across the field than the distance along two sides?
≈ 586 m

42. A hiker can walk on a road around the field described in Exercise 41 at the rate of 6 km/h. Walking diagonally across the field, the hiker walks at a rate of 4 km/h. Which route from one corner of the field to the opposite corner is faster? How much faster? Around the field; ≈ 1.2 min

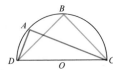

Triangles ACD and BCD are formed by joining points A and B on circle O to the ends of diameter DC. The angles at A and B are right angles. The diameter of the circle is 20 cm. The length of side AD is 10 cm and the length of side BD is 14 cm.

43. Find the perimeter and area of triangle ACD. ≈ 47.32 cm, ≈ 86.6 cm²

44. Find the perimeter and area of triangle BCD. ≈ 48.28 cm, ≈ 100.0 cm²

C 45. A room is 12 m long and 4 m wide. The ceiling is 3 m above the floor. How far is one corner of the floor from the opposite corner of the ceiling? 13 m

46. Can a 1-m stick be put in a box that measures 33 cm by 56 cm by 72 cm? What is the length of the longest stick that can fit in the box? No; 97 cm

47. The sides of an acute triangle (each angle less than 90°) are a, b, and c with c being the longest side. How is $a^2 + b^2$ related to c^2? $a^2 + b^2 > c^2$

48. The sides of an obtuse triangle (one angle greater than 90°) are a, b, and c with c being the longest side. How is $a^2 + b^2$ related to c^2? $a^2 + b^2 < c^2$

■ REVIEW EXERCISES

1. Solve this system by graphing.
$x + y = 2$ {(0, 2)}
$x - 2y = -4$

2. Solve this system by substitution. [6–1, 6–2]
$y = 5x$ {(4, 20)}
$25x + 10y = 300$

3. State whether this system has 0, 1, or infinitely many solutions. [6–3]
$y = 2x + 2$ 1
$y = 3x + 2$

Self-Quiz 1

10–1 Simplify.

1. $\sqrt{\dfrac{49}{25}}$ $\dfrac{7}{5}$
2. $-\sqrt{8100}$ -90
3. $\pm\sqrt{0.36}$ ± 0.6

Solve these equations.

4. $x^2 = 144$ {12, −12}
5. $x^2 = 225$ {15, −15}
6. $x^2 = -16$ ∅

10–2 Use the table on page 641 to find these square roots to the nearest tenth.

7. $\sqrt{12}$ 3.5
8. $\sqrt{19{,}600}$ 140
9. $\sqrt{169}$ 13

10–3 Find the missing lengths.

10.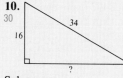
11.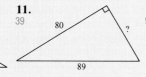
12.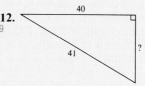

Solve.

13. What length of wire is needed to reach from the top of a 52-ft antenna to a point on the ground 20 ft from its base? 48 ft

---

x cm^2

ADDITIONAL ANSWER

■ **Review Exercises**

1.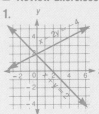

Is a triangle a right triangle if its sides have these lengths?

1. 40 m, 42 m, 58 m Yes
2. 30 m, 32 m, 48 m No

Find the missing length in these right triangles.

3.

4.
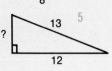

5.
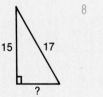

PURPOSE

To improve communication of mathematical ideas, standard notation, symbols, and forms have been agreed upon. It is important for students to understand conventional notation for radicals.

PREVIEW

Historically, the reason for considering $2\sqrt{2}$ to be simpler than $\sqrt{8}$ is related to the "paper and pencil" computation used to find a decimal approximation of $\sqrt{8}$. It was easier to compute an approximation of $\sqrt{2}$ and then use that to find approximations of $\sqrt{8}$, $\sqrt{18}$, $\sqrt{50}$, and the like, than to compute those approximations directly.

However, if students are using calculators, $\sqrt{8}$ would be considered simpler, since it requires fewer key strokes to compute.

OBJECTIVE 10–4

To simplify expressions involving sums, products, and differences of radicals.

10–4 Simplifying Square Roots

Preview

• Which of these equivalent algebraic expressions is simplest?

$$5x - 3x - x \qquad \frac{10x}{10} \qquad x \qquad 1x$$

Most people would agree that x is simpler than the others.

• Which of these expressions is simplest?

$$\sqrt{8} \qquad 2\sqrt{2} \qquad \sqrt{\frac{24}{3}} \qquad \frac{4}{\sqrt{2}}$$

Although both $\sqrt{8}$ and $2\sqrt{2}$ are simple expressions, mathematicians have generally agreed that $2\sqrt{2}$ is "simpler" than $\sqrt{8}$.

In this lesson you will study how to simplify expressions that include radicals.

■ LESSON

Notice that

$$\sqrt{4} \cdot \sqrt{9} = 2 \cdot 3 = 6$$

and that

$$\sqrt{4 \cdot 9} = \sqrt{36} = 6;$$

therefore,

$$\sqrt{4} \cdot \sqrt{9} = \sqrt{4 \cdot 9}.$$

The last equation is an example of the multiplication property for radicals.

The Multiplication Property for Radicals

For all nonnegative numbers a and b,

$$\sqrt{ab} = \sqrt{a} \cdot \sqrt{b}$$

In the property above, the values of a and b must be restricted to 0 or the positive numbers. If only one of a and b is a negative number, then the expression $\sqrt{ab}$ is not a real number. If both a and b are negative numbers, then the expression $\sqrt{ab}$ is a real number, but the expressions $\sqrt{a}$ and $\sqrt{b}$ are not.

This property can be used to simplify some radicals. For example, consider simplifying $\sqrt{18}$.

Factor the radicand.	$\sqrt{18} = \sqrt{2 \cdot 3^2}$
Use the multiplication property for radicals.	$= \sqrt{2} \cdot \sqrt{3^2}$
Simplify.	$= 3\sqrt{2}$

Listening and speaking mathematics should receive as much emphasis in algebra classes as reading and writing mathematics. Therefore, provide opportunities to communicate mathematics in peer tutoring.

In the multiplication property for radicals, $\sqrt{ab} = \sqrt{a} \cdot \sqrt{b}$ is restricted to nonnegative values. It is not true if a and b are negative numbers. For example, $\sqrt{(-4)(-9)}$ is a real number, while $\sqrt{-4}$ and $\sqrt{-9}$ are not real numbers.

Mention that it is customary to write $4 + \sqrt{6}$ rather than $\sqrt{6} + 4$. Also, $4\sqrt{5}$ is preferred to $\sqrt{5} \cdot 4$. In both examples, the preferred notation will not inadvertently extend the vinculum over an addend or factor (as in $\sqrt{6 + 4}$ or $\sqrt{5 \cdot 4}$).

When the radicand does not contain any perfect-square factors, we say that it is in **simplest form**.

The simplest form of $\sqrt{18}$ is $3\sqrt{2}$.

Example 1 Simplify. $\sqrt{48}$

Solution
$$\begin{aligned}\sqrt{48} &= \sqrt{2^4 \cdot 3}\\ &= \sqrt{(2^2)^2} \cdot \sqrt{3}\\ &= 2^2 \cdot \sqrt{3}\\ &= 4\sqrt{3}\end{aligned}$$

Answer $\sqrt{48} = 4\sqrt{3}$

Example 2 Simplify. $\sqrt{360}$

Solution
$$\begin{aligned}\sqrt{360} &= \sqrt{2^3 \cdot 3^2 \cdot 5}\\ &= \sqrt{2^2 \cdot 3^2 \cdot 2 \cdot 5}\\ &= \sqrt{(2 \cdot 3)^2} \cdot \sqrt{2 \cdot 5}\\ &= 6\sqrt{10}\end{aligned}$$

Answer $\sqrt{360} = 6\sqrt{10}$

The multiplication property for radicals is also used to simplify expressions involving the product of radicals.

Example 3 Simplify. $-\sqrt{24} \cdot \sqrt{30}$

Solution
$$\begin{aligned}-\sqrt{24} \cdot \sqrt{30} &= -\sqrt{24 \cdot 30}\\ &= -\sqrt{2^3 \cdot 3 \cdot 2 \cdot 3 \cdot 5}\\ &= -\sqrt{2^4 \cdot 3^2 \cdot 5}\\ &= -\sqrt{(2^2 \cdot 3)^2} \cdot \sqrt{5}\\ &= -(2^2 \cdot 3) \cdot \sqrt{5}\\ &= -12\sqrt{5}\end{aligned}$$

Answer $-\sqrt{24} \cdot \sqrt{30} = -12\sqrt{5}$

Example 4 Simplify. $\sqrt{3}(\sqrt{3} + \sqrt{8})$

Solution
$$\begin{aligned}\sqrt{3}(\sqrt{3} + \sqrt{8}) &= \sqrt{3} \cdot \sqrt{3} + \sqrt{3} \cdot \sqrt{8}\\ &= \sqrt{3^2} + \sqrt{3} \cdot 2\sqrt{2}\\ &= 3 + 2\sqrt{6}\end{aligned}$$

Answer $\sqrt{3}(\sqrt{3} + \sqrt{8}) = 3 + 2\sqrt{6}$

Example 1. Simplify. $\sqrt{80}$
$$\sqrt{80} = \sqrt{4^2 \cdot 5} = 4\sqrt{5}$$

Example 2. Simplify. $\sqrt{500}$
$$\sqrt{500} = \sqrt{10^2 \cdot 5} = 10\sqrt{5}$$

Example 3. Simplify. $-\sqrt{15} \cdot \sqrt{5}$
$$\begin{aligned}-\sqrt{15} \cdot \sqrt{5} &= -\sqrt{15 \cdot 5}\\ &= -\sqrt{5^2 \cdot 3} = -5\sqrt{3}\end{aligned}$$

Example 4. Simplify. $\sqrt{2}(\sqrt{3} + \sqrt{8})$
$$\begin{aligned}\sqrt{2}(\sqrt{3} + \sqrt{8}) &= \sqrt{2} \cdot \sqrt{3} + \sqrt{2} \cdot \sqrt{8}\\ &= \sqrt{6} + \sqrt{16} = 4 + \sqrt{6}\end{aligned}$$

- What property is used to simplify radicals? ($\sqrt{ab} = \sqrt{a} \cdot \sqrt{b}$)
- How is the property used to simplify $\sqrt{18}$? (18 is factored to $9 \cdot 2$. Then the property is used to write $\sqrt{18}$ as the product of $\sqrt{9}$ and $\sqrt{2}$. $\sqrt{9}$ can then be written as 3. The key point is to factor the radicand so that one factor is a perfect square.)
- Factor 50 so that one factor is a perfect square. $(25 \cdot 2)$

CLASSROOM EXERCISES

In exercises 1 and 2, emphasize that a radical can be simplified if the radicand contains any prime factor more than once.

ASSIGNMENT GUIDE

Basic   1–39 odd, Review Exercises
Average   3–39 multiples of 3, 40–48 all,
              Review Exercises
Enriched 3–48 multiples of 3, 49–53 all,
              Review Exercises

PRACTICE WORKSHEET 54

10-4 SIMPLIFYING SQUARE ROOTS

■ Simplify.

1. $\sqrt{150}$ $5\sqrt{6}$
2. $\sqrt{700}$ $10\sqrt{7}$
3. $-\sqrt{44}$ $-2\sqrt{11}$
4. $\sqrt{90}$ $3\sqrt{10}$
5. $-\sqrt{180}$ $-6\sqrt{5}$
6. $\sqrt{96}$ $4\sqrt{6}$
7. $\sqrt{3}(\sqrt{3} + \sqrt{5})$ $3 + \sqrt{15}$
8. $\sqrt{2}(\sqrt{5} + \sqrt{6})$ $\sqrt{10} + 2\sqrt{3}$
9. $-\sqrt{5}(\sqrt{10} + \sqrt{15})$ $-5\sqrt{2} - 5\sqrt{3}$
10. $\sqrt{7}(\sqrt{14} + 6)$ $7\sqrt{2} + 6\sqrt{7}$
11. $(5 - \sqrt{2})(5 + \sqrt{2})$ 23
12. $\sqrt{3}(2\sqrt{3} - 1)$ $6 - \sqrt{3}$
13. $\sqrt{6}(\sqrt{15} + \sqrt{14})$ $3\sqrt{10} + 2\sqrt{21}$
14. $\sqrt{15}(\sqrt{21} - \sqrt{10})$ $3\sqrt{35} - 5\sqrt{6}$
15. $(\sqrt{3} - 1)(\sqrt{3} + 1)$ 2
16. $(4 - \sqrt{3})(4 + \sqrt{3})$ 11

CONCEPT EXTENSION

Discuss with students why it is important to be able to write an expression in simplest form. Some possible answers include these:
a. To communicate more easily
b. To compare results
c. To simplify calculations
d. To combine similar expressions that may not be in the same form (For example, $\sqrt{8} + \sqrt{32} = 2\sqrt{2} + 4\sqrt{2} = 6\sqrt{2}$.)
e. To discover relationships among numbers (For example, $\sqrt{18}$ is 3 times $\sqrt{2}$ because $\sqrt{18} = \sqrt{9 \cdot 2} = 3\sqrt{2}$.)

508

EXTRA PRACTICE, page 638

■ CLASSROOM EXERCISES

Write the prime factorization.

1. 18 $2 \cdot 3^2$
2. 150 $2 \cdot 3 \cdot 5^2$

Simplify.

3. $\sqrt{8}$ $2\sqrt{2}$
4. $\sqrt{12}$ $2\sqrt{3}$
5. $\sqrt{16}$ 4
6. $\sqrt{24}$ $2\sqrt{6}$
7. $\sqrt{40}$ $2\sqrt{10}$
8. $\sqrt{160}$ $4\sqrt{10}$
9. $\sqrt{2}(\sqrt{8} - 2\sqrt{3})$ $4 - 2\sqrt{6}$
10. $(\sqrt{10} + \sqrt{20})\sqrt{5}$ $5\sqrt{2} + 10$

■ WRITTEN EXERCISES

Write the prime factorization.

A

1. 20 $2^2 \cdot 5$
2. 50 $2 \cdot 5^2$
3. 300 $2^2 \cdot 3 \cdot 5^2$
4. 450 $2 \cdot 3^2 \cdot 5^2$
5. 75 $3 \cdot 5^2$
6. 45 $3^2 \cdot 5$
7. 200 $2^3 \cdot 5^2$
8. 72 $2^3 \cdot 3^2$

Simplify.

9. $\sqrt{50}$ $5\sqrt{2}$
10. $\sqrt{20}$ $2\sqrt{5}$
11. $-\sqrt{450}$ $-15\sqrt{2}$
12. $-\sqrt{300}$ $-10\sqrt{3}$
13. $\sqrt{15} \cdot \sqrt{3}$ $3\sqrt{5}$
14. $\sqrt{15} \cdot \sqrt{5}$ $5\sqrt{3}$
15. $\sqrt{24} \cdot \sqrt{3}$ $6\sqrt{2}$
16. $-\sqrt{10} \cdot \sqrt{20}$ $-10\sqrt{2}$
17. $\sqrt{2}(\sqrt{2} + \sqrt{3})$ $2 + \sqrt{6}$
18. $\sqrt{3}(\sqrt{2} + \sqrt{3})$ $\sqrt{6} + 3$
19. $\sqrt{5}(2 + \sqrt{5})$ $2\sqrt{5} + 5$
20. $\sqrt{7}(1 + \sqrt{7})$ $\sqrt{7} + 7$
21. $\sqrt{3}(\sqrt{3} - 1)$ $3 - \sqrt{3}$
22. $\sqrt{5}(\sqrt{5} - 1)$ $5 - \sqrt{5}$
23. $\sqrt{2}(2\sqrt{2} + \sqrt{6})$ $4 + 2\sqrt{3}$
24. $\sqrt{3}(\sqrt{6} + 2\sqrt{3})$ $3\sqrt{2} + 6$
25. $\sqrt{5}(\sqrt{20} + \sqrt{45})$ 25
26. $\sqrt{2}(\sqrt{50} + \sqrt{18})$ 16
27. $(2 + \sqrt{3})(2 - \sqrt{3})$ 1
28. $(3 + \sqrt{2})(3 - \sqrt{2})$ 7
29. $(4 + \sqrt{5})^2$ $21 + 8\sqrt{5}$
30. $(5 - \sqrt{3})^2$ $28 - 10\sqrt{3}$

a	b
3	$\sqrt{3}$

Substitute and simplify.

31. $\sqrt{3 + a^2}$ $2\sqrt{3}$
32. $\sqrt{a^2 - 1}$ $2\sqrt{2}$
33. $\sqrt{15 + b^2}$ $3\sqrt{2}$
34. $\sqrt{25 + b^2}$ $2\sqrt{7}$
35. $(ab)^2$ 27
36. ab^2 9
37. $(a - b)(a + b)$ 6
38. $(a + b)^2$ $12 + 6\sqrt{3}$
39. $(a - b)^2$ $12 - 6\sqrt{3}$

B Use the Pythagorean theorem to find the length x. Write the answer in simplest form.

40. $4\sqrt{5}$

41. $3\sqrt{10}$

42. $8\sqrt{2}$

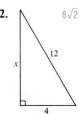

Use the Pythagorean theorem to find the length x. Write the answer in simplest form.

43. 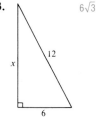 $6\sqrt{3}$

12

x

6

44. 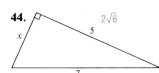 $2\sqrt{6}$

x

5

7

45. $4\sqrt{3}$

1

x

7

46. $\sqrt{17}$

$\sqrt{10}$

x

$\sqrt{7}$

47. 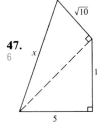 $\sqrt{10}$

6

x

1

5

48. $2\sqrt{7}$

x

$\sqrt{13}$

$\sqrt{15}$

Approximate these radicals to the nearest hundredth. Use the table on page 641.

Sample Approximate the square root of 300 correct to the nearest hundredth.

Solution Simplify radicals before finding decimal approximations.

$$\sqrt{300} = 10\sqrt{3}$$
$$\approx 10(1.732) = 17.32$$

C **49.** $\sqrt{316}$ 17.78   **50.** $\sqrt{320}$ 17.89   **51.** $\sqrt{500}$ 22.36   **52.** $\sqrt{775}$ 27.84

53. Explain what is wrong with this demonstration that $-4 = 4$.

$-4 = \sqrt{-4} \cdot \sqrt{-4}$ $\sqrt{-4}$ is not a real number.
$= \sqrt{(-4)(-4)}$
$= \sqrt{16}$
$= 4$

■ REVIEW EXERCISES

1. List all the positive integer factors of 18.   1, 2, 3, 6, 9, 18   [7–1]

2. Write the prime factorization of 42. $2 \cdot 3 \cdot 7$ [7–1]

3. State the greatest common factor of 18 and 36.   18   [7–2]

4. State the greatest common factor of $8ab$ and $12a^2$.   4a   [7–2]

Solve.

5. $x(x + 5) = 0$ (0, −5)   **6.** $3(2x + 4)(x − 5) = 0$ (5, −2)   [7–3]

7. Factor completely. $4a^2 − 6a$ 2a(2a − 3)   [7–4]

8. The square of a number is 9 times the number. What is the number?   0 or 9   [7–4]

- True or false?
  For each real number x, $\sqrt{x^2} = x$.
  False. Substitute -2 for x.

- Note that
  $\sqrt{256} = 16$, $\sqrt{16} = 4$, and $\sqrt{4} = 2$.

  So, $\sqrt{\sqrt{\sqrt{256}}} = 2$.

  Use a calculator. Start with 1,000,000 and count how many consecutive square roots must be taken
  a. to get a value less than 2.
       5
  b. to get a value less than 1.
  No number of square roots will give a value less than 1. The calculator will eventually round the value to 1.0000000 or 1.

Class Starter Quiz
on previous section

Simplify.

1. $\sqrt{12}$ $2\sqrt{3}$

2. $-\sqrt{75}$ $-5\sqrt{3}$

3. $\sqrt{600}$ $10\sqrt{6}$

4. $\sqrt{3}(\sqrt{2} + \sqrt{3})$ $3 + \sqrt{6}$

5. $(\sqrt{5} + \sqrt{3})(\sqrt{5} - \sqrt{3})$ 2

PURPOSE

It is important to compute with radicals and express results in simplest form. If two radical expressions are not expressed in the same form, it is not clear whether they are names for the same number. By agreement, an expression containing radicals in the denominator is not considered to be in simplest form.

PREVIEW

The Preview points out the historical reason for considering $\frac{\sqrt{6}}{6}$ to be simpler than $\frac{1}{\sqrt{6}}$. The existence of calculators has eliminated ease of calculation as a reason for considering one form as simpler than another. However, there are still important reasons for agreeing to write radicals in a standard form. One reason is to make it easier to recognize relationships among numbers when they are all written in the same form.

OBJECTIVE 10–5

To simplify expressions involving quotients of radicals.

10–5 Simplifying Quotients of Square Roots

Preview

Before the invention of calculators and computers, most computations were done using paper and pencil. Thus it was important to use efficient techniques.

If we know that $\sqrt{6} \approx 2.449489743$, how can we find an approximation for $\frac{1}{\sqrt{6}}$ to the nearest hundredth?

We could divide 1 by 2.449489743, but there is a method that is less cumbersome.

In this lesson we will study how to simplify expressions with radicals in denominators. The decimal approximation for expressions like $\frac{1}{\sqrt{6}}$ can then be found efficiently.

■ LESSON

Notice that

$$\sqrt{\frac{36}{9}} = \sqrt{4} = 2$$

and that

$$\frac{\sqrt{36}}{\sqrt{9}} = \frac{6}{3} = 2.$$

Therefore,

$$\sqrt{\frac{36}{9}} = \frac{\sqrt{36}}{\sqrt{9}}.$$

The last equation is an example of the division property for radicals.

The Division Property for Radicals

For all nonnegative numbers a and b, $b \neq 0$,

$$\sqrt{\frac{a}{b}} = \frac{\sqrt{a}}{\sqrt{b}}$$

The division property for radicals can be used to simplify radical expressions that contain fractions. For example, consider simplifying $\sqrt{\frac{27}{4}}$.

Use the division property for radicals. $\sqrt{\frac{27}{4}} = \frac{\sqrt{27}}{\sqrt{4}}$

Simplify each radical. $= \frac{3\sqrt{3}}{2}$

The simplest form of $\sqrt{\frac{27}{4}}$ is $\frac{3\sqrt{3}}{2}$.

The process of putting their ideas into words helps students to clarify those ideas. Therefore, ask your students to verbalize the problem-solving strategies that they use. Students will also enrich each other through sharing various ways to solve individual problems.

Definition: The Simplest Form of a Radical Expression

A radical expression is in simplest form if:

1. the radicand does not contain a fraction;
2. the radicand has no perfect-square factor other than 1;
3. no radicals appear in the denominator.

Example 1   Simplify. $\sqrt{\dfrac{1}{3}}$

Solution

$$\sqrt{\frac{1}{3}} = \frac{\sqrt{1}}{\sqrt{3}}$$

$$= \frac{1}{\sqrt{3}}$$

Multiply the numerator and denominator by $\sqrt{3}$ to make the denominator an integer.

$$= \frac{1}{\sqrt{3}} \cdot \frac{\sqrt{3}}{\sqrt{3}}$$

$$= \frac{\sqrt{3}}{3}$$

Answer $\sqrt{\dfrac{1}{3}} = \dfrac{\sqrt{3}}{3}$

The process of changing the form of a fraction from one with a radical in the denominator to an equivalent fraction without a radical in the denominator is called **rationalizing the denominator**. To rationalize a denominator, first write the denominator in simplest radical form. Then multiply the numerator and denominator by the remaining radical.

Example 2   Rationalize the denominator and simplify. $\dfrac{4}{\sqrt{80}}$

Solution   *Simplify the denominator.*

$$\frac{4}{\sqrt{80}} = \frac{4}{4\sqrt{5}}$$

Simplify the fraction.

$$= \frac{1}{\sqrt{5}}$$

Multiply the numerator and denominator by $\sqrt{5}$.

$$= \frac{1}{\sqrt{5}} \cdot \frac{\sqrt{5}}{\sqrt{5}}$$

Simplify the numerator and denominator.

$$= \frac{\sqrt{5}}{5}$$

Answer $\dfrac{4}{\sqrt{80}} = \dfrac{\sqrt{5}}{5}$

Emphasize the need to carefully draw radical signs in rational expressions to clearly indicate the appropriate radicand. For example, the fraction bar in $\dfrac{\sqrt{2}}{3}$ could be drawn a little longer than usual to distinguish the number from $\sqrt{\dfrac{2}{3}}$.

In approximating an expression such as $\dfrac{\sqrt{23}}{\sqrt{3}}$ to the nearest hundredth, review with students how to find $\sqrt{69}$ in the table of squares and square roots. Some students may elect (or be permitted) to use calculators to find square roots. Since an answer accurate to hundredths is required, it is appropriate to discuss with students the rounding of the 8-digit or 10-digit calculator result before dividing. One more decimal position than that required in the final result is usually appropriate.

ADDITIONAL EXAMPLES

Example 1. Simplify. $\sqrt{\dfrac{5}{6}}$

$$\sqrt{\frac{5}{6}} = \frac{\sqrt{5}}{\sqrt{6}} \cdot \frac{\sqrt{6}}{\sqrt{6}} = \frac{\sqrt{30}}{6}$$

Example 2.
Rationalize the denominator and simplify.
$\dfrac{5}{\sqrt{50}}$

$$\frac{5}{\sqrt{50}} = \frac{5}{5\sqrt{2}} = \frac{1}{\sqrt{2}} = \frac{\sqrt{2}}{2}$$

Example 3.

Write a decimal approximation of $\dfrac{\sqrt{18}}{\sqrt{5}}$ to the nearest hundredth.

The decimal approximation of $\dfrac{\sqrt{18}}{\sqrt{5}}$ may be found in more than one way:

a. $\dfrac{\sqrt{18}}{\sqrt{5}} = \dfrac{3\sqrt{2}}{\sqrt{5}} = \dfrac{3\sqrt{10}}{5} \approx \dfrac{3(3.162)}{5} =$

$1.897 \approx 1.90$

b. $\dfrac{\sqrt{18}}{\sqrt{5}} = \dfrac{\sqrt{90}}{5} \approx \dfrac{9.487}{5} = 1.897 \approx 1.90$

Example 4. Simplify. $\sqrt{7\frac{1}{2}}$

$\sqrt{7\frac{1}{2}} = \sqrt{\dfrac{15}{2}} = \dfrac{\sqrt{30}}{2}$

CHECK UNDERSTANDING

- Is the denominator of $\dfrac{3}{\sqrt{2}}$ rational? (No)

- Is the denominator of $\dfrac{5}{\sqrt{4}}$ rational? (Yes)

- What can $\sqrt{2}$ be multiplied by to give a rational number? ($\sqrt{2}$)

- What should both numerator and denominator be multiplied by to produce a rational denominator? $\dfrac{3}{\sqrt{5}}$ $(\sqrt{5})$

CLASSROOM EXERCISES

There are three possible methods of simplifying the radicals in exercise 4:

a. $\dfrac{\sqrt{6}}{\sqrt{8}} = \sqrt{\dfrac{6}{8}} = \sqrt{\dfrac{3}{4}} = \dfrac{\sqrt{3}}{2}$

b. $\dfrac{\sqrt{6}}{\sqrt{8}} = \dfrac{\sqrt{6}}{\sqrt{8}} \cdot \dfrac{\sqrt{2}}{\sqrt{2}} = \dfrac{\sqrt{12}}{\sqrt{16}} = \dfrac{2\sqrt{3}}{4} = \dfrac{\sqrt{3}}{2}$

c. $\dfrac{\sqrt{6}}{\sqrt{8}} = \dfrac{\sqrt{6}}{2\sqrt{2}} = \dfrac{\sqrt{6}}{2\sqrt{2}} \cdot \dfrac{\sqrt{2}}{\sqrt{2}} = \dfrac{\sqrt{12}}{2 \cdot 2}$

$= \dfrac{2\sqrt{3}}{4} = \dfrac{\sqrt{3}}{2}$

Example 3 Write a decimal approximation of $\dfrac{\sqrt{27}}{\sqrt{2}}$ to the nearest hundredth.

Solution $\qquad \dfrac{\sqrt{27}}{\sqrt{2}} = \dfrac{3\sqrt{3}}{\sqrt{2}}$

Rationalize the denominator. $\qquad = \dfrac{3\sqrt{3}}{\sqrt{2}} \cdot \dfrac{\sqrt{2}}{\sqrt{2}}$

$\qquad = \dfrac{3\sqrt{6}}{2}$

Use the table of square roots. $\qquad \approx \dfrac{3(2.449)}{2}$

$\qquad = \dfrac{7.347}{2}$

$\qquad = 3.674$

Answer $\quad \dfrac{\sqrt{27}}{\sqrt{2}} = 3.67$ to the nearest hundredth

---

Example 4 Simplify. $\sqrt{15\frac{1}{2}}$

Solution *Write the radicand as a fraction.* $\quad \sqrt{15\frac{1}{2}} = \sqrt{\dfrac{31}{2}}$

Use the division property for radicals. $\quad = \dfrac{\sqrt{31}}{\sqrt{2}}$

Rationalize the denominaor. $\quad = \dfrac{\sqrt{31}}{\sqrt{2}} \cdot \dfrac{\sqrt{2}}{\sqrt{2}}$

$\quad = \dfrac{\sqrt{62}}{2}$

Answer $\quad \sqrt{15\frac{1}{2}} = \dfrac{\sqrt{62}}{2}$

■ CLASSROOM EXERCISES

Simplify.

1. $\sqrt{\dfrac{8}{25}}$ $\quad \frac{2\sqrt{2}}{5}$ **2.** $\sqrt{\dfrac{3}{5}}$ $\quad \frac{\sqrt{15}}{5}$ **3.** $\dfrac{\sqrt{5}}{\sqrt{2}}$ $\quad \frac{\sqrt{10}}{2}$ **4.** $\dfrac{\sqrt{6}}{\sqrt{8}}$ $\quad \frac{\sqrt{3}}{2}$ **5.** $\sqrt{\dfrac{5}{12}}$ $\quad \frac{\sqrt{15}}{6}$

6. Give a decimal approximation to the nearest thousandth of $\dfrac{\sqrt{19}}{\sqrt{3}}$.   2.517

Simplify.

7. $\sqrt{3\frac{1}{2}}$ $\quad \frac{\sqrt{14}}{2}$ **8.** $\sqrt{2\frac{1}{2}}$ $\quad \frac{\sqrt{10}}{2}$ **9.** $\sqrt{1\frac{1}{5}}$ $\quad \frac{\sqrt{30}}{5}$ **10.** $\sqrt{1\frac{2}{3}}$ $\quad \frac{\sqrt{15}}{3}$ **11.** $\sqrt{6\frac{2}{3}}$ $\quad \frac{2\sqrt{15}}{3}$

ASSIGNMENT GUIDE

Basic	1–41 odd, Review Exercises
Average	3–42 multiples of 3, 43–53 odd, Review Exercises
Enriched	3–54 multiples of 3, 55–61 odd, Review Exercises

EXTRA PRACTICE, page 638

■ WRITTEN EXERCISES

Simplify.

A

1. $\sqrt{\dfrac{6}{25}}$ $\dfrac{\sqrt{6}}{5}$

2. $\sqrt{\dfrac{3}{16}}$ $\dfrac{\sqrt{3}}{4}$

3. $\sqrt{\dfrac{7}{9}}$ $\dfrac{\sqrt{7}}{3}$

4. $\sqrt{\dfrac{3}{4}}$ $\dfrac{\sqrt{3}}{2}$

5. $\dfrac{2}{\sqrt{7}}$ $\dfrac{2\sqrt{7}}{7}$

6. $\dfrac{3}{\sqrt{10}}$ $\dfrac{3\sqrt{10}}{10}$

7. $\dfrac{\sqrt{2}}{\sqrt{5}}$ $\dfrac{\sqrt{10}}{5}$

8. $\dfrac{\sqrt{2}}{\sqrt{3}}$ $\dfrac{\sqrt{6}}{3}$

9. $\dfrac{\sqrt{7}}{\sqrt{2}}$ $\dfrac{\sqrt{14}}{2}$

10. $\dfrac{\sqrt{10}}{\sqrt{3}}$ $\dfrac{\sqrt{30}}{3}$

11. $\sqrt{\dfrac{7}{3}}$ $\dfrac{\sqrt{21}}{3}$

12. $\sqrt{\dfrac{10}{7}}$ $\dfrac{\sqrt{70}}{7}$

13. $\dfrac{\sqrt{12}}{\sqrt{10}}$ $\dfrac{\sqrt{30}}{5}$

14. $\dfrac{\sqrt{6}}{\sqrt{15}}$ $\dfrac{\sqrt{10}}{5}$

15. $\dfrac{\sqrt{8}}{\sqrt{27}}$ $\dfrac{2\sqrt{6}}{9}$

16. $\dfrac{\sqrt{18}}{\sqrt{125}}$ $\dfrac{3\sqrt{10}}{25}$

17. $\dfrac{\sqrt{12}}{\sqrt{27}}$ $\dfrac{2}{3}$

18. $\dfrac{\sqrt{18}}{\sqrt{50}}$ $\dfrac{3}{5}$

19. $\dfrac{\sqrt{50}}{\sqrt{72}}$ $\dfrac{5}{6}$

20. $\dfrac{\sqrt{45}}{\sqrt{20}}$ $\dfrac{3}{2}$

Give a decimal approximation to the nearest hundredth.

21. $\dfrac{1}{\sqrt{3}}$ 0.58

22. $\dfrac{1}{\sqrt{2}}$ 0.71

23. $\dfrac{1}{\sqrt{10}}$ 0.32

24. $\dfrac{1}{\sqrt{6}}$ 0.41

25. $\dfrac{\sqrt{21}}{\sqrt{2}}$ 3.24

26. $\dfrac{\sqrt{17}}{\sqrt{5}}$ 1.84

27. $\sqrt{\dfrac{13}{6}}$ 1.47

28. $\sqrt{\dfrac{23}{3}}$ 2.77

29. $\dfrac{\sqrt{21}}{\sqrt{3}}$ 2.65

30. $\dfrac{\sqrt{21}}{\sqrt{7}}$ 1.73

31. $\dfrac{\sqrt{500}}{\sqrt{3}}$ 12.91

32. $\dfrac{\sqrt{700}}{\sqrt{11}}$ 7.98

33. $\sqrt{8\dfrac{1}{3}}$ 2.89

34. $\sqrt{5\dfrac{1}{3}}$ 2.31

35. $\sqrt{6\dfrac{2}{5}}$ 2.53

36. $\sqrt{8\dfrac{4}{5}}$ 2.97

Find the length of the rectangle having the given area and width. Write the answer in simplest form.

37. area: 7 cm²   width: $\sqrt{2}$ cm $\dfrac{7\sqrt{2}}{2}$ cm

38. area: 8 cm²   width: $\sqrt{3}$ cm $\dfrac{8\sqrt{3}}{3}$ cm

39. area: $\sqrt{15}$ m²   width: $\sqrt{2}$ m $\dfrac{\sqrt{30}}{2}$ m

40. area: $\sqrt{40}$ m²   width: $\sqrt{3}$ m $\dfrac{2\sqrt{30}}{3}$ m

41. area: 12 km²   width: $\sqrt{18}$ km $2\sqrt{2}$ km

42. area: 24 km²   width: $\sqrt{20}$ km $\dfrac{12\sqrt{5}}{5}$ km

a	b	c
2	3	5

Substitute and simplify.

B

43. $\sqrt{\dfrac{a}{b}}$ $\dfrac{\sqrt{6}}{3}$

44. $\sqrt{\dfrac{b}{a}}$ $\dfrac{\sqrt{6}}{2}$

45. $\dfrac{\sqrt{a^2}}{\sqrt{b}}$ $\dfrac{2\sqrt{3}}{3}$

46. $\dfrac{\sqrt{b^2}}{\sqrt{a}}$ $\dfrac{3\sqrt{2}}{2}$

47. $\sqrt{\dfrac{a^2b}{ab^2}}$ $\dfrac{\sqrt{6}}{3}$

48. $\sqrt{\dfrac{ab^2}{a^2b}}$ $\dfrac{\sqrt{6}}{2}$

49. $\dfrac{\sqrt{a^2c}}{\sqrt{ab}}$ $\dfrac{\sqrt{30}}{3}$

50. $\dfrac{\sqrt{b^2}}{\sqrt{abc}}$ $\dfrac{\sqrt{30}}{10}$

ENRICHMENT PROBLEM

• True or false?
For all *admissible* values of x,
$$\dfrac{1}{\sqrt{x}} = \dfrac{\sqrt{x}}{x}.$$
True.
(The admissible values are all real numbers x such that $x > 0$.)

Find the missing lengths.

51.
$\frac{\sqrt{89}}{10}$
x
0.8
0.5

52. 0.8
1
0.6
x

53. $\frac{1}{2}$
$\frac{\sqrt{3}}{2}$
1
x

54. $\frac{\sqrt{2}}{2}$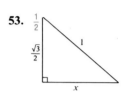
x
$\frac{1}{2}$
$\frac{1}{2}$

If $\sqrt{y}$ is an irrational number, then the two binomials of the form $x + \sqrt{y}$ and $x - \sqrt{y}$ are **conjugates** of each other. A conjugate can be used to rationalize a binomial denominator.

> **Example 5** Simplify. $\dfrac{5}{4 + \sqrt{3}}$
>
> *Solution* *Multiply the numerator and denominator by the conjugate of the denominator.*
>
> $\dfrac{5}{4 + \sqrt{3}} = \dfrac{5}{4 + \sqrt{3}} \cdot \dfrac{4 - \sqrt{3}}{4 - \sqrt{3}}$
>
> *Simplify.*
>
> $= \dfrac{20 - 5\sqrt{3}}{16 - 3}$
>
> $= \dfrac{20 - 5\sqrt{3}}{13}$
>
> *Answer* $\dfrac{5}{4 + \sqrt{3}} = \dfrac{20 - 5\sqrt{3}}{13}$

Use conjugates to simplify.

C **55.** $\dfrac{6}{3 - \sqrt{2}}$ $\frac{18 + 6\sqrt{2}}{7}$ **56.** $\dfrac{5}{2 + \sqrt{3}}$ $10 - 5\sqrt{3}$ **57.** $\dfrac{10}{4 + \sqrt{6}}$ $4 - \sqrt{6}$ **58.** $\dfrac{2}{5 - \sqrt{5}}$ $\frac{5 + \sqrt{5}}{10}$

Give a decimal approximation to the nearest hundredth.

59. $\dfrac{2}{2 - \sqrt{2}}$ 3.41   **60.** $\dfrac{2}{2 + \sqrt{2}}$ 0.59   **61.** $\dfrac{\sqrt{2}}{\sqrt{2} - 2}$ −2.41   **62.** $\dfrac{\sqrt{2}}{2 + \sqrt{2}}$ 0.41

■ REVIEW EXERCISES

Factor.

1. $x^2 - 100$ (x + 10)(x − 10)   **2.** $x^2 + 12x + 36$ (x + 6)²   [7–6, 7–7]

3. $x^2 - 7x + 12$ (x − 3)(x − 4)   **4.** $x^2 - x - 42$ (x − 7)(x + 6)   [7–8, 7–9]

Solve.

5. $2x^2 - 50 = 0$ (5, −5)   **6.** $x^2 + 10x + 25 = 0$ (−5)   [7–6, 7–7]

7. $x^2 + 12x + 20 = 0$ (−2, −10)   **8.** $x^2 + 4x - 12 = 0$ (2, −6)   [7–8, 7–9]

Class Starter Quiz
on previous section

Simplify.

1. $\sqrt{\dfrac{17}{36}}$ $\dfrac{\sqrt{17}}{6}$

2. $\sqrt{\dfrac{2}{3}}$ $\dfrac{\sqrt{6}}{3}$

3. $\sqrt{\dfrac{15}{8}}$ $\dfrac{\sqrt{30}}{4}$

4. $\dfrac{5}{\sqrt{10}}$ $\dfrac{\sqrt{10}}{2}$

5. $\dfrac{\sqrt{8}}{\sqrt{27}}$ $\dfrac{2\sqrt{6}}{9}$

10-6 Adding and Subtracting Radicals

Preview   A model for adding radicals

What is the total area of these two rectangles?

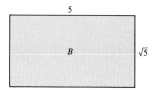

The area of rectangle *A* is $2\sqrt{5}$ and the area of rectangle *B* is $5\sqrt{5}$. The total area can be written as

$$2\sqrt{5} + 5\sqrt{5}$$

The diagram below suggests another way to express the area.

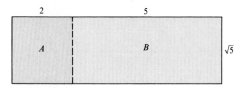

Find the combined area of rectangles *C* and *D*. $11\sqrt{7}$

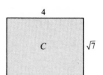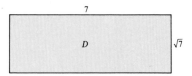

How much greater is the area of rectangle *D* than the area of rectangle *C*? $3\sqrt{7}$

In this lesson we will study how to add, subtract, and simplify expressions containing radicals.

■ LESSON

Here are two sums that involve radicals:

$$3\sqrt{2} + 5\sqrt{2} \qquad 4\sqrt{7} + 2\sqrt{5}$$

PURPOSE

Skill in working with radicals requires students to be able to simplify expressions involving addition and subtraction of radicals as well as multiplication and division.

PREVIEW

The geometric model presented in the Preview is a specific case of a more general representation that can be used to illustrate the distributive property.

LESSON

Point out that $3\sqrt{2} + 5\sqrt{2}$ has the same form as $3x + 5x$ where $x = \sqrt{2}$. Therefore, the distributive property can be applied.

$$3\sqrt{2} + 5\sqrt{2} = (3 + 5)\sqrt{2} = 8\sqrt{2}$$

The sum of $4\sqrt{7} + 2\sqrt{5}$ has the form $4x + 2y$ where $x = \sqrt{7}$ and $y = \sqrt{5}$. There is no common factor, so the distributive property cannot be applied.

ADDITIONAL EXAMPLES

Example 1. Simplify. $6\sqrt{3} + 2\sqrt{3}$
$$6\sqrt{3} + 2\sqrt{3} = 8\sqrt{3}$$

Example 2. Simplify. $\sqrt{3} + 2\sqrt{27} + \sqrt{75}$
$$\sqrt{3} + 2\sqrt{27} + \sqrt{75} = 12\sqrt{3}$$

Example 3. Simplify. $\sqrt{48} - \sqrt{18} - \sqrt{12}$
$$\sqrt{48} - \sqrt{18} - \sqrt{12} = 2\sqrt{3} - 3\sqrt{2}$$

The first can be simplified using the distributive property.

$$3\sqrt{2} + 5\sqrt{2} = (3 + 5)\sqrt{2}$$
$$= 8\sqrt{2}$$

The second sum $(4\sqrt{7} + 2\sqrt{5})$ cannot be simplified. In order to combine radical terms by adding or subtracting, we must be sure that the radical factors of the terms are the same.

To simplify sums or differences of square roots:

1. Write each radical in simplest form.
2. Use the distributive property to add or subtract terms with like radicands.

Example 1 Simplify. $8\sqrt{5} - 2\sqrt{5} + 4$

Solution
$$8\sqrt{5} - 2\sqrt{5} + 4 = (8 - 2)\sqrt{5} + 4$$
$$= 6\sqrt{5} + 4$$

Answer $8\sqrt{5} - 2\sqrt{5} + 4 = 6\sqrt{5} + 4$

Be sure to write all radicals in simplest form before trying to simplify further.

Example 2 Simplify. $7\sqrt{2} - 4\sqrt{8} + \sqrt{18}$

Solution
$$7\sqrt{2} - 4\sqrt{8} + \sqrt{18} = 7\sqrt{2} - 4(2\sqrt{2}) + 3\sqrt{2}$$
$$= 7\sqrt{2} - 8\sqrt{2} + 3\sqrt{2}$$
$$= 2\sqrt{2}$$

Answer $7\sqrt{2} - 4\sqrt{8} + \sqrt{18} = 2\sqrt{2}$

Example 3 Simplify. $2\sqrt{27} + \sqrt{50} + 4\sqrt{75}$

Solution
$$2\sqrt{27} + \sqrt{50} + 4\sqrt{75} = 2 \cdot 3\sqrt{3} + 5\sqrt{2} + 4 \cdot 5\sqrt{3}$$
$$= 6\sqrt{3} + 20\sqrt{3} + 5\sqrt{2}$$
$$= 26\sqrt{3} + 5\sqrt{2}$$

Answer $2\sqrt{27} + \sqrt{50} + 4\sqrt{75} = 26\sqrt{3} + 5\sqrt{2}$

Frequently ask students to justify their answers (both right and wrong answers) by saying "Convince me that you are right" or "Why do you believe that?"

Example 4. Simplify. $\sqrt{\frac{3}{4}} - \sqrt{\frac{3}{8}}$

$$\sqrt{\frac{3}{4}} - \sqrt{\frac{3}{8}} = \frac{2\sqrt{3} - \sqrt{6}}{4}$$

CHECK UNDERSTANDING

- State the distributive property for multiplication over addition. (For all real numbers a, b, and c $ab + cb = (a + c)b$.)
- What is the common factor of the terms of $3\sqrt{2} - 5\sqrt{2}$? ($\sqrt{2}$)
- Simplify. $3\sqrt{2} - 5\sqrt{2}$ ($-2\sqrt{2}$)

Example 4   Simplify. $\sqrt{\frac{2}{3}} + \sqrt{\frac{3}{8}}$

Solution

$$\sqrt{\frac{2}{3}} + \sqrt{\frac{3}{8}} = \frac{\sqrt{2}}{\sqrt{3}} + \frac{\sqrt{3}}{\sqrt{8}}$$

$$= \frac{\sqrt{2}}{\sqrt{3}} \cdot \frac{\sqrt{3}}{\sqrt{3}} + \frac{\sqrt{3}}{2\sqrt{2}} \cdot \frac{\sqrt{2}}{\sqrt{2}}$$

$$= \frac{\sqrt{6}}{3} + \frac{\sqrt{6}}{4}$$

$$= \frac{4\sqrt{6}}{12} + \frac{3\sqrt{6}}{12}$$

$$= \frac{7\sqrt{6}}{12}$$

Answer $\sqrt{\frac{2}{3}} + \sqrt{\frac{3}{8}} = \frac{7\sqrt{6}}{12}$

CLASSROOM EXERCISES

In exercise 3, it is important to know when the simplifying process is complete. Once an expression is in simplest form, to continue manipulating will result in a more complex expression or might result in an expression that is not equivalent.

ASSIGNMENT GUIDE

Basic   1–27 odd, Review Exercises, Self-Quiz 2

Average   1–41 odd, Review Exercises, Self-Quiz 2

Enriched   3–42 multiples of 3, 43–48 all, Review Exercises, Self-Quiz 2

PRACTICE WORKSHEET 55

■ **CLASSROOM EXERCISES**

Simplify. Write "simplest form" if the expression cannot be simplified.

1. $5\sqrt{3} + 2\sqrt{3}$ $7\sqrt{3}$

2. $4\sqrt{2} - 9\sqrt{2}$ $-5\sqrt{2}$

3. $6\sqrt{3} - 7\sqrt{2}$ Simplest form

4. $2\sqrt{27} + 3\sqrt{12} - \sqrt{24}$ $12\sqrt{3} - 2\sqrt{6}$

5. $\sqrt{8} + \sqrt{75} - \sqrt{48} - \sqrt{50}$ $-3\sqrt{2} + \sqrt{3}$

6. $\sqrt{\frac{1}{5}} + \frac{\sqrt{5}}{3}$ $\frac{8\sqrt{5}}{15}$

■ **WRITTEN EXERCISES**

Simplify. Write "simplest form" if the expression cannot be simplified.

1. $3\sqrt{2} + 7\sqrt{2}$ $10\sqrt{2}$

2. $5\sqrt{2} + 6\sqrt{2}$ $11\sqrt{2}$

3. $6\sqrt{3} + \sqrt{3}$ $7\sqrt{3}$

4. $5\sqrt{7} + \sqrt{7}$ $6\sqrt{7}$

5. $4\sqrt{7} - 6\sqrt{7}$ $-2\sqrt{7}$

6. $7\sqrt{3} - 10\sqrt{3}$ $-3\sqrt{3}$

7. $8\sqrt{5} - \sqrt{5}$ $7\sqrt{5}$

8. $4\sqrt{6} - \sqrt{6}$ $3\sqrt{6}$

9. $5\sqrt{3} + 3\sqrt{2} + 2\sqrt{3}$ $7\sqrt{3} + 3\sqrt{2}$

10. $3\sqrt{2} + 2\sqrt{3}$ Simplest form

11. $\sqrt{21} - \sqrt{4}$ $\sqrt{21} - 2$

12. $2\sqrt{3} + 5\sqrt{2} + 3\sqrt{2}$ $2\sqrt{3} + 8\sqrt{2}$

13. $\sqrt{8} + \sqrt{18}$ $5\sqrt{2}$

14. $\sqrt{12} + \sqrt{27}$ $5\sqrt{3}$

15. $\sqrt{10} + \sqrt{21}$ Simplest form

16. $\sqrt{15} + \sqrt{14}$ Simplest form

17. $\sqrt{45} - \sqrt{20}$ $\sqrt{5}$

18. $\sqrt{125} - \sqrt{80}$ $\sqrt{5}$

19. $\sqrt{48} - \sqrt{75}$ $-\sqrt{3}$

20. $\sqrt{50} - \sqrt{98}$ $-2\sqrt{2}$

Find the perimeter of the triangle. Simplify the answer.

21.

22.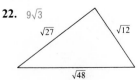

23.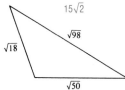
$15\sqrt{2}$
$\sqrt{98}$
$\sqrt{18}$
$\sqrt{50}$

24. $10\sqrt{5}$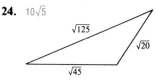
$\sqrt{125}$
$\sqrt{20}$
$\sqrt{45}$

Find the perimeter and area of the rectangle. Simplify the answers.

25.
$\sqrt{3}$
$2\sqrt{5}+2\sqrt{3}, \sqrt{15}$ $\quad \sqrt{5}$

26.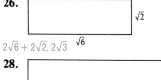
$\sqrt{2}$
$2\sqrt{6}+2\sqrt{2}, 2\sqrt{3}$ $\quad \sqrt{6}$

27.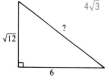
$\sqrt{45}$
$24\sqrt{5}, 135$ $\quad \sqrt{405}$

28.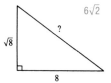
$\sqrt{32}$
$32\sqrt{2}, 96$ $\quad \sqrt{288}$

Simplify.

B **29.** $\sqrt{2}+\dfrac{3}{\sqrt{2}}$ $\quad \frac{5\sqrt{2}}{2}$

30. $\dfrac{\sqrt{3}}{6}+\dfrac{2}{\sqrt{3}}$ $\quad \frac{5\sqrt{3}}{6}$

31. $\dfrac{4}{\sqrt{6}}+\dfrac{\sqrt{2}}{\sqrt{3}}$ $\quad \sqrt{6}$

32. $5\sqrt{\dfrac{2}{3}}-4\sqrt{\dfrac{3}{2}}$ $\quad -\frac{\sqrt{6}}{3}$

33. $\dfrac{2\sqrt{5}}{12}-\sqrt{\dfrac{3}{20}}$ $\quad \frac{5\sqrt{5}-3\sqrt{15}}{30}$

34. $\dfrac{6}{\sqrt{6}}+4\sqrt{\dfrac{5}{6}}$ $\quad \frac{3\sqrt{6}+2\sqrt{30}}{3}$

Find the length of the hypotenuse of the triangle.

35.
$4\sqrt{3}$
?
$\sqrt{12}$
6

36.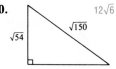
$6\sqrt{2}$
?
$\sqrt{8}$
8

37. What is the perimeter of the triangle in Exercise 35? $\quad 6\sqrt{3}+6$

38. What is the perimeter of the triangle in Exercise 36? $\quad 8\sqrt{2}+8$

Find the perimeter of the triangle.

39.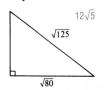
$12\sqrt{5}$
$\sqrt{125}$
$\sqrt{80}$

40.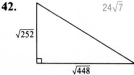
$12\sqrt{6}$
$\sqrt{150}$
$\sqrt{54}$

41.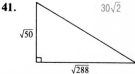
$30\sqrt{2}$
$\sqrt{50}$
$\sqrt{288}$

42.
$24\sqrt{7}$
$\sqrt{252}$
$\sqrt{448}$

43. Find the perimeter of this parallelogram.

$4 + 2\sqrt{2}$

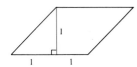

44. Find the area of this square.   2

In each of the following, is the equation true for all positive values of a and b? If not, write a counterexample to show that it is false.   No, $\sqrt{25} + \sqrt{16} \neq \sqrt{25 + 16}$

C **45.** $\sqrt{a^2 - b^2} = a - b$ No, $\sqrt{5^2 - 4^2} \neq 5 - 4$ **46.** $\sqrt{a} + \sqrt{b} = \sqrt{a + b}$

47. $(\sqrt{a} - \sqrt{b})^2 = a - b$ No, $(\sqrt{25} - \sqrt{16})^2 \neq 25 - 16$ **48.** $\dfrac{1}{\sqrt{a}} \cdot \dfrac{1}{\sqrt{b}} = \dfrac{1}{\sqrt{ab}}$ Yes

■ REVIEW EXERCISES

1. Are these fractions equivalent for admissible values of x?   [8–1]

$\dfrac{3x + 2}{4x + 2}$ and $\dfrac{3x}{4x}$ No

2. Which values of x are not admissible? $\dfrac{x(x + 3)}{(x - 1)(x + 2)}$ $1, -2$ [8–1]

Simplify. Assume that no denominators are zero.

3. $\dfrac{3a}{4b} \cdot \dfrac{6ab}{c}$ $\dfrac{9a^2}{2c}$ **4.** $\dfrac{x(x + 1)}{x(x + 2)} \div \dfrac{x + 1}{2}$ $\dfrac{2}{x + 2}$ [8–2]

5. $\dfrac{2}{x} + \dfrac{3}{x^2}$ $\dfrac{2x + 3}{x^2}$ **6.** $\dfrac{1}{2x} + \dfrac{2}{3x}$ $\dfrac{7}{6x}$ [8–4]

Solve.

7. $\dfrac{24}{18} = \dfrac{36}{x}$ (27)   **8.** $\dfrac{1}{12} = \dfrac{1}{r} + \dfrac{1}{20}$ (30)   [8–5]

9. It takes one machine 10 h to complete a job and it takes another machine 15 h to complete the same job. How long will it take both machines working together to complete the job?   6 h   **10.** What is the resistance in a circuit that contains a 10-ohm resistance and a 20-ohm resistance connected in parallel?   [8–6]

$\left[\text{Use the equation } \dfrac{1}{R} = \dfrac{1}{r_1} + \dfrac{1}{r_2}. \right]$

$6\frac{2}{3}\Omega$

Simplify.   [4–6]

11. $3x(x^2 - 5x + 4)$ $3x^3 - 15x^2 + 12x$ **12.** $(2xy^2)^3(x + y)$ $8x^4y^6 + 8x^3y^7$

Solve by making and using a table.   [2–9]

13. What number can be added to the numerator and denominator of $\frac{1}{4}$ so that the new fraction will equal $\frac{4}{5}$?   11

The importance of simplifying radicals becomes more apparent in this lesson. Expressions such as $\sqrt{48} + \sqrt{18} - \sqrt{12}$ cannot be easily simplified until each radical is written in simplest form. In the form $4\sqrt{3} + 3\sqrt{2} - 2\sqrt{3}$ similar terms can be identified. Relating a radical expression to an algebraic problem students already know how to solve is an application of the problem-solving strategy, solve a similar-but-simpler problem.

$$4a + 3b - 2a$$
$$= (4a - 2a) + 3b$$
$$= 2a + 3b$$

$$4\sqrt{3} + 3\sqrt{2} - 2\sqrt{3}$$
$$= (4\sqrt{3} - 2\sqrt{3}) + 3\sqrt{2}$$
$$= 2\sqrt{3} + 3\sqrt{2}$$

Emphasizing how new problems can be solved by relating them to previous problems whose solution process is already known helps students assimilate new ideas and appreciate the interrelatedness of mathematics.

ENRICHMENT PROBLEMS

• Show that the square-root operation is not distributive over addition.

$\sqrt{36 + 25} \neq \sqrt{36} + \sqrt{25}$ because

$\sqrt{36} + \sqrt{25} = 6 + 5 = 11$, whereas

$\sqrt{36 + 25} = \sqrt{61}$, and $\sqrt{61} \neq 11$.

• Which of the following are true statements?

   a. $\sqrt{6^2 + 8^2} = 6 + 8$
   b. $\sqrt{8^2 - 6^2} = 8 - 6$
   c. $\sqrt{8^2 - 6^2} = \sqrt{2^2}$
   d. $\sqrt{(6 + 8)^2} = 6 + 8$
   e. $\sqrt{8^2 + 6^2} = 8 + 6$

   Statements b, d, and e are true.

Self-Quiz 2

10-4,
10-5, Simplify.
10-6

1. $\sqrt{72}$ $6\sqrt{2}$ **2.** $\sqrt{5}(\sqrt{10} - \sqrt{15})$ **3.** $\sqrt{42} \cdot \sqrt{56}$ $28\sqrt{3}$ **4.** $\sqrt{\dfrac{4}{7}}$ $\dfrac{2\sqrt{7}}{7}$

$5\sqrt{2} - 5\sqrt{3}$

5. $\dfrac{\sqrt{96}}{\sqrt{18}}$ $\dfrac{4\sqrt{3}}{3}$ **6.** $\dfrac{2}{\sqrt{6}}$ $\dfrac{\sqrt{6}}{3}$ **7.** $5\sqrt{8} - \sqrt{18}$ $7\sqrt{2}$ **8.** $\dfrac{2}{\sqrt{12}} + \dfrac{1}{\sqrt{3}}$ $\dfrac{2\sqrt{3}}{3}$

10-4,
10-5

Substitute and simplify.

a	b	c
$\sqrt{6}$	$\sqrt{18}$	$\sqrt{24}$

9. $a^2 + b^2$ 24   **10.** $\dfrac{1}{a+c}$ $\dfrac{\sqrt{6}}{18}$ **11.** $\sqrt{b^2 - 2}$ 4

12. $-\sqrt{a^2 - 2}$ -2 **13.** $\dfrac{1}{c-a}$ $\dfrac{\sqrt{6}}{6}$ **14.** $a(c - b)$ $12 - 6\sqrt{3}$

10-6 Find the perimeter of each figure.

15. $12\sqrt{2}$

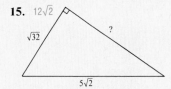

$\sqrt{32}$? $5\sqrt{2}$

16.

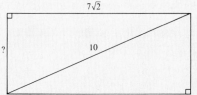

$16\sqrt{2}$ $7\sqrt{2}$?   10

Mathematics and Your Future

Today students rarely decide on a career by their first year in high school. In fact, college students typically change majors several times. Therefore, even if you have a career in mind, you should take enough mathematics to keep your options open for other careers. For example, with fewer than four years of precollege high school mathematics you eliminate your options for college-level programs in science or engineering. With fewer than three years you eliminate your options for most college majors, while with fewer than two years you eliminate your options for many vocational and technical school programs. The best way to keep your options open is to take as many mathematics courses as you can.

520

Class Starter Quiz
on previous section

Simplify. Write "simplest form" if the expression cannot be simplified.

1. $7\sqrt{2} - 3\sqrt{2}$ $4\sqrt{2}$
2. $\sqrt{8} + \sqrt{18}$ $5\sqrt{2}$
3. $\sqrt{30} - \sqrt{14}$ simplest form

Find the perimeters of these figures and simplify the answers.

4. 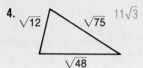 $11\sqrt{3}$

$\sqrt{12}$ $\sqrt{75}$

$\sqrt{48}$

5.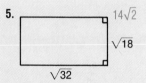

$14\sqrt{2}$

$\sqrt{18}$

$\sqrt{32}$

10–7 Radicands with Variables

Preview

Consider this equation.

$$\sqrt{x^2} = x$$

• Substitute 6 for x. Is the sentence that you get true or false?   T

• Substitute 0 for x. Is the sentence that you get true or false?   T

• Substitute -3 for x. Is the sentence that you get true or false?   F

• Which of the following statements is always true?   c

   a. For all real numbers a, $\sqrt{a^2} = a$.

   b. For all real numbers a, $\sqrt{a^2} = -a$.

   c. For all nonnegative real numbers a, $\sqrt{a^2} = a$.

• Complete this equation to obtain a true sentence.

$$\text{For all real numbers } a, \sqrt{a^2} = ?\quad |a|$$

In this lesson you will learn to simplify a radical when the radicand contains a variable.

■ LESSON

Radicals that contain variables are simplified by the same techniques used to simplify other radicals. For example, consider simplifying $\sqrt{54x^2y^5}$. Since it is difficult to simplify when the values of variables in radicals are negative numbers, we will assume at first that domains of the variables are restricted to the set of nonnegative numbers.

First write the radicand as two factors, one of which contains all square factors.

$$\sqrt{54x^2y^5} = \sqrt{9x^2y^4} \cdot \sqrt{6y}$$

Then simplify.

$$= 3xy^2 \sqrt{6y}$$

> **Example 1**   Simplify. $\sqrt{25a^2b^3}$, $a \geq 0$, $b \geq 0$
>
>   *Solution* $\sqrt{25a^2b^3} = \sqrt{25a^2b^2} \cdot \sqrt{b}$
>
> $= 5ab\sqrt{b}$
>
>   *Answer* $\sqrt{25a^2b^3} = 5ab\sqrt{b}$, $a \geq 0$, $b \geq 0$

PURPOSE

Many formulas contain radicals with variable radicands. Equations containing radicals with variables frequently arise in the solution of problems. In these applications, it is important to be able to simplify expressions containing radicals with variables.

PREVIEW

As students try to determine whether the general statements are true, they should be sure to consider positive numbers, negative numbers, and zero. A hint may be needed to complete the last generalization.

• What operation always results in a number that is not negative?

Taking the
absolute value

Briefly review absolute value by pointing out that absolute value of a number is never negative. For example, $|-5| = 5$, $|0| = 0$, and $|2\frac{1}{2}| = 2\frac{1}{2}$. A formal definition may be given: The absolute value of a negative number is the opposite of the number; the absolute value of a nonnegative number is the number itself.

The difficulties involved in determining what restrictions are needed and when absolute values must be used can be overwhelming for less able students. You may wish such students to assume that variables in radicands always represent positive numbers, thus eliminating those difficulties.

ADDITIONAL EXAMPLES

Example 1.
Simplify. $\sqrt{16x^3y^2}$, $x \geq 0$, $y \geq 0$
$\sqrt{16x^3y^2} = 4xy\sqrt{x}$, $x \geq 0$, $y \geq 0$

Example 2.
Simplify. $\sqrt{\dfrac{32}{y}}$, $y > 0$
$$\sqrt{\dfrac{32}{y}} = \dfrac{4\sqrt{2y}}{y}, \; y > 0$$

Example 3.
Simplify, stating any necessary restrictions.
$\sqrt{50a^2b^3}$
The restriction is $b \geq 0$.
$50a^2b^3 = 5|a|b\sqrt{2b}$, $b \geq 0$

Example 2 Simplify. $\sqrt{\dfrac{48}{x^3}}$, $x > 0$

Solution Note that x is restricted to positive values because the denominator cannot be 0.

$$\sqrt{\dfrac{48}{x^3}} = \dfrac{4\sqrt{3}}{x\sqrt{x}}$$

Rationalize the denominator.
$$= \dfrac{4\sqrt{3}}{x\sqrt{x}} \cdot \dfrac{\sqrt{x}}{\sqrt{x}}$$

$$= \dfrac{4\sqrt{3x}}{x^2}$$

Answer $\sqrt{\dfrac{48}{x^3}} = \dfrac{4\sqrt{3x}}{x^2}$, $x > 0$

Now consider the difficulties caused when the values of variables in radicands are negative or zero.

1. The value of a square-root radicand cannot be negative. The domains of variables must be restricted to values that make the radicand positive or zero; for example,

$$\sqrt{3x^2y}, \quad y \geq 0.$$

The domain of x is not restricted since x^2 is nonnegative for all values of x.

2. The principal square root of a quantity cannot be negative, so absolute value must be used whenever necessary to ensure that the principal square root is not negative.

$$\sqrt{x^2} = |x|, \quad \text{where } x \text{ is a real number}$$

Note that without using absolute value we would have a false statement if a negative number is substituted for x. For example, the principal square root of $\sqrt{(-3)^2}$ is 3, not -3.

$$\sqrt{(-3)^2} = |-3| = 3$$

3. Division by zero is never allowed. Thus, values of variables that make denominators in radicands zero are not allowed; for example,

$$\sqrt{\dfrac{5}{y^2}}, \quad y \neq 0.$$

Example 3 Simplify, stating any necessary restrictions. $\sqrt{x^2y}$

Solution First state the restrictions. The restriction is $y \geq 0$.
$$\sqrt{x^2y} = \sqrt{x^2}\sqrt{y}$$
$$= |x|\sqrt{y}$$

Answer $\sqrt{x^2y} = |x|\sqrt{y}$, $y \geq 0$

One weakness of an oral response to a question in a class discussion is that you get verbal feedback from only one student. Therefore, you may occasionally wish to have all students write answers to a discus-sion question on scratch paper. You can get feedback from all students by reading their answers as you move about the room.

Example 4   Simplify, stating any necessary restrictions. $\sqrt{y^4}$

Solution   No restrictions on the values of the variable are necessary since y^4 is never negative.

$$\sqrt{y^4} = y^2$$

Absolute values are not needed in the answer since y^2 is never negative.

Answer $\sqrt{y^4} = y^2$

■ CLASSROOM EXERCISES

Simplify. Assume that the domain of each variable is the set of positive numbers.

1. $\sqrt{25x}$ $5\sqrt{x}$ 2. $\sqrt{49y}$ $7\sqrt{y}$ 3. $\sqrt{12x^2y}$ $2x\sqrt{3y}$ 4. $\sqrt{48a^3b^2}$ $4ab\sqrt{3a}$ 5. $\sqrt{\dfrac{1}{x}}$ $\dfrac{\sqrt{x}}{x}$

State restrictions, if any, on the values of the variables.

6. $\sqrt{x}$ $x \geq 0$ 7. $\sqrt{y^2}$ None   8. $\sqrt{c^3}$ $c \geq 0$ 9. $\sqrt{\dfrac{10}{b}}$ $b > 0$ 10. $\sqrt{\dfrac{a}{b^2}}$ $a \geq 0, b \neq 0$

Simplify, stating restrictions where necessary.

11. $\sqrt{a^2}$ $|a|$ 12. $\sqrt{\dfrac{1}{a^2}}$ $\dfrac{1}{|a|}, a \neq 0$ 13. $\sqrt{b^3}$ $b\sqrt{b}, b > 0$ 14. $\sqrt{c^4}$ c^2 15. $\sqrt{24x^4y^2}$ $2x^2|y|\sqrt{6}$

■ WRITTEN EXERCISES

Simplify. Assume that the domain of each variable is the set of positive numbers.

A 1. $\sqrt{36y}$ $6\sqrt{y}$ 2. $\sqrt{16x}$ $4\sqrt{x}$ 3. $\sqrt{18ab^2}$ $3b\sqrt{2a}$ 4. $\sqrt{8a^2b}$ $2a\sqrt{2b}$

5. $\sqrt{\dfrac{5}{x}}$ $\dfrac{\sqrt{5x}}{x}$ 6. $\sqrt{\dfrac{7}{y}}$ $\dfrac{\sqrt{7y}}{y}$ 7. $\sqrt{\dfrac{45c^4}{a^3}}$ $\dfrac{3c^2\sqrt{5a}}{a^2}$ 8. $\sqrt{\dfrac{44c^2}{a^5}}$ $\dfrac{2c\sqrt{11a}}{a^3}$

State restrictions, if any, on the values of the variables.

9. $\sqrt{r}$ $r \geq 0$ 10. $\sqrt{s^2}$ None   11. $\sqrt{t^4}$ None   12. $\sqrt{w^3}$ $w \geq 0$

13. $\sqrt{\dfrac{2}{x}}$ $x > 0$ 14. $\sqrt{\dfrac{1}{y}}$ $y > 0$ 15. $\sqrt{-3s}$ $s \leq 0$ 16. $\sqrt{-2t}$ $t \leq 0$

Suppose that x represents a positive real number. Simplify. Write x or $-x$.

17. $\sqrt{x^2}$ x 18. $-\sqrt{x^2}$ $-x$ 19. $-\sqrt{(-x)^2}$ $-x$ 20. $\sqrt{(-x)^2}$ x

Suppose that x represents any real number. Simplify. Write x, $-x$, $|x|$ or $-|x|$.

21. $-\sqrt{x^2}$ $-|x|$ 22. $\sqrt{x^2}$ $|x|$ 23. $\sqrt{(-x)^2}$ $|x|$ 24. $-\sqrt{(-x)^2}$ $-|x|$

ADDITIONAL EXAMPLES

Example 4.

Simplify, stating any necessary restrictions.
$\sqrt{c^6}$

$$\sqrt{c^6} = |c^3|$$

CHECK UNDERSTANDING

- Simplify $\sqrt{x^5}$ for $x \geq 0$. ($x^2\sqrt{x}$)
- State restrictions for $\sqrt{xy^2}$. ($x \geq 0$)
- Simplify $\sqrt{x^3y^2}$, stating any necessary restrictions. ($\sqrt{x^3y^2} = x|y|\sqrt{x}, x \geq 0$)

CLASSROOM EXERCISES

Contrast exercises 6 and 7 by noting that there are no restrictions on the domain in exercise 7. However, the domain of the variable in exercise 6 must be nonnegative.

In exercises 9 and 10, point out that the restrictions on b are necessary for different reasons. In both exercises, $b \neq 0$ because the denominator of a fraction cannot be 0. In exercise 9, b cannot be negative because a radicand cannot be negative. In exercise 10, b can be positive or negative, but not 0. In exercises 11–15, emphasize those situations for which absolute values are necessary in the answers.

ASSIGNMENT GUIDE

Basic   1–39 odd, Review Exercises
Average   3–45 multiples of 3, 47–54 all, Review Exercises
Enriched   18–54 multiples of 3, 55–63 all, Review Exercises

PRACTICE WORKSHEET 55

10-7 RADICANDS WITH VARIABLES

■ Simplify. Assume that the domain of each variable is the set of positive numbers.

1. $\sqrt{x^3}$ $x\sqrt{x}$ 2. $\sqrt{36x}$ $6\sqrt{x}$ 3. $\sqrt{\dfrac{2}{x}}$ $\dfrac{\sqrt{2x}}{x}$

4. $\sqrt{\dfrac{t}{t^2}}$ $\dfrac{\sqrt{t}}{t}$ 5. $\sqrt{\dfrac{2}{t}}$ $\dfrac{\sqrt{2t}}{t}$ 6. $\sqrt{\dfrac{b^4}{3c^3}}$ $\dfrac{b^4\sqrt{3c}}{3c^2}$

■ Simplify, stating restrictions where necessary.

7. $\sqrt{a^4}$ a^2 8. $\sqrt{d^7}$ $d^3\sqrt{d}, d \geq 0$ 9. $\sqrt{h^2}$ $|h|$

10. $-\sqrt{\dfrac{j}{3}}$ $-\dfrac{\sqrt{3j}}{3}, j \geq 0$ 11. $\sqrt{\dfrac{5}{k}}$ $\dfrac{\sqrt{5k}}{k}, k > 0$ 12. $\sqrt{\dfrac{1}{m^2}}$ $\dfrac{\sqrt{3}}{|m|}, m \neq 0$

13. $\sqrt{\dfrac{10}{p}}$ $\dfrac{\sqrt{10p}}{p}, p > 0$ 14. $-\sqrt{\dfrac{q^4}{2}}$ $-\dfrac{q^2\sqrt{2}}{2}$ 15. $\sqrt{\dfrac{t^2}{t^4}}$ $\dfrac{|t|}{t^2}, t \neq 0$

This lesson links three somewhat difficult ideas for students: principal square roots, absolute value, and restricted domains. To assist students having difficulty, encourage them to substitute specific numbers for radicand variables to check whether their simplified expression is correct. Their substitutions should include negative numbers and zero.

For example, are these equations true or false?

a. $\sqrt{x^3} = x\sqrt{x}$

    False; substitute -2 for x.

$$\sqrt{(-2)^3} \neq -2\sqrt{-2}$$
$$\sqrt{x^3} = x\sqrt{x}, x \geq 0$$

b. $\sqrt{x^2 y} = x\sqrt{y}$

    False; substitute -1 for x and -3 for y.

$$\sqrt{(-1)^2(-3)} \overset{?}{=} -1\sqrt{-3}$$
$$\sqrt{-3} \neq -\sqrt{-3}$$
$$\sqrt{x^2 y} = |x|\sqrt{y}, y \geq 0$$

ENRICHMENT PROBLEM

• State the restrictions on the domain of the variables x and y for these expressions.

a. $\dfrac{1}{\sqrt{x-y}}$
   $x > y$

b. $\dfrac{1}{\sqrt{(x-y)^2}}$
   $x \neq y$

524

EXTRA PRACTICE, page 639

Simplify, stating restrictions where necessary.

25. $\sqrt{x^6}$ $|x^3|$

26. $\sqrt{x^{10}}$ $|x^5|$

27. $\sqrt{x^3}$ $x\sqrt{x}, x \geq 0$

28. $\sqrt{x^5}$ $x^2\sqrt{x}, x \geq 0$

29. $\sqrt{\dfrac{1}{x^{10}}}$ $\dfrac{1}{|x^5|}, x \neq 0$

30. $\sqrt{\dfrac{1}{x^6}}$ $\dfrac{1}{|x^3|}, x \neq 0$

31. $\sqrt{5x^2}$ $\sqrt{5}|x|$

32. $\sqrt{7x^2}$ $\sqrt{7}|x|$

33. $\sqrt{\dfrac{4}{x}}$ $\dfrac{2\sqrt{x}}{x}, x > 0$

34. $\sqrt{\dfrac{25}{x}}$ $\dfrac{5\sqrt{x}}{x}, x > 0$

35. $\sqrt{\dfrac{x}{2}}$ $\dfrac{\sqrt{2x}}{2}, x \geq 0$

36. $\sqrt{\dfrac{x}{3}}$ $\dfrac{\sqrt{3x}}{3}, x \geq 0$

37. $\sqrt{\dfrac{a^2}{b}}$ $\dfrac{|a|\sqrt{b}}{b}, b > 0$

38. $\sqrt{\dfrac{a}{b^2}}$ $\dfrac{\sqrt{a}}{|b|}, a \geq 0, b \neq 0$

39. $\sqrt{\dfrac{a^3}{b^4}}$ $\dfrac{a\sqrt{a}}{b^2}, a \geq 0, b \neq 0$

40. $\sqrt{\dfrac{a^4}{b^3}}$ $\dfrac{a^2\sqrt{b}}{b^2}, b > 0$

Find the missing length and simplify. List any restrictions on the variable.

B **41.** $2\sqrt{a}, a > 0$

42. $2a, a > 0$

43. 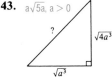 $a\sqrt{5a}, a > 0$

44. 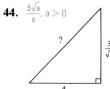 $\dfrac{5\sqrt{a}}{a}, a > 0$

45. 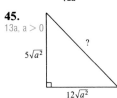 $13a, a > 0$

46. 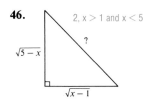 $2, x > 1$ and $x < 5$

True or false? If the statement is false, write a counterexample to show that it is false.

47. For all real numbers x, $\sqrt{16x^2} = 4x$.   F, If $x = -1$, $\sqrt{16} \neq -4$.

48. For all real numbers x, $\sqrt{16x^2} = 4|x|$.   T

49. For all positive numbers x, $\sqrt{16x^2} = 4x$.   T

50. For all positive numbers x, $\sqrt{16x^2} = -4x$.   F, If $x = 1$, $\sqrt{16} \neq -4$

51. For $x = 0$, $\sqrt{16x^2} = 4$.   F, If $x = 0$, $\sqrt{0} \neq 4$

52. For all real numbers x, $\sqrt{x^4} = x^2$.   T

53. For all real numbers x, $\dfrac{3}{\sqrt{x}} = \dfrac{3\sqrt{x}}{x}$.   F, If $x = 0$, $\dfrac{3}{\sqrt{x}}$ is undefined.

54. For all positive numbers x, $\dfrac{3}{\sqrt{x}} = \dfrac{3\sqrt{x}}{x}$.   T

Simplify. List any restrictions on the variables.

C **55.** $\sqrt{\dfrac{x}{16} + \dfrac{x}{9}}$ $\dfrac{5\sqrt{x}}{12}, x \geq 0$

56. $\sqrt{\dfrac{x^3}{25} + \dfrac{x^3}{144}}$ $\dfrac{13x\sqrt{x}}{60}, x \geq 0$

57. $\sqrt{\dfrac{5}{x} - \dfrac{1}{x}}$ $\dfrac{2\sqrt{x}}{x}, x > 0$

58. $\sqrt{\dfrac{a}{b^2} + \dfrac{7a}{b^2}}$ $\dfrac{2\sqrt{2a}}{|b|}, a \geq 0, b \neq 0$

Consider the expression $\sqrt{b^2 - 4ac}$.

59. If $b = 4$ and $a = 1$, what are the restrictions on c? $c \le 4$

60. If $a = 1$ and $c = 9$, what are the restrictions on b? $b \ge 6$ or $b \le -6$

61. If $a = 2$ and $c = -2$, what are the restrictions on b? None

62. Use the Pythagorean theorem to express the length of the diagonal d of a square in terms of the length of a side s.

$d = \sqrt{2}s$

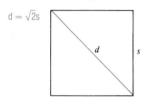

63. Use the Pythagorean theorem to express the altitude h of an equilateral triangle in terms of the length of a side e.

$h = \dfrac{\sqrt{3}e}{2}$

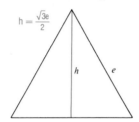

■ REVIEW EXERCISES

Solve.

1. $x\%$ of $50 = 20$ (40)

2. 75% of $x = 60$ (80) [8–8]

3. What is the simple interest earned on $400 invested for 4 years at 8%? $128 [8–8]

4. Jennifer had 24 problems correct on a test and received a score of 75%. How many questions were on the test? 32 [8–9]

5. If Jane and Sarah earned $18 washing cars in 2 h, how much could they expect to earn in 5 h? $45 [8–9]

6. If y varies directly as x and $y = 20$ when $x = 8$, find y when $x = 36$. 90 [8–10]

7. Does y vary directly as x if $y = 2x + 10$? No [8–10]

8. If y varies inversely as x and $y = 20$ when $x = 5$, find the value of y when $x = 10$. 10 [8–11]

9. If y varies inversely as x and $y = 10$ when $x = 6$, find y when $x = 20$. 3 [8–11]

Mathematics and Your Future

Succeeding in mathematics takes ability and hard work. You probably have more ability in mathematics than you think. The fact that you have progressed as far as you have in mathematics indicates that you have ability. If you work hard and seek help when you need it, you will probably be successful in mathematics.

List the restrictions, if any, on the values of x.

1. $\sqrt{x}$ $x \geq 0$

2. $\sqrt{\dfrac{3}{x}}$ $x > 0$

3. $\sqrt{\dfrac{4}{x^2}}$ $x \neq 0$

Simplify, stating any necessary restrictions.

4. $\sqrt{a^2 b^2}$ $|ab|$

5. $\sqrt{a^3 b^4}$ $ab^2\sqrt{a}, \; a \geq 0$

PURPOSE

Radicals sometimes arise in practical problems and formulas. Therefore, it is important to be able to solve equations containing radicals.

PREVIEW

Point out that new roots are not introduced when both sides of an equation are multiplied by a number. For example, $x = 3$ and $5x = 5 \cdot 3$ are equivalent. However, when one or both sides of an equation are multiplied by a variable, new roots may be introduced. For example, $x = 2$ and $x \cdot x = 2 \cdot x$ are not equivalent (the new root 0 is introduced). Moreover, squaring both sides of an equation may introduce new roots. For example, $x = 3$ is not equivalent to $x^2 = 9$ (the new root -3 has been introduced).

LESSON

Emphasize the importance of checking solutions. In checking, note that radicands cannot be negative.

Equations containing two radicals are not presented in the lesson, but they are encountered in B-level and C-level exercises.

In Example 3, point out that the solution ($\emptyset$) may be found quickly.

$$\sqrt{x + 5} + 16 = 4$$

Isolate the radical on one side. ($\sqrt{x + 5} = -12$) Note that the left side is a radical and therefore not negative. The right side is negative. The equation, therefore, has no real roots.

526

OBJECTIVE 10–8

To solve equations containing radicals.

You may wish to spend two days on this section. Refer to the Pacing Chart.

10–8 Solving Radical Equations

Preview

An equivalent equation results when the same number is added to both sides of an equation. An equivalent equation is also formed when both sides of an equation are multiplied by the same nonzero number. Examine what happens when both sides of an equation are squared.

Equation	Solution	Equation	Solution	Equation	Solution
$x = -3$ $x^2 = 9$	$\{-3\}$ $\{3, -3\}$	$\sqrt{x} = 2$ $x = 4$	$\{4\}$ $\{4\}$	$\sqrt{4 - x} = -2$ $4 - x = 4$	$\emptyset$ $\{0\}$

The tables show that squaring does not always produce an equivalent equation. Sometimes "extra" or extraneous solutions are introduced. However, the solutions of the original equation are not "lost." Therefore, squaring both sides of an equation can help us simplify radical equations, but we must be especially alert to check the solutions.

■ LESSON

An equation that contains a radical with a variable in the radicand is called a **radical equation**. The following are radical equations.

$$\sqrt{2x - 4} = 8 \qquad \sqrt{a + 2} = a \qquad \sqrt{2a} + 4 = a$$

In mathematics, when we are confronted with a new equation to solve, we try to change the equation to one that we already know how to solve. We can change radical equations by squaring both sides of the equation.

Example 1   Solve. $\sqrt{2x - 4} = 8$

Solution

Square both sides.
$$\sqrt{2x - 4} = 8$$
$$2x - 4 = 64$$
$$2x = 68$$
$$x = 34$$

Check   Since squaring does not always produce an equivalent equation, the solution of the equation must be checked in the original equation.

$$\sqrt{2x - 4} = 8$$
$$\sqrt{2 \cdot 34 - 4} \overset{?}{=} 8$$
$$\sqrt{68 - 4} \overset{?}{=} 8$$
$$\sqrt{64} \overset{?}{=} 8$$
$$8 = 8 \qquad \text{True}$$

Answer $\{34\}$

Example 2   Solve. $\sqrt{y + 2} = y - 4$

Solution

$$\sqrt{y + 2} = y - 4$$
$$y + 2 = y^2 - 8y + 16$$
$$0 = y^2 - 9y + 14$$
$$0 = (y - 2)(y - 7)$$
$$y - 2 = 0 \quad \text{or} \quad y - 7 = 0$$
$$y = 2 \quad \text{or} \qquad y = 7$$

Check   Check each solution in the original equation.

$$\sqrt{y + 2} = y - 4 \qquad\qquad \sqrt{y + 2} = y - 4$$
$$\sqrt{2 + 2} \stackrel{?}{=} 2 - 4 \qquad\qquad \sqrt{7 + 2} \stackrel{?}{=} 7 - 4$$
$$\sqrt{4} \stackrel{?}{=} -2 \qquad\qquad\qquad \sqrt{9} \stackrel{?}{=} 3$$
$$2 = -2 \quad \text{False} \qquad\qquad 3 = 3 \quad \text{True}$$

Answer $\{7\}$

Note how important it is to test possible answers in the original equation. In Example 2, the solution 2 satisfies the equation $y + 2 = y^2 - 8y + 16$, but it does not satisfy the original equation.

Example 3   Solve. $\sqrt{x + 5} + 16 = 4$

Solution

Isolate the radical on one side of the equation.
Square both sides.

$$\sqrt{x + 5} + 16 = 4$$
$$\sqrt{x + 5} = -12$$
$$x + 5 = 144$$
$$x = 139$$

Check

$$\sqrt{x + 5} + 16 = 4$$
$$\sqrt{139 + 5} + 16 \stackrel{?}{=} 4$$
$$\sqrt{144} + 16 \stackrel{?}{=} 4$$
$$12 + 16 = 4 \quad \text{False}$$

Answer $\emptyset$ (No number satisfies the equation.)

The following steps can be used to solve a radical equation.

1. Rewrite the equation with the radical isolated on one side.
2. Square both sides of the equation to eliminate the radical.
3. Solve the new equation.
4. Check possible answers in the original equation.

CLASSROOM EXERCISES

In classroom exercises 9 and 10, review the FOIL method in squaring binomials such as $x - 1$ and $x - 2$.

Basic   1–27 odd, 28, Review Exercises, Self-Quiz 3

Average   1–39 odd, 28, Review Exercises, Self-Quiz 3

Enriched   3–39 multiples of 3, 28, 41–46 all, Review Exercises, Self-Quiz 3

PRACTICE WORKSHEET 56

10-8 SOLVING RADICAL EQUATIONS

■ Simplify. Write ∅ if there is no solution.

1. $\sqrt{v+7} = 3$ {2}
2. $\sqrt{1-w} = 2$ {-3}
3. $\sqrt{2y+1} = -3$ ∅
4. $\sqrt{4z+2} = 2$ {1/2}
5. $\sqrt{4a+1} = a - 1$ {6}
6. $\sqrt{12b+5} = 3$ {1/3}
7. $\sqrt{2x+1} + 7 = 3$ ∅
8. $\sqrt{6c-5} = c$ {1,5}
9. $\sqrt{d+5} = d + 5$ {-5, -4}
10. $\sqrt{5h+1} - h = 1$ {0, 3}
11. $\sqrt{6k+10} = k + 3$ {-1,1}
12. $\sqrt{6-m} = -m$ {-3}

PROBLEM-SOLVING NOTES
Using estimation

Exercises 25–27 illustrate an important activity in the solution of many equations or problems—that of making a reasonable estimate before formally solving the problem. Such a view of radical equations may immediately disclose there is no solution (as in exercises 25 and 26), indicate only one solution (as in exercise 27), or give the answer by inspection.

528

EXTRA PRACTICE, page 639

■ CLASSROOM EXERCISES

Solve.

1. $\sqrt{x} = 4$ (16)
2. $\sqrt{n} = 9$ (81)
3. $\sqrt{a-7} = 0$ (7)
4. $\sqrt{5m-1} = 7$ (10)
5. $\sqrt{x+8} = 2$ (-4)
6. $\sqrt{4n+4} = 8$ (15)
7. $\sqrt{2n+2} = 4$ (7)
8. $\sqrt{5n+1} = 6$ (7)
9. $2\sqrt{x-1} = x - 1$ (1, 5)
10. $\sqrt{x+10} + 2 = x$ (6)

■ WRITTEN EXERCISES

Solve.

Ⓐ
1. $\sqrt{t} = 5$ (25)
2. $\sqrt{t} = 7$ (49)
3. $\sqrt{3x-2} = 4$ (6)
4. $\sqrt{2x-3} = 5$ (14)
5. $\sqrt{3y+9} = 6$ (9)
6. $\sqrt{4y+1} = 3$ (2)
7. $\sqrt{c+6} = c$ (3)
8. $\sqrt{c+12} = c$ (4)
9. $\sqrt{3x-8} = x - 2$ (3, 4)
10. $\sqrt{3x-5} = x - 1$ (2, 3)
11. $\sqrt{r+14} = r + 2$ (2)
12. $\sqrt{9r+19} = r + 3$ (5, -2)
13. $\sqrt{x+6} = x$ (3)
14. $\sqrt{x} + 2 = x$ (4)
15. $\sqrt{2x} + 3 = 8$ (12.5)
16. $\sqrt{3x} + 1 = 7$ (2√3)
17. $\sqrt{5p-1} + p = 3$ (1)
18. $\sqrt{3p+1} + p = 9$ (5)
19. $\sqrt{a+1} = a - 5$ (8)
20. $\sqrt{5a+6} = a + 2$ (2, -1)
21. $x + \sqrt{5} = 4$ (4 - √5)
22. $x - \sqrt{3} = 6$ (6 + √3)
23. $\sqrt{10q+4} - q = 2$ (0, 6)
24. $\sqrt{10q-6} - q = 1$ (1, 7)

Sometimes it is helpful to examine the original radical equation before solving. Use your knowledge of principal square roots to solve these equations easily.

25. $\sqrt{x+4} = -3$ ∅
26. $\sqrt{y} - \sqrt{2y} = 5$ ∅
27. $\sqrt{a} + \sqrt{-a} = 0$ (0)

28. Why is it inappropriate to square both sides as the first step in solving this equation?

$$2\sqrt{x} - 1 = x$$ The term with the radical should be isolated first.

Solve these equations containing two radicals. If there is no solution, write ∅.

Ⓑ
29. $\sqrt{x} = \sqrt{5x-8}$ (2)
30. $\sqrt{5x} = \sqrt{3x+6}$ (3)
31. $\sqrt{6x} = \sqrt{2x-8}$ ∅
32. $\sqrt{7x} = \sqrt{8x+6}$ ∅
33. $\sqrt{x^2+2} = \sqrt{3x}$ (1, 2)
34. $\sqrt{x^2+4} = \sqrt{5x}$ (1, 4)
35. $\sqrt{x^2-10} = \sqrt{3x}$ (5)
36. $\sqrt{2x} = \sqrt{15-x^2}$ (3)
37. $\sqrt{5x} = \sqrt{2x^2+3}$ $\left\{1, \frac{3}{2}\right\}$
38. $\sqrt{13x} = \sqrt{3x^2+4}$ $\left\{\frac{1}{3}, 4\right\}$
39. $\sqrt{5x^2+x} = \sqrt{3-x}$ $\left\{\frac{3}{5}, -1\right\}$
40. $\sqrt{5x^2+x} = \sqrt{2-x^2}$ $\left\{\frac{1}{2}, -\frac{2}{3}\right\}$

528   Chapter 10   Rational and Irrational Numbers

• The symbol $\sqrt[3]{x}$ represents the cube
root of x; that is, $(\sqrt[3]{x})^3 = x$.
Solve. $\sqrt[3]{(x-2)} = 3$

$$(\sqrt[3]{x-2})^3 = (3)^3$$
$$x - 2 = 27$$
$$x = 29$$
Solution: {29}

To solve some equations containing two radicals, we must square both sides of the equation twice.

Example 4   Solve. $\sqrt{x} + 1 = \sqrt{2x - 2}$

Solution
$$\sqrt{x} + 1 = \sqrt{2x - 2}$$

Square both sides.
$$(\sqrt{x} + 1)^2 = (\sqrt{2x - 2})^2$$
$$x + 2\sqrt{x} + 1 = 2x - 2$$
$$2\sqrt{x} = x - 3$$

Square both sides.
$$4x = x^2 - 6x + 9$$
$$0 = x^2 - 10x + 9$$
$$0 = (x - 9)(x - 1)$$
$$x - 9 = 0 \quad \text{or} \quad x - 1 = 0$$
$$x = 9 \quad \text{or} \qquad x = 1$$

Check

$\sqrt{x} + 1 = \sqrt{2x - 2}$	$\sqrt{x} + 1 = \sqrt{2x - 2}$
$\sqrt{9} + 1 \overset{?}{=} \sqrt{2(9) - 2}$	$\sqrt{1} + 1 \overset{?}{=} \sqrt{2(1) - 2}$
$3 + 1 \overset{?}{=} \sqrt{16}$	$1 + 1 \overset{?}{=} \sqrt{0}$
$4 = 4$ True	$2 = 0$ False

Answer   {9}

Solve these equations containing two radicals. If there is no solution, write $\emptyset$.

41. $\sqrt{x - 1} + 3 = \sqrt{4x + 5}$ {1, 5}

42. $\sqrt{x + 10} + 2 = \sqrt{x + 26}$ {−1}

43. $\sqrt{2x - 7} - 1 = \sqrt{x - 4}$ {4, 8}

44. $\sqrt{x} + \sqrt{x + 5} = 5$ {4}

45. $\sqrt{x + 2} + \sqrt{x - 3} = -5$ $\emptyset$

46. $\sqrt{2x + 4} - \sqrt{x - 2} = 2$ {6}

■ REVIEW EXERCISES

Graph these inequalities on a number line.

1. $2x + 3 > x + 5$

2. $3x + 5 < 2x + 6$

3. $4 - 2x > 10$ [9–3, 9–5]

 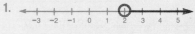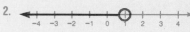
Self-Quiz 3

10–7   Simplify each expression. Assume that the variables are all positive.

1. $\sqrt{121y^3z^2}$ $11yz\sqrt{y}$

2. $\sqrt{\dfrac{a^4}{b}}$ $\dfrac{a^2\sqrt{b}}{b}$

3. $\dfrac{\sqrt{y^5}}{\sqrt{x^3}}$ $\dfrac{y^2\sqrt{xy}}{x^2}$

State restrictions, if any, on the values of the variables. Then simplify.

4. $\sqrt{x^3y^4}$ $xy^2\sqrt{x}, x \geq 0$

5. $\sqrt{\dfrac{36}{z}}$ $\dfrac{6\sqrt{z}}{z}, z > 0$

6. $\sqrt{-2x^5}$ $x^2\sqrt{-2x}, x \leq 0$

10–8   Solve each equation for x.

7. $\sqrt{2x} = \sqrt{x - 4}$ $\emptyset$

8. $\sqrt{y} + 2 = y$ {4}

9. $\sqrt{x^2 - 5} = 2\sqrt{x}$ {5}

Solve. If there is no solution, write ∅.

1. $\sqrt{x} = 10$ {100}

2. $\sqrt{2x + 1} = 3$ {4}

3. $\sqrt{x - 1} = -5$ ∅

4. $\sqrt{10x + 5} = x + 3$ {2}

5. $\sqrt{x + 7} = x + 5$ {−3}

PURPOSE

The Pythagorean theorem can be used to derive a formula for determining the distance between two given points of the coordinate plane. The distance formula is an important tool in working with figures drawn on the coordinate plane.

PREVIEW

Point out that the triangles pictured in the Preview are right triangles. This is evident since the legs are horizontal and vertical line segments. Once the lengths of a triangle's legs are known, the length of its hypotenuse can be determined by applying the Pythagorean theorem.

LESSON

Have students make a sketch of two given points and the segment joining them before setting about finding its length. Point out that the sketch helps organize the information and can give them an idea of a reasonable value for the answer.

Emphasize that the *difference* in the x-coordinates is the length of a horizontal segment; the *difference* in the y-coordinates is the length of a vertical segment. The distance formula is an application of the Pythagorean theorem.

OBJECTIVE 10–9

To use the distance formula to find the distance between two points.

10–9 The Distance Formula

Preview

What is the distance between the two points?

A and C 6

B and C 4

A and B $\sqrt{52}$ or $2\sqrt{13}$

F and D 3

E and F 5

D and E $\sqrt{34}$

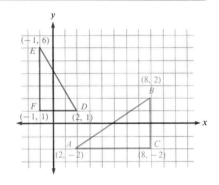

In this lesson you will learn to use a formula to find the distance between any two points whose coordinates are known.

■ LESSON

The distance between two points on the same horizontal line or the same vertical line is easy to compute.

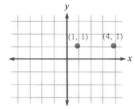
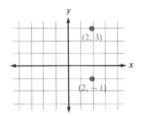

The distance d is the difference between the x-coordinates.

$$d = 4 - 1 = 3$$

In general, for points (x_1, y_1) and (x_2, y_2), when $y_1 = y_2$, $d = |x_2 - x_1|$.

The distance d is the difference between the y-coordinates.

$$d = 3 - (-1) = 4$$

In general, for points (x_1, y_1) and (x_2, y_2), when $x_1 = x_2$, $d = |y_2 - y_1|$.

The absolute value ensures that the positive difference is used to denote the distance.

When two points are not on the same horizontal or vertical line, the Pythagorean theorem is used to find the distance between them.

530

One major goal of education is to teach students to be independent learners. Therefore, gradually give students more and more responsibility for their own instruction by giving them reading assignments.

To find the distance d between points (2, 3) and (4, 7), draw a horizontal line through one point and a vertical line through the other. Note that a right triangle is formed, and the Pythagorean theorem can now be used.

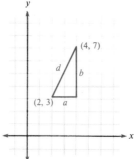

$$d^2 = a^2 + b^2$$
$$d^2 = |4 - 2|^2 + |7 - 3|^2$$
$$d^2 = 2^2 + 4^2$$
$$d^2 = 20$$
$$d = \sqrt{20} \quad [d \neq -\sqrt{20} \text{ because the distance cannot}$$
$$\qquad\qquad\quad \text{be negative.}]$$
$$d = 2\sqrt{5}$$

Since the differences above are squared, parentheses can be used instead of absolute value signs.

The distance between two points can be found by using this formula.

The Distance Formula

The distance d between two points

$$(x_1, y_1) \text{ and } (x_2, y_2)$$

is

$$d = \sqrt{(x_2 - x_1)^2 + (y_2 - y_1)^2}.$$

Example 1   Find the distance between points (2, -3) and (5, 1).

Solution
$$d = \sqrt{(x_2 - x_1)^2 + (y_2 - y_1)^2}$$
$$= \sqrt{(5 - 2)^2 + [1 - (-3)]^2}$$
$$= \sqrt{3^2 + 4^2}$$
$$= \sqrt{9 + 16}$$
$$= \sqrt{25}$$
$$= 5$$

Answer   The distance between (2, -3) and (5, 1) is 5.

Example 2   Find the value of y such that the distance between point A and point B is $2\sqrt{5}$.

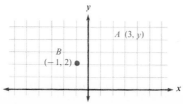

Example 1.
Find the distance between $(-3, -6)$ and (2, 6).

The distance is 13.

Example 2.
Find the value of x so that the distance between the two points $(x, 3)$ and (4, 5) is $\sqrt{13}$.

$x = 7$ or $x = 1$

CHECK UNDERSTANDING

• Find c.

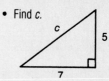

$(5^2 + 7^2 = 74$
$c = \sqrt{74})$

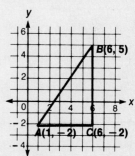

• What is the distance between A and C? (5)
• What is the distance between B and C? (7)
• What is the distance between A and B? ($\sqrt{74}$)

531

In exercises 4–6, discuss why the choice of points for (x_1, y_1) and (x_2, y_2) does not matter. Since the differences between coordinates are squared, the results are the same.

ASSIGNMENT GUIDE

Basic   1–23 odd, Review Exercises
Average   3–39 multiples of 3, 41–47 odd,
        Review Exercises
Enriched   9–39 multiples of 3, 41–47 odd,
        48–51 all, Review Exercises

PRACTICE WORKSHEET 56

10-9 THE DISTANCE FORMULA

■ Find the distance between the two points. Simplify the distance.

1. (4, 4), (6, 8) $2\sqrt{5}$ 2. (0, 0), (3, 6) $3\sqrt{5}$

3. (2, 3), (11, 15) 15 4. (7, 6), (1, 2) $2\sqrt{13}$

5. (5, −4), (2, −5) $\sqrt{10}$ 6. (2, −5), (7, 7) 13

7. (−6, −3), (2, 3) 10 8. (6, −2), (−2, 2) $4\sqrt{5}$

9. (−2, −1), (5, −2) $5\sqrt{2}$ 10. (−5, 9), (3, −6) 17

EXTRA PRACTICE, page 639
COMPUTER WORKSHEET 15

Example 2   (continued)

Solution

$$d = \sqrt{(x_2 - x_1)^2 + (y_2 - y_1)^2}$$
$$2\sqrt{5} = \sqrt{[3 - (-1)]^2 + (y - 2)^2}$$
$$2\sqrt{5} = \sqrt{16 + (y^2 - 4y + 4)}$$
$$2\sqrt{5} = \sqrt{y^2 - 4y + 20}$$
$$(2\sqrt{5})^2 = (\sqrt{y^2 - 4y + 20})^2$$
$$20 = y^2 - 4y + 20$$
$$0 = y^2 - 4y$$
$$0 = y(y - 4)$$
$$y = 0 \quad \text{or} \quad y = 4$$

Check   The check is left to the student.

Answer   {0, 4}

■ CLASSROOM EXERCISES

State the values of x_1, x_2, y_1, and y_2.

1. (4, 2), (5, 1) 4, 5, 2, 1   **2.** (−3, 4), (2, 8) −3, 2, 4, 8   **3.** (−1, −3), (−5, −6) −1, −5, −3, −6

State the values of $|x_2 - x_1|$ and $|y_2 - y_1|$.

4. (−8, 1), (0, −5) 8, 6   **5.** (1, 4), (6, −8) 5, 12   **6.** (3, 7), (1, −9) 2, 16

Find the distance between the two points.

7. (2, 4), (2, −5) 9   **8.** (3, 3), (5, 3) 2   **9.** (−3, −2), (3, −10) 10

■ WRITTEN EXERCISES

Find $|x_2 - x_1|$ and $|y_2 - y_1|$ for each pair of points.

Ⓐ **1.** (2, 2), (6, 8) 4, 6   **2.** (3, 3), (9, 7) 6, 4

3. (10, 3), (4, 6) 6, 3   **4.** (9, 1), (2, 10) 7, 9

5. (−2, 3), (4, −10) 6, 13   **6.** (5, −3), (−1, 7) 6, 10

7. (0, 0), (−2, −10) 2, 10   **8.** (−3, −15), (0, 0) 3, 15

Find the distance between the two points. Simplify the distances.

9. (2, −3), (2, 7) 10   **10.** (−3, 5), (−3, 1) 4

11. (4, −2), (−1, −2) 5   **12.** (−3, 6), (2, 6) 5

13. (2, 4), (6, 7) 5   **14.** (3, 6), (7, 9) 5

15. (3, 7), (15, 2) 13   **16.** (3, 9), (9, 1) 10

17. (10, 10), (−6, −2) 20   **18.** (4, 4), (−11, −4) 17

19. (4, 3), (4, 10) 7   **20.** (6, 2), (6, 11) 9

Find the distance between the two points. Simplify the distances.

21. $(5, -2)$, $(6, -2)$ 1

22. $(7, -3)$, $(4, -3)$ 3

23. $(100, 100)$, $(114, 52)$ 50

24. $(50, 50)$, $(74, 18)$ 40

Find the value of x or y given the distance d between the two points.

B **25.** $(11, 7)$, $(3, y)$; $d = 10$ 1 or 13

26. $(7, 10)$, $(x, 4)$; $d = 10$ 15 or -1

27. $(5, -5)$, $(x, 7)$; $d = 13$ 0 or 10

28. $(10, 10)$, $(-5, y)$; $d = 17$ 2 or 18

29. $(2, 3)$, $(4, y)$; $d = \sqrt{5}$ 2 or 4

30. $(5, 1)$, $(x, 5)$; $d = 4\sqrt{2}$ 1 or 9

31. $(x, 4)$, $(5, 9)$; $d = 5\sqrt{2}$ 0 or 10

32. $(3, y)$, $(7, 1)$; $d = 2\sqrt{5}$ 3 or -1

Find the distance between the two points. Write the approximation of the distance to tenths.

33. $(5, 4)$, $(7, 9)$ 5.4

34. $(-3, 7)$, $(2, 4)$ 5.8

35. $(-2, -3)$, $(5, 3)$ 9.2

36. $(-2, -3)$, $(-6, 2)$ 6.4

37. Find the length of side BC. 10

38. Find the length of the longer diagonal. $12\sqrt{10}$

39. Find the length of the shorter diagonal. 20

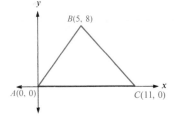

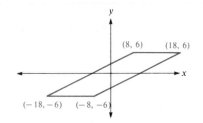

40. Use the distance formula to show that the triangle with the following vertices is isosceles: $A(3, 1)$, $B(3, 9)$, and $C(8, 5)$. $AC = BC = \sqrt{41}$

41. Use the distance formula to show that the triangle with the following vertices is isosceles: $A(-4, 3)$, $B(5, 1)$, and $C(-2, -5)$. $AB = BC = \sqrt{85}$

Find the perimeter of triangle ABC given the coordinates of A, B, and C.

42. $A(7, 10)$ 12
$B(10, 14)$
$C(10, 10)$

43. $A(-3, 5)$ 30
$B(2, 17)$
$C(2, 5)$

44. $A(10, 6)$ $9 + 3\sqrt{5}$
$B(10, 12)$
$C(7, 6)$

Find the length of each diagonal of quadrilateral $ABCD$.

45. $A(10, 0)$ $17\sqrt{2}, 17\sqrt{2}$
$B(2, 15)$
$C(17, 23)$
$D(25, 8)$

46. $A(-10, -10)$ 29, 29
$B(-10, 11)$
$C(10, 11)$
$D(10, -10)$

47. $A(35, 12)$ 13, 37
$B(21, 0)$
$C(0, 0)$
$D(16, 12)$

- Show that line AM is the perpendicular bisector of segment CD.

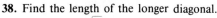

$\overleftrightarrow{AM}$ is the perpendicular bisector of $\overline{CD}$

a. if $CM = MD$ and

b. if the product of the slopes of $\overleftrightarrow{AM}$ and $\overleftrightarrow{CD}$ is -1.

a. $CM = \sqrt{3^2 + 3^2} = 3\sqrt{2}$

$MD = \sqrt{3^2 + 3^2} = 3\sqrt{2}$

$CM = MD$

b. Slope of $\overleftrightarrow{AM}$ is $\dfrac{9 - 5}{0 - 4} = -1$

Slope of $\overleftrightarrow{CD}$ is $\dfrac{8 - 2}{7 - 1} = 1$

$-1 \cdot 1 = -1$

2.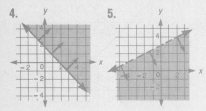

3.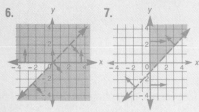

4. **5.**

6. **7.**

C **48.** Show that ABC is a right triangle.

$$\sqrt{53}^2 + \sqrt{53}^2 = \sqrt{106}^2$$

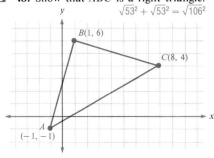

49. Find the area of rectangle $MNOP$.

41 square units

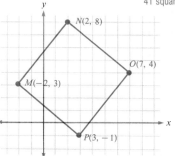

50. Show that the lengths of the diagonals of the square $PQRS$ are equal. $5\sqrt{2}, 5\sqrt{2}$

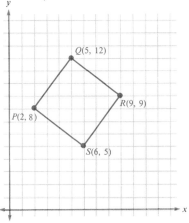

51. The point M is on a coordinate axis, a distance of 5 units from $N(-3, 4)$. What are the possible coordinates of M? $(0, 0), (0, 8),$ or $(-6, 0)$

■ REVIEW EXERCISES

1. Use absolute values to write an inequality that describes this graph. $|x| > 1$ [9–6]

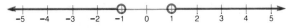

Graph on a number line.

2. $|2 + x| < 4$ **3.** $|x - 2| > 3$ [9–6]

Graph on a coordinate plane.

4. $x + y \geq 2$ **5.** $y < \frac{1}{2}x + 3$ [9–7]

6. $y < x$ or $y \geq 0$ **7.** $y > x - 1$ and $x \geq 0$ [9–8]

EXTENSION   Using the distance formula on a computer

Number pairs (x,y) that satisfy the equation $4 = \sqrt{(1-x)^2 + (2-y)^2}$ are coordinates of points that are a distance of 4 units from the point $(1, 2)$. The following program takes any value of x between -3 and 5 and computes the corresponding value(s) of y. The BASIC function SQR instructs the computer to take a square root.

```
 10   PRINT "ENTER A NUMBER BETWEEN − 3 AND 5."
 20   INPUT X
 30   Y = 2 + SQR (16 − (1 − X) ↑ 2)
 40   Y = INT(Y * 10 + .5)/10
 50   PRINT "X =     "; X, "Y =     "; Y
 60   Y = 2 − SQR (16 − (1 − X) ↑ 2)
 70   Y = INT(Y * 10 + .5)/10
 80   PRINT "X =     "; X, "Y =     "; Y
 90   PRINT "ANY MORE NUMBERS? (Y/N)"
100   INPUT P$
110   IF P$ = "N" THEN 130
120   GOTO 10
130   END
```

1. Use the program to find many (x, y) pairs that satisfy the given equation.

2. Graph the equation.   The graph is a circle with radius 4 centered at $(1, 2)$.

3. Enter a value of x that is either less than -3 or greater than 5. What happens? Why?   ILLEGAL QUANTITY ERROR IN 30; If $x < -3$ or $x > 5$, then $(16 - (1\ x)^2)$
< 0 and has no real-number square root.

4. How can you change lines 10, 30, and 60 to define a circle with radius 4 centered at $(-2, 3)$?   10   PRINT "ENTER A NUMBER BETWEEN − 6 AND 2."
30   $Y = 3 + SQR (16 - (-2 - X) ↑ 2)$
60   $Y = 3 - SQR (16 - (-2 - X) ↑ 2)$

Mathematics and Your Future

Counselors have information about admissions and scholarships to colleges and universities. They also know about vocational schools and employment opportunities. Ask your counselor for information about entrance requirements for the schools you may be considering. Be sure to find out the mathematics requirements for major fields that you may wish to study. The amount of mathematics needed for a specific major is frequently greater than the amount of mathematics you will need to get admitted to the institution. You will find that if you take plenty of mathematics, you will keep your options open.

■ CHAPTER SUMMARY

- **Vocabulary**

- If $x^2 = y$, then x is a *square root* of y.   [10–1]

- An *irrational number* is a real number that cannot be expressed as a quotient   [10–2]
  of two integers.

- The Pythagorean Theorem   [10–3]

  For a right triangle, the square of the hypotenuse
  is equal to the sum of the squares of the legs.

  $$a^2 + b^2 = c^2$$

  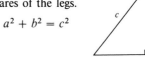

- Converse of the Pythagorean Theorem   [10–3]

  If sides a, b, and c of a triangle are such that $a^2 + b^2 = c^2$, then the triangle
  is a right triangle. The right angle is opposite the longest side.

- The Multiplication Property for Radicals   [10–4]

  For all nonnegative numbers a and b,

  $$\sqrt{ab} = \sqrt{a} \cdot \sqrt{b}.$$

- The Division Property for Radicals   [10–5]

  For all nonnegative numbers a and b, $b \neq 0$,

  $$\sqrt{\frac{a}{b}} = \frac{\sqrt{a}}{\sqrt{b}}.$$

- Simplest Form of a Radical Expression   [10–5]

  A radical expression is in simplest form if:

  1. the radicand does not contain a fraction;
  2. the radicand has no perfect-square factor other than 1;
  3. no radicals appear in the denominator.

- For all real numbers x,   [10–7]

  $$\sqrt{x^2} = |x|.$$

- When working with square roots and variables: [10–7]

  1. The value of the radicand cannot be negative, so the domains of the variables must be properly restricted.

  2. The principal square root of a quantity cannot be negative. Absolute value must be used whenever necessary to be sure that the principal square root is not negative.

  $$\sqrt{x^2} = |x|, \text{ where } x \text{ is a real number}$$

  3. Division by zero is never allowed. Thus, values of variables that make denominators in radicands zero are not allowed.

- The following general steps are used to solve radical equations. [10–8]

  1. Rewrite the equation with the radical isolated on one side.
  2. Square both sides of the equation to eliminate the radical.
  3. Solve the new equation.
  4. Check possible answers in the original equation.

- The Distance Formula [10–9]

  The distance d between two points (x_1, y_1) and (x_2, y_2) is

  $$d = \sqrt{(x_2 - x_1)^2 + (y_2 - y_1)^2}.$$

■ CHAPTER REVIEW

10–1 Objective: To simplify expressions containing square roots of perfect squares.

    1. Simplify. $-\sqrt{1.44}$ **2.** Find the square roots of 3600.   **3.** Solve. $x^2 = 81$
                −1.2   60, −60   (9, −9)

10–2 Objective: To use a table to find approximations for square roots of numbers.

    Use the table of square roots on page 641. Give your answers to the nearest hundredth.

    4. $\sqrt{24}$ 4.90   **5.** $x^2 = 40$ (6.33, −6.33)

    6. The area of a square is 50 cm². What is the length of each side of the square to the nearest hundredth of a centimeter?   7.07 cm

10–3 Objective: To use the Pythagorean theorem to find a missing length of a side in a right triangle.

    Find the missing length.

    7.   13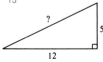

    8.   9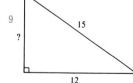

    9. A rectangle is 4 cm long and 2 cm wide. Use a table to find the length of the diagonal of the rectangle to the nearest tenth of a centimeter.   4.5 cm

10-4 Objective: To simplify expressions involving sums, products, and differences of radicals.

Simplify.

10. $\sqrt{18}$ $3\sqrt{2}$

11. $\sqrt{2}(\sqrt{5} + \sqrt{2})$ $\sqrt{10} + 2$

12. $(3 + \sqrt{5})(3 - \sqrt{5})$ 4

10-5 Objective: To simplify expressions involving quotients of radicals.

Simplify.

13. $\sqrt{\dfrac{5}{9}}$ $\dfrac{\sqrt{5}}{3}$

14. $\dfrac{\sqrt{12}}{\sqrt{75}}$ $\dfrac{2}{5}$

15. The area of a rectangle is 20 cm² and its width is $\sqrt{5}$ cm. Write the length of the rectangle in simplest form. $4\sqrt{5}$ cm

10-6 Objective: To simplify sums and differences of square roots.

Simplify. Write "simplest form" if the expression cannot be simplified.

16. $3\sqrt{5} + \sqrt{5}$ $4\sqrt{5}$

17. $\sqrt{27} - \sqrt{18}$ $3\sqrt{3} - 3\sqrt{2}$

18. Find the perimeter and area of the rectangle. Simplify the answer. $8\sqrt{2}$, 6

10-7 Objective: To simplify radicals containing variables.

Simplify. State restrictions, if any, on the values of the variables.

19. $\sqrt{4x^2}$ $2|x|$

20. $\sqrt{\dfrac{x}{4}}$ $\dfrac{\sqrt{x}}{2}$, $x \geq 0$

21. $\sqrt{\dfrac{a^3}{b^2}}$ $\dfrac{a\sqrt{a}}{|b|}$, $a \geq 0$, $b \neq 0$

10-8 Objective: To solve equations containing radicals.

Solve.

22. $\sqrt{x} = 9$ (81)

23. $\sqrt{2x + 5} = 3$ (2)

24. $\sqrt{4x} + 3 = x$ (9)

10-9 Objective: To use the distance formula to find the distance between two points.

Find the distance between the two points. Simplify all radicals.

25. $(2, 4)$, $(6, 7)$ 5

26. $(4, -3)$, $(4, 6)$ 9

27. Find the value of x such that the distance between the points $(3, 0)$ and $(x, -2)$ is $2\sqrt{5}$. -1 or 7

28. Find the perimeter of triangle ABC with the following coordinates.
  A $(-2, 0)$ B $(-2, -5)$ C $(-6, -5)$ $9 + \sqrt{41}$

■ CHAPTER 10 SELF-TEST

10-1 Simplify, if possible. Write "NR" if not a real number.

    1. $\sqrt{-64}$ NR   **2.** $-\sqrt{0.36}$ -0.6 **3.** $\sqrt{\dfrac{9}{4}}$ $\dfrac{3}{2}$

Solve.

    4. $x^2 = 0.16$ $\{0.4, -0.4\}$ **5.** $y = -\sqrt{81}$ $\{-9\}$

10-2   **6.** State the consecutive integers that $\sqrt{59}$ is between.   7, 8

Write the exact solution in simplest form.

    7. $x^2 = 76$ $\{2\sqrt{19}, -2\sqrt{19}\}$ **8.** $y = -\sqrt{180}$ $\{-6\sqrt{5}\}$

10-3 Find the missing length.

9.
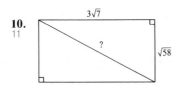
40   58   ?   42

10.
$3\sqrt{7}$? $\sqrt{58}$ 11

    11. A flagpole 30 ft high has a rope attached to raise the flag. If the rope is 34 ft long, how far away from the base of the pole can the rope be stretched and still touch the ground?   16 ft

10-4 Simplify.

    12. $\sqrt{54}$ $3\sqrt{6}$ **13.** $\sqrt{7}(\sqrt{35} - 2\sqrt{7})$ $7\sqrt{5} - 14$ **14.** $(\sqrt{2} + \sqrt{3})^2$ $5 + 2\sqrt{6}$

10-5

a	b	c
5	8	11

Substitute and simplify.

    15. $\dfrac{\sqrt{a+c}}{\sqrt{b^2}}$ $\dfrac{1}{2}$ **16.** $\dfrac{\sqrt{b+2c}}{\sqrt{ab}}$ $\dfrac{\sqrt{3}}{2}$

10-6 Write in simplest form.

    17. $\sqrt{\dfrac{9}{5}}$ $\dfrac{3\sqrt{5}}{5}$ **18.** $\dfrac{\sqrt{35}}{\sqrt{15}}$ $\dfrac{\sqrt{21}}{3}$

    19. $\sqrt{98} - \sqrt{50}$ $2\sqrt{2}$ **20.** $\sqrt{18} + \sqrt{12} - \sqrt{3}$ $3\sqrt{2} + \sqrt{3}$

10-7 Simplify if possible. State any restrictions on the values of the variables.

    21. $\sqrt{\dfrac{5}{x^2}}$ $\dfrac{\sqrt{5}}{|x|}, x \neq 0$ **22.** $\sqrt{\dfrac{b^4}{a}}$ $\dfrac{b^2\sqrt{a}}{a}, a > 0$

Chapter 10   Self-Test   **539**

539

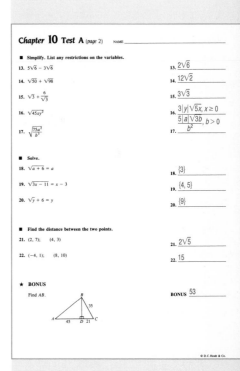

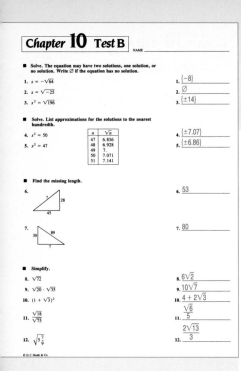

■ Solve. The equation may have two solutions, one solution, or
no solution. Write ∅ if the equation has no solution.

1. $x = -\sqrt{64}$ 1. $\{-8\}$ _____

2. $x = \sqrt{-25}$ 2. $\varnothing$ _____

3. $x^2 = \sqrt{196}$ 3. $\{\pm 14\}$ _____

■ Solve. List approximations for the solutions to the nearest
hundredth.

n	$\sqrt{n}$
47	6.856
48	6.928
49	7.
50	7.071
51	7.141

4. $x^2 = 50$ 4. $\{\pm 7.07\}$ _____

5. $x^2 = 47$ 5. $\{\pm 6.86\}$ _____

■ Find the missing length.

6.   6. 53 _____

7.   7. 80 _____

■ Simplify.

8. $\sqrt{72}$ 8. $6\sqrt{2}$ _____

9. $\sqrt{20} \cdot \sqrt{35}$ 9. $10\sqrt{7}$ _____

10. $(1 + \sqrt{3})^2$ 10. $4 + 2\sqrt{3}$ _____

11. $\dfrac{\sqrt{18}}{\sqrt{75}}$ 11. $\dfrac{\sqrt{6}}{5}$ _____

12. $\sqrt{\dfrac{7}{9}}$ 12. $\dfrac{2\sqrt{13}}{3}$ _____

© D.C. Heath & Co.

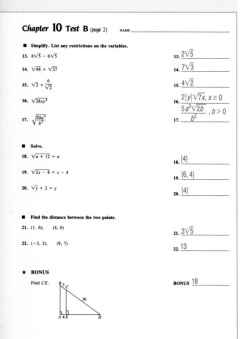

■ Simplify. List any restrictions on the variables.

13. $8\sqrt{5} - 6\sqrt{5}$ 13. $2\sqrt{5}$ _____

14. $\sqrt{48} + \sqrt{27}$ 14. $7\sqrt{3}$ _____

15. $\sqrt{2} + \dfrac{6}{\sqrt{2}}$ 15. $4\sqrt{2}$ _____

16. $\sqrt{28xy^2}$ 16. $2|y|\sqrt{7x}, x \geq 0$ _____

17. $\sqrt{\dfrac{50a^4}{b^3}}$ 17. $\dfrac{5a^2\sqrt{2b}}{b^2}, b > 0$ _____

■ Solve.

18. $\sqrt{a + 12} = a$ 18. $\{4\}$ _____

19. $\sqrt{2x - 8} = x - 4$ 19. $\{6, 4\}$ _____

20. $\sqrt{y} + 2 = y$ 20. $\{4\}$ _____

■ Find the distance between the two points.

21. $(1, 6); \quad (4, 0)$ 21. $3\sqrt{5}$ _____

22. $(-3, 2); \quad (9, 7)$ 22. 13 _____

★ BONUS

Find CE.   BONUS 18 _____

© D.C. Heath & Co.

10–8   Solve.

23. $\sqrt{1 - 2a} = 7$ (-24) 24. $x = \sqrt{15 - 2x}$ (3)

10–9   **25.** Find the distance between $(-3, 4)$ and $(2, -6)$. $5\sqrt{5}$

26. Find y such that the distance between $(2, y)$ and $(7, -5)$ is $\sqrt{29}$. -3 or -7

■ PRACTICE FOR COLLEGE ENTRANCE TESTS

Each question consists of two quantities, one in column A and one in column B. Compare the two quantities and select one of the following answers:

A   if the quantity in column A is greater

B   if the quantity in column B is greater

C   if the two quantities are equal

D   if the relationship cannot be determined from the information given

Comments:

● Letters such as a, b, x, and y are variables that can be replaced by real numbers.

● A symbol that appears in both columns in a question stands for the same thing in column A as in column B.

● In some questions information that applies to quantities in both columns is centered above the two columns.

	Column A	*Column B*	
1.	The length of the hypotenuse of a right triangle with legs of lengths 1 and 3	The length of the hypotenuse of a right triangle with legs of lengths 2 and 2	A
2.	$\sqrt{a} = \sqrt{b}$		
	ab	b^2	C
3.	$a > 0, b > 0$		
	$\sqrt{a + b}$	$\sqrt{a} + \sqrt{b}$	B
4.	$3x \leq 15$		
	$2x \geq 10$		
	x	5	C

	Column A	Column B	

5.

A, B, and C are vertices of a cube.

The length of diagonal AB (not shown)	The length of diagonal BC (not shown)	C

6.

The length of the diagonal of a square with side 5.	7	A

7.

0.2	$\sqrt{0.4}$	B

8.

ABC is a right triangle with legs of length a.

The area of square $ACDE$	$2a^2$	C

9.

$$a > 0$$

$\sqrt{a}$	$\dfrac{a}{2}$	D

10.

$$y + \sqrt{8} = \sqrt{18}$$

y	2	B

11.

$$x > 0$$

$\sqrt{x}$	$\sqrt{x+1}$	B

12.

$3\sqrt{2}$	$2\sqrt{3}$	A

13.

$$0 < a < b = c$$

$\sqrt{ac}$	b	B

14.

For $x \neq 0$, let $\boxed{\nabla x} = \dfrac{x+1}{x}$

$\nabla{-1}$ ∇x $\nabla{-2}$

		B

CHAPTER OVERVIEW

Students learn to graph quadratic functions and use the graphs to solve quadratic equations. Students learn to solve quadratic equations by using square roots, by completing the square, and by using the quadratic formula. Students learn to use a part of the quadratic formula called the discriminant to determine the number and kind of roots of a quadratic equation. In this chapter, students use a combination of the algebra skills they acquired in Chapters 1, 2, 3, 4, 5, 7, 8, and 10.

In advanced algebra, solutions of quadratic equations will be extended to the complex numbers, a set of numbers that includes square roots of negative real numbers. Advanced algebra and later courses will address solutions of polynomial equations of degrees higher than two.

11 Solving Quadratic Equations

Under the influence of gravity, a projectile follows a curved path called a parabola. The height (h) of a projectile at any time (t) is described by a second-degree (quadratic) equation.

For example, the equation $h = 80t - 16t^2$ describes the height of an object t seconds after it has been projected upward at a speed of 80 feet per second.

Imagine that a pitcher throws a baseball upward at a speed of 80 feet per second from the rim of the Grand Canyon. If the baseball falls to the base of the canyon one mile below, how long is the ball in the air?

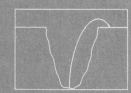

PURPOSE

To understand quadratic functions, it is important to be able to relate coefficients in the defining equation to characteristics of the graph of the function. Two important characteristics of the graph of a quadratic function (a parabola) are the equation of its axis of symmetry and the coordinates of its vertex.

11–1 Quadratic Functions

PREVIEW

Have students describe the pattern in the *Number of matches* column. The numbers increase by 1, 2, 3, 4, and so on. The pattern could easily be extended to find the number of matches for 6 players (15 matches), but it would be cumbersome to use that pattern to find the number of matches for 25 players (300 matches) or 100 players (4950 matches).

There are several ways to develop the formula given. One way is to say that each of the players (p) plays each of the other ($p - 1$) players for total of $p(p - 1)$ matches. But this counts each match twice. So the number of matches (M) is

$$M = \frac{p(p - 1)}{2} = \frac{p^2 - p}{2} = \frac{1}{2}p^2 - \frac{1}{2}p$$

Preview

The 25 members of a tennis club organized a round-robin tournament in which each player played against each of the other players. To find the number of required matches, one member looked at simpler problems and made a table.

Number of players	1	2	3	4	5	6	$\cdots$	25
Number of matches	0	1	3	6	10	?	$\cdots$	?

- How many matches would be played if there were only 6 players? 15
- Describe a way to find the number of matches to be played for all 25 players. As number of players increases by 1, number of matches increases by 1, 2, 3, 4, 5, . . . ,24.

Another tennis club member found an equation for the number of matches (M) for any number of players (p).

$$M = \frac{1}{2}p^2 - \frac{1}{2}p$$

- Does the equation give the results shown in the table? Yes
- Use the equation to find the number of matches required for 25 players. 300

Equations like the one above are called quadratic equations.

In this lesson you will learn about functions defined by quadratic equations.

■ LESSON

Polynomial equations of degree 2 are called **quadratic equations**. Here are examples of quadratic equations in two variables. In each equation, for a given value of x, there is a unique value of y. Therefore, each equation describes a function.

$$y = x^2 + 2x - 3 \qquad y = -2x^2 + 5x \qquad y = (x - 2)^2$$

$$y = x^2 + 6 \qquad y = \frac{1}{2}x^2 \qquad y - 5 = -3(x + 4)^2$$

The solution of each equation is the set of (x, y) number pairs that satisfies the equation. The set of solutions of each of the above equations is a **quadratic function**.

Emphasize that points of a parabola are joined by a smooth curve. If one point in the graph seems to be out of place, check the coordinates to determine whether there has been a computation error. The curve should be rounded at the vertex, not V-shaped.

It is visually difficult to determine that the domain of a quadratic function is the set of *all* real numbers. That is, no matter how great or small the number *n*, the parabola crosses the vertical line $x = n$; a parabola is infinitely "wide."

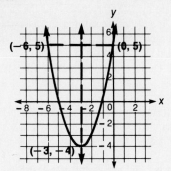

You may wish to expand on the symmetry of the parabola. For example, the parabola above has the minimum point $(-3, -4)$. The vertical line through the minimum point is the axis of symmetry. All other points of the parabola are in pairs. A segment joining the points of a pair is horizontal and bisected by the axis of symmetry. For example, one pair of such points is $(-6, 5)$ and $(0, 5)$. Note that both points are 3 units horizontally from and 9 units above the minimum point.

The equation of the axis of symmetry is stated without explanation. A detailed explanation will be possible after Section 11-4 on completing the square.

Definition: Quadratic Function

A *quadratic function* is a set of ordered pairs (x, y) described by an equation that can be written in the form

$$y = ax^2 + bx + c, \text{ where } a \neq 0.$$

Here is a table of some solutions of the equation $y = x^2 + 2x - 3$ and a graph of the function.

$$y = x^2 + 2x - 3$$

x	y
2	5
1	0
0	-3
-1	-4
-2	-3
-3	0
-4	5
-5	12

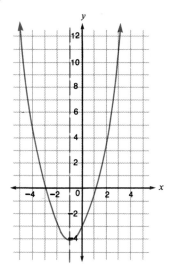

The graph of the equation is a **parabola**. Note these characteristics of the function and its graph.

- There is a "lowest" point, called the **minimum** of the function. The minimum of this quadratic function is $(-1, -4)$.
- The graph extends infinitely far up and to the right and left.
- If the graph is "folded" on the line $x = -1$, the two parts of the graph match each other. The line $x = -1$ is called the **axis of symmetry** of the function. The minimum is on the axis of symmetry.
- The graph crosses the *y*-axis at $(0, -3)$. The *y*-intercept is -3.
- The graph crosses the *x*-axis at $(-3, 0)$ and $(1, 0)$. The *x*-intercepts are -3 and 1.

By inspecting the *y*-values in the table, we can predict that $(-1, -4)$ is the minimum point and that the graph is symmetric about $x = -1$.

Example 1 Draw the graph of the quadratic function $y = -x^2 + 2x + 1$.

Solution To graph the function, first make a table of solutions. Then graph a point for each solution. Join the points with a smooth curve.

$$y = -x^2 + 2x + 1$$

x	y
3	-2
2	1
1	2
0	1
-1	-2
-2	-7

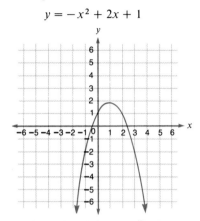

In Example 1 the function has a **maximum** point at $(1, 2)$. In general, a quadratic function described by the equation $y = ax^2 + bx + c$ has a *maximum* point if a is negative and a *minimum* point if a is positive.

The axis of symmetry is the line $x = 1$. The maximum or minimum point is always on the axis of symmetry.

Example 2 Graph the quadratic function $y = 2x^2 - 2x - 1$, and give the maximum or minimum point and the axis of symmetry.

Solution

$$y = 2x^2 - 2x - 1$$

x	y
3	11
2	3
1	-1
0	-1
-1	3
-2	11

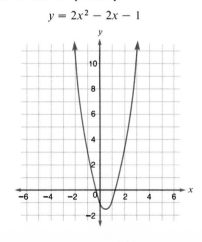

ADDITIONAL EXAMPLES

Example 1.

Draw the graph of the quadratic function $y = -x^2 - 2x + 1$.

x	y
-5	-14
-2	1
-1	2
0	1
3	-14

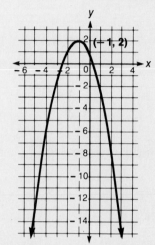

Noting the symmetry, students are best advised to plot the vertex first and then plot symmetric points on either side of that table entry.

Example 2. Graph $y = \frac{1}{2}x^2 - 2x - 1$ and give the maximum or minimum point and the axis of symmetry.

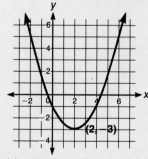

The minimum point is $(2, -3)$. The axis of symmetry is $x = 2$.

Example 3.

Give the axis of symmetry and the maximum or minimum point of $y = -\frac{1}{2}x^2 + 4x + 6$.

The axis of symmetry is $x = 4$. The maximum point is $(4, 14)$.

CHECK UNDERSTANDING

The following equations are in the form $y = ax^2 + bx + c$, $a \neq 0$. State the values of a, b, and c.

- $y = 7x^2 + 3x + 9$
  ($a = 7$, $b = 3$, $c = 9$)
- $y = -3x^2 - 8x + 4$
  ($a = -3$, $b = -8$, $c = 4$)
- $y = x^2 + 5$
  ($a = 1$, $b = 0$, $c = 5$)
- $y = x^2 - x$
  ($a = 1$, $b = -1$, $c = 0$)
- Is $y = x^2 + 3x - x^2 - 1$ the equation of a quadratic function? (No)

ADDITIONAL ANSWERS

■ **Written Exercises**

19. 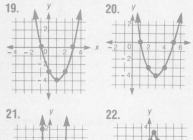 20.

21. 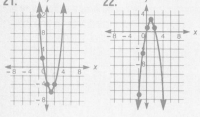 22.

Example 2 (continued)

A minimum point does not appear in the table. However, we can see that the axis of symmetry passes midway between the points $(1, -1)$ and $(0, -1)$.

The average of the x-values for these points is $\frac{1}{2}$. This means that the line of symmetry is $x = \frac{1}{2}$.

Now we can find the y-coordinate of the minimum point by substituting $\frac{1}{2}$ for x in the equation $y = 2x^2 - 2x - 1$.

$$y = 2\left(\frac{1}{2}\right)^2 - 2\left(\frac{1}{2}\right) - 1$$

$$y = -\frac{3}{2}$$

Answer The minimum point is $\left(\frac{1}{2}, -\frac{3}{2}\right)$. The axis of symmetry is the line $x = \frac{1}{2}$.

In general, the equation for the axis of symmetry of the quadratic function $y = ax^2 + bx + c$ is $x = -\frac{b}{2a}$, where $a \neq 0$.

Example 3 Give the axis of symmetry and the minimum or maximum point of the quadratic function $y = 3x^2 - 2x - 4$.

Solution The axis of symmetry is

$$x = -\frac{b}{2a}$$

$$x = -\frac{-2}{2 \cdot 3}$$

$$x = \frac{1}{3}$$

Substitute $\frac{1}{3}$ for x in the quadratic equation. $y = 3x^2 - 2x - 4$

$$y = 3\left(\frac{1}{3}\right)^2 - 2\left(\frac{1}{3}\right) - 4$$

$$y = \frac{1}{3} - \frac{2}{3} - 4$$

$$y = -\frac{13}{3}$$

Answer The axis of symmetry is $x = \frac{1}{3}$, and the minimum point is $\left(\frac{1}{3}, -\frac{13}{3}\right)$. The point $\left(\frac{1}{3}, -\frac{13}{3}\right)$ is a minimum, rather than a maximum, because the coefficient of x^2 in $y = 3x^2 - 2x - 4$ is positive.

■ CLASSROOM EXERCISES

The following quadratic equations can be written in the form $y = ax^2 + bx + c$.
State the values of a, b, and c.

1. $y = 3x^2 + 2x - 4$ 3, 2, −4

2. $y = -2x^2 - x + 5$ −2, −1, 5

3. $y = -x^2 + x$ −1, 1, 0

4. $y = 0.5x^2 - 6$ 0.5, 0, −6

5. $y = (x + 5)(x + 6)$ 1, 11, 30

6. $y = 2(x^2 - 7x - 1)$ 2, −14, −2

Give the axis of symmetry and the minimum or maximum point.

7. $y = x^2 - 6x + 5$ $x = 3$, minimum: (3, −4)

8. $y = x^2 + 3x - 1$ $x = -\frac{3}{2}$, minimum: $\left(-\frac{3}{2}, -\frac{13}{4}\right)$

9. $y = (x - 1)(x - 3)$ $x = 2$, minimum: (2, −1)

10. $y = (x + 4)^2$ $x = -4$, minimum: (−4, 0)

11. What kind of function is the equation $y = 0x^2 + 2x + 4$?   Linear

■ WRITTEN EXERCISES

State whether the equation describes a quadratic function.

A

1. $y = 5x + 3$ No

2. $y = 3x - 2$ No

3. $y = \frac{1}{2}x^2 + 3x + 5$ Yes

4. $y = \frac{1}{3}x^2 + 2x + 1$ Yes

5. $y = (x + 1)(x - 1)$ Yes

6. $y = (x - 3)(x + 3)$ Yes

7. $y = x^2 - x$ Yes

8. $y = 2x^2 - 2x$ Yes

9. $y = x(x + 5)$ Yes

10. $y = x(x + 1)$ Yes

11. $y = x^2 + x - x^2$ No

12. $y = x^2 - 3x - x^2$ No

Write each equation in the form $y = ax^2 + bx + c$. Then give the values of a, b, and c.

13. $y = x^2 + 2x + 3$ 1, 2, 3

14. $y = 3x^2 + x + 6$ 3, 1, 6

15. $y = -3x^2 + 2x$ −3, 2, 0

16. $y = -4x^2 + 3x$ −4, 3, 0

17. $y = (x + 2)(x + 4)$ $y = x^2 + 6x + 8$; 1, 6, 8

18. $y = (x + 3)(x + 6)$ $y = x^2 + 9x + 18$; 1, 9, 18

Copy and complete each table of solutions. Then graph the function.

19. $y = x^2 - 2x - 3$

x	−1	0	1	2	3
y	?	?	?	?	?

0, −3, −4, −3, 0

20. $y = x^2 - 6x + 5$

x	1	2	3	4	5
y	?	?	?	?	?

0, −3, −4, −3, 0

21. $y = 2x^2 - 4x - 4$

x	−2	−1	0	1	2
y	?	?	?	?	?

12, 2, −4, −6, −4

22. $y = -2x^2 + 4x + 1$

x	−2	−1	0	1	2
y	?	?	?	?	?

−15, −5, 1, 3, 1

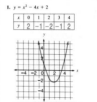
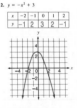

23.

24.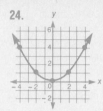

25.

26.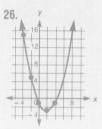

31.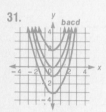

32.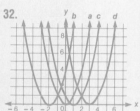

33. 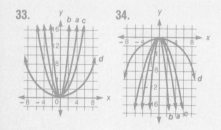   **34.**

Copy and complete each table of solutions. Then graph the function.

23. $y = \frac{1}{2}x^2$

x	-4	-2	0	2	4
y	?	?	?	?	?

8   2   0   2   8

24. $y = \frac{1}{4}x^2$

x	-4	-2	0	2	4
y	?	?	?	?	?

4   1   0   1   4

25. $y = \frac{1}{4}x^2 - x - 3$

x	-4	-2	0	2	4
y	?	?	?	?	?

5   0 -3 -4 -3

26. $y = \frac{1}{2}x^2 - 2x - 1$

x	-4	-2	0	2	4
y	?	?	?	?	?

15   5 -1 -3 -1

Give the axis of symmetry and the minimum or maximum point.

27. $y = x^2 - 2x - 3$ $x = 1$, minimum: $(1, -4)$

28. $y = x^2 - 6x + 5$ $x = 3$, minimum: $(3, -4)$

29. $y = 2x^2 + 3x - 2$ $x = -\frac{3}{4}$, minimum: $\left(-\frac{3}{4}, -\frac{25}{8}\right)$

30. $y = 2x^2 - 3x - 2$ $x = \frac{3}{4}$, minimum: $\left(\frac{3}{4}, -\frac{25}{8}\right)$

In each exercise, graph the four functions using the same coordinate axes. Label the graphs a, b, c, and d.

B **31.** **a.** $y = x^2$
   b. $y = x^2 + 2$
   c. $y = x^2 - 1$
   d. $y = x^2 - 3$

32. **a.** $y = x^2$
   b. $y = (x + 2)^2$
   c. $y = (x - 1)^2$
   d. $y = (x - 3)^2$

33. **a.** $y = x^2$
   b. $y = 3x^2$
   c. $y = \frac{1}{2}x^2$
   d. $y = 0.1x^2$

34. **a.** $y = -x^2$
   b. $y = -2x^2$
   c. $y = -\frac{1}{2}x^2$
   d. $y = -0.1x^2$

35. Describe how the value of c in the equation $y = x^2 + c$ affects the graph of the function. (See Exercise 31.)   The greater c is, the higher the graph is.

36. Describe how the value of h in the equation $y = (x - h)^2$ affects the graph of the function. (See Exercise 32.)   The greater h is, the farther to the right the graph is.

37. Describe how the value of a in the equation $y = ax^2$ affects the graph of the function when a is positive. (See Exercise 33.)
The greater a is, the narrower the graph is.

38. Describe how the value of a in the equation $y = ax^2$ affects the graph of the function when a is negative. (See Exercise 34.)
The greater a is, the wider the graph is.

548

	axis	min.	max.	y-int.	x-int.
39.	$x = 2$	$(2, -2)$		6	1, 3
40.	$x = 1$	$(1, -8)$		-6	$-1, 3$
41.	$x = 2$	$\left(2, -\frac{9}{2}\right)$		$-\frac{5}{2}$	$-1, 5$
42.	$x = 2$		$\left(2, \frac{9}{2}\right)$	$\frac{5}{2}$	$-1, 5$
43.	$x = -2$	$(-2, -1)$		3	$-3, -1$
44.	$x = -1$	$(-1, -4)$		-3	$-3, 1$

For each exercise, copy and complete the table of solutions, graph the function, give the axis of symmetry, the minimum or maximum point, the y-intercept, and the x-intercepts.

39. $y = 2x^2 - 8x + 6$

x	-1	0	1	2	3	4	5
y	?	?	?	?	?	?	?

16 6 0 -2 0 6 16

40. $y = 2x^2 - 4x - 6$

x	-2	-1	0	1	2	3	4
y	?	?	?	?	?	?	?

10 0 -6 -8 -6 0 10

41. $y + \frac{9}{2} = \frac{1}{2}(x - 2)^2$

x	-1	0	1	2	3	4	5
y	?	?	?	?	?	?	?

0 $-\frac{5}{2}$ -4 $-\frac{9}{2}$ -4 $-\frac{5}{2}$ 0

42. $y - \frac{9}{2} = -\frac{1}{2}(x - 2)^2$

x	-1	0	1	2	3	4	5
y	?	?	?	?	?	?	?

0 $\frac{5}{2}$ 4 $\frac{9}{2}$ 4 $\frac{5}{2}$ 0

43. $y = (x + 3)(x + 1)$

x	-5	-4	-3	-2	-1	0	1
y	?	?	?	?	?	?	?

8 3 0 -1 0 3 8

44. $y = (x + 3)(x - 1)$

x	-4	-3	-2	-1	0	1	2
y	?	?	?	?	?	?	?

5 0 -3 -4 -3 0 5

45. Is it possible for a parabola to lie entirely in one quadrant? in two quadrants? in three quadrants? in four quadrants? No, yes, yes, yes

46. Is it possible for the graph of a quadratic function to have two y-intercepts? no y-intercepts? No, no

47. Is it possible for the graph of a quadratic function to have three x-intercepts? one x-intercept? no x-intercepts? No, yes, yes

C **48.** Graph the function $M = \frac{1}{2}p^2 - \frac{1}{2}p$ (described in the Preview) for this set of values of p: {0, 1, 2, 3, 4, 5}. The graph for Exercise 48 consists of only 6 points.

49. How does the graph in Exercise 48 differ from the graph of $y = \frac{1}{2}x^2 - \frac{1}{2}x$?

[*Hint:* The variable x can be any real number. The variable p is restricted to what kind of numbers?] p must be a whole number.

Answer these questions about the quadratic function $y = ax^2 + bx + c$, where $a \neq 0$.

50. What is the y-intercept? c

51. What are the coordinates of the minimum (or maximum) point?

$\left[Hint: \text{The point is on the line } x = -\frac{b}{2a}. \right]$ $\left(-\frac{b}{2a}, \frac{-b^2 + 4ac}{4a} \right)$

39.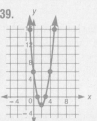

40.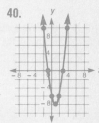

41.

42.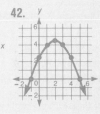

43.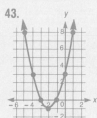

44.

48.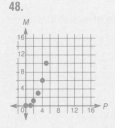

Emphasis placed on the symmetry of quadratic graphs can help students better relate table values to important curve characteristics. For example, consider this table:

x	−3	−2	−1	0	1	2	3	4
y	12	5	0	−3	−4	−3	0	5

The table displays some coordinate pairs satisfying the quadratic function $y = x^2 - 2x - 3$. Rather than plot points from left to right in the table, a student should take a moment to inspect the table. Since the x-values are written in increasing order, the y-values can be examined for graph information. Clearly the y-values occur symmetrically on either side of −4 (smallest y-value). Therefore, the vertex of the parabola occurs at (1, −4) and is a minimum. The axis of symmetry is $x = 1$. We also note two x-intercepts and one y-intercept. The x-intercepts (occurring when $y = 0$) are important in the next lesson; they are solutions of the quadratic equation $0 = x^2 - 2x - 3$.

ENRICHMENT PROBLEM

- The axis of symmetry of the parabola $y = ax^2 + bx + c$ is $x = -\dfrac{b}{2a}$. This means that the first coordinate of the minimum (maximum) point is $-\dfrac{b}{2a}$. Find the second coordinate of the point.

Substitute $-\dfrac{b}{2a}$ for x, then solve for y.

$$y = \frac{-b^2 + 4ac}{4a}$$

ADDITIONAL ANSWER

■ Review Exercise

3.
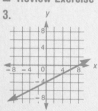

Answer these questions about the quadratic function $y = ax^2 + bx + c$, where $a \neq 0$.

52. Suppose that the minimum point is (3, −4) and that the graph crosses the x-axis at (0, 0). At what other point does the graph cross the x-axis? [*Hint:* Sketch the graph.] (6, 0)

53. Suppose that the minimum point is (3, −4) and that the graph crosses the x-axis at (1, 0). At what other point does the graph cross the x-axis? (5, 0)

54. Suppose that the minimum point is (3, −4) and that the graph crosses the x-axis at two points. Is *a* positive or negative? Positive

■ REVIEW EXERCISES

1. Simplify. $2x(x - 3) - x(2x + 4)$ $-10x$ [4–6]

2. Write the equation $2x - 3y = 6$ in slope–intercept form. $y = \frac{2}{3}x - 2$ [5–6]

3. Graph. $y = \frac{1}{2}x - 4$ [5–4]

4. Solve this system. $2x + 3y = 10$ ((2, 2))   [6–6]
$3x + 2y = 10$

5. Nuts that cost $4 per lb are mixed with nuts that cost $5 per lb. How many pounds of each kind must be used to obtain a 20-lb mixture worth $4.75 per lb? $4/lb:5, $5/lb:15   [6–7]

Factor completely.

6. $2x^2 - 50$ $2(x + 5)(x - 5)$ [7–4]

7. $2x^2 + 4x - 30$ $2(x + 5)(x - 3)$ [7–10]

8. Solve. $x^2 - 7x = 18$ (9, −2)   [7–9]

Mathematics and Your Future

Your teacher knows both your mathematical background and the courses that are offered in your school. He or she has probably also received feedback from former students about how well prepared they were for college, vocational school, or employment. Students rarely return to thank teachers for letting them slide by; they often thank teachers for motivating them to apply themselves. Talk to your teacher about mathematics and your future. You will gain useful information.

You may wish to spend two days on this section. Refer to the Pacing Chart.

Class Starter Quiz
on previous section

Answer these questions about the function $y = x^2 - 6x + 7$.

1. Is the function a quadratic function?   Yes
2. Complete the table of values.

x	−1	1	3	5
y				

14 2 −2 2

3. What are the coordinates of the minimum point? $(3, -2)$
4. What is the axis of symmetry? $x = 3$
5. Graph the function for $0 \le x \le 6$.

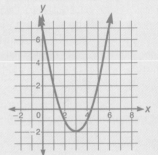

11–2 Solving Quadratic Equations by Graphing

Preview

The height h (in meters) of a projectile with an initial vertical velocity of 40 meters per second is given by the formula

$$h = -5t^2 + 40t,$$

where t is the number of seconds after launch.

- How many seconds after launch does the projectile return to the ground?   8
- How many seconds after launch is the projectile 60 m above the ground?   2 and 6

The graph of the function can be used to answer these questions.

In this lesson you will learn how to use graphs to solve quadratic equations.

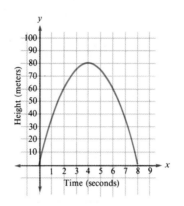

■ LESSON

In the study of linear functions, finding the y-intercept was helpful in determining the graph. Consider the equation $y = 2x - 4$, which is written in slope–intercept form $y = mx + b$. The y-intercept is the value of y when $x = 0$.

$$y = 2(0) - 4$$
$$y = -4$$

It is the constant term when the equation is in slope–intercept form.

Substitute other values for x to complete the table and graph the equation.

The x-intercept is the value of x when $y = 0$. The graph shows that the line crosses the x-axis at the point $(2, 0)$. Thus the x-intercept is 2.

$$y = 2x - 4$$

x	0	−1	3
y	−4	−6	2

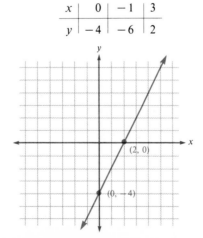

PURPOSE

Quadratic equations in one variable $ax^2 + bx + c = 0$ can be solved graphically by considering the equation as a special case of the function $ax^2 + bx + c = y$. The solutions of the given equation can be found by using the graph of the quadratic function to estimate x-intercepts.

PREVIEW

The graph of the formula should be used to answer the questions. Point out that in the questions, a value of h is given and the values of t are to be found. Note that $0 \le h \le 80$.

Finding the x-intercepts of a quadratic function by graphing is a special case of a more general problem. We could find the values of x for *any* given value of y. However, the process of finding the x-intercepts of a function can be used in the other cases as well. For example, to find the values of x for which y is 3 for the function $y = x^2 + 4x + 8$, you could find the x-intercepts of the function $y = x^2 + 4x + 5$. That is, $3 = x^2 + 4x + 8$ is equivalent to $0 = x^2 + 4x + 5$.

Finding non-integer solutions by graphing requires estimation and, in some instances, may not identify exact solutions. Graphing may clearly establish the existence of x-intercepts and provide reasonable approximations for their values. But exact solutions may not be possible until other methods are developed in the next sections.

ADDITIONAL EXAMPLES

Example 1.

Solve by graphing. $0 = \dfrac{1}{2}x^2 + x - 4$

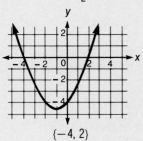

$\{-4, 2\}$

Consider the equation $y = x^2 - 2x - 3$.

The y-intercept is the value of y when $x = 0$.

$$y = (0)^2 - 2(0) - 3$$
$$y = -3$$

The y-intercept is the constant term c when the equation is in the form $y = ax^2 + bx + c$.

Substitute other values for x to complete the table and graph the equation.

x	y
-2	5
-1	0
0	-3
1	-4
2	-3
3	0

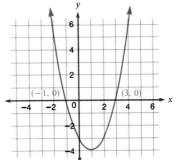

The x-intercepts are the values of x when $y = 0$. To find the x-intercepts we could let $y = 0$ and solve the equation $x^2 - 2x - 3 = 0$. However, since we have the graph of the equation $y = x^2 - 2x - 3$, we can determine the x-intercepts by noting where the graph crosses the x-axis. The graph crosses the x-axis at the points $(-1, 0)$ and $(3, 0)$, so the x-intercepts are -1 and 3.

Check by substituting these values in the equation $x^2 - 2x - 3 = 0$.

$$x^2 - 2x - 3 = 0 \qquad\qquad x^2 - 2x - 3 = 0$$
$$(-1)^2 - 2(-1) - 3 \overset{?}{=} 0 \qquad 3^2 - 2(3) - 3 \overset{?}{=} 0$$
$$1 + 2 - 3 \overset{?}{=} 0 \qquad\qquad 9 - 6 - 3 \overset{?}{=} 0$$
$$0 = 0 \quad \text{True.} \qquad\qquad 0 = 0 \quad \text{True.}$$

This example shows a method of solving quadratic equations in one variable: graph the related quadratic function and find the x-intercepts.

Example 1 Solve by graphing. $2x^2 - 7x + 3 = 0$

Solution The x-intercepts of the function $y = 2x^2 - 7x + 3$ are the solutions of the equation $0 = 2x^2 - 7x + 3$.

Graph the quadratic function $y = 2x^2 - 7x + 3$.

x	y
0	3
1	-2
2	-3
3	0
4	7

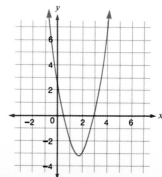

As an aid to developing understanding, frequently pose problems that are the "reverse" of the problems on which you are working. For example, give an equation and ask students to make up a problem for it. Or give a pair of numbers and ask students to make up a quadratic equation with those numbers as roots.

Example 1   (continued)

One of the x-intercepts of the function is 3. Another x-intercept is between 0 and 1, or approximately $\frac{1}{2}$. To check, substitute $\frac{1}{2}$ for x.

$$y = 2\left(\frac{1}{2}\right)^2 - 7\left(\frac{1}{2}\right) + 3$$

$$y = \frac{1}{2} - 3\frac{1}{2} + 3$$

$$y = 0$$

The other x-intercept of the function is $\frac{1}{2}$.

Answer $\left\{\frac{1}{2}, 3\right\}$

Example 2   Between which consecutive integers do the solutions of $x^2 - 4x - 1 = 0$ lie?

Solution   Graph the quadratic function $y = x^2 - 4x - 1$.

x	y
-1	4
0	-1
1	-4
2	-5
3	-4
4	-1
5	4

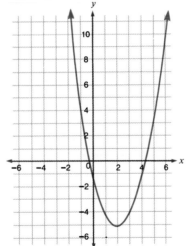

Answer   The x-intercepts are between -1 and 0 and between 4 and 5. Therefore, one of the solutions is between -1 and 0, and another is between 4 and 5.

■ CLASSROOM EXERCISES

Solve by graphing.

1. $x^2 - 3x + 2 = 0$ (1, 2)
2. $x^2 - 4 = 0$ $(2, -2)$
3. $x^2 - 4x + 4 = 0$ (2)

Example 2.

Between which consecutive integers do the solutions of $x^2 - 4x + 1 = 0$ lie?

> One solution is between 0 and 1 and another is between 3 and 4.

CHECK UNDERSTANDING

The equation of the graph is $y = x^2 + x - 12$.

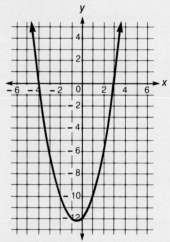

- State the solutions of $x^2 + x - 12 = 0$. $(\{-4, 3\})$
- State the solutions of $x^2 + x - 12 = -6$. $(\{-3, 2\})$

ADDITIONAL ANSWERS
■ Classroom Exercises

1.
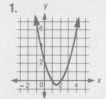

2.
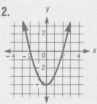

3.
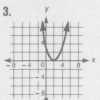

PRACTICE WORKSHEET 58

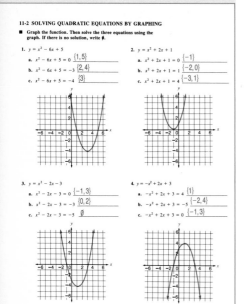

11-2 SOLVING QUADRATIC EQUATIONS BY GRAPHING

■ Graph the function. Then solve the three equations using the graph. If there is no solution, write ∅.

1. $y = x^2 - 6x + 5$
a. $x^2 - 6x + 5 = 0$ $\{1, 5\}$
b. $x^2 - 6x + 5 = -3$ $\{2, 4\}$
c. $x^2 - 6x + 5 = -4$ $\{3\}$

2. $y = x^2 + 2x + 1$
a. $x^2 + 2x + 1 = 0$ $\{-1\}$
b. $x^2 + 2x + 1 = 1$ $\{-2, 0\}$
c. $x^2 + 2x + 1 = 4$ $\{-3, 1\}$

3. $y = x^2 - 2x - 3$
a. $x^2 - 2x - 3 = 0$ $\{-1, 3\}$
b. $x^2 - 2x - 3 = -3$ $\{0, 2\}$
c. $x^2 - 2x - 3 = -5$ $\emptyset$

4. $y = -x^2 + 2x + 3$
a. $-x^2 + 2x + 3 = 4$ $\{1\}$
b. $-x^2 + 2x + 3 = -5$ $\{-2, 4\}$
c. $-x^2 + 2x + 3 = 0$ $\{-1, 3\}$

WRITTEN EXERCISES

In exercise 1a, point out that you are looking for the x-intercepts of the function $y = x^2 + 2x - 3$. That is, look for the first coordinates of the points where the parabola crosses the line $y = 0$ (the x-axis). Similarly in exercise 1b (and exercise 1c) look for the first coordinates of the points where the parabola crosses the line $y = -3$ (the line $y = -4$).

554

EXTRA PRACTICE, page 639

In the following exercises, use the graph of the function $y = ax^2 + bx + c$ to determine the number of real-number solutions (0, 1, or 2) of the quadratic equation $ax^2 + bx + c = 0$.

4. 2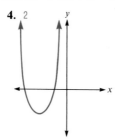

5. 1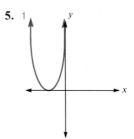

6. 0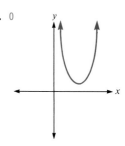

7. Use a graph of a quadratic function to find the consecutive integers between which the solutions of the equation $x^2 + 4x + 2 = 0$ lie. -3 and -4, 0 and -1

■ WRITTEN EXERCISES

For each exercise, graph the function. Then solve the three equations using the graph.

Ⓐ 1. $y = x^2 + 2x - 3$
a. $x^2 + 2x - 3 = 0$ $\{1, -3\}$
b. $x^2 + 2x - 3 = -3$ $\{0, -2\}$
c. $x^2 + 2x - 3 = -4$ $\{-1\}$

2. $y = x^2 + 4x + 3$
a. $x^2 + 4x + 3 = 0$ $\{-1, -3\}$
b. $x^2 + 4x + 3 = 3$ $\{0, -4\}$
c. $x^2 + 4x + 3 = -1$ $\{-2\}$

3. $y = x^2 - 6x + 8$
a. $x^2 - 6x + 8 = 0$ $\{2, 4\}$
b. $x^2 - 6x + 8 = 3$ $\{1, 5\}$
c. $x^2 - 6x + 8 = -1$ $\{3\}$

4. $y = x^2 - 4x + 3$
a. $x^2 - 4x + 3 = 0$ $\{1, 3\}$
b. $x^2 - 4x + 3 = 3$ $\{0, 4\}$
c. $x^2 - 4x + 3 = -1$ $\{2\}$

5. $y = -x^2 + 2x + 3$
a. $-x^2 + 2x + 3 = 0$ $\{3, -1\}$
b. $-x^2 + 2x + 3 = 3$ $\{0, 2\}$
c. $-x^2 + 2x + 3 = 4$ $\{1\}$

6. $y = -x^2 - 2x + 3$
a. $-x^2 - 2x + 3 = 0$ $\{1, -3\}$
b. $-x^2 - 2x + 3 = 3$ $\{0, -2\}$
c. $-x^2 - 2x + 3 = 4$ $\{-1\}$

Solve by graphing. If there is no solution, write ∅.

7. $x^2 - 5x + 6 = 0$ $\{2, 3\}$

8. $x^2 - 3x + 2 = 0$ $\{1, 2\}$

9. $x^2 - 6x + 8 = 0$ $\{2, 4\}$

10. $x^2 - 4x + 3 = 0$ $\{1, 3\}$

11. $x^2 + 2x + 2 = 0$ $\emptyset$

12. $x^2 - 4x + 5 = 0$ $\emptyset$

Solve by graphing. State the consecutive integers between which the solutions lie.

13. $x^2 - 2x - 2 = 0$ 2, 3; -1, 0

14. $x^2 - 4x + 2 = 0$ 3, 4; 0, 1

15. $x^2 + 3x + 1 = 0$ -1, 0; -3, -2

16. $x^2 + x - 1 = 0$ 0, 1; -2, -1

17. $\frac{1}{2}x^2 - 2x + 1 = 0$ 3, 4; 0, 1

18. $\frac{1}{2}x^2 - 2x - 1 = 0$ 4, 5; -1, 0

Solve by graphing. Some solutions are not integers. Check your answers.

19. $2x^2 - 10x + 12 = 0$ $\{2, 3\}$

20. $2x^2 - 13x + 20 = 0$ $\left\{\frac{5}{2}, 4\right\}$

21. $3x^2 - x - 4 = 0$ $\left\{\frac{4}{3}, -1\right\}$

22. $2x^2 - 6x - 20 = 0$ $\{5, -2\}$

23. $4x^2 - 4x - 3 = 0$ $\left\{\frac{3}{2}, -\frac{1}{2}\right\}$

24. $6x^2 + x - 2 = 0$ $\left\{\frac{1}{2}, -\frac{2}{3}\right\}$

Use the graph in the Preview to answer Exercises 25 and 26. A projectile is launched with an initial vertical velocity of 40 m/s. After how many seconds will the projectile reach these heights?

25. 50 m   ≈ 1.5, ≈ 6.5   **26.** 70 m   ≈ 2.5, ≈ 5.5

Suppose that a projectile is launched with an initial velocity of 100 m/s. Its height h (in meters) after t seconds is given by the formula $h = -5t^2 + 100t$.

B **27.** Draw a graph of the function.

28. After how many seconds will the projectile return to the ground?   20

29. After how many seconds will the projectile reach its maximum height?   10

30. When will the projectile reach a height of 320 m?   4 s, 16 s

31. When will the projectile reach a height of 480 m?   8 s, 12 s

32. Estimate when the projectile will reach a height of 200 m.   2.25 s, 17.75 s

33. Estimate when the projectile will reach a height of 300 m.   3.5 s, 16.5 s

For each exercise, write an equation that fits the situation. Let x represent the number of meters in the width of the rectangle. Graph the related quadratic function. Use the graph to answer the question.

34. The length of a rectangle is 2 m more than the width. What is the width of the rectangle if its area is 11.25 m²?
[*Hint:* $x(x + 2) = 11.25$. Graph $y = x^2 + 2x - 11.25$.]   2.5 m

35. The length of a rectangle is 3 m more than the width. What is the width of the rectangle if its area is 8.64 m²?   1.8 m

36. A rectangle is twice as long as it is wide. Find the width of the rectangle if its area is 26 m².   About 3.6 m

Solve.

37. Bob wants to enlarge a 4-m by 1-m flower bed to twice its area by increasing the length and width by the same amount. By how much should each be increased?   By about 0.7 m

38. The altitude of a triangle is 1.5 cm less than the base. Find the altitude and base if the area of the triangle is 26 cm².   Altitude: 6.5 cm, base: 8 cm

The graphing method can be used to find the approximate solutions of any quadratic equation in one variable, but it does have some limitations. Describe the difficulties encountered in solving these equations by graphing.

C **39.** Equation: $8x^2 + 6x - 5 = 0$
Graph: $y = 8x^2 + 6x - 5$ Very narrow graph

40. Equation: $x^2 + 14x - 240 = 0$
Graph: $y = x^2 + 14x - 240$
Very wide graph

41. Equation: $x^2 + 3x - 1 = 0$
Graph: $y = x^2 + 3x - 1$ Approximate x-intercepts

42. Equation: $\frac{1}{8}x^2 - \frac{1}{4}x - 1 = 0$

Graph: $y = \frac{1}{8}x^2 - \frac{1}{4}x - 1$
Difficult to get table of values

Exercise 27–33 should be discussed in depth. These additional questions could be asked:

• Over what time interval is the projectile rising? ($0 < t < 10$)
• Over what time interval is the height of the projectile decreasing? ($10 < t < 20$)
• What is the height of the projectile when $t \le 0$ or $t \ge 20$? ($h = 0$)

ADDITIONAL ANSWERS
■ **Written Exercises**

1.   **2.**

3. 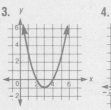   **4.**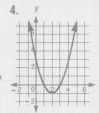

5. 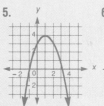   **6.**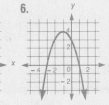

7. 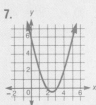   **8.**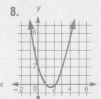

Graphs for exercises 9–24, 27, 34–36 are on pages 654 and 655.

CONCEPT EXTENSION

Care is needed to help students fully understand the relationship of the graph of a quadratic function, its table of values, and solving the corresponding quadratic equation. The projectile example of the Preview can be extended to enable students to understand these interrelationships.

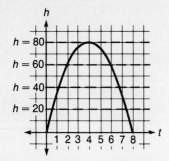

$$80 = -5t^2 + 40t$$

$$60 = -5t^2 + 40t$$

$$40 = -5t^2 + 40t$$

$$20 = -5t^2 + 40t$$

$$0 = -5t^2 + 40t$$

(*Note:* The coordinates are approximate values)

t	0	1	2	3	4	5	6	7	8
h	0	35	60	75	80	75	60	35	0

Discuss with students how information can be obtained from the graph.

• When is the projectile 50 meters high? (When *t* is about 1.6 and 6.4)
• Does the equation $90 = -5t^2 + 40t$ have any solutions? (No)

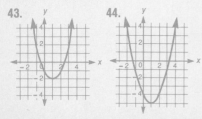
556

Solve by graphing. Estimate the solutions to the nearest tenth. Do not check.

43. $x^2 - 2x - 1 = 0$ (2.4, −0.4)

44. $x^2 - 2x - 4 = 0$ (3.2, −1.2)

45. $x^2 - 4x + 2 = 0$ (3.4, 0.6)

46. $x^2 + 6x + 6 = 0$ (−1.3, −4.7)

47. A farmer has 100 ft of fencing to make three sides of a rectangular pig pen beside the barn. The barn will serve as the fourth side. What should be the length and width of the pen in order to enclose the maximum area? [*Hint:* Let x be the width and $100 - 2x$ the length. If the area is y, then $y = x(100 - 2x)$. Graph this function.]   Length: 50 ft, width: 25 ft

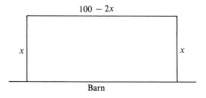

■ REVIEW EXERCISES

1. Which values of x are not admissible? $\dfrac{x-2}{x(x+1)}$ 0, −1   [8–1]

Simplify. Assume that no denominator is zero.

2. $\dfrac{2a}{5b} \cdot \dfrac{10b}{3c}$ $\frac{4a}{3c}$

3. $\dfrac{6(a+b)}{3} \div \dfrac{a^2 - b^2}{9}$ $\frac{18}{a-b}$ [8–2]

Solve.

4. $\dfrac{1}{5} = \dfrac{1}{R_1} + \dfrac{1}{10}$ (10)

5. $\dfrac{3}{5} = \dfrac{15}{x}$ (25)   [8–5]

6. $80\% = \dfrac{400}{x}$ (500)

7. $8 = x\%$ of 9 $\left\{88\frac{8}{9}\right\}$

8. A circuit is made up of a 10-ohm resistance and a 50-ohm resistance connected in parallel. What is the total resistance of the circuit? $\left(\text{Use the equation } \dfrac{1}{R} = \dfrac{1}{r_1} + \dfrac{1}{r_2}.\right)$ $8\frac{1}{3}\,\Omega$ [8–6]

9. One machine can complete a job in 8 h. Another machine can complete the job in 10 h. How long will it take both machines working together to complete the job? $4\frac{4}{9}$ h   [8–6]

10. If a coin is flipped 10 times and it comes up heads 7 times, what is the ratio of heads to tails for 10 flips? $\frac{7}{3}$ [8–7]

Find the missing length.   [10–3]

11.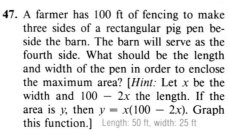

12.

Self-Quiz 1

11–1   **1.** Write the equation $y - 3 = (x - 2)(x + 5)$ in the form $y = ax^2 + bx + c$ and give the values of a, b, and c. $y = x^2 + 3x - 7;\ 1,\ 3,\ -7$

Given the quadratic function $y = x^2 + 4x + 1$.

2. Sketch its graph.

3. Give its axis of symmetry. $x = -2$

4. Give the maximum or minimum point, identifying which it is.
   Minimum: $(-2, -3)$

11–2   State the y-intercepts for these equations.

5. $y = x^2 - 5x + 6$ 6 **6.** $y = -x^2 - x + 2$ 2

7. $y = x^2 + 5x - 1$ **8.** $y = -x^2 - 3x + 1$

Solve by graphing. Write $\emptyset$ if there is no solution.

9. $2x^2 - 7x + 3 = 0$ $\left\{\frac{1}{2}, 3\right\}$ **10.** $x^2 + x + 4 = 0$ $\emptyset$

Solve.

11. The height h in meters of a rocket after t seconds is given by the formula $h = -5t^2 + 60t$. In how many seconds after its launch will the rocket return to the ground?   12

12. A rectangle is three times as long as it is wide. Find the width of the rectangle if its area is 27 m².   3 m

Mathematics and Your Future

People used to think that mathematics was necessary only for those who planned careers in such areas as science, engineering, and mathematics. However, with today's increasing use of computers and greater analysis of numerical data, knowledge of mathematics is important to those working in virtually every field. Mathematical applications in such fields as agriculture, business, home economics, and psychology can be expected to continue to grow. As you continue to study mathematics, you will be preparing yourself for opportunities in a wide range of fields.

ENRICHMENT PROBLEM

A line is *tangent to a curve* if it touches the curve at just one point and all other points of the curve are on the same side of the line.

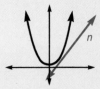

For example, line m is tangent to circle O and line n is tangent to the parabola $y = x^2$.

• Suppose points A, B, and C are on the parabola as shown.

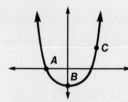

a. At what point does the slope of the tangent line to the curve at that point change from negative to positive?

   At point B, the minimum

b. What is the slope of the line tangent to the minimum point?

   The slope is 0.

ADDITIONAL ANSWERS

■ Self-Quiz 1

2.    **9.**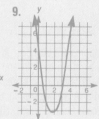

10.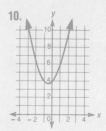

Graph the function. Then solve the three equations using the graph.

$$y = x^2 - 2x - 3$$

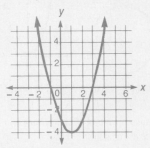

1. $x^2 - 2x - 3 = 0$ $\{-1, 3\}$
2. $x^2 - 2x - 3 = 5$ $\{-2, 4\}$
3. $x^2 - 2x - 3 = -4$ $\{1\}$

Solve by graphing. If there is no solution, write ∅.

4. $-x^2 + 3x - 2 = 0$ $\{1, 2\}$
5. $x^2 + 2x + 4 = 0$ ∅

PURPOSE

More than one technique is used to solve quadratic equations efficiently. The square root property is useful in solving some simple equations. It is also used in subsequent lessons to develop more general methods such as completing the square and the quadratic formula.

PREVIEW

Important advances in mathematics have been made by men and women representing many different cultures. The Preview mentions Arab and Hindu mathematicians; previous lessons have cited contributions of European and Chinese mathematicians. Impress upon students that mathematics is a world wide "language." Because of this, results discovered in one area of the world are easily transmitted to other countries around the globe.

11–3 Solving Quadratic Equations Using Square Roots

Preview **Historical note**

In A.D. 825 the Arab mathematician al-Khowarizmi wrote the first textbook on algebra. Its title was

ilm al-jabr wa'l muqabalah

which means roughly "the art of bringing together unknowns to match a known quantity." The key word in the title is "al-jabr," or "bring together," which became our word "algebra." Curiously, in those times, the term "algebraist" could refer either to someone who "brought bones together" (a surgeon) or to a specialist in equations.

The most significant problem left unanswered by al-Khowarizmi and his predecessors was how to interpret negative numbers. It is believed that the Hindus were among the first to realize that quadratic equations can have negative solutions. For instance, the equation $x^2 = 9$ has the solution $x = -3$ as well as the obvious solution $x = 3$.

You already know two methods of solving quadratic equations: factoring and graphing. In this lesson you will learn how to use the square root property of equations in solving quadratic equations.

■ LESSON

We can solve quadratic equations by factoring as shown in the following examples.

$$x^2 = 9$$
$$x^2 - 9 = 0$$
$$(x + 3)(x - 3) = 0$$
$$x + 3 = 0 \quad \text{or} \quad x - 3 = 0$$
$$x = -3 \quad \text{or} \quad x = 3$$

$$x^2 = 10$$
$$x^2 - (\sqrt{10})^2 = 0$$
$$(x + \sqrt{10})(x - \sqrt{10}) = 0$$
$$x + \sqrt{10} = 0 \quad \text{or} \quad x - \sqrt{10} = 0$$
$$x = -\sqrt{10} \quad \text{or} \quad x = \sqrt{10}$$

The symbol $\pm$ can be used to shorten the solutions to

$$x = \pm 3 \qquad\qquad x = \pm \sqrt{10}$$

Since both of the quadratic equations above are of the form $x^2 = c$, where $c > 0$, we can use a shorter method, called the **square root property of equations**, to solve them.

The Square Root Property of Equations

For each real number c, $c > 0$,

$$\text{if } x^2 = c, \text{ then } x = \pm\sqrt{c}.$$

Constantly review. Reviewing concepts deepens students' understanding of them and underscores their importance.

Remind students that the plus-or-minus sign ($\pm$) can be used to shorten a compound sentence such as "$x = 3$ *or* $x = -3$" to simply "$x = \pm 3$." The solutions of $x^2 = 9$ are 3 *and* -3; therefore $x = 3$ *or* $x = -3$. Emphasize that c cannot be negative in the statement of the square-root property of equations, "If $a^2 = c$, then $a = \pm\sqrt{c}$."

Applying this property gives the following.

$$\text{If } x^2 = 16, \text{ then } x = \pm 4.$$
$$\text{If } x^2 = 17, \text{ then } x = \pm\sqrt{17}.$$

There are many other quadratic equations that can be solved using this property.

Point out that decimals used to represent irrational numbers are approximations. If exact solutions are needed, radicals should be used. For example,

$$x^2 = 5$$
$$x = \pm\sqrt{5}$$
$$x \approx \pm 2.236$$

Example 1   Solve. $(x + 2)^2 = 9$

Solution

Use the square root property.

$$(x + 2)^2 = 9$$
$$x + 2 = \pm 3$$
$$x + 2 = 3 \quad \text{or} \quad x + 2 = -3$$
$$x = 1 \quad \text{or} \quad x = -5$$

Answer $\{1, -5\}$

Check

$(x + 2)^2 = 9$	$(x + 2)^2 = 9$
$(1 + 2)^2 \overset{?}{=} 9$	$(-5 + 2)^2 \overset{?}{=} 9$
$3^2 \overset{?}{=} 9$	$(-3)^2 \overset{?}{=} 9$
$9 = 9$ It checks.	$9 = 9$ It checks.

Example 1. Solve $(x - 5)^2 = 16$
$$\{1, 9\}$$

Example 2. Solve. $(x - 3)^2 = 13$
$$\{3 + \sqrt{13}, 3 - \sqrt{13}\}$$

Example 3. Solve. $x^2 + 10x + 25 = 4$
$$x^2 + 10x + 25 = 4$$
$$(x + 5)^2 = 4$$
$$x + 5 = \pm 2$$
$$x = -3 \text{ or } x = -7$$
$$\{-3, -7\}$$

Example 2   Solve. $(x - 3)^2 = 7$

Solution

$$(x - 3)^2 = 7$$
$$x - 3 = \pm\sqrt{7}$$
$$x - 3 = \sqrt{7} \quad \text{or} \quad x - 3 = -\sqrt{7}$$
$$x = 3 + \sqrt{7} \quad \text{or} \quad x = 3 - \sqrt{7}$$

Answer $\{3 + \sqrt{7}, 3 - \sqrt{7}\}$

Check

$(x - 3)^2 = 7$	$(x - 3)^2 = 7$
$[(3 + \sqrt{7}) - 3]^2 \overset{?}{=} 7$	$[(3 - \sqrt{7}) - 3]^2 \overset{?}{=} 7$
$(\sqrt{7})^2 \overset{?}{=} 7$	$(-\sqrt{7})^2 \overset{?}{=} 7$
$7 = 7$ It checks.	$7 = 7$ It checks.

Example 3   Solve. $x^2 - 2x + 1 = 4$

Solution

Factor the left side of the equation.
Use the square root property.

$$x^2 - 2x + 1 = 4$$
$$(x - 1)^2 = 4$$
$$x - 1 = \pm 2$$
$$x = 1 \pm 2$$
$$x = 3 \quad \text{or} \quad x = -1$$

Answer $\{3, -1\}$

Check   The check is left to the student.

Example 4. Solve. $x^2 = -9$

$\emptyset$. No real number squared is negative.

Example 5.

Solve. Write the solution as a decimal correct to the nearest thousandth. $(x + 2)^2 = 10$

$\{-5.162, 1.162\}$ (The exact solution is $\{-2 + \sqrt{10}, -2 - \sqrt{10}\}$.)

CHECK UNDERSTANDING

- Simplify 3 ± 5. (8 and -2)
- Solve $x^2 = 100$. ($\{-10, 10\}$)
- Solve $x^2 = 17$. ($\{-\sqrt{17}, \sqrt{17}\}$)

CLASSROOM EXERCISES

Point out the different types of solutions—for example, exercises 1 and 3 have two integer solutions, one positive and one negative; exercises 2 and 4 have two irrational solutions, one positive and one negative; exercise 5 has two irrational solutions, both positive; exercise 6 has no solution.

ASSIGNMENT GUIDE

Basic	1–47 odd, Review Exercises
Average	3–48 multiples of 3, 49–61 odd, Review Exercises
Enriched	3–60 multiples of 3, 63–68 all, Review Exercises

PRACTICE WORKSHEET 59

11-3 SOLVING QUADRATIC EQUATIONS BY USING SQUARE ROOTS

■ Solve. If the equation has no solution, write $\emptyset$.

1. $x^2 = 25$ $\{-5,5\}$
2. $(x + 10)^2 = 1$ $\{-11,-9\}$
3. $(x - 1)^2 = -100$ $\emptyset$
4. $4x^2 = 36$ $\{-3,3\}$
5. $x^2 - 12 = 37$ $\{-7,7\}$
6. $x^2 + 10 = 26$ $\{-4,4\}$
7. $\frac{1}{4}x^2 = 25$ $\{-10,10\}$
8. $x^2 + 5 = 4$ $\emptyset$
9. $2(x - 3)^2 = 242$ $\{-8,14\}$
10. $x^2 - 6x + 9 = 0$ $\{3\}$
11. $x^2 + 8x + 16 = 1$ $\{-5,-3\}$
12. $x^2 - 12x + 36 = -20$ $\emptyset$

Example 4 Solve. $(x - 4)^2 = -5$

Solution The square root property of equations cannot be used because the right side of the equation is negative.

Answer $\emptyset$. No real number squared is negative.

Example 5 Solve. $(x - 5)^2 = 5$

Write the solution as a decimal correct to the nearest thousandth.

Solution
$$(x - 5)^2 = 5$$
$$x - 5 = \pm \sqrt{5}$$
$$x = 5 \pm \sqrt{5}$$

Use a table of square roots or a calculator to approximate $\sqrt{5}$.

$$\sqrt{5} \approx 2.236 \qquad x \approx 5 \pm 2.236$$

Answer $\{7.236, 2.764\}$

■ CLASSROOM EXERCISES

Solve.

1. $x^2 = 25$ (± 5)
2. $x^2 = 6$ $(\pm \sqrt{6})$
3. $(x + 3)^2 = 16$ $(1, -7)$
4. $(x + 1)^2 = 5$ $(-1 \pm \sqrt{5})$
5. $x^2 - 6x + 9 = 8$ $(3 \pm 2\sqrt{2})$
6. $(x + 2)^2 = -2$ $\emptyset$

■ WRITTEN EXERCISES

Solve. If the equation has no solution, write $\emptyset$.

A
1. $x^2 = 49$ (± 7)
2. $x^2 = 81$ (± 9)
3. $(x - 2)^2 = 100$ $(12, -8)$
4. $(x - 3)^2 = 64$ $(11, -5)$
5. $x^2 = -81$ $\emptyset$
6. $x^2 = -16$ $\emptyset$
7. $(x + 5)^2 = 4$ $(-3, -7)$
8. $(x + 4)^2 = 1$ $(-3, -5)$
9. $(x + 3)^2 = -36$ $\emptyset$
10. $(x + 2)^2 = -25$ $\emptyset$
11. $(x - 9)^2 = 0$ (9)
12. $(x - 7)^2 = 0$ (7)
13. $3x^2 = 75$ (± 5)
14. $2x^2 = 72$ (± 6)
15. $x^2 + 22 = 122$ (± 10)
16. $x^2 + 26 = 170$ (± 12)
17. $2x^2 + 36 = 164$ (± 8)
18. $3x^2 + 42 = 150$ (± 6)
19. $4x^2 - 40 = 104$ (± 6)
20. $5x^2 - 30 = 50$ (± 4)
21. $4(x - 3)^2 = 36$ $(0, 6)$
22. $5(x - 2)^2 = 20$ $(0, 4)$
23. $4x^2 = 9$ $\left\{\pm \frac{3}{2}\right\}$
24. $9x^2 = 25$ $\left\{\pm \frac{5}{3}\right\}$
25. $x^2 + 6x + 9 = 100$ $(7, -13)$
26. $x^2 + 10x + 25 = 36$ $(1, -11)$
27. $x^2 - 12x + 36 = 4$ $(4, 8)$
28. $x^2 - 8x + 16 = 1$ $(3, 5)$
29. $x^2 - 20x + 100 = 0$ (10)
30. $x^2 - 16x + 64 = 0$ (8)

Solve. Write the solutions as simplified radicals.

31. $x^2 = 18$ $\{\pm 3\sqrt{2}\}$ **32.** $x^2 = 12$ $\{\pm 2\sqrt{3}\}$ **33.** $x^2 = 13$ $\{\pm \sqrt{13}\}$

34. $x^2 = 17$ $\{\pm \sqrt{17}\}$ **35.** $(x - 5)^2 = 7$ $\{5 \pm \sqrt{7}\}$ **36.** $(x - 7)^2 = 5$ $\{7 \pm \sqrt{5}\}$

37. $x^2 - 2x + 1 = 3$ $\{1 \pm \sqrt{3}\}$ **38.** $x^2 - 4x + 4 = 10$ $\{2 \pm \sqrt{10}\}$**39.** $x^2 + 8x + 16 = 8$ $\{-4 \pm 2\sqrt{2}\}$

40. $x^2 + 6x + 9 = 27$ $\{-3 \pm 3\sqrt{3}\}$**41.** $(2x - 1)^2 = 6$ $\left\{\dfrac{1 \pm \sqrt{6}}{2}\right\}$ **42.** $(3x - 2)^2 = 11$ $\left\{\dfrac{2 \pm \sqrt{11}}{3}\right\}$

Solve. Write the solutions as decimals to the nearest thousandth.

43. $(x - 2)^2 = 5$ $\{4.236, -0.236\}$ **44.** $(x - 3)^2 = 7$ $\{0.354, 5.646\}$ **45.** $(x + 3)^2 = 70$ $\{5.367, -11.367\}$

46. $(x + 2)^2 = 60$ $\{5.746, -9.746\}$ **47.** $(x - 1.1)^2 = 10$ $\{4.262, -2.062\}$ **48.** $(x - 2.1)^2 = 90$ $\{11.587, -7.387\}$

Write an equation that fits the situation. Solve the equation and answer the question. Write the solutions as simplified radicals.

49. A lot in the shape of a square has an area of 400 m². What is the length of each side of the square? 20 m

50. Each side of a square is increased by 5 cm in order to make a square with an area of 80 cm². What is the length of each side of the original square? $(-5 + 4\sqrt{5})$ cm

51. A square has an area of 50 cm². By how much should each of its sides be increased in order to double its area? $(10 - 5\sqrt{2})$ cm

52. A square has an area of 200 m². By how much should each of its sides be decreased in order to form a square with half the area of the original square? $(10\sqrt{2} - 10)$ m

53. A square garden has an area of 90 m². How long is the fence that completely encloses the garden? $12\sqrt{10}$ m

54. A square room has a ceiling area of 14 m². How many meters of trim are needed to cover the edges where the ceiling joins the wall? $4\sqrt{14}$ m

Solve. Write the solution as a decimal correct to the nearest thousandth.

55. The distance d in feet that an object falls in t seconds is given by the formula $d = 16t^2$. How long will it take an object to fall 1000 ft? 7.906 s

56. If the square of 3 more than a number equals 10, what is the number? 0.162 or −6.162

57. A number is subtracted from 50 and the difference is squared. If the result is 100, what is the number? 40 or 60

58. The area of a circle is 100π cm². If the area is doubled, how much is added to the circumference? 26.026 cm (Answer will vary with values used for $\sqrt{2}$ and π.)

Solve. Write the solutions as simplified radicals.

59. $x^2 + 7x + 6 = 7x + 24$ $\{\pm 3\sqrt{2}\}$ **60.** $x^2 + 9x + 10 = 9x + 34$ $\{\pm 2\sqrt{6}\}$

61. $(x + 2)(x - 5) = 3(6 - x)$ $\{\pm 2\sqrt{7}\}$ **62.** $(x + 6)(x - 2) = 4(x + 9)$ $\{\pm 4\sqrt{3}\}$

CONCEPT EXTENSION

The equation $(x - 4)^2 = -5$ (Example 4) cannot be solved by using the square-root property. Understanding a new idea can often be enhanced by considering examples that do not "fit" a new definition or technique. A worthwhile learning activity is to have students propose examples for the following table through class discussion.

Quadratic Equations		
Solvable by square-root property	Not solvable by square-root property	Why not solvable?

For example, the following equations are not solvable by using the square-root property:

$(x - 2)^2 = -3$ (The equation has no real-number solutions.)

$(x - 3)^2 + x = 6$ (The equation is not in the form $(x + m)^2 = n$.)

ENRICHMENT PROBLEM

- Change each of these equations to an equivalent equation that can be solved by using the square-root property. Then solve the equation.

  a. $x^2 + 4x = -4$
  b. $x^2 + 4x = -3$
  c. $x^2 + 4x = 6$

  a. $x^2 + 4x + 4 = 0$
  $(x + 2)^2 = 0$; $\{-2\}$
  b. $x^2 + 4x + 4 = -3 + 4$
  $(x + 2)^2 = 1$; $\{-1, -3\}$
  c. $x^2 + 4x + 4 = 6 + 4$
  $(x + 2)^2 = 10$; $\{-2 \pm \sqrt{10}\}$

Describe the values of k for which the equation has the given number of solutions.

C **63.** $x^2 = k$; 2 solutions $k > 0$ **64.** $x^2 = k$; 1 solution $k = 0$

65. $x^2 = k$; 0 solutions $k < 0$ **66.** $kx^2 = -2$; 2 solutions $k < 0$

67. $(x - k)^2 = 5$; 2 solutions Any real number   **68.** $(x - 5)^2 + k = 7$; 1 solution $k = 7$

■ REVIEW EXERCISES

Solve.

1. How much did Tom earn on $500 invested at 10% simple interest for two years? $100   [8–8]

2. Sarah answered 21 of 25 problems correctly on an algebra test. What percent of the problems did she answer correctly? 84%   [8–9]

3. If Isabel can ride her bike 10 km in 40 min, how far will she ride at the same rate in 2 h? 30 km   [8–9]

4. Does y vary directly as x if $10y = 25x$? Yes   [8–10]

5. If Henri solves 10 problems in 15 minutes, how long should it take him to complete a 30-problem assignment if he is solving at the same rate? 45 min   [8–10]

6. Suppose x and y vary inversely. If $y = 12$ when $x = 4$, what is the value of y when $x = 6$? 8   [8–11]

7. The electrical current I varies inversely as the resistance R. If the current is 5 amperes when the resistance is 20 ohms, what is the current when the resistance is 50 ohms? 2 amperes   [8–11]

8. Evaluate $x^2 + 2x - 3$ for these values of x.   [10–4]

   a. $x = -1 + \sqrt{5}$ 1   **b.** $x = -1 - \sqrt{5}$ 1

9. Evaluate $x^2 - 3x + 1$ for these values of x.   [10–4]

   a. $\dfrac{3 + \sqrt{33}}{2}$ 7   **b.** $\dfrac{3 - \sqrt{33}}{2}$ 7

Mathematics and Your Future _____

There tend to be more desirable job opportunities in positions that require a strong background in mathematics. Even in times of high unemployment, many higher-level jobs remain unfilled because of a lack of applicants with the necessary qualifications. Those qualifications often include a sound knowledge of mathematics. If you continue to take mathematics in high school you will be in a better position to compete for the best job opportunities.

562

To solve quadratic equations by completing the square.

You may wish to spend two days on this section. Refer to the Pacing Chart.

11–4 Solving Quadratic Equations by Completing the Square

Preview Historical note

More than 2500 years ago the Greeks had already made great discoveries in geometry. Some of their discoveries were related to algebra, although they did not have the notation that we use today. For example, whereas we might write the algebraic expression $x^2 + 2xy$, the Greek mathematicians might represent the quantity geometrically as shown at the right.

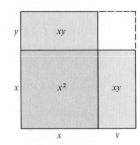

- What are the dimensions of the small square at the upper right that completes the square? y by y
- What are the dimensions of the sides of the completed square? (x + y) by (x + y)
- Write the area of the completed square as the square of a binomial. $(x + y)^2$

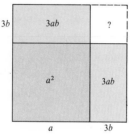

How would you answer the questions above for the geometric representation of $a^2 + 6ab$? 3b by 3b; (a + 3b) by (a + 3b); $(a + 3b)^2$

In this lesson you will learn another method of solving quadratic equations: completing the square.

■ LESSON

Some quadratic equations can be solved by factoring, while some can be solved by graphing. But neither of these methods gives exact solutions for all quadratic equations.

In Section 11–3 we learned an interesting fact: It is possible to solve any quadratic equation that is in the form

$$(x + a)^2 = c, \quad c \geq 0$$

Furthermore, every quadratic equation that has real-number solutions can be written in that form. For example, consider the equation:

$$x^2 + 6x = 7$$

We would like to factor the left side as the square of a binomial. Unfortunately, the expression is not a perfect square. If the left side were

$$x^2 + 6x + 9$$

we could factor it as we wish. By adding 9 to the left side (and to the right side), we will have what we need.

$$x^2 + 6x + 9 = 7 + 9$$

PURPOSE

To solve any quadratic equation with real roots, a general technique is needed. Completing the square provides such a technique. Completing the square is the method used in the derivation of the quadratic formula that is presented in the next section.

PREVIEW

An overhead projector can be used to present the problems used in the Preview. Cut out a 10-cm by 10-cm square and two 10-cm by 5-cm rectangles for the first figure. For the second figure, use the 10-cm by 10-cm square and a 3-cm by 3-cm square.

LESSON

Completing the square is a powerful method because it can be used to solve any quadratic equation. It is not limited to special cases such as equations written in a certain form. In more advanced work (second-year algebra), completing the square will be used again to write standard-form equations for ellipses and hyperbolas.

This process is called **completing the square**. Now we can use the square root property of equations to solve the equation.

$$x^2 + 6x + 9 = 16$$
$$(x + 3)^2 = 16$$
$$x + 3 = \pm 4$$
$$x = 1 \quad \text{or} \quad x = -7$$

We can use completing the square to solve any quadratic equation.

To complete the square of any equation in the form $x^2 + bx = c$:

1. find $\frac{1}{2}$ of the coefficient of x: $\frac{b}{2}$;

2. square the result of step 1: $\left(\frac{b}{2}\right)^2$; and

3. add the result of step 2 to both sides of the equation.

Example 1 Solve by completing the square. $x^2 - 4x = -3$

Solution $x^2 - 4x = -3$

Complete the square: $\left(\frac{-4}{2}\right)^2 = 4.$ $x^2 - 4x + 4 = -3 + 4$

Factor. $(x - 2)^2 = 1$
$$x - 2 = \pm 1$$
$$x = 3 \quad \text{or} \quad x = 1$$

Answer $\{3, 1\}$

Check
$$x^2 - 4x = -3 \qquad\qquad x^2 - 4x = -3$$
$$3^2 - 4 \cdot 3 \stackrel{?}{=} -3 \qquad\quad 1^2 - 4 \cdot 1 \stackrel{?}{=} -3$$
$$9 - 12 \stackrel{?}{=} -3 \qquad\qquad 1 - 4 \stackrel{?}{=} -3$$
$$-3 = -3 \quad \text{It checks.} \qquad -3 = -3 \quad \text{It checks.}$$

Example 2 Solve by completing the square. $x^2 + 2x - 3 = 1$

Solution $x^2 + 2x - 3 = 1$

Collect constants on the right side. $x^2 + 2x = 4$
Complete the square. $x^2 + 2x + 1 = 4 + 1$
Factor. $(x + 1)^2 = 5$
$$x + 1 = \pm \sqrt{5}$$
$$x = -1 \pm \sqrt{5}$$

Answer $\{-1 + \sqrt{5}, -1 - \sqrt{5}\}$

Check   The check is left to the student.

The most commonly requested teaching materials are enrichment materials. Ideas for enrichment are often the subject of sessions at meetings of the National Council of Teachers of Mathematics and state and local councils.

Example 3   Solve. $x^2 - 3x + 1 = 7$

Solution

$$x^2 - 3x + 1 = 7$$

Collect constants on the right side. $x^2 - 3x = 6$

Complete the square. $x^2 - 3x + \dfrac{9}{4} = 6 + \dfrac{9}{4}$

Factor. $\left(x - \dfrac{3}{2}\right)^2 = \dfrac{33}{4}$

Simplify the radical. $x - \dfrac{3}{2} = \pm\sqrt{\dfrac{33}{4}}$

$$x - \dfrac{3}{2} = \pm\dfrac{\sqrt{33}}{2}$$

$$x = \dfrac{3}{2} \pm \dfrac{\sqrt{33}}{2}$$

$$x = \dfrac{3 \pm \sqrt{33}}{2}$$

Answer $\left\{\dfrac{3 + \sqrt{33}}{2}, \dfrac{3 - \sqrt{33}}{2}\right\}$

Check   The check is left to the student.

Example 4   Solve. $2x^2 + 8x = 9$

Solution

$$2x^2 + 8x = 9$$

Divide both sides by 2. $x^2 + 4x = \dfrac{9}{2}$

Complete the square. $x^2 + 4x + 4 = \dfrac{9}{2} + 4$

Factor. $(x + 2)^2 = \dfrac{17}{2}$

$$x + 2 = \pm\sqrt{\dfrac{17}{2}}$$

Simplify the radical. $x + 2 = \pm\sqrt{\dfrac{34}{4}}$

$$x + 2 = \pm\dfrac{\sqrt{34}}{2}$$

Solve for x. $x = -2 \pm \dfrac{\sqrt{34}}{2}$

Answer $\left\{-2 + \dfrac{\sqrt{34}}{2}, -2 - \dfrac{\sqrt{34}}{2}\right\}$

Check   The check is left to the student.

ADDITIONAL EXAMPLES

Example 3.

Solve. $x^2 - 7x - 5 = -3$

$$x^2 - 7x + \dfrac{49}{4} = 5 - 3 + \dfrac{49}{4}$$

$$\left(x - \dfrac{7}{2}\right)^2 = \dfrac{57}{4};$$

$$\left\{\dfrac{7}{2} \pm \dfrac{\sqrt{57}}{2}\right\}$$

Example 4.

Solve. $3x^2 + 6x = 8$

$$x^2 + 2x = \dfrac{8}{3}$$

$$x^2 + 2x + 1 = \dfrac{8}{3} + 1$$

$$(x + 1)^2 = \dfrac{11}{3};$$

$$\left\{-1 \pm \dfrac{\sqrt{33}}{3}\right\}$$

CHECK UNDERSTANDING

Is the expression the square of a binomial?

- $x^2 + 10x + 25$ (Yes)
- $x^2 - 10x + 25$ (Yes)
- $x^2 + 12x + 144$ (No)
- $x^2 + 5x + {}^{25}/_4$ (Yes)
- $x^2 - 2x - 1$ (No)

In exercises 1–3, emphasize that the number added is positive because the last term in the expansion of a squared binomial of the form $(x + a)^2$ is always positive (namely, a^2).

ASSIGNMENT GUIDE

Basic   1–35 odd, Review Exercises, Self-Quiz 2
Average 3–36 multiples of 3, 37–49 odd, Review Exercises, Self-Quiz 2
Enriched 3–48 multiples of 3, 50–56 all, Review Exercises, Self-Quiz 2

PRACTICE WORKSHEET 59

11-4 SOLVING QUADRATIC EQUATIONS BY COMPLETING THE SQUARE

■ Solve by completing the square. Write the solutions as simplified radicals.

1. $x^2 - 2x = 1$ $\{1 \pm \sqrt{2}\}$
2. $x^2 + 8x = 4$ $\{-4 \pm 2\sqrt{5}\}$
3. $x^2 - 10x = -13$ $\{5 \pm 2\sqrt{3}\}$
4. $x^2 + 7x = 0$ $\{-7, 0\}$
5. $x^2 - 3x = 1$ $\left\{\frac{3}{2} \pm \frac{\sqrt{13}}{2}\right\}$
6. $x^2 + 5x = 6$ $\{-6, 1\}$
7. $x^2 - 4x + 2 = 0$ $\{2 \pm \sqrt{2}\}$
8. $x^2 + 6x + 3 = 2$ $\{-3 \pm 2\sqrt{2}\}$
9. $x^2 - 24x + 150 = 26$ $\{12 \pm 2\sqrt{5}\}$
10. $x^2 - 20x + 96 = 2$ $\{10 \pm \sqrt{6}\}$
11. $x^2 + 40x + 350 = 0$ $\{-20 \pm 5\sqrt{2}\}$
12. $x^2 - x + \frac{1}{8} = \frac{7}{8}$ $\left\{-\frac{1}{2}, \frac{3}{2}\right\}$

EXTRA PRACTICE, page 640

These steps are used to solve a quadratic equation by completing the square.

1. Divide both sides of the equation by the coefficient of x^2. The coefficient of x^2 will then be 1.
2. Isolate the x^2- and x-terms on one side of the equation.
3. Add the square of half the coefficient of x to both sides.
4. Factor.
5. Use the square root property of equations.
6. Simplify all radicals.
7. Write the solutions.

■ CLASSROOM EXERCISES

What number added to the expression will complete the square?

1. $x^2 + 6x$ 9
2. $x^2 - 6x$ 9
3. $x^2 + 12x$ 36

What number must be added to both sides of the equation to complete the square?

4. $x^2 - 8x - 4 = 2$ 16
5. $x^2 + 3x - 5 = 1$ $\frac{9}{4}$
6. $x^2 + 7x = 10$ $\frac{49}{4}$

Solve by completing the square.

7. $x^2 + 4x = 12$ $(2, -6)$
8. $x^2 - 6x + 4 = 11$ $(7, -1)$
9. $3x^2 + 12x = 8$ $\left\{-2 \pm \frac{2\sqrt{15}}{3}\right\}$

■ WRITTEN EXERCISES

What number added to the expression will complete the square?

A 1. $x^2 + 10x$ 25
2. $x^2 + 8x$ 16
3. $x^2 - 6x$ 9
4. $x^2 - 12x$ 36
5. $x^2 + 5x$ $\frac{25}{4}$
6. $x^2 + 3x$ $\frac{9}{4}$

What number must be added to both sides of the equation to complete the square?

7. $x^2 - 4x = 3$ 4
8. $x^2 - 14x = 40$ 49
9. $x^2 + \frac{4}{5}x = 0$ $\frac{4}{25}$
10. $x^2 + \frac{2}{3}x = 0$ $\frac{1}{9}$
11. $x^2 - 8x = 6$ 16
12. $x^2 - 10x = 5$ 25

Solve by completing the square.

13. $x^2 + 10x = 11$ $(1, -11)$
14. $x^2 + 8x = 20$ $(2, -10)$
15. $x^2 - 6x = 16$ $(8, -2)$
16. $a^2 - 12a = 28$ $(14, -2)$
17. $x^2 - 6x + 12 = 4$ $(2, 4)$
18. $b^2 - 8b + 18 = 3$ $(3, 5)$
19. $t^2 + 5t + 10 = 4$ $(-2, -3)$
20. $p^2 + 3p + 1 = 5$ $(1, -4)$
21. $n^2 + 4n - 20 = 12$ $(4, -8)$
22. $x^2 + 4x - 8 = 4$ $(2, -6)$
23. $q^2 - 6q - 3 = 4$ $(7, -1)$
24. $x^2 - 8x - 20 = 13$ $(11, -3)$

• If possible, use *completing the square* to solve $5 + 4x - x^2 = 0$.

You can use completing the square to solve any quadratic equation.

$$5 + 4x - x^2 = 0$$
$$-x^2 + 4x + 5 = 0$$
$$x^2 - 4x = 5$$
$$x^2 - 4x + 4 = 9$$
$$(x - 2)^2 = 9$$
$$x - 2 = \pm 3$$
$$x = 5 \text{ or } x = -1$$
$$\{-1, 5\}$$

Solve by completing the square. Write the solutions as simplified radicals.

25. $x^2 + 4x = 14$ $(-2 \pm 3\sqrt{2})$

26. $x^2 + 6x = 15$ $(-3 \pm 2\sqrt{6})$

27. $x^2 - 10x = 15$ $(5 \pm 2\sqrt{10})$

28. $x^2 - 8x = 29$ $(4 \pm 3\sqrt{5})$

29. $x^2 - 20x + 25 = 0$ $(10 \pm 5\sqrt{3})$

30. $x^2 - 12x + 26 = 40$ $(6 \pm 5\sqrt{2})$

Solve by completing the square. Write the solutions as decimals correct to the nearest thousandth.

31. $x^2 - 6x = 17$ $(8.099, -2.099)$

32. $x^2 - 4x = 7$ $(5.317, -1.317)$

33. $x^2 + 8x - 3 = 66$ $(5.220, -13.220)$

34. $x^2 + 10x - 4 = 36$ $(3.062, -13.062)$

35. $x^2 - 7x + 2.25 = 16$ $(8.599, -1.599)$

36. $x^2 - 5x + 1.25 = 85$ $(11.987, -6.987)$

Write an equation that fits the problem. Then solve the equation by completing the square. Answer the question with a simplified radical.

B **37.** One positive number is 2 greater than another positive number. The product of the two numbers is 11. What is the smaller number?
$-1 + 2\sqrt{3}$

38. A rectangle is 10 cm longer than it is wide. Its area is 38 cm². What are the length and width of the rectangle? [*Note:* Both must be positive.]
$(5 + 3\sqrt{7})$ cm, $(-5 + 3\sqrt{7})$ cm

39. The length and width of a 5-cm by 7-cm rectangle are both increased by the same amount in order to form a rectangle with an area of 59 cm². By how much were the length and width increased? $(-6 + 2\sqrt{15})$ cm

Solve by completing the square.

40. $3x^2 - x = 2$ $\left\{1, -\frac{2}{3}\right\}$

41. $2x^2 + x = 15$ $\left\{\frac{5}{2}, -3\right\}$

42. $4x^2 + 8x + 1 = 4$ $\left\{-1 \pm \frac{\sqrt{7}}{2}\right\}$

43. $9x^2 + 18x - 3 = 4$ $\left\{\frac{1}{3}, -\frac{7}{3}\right\}$

44. $4x^2 - 12x - 2 = 25$ $\left\{\frac{9}{2}, -\frac{3}{2}\right\}$

45. $5x^2 + 5x + 1 = 0$ $\left\{\frac{-5 \pm \sqrt{5}}{10}\right\}$

46. $2x^2 - 6x + 1 = 0$ $\left\{\frac{3 \pm \sqrt{7}}{2}\right\}$

47. $3x^2 - 8x + 2 = 0$ $\left\{\frac{4 \pm \sqrt{10}}{3}\right\}$

48. $2x^2 - 8x - 3 = 0$ $\left\{\frac{4 \pm \sqrt{22}}{2}\right\}$

49. The base of a triangle is 4 cm more than its altitude. If the area of the triangle is 100 cm², find the base and altitude. $(2 + 2\sqrt{51})$ cm, $(-2 + 2\sqrt{51})$ cm

Solve by completing the square.

C **50.** $x^2 + 10x + c = 0$ Express the answer in terms of c. $-5 \pm \sqrt{-c + 25}$

51. $x^2 + bx + 2 = 0$ Express the answer in terms of b. $\dfrac{-b \pm \sqrt{b^2 - 8}}{2}$

52. $ax^2 + 6x + 3 = 0$ Express the answer in terms of a. $\dfrac{-3 \pm \sqrt{9 - 3a}}{a}$

53. $ax^2 + bx + c = 0$ Express the answer in terms of a, b, and c. $\dfrac{-b \pm \sqrt{b^2 - 4ac}}{2a}$

54. For Exercises 50–53, describe the restrictions on a, b, and c so that the equation has real-number solutions.
50. $c \geq 25$ **51.** $|b| \geq 2\sqrt{2}$ **52.** $a \leq 3$, $a \neq 0$ **53.** $a \neq 0$, $b^2 \geq 4ac$

2.
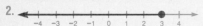

3.

4.

5.

The formula $h = vt - 5t^2$ gives the height in meters of an object projected vertically at v meters per second after t seconds. Solve and give the answer to the following to the nearest tenth of a second.

55. How long will it take an object projected vertically at a speed of 100 m/s to reach a height of 200 m?   2.3 s

56. How long will it take an object projected vertically at a speed of 50 m/s to reach a height of 100 m?   2.8 s

■ REVIEW EXERCISES

1. Write the inequality that is graphed on this number line. $x > -2$ [9–1]

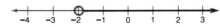

Graph on a number line.

2. $x \leq 3$ **3.** $x \neq 1$ [9–1]

4. $x \geq -3$ and $x \leq 0$ **5.** $x < 0$ or $x > 2$ [9–2]

Solve.

6. $x + 6 \leq 4$ $x \leq -2$ **7.** $2x - 5 < x + 4$ $x < 9$ [9–3]

Evaluate each of the expressions for the following values of a, b, and c.   [10–4]

i. $\dfrac{-b + \sqrt{b^2 - 4ac}}{2a}$ ii. $\dfrac{-b - \sqrt{b^2 - 4ac}}{2a}$

8. $a = 1$, $b = -2$, $c = -3$ **9.** $a = 2$, $b = -1$, $c = 5$ **10.** $a = 1$, $b = -6$, $c = 9$
i. 3   i. ∅   i. 3
ii. −1   ii. ∅   ii. 3

Self-Quiz 2

11–3   Solve. Write ∅ if there is no solution.

    1. $x^2 = 125$ $(\pm 5\sqrt{5})$ **2.** $(x + 6)^2 = 4$ $\{-4, -8\}$

    3. $y^2 + 49 = 0$ ∅   **4.** $y^2 - 14y + 49 = 100$ $(17, -3)$

11–4   Solve by completing the square.

    5. $x^2 + 8x - 4 = 0$ **6.** $y^2 - 3y + 1 = 0$ **7.** $2x^2 + 8x - 5 = 0$
       $\{-4 \pm 2\sqrt{5}\}$ $\left\{\dfrac{3 \pm \sqrt{5}}{2}\right\}$ $\left\{\dfrac{-4 \pm \sqrt{26}}{2}\right\}$

    8. One side of a square is increased by 3 cm. An adjacent side is decreased by 5 cm. The area of the rectangle formed is 32 cm². What is the length of a side of the original square? $(1 + 4\sqrt{3})$ cm

You may wish to spend two days on this
section. Refer to the Pacing Chart.

What must be added to both sides of the equation to complete the square?

1. $x^2 - 6x = 8$ 9
2. $x^2 + 10x + 15 = 3$ 10

Solve by completing the square.

3. $x^2 + 4x = 12$ {−6, 2}
4. $x^2 - 5x + 4 = -2$ {2, 3}
5. $x^2 + 6x + 1 = 5$ {−3 ± $\sqrt{13}$}

11-5 The Quadratic Formula

Preview

Suppose we wish to solve the following equations:

1. $(x - 3)^2 = 7$ **2.** $(x - 4)^2 = 9$ **3.** $(x - 5)^2 = 10$

These equations have the same form:

$$(x - h)^2 = k, \text{ where } k > 0$$

Each can be solved in exactly the same way. In such situations, mathematicians prefer to solve the general equation to obtain a "formula." The formula can then be used to solve any equation that has the form of the general equation.

$$(x - h)^2 = k$$
$$x - h = \pm \sqrt{k}$$
$$x = h \pm \sqrt{k}$$

- In equation 1, what are the values of h and k?   h = 3, k = 7
- In equation 2, what are the values of h and k?   h = 4, k = 9
- Use the formula to solve equations 1–3.   **1.** {3 ± $\sqrt{7}$} **2.** {1, 7} **3.** {5 ± $\sqrt{10}$}

In this lesson you will learn a formula that can be used to solve any quadratic equation in the form $ax^2 + bx + c = 0$.

PURPOSE

The expression of a general process (or algorithm) as a formula or equation makes the process easy to apply. Solutions to quadratic equations can be found in one step by making appropriate substitutions in the formula.

PREVIEW

In the previous section, all solutions of quadratic equations had a step in which one side of the equation was written as the square of a binomial and the other side as a constant.

In the general form $(x - h)^2 = k$, point out that h could be any real number and that k could be any nonnegative real number.

LESSON

Emphasize that the quadratic formula applies to all quadratic equations *written in a certain form*. The first step in using the formula is to check that the equation is in the form $ax^2 + bx + c = 0$. Most students should not be expected to develop the quadratic formula on their own. However, they should note that each step in the development of the formula uses a property with which they are already familiar.

■ LESSON

Instead of completing the square each time that we wish to solve a quadratic equation, we can solve the general form of a quadratic equation $ax^2 + bx + c = 0$ and obtain a formula for the solutions.

Consider this equation.	$ax^2 + bx + c = 0$
Isolate the x^2- and x-terms on one side of the equation.	$ax^2 + bx = -c$
Multiply both sides by $\frac{1}{a}$ so the coefficient of x^2 will then be 1.	$x^2 + \left(\frac{b}{a}\right)x = -\frac{c}{a}$
Complete the square by adding $\left(\frac{b}{2a}\right)^2$ to both sides of the equation.	$x^2 + \left(\frac{b}{a}\right)x + \left(\frac{b}{2a}\right)^2 = \left(\frac{b}{2a}\right)^2 - \frac{c}{a}$
Factor.	$\left(x + \frac{b}{2a}\right)^2 = \frac{b^2}{4a^2} - \frac{c}{a}$

CONCEPT EXTENSION

Developing the quadratic formula seems very abstract for most students. To aid their understanding, a specific example taken through the same steps as the general equation is helpful. This will also emphasize the quadratic formula as a generalization of the same completing-the-square process used in the preceding lesson.

Specific Example

$$2x^2 + 8x - 5 = 0$$
$$2x^2 + 8x = 5$$
$$x^2 + 4x = \frac{5}{2}$$
$$x^2 + 4x + 4 = \frac{5}{2} + 4$$

General Equation

$$ax^2 + bx + c = 0$$
$$ax^2 + bx = -c$$
$$x^2 + \frac{b}{a}x = -\frac{c}{a}$$
$$x^2 + \frac{b}{a}x + \frac{b^2}{4a^2} = -\frac{c}{a} + \frac{b^2}{4a^2}$$

ADDITIONAL EXAMPLES

Example 1.
Solve using the quadratic formula.
$$x^2 - 4x + 3 = 0 \quad \{1, 3\}$$

Example 2.
Solve using the quadratic formula.
$$3x^2 + 2x + 4 = 0 \quad \emptyset$$

Example 3.
Solve using the quadratic formula.
$$2x^2 + 1 = 7x + 4$$
$$2x^2 - 7x - 3 = 0$$
$$x = \frac{7 \pm \sqrt{49 + 24}}{4}$$
$$\left\{\frac{7 \pm \sqrt{73}}{4}\right\}$$

Subtract the fractions.

$$\left(x + \frac{b}{2a}\right)^2 = \frac{b^2 - 4ac}{4a^2}$$

Use the square root property of equations.

$$x + \frac{b}{2a} = \pm\sqrt{\frac{b^2 - 4ac}{4a^2}}$$

Simplify the radical.

$$x + \frac{b}{2a} = \pm\frac{\sqrt{b^2 - 4ac}}{2a}$$

Add $-\dfrac{b}{2a}$ to both sides.

$$x = -\frac{b}{2a} \pm \frac{\sqrt{b^2 - 4ac}}{2a}$$

Simplify the right side.

$$x = \frac{-b \pm \sqrt{b^2 - 4ac}}{2a}$$

The last equation is called the **quadratic formula**. This formula can be used to solve any quadratic equation.

The Quadratic Formula

If $ax^2 + bx + c = 0$, $a \neq 0$, then

$$x = \frac{-b \pm \sqrt{b^2 - 4ac}}{2a}.$$

Example 1 Solve using the quadratic formula. $x^2 - 2x - 3 = 0$

Solution

$$x = \frac{-b \pm \sqrt{b^2 - 4ac}}{2a}$$

Substitute 1 for a, -2 for b, and -3 for c in the quadratic formula.

$$x = \frac{-(-2) \pm \sqrt{(-2)^2 - 4 \cdot 1 \cdot (-3)}}{2 \cdot 1}$$

$$x = \frac{2 \pm \sqrt{4 + 12}}{2}$$

$$x = \frac{2 \pm \sqrt{16}}{2}$$

$$x = \frac{2 \pm 4}{2}$$

$$x = 3 \quad \text{or} \quad x = -1$$

Answer $\{3, -1\}$

Check The check is left to the student.

Promote student-student as well as student-teacher interactions during class discussions. For example, encourage students to listen and respond to each other by having students "field" other students' questions.

Example 2   Solve using the quadratic formula. $2x^2 - x + 5 = 0$

Solution

$$x = \frac{-b \pm \sqrt{b^2 - 4ac}}{2a}$$

Substitute 2 for *a*, -1 for *b*, and 5 for *c*. $x = \frac{-(-1) \pm \sqrt{(-1)^2 - 4(2)(5)}}{2(2)}$

$$x = \frac{1 \pm \sqrt{1 - 40}}{4}$$

$$x = \frac{1 \pm \sqrt{-39}}{4}$$

Since $\sqrt{-39}$ is not defined, there are no real-number solutions of the equation.

Answer $\emptyset$

Example 3   Solve using the quadratic formula. $x^2 + 4 = 6x - 5$

Solution $x^2 + 4 = 6x - 5$

Collect all terms on the left side. $x^2 - 6x + 9 = 0$

Use the quadratic formula. $x = \frac{-(-6) \pm \sqrt{(-6)^2 - 4(1)(9)}}{2(1)}$

$$x = \frac{6 \pm 0}{2}$$

$$x = 3$$

Answer $\{3\}$

Check   The check is left to the student.

The three examples above illustrate that quadratic equations may have zero, one, or two solutions.

■ CLASSROOM EXERCISES

Write each equation in the form $ax^2 + bx + c = 0$.

1. $2x^2 - 3x = 7$ $2x^2 - 3x - 7 = 0$ **2.** $3x^2 + 4 = x^2 + 6x$ $2x^2 - 6x + 4 = 0$ **3.** $x(x - 1) = 5(x + 2)$ $x^2 - 6x - 10 = 0$

What are the values of *a*, *b*, and *c*?

4. $5x^2 - 3x + 4 = 0$ $5, -3, 4$ **5.** $6x^2 - 2x = 0$ $6, -2, 0$ **6.** $3x^2 - 4 = 2x - 3$ $3, -2, -1$

Solve using the quadratic formula.

7. $3x^2 + 2x - 4 = 0$ $\left\{\frac{-1 \pm \sqrt{13}}{3}\right\}$ **8.** $x^2 - 3x + 6 = 0$ $\emptyset$ **9.** $2(2x^2 + 3) = 7$ $\left\{\pm\frac{1}{2}\right\}$

CHECK UNDERSTANDING

- Write the quadratic formula.
$$\left(x = \frac{-b \pm \sqrt{b^2 - 4ac}}{2a}\right)$$
- Is the equation $2x^2 - 5x - 7 = 9$ in the form necessary to determine *a*, *b*, and *c* in the quadratic formula? (No)
- What are the values of *a*, *b*, and *c* of the equation $-x^2 - 7x = 0$?   ($a = -1$, $b = -7$, $c = 0$)

CLASSROOM EXERCISES

In exercises 6 and 9, point out that the equation should first be written in the form $ax^2 + bx + c = 0$.

ASSIGNMENT GUIDE

Basic   1–35 odd, Review Exercises
Average   1–43 odd, 45–49 all, Review Exercises
Enriched   3–36 multiples of 3, 37–49 odd, 50–54 all, Review Exercises

PRACTICE WORKSHEET 60

11-5 THE QUADRATIC FORMULA

■ Solve using the quadratic formula. Simplify the solutions.

1. $x^2 + 6x + 4 = 0$ $\{-3 \pm \sqrt{5}\}$ 2. $x^2 - 5x + 1 = 0$ $\left\{\frac{5 \pm \sqrt{21}}{2}\right\}$

3. $x^2 + x - 4 = 0$ $\left\{\frac{-1 \pm \sqrt{17}}{2}\right\}$ 4. $2x^2 - 7x + 5 = 0$ $\left\{\frac{5}{2}, 1\right\}$

5. $3x^2 + 2x - 2 = 0$ $\left\{\frac{-1 \pm \sqrt{7}}{3}\right\}$ 6. $3x^2 + 4x - 5 = 0$ $\left\{\frac{-2 \pm \sqrt{19}}{3}\right\}$

7. $-2x^2 + 3x + 4 = 0$ $\left\{\frac{3 \pm \sqrt{41}}{4}\right\}$ 8. $-3x^2 + x + 1 = 0$ $\left\{\frac{1 \pm \sqrt{13}}{6}\right\}$

9. $x^2 + 10x + 9 = 0$ $\{-1, -9\}$ 10. $x^2 - 8x + 6 = 0$ $\{4 \pm \sqrt{10}\}$

11. $2x^2 - 4x + 1 = 0$ $\left\{\frac{2 \pm \sqrt{2}}{2}\right\}$ 12. $3x^2 - 2x - 2 = 0$ $\left\{\frac{1 \pm \sqrt{7}}{3}\right\}$

COMPUTER EXTENSION

Write a computer program that uses the quadratic formula to solve any equation of the form $ax^2 + bx + c = 0$.

```
10  PRINT "THIS PROGRAM SOLVES"
20  PRINT "QUADRATIC
    EQUATIONS"
30  PRINT "OF THE FORM"
40  PRINT "AX ∧ 2 + BX + C = 0"
50  PRINT
60  PRINT "ENTER A"
70  INPUT A
80  IF A < > 0 THEN 120
90  PRINT "WHEN A = 0 THE
    EQUATION"
100 PRINT "IS NOT A QUADRATIC"
110 GOTO 270
120 PRINT "ENTER B"
130 INPUT B
140 PRINT "ENTER C"
150 INPUT C
160 PRINT A; "X ∧ 2 +"; B;
    "X + "; C; "= 0";
170 D = B * B - 4 * A * C
180 IF D > = 0 THEN 210
190 PRINT "HAS NO REAL ROOTS"
200 GOTO 270
210 IF D > 0 THEN 240
220 PRINT "HAS ONE REAL ROOT,
    "; - B / (2 * A)
230 GOTO 270
240 PRINT "HAS TWO REAL ROOTS, "
250 PRINT ( - B + SQR (D))/
    (2 * A);" AND ";
260 PRINT ( - B - SQR (D))/
    (2 * A)
270 END
```

EXTRA PRACTICE, page 640

■ WRITTEN EXERCISES

Write each equation in the form $ax^2 + bx + c = 0$.

A 1. $x^2 + 5x = 2$ $x^2 + 5x - 2 = 0$ 2. $x^2 + 6x = 3$ $x^2 + 6x - 3 = 0$ 3. $2x^2 = x - 6$
$2x^2 - x + 6 = 0$

4. $2x^2 = 3x - 5$ $2x^2 - 3x + 5 = 0$ 5. $3x^2 + 5x = 6 - x$ 6. $4x^2 + x = x^2 + 2$
$3x^2 + 6x - 6 = 0$ $3x^2 + x - 2 = 0$

What are the values of a, b, and c?

7. $5x^2 + 7x + 2 = 0$ $5, 7, 2$ 8. $3x^2 + 6x + 2 = 0$ $3, 6, 2$ 9. $x^2 + x - 1 = 0$ $1, 1, -1$

10. $x^2 - x + 1 = 0$ $1, -1, 1$ 11. $2x^2 - 11 = 0$ $2, 0, -11$ 12. $3x^2 - 8x = 0$ $3, -8, 0$

13. $2 + 3x + x^2 = 0$ $1, 3, 2$ 14. $1 + 4x + 5x^2 = 0$ $5, 4, 1$ 15. $\frac{1}{2}x^2 - x - \frac{1}{3} = 0$
$\frac{1}{2}, -1, -\frac{1}{3}$

16. $\frac{1}{3}x^2 + x - \frac{1}{4} = 0$ $\frac{1}{3}, 1, -\frac{1}{4}$ 17. $x^2 = 5x + 2$ $1, -5, -2$ 18. $x^2 = 6x$ $1, -6, 1$

Solve using the quadratic formula. Simplify the solutions.

19. $x^2 + 2x - 15 = 0$ $\{3, -5\}$ 20. $x^2 - 2x - 15 = 0$ $\{5, -3\}$ 21. $5x^2 + 7x + 2 = 0$
$\left\{-\frac{2}{5}, -1\right\}$

22. $4x^2 + 9x + 2 = 0$ $\left\{-\frac{1}{4}, -2\right\}$ 23. $x^2 - 3x + 2 = 0$ $\{1, 2\}$ 24. $x^2 + 3x + 2 = 0$ $\{-1, -2\}$

25. $6x^2 + x - 2 = 0$ $\left\{\frac{1}{2}, -\frac{2}{3}\right\}$ 26. $6x^2 - 5x - 6 = 0$ $\left\{\frac{3}{2}, -\frac{2}{3}\right\}$ 27. $4x^2 - 4x - 3 = 0$ $\left\{\frac{3}{2}, -\frac{1}{2}\right\}$

28. $5x^2 - x - 4 = 0$ $\left\{1, -\frac{4}{5}\right\}$ 29. $x^2 - 10x + 25 = 0$ $\{5\}$ 30. $x^2 - 8x + 16 = 0$ $\{4\}$

31. $x^2 - 5x = 0$ $\{0, 5\}$ 32. $x^2 - 7x = 0$ $\{0, 7\}$

Solve. Give answers to the nearest thousandth.

33. $x^2 + 5x + 2 = 0$ $\{-0.438, -4.562\}$ 34. $x^2 + 6x + 2 = 0$ $\{-0.354, -5.646\}$

35. $x^2 + 2x - 5 = 0$ $\{1.449, -3.449\}$ 36. $x^2 + 3x - 1 = 0$ $\{0.303, -3.303\}$

Write the equation in the form $ax^2 + bx + c = 0$. Then solve the equation using the quadratic formula and simplify the solutions. Write $\emptyset$ if there are no solutions.

B 37. $3x^2 + 5x + 6 = 2x^2 + 4x + 7$ $\left\{\frac{-1 \pm \sqrt{5}}{2}\right\}$ 38. $5x^2 + 2x + 3 = 4x^2 - x + 4$ $\left\{\frac{-3 \pm \sqrt{13}}{2}\right\}$
$x^2 + x - 1 = 0;$ $x^2 + 3x - 1 = 0;$

39. $(2x + 3)(x + 4) = (x - 4)(x - 5)$ 40. $(2x - 3)(3x + 4) = 2x^2 - 12x + 11$
$x^2 + 20x - 8 = 0; \{-10 \pm 6\sqrt{3}\}$ $4x^2 + 11x - 23 = 0; \left\{\frac{-11 \pm \sqrt{489}}{8}\right\}$

41. $x^2 + 2x + 2 = 0$ $\emptyset$ 42. $x^2 + 2x + 10 = 0$ $\emptyset$

43. $-x^2 + 5x - 7 = 0$ $\emptyset$ 44. $x^2 + 4x + 1 = 3x^2 + 2x + 3$
$2x^2 - 2x + 2 = 0; \emptyset$

Write an equation that fits the problem. Solve the equation using the quadratic formula and answer the question.

45. One number is 2 more than another number. The product of the two numbers is 3. What are the two numbers? (There are two possibilities.)
$x(x + 2) = 3; 1, 3$ or $-1, -3$

46. The length of a rectangle is 10 cm greater than its width. What is the length of the rectangle if its area is 12 cm²? $l(l - 10) = 12; (5 + \sqrt{37})$ cm

47. The length of a rectangle is 10 cm greater than its width. What is the length of the rectangle if its diagonal is 11 cm? $l^2 + (l - 10)^2 = 11^2; \left(\frac{10 + \sqrt{142}}{2}\right)$ cm

• What part of the quadratic formula do you examine to determine whether an equation has real solutions, rational solutions, one solution?

$$b^2 - 4ac$$

• Can you write a rule for determining what kind of solutions the equation will have by looking at part of the quadratic formula?

If $b^2 - 4ac < 0$, there are no real-number solutions.

If $b^2 - 4ac = 0$, there is one rational solution.

If $b^2 - 4ac > 0$ and a perfect square, there are two rational solutions.

If $b^2 - 4ac > 0$ and not a perfect square, there are two irrational solutions.

48. A rectangular garden borders a building along the garden's length. The length of the garden is 2 m more than its width. The area of the garden is 16 m². How long is the fence that is needed to enclose the garden? (No fence is needed on the building side of the garden.)

$w(w + 2) = 16; (-1 + 3\sqrt{17})$ m

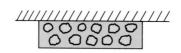

49. The surface area of a prism with a square base of side s and height h is given by the formula $S = 2s^2 + 4hs$. If the surface area is 200 square units and the height is 10, what is the length of the base?

$-10 + 10\sqrt{2}$

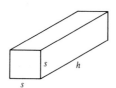

Find the two solutions of each equation, the sum of the solutions, and the product of the solutions.

	Equation	Smaller solution	Larger solution	Sum of solutions	Product of solutions
	Sample: $2x^2 + 5x - 2 = 0$	$\dfrac{-5 - \sqrt{41}}{4}$	$\dfrac{-5 + \sqrt{41}}{4}$	$-\dfrac{5}{2}$	-1
50.	$x^2 + 3x - 2 = 0$	$\dfrac{-3 - \sqrt{17}}{2}$	$\dfrac{-3 + \sqrt{17}}{2}$	-3	-2
51.	$3x^2 + 6x + 2 = 0$	$\dfrac{-3 - \sqrt{3}}{3}$	$\dfrac{-3 + \sqrt{3}}{3}$	-2	$\dfrac{2}{3}$
52.	$6x^2 - 7x + 2 = 0$	$\dfrac{1}{2}$	$\dfrac{2}{3}$	$\dfrac{7}{6}$	$\dfrac{1}{3}$
53.	$2x^2 - 11x + 12 = 0$	$\dfrac{3}{2}$	4	$\dfrac{11}{2}$	6
54.	$ax^2 + bx + c = 0$	$\dfrac{-b - \sqrt{b^2 - 4ac}}{2a}$	$\dfrac{-b + \sqrt{b^2 - 4ac}}{2a}$	$\dfrac{-b}{a}$	$\dfrac{c}{a}$

■ REVIEW EXERCISES

Solve. Graph the solution on a number line.

1. $3x - 4 > 4x - 7$ $x < 3$

2. $3x + 1 < 2x - 3$ $x < -4$ [9–3]

3. $-2x \le -6$ $x \ge 3$

4. $-4x > 12$ $x < -3$ [9–4]

5. $3(2 - x) > x$ $x < \dfrac{3}{2}$

6. $5x - 12 \le 8$ $x \le 4$ [9–5]

7. $|x + 1| > 3$ $x > 2$ or $x < -4$

8. $|x - 2| \le 1$ $1 \le x \le 3$ [9–6]

Graph the inequalities on the coordinate plane.

9. $x + 2y \le 4$ [9–7]

10. $x + y > 2$ and $y > 1$ [9–8]

 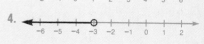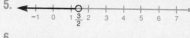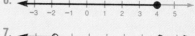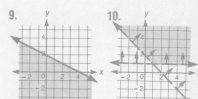

(If students are expected to have memorized the quadratic formula, the formula need not be stated.)
Solve using the quadratic formula: if $ax^2 + bx + c = 0$, then

$$x = \frac{-b \pm \sqrt{b^2 - 4ac}}{2a}$$

1. $x^2 + 5x + 4 = 0$ $\{-4, -1\}$
2. $x^2 - 8x - 20 = 0$ $\{-2, 10\}$

3. $x^2 + 5x + 1 = 0$ $\left\{\dfrac{-5 \pm \sqrt{21}}{2}\right\}$

4. $2x^2 - 3x - 1 = 0$ $\left\{\dfrac{3 \pm \sqrt{17}}{4}\right\}$

5. $x^2 + 4x + 6 = x + 9$ $\left\{\dfrac{-3 \pm \sqrt{21}}{2}\right\}$

PURPOSE

To avoid rote use of the quadratic formula, it is important to think of the expressions it generates. Some expressions can be simplified. Some name one number and others name two numbers. Some do not name any real number at all. Examination of the discriminant portion of the quadratic formula can indicate the number and nature of the roots of the quadratic equation. It can also provide information about the graph of the corresponding quadratic function.

PREVIEW

Remind students that the solutions of a quadratic equation in one variable are numbers, while the solutions of a quadratic equation in two variables are ordered pairs. The x-intercepts of the equation in two variables $y = ax^2 + bx + c$ are the solutions of the corresponding equation in one variable $0 = ax^2 + bx + c$.

The graph of $x^2 - 6x + 7 = 0$ on the number line identifies two points, $3 + \sqrt{2}$ and $3 - \sqrt{2}$. The x-intercepts of the graph of the function $y = x^2 - 6x + 7$ are the same points, $(3 + \sqrt{2}, 0)$ and $(3 - \sqrt{2}, 0)$.

To determine the number and nature of the roots of quadratic equations from the value of the discriminant.

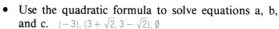

11–6 The Discriminant

Preview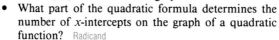

Recall that the solutions of these equations:

   a. $x^2 + 6x + 9 = 0$
   b. $x^2 - 6x + 7 = 0$
   c. $x^2 - 6x + 12 = 0$

are the x-intercepts of their respective functions:

   A. $y = x^2 + 6x + 9$
   B. $y = x^2 - 6x + 7$
   C. $y = x^2 - 6x + 12$

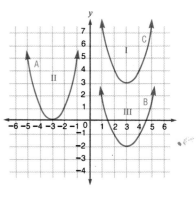

- Use the quadratic formula to solve equations a, b, and c. $(-3), (3 + \sqrt{2}, 3 - \sqrt{2}), \emptyset$
- Use your solutions to the equations to match functions A, B, and C with the graphs.   See above.
- What part of the quadratic formula determines the number of x-intercepts on the graph of a quadratic function?   Radicand

■ LESSON

The solutions of an equation are called the **roots** of the equation. The quadratic formula tells us that the roots of the equation $ax^2 + bx + c = 0$ are

$$\frac{-b + \sqrt{b^2 - 4ac}}{2a} \quad \text{and} \quad \frac{-b - \sqrt{b^2 - 4ac}}{2a}$$

The number and kind of roots of the equation depend on the value of the radicand, $b^2 - 4ac$. Four possibilities for the value of $b^2 - 4ac$ are shown in the following examples.

The value of $b^2 - 4ac$ is a positive perfect square, and there are two rational roots of the equation.

Example 1   Solve. $x^2 - 2x - 8 = 0$

     Solution $x = \dfrac{-(-2) \pm \sqrt{(-2)^2 - 4(1)(-8)}}{2(1)}$

                 $x = \dfrac{2 \pm \sqrt{36}}{2}$

                 $x = -2 \quad \text{or} \quad x = 4$

     Answer $\{-2, 4\}$

The value of $b^2 - 4ac$ is positive but not a perfect square, and there are two irrational roots.

Example 2   Solve. $2x^2 - 3x - 1 = 0$

Solution

$$x = \frac{-(-3) \pm \sqrt{(-3)^2 - 4(2)(-1)}}{2(2)}$$

$$x = \frac{3 \pm \sqrt{17}}{4}$$

Answer $\left\{ \dfrac{3 + \sqrt{17}}{4}, \dfrac{3 - \sqrt{17}}{4} \right\}$

The value of $b^2 - 4ac$ is 0, and there is one rational root.

Example 3   Solve. $x^2 - 4x + 4 = 0$

Solution

$$x = \frac{-(-4) \pm \sqrt{(-4)^2 - 4(1)(4)}}{2(1)}$$

$$x = \frac{4 \pm \sqrt{0}}{2}$$

$$x = 2$$

Answer $\{2\}$

The value of $b^2 - 4ac$ is negative, and there are no real roots of the equation.

Example 4   Solve. $x^2 + 3x + 5 = 0$

Solution

$$x = \frac{-3 \pm \sqrt{3^2 - 4(1)(5)}}{2(1)}$$

$$x = \frac{-3 \pm \sqrt{-11}}{2}$$

Answer $\emptyset$ There are no real roots.

Mathematics and Your Future

As we move from the industrial age into the information age, the number of jobs in the industrial sector are diminishing and the number in the information sector is increasing. Many of the new jobs in both the industrial and the information sectors require more education, including knowledge of mathematics. To prepare yourself for opportunities in the future, be sure that you take enough mathematics.

LESSON

The graphs in the Preview can be used to further analyze quadratic functions. If a quadratic function is written in the form $y = ax^2 + bx + c$, the values of its x-intercepts are $\dfrac{-b \pm \sqrt{b^2 - 4ac}}{2a}$. This expression can also be written $\dfrac{-b}{2a} \pm \dfrac{\sqrt{b^2 - 4ac}}{2a}$. The quantity $\dfrac{\sqrt{b^2 - 4ac}}{2a}$ is the distance the x-intercepts are to the left and right of the axis of symmetry.

Briefly review the definition of rational number. A *rational* number can be written in the form $\dfrac{m}{n}$ where m and n are integers, $n \neq 0$. An *irrational* number cannot be written in this form. Note that the discriminant is the expression $b^2 - 4ac$, not $\sqrt{b^2 - 4ac}$. It is the radicand, not the radical.

ADDITIONAL EXAMPLES

Example 1. Solve. $x^2 + 2x - 15 = 0$
$\{-5, 3\}$
Are the roots rational or irrational?
Rational

Example 2. Solve. $6x^2 - x - 12 = 0$
$\{-\frac{4}{3}, \frac{3}{2}\}$
Are the roots rational or irrational?
Rational

Example 3. Solve. $x^2 + 6x + 9 = 0$
$\{-3\}$
Are the roots rational or irrational?
One rational root

Example 4. Solve. $x^2 + 6x + 6 = 0$
$\{-3 \pm \sqrt{3}\}$
Are the roots rational or irrational?
Irrational

Example 5. Solve. $x^2 + 6x + 10 = 0$

∅. There are no real roots.

CHECK UNDERSTANDING

• State the formula for the discriminant.
  $(b^2 - 4ac)$
• When the discriminant is 0, there is one
  solution. Explain. (When the discriminant
  is 0, the quadratic formula gives the solutions as $\dfrac{-b \pm 0}{2a}$. The numbers $-b + 0$
  and $-b - 0$ are equal.)
• If the discriminant of a quadratic equation
  is 13, are the roots of the equation real
  numbers? (Yes) Are they rational or irrational? (Irrational)

CLASSROOM EXERCISES

Point out that the table of squares and
square roots on page 641 may be used to determine whether a discriminant is a perfect
square.

ASSIGNMENT GUIDE

Basic   1–37 odd, Review Exercises, Self-
         Quiz 3
Average 3–42 multiples of 3, 45–55 odd,
         Review Exercises, Self-Quiz 3
Enriched 3–54 multiples of 3, 57–62 all,
         Review Exercises, Self-Quiz 3

PRACTICE WORKSHEET 60

11-6 THE DISCRIMINANT

■ State the number and kind of roots for a quadratic equation
  with the given discriminant.

1. 64 _2 rational_   2. –4 _None_   3. 0 _1 rational_   4. 18 _2 irrational_

5. 0.16 _2 rational_ 6. 81 _2 rational_ 7. –25 _None_ 8. $\frac{1}{9}$ _2 rational_

■ Solve using the quadratic formula. Simplify all solutions. Write
  ∅ if there is no solution.

9. $6x^2 - 7x + 2 = 0$ $\left\{\frac{1}{2}, \frac{2}{3}\right\}$ 10. $x^2 - 8x + 16 = 0$ $\{4\}$

11. $3x^2 - 5x + 4 = 0$ ∅   12. $x^2 + 3x - 1 = 0$ $\frac{-3 \pm \sqrt{13}}{2}$

13. $2x^2 + 4x + 3 = 0$ ∅   14. $x^2 + x - 1 = 0$ $\frac{-1 \pm \sqrt{5}}{2}$

EXTRA PRACTICE, page 640

The expression $b^2 - 4ac$ is called the **discriminant**. Its value determines the
number and kind of roots of the equation. The table below summarizes the relationship between the value of the discriminant and the number and kinds of
real roots.

Value of discriminant $b^2 - 4ac$	Number of real roots of $ax^2 + bx + c = 0$	Kind of real roots (when a, b, and c are rational numbers.)
Positive and a perfect square	2	Rational
Positive but not a perfect square	2	Irrational
Zero	1	Rational
Negative	0	—

Example 5 Use the discriminant to find the number and kind of roots, and then
solve. $3x^2 + 2x - 5 = 0$

Solution Evaluate the discriminant. $b^2 - 4ac = 2^2 - 4(3)(-5)$
$$= 4 + 60$$
$$= 64$$

The value of the discriminant is a positive perfect square, so there are two
rational roots.

Use the quadratic formula to solve. $x = \dfrac{-b \pm \sqrt{b^2 - 4ac}}{2a}$

$$x = \dfrac{-2 \pm \sqrt{64}}{6}$$

$$x = \dfrac{-2 \pm 8}{6}$$

$$x = 1 \quad \text{or} \quad x = -\dfrac{5}{3}$$

Answer $\left\{1, -\dfrac{5}{3}\right\}$

■ CLASSROOM EXERCISES

1. What is the discriminant of the equation $ax^2 + bx + c = 0$? $b^2 - 4ac$

In each of Exercises 2–7, the value of the discriminant of a quadratic equation
is given. State the number and kind of roots.

2. Discriminant = 25 2, rational   **3.** Discriminant = 7 2, irrational   **4.** Discriminant = -9 None

5. Discriminant = 0 1, rational   **6.** Discriminant = 12 2, irrational   **7.** Discriminant = 100
2, rational

State the number and kind of roots.

8. $x^2 - 6x + 8 = 0$ 2, rational **9.** $x^2 - 6x + 7 = 0$ 2, irrational **10.** $x^2 + 6x + 10 = 0$ None

11. $9x^2 - 3x + 1 = 0$ None **12.** $x^2 + x + 1 = 0$ None **13.** $x^2 - 10x - 9 = 0$
2, irrational

14. $x^2 + 4x - 8 = 0$ 2, irrational **15.** $x^2 + 3x - 2 = 0$ 2, irrational **16.** $x^2 - 2x + 1 = 0$
1, rational

■ WRITTEN EXERCISES

Write the discriminant of each equation in simplest form.

A **1.** $x^2 - 2x + 3 = 0$ -8 **2.** $x^2 - 3x + 4 = 0$ -7

3. $x^2 - 3x - 4 = 0$ 25 **4.** $x^2 - 2x - 3 = 0$ 16

5. $x^2 - 4x + 4 = 0$ 0 **6.** $x^2 + 2x + 1 = 0$ 0

7. $4x^2 + 8x + 3 = 0$ 16 **8.** $4x^2 + 13x + 3 = 0$ 121

State the number and kind of roots for a quadratic equation with the given discriminant.

9. 100 2, rational **10.** 50 2, irrational **11.** 75 2, irrational **12.** 25 2, rational

13. -16 None **14.** -36 None **15.** 0 1, rational **16.** 3 2, irrational

17. 5 2, irrational **18.** 8 2, irrational **19.** 0.64 2, rational **20.** 0.16 2, rational

State the number and kind of roots.

21. $x^2 - 20x + 100 = 0$ 1, rational **22.** $x^2 + 20x + 100 = 0$ 1, rational

23. $x^2 + 20x - 100 = 0$ 2, irrational **24.** $x^2 - 20x - 100 = 0$ 2, irrational

25. $x^2 - 20x + 99 = 0$ 2, rational **26.** $x^2 + 20x + 99 = 0$ 2, rational

Solve using the quadratic formula. Simplify all solutions. If there is no solution, write ∅.

27. $x^2 + 8x + 6 = 0$ $\{-4 \pm \sqrt{10}\}$ **28.** $x^2 + 6x + 4 = 0$ $\{-3 \pm \sqrt{5}\}$

29. $x^2 + 6x - 4 = 0$ $\{-3 \pm \sqrt{13}\}$ **30.** $x^2 + 8x - 6 = 0$ $\{-4 \pm \sqrt{22}\}$

31. $x^2 + 6x + 10 = 0$ ∅ **32.** $x^2 + 5x + 8 = 0$ ∅

33. $x^2 - x - 6 = 0$ $\{3, -2\}$ **34.** $x^2 - x - 12 = 0$ $\{4, -3\}$

35. $3x^2 + x + 1 = 0$ ∅ **36.** $3x^2 - x + 2 = 0$ ∅

37. $4x^2 - 12x + 9 = 0$ $\{\frac{3}{2}\}$ **38.** $4x^2 - 4x + 1 = 0$ $\{\frac{1}{2}\}$

State the number of x-intercepts of each quadratic function.

B **39.** $y = x^2 + 6x + 100$ None **40.** $y = x^2 - 5x + 80$ None

41. $y = 5x^2 - 4x - 100$ 2 **42.** $y = 8x^2 - 5x - 80$ 2

43. $y = -2x^2 + 3x + 100$ 2 **44.** $y = -5x^2 + 2x + 80$ 2

CONCEPT EXTENSION

Effort should be made to consolidate students' understanding of quadratic functions, the relationship of roots and intercepts, and the nature of the discriminant. Questions of the following type can be helpful.

Graphs of equations of the form

$$y = ax^2 + bx + c$$

Graph A

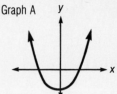

Graph B

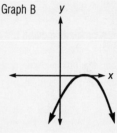

Graph C

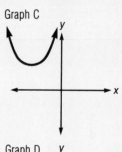

Graph D

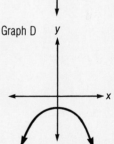

a. For which graph(s) will the discriminant of $ax^2 + bx + c = 0$ be negative? (C and D) Positive? (A) Zero? (B)

b. From each graph above, what can be determined about the nature and number of the roots of $ax^2 + bx + c = 0$? (A: 2 real roots; B: 1 real root; C and D: no real roots)

ENRICHMENT PROBLEM

- If an equation $ax^2 + bx + c = 0$ has one rational root, then $b^2 - 4ac = 0$ and $b = \pm 2\sqrt{ac}$.

  a. Suppose you wish to write a quadratic equation with *integer* coefficients and one *rational root*. What do you know about b that would help you determine its possible values?

  The value of b must be even. It could be positive or negative.

  b. What do you know about the values of a and c?

  The product of a and c is a perfect square, and the values of a and c agree in sign.

  c. Use your answer to parts a and b to write five equations that have integer coefficients and one rational root.

  For example, if $b = 6$, then
  $$6 = 2\sqrt{ac}$$
  $$3 = \sqrt{ac}$$
  So, $ac = 9$.
  Let $a = -3$ and $c = -3$.
  The equation is
  $$-3x^2 + 6x - 3 = 0.$$
  It has one rational root, {1}.

For what value of k ($k \neq 0$) will the equation have exactly one root?

45. $3x^2 + 4x + k = 0$ $\quad \frac{4}{3}$

46. $kx^2 + 2x + 5 = 0$ $\quad \frac{1}{5}$

47. $kx^2 - 2x + 5 = 0$ $\quad \frac{1}{5}$

48. $kx^2 + 2x - 5 = 0$ $\quad -\frac{1}{5}$

49. $3x^2 - 4x + k = 0$ $\quad \frac{4}{3}$

50. $3x^2 + 4x - k = 0$ $\quad -\frac{4}{3}$

For what values of k (if any) will the equation have two roots?

51. $3x^2 + 5x + k = 0$ $\quad k < \frac{25}{12}$

52. $3x^2 + 4x - k = 0$ $\quad k > -\frac{4}{3}$

53. $kx^2 + 4x + 3 = 0$ $\quad k < \frac{4}{3}$

54. $kx^2 + 4x - 3 = 0$ $\quad k > -\frac{4}{3}$

55. $4x^2 + kx + 4 = 0$ $\quad |k| > 8$

56. $3x^2 + kx - 3 = 0$ $\quad$ All values of k

Given $ax^2 + bx + c = 0$ and $a \neq 0$, is each of the following true or false?

C **57.** If $a > 0$ and $c < 0$, the equation has two roots. True

58. If $a < 0$ and $c > 0$, the equation has two roots. True

59. If $ac = b^2$, the equation has exactly one root. False

60. If $ac = \frac{1}{4}b^2$, the equation has exactly one root. True

Given $y = ax^2 + bx + c$ and $a \neq 0$, is each of the following true or false?

61. If $a > 0$ and $c < 0$, the graph crosses the x-axis twice. True

62. If $a < 0$ and $c > 0$, the graph crosses the x-axis twice. True

■ REVIEW EXERCISES

Simplify.

1. $\sqrt{\dfrac{9}{25}}$ $\quad \frac{3}{5}$

2. $-\sqrt{64}$ $\quad -8$

3. $\sqrt{75}$ $\quad 5\sqrt{3}$

4. $\sqrt{2}(\sqrt{2} + \sqrt{6})$ $\quad$ [10–1, 10–4]
$2 + 2\sqrt{3}$

Self-Quiz 3

11–5 Solve using the quadratic formula. Write $\emptyset$ if there is no solution.

    1. $x^2 - 6x + 3 = 0$ $\quad (3 \pm \sqrt{6})$
    2. $x(x + 5) = 1$ $\quad \left\{\dfrac{-5 \pm \sqrt{29}}{2}\right\}$

    3. $5x^2 + 10x = x^2 + x - 2$ $\quad \left\{-\dfrac{1}{4}, -2\right\}$
    4. $3x^2 + 7 = x^2 - 5x + 4$ $\quad \left\{-1, -\dfrac{3}{2}\right\}$

11–6 Use the discriminant to give the number and kind of roots.

    5. $16x^2 + 6x - 1 = 0$ $\quad$ 2, rational
    6. $x^2 - 2x + 7 = 0$ $\quad$ None

    For what values of k will the equation have one root?

    7. $x^2 + kx + 4 = 0$ $\quad 4, -4$
    8. $kx^2 - 6x + 1 = 0$ $\quad 9$

To solve quadratic equations using the most efficient method.

11–7 Choosing a Method of Solving Quadratic Equations

Preview

Five students in the Freedom High School algebra classes are specialists in solving quadratic equations.

Amy solves quadratic equations by using a graph.
Brad guesses the solutions and then checks his guesses.
Carla solves the equations by factoring.
David uses the method of completing the square.
Ellie applies the quadratic formula.

- Which students can solve any quadratic equation they are given? David, Ellie
- In a contest to determine who can solve quadratic equations fastest, who would probably finish first for each of these equations?

  a. $x^2 + 6x + 8 = 0$ Carla
  b. $x^2 + 4x = 6$ David

In this lesson you will study further the advantages of some of the methods of solving quadratic equations.

■ LESSON

We now know several methods of solving a quadratic equation including factoring, completing the square, graphing, and using the quadratic formula. Each time we wish to solve a quadratic equation we must choose one of the methods. We can, of course, use the quadratic formula for solving every quadratic equation. But in some cases one of the other methods may be easier to use.

When the coefficient of x^2 is 1 and the other coefficients are small, we can save time if the quadratic expression can be easily factored.

Example 1 Solve. $x^2 + x - 12 = 0$

Solution *Factoring*

$$x^2 + x - 12 = 0$$
$$(x + 4)(x - 3) = 0$$
$$x + 4 = 0 \quad \text{or} \quad x - 3 = 0$$
$$x = -4 \quad \text{or} \qquad x = 3$$

Quadratic formula

$$x^2 + x - 12 = 0$$

$$x = \frac{-b \pm \sqrt{b^2 - 4ac}}{2a}$$

$$x = \frac{-1 \pm \sqrt{1^2 - 4(1)(-12)}}{2(1)}$$

$$x = \frac{-1 \pm \sqrt{49}}{2}$$

$$x = \frac{-1 \pm 7}{2}$$

$$x = -4 \quad \text{or} \quad x = 3$$

Answer $\{-4, 3\}$

Class Starter Quiz
on previous section

Give the number (0, 1, or 2) and nature of the roots (rational or irrational).

1. $x^2 + 16x + 64 = 0$ 1; rational
2. $2x^2 + 6x + 3 = 0$ 2; irrational
3. $4x^2 - 12x + 9 = 0$ 1; rational

Solve using the quadratic formula. If there is no solution, write $\emptyset$.

4. $x^2 - 5x + 7 = 0$ $\emptyset$
5. $x^2 + 5x - 7 = 0$ $\left\{\dfrac{-5 \pm \sqrt{53}}{2}\right\}$

PURPOSE

Students should recognize the strengths and weaknesses of various methods when more than one method may be used. It is sensible to use the simplest, most efficient method for a given equation.

PREVIEW

There is no hard-and-fast rule about which method is most easily applied to a given quadratic equation. The choice of method depends to some extent on the equation and to some extent on the personal preference of the person who is solving the equation.

Discuss with the students the advantages and disadvantages of each method:

(1) Graphing provides a visual picture, but it is time-consuming and not well suited to exercises with solutions that are not integers.

(2) Guessing and checking provides an immediate verification of the accuracy of the solutions, but it is cumbersome to use when the solutions are not integers.

(3) Factoring is an efficient method to use when the expression is easily factored, but some expressions cannot be factored over the integers or rational numbers.

(4) Completing the square can be used to solve any quadratic equation, but the quadratic formula is usually more efficient.

(5) The quadratic formula can be used to solve any quadratic equation, but factoring is often easier and quicker for simple, factorable expressions.

LESSON

The choice of methods in solving quadratic equations comes down to these three: factoring, completing the square, and the quadratic formula. (Graphing and guess-and-check methods are too cumbersome.) Students may choose to use the quadratic formula for *every* quadratic equation. While this will provide solutions, it may be less efficient than factoring for some exercises.

ADDITIONAL EXAMPLES

Example 1. Solve. $x^2 - 3x - 18 = 0$

By factoring:
$x^2 - 3x - 18 = 0$
$(x - 6)(x + 3) = 0$
$x = 6$ or $x = -3$
$\{-3, 6\}$

Example 2. Solve. $x^2 + 18x = -76$

By completing the square:
$x^2 + 18x = -76$
$x^2 + 18x + 81 = -76 + 81$
$(x + 9)^2 = 5$
$x = -9 \pm \sqrt{5}$
$\{-9 \pm \sqrt{5}\}$

Example 3. Solve. $3x^2 - 5x + 1 = 0$

By the quadratic formula:
$3x^2 - 5x + 1 = 0$
$x = \dfrac{5 \pm \sqrt{25 - 12}}{6}$
$x = \dfrac{5 \pm \sqrt{13}}{6}$
$\left\{ \dfrac{5 \pm \sqrt{13}}{6} \right\}$

CHECK UNDERSTANDING

• Which methods can be used to solve every quadratic equation? (Completing the square and the quadratic formula)

CLASSROOM EXERCISES

In exercises such as 4, 5, and 6, students should carefully consider their choice of method but not use too much time in doing so. If factors are not apparent within 10–15 seconds, another method should be used.

In Example 1 the factoring method is shorter and involves less computation than using the quadratic formula.

If the coefficient of x^2 is 1 and the coefficient of x is even, completing the square may be easier.

Example 2 Solve. $x^2 + 20x - 8 = 0$

Solution *Completing the square*

$x^2 + 20x - 8 = 0$
$x^2 + 20x = 8$
$x^2 + 20x + 100 = 8 + 100$
$(x + 10)^2 = 108$
$x + 10 = \pm\sqrt{108}$
$x + 10 = \pm 6\sqrt{3}$
$x = -10 \pm 6\sqrt{3}$

Quadratic formula

$x^2 + 20x - 8 = 0$

$x = \dfrac{-20 \pm \sqrt{20^2 - 4(1)(-8)}}{2 \cdot 1}$

$x = \dfrac{-20 \pm \sqrt{432}}{2}$

$x = \dfrac{-20 \pm 12\sqrt{3}}{2}$

$x = -10 \pm 6\sqrt{3}$

Answer $\{-10 + 6\sqrt{3}, -10 - 6\sqrt{3}\}$

In Example 2 completing the square is easier than using the quadratic formula.

Remember that the quadratic formula can be used to solve any quadratic equation. If the coefficient of x^2 is not 1 or if the other constants are large, it may be the easiest method.

Example 3 Solve. $2x^2 - 3x - 6 = 0$

Solution $2x^2 - 3x - 6 = 0$

$x = \dfrac{-b \pm \sqrt{b^2 - 4ac}}{2a}$

$x = \dfrac{-(-3) \pm \sqrt{(-3)^2 - 4(2)(-6)}}{2(2)}$

$x = \dfrac{3 \pm \sqrt{57}}{4}$

Answer $\left\{ \dfrac{3 + \sqrt{57}}{4}, \dfrac{3 - \sqrt{57}}{4} \right\}$

Here is a suggested strategy for solving quadratic equations of the form

$$ax^2 + bx + c = 0, \qquad a \neq 0.$$

• If $a = 1$ and b and c are small integers, try factoring.
• If $a = 1$ and b is even, try completing the square.
• If the solution cannot be found quickly by either of the above methods, then use the quadratic formula.

Reinforcement and review are large parts of instruction. In particular, cumulative reviews help students see how individual lessons and units fit together into larger mathematical ideas. Therefore, it is important to take advantage of some of the many review features in the student text.

ASSIGNMENT GUIDE

Basic   1–35 odd, Review Exercises
Average   1–35 odd, 37–40 all, Review
          Exercises
Enriched 1–47 odd, Review Exercises

PRACTICE WORKSHEET 61

■ CLASSROOM EXERCISES

1. Solve by factoring. $x^2 + 7x - 8 = 0$ $(1, -8)$

2. Solve by completing the square. $x^2 + 24x + 9 = 0$ $(-12 \pm 3\sqrt{15})$

3. Solve by using the quadratic formula. $3x^2 + 4x - 3 = 0$ $\left\{ \dfrac{-2 \pm \sqrt{13}}{3} \right\}$

Solve.

4. $2x^2 + 5x - 4 = 0$ $\left\{ \dfrac{-5 \pm \sqrt{57}}{4} \right\}$ **5.** $x^2 + 8x + 2 = 0$ $(-4 \pm \sqrt{14})$ **6.** $x^2 + 8x - 16 = 0$
$(-4 \pm 4\sqrt{2})$

■ WRITTEN EXERCISES

Solve by factoring.

1. $x^2 - 3x - 28 = 0$ $(7, -4)$ **2.** $x^2 - 5x - 24 = 0$ $(8, -3)$ **3.** $x^2 - 9x + 18 = 0$ $(3, 6)$

4. $x^2 - 11x + 18 = 0$ $(2, 9)$ **5.** $x^2 + 15x + 14 = 0$ $(-1, -14)$ **6.** $x^2 + 16x + 15 = 0$
$(-1, -15)$

Solve by completing the square.

7. $x^2 + 4x = 6$ $(-2 \pm \sqrt{10})$ **8.** $x^2 + 6x = 4$ $(-3 \pm \sqrt{13})$ **9.** $x^2 - 8x = 5$ $(4 \pm \sqrt{21})$

10. $x^2 - 2x = 6$ $(1 \pm \sqrt{7})$ **11.** $x^2 - 12x + 12 = 0$ $(6 \pm 2\sqrt{6})$ **12.** $x^2 - 10x + 7 = 0$
$(5 \pm 3\sqrt{2})$

Solve by using the quadratic formula.

13. $x^2 + 5x - 4 = 0$ $\left\{ \dfrac{-5 \pm \sqrt{41}}{2} \right\}$ **14.** $x^2 + 7x - 4 = 0$ $\left\{ \dfrac{-7 \pm \sqrt{65}}{2} \right\}$ **15.** $3x^2 - 3x - 5 = 0$
$\left\{ \dfrac{3 \pm \sqrt{69}}{6} \right\}$

16. $3x^2 - 5x - 3 = 0$ $\left\{ \dfrac{5 \pm \sqrt{61}}{6} \right\}$ **17.** $5x^2 + 10x + 2 = 0$ **18.** $5x^2 + 10x + 4 = 0$
$\left\{ \dfrac{-5 \pm \sqrt{15}}{5} \right\}$ $\left\{ \dfrac{-5 \pm \sqrt{5}}{5} \right\}$

Solve by any method.

19. $x^2 - 3x = 0$ $(0, 3)$ **20.** $x^2 - 5x = 0$ $(0, 5)$ **21.** $x^2 - x - 1 = 0$ $\left\{ \dfrac{1 \pm \sqrt{5}}{2} \right\}$

22. $x^2 - x - 3 = 0$ $\left\{ \dfrac{1 \pm \sqrt{13}}{2} \right\}$ **23.** $x^2 + 6x + 8 = 0$ $(-2, -4)$ **24.** $x^2 + 4x + 3 = 0$ $(-1, -3)$

25. $4x^2 - 16x + 15 = 0$ $\left\{ \dfrac{3}{2}, \dfrac{5}{2} \right\}$ **26.** $4x^2 - 19x + 15 = 0$ $\left\{ 1, \dfrac{15}{4} \right\}$ **27.** $2x^2 + 3x - 1 = 0$
$\left\{ \dfrac{-3 \pm \sqrt{17}}{4} \right\}$

28. $3x^2 + 2x - 2 = 0$ $\left\{ \dfrac{-1 \pm \sqrt{7}}{3} \right\}$ **29.** $x^2 - 8x = 33$ $(11, -3)$ **30.** $x^2 - 6x = 27$
$(9, -3)$

Write an equation that fits the problem. Solve the equation and answer the question.

31. The length of a rectangle is 3 m more than its width. What is the length of the rectangle if its area is 3 m²? $l(l - 3) = 3; \dfrac{3 + \sqrt{21}}{2}$ m

32. The length of a rectangle is 2 m more than its width. What is the length of the rectangle if its area is 2 m²? $l(l - 2) = 2; (1 + \sqrt{3})$ m

33. The square of a number is 6 more than the number. What is the number? $n^2 = n + 6;$ 3 or -2

34. The square of a number is 12 more than the number. What is the number? $n^2 = n + 12;$ 4 or -3

COMPUTER EXTENSION

Write a computer program that gives the number and nature of the roots of a quadratic equation of the form $ax^2 + bx + c = 0$.

```
 5 PRINT "THIS PROGRAM GIVES
   THE "
10 PRINT "NUMBER AND NATURE
   OF ROOTS OF "
20 PRINT "QUADRATIC EQUATIONS
   OF "
30 PRINT " THE FORM "
40 PRINT "AX ∧ 2 + BX + C = 0"
50 PRINT
60 PRINT "ENTER A"
70 INPUT A
80 IF A < > 0 THEN 120
90 PRINT "WHEN A = 0 THE
   EQUATION "
100 PRINT "IS NOT A QUADRATIC."
110 GOTO 280
120 PRINT "ENTER B"
130 INPUT B
140 PRINT "ENTER C"
150 INPUT C
160 PRINT A; "X ∧ 2 + "; B;
    "X + "; C; " = 0";
170 D = B * B − 4 * A * C
180 IF D = 0 THEN 210
190 PRINT "HAS NO REAL ROOTS"
200 GOTO 280
210 IF D > 0 THEN 240
220 PRINT "HAS ONE RATIONAL
    ROOT"
230 GOTO 280
240 IF INT (SQR (D)) < >
    SQR (D) THEN 270
250 PRINT "HAS TWO RATIONAL
    ROOTS"
260 GOTO 280
270 PRINT "HAS TWO IRRATIONAL
    ROOTS"
280 END
```

EXTRA PRACTICE, page 640

35. Find the number such that its square is 3 more than the number. $n^2 = n + 3;\ \dfrac{1 \pm \sqrt{13}}{2}$

36. Find the number such that its square is 1 more than the number. $n^2 = n + 1;\ \dfrac{1 \pm \sqrt{5}}{2}$

B 37. The sum S of the first n positive integers is given by the formula $S = \dfrac{1}{2}n^2 + \dfrac{1}{2}n$. How many consecutive integers, starting with 1, were added if their sum is 2556? $2556 = \dfrac{1}{2}n^2 + \dfrac{1}{2}n;\ 71$

38. A vegetable garden is in the shape of a rectangle 6 m long and 4 m wide. It is surrounded by a border of flowers. What is the width of the border if the *total* area of the garden (including the flower border) is 30 m²? $(4 + 2x)(6 + 2x) = 30;\ \dfrac{-5 + \sqrt{31}}{2}$ m

39. A rocket shot in the air with a velocity of 24 m/s reaches a height of h meters in t seconds as given by the formula $h = -5t^2 + 24t$. After how many seconds is the rocket at each of the following heights?
   a. 10 m $\dfrac{12 \pm \sqrt{94}}{5}$ b. 20 m $\dfrac{12 \pm 2\sqrt{11}}{5}$ c. 25 m $\dfrac{12 \pm \sqrt{19}}{5}$ d. 30 m Never

40. What is the perimeter of a right triangle if its hypotenuse is 15 cm and one of its legs is 3 cm longer than the other leg? $x^2 + (x - 3)^2 = 15^2;\ 36$ cm

C 41. Two cars leave a gas station at the same time. One travels west at 55 mph and the other travels south at 45 mph. After how many hours are the two cars 100 mi apart? $(55t)^2 + (45t)^2 = 100^2;\ \dfrac{10\sqrt{202}}{101}$ h   42. $(3k)^2 + [3(k + 5)]^2 = 350^2;\ \dfrac{-15 + 5\sqrt{9791}}{6}$ km/h

42. Two cars leave the same place at the same time. One travels east at a constant speed. The other travels north at a speed that is 5 km/h faster than the other car. When they have driven for 3 h, the two cars are 350 km apart. What was the average speed of the slower car?

43. A number is 4 more than its reciprocal. Find the number. $n = 4 + \dfrac{1}{n};\ 2 + \sqrt{5}$ or $2 - \sqrt{5}$

44. The height h in meters of a rocket t seconds after it is fired upward with an initial velocity of 130 m/s is given by the formula $h = -5t^2 + 130t$. Find the maximum height reached by the rocket? [Hint: First find the axis of symmetry.] 845 m

Solve by any method.

45. $3(x + 2)(x + 1) = x(2x + 3) + 7$ $(-3 \pm \sqrt{10})$

46. $8x^2 - 12x - 3 = (2x - 1)(x - 3)$ $\left\{\dfrac{3}{2}, -\dfrac{2}{3}\right\}$

47. $(x^2 - 5x + 6)(x^2 - 5x + 5) = 0$ $\left\{2, 3, \dfrac{5 \pm \sqrt{5}}{2}\right\}$

48. $(x^2 - 7)x - (x^2 - 7)5 = 0$ $(5, \pm \sqrt{7})$

■ REVIEW EXERCISES

Simplify. List any restrictions on the variables.

1. $\sqrt{32} - \sqrt{18}$ $\;\sqrt{2}$

2. $4\sqrt{2} - \sqrt{2}$ $\;3\sqrt{2}$ [10–6]

3. $\sqrt{x^2}$ $\;|x|$

4. $\sqrt{12a^2b^3}$ $\;2|a|b\sqrt{3b},\ b \geq 0$ [10–7]

Solve.

5. $\sqrt{3x - 2} = 5$ $\;(9)$

6. $\sqrt{2x} + 4 = x$ $\;(8)$ [10–8]

Find the distance between the points. Simplify.

7. $(2, 5)$ and $(6, 8)$ $\;5$

8. $(-1, -1)$ and $(-2, 1)$ $\;\sqrt{5}$ [10–9]

Factor completely.

9. $x^2 + 5x - 14$ $\;(x + 7)(x - 2)$

10. $2x^2 + 5x + 2$ $\;(2x + 1)(x + 2)$ [7–9, 7–10]

■ CHAPTER SUMMARY

• **Vocabulary**

quadratic equation	[page 543]	x-intercept	[page 551]
quadratic function	[page 543]	completing the square	[page 564]
parabola	[page 544]	quadratic formula	[page 569]
minimum		roots of an equation	[page 574]
(of a quadratic function)	[page 544]	discriminant	[page 576]
axis of symmetry	[page 544]		
maximum			
(of a quadratic function)	[page 545]		

• The axis of symmetry of the function $y = ax^2 + bx + c\ (a \neq 0)$ is the line
$$x = -\frac{b}{2a}.$$

• The solutions of $ax^2 + bx + c = 0$ are the x-intercepts of the graph of $y = ax^2 + bx + c$.   [11–2]

• The Square Root Property of Equations   [11–3]

For each real number c, $c > 0$,
if $x^2 = c$, then $x = \pm\sqrt{c}$.

• The Quadratic Formula   [11–5]

If $ax^2 + bx + c = 0$, $a \neq 0$, then
$$x = \frac{-b \pm \sqrt{b^2 - 4ac}}{2a}.$$

ENRICHMENT PROBLEMS

• Write a quadratic equation that has $2 + \sqrt{5}$ and $2 - \sqrt{5}$ as roots.

If $x = 2 + \sqrt{5}$ and $x = 2 - \sqrt{5}$, then
$$(x - (2 + \sqrt{5}))(x - (2 - \sqrt{5})) = 0$$
$$((x - 2) - \sqrt{5})((x - 2) + \sqrt{5}) = 0$$
$$(x - 2)^2 - (\sqrt{5})^2 = 0$$
$$x^2 - 4x + 4 - 5 = 0$$
$$x^2 - 4x - 1 = 0$$

• Write a quadratic equation that has $2 + \sqrt{5}$ as a root by reversing the steps for completing the square. Will this equation also have $2 - \sqrt{5}$ as a root?

If $x = 2 + \sqrt{5}$, then
$$x - 2 = \sqrt{5}$$
$$(x - 2)^2 = (\sqrt{5})^2$$
$$x^2 - 4x + 4 = 5$$
$$x^2 - 4x + 4 - 4 = 5 - 4$$
$$x^2 - 4x = 1$$
$$x^2 - 4x - 1 = 0$$

Since this equation is the same as the result of the previous problem, $2 - \sqrt{5}$ is also a root.

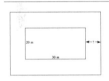

Enrichment Worksheet 23

NAME _____

QUADRATIC EQUATIONS

1. The area of the flower border around a rectangular lawn is equal to the area of the lawn. The flower border has a uniform width, and the lawn is 20 m by 30 m. How wide is the flower border.
   5 m

2. Pete uses the quadratic function
   $$P = 3d^2 - 2d + 450$$
   to determine the prices of the pizzas he sells at his restaurant. P is the price in cents, and d is the diameter of the pizza. Use the function to fill in the table.

Diameter (in inches)	Price (in cents)
8	626
10	730
13	931
20	1610

3. What is the fixed cost? $4.50

4. What kinds of things might be included in the fixed cost?
   salaries, rent, equipment, supplies

Can be used after Section 11-7

© D.C. Heath & Co.

ADDITIONAL ANSWERS

■ **Chapter Review**

3.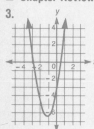

4.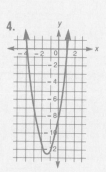

5.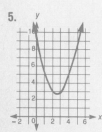

6.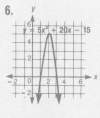

• The following table lists the number and kind of roots of the quadratic equation $ax^2 + bx + c = 0$, $a \ne 0$. [11–6]

Value of discriminant $b^2 - 4ac$	Number of real roots	Kind of real roots (when a, b, and c are rational numbers)
Positive and a perfect square	2	Rational
Positive but not a perfect square	2	Irrational
Zero	1	Rational
Negative	0	—

• A suggested strategy for solving $ax^2 + bx + c = 0$ [11–7]

  • If $a = 1$ and b and c are small integers, try factoring.
  • If $a = 1$ and b is even, try completing the square.
  • If the solution cannot be found quickly by either of the above methods, then use the quadratic formula.

■ CHAPTER REVIEW

11–1 Objective: To graph a quadratic function and find its axis of symmetry and minimum or maximum point.

  1. Write the equation in the form $y = ax^2 + bx + c$ and give the values of a, b, and c.

  $$y = (x - 2)(x + 4) \quad y = x^2 + 2x - 8; \, 1, \, 2, \, -8$$

  2. Give the axis of symmetry and the maximum or minimum point.

  $$y = x^2 - 2x - 3 \quad x = 1, \text{ minimum: } (1, -4)$$

  3. Graph. $y = 2x^2 + 5x - 3$

11–2 Objective: To solve quadratic equations by graphing.

  Solve by graphing. If there is no solution, write ∅.

  4. $2x^2 + 6x - 8 = 0$ (1, -4)   **5.** $x^2 - 5x + 9 = 0$ ∅

  6. The height h in meters of a football t seconds after it has been kicked upward is given by the formula $h = -5t^2 + 20t$. When will the football be at a height of 15 m? 1 s, 3 s

3. 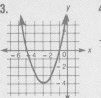 4.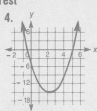

5.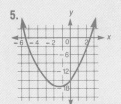

11-3 Objective: To solve quadratic equations by using the square root property for equations.

Solve.

7. $(x - 3)^2 = 49$ $(10, -4)$ **8.** $x^2 + 12x + 36 = 4$ **9.** $(x + 2)^2 = 5$ $(-2 \pm \sqrt{5})$
$\{-4, -8\}$

11-4 Objective: To solve quadratic equations by completing the square.

10. To complete the square, what number must be added to $x^2 - 8x$? 16

11. Solve $x^2 + 4x + 1 = 0$ by completing the square. Write the solutions as simplified radicals. $\{-2 \pm \sqrt{3}\}$

12. Solve $x^2 - 10x = 7$ by completing the square. Write the solutions as decimals to the nearest thousandth. $(10.657, -0.657)$

11-5 Objective: To use the quadratic formula to solve quadratic equations.

Solve using the quadratic formula.

13. $2x^2 - 7x + 6 = 0$ $\left\{\frac{3}{2}, 2\right\}$ 14. $x^2 + 1 = 4x$ $\{2 \pm \sqrt{3}\}$

15. The length of a rectangle is 6 cm more than the width. What are the length and width if the area is 30 cm²? $(3 + \sqrt{39})$ cm, $(-3 + \sqrt{39})$ cm

11-6 Objective: To determine the number and kind of roots of a quadratic equation from the value of the discriminant.

16. Write the discriminant of the equation $x^2 + 3x - 9 = 0$ in simplest form. 45

Give the number and kind of roots for the following.

17. An equation with discriminant -9 None

18. The equation $x^2 - 7x - 25 = 0$ 2, irrational

11-7 Objective: To solve quadratic equations using the easiest method.

Solve.

19. $x^2 - 3x = 0$ $(0, 3)$ 20. $x^2 + 4x = 1$ $\{-2 \pm \sqrt{5}\}$

21. The square of a number is 9 more than twice the number. What is the number?
$1 + \sqrt{10}$ or $1 - \sqrt{10}$

■ CHAPTER 11 SELF-TEST

11-1 1. State whether the function described by this equation is a quadratic function.

$$y = (x + 4)(x - 1) - x^2 \quad \text{No}$$

2. Write the equation $y = 4x(2 - x) + 3$ in the form $y = ax^2 + bx + c$.
$y = -4x^2 + 8x + 3$
3. Sketch the graph of the function defined by $y = x^2 + 6x + 5$ and identify its axis of symmetry and minimum point. $x = -3, (-3, -4)$

■ Given the function $y = x^2 - 4x + 3$:

1. Draw the graph.

1.

2. Give the axis of symmetry.

2. $x = 2$

3. State whether there is a maximum or minimum point, and give its coordinates.

3. Minimum, (2, −1)

■ Given the function $x^2 - 4x - 2 = 0$:

4. Draw the graph.

4.

5. State the consecutive integers between which the solutions lie.

5. −1 and 0, 4 and 5

■ Solve.

6. $(x + 3)^2 = 64$

6. {−11, 5}

7. $x^2 - 2x + 1 = 7$

7. {1 ± √7}

8. $x^2 - 12x = 4$

8. {6 ± 2√10}

9. $x^2 + 10x = 3$

9. {−5 ± 2√7}

© D.C. Heath & Co.

■ Solve.

10. $x^2 - 4x + 2 = 0$

10. {2 ± √2}

11. $6x^2 + 7x - 3 = 0$

11. {1/3, −3/2}

12. $x^2 - x - 1 = 0$

12. {(1 ± √5)/2}

13. $2x^2 + 4x - 3 = 0$

13. {(−2 ± √10)/2}

■ Write the discriminant of each equation in simplest form.

14. $x^2 + 6x + 10 = 0$

14. −4

15. $2x^2 + 6x - 3 = 0$

15. 60

■ State the number and kind of real roots for each equation.

16. $x^2 + 6x + 10 = 0$

16. None

17. $2x^2 + 6x - 3 = 0$

17. Two, irrational

■ Solve.

18. The square of a number is 1 more than twice the number. What is the number?

18. 1 ± √2

★ BONUS

A positive number is 4 less than its reciprocal. What is the number?

BONUS −2 + √5

© D.C. Heath & Co.

586

11–2

4. Graph the equation $y = 2x^2 - 9x - 5$ to determine the x- and y-intercepts. x-int.: 5, −1/2; y-int.: −5

5. Solve $x^2 + 3x - 15 = 0$ by graphing. Find the consecutive integers between which the roots lie. 2, 3; −6, −5

6. What are the x-intercepts of the function $y = x^2 + x - 12$? 3, −4

11–3 Solve. Write ∅ if there is no solution.

7. $x^2 = -144$ ∅

8. $x^2 + 20 = 120$ (± 10)

9. $9x^2 = 36$ (± 2)

10. $x^2 - 6x + 9 = 8$ (3 ± 2√2)

11–4 Solve by completing the square.

11. $w^2 + 4w = 60$ (6, −10)

12. $x^2 - 5x + \frac{1}{4} = 0$ {(5 ± 2√6)/2}

13. $m^2 + 10m = 11$ (1, −11)

14. $a^2 - 6a + 12 = 4$ (2, 4)

11–5 Solve using the quadratic formula.

15. $2x^2 + 3x - 1 = 0$ {(−3 ± √17)/4}

16. $x^2 - 6x + 2 = 0$ (3 ± √7)

17. $5a^2 - a - 4 = 0$ {1, −4/5}

18. $a^2 - 8a + 16 = 0$ (4)

11–6

19. Complete this table by describing the discriminant of the quadratic equation $ax^2 + bx + c = 0$, $a \neq 0$.

Kind of roots	Number of solutions	Value of the discriminant $b^2 - 4ac$
Rational	2	? Positive, perfect square
Irrational	2	? Positive, not perfect square
Rational	1	? 0
—	0	? Negative

11–7 Solve using any method.

20. $x^2 + 20x - 44 = 0$ (2, −22)

21. $4(x - 1)^2 = 9$ {5/2, −1/2}

22. $5x^2 + x - 18 = 0$ {9/5, −2}

23. $x^2 + 2x = 7$ (−1 ± 2√2)

11–7 Solve.

24. A rectangular pool is twice as long as it is wide. There is a 2-m wide concrete walk around the outside of the pool. The pool and walk cover a combined area of 160 m². Find the dimensions of the pool. 6 m by 12 m

25. The height h in meters of a rocket t seconds after it has been fired upward with an initial velocity of 120 m/s is given by the formula $h = -5t^2 + 120t$. After how many seconds is the rocket 640 meters high? 8 s and 16 s

■ PRACTICE FOR COLLEGE ENTRANCE TESTS

Each question consists of two quantities, one in column A and one in column B. Compare the two quantities and select one of the following answers:

A   if the quantity in column A is greater;
B   if the quantity in column B is greater;
C   if the two quantities are equal;
D   if the relationship cannot be determined from the information given.

Comments:

- Letters such as a, b, x, and y are variables that can be replaced by real numbers.
- A symbol that appears in both columns in a question stands for the same thing in column A as in column B.
- In some questions information that applies to quantities in both columns is centered above the two columns.

	Column A	Column B	
1.	y is the least possible value of $x^2 + 4$.		C
	y	4	
2.	The surface area of a cube is $24s^2$.		B
	The volume of the cube	$64s^3$	
3.	$x > 0$		D
	$x^3 - 8$	x^2	
4.	$y = x^2 - 4x + 4$		A
	The value of y when $x = 0$	The value of y when $x = 2$	
5.	$2^n = 2^5 - 2^4$		B
	3	n	
6.	a and b are integers and $a^b = 16$.		D
	a	b	
7.	$x < 0$		B
	x^2	$(x - 1)^2$	
8.	$x^2 + 1 > y^2$		D
	x	y	
9.	a is a positive integer.		C
	$2^{(a+1)}$	$2 \cdot 2^a$	

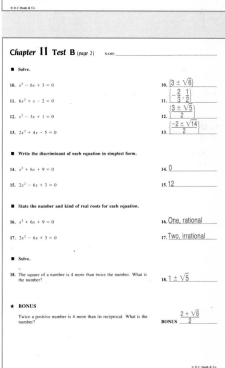

29.

30.

31.

37.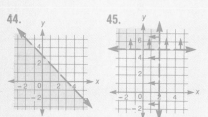

38.

39.

44. 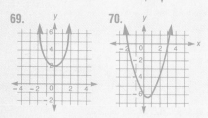   45.

69.   70.

■ CUMULATIVE REVIEW (Chapters 7–11)

7–1   **1.** Write the prime factorization of 84. $2^2 \cdot 3 \cdot 7$

7–2   **2.** State the greatest common factor of $4a^2b$ and $8ab$. $4ab$

7–3   **3.** Solve. $(a + 4)(2a - 1) = 0$ $\left\{-4, \frac{1}{2}\right\}$

7–5   Expand and simplify.

  4. $(x + 7)(x - 2)$ $x^2 + 5x - 14$ **5.** $(c - 5)^2$ $c^2 - 10c + 25$

7–4,   Factor.
7–6,
7–7,   **6.** $6x + 12y$ $6(x + 2y)$ **7.** $y^2 - 64$ $(y + 8)(y - 8)$
7–8,   **8.** $a^2 + 6a + 9$ $(a + 3)^2$ **9.** $x^2 - 8x + 15$ $(x - 5)(x - 3)$
7–9,
7–10   **10.** $y^2 + 2y - 8$ $(y + 4)(y - 2)$ **11.** $2x^2 + 7x - 4$ $(2x - 1)(x + 4)$

7–8,   Solve.
7–9
  12. $w^2 - 5w + 6 = 0$ $(2, 3)$ **13.** $t^2 + 2t = 15$ $(-5, 3)$

8–1   **14.** List the value(s) of x for which the fraction is undefined.

$$\frac{x + 4}{x - 1} \quad x = 1$$

8–1,   Simplify. Assume that no denominator is zero.
8–2,
8–3,   **15.** $\frac{25ab}{5b}$ $5a$ **16.** $\frac{3x}{y} \cdot \frac{5y}{9}$ $\frac{5x}{3}$
8–4

  17. $\frac{18xy}{7} \div \frac{3x}{14}$ $12y$ **18.** $\frac{7y}{3} + \frac{14y}{3}$ $7y$

  19. $\frac{x}{4} - \frac{x}{6}$ $\frac{x}{12}$ **20.** $\frac{8}{x - 1} + \frac{2}{x + 1}$ $\frac{10x + 6}{x^2 - 1}$

8–5,   Solve.
8–7,
8–8   **21.** $\frac{1}{x} + \frac{7}{2x} = 9$ $\left\{\frac{1}{2}\right\}$ **22.** $\frac{x}{16} = \frac{15}{64}$ $\left\{\frac{15}{4}\right\}$ **23.** 30% of $x = 18$ (60)

8–7   **24.** Write the measurements in the same units and then simplify the ratio.
       24 in. to 2 yd $\frac{24}{72} = \frac{1}{3}$

8–9   **25.** A 15-oz box of cereal costs 87¢. What does a 25-oz box cost if the price per ounce is the same? $1.45

8–10 **26.** Suppose y varies directly as x. If $x = 12$ when $y = 16$, find y when $x = 21$. 28

8–11 **27.** Suppose y varies inversely as x. If $y = 6$ when $x = 36$, find y when $x = 18$. 12

9–1 **28.** Write an inequality for this statement.

The number n is not more than 17. $n \le 17$

9–1, Graph on a number line.
9–2
29. $x < -3$ **30.** $y < 2$ and $y > 0$ **31.** $x \ge 5$ or $x = 1$

32. Write a compound inequality for this graph. $-2 \le x \le 3$

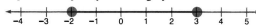

9–3 Solve.

33. $b + 3 > -2$ b > -5   **34.** $5x + 1 < 6x - 2$ x > 3

9–3 Write an inequality for the situation and solve.

35. If Glenda gained 15 lb, she would be at least 128 lb. What is Glenda's present weight (w)? w + 15 ≥ 128; 113 lb or more

9–4 **36.** The price of $\frac{1}{3}$ lb of imported cheese is slightly more than $1.50. What is the price (p) per pound? $\frac{1}{3}$ p > 1.50; more than $4.50

9–4, Solve and graph on a number line.
9–5
37. $-3a > 12$ a < -4   **38.** $\frac{1}{2} d \ge 2$ d ≥ 4   **39.** $-2y + 1 < 5$ y > -2

9–5 Solve.

40. The length of a rectangle is 4 cm more than its width. What is the width if the perimeter is less than 48 cm? w < 10 cm

9–6 Write as a compound inequality without absolute value.

41. $|x| > 11$ x > 11 or x < -11   **42.** $|b - 2| < 4$ b > -2 and b < 6

9–7 **43.** State whether the point $(2, -3)$ is on the graph of $y > 2x - 6$. No

44. Graph. $x + y < 3$

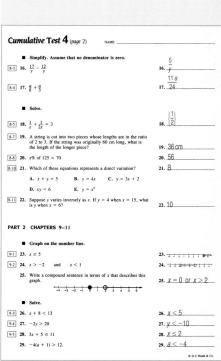

589

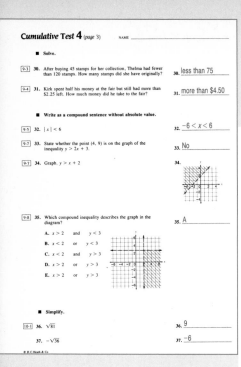

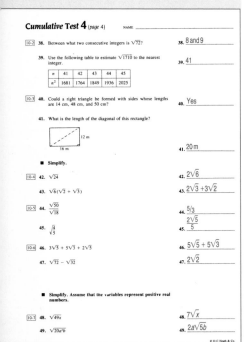

45. Graph the compound inequality
$y > 5$ and $x < 2$.

46. Which region of the plane satisfies the graph of the compound ineqality
$y < x$ and $y < -3$? III

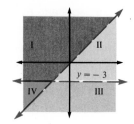

10-1 Simplify.

47. $\sqrt{81}$ 9

48. $-\sqrt{36}$ -6

49. The area of a square is 49 cm². What is the length of a side of the square? 7 cm

10-2 **50.** Between what two consecutive integers does $\sqrt{31}$ lie? 5 and 6

51. The square root of an integer is 8.3 (accurate to the nearest tenth). What is the integer? 69

10-3 **52.** Could 10 cm, 24 cm, and 26 cm be the lengths of the sides of a right triangle? Yes

53. Find the missing length in the right triangle. 20

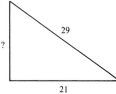

10-4, Simplify.
10-5,
10-6

54. $\sqrt{72}$ $6\sqrt{2}$

55. $-\sqrt{48}$ $-4\sqrt{3}$

56. $\sqrt{2}(\sqrt{6} + \sqrt{2})$ $2\sqrt{3} + 2$

57. $\sqrt{\dfrac{9}{16}}$ $\dfrac{3}{4}$

58. $\dfrac{\sqrt{25}}{\sqrt{27}}$ $\dfrac{5\sqrt{3}}{9}$

59. $8\sqrt{7} - \sqrt{7}$ $7\sqrt{7}$

60. $\sqrt{75} + \sqrt{12}$ $7\sqrt{3}$

10-6 **61.** Find the perimeter of the triangle. $10\sqrt{5}$

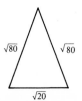

10–7 Simplify. Assume that all variables are positive.

62. $\sqrt{9xy^2}$ $3y\sqrt{x}$

63. $\sqrt{32x^5}$ $4x^2\sqrt{2x}$

10–8 Solve.

64. $\sqrt{y-2} = 6$ (38)

65. $\sqrt{12+c} = c$ (4)

10–9 **66.** Find the distance between the points $(0, 7)$ and $(8, 1)$.   10

67. Find the value(s) of y that makes the distance between the points $(5, 2)$ and $(3, y)$ equal to $2\sqrt{5}$. -2 and 6

11–1 **68.** Write the equation $y = (x - 4)(2x + 1)$ in the form $y = ax^2 + bx + c$ and state the values of a, b, and c. $y = 2x^2 - 7x - 4$; $a = 2$, $b = -7$, $c = -4$

69. Graph the equation $y = x^2 + 2$.

11–2 **70.** Graph the function $y = x^2 - x - 6$ to solve the equation $x^2 - x - 6 = 0$. $(-2, 3)$

11–3 Solve. If there is no solution, write $\emptyset$.

71. $x^2 = -25$ $\emptyset$

72. $(x - 2)^2 = 100$ $\{-8, 12\}$

11–4 **73.** What number will complete the square when added to the expression $x^2 - 8x$?   16

74. Solve by completing the square. $x^2 - 2x = 24$ $\{-4, 6\}$

11–5 **75.** In applying the quadratic formula to solve the equation $6x^2 - x + 1 = 0$, what values should be substituted for a, b, and c? $a = 6$, $b = -1$, $c = 1$

Solve using the quadratic formula.

76. $x^2 - 14x + 48 = 0$ $\{6, 8\}$

77. $2x^2 - x - 10 = 0$ $\left\{-2, \dfrac{5}{2}\right\}$

11–6 **78.** Use the discriminant to state the number and kind of roots of the equation $4x^2 - 20x + 25 = 0$.   1 rational root

79. Write the discriminant in simplest form for the equation $x^2 - 8x + 4 = 0$.   48

11–7 Solve.

80. A picture is 4 in. wide and 6 in. long. It has a white border around it. What is the width of the border if the total area of the picture, including the border, is 29 square inches? $\dfrac{-5 + \sqrt{30}}{2}$ in.

81. A rocket shot in the air with a velocity of 40 m/s reaches a height of h meters in t seconds, as given by the formula $h = -5t^2 + 40t$. After how many seconds will the rocket be at a height of 80 m?   4 s

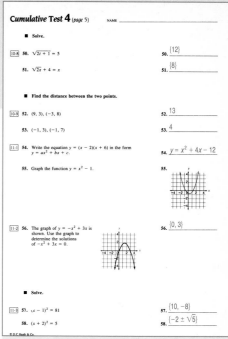

■ Solve.

10-8 **50.** $\sqrt{2t + 1} = 5$ **50.** $\{12\}$

51. $\sqrt{2x + 4} = x$ **51.** $\{8\}$

■ Find the distance between the two points.

10-9 **52.** $(9, 3)$, $(-3, 8)$ **52.** 13

53. $(-1, 3)$, $(-1, 7)$ **53.** 4

11-1 **54.** Write the equation $y = (x - 2)(x + 6)$ in the form $y = ax^2 + bx + c$.   **54.** $y = x^2 + 4x - 12$

55. Graph the function $y = x^2 - 1$.   **55.**

56. The graph of $y = -x^2 + 3x$ is shown. Use the graph to determine the solutions of $-x^2 + 3x = 0$.   **56.** $\{0, 3\}$

■ Solve.

11-3 **57.** $(x - 1)^2 = 81$ **57.** $\{10, -8\}$

58. $(x + 2)^2 = 5$ **58.** $\{-2 \pm \sqrt{5}\}$

© D.C. Heath & Co.

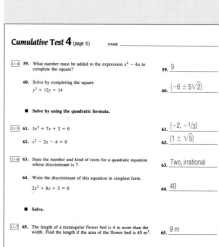

11-4 **59.** What number must be added to the expression $x^2 - 6x$ to complete the square?   **59.** 9

60. Solve by completing the square. $y^2 + 12y = 14$ **60.** $\{-6 \pm 5\sqrt{2}\}$

■ Solve by using the quadratic formula.

11-5 **61.** $3x^2 + 7x + 2 = 0$ **61.** $\{-2, -\frac{1}{3}\}$

62. $x^2 - 2x - 4 = 0$ **62.** $\{1 \pm \sqrt{5}\}$

11-6 **63.** State the number and kind of roots for a quadratic equation whose discriminant is 7.   **63.** Two, irrational

64. Write the discriminant of this equation in simplest form. $2x^2 + 8x + 3 = 0$ **64.** 40

■ Solve.

11-7 **65.** The length of a rectangular flower bed is 4 m more than the width. Find the length if the area of the flower bed is 45 m².   **65.** 9 m

© D.C. Heath & Co.

OVERVIEW

The quadratic formula is the final topic of the standard first year algebra course. If additional time remains after the completion of Chapter 11, the supplementary topics included in this section may be selected for study.

The probability and statistics lessons give an introduction to this increasingly important area of mathematics.

In the trigonometry lessons, students learn to use trigonometric ratios to find missing measures of parts of right triangles. These lessons prepare students for later study of trigonometry.

PURPOSE

Few events in our lives are either certain to occur or impossible. Therefore, we must often make decisions by estimating the likelihood of an event's occurring and determining the consequences of that event if it does occur. Often these estimates are made intuitively, based on experience. A rudimentary knowledge of probability can help us make more accurate estimates.

LESSON

It is worthwhile to do experiments to test probability statements about events such as coin tossing. However, there are also dangers. Physical objects are not perfectly made—a die is not perfectly balanced with perfectly square sides. Therefore, empirical (experimental) probabilities may not agree exactly with theory, particularly for a small number of trials. Determining that the probability of getting heads on the toss of a coin is ½ does not mean that heads *must* occur in ½ the tosses. When doing real experiments, help students to understand that their results neither prove nor disprove statements about probabilities. However, experiments can be effective ways to estimate the solution to probability problems, particularly for large numbers of trials.

Supplementary Topic
Probability and Statistics

Probability

Consider the experiment of tossing a "fair" coin into the air. The coin is just as likely to land heads up as tails up. Since there are 2 equally likely outcomes, we say that the **probability** of obtaining heads is $\frac{1}{2}$. We write $P(\text{heads}) = \frac{1}{2}$. Similarly, $P(\text{tails}) = \frac{1}{2}$.

Now consider a more complex situation. Suppose a jar contains 4 red marbles and 2 white marbles. The probability of selecting any given marble without looking is $\frac{1}{6}$, but what is the probability of selecting a red marble without looking?

$$P(\text{red}) = \frac{\text{Number of red marbles}}{\text{Total number of marbles}} = \frac{4}{6} = \frac{2}{3}$$

An event is a collection of one or more outcomes of an experiment. If all outcomes are equally likely, the probability of an event is the quotient of the number of outcomes in the event (called successes) divided by the total number of outcomes.

> ## Definition: Probability of an Event
>
> $$P(\text{event}) = \frac{\text{Number of successes}}{\text{Number of outcomes}}$$

Example 1   In the throw of a die, what is the probability that the number of dots on the top face will be fewer than 3?

Solution   There are 6 different faces that can be up.

Two of those faces have fewer than 3 dots.

Answer $P(\text{fewer than 3 dots}) = \frac{2}{6} = \frac{1}{3}$

Example 1.
In the throw of a die, what is the probability that the top number will be prime?
$$P(\text{prime}) = \frac{3}{6} = \frac{1}{2}$$
Example 2.
What is the probability of randomly drawing a king from a regular deck of playing cards?
$$P(\text{king}) = \frac{4}{52} = \frac{1}{13}$$
Example 3.
A jar has 4 red marbles, 3 blue marbles, and 2 black marbles. A marble is selected without looking. Find $P(\text{red})$.
$$P(\text{red}) = \frac{4}{9}$$
Example 4.
In Example 4, what is the probability of the spinner landing on orange?
$$P(\text{orange}) = \frac{180}{360} = \frac{1}{2}$$

CHECK UNDERSTANDING

- What is the probability of an event that is certain to occur? (1)
- What is the probability of an event that cannot happen? (0)
- There are 5 people on a committee, 3 girls and 2 boys. One person will be chosen at random to be chairperson. What is the probability that the chairperson will be a girl? ($\frac{3}{5}$)

Example 2   A deck of playing cards has 52 cards. There are 13 cards in each of four suits. Two of the suits (hearts and diamonds) are red and two of the suits (spades and clubs) are black. What is the probability that one card drawn at random from a deck will be a red ace?

Solution   There are 2 red aces in the 52 cards so there are 2 ways of drawing a red ace. There are 52 possible ways of drawing one card.

$$P(\text{red ace}) = \frac{2}{52} = \frac{1}{26}$$

Answer   The probability of drawing a red ace is $\frac{1}{26}$.

Consider rolling a die. What is the probability of getting a 7? What is the probability of getting a number less than 7? In the first case, there is no face with 7 dots. Therefore,

$$P(7) = \frac{0}{6} = 0.$$

In the second case, all faces have fewer than 7 dots. Therefore,

$$P(\text{less than } 7) = \frac{6}{6} = 1.$$

The first case is an example of an **impossible event**. The second is an example of a **certain event**.

Definitions: Impossible and Certain Events

The probability of an impossible event is 0.
The probability of a certain event is 1.

Note that the probability of an event occurring plus the probability of the event not occurring is 1.

Example 3   A jar has 5 red marbles, 4 green marbles, and 3 white marbles. A marble is selected without looking. Find $P(\text{red})$ and $P(\text{not red})$.

Solution $P(\text{red}) = \dfrac{\text{Number of red marbles}}{\text{Number of marbles}} = \dfrac{5}{12}$

$P(\text{not red}) = \dfrac{\text{Number of not red marbles}}{\text{Number of marbles}} = \dfrac{7}{12}$

Check $P(\text{red}) + P(\text{not red}) = \dfrac{5}{12} + \dfrac{7}{12} = 1$ It checks.

CLASSROOM EXERCISES

Exercise 4 and some Written Exercises assume that students are at least slightly acquainted with regular playing cards. If they are not, you may wish to show and explain a deck of cards or omit those exercises.

ASSIGNMENT GUIDE

Basic   1–15 all
Average   1–15 odd, 16–24 all
Enriched   1–15 odd, 16–25 all

ENRICHMENT PROBLEM

- Assume the probability of an event occurring is p.
  a. What is the probability of the event not occurring?
  b. What is the probability of the event occurring twice in succession?

  a. $1 - p$ **b.** p^2

Example 4 What is the probability of this spinner landing on blue?

Solution The blue section is a 90-degree section of the circle.

$$P(\text{blue}) = \frac{90}{360} = \frac{1}{4}$$

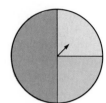

■ CLASSROOM EXERCISES

In a jar of 15 marbles, 5 of the marbles are red and 6 are black. Find the probability.

1. $P(\text{red})$ $\frac{1}{3}$ **2.** $P(\text{not red})$ $\frac{2}{3}$ **3.** $P(\text{neither red nor black})$ $\frac{4}{15}$

4. A deck of playing cards has 52 cards, 13 in each of 4 suits (hearts, spades, diamonds, and clubs). What is the probability of selecting a spade? $\frac{1}{4}$

■ WRITTEN EXERCISES

Twenty identical slips of paper are marked with the numbers 1 to 20, put in a box, and thoroughly mixed. A slip of paper is randomly drawn. Find each probability, where n represents the number that was randomly drawn.

A **1.** $P(n = 7)$ $\frac{1}{20}$ **2.** $P(n > 12)$ $\frac{2}{5}$ **3.** $P(n$ is a multiple of 3) $\frac{3}{10}$

4. $P(n$ is odd) $\frac{1}{2}$ **5.** $P(n$ is prime) $\frac{2}{5}$ **6.** $P(n$ is a 2-digit number) $\frac{11}{20}$

A die is rolled and the number on the top face is observed. Find each probability.

7. $P(2)$ $\frac{1}{6}$ **8.** $P(\text{less than 10})$ 1 **9.** $P(\pi)$ 0

10. $P(\text{multiple of 3})$ $\frac{1}{3}$ **11.** $P(\text{not prime})$ $\frac{1}{2}$ **12.** $P(\text{factor of 60})$ 1

A card is selected at random from a deck of 52 thoroughly shuffled playing cards. Find each probability.

13. $P(\text{club})$ $\frac{1}{4}$ **14.** $P(\text{not club})$ $\frac{3}{4}$ **15.** $P(\text{king or queen})$ $\frac{2}{13}$

The possible outcomes of tossing two coins are HH, HT, TH, TT. State the probability of the following outcomes.

B **16.** both heads $\frac{1}{4}$ **17.** heads on at least one coin $\frac{3}{4}$ **18.** no heads $\frac{1}{4}$

List the possible outcomes of tossing three coins. State the probabilities of the following outcomes.

19. three tails $\frac{1}{8}$ **20.** no tails $\frac{1}{8}$ **21.** two heads and one tail $\frac{3}{8}$

22. more tails than heads $\frac{1}{2}$ **23.** at least one tail $\frac{7}{8}$ **24.** half tails and half heads 0

C **25.** What is the probability of getting more than two heads when you toss four coins? $\frac{5}{16}$

Compound Events

Consider tossing a "fair" coin three times. What is the probability of getting heads on each toss? To answer the question we can list all possible outcomes.

HHH   HHT   HTH   HTT   THH   THT   TTH   TTT

Since the eight outcomes are equally likely, the probability of each outcome is $\frac{1}{8}$. Therefore, $P(\text{HHH}) = \frac{1}{8}$. Note that

$$P(\text{HHH}) = \frac{1}{8} = \frac{1}{2} \cdot \frac{1}{2} \cdot \frac{1}{2} = P(\text{H}) \cdot P(\text{H}) \cdot P(\text{H})$$

This fact illustrates the following property.

Probability—Independent Events

For two independent events A and B, if $P(A)$ is the probability of A occurring and $P(B)$ is the probability of B occurring, then

$$P(A \text{ and } B) = P(A) \cdot P(B)$$

Example 1   What is the probability of rolling a die twice and getting 6 on the first roll and 3 on the second roll?

Solution $P(6 \text{ on the first roll}) = \frac{1}{6}$

$P(3 \text{ on the second roll}) = \frac{1}{6}$

$$P(6, 3) = P(6) \cdot P(3) = \frac{1}{6} \cdot \frac{1}{6} = \frac{1}{36}$$

Answer $P(6, 3) = \frac{1}{36}$

Check   List all the possible outcomes:

(1, 1)	(1, 2)	(1, 3)	(1, 4)	(1, 5)	(1, 6)
(2, 1)	(2, 2)	(2, 3)	(2, 4)	(2, 5)	(2, 6)
(3, 1)	(3, 2)	(3, 3)	(3, 4)	(3, 5)	(3, 6)
(4, 1)	(4, 2)	(4, 3)	(4, 4)	(4, 5)	(4, 6)
(5, 1)	(5, 2)	(5, 3)	(5, 4)	(5, 5)	(5, 6)
(6, 1)	(6, 2)	(6, 3)	(6, 4)	(6, 5)	(6, 6)

One of the 36 outcomes is (6, 3). The answer checks.

PURPOSE

Many events are combinations of simple events for which probabilities can be estimated. The probabilities of the simple events can be used to obtain the probability of the compound event.

LESSON

The equation for computing the probability of the occurrence of independent events has wider application than may first appear. For example, consider drawing two cards from a deck without replacing the first card. The two events, drawing a first card and drawing a second card, are not independent—the first draw affects the second. The probability of drawing the ace of spades is $\frac{1}{52}$ and the probability of drawing the ace of hearts is $\frac{1}{52}$. However, the probability of drawing the ace of spades followed by the ace of hearts is not $(\frac{1}{52})(\frac{1}{52})$. On the other hand, we can redefine the two events so that they are independent. The first event is drawing the ace of spades. The second event is drawing the ace of hearts from a deck of 51 cards. These two events are independent. The probability of the first is $\frac{1}{52}$ and the probability of the second is $\frac{1}{51}$. The probability of both is $(\frac{1}{52})(\frac{1}{51})$.

Example 1.
What is the probability of rolling a die twice and getting a number less than 3 each time?

P(first die < 3 and second die < 3) =

$$\frac{1}{3} \cdot \frac{1}{3} = \frac{1}{9}$$

Example 2.
What is the probability of drawing two red cards from a deck (without replacement)?

$$P(\text{red, red}) = \frac{1}{2} \cdot \frac{25}{51} = \frac{25}{102}$$

CHECK UNDERSTANDING

- What is the probability of tossing heads on one toss of a coin? (½)
- What is the probability of tossing tails on a second toss of a coin? (½)
- What is the probability of tossing heads followed by tails in two tosses of a coin?

$(\frac{1}{2} \cdot \frac{1}{2},$ or ¼)

ASSIGNMENT GUIDE

Basic   1–25 odd
Average   1–25 odd, 26–31 all
Enriched 5–31 odd, 32–35 all

PROBLEM-SOLVING NOTES

- What is the probability of getting a 6 at least once in 4 tosses of a single die?

Solving this problem is difficult because the sample space is large and there are so many possibilities; that is, the favorable outcomes include one 6, two 6's, three 6's, and four 6's.

A simple way of doing the problem is to compute the probability of not getting a 6 on any of the rolls.

The probability of not getting a 6 on one toss is $1 - \frac{1}{6}$, or $\frac{5}{6}$. The probability of not getting a 6 on each of 4 tosses is $\left(\frac{5}{6}\right)^4 = \frac{625}{1296} \approx 0.48$. So, the probability of getting at least one 6 is $1 - 0.48 = 0.52$.

This technique can be used to solve the birthday problem given below.

In rolling dice, an outcome of one roll does not affect an outcome of another roll. Therefore, the probability of getting a given number is the same on every roll. However, there are situations in which the outcome of a first event may change the probability of a second event.

Example 2 A deck of playing cards has 52 cards. If two cards are selected by chance, what is the probability of getting the ace of hearts followed by the ten of clubs? The first card is not replaced before the second selection.

Solution On the first draw there are 52 cards in the deck. Therefore, the probability of getting any specific card is $\frac{1}{52}$. On the second draw there are only 51 cards. The probability of getting any specific one of the remaining cards is $\frac{1}{51}$.

$$P(\text{ace of hearts, ten of clubs}) = \frac{1}{52} \cdot \frac{1}{51}$$

$$= \frac{1}{2652}$$

Answer $P(\text{ace of hearts, ten of clubs}) = \frac{1}{2652}$

■ CLASSROOM EXERCISES

There are 5 red beads, 6 green beads, and 9 white beads in a jar. Two beads are drawn by chance.

1. What is the probability of getting red on the first draw and green on the second draw if the first bead is replaced before the second draw? $\frac{3}{40}$

2. What is the probability of getting white on the first draw and white on the second draw if the first bead is not replaced before the second draw? $\frac{18}{95}$

■ WRITTEN EXERCISES

Two coins are tossed. Find each probability.

A 1. $P(\text{2 heads})$ $\frac{1}{4}$

2. $P(\text{same outcome})$ $\frac{1}{2}$

3. $P(\text{different outcomes})$ $\frac{1}{2}$

4. $P(\text{heads on first, tails on second})$ $\frac{1}{4}$

A card is randomly selected from a deck of 52 playing cards, observed, and returned to the deck. Then another card is randomly selected and observed. Find each probability.

5. $P(\text{both red})$ $\frac{1}{4}$

6. $P(\text{red, club})$ $\frac{1}{8}$

7. $P(\text{diamond, heart})$ $\frac{1}{16}$

8. $P(\text{first card is a 2, 3, or 4 and second card is a 2 or 3})$ $\frac{6}{169}$

9. $P(\text{first card is a 5, 6, 7, or 8 and second card is a 5 or 6})$ $\frac{8}{169}$

A card is randomly selected from a deck of 52 playing cards and not replaced. Then a second card is randomly selected. Find each probability.

10. $P(\text{both red})$ $\frac{25}{102}$

11. $P(\text{first card is black and second card is red})$ $\frac{13}{51}$

12. $P(\text{first card is an ace and second card is a king})$ $\frac{4}{663}$

13. $P(\text{first card is the ace of spades and second card is the ace of spades})$ 0

The 36 equally likely outcomes of rolling two dice are given at the right. Find each probability.

(1, 1)	(1, 2)	(1, 3)	(1, 4)	(1, 5)	(1, 6)
(2, 1)	(2, 2)	(2, 3)	(2, 4)	(2, 5)	(2, 6)
(3, 1)	(3, 2)	(3, 3)	(3, 4)	(3, 5)	(3, 6)
(4, 1)	(4, 2)	(4, 3)	(4, 4)	(4, 5)	(4, 6)
(5, 1)	(5, 2)	(5, 3)	(5, 4)	(5, 5)	(5, 6)
(6, 1)	(6, 2)	(6, 3)	(6, 4)	(6, 5)	(6, 6)

14. $P(\text{sum} = 6)$ $\frac{5}{36}$

15. $P(\text{sum} > 3)$ $\frac{11}{12}$

16. $P(\text{first die} < 3 \text{ and second die} < 4)$ $\frac{1}{6}$

17. $P(\text{first die} < 3 \text{ or second die} < 4)$ $\frac{2}{3}$

18. $P(\text{first die} > 2 \text{ and sum} = 7)$ $\frac{1}{9}$

19. $P(\text{first die} < 3 \text{ or sum} = 7)$ $\frac{4}{9}$

20. $P(\text{sum} > 1)$ 1

21. $P(\text{sum} > 12)$ 0

A jar contains 6 blue beads, 3 green beads, and 1 brown bead. Two beads are drawn at random without replacement. Find each probability.

22. $P(\text{both blue})$ $\frac{1}{3}$

23. $P(1 \text{ blue and } 1 \text{ brown})$ $\frac{1}{15}$

24. $P(\text{neither blue})$ $\frac{2}{15}$

25. $P(\text{neither green})$ $\frac{7}{15}$

B In an experiment a card is drawn at random from a deck of 52 playing cards and a die is rolled. Find each probability.

26. $P(\text{the card is a heart and the die shows one})$ $\frac{1}{24}$

27. $P(\text{red card and number less than 5})$ $\frac{1}{3}$

28. $P(\text{ace and one})$ $\frac{1}{78}$

29. $P(\text{not ace and not one})$ $\frac{10}{13}$

30. $P(\text{club and odd number})$ $\frac{1}{8}$

31. $P(\text{not club and even number})$ $\frac{3}{8}$

C The 200 students in a small school may be enrolled in mathematics (M), in social studies (S), in both, or in neither. The diagram at the right shows that 130 students are enrolled in mathematics and 120 are enrolled in social studies. A student is selected at random. Find each probability.

32. $P(\text{enrolled in mathematics or in social studies})$ $\frac{17}{20}$

33. $P(\text{not enrolled in mathematics})$ $\frac{7}{20}$

34. $P(\text{enrolled in mathematics but not in social studies})$ $\frac{1}{4}$

35. $P(\text{enrolled neither in mathematics nor in social studies})$ $\frac{3}{20}$

ENRICHMENT PROBLEM
The Birthday Problem

- There are 20 people in a room. Ignoring February 29, what is the probability that two of these people have the same birthday, that is, have their birthdays on the same day and month of the year? Use a calculator to give your answer to the nearest hundredth. [*Hint:* First, find the probability of no two of the 20 people having the same birthday.]

The probability of no two of the people having the same birthday is as follows:

First Second Third. . .Twentieth
person person person person

$$\frac{365}{365} \cdot \frac{364}{365} \cdot \frac{363}{365} \cdots \frac{346}{365}$$

$$= \frac{365 \cdot 364 \cdot 363 \cdots 346}{365^{20}}$$

$$\approx 0.59$$

So the probability of two people having the same birthday is $1 - 0.59 = 0.41$.

Note: The table below gives some values for the birthday problem. With as few as 23 people in the room there is a better than even chance that two people have identical birthdays!

Number of people in room	Probability of at least 2 birthdays the same
5	0.027
10	0.0117
20	0.411
23	0.507
30	0.706
40	0.891
60	0.994

1. A card is randomly selected from a deck of 52 cards, observed, and returned to the deck. Then another card is randomly selected and observed. Find P(both black).

$$P(\text{both black}) = \frac{1}{2} \cdot \frac{1}{2} = \frac{1}{4}$$

2. In exercise 1, the first card is not returned. Find P(both black).

$$P(\text{both black}) = \frac{1}{2} \cdot \frac{25}{51} = \frac{25}{102}$$

3. Two dice are tossed. What is the probability of less than 2 on the first die and more than 3 on the second?

$$\frac{1}{6} \cdot \frac{1}{2} = \frac{1}{12}$$

A jar contains 3 red beads, 4 green beads, and 5 blue beads. Two beads are drawn at random without replacement. Find each probability.

4. P(both red) $\frac{3}{12} \cdot \frac{2}{11} = \frac{1}{22}$

5. P(neither red) $\frac{9}{12} \cdot \frac{8}{11} = \frac{6}{11}$

PURPOSE

When a set of data is large, it is difficult to deal with the individual numbers. It becomes necessary to describe characteristics of the set as a whole. One kind of useful description is a **measure of central tendency,** that is, a number about which the data "cluster." Three commonly used measures of central tendency are the mean, median, and mode.

LESSON

Be sure that students understand that each tally mark in the frequency table represents one student score. Have students use calculators to check the total of the scores.

See *How to Lie with Statistics,* © 1954, by Darrell Huff for actual examples of misuses of statistics. [This paperback book is available from the Norton College Division of W. W. Norton & Company, Inc., New York.]

OBJECTIVE

To compute the mean, median, and mode of a frequency distribution.

Statistics

The **frequency** table at the right shows student scores on an algebra test. Each **tally mark** represents one student score. The most common score is 86, achieved by 4 students. The most common score is called the **mode.**

There are 25 scores in all. The middle score is 85. The middle score is called the **median.** The median is found by arranging the scores in order from largest to smallest and locating the middle score. If there is an even number of scores, the median is midway between the two middle scores. For example, the median of these four scores is 6.

$$1, \quad 5, \quad 7, \quad 18$$
$$\text{Median} = 6$$

The **arithmetic mean** of a set of scores is the quotient of the sum of the scores divided by the number of scores.

$$\text{Mean} = \frac{\text{Total of scores}}{\text{Number of scores}} = \frac{2121}{25} \approx 84.8$$

Score	Tallies	Frequency
95	/	1
92	//	2
90	/	1
89	/	1
87	//	2
86	////	4
85	///	3
84	/	1
83	///	3
82	/	1
81	//	2
80	//	2
78	/	1
75	/	1
Total		25
Total of scores	=	2121

Note that the test scores are correct to the nearest whole-number integer and the mean is given to the nearest tenth. Means are usually given to one more place of accuracy than the score themselves.

The mean, median, and mode are called **averages,** or **measures of central tendency**.

Example 1 Find the mean, median, and mode of this set of kilogram weights.

$$81, \quad 84, \quad 75, \quad 58, \quad 75, \quad 82, \quad 84, \quad 75$$

Solution Arrange the numbers in order.

$$58, \quad 75, \quad 75, \quad 75, \quad 81, \quad 82, \quad 84, \quad 84$$

To find the mean, first find the sum of the scores: 614.
Then divide by the number of scores: 8.

$$\text{Mean} = \frac{614}{8} = 76.8$$

The median, midway between 75 and 81, is 78.
The mode is the most frequent score, 75.

Answer Mean = 76.8 kg   Median = 78 kg   Mode = 75 kg

Example 1.
Find the mean, median, and mode of this set of heights (in inches) of members of a basketball team:

65, 70, 71, 72, 72, 72, 74, 76, 77

The mean is 72.1. The median is 72. The mode is 72.

Example 2.
Ken averaged 85 on his first two algebra tests. What will he have to score on the third test in order to have a mean of 90?

Let x = the next test score

$$\frac{2(85) + x}{3} = 90$$

$$\frac{170 + x}{3} = 90$$

$$x = 100$$

Ken must score 100 on his next test in order to have a mean of 90.

Example 2   Carrie scores 87, 84, and 93 on her first three algebra tests. What does she have to score on the next test in order to have a mean of at least 90?

Solution   Let x = the next test score.

$$\frac{87 + 84 + 93 + x}{4} \geq 90$$

$$\frac{264 + x}{4} \geq 90$$

$$264 + x \geq 360$$

$$x \geq 96$$

Answer   Carrie must score 96 or more in order to have a mean of at least 90.

The fact that the mean, median, and mode are called averages can create confusion. For example, these are the yearly salaries of the seven employees of a small company.

$200,000 $20,000 $18,000 $15,000 $12,000 $12,000 $12,000

The mean salary is $41,286.
The median salary is $15,000.
The mode salary is $12,000.

During salary negotiations a union representative might claim that the average salary is $12,000. The owner might claim that the average salary is over $41,000. Both claims are correct, but communication will be clear only if the words "mode" and "mean" are used in place of the word "average."

CHECK UNDERSTANDING

How does one find the
• mean of a set of data? (Divide the sum of the numbers by the number of numbers.)
• median? (Order the numbers and find the one in the middle.)
• mode? (Find the most common number.)

■ CLASSROOM EXERCISES

1. In the example of the yearly salaries given above, which best describes the "average" salary: the mean salary, the median salary, or the mode salary? Why?   The median, because all but one of the salaries are close to it.

2. Compute the mean, median, and mode of the frequency distribution shown here.   177.2, 175, 175

Score	Frequency
135	1
145	2
155	4
165	5
175	8
185	7
195	6
205	4

CLASSROOM EXERCISES

In Exercise 1 there is no clear-cut "best" average to use. However, the median is perhaps less distorted than the other two.

ASSIGNMENT GUIDE

Basic   1–11 all
Average   1–13 all
Enriched   1–15 all

CONCEPT EXTENSION

Students may not be convinced of the need for the mode and median until they appreciate the role of a particular number in describing the characteristics of the whole set. Emphasize that the mean, median, and mode each describe a different measure of central tendency, that is, behavior near the middle. We select the statistic that best meets our purpose. Discuss numerous examples with students where each "average" is the best description of a particular set of data.

Mean
Used for situations in which continuous variation of the data makes sense, for example,
- scores
- temperatures
- weights

Mode
Used for situations in which the data cluster about particular values, for example,
- shoe sizes
- clothing sizes

Median
Used for any situation in which the data must be whole numbers to make sense, for example,
- number of children per family
- number of visits to a doctor per person per year

ENRICHMENT PROBLEM

- In a gymnastics meet, four judges score each gymnast from 0 to 10 on an exercise. The high and low scores are discarded. The mean of the two middle scores is the official score of the gymnast. Three judges gave these scores to Deana on the balance beam: 8.3, 8.8, 9.0. What is the highest possible score Deana can have after the fourth judge's score is given?

  8.9

■ WRITTEN EXERCISES

Compute the mean, median, and mode of each set of numbers.

A
1. 3, 6, 2, 3, 8, 2, 5, 5, 2   4, 3, 2

2. 7, 9, 6, 37, 5, 9, 6, 9   11, 8, 9

3. 23, 26, 27, 27, 28, 30   26.8, 27, 27

4. 2, 2, 2, 6, 7, 10, 11, 20   7.5, 6.5, 2

Compute the mean, median, and mode of each frequency distribution.

5.
Score	Frequency
10	1
13	2
15	1
18	2
20	3
23	1

17, 18, 20

6.
Score	Frequency
50	3
51	2
55	2
59	1
65	1

54, 51, 50

7.
Score	Frequency
65	2
70	4
72	2
73	1
78	1

70.5, 70, 70

Solve.

8. Eva had scores of 127 and 139 in her first two bowling games. What score must she get in her third game in order to have a mean score of 150?   184

9. On his fifth test, Zach's score was 40, which made the mean of his scores 50. What was the mean of Zach's scores for the first four tests?   52.5

10. The mean score on a recent test was 56 when one student was absent. When the absent student returned and took the test, the class mean was 57. What was the absent student's score if there are 25 students in the class?   81

11. Three of the most popular shows in the winter series of the Nurnberg Music Theater were "Die Fledermaus" (297 performances; 182,000 attending), "The Marriage of Figaro" (216 performances; 183,000 attending), and "La Boheme" (216 performances; 172,000 attending). Which of the three shows was most popular, on the basis of average attendance? Explain.
The Marriage of Figaro; average attendances are 613, 847, and 796.

Compute the mean, median, and mode of each frequency distribution. Consider the height for each frequency to be at the midpoint of the interval.

B
12.
Height (in cm)	Frequency
136–140	4
141–145	3
146–150	13

145.3, 148, 148

13.
Height (in cm)	Frequency
150–154.9	5
155–159.9	5
160–164.9	10

158.7, 159.95, 162.45

Find the frequency distribution that satisfies each set of conditions.

C
14. Ten players.
Points scored are 1, 3, and 6.
Mean is 4 points.
Mode is 3 points.

Points	Frequency
1	1
3	5
6	4

15. Ten players.
Points scored are 1, 3, and 6.
Mean is 4 points.
Median is 3 points.

Points	Frequency
1	1
3	5
6	4

OBJECTIVE

To compute the range and standard deviation of a frequency distribution.

Class Starter Quiz
on previous section

Use this distribution:
3, 9, 6, 8, 8, 5, 4, 8

1. Find the mean. 6.4
2. Find the median. 7
3. Find the mode. 8
4. Sharon has a mean of 75 after the first three French tests. What does she have to score on the fourth test to bring her mean score to 80?
   95
5. What is the mean of the following distribution? 4.9

Score	3	4	5	6	7
Tally	//	//	/////	/	//

Variation

These two sets of data have the same mean, 60, but are very different from each other.

$$59, \quad 60, \quad 61 \qquad 1, \quad 2, \quad 177$$

In the first set, the data are nearly the same whereas in the second, they vary widely. It is often useful to measure the variation of the data.

One measure of variation is the **range**, the difference between the least number and the greatest number in the set. The range of the first set of data given above is $61 - 59$, or 2. The range of the second set is $177 - 1$, or 176. The range is the difference between the extremes of a set of data, but it tells nothing about how the data are distributed between the extreme values.

The following two sets of data have the same mean (60) and the same range (40). But note that in Set 1 the data "cluster" near the mean, whereas in Set 2 the data are near the extreme values.

Set 1					Set 2				
40	59	60	61	80	40	41	60	79	80
	59	60	61		40	41		79	80
	59	60	61		40				80

This example shows another component of variation: the amount of dispersion from the mean of numbers in the set.

A commonly used statistic that describes this characteristic is called the **standard deviation**. The standard deviation of the data in Set 1 is computed as follows.

1. Compute the sum of the squares of the differences from the mean.

$$(40 - 60)^2 + 3(59 - 60)^2 + 3(60 - 60)^2 + 3(61 - 60)^2 + (80 - 60)^2 = 806$$

2. Compute the mean of the squares. $806 \div 11 \approx 73.27$

3. Compute the square root of the mean of the squares. $\sqrt{73.27} \approx 8.6$

The standard deviation of Set 1 is about 8.6. Using the same method, we can compute the standard deviation of Set 2. The standard deviation of Set 2 is about 18.7. The larger standard deviation of Set 2 indicates that its scores vary more from the mean than those in Set 1.

PURPOSE

Sets of data that have the same mean can be widely different from each other. Therefore, another measure of the set is desirable—a measure of the dispersion (how widely "scattered" the scores are). Two measures of dispersion are given, range and standard deviation.

LESSON

Students should realize that the range describes only two scores of the distribution. The standard deviation, on the other hand, involves all scores.

ADDITIONAL EXAMPLE

Give the mean, range, and standard deviation of this distribution:
12, 12, 13, 15, 17, 17, 17, 18
Mean = 15.125
Range = 6
S.D. = 2.315

Example   Compute the mean, range, and standard deviation of this set of scores from a sharpshooter's competition.

$$60, \quad 65, \quad 68, \quad 68, \quad 68, \quad 70, \quad 70, \quad 71, \quad 75$$

Solution   Mean $= \dfrac{60 + 65 + 68 + 68 + 68 + 70 + 70 + 71 + 75}{9} = \dfrac{615}{9} \approx 68.3$

Range $= 75 - 60 = 15$

- How is the range computed? (Subtract the smallest score from the largest.)
- Two frequency distributions have the same mean. The first has a larger standard deviation than the other. How are the data in the first set different from the data in the second set? (The data in the first set are more scattered.)

ASSIGNMENT GUIDE

Basic 1–9*
Average 1–9 odd, 10–15 all
Enriched 1–9 odd, 10–16 all
Note: *Students should not be required to compute standard deviations of more than one or two small distributions without a calculator.

CONCEPT EXTENSION

The focus in the lesson is upon computing the range and standard deviation of a given set of data. Students also need to realize that we can make judgments about a set of data that is not present from the statistics studied thus far. Ask students what they can tell about the sets of data having these statistics. (Let N = number of data in the set):

a. $N = 12$
mean = 80.3
range = 14
S.D. = 8.5
Since the range is low and the standard deviation is high, the scores cluster at both ends of the range.

b. $N = 100$
median = 42
range = 8
S.D. = 2.1
Since the range and the standard deviation are both low, the scores probably cluster somewhere around the median.

c. $N = 25$
mode = 80
median = 60.5
S.D. = 15
Since the median and mode vary by 19.5 points, and since there is a very high standard deviation and no indication of the range, the scores are probably scattered from low to high.

Example (continued)

Compute the standard deviation.
1. Square the differences from the mean. (Use a calculator.)

$$(68.3 - 60)^2 = 68.89$$
$$(68.3 - 65)^2 = 10.89$$
$$(68.3 - 68)^2 = 0.09 \qquad 3(0.09) = 0.27$$
$$(68.3 - 70)^2 = 2.89 \qquad 2(2.89) = 5.78$$
$$(68.3 - 71)^2 = 7.29$$
$$(68.3 - 75)^2 = 44.89$$

2. Compute the sum of the squares.

$$138.01$$

3. Compute the mean of the sum of the squares.

$$\frac{138.01}{9} \approx 15.33$$

4. Compute the square root of the mean of the sum of the squares. (Use a calculator.)

$$\sqrt{15.33} \approx 3.9$$

Answer The mean is 68.3, the range is 15, and the standard deviation is 3.9.

■ CLASSROOM EXERCISES

Match each standard deviation with the correct set of data.

Standard deviations: 1.6 1.1

1. Set A 1.6

Score	20	19	18	17	16	15
Number	3	3	4	4	3	3

2. Set B 1.1

Score	20	19	18	17	16	15
Number	1	2	6	8	2	1

3. What is the range of data in Set A? 5

■ WRITTEN EXERCISES

Three sets of data are given. Without computing, state which set has the greatest standard deviation and which set has the least standard deviation.

A **1.** Set A: {91, 94, 97, 100, 103, 106, 109} Greatest: A, least: C
Set B: {94, 96, 98, 100, 102, 104, 106}
Set C: {97, 98, 99, 100, 101, 102, 103}

Find the range and standard deviation of each set of data. (Use a calculator.)

2. {10, 16, 17, 20, 21, 28, 28} 18, 6.0

3. {-15, -17, -17, -18, -24, -24, -25} 10, 3.9

4. {35, 35, 45, 45} 10, 5

5. {36, 39, 39, 40, 40, 40, 41, 41, 44} 8, 2

6. {34, 34, 40, 40, 40, 40, 40, 46, 46} 12, 4

7. {63, 72, 72, 75, 75, 75, 78, 78, 87} 24, 6

Find the mean, range, and standard deviation of each frequency distribution. (Use a calculator.)

8.

Score	9	22	23	24	26	27
Frequency	1	2	1	2	2	2

23, 18, 5

9.

Score	-9	-22	-23	-24	-26	-27
Frequency	10	20	10	20	20	20

-23, 18, 5

True or false?

B 10. If 10 is added to each score in a frequency distribution, the mean, median, and mode are each increased by 10. T

11. If 10 is added to each score in a frequency distribution, the range and standard deviation are increased by 10. F

12. If each score in a frequency distribution is doubled, the mean, median, and mode are doubled. T

13. If each score in a frequency distributuion is doubled, the range and standard deviation are doubled. T

14. The standard deviation of a set of numbers is never negative. T

15. There are as many numbers larger than the mean as there are smaller than the mean. F

In many frequency distributions, approximately 68% of the scores are within one standard deviation of the mean and approximately 95% are within two standard deviations of the mean.

The distribution of heights for a class of students is given.

Height of students (in.) (midpoint of interval)	54	57	60	63	66	69	72	75	78
Number of students	2	8	22	32	72	32	23	6	3

C 16. Describe the heights using the following statistics.

a. The mean. 66
b. The standard deviation (rounded to the nearest tenth). 4.5
c. The percent of heights within one standard deviation of the mean. 68%

• A set of data has these statistics:
   The median is 42.
   The lowest score is 14.
   The range is 60.

a. What is the highest score for the set of data?

$$14 + 60 = 74$$

b. Assume that the set of data contains 7 scores. Write two examples to show that the mean could be on "either side" of the median.

Answers will vary. For example,

Set 1	Set 2
14	14
21	28
28	42
42	42
42	56
56	63
74	74
mean: 39 4/7	mean: 45 4/7

c. Which of your sets has the greater standard deviation?

Set 1: 19.3
Set 2: 19.1

PURPOSE

Many distances can be measured directly. For example, we can measure the length of a house using a steel tape, the distance between cities using the odometer of a car, or the thickness of a piece of paper using a micrometer. Other distances are difficult or impossible to measure directly. For example, we cannot directly measure the distance between two stars because we cannot travel there, or the height of a mountain because we cannot drill a hole from the peak of the mountain down to its base. Such distances are measured indirectly by measuring other distances and using those other distances to compute the desired distance. One commonly used indirect-measurement technique involves similar triangles.

LESSON

The angle-sum property can be physically demonstrated. Carefully cut a large triangle from a piece of paper. Then tear off the corners and place them together as illustrated. The three corners together fill half the space about a point.

Students should realize that the above demonstration is not a proof, but it does make the property seem reasonable.

The concepts of corresponding sides and corresponding angles of similar triangles are not formally defined. Corresponding angles, which are congruent, are easy to locate in a figure. Students can then determine which sides are corresponding by mentally turning and/or flipping one triangle until its congruent angles "match up." The sides that have the same positions are corresponding sides.

OBJECTIVE

To compute the missing measures of sides of similar triangles.

Supplementary Topic
Trigonometry

Similar Triangles

Triangles exist in a variety of shapes and sizes. However, the sum of the degree measures of the angles of a triangle is constant.

Angle-Sum Property

The sum of the measures of the angles of a triangle is 180°.

The two triangles below have the same shape. They are called **similar** triangles. Angle A and angle D are **congruent** angles. (The angles are the same size.) Angle B is congruent to angle E, and angle C is congruent to angle F.

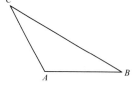

Definition: Similar Triangles

Two triangles are similar if and only if their corresponding angles are congruent.

604

Example 1 Determine whether triangle *MNO* and triangle *RST* are similar.

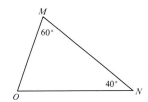

Solution Since each triangle has a 40°-angle and a 60°-angle, the third angles are [180 − (60 + 40)]° angles or 80°-angles. Corresponding angles of the two triangles are congruent.

Answer The triangles are similar.

The two triangles at the right are similar. Note that the ratios of the lengths of corresponding sides are equal.

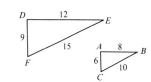

$$\frac{AB}{DE} = \frac{8}{12} = \frac{2}{3} \qquad \frac{BC}{EF} = \frac{10}{15} = \frac{2}{3} \qquad \frac{CA}{FD} = \frac{6}{9} = \frac{2}{3}$$

Property of Corresponding Sides of Similar Triangles

Corresponding sides of similar triangles are proportional.

The fact that corresponding sides of similar triangles are proportional gives us a method of computing missing lengths of triangles.

Example 2 Find the length of side *GH*.

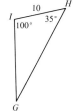
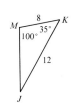

Solution Since two angles of one triangle are congruent to two angles of the other triangle, the triangles are similar and corresponding sides are proportional.

$$\frac{GH}{JK} = \frac{IH}{MK}$$

Substitute. $\dfrac{GH}{12} = \dfrac{10}{8}$

$$GH = \frac{10}{8} \cdot 12$$

$$GH = 15$$

Answer The length of side *GH* is 15.

Example 1.
Determine whether triangles *ABC* and *DEF* are similar.

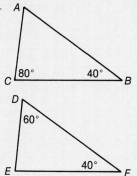

Angle *A* is a 60° angle, and angle *E* is an 80° angle. Since corresponding angles are congruent, the triangles are similar.

Example 2.
Triangles *ABC* and *XYZ* are similar.

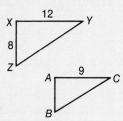

Find the length of side *AB*.

$$\frac{AB}{XZ} = \frac{AC}{XY}$$

$$\frac{AB}{8} = \frac{9}{12}$$

$$AB = 6$$

The length of side *AB* is 6.

Example 3.
A person 5 ft tall casts a 3-ft shadow at the same time a flagpole casts a 10-ft shadow. How tall is the flagpole?

$$\frac{5}{x} = \frac{3}{10}$$

$$3x = 50$$

$$x = 16\tfrac{2}{3}$$

The flagpole is 16⅔ feet tall.

CHECK UNDERSTANDING

- State two important characteristics of similar triangles. (Corresponding angles are congruent, and corresponding sides are proportional.)
- What is the sum of the angle measures of a triangle? (180°)

ASSIGNMENT GUIDE

Basic   1–10 all
Average   1–12 all
Enriched   5–18 all

ENRICHMENT PROBLEM

- Right triangle *ABC* is inscribed in a semicircle as shown.

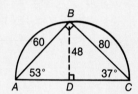

a. How many pairs of similar triangles can you find in the figure?

3 (*ABD* and *BDC*, *ABD* and *ABC*, *BDC* and *ABC*)

b. What is the length of $\overline{AD}$? of $\overline{DC}$?

AD = 36 and DC = 64

c. Find *AC* directly and show that *AC* = *AD* + *DC*.

$(AC)^2 = (AB)^2 + (BC)^2$
$= 60^2 + 80^2$
$= 3600 + 6400$
$= 10000$
$AC = 100$

$AC = AD + BC$
$= 36 + 64$
$= 100$
It checks.

Similar triangles can be used to solve some practical problems.

Example 3 A person 2 m tall casts a 3-m shadow at the same time that a tree casts a 10-m shadow. How tall is the tree?

Solution Sketch a picture. The two triangles are similar.

$$\frac{2}{x} = \frac{3}{10}$$

$$3x = 20$$

$$x = 6\frac{2}{3}$$

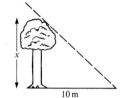

Answer The tree is about 6.7 m tall.

■ CLASSROOM EXERCISES

1. The measures of two angles of a triangle are 56° and 39°. What is the measure of the third angle? 85°

Find the missing lengths in these similar triangles.

2. $a = 5, b = 7$

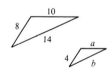

3. $a = 6\frac{6}{13}, b = 16\frac{5}{7}$

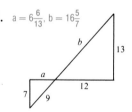

■ WRITTEN EXERCISES

The measures of two angles of a triangle are given. Find the measure of the third angle.

A 1. 25°, 100° 55° **2.** 90°, 12° 78° **3.** 16°, 56° 108° **4.** 62.6°, 72° 45.4°

Find the missing lengths in these similar triangles.

5.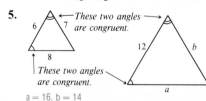

a = 16, b = 14

6.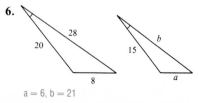

a = 6, b = 21

606

7. 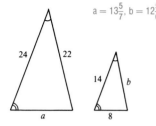 $a = 13\frac{5}{7}$, $b = 12\frac{5}{6}$

8. $a = 16$, $b = 16$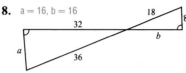

Solve.

9. At the time a 2-m pole casts a 3-m shadow, the shadow of a building is 15 m. What is the height of the building? 10 m

10. A scale model of a building is 7 cm tall and 15 cm long. If the actual building is 6 m long, what is the height of the building? 2.8 m

Triangles *ABC* and *DEF* are similar. Find the missing measures of the angles and sides.

B **11.** 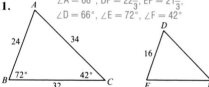 $\angle A = 66°$, $DF = 22\frac{2}{3}$, $EF = 21\frac{1}{3}$, $\angle D = 66°$, $\angle E = 72°$, $\angle F = 42°$

12. 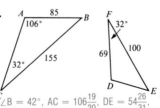 $\angle B = 42°$, $AC = 106\frac{19}{20}$, $DE = 54\frac{26}{31}$, $\angle D = 106°$, $\angle E = 42°$

A **regular polygon** has all angles congruent and all sides congruent. An equilateral triangle and a square are examples of regular polygons. The sum *S* of the degree measures of the angles of an *n*-sided regular polygon is given by the formula $S = (n - 2) \cdot 180$. Find the measure of each angle of these regular polygons.

C **13.** Regular pentagon 108°

14. Regular hexagon 120°

15. Regular octagon 135°

16. Regular decagon 144°

17. Regular 20-sided polygon 162°

18. Regular 100-sided polygon 176.4°

Mathematics and Your Future

Many entry-level jobs require only a limited knowledge of mathematics. Opportunities for promotion are often tied to education or training with a strong mathematics component. If you acquire a good background in mathematics you will increase your opportunities for employment and advancement.

1. Two angles of a triangle   57°
   measure 43° and 80°
   respectively. What
   is the measure of the
   third angle?

2. Are the triangles similar?   Yes

The triangles below are similar:

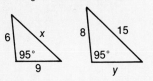

3. Find *x*. $x = 11\frac{1}{4}$
4. Find *y*. $y = 12$
5. A 6-ft shrub casts a 4-ft shadow
   at the same time that a tree
   casts a 15-ft shadow. How tall
   is the tree?   22.5 ft

PURPOSE

The tangent ratio and other trigonometric ratios can be used to find missing lengths and measures of angles given a single right triangle. This frees us from the need to have *two similar* triangles in order to make indirect measurements.

LESSON

Adjacent may be a new term for some students. The term itself is not important at this time; the concept is important. If you wish, feel free to substitute another more descriptive term such as *next to.*

   Emphasize that except for tan 45°, the tangent ratios given in the table are approximations. Therefore, we use "≈" instead of "=" when writing "equations" after values from the table are substituted.

OBJECTIVE

To use the tangent ratio to compute missing length and angle measures in right triangles.

The Tangent Ratio

Recall that a right triangle has a right (or 90°) angle and two acute angles. The side opposite the right angle is called the **hypotenuse**. Side *BC* is called the **side opposite angle *A*** and the **side adjacent to angle *B***. Similarly, side *AC* is called the **side opposite angle *B*** and the **side adjacent to angle *A***.

   Right triangles can be thought of as belonging to "families." For example, all right triangles with a 40° angle are similar, and all right triangles with a 30° angle are similar. For the triangles in any "family" of similar right triangles, the corresponding sides are proportional. For each right triangle "family," this ratio is constant:

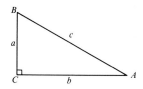

$$\frac{\text{Length of side opposite an acute angle}}{\text{Length of side adjacent to that acute angle}}$$

The ratio is called the **tangent** (or **tan**) of the acute angle. In triangle *ABC*:

$$\text{Tangent of angle } A = \frac{\text{Length of side opposite angle } A}{\text{Length of side adjacent to angle } A} \quad \tan A = \frac{a}{b}$$

$$\text{Tangent of angle } B = \frac{\text{Length of side opposite angle } B}{\text{Length of side adjacent to angle } B} \quad \tan B = \frac{b}{a}$$

Example 1 For triangle *XYZ* compute tan *X* and tan *Y* correct to the nearest hundredth.

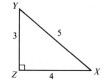

Solution $\tan X = \frac{3}{4} = 0.75$ $\tan Y = \frac{4}{3} = 1.33$

The tangent of an angle depends on the size of the angle. The following table lists the tangents of some acute angles. A complete table of tangents is on page 642. These ratios can be used to compute the missing measures of a right triangle.

Angle	Tangent	Angle	Tangent
5°	0.0875	50°	1.1918
10°	0.1763	55°	1.4281
15°	0.2679	60°	1.7321
20°	0.3640	65°	2.1445
25°	0.4663	70°	2.7475
30°	0.5774	75°	3.7321
35°	0.7002	80°	5.6713
40°	0.8391	85°	11.4301
45°	1.0000		

Example 1.

For triangle *ABC*, compute tan *A* and tan *B* correct to the nearest hundredth.

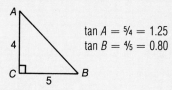

$$\tan A = \tfrac{5}{4} = 1.25$$
$$\tan B = \tfrac{4}{5} = 0.80$$

Example 2.
Find the length of side *PQ* to the nearest tenth.

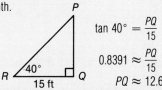

$$\tan 40° = \frac{PQ}{15}$$
$$0.8391 \approx \frac{PQ}{15}$$
$$PQ \approx 12.6$$

Side *PQ* is about 12.6 ft long.

Example 3.
The angle of elevation to the top of a building from a point on the ground 200 ft from the base of the building is 50°. How tall is the building?

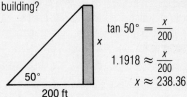

$$\tan 50° = \frac{x}{200}$$
$$1.1918 \approx \frac{x}{200}$$
$$x \approx 238.36$$

The building is about 238 ft tall.

CHECK UNDERSTANDING

- For triangle *ABC*, state tan *A* and tan *B* as fractions.
  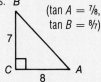
  ($\tan A = \tfrac{7}{8}$, $\tan B = \tfrac{8}{7}$)

- Use the table on page 608 to state the measure of the angle whose tangent is 1.4281. (55°)

- Find the tan 70° in the table on page 608. (2.7475)

Example 2 Find the length of side *MN* to the nearest tenth.

Solution

$$\tan 35° = \frac{l}{12}$$

Find tan 35° in the table and substitute.

$$0.7002 \approx \frac{l}{12}$$
$$l \approx 12(0.7002)$$
$$\approx 8.4$$

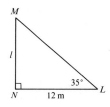

Answer Side *MN* is about 8.4 m long.

Example 3 A fire ranger in a 100-ft tower spotted smoke near the ground. The angle of depression was 5°. About how far from the base of the tower was the fire?

Solution Make a sketch. If the angle of depression is 5°, then angle *A* of the triangle is 85°.

$$\tan 85° = \frac{d}{100}$$
$$11.4301 \approx \frac{d}{100}$$
$$d \approx 1143$$

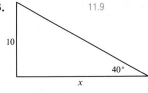

Answer The fire is about 1143 ft from the base of the tower.

■ CLASSROOM EXERCISES

1. Compute tan *A* and tan *B* to the nearest hundredth.

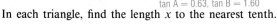

tan A = 0.63, tan B = 1.60

In each triangle, find the length *x* to the nearest tenth.

2.   8.4

3. 11.9

4. 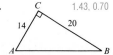 18.7

■ WRITTEN EXERCISES

Compute tan *A* and tan *B* to the nearest hundredth.

 1. 0.56, 1.80

2. 1.50, 0.67

3. 1.43, 0.70

ASSIGNMENT GUIDE

Basic   1–11 all
Average   1–14 all
Enriched 1–9 odd, 10–18 all

CONCEPT EXTENSION

The tangent of an angle of elevation is sometimes defined as the ratio $\frac{\text{rise}}{\text{run}}$.

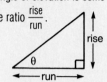

The steepness of a hill can be expressed in terms of its angle of elevation. However, in surveying, the more common term is **percent grade,** where a 1% grade refers to a rise of 1 unit for a run of 100 units. A frequent mistake students make is assuming that a 100% grade refers to a vertical plane. It is actually the ratio $\frac{\text{rise}}{\text{run}} = \frac{100 \text{ units}}{100 \text{ units}} = 1$. This corresponds to $\tan \theta = 1$ where θ is the angle of elevation. In this case $\theta = 45°$. Any angle of elevation can be converted to a percent grade by multiplying the tangent of the angle by 100 percent.

ENRICHMENT PROBLEM

• Use the definition of tangent to show that the following statements are true for triangle XYZ.

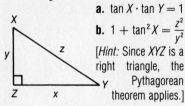

  a. $\tan X \cdot \tan Y = 1$

  b. $1 + \tan^2 X = \frac{z^2}{y^2}$

  [*Hint:* Since XYZ is a right triangle, the Pythagorean theorem applies.]

a. $\tan X = \frac{x}{y}$, $y \neq 0$, and $\tan Y = \frac{y}{x}$, $x \neq 0$

$\tan X \cdot \tan Y = \frac{x}{y} \cdot \frac{y}{x} = 1$

b. $1 + \tan^2 X = 1 + \frac{x^2}{y^2}$, $y \neq 0$

$= \frac{y^2 + x^2}{y^2}$

$= \frac{z^2}{y^2}$

610

Find the length x to the nearest tenth.

4. 42.9

5. 50.1

6. 71.5

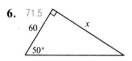

Find the measures of angle A and angle B to the nearest degree.

7.

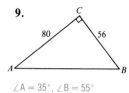

$\angle A = 20°, \angle B = 70°$

8.

$\angle A = 45°, \angle B = 45°$

9.

$\angle A = 35°, \angle B = 55°$

Solve. Give each answer to the nearest tenth.

10. From a point 20 m from the base of a tree, the angle of elevation to the top of the tree is 30°. What is the height of the tree?   11.5 m

11. A lighthouse has a telescope mounted 120 m above the surface of the ocean. A ship was sighted at an angle of depression of 5°. How far was the ship from the lighthouse?   1371.6 m

Find the lengths x and y to the nearest tenth.

B **12.** $x = 3.5, y = 8.4$ **13.**

$x = 57.2, y = 50$ **14.**

$x = 136.8, y = 36.4$

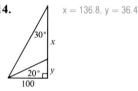

Find α and β in each figure to the nearest degree. The letters α (alpha) and β (beta) are the Greek letter equivalents of a and b.

C **15.** $\alpha = 45°, \beta = 20°$ **16.**

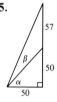

$\alpha = 30°, \beta = 45°$ **17.** $\alpha = 20°, \beta = 20°$

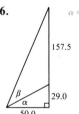

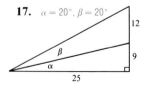

Solve. Give the answer to the nearest tenth.

18. Looking due north from the observation deck of a lighthouse 60 m above the sea, a lighthouse keeper sees two ships. The angles of depression to the ships are 5° and 10°. How far apart are the ships?   345.5 m

Class Starter Quiz
on previous section

1. Write tan *A* as a fraction. ⅔
2. Write tan *B* as a decimal. 1.5

Use the table on page 642.
3. Find the measure of angle *X*. 35°
4. Find the measure of angle *Y*. 55°

5. Find the length of side *PQ* to 15.1
   the nearest tenth.

Sine and Cosine

The tangent ratio is an example of a **trigonometric ratio**. Two other trigonometric ratios are the **sine ratio (sin)** and **cosine ratio (cos)**.

Sine of angle $A = \dfrac{\text{Length of side opposite angle } A}{\text{Length of hypotenuse}}$ $\quad \sin A = \dfrac{a}{c}$

Cosine of angle $A = \dfrac{\text{Length of side adjacent to angle } A}{\text{Length of hypotenuse}}$ $\quad \cos A = \dfrac{b}{c}$

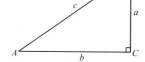

Example 1 Compute sin *R*, cos *R*, sin *T*, and cos *T* to the nearest hundredth.

Solution

$\sin R = \dfrac{5}{13}$ $\qquad \cos R = \dfrac{12}{13}$

≈ 0.38 $\qquad\quad \approx 0.92$

$\sin T = \dfrac{12}{13}$ $\qquad \cos T = \dfrac{5}{13}$

≈ 0.92 $\qquad\quad \approx 0.38$

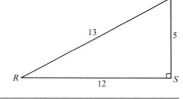

Example 1 illustrates the facts that $\sin A = \cos (90 - A)$ and $\cos A = \sin (90 - A)$. A table of trigonometric ratios for angles 0° to 90° is on page 642.

The sine and cosine ratios can be used to solve problems involving right triangles.

Example 2 Find the lengths of sides *ST* and *RS* to the nearest tenth.

Solution Solve for *r*.

$$\sin 35° = \frac{r}{18}$$

$$0.5736 \approx \frac{r}{18}$$

$$r \approx 10.3$$

Solve for *t*.

$$\cos 35° = \frac{t}{18}$$

$$0.8192 \approx \frac{t}{18}$$

$$t \approx 14.7$$

Answer The length of side *ST* is about 10.3 m.
The length of side *RS* is about 14.7 m.

PURPOSE

The sine and cosine ratios, along with the tangent ratio, are the most commonly used trigonometric ratios.

LESSON

Students should notice that the sine of one acute angle of a right triangle is the cosine of the other acute angle.

Emphasize again that most trigonometric ratios given in the table are approximations.

ADDITIONAL EXAMPLES

Example 1.
For triangle *ABC* compute sin *A*, sin *B*, cos *A*, and cos *B* correct to the nearest hundredth.

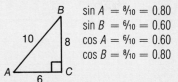

$\sin A = {}^{8}/_{10} = 0.80$
$\sin B = {}^{6}/_{10} = 0.60$
$\cos A = {}^{6}/_{10} = 0.60$
$\cos B = {}^{8}/_{10} = 0.80$

ADDITIONAL EXAMPLES

Example 2.

Find the lengths of sides *PQ* and *QR* to the nearest tenth.

$\sin 50° \approx 0.7660 \quad \cos 50° \approx 0.6428$

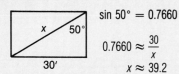

$\cos 50° \approx \dfrac{PQ}{10}$

$PQ \approx 6.4$

$\sin 50° = \dfrac{QR}{10}$

$QR \approx 7.7$

Example 3.

The diagonal of a rectangle forms a 50° angle with the shorter side. How long is the diagonal if the longer side of the rectangle is 30 ft?

$\sin 50° = 0.7660$

$0.7660 \approx \dfrac{30}{x}$

$x \approx 39.2$

The diagonal is about 39.2 ft long.

CHECK UNDERSTANDING

- State sin *A* and sin *B* as fractions.
  ($\sin A = {}^{40}\!/_{41}$, $\sin B = {}^{9}\!/_{41}$)
- State cos *A* and cos *B* as fractions.
  ($\cos A = {}^{9}\!/_{41}$, $\cos B = {}^{40}\!/_{41}$)

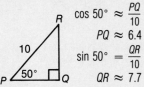

- Find sin 70° and cos 35° in the table on page 642.
  ($\sin 70° \approx 0.9397$, $\cos 35° \approx 0.8192$)

ASSIGNMENT GUIDE

Basic   1–12 all
Average   1–5 odd, 7–17 all
Enriched   1–9 odd, 10–20 all

612

Example 3   A ladder is needed to reach a window that is 15 ft above the ground. How long must the ladder be if the angle that it makes with the ground is 60°?

Solution $\sin 60° = \dfrac{15}{x}$

$0.8660 \approx \dfrac{15}{x}$

$0.8660x \approx 15$

$x \approx 17.3$

Answer   The ladder must be at least 17.3 ft long.

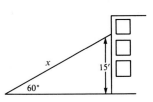

■ CLASSROOM EXERCISES

1. Compute sin *A*, cos *A*, sin *B*, and cos *B* to the nearest hundredth.   0.38, 0.92, 0.92, 0.38

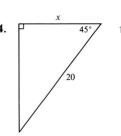

Find the length *x* to the nearest tenth.

2.   24.9   **3.**   20.9   **4.**   45°   14.1

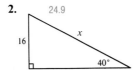 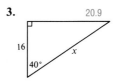 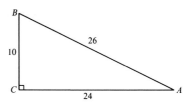

■ WRITTEN EXERCISES

Compute sin *A*, cos *A*, sin *B*, and cos *B* to the nearest hundredth.

A   **1.**   **2.**   **3.**

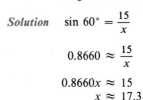

0.80, 0.60, 0.60, 0.80

0.28, 0.96, 0.96, 0.28

0.98, 0.22, 0.22, 0.98

Find the length *x* to the nearest tenth.

4.   11.5   **5.**   47.0   **6.**   53.6

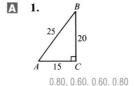 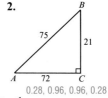   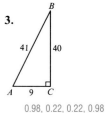 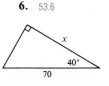

612   Supplementary Topic   Trigonometry

a. $\sin X = \cos Y$
b. $(\sin X)^2 + (\cos X)^2 = 1$
c. $(\cos Y)^2 + (\cos X)^2 = (\sin X)^2 + (\sin Y)^2$

a. $\sin X = \dfrac{x}{z}$, $\cos Y = \dfrac{x}{z}$
So, $\sin X = \cos Y$

b. $\sin X = \dfrac{x}{z}$, $\cos X = \dfrac{y}{z}$

$\left(\dfrac{x}{z}\right)^2 + \left(\dfrac{y}{z}\right)^2 = \dfrac{x^2 + y^2}{z^2}$

By the Pythagorean theorem,
$x^2 + y^2 = z^2$

So, $\dfrac{x^2 + y^2}{z^2} = \dfrac{z^2}{z^2} = 1$

c. $(\cos Y)^2 + (\cos X)^2 \overset{?}{=}$
$(\sin X)^2 + (\sin Y)^2$

$\dfrac{x^2}{z^2} + \dfrac{y^2}{z^2} \overset{?}{=} \dfrac{x^2}{z^2} + \dfrac{y^2}{z^2}$

$\dfrac{x^2 + y^2}{z^2} = \dfrac{x^2 + y^2}{z^2}$

Find the measures of angle *A* and angle *B* to the nearest degree.

7. $\angle A = 30°$, $\angle B = 60°$

8. $\angle A = 75°$, $\angle B = 15°$

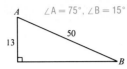

9. $\angle A = 65°$, $\angle B = 25°$

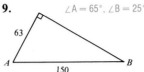

Solve. Give each answer to the nearest tenth.

10. A 15-ft ladder leaning against a building forms a 60° angle with the ground. How high above the ground does the ladder touch the building? 13.0 ft

11. A 12-ft ladder leaning against a wall forms a 65° angle with the ground. How far from the wall is the foot of the ladder? 5.1 ft

12. The diagonal of a rectangle forms a 35° angle with the longer side. How long is the diagonal if the longer side of the rectangle is 150 cm long?
183.1 cm

Find the lengths *x* and *y* to the nearest tenth.

B **13.**

$x = 76.6$, $y = 81.5$

14.

$x = 64.3$, $y = 53.2$

15.

$x = 57.4$, $y = 33.8$

Solve. Give each answer to the nearest tenth.

16. The diagonal of a rectangle forms a 25° angle with the longer side. If the rectangle is 100 cm long, what is the perimeter of the rectangle? 293.3 cm

17. There are two routes from *A* to *B*, as shown in the figure. The direct route is 100 mi long at an angle of 35° south of east. The other route is east to point *C*, then south to *B*. How much longer is the route by way of *C*?
39.3 mi

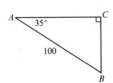

Find the measures of angles α and β to the nearest degree.

C **18.** $\alpha = 30°$, $\beta = 35°$

19. $\alpha = 35°$, $\beta = 35°$

20.

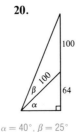

$\alpha = 40°$, $\beta = 25°$

Class Starter Quiz
on previous section

1. Write sin A as a fraction.   ½
2. Write cos B as a decimal.   0.5
3. Use the table on page 642.
   If cos $T \approx 0.9063$, state the   25°
   measure of angle T.

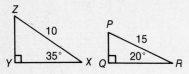

4. Find the length of side XY.   8.2
5. Find the length of side PQ.   5.1

PURPOSE

Many practical applications of trigonometric ratios involving right triangle problems.

LESSON

If students are allowed to use calculators, all calculations are equally simple. However, if students are required to use paper and pencil calculations, they should plan ahead to avoid dividing by four-place decimals from the trigonometric ratio tables.

ADDITIONAL EXAMPLES

Example 1.
Find the length of side AB.

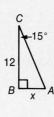

Let x = the length of side AB.

$$\tan 15° = \frac{x}{12}$$

$$0.2679 \approx \frac{x}{12}$$

$$x \approx 3.2$$

OBJECTIVE

To use trigonometric ratios to solve problems.

Using Trigonometric Ratios

If the measures of an acute angle and one side of a right triangle are known, the other measures can be computed.

Example 1 Find the length of side AC.

Solution Let x = the length of side AC in meters.

$$\tan B = \frac{x}{5}$$

$$\tan 30° = \frac{x}{5}$$

$$0.5774 \approx \frac{x}{5}$$

$$x \approx 2.9$$

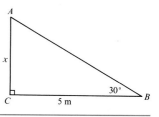

Answer The length of side AC is about 2.9 m.

Example 2 Find the missing measures of the angle and sides in the triangle below.

Solution *Find angle A.*   Measure of angle $A = 90° - 35° = 55°$

Find side BC. $\tan A = \dfrac{a}{18}$

$$\tan 55° = \frac{a}{18}$$

$$1.4281 \approx \frac{a}{18}$$

$$a \approx 25.7$$

Find side AB. $\sin B = \dfrac{18}{c}$

$$\sin 35° = \frac{18}{c}$$

$$0.5736 \approx \frac{18}{c}$$

$$0.5736c \approx 18$$

$$c \approx 31.4$$

Answer The measure of angle A is 55°. Side BC is about 25.7 m long. Side AB is about 31.4 m long.

Example 3 Find the area of a right triangle in which one acute angle measures 40° and the side opposite that angle is 30 m long.

Solution The area of a right triangle is equal to one half the product of the lengths of the perpendicular sides.

Find x.
$$\tan 40° = \frac{30}{x}$$

$$0.8391 \approx \frac{30}{x}$$

$$x \approx 36$$

Find the area.
$$A \approx \frac{1}{2} \cdot 30 \cdot 36$$

$$\approx 540$$

Answer The area of the triangle is about 540 m².

CLASSROOM EXERCISES

1. Find the missing measures to the nearest tenth. $\angle B = 65°$, AC = 21.4, AB = 23.7

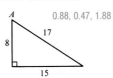

2. A flagpole casts a shadow 30 m long when the angle of elevation of the sun is 60°. How tall is the flagpole? ≈ 52.0 m

WRITTEN EXERCISES

Find sin A, cos A, and tan A to the nearest hundredth.

A **1.** 0.60, 0.80, 0.75

2. 0.88, 0.47, 1.88

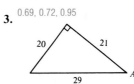

3. 0.69, 0.72, 0.95

Find α and compute a and b to the nearest tenth.

4. 60°; 17.3, 10

5. 35°; 45.9, 65.5

6. 50°; 30.6, 25.7

ADDITIONAL EXAMPLES

Example 2.
Find the missing measure of the angle and sides in triangle *PQR*.

Find angle *Q*. Angle *Q* is 60°.

Find side *PQ* (*x*).

$$\sin 60° = \frac{25}{x}$$

$$0.8660 = \frac{25}{x}$$

$$x \approx 29$$

Find side *QR* (*y*).

$$\tan 30° = \frac{y}{25}$$

$$0.5774 \approx \frac{y}{25}$$

$$y \approx 14.4$$

Example 3.
Find the area of a right triangle in which one acute angle measures 50° and the side adjacent to the angle is 20 m long.

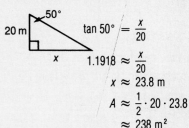

$$\tan 50° = \frac{x}{20}$$

$$1.1918 \approx \frac{x}{20}$$

$$x \approx 23.8 \text{ m}$$

$$A \approx \frac{1}{2} \cdot 20 \cdot 23.8$$

$$\approx 238 \text{ m}^2$$

The area is about 238 m².

CHECK UNDERSTANDING

• Write an equation for finding the length of side *AB*.

$$\left(\sin 40° = \frac{7}{x} \text{ or } \cos 50° = \frac{7}{x}\right)$$

ASSIGNMENT GUIDE

Basic   1–15 all
Average   1–9 odd, 10–22 all
Enriched 1–11 odd, 12–25 all

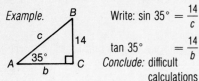
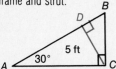
616

Find α and compute b and c to the nearest tenth.

7. 80°; 7.1, 40.6

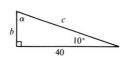

8. 50°; 25.2, 39.2

9. 55°; 10.5, 18.3

Solve. Give each answer to the nearest whole number.

10. From a point 20 mi from the base of a mountain, the angle of elevation to the summit of the mountain is 5°. How many miles is the summit above the base of the mountain?   2

11. A scout found an angle of elevation to the tip of a tree to be 40° at a point 50 ft from the tree. What is the height of the tree?   42 ft

12. A 50-ft supporting cable attached to the top of a 41-ft pole is anchored to the ground. What angle does the cable make with the ground?   55°

13. The base of a 25-ft ladder leaning against a building is 16 ft from the building. What angle does the ladder make with the ground?   50°

14. In a right triangle, the side opposite a 35° angle is 28 cm. What is the area of the triangle?   560 cm²

15. A side 18 cm long is opposite a 20° angle in a right triangle. What is the area of the triangle?   445 cm²

True or false? Refer to triangle ABC.

B **16.** $\sin A = \dfrac{a}{c}$ T

17. $\sin A = \cos B$ T

18. $(\sin A)^2 + (\cos A)^2 = 1$ T

19. Area $= \dfrac{ac \cdot \sin B}{2}$ T

Find the missing length in each right triangle. Then compute $\sin A$ to the nearest hundredth.

20. 30, 0.88

21. 12, 0.32

22. 50, 0.28

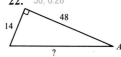

Find the measure of α to the nearest degree.

C **23.** 53°

24. 67°

25. 28°

EXTRA PRACTICE

There is a set of Extra Practice exercises for each section in the textbook. These exercises are at the A-level of difficulty and can be used whenever a student needs additional basic practice.

■ EXTRA PRACTICE

Chapter 1

1–1

j	k	K	r	R
$\frac{1}{3}$	$\frac{1}{2}$	2	0	3

Substitute and simplify.

1. $k \times K$ 1 **2.** $r \times R$ 0 **3.** $R - K$ 1 **4.** $k - r$ $\frac{1}{2}$ **5.** $j \times k$ $\frac{1}{6}$

6. $\frac{1}{4} \times j$ $\frac{1}{12}$ **7.** $\frac{1}{4} + k$ $\frac{3}{4}$ **8.** $R - k$ $2\frac{1}{2}$ **9.** $\frac{r}{k}$ 0 **10.** $\frac{R}{j}$ 9

w	y	t	s	r
4	16	0.25	12	0.75

Substitute and simplify.

11. $\frac{w}{y}$ $\frac{1}{4}$ **12.** $\frac{y}{w}$ 4 **13.** $r - t$ 0.5 **14.** $w - r$ 3.25 **15.** $\frac{s}{w}$ 3

16. $\frac{y}{t}$ 64 **17.** $1.3 - r$ 0.55 **18.** $\frac{s}{0.6}$ 20 **19.** $1.5 \times w$ 6 **20.** $y \times y$ 256

1–2 Write $+$, $-$, $\times$, or $\div$ to tell which operation is done first.

1. $7 \times 9 + 10$ $\times$ **2.** $7 + 9 \times 10$ $\times$ **3.** $\frac{5 + 10}{3}$ $+$ **4.** $6 + 4 \div 2$ $\div$

5. $(7 + 3) \times 9$ $+$ **6.** $9 \times (10 - 2)$ $-$ **7.** $12 \div (6 - 2)$ $-$ **8.** $12 \div 6 - 2$ $\div$

Simplify.

9. $(7 + 5) \times 3$ 36 **10.** $30 \div (6 - 1)$ 6 **11.** $5 + 3 \times 10$ 35 **12.** $(48 - 8) \div 5$ 8

13. $(18 - 3) \times 2$ 30 **14.** $36 + 6 \div 3$ 38 **15.** $(6.8 - 1.8) \times 3$ 15 **16.** $4.2 + 2.4 \div 6$ 4.6

17. $(4.3 + 2.1) \times 5$ 32 **18.** $\frac{12 + 18}{6 + 4}$ 3 **19.** $\left(\frac{7}{8} - \frac{1}{4}\right) \times \frac{1}{2}$ $\frac{5}{16}$ **20.** $8 + 12 \div \frac{1}{2}$ 32

1–3 Evaluate for $a = 12$.

1. $5(a + 3)$ 75 **2.** $7(a - 4)$ 56 **3.** a^2 144 **4.** $3a$ 36 **5.** $\frac{1}{4}a$ 3

6. $2a - 7$ 17 **7.** $3a + 4$ 40 **8.** 1^a 1 **9.** $(a - 2)^3$ 1000 **10.** $0.4a$ 4.8

x	y	a	b	c
$\frac{1}{3}$	$\frac{1}{2}$	0	2	6

Substitute and simplify.

11. bc 12 **12.** $(c - b)y$ 2 **13.** $xc + 5$ 7

14. $c\left(x + \frac{2}{3}\right)$ 6 **15.** $(10 - c)y$ 2 **16.** $(b + c)^2$ 64

17. $b^4 + c$ 22 **18.** $xyabc$ 0 **19.** $c(y - x)$ 1

1-4 For each pair of expressions, substitute numbers for the variable and simplify the expressions. State whether you think the expressions in each pair are equivalent.

1. $2x + x$
$3x$ Yes

2. $(2a)^2$
$2a^2$ No

3. $7 + r$
$r + 7$ Yes

4. $7(8y)$
$(7 \cdot 8)y$ Yes

5. $9(b - 3)$
$9b + 6$ No

6. $20 - (s - 4)$
$(20 - s) - 4$ No

7. $50 - (z - 10)$
$(50 - z) + 10$ Yes

8. $(c + 1)^2$
$c^2 + 2c + 1$ Yes

9. $t \cdot 6$
$6t$ Yes

10. $12(8 + k)$
$96 + 12k$ Yes

11. $1 \cdot m$
m Yes

12. d^3
$d^2 + d$ No

13. $(j + 2)(j + 3)$
$j^2 + 6$ No

1-5 Name the property illustrated in each equation.

1. $(5 + 3) + 0 = 5 + 3$
Identity Property for Addition

2. $(1 + 5) + 2 = 2 + (1 + 5)$
Commutative Property of Addition

3. $4 + (1 + 8) = (4 + 1) + 8$
Associative Property of Addition

4. $7(9 + 6) = 63 + 42$ Distributive Property

5. $24(5a) = (24 \cdot 5)a$
Associative Property of Multiplication

6. $13(7r) = (7r) \cdot 13$
Commutative Property of Multiplication

7. $10(1.3 + 0.5d) = 13 + 5d$
Distributive Property

8. $1q = q$ Identity Property for Multiplication

9. $(0 + m) + 6 = m + 6$
Identity Property for Addition

10. $12r + 36 = 12(r + 3)$ Distributive Property

11. $20(5n) = (20 \cdot 5)n$
Associative Property of Multiplication

12. $(z + 36) + 64 = z + (36 + 64)$
Associative Property of Addition

1-6 Simplify each expression.

1. $3p + 7p$ 10p

2. $4r - r$ 3r

3. $2(m + 3) - 1$ 2m + 5

4. $6(3z) - 3z$ 15z

5. $3(c + 9) - 4$ 3c + 23

6. $12y - 10y$ 2y

7. $5(n + 2) - 2n$ 3n + 10

8. $2(r + s) - 2r$ 2s

9. $7 - g - 5$ 2 - g

10. $2.5z - 2 - 0.5z$ 2z - 2

11. $2.3w - 2w - x$ 0.3w - x

12. $\frac{1}{6}c + \frac{5}{6}c$ c

13. $2(5a) + 3(4a)$ 22a

14. $7h + 8h + 9$ 15h + 9

15. $7(10b) - 2(3b)$ 64b

16. $5 + 6p + 3p$ 5 + 9p

17. $w + 3(w - 1)$ 4w - 3

18. $12j + 6j + j$ 19j

19. $k + 10k + 12k$ 23k

20. $4(x + y) - 4y$ 4x

1-7 Write an expression for each.

1. Mr. Adams is 3 years older than Mrs. Adams.

a. Let x be Mr. Adams' age in years. What is Mrs. Adams' age? x − 3
b. Let y be Mrs. Adams' age in years. What is Mr. Adams' age? y + 3

2. A rectangle is 4 times as long as it is wide.

a. Let w be the width. What is the length? 4w
b. Let l be the length. What is the width? l ÷ 4

3. There are c coins in a case.

a. If the average weight of a coin is 4.3 g, what is the total weight of the coins? 4.3c
b. If the total weight of the coins is 128 g, what is the average weight of one coin? 128 ÷ c

Chapter 2

2–1 Replace ⑦ with <, >, or = to make a true statement.

1. $+4.7$ ⑦ -5.1 $>$ **2.** $-2\frac{1}{2}$ ⑦ $-\frac{5}{2}$ $=$ **3.** -1.7 ⑦ -1.8 $>$

4. $-\frac{3}{8}$ ⑦ $-\frac{5}{7}$ $>$ **5.** $-\frac{5}{4}$ ⑦ $-\frac{4}{5}$ $<$ **6.** $\frac{3}{4}$ ⑦ $\frac{2}{3}$ $>$

7. -2.5 ⑦ -1.9 $<$ **8.** -4.9 ⑦ 3.2 $<$ **9.** $\frac{5}{4}$ ⑦ $-1\frac{1}{4}$ $>$

Simplify.

10. $-(-4.7)$ 4.7   **11.** $|9.2|$ 9.2   **12.** $|-2.5|$ 2.5   **13.** $-|0.5|$ -0.5

14. $-|-6.2|$ -6.2 **15.** $-(-5.3)$ 5.3   **16.** $|0.6|$ 0.6   **17.** $|-19.3|$ 19.3

18. $-|7|$ -7 **19.** $-\left|-\frac{7}{2}\right|$ $-\frac{7}{2}$ **20.** $-\left|\frac{4}{3}\right|$ $-\frac{4}{3}$ **21.** $|-12.8|$ 12.8

2–2 Simplify.

1. $5 + (-2)$ 3   **2.** $-9 + (-9)$ -18 **3.** $7 + (-10)$ -3 **4.** $-12 + (-6)$ -18

5. $-16 + (-23)$ -39 **6.** $12 + (-4)$ 8   **7.** $-28 + (-75)$ -103 **8.** $15 + (-45)$ -30

9. $-4.93 + (-2.85)$ -7.78 **10.** $4.75 + (-5.5)$ -0.75 **11.** $-9.53 + 2.2$ -7.33

12. $-6.4 + 8.2$ 1.8   **13.** $1.7 + (-1.2)$ 0.5   **14.** $-5.4 + 1.18$ -4.22

15. $\frac{1}{2} + \left(-\frac{2}{3}\right)$ $-\frac{1}{6}$ **16.** $\frac{5}{3} + \left(-\frac{3}{4}\right)$ $\frac{11}{12}$ **17.** $-\frac{1}{3} + \frac{1}{2}$ $\frac{1}{6}$

18. $1\frac{1}{2} + \left(-3\frac{1}{4}\right)$ $-1\frac{3}{4}$ **19.** $2\frac{5}{8} + \left(-1\frac{5}{6}\right)$ $\frac{19}{24}$ **20.** $-5\frac{3}{4} + 1\frac{2}{3}$ $-4\frac{1}{12}$

21. $-10 + (-4) + 3$ -11 **22.** $-1.3 + 5.4 + (-1.2)$ 2.9

23. $-\frac{2}{3} + \left(-\frac{1}{2}\right) + \left(-\frac{1}{3}\right)$ $-\frac{3}{2}$ **24.** $-\frac{5}{4} + \left(-\frac{2}{3}\right) + \frac{1}{4}$ $-\frac{5}{3}$

25. $|1.2 + (-3.6)| + (-2)$ 0.4   **26.** $|-2.8 + 5.3| + 7$ 9.5

2–3 Simplify.

1. $-3 - (-10)$ 7   **2.** $43 - 27$ 16   **3.** $26 - 30$ -4

4. $-43 - 20$ -63 **5.** $-1.5 - (-2.5)$ 1   **6.** $3.7 - 4.2$ -0.5

7. $6.4 - (-4.2)$ 10.6   **8.** $-17.2 - 12.8$ -30 **9.** $\frac{1}{2} - \left(-\frac{1}{2}\right)$ 1

10. $-\frac{2}{3} - \frac{2}{3}$ $-\frac{4}{3}$ **11.** $\frac{3}{4} - \left(-\frac{1}{2}\right)$ $\frac{5}{4}$ **12.** $-\frac{2}{3} - \frac{1}{2}$ $-\frac{7}{6}$

13. $-5 - 2 - 6$ -13 **14.** $-7 + 10 - 2$ 1   **15.** $8 - 10 - 5$ -7

16. $-7 - 6 + 2$ -11 **17.** $12 - (8 - 3)$ 7   **18.** $2 - (10 - 7)$ -1

2-4 Simplify.

1. $-4 \cdot 7$ -28 **2.** $-9 \cdot -3$ 27 **3.** $10 \cdot -4$ -40

4. $-1.5 \cdot -4$ 6 **5.** $\dfrac{1}{2} \cdot -\dfrac{1}{3}$ $-\dfrac{1}{6}$ **6.** $-\dfrac{3}{4} \cdot -\dfrac{2}{3}$ $\dfrac{1}{2}$

w	x	y	z
$-\dfrac{5}{4}$	$\dfrac{2}{3}$	-12	-1

Substitute and simplify.

7. wx $-\dfrac{5}{6}$ **8.** wy 15 **9.** $wxyz$ -10 **10.** $(-x)y$ 8

11. $w(9 + z)$ -10 **12.** $w(9 - z)$ $-\dfrac{25}{2}$ **13.** $z(y - z)$ 11 **14.** $(yz)(yz)$ 144

2-5 Write each division as a multiplication and simplify.

1. $2 \div 3$ $\dfrac{2}{3}$ **2.** $\dfrac{3}{4} \div \dfrac{2}{3}$ $\dfrac{9}{8}$ **3.** $-\dfrac{1}{2} \div \dfrac{1}{3}$ $-\dfrac{3}{2}$ **4.** $0 \div 4$ 0

5. $-6 \div -3$ 2 **6.** $-\dfrac{1}{2} \div 5$ $-\dfrac{1}{10}$ **7.** $2\dfrac{1}{3} \div -2$ $-\dfrac{7}{6}$ **8.** $-1\dfrac{1}{4} \div -1\dfrac{1}{8}$ $\dfrac{10}{9}$

A	r	R	c
-8	-12	$\dfrac{3}{2}$	$-\dfrac{2}{3}$

Substitute and simplify.

9. $\dfrac{r}{A}$ $\dfrac{3}{2}$ **10.** $\dfrac{A}{r}$ $\dfrac{2}{3}$ **11.** $\dfrac{R}{r}$ $-\dfrac{1}{8}$ **12.** $\dfrac{r}{R}$ -8

13. $\dfrac{A + r}{R}$ $-\dfrac{40}{3}$ **14.** $\dfrac{A - r}{c}$ -6 **15.** $\dfrac{Ar}{Rc}$ -96 **16.** $\dfrac{r}{R + c}$ $-\dfrac{72}{5}$

2-6 Simplify.

1. $6 + (-a)$ $6 - a$ **2.** $5 - (-2b)$ $5 + 2b$ **3.** $-c + (-2c)$ $-3c$ **4.** $-2c - (-c)$ $-c$

5. $t + (-r) + s$ $t - r + s$ **6.** $7 - (-x) - y$ $7 + x - y$

7. $5 + (-p) + (-q)$ $5 - p - q$ **8.** $4 - (-a) - (-b)$ $4 + a + b$

2-7 State the property illustrated in each equation.

1. $p + q = q + p$
Commutative (Add.)

2. $(2k)r = 2(kr)$
Associative (Mult.)

3. $5(m + n) = 5m + 5n$
Distributive

4. $3a + 0 = 3a$
Identity (Add.)

5. $t + (-t) = 0$
Inverse (Add.)

6. $(2 + r) + t = 2 + (r + t)$
Associative (Add.)

Simplify.

7. $3t + t$ $4t$ **8.** $4r - r$ $3r$ **9.** $2a + 3 + 7a$ $9a + 3$

10. $3z - 7 - 7 - 3z$ -14 **11.** $-5t + v + t + v$ $-4t + 2v$ **12.** $14w + 6 + 6w - w$ $19w + 6$

13. $b + 3a + 5 + a$ $b + 4a + 5$ **14.** $b + 2a + 2b - 4$ $3b + 2a - 4$ **15.** $4 + 7v - 16w - 6v - w$ $4 + v - 17w$

620

2–8 Write an equivalent expression without parentheses.

1. $3(c + 10)$ $3c + 30$ **2.** $-4(t + 8)$ **3.** $7(t - 9)$ $7t - 63$ **4.** $-8(b - 3)$
$-4t - 32$ $-8b + 24$
5. $2(3r - 7)$ $6r - 14$ **6.** $6(a + 5)$ $6a + 30$ **7.** $-1(4c + 2)$ **8.** $-4(b + 1)$
$-4c - 2$ $-4b - 4$

Simplify.

9. $2(q + 3) + 4$ $2q + 10$ **10.** $3(h - 6) + 9$ $3h - 9$ **11.** $-2(k - 3) + 10$
$-2k + 16$
12. $-4(2 - j) - 3$ $4j - 11$ **13.** $5(x + 2) + x$ $6x + 10$ **14.** $3(y - 4) + 2y$ $5y - 12$

15. $-8a + 3(2a + 3)$ **16.** $3a - 5(a - 2) + 7$ **17.** $-4 + 6(b + 2) - b$
$-2a + 9$ $-2a + 17$ $5b + 8$
18. $2(c + 3) + 4(c + 5)$ $6c + 26$ **19.** $6(p - 2) + 2(2p + 3)$ $10p - 6$

20. $4(q + 3) - 3(q - 1)$ $q + 15$ **21.** $5(r + 2) - (r - 10)$ $4r + 20$

2–9 Make a table to solve each problem.

1. Andrew Rose has 20 coins consisting of nickels and dimes. How many of the coins are nickels if the total value of the coins is $1.30? 14

2. Machine A produces 8 units per hour and machine B produces 10 units per hour. Machine A starts producing at 9:00 A.M. and machine B starts producing 2 h later. At what time will they have produced a total of 115 units? 4:30 P.M.

3. A painter can paint $\frac{1}{30}$ of a house in 1 h. The painter's assistant can paint $\frac{1}{60}$ of the house in 1 h. Working together, how long would it take them to paint the house? 20 h

4. What number added to the numerator and to the denominator of $\frac{2}{11}$ makes a new fraction equal to $\frac{1}{2}$? 7

5. Russ Fullbright's light truck goes 25 mi on 1 gal of gasoline. He drives at a rate of 55 mph. How many hours can he drive using 11 gal of gasoline? 5

6. Mama's Deli makes a profit of $225 per day on Fridays and Saturdays. It makes a $175 profit on Mondays and Wednesdays. On Tuesdays and Thursdays it makes a $50 profit. What is the profit for a 50-week period? $45,000

Chapter 3

3–1 Which of the numbers 0, 1, 2, 3, and 4 are solutions of these equations?

1. $2x + 5 = 13$ 4   **2.** $-x + 3 = 1$ 2   **3.** $3x + 1 = 1$ 0

4. $3(x + 1) = 6$ 1   **5.** $x^2 + 2 = 3x$ 1, 2   **6.** $x^2 + 12 = 7x$ 3, 4

7. $2 - (x - 1) = 0$ 3   **8.** $4 - (3 - x) = 5$ 4   **9.** $x^3 + 4x = 5x^2$ 0, 1, 4

Solve these equations for the replacement set $\{-2, -1, 0, 1, 2\}$.
Write $\emptyset$ if there is no solution.

10. $5 - x = 6$ -1 **11.** $2x - 1 = 5$ $\emptyset$ **12.** $10x + 5 = 25$ 2

13. $x - 10 = -8$ 2   **14.** $3x - x = 2$ 1   **15.** $7 - x = 7$ 0

16. $5x = 0$ 0   **17.** $x^2 + x = 2$ $-2, 1$ **18.** $x^2 = x + 2$ $-1, 2$

3–2 What equations result from following these directions in order?

1. $-3x + 2 = 10$

    a. Subtract 2 from both sides. $-3x = 8$

    b. Multiply both sides by $-\frac{1}{3}$. $x = -\frac{8}{3}$

3. $2x + 3x = 8$

    a. Combine the x-terms. $5x = 8$

    b. Divide both sides by 5. $x = \frac{8}{5}$

2. $\frac{3}{4}x - 3 = -15$

    a. Multiply both sides by 4. $3x - 12 = -60$

    b. Add 12 to both sides. $3x = -48$

    c. Divide both sides by 3. $x = -16$

4. $4x + 3 + 2x = 7$

    a. Add -3 to both sides. $4x + 2x = 4$

    b. Combine the x-terms. $6x = 4$

    c. Multiply both sides by $\frac{1}{6}$. $x = \frac{2}{3}$

5. $\frac{1}{2}x + 2 + \frac{1}{3}x = 2\frac{1}{6}$

    a. Combine the x-terms. $\frac{5}{6}x + 2 = 2\frac{1}{6}$

    b. Subtract 2 from both sides. $\frac{5}{6}x = \frac{1}{6}$

    c. Multiply both sides by $\frac{6}{5}$. $x = \frac{1}{5}$

6. $x - 5 - 4x = -7$

    a. Add 5 to both sides. $x - 4x = -2$

    b. Combine the x-terms. $-3x = -2$

    c. Multiply both sides by $-\frac{1}{3}$. $x = \frac{2}{3}$

3–3 Solve each equation by writing a series of equivalent equations.

1. $x + 8 = -3$ (-11) **2.** $y - 4 = 10$ (14) **3.** $2z = z + 3$ (3)

4. $6a = 5a - 4$ (-4) **5.** $7 + b = 2b$ (7) **6.** $6 + 3p = 4p$ (6)

7. $5r + 2 = 4r + 12$ (10) **8.** $7s - 5 = 6s - 1$ (4) **9.** $-7 + s = 2s + 3$ (-10)

10. $x + \frac{1}{3} = \frac{5}{3}$ $\left\{\frac{4}{3}\right\}$ **11.** $x - \frac{1}{2} = 5$ $\left\{\frac{11}{2}\right\}$ **12.** $4v + \frac{1}{2} = 3v + 1$ $\left\{\frac{1}{2}\right\}$

13. $-\frac{1}{2}w + \frac{4}{5} = \frac{1}{2}w + \frac{1}{5}$ $\left\{\frac{3}{5}\right\}$ **14.** $\frac{1}{3}y + 1 = \frac{4}{3}y + \frac{1}{6}$ $\left\{\frac{5}{6}\right\}$

3–4 Solve.

1. $4c = 7$ $\left\{\frac{7}{4}\right\}$ **2.** $-3k = 16$ $\left\{-\frac{16}{3}\right\}$ **3.** $\frac{1}{4}p = -3$ (-12) **4.** $-\frac{1}{3}r = 9$ (-27)

5. $\frac{v}{4} = 1.3$ (5.2) **6.** $0.3s = 30$ (100) **7.** $\frac{5}{8}w = \frac{3}{4}$ $\left\{\frac{6}{5}\right\}$ **8.** $5a = -15$ (-3)

9. $\frac{y}{2.5} = -20$ (-50) **10.** $-7b = -21$ (3) **11.** $0.4z = 5$ (12.5) **12.** $-\frac{1}{8}m = -8$ (64)

13. $1.5t = 21$ (14) **14.** $\frac{4}{3}d = 12$ (9) **15.** $-\frac{1}{3}c = -\frac{1}{2}$ $\left\{\frac{3}{2}\right\}$ **16.** $\frac{k}{0.3} = 4$ (1.2)

3–5 Solve.

1. $4x - 3 = 2$ $\left\{\frac{5}{4}\right\}$ **2.** $\frac{2x + 5}{3} = 4$ $\left\{\frac{7}{2}\right\}$ **3.** $\frac{1}{2}x - 2 = 3$ (10) **4.** $6x + 2 = 2x + 10$

                                                                                                    (2)

5. $3 + \frac{1}{3}x = 4$ (3) **6.** $3x - 5 = 9$ $\left\{\frac{14}{3}\right\}$ **7.** $4x + 7 = 2$ $\left\{-\frac{5}{4}\right\}$ **8.** $\frac{x - 1}{2} = 12$ (25)

3–6 Solve.

1. $4 - 3x = 13$ (-3)

2. $2 - 4x = -10$ (3)

3. $-5 - 6x = 7$ (-2)

4. $7 - \frac{1}{5}x = 9$ (-10)

5. $-2 - \frac{1}{4}x = 2$ (-16)

6. $-10 - \frac{2x}{3} = -4$ (-9)

7. $\frac{x}{4} - 2 = 3$ (20)

8. $4x - 5 = 20$ $\left\{\frac{25}{4}\right\}$

9. $4(2 - x) = 3$ $\left\{\frac{5}{4}\right\}$

10. $3(x - 4) = 1$ $\left\{\frac{13}{3}\right\}$

11. $-2(x - 5) = 3$ $\left\{\frac{7}{2}\right\}$

12. $-6(3 - x) = 5$ $\left\{\frac{23}{6}\right\}$

3–7 Solve.

1. $3(t - 4) = 15$ (9)

2. $6(v + 2) = -12$ (-4)

3. $\frac{1}{3}(w + 4) = 4$ (8)

4. $\frac{1}{5}(y - 10) = 3$ (25)

5. $-\frac{1}{2}(z + 4) = -3$ (2)

6. $-\frac{1}{4}(a - 6) = 1$ (2)

7. $2c + 3(c + 2) = -4$ (-2)

8. $7s + 2(6 - s) = 7$ (-1)

9. $5x - 3(x - 2) = 18$ (6)

10. $3(b + 1) + 2(b + 3) = 34$ (5)

3–8 Solve the literal equation for the variable indicated.

1. $pq = r$, for p $p = \frac{r}{q}$

2. $3 + a = b$, for a $a = b - 3$

3. $p - 4 = q$, for p $p = q + 4$

4. $\frac{2}{3}t = d$, for t $t = \frac{3}{2}d$

5. $7jk = 28$, for k $k = \frac{4}{j}$

6. $2x + 3y = 12$, for y $y = \frac{12 - 2x}{3}$

7. $2x - 3y = 12$, for x $x = \frac{12 + 3y}{2}$

8. $a(2 + b) = 7$, for b $b = \frac{7 - 2a}{a}$

9. $(3 + r)s = 2$, for r $r = \frac{2 - 3s}{s}$

10. $(7 - t)2 = v$, for t $t = \frac{-v + 14}{2}$

11. $2(t + 3) = 3(r + 5)$, for r $r = \frac{2t - 9}{3}$

12. $4(w - z) = z$, for w $w = \frac{5}{4}z$

13. $2j + 3k = 3j - 3k$, for j $j = 6k$

14. $\frac{7 - 2y}{3} = x - 1$, for y $y = \frac{3x - 10}{-2}$

3–9 For each problem, write (a) what the variable represents, (b) an equation that fits the problem, (c) the solution to the equation, and (d) the answer to the question.

1. The length of a rectangle is 5 cm more than its width. What is the width if the length is 6.8 cm? $w + 5 = 6.8$; 1.8 cm

2. Lance has 4 times as many dimes as quarters. How many quarters does he have if he has 44 dimes? $4q = 44$; 11

3. Amy is 4 cm taller than Christa. How tall is Amy if Christa is 165 cm tall? $a = 165 + 4$; 169 cm

4. Mark saved $\frac{1}{5}$ the price of a camera. He saved \$24. What is the cost of the camera? $\frac{1}{5}c = 24$; \$120

5. Sabrina scored 8 points more on the second test than she scored on the first test. What was her score on the first test if she scored 98 points on the second test? $f + 8 = 98$; 90 points

6. Matt is 6 lb heavier than Scott. How much does Scott weigh if Matt weighs 150 lb? $s + 6 = 150$; 144 pounds

3–10 For each problem, write (a) what the varible represents, (b) a figure that helps organize the information, (c) an equation that fits the problem, (d) the solution to the equation, and (e) the answer to the question.

1. A wire 100 cm long is bent to form a triangle. The middle-sized side of the triangle is 2 cm longer than one side and 6 cm shorter than the other side. What are the lengths of the three sides? $x + (x - 2) + (x + 6) = 100$; 32 cm, 30 cm, 38 cm

2. A 12-ft board is cut so that one piece is 5 ft longer than the other piece. How long is each piece? $s + (s + 5) = 12$; $3\frac{1}{2}$ ft, $8\frac{1}{2}$ ft

3. The body of a fish is 4 times the length of its head. Its tail is 2 cm longer than the head. The total length of the fish is 20 cm. How long are the head, body, and tail of the fish? $h + (4h) + (h + 2) = 20$; 3 cm, 12 cm, and 5 cm

4. The perimeter of a triangle is 50 cm. The longest side is twice the length of the shortest side. The other side is 5 cm shorter than the longest side. Find the length of each side. $x + \left(\frac{1}{2}x\right) + (x - 5) = 50$; 22 cm, 11 cm, 17 cm

Chapter 4

4–1 Add these polynomials.

1. $5a + 6b - 2c$
$\underline{2a - 8b - 4c}$
$7a - 2b - 6c$

2. $3r + 7s$
$\underline{\quad 5s + 4t}$
$3r + 12s + 4t$

3. $x^2 - 2x - 9$
$\underline{x^2 - 5x + 4}$
$2x^2 - 7x - 5$

Subtract these polynomials.

4. $5x^2 + 6x + 7$
$\underline{x^2 + 2x + 9}$
$4x^2 + 4x - 2$

5. $a + b - c$
$\underline{a - b + c}$
$2b - 2c$

6. $3a^2 - 6a - 9$
$\underline{a^2 + 4a + 1}$
$2a^2 - 10a - 10$

Simplify each sum or difference.

7. $(x^2 - x - 10) - (x^2 + x - 20)$
$-2x + 10$

8. $(p - q - r) - (2p - 2q - 2r)$ $-p + q + r$

9. $(2a - 3b + 4c) + (a + b - c)$
$3a - 2b + 3c$

10. $(7x + 10y + z) + (3x - 10y + z)$
$10x + 2z$

11. $(a^2 + 5a + 8) - (5a - 2)$ $a^2 + 10$

12. $(t^2 - 16t) - (5t + 4)$ $t^2 - 21t - 4$

4–2 State whether each polynomial is a monomial, binomial, or trinomial.

1. $2a + 3b$ Binomial
2. $7rst$ Monomial
3. $2 + c$ Binomial
4. $a^2 + a + 1$ Trinomial

5. $p + q - r$ Trinomial
6. $0.5x^2$ Monomial
7. $a^4 - a^3$ Binomial
8. $5x^2 - 5xy + y^2$ Trinomial

State the degree of each polynomial.

9. $5 + 4x$ 1
10. $2t^3 + 4t$ 3
11. $-2x^2 + 3x + 7$ 2
12. 7 0

13. $2x^2y^3$ 5
14. $xy + x - y$ 2
15. $r^2 + rs^2$ 3
16. $2a^2 - 3ab + 4b^2$ 2

Write each polynomial in descending order.

17. $2 + 3a + 4a^2$
$4a^2 + 3a + 2$
18. $7a - 6a^2 - 4$
$-6a^2 + 7a - 4$
19. $r + 2 + r^2$
$r^2 + r + 2$
20. $7x^2 - 2 - x$
$7x^2 - x - 2$

21. $4p + 5p^2 + 1$
$5p^2 + 4p + 1$
22. $7 - a - 2a^2$
$-2a^2 - a + 7$
23. $x^2 + x^3 + 4x$
$x^3 + x^2 + 4x$
24. $r^2 + 2r^3 - r^4$
$-r^4 + 2r^3 + r^2$

4–3 Complete.

1. $5^7 \cdot 5^6 = 5^?$ 13

2. $(0.7)(0.7)^2 = (0.7)^?$ 3

3. $12 \cdot 12 = 12^?$ 2

4. $6^? \cdot 6^3 = 6^{12}$ 9

5. $(-4)^2(-4)^3 = (-4)^?$ 5

6. $\left(\frac{1}{2}\right)^{10}\left(\frac{1}{2}\right)^{20} = \left(\frac{1}{2}\right)^?$ 30

Simplify.

7. $p^3 \cdot p^2$ p^5

8. $q^5 \cdot q$ q^6

9. $(2r)(3r)$ $6r^2$

10. $(6s^2)(5s^4)$ $30s^6$

11. $(0.5t)(7t)$ $3.5t^2$

12. $\left(\frac{1}{2}v^2\right)\left(\frac{1}{2}v^3\right)$ $\frac{1}{4}v^5$

13. $(3w^2)(w^{10})$ $3w^{12}$

14. $xy \cdot x^2y^3$ x^3y^4

15. $(2yz^2)(5z^3)$ $10yz^5$

4–4 Write each product in scientific notation.

1. $(3 \times 10^2)(3.1 \times 10^4)$ 9.3×10^6

2. $(2 \times 10^4)(8 \times 10^5)$ 1.6×10^{10}

3. $(2.5 \times 10)(6 \times 10^8)$ 1.5×10^{10}

4. $(7.3 \times 10^4)(4 \times 10^5)$ 2.92×10^{10}

5. $(8.2)(2 \times 10^6)$ 1.64×10^7

6. $(4 \times 10^9)(5)$ 2×10^{10}

7. $(2 \times 10^4)^3$ 8×10^{12}

8. $(3 \times 10^5)^2$ 9×10^{10}

9. $(4 \times 10^6)^3$ 6.4×10^{19}

10. $2,500 \times 50,000$ 1.25×10^8

11. $73,000,000 \times 2,000$ 1.46×10^{11}

12. $8,500,000 \times 4,000,000$ 3.4×10^{13}

13. $340 \times 2,000,000$ 6.8×10^8

4–5 Simplify.

1. $(c^4)^3$ c^{12}

2. $(2k)^4$ $16k^4$

3. $(3m)^2$ $9m^2$

4. $(z^4)^5$ z^{20}

5. $(-2x^3)^2$ $4x^6$

6. $(-2x^2)^3$ $-8x^6$

7. $\left(\frac{1}{2}a^4\right)^4$ $\frac{1}{16}a^{16}$

8. $(r^3s^4)^5$ $r^{15}s^{20}$

9. $(2a^2b^3)^4$ $16a^8b^{12}$

10. $(0.2jk^2)^2$ $0.04j^2k^4$

11. $(5m^2n)^4$ $625m^8n^4$

12. $(10rs^2t^3)^3$ $1000r^3s^6t^9$

State which number is larger.

13. $(3^3)^4$ or $3^3 \cdot 3^4$ $(3^3)^4$

14. 6^{10} or $(6^7)^3$ $(6^7)^3$

15. 10^{10} or 100^1 10^{10}

16. $\left(\frac{1}{3} \cdot 3\right)^4$ or $\frac{1}{3} \cdot 3^4$ $\frac{1}{3} \cdot 3^4$

17. $(-2)^4$ or $(-2)^5$ $(-2)^4$

18. $\left(\frac{1}{2}\right)^{10}$ or $\left(\frac{1}{2}\right)^{11}$ $\left(\frac{1}{2}\right)^{10}$

4–6 Simplify.

1. $8(a + 3)$ $8a + 24$

2. $-7(b - 4)$ $-7b + 28$

3. $\frac{1}{2}(c + 6)$ $\frac{1}{2}c + 3$

4. $5(2d + 3)$ $10d + 15$

5. $10(0.1m - 2.4)$ $m - 24$

6. $-1(-p - 2)$ $p + 2$

7. $t(t + 3)$ $t^2 + 3t$

8. $v(v^2 - 3)$ $v^3 - 3v$

9. $w(6w - 3)$ $6w^2 - 3w$

10. $2x(x - 4)$ $2x^2 - 8x$

11. $3y(x + y)$ $3xy + 3y^2$

12. $-z(2 - z)$ $-2z + z^2$

13. $2a(a - 3b)$ $2a^2 - 6ab$

4–7 The distances for A and B are equal. Write an equation for each problem, and solve for x.

1. **A:** Rate is x km/h, and time is 17 h.
   B: Rate is $(x + 20)$ km/h, and time is 13 h. $17x = 13(x + 20); 65$

2. **A:** Rate is 800 km/h, and time is x h.
   B: Rate is 750 km/h, and time is $(x + 1)$ h. $800x = 750(x + 1); 15$

The sum of the distances for A and B is 400 km. Write an equation for each problem, and solve for x.

3. **A:** Rate is 50 km/h, and time is x h.
   B: Rate is 40 km/h, and time is $(x - 3.5)$ h. $50x + 40(x - 3.5) = 400; 6$

4. **A:** Rate is 600 km/h, and time is x h.
   B: Rate is 500 km/h, and time is $2x$ h. $600x + 500(2x) = 400; \frac{1}{4}$

4–8 Simplify. Assume that no variable is equal to zero.

1. $\dfrac{p^{12}}{p^4}$ p^8

2. $\dfrac{6r^8}{3r^6}$ $2r^2$

3. $\dfrac{24t^4}{-18t^6}$ $-\dfrac{4}{3t^2}$

4. $\dfrac{-14jk^2}{21j^2k}$ $-\dfrac{2k}{3j}$

Solve.

5. $\dfrac{7^6}{7^2} = 7^x$ (4)

6. $\dfrac{3^{10}}{3^2} = 3^x$ (8)

7. $\dfrac{2^{20}}{2^{17}} = x$ (8)

8. $\dfrac{5^6}{5^8} = x$ $\left(\dfrac{1}{25}\right)$

Write the quotient in scientific notation.

9. $\dfrac{9 \times 10^8}{2 \times 10^2}$ 4.5×10^6

10. $\dfrac{4.8 \times 10^6}{3.0 \times 10^5}$ 1.6×10

11. $\dfrac{9.6 \times 10^{12}}{4.8 \times 10}$ 2×10^{11}

12. $\dfrac{2 \times 10^{15}}{5 \times 10^{10}}$ 4×10^4

4–9 Solve.

1. The cost of 5 soccer balls including a $3.75 delivery charge is $128.70. What is the cost of 1 soccer ball not including a delivery charge? $24.99

2. Ranson's Rapid Repair charges for parts plus $25 per hour for labor. A vacuum-cleaner repair bill was $16.25 including $3.75 for parts. How many hours of labor were needed? $\frac{1}{2}$

3. The four members of the Peterson family all ordered the Breakfast Special at the Blue Diner. They paid $2.20 for beverages not included in the Breakfast Special. Their bill, including the beverages, was $11.20. What was the cost of one Breakfast Special? $2.25

4–10 Let n represent an integer. Express each of these numbers.

1. The next integer $n + 1$

2. The preceding integer $n - 1$

3. The preceding odd number if n is odd $n - 2$

4. The next three consecutive integers $n + 1, n + 2, n + 3$

Solve.

5. The sum of three consecutive integers is 369. What is the smallest integer?   122

6. The sum of four consecutive even integers is 348. What are the integers?   84, 86, 88, 90

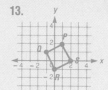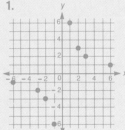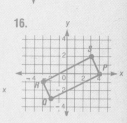
Chapter 5

5-1 Identify the quadrant that each point is in or the axis that it is on. Then state the coordinates of each point.

1. *A*   **2.** *B*   **3.** *C*   **4.** *D*

II, (−4, 2)   II, (−1, 2)   y-axis, (0, 3)   I, (1, 4)

5. *E*   **6.** *F*   **7.** *G*   **8.** *H*

I, (4, 1)   x-axis, (1, 0)   IV, (3, −2)   IV, (4, −4)

9. *I*   **10.** *J*   **11.** *K*   **12.** *L*

IV, (1, −3)   y-axis, (0, −2)   III, (−3, −2)   x-axis, (−3, 0)

Graph the points *P*, *Q*, *R*, and *S*. Draw line segments from *P* to *Q*, *Q* to *R*, *R* to *S*, and *S* to *P*.

13. $P(1, 2)$, $Q(-1, 1)$, $R(0, -1)$, $S(2, 0)$ (a square)

14. $P(2, 1)$, $Q(6, 2)$, $R(5, 4)$, $S(1, 3)$ (a parallelogram)

15. $P(-1, -1)$, $Q(-2, 3)$, $R(2, 3)$, $S(1, -1)$ (an isosceles trapezoid)

16. $P(4, 0)$, $Q(-2, -3)$, $R(-3, -1)$, $S(3, 2)$ (a rectangle)

5-2 Each exercise describes a relation.

a. List the ordered pairs.   **c.** List the range.

b. List the domain.   **d.** Draw the graph.

1. The set of ordered pairs in which the components are integers and the product of the components is 6. (1, 6), (2, 3), (3, 2), (6, 1), (−1, −6), (−2, −3), (−3, −2), (−6, −1)

2. The set of ordered pairs in which the components are positive integers having a product of 6 or less.
(1, 1), (1, 2), (1, 3), (1, 4), (1, 5), (1, 6), (2, 1), (2, 2), (2, 3), (3, 1), (3, 2), (4, 1), (5, 1), (6, 1)

3. The set of ordered pairs in which the components are negative integers having a sum greater than −6.
(−1, −1), (−1, −2), (−1, −3), (−1, −4), (−2, −1), (−2, −2), (−2, −3), (−3, −1), (−3, −2), (−4, −1)

4. The set of ordered pairs in which the first component is a positive integer less than 6, and the second component is 1 less than the first component.
(1, 0), (2, 1), (3, 2), (4, 3), (5, 4)

5. The set of ordered pairs in which the first component is a positive even integer less than 10, and the second component is half the first component. (2, 1), (4, 2), (6, 3), (8, 4)

5-3 Copy and complete each table.

1. $y = 4 - x$

x	0	2	4	6
y	?	?	?	?
	4	2	0	−2

2. $y = -2x + 4$

x	−1	0	1	2
y	?	?	?	?
	6	4	2	0

3. $2x + 3y = 24$

x	?	?	0	12
y	4	6	?	?
	6	3	8	0

4. $2x - 3y = 24$

x	6	9	?	?
y	?	?	0	1
	−4	−2	12	$\frac{27}{2}$

5. $4x - 3y = 5$

x	1	?	0	?
y	?	0	?	1
	$-\frac{1}{3}$	$\frac{5}{4}$	$-\frac{5}{3}$	2

6. $6x + 2y = -3$

x	0	?	2	?
y	?	0	?	2
	$-\frac{3}{2}$	$-\frac{1}{2}$	$-\frac{15}{2}$	$-\frac{7}{6}$

 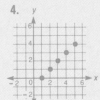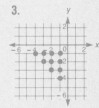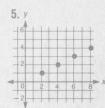

1.

2.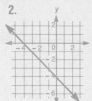

3.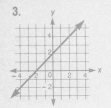

4.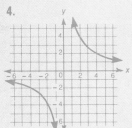

5.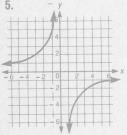

6.

7.

5-4 Graph each equation.

1. $x + y = 4$ **2.** $x + y = -4$ **3.** $x - y = -2$

4. $xy = 8$ **5.** $xy = -6$ **6.** $2x - 4y = 5$

7. $3y - 4x = 24$ **8.** $y = 0.1x^3$ **9.** $y = -x$

10. $y = 0x + 2$ **11.** $y = -x^2$ **12.** $y = 2(x + 1)$

5-5 Graph the point. Then draw lines with the stated slopes through the point. Label the lines a, b, and c.

1. Point $(4, 2)$ **a.** Slope 1   **b.** Slope 2   **c.** Slope $\frac{1}{4}$

2. Point $(1, -3)$ **a.** Slope 0   **b.** Slope -3 **c.** Slope $\frac{1}{2}$

3. Point $(-3, 3)$ **a.** Slope $-\frac{1}{3}$ **b.** Slope -1 **c.** Slope -2

5-6 Write an equation in slope–intercept form. State the slope and y-intercept of the line.
y = mx + b where m is slope and b is y-intercept.

1. $2x - 3y = 12$ **2.** $\frac{1}{2}y = x + 4$ m = 2, b = 8   **3.** $4y - 6x = 9$ m = $\frac{3}{2}$, b = $\frac{9}{4}$
m = $\frac{2}{3}$, b = -4

4. $10y + x = 20$ **5.** $y - \frac{3}{4}x = 7$ m = $\frac{3}{4}$, b = 7   **6.** $\frac{1}{3}y = \frac{1}{2}x - 1$ m = $\frac{3}{2}$, b = -3
m = $-\frac{1}{10}$, b = 2

7. $5x + 2y = 10$ m = $-\frac{5}{2}$, b = 5   **8.** $-2x - 3y = 6$ m = $-\frac{2}{3}$, b = -2

State whether the graphs of these pairs of equations are parallel, perpendicular, or neither.

9. $x + y = 6$ **10.** $2x - 4y = 13$ **11.** $2y - 3x = 4$ **12.** $5x + 6y = 30$
$y = -x + 3$ $4x - 8y = 5$ $3y + 2x = 6$ $4x + 5y = 20$
Parallel   Parallel   Perpendicular   Neither

5-7 Write an equation in the form $y = mx + b$ for the line with the given characteristics.

1. Has slope 2 and passes through $(3, 1)$ y = 2x − 5

2. Has slope 0 and passes through $(1, -5)$ y = −5

3. Has no slope and passes through $(-2, -6)$ x = −2

4. Has slope $-\frac{1}{2}$ and passes through $(8, 3)$ y = −$\frac{1}{2}$x + 7

5. Has slope -10 and passes through $(3, 3)$ y = −10x + 33

Write an equation in the form $y = mx + b$ for the line that passes through the two points.

6. $(6, 6)$, $(12, 10)$ y = $\frac{2}{3}$x + 2 **7.** $(6, -6)$, $(3, -5)$ **8.** $(4, 1)$, $(-4, -1)$ y = $\frac{1}{4}$x
y = −$\frac{1}{3}$x − 4

9. $(-2, 10)$, $(-1, 6)$ **10.** $(4, 1)$, $(-2, 4)$ **11.** $(8, 12)$, $(-4, 3)$
y = −4x + 2   y = −$\frac{1}{2}$x + 3   y = $\frac{3}{4}$x + 6

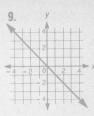
5–8 State whether the equation defines a function.

1. $y = x^2$ Yes
2. $x = y^2$ No
3. $x = |y|$ No
4. $y = |x|$ Yes

5. $y = 2x$ Yes
6. $x = 2y$ Yes
7. $y = (x - 1)^2$ Yes
8. $xy = 1$ Yes

State whether the equation defines a *linear* function.

9. $y = \frac{1}{2}x^2$ No
10. $y = 2x$ Yes
11. $y = x + 2$ Yes
12. $y = \frac{2}{x}$ No

13. $y = x^3$ No
14. $y = \frac{1}{3}x$ Yes
15. $y = 3 - x$ Yes
16. $y = -\frac{3}{x}$ No

5–9 For the linear functions, determine the slope, y-intercept, and equation in slope–intercept form. $y = mx + b$ where m is slope and b is y-intercept.

1.

x	-1	0	1	2
y	7	4	1	-2

$m = -3$, $b = 4$

2.

x	-1	1	3	5
y	-9	-1	7	15

$m = 4$, $b = -5$

3.

x	-10	-9	-8	-7
y	4	3	2	1

$m = -1$, $b = -6$

4.

x	4	8	12	16
y	6	8	10	12

$m = \frac{1}{2}$, $b = 4$

Each table shows the number of spectators at a game and the revenue at the concession stands. State whether the number pairs belong to a *linear* function.

5.

Spectators	500	750	1000
Revenue (in dollars)	750	1125	1500

Yes

6.

Spectators	1000	2000	3000
Revenue (in dollars)	2000	3500	4500

No

Chapter 6

6–1 Solve each system of equations by graphing.

1. $x + 2y = 4$
$x - y = -5$
$\{(-2, 3)\}$

2. $2x - y = 0$
$x - y = 2$
$\{(-2, -4)\}$

3. $2x + y = 1$
$3x + y = 3$
$\{(2, -3)\}$

4. $y = x + 6$
$y = \frac{1}{2}x + 4$
$\{(-4, 2)\}$

5. $y = \frac{1}{3}x$
$y = x + 2$
$\{(-3, -1)\}$

6. $x + 2y = -4$
$x - y = -4$
$\{(-4, 0)\}$

7. $y = -x - 2$
$y = 2x - 2$
$\{(0, -2)\}$

8. $-x + y = 4$
$-2x - y = 5$
$\{(-3, 1)\}$

6–2 Solve by substitution.

1. $y = 6x$
$4x + 3y = 11$
$\left\{\left(\frac{1}{2}, 3\right)\right\}$

2. $x = -3y$
$5x - 6y = 7$
$\left\{\left(1, -\frac{1}{3}\right)\right\}$

3. $y = 2x - 4$
$5x - 2y = 4$
$\{(-4, -12)\}$

4. $x = y + 3$
$2x + 2y = -1$
$\left\{\left(\frac{5}{4}, -\frac{7}{4}\right)\right\}$

5. $3x = y - 10$
$6x + 5y = -6$
$\left\{\left(-\frac{8}{3}, 2\right)\right\}$

6. $y = 1 - 3x$
$4x + y = 4$
$\{(3, -8)\}$

7. $2x = y - 2$
$2x - 3y = -9$
$\left\{\left(\frac{3}{4}, \frac{7}{2}\right)\right\}$

8. $3x + y = 3$
$5x + y = 1$
$\{(-1, 6)\}$

10. 11.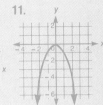

12.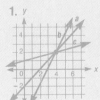

ADDITIONAL ANSWERS

5–5

1. 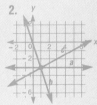 2.

3.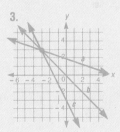

ADDITIONAL ANSWERS

6–1

1.

2.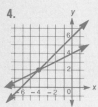

3.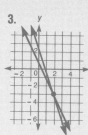

4.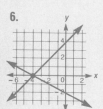

5.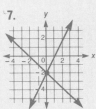

6.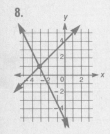

7.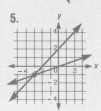

8.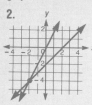

6–3 If possible, solve the system by substituting from the first equation into the second equation. State the number of solutions that each system has.

1. $y = 2x + 3$
$y = 2x + 5$
None

2. $y = x + 4$
$2y = 2x + 8$
Infinitely many

3. $x = 2y + 3$
$2x + 3 = 4y$
None

4. $x = -2y + 1$
$3x + 6y = 3$
Infinitely many

5. $2y = 3x - 7$
$2y + 3x = 11$
$\{(3, 1)\}$, one

6. $3x = 2y - 2$
$y + 6x = -4$
$\left\{\left(-\frac{2}{3}, 0\right)\right\}$, one

7. $y = -2x$
$x = -2y$
$\{(0, 0)\}$, one

8. $y = -x + 4$
$x + 2y = 8$
$\{(0, 4)\}$, one

6–4 For each problem, let t represent the tens digit and u represent the ones digit of a two-digit number. Write two equations. Solve the system and answer the question.

1. The tens digit is 1 more than the ones digit. The tens digit plus twice the ones digit is 13. What is the number? $t = u + 1, t + 2u = 13$; 54

2. The ones digit is 1 more than the tens digit. If the digits are reversed and the new number is doubled, the result is 41 more than the original number. What is the original number? $u = t + 1, 2(10u + t) = 10t + u + 41$; 23

Solve.

3. One number is 3 less than another number. Their sum is 53. What are the numbers? 25 and 28

4. One number is 12 more than another number. If twice the smaller number is subtracted from the larger number, the result is 16. What are the numbers? -4 and 8

6–5 Solve by addition.

1. $x + y = 6$
$x - y = 9$
$\left\{\left(\frac{15}{2}, -\frac{3}{2}\right)\right\}$

2. $x - 2y = 6$
$3x + 2y = -14$
$\{(-2, -4)\}$

3. $3x + 5y = -1$
$-5x - 5y = 0$
$\left\{\left(\frac{1}{2}, -\frac{1}{2}\right)\right\}$

4. $3x + y = 1$
$-3x - 2y = 4$
$\{(2, -5)\}$

5. $3x + 2y = 2$
$-3x + 2y = 6$
$\left\{\left(-\frac{2}{3}, 2\right)\right\}$

6. $x = 4y - 2$
$12y = x + 8$
$\left\{\left(1, \frac{3}{4}\right)\right\}$

7. $-2x + 5y = 12$
$2x + 3y = -12$
$\{(-6, 0)\}$

8. $x + 8y = 1$
$-x + 4y = 2$
$\left\{\left(-1, \frac{1}{4}\right)\right\}$

6–6 Solve each system by multiplication and addition.

1. $2x - 3y = 18$
$4x - 2y = 4$
$\{(-3, -8)\}$

2. $x + 3y = 2$
$2x + 5y = 2$
$\{(-4, 2)\}$

3. $4x - y = 4$
$6x - 3y = 3$
$\left\{\left(\frac{3}{2}, 2\right)\right\}$

4. $3x - y = 7$
$5x - y = 5$
$\{(-1, -10)\}$

5. $x - 3y = 5$
$2x - 9y = 9$
$\left\{\left(6, \frac{1}{3}\right)\right\}$

6. $3x + 4y = 9$
$5x + 8y = 14$
$\left\{\left(4, -\frac{3}{4}\right)\right\}$

7. $3x + 4y = -15$
$-2x + 3y = 10$
$\{(-5, 0)\}$

8. $5x - 4y = 6$
$10x - 5y = 5$
$\left\{\left(-\frac{2}{3}, -\frac{7}{3}\right)\right\}$

9. $9x - 8y = 1$
$3x - 4y = 11$
$\{(-7, -8)\}$

10. $7x - 4y = 3$
$8x - 5y = 4$
$\left\{\left(-\frac{1}{3}, -\frac{4}{3}\right)\right\}$

11. $6x - 2y = 12$
$-4x - 3y = 18$
$\{(0, -6)\}$

12. $9x + 4y = 8$
$3x + 5y = 43$
$\{(-4, 11)\}$

1. $x + y = 20$
$1.50x + 2.50y = 1.90(20)$
$\{(12, 8)\}$
2. $x + y = 200$
$50x + 75y = 55(200)$
$\{(160, 40)\}$
3. $x + y = 10$
$2.00x + 2.75y = 21.05$
$\{(8.6, 1.4)\}$
4. $x + y = 50$
$0.05x + 0.01y = 0.02(50)$
$\{(12.5, 37.5)\}$

6–7 Write two equations. Solve the system, and answer the question.

1. Some \$1.50-per-oz spice and some \$2.50-per-oz spice are to be mixed to produce 20 oz of a mixture worth \$1.90 per oz. How many ounces of each should be used? \$1.50: 12 oz, \$2.50: 8 oz

2. Bird feed worth 50¢ per lb is mixed with bird feed worth 75¢ per lb to produce 200 lb of a mixture worth 55¢ per lb. How many pounds of each type of bird feed are used? 50¢: 160 lb, 75¢: 40 lb

3. Cheeses costing \$2.00 per lb and \$2.75 per lb are mixed to produce a 10-lb package worth \$21.05. How many pounds of each type of cheese are used? \$2.75: 1.4 lb, \$2: 8.6 lb

4. Milk that is 5% butterfat is mixed with milk that is 1% butterfat to produce 50 gal of milk that is 2% butterfat. How much milk of each type is used? 5%: 12.5 gal, 1%: 37.5 gal

Chapter 7

7–1 List all positive integer factors of the given number.

1. 28 1, 2, 4, 7, 14, 28 **2.** 45 1, 3, 5, 9, 15, 45 **3.** 57 1, 3, 19, 57 **4.** 46 1, 2, 23, 46

5. 75 1, 3, 5, 15, 25, 75 **6.** 81 1, 3, 9, 27, 81 **7.** 64 1, 2, 4, 8, 16, 32, 64 **8.** 60 1, 2, 3, 4, 5, 6, 10, 12, 15, 20, 30, 60

Write the prime factorization of each number. List the factors in increasing order.

9. 92 $2^2 \cdot 23$ **10.** 48 $2^4 \cdot 3$ **11.** 52 $2^2 \cdot 13$ **12.** 84 $2^2 \cdot 3 \cdot 7$

13. 80 $2^4 \cdot 5$ **14.** 72 $2^3 \cdot 3^2$ **15.** 68 $2^2 \cdot 17$ **16.** 96 $2^5 \cdot 3$

7–2 List the common factors of each pair of monomials.

1. $10a, 15a^2$ 1, 5, a, 5a **2.** $b^2c, 2bc^2$ 1, b, c, bc **3.** $3st^2, 6s^2$ 1, 3, s, 3s

4. ab^3, b^2c 1, b, b^2 **5.** $7a, 8b$ 1 **6.** $18m^2, 27mn$ 1, 3, 9, m, 3m, 9m

List the greatest common factor of each pair of monomials.

7. $2a^2, 6a$ 2a **8.** $4bc, 10cd$ 2c **9.** $6e^2g^2, 9eg^2$ 3eg^2

10. $3j^2k, jk^2$ jk **11.** $9a, 4b^2$ 1 **12.** $24pq^2, 36q$ 12q

7–3 Solve.

1. $(n - 2)(n - 7) = 0$ $\{2, 7\}$ **2.** $(m + 4)(m + 9) = 0$ $\{-4, -9\}$

3. $p(p - 10) = 0$ $\{0, 10\}$ **4.** $q(q + 8) = 0$ $\{0, -8\}$

5. $(s - 1)(s + 1) = 0$ $\{1, -1\}$ **6.** $(t + 12)(t + 12) = 0$ $\{-12\}$

7. $(2a - 5)(3a - 2) = 0$ $\left\{\frac{5}{2}, \frac{2}{3}\right\}$ **8.** $(b - 7)(2b - 1) = 0$ $\left\{7, \frac{1}{2}\right\}$

9. $(5d + 3)(3d + 5) = 0$ $\left\{-\frac{3}{5}, -\frac{5}{3}\right\}$ **10.** $4(c + 7)(2c - 13) = 0$ $\left\{-7, \frac{13}{2}\right\}$

11. $(s + 4)(s + 4) = 0$ $\{-4\}$ **12.** $3 \cdot 4 \cdot 5 \cdot x = 0$ $\{0\}$

7–4 Factor. If the expression cannot be factored, write "not factorable."

1. $5x + 5y$ $5(x + y)$ **2.** $a^2 + 3a$ $a(a + 3)$ **3.** $x^2 + x$ $x(x + 1)$ **4.** $a^2 + 4$
Not factorable

5. $14x^2 - 21x$ **6.** $3a - 4b$ **7.** $x^2y^2 - xy^3$ **8.** $16 - 16t$ $16(1 - t)$
$7x(2x - 3)$ Not factorable $xy^2(x - y)$

Solve.

9. $t^2 - 4t = 0$ $\{0, 4\}$ **10.** $w^2 + 3w = 0$ **11.** $2p^2 - 3p = 0$ **12.** $3q^2 - 6q = 0$
$\{0, -3\}$ $\left\{0, \frac{3}{2}\right\}$ $\{0, 2\}$

13. $z^2 = 10z$ $\{0, 10\}$ **14.** $2c^2 = -3c$ **15.** $b = b^2$ $\{0, 1\}$ **16.** $-a = a^2$ $\{0, -1\}$
$\left\{0, -\frac{3}{2}\right\}$

7–5 Expand and simplify.

1. $(n + 2)(n + 6)$ **2.** $(p + 7)(p - 1)$ $p^2 + 6p - 7$ **3.** $(a - 3)(a - 4)$
$n^2 + 8n + 12$ $a^2 - 7a + 12$

4. $(m - 8)(m + 3)$ **5.** $(q - 10)(q + 10)$ $q^2 - 100$ **6.** $(b + 3)^2$ $b^2 + 6b + 9$
$m^2 - 5m - 24$

7. $(r - 5)^2$ $r^2 - 10r + 25$ **8.** $(2c + 1)(c + 2)$ **9.** $(3v - 4)(3v + 4)$ $9v^2 - 16$
$2c^2 + 5c + 2$

10. $(d - 4)(3d - 2)$ **11.** $(2s + 1)(3s + 2)$ **12.** $(2h - 3)^2$ $4h^2 - 12h + 9$
$3d^2 - 14d + 8$ $6s^2 + 7s + 2$

7–6 Factor.

1. $a^2 - 16$ **2.** $x^2 - 100$ **3.** $c^2 - 1$ **4.** $2n^2 - 50$
$(a + 4)(a - 4)$ $(x + 10)(x - 10)$ $(c + 1)(c - 1)$ $2(n + 5)(n - 5)$

5. $3p^2 - 12$ **6.** $24 - 6t^2$ **7.** $25k^2 - 36$ **8.** $d^2 - 144$
$3(p + 2)(p - 2)$ $6(2 + t)(2 - t)$ $(5k + 6)(5k - 6)$ $(d + 12)(d - 12)$

9. $49m^2 - 4$ **10.** $9j^2 - 1$ **11.** $p^2q^2 - 81$ **12.** $5r^2s^2 - 5$
$(7m + 2)(7m - 2)$ $(3j + 1)(3j - 1)$ $(pq + 9)(pq - 9)$ $5(rs + 1)(rs - 1)$

Solve.

13. $c^2 - 25 = 0$ **14.** $j^2 - 64 = 0$ **15.** $g^2 = 400$ **16.** $m^2 - 4 = 0$
$\{5, -5\}$ $\{8, -8\}$ $\{20, -20\}$ $\{2, -2\}$

17. $a^2 - 121 = 0$ **18.** $4n^2 - 36 = 0$ **19.** $2b^2 - 200 = 0$ **20.** $3h^2 - 3 = 0$
$\{11, -11\}$ $\{3, -3\}$ $\{10, -10\}$ $\{1, -1\}$

21. $5k^2 = 45$ $\{3, -3\}$ **22.** $4p^2 = 9$ $\left\{\frac{3}{2}, -\frac{3}{2}\right\}$ **23.** $4d^2 = 100$ $\{5, -5\}$ **24.** $25q^2 - 36 = 0$
$\left\{\frac{6}{5}, -\frac{6}{5}\right\}$

7–7 Factor.

1. $a^2 - 10a + 25$ $(a - 5)^2$ **2.** $d^2 + 18d + 81$ $(d + 9)^2$ **3.** $p^2 + 2pq + q^2$ $(p + q)^2$

4. $r^2 - 4rs + 4s^2$ $(r - 2s)^2$ **5.** $b^2 - 14b + 49$ $(b - 7)^2$ **6.** $c^2 + 16c + 64$ $(c + 8)^2$

7. $g^2 + 22g + 121$ $(g + 11)^2$ **8.** $4t^2 + 16t + 16$ $4(t + 2)^2$ **9.** $w^2 - 100$ $(w + 10)(w - 10)$

Solve.

10. $t^2 - 2t + 1 = 0$ $\{1\}$ **11.** $s^2 - 18s + 81 = 0$ $\{9\}$

12. $v^2 - 16 = 0$ $\{4, -4\}$ **13.** $r^2 + 10r + 25 = 0$ $\{-5\}$

14. $b^2 - 100 = 0$ $\{10, -10\}$ **15.** $c^2 - \frac{2}{3}c + \frac{1}{9} = 0$ $\left\{\frac{1}{3}\right\}$

16. $j^2 + j + \frac{1}{4} = 0$ $\left\{-\frac{1}{2}\right\}$ **17.** $k^2 - 49 = 0$ $\{7, -7\}$

7–8 Factor.

1. $m^2 - 5m + 6$
$(m - 2)(m - 3)$

2. $h^2 - 3h + 2$ $(h - 1)(h - 2)$

3. $c^2 + 9c + 8$ $(c + 1)(c + 8)$

4. $a^2 + 9a + 20$
$(a + 4)(a + 5)$

5. $k^2 - 13k + 42$
$(k - 6)(k - 7)$

6. $t^2 - 12t + 20$
$(t - 2)(t - 10)$

7. $w^2 - 7w + 10$
$(w - 2)(w - 5)$

8. $d^2 - 14d + 24$
$(d - 2)(d - 12)$

9. $t^2 + 11t + 18$
$(t + 2)(t + 9)$

Solve.

10. $k^2 + 13k + 30 = 0$ $\{-3, -10\}$

11. $a^2 + 5a + 4 = 0$ $\{-1, -4\}$

12. $s^2 - 13s + 12 = 0$ $\{1, 12\}$

13. $t^2 - 10t + 9 = 0$ $\{1, 9\}$

14. $j^2 - 11j + 24 = 0$ $\{3, 8\}$

15. $c^2 - 16c + 64 = 0$ $\{8\}$

16. $w^2 + 15w + 54 = 0$ $\{-6, -9\}$

17. $h^2 - 10h + 24 = 0$ $\{4, 6\}$

7–9 Factor.

1. $g^2 + 4g - 12$
$(g + 6)(g - 2)$

2. $z^2 - 16$ $(z + 4)(z - 4)$

3. $x^2 + 3x - 10$
$(x + 5)(x - 2)$

4. $m^2 - 3m - 28$
$(m + 4)(m - 7)$

5. $c^2 + c - 30$ $(c + 6)(c - 5)$

6. $y^2 - 11y - 12$
$(y + 1)(y - 12)$

7. $a^2 + 5a - 36$
$(a + 9)(a - 4)$

8. $h^2 + 6h - 16$
$(h + 8)(h - 2)$

9. $k^2 - 5k - 24$
$(k + 3)(k - 8)$

Solve.

10. $c^2 + 6c - 27 = 0$ $\{3, -9\}$

11. $j^2 + 10j - 11 = 0$
$\{1, -11\}$

12. $p^2 + p - 56 = 0$ $\{7, -8\}$

13. $s^2 - 2s - 15 = 0$ $\{5, -3\}$

14. $u^2 - 3u - 18 = 0$ $\{6, -3\}$

15. $d^2 - 10d - 24 = 0$
$\{12, -2\}$

16. $m^2 + 2m - 24 = 0$
$\{4, -6\}$

17. $k^2 - 2k - 8 = 0$ $\{4, -2\}$

18. $v^2 - 2v - 35 = 0$ $\{7, -5\}$

19. $x^2 - 36 = 0$ $\{6, -6\}$

20. $z^2 + 3z - 54 = 0$ $\{6, -9\}$

21. $g^2 + 8g - 48 = 0$
$\{4, -12\}$

22. $w^2 + 6w - 40 = 0$
$\{4, -10\}$

23. $h^2 - 7h - 60 = 0$
$\{12, -5\}$

24. $k^2 + 8k - 20 = 0$
$\{2, -10\}$

7–10 Factor.

1. $2a^2 + 5a + 2$
$(2a + 1)(a + 2)$

2. $3m^2 - 20m - 7$
$(3m + 1)(m - 7)$

3. $3b^2 - 11b + 6$
$(3b - 2)(b - 3)$

4. $2g^2 + 7g - 4$
$(g + 4)(2g - 1)$

5. $7t^2 - 10t + 3$
$(7t - 3)(t - 1)$

6. $5n^2 - 13n - 6$
$(5n + 2)(n - 3)$

7. $4c^2 + 11c - 3$
$(c + 3)(4c - 1)$

8. $6q^2 + q - 12$
$(2q + 3)(3q - 4)$

9. $4d^2 - 4d - 3$
$(2d + 1)(2d - 3)$

10. $8p^2 - 2p - 15$
$(4p + 5)(2p - 3)$

11. $3h^2 - 7h + 2$
$(3h - 1)(h - 2)$

12. $4k^2 - 4k - 15$
$(2k + 3)(2k - 5)$

Solve.

13. $5z^2 - 13z - 6 = 0$ $\left\{3, -\frac{2}{5}\right\}$

14. $7a^2 + 19a - 6 = 0$ $\left\{\frac{2}{7}, -3\right\}$

15. $4m^2 + 15m - 4 = 0$ $\left\{\frac{1}{4}, -4\right\}$

16. $4h^2 - 12h + 9 = 0$ $\left\{\frac{3}{2}\right\}$

17. $4y^2 + 23y - 6 = 0$ $\left\{\frac{1}{4}, -6\right\}$

18. $6n^2 - 19n + 15 = 0$ $\left\{\frac{5}{3}, \frac{3}{2}\right\}$

19. $8b^2 + 37b - 15 = 0$ $\left\{\frac{3}{8}, -5\right\}$

20. $8c^2 - 2c - 15 = 0$ $\left\{\frac{3}{2}, -\frac{5}{4}\right\}$

21. $8d^2 + 14d - 15 = 0$ $\left\{\frac{3}{4}, -\frac{5}{2}\right\}$

22. $9j^2 - 16 = 0$ $\left\{\frac{4}{3}, -\frac{4}{3}\right\}$

8-1 Simplify. List any necessary restrictions on the variables.

1. $\dfrac{12x}{18x}$ $\frac{2}{3}$; $x \neq 0$

2. $\dfrac{20a^2}{15a^3}$ $\frac{4}{3a}$; $a \neq 0$

3. $\dfrac{16b^4}{24b}$ $\frac{2b^3}{3}$; $b \neq 0$

4. $\dfrac{3x-6}{3x+12}$ $\frac{x-2}{x+4}$; $x \neq -4$

5. $\dfrac{2t}{t^2-4t}$ $\frac{2}{t-4}$; $t \neq 0, 4$

6. $\dfrac{c^2-c}{c^2}$ $\frac{c-1}{c}$; $c \neq 0$

7. $\dfrac{h^2+3h+2}{h^2+6h+8}$ $\frac{h+1}{h+4}$; $h \neq -2, -4$

8. $\dfrac{k^2-25}{k^2+10k+25}$ $\frac{k-5}{k+5}$; $k \neq -5$

9. $\dfrac{4t+20}{t^2+t-20}$ $\frac{4}{t-4}$; $t \neq 4, -5$

8-2 Write each product in simplest form. Assume that no denominator is zero.

1. $\dfrac{2}{r} \cdot \dfrac{r^2}{8}$ $\frac{r}{4}$

2. $\dfrac{15h}{7} \cdot \dfrac{2}{5h}$ $\frac{6}{7}$

3. $12\left(\dfrac{x}{3}+\dfrac{1}{4}\right)$ $4x+3$

4. $6a\left(\dfrac{4}{3a}+\dfrac{1}{2a^2}\right)$ $8+\frac{3}{a}$

5. $\dfrac{r(s-2)}{s} \cdot \dfrac{s}{r(r+2)}$ $\frac{s-2}{r+2}$

6. $\dfrac{2(w+3)}{3} \cdot \dfrac{9}{4(w+3)}$ $\frac{3}{2}$

Write each quotient in simplest form. Assume that no denominator is zero.

7. $\dfrac{r^3}{s^2} \div \dfrac{r}{s}$ $\frac{r^2}{s}$

8. $\dfrac{6mn^4}{5} \div \dfrac{4n^3}{15m}$ $\frac{9m^2n}{2}$

9. $\dfrac{a^2b^2}{c} \div \dfrac{ab^3}{c^2}$ $\frac{ac}{b}$

10. $\dfrac{3x^3y}{6x} \div \dfrac{2x^3y^2}{5x}$ $\frac{5}{4y}$

11. $\dfrac{b(c+2)}{c+3} \div \dfrac{c}{b(c+3)}$ $\frac{b^2(c+2)}{c}$

12. $\dfrac{h}{k+1} \div \dfrac{h^3}{k+1}$ $\frac{1}{h^2}$

13. $\dfrac{(r-3)^2}{r} \div \dfrac{r-3}{r^3}$ $r^2(r-3)$

14. $\dfrac{5(s-3)}{s} \div \dfrac{s+3}{s^2}$ $\frac{5s(s-3)}{s+3}$

15. $\dfrac{7(t-4)}{t} \div \dfrac{5(t-4)}{t}$ $\frac{7}{5}$

8-3 Simplify. Assume that no denominator is zero.

1. $\dfrac{3t}{2}+\dfrac{5t}{2}$ $4t$

2. $\dfrac{b}{a}-\dfrac{5b}{a}$ $-\frac{4b}{a}$

3. $\dfrac{7}{3c}+\dfrac{5}{3c}$ $\frac{4}{c}$

4. $\dfrac{h}{h-4}-\dfrac{2}{h-4}$ $\frac{h-2}{h-4}$

5. $\dfrac{4j+3}{2j+1}-\dfrac{2j+3}{2j+1}$ $\frac{2j}{2j+1}$

6. $\dfrac{2r-4}{5r-20}+\dfrac{-r}{5r-20}$ $\frac{1}{5}$

7. $\dfrac{t}{t^2-9}-\dfrac{3}{t^2-9}$ $\frac{1}{t+3}$

8. $\dfrac{z}{(z+2)^2}+\dfrac{2}{(z+2)^2}$ $\frac{1}{z+2}$

9. $\dfrac{3c}{(c+2)(c-3)}+\dfrac{6}{(c+2)(c-3)}$ $\frac{3}{c-3}$

10. $\dfrac{5r}{(r-4)(r-5)}-\dfrac{4r+4}{(r-4)(r-5)}$ $\frac{1}{r-5}$

8-4 Simplify. Assume that no denominator is zero.

1. $\dfrac{2}{5r}+\dfrac{3}{r}$ $\frac{17}{5r}$

2. $\dfrac{4}{w}-\dfrac{5}{6}$ $\frac{24-5w}{6w}$

3. $\dfrac{7}{v^2}+\dfrac{5}{v}$ $\frac{7+5v}{v^2}$

4. $\dfrac{2}{3b}+\dfrac{5}{3b^2}$ $\frac{2b+5}{3b^2}$

5. $\dfrac{7}{2a}-\dfrac{10}{3a^2}$ $\frac{21a-20}{6a^2}$

6. $\dfrac{a}{4}-\dfrac{b}{a}$ $\frac{a^2-4b}{4a}$

7. $\dfrac{2}{x}+\dfrac{2}{x+3}$ $\frac{2(2x+3)}{x(x+3)}$

8. $\dfrac{1}{x+2}+\dfrac{2}{x+3}$ $\frac{3x+7}{(x+2)(x+3)}$

9. $\dfrac{4}{x^2+7x+12}+\dfrac{4}{x+4}$ $\frac{4}{x+3}$

8-5 Solve. Write ∅ if there is no solution.

1. $\dfrac{3}{x} = \dfrac{9}{12}$ {4}

2. $\dfrac{21}{35} = \dfrac{a}{5}$ {3}

3. $\dfrac{c}{2} + \dfrac{1}{2} = 4$ {7}

4. $\dfrac{x}{3} - \dfrac{x}{5} = \dfrac{2}{3}$ {5}

5. $\dfrac{2}{y} + \dfrac{3}{4} = \dfrac{11}{4}$ {1}

6. $\dfrac{3}{2} - \dfrac{7}{k} = 5$ {−2}

7. $\dfrac{1}{8}n - \dfrac{7}{8}n = 3$ {−4}

8. $\dfrac{1}{3}x + \dfrac{1}{2}x = 5$ {6}

9. $\dfrac{1}{b} + \dfrac{3}{2b} = 5$ $\left\{\dfrac{1}{2}\right\}$

10. $\dfrac{7}{x} - \dfrac{9}{x} = 1$ {−2}

11. $\dfrac{3}{4}r + \dfrac{9}{4}r = 2$ $\left\{\dfrac{2}{3}\right\}$

12. $\dfrac{2}{3p} - \dfrac{6}{p} = 16$ $\left\{-\dfrac{1}{3}\right\}$

8-6 Solve these work problems. Write an equation that fits the problem. Solve the equation and answer the question.

1. Working together, Chrystal and Gayle can clean their house in 3 h. Working alone, Chrystal takes twice as long to clean the house as Gayle takes when she cleans it by herself. How long does Gayle take to clean the house by herself? $4\dfrac{1}{2}$ hours

2. Steve can deliver the newspapers in his neighborhood in 2 h. Alexander takes 3 h to do the same job. How long does it take Steve and Alexander to deliver the papers if they work together? $1\dfrac{1}{5}$ hours

3. Libby takes 2 h to mow the lawn. When her sister helps her, the job takes $\dfrac{5}{4}$ h. How long does it take Libby's sister to mow the lawn by herself? $3\dfrac{1}{3}$ hours

4. Machine A and machine B produce the same item. Machine A produces 3 times as many items as machine B in the same time. When both machines work, they produce the day's quota in 4 h. How long would it take machine B alone to produce the quota? How long would it take machine A alone to produce the quota? $5\dfrac{1}{3}$ hours, $1\dfrac{7}{9}$ hours

5. A small pipe, a large pipe, or both pipes can be used to fill a pool. The large pipe takes 20 h to fill the pool. When both pipes are used, the pool is filled in 18 h. How long does it take the small pipe alone to fill the pool? 180 hours

8-7 Solve these proportions.

1. $\dfrac{8}{11} = \dfrac{x}{5.5}$ {4}

2. $\dfrac{10}{15} = \dfrac{12}{x}$ {18}

3. $\dfrac{35}{x} = \dfrac{40}{32}$ {28}

4. $\dfrac{x}{24} = \dfrac{15}{40}$ {9}

5. $\dfrac{2.5}{x} = \dfrac{15}{24}$ {4}

6. $\dfrac{3.5}{6} = \dfrac{1.4}{x}$ {2.4}

7. $\dfrac{2}{3} = \dfrac{x+4}{x+9}$ {6}

8. $\dfrac{7}{4} = \dfrac{x+9}{x}$ {12}

Solve.

9. A 12-ft board is cut into two pieces whose lengths are in the ratio of 1 to 5. How long are the pieces? 2 ft, 10 ft

10. A prize of $6000 is divided between two people in the ratio of 3 to 5. How much does each person get? $2250, $3750

11. The ratio of student tickets to adult tickets for a drama production is 4 to 3. How many of each kind were sold if 840 tickets were sold in all? 480 student, 360 adult

1. Let t = Gayle's time in hours and $2t$ = Chrystal's time in hours. Then $\dfrac{1}{t}$ = Gayle's rate in jobs per hour, and $\dfrac{1}{2t}$ = Chrystal's rate in jobs per hour. $\dfrac{3}{2t} + \dfrac{3}{t} = 1$; $\left\{4\dfrac{1}{2}\right\}$

2. Let t = the time in hours they work together. $\dfrac{t}{2} + \dfrac{t}{3} = 1$; $\left\{\dfrac{6}{5}\right\}$

3. Let t = the time in hours it takes Libby's sister. Then her rate in jobs per hour is $\dfrac{1}{t}$. $\left(\dfrac{5}{4}\right)\left(\dfrac{1}{2}\right) + \dfrac{5}{4}\left(\dfrac{1}{t}\right) = 1$; $\left\{3\dfrac{1}{3}\right\}$

4. Let t = time in hours it takes machine B. Then its rate in jobs per hour is $\dfrac{1}{t}$. Machine A's rate in jobs per hour is $\dfrac{1}{3t}$. $\dfrac{4}{t} + \dfrac{4}{3t} = 1$; $\left\{5\dfrac{1}{3}\right\}$

5. Let t = the time in hours it takes the smaller pipe. Then the smaller pipe's rate in jobs per hour is $\dfrac{1}{t}$. $\dfrac{18}{20} + \dfrac{18}{t} = 1$; {180}

635

1.

2.
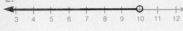

3.

4.

5.

6.

7.
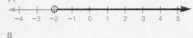

8.

9.

10.

1.

2.

3.

4.
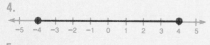

5.

6.

7.

8–8 Solve.

1. 15% of 260 = x (39) **2.** 10% of x = 320 (3200) **3.** x% of 450 = 99 (22)

4. 3% of 20 = x $\left\{\frac{3}{5}\right\}$ **5.** 2% of x = 500 (25,000) **6.** x% of 540 = 27 (5)

7. 125% of 16 = x (20) **8.** 150% of x = 375 (250) **9.** x% of 56 = 42 (75)

Solve.

10. Owen Lott borrowed $7000 for 3 years at an annual rate of 15%. How much interest did he pay on his loan? $3150

11. A television station reported that 45% of the registered voters questioned favored candidate Lincoln. If 81 of the voters questioned favored Lincoln, how many voters were questioned in all? 180

12. A convenience store reported that 156 out of 240 customers spent more than $10. What percent of the customers spent more than $10? 65%

8–9 Write a proportion for each problem. Solve the proportion, and answer the question.

1. How much will 10 oz of cheese cost if it sells for $3.60 per lb? $\frac{x}{10} = \frac{3 \cdot 60}{16}$; (2.25); $2.25

2. Mr. VanBuren drove at a constant rate for $1\frac{1}{2}$ h and traveled 81 mi. What was his rate in miles per hour? $\frac{81}{1\frac{1}{2}} = \frac{x}{1}$; (54); 54 mph

3. Catherine Harrison received 52% of the votes in an election in which 2575 persons voted. How many votes did she get? $\frac{x}{2575} = \frac{52}{100}$; (1339); 1339

4. Robert Stewart got 44% of the votes in an election. If he got 1463 votes, how many people voted? $\frac{1463}{x} = \frac{44}{100}$; (3325); 3325

5. On a map of Idaho, 3.2 cm represents 40 km. How far is Payette from Gooding if the distance is 8.4 cm on the map? $\frac{3.2}{40} = \frac{8.4}{x}$; (105); 105 km

6. Mrs. Spruce drove 391 mi and used 11.5 gal of gasoline. What was her average fuel consumption (in miles per gallon)? $\frac{391}{11.5} = \frac{x}{1}$; (34); 34 miles per gallon

8–10 Suppose that y varies directly as x in the following exercises.

1. If y = 2.5 when x = 4, what is y when x = 20? 12.5

2. If y = 6 when x = 3.5, what is y when x = 28? 48

3. If y = 200 when x = 15, what is x when y = 50? 3.75

4. If y = 3 when x = 125, what is x when y = 4.5? 187.5

Suppose that the quantities in the following exercises vary directly. Write an equation that fits the problem. Solve the equation, and answer the question.

5. A 50-ft length of wire weighs 20 oz. How long is a wire that weighs 5 lb? $\frac{50}{20} = \frac{x}{80}$; (200); 200 ft

6. A 10.75-oz can of cream of chicken soup contains 2.75 servings. Each can has 302.5 calories. How many calories are in each serving? $\frac{302.5}{2.75} = \frac{x}{1}$; (110); 110

8.

9.

Chapter 9

9–1 Graph on a number line.

1. $x > 6$ **2.** $x < 10$ **3.** $x \geq 2$ **4.** $x \leq 4$ **5.** $x \neq 3$

6. $x \neq -2$ **7.** $x > -2$ **8.** $x < -5$ **9.** $x \geq -10$ **10.** $x \leq -7$

9–2 Graph on a number line.

1. $a < 1$ or $a > 5$ **2.** $b > 3$ and $b < 8$ **3.** $c \leq -2$ or $c \geq 2$

4. $d \geq -4$ and $d \leq 4$ **5.** $h \neq 3$ and $h \leq 5$ **6.** $j \geq -5$ and $j \neq 0$

7. $k = 0$ or $k > 4$ **8.** $q < -3$ and $q < -6$ **9.** $r < -3$ or $r < -6$

9–3 Solve.

1. $a - 2 \geq 3$ $a \geq 5$ **2.** $d - 1 \leq -4$ $d \leq -3$ **3.** $h - 5 > -3$ $h > 2$

4. $2m + 3 \geq 3m$ $m \leq 3$ **5.** $4p + 8 < 3p + 10$ $p < 2$ **6.** $7r - 1 > 8r + 5$ $r < -6$

Solve the compound sentence. Graph the solutions on a number line.

7. $s + 1 \geq 4$ or $s + 4 \leq 4$ $s \geq 3$ or $s \leq 0$ **8.** $t - 2 \leq 6$ and $t + 2 \geq 6$ $t \leq 8$ and $t \geq 4$

9. $2x - 3 \leq 3x + 4$ and $3x + 4 \leq 2x + 2$ $x \geq -7$ and $x \leq -2$

9–4 Solve and graph on a number line.

1. $3a \leq 15$ $a \leq 5$ **2.** $4b \geq 12$ $b \geq 3$ **3.** $-2c \leq 8$ $c \geq -4$

4. $-5d \geq -30$ $d \leq 6$ **5.** $\frac{1}{2}h > -4$ $h > -8$ **6.** $-\frac{1}{3}j < 6$ $j > -18$

9–5 Solve and graph on a number line.

1. $3v + 2 \leq 14$ $v \leq 4$ **2.** $2w - 3 \geq 7$ $w \geq 5$ **3.** $\frac{1}{2}x - 1 > 5$ $x > 12$

4. $3c + 5 \leq 5c - 7$ $c \geq 6$ **5.** $-4d + 2 \geq d - 8$ $d \leq 2$ **6.** $2(j + 3) \leq 4(j - 1)$ $j \geq 5$

9–6 Write a compound sentence without absolute value.

1. $|a| \geq 5$ **2.** $|b| \leq 3$ **3.** $|c| < 4$ $-4 < c < 4$ **4.** $|d| > 6$
   $a \geq 5$ or $a \leq -5$ $-3 \leq b \leq 3$ $d > 6$ or $d < -6$
5. $|h + 3| \leq 2$ **6.** $|j - 4| \geq 7$ **7.** $|k - 2| > 1$ **8.** $|m + 4| < 4$
   $-5 \leq h \leq -1$ $j \geq 11$ or $j \leq -3$ $k > 3$ or $k < 1$ $-8 < m < 0$
Graph on a number line.

9. $|r + 3| < 8$ **10.** $|2t| > 7$ **11.** $\left|-\dfrac{y}{4}\right| \geq 2$ **12.** $|-u + 2| \geq 5$

9–7 Graph.

1. $y \geq 2x + 3$ **2.** $y > -\dfrac{1}{2}x - 2$ **3.** $x + y \geq -2$ **4.** $y \geq \dfrac{1}{3}x^2$

9–8 Graph.

1. $y \geq 2x$ or $y \leq -2x$ **2.** $y \geq 2x$ and $y \leq -2x$ **3.** $y \leq 2$ and $x \geq 3$

5.

6.

9.

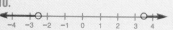

10.

11.

12.

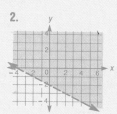

1. 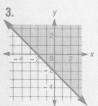   **2.**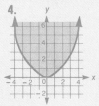

3.   **4.**

1.

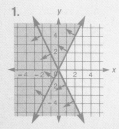

638

Chapter 10

10–1 Simplify.

1. $\sqrt{64}$ 8   **2.** $-\sqrt{81}$ -9 **3.** $\sqrt{0.36}$ 0.6   **4.** $-\sqrt{1.96}$ -1.4

5. $\sqrt{\dfrac{16}{25}}$ $\dfrac{4}{5}$ **6.** $-\sqrt{\dfrac{9}{100}}$ $-\dfrac{3}{10}$ **7.** $\dfrac{-\sqrt{4}}{-\sqrt{81}}$ $\dfrac{2}{9}$ **8.** $\dfrac{\sqrt{25}}{-\sqrt{36}}$ $-\dfrac{5}{6}$

Solve. The equations may have two solutions, one solution, or no solutions. Write $\emptyset$ if the equation has no solution.

9. $x = \sqrt{100}$ (10)   **10.** $x^2 = 100$ (10, −10)   **11.** $x = \sqrt{-100}$ $\emptyset$ **12.** $x^2 = -100$ $\emptyset$

13. $\sqrt{x} = 16$ (256)   **14.** $x = \sqrt{-9}$ $\emptyset$ **15.** $x^2 = 81$ (9, −9)   **16.** $x = -\sqrt{81}$ (−9)

10–2 State the consecutive integers between which the given number lies.

1. $\sqrt{70}$ 8, 9   **2.** $\sqrt{25.4}$ 5, 6   **3.** $\sqrt{3.61}$ 1, 2   **4.** $\sqrt{40.32}$ 6, 7   **5.** $\sqrt{90.67}$ 9, 10

Use the table on page 641 to find a decimal approximation to the nearest hundredth.

6. $\sqrt{5}$ 2.24   **7.** $-\sqrt{30}$ -5.48 **8.** $-\sqrt{87}$ -9.33 **9.** $\sqrt{75}$ 8.66   **10.** $\sqrt{40}$ 6.32

Solve. List approximations for the solutions to the nearest hundredth.

11. $x^2 = 45$ (6.71, −6.71)   **12.** $x^2 = 68$ (8.25, −8.25)   **13.** $x = -\sqrt{83}$ (−9.11)

14. $x^2 = 90$ (9.49, −9.49)   **15.** $x^2 = 7$ (2.65, −2.65)   **16.** $x^2 = 200$ (14.14, −14.14)

10–3 Find the length of the diagonal of a rectangle with the given length and width. Use the table on page 641 to approximate to the nearest tenth.

1. length: 4 cm 4.5 cm   **2.** length: 9 cm 9.8 cm   **3.** length: 6 m 8.5 m
    width: 2 cm   width: 4 cm   width: 6 m

4. length: 8 m 9.4 m   **5.** length: 23 km 25.9 km   **6.** length: 40 km 47.2 km
    width: 5 m   width: 12 km   width: 25 km

10–4 Simplify.

1. $\sqrt{98}$ $7\sqrt{2}$ **2.** $\sqrt{48}$ $4\sqrt{3}$ **3.** $-\sqrt{108}$ $-6\sqrt{3}$ **4.** $\sqrt{162}$ $9\sqrt{2}$

5. $-\sqrt{500}$ $-10\sqrt{5}$ **6.** $\sqrt{288}$ $12\sqrt{2}$ **7.** $\sqrt{5}(3 + \sqrt{5})$ $3\sqrt{5}+5$ **8.** $\sqrt{2}(\sqrt{8} + \sqrt{3})$ $4+\sqrt{6}$

9. $\sqrt{3}(\sqrt{27} - \sqrt{3})$ 6   **10.** $(3 + \sqrt{5})(3 - \sqrt{5})$ 4   **11.** $(4 - \sqrt{3})^2$ $19 - 8\sqrt{3}$ **12.** $(3 + \sqrt{2})^2$ $11 + 6\sqrt{2}$

10–5 Simplify.

1. $\sqrt{\dfrac{5}{36}}$ $\dfrac{\sqrt{5}}{6}$ **2.** $\sqrt{\dfrac{17}{64}}$ $\dfrac{\sqrt{17}}{8}$ **3.** $\sqrt{\dfrac{5}{3}}$ $\dfrac{\sqrt{15}}{3}$ **4.** $\sqrt{\dfrac{9}{2}}$ $\dfrac{3\sqrt{2}}{2}$ **5.** $\sqrt{\dfrac{7}{8}}$ $\dfrac{\sqrt{14}}{4}$

6. $\dfrac{\sqrt{10}}{\sqrt{2}}$ $\sqrt{5}$ **7.** $\dfrac{\sqrt{12}}{\sqrt{8}}$ $\dfrac{\sqrt{6}}{2}$ **8.** $\dfrac{\sqrt{20}}{\sqrt{24}}$ $\dfrac{\sqrt{30}}{6}$ **9.** $\dfrac{\sqrt{27}}{\sqrt{18}}$ $\dfrac{\sqrt{6}}{2}$ **10.** $\dfrac{\sqrt{54}}{\sqrt{12}}$ $\dfrac{3\sqrt{2}}{2}$

Write a decimal approximation to the nearest hundredth.

11. $\dfrac{1}{\sqrt{5}}$ 0.45   **12.** $\dfrac{\sqrt{2}}{\sqrt{3}}$ 0.82   **13.** $\sqrt{\dfrac{7}{2}}$ 1.87   **14.** $\sqrt{4\dfrac{4}{5}}$ 2.19   **15.** $\sqrt{2\dfrac{1}{7}}$ 1.46

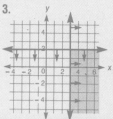

10–6 Simplify. Write "simplest form" if the expression cannot be simplified.

1. $\sqrt{8} + \sqrt{2}$ $3\sqrt{2}$ **2.** $2\sqrt{5} - 5\sqrt{5}$ $-3\sqrt{5}$ **3.** $\sqrt{18} - \sqrt{3}$ $3\sqrt{2} - \sqrt{3}$ **4.** $\sqrt{18} - \sqrt{2}$ $2\sqrt{2}$

5. $\sqrt{72} - \sqrt{2}$ $5\sqrt{2}$ **6.** $\sqrt{20} + \sqrt{5}$ $3\sqrt{5}$ **7.** $\sqrt{10} + \sqrt{6}$ Simplest form **8.** $\sqrt{108} + \sqrt{48}$ $10\sqrt{3}$

10–7 Simplify. Assume that the domain of each variable is the set of positive numbers.

1. $\sqrt{b^3}$ $b\sqrt{b}$ **2.** $\sqrt{\dfrac{c}{d}}$ $\dfrac{\sqrt{cd}}{d}$ **3.** $\sqrt{25h}$ $5\sqrt{h}$ **4.** $\sqrt{\dfrac{3}{j^2}}$ $\dfrac{\sqrt{3}}{j}$ **5.** $\sqrt{\dfrac{m^3}{2}}$ $\dfrac{m\sqrt{2m}}{2}$

Simplify, stating restrictions where necessary.

6. $\sqrt{x^2}$ $|x|$ **7.** $\sqrt{z^5}$ $z^2\sqrt{z};\ z \ge 0$ **8.** $\sqrt{\dfrac{n}{2}}$ $\dfrac{\sqrt{2n}}{2};\ n \ge 0$ **9.** $\sqrt{\dfrac{8}{p}}$ $\dfrac{2\sqrt{2p}}{p};\ p > 0$ **10.** $\sqrt{\dfrac{u^4}{v^5}}$ $\dfrac{u^2\sqrt{v}}{v^3};\ v > 0$

10–8 Solve. If there is no solution, write $\emptyset$.

1. $\sqrt{q + 11} = 3$ $\{-2\}$ **2.** $\sqrt{r + 5} = 2$ $\emptyset$ **3.** $\sqrt{3s - 5} = s - 1$ $\{2, 3\}$

4. $\sqrt{2t + 24} = t + 8$ $\{-4\}$ **5.** $\sqrt{4v - 1} = 2v$ $\left\{\dfrac{1}{2}\right\}$ **6.** $\sqrt{6w + 6} + 3 = w + 4$ $\{5, -1\}$

7. $6 = \sqrt{y + 1}$ $\{35\}$ **8.** $\sqrt{2 - z} + 3 = 7$ $\{-14\}$ **9.** $a - 1 = \sqrt{4a + 1}$ $\{6\}$

10–9 Find the distance between the two points. Simplify the distances.

1. $(-12, 3), (12, 10)$ 25 **2.** $(3, 2), (8, 14)$ 13 **3.** $(10, -5), (-5, 3)$ 17

4. $(6, 10), (8, 6)$ $2\sqrt{5}$ **5.** $(-2, 3), (1, 6)$ $3\sqrt{2}$ **6.** $(6, 5), (2, -1)$ $2\sqrt{13}$

Chapter 11

11–1 State the axis of symmetry and the minimum or maximum point.

1. $y = x^2 - 8x + 10$ $x = 4$, minimum: $(4, -6)$ **2.** $y = x^2 - 3x - 2$ $x = \dfrac{3}{2}$, minimum: $\left(\dfrac{3}{2}, -\dfrac{17}{4}\right)$

3. $y = x^2 + 5x + 2$ $x = -\dfrac{5}{2}$, minimum: $\left(-\dfrac{5}{2}, -\dfrac{17}{4}\right)$ **4.** $y = -x^2 + 6x$ $x = 3$, maximum: $(3, 9)$

5. $y = -x^2 - 2x$ $x = -1$, maximum: $(-1, 1)$ **6.** $y = 2x^2 + 11x + 14$ $x = -\dfrac{11}{4}$, minimum: $\left(-\dfrac{11}{4}, -\dfrac{9}{8}\right)$

11–2 Graph the function. Then solve the three equations using the graph. If there is no solution, write $\emptyset$.

1. $y = x^2 - 5x + 6$

   a. $x^2 - 5x + 6 = 0$ $\{2, 3\}$
   b. $x^2 - 5x + 6 = -1$ $\emptyset$
   c. $x^2 - 5x + 6 = 2$ $\{1, 4\}$

2. $y = x^2 + x - 12$

   a. $x^2 + x - 12 = 0$ $\{3, -4\}$
   b. $x^2 + x - 12 = -6$ $\{2, -3\}$
   c. $x^2 + x - 12 = 8$ $\{4, -5\}$

3. $y = x^2 - 2x - 8$

   a. $x^2 - 2x - 8 = 0$ $\{4, -2\}$
   b. $x^2 - 2x - 8 = 7$ $\{5, -3\}$
   c. $x^2 - 2x - 8 = -9$ $\{1\}$

4. $y = -x^2 + 6x - 5$

   a. $-x^2 + 6x - 5 = 0$ $\{1, 5\}$
   b. $-x^2 + 6x - 5 = 4$ $\{3\}$
   c. $-x^2 + 6x - 5 = 6$ $\emptyset$

ADDITIONAL ANSWERS

11–2

1.    **2.**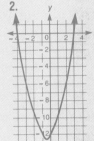

3.   **4.**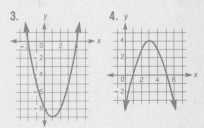

11–3 Solve. If the equation has no solution, write $\emptyset$.

1. $x^2 = 64$ $\{8, -8\}$ **2.** $(x - 3)^2 = 4$ $\{1, 5\}$ **3.** $(x + 5)^2 = -1$ $\emptyset$

4. $(x + 4)^2 = 36$ $\{2, -10\}$ **5.** $(x - 1)^2 = 0$ $\{1\}$ **6.** $(x + 6)^2 = 2$ $\{-6 \pm \sqrt{2}\}$

7. $3(x + 2)^2 = 12$ $\{0, -4\}$ **8.** $2(x - 5)^2 = 36$ $\left\{\frac{5 \pm 3\sqrt{2}}{}\right\}$ **9.** $x^2 + 7 = 23$ $\{4, -4\}$

10. $(2x - 7)^2 = 36$ $\left\{\frac{1}{2}, \frac{13}{2}\right\}$ **11.** $(x - 4)^2 = 20$ $\{4 \pm 2\sqrt{5}\}$ **12.** $x^2 + 4x + 4 = 9$ $\{1, -5\}$

13. $x^2 - 6x + 9 = 25$ $\{8, -2\}$ **14.** $x^2 - 4x + 4 = 18$ $\{2 \pm 3\sqrt{2}\}$ **15.** $x^2 - 8x + 16 = 11$ $\{4 \pm \sqrt{11}\}$

11–4 Solve by completing the square. Write the solutions as simplified radicals.

1. $x^2 + 8x = 9$ $\{1, -9\}$ **2.** $x^2 + 7x = 8$ $\{1, -8\}$ **3.** $x^2 - 6x = -8$ $\{2, 4\}$

4. $x^2 - 4x = 5$ $\{5, -1\}$ **5.** $x^2 - 2x = 4$ $\{1 \pm \sqrt{5}\}$ **6.** $x^2 + 6x + 2 = 5$ $\{-3 \pm 2\sqrt{3}\}$

7. $x^2 + 2x + 5 = 4$ $\{-1\}$ **8.** $x^2 - 9x = 2$ $\left\{\frac{9 \pm \sqrt{89}}{2}\right\}$ **9.** $x^2 - 5x = 3$ $\left\{\frac{5 \pm \sqrt{37}}{2}\right\}$

11–5 Solve using the quadratic formula. Simplify the solutions. If there is no solution, write $\emptyset$.

1. $x^2 - 6x + 4 = 0$ $\{3 \pm \sqrt{5}\}$ **2.** $x^2 + 3x + 1 = 0$ $\left\{\frac{-3 \pm \sqrt{5}}{2}\right\}$

3. $x^2 + 5x + 3 = 0$ $\left\{\frac{-5 \pm \sqrt{13}}{2}\right\}$ **4.** $2x^2 + 5x + 5 = 0$ $\emptyset$

5. $3x^2 + x - 2 = 0$ $\left\{\frac{2}{3}, -1\right\}$ **6.** $x^2 + 6x - 2 = 0$ $\{-3 \pm \sqrt{11}\}$

7. $x^2 - 4x - 3 = 0$ $\{2 \pm \sqrt{7}\}$ **8.** $3x^2 + x - 1 = 0$ $\left\{\frac{-1 \pm \sqrt{13}}{6}\right\}$

9. $x^2 + 6x = 0$ $\{0, -6\}$ **10.** $x^2 - 2 = 0$ $\{\pm\sqrt{2}\}$

11–6 Solve using the quadratic formula. Simplify all solutions. If there is no solution, write $\emptyset$.

1. $x^2 + 6x + 10 = 0$ $\emptyset$ **2.** $x^2 - 4x + 4 = 0$ $\{2\}$

3. $4x^2 - 5x - 6 = 0$ $\left\{2, -\frac{3}{4}\right\}$ **4.** $3x^2 - 4x + 2 = 0$ $\emptyset$

5. $4x^2 - 4x + 1 = 0$ $\left\{\frac{1}{2}\right\}$ **6.** $3x^2 - 5x + 1 = 0$ $\left\{\frac{5 \pm \sqrt{13}}{6}\right\}$

7. $2x^2 + 6x - 3 = 0$ $\left\{\frac{-3 \pm \sqrt{15}}{2}\right\}$ **8.** $-2x^2 + 3x + 1 = 0$ $\left\{\frac{-3 \pm \sqrt{17}}{-4}\right\}$

11–7 Solve by any method. If there is no solution, write $\emptyset$.

1. $x^2 - 2x - 1 = 0$ $\{1 \pm \sqrt{2}\}$ **2.** $x^2 + 8x - 15 = 0$ $\{-4 \pm \sqrt{31}\}$

3. $x^2 - 3x = 0$ $\{0, 3\}$ **4.** $x^2 - 16 = 0$ $\{4, -4\}$

5. $x^2 - 4x + 2 = 0$ $\{2 \pm \sqrt{2}\}$ **6.** $x^2 - x - 12 = 0$ $\{4, -3\}$

7. $x^2 + 5x + 2 = 0$ $\left\{\frac{-5 \pm \sqrt{17}}{2}\right\}$ **8.** $x^2 - 3x + 8 = 0$ $\emptyset$

9. $x^2 + 7x = 0$ $\{0, -7\}$ **10.** $x^2 - 3x - 18 = 0$ $\{6, -3\}$

11. $x^2 + 7x + 5 = 0$ $\left\{\frac{-7 \pm \sqrt{29}}{2}\right\}$ **12.** $2x^2 - 5x - 2 = 0$ $\left\{\frac{5 \pm \sqrt{41}}{4}\right\}$

13. $2x^2 - 5x + 2 = 0$ $\left\{\frac{1}{2}, 2\right\}$ **14.** $2x^2 - 9x + 7 = 0$ $\left\{1, \frac{7}{2}\right\}$

15. $3x^2 + 2x = 0$ $\left\{0, -\frac{2}{3}\right\}$ **16.** $6x^2 + 5x - 21 = 0$ $\left\{\frac{3}{2}, -\frac{7}{3}\right\}$

Table of Squares and Approximate Square Roots

n	n^2	$\sqrt{n}$	$\sqrt{10n}$	n	n^2	$\sqrt{n}$	$\sqrt{10n}$
1	1	1.000	3.162	51	2601	7.141	22.583
2	4	1.414	4.472	52	2704	7.211	22.804
3	9	1.732	5.477	53	2809	7.280	23.022
4	16	2.000	6.325	54	2916	7.348	23.238
5	25	2.236	7.071	55	3025	7.416	23.452
6	36	2.449	7.746	56	3136	7.483	23.664
7	49	2.646	8.367	57	3249	7.550	23.875
8	64	2.828	8.944	58	3364	7.616	24.083
9	81	3.000	9.487	59	3481	7.681	24.290
10	100	3.162	10.000	60	3600	7.746	24.495
11	121	3.317	10.488	61	3721	7.810	24.698
12	144	3.464	10.954	62	3844	7.874	24.900
13	169	3.606	11.402	63	3969	7.937	25.100
14	196	3.742	11.832	64	4096	8.000	25.298
15	225	3.873	12.247	65	4225	8.062	25.495
16	256	4.000	12.649	66	4356	8.124	25.690
17	289	4.123	13.038	67	4489	8.185	25.884
18	324	4.243	13.416	68	4624	8.246	26.077
19	361	4.359	13.784	69	4761	8.307	26.268
20	400	4.472	14.142	70	4900	8.367	26.458
21	441	4.583	14.491	71	5041	8.426	26.646
22	484	4.690	14.832	72	5184	8.485	26.833
23	529	4.796	15.166	73	5329	8.544	27.019
24	576	4.899	15.492	74	5476	8.602	27.203
25	625	5.000	15.811	75	5625	8.660	27.386
26	676	5.099	16.125	76	5776	8.718	27.568
27	729	5.196	16.432	77	5929	8.775	27.749
28	784	5.292	16.733	78	6084	8.832	27.928
29	841	5.385	17.029	79	6241	8.888	28.107
30	900	5.477	17.321	80	6400	8.944	28.284
31	961	5.568	17.607	81	6561	9.000	28.460
32	1024	5.657	17.889	82	6724	9.055	28.636
33	1089	5.745	18.166	83	6889	9.110	28.810
34	1156	5.831	18.439	84	7056	9.165	28.983
35	1225	5.916	18.708	85	7225	9.220	29.155
36	1296	6.000	18.974	86	7396	9.274	29.326
37	1369	6.083	19.235	87	7569	9.327	29.496
38	1444	6.164	19.494	88	7744	9.381	29.665
39	1521	6.245	19.748	89	7921	9.434	29.833
40	1600	6.325	20.000	90	8100	9.487	30.000
41	1681	6.403	20.248	91	8281	9.539	30.166
42	1764	6.481	20.494	92	8464	9.592	30.332
43	1849	6.557	20.736	93	8649	9.644	30.496
44	1936	6.633	20.976	94	8836	9.695	30.659
45	2025	6.708	21.213	95	9025	9.747	30.822
46	2116	6.782	21.448	96	9216	9.798	30.984
47	2209	6.856	21.679	97	9409	9.849	31.145
48	2304	6.928	21.909	98	9604	9.899	31.305
49	2401	7.000	22.136	99	9801	9.950	31.464
50	2500	7.071	22.361	100	10000	10.000	31.623

Table of Trigonometric Ratios

Angle	Sine	Cosine	Tangent	Angle	Sine	Cosine	Tangent
1°	0.0175	0.9998	0.0175	46°	0.7193	0.6947	1.0355
2°	0.0349	0.9994	0.0349	47°	0.7314	0.6820	1.0724
3°	0.0523	0.9986	0.0524	48°	0.7431	0.6691	1.1106
4°	0.0698	0.9976	0.0699	49°	0.7547	0.6561	1.1504
5°	0.0872	0.9962	0.0875	50°	0.7660	0.6428	1.1918
6°	0.1045	0.9945	0.1051	51°	0.7771	0.6293	1.2349
7°	0.1219	0.9925	0.1228	52°	0.7880	0.6157	1.2799
8°	0.1392	0.9903	0.1405	53°	0.7986	0.6018	1.3270
9°	0.1564	0.9877	0.1584	54°	0.8090	0.5878	1.3764
10°	0.1736	0.9848	0.1763	55°	0.8192	0.5736	1.4281
11°	0.1908	0.9816	0.1944	56°	0.8290	0.5592	1.4826
12°	0.2079	0.9781	0.2126	57°	0.8387	0.5446	1.5399
13°	0.2250	0.9744	0.2309	58°	0.8480	0.5299	1.6003
14°	0.2419	0.9703	0.2493	59°	0.8572	0.5150	1.6643
15°	0.2588	0.9659	0.2679	60°	0.8660	0.5000	1.7321
16°	0.2756	0.9613	0.2867	61°	0.8746	0.4848	1.8040
17°	0.2924	0.9563	0.3057	62°	0.8829	0.4695	1.8807
18°	0.3090	0.9511	0.3249	63°	0.8910	0.4540	1.9626
19°	0.3256	0.9455	0.3443	64°	0.8988	0.4384	2.0503
20°	0.3420	0.9397	0.3640	65°	0.9063	0.4226	2.1445
21°	0.3584	0.9336	0.3839	66°	0.9135	0.4067	2.2460
22	0.3746	0.9272	0.4040	67°	0.9205	0.3907	2.3559
23°	0.3907	0.9205	0.4245	68°	0.9272	0.3746	2.4751
24°	0.4067	0.9135	0.4452	69°	0.9336	0.3584	2.6051
25°	0.4226	0.9063	0.4663	70°	0.9397	0.3420	2.7475
26°	0.4384	0.8988	0.4877	71°	0.9455	0.3256	2.9042
27°	0.4540	0.8910	0.5095	72°	0.9511	0.3090	3.0777
28°	0.4695	0.8829	0.5317	73°	0.9563	0.2924	3.2709
29°	0.4848	0.8746	0.5543	74°	0.9613	0.2756	3.4874
30°	0.5000	0.8660	0.5774	75°	0.9659	0.2588	3.7321
31°	0.5150	0.8572	0.6009	76°	0.9703	0.2419	4.0108
32°	0.5299	0.8480	0.6249	77°	0.9744	0.2250	4.3315
33°	0.5446	0.8387	0.6494	78°	0.9781	0.2079	4.7046
34°	0.5592	0.8290	0.6745	79°	0.9816	0.1908	5.1446
35°	0.5736	0.8192	0.7002	80°	0.9848	0.1736	5.6713
36°	0.5878	0.8090	0.7265	81°	0.9877	0.1564	6.3138
37°	0.6018	0.7986	0.7536	82°	0.9903	0.1392	7.1154
38°	0.6157	0.7880	0.7813	83°	0.9925	0.1219	8.1443
39°	0.6293	0.7771	0.8098	84°	0.9945	0.1045	9.5144
40°	0.6428	0.7660	0.8391	85°	0.9962	0.0872	11.4301
41°	0.6561	0.7547	0.8693	86°	0.9976	0.0698	14.3007
42°	0.6691	0.7431	0.9004	87°	0.9986	0.0523	19.0811
43°	0.6820	0.7314	0.9325	88°	0.9994	0.0349	28.6363
44°	0.6947	0.7193	0.9657	89°	0.9998	0.0175	57.2900
45°	0.7071	0.7071	1.0000	90°	1.0000	0.0000	.....

■ GLOSSARY

abscissa (p. 198)   The first number in the ordered pair for a point in the coordinate plane.

absolute value (p. 40)   On the number line, the distance of a number from zero is called the absolute value of that number. The absolute value of any number (except zero) is a positive number, and the absolute value of zero is zero. Absolute value is indicated by the symbol, $|\ |$.

absolute value property of inequalities (p. 464)   For all real numbers x and a, if a is 0 or positive, $|x| < a$ is equivalent to $-a < x$ and $x < a$, which is equivalent to $-a < x < a$. For all real numbers x and a, if a is 0 or positive, $|x| > a$ is equivalent to $x < -a$ or $x > a$.

addition property of equality (p. 279)   For all numbers a, b, c, and d, if $a = b$ and $c = d$, then $a + c = b + d$.

addition property of equations (p. 98)   An equivalent equation is obtained when the same number is added to (or subtracted from) both sides of an equation. For all real numbers a, b, and c, if $a = b$, then $a + c = b + c$.

addition property of exponents (p. 153)   For all real numbers a, and all positive numbers m and n, $a^m \cdot a^n = a^{m+n}$.

additional property of inequalities (p. 447)   For all numbers a, b, and c, if $a < b$, then $a + c < b + c$ and if $a > b$, then $a + c > b + c$.

admissible values (p. 359)   The values of the variables for which a fraction is defined.

algebraic fractions (p. 359)   Fractions that contain variables.

angle-sum property (p. 604)   The sum of the measures of the angles of a triangle is $180°$.

arithmetic mean (p. 598)   For a set of numbers, the arithmetic mean is the quotient of the sum of the numbers divided by the number of numbers.

ascending order (p. 149)   The order of the terms of a polynomial when written in order of their degrees from lowest to highest.

associative property of addition (p. 20)   For all numbers a, b, and c, $(a + b) + c = a + (b + c)$.

associative property of multiplication (p. 20)   For all numbers a, b, and c, $(ab)c = a(bc)$.

averages (p. 598)   The mean, median, and mode.

axes (p. 197)   Two perpendicular lines selected in a plane.

axis of symmetry (p. 544)   The line at which, if the graph of a quadratic equation is folded, the two parts of the graph will match each other.

base (of an exponent) (p. 11)   The number that is used as a factor.

binomial (p. 148)   A polynomial with exactly two terms.

braces (p. 1)   Symbols, { }, used to indicate a set of numbers.

brackets (p. 6)   Grouping symbols, [ ], similar to parentheses.

certain event (p. 593)   An event that will always occur. The probability of a certain event is 1.

coefficient (p. 10)   The number in a product that includes a number and variables.

common factors (p. 310)   Numbers that are factors of more than one number.

commutative property of addition (p. 19)   For all real numbers a and b, $a + b = b + a$.

commutative property of multiplication (p. 19)   For all real numbers a and b, $ab = ba$.

completing the square (p. 564)   A process used to solve any quadratic equation.

composite number (p. 305)   A positive number with more than two factors.

compound inequality (p. 435)   An inequality with $\geq$ or $\leq$.

congruent angles (p. 604)   Angles that are the same size.

conjugates (p. 514)   If $\sqrt{y}$ is an irrational number, then the two binomials of the form $x + \sqrt{y}$ and $x - \sqrt{y}$ are conjugates of each other.

consecutive integers (p. 185)   Integers that "follow" one after another.

constant (p. 148)   A monomial that is a number.

constant of variation (p. 411)   The constant k in the relationships of variation.

converse of the Pythagorean theorem (p. 501)   If sides a, b, and c of a triangle are such that $a^2 + b^2 = c^2$, then the triangle is a right triangle. The right angle is opposite the longest side.

coordinate (of a point) (p. 197)   The number associated with a particular point on a number line.

corresponding sides of similar triangles property (p. 605)   Corresponding sides of similar triangles are proportional.

cosine of an angle (p. 611)   In a right triangle, the ratio of the length of the side adjacent to an acute angle to the length of the hypotenuse.

cross-multiplication property (p. 395)   For all numbers a, b, c, and d ($b \neq 0$ and $d \neq 0$), if $\frac{a}{b} = \frac{a}{d}$, then $ad = bc$.

degree of monomial (p. 148)   The sum of the exponents of a monomial's variables.

degree of a polynomial (p. 149)   The highest degree of any of a polynomial's terms *after* the polynomial has been simplified.

descending order (p. 149)   The order of the terms of a polynomial when written in order of their degrees from highest to lowest.

difference of squares property (p. 327)   For all numbers a and b, $(a+b)(a-b) = a^2 - b^2$.

direct variation (p. 411)   A function such that $y = kx$ or $\frac{y}{x} = k$ is called direct variation, where y varies directly with x and k is called the consonant of variation.

discriminant (p. 576)   The expression $b^2 - 4ac$.

distance formula (p. 531)   The distance d between two points (x_1, y_1) and (x_2, y_2) is $d = \sqrt{(x_2 - x_1)^2 + (y_2 - y_1)^2}$.

distributive property of exponents over multiplication (p. 163)   For all real numbers a and b, and all positive integers n, $(ab)^n = a^n b^n$.

distributive property of multiplication over addition (p. 20)   For all numbers a, b, and c, $ab + ac = a(b + c)$ and $ba + ca = (b + c)a$.

distributive property of multiplication over subtraction (p. 24)   For all numbers a, b, and c, $ca - cb = c(a - b)$ and $ac - bc = (a - b)c$.

distributive property of opposites (p. 67)   For all real numbers a and b, $-(a + b) = -a + (-b)$.

dividing opposites property (p. 67)   For all real numbers a and b, $b \neq 0$, $\frac{-a}{b} = -\frac{a}{b} = \frac{a}{-b}$.

division property for equivalent fractions (p. 360)   For all admissible values of a, b, and c, $\frac{a}{b} = \frac{a \div c}{b \div c}$.

division property for radicals (p. 510)   For all nonnegative numbers a and b ($b \neq 0$), $\sqrt{\frac{a}{b}} = \frac{\sqrt{a}}{\sqrt{b}}$.

domain (of a relation) (p. 201)   The set of first components of a relation.

domain (of a variable) (p. 1)   The set of numbers to be substituted for a variable.

empty set (p. 89)   The solution set of equations that have no solutions given in the replacement set.

equal ordered pairs (p. 198)   Pairs that have the same first coordinates and the same second coordinates. For all real numbers a, b, c, and d, $(a, b) = (c, d)$ if and only if $a = c$ and $b = d$.

equivalent equations (p. 92)   Equations that have the same solution set.

equivalent expressions (p. 15)   Two expressions that have the same values for every possible substitution.

equivalent fractions (p. 360)   Two fractions are equivalent if one of them can be transformed into the other by multiplication or division by a number or expression equal to 1.

equivalent inequalities (p. 447)   Inequalities with the same set of solutions.

evaluate (p. 2)   To substitute for a variable and then simplify the resulting numerical expression.

expanding (p. 318)   The process of changing from factored form to polynomial form.

exponent (p. 11)   The number that indicates how many times the base number is used as a factor.

factor (*noun*) (p. 10)   In a multiplication expression, a number that is multiplied.

factor (*verb*) (p. 306)   To write a number or an expression as the product of two or more of its factors.

factoring (p. 318)   The process of changing from polynomial form to factored form.

first component (p. 198)   The x-coordinate of an ordered pair.

frequency table (p. 598)   A list of the number of outcomes of an experiment that shows the frequency with which each outcome occurs.

function (p. 234)   A relation that has no two ordered pairs with the same first component. A relation is a function if and only if each first component in the relation is paired with exactly one second component.

graph of the equation (p. 211)   The graph of the set of all solutions of an equation.

graph (of an ordered number pair) (p. 197)   A point indicating the location of an ordered pair in the plane.

greatest common factor of two or more integers (GCF) (p. 310)   The greatest integer that is a factor of each given integer.

greatest common factor of two or more monomials (p. 311)   A monomial whose coefficient is the greatest common factor of the coefficients of the given monomials and whose variables have the greatest common degree of each variable in the given monomials.

horizontal line (p. 217)   A line parallel to the x-axis.

hyperbola (p. 419)   The graph of a second-degree equation formed by inverse variation.

hypotenuse (p. 500)   The longest side of a right triangle.

identity property for addition (p. 21)   For all numbers a, $a + 0 = a$ and $0 + a = a$.

identity property for multiplication (p. 21)   For all numbers a, $1a = a$ and $a \cdot 1 = a$.

impossible event (p. 593)   An event that will never occur. The probability of an impossible event is 0.

independent events (p. 595)   Two events where either event can occur without affecting the other.

inequality (p. 435)   A mathematical sentence stating that two quantities are not equal.

integers (p. 39)   The numbers . . . , $^-5$, $^-4$, $^-3$, $^-2$, $^-1$, 0, $^+1$, $^+2$, $^+3$, $^+4$, $^+5$, . . . are integers.

interest (p. 402)   The amount of money earned (or paid) from (for) an investment (loan).

inverse operation (p. 108)   The operation that will "undo" an operation.

inverse property of addition (p. 66)   For all real members a, $a + (-a) = 0$.

inverse property of multiplication (p. 66)   For all real numbers a, $a\left(\dfrac{1}{a}\right) = 1$ $(a \neq 0)$.

inverse variation (p. 419)   A function defined by an equation of the form $xy = k$ or $y = \dfrac{k}{x}$, where k is a constant greater than 0, y is said to vary inversely as x, and k is called the constant of variation.

irrational number (p. 494)   A real number that cannot be expressed as the quotient of two integers.

least common denominator (p. 376)   The least common multiple of the denominators of two or more fractions.

legs (p. 500)   The two shorter sides of a right triangle.

like terms (p. 24)   Terms that contain the same variable factors.

linear equation in two variables (p. 235)   Equations that define linear functions.

linear function (p. 235)   A function whose graph is a straight line.

literal equation (p. 123)   Formula or other equation containing more than one variable.

maximum (of a quadratic function) (p. 545)   The highest point on the graph of a quadratic function.

measures of central tendency (p. 598)   The mean, median, and mode.

median (p. 598)   For a set of numbers, the median is found by arranging the numbers in order from greatest to least and locating the middle number. If there is an even number of numbers, the median is midway between the two middle numbers.

minimum (of a quadratic function) (p. 544)   The lowest point on the graph of a quadratic function.

mode (p. 598)   For a set of numbers, the most frequently occurring number.

monomial (p. 143)   A number, a variable, or the product of numbers and/or variables.

multiplying opposites property (p. 67)   For all real numbers a and b, $(-a)b = a(-b) = -(ab)$ and $(-a)(-b) = ab$.

multiplication property of equations (p. 103)   An equivalent equation is obtained when both sides of an equation are multiplied (or divided) by the same number. For all real numbers a, b, and c, if $a = b$, then $ac = bc$.

multiplication property for equivalent fractions (p. 360)   For all admissible values of a, b, and c, $\dfrac{a}{b} = \dfrac{ac}{bc}$.

multiplication property of exponents (p. 162)   For all numbers a, and all positive integers m and n, $(a^m)^n = a^{mn}$.

multiplication property of inequalities (p. 452)   For all numbers a, b, and c, $c > 0$, if $a > b$, then $ca > cb$, and if $a < b$, then $ca < cb$. For all numbers a, b, and c, $c < 0$, if $a > b$, then $ca < cb$, and if $a < b$, then $ca > cb$.

multiplication property for radicals (p. 506)   For all numbers a and b, $\sqrt{ab} = \sqrt{a}\sqrt{b}$.

negative numbers (p. 39)   Numbers that are to the left of zero on the number line.

negative one (-1) **property of multiplication** (p. 67)   For all real numbers a, $(-1)a = -a$.

number line (p. 39)   A model in which real numbers are represented as points.

numerical coefficient (p. 10)   The number in a product that includes a number and variables.

opposite directions (p. 39)   Numbers involved in measurements that can be described by positive and negative numbers.

opposite of an opposite property (p. 67)   For all real numbers a, $-(-a) = a$.

opposites (p. 40)   Numbers that have the same absolute value and opposite signs. Zero is the opposite of zero.

order of operations (p. 5)   Rules used in simplifying numerical expressions. Mathematicians have agreed on the following rules for the order of operations:
1. Simplify inside parentheses and other grouping symbols first.
2. Do multiplications and divisions next, in order from left to right.
3. Do additions and subtractions next, in order from left to right.

order of real numbers (p. 39)   The way in which the real numbers are set up on the number line.

ordered pair (p. 197)   A pair of numbers that has a graph in the plane.

ordinate (p. 198)   The second number in the ordered pair for a point in the coordinate plane.

origin (p. 197)   The point of intersection of the two axes.

parabola (p. 544)   The graph of a quadratic equation.

percent (p. 400)   A term meaning "hundredth," usually denoted by the symbol %.

perfect square property (page 332)   For all numbers a and b, $(a + b)^2 = a^2 + 2ab + b^2$ and $(a - b)^2 = a^2 - 2ab + b^2$.

polynomial (p. 143)   The sum (or difference) of monomials. Monomials are also polynomials.

positive numbers (p. 39)   Numbers that are to the right of zero on the number line.

prime factorization (p. 306)   A factorization of a number such that all of its factors are prime numbers.

prime number (p. 305)   A number that has exactly two factors.

principal (p. 402)   An amount of money borrowed or invested in dollars.

principal square root (p. 489)   The positive square root of a number, and indicated by the radical sign.

probability (p. 592)   The quotient of the number of outcomes in an event divided by the total number of outcomes.

product (p. 10)   The result obtained when factors are multiplied.

proportion (p. 394)   An equation that states that two ratios are equal.

Pythagorean theorem (p. 500)   For a right triangle, the square of the hypotenuse is equal to the sum of the squares of the legs.

quadrants (p. 197)   The four regions in the plane formed by the axes.

quadratic equation (p. 543)   A polynomial equation of degree two.

quadratic formula (p. 569)   If $ax^2 + bx + c = 0$, $a \neq 0$, then $x = \dfrac{-b \pm \sqrt{b^2 - 4ac}}{2a}$.

quadratic function (p. 543)   A set of solutions of a polynomial function of degree two. A quadratic function is a set of ordered pairs (x, y) described by an equation that can be written in the form $y = ax^2 + bx + c$, $a \neq 0$.

radical (p. 489)   An expression that includes a radical sign ($\sqrt{}$) and the expression under the radical sign called the radicand.

radical equation (p. 526)   An equation that contains a radical with a variable in the radicand.

radical sign ($\sqrt{}$) (p. 489)   The symbol used for taking a square root.

radicand (p. 489)   The expression under the radical sign.

raise to a power (p. 11)   To evaluate numbers with exponents.

range (measure of central tendency) (p. 601)   The difference between the least number and the greatest number in a set of numbers.

range (of a relation) (p. 201)   The set of second components of the relation.

ratio (p. 394)   A comparison of two numbers by division.

rate (p. 402)   A comparison of two quantities by division; for example, 5 miles per hour, 6% per year.

rational number (p. 494)   A number that can be expressed as the quotient of two integers.

rationalizing the denominator (p. 511)   The process of eliminating a radical from the denominator of a fraction.

real numbers (p. 39)   The set of numbers consisting of the positive numbers, the negative numbers, and zero.

reciprocals (p. 56)   The numbers whose product is 1.

regular polygon (p. 607)   A polygon that has all angles congruent and all sides congruent.

relation (p. 201)   A set of ordered pairs.

replacement set (p. 89)   The set of numbers that can be substituted for the variable. Also called the domain of the variable.

roots of an equation (p. 574)   The solutions of an equation.

scientific notation (p. 157)   A method of writing a number as the product of two factors. One factor is a number greater than or equal to 1 and less than 10, and the other factor is a power of 10 written in exponential form.

second component (p. 198)   The y-coordinate of an ordered pair.

sense (p. 452)   The inequalities $a > b$ and $c > d$ are said to be inequalities in the *same sense*, whereas $a < b$ and $c > d$ are said to be inequalities of the *opposite sense*.

similar triangles (p. 604)   Two triangles are similar if and only if their corresponding angles are congruent.

simplest expression (p. 2)   A numerical or variable expression that most closely represents a number.

simplest form (of a radical) (p. 507)   When a radicand does not contain a fraction, has no perfect-square factors other than 1, and has no radicals in the denominator, we say that it is in simplest form.

simplify (p. 2)   To write the simplest expression that represents the number.

sine of an angle (p. 611)   In a right triangle, the ratio of the length of the side adjacent to an acute angle to the length of the hypotenuse.

slope–intercept form (of a linear equation) (p. 223)   The equation $y = mx + b$. The graph of the equation is a straight line with slope m and y-intercept b.

slope of a line (p. 216)   The ratio of the vertical change to the horizontal change. The slope of a line is the ratio of the change in y to the corresponding change in x between two points on the line (x_1, y_1) and (x_2, y_2).

$$m = \frac{y_2 - y_1}{x_2 - x_1} = \frac{y_1 - y_2}{x_1 - x_2}$$

slopes of parallel lines property (p. 225) Two lines are parallel if and only if they have the same slope or they have no slope.

slopes of perpendicular lines property (p. 226) Two lines are perpendicular if and only if the product of their slopes is -1, or if one slope is zero and the other is undefined.

solution (p. 89) The number that changes an equation into a true statement when it is substituted for the variable.

solution set (p. 89) The set of numbers from the replacement set that are solutions of the equation.

solution of a system of equations (p. 258) An ordered pair that is a solution of each of the two equations.

solutions of inequalities (p. 436) Those numbers that make the inequality true when they are substituted for the variable.

solve (p. 89) To find all the solutions of an equation.

solve an inequality (p. 447) To change to simpler equivalent inequalities until the variable is alone on one side.

square (p. 489) The square of a number is the product of the number multiplied by itself.

square root (p. 489) If $x^2 = y$, then x is a square root of y.

square root property of equations (p. 558) For each real number c, $c > 0$, if $x^2 = c$, then $x = \pm \sqrt{x}$.

standard deviation (p. 601) A commonly used statistic that describes the amount of dispersion from the mean numbers in the set.

subscript (p. 123) A number that indicates that variables are related but different.

substitution (p. 1) The process by which variables are replaced by numbers.

subtraction property of exponents (p. 175) For all numbers a, $a \neq 0$, and for all positive integers m and n, if $m > n$, then $\frac{a^m}{a^n} = a^{m-n}$ and if $m < n$, then $\frac{a^m}{a^n} = \frac{1}{a^{n-m}}$.

symmetric property of equations (p. 93) For all real numbers a and b, if $a = b$, then $b = a$.

system of equations (p. 258) A pair of equations.

tangent of an angle (p. 608) In a right triangle, the ratio of the length of the side opposite an acute angle to the length of the side adjacent to the acute angle.

terms (p. 24) Parts of an expression "connected" by addition or subtraction signs.

trigonometric ratios (p. 608) Ratios related to triangles, such as the sine, cosine, and tangent ratios.

trinomial (p. 148) A polynomial with exactly three terms.

uniform motion (p. 169) When motion is uniform, the relationship among distance (d), rate of speed traveled (r), and time traveled (t) is given by the formula $d = rt$.

unlike terms (p. 143) Terms that have different variable expressions.

variable (p. 1) A letter such as x, y, A, and g that is used in an expression in place of a number.

vertical line (p. 217) A line parallel to the y-axis.

vertical-line test (p. 235) A test used to determine whether a relation is a function. A vertical line can never cross the graph of a function more than once since there are no two ordered pairs with the same first coordinate.

x-axis (p. 197) The horizontal axis.

x-coordinate (p. 198) The first coordinate in an ordered pair.

x-intercept (p. 229) The x-coordinate of the point at which a line crosses the x-axis.

y-axis (p. 197) The vertical axis.

y-coordinate (p. 198) The second coordinate in an ordered pair.

y-intercept (p. 223) The y-value of the point at which a graph line crosses the y-axis.

zero exponent (p. 176) For all numbers a ($a \neq 0$), $a^0 = 1$.

zero (0) property of multiplication (p. 67) For all real numbers a, $0a = 0$.

zero-product property (p. 314) For all numbers a and b, if $ab = 0$, then $a = 0$ or $b = 0$.

■ SYMBOLS

{ }	Set
$\emptyset$	Empty set
=	Is equal to
$\neq$	Is not equal to
>	Is greater than
<	Is less than
$\geq$	Is greater than or equal to
$\leq$	Is less than or equal to
$\approx$	Is approximately equal to
$5 \cdot 4$	5 times 4
$^{-}5$	Negative 5
$^{+}5$	Positive 5
5^4	5 to the fourth power ($5 \cdot 5 \cdot 5 \cdot 5$)
$-n$	Opposite or additive inverse of a number n
$\|n\|$	Absolute value of a number n
$x \stackrel{?}{=} y$	Does $x = y$?
π	Pi

°	Degree
%	Percent
(x, y)	Ordered pair x, y
$A(x, y)$	Point A with coordinates x, y
$x : y$	Ratio of x to y
$\sqrt{x}$	Principal or positive square root of x
$\pm\sqrt{5}$	Positive or negative $\sqrt{5}$
$3 \pm \sqrt{5}$	3 plus or minus $\sqrt{5}$
$\overleftrightarrow{AB}$	Line AB
$\overline{AB}$	Segment AB
AB	Measure of segment AB
$\angle A$	Angle A
$P(A)$	The probability of the outcome A
tan A	Tangent of angle A
sin A	Sine of angle A
cos A	Cosine of angle A

■ FORMULAS

$P = a + b + c$	Perimeter of a triangle
$P = 4s$	Perimeter of a square
$P = 2(l + w)$	Perimeter of a rectangle
$C = \pi d$	Circumference of a circle
$A = lw$	Area of a rectangle
$A = s^2$	Area of a square
$A = bh$	Area of a parallelogram
$A = \frac{1}{2}bh$	Area of a triangle
$A = \frac{1}{2}h(b_1 + b_2)$	Area of a trapezoid
$A = \pi r^2$	Area of a circle
$S = 4\pi r^2$	Surface area of a sphere
$S = \pi rs$	Area of the slant surface of a cone

$V = lwh$	Volume of a rectangular prism
$V = Bh$	Volume of a prism
$V = \frac{1}{3}Bh$	Volume of a pyramid
$V = \frac{1}{3}\pi r^2 h$	Volume of a cone
$V = \frac{4}{3}\pi r^3$	Volume of a sphere
$V = \pi r^2 h$	Volume of a cylinder
$i = prt$	Interest
$d = rt$	Distance
$F = \frac{9}{5}(C + 32)$	Temperature conversion to Fahrenheit
$C = \frac{5}{9}(F - 32)$	Temperature conversion to Celsius
$a^2 + b^2 = c^2$	Pythagorean theorem

■ METRIC SYSTEM

1 kilometer (km) = 1000 meters (m)
1 centimeter (cm) = 0.01 meter
1 millimeter (mm) = 0.001 meter

1 kilogram (kg) = 1000 grams (g)
1 milligram (mg) = 0.001 gram

1 kiloliter (kL) = 1000 liters (L)
1 milliliter (mL) = 0.001 liter

km/h	Kilometers per hour
m/s	Meters per second
°C	Degrees Celsius
m^2	Square meter
cm^2	Square centimeter
m^3	Cubic meter
cm^3	Cubic centimeter

ADDITIONAL ANSWERS

■ Written Exercises SECTION 5–2

25.

26.

27.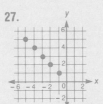

28.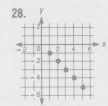

29.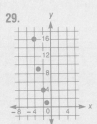

30.

31.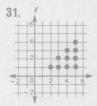

32.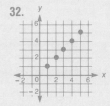

33.

34.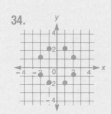

35.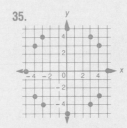

■ Classroom Exercises SECTION 5–4

1.

2.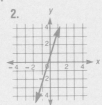

3.

4.

5.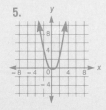

6.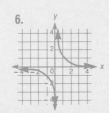

1.

2.

3.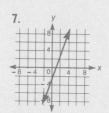

4.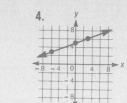

5.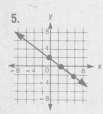

6.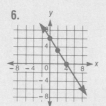

7.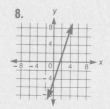

8.

9.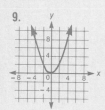

10.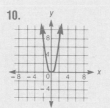

11.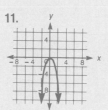

12.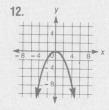

13.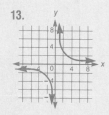

14.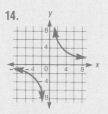

15.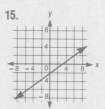

16.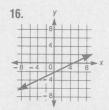

17.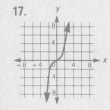

18.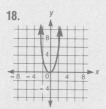

19.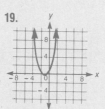

20.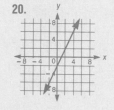

21.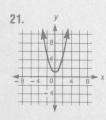

22.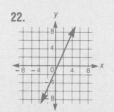

23.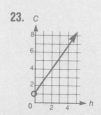

24.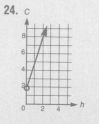

650

25.

26.

27.

28.

29.

30.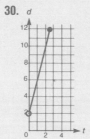

■ **Written Exercises SECTION 6-1**

26.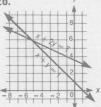

27.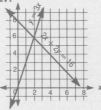

28.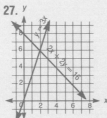

29.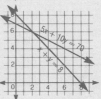

30.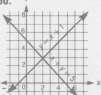

31.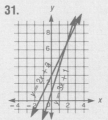

32.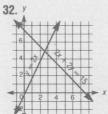

33.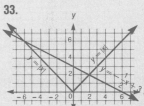

34.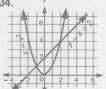

35.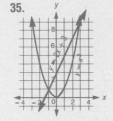

36.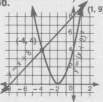

37.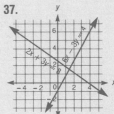

38.

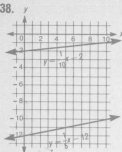

$y = \frac{1}{10}x - 2$

$y = \frac{1}{6}x - 12$

39.

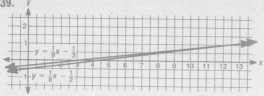

$y = \frac{1}{9}x - \frac{1}{3}$

$y = \frac{1}{8}x - \frac{1}{2}$

■ **Written Exercises SECTION 6-3**

9.

10.

11.

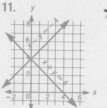

12.

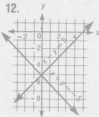

13.

14.

15.

16.

■ **Review Exercises SECTION 9-3**

2.

3.

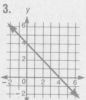

4.

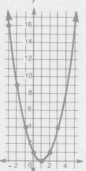

5.

■ **Written Exercises SECTION 9-4**

55.

56.

57.

58.

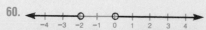

59.

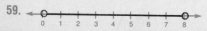

60.

■ **Review Exercises SECTION 9-4**

1.

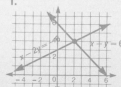

$x - y = 6$

■ Written Exercises SECTION 9–5

32.

33.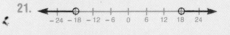

34.

35.

36.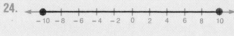

43.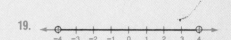

44.

45.

46.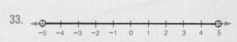

■ Written Exercises SECTION 9–6

17.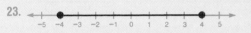

18.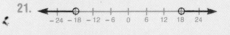

19.

20.

21.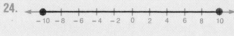

22.

23.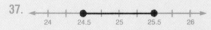

24.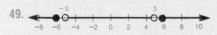

33.

34.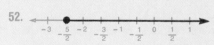

35.

36.

37.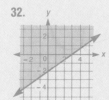

38.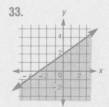

48.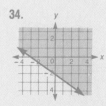

49.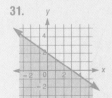

50.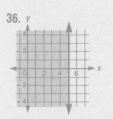

51.

52.

53.

54.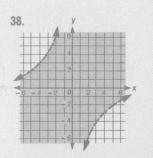

55.

56.

■ Written Exercises SECTION 9–7

31.

32.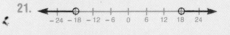

33.

34.

35.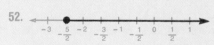

36.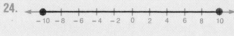

37.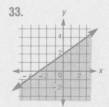

38.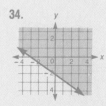

653

39.

40.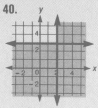

41.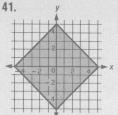

42.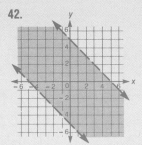

43.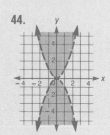

44.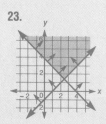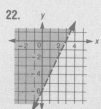

■ **Chapter 9 Self-Test**

3.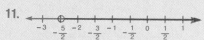

4.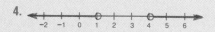

5.

10.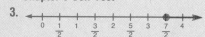

11.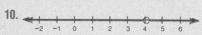

12.

13.

22.

23.

■ **Written Exercises SECTION 11–2**

9.

10.

11.

12.

13.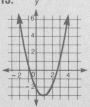

14.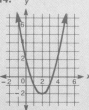

15.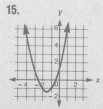

16.

17.

18.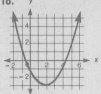

19.

20.

21.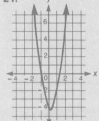

22.

23.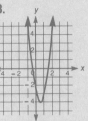

24.

27.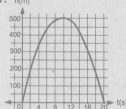

34.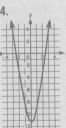

35.

36.

45.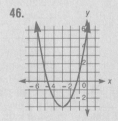

46.

47.

■ INDEX

*Boldfaced numerals indicate the pages
that contain formal or informal
definitions.*

CREDITS

Design   *Cover:* Barbara Tonnesen   *Text:* Volney Croswell

Illustrations   *Cover:* Jeff Stock   *Text:* RoseDesign

Photography   *Research:* Linda Finigan

x: Guy Sauvage (Photo Researchers). *5:* Paul Johnson. *15:* Clive Russ. *28:* Bill Gallery (Stock, Boston). *30:* Arthur Grace (Stock, Boston). *30:* Scott Ransom (Taurus Photos). *38:* Ed Robinson (Tom Stack & Associates). *41:* Peter Menzel (Stock, Boston). *47:* James Holland (Stock, Boston). *61:* Joseph Martin/Scala (Art Resource). *66:* The Bettmann Archive. *76:* Gabor Demjen (Stock, Boston). *88:* Porterfield/Chickering (Photo Researchers). *92:* Clive Russ. *103:* Heinz Klutemeir/Sports Illustrated (Time, Inc.). *107:* P.J. Crowley. *118:* Owen Franken. *124:* Edward Jones (Photo Researchers). *131:* Culver Pictures. *142:* John Sutton (Alberta Color Productions). *157:* National Optical Astronomy Observatories. *167:* Richard Paisley. *172:* Dan McCoy (Rainbow). *174:* P.J. Crowley. *174, 178:* Z. Leszczynski (Animals, Animals/Earth Scenes). *179:* Mike Mazzaschi (Stock, Boston). *181:* Edith Haun (Stock, Boston). *184:* Will McIntyre (Photo Researchers). *185:* Tom Stack (Tom Stack & Associates). *189:* Ralph Mercer. *196:* Doug Lee (Tom Stack & Associates) *206:* The Granger Collection. *229:* Steve Allen (Peter Arnold). *234:* Ralph Mercer. *256:* Brian Parker (Tom Stack & Associates). *274:* Dave Schaefer (The Picture Cube). *289:* Michael Heron. *304:* John Zoiner (Peter Arnold). *316:* Sissac (Nawrocki Stock Photo). *341:* C.T. Seymour (Photo Researchers). *342:* P.J. Crowley. *351:* Les Van (Nawrocki Stock Photo). *358:* Peter Menzel (Stock, Boston). *381:* Clive Russ. *394:* Sheryl McNee (Tom Stack & Associates). *403:* Tom Hannon (The Picture Cube). *406:* Dave Schaefer (The Picture Cube). *409:* Tom Stack (Tom Stack & Associates). *423:* Ralph Mercer. *434:* Larry Lefever (Grant Heilman). *447:* Clive Russ. *488:* Runk/Schoenberger (Grant Heilman). *492:* Hugh Patrick Brown (Photo Researchers). *494:* The University Museum, University of Pennsylvania. *497:* Robert Dowling (Nawrocki Stock Photo). *504:* H. Silvester (Photo Researchers). *542:* Du Puy (Monkmeyer Press). *582:* NASA (Grant Heilman).